A TOPOGRAPHICAL LIST OF THE INSCRIPTIONS OF THE MADRAS PRESIDENCY

A TOPOGRAPHICAL LIST
OF THE
INSCRIPTIONS OF THE MADRAS PRESIDENCY

(Collected till 1915)

WITH NOTES AND REFERENCES

BY

V. RANGACHARYA, M.A., L.T.

ASSISTANT PROFESSOR OF HISTORY, PRESIDENCY COLLEGE, MADRAS.

VOLUME I.

GYAN

Published by

Gyan Publishing House
5, Ansari Road
Daryaganj, New Delhi-110002
Phone: 011-47034999, 9811692060
E-mail: books@gyanbooks.com

Distribution Network
gyanbooks.com
India, USA, Canada, UK, Australia, France

ISBN : 978-81-212-4129-8 (Set)
ISBN : 978-81-212-4902-7 (PB)
First Published, 1919

2nd Impression 2020

Printed at: Gyan Press, Delhi.

Inscriptions of the Madras Presidency Vol. I
Author: V. Rangacharya

A TOPOGRAPHICAL LIST

OF THE

INSCRIPTIONS OF THE MADRAS PRESIDENCY

(Collected till 1915)

WITH NOTES AND REFERENCES

BY

V. RANGACHARYA, M.A., L.T.,

ASSISTANT PROFESSOR OF HISTORY, PRESIDENCY COLLEGE, MADRAS.

VOLUME I.

MADRAS:

PRINTED BY THE SUPERINTENDENT, GOVERNMENT PRESS.

1919.

PREFACE.

IT was in the month of January 1916 that, in the course of an interview I had with Sir John Marshall, the Director-General of Archæology, who was then on a flying visit to Madras, the question of compiling a list of the inscriptions which had been published by the Department of Epigraphy in the Madras Presidency, was first mooted. The idea had been suggested by Mr. F. J. Richards, I.C.S., whose labours in the compilation of the "Salem Gazetteer" and whose researches in the field of South Indian history, ethnology and customs had taught him the necessity of a handbook, which could give in short and succinct compass the inscriptions contained in the annual reports of the department. The epigraphical reports are a veritable mine of information, but unfortunately the information they give have not been arranged according to any definite plan. The exact situation of the villages from which the inscriptions have been copied has been omitted in a large number of cases and the student of research has to spend a lot of time in tracing the exact topographies for which he has not often got the proper books of reference. The inscriptions of a single locality, moreover, have been published in a number of reports so that a scholar who is in need of the epigraphical data of a local history has to waste an enormous amount of time by going through all the reports. The inscriptions of Tanjore, for instance, are to be seen in half a dozen reports, and references to them have been given in almost every page of every report. The difficulties which have arisen in consequence of these defects can be appreciated only by people who have been actually engaged in the work of research. Mr. Richards saw them and suggested to Sir Alexander Cardew the possible usefulness of a publication which, in a convenient form, could give a topographical arrangement of the inscriptions. His proposal was tantamount to the publication of a list similar to that of Mr. Sewell's "Antiquities"; only what Mr. Sewell had done for antiquities as a whole was to be done for inscriptions in particular. It was to be a more specialized work but necessarily fuller and more detailed. Sir Alexander sympathized with the proposal and suggested it to Sir John Marshall who, as has been already said, asked me to undertake it.

When Sir John Marshall offered this task to me, I took the liberty to make certain suggestions in regard to the scope and aims of the treatise. I pointed out to him that there were inscriptions in the Presidency other than those published by the department. There are, for instance, the "Nellore Inscriptions" of Messrs. Butterworth and Venugopal Chetti; the "Tamil and Sanskrit Inscriptions" of Burgess and Natesa Sastri; the "Elliot Collections" and local inscriptions referred to by Mr. Sewell in his "Antiquities"; the "Travancore Inscriptions" of the late Sundaram Pillai; the "Travancore Archæological Series" which contains, in addition to the inscriptions copied by the Madras office, certain new ones; and the "Mackenzie Collections." The Director-General and the Madras Government agreed to my proposal and the present work in consequence includes the inscriptions contained in all these. The inscriptions collected by Mackenzie have indeed given me trouble. Their geographical spellings are so crude and part of their contents themselves so suspicious that I came to feel that their inclusion in the body of the volume might, in the eyes of some, be a defect. At the same time the world of scholarship, I felt, should know what had been done by that great pioneer, Colonel Mackenzie, more than a century back. I have, therefore, adopted a compromise and given the Mackenzie inscriptions, as a rule, in footnotes. Scholars will now be able to see what they contain and be in a position to compare the information therein with that of more scientific methods of later days.

It is not the attempt at the complete utilization of all epigraphical materials, however that is likely to be the characteristic of the present work. Its merit, if any, lies more in the method adopted. Not only have the summaries of the inscriptions been given, but their importance and significance, political, social, financial, etc., have been pointed out and their interconnexions shown by numerous cross-references, the notation of which has cost a labour the amount of which can hardly be imagined or appreciated by laymen. References to the *Epigraphia Indica*, the "South

Indian Inscriptions," the "Tamil and Sanskrit Inscriptions," the "Travancore Archæological Series," the "Antiquities," the *Indian Antiquary*, the *Journal of Royal Asiatic Society*, the *Mythic Journal*, *Madras Journal*, the District Manuals and Gazetteers are given wherever possible. An attempt has also been made to append bibliographical notes on literary and religious persons or events occurring in inscriptions based on Taylor's "Rais Catalogue," the publications of Professors Seshagiri Sastriyar and Ranga Acharya, the Vaishnava "Guruparamparas," the Tamil "Abhidhānachintāmani," "Abhidhānakōsam," "Pāvalar-Charitradīpaka," the Telugu Biographies of Poets by Viresalingam Pantulu and Guruzada Sriramamurti, etc.

It will be seen that the result of my proposals and suggestions was to make the publication a much more complete and comprehensive book of reference than the Government at first intended it to be. It gives not only the list of inscriptions, their summaries and references to them in research journals, but it attempts to show their bearings on the literary, social, religious and economic history of the land and bibliographical references thereon. I trust that the students of history will find the publication useful and look upon the incompleteness which is bound to exist in a work of such a gigantic scope with indulgence. More than 12,100 inscriptions have been entered in the list and a complete exhaustiveness of references and notes, in the midst of heavy college work, is impossible; but a sincere attempt has been made at thoroughness. I intended to give the ancient geographical divisions of each district as far as they can be gathered from epigraphy as introduction to each, but I gave it up, as it forms a chapter in a monograph I am preparing on South Indian History. The Mysore and Bastar inscriptions copied by the department have been omitted as they do not belong to the Presidency. The index and glossary at the end of the volume will, I believe, highly facilitate the reading of the inscriptions in each district.

It only remains for me to express my obligations to those who have lightened my task with their assistance or sympathy. I am much obliged to Rao Sahib H. Krishna

Sastriyar Avargal, the Assistant Superintendent of Archæology for Epigraphy, for his never-failing courtesy and for the ready willingness with which he gave me facilities in the ways of books of reference, copies of inscriptions, etc., whenever I wanted them. I must thank Mr. Richards, I.C.S., for his valuable suggestions in regard to the manner of arrangement of inscriptions. The idea of a general number for each district and of a short notation of the same is his. I am obliged to Sir Alexander Cardew for the cordial manner in which he encouraged me, and I am deeply indebted to Sir John Marshall for the honour he did me in entrusting this work to me and for the volumes of the *Epigraphia Indica* he placed at my disposal. Mr. S. Kuppuswami Sastrigal, Professor of Sanskrit and Comparative Philology in the Presidency College, gave me every facility for consulting the manuscripts in the Oriental Manuscripts Library and Mr. N. Ramani, Lecturer at Anantapur College, rendered me occasional help in the arrangement of the index slips. To these gentlemen and to a few students of mine, both in Madras and Anantapur, who helped me in the mechanical part of the work I am obliged. I am indebted above all to the Government for its generous recognition of the difficulties of the work and its ready sanction of the facilities for me.

OOTACAMUND,
6th June 1917.

V. RANGACHARYA.

GENERAL CONTENTS.

VOLUME I.

VOLUME II.

VOLUME III.

TOPOGRAPHICAL INSCRIPTIONS.

ANANTAPŪR DISTRICT.

ANANTAPŪR TALUK.

No inscriptions have been copied in this taluk. The *Mack. MSS.* (*Inscriptions of Ceded Districts*, pp. 13—16) give notices of seven places containing inscriptions under the heading Anantapuram; but of these, four do not certainly belong to Anantapūr taluk; two (Janakumpulla and Pulladaravu) are not found in the alphabetical list of villages of the taluk. The only place which can be certainly attributed to it is Bukkarāyasamudram, the tank at Anantapūr.

Anantapūr.

1. On a stone at Bukkarāyasamudram. A Kanarese record dated Śaka 1286 Krōdhi, in the reign of Bukka Rāya of Vijayanagar. Records that his Minister Anantarasa Uḍayār excavated the tank and built a temple of Śaṅkara on its banks. [See Brown's *Wars of the Rajahs* and Mr. Sewell's *Antiquities*, p. 117.]

DHARMAVARAM TALUK.

Chennakottapalle.

2. 65 *of* 1912.—(Telugu.) On a rock south of the village. A damaged record dated Śaka 1539, Piṅgaḷa. Refers to the rule at Kalyāṇadurga, of a certain Veṅkaṭapati-Nāyanayyavāru, son of Rāya Daḷavāyi Kōnēṭi-Nāyuḍu and to the gift of the village Kottapalle to a certain Dāsappa-Nāyuḍu as a feudal tenure in fee (*pālepaṭṭu*). This latter seems to have induced a merchant of Chēlūru to dig a canal at Kottapalle.

Dādalūru.

3. 61 *of* 1912.—(Telugu.) On a slab set up in the Pōtularāju temple. A mutilated record dated Śaka 1630, Sarvadhāṛin. Registers that two tanks breached on the night of Sunday, the 10th of the dark fortnight of Bhādrapada in this year and that the compound wall (*parikōṭa*) ? of the temple of Pōtularāju was washed away. A certain Veṅkaṭapati-Nāyaniṅgāru appears to have restored it. See Mr. Sewell's *Antiquities*, I, 117.

4. 62 *of* 1912.—(Telugu.) On another slab set up in the same temple. Records in Śaka 1439, Īśvara, gift of land at Dādalūru to the temple of Pōtularāju for offerings and lamps, by a certain Koṇḍama-Nāyaniṅgāru, son of Chāki Chennama Nāyuḍu. Mentions the tank Nāgalādēvicheruvu. [Mr. Sewell refers to this, but gives the wrong date Śaka 1434.]

5. 63 *of* 1912.—(Telugu.) On the third slab set up in the same place. A damaged record dated Śaka 1707, Viśvāvasu. Mentions the temple of Pōtapa at Dādalūru and the repairs executed therein by a certain Pōtanna.

6. 64 *of* 1912.—(Kanarese.) On the fourth slab set up in the same place. Records gift of land at Dādalūru to a certain Krishṇadāsa by Timmapa-Nāyaka for the worship of Tiruvēṅgalanātha.

Dharmavaram.

7 a & b.—Mr. Sewell refers to two copper plate grants in this place belonging to the reign of Prauḍhadēva of Vijayanagar, but the dates of which were wrongly reported to him to be A.D. 1153 and 1163. [For the later history of the place see *Anantapur Gazetteer*, p. 150.]

Kānaganapalle.

8. Mr. Sewell refers to four inscriptions in this place, of which he gives the details of one. This is dated in Śaka 1455 and is said to be a private grant in the reign of Achyuta Rāya of Vijayanagar.

Kanumukkala.

9. 67 *of* 1912.—(Telugu.) On a rock to the west of the village. A much damaged record dated Śaka 1637, Manmatha. Seems to record an agreement made among themselves by the Karṇams, Reḍḍis and other residents of Kanumukkala.

Mallināyanipalle

(four miles north-east of Dharmāvaram.)

10. 51 *of* 1912.—(Telugu.) On a slab set up in the village. An unfinished record of the Vijayanagara king Vīrapratāpa Achyutarāya-Mahārāya, dated Śaka 1455, Vijaya. Records that the Mahāmaṇḍalēśvara Sālakarāja China or Pina—Tirumalayyadēva-Mahārāja, the king's brother-in-law and minister (who led the Tiruvaḍi campaign in 1531-2) gave for offerings to the God Mandem Narasimhadēva, 'who was pleased to manifest himself in a field near Dharmāvaram,' the village of Mallapanāyanipalle which he had founded, for the merit of his father Sālakarāja and his mother Tippājamma.

Mēlāpuram (or Mēḍāpuram).

11. 66 *of* 1912.—(Telugu.) On a stone set up in front of the Añjanēyasvāmin temple. A damaged record of the Vijayanagara king Vīrapratāpa Vijayabukkarājayya-Mahārāya; dated Śaka 1473, Virōdhikrit. Mentions Maṅgamārepalli surnamed Mēḷāpura and the temple of Prasanna-Varadarāja. Certain Reḍḍis appear to have made a grant to the temple.

Rāghavampaḷḷi.

12. A Telugu paper grant in charge of a local Brahman. Records gift of the village to one Kṛishṇamāchārya by Tirumalappa Nāyuḍu, son of Koṇḍappa Nāyuḍu, in Śaka 1637. *Ins., Ceded Dts.* in *Mack. MSS.*, p. 208, No. 5.

13. A Telugu paper grant in charge of the local Brāhmaṇas. Records that the village was restored by Sivarām Bāba Ghorpaḍe to one Nrisimhāchārya in Jaya. *Ibid.*, No. 9.

Rāvulacheruvu.

14. A. C.P. grant of Śrī Vīrapratāpa Vijaya Bukka Rāya, but date wrongly reported as Śaka 1109. [See *Antiquities*, I, 118.]

*Tāḍimarri.**

15. On the third gate of the fort at Tāḍimarri (Telugu). A record of Immaḍi Koṇḍappa Nāyuḍu saying that the fort with its stone gates, etc., was built in Śaka 1628 Vijaya. *Mack. Ins., Ced. Dts.*, p. 208, No. 3.

16. On a stone in the fort. Records in Śaka 1448, Vijaya, that some land was given as free gift to the drummers and pipers of the local Chennakēśava temple by Śaṅkarappa. *Ibid.*, No. 4.

17. A paper grant in the hands of Chinnappa. A Telugu record, dated Śaka 1680, Bahudhānya, saying that Rāmappa Nāyuḍu, son of Chinnappa Nāyuḍu, the Polygar of "Cheyatidurgam"

* Under this heading the *Mack. MSS.* (*Ins. Ced. Dts.*, p. 207–12) give twelve inscriptions. Of these three (1, 10 and 11) are at "Chetidurgam" (Chitaldrug ?); three at Tādimarri (given above), two at Rāghavapalle (given above); two at Chelavāripalle (see Tādpatri taluk); and the other three at the villages of Tumpara (No. 6), Vilivutta (No. 8) and Singammalla (No. 12). I have not identified the last three. The inscription at Tumpara records that in Śaka 1186, two persons (Rāma Rao and Subba Rao) granted an allowance of 3 pagodas and 1 *fanam* from the revenue of Ganganapalle for the local Ānjanēya temple. The Vilivutta epigraph records a gift of land to one Tummana Śurappa in Śaka 1598, Naḷa, in the reign of Rāmadēva Mahārāya, by Veṅkaṭagiri Veṅkaṭādri. The "Singun-mulla" inscription is dated in Śaka 1475, Pramādīcha, in the reign of Śrīraṅga Rāya and grants this village and another (Maderapalle) to a Vaishnava Brahman for worship of the local deity. See *Mack. Ins., Ced. Dts.*, p. 210.

re-established the Chennakēśava shrine on the hill fort and granted a *tūm* of dry land, besides a *fanam* from "Cheyatidurgam" for offerings to the deity. *Ibid*, No. 7.

Togarakunṭa.

18. Mr. Sewell mentions a C.P. in the possession of the karṇam, dated in Śaka. 1688, recording private charities.

GOOTY TALUK.*

Anumpalli.

19. On a stone in the village. A Telugu record of the reign of Vīra Rāmadēva Rāya at Penukoṇḍa, dated in Śaka 1548, *Prabhava*. Records gift of five *tūms* of paddy fields to the Gōpālasvāmi temple. *Mack. Ins., Ced. Dts.*, p. 141, No. 3.

Gooty.

20. 83 *of* 1903.—(Kanarese.) On a rock near the deserted Narasiṃhasvāmi temple on the local hill. A damaged epigraph, dated Śaka 1429, *Prabhava*, mentioning several Gauṇḍas.

21. 84 *of* 1903.—(Kanarese.) In the same place. A damaged record of the fifth year of the W. Chāḷukyan king Pratāpachakravartin Jagadēkamalla, Śaka 1065, *Dundubhi*, mentioning Kalyāṇapura as the capital (*Nelvidu*).

22. 85 *of* 1903.—(Sanskrit.) On the same rock. A record of the Vijayanagara king Bukka. See *S. Ind. Inscriptions, Vol. I*, p. 167. Also *Anantapur Gazetteer*, p. 156.

23. 86 *of* 1903.—(Kanarese.) On the same rock. Damaged.

24. 87 *of* 1903.—(Kanarese.) On the same rock. Damaged.

25. 88 *of* 1903.—(Kanarese.) On the same rock. Damaged.

26. 89 *of* 1903.—(Kanarese.) On the same rock. A record of the W. Chāḷukya Tribhuvanamalladēva (i.e., Vikramāditya VI) dated in Chāḷukya-Vikramā 46, *Plava*. See *S. Ind. Inscriptions*, I, p. 167.—As this era began, according to Dr. Fleet in Śaka 997, Hultzsch attributes the present epigraph to Śaka 1043 or A.D. 1121–2.

27. 90 *of* 1903.—(Kanarese.) On the same rock. A record of the same king (as in 7) with date 47 of the C. V. era, i.e., A.D. 1122–3. See *Ibid.*, p. 167. [These records show that Vikramāditya's power was recognized in the Anantapūr district.]

---

* The *Mack. MSS.* (*Ins., Ced. Dts.*, p. 141–4) mention ten inscriptions under this heading. Two villages Buradalu (No. 7) and Narasapuram I am unable to identify. The latter might be the place of that name in Anantapūr taluk or Tādpatri. The epigraph at Buradalu records that in Śaka 1439, Īśvara, in the reign of Kṛishṇadēva Rāya, one Narapa Gōvinda granted Māture village to the local God Vighnēśvara. The Narasāpuram inscription is dated in Śaka 1477, Rākshasa, in the reign of Sadāśiva Rāya of Vijayanagar, and records a grant of allowance by the Vīpravinōdins for the worship of God Virūpākshēsvara. All the other inscriptions have been included in the text.

28. *C.P. No.* 9 *of* 1915.—A record of Sadāśiva Mahārāya in Śaka 1470, *Kilaka*, Āshāḍha śuddi 12, Sunday. Registers the king's gift, of the village of Kanuma in Mundimaḍugu śīma in Gutti valita to a number of Brahmans to perform worship to God Chennakēśavadēva at Mundimaḍugu. The grant was made at the request of Appala Rāja, son of Kṛishṇa Rāja and grandson of Timma Rāja of the Solar race. [Mundimaḍugu is in Anantapūr taluk.]

Kōnakondla.

29. 76 *of* 1912.—(Kanarese.) On a slab set up in front of the Bhōgīśvara temple. A much damaged record of the Vijayanagara king Vīrapratāpa Kṛishṇadēva-Mahārāya dated Śaka 1448, *Pārthiva.* The king receives the title *samasthabhuvanāsraya*, 'the asylum of the whole world.' Mentions Ādapa Nāyaka and Kondakunte (i.e., Kōnakoṇḍḷa).

30. 77 *of* 1912.—(Sanskrit and Telugu.) On another slab set up in the same place. Records for the merit of the Qutb Shahi king, Hajarati Sultānu Abdula Hassanu Kudupusāha, that in Śaka 1662, *Siddhārtin*, a certain Konḍamayya got the privilege of worshipping in the temple of Kēśavanātha at Kōnakoṇḍḷapēṭa and of enjoying as such, all the property belonging to the temple. The donor was Timmāji, also called Rāmadāsu Timmarsu. Abdul Hassan died in 1688. So this grant should have been made long after his death. For discussion see *Ep. Rep.*, 1912, p. 91.

31. 78 *of* 1912.—(Kanarese.) On a slab set up near a mosque in the bazaar of the same village. A damaged record of the Western Chāḷukya king Pratāpachakravartin Jagadēkamalla II, dated 2nd year, *Siddhārthin*. Mentions the Mahāmaṇḍalēśvara Iruṅgōḷarasa and seems to register a gift of land to the temple of Kēśavadēva. [Iruṅgōḷa was evidently a Telugu-chōḷa chief said to be a descendant of Karikāl-chōḷa and of the solar race. (See *Mys. & Coorg*, p. 163. Also Ap. 120, Ap. 122, Ap. 124. *Ep. Rep.*, 1907, p. 75.

32. 79 *of* 1912.—(Kanarese.) On a pillar set up near a pond in the same village. A record in archaic characters. "Hail! (This is) the tank of (i.e., built by) the glorious Sarvāditya-Sōmayājin."

Maranapalli.

33. On a marble stone in the pagoda. A record of Vīra Veṅkaṭapatidēva in Śaka 1525, *Subhakrit*. Mentions Āluḍa Rāmarājayya dēva Mahārāja and records the gift of the village of Maranapalli to God Raghunāyaka on the hill-fort of Gutti. See *List Ins., Ced. Dts.*, p. 142, No. 6.

Miḍatur.

34. On a stone near the pagoda of Vīrabhadra. A record of the time of Kṛishṇadēva Mahārāya in Śaka 1439, Īśvara. Records the grant of the village of Miḍatūru to the pagoda. Mentions "Nayava Govindaya." See *Ins.*, *Ced. Dts.* (*Mack. MSS.*), p. 141, No. 1.

Nārimetla.

35. "At the temple of Anjanēya is an inscription dated Śaka 1558 (A.D. 1636), recording a grant to a temple by private parties." (*Antiquities*, I, 116).

Pātachēruvu.

36. On a stone on the bank "Mannvagu" in the village. A record of the time of Sadāśiva Mahārāya in Śaka 1479, *Kāḷayukti*. Mentions Tirumala Rājayya and records gift of one *tūm* of land to a water-keeper in the local choultry. *Ibid.*, p. 143, No. 9.

37. On a stone south of the village. A record of the time of Sadāśiva Mahārāya, dated in Śaka 1440, *Pramādi*. Records gift of ½ *puṭṭi* of dry field in Pātacheruvu or Lakshmīpuram village as free gift to Guṭṭi Nārāyaṇa Bhaṭṭa by "Chirutena Kesva Rāju." *Ibid.*, No. 8.

Penna-Ahōbilam.

38. "On a stone in the temple is an inscription, dated Śaka 1478 (A.D. 1556), recording a grant by a chief in the reign of Sadāśiva of Vijayanagar." [*Antiquities*, p. 116]. The *Anantapur Gazetteer* mentions two other inscriptions in 1552 and 1559. See p. 164.

[The chief mentioned in the inscription of 1556, was evidently Timma Nāyuḍu, the son of Jyōgi Nāyuḍu, the Polegar of Uḍiripikoṇḍa. For a history of these Poligars see *Ibid.*, p. 165–6. See also *Ins.*, *Ced. Dts.*, p. 143, No. 10.]

Rāmpuram.

39. In the temple of Rāmēśvarasvāmi is "an inscription, dated Śaka 1419 (A.D. 1497), commemorating the grant of a village by Sāḷuva Immaḍi Narasimha Rāya Mahārāya" and others. [Mr. Sewell says that this might be the father of Kṛishṇadēva Rāya. He is of course wrong.]

Tummadipulla (Tambalapalle?)

40. On a stone in the village. A record of Kṛishṇadēva Rāya making the gift of Tummaḍipulla village to "Ramesibhoga Deva." *Ins.*, *Ced. Dts.*, p. 141, No. 2.

Yerratimmacheruvu.

41. On a stone west of the village. Records that in Śaka 1481, *Siddhārti*, Tirumala Rājayya remitted the tax on some land of Īśvaradēva. *Ibid.*, p. 142, No. 4.

HINDUPUR TALUK.

Bichagānipalle.

42. 589 *of* 1912.—(Kanarese.) On a stone set up near the Añjanēya temple. Records in Plava the exemption of fishing (?) taxes granted to the Besta-bōya (i.e., fishermen) community of Ūṭukūru by Mummaḍi-Reḍḍi, the agent of Peḍirājaya, and the Gauḍa and Sēnabova of Ūtukūru.

Chaulūru.

43. 585 *of* 1912.—(Kanarese.) On a stone set up in front of the Añjanēya temple. Records in Śaka 1471, *Saumya, Nija-Vaiśākha, ba. di.* 6, Friday (Friday 17 May, A.D. 1549) that a certain Jakkarāsa, son of Kuppa-Nāyaka of the Haragumodalēri (i.e., Mudaliyars of Parigi) family, constructed a maṇṭapa in front of the temple of Hanumantadēva at Chauḷūru and made some grants to it.

44. 586 *of* 1912.—(Telugu.) On a second stone set up near the same temple. A damaged record of the Vijayanagara king Vīrapratāpa Sadāśivadēva-Mahārāya, dated Śaka 1478, *Naḷa, Aśvija, su. di.* 2. Seems to record a gift to the Mahājanas of Chauḷūru by a number of Vipravinōdins who belonged to various śākhas and sūtrās. The Vipravinōdins were Brahman jugglers who, on account of their occupation, have now socially degenerated. See Ap. 94.

Chilumuttūru.

45. "On the bund of the tank is an inscription, dated A.D. 1367, which mentions king Bukka I of Vijayanagar." See *Antiquities*, I, 121 and *Anantapur Gazetteer*, 169.

Chōḷasamudram.

46. 86 *of* 1912.—(Kanarese). On the wall, right of main entrance into the Chauḍēśvari temple. A damaged record in Vikriti, refers to the building of the temple of Chauḍēśvari-Amma at Chōḷasamudra and to a tax fixed on each loom (*magga*) by Timmarasa and others.

47. 87 *of* 1912.—(Kanarese.) On a slab set up in the court-yard of the same temple. An unfinished record of the Vijaya-nagara king Kṛishṇarāya-Mahārāya, dated Śaka 1439, Īśvara. Records a gift to the temple of Chauḍēśvari at Chōlasamudra by Rāyasam Koṇḍamarasayya, son of Timmarasamantri who was one of the sons of Śrīpatyāchārya, chief of Podatūru in Drāviḍa-dēśa and the ornament of the Udayagiri-Kannaḍiga sect. The gift was made in order that the king may be blessed with children. [Koṇ-ḍamarasayya (Comdamara of Nuniz) is said to have actually planted the Vijayanagara colours on the Simhādri and Śrikūrmam during Kṛishṇadēva's celebrated campaign in the north. It was evidently after this that Tirumala was born. See Ap. 48.]

Gōraṇṭla.

(This place was so important in the mediæval period that it gave its name to one of the gates of the Penukoṇḍa fort.)

48. 91 *of* 1912.—(Telugu.) On a slab set up at the entrance into the Īśvara temple. The Vijayanagara king Vīrapratāpa Tirumaladēva-Mahārāya (son of Kṛishṇadēva Rāya) records in Śaka 1446, Tāraṇa, that Śūraparāja, the agent of Vākiṭi Aṭappa-Nāyaniṅgāru freed the *Tammala* servants of the temple of Sōmēśvara at Gōraṇṭla from supplying leaves (used in eating food) to that temple free of cost, on the condition that they repaired the temple, built the śikhara, and constructed a compound wall of mud. [This is evidently the prince who, according to Nuniz, died prematurely. He was born evidently after Śaka 1440. See Ap. 47, above.]

49. 92 *of* 1912.—(Sanskrit and Telugu.) On a slab lying in the Mādhavarāyasvāmin temple in the same village. Records in Śaka 1276, Jaya, that a certain king Naraśinga of the Sāḷuva family (and son of Sāḷuva Maṅgi) built the temple of Vishṇu. His ancestors had the *birudas* Mēdinimisaragaṇḍa Kaṭhāri-Sāḷuva and Dharaṇīvarāha. [The genealogy of the Sāḷuvas given here is different from that given in the Dēvulapalle plates and Telugu Literature. See *Ep. Rep.* 1912, p. 79 for details.]

50. 181 *of* 1913.—(Telugu.) On the west wall of the maṇṭapa in the Mādhavarāyasvāmin temple. A much damaged record of the Vijayanagara king Vīrapratāpa Tirumaladēvarāya-Mahārāya, dated Śaka 1446, Tāraṇa, Kārttika, śu. di. 12, Monday, Utthānadvādaśi, Chitrānakshatra. Records that the agent of Vākiṭi Ādapa-Nāyuḍu granted land to the Vishṇu (Perumāḷ) temple at Gōraṇṭla for maintaining festive processions on the *daśami* days of the month. The date corresponded, according to Mr. Swamikannu Pillai, to Monday, November 7, 1524. "Nakshatra wrong. The day was Utthānadvādaśi." See note to 47 and 48 above.

51. 182 *of* 1913.—(Telugu.) On the same wall. A much damaged record of the Vijayanagara king Achyutarāya-Mahārāya, dated Śaka 1452, Vikrita (Maghi śu. di. 14, Monday). Mentions Gōraṇṭla-śīma which was conferred as a fief (*nāyankara*) on the son of Vākiṭi Mallapa-Nāyuḍu. As to date Mr. Swamikannu Pillai says: "In Vikriti-Samvat—A.D. 1530, Magha śu. 14 ended on Tuesday, January 31·77, so that on Monday, January 30, the *tithi* was current for less than 15 *ghaṭikas.* The reading does not however appear to be quite certain. The text may after all be Śukla 13. The week-day in A.D. 1532-33 (—Śaka 1454) was Saturday not Monday."

52. 183 *of* 1913.—(Telugu.) On the same wall. A damaged record of the Vijayanagara king Achyutarāya-Mahārāya dated Śaka 1455, Vijaya, śu. di. 15, Monday. Records that Timmapa-Nāyuḍu, son of Vākiṭi-Mallapa-Nāyuḍu ordered the *sthānikas*, citizens and the temple cook to revive the processions in the Perumāḷ temple at Gōraṇṭla which had been neglected till then. As to date Mr. Swamikannu Pillai says that details are not enough for calculation.

53. 184 *of* 1913.—(Telugu.) On a stone built into the floor of a maṇṭapa in the same temple. A damaged record of the Vijayanagara king Vīra-Veṅkaṭapatidēva-Mahārāya, ruling at Penugoṇḍa, dated Śaka 1532, Sādhāraṇa, Pushya, śu. di. 2, Friday. Seems to register the grant of certain taxes (?) to the temple of Mādhavēśvara at Gōraṇṭla for the merit of the king and of Chikka-Veṅkaṭappa-Nāyuḍu. [The date corresponded, according to Mr. Swamikannu Pillai, to Friday, December 7.41, A.D. 1610. The Government Epigraphist believes that Veṅkaṭappa was "evidently one of the two Veṅkaṭas of the Hemrāj line." *Ep. Ind.*, Vol. III, p. 238.

54. 185 *of* 1913.—(Telugu.) On the capital of a pillar in the same maṇṭapa. Records that the four pillars on the east side of the platform (*jagali*) were the gift of Tirupati-vāru.

Gorrepalle

(Goravanahalle near Hindupūr).

55. 68 *of* 1912.—(Sanskrit and Kanarese.) On the south wall of the prākāra in the Lakshmidēvi temple. Dated in the reign of the Vijayanagara king Vīrapratāpa Achyutadēva-Mahārāya in Śaka 1460, Viḷambi. Records that a certain Vīraṇa-Nāyaka, younger brother of Virūpaṇṇayya of Penugoṇḍe, dug up a spring *(talaparigi)* with an irrigation channel called Nūtana-Tungabhadra, in the village of Mōdaya surnamed Achyutarāya-pura and got certain lands watered by it (which belonged to Antayyana Koḍigēhaḷḷi in Goyyalūra-śīme), presented to the temple of Mahālakshmidēvi at Haruhe-Lakkhaṇapura.

56. 69 *of* 1912.—(Kanarese.) On the same wall. Dated in the reign of the Vijayanagara king Vīrapratāpa Achyutadēva-Mahārāya, in Śaka 1459, Hēmalambi. Records that the same Vīraṇa-Nāyaka presented to the temple of Mahālakshmidēvi at Lakkhaṇapura in Haruhe-sthala the offerings made to that temple in the form of coin, clothes, gold, etc., during festivals, by the people assembled together for the occasion.

57. 70 *of* 1912.—(Kanarese.) On the same wall. Dated in the reign of the Vijayanagara king Vīrapratāpa Achyutadēva-Mahārāya in Śaka 1460, Vilambi. Records the gift of income from tolls collected by merchants (śeṭṭis and paṭṭanasvāmis) on every Friday market held at Haruhē-Lakkhaṇapura, to the temple by the same Vīrana-Nāyaka.

58. 71 *of* 1912.—(Kanarese.) On the same wall. Dated in the reign of the Vijayanagara king Vīrapratāpa Achyutadēva Mahārāya in Śaka 1460, Viḷambi. Records the buildings constructed in the same temple by the brothers Vīraṇa-Nāyaka and Virappaṇṇa of Ponugoṇḍe. These were: (1) the stone prākāra wall, (2) the eastern and the southern gōpuras, (3) the gates (?), (4) the kitchen and the verandah in front of it, (5) the assembly-hall, (6) the paving of the courtyard, (7) shrines for Rāma, Lakshmaṇa, Hanūmān, Bhairava, Vighnēśvara, etc.

59. 72 *of* 1912.—(Sanskrit and Kanarese.) On the same wall. Dated in the reign of the Vijayanagara king Vīrapratāpa Achyutadēva Mahārāya in Śaka 1456, Jaya. A copy of the deed by which Muttakadahalli surnamed Mahālakshmīpura was granted to the temple of Mahālakshmi by Timmarasa, son of Apparasa of the treasury, at the instance of Vīrappaṇṇayya of Penugoṇḍe.

60. 73 *of* 1912.—(Sanskrit and Kanarese.) Dated in the reign of the Vijayanagara king Vīrapratāpa Achyutadēva Mahārāya in Śaka 1458, Durmukhi. Records gift of the village of Goravanahaḷḷi surnamed Lakshmīsāgara, in Antayyana Koḍagihaḷḷi-sthala, of Guyyalūru-śīme in Rodda-nāḍu which was a district of Penugoṇḍe-rājya, to the same temple by Kṛishṇappa-Nāyaka, son of Sani Chinnappa-Nāyaka, at the instance of Vīrappaṇṇayya.

61. 74 *of* 1912.—(Sanskrit and Kanarese.) On the same wall. Records that the above documents were caused to be engraved by Basavana-Sōmayājin of Chauṭakūru and Vīrappaṇṇa's clerk (*Sēnabōva*) Timmappa of Goranṭḷa with the approval of Vīrappaṇṇayya of Penugoṇḍa.

Hindupur.

A purely modern town (see *Anantapur Gazetteer*, I, 170-1), it has got the following inscriptions in the neighbourhood:—

62. 587 *of* 1912.—(Kanarese.) On a stone set up in a field below the tank bund. The Noḷamba (Pallava) king Dilīpayya Iṛiva-Noḷamba (grandson of Mahēndrādhirāja) records gift of land to a certain Duggaśeṭṭi, a member of the Pasundi-Bōya (community ?) by the 300 great men of Kagūru.

63. 588 *of* 1912.—(Kanarese.) On a stone set up near the Āñjanēya temple below the same tank-bund. A record of the western king Eragaṅga Permānaḍi. Seems to refer in Śaka 775 to the Noḷamba who ruled the country extending up to Kānchi. [This Noḷamba was either Noḷambādhirāja Poḷalchōra or his son Mahēndrādhirāja. Eragaṅga's position in the Gaṅga family is unknown. See *Ep. Ind.*, VI, p. 59.]

64. *C.P. No.* 15 *of* 1912–13. A record in Sanskrit of the Vijâyanagara king Raṅga VI.—Incomplete. The beginning is identical with that of the Kaḷḷakkuruchchi grant.

65. *C.P. No.* 16 *of* 1912–13.—A forged grant of alleged date Ś. 1109, Jaya (wrong), Aśvija, *Su di* 10, in Telugu. Registers the advent of a number of Gavuṇḍas from Nagara śīma with their baggages to settle in the country ruled by Sōmaśaṅkara Nāyaka of Ratnagiri. Three new villages were founded and village officers appointed. Also mentions *malika bharama varāha* (the pagoda issued by the Golconda king Malik Ibrahim). [The grant pretends to be dated in the reign of Vijaya Bukkarāya. Ratnagiri is an ancient place as it is referred to in a C.P. grant of the W. Chāḷukya Vikramāditya I (655–80); but the local chronicle gives its history only after it came under the Nāyuḍu chiefs of Sera in the time of Bijapūr supremacy. Śōmaśaṅkara was evidently one of them.]

Kaggallu.

66. 84 *of* 1912.—(Kanarese.) On a slab set up in a garden. A damaged record of the Vijayanagara king Vīrapratapa Sadāśivadēva-Mahāraya dated 1475, Pramādin. Seems to register the gift of the village of Kaggallu, surnamed Timmasamudra, to the temple of Mallikārjuna.

Kambaladinne.

67. On a stone in the pagoda of "Mantraula natha" in the village. A record dated in Ś. 1457 Manmatha. Records that one Vīrappanāyaṅgar granted the village of Kambaladinne to "the God Singaswamy of Gangıuntoo." (*Mack. Ins. Ced. Dts.*, p. 68, No. 31.)

Kirikera.

68. 591 *of* 1912.—(Kanarese.) On a stone set up in a field near the ruined Īśvara temple. A record in archaic characters. Registers that four Gavuṇḍas (mentioned by name) undertook to protect certain privileges (?) pertaining to Eradukēre in the presence of Bīrayya.

Koḍigēpalle.

69. 80 *of* 1912.—(Telugu.) On a slab built into the wall of a ruined maṇṭapa near the Āñjanēya temple. A damaged record of the Vijayanagara king Vīrapratāpa Śrīraṅgayadēva Mahārāya (VI) dated Śaka 1567, Pārthiva. Records that a certain Obalarāya Kōnēṭi Nāyaniṅgāru repaired the temple of Pala-Veṅkaṭēśvara at Dinnamiḍi-Koḍigēpalle alias Pala-Veṅkaṭapura in Guyyulūru-nāḍu, included in (the territory of) Penugoṇḍa-durga, and presented the village to that temple under orders of Peda-Veṅkaṭapatirāya (Veṅkaṭa II ?). Mr. Krishna Sastri believes it might be Veṅkaṭa II, but it is doubtful.

70. 81 *of* 1912.—(Kanarese.) On a slab built into the wall of a private house in the same village. The Hoysaḷa king

Vīra-Ballāḷadēvarasa (Ballāla III, 1291–1342), son of Vishṇuvardhana Pratāpachakravartin Vīranarasimhadēvarasa (Narasimha III, 1254–91), records in Śaka 1250, Vibhava, that the Māhāpradhāna (Kōṭeya Māchaya-Daṇṇāyaka) was ruling at Penugoṇḍēya-nelavīḍu and gave the village of Benagūru as a koḍagi-gift to a certain Gauḍa. [The inscription shows the extent of Ballāḷa territory. Penukoṇḍa apparently was included in it, but was soon to be ruled by Bukka I.]

71. 82 *of* 1912.—(Kanarese.) On a slab in a field near the Siva temple of the same village. A mutilated record in archaic characters. Mentions in the beginning a certain Mahārājādhirāja whose name is not clear on the impression. Registers perhaps the gift of the village of Vannaṅgūru.

Koṭnūru.

72. 590 *of* 1912.—(Kanarese.) On a stone set up in front of the Chauḍēśvari temple. A much damaged record of the Vijayanagara king Vīrapratāpa Vīra-Sadāśiva-Mahārāya, dated in year Sādhāraṇa. Seems to register a gift to the temple of Chauḍēśvari, for the merit of Daḷavāy Kṛishṇama-Nāyaka.

Lēpākshi.

For an excellent description of the local Vīrabhadra temple, its history. etc., see *Anantapūr Gazetteer*, 172–4. The Vishṇu temple of this place which contains the finest sculptures in the Anantapūr district is commemorated by a Telugu bard who wrote the Telugu dramatic poem *Lēpākshi-Rāmāyaṇamu*, which, I understand, is largely sung on occasions of puppet shows.

73. 88 *of* 1912.—(Sanskrit and Kanarese.) The Vijayanagara king Vīrapratāpa Achyutadēva-Mahārāya records in Śaka 1460, Viḷambi, gift of Chikanandichervu surnamed Dēvarāyapura, a village near Deppāru in Sādali-sthala of Chelurachāvaḍi to the temple of Vīrēśvara on the Kūrmaśaila hill at Lēpākshipura, by Vīrappannayya of Penugoṇḍe. It is stated that the donor purchased it from four Brāhmaṇas who had acquired the village as a *sarvamānya* grant from king Prauḍhadēva-Mahārāya.

74. 89 *of* 1912.—(Sanskrit and Kanarese.) On the same wall. Records in Śaka 1460, Viḷambi, that half of the village of Sadāśivapura surnamed Dēvarāyapura, also near Dēppāru, was purchased from two Brāhmaṇas and granted to the same temple by Vīrapannayya. As in the previous instance the Brāhmaṇas had acquired it from Prauḍhadēva-Mahārāya. [See *Antiquities*.]

75. 90 *of* 1912.—(Sanskrit and Kanarese.) On the same wall. A record of the Vijayanagara king Vīrapratāpa Achyutadēva-Mahārāya. Records in Śaka 1460, Viḷambi, gift of some *vriṭṭi*-lands, by purchase, in the sarvamānya-agrahāra Nagaragēre, surnamed

Krishnarāyasamudra, to the same temple, by Vīrapannayya and his brother Vīraṇa-Nāyaka. Nagaragēre is stated to have belonged to Tumbekalla-sthala in Rodda-nāḍu which was a subdivision of Penugoṇḍe-rājya.

76. 569 *of* 1912.—(Sanskrit and Kanarese.) On the east wall of the second prākāra in the Vīrabhadra temple. A damaged record in Śaka 1459, Hēmalambi, Phalguna, ba. di. 2, Thursday (Thursday, 21, Feb. A.D. 1538). Records a gift to the shrines of Pāpavināśadēva, Raghunāthadēva and Vīrēśvaradēva, by the Mahājanas of Nagaragēre *alias* Krishṇarāya-samudra-agrahāra, a village in Rodda-nāḍu which was a subdivision of Penugoṇḍe-rājya. The gift consisted of a *talaparigi* channel below the tank of Nagaragēre and of a tank called *Gūḷiseṭikuṇṭe* in Āḍabārahalli village. Mentions Vīrabhūpa, the brother of Penugoṇḍe Vīrappanna, who was the son of Nandi-Lakiśeṭi of Lēpākshi.

77. 570 *of* 1912.—(Sanskrit and Kanarese.) A record of the Vijayanagara king Vīrapratāpa Achyutadēva-Mahārāya in Śaka 1456, *Jaya, Vaiśākha*, śu. di. 15. Gift of tolls collected by the merchants at the market held every Sunday in the hamlet of Vīrēśvaradēvarapura belonging to Lēpākshi, of tolls raised in Haru-ṇāḍu and Hosūra-nāḍu and of other income, for oblations to be offered in the three shrines mentioned above. The grant was made at the instance of Vīraṇa Nāyaka, brother of Vīrapaṇṇaya of Penugoṇḍe. [This is No. 4 in Sewell's List.]

78. 571 *of* 1912.—(Sanskrit and Kanarese.) On the east wall of the second prākāra in the Vīrabhadra temple. The Vijayanagara king Vīrapratāpa Vīra Achyutadēvarāya Mahārāya records in Śaka 1459, *Hēmalambi, Jyēshṭha*, ba. di. 10, Monday, a sale of land to the same three shrines by the mahājanas of the sarvamānya-agrahāra village Kāñchasamudra *alias* Pratāpadēva-rāyapura which was given to them as a free gift by Pratāpadēva-Mahārāya (i.e., Dēvarāya II) when he made the great gifts named *kāmadhēnu, kalpavriksha* and *viśvachakra* in the presence of the god-Virūpāksha on the banks of the Tungabhadra river. Lēpākshi is stated to have been a village in Sādali-vēṇṭe which belonged to Rodda-nāḍu, a subdivision of Penugoṇḍe-rājya. [This is No. 1 in Sewell's List.]

79. 572 *of* 1912.—(Sanskrit and Kanarese.) On the east wall of the second prākāra in the Vīrabhadra temple. A record of the Vijayanagara king Vīrapratāpa Achyutadēva-Mahārāya dated in Saka 1459, *Hēmalambi, Kārttika*, śu. di. 12, Monday (Utthānadvādaśi), corresponding to 15th October 1537. Seems to refer to the grant of two villages to the temple of Vīrēśvara, made by the king in the presence of Viṭhalēśvara on the banks of the Tungabhadra river. [No. 2 of Sewell's List.]

80. 573 *of* 1912.—(Sanskrit and Kanarese.) On the east wall of the second prākāra in the Vīrabhadra temple. A preface to the inscriptions on the east wall which record gifts made to the shrines of Vīrabhadra, Pāpanāśēśvara and Rāma at Lēpākshi. It is stated that these were engraved by Basavaṇa Sōmayājin of Chāṭakūru and Timmapa of Gōraṅṭla who was the *sēnabōva* (clerk or shroff) of Vīrapaṇṇayya, under orders from Vīrapaṇṇa.

81. 574 *of* 1912.—(Sanskrit and Kanarese.) On the east wall of the second prākāra in the Vīrabhadra temple. An incomplete record of the Vijayanagara king Vīrapratāpa Achyutadēva Mahārāya, dated Śaka 1455, *Vijaya, Kārttika,* śu. di. 12, Monday (Utthānadvādaśi). The Sanskrit portion at the beginning registers the grant of three villages named Hampaṇapalli, Kancharlahaḷḷi and Timagoṇḍanahaḷḷi to the shrine of Vīrabhadra at Lēpākshi. The villages were all surnamed Vēṅkaṭādri-samudra after prince Kumāra-Veṅkaṭādri, the son of Achyuta Rāya. [The date is not quite consistent as the week day should be Thursday.]

82. 575 *of* 1912.—(Sanskrit and Kanarese.) A much damaged record of the Vijayanagara king Vīra-Achyutarāya, dated Śaka 1456, *Manmatha.* Seems to register the gift of a village by the king for the worship of Vīrabhadra of Lēpākshi.

83. 576 *of* 1912.—(Sanskrit and Kanarese.) On the east wall of the second prākāra in the Vīrabhadra temple. The Vijayanagara king Vīrapratāpa Achyutadēva-Mahārāya records in Śaka 1459, *Hēmalambi, Ashāḍha,* śu. di. 12, Monday, corresponding to 15th October 1537, gift by purchase from Bhaṇḍāra Timmapa, of the village Nandichērla *alias* Virūpākshapura, near Kārakalike in Buruḍakuṇṭe rājya, to the god Vīrēśa who had bestowed favours on Vīrapaṇṇa, by the chief Achyutarāya Mallapaṇṇa, devotee of Mallikārjuna. The village was originally granted in Śaka 1389, *Sarvajit, Pushya,* śu. di. 2, Monday, Makara Saṁkrānti, to Timmapa's grandfather Vīramarsa by Virūpākshadēva-Mahārāya II, son of Prauḍhapratāpa-Dēvamahārāya (i.e., Dēvarāya II). [No. 3 in Sewell's list.]

84. 577 *of* 1912.—(Sanskrit and Kanarese.) On the east wall of the second prākāra in the Vīrabhadra temple. The Vijayanagara king Vīrapratāpa Vīra-Achyutadēva-Mahārāya records in Śaka 1459, Hēmalambi, Aśvija, ba. di. 5, Monday (Monday, 24th Sep. A.D. 1537) gift of lands at Kalanūra-agrahāra, which were purchased by Vīrapaṇṇa for the temple of Vīrabhadra at Lēpākshi.

85. 578 *of* 1912.—(Kanarese.) On the rocky floor of the same prākāra. A damaged record of the Vijayanagara king Vīrapratāpa Vīra-Achyutarāya-Mahārāya in Khara. Records gift of the village of Chaluvinḍla (*lit.* water-shed) surnamed Komāra-Veṅkaṭādripura, to the temple of Pāpavināśanadēva at Lēpākshi. See Ap. 58 for reference to the same prince.

86. 579 *of* 1912.—(Sanskrit and Kanarese.) In the same place. A much damaged record of the Vijayanagara king Achyuta, dated

Śaka 1455, Khara. Gives the usual long genealogy commencing with the moon.

87. 580 *of* 1912.—(Sanskrit and Kanarese.) On the north wall of the same prākāra. The Vijayanagara king Achyuta records that what follows is a copy of a copper plate document of Vīrēśvaradēva. After the long praśasti which is identically the same as that of the Unamanjēri plates, it is recorded that the king weighed himself against pearls at Kāñchi in the Śaka year 1455, Nandana, and that he made the gift called *Kānchanamēru* in Śaka 1456, Vijaya.

88. 581 *of* 1912.—(Telugu.) On the east wall, right of entrance into the Īśvara temple at old Lēpākshi near the same village. Records in Śaka 1603, Durmati, Vaiśākha, śu. di. 3, Monday, solar eclipse (Monday, 9 May A.D. 1681), gift of tolls by the merchants of all countries headed by Prithvīśeṭṭi Rāyana-Bhāskara, to the temple of Śānta-Nañjuṇḍēśvara at Lēpākshi. [This princely merchant was the contemporary of the Kārvēṭinagar chief Sāḷuva Mākarāja Tirumalarājayyadēva mahārāja. See *Ep. Rep*., 1912, p. 60 and 83–4 for details.]

89. 582 *of* 1912.—(Telugu.) On the same wall, left of entrance, Hajuratu Sultānu Abdula Hasānu Alamgiru Pannāha (i.e., Hajarat Sultan Abdul Hassan Alamghyr Pādshah) records in Śaka 1602, Raudri Vaiśākha, śu. di. 3 Monday, gift of fields and gardens to the temple of Śānta-Nañjunḍēśvara, by the Reḍḍis and Karṇams of old Lēpākshi, for the merit of the king. [This was Abul Hassan of Golcoṇḍa who ruled from 1672 to 1688.]

90. 583 *of* 1912.—(Kanarese.) On the Nāgalabaṇḍa rock near the Peddacheruvu tank in the same village. A damaged and unfinished record of the Vijayanagara king Vīrapratāpa-Sadāśiva-Mahārāya in Śaka 1471, Kīlaka, Bhādrapada śu. di. 1. Records a gift (not specified) for the merit of the Mahāmaṇḍalēśvara Rāmarāja-Viṭhaladēva (the conqueror of the south in the campaign of 1544–5).

Malagūru.

91. 95 *of* 1912.—(Kanarese.) On a slab near the Siva temple. A much-damaged record dated Śaka 1107, Viśvāvasu. Begins with an introduction which is generally found at the beginning of the Telugu and Kanarese-Chōḷa inscriptions and mentions Māchadēva (a Telugu-Chōḷa).

Mānēpalle.

92. 592 *of* 1912.—(Kanarese.) On a stone lying near the Īśvara temple in the bed of the tank. The Noḷamba (Pallava) king Ayyadēva (son of Mahēndra Noḷambādhirāja) records that Chōrayya, son of Śrīpurushayya and other Gamuṇḍas of Eṛaḍumūru obtained certain privileges (?).

Māṇesandra. (*Mēnāsamudram.*)

93. 96 *of* 1912.—(Kanarese.) On a slab set up on the way to Ūṭukūru. Records in Jaya, the gift of Chauḍapura as a sarvamānya grant to the goddess Chauḍēśvaramma of Ūṭukūru, by a certain Nallamāchi-Nāyaka under the orders of Kṛishṇapa Nāyaka, son of Chinnapa Nāyaka.

94. 97 *of* 1912.—(Telugu.) On another slab set up near a well in the same village. The Vijayanagara King Vīrapratāpa Sadāśivarāya-Mahārāya records a gift of lamps to the temple of Hanumantadēva at Maṇṇēyasamudra surnamed Dēvarāyapura, an agrahāra in Rodda-nāḍu, a district of Penugoṇḍa-rājya, for the merit of all Vipravinōdins. Date doubtful. [Brown explains Vipravinōdins as Brahman Jugglers. Mr. Krishna Sastri points out that they are, in the Ganjām and Vizagapatam districts, no longer Brahmans but Śūdras, a phenomenon which he attributes to the demoralising effect of the occupation. See Ap. 44 for another reference to them.]

Mōḍa.

95. 75 *of* 1912.—(Tamil.) On stone beams in the Īśvara temple. A record of the Chōḷa King Rājēndra-Chōḷa I. The major portion of the historical introduction beginning with *tirumanni vaḷara.*

Morsalapalle.

96. "There is a copper-plate grant in this village, in the possession of Sukha Reḍḍi and Hanumanta Reḍḍi, residents. It is dated Ś. 1276 (A.D. 1354), and records a grant by Vijaya Bukka Rāya, Narasa Rāya and Srī Kṛishṇa Rāya." [*Antiquities*, I, 122.]

Parigi.

This place has been identified with Parivi, the capital of the early Bāṇa Kings. No epigraphical evidences are available, but the three temples of Dharmēśvara, Bhīmēśvara and Saptamātrikas, together with the fine sculptures of the place where the old town is supposed to have been located, suggest its early importance.

97. 83 *of* 1912.—(Kanarese.) On two fragments of a slab near the Honnāṭikamma temple. The Hoysaḷa King Vīra-Ballāḷa II, ruling at Dorasamudra with Śāntaladēvi, records in Śaka 1100, Viḷambi, the presentation of a bell to the temple of Bhīmēśvara at Guruguñjikōla-bayalu below the tank of Haruve (i.e., Parigi) in Haruhe-nāḍu and the gift of 800 . . . of land measured by the rod called (evidently after the king) *drōharamalla*, for oblations, lamps, etc. A piece of stone is, evidently, missing in the middle.

Pūlaguṇṭa.

98. 85 *of* 1912.—(Kanarese.) On the Garuḍakambha in front of the Āñjanēya temple. Records in Saumya, gift of the pillar by a bōya.

Vānavōlu.

99. 93 *of* 1912.—(Kanarese.) On a slab lying in a field. Records that Gaṅgasāni, daughter of Payiḍiśeṭṭi of Pāmiḍi entered into the fire (i.e., performed suttee) at Penugoṇḍa. To her memory was, perhaps, erected ? a *brindāvana* at Vānavōlu.

100. 94 *of* 1912.—(Telugu.) On a rock in another field in the same village. A much damaged record of the Vijayanagara King Vīrapratāpa Rāmarāju-Veṅkaṭapatirāyadēva-Mahārāya, dated Śaka 1555, Śrīmukha.

KADIRI TALUK.*

Kadiri.

101. 520 *of* 1906.—(Telugu.) On a slab lying near a tamarind tree west of the Lakshminarasimhasvāmin temple. Records the reconstruction of a street, to the west of the Narasimha temple at Kadiri, in the name of Saṅgayadēva-Mahārāju, son of Chōḍarāya-gurudēva-Mārāju.

102. 521 *of* 1906.—(Kanarese.) On four faces of a pillar lying at the western entrance into the same temple. A record of the Vijayanagara King Vīrapratāpa Dēvarāya-Mahārāya; refers in Hēmalamba to Harihara-Mahārāya. [*Mack. Ins., Ced. Dts.*, p. 122, No. 9.]

103. 522 *of* 1906.—(Telugu.) On a slab set up near the south wall of the maṇṭapa in front of the central shrine in the same temple. Dated in the reign of the Vijayanagara King Vīra-Bukkaṇa-Voḍayalu. Records in Śaka 1274, Nanḍana, that while the king was ruling at Dhorasamudra and Penugoṇḍa, the temple of Avubhaladēva at Kadiri was built by a Nāyaka. [See *Mack. Ins., Ced. Dts.*, p. 120, No. 7.]

104. 523 *of* 1906.—(Kanarese and Sanskrit.) On another slab set up in the same place. A record dated in Śaka 1275, Vijaya, consisting of a Sanskrit verse with two meanings (*ślēsha*) composed by the pradhāni Sovappagalu on the occasion of the gift of an ornament to the temple at Kadiri by Gōpaṇa, an officer of Kumāra-Kampaṇa II, i.e., Goppaṇa Rāya, the restorer of

---

* The *Mack. MSS.* (*List of Inscrns., Ceded districts*, pages 119—25) gives nineteen inscriptions in the "Cadari district." These are at Tummala (No. 2), Sōmapulla (Nos. 3-4), Chakibunda (No. 5), Pulichurlu (No. 6), Kadiri (7—9), Guryāla (10-11) Parlapulla (12), Curumala (13—16) and Yurrabulla (17—19). I am able to identify the villages Tummala, Kadiri and Curumala. The inscriptions of these three places I have included in the epigraphs of this taluk. Of the other villages Sōmapulla (Sōmapaḷḷi) is in Madanapalli taluk (Chittoor district); Guryāla, Parlapulla (i.e., Parnapaḷḷi) and Yerrabulla are in Pulivendla taluk, Cuddapah district. See these taluks for their inscriptions. I am unable to locate Chakibunda and Pulichurlu. The inscription in the first of these is dated in Ś. 1569, Virōdhi, and records the repair of the local tank by Chili Nāyuḍu in the reign of Tiruvēngalanātha Rāja Chōḍa Dēva. The Pulichurla epigraph is a grant by "Luckki Naidu" in Ś. 1431, Bhava, to the local deity Nṛisimhasvāmi. See *Mack. Ins., Ced. Dts.*, p. 120.

Srīrangam and the contemporary of Vēdānta Dēśika. [*Mack. Ins., Ced. Dts.*, p. 120, No. 8. But here the year is given as Pramōdūta.]

105. 524 *of* 1906.—(Telugu.) On a slab built into the floor of the court-yard of the same temple. Records in Khara, a charter granted to potters by a Nāyaka.

106. 525 *of* 1906.—(Telugu.) On a slab built into the floor of the kitchen in the same temple. A damaged record of the Vijayanagara king Vīrapratāpa Kṛishṇadēvarāya-Mahārāya, dated Saka 1452, Virōdhin. Records gift of land to the temple of Narasimhadēva of Kadiri by a relation of the king.

107. 526 *of* 1906.—(Telugu.) On a slab set up below a peepul tree in the court-yard of the same temple. A damaged record of the Vijayanagara king Vīra-Kumāra-Dēvarāya-Mahārāya, son of Vīra-Harihararāya, dated Saka 1339, Hēmalamba. Seems to mention the *Mālas* and *Mādigas.* See Thurston's *Castes* and *Tribes*, pp. 329—87 and 292—325 for a description of these.

108. 527 *of* 1906.—(Telugu.) On a slab set up near the big gōpura of the same temple. Records in Śaka 1380, Kāḷayukta, gift of land to the *Rāmānujakūṭā* in the Kadiri temple.

109. 528 *of* 1906.—(Sanskrit in Telugu characters.) On the base of the same gōpura, right and left sides. A mutilated record, the date and the name of the king of which are lost. Gives a genealogy of the first Vijayanagara dynasty. Seems to record the building of the gōpura by Viṭhalāmātya, son of Dēvapāmātya.

110. 529 *of* 1906.—(Telugu.) On the base of a platform in the 1,000 pillared maṇṭapa of the same temple. An incomplete record, dated Śaka 1451, Virōdhin. Records a gift by a merchant from Tāḍiparati (Tāḍpatri).

111. 530 *of* 1906.—(Telugu.) On a lamp pillar lying in front of the same temple. Records in Śaka 1391, Virōdhin, gift of the pillar.

112. 531 *of* 1906.—(Telugu.) . On another pillar set up in the same place. A record, dated in Śaka 1337, Jaya.

113. 532 *of* 1906.—(Telugu). On a boulder near the Vishṇu temple at the foot of the Narasimhakoṇḍa hill, east of Kadiri. Records in Sarvadhāri, gift of a garden.

Kurumāla.

114. On a stone in the village. A record of the reign of Achyuta Rāya of Vijayanagar, dated in Virōdhikrit. Mentions Mahārājalu 'Rāmachandra Dīkshit and grants the village to God Nrisimhaswāmi for food offering. [*Mack. Ins., Ced. Dts.*, p. 123, No. 13.]

115. A record of the time of Kṛishṇadēva Rāya in Śaka 1436, Bhava. Mentions "Lucki Naidu" and records the gift of the village of "Pubichurla" for food offering to God Nrisimha. *Ibid.*, No. 14.

116. A record of the time of Sadāśiva Rāya of Vijayanagar, dated in Śaka 1468, Parābhava. Records that one Rāyulu Gunji Reḍḍi purchased 19 *tūms* of land (for 60 pagodas) below the tank at Malacalacheruvu and granted it to God Tiruvēṅgalanātha. *Ibid.*, No. 15.

117. A record of the time of Vikrama Rāya, dated in Śaka 730, Nandana. Grants the village of Vikramarāyapuram or Dēvarāyapuram to "Nundavighala." *Ibid.*, No. 16.

Tummala.

118. On a stone below the tank at the village. A record, dated in Śaka 1598, Naḷa. Mentions Haji Muhammad and records grant of lands to the tank-diggers, the karṇam, etc. *Ibid.*, No. 2.

KALYĀNDRUG TALUK.

Chintalapalle (Chintaralapalle).

119. Mr. Sewell mentions two copper plate grants in this place, of which one is dated Śaka 1580 and records a grant by Rāya Daḷavāi Kōnēṭi Nāyani Veṅkaṭapati Nāyaḍu. [See *Antiquities* I, 117.]

Eraḍukera.

120. 83 *of* 1913.—(Kanarese.) On a slab set up in the courtyard of the Saṅkarēśvarasvāmi temple. Dated in the reign of the Western Chāḷukya king Jagadēkamalla (II), in Śaka 1051, Siddhārthi, Mārgasira, su. di. 5, Sunday, Uttarāyaṇa Saṁkramaṇa. Records gifts of land and of taxes by a certain Kētanavergḡaya who was the mahāpradhāna and military officer of the chief Irungōḷa Chōḷa I, ruling at Goydavāḍi, to the temple of Śaṁkaradēva at Eraḍukera, a village in Suḷiyanūr Seventy, which was a district of Sīr-nāḍu. The date is irregular and the Uttarāyaṇa Saṅkramaṇa in 1139-40 fell, says Mr. Swamikannu Pillai, on Monday, 25th December. [*See* Ap. 31 and 122 for further references to this chief.]

121. 84 *of* 1913.—(Kanarese.) On another slab in the same place. Rōdadamalla Mallidēvarasa records in Sārvari, a gift of oil for lamps by the mercantile community of Eraḍukera to the same temple. The epigraphist surmises that Mallidēva was the son of Iruṅgōḷa I and possibly became the feudatory of Kulōttuṇgachōḷa. [*See* at p. 112 for the authority on which he bases his opinion.]

122. 85 *of* 1913.—(Kanarese.) On another slab in the same place. Iruṅgōḷa-Chōḷa Mahārāja records in Śaka 1065, Dundubhi, the death of a certain Gaṅgaṇavergaḍe and his follower in a *dhāli*. The chief mentioned here is Iruṇgōḷa I, whose inscriptions are in Ap. 31, Ap. 120, etc.

(95) 86 *of* 1913.—(Kanarese.) On a broken slab in the same place. This is a *viragal* which states that Vaiḍumba Chūḍāmaṇi captured the cows of the 96,000 (people ?) of Bēvinabīḍu.

Kambadūru.

123. 89 *of* 1913.—(Sanskrit and Kanarese.) On a pillar in the inner court-yard of the Mallikārjuna temple. Iruṇgōḷadēva Chōla-Mahārāja (II), ruling at Niḍugallu, records in Śaka 1171, Kīlaka, Chaitra, ba. di. 13, Tuesday, Uttarāyaṇa-Vishusamkramaṇa, corresponding to 24th March A.D. 1258, gift of land to the temple of Mallikārjunadēva at Kambadahola, after repairing it. This chief was the great-grandson of Iruṅgōḷa I. Some of his inscriptions in the Tumkūr and Chitaldroog districts have been printed in Rice's *Ep. Carṅa.*

124. 90 *of* 1913.—(Kanarese.) On the same pillar. Records in Sarvadhāri, Māgha, ba. di. 14, Monday, gift of land to the same temple by the crown prince, the son of Iruguṇadēva (i.e., Iruṅgōḷadēva).

125. 91 *of* 1913.—(Kanarese.) On another pillar in the same place. A record of the Noḷamba (Pallava) king Noḷambarāja-Mahēndra-Tribhuvanadhīra. Records in Śaka 805 (A.D. 883) a gift of land and paddy by the *gāmuṇḍas* and *pārvas* (Brahmans) of Beddugoṇḍe to a temple of the Sun (Ādityagriha). [See *Ep. Ind.*, Vol. X, pp. 54-70.]

126. 92 *of* 1913.—(Kanarese.) On the same pillar. A much mutilated record of Iruṅgōḷadēva. Mentions the repairs made to the temple of Mallikārjunadēva.

127. 93 *of* 1913.—(Kanarese.) On the third pillar lying in the same place. The Noḷamba (Pallava) king Iruva-Noḷambādhirāja records in Śaka 887, Krōdhana, Phalguna, Amāvāsya, Sunday, solar eclipse, corresponding to 6th March 965, a gift of land for maintaining a tank, by prince Poḷalchōra, a grandson of the king and 'the lord of Kānchi.' The pillar was set up by Chāvuṇḍayya of the Śrīvatsa-gōtra, the favourite minister of Poḷalchōra II, father of Vīramahēndra, sixth in descent from Mahēndra I and lieutenant of the Rāshṭrakūṭa Kṛishṇa III in the conquest of Chōḷa land in the weak times which followed the death of Parāntaka I.

128. 94 *of* 1913.—(Kanarese.) On a slab set up in the same place. Dated in the reign of the Vijayanagara king Vīrapratāpa-Sadāśivarāya-Mahārāya, in Śaka 1478, Nala. Records gift of 50 *varāhas* (till now appropriated by the overseers of temple affairs) to the temple of Mallikārjuna-dēva at Kambadūru, by Virūpaṇa-Nāyaka, for the merit of his father Tammapa-Nāyaka. [This is the only inscription which Mr. Sewell refers to in his local list.]

129. 95 *of* 1913.—(Kanarese.) On a pillar built into the floor at the entrance into the same temple. A seriously damaged record. Seems to be a Vijayanagara record and register the gift of the village Tenegalapura surnamed Mallāpura, for the merit of Achyutadēva-Mahārāya, on the auspicious occasion of Mahā-Viśākha. Date lost.

130. 96 *of* 1913.—(Kanarese.) On a pillar lying in the outer prākāra wall of the same temple. Dated in the reign of the Vijayanagara king Vīrapratāpa-Kṛishṇarāya Mahārāya in Śaka 1434, Āṅgirasa, Kārttika, śu. di. 12, corresponding to Friday, 22nd October 1512. Records gift of land by Rāyasa Koṇḍamarassayya to the temple of Mallikārjunadēva at Kambadūru, for the merit of the king. The land was situated below the tank of Kambadūru in Kuṇḍurupiyaśīme which was the Jāghir of the chief.

131. 97 *of* 1913.—(Kanarese.) On the same pillar. Dated in the reign of the Vijayanagara king Vīrapratāpa Kṛishṇadēva-Mahārāya in Śaka 1447, Pārthiva. Records gift of the village Jalavati to the same temple by Rāyasa Ayyaparasayya 'in order that Rāyasa Koṇḍamarasayya may dwell in heaven.'

132. 98 *of* 1913.—(Kanarese.) On a pillar in a field to the east of the same temple. The Noḷamba (Pallava) king Noḷambādhirāja (probably Poḷalchōra, the father of Mahēndra I) records that while the tank of Benḍugoṇḍe was constructed, a temple for Mahādēva was also built, and pinnacles were placed over it (for the merit of) Śiṅgapōta, Ponnēra and Dharma-mahādēvi (early Noḷamba names).

133. 99 *of* 1913.—(Kanarese). On a slab set up in a field to the west of the same temple. The Vijayanagara king Vīrapratāpa Achyutarāya-Mahārāya records in Śaka 1458, Durmukhi, Jyēshṭha, ba. di. 30, Sunday, the village and lands owned by the temple of Mallikārjunadēva at Kambadūru in Kuṇḍurupiyaśīme which was the fief *(nāyakatana)* of Bayyapa-Nāyaka.

134. 100 *of* 1913.—(Kanarese.) On a slab set up in front of the Akkataṅgēru-guḍi in the same village. A much damaged record of a Western Chāḷukya king, dated 1108, Viśvāvasū, Chaitra, Paurṇami, Monday, lunar eclipse. Records gift of land to the temple of Atteradēva at Kuḍarpi-durga. The date probably refers to Tuesday, 16th April 1185, says Mr. Swamikannu Pillai.

135. 101 *of* 1913.—(Kanarese.) On a boulder in a field in the same village. Records in Naḷa, a gift of land granted by Timmaṇa-Nāyaka of Kuṇḍurpe, to a certain Vīrayya of his own caste (?).

136. Mr. Sewell says that there is a copper plate inscription in this place recording a grant by Vijaya Bukka Rāja, the date of which was wrongly reported to him as Śaka 1109.

Mulakalēḍu.

137. 87 *of* 1913.—(Kanarese.) On a slab set up near a well. Records in Śaka 1574, Nandana, an endowment by a Muhammadan chief whose name is not clear. Refers to Kuṇḍurpi-durga.

138. 88 *of* 1913.—(Kanarese.) On a fallen pillar lying down in front of the Kāli-Amma temple in the same village. Records in Virōdhi gift of land to a merchant of Mulukalēḍu by an agent of Ayyaparasayya.

MADAKASIRA TALUK.

In his *lists* of antiquities Mr. Sewell mentions as many as eight villages of epigraphical interest in this taluk. Of these, the following are given as they alone are definite.

Hēmāvati.

139. Besides three inscriptions at the Śiva temple, one at Basavannaguḍi, Mr. Sewell gives three at the temple of Siddhēśvarasvāmi. One of these is undated and mentions "Srīman Mahāmaṇḍalēśvara Tribhuvanamalla Mallidēva Chōḍa Mahārāja," The second, dated Śaka 1090, is a grant by the same king, The third, dated Śaka 1127, records 'a grant by Vīra Ballāḷadēva of the Hoysaḷa Ballāla dynasty. See *Antiq.*, I, 121.

Tammaḍihaḷḷi.

140. "An inscription on a stone on the tank-bund south of the village. It is dated Śaka 1463 (A.D. 1541) and records a grant by a private person in the reign of Achyutadēva." See *Antiq.* I, 121.

PENUKOṆḌA TALUK.

Bukkapaṭṇam.

141. 176 *of* 1913.—(Telugu.) On a slab set up at the entrance into the Lakshminārāyaṇasvāmin temple. The Vijayanagara king Achyuta-Mahārāya records in Śaka 1463, Plava, Āśvija, ba. di. 13, Monday, that Peddirājayya, under orders of Rāmabhaṭlayavāru, remitted the *rāiulagutta* tax ? in the *māgāna* of Krottacheruvu, for the merit of the king. The date corresponded, according to Mr. Swamikannu Pillai, to Monday, October 1740, A.D. 1541.

142. 177 *of* 1913.—(Telugu.) The Vijayanagara king Achyuta Mahārāya records in Śaka 1464, Subhakrit, Chaitra, ba. di. 6, Wednesday, the remission of taxes on marriages and the taxes on the earnings of Brāhmans for the merit of the king. Rāmabhaṭlayya issued the orders and Peddirājayya conveyed them to the Reḍḍis and Karṇams of the village of Krottacheruvu. The date corresponded, according to Mr. Swamikannu Pillai, to Wednesday, April 5, A.D. 1542.

143. 178 *of* 1913.--(Telugu.) On the rock below the dhvajastambha in the Chauḍēśvari temple in the same village. The Vijayanagara king Vīrapratāpa Srīraṅgarāyadēva-Mahāraya records in Śaka 1503, Vrisha, Bhādrapada, ba. di. 12, Sunday, that Daḷavāyi Veṅkaṭappa-Nāyuḍu, under orders of Mēgōṭi Timma Nāyuḍu, the agent and minister of the king, remitted the taxes *nāgaribirāda Asavechchālu* and *birudulu* due on the lands owned at Bukkasāgaram and Anantapuram by the temple of Chavuḍēśvari of Krottacheruvu Bukkasāgaram. The date corresponded, according to Mr. Swamikannu Pillai, to Sunday, September 24, A.D. 1581. The inscription has been noted in *Mack. Ins. Ced. Dts.*, p. 13, No. 4.

144. 179 *of* 1913.—(Kanarese.) On a slab lying near a sluice of the tank, in the same village. The Vijayanagara king Vīrapratāpa Achyutadēvarāya records in Śaka 1455, Vijaya, Phalguna, śu. di. 15, Saturday, that Bhandarāda Timmarasa, son of Apparasayya, made rent-free, the dēvadāya and brahmadāya lands below the tank of Hosakere, included in Penugoṇḍa, a district of Yeramanti-rājya. These had been so enjoyed since the time of Chikka-Oḍeya (probably Bukka I suggests Mr. Krishna Sastri), but had been assessed in corn and in coin owing to disturbances in the interval. The grant was made on the occasion when the king performed the *Lakshahōma* ceremony at Varadarājammana-pēṭhe. The stone was put up by Koṇḍapa under orders of Timmarasa at the elephant-sluice of the tank. The date corresponded, according to Mr. Swamikannu Pillai, to Saturday, February 28, A.D. 1534. See *Mack. Ins. Ced. Dts.*, p. 14, No. 5.

145. 180 *of* 1913.—(Telugu.) On a rock near the tank in the same village. Partially damaged record of the Vijayanagara king Kṛishṇarāya-Mahārāya, dated Śaka, *Angirasa*, śu. di. 12, Wednesday. Registers that the dēvadāya and brahmadāya lands under the tank Krottacheruvu in Penugoṇḍa-rājya which had been held rent-free (sarvamānya) from the time of Chikka-Oḍayalu had been re-assessed on account of certain disturbances in the interval. The king, now at Sivanasamudram on state business, ordered that the lands might be restored as before, and this was announced on the occasion of the Lakshahōma ceremony conducted at Penugoṇḍa. Kunama Nāyuḍu had this inscription engraved under orders of Rāyasam Koṇḍamarasayya Dēmarasayya. As to the date, Mr. Swamikannu Pillai says that the details are not enough for calculation. See *Mack. Ins. Ced. Dts.*, p. 13, No. 1.

Kottacheruvu.

146. On a stone situated in the fort at Kottacheruvu. A record of Sadāśivarāya of Vijayanagar, dated in Śaka 1489, Prabhava, mentions Nāgappa Nāyaḍu and records the remission of rent to a Brahman Bhāgavatulu Chāyappa. See *Ins. Ced. Dts.*, p. 14, No. 7.

Nallūru.

147. "In a small reservoir is a stone bearing an inscription, dated Śaka 1475 (A.D. 1553), recording the settlement of a water dispute by Rāma Rāju Kōnappadēva Mahārāju in the reign of Sadāśiva of Vijayanagar." See *Antiq.* I, 189.

Penukoṇḍa.

The fort of this historic place was built by Bukka I in 1354. For its description as well as the history of the place. See *Mad. Jour.* 1878, p. 166 ff; *Anantapur Gaz.*

148. 326 *of* 1901.—(Kanarese.) Dated in a *Sarvadhārin.* Gift by Bommarasa to the temple of Mailāradēva.

149. 327 *of* 1901.—(Telugu.) On the wall of the east gate of the fort, right of entrance. A much damaged record of Sadāśiva Rāya.

150. 328 *of* 1901.—(Kanarese.) On the same wall. A record of the time of Śrīraṅgarāya, dated in *Krōdhin*, making gift of tolls to the temple of Tiruvēṅgalanātha.

151. 329 *of* 1901.—(Telugu.) On the same wall. A much damaged record of Sadāśiva Rāya, dated in *Siddhārtin.*

152. 330 *of* 1901.—(Telugu.) On a boulder by the side of the path leading to the Narasimha temple on the top of the hill. A damaged private grant dated in Śaka 1558.

153. 331 *of* 1901.—(Telugu.) On a slab built into the floor of the same temple. A record of Śaka 1778, *Naḷa*, recording repairs, "when the glorious Mahārājadhirāja Rājaśrī Arbuthnot Sahib, born of the Hūṇa (European) race, was administering the 5 purganas beginning with the throne of the kingdom of Ghānagiri, *i.e.*, Penukoṇḍa.

154. 332 *of* 1901.—(Telugu.) On the gōpura of the same temple. A record of Śrīraṅgadēva dated in Śaka 1503, *Vikramā.* [The name of the king is misread as Jagadēva and date as 1183 by Mr. Sewell. See *Antiq.* I, pp. 103 and 120.]

155. 333 *of* 1901.—On the wall of the east gate of the fort, left entrance. A record of the time of Sadāśiva Rāya, dated in Śaka 1487, *Krōdhana*, recording gift of tolls by Rāmarāja, son of Tirumalrāja to a temple of Hanūmat.

156. 334 *of* 1901.—(Telugu.) On a slab built into the floor of the Sher Sahib mosque. A record of Sadāśiva Rāya, dated in Śaka 1487, *Krōdhana*, recording gift of land by the same to the Sōmēśvara temple. Incomplete.

157. 335 *of* 1901.—(Telugu.) A record of Rāmarāja, son of Tirumalarāja (date lost), making gift of a village.

158. 336 *of* 1901.—(Telugu.) On the south wall of the Āñjanēya temple at the north gate of the fort. A record of the time of

Śrīraṅga Rāya, dated Ś. 1499, *Dhātu*. Records that Chennappa Nāyuḍu, an officer of Tirumaladēva, repaired and extended the fort and defeated several Musalmān chiefs.

159. 337 *of* 1901.—(Telugu.) On the same wall. A record of the time of Sadāśiva Rāya, dated in Ś. 1489, *Prabhava*. Mentions Tirumalarāja, the son of Śrīraṅgarāja.

160. 338 *of* 1901.—(Kanarese and Sanskrit.) On the west wall of the same temple. A record of Vīra Harihara II, dated Ś. 1314, *Āṅgiras*, recording the building of the gōpura of the temple of Vīrabhadra by Marilapa.

161. 339 *of* 1901.—(Kanarese.) On the wall of a bastion at the north gate of the fort. A record of Ś. 1276, *Jaya*, in the reign of Vīra Bukhaṇa Uḍaiyar (I). See *Ep. Ind.*, Vol. VI, p. 327.

162. 340 *of* 1901.—(Kanarese.) On the wall of the same gate. A record of the reign of Sadāśiva Rāya, dated in Ś. 1466, *Krōdhin*, recording that Rāmarāja Viṭṭhalēśvara remitted certain taxes to the barbers.

163. 341 *of* 1901.—(Telugu.) On a slab set up in the compound of the reading room (the old site of the Kēśavasvāmi temples). Dated in the reign of Śrīraṅgadēva in Ś. 1502, Vikrama. Records gifts to a temple which had been built by Chennappa Nāyuḍu, an officer of Tirumaladēva.

164. 342 *of* 1901.—(Sanskrit.) On the wall of the maṇṭapa in front of the Avimuktēśvara temple. Much damaged. Mentions Dēvarāya.

165. 343 *of* 1901.—(Telugu.) On the south wall of the Rāmasvāmi temple. Records gift of a lamp by Kōnappaiyadēva mahārāja to the temple of Lakshmi Narasimha.

166. 344 *of* 1901.—On the rock close to the pond *(nāgarabhāvi)* on the top of the hill. In Nāgari. Illegible.

167. 345 *of* 1901.—(Kanarese.) On a slab placed by the side of the well in the Pārśvanātha temple. Records that it is the tombstone of Nāgaya, the lay disciple of Jinabhūshaṇabhaṭṭāraka dēva.

168. 584 *of* 1912.—(Kanarese.) On a pillar in the compound of the Sub-Collector's Office. Dated in Ś. 1339. A portion of the pillar on the right side has been apparently cut off. Seems to record the gift of this lamp-pillar.

169. *C.P. No.* 12 *of* 1914.—These register the gift by the Gaṅga King Mādhava of 65 paddy fields *(Kēdāra)* sowable with 25 *Kaṇḍukas* of paddy below the big tank of Paruvi in Paravivishaya, to the Brahman Kumāraśarman of the Vatsa gōtra and Taittirīya-charaṇa, on a full moon day of the lunar month of *Chaitra*. [The inscription gives the relative chronology of the Gaṅga and Pallava chiefs and is therefore of very great value. See *Mad. Ep. Rep.*, 1914, 83-4, for discussion and *J.R.A.S.*, Jan. 1915, where Dr. Fleet discusses it and shows how its evidences are supported by a Jain work on cosmography called *Lōkavibhāga*, discovered by Mr. R. Narasimhāchar of Mysore].

170. *C.P. No.* 17 *of* 1911.—A grant of Veṅkaṭa II, dated Ś. 1560, Pramāthin, which agrees word for word with the Kūniyūr grant. Records the restoration of certain villages originally granted by Vīra Naraśiṅga Rāya, Sadāśiva and Veṅkaṭa I, to the Daraga of Bābayya in Penukoṇḍa. The renewal of the grants was necessitated by the loss of the original documents on the occasion of the seizure of Penukoṇḍa by Immaḍi Hāvadi Baire Gauḍa of Peddarāya. [Mr. Krishna Sastri points out that Baire Gauḍa was the ruler of Doḍ-Ballapura, referred to by Rice in his *Gazr.*, Vol. II, p. 69. The chiefs of the line were of course feudatories of Penukoṇḍa, but evidently about 1630 a chief proved a rebel and seized Penukoṇḍa, itself for some time. As for Bābayya Durga Mr. Krishna Sastri believes it was the same as the shrine of the Mahomedan Saint Bābanatta to which much veneration was paid by all people for the success of its astrological forecasts. Hence the villages granted were known as *hōra* villages. The reputation of the shrine reached the far south and brought grants from such distant and orthodox rulers as Rāni Maṅgammāḷ of Madura. See C.P. No. 19 of 1911.]

171. *C.P.* 23 *of* 1911.—A grant of Śrīraṅga I (157-886), dated in Ś. 1498, Dhātri, saying that while he was at Udayagiri he conquered the inaccessible fortresses of Koṇḍavīḍu, Vinukoṇḍa, etc., and that he was at the time of the inscription abiding with all insignia of royalty at Penukoṇḍa. The grant registers the village of U (ra) jānchēre, surnamed Vengalāmbāpura, to a certain Lakshmīpati bhaṭṭa. [*See* Dēvanahalli plates of Śrīraṅga Rāya, Ś. 1506, *Mys. Arch. Rep.*, 1910, for details.]

Siddharāmpuram.

172. On a stone north of the village. A Telugu record dated in Ś. 1680, Bahudhānya, mentions Haṇḍe Rāmappa Nāyudu and records establishment of Śiva and Āñjanēya in the village. See *Mack. Ins., Ced. Dts.*, p. 15, No. 8.

TĀDPATRI TALUK.

Arkativemula.

173. On the southern gate of the Veṅkatēśvar pagoda. A grant of the village in Ś. 1481, *Raudri*, to the Brahmans of the place by Achyuta Rāya of the Vijayanagar dynasty. See *Mack. Ins., Ced. Dts.*, p. 129, No. 1.

174. In the same place. A Telugu record dated in Ś. 1481, Raudri, in the reign of Sadāśiva Mahārāya. Records that the Vīramushṭivāru granted an allowance to the local deity Rāmēśvara. *Ibid.*, No. 2.

175. Opposite the above inscription. A record dated in Hēvilambī granting some land to God " Beyapaka Devaru " by Jagadala Bōgarāya Dēva Mahārāya. See *Mack. Ins., Ced. Dts.*, p. 129, No. 3.

Challavarāpalle.

176. Mr. Sewell mentions on a stone in front of the Siva temple an inscription purporting to settle a dispute between this village and Dāditōṭa, 3 miles to the south-east.

Chilamakūru.

177. On a stone east of the village. A record of Gutti Erratimma Rāju in Ś. 1468, Parābhava, exempting the tax of the local barbers. See *Mack. Ins., Ced. Dts.*, p. 139, No. 38.

Chinnapolamāḍa.

178. On a stone near the old fort. A Telugu record in year Vishu, regarding the settlement of a dispute about a garden by the Brahmans of Timmapuram. *Ibid.*, p. 132, No. 12. [The inscription is of interest in showing the friendly spirit of villages.]

179. On a stone near the above. A record in *Krōdhana* in the time of Gutti " Hamagaudu Pamagaudu," saying that the boundary between the villages of Heralpolamāḍa and Chinnapolamāḍa were settled by the inhabitants and the land-mark stone was put up. *Ibid.*, No. 13.

180. On a stone in the bank of the Pinākini river. A record dated in Ś. 1210, Pārthiva. Records that Jagajini Raṅga Rāya Dēva Mahārāya granted a piece of land to God Sāmbaśiva. *Ibid.*, p. 134, No. 14.

Chintakuṇṭa.

181. On a stone in the pagoda of Paṭuchintakuṇṭa. A record of the reign of Pratāpa Jayadēva Mahārāya dated in Ś. 1449, Sarvajit. Records that " Casinani Vabal Naidu " set up the image of Obalēśvara and granted some land to it. *Ibid.*, p. 131, No. 7.

Dosalēḍu (Dāsalūr ?)

182. On a stone in the pagoda. Records that in a certain Raudri Nandyāla Timma Rāju and Koṇḍarāju granted one *puṭṭi* of dry land to the drummers and pipers of the Chennakēśava pagoda. *Ibid.*, p. 132, No. 11.

Goḍḍumarri.

183. In possession of Nārāyana Reḍḍi, a resident of the village. A.C.P. which is a copy of the inscription at Pārnapalle in Pulivenḍla taluk, Cuddapah district. See *Antiquities*, I, p. 116.

Kāḍavakallu.

184. On a stone in the local Chennakēśava pagoda. Records in Ś. 1438, Yuva, in the reign of Kṛishṇadēva Rāya, the construction of a maṇṭapa, compound wall, and a well in the temple by Timma Nāyuḍu, son of Channama Nāyuḍu. See *Mack. Ins., Ced. Dts.*, p. 130, No. 4.

185. On a stone near the round pagoda. A record of the Vijayanagara king Veṅkaṭapaṭi Rāya, dated in Ś. 1569, Sarvajit, mentions Penukoṇḍa Abba Bhaṭlu and his grant of four *tūms* of land to God Rāmēśvara. *Ibid.*, No. 5.

Mēdikurti.

186. On a stone in the village. A record in 'Hala Canara,' dated Ś. 1143, Vikrama, in the reign of Praṭāpa Chakravartin Siṅgaṇadēva at "Villanore." Records that Mallaya Sāhini, the chief of the merchants, set up an image of Jaṅgamēśvarā at Yellanore and granted three *vrittis* of land. See *Mack. Ins., Ced. Dts.*, p. 136, No. 28.

187. A record of Narasimha Rāya Uḍaiyār in Ś. 1428, *Vijaya*. Records that Tirumalayya dēva Mahārāja granted the village as free gift to God Nīlakaṇṭha at Naṭṭūr. *Ibid.*, p. 137, No. 29.

Nandulapād (Nandipād).

188. In the Garuḍasthamba pillar in the local Chennakēśava temple. A certain Timmarāju of "Palapullah" (Pātapalli ?) gave some land to Timmāji, son of Gopāji, for building a hall, in Ś. 1449, Sarvajit. *Mack. Ins., Ced. Dts.*, p. 91, No. 132.

Nittur.

189. On a stone in the local pagoda. Dated in the reign of Kṛishṇadēva Rāya in Ś. 1445, Svabhānu. Records that one "Vadamallunna" prevented the custom of supplying leaves to the 'circar' people and arranged for the *abhishēka* of the God with the water of the Chiranadi river. *Mack. Ins., Ced. Dts.*, p. 136, No. 30.

190. On a pillar in the temple. Records the gift of a *puṭṭi* of land to God Nīlakaṇṭha, by Timma Nāyuḍu in the time of Sadāśiva Rāya in Ś. 1466, Śōbhakrit. *Ibid.*, No. 31.

191. In the same pagoda. An effaced Kanarese record of Bhuvanēka-malla Dēva. *Ibid.*, No. 32.

192. In the "down-stone" of the temple. A grant of five *tūms* of land and allowances to the deity by the *Viramushṭi* disciples of Śiva. *Ibid.*, No. 33.

193. On a pillar of the Chennakēśava pagoda. A record of Ś. 1472, Saumya, making a gift of land to the God by Tirumala Nāyuḍu, in the reign of Sadāśiva Mahārāya. *Ibid.*, No. 34.

194. On a stone opposite to the above. A Kanarese grant of Praṭāpa Dēva Mahārāya in Hēvilambi. *Ibid.*, No. 35, page 138.

195. In the same place. A grant of 13½ *puṭṭis* of land to God Chenna Kēśava by "Jukkumpudi Tirumala Nāyuḍu" in the reign of Sadāśiva Rāya in Ś. 1472, Saumya. *Ibid.*, No. 36.

Pātapalli.

196. In a stone opposite to the Veṅkaṭāchalapati pagoda. A record in Ś. 1592, Sādhāraṇa, in which the inhabitants of 'Villalūr' allowed 3 *paṇams* per 100 on their revenue collections, to the deity. *Mack. Ins., Ced. Dts.*, p. 139, No. 40.

197. On a stone near Rāmēśvara shrine. The gift of one *Tūm* of land at Vellalore to the deity by the inhabitants of a village in Ś. 1671, Krōdhana. *Ibid.*, No. 41.

198. On the other side of the above inscription. A record dated in Ś. 1668, Śubhakrit, making the grant of one *Tūm* of land to God Rāmaliṅga by the inhabitants of Simhādripalle. *Ibid.*, No. 42.

Peddamallēpalli.

199. On the well of the Āñjanēya pagoda. A record dated in Ś. 1477, Krōdhi, regarding the raising up of the village boundary stones. Sadāśiva Rāya and a Dāsappa Nāyuḍu are mentioned. See *Ibid.*, No. 37, p. 137.

Sajjaladinne.

200. On a stone in the Vīrabhadra pagoda. Records gift of the village to the people (?) by Pammasāni Rāmaliṅga Nāyuḍu in Ś. 1486 in the reign of " Vīrapratāpa Dēva Mahārāyalu. " *Ibid.*, p. 130, No. 6.

201. On a stone between the Vīrabhadra and Āñjanēya shrines. A record of Ś. 1466, Krōdhi, in the reign of Vīra Narasimhadēva Mahārāya. A grant of taxes by Aliya Rāmarāja. *Ibid.*, No. 7.

202. On a stone north-east of the village. Records that Appaya and Goppaya built in Ś. 1438, Dhātu, in the reign of Kṛishnādēva Rāya, the pagoda of Bilvēśvara and granted the village of Lakshmīsamudram (besides 3 chakrams for each house) for worship. *Ibid.*, p. 131, No. 8.

Tāḍpatri.

See Fergusson's *Ind. and East. Arch.*, page 375, for a description of the local temples. Also Kelsall's *Bellary Manual*, pp. 48–9.

203. 338 *of* 1892.—(Kanarese.) In the north-west corner of the prākāra of the Rāmēśvara temple, first stone. A Jain record of Udayāditya, son of Sōmidēva and Kānchelādēvi, in Ś. 1120 expired, Kāḷayukta. The donor resided at Tāṭipara Tāḍpatri. Dr. Hultzsch suggests that the stone was probably transferred from some Jain building, of which no traces remain.

204. 339 *of* 1892.—(Telugu.) Third stone at the same place. A record in Paridhāvin. Mentions Pemmaya Dēva. See *Ins., Ced. Dts.*, p. 135, No. 24.

205. 340 *of* 1892.—(Telugu.) Fifth stone at the same place. A record of the Vijayanagara king Kṛishṇarāya, dated Ś. 1435 expired, Śrīmukha. A gift of land by Sāḷuva Gōvindayya. See *Ins., Ced. Dts.*, p. 135, No. 22.

206. 341 *of* 1892.—(Telugu.) Sixth stone at the same place. A record of the Vijayanagara king Achyutadēva, dated Ś. 1453 expired, Khara. See *Ins., Ced. Dts.*, p. 135, No. 28.

207. 342 *of* 1892.—(Telugu.) Seventh stone at the same place. A record of the Vijayanagara king Vīra-Narasimharāya in Ś. 1431 expired, Śukla. Mentions the minister Sāḷuva-Timma. See *Mack. Ins., Ced. Dts.*, p. 134, No. 20.

208. 343 *of* 1892.—(Telugu.) Eighth stone at the same place. A record of the Vijayanagara king Vīra-Narasimharāya. Mentions in Ś. 1429 expired, Prabhava, the minister Sāḷuva-Timma. This inscription is in *Ins., Ced. Dts.*, p. 135, No. 23.

209. On a stone in the pagoda of Raṅgaswāmi on the banks of the Pinākini. A gift of land to the temple warden by Timma Nāyanigāru in Ś. 1585, Vijaya. *Ins., Ced. Dts.*, p. 35, No. 825.

210. In a street at Tāḍpatri. Gift of one "Dharanum" for every 100 pagodas of the Tādipurti revenue by the inhabitants, to God Tiruvēṅgalanātha, in Ś. 1585, Śōbhakrit. *Ibid.*, p. 836, No. 27.

211. In a stone in the pagoda of Chintalarāya. A gift of 3 puṭṭis of land in Ś. 1500, Bahudhānya, by Pammasāni Timma Nāyuḍu, in the reign of Śrīraṅgadēva Mahārāya of Karnāṭaka. *Ibid.*, p. 833, No. 85.

212. In the same place. Gift of 5 *Tūms* of land in Villalore to the deity by Liṅgaṇṇa, son of Kṛishṇama Rāju in Ś. 1586, Vijaya. *Ibid.*, No. 86.

213. In the same place. Gift of land by Mādhava Dāsa in Ś. 1486, Raktākshi. *Ibid.*, No. 87.

214. On the stone in the same temple. Gift of allowances for Tiruvēṅgalanāthaswāmi in Ś. 1509, Sarvajit, by Pammasāni Nāyuḍu. *Ibid.*, No. 88.

215. On a stone in the same. Records that in Ś. 1485, Rudhirōtkāri, one Kampaṇa Yellappa purchased and give away one Tūm land to the deity. *Ibid.*, No. 89.

Velamakūru.

216. Near the local Hanūmat pagoda. A record in Ś. 1421, Virōdhin, in the reign of Kṛishṇadēva Rāya, saying that Dāsappa Nāyuḍu granted 10 Tūms of paddy and fixed a fee of 4 *Gāruḍakāsu* per day to God Āñjanēya. *Ibid.*, p. 132, No. 80.

Yellanore.

217. A paper grant of a Mullapulla Rāmakṛishṇappa in Ś. 1679, Īśvara, allowing 3 pagodas per annum on the custom house at "Vellore" to one Śēshāchārya. *Ibid.*, p. 140, No. 43.

ARCOT NORTH DISTRICT.

ARCOT NORTH GENERAL.

These plates are given in Mr. Sewell's *Antiquities*, Vol. II. Almost all of them are either in the office of the Collector or Judge, or in the Madras Museum.

(*A*) *No. 4 of Sewell's List of Copper Plates.*—Records grants by a Chōḷa sovereign in the years Ś. 1008 or 1011 (A.D. 1086 or 1089), to which period they cannot, palaeographically, belong. "Moreover they bear a seal at the top in characters resembling the Persian, but which no one whom I have yet met with can decipher; and this would seem to be a clear anachronism. This grant is on a leaden plate, coated with a thin sheet of copper. It purports to be a grant by Rāja Vīra Chōḷa in Ś. 1011 (A.D. 1089) in the year of the Kaliyuga 4190 and cyclic year Plavaṅga. But Ś. 1011 corresponds to the cyclic year Śukla, twenty-two years subsequent to Plavaṅga. It seems difficult to suppose that all these plates can be forgeries, partly from their number, and partly because no forger would be so foolish as to annex the Persian seal to such a document." See Madras Lists for details.

(*B*) *Nos. 177* and *178 of Sewell's List.*—These are exact facsimiles of the inscription above. *Ibid.*

(*C*) *No. 205 of Sewell's List.*—A private grant to a maṭham. No date or Sovereign's name. Modern.

(*D*) *No. 206 of Sewell's List.*—A Vijayanagar grant by Achyutadēva, having the usual Vijayanagar emblems on the seal. The grant is one of lands to the Tirupati temple in Ś. 1466 ("Rasarasāvabdīndu"), year Vikāri. The document mentions that Achyuta began to make grants for charitable purposes in Ś. 1455 (A.D. 1533).

(*E*) *No. 207 of Sewell's List.*—A Vijayanagar grant executed by and in the reign of Achyutadēva. The document testifies to the grant of the village of Nārāyaṇapuram to a Brahman in Ś. 1459 (A.D. 1537). The document is a very important one in one respect, as it fixes Achyuta's relationship 'as younger brother' to Krishṇadēva.

(*F*) *No. 208 of Sewell's List.*—Records a grant by Vijayadeva or Vijaya Bhūpati, son of Dēvarāya (I). The name of the year Vikriti being clear, the Śaka era being mentioned without any figures. The inscription is thus very irregular.]

(*G*) *No. 209 of Sewell's List.*—(Sanskrit in old Grantha characters.) The Pallava sovereign Nripatuṅga, son of Dantivarman, grants, in the sixth year of his reign, some lands to Brāhmans in the village of Pratimā Dēvi Chaturvēdimaṅgalam. No date is given. Nripatuṅga is said to have married Prithvīmāṇikka, daughter of Bhānumāli. [Mr. Sewell is unaware of Nripatuṅga's position in Pallava genealogy.]

(*H*) In possession of the North Arcot Collector. A record in Sanskrit (Grantha) and Tamil, of the Chōḷa king Parakēsarivarman Rājēndra Chōḷa I in his sixth year. See *S.I.I.* III, Part III. Also No. 30 of 1905–06.

ARKŌNAM TALUK.

Aṇaikkaṭṭattūr near Kaḍambattūr.

1. 288 *of* 1895.—(Tamil.) On a stone. A much damaged record in the ninth year of Pārthivēndravarman, recording a private grant of land to a temple of Ādityadēva which has now disappeared. [Parthivēndravarman was a contemporary of Āditya II. Was the deity named after the latter ?]

Kāvērippākkam.

2. 381 *of* 1905.—(Tamil.) On the north wall of the central shrine in the Sundara-Varada-Perumāḷ temple. An unfinished record in the sixth year of the Chōḷa king Rājakēsarivarman.

3. 382 *of* 1905.—(Tamil.) On the west and south walls of the same shrine. An incomplete record in the sixth year of the Chōḷa king Rājakēsarivarman (Ariñjaya ?) Records gift of 90 sheep for a lamp by a merchant of Kīrttimāṭṭāṇḍa-Kālapriyam, a village in Śiru-Timiri-nāḍu, a district of Paḍuvūr-kōṭṭam. The deity is called Kīrttimārttāṇḍa Kālapriyadēva. [The Government Epigraphist points out, on the authority of Karhād inscription, that the temple should have been built by the Rāshṭrakūṭa Kṛishṇa III (939-68). For while encamped at Mēlpādi, it says, he established his followers in the southern provinces and built shrines to Kālapriya, Gaṇḍamārttāṇḍa, Kṛishṇa and others.]

4. 383 *of* 1905.—(Tamil.) On the south wall of the central shrine in the Sundara-Varada-Perumāḷ temple. A record of the Vijayanagara king Mallikārjunarāya, son of Vīrapratāpa-Dēvarāya II, in Ś. 1377, Yuvan. Records a private agreement among certain merchants that, on marriage occasions, a certain amount of money should be set apart to meet the repairs of the Kēśava-Perumāḷ temple at Kāvērippākkam *alias* Vikrama-śōḷa-chaturvēdimaṅgalam.

5. 384 *of* 1905.—(Tamil.) On the same wall. A fragment of record in the eleventh year. Mentions Karaivaḷi-kaṇḍapurappēṭṭai in Paḍuvūr-kōṭṭam and the citizens of Lōkamahādēvipuram.

6. 385 *of* 1905.—(Tamil.) On the north wall of the central shrine in the Varadarāja-Perumāḷ temple in the same village. A record of the Vijayanagara king Veṅkaṭapatidēva-Mahārāya (I) in Ś. 1514, Nandana. Registers certain arrangements made for celebrating a festival in the temple of Aḷagiyarāma-Perumāḷ.

7. 386 *of* 1905.—(Tamil.) On the north and west walls of the same shrine. A record of the Vijayanagara king Vīra-Kampaṇa-Uḍaiyār II, son of Vīra-Bokkaṇa-Uḍaiyār in Ś. 1292, Sādhāraṇa. Mentions the free village (*taniyūr*) of Kāvērippākkam *alias* Vikrama-śōḷa-chaturvēdimaṅgalam in Paḍuvūr-kōṭṭam, a district of

Jayaṅgoṇḍa Chōḷa-manḍalam. Records the sale of the village of Kaḍappēri in Kalavaippaṟṟu of the same kōṭṭam. Mentions a coin named *Virachampaṅ-kuligai*.

8. 387 *of* 1905.—(Tamil.) On the west wall of the same shrine. A record in the eighth year of Tribhuvanachakravartin Kōnērinmēlkoṇḍān. Records gift of land for the celebration of a festival called Sundara-Pāṇḍyanśandi. Mentions Kāvērippākkam in Toṇḍaimaṇḍalam and the temple of Aruḷāḷa Perumāḷ at Tiruvattiyūr (i.e., Conjeeveram). The land was to be used for growing red water-lilies, garlands of which had to be offered to the god on the occasion.

9. 388 *of* 1905.—(Tamil.) On the same wall. A damaged record of the Vijayanagara king Śrīraṅgadēva-Mahārāya (Raṅga VI) in Ś. 1559. The cyclic year is not distinct. The Kallakkuruchchi grant is by the same king in A.D. 1644-45. See *Ep. Ind.* VII, Appendix No. 545.

10. 389 *of* 1905.—(Tamil.) On the south wall of the same shrine. A record in the nineteenth year of Tribhuvanachakravartin Vijaya-Gaṇḍagōpāladēva (1250—83). Registers a gift of land for the temple of Aḷagiya-Perumāḷ at Kāvērippākkam *alias* Vijayagaṇḍagōpālachaturvēdimaṅgalam by Sāḷukki-Nārāyaṇan Alluvimarśan.

11. 390 *of* 1905.—(Tamil.) On the same wall. A record of the Vijayanagara king Kampaṇa-Uḍaiyār II, son of Vīra-Bokkaṇa-Uḍaiyār I in Ś. 1295, Ānanda. Records sale of land. Mentions the free village (taniyur) of Kāvērippākkam *alias* Vikrama-Sōḷachaturvēdimaṅgalam in Paḍuvūr-kōṭṭam. Refers to a gift made by Malli-nāḍan Śambuvarāyar.

12. 391 *of* 1905.—(Tamil.) On a stone built into the floor close to the south wall of the same shrine. A record in the seventeenth year of the so-called Gaṅga-Pallava king Vijaya-Kampavarman. Records gift of gold. Mentions Kāvirippākkam *alias* Avaninārāyaṇachaturvēdimaṅgalam.

13. 392 *of* 1905.—(Tamil.) On the south wall of the inner maṇṭapa of the same temple. A record of the Vijayanagara king Mallikārjunadēva Mahārāya, son of Vīra-Pratāpa Dēvarāya II,* in Ś. 1381, Pramādin. Records a gift for the merit of Naraśiṅgarāja-Uḍaiyār. Mentions the great assembly (mahāsabhai) of Kāvirippākkam. In *Madr. Ep. Rep.*, 1906, p. 82, paragraph 47, the epigraphist identifies Vīrapratāpa Dēvarāya, Mallikārjūna's father, with the younger brother of Dēvarāya II known as Srīgiri. He is mentioned in the 2nd Act of the Sanskrit drama composed by Gaṅgādhara.

14. 393 *of* 1905.—(Tamil.) On a stone built into the south wall of the first prākāra of the same temple. Fragment of a record. Mentions three village committees, viz., 'the great men of the

annual committee,' 'the great men of the garden committee' and 'the great men of the tank committee.'

15. 394 *of* 1905.—(Tamil.) On a stone built into the north wall of the maṇṭapa in front of the same temple. A fragment of record of the "Gaṅga-Pallava" king Nripatuṅgavarman, the date of which is lost. Mentions Māṅgāḍu-nāḍu, a subdivision of Paḍuvūr-kōṭṭam and Kāviḍippākkam *alias* Amaninārāyaṇa-chaturvēdi-maṅgalam in the same kōṭṭam. [For a fanciful origin of the place see *N.A. Manual*, p. 438.]

16. 395 *of* 1905.—(Tamil.) On another stone built into the same wall. Fragment of a record. Mentions Kāviḍippākkam *alias* Avaninārāyaṇa-chaturvēdimaṅgalam and '*the great men of the wards committee.' The 'tank committee' was appointed to look after a lamp gift.* See No. 14 for other committees.

17. 396 *of* 1905.—(Tamil.) On a stone built into the west wall of the same maṇṭapa. Fragment of a record. Mentions the big tank *(periya-ēri)* and the '*tank committee' (ēri vārigam).*

18. 397 *of* 1905.—(Tamil.) On a stone built into the ceiling of the same maṇṭapa. A fragment of record in the twenty-fifth year of the "Gaṅga Pallava" king Vijaya Nripatuṅgavikramavarman. Records gift of gold.

19. 398 *of* 1905.—(Tamil.) On another stone built into the same ceiling. Fragment of a record of the sixth year of the "Gaṅga-Pallava" king Vijaya Kampavarman.

20. 399 *of* 1905.—(Tamil.) On a pillar in the same maṇṭapa. A much damaged record the king's name in which is lost. Mentions the temple called Tiruppanṟīśvaram.

21. 400 *of* 1905.—(Tamil.) On another pillar in the same maṇṭapa. A damaged record in the twenty-fifth year of the Chōḷa king Rājakēsarivarman.

22. 401 *of* 1905.—(Tamil.) On the third pillar in the same maṇṭapa. A damaged record in the twenty-fourth year of the Chōḷa king Rājakēsarivarman.

23. 402 *of* 1905.—(Tamil.) On the fourth pillar in the same maṇṭapa. A record in the fourteenth year of the Pāṇḍya king Perumāl Sundara-Pāṇḍyadēva, 'who was pleased to take every country' (i.e.), Jatāvarman Sundara Pāṇḍya I (1251–64). Mentions Miḷalaikkūṟṟam in Pāṇḍināḍu.

24. 403 *of* 1905.—(Telugu.) On a slab set up in front of the masjid. A record of Sultan Abdula Pātasaha in Ś. 1591, Kīlaka. Records the building of the masjid. At the top of this slab is an inscription in Hindustani, which is perhaps another copy of the same.

25. 404 *of* 1905.—(Tamil.) At the foot of the entrance into the Amman shrine in the Koṅkaṇīśvara temple in the same village. A fragment of record in the fifteenth year of the "Gaṅga-Pallava" king Nripatuṅgavarman. Mentions the temple of Tirumēṟṟali at Kāvaḍipākkam.

26. 405 *of* 1905.—(Tamil.) On the south wall of the central shrine in the Muktīśvara temple in the same village. A damaged record in the twelfth year of the Chōla king Tribhuvanachakravartin Kulōttuṅga-Chōladēva III. Mentions Śeṅgēṇi Ammayappan Vīramiṇḍan *alias* Attimallan Vikrama-Chōḷa Śambuvarāyan.

27. 406 *of* 1905.—(Tamil.) At the entrance into the gōpura of the same temple. A mutilated record in the thirteenth year of the Pallava king Nandivarman.

28. 407 *of* 1905.—(Tamil.) On a stone built into the bund of the tank in the same village. A fragment of record in the tenth year of the Chōla king Parakēsarivarman. Mentions the temple of Tiruvākkīśvaram.

29. 408 *of* 1905.—(Tamil.) On another stone built into the same bund. A record of the Chōla king Rājakēsarivarman Vīrarājēndradēva. A fragment of the historical introduction of the king.

30. 409 *of* 1905.—(Tamil.) On a third stone built into the same bund. A mutilated record.

31. 410 *of* 1905.—(Tamil.) On a fourth stone built into the same bund. A fragmentry record. Appears to register an endowment for offerings and for burning a perpetual lamp.

32. 411 *of* 1905.—(Tamil.) On a fifth stone built into the same bund. A fragment of record in the sixteenth year of the Chōla king Parakēsarivarman Rājēndra-Chōḷadēva I.

33. 412 *of* 1905.—(Tamil.) On one of the inscribed stones kept in the Public Works Department bungalow in the same village. A fragmentary record. Seems to contain a Śaka date, the first figure of which is 8, and the second 2, while the third is lost.

34. 413 *of* 1905.—(Tamil.) On another stone in the same place. A fragmentary record. Mentions a temple called Tirunattapperumānaḍigal and Kāvaḍippākkam.

35. 414 *of* 1905.—(Grantha.) On the third stone in the same place. A fragmentary record. Mentions a Chōḷa feudatory named Parāntakapallavarāyan of Umbala-nāḍu and the Chōḷa kings Jananātha and Mummaḍi-Chōla.

***36.** 415 *of* 1905.—(Tamil.) On the fourth stone in the same place. A fragmentary record of the Chōḷa king Kulōttuṅga-Chōḷadēva.

---

* It may be pointed out that the *Mack. Mss.* (*Inscrns. South Dts.*, p. 68) contain an inscription under "Cauvaripaukum District." It records the grant of the village of "Vadacara paroombacum" to a Brahman named "Sooreyana Dechter" in Ś. 1526, Krōdhin, in the time of Venkatapati I (1586–1614).

Kilpākkam.

37. 35 *of* 1911.—(Tamil.) On the north base of the Narēndrēśvara temple. A record in the twelfth year of Tribhuvanachakravartin Śrīraṅganātha Yādavarāya. Records that a son of Kāḷiṅgarāya named Āpatsahāya Pallavaraiyan renovated with stone the dilapidated wooden roof of the Ardhamaṇṭapa in the temple and plastered it with flat tiles.

38. 36 *of* 1911.—(Tamil.) On the north and west bases of the same temple. A record of the Vijayanagara king Sadāśivarāya in Piṅgala (i.e., Ś. 1470). Records gift of a dancing girl by a certain Śellappar, to the temple of Rājākkaḷ-Nāyanār Rājēndraśōḷa-Perumān. [Śellappa is not improbably the Sāluva chief who figures in the troubles of Achyuta Rāya in the early part of his reign.]

39. 37 *of* 1911.—(Tamil.) On the south base of the same temple. An incomplete record in the nineteenth year of the Chōla king Rājēndra-Chōla. Seems to register a gift of land and refers to Kīḷpākkam, the eastern hamlet of Nittavinōda-chaturvēdimaṅgalam and to the god Rājāditta-Viṭaṅka in the temple of Rājādittēśvara.

40. 38 *of* 1911.—(Tamil.) On the south wall of the same temple. A record in the seventeenth year of the Chōḷa king Parakēsarivarman alias Uḍaiyār Śrī-Rājēndra-Chōladēva (I) records that the great assembly of Nityavinōda-chaturvēdimaṅ galam in Mēnmalai-Mēlūrnāḍu in Jayaṅgoṇḍachōlamaṇḍalam, having assembled in the temple of Śrīkailāsa alias Mummaḍiśōḷa-Īśvaramuḍaiyār (modern Narēndrēśvara?) in that village, borrowed 20 *kaḷanju* of gold from the temple of Rājāditta-Īsvaramuḍaiyār (named evidently after Rājāditya) and placed it in the hands of the village committee (*ūr-vāriyam*) to supply oil, as interest on the amount borrowed.

Mahēndravāḍi.

41. 13 *of* 1896.—(Grantha.) On a pillar in the rock-cut temple near Sholinghur Railway station. A record of the Pallava king Guṇabhara. See *Ep. Ind. IV*, 152 ff, where Dr. Hultzsch edits the inscription. It records that king Guṇabhara caused to be made on the bank of the Mahēndra-taṭāka, in the city of Mahēndrapura, this temple of Murāri or Mahēndra vishṇugriha. [The king is Mahēndravarman I, the excavator of the Trichinopoly and Vallam caves also. See *Ep. Rep.* 1896, p. 4, para. 9; *S. Ind. Inscns.*, vol. II, No. 72; *Ibid* I, Nos. 33 and 34; *Manual of North Arcot*, vol. II, p. 438.]

Mudūr.

42. 30 *of* 1911.—(Tamil.) On two broken slabs lying near the Tiruvēndīśvara temple. A record of .
kiramavarman, the date of which is lost. Seems to record a gift of land which the donees were required not to mortgage.

Takkōlam.

The temple of Jalanāthēśvara in this village has been called *ūral* (fountain) in its inscriptions and in the *Periapurāṇa.* It is also known as Nanditīrtha, a name which occurs in the inscriptions of the Vijayanagara kings. All these names are derived from a natural spring which is conducted through the mouth of a stone *nandi* into a small tank.

43. 1 *of* 1897.—(Tamil.) On the south wall of the central shrine of the Jalanāthēśvara temple. A record in the second year of Kō-Vimalādityavarman. Records gift of sheep for a lamp.

44. 2 *of* 1897.—(Tamil.) On the same wall. A record in the 27th year of the Rāshṭrakūṭa king Kaṇṇaradēva (i.e. Kṛishṇa III) "who conquered Kachchi and Tanjai." Records gift of sheep for a lamp. [This corroborates the Ātakūr inscription which says that at Takkōlam the feudatory of Kṛishṇa III, Bhūtuga, killed the Chōḷa Rājāditya in 949–50.]

45. 3 *of* 1897.—(Tamil.) On the same wall. A record in the eleventh year of the Chōḷa king Kō-Rājarājakēsarivarman. Records gift of gold.

46. 4 *of* 1897.—(Tamil.) On the west wall of the same shrine. A record in the seventh year of Ko-Pārthivēndrādhipativarman. Records gift of sheep for a lamp. See 49 and 56 below, and 288 of 1895 at Kaḍambattūr.

47. 5 *of* 1897.—(Tamil.) On the same wall. A record in the 24th year of the Chōḷa king Ko-Rājakēsarivarman. Records gift of a silver vessel by Piridipati, the son of Māramaraiyar, "who must be identical with one of the two Gaṅga kings named Prithvīpati." The Rājakēsarivarman here referred to "was probably Āditya I."

48. 6 *of* 1897.—(Tamil). On the same wall. A record in the fifth year of the Chōḷa king Kō-Parakēsarivarman. Records gift of sheep for a lamp.

49. 7 *of* 1897.—(Tamil.) On the north wall of the same shrine. A record in the third year of Kō-Pārthivēndravarman. Records gift of couch by his queen Arumoḷinaṅgai. See No. 4 above.

50. 8 *of* 1897.—(Tamil.) On the same wall. A record in the nineteenth year of the Chōḷa king Madiraikoṇḍa Kō-Parakēsari-varman (Parāntaka I). Records gift of paddy.

51. 9 *of* 1897.—(Tamil.) On the same wall. A record in the 28th year of the Chōḷa king Madiraikoṇḍa Kō-Parakēsarivarman (Parāntaka I). Records gift of sheep for a lamp.

52. 10 *of* 1897.—(Tamil.) On the same wall. A record in the 21st year of the Chōḷa king Madiraikoṇḍa Kō-Parakēsarivarman (Parāntaka I). Records gift of sheep for a lamp.

53. 11 *of* 1897.—(Tamil.) On the same wall. A record in the 20th year of the Chōḷa king Madiraikoṇḍa Kō-Parakēsarivarman (Parāntaka I). Records gift of sheep for a lamp.

54. 12 *of* 1897.—(Tamil.) On the same wall. A record in the 21st year of the Chōḷa king Madiraikoṇḍa Kō-Parakēsarivarman (Parāntaka I). Records gift of paddy and gold.

55. 13 *of* 1897.—(Tamil.) On the same wall. A record in the tenth year of Kō-Pārthivēndravarman. Records gift of gold. See No. 46 above.

56. 14 *of* 1897.—(Tamil.) On the same wall. A record in the fourth year of Kō-Pārthivēndravarman. Records gift of sheep for a lamp to an image of Durga. See No. 46 above.

57. 15 *of* 1897.—(Tamil.) On the same wall. A record in the third year of the Chōḷa king Kō-Parakēsarivarman *alias* Rājēndra-Chōḷadēva (I). End built in.

58. 16 *of* 1897.—(Tamil.) On the same wall. A record in the seventeenth year of the Chōḷa king Tribhuvanachakravartin Kulōttuṅga-Chōḷadēva (III). Records gift of land by Tirukkāḷattidēva *alias* Yādavarāya. [This chief was, like Vīra Narasimha Yādavarāya and Tammusiddhi, the feudatory of Kulōttuṅga III. For these chiefs see Tiruvoṟṟiyūr, Tiruppāśūr and Conjeeveram lists.]

59. 17 *of* 1897.—(Tamil.) On the same wall. A record in the twelfth year of the Chōḷa king Tribhuvanachakravartin Kulōttuṅga-Chōḷadēva (III). Records gift of money for a lamp.

60. 18 *of* 1897.—(Tamil.) On the east wall of the second prākāra of the same temple. A record in the 36th year of the Chōḷa king Kō-Rājakēsarivarman *alias* Kulōttuṅga-Chōladēva (I ?). Records gift of land.

61. 19 *of* 1897.—(Tamil.) On a pillar in front of the shrine of the goddess in the same temple. An incomplete record of the Chōḷa king Kō-Rājakēsarivarman *alias* Vīra-Rājēndradēva. (I ?).

Taṇḍālam.

62. *Inscription* 1 *of* 1892.—(Tamil.) On a rock near the local tank. Records that a Pallava Mahārāja who ruled over the Tamil country built a sluice for the tank at Taṇḍālam.

Tirumalāpuram (Tirumālpūr).

63. 265 *of* 1906.—(Tamil.) On the south wall of the central shrine in the Maṇikaṇṭhēśvara temple. A record in the fourth year of the Chōḷa king Rājakēsarivarman *alias* Śrī-Mummaḍi-Chōḷadēva. Records gift of gold. [The king referred to is Rājarāja I (985—1013) who took the title Mummuḍichōḷa in the third year of his rule, i.e., 988 A.D.]

64. 266 *of* 1906.—(Tamil.) On the same wall. A record in the thirteenth year of Pārthivēndrādivarman, 'who took the head of

Vīra-Pāṇḍya.' Records gift of two lamps by Vijjavai-Mahādēviyār, daughter of Nandi-varma-Kāḍupaṭṭigaḷ. (Nandivarman III?).

65. 267 *of* 1906.—(Tamil and Grantha.) On the same wall. A damaged record in the third year of Pārthivēndrādhipativarman. Records the building of the temple and the enclosing verandah by the Virāṭa king Anayamān *alias* Paramaṇḍalāḍitya.

66. 268 *of* 1906.—(Tamil.) On the same wall. A record in the sixth year of the Chōḷa king Rājakēsarivarman (985—1013). Records a gift by Madurāntakan Kaṇḍarāḍittan, i.e., Gaṇḍarāditya, son of Madhurāntaka Chōḷa. See No. 78.

67. 269 *of* 1906.—(Tamil.) On the same wall. A damaged record of the Chōḷa king Rājarāja I, the date of which is lost. Records gift of a lamp.

68. 270 *of* 1906.—(Tamil.) On the same wall. A record in the 27th year of the Chōḷa king Kulōttuṅga-Chōḷadēva. Records gift of land.

69. 271 *of* 1906.—(Tamil.) On the same wall. A record in the 46th year of the Chōḷa king Rājakēsarivarman *alias* Chakravartin-Kulōttuṅga-Chōḷadēva (I). Records gift of money for ten lamps to the temple of Tirumarpēruḍaiyār in Valla-nāḍu, a district of Dāmar-kōṭṭam in Jayaṅkoṇḍa-Chōḷamaṇḍalam.

70. 272 *of* 1906.—(Tamil.) On the same wall. A record in the seventh year of the Chōḷa king Parakēsarivarman *alias* Tribhuvana-chakravartin Vikrama-Chōḷadēva (1118–35). Records sale of land. Mentions the temples of Āḷuḍaiyār, Tirumarpēruḍaiyār, Uttama-Chōḷīśvaram uḍaiyār and Avimuttīśvaramuḍaiyār.

71. 273 *of* 1906.—(Tamil.) On the same wall. A record in the sixth year of the Chōḷa king Tribhuvanachakravartin Vīrarājēndra-Chōḷadēva. Records gift of 32 sheep for a lamp.

72. 274 *of* 1906.—(Tamil.) On the same wall. A record in the 38th year of the Chōla king Rājakēsarivarman *alias* Chakravartin Kulōttuṅga-Chōladēva (I). Records gift of 30 cows for a lamp.

73. 275 *of* 1906.—(Tamil.) On the same wall. A record in the fifteenth year of the Chōḷa king Tribhuvanachakravartin Rājarāja-dēva. Records gift of 64 cows for two lamps and of ornaments.

74. 276 *of* 1906.—(Tamil.) On the same wall. An incomplete record in the eighth year of the Chōḷa king Tribhuvanachakravartin Rājarājadēva.

75. 277 *of* 1906.—(Tamil.) On the same wall. A record in the 34th year of the Chōḷa king Tribhuvanachakravartin Kōnērinmai-koṇḍān Tribhuvanavīradēva (i.e., Kulōttuṅga III). Records gift of land to the image of Uttama-Chōḷīśvaramuḍaiyār set up by a certain Chēdirāyan.

76. 278 *of* 1906.—(Tamil.) On the same wall. A much damaged record of the Chōḷa king Rājakēsarivarman (985—1013)

'who destroyed the ships at Kāndaḷūr-Śālai,' the date of which is lost.

77. 279 *of* 1906.—(Tamil.) On the same wall. A record in the twelfth year of the Chōḷa king Rājarājakēsarivarman (985—1013) 'who destroyed the ships at Kāndaḷūr-Śālai.' Records gift of 90 sheep for a lamp.

78. 280 *of* 1906.—(Tamil.) On the same wall. A partially damaged record in the fourteenth year of the Chōḷa king Parakēsarivarman. Provides for the bathing every month of the image of the god with 108 pots. The provision was made by Madurāntakan Kaṇḍarādittar, i.e., Gaṇḍarāditya, son of Madurāntaka (970—85).

79. 281 *of* 1906.—(Tamil.) On the same wall. A record in the twelfth year of the Chōḷa king Rājarājakēsarivarman, (985—1013) 'who destroyed the ships at Kāndaḷūr-Śālai.' Registers an agreement of the sabha of Prithivīmahādēvi-chaturvēdimaṅgalam.

80. 282 *of* 1906.—(Tamil.) On the west wall of the same shrine. A record in the twelfth year of the Chōḷa king Rājarājakēsarivarman (985—1013), 'who destroyed the ships at Kāndalūr-Śālai.' Registers an agreement of the villagers of Paḷugūr to pay 60 *kaḷanjus* or 225 *kāḍis* of paddy every year in Paḷugūr-nāḍu, a subdivision of Maṇaiyir-kōṭṭam. Refers to the fact that Madurāntakan Kaṇḍarādittar had fined the men in charge of the store-room in the fourth year of the king's reign. Mentions also the fourteenth year of some king whose name is lost. The fine was evidently the result of the inquiry referred to in No. 81.

81. 283 *of* 1906.—(Tamil.) On the same wall. A record in the fourth year of the Chōḷa king Rājakēsarivarman *alias* Mummaḍi-Chōḷadēva (985—1013). Refers to an enquiry with a committee of five men (amidst whom were Adikāri Śiṟṟadikāri) made by Madurāntakan Kaṇḍarādittanār into the affairs of the Agnīśvara temple at Tirumalpēru, as the temple lands had been misappropriated and the offerings reduced to two *nāḷis* of rice. For a similar enquiry three years later at Tiruvallam see *S.I.I.*, III, p. 102; *Ep. Rep.* 1911, p. 69.

82. 284 *of* 1906.—(Tamil.) On the same wall. A record in the eleventh year of the Chōḷa king Rājarājakēsarivarman (985—1013) 'who destroyed the ships at Kāndalūr-Śālai.' Refers to the setting up of an image of Umābhaṭṭārakiyār *also* called Ādisundaradēva-dēviyār and records a gift of land to it. 500 *kuḷis.*

83. 285 *of* 1906.—(Tamil.) On the same wall. A record in the third year of the Chōḷa king Rājakēsarivarman. Records gift of 15 *kaḷanjus* for a lamp by Madurāntakan Kaṇḍarādittan. [1 *Tirunārāṇa Uḷakku,* 1/8 Int.] See N.A. 78.

84. 286 *of* 1906.—(Tamil.) On the north wall of the same shrine. A record in the fourteenth year of the Chōḷa king

Kō-Nōinmēl-koṇḍān. Records gift of the village Śiṟṟiyaṟṟūr, to the temple at Tirumālpēru. Says that the village assembly misappropriated some temple property, and the temple authorities complained to the king, while at Conjeeveram. The king sent for both the parties and, after enquiry, fined the assembly and restored the property. See N.A. 81.

85. 287 *of* 1906.—(Tamil.) On the same wall. A record in the forty-first year of the Chōḷa king Rājakēsarivarman *alias* Chakravartin śrī-Kulōttuṅga-Chōḷaḍēva. Records sale of land by the villagers of Nittavinōdanallūr in Dāmar-nāḍu, a district of Dāmarkōṭṭam in Jayaṅgoṇḍa-Chōḷamaṇḍalam.

86. 288 *of* 1906.—(Tamil.) On the same wall. A record in the twelfth year of the Chōḷa king Rājarājakēsarivarman (985—1013) 'who destroyed the ships at Kāndaḷūr-Śālai.' Registers an agreement of the villagers of Maṇavil in Maṇavil-nāḍu, a district of Maṇavilkōṭṭam.

87. 289 *of* 1906.—(Tamil.) On the same wall. A damaged record of the Chōḷa king Rājarājakēsarivarman (985—1013) 'who destroyed the ships at Kāndaḷūr-Śālai,' the date of which is lost.

88. 290 *of* 1906.—(Tamil.) On the same wall. A record in the twenty-sixth year of the Chōḷa king Rājakēsarivarman *alias* Chakarvartin Śrī-Kulōttuṅga-Chōḷadēva. Records sale of land. At the bottom of this is an inscription of the twenty-seventh year of the same king.

89. 291 *of* 1906.—(Tamil.) On the north, west and south walls of the same shrine. A record in the twenty-first year of the Chōḷa king Parakēsarivarman *alias* Uḍaiyār śrī-Rājēndra-Chōḷadēva (I, 1012—43). Records sale of land by the *sabha* of Puduppākkam in Puriśaināḍu, a district of Maṇaiyil-kōṭṭam.

90. 291-*A of* 1906.—(Tamil.) On the north, west and south walls of the same shrine. A record in the twenty-first year of the Chōḷa king Parakēsarivarman *alias* Uḍaiyār śrī-Rājēndra-Chōḷadēva (I, 1012—43). Records sale of land.

91. 292 *of* 1906.—(Tamil.) On the same wall. A record in the tenth year of the Chōḷa king Parakēsarivarman *alias* śrī-Rājēndra-Chōḷadēva (I). Records gift of money for supplying four *kaḷanju* of *sidari* by a native of the Chōla country. Mentions Punnai *alias* Parakulāntaka-Chaturvēdimaṅgalam in Vallanāḍu, a district of Dāmar-kōṭṭam in Jayaṅgoṇḍa-Chōḷamaṇḍalam.

92. 292-*A of* 1906.—(Tamil.) On the same wall. A record in the third year of the Chōḷa king Rājakēsarivarman. Records gift of a lamp by Madurāntakan Kaṇḍarādittan. See N.A. 78.

93. 293 *of* 1906.—(Tamil.) On the same wall. A record in the fifteenth year of the Chōḷa king Rājarāja-Rājakēsarivarman (i.e., A.D. 1000). Records gift of gold (15½ *kaḷanju*).

94. 294 *of* 1906.—(Tamil.) On the same wall. A record in the third year of the Chōḷa king Rājakēsarivarman. Records sale of land. Mentions Madurāntakan Kaṇḍarādittan and Śōḷamādēviyār *alias* Panchavanmādēviyār, queen of Mummuḍi-Chōla (i.e., Rajarāja I).

95. 295 *of* 1906.—(Tamil.) On the same wall. A record in the third year of the Chōḷa king Rājakēsarivarman. Records gift of gold (15 *kaḷanjus*) by Madurāntakan Kaṇḍarādittan for lamp. [Daily 1 *ulakku* of oil was to be supplied by Śerukūr people; ⅛ pon penalty.] See N.A. 78.

96. 295-*A of* 1906.—(Tamil.) On the same wall. An incomplete record in the thirteenth year of the Chōḷa king Rājarāja-Rājakēsarivarman (985—1013). Above this is another damaged Chōḷa inscription.

97. 296 *of* 1906.—(Tamil.) On the north wall of the first prākāra of the same temple. A record in the eleventh year of the Chōḷa king Rājakēsarivarman *alias* Uḍaiyār śrī-Kulōttuṅga-Chōḷadēva. Built in at the end. Records gift of a lamp.

98. 297 *of* 1906.—(Tamil.) On the west and north walls of the same prākāra. A record in the thirtieth year of the Chōḷa king Parakēsarivarman *alias* Uḍaiyār śrī-Rājēndra-Chōḷadēva (I, 1012—43). Records sale of land by the Sabhā of Kūram *alias* Śōḷamāttāṇḍa chaturvēdimaṅgalam in Nirvēlūr-nāḍu, a district of Ūṟṟukkāṭṭukōṭṭam. Mentions *Rājarājan-kāśu*.

99. 298 *of* 1906.—(Tamil.) On the west wall of the same prākāra. A record in the thirty-seventh year of the Chōḷa king Madiraikoṇḍa Parakēsarivarman (i.e., Parāntaka I, 905—47). Records sale of land.

100. 299 *of* 1906.—(Tamil.) On the south, west and north walls of the same prākāra. A mutilated and damaged record of the Chōḷa king Parakēsarivarman *alias* Uḍaiyār śrī-Rājēndra-Chōḷa dēva (I, 1012—43), the date of which is lost.

101. 300 *of* 1906.—(Tamil.) On the east wall of the central shrine in the ruined Vishṇu temple in the same village, right of entrance. A record in the twenty-sixth year of the Chōḷa king Madiraikoṇḍa Parakēsarivarman (Parāntaka I). Records gift of a lamp.

102. 301 *of* 1906.—(Tamil.) On the same wall. A record of the Chōḷa king Madiraikoṇḍa Parakēsarivarman (Parāntaka I), the date of which is lost. Records gift of gold for a lamp by Prince Parāntakan Uttamaśīli. See *Ep. Rep.*, 1909, p. 89.

103. 302 *of* 1906.—(Tamil.) On the same wall. A record in the thirty-ninth year of the Chōḷa king Madiraikoṇḍa Parakēsarivarman (Parāntaka I). Records gift of 96 sheep for a lamp.

104. 303 *of* 1906.—(Tamil.) On the same wall. A record in the thirty-first year of the Chōḷa king Madiraikoṇḍa Parakēsarivarman (Parāntaka I). Records gift of a lamp to the temple of

Ninraruḷina-Perumanaḍigaḷ at Gōvindapāḍi in Valla-nāḍu, a district of Dāmarkōṭṭam by the Chōḷa queen Amudan Perrāḷ *alias* Pallavan Mādēviyār of Kānattūr in Umbaḷa-nāḍu.

105. 304 *of* 1906.—(Tamil.) On the south wall of the same shrine. A record in the third year of Parthivēndravarman. Records a gift by Nārāyaṇakramavittan *alias* Vaiḍumbarāditta Brahmādhirājan.

106. 305 *of* 1906.—(Tamil.) On the same wall. A damaged record in the tenth year of the Chōḷa king Rājarājakēsarivarman (Rājarāja I).

107. 306 *of* 1906.—(Grantha and Tamil.) On the same wall. An unfinished record in the third year of the Chōḷa king Rājakēsarivarman. Records gift of gold for feeding Brāhmaṇas by Madurāntakam Achchapiḍāran (Aditya in the Sanskrit portion), son of Vīrachōḷā-Iḷaṅgōvēḷār of Koḍumbāḷūr in Kōnāḍu.

108. 307 *of* 1906.—(Tamil.) On the same wall. An unfinished record in the seventeenth year of the Chōḷa king Madiraikoṇḍa Rājakēsarivarman (not identified, but probably Gaṇḍarāditya). Records gift of a lamp. The characters do not seem to belong to the period of Parāntaka I. [In *Ep. Ind. IV*, p. 331, Dr. Hultzsch identifies the king bearing this name and title with Madurāntaka, son of Gaṇḍarāditya, but Venkayya points out that this is untenable as the latter was a Parakēsarivarman and called Uttama Chōḷa.]

109. 308 *of* 1906.—(Tamil.) On the same wall. A record in the seventeenth year of the Chōḷa king Madiraikoṇḍa Rājakēsarivarman (Gaṇḍarāditya ?) Records gift of 96 sheep for a lamp. The characters do not seem to belong to the period of Parāntaka I. See No. 108.

110. 309 *of* 1906.—(Tamil.) On the same wall. A damaged record in the thirty-first year of the Chōḷa king Madiraikoṇḍa Parakēsarivarman (Parāntaka I). Records a gift made on the day of a solar eclipse.

111. 310 *of* 1906.—(Tamil.) On the same wall. A damaged record in the fortieth year of the Chōḷa king Parakēsarivarman, 'who took Madirai and Īḷam (Ceylon)' (i.e., Parāntaka I). Records gift of land for a lamp. [Parāntaka undertook his invasion of Ceylon about his thirty-seventh year, i.e., A.D. 942.]

112. 311 *of* 1906.—(Tamil.) On the same wall. A record in the thirty-fourth year of the Chōḷa king Madiraikoṇḍa-Parakēsarivarman (Parāntaka I). Records gift of gold.

113. 312 *of* 1906.—(Grantha and Tamil.) On the same wall. A record in the third year of the Chōḷa king Rājakēsarivarman. Records gift of a lamp.

114. 313 *of* 1906.—(Tamil.) On the same wall. A record in the forty-first year of the Chōḷa king Parakēsarivarman 'who took Madurai and Īḷam (Ceylon)' (i.e., Parāntaka I). Records gift of sheep for a lamp by Pūvan Māran of Neḍiyataḷi in Koduṅgōḷūr, a town in Malai-nāḍu. [This corroborates Parāntaka's mastery over the Chēras.]

115. 314 *of* 1906.—(Tamil.) On the same wall. A record in the thirty-first year of the Chōḷa king Madiraikoṇḍa Parakēsarivarman (Parāntaka I). Records gift of a lamp by the Chōḷa queen Amanimādēviyār. The temple is called Ninṟaruḷina-Perumanāḍigal at Gōvindapāḍi in Valla-nāḍu, a subdivision of Dāmar-kōṭṭam, a district of Tanḍaiya-nāḍu.

116. 315 *of* 1906.—(Tamil.) On the same wall. An incomplete record of the Chōḷa king Tribhuvanachakravartin śrī-Rājarājadēva, the date of which is lost. Records gift of a lamp.

117. 316 *of* 1906.—(Tamil.) On the same wall. A damaged record in the tenth year of the Chōla king Tribhuvanachakravartin Rājarājadēva.

118. 317 *of* 1906.—(Tamil.) On the same wall. An incomplete record in the twenty-first year of the Chōla king Parakēsarivarman *alias* Uḍaiyār śrī-Rājēndra-Chōḷadēva I (1012–43).

119. 318 *of* 1906.—(Tamil.) On the same wall. A record of the Chōḷa king Madiraikoṇḍa Parakēsarivarman (Parāntaka I, 905—47), the date of which is lost; built in at the end.

120. 319 *of* 1906.—(Tamil.) On the same wall. A record in the twelfth year of the Chōḷa king Madiraikoṇḍa Parakēsarivarman (905–47). The temple is called Perumanāḍigal of Gōvindapāḍi in Tonḍai-nāḍu.

121. 320 *of* 1906.—(Tamil.) On the same wall. A damaged record in the fourteenth year of the Chōḷa king Parakēsarivarman. Seems to record a gift of land for offerings.

122. 321 *of* 1906.—(Tamil.) On the same wall. A record in the fourteenth year of the Chōḷa king Parakēsarivarman. Refers to the setting up of an image of Maṇavāḷa Perumāḷ and registers an endowment for offerings to it.

123. 322 *of* 1906.—(Tamil.) On the same wall. A record in the nineteenth year, 152nd day of the Chōḷa king Rāja-rāja-Rājakēsarivarman (985–1013 A.D.). Records gift of land. Reference to the Śrī-Vaishṇavas of 18 nāḍs. The inscription refers to the silting of lands on the Śiṟṟāṟṟūr on account of the Pālār floods. Of this 1,000 *kulis* by the 12-span-pole were reclaimed by a person, named Rājarāja-viśākam and given away to the temple for the offering of 4 nāḷis. Details of offerings given. [The interesting point in the inscription is the mention of the traditional Śrī-Vaishṇavas of the 18 Nāḍs in such an early age.]

124. 323 *of* 1906.—(Tamil prose and verse.) On the west wall of the same shrine. A damaged record in the twelfth year of Pārthivēndravarman. Records that Anaiyaman Paramaṇḍalādittan built a manṭapa in the temple.

125. 324 *of* 1906.—(Grantha and Tamil.) On the same wall. A damaged record in the twelfth year of Pārthivēndravarman. Records a gift by the Virāṭa king Anaiyamān. His ancestors are mentioned as in N.A. 65.

126. 325 *of* 1906.—(Tamil.) On the same wall. A damaged record of the Chōḷa king Rājakēsarivarman, the date of which is lost. Records gift of sheep for a lamp.

127. 326 *of* 1906.—(Tamil.) On the same wall. The beginning of this inscription has not been traced. Provision is here made for the recitation of *Tiruvāymoli*, the *prabandha* of Nammāḷvār. [For a discussion of his date see *Jour. S. Ind. Assocn.*, June 1914.]

128. 327 *of* 1906.—(Tamil.) On the north wall of the same shrine. A record in the tenth year of Pārthivēndradivarman, "who took the head of Vīra-Pāṇḍya." Records gift of 96 sheep for a lamp by the Vānarāja Aḷagamaiyan. See N.A. 65 and 125.

129. 328 *of* 1906.—(Tamil.) On the same wall. A record in the thirteenth year of Pārthivēndrādivarman. Records gift of land for feeding Brāhmaṇas. The temple is called Gōvindapāḍi-Āḷvār at Śiṟṟiyāṟṟūr in Mēl-Paḷugūr-nāḍu, a subdivision of Maṇavilkōṭṭam.

130. 329 *of* 1906.—(Tamil.) On the same wall. A damaged record in the fifth year of the Chōḷa king Rājakēsarivarman. Records gift of 96 sheep for a lamp.

131. 330 *of* 1906.—(Tamil.) On the same wall. A record in the thirty-second year of the Chōḷa king Rājakēsarivarman *alias* Śrī-Rājādhirājadēva (1018—53). Records sale of land to the temple of Uyyakkoṇḍāḷvār at Gōvindapāḍi.

132. 331 *of* 1906.—(Tamil.) On the same wall. Built in at the beginning.

133. 332 *of* 1906.—(Tamil.) On the same wall. An unfinished record in the thirteenth year of the Chōḷa king Tribhuvanachakravartin Rājarājadēva.

134. 333 *of* 1906.—(Tamil.) On the same wall. A record in the tenth year of the Chōḷa king Rājarājakēsarivarman, 'who destroyed the ships at Kāndaḷūr-Śālai (985—1013).' Records gift of gold by Kulakkuḍaiyan Arunilai Śrī-Krishnan *alias* Mūvēnda Piḍavūr vēḷār. A *tiruppadiyam* beginning with *kolanār-kulal* composed by the donor's father in praise of Gōvindapāḍi-Āḷvār had to be sung on the occasion of a festival.

135. 334 *of* 1906. (Tamil.) On the same wall. A record in the thirtieth year of the Chōḷa king Rājakēsarivarman *alias* Uḍaiyār Śrī-Rājādhirājadēva. Records loan of money.

136. 335 *of* 1906.—(Tamil.) On the same wall. A record in the eleventh year of the Chōḷa king Rājarājakēsarivarman, 'who destroyed the ships at Kāndaḷūr-Śālai (985—1013). Records gift of 96 sheep for a lamp by a native of the Chōla country to the image of

Anumadēva set up by him at Gōvindapāḍi in Toṇḍaināḍu. [Venkayya notes that this epigraph is interesting for the fact that the worship of Hanūmān prevailed as early as the tenth century.]

137. 336 *of* 1906.—(Tamil.) On the same wall. Built in at the beginning. Records gift of gold.

138. 337 *of* 1906.—(Tamil.) On the same wall. A record in the third year of the Chōḷa king Parakēsarivarman *alias* Śrī-Rājēndra-Chōḷadēva (I, 1012—43). Seems to record a gift of gold. A fragmentary inscription of Rājarāja I. is found close to this.

139. 338 *of* 1906.—(Tamil.) On the same wall. A record of the Chōḷa king Parakēsarivarman, the date of which is lost. Records gift of 120 sheep for a lamp by the Chōḷa queen Panchavanmahādēvi.

140. 339 *of* 1906.—(Tamil.) On the same wall. A record of the Chōḷa king Parakēsarivarman, the date of which is lost. Records gift of 96 sheep for a lamp.

141. 340 *of* 1906.—(Tamil.) On the west and south walls of the same shrine. A damaged record of the Chōḷa king Rājarāja-Rājakēsarivarman *alias* śrī-Rājarājadēva (I, 985—1013), the date of which is lost. Records gift of land.

142. 341 *of* 1906.—(Tamil.) On the same walls. A record in the thirty-ninth year of the Chōḷa king Parakēsarivarman, 'who took Madirai and Iḷam (Ceylon)' (i.e., Parāntaka I, 905—47). Records sale of land.

143. 342 *of* 1906.—(Tamil.) On the north, west and south walls of the same shrine. A record in the twenty-third year of the Chōḷa king Rājarāja-Rājakēsarivarman *alias* Śrī-Rājarājadēva (I, 985—1013). Records gift of gold by a native of the Pāṇḍya country.

144. 343 *of* 1906.—(Tamil.) On the same walls. A record in the twelfth year of the Chōḷa king Parakēsarivarman. Records gift of ninety-six sheep for a lamp.

145. 344 *of* 1906.—(Tamil.) On the same walls. A record in the ninth year of the Chōḷa king Parakēsarivarman. Records gift of gold.

Valarpuram.

146. 26 *of* 1911.—(Tamil.) On the east wall of the maṇtapa in front of the central shrine in the Toṇḍīśvara temple; right of entrance. A damaged record in the eighteenth year of the Pāṇḍya king Jaṭāvarman Tribhuvanachakravartin Kōnērimēlkoṇḍān Sundara-Pāṇḍyadēva. Records gift of land to the temple of Nāgīsuramuḍaiya-Nāyanār at Valaikuḷam *alias* Pattarsuravalli-Saṅgraonarāma-chaturvēdimaṅgalam in Mēlūr-nāḍu, a subdivision of Mēlūrkōṭṭam, which was a district of Jayaṅgoṇḍa-Chōḷamaṇḍalam. [It is difficult to identify the Pāṇḍya king.]

147. 27 *of* 1911.—(Tamil.) On the south wall of the central shrine of the Sundararājaperumāḷ temple in the same village. An unfinished record of the Vijayanagara king Vīrapratāpa Achyutayyadēva-Mahārāya, 'who took all countries,' in Ś. 1457, Durmukhi. Records the privileges granted to certain priests in the temple of Aḷagiya Maṇavāḷa-Perumāḷ at Valaikuḷam in Vēlūrnāḍu, in Nārāyaṇapura-paṟṟu, in Kunṟavarttana-kōṭṭam of Chandragiri rājya in Jayaṅgoṇḍa-Chōḷamaṇḍalam.

148. 28 *of* 1911.—(Tamil.) On the north wall of the same shrine. An unfinished record of the Vijayanagara king Vīra-pratāpa-Sadāśivadēva-Mahārāya in Ś. 1470, Piṅgaḷa. Records that Ondari Vasava-Nāyakkar, son of Śennama-Nāyakkar, agent of Doratta Vāsavāyadēva-Mahārāja, presented an image of Śēnai-mudaliyār to the temple of Aḷagiyamaṇavāḷa-Perumāḷ at Vala-kulam and built a maṇtapa for the merit of Vasavarāja [who was evidently an important chief like Chinna Timmaiyadēva Mahārāja, etc. See Naraśiṅgapuram inscription, 250 of 1910, in the time of Sadāśiva. He was perhaps connected with Immaḍi Doratta Sindaya Dēva of 294 and 295 of 1897 at Maṇimaṅgalam].

149. 29 *of* 1911.—(Tamil.) On the base of the same shrine. An unfinished record of the Vijayanagara king Harihara II (Ariyaṇa Uḍaiyār) in Prabhava (i.e., Ś. 1310). Mentions the assembly of Sēnaikuḷam and the temple Śittiramēḷi-Viṇṇagar-Emberumān.

Vēlūrpālaiyam.

150. A Copper Plate grant of the sixth year of the Pallava king Ko-Vijaya Nandivikramavarman (III), the son of Dantivarman (by the Kadamba princess Aggaḷa-Nimmaḍi) who was the son of Nandivarman II (by his queen Rēvā). The record says that Nandi-varman's minister, a certain Yagñabhaṭṭa *alias* Bappa Bhaṭṭāraka, built a temple for Śiva in the village of Tirukkāṭṭuppaḷḷi, which the king granted to the temple at the request of Kumārāṅkuśa, 'a jewel of the Chōḷa race,' for maintaining daily worship and a feeding institute. The village granted was in Nāyaru-nāḍu in Puḷar-kōṭṭam. The inscription details the *parihāras* (redemptions) and privileges granted to the deity as the owner of the village. See *Ep. Rep.*, 1911, p. 60–4 and *Ep. Ind.*, Vol. II, pt. V, where Mr. Krishna Sastri edits it.

ARNI TALUK.

Aḍaipālam.

151. 395 *of* 1911.—(Grantha and Tamil.) On the south wall of the central shrine in the Kālakaṇṭhēśvara temple. A record of Chinna-Bomma-Nāyaka of Vēlūr in Ś. 1504, Chitrabhānu. Registers that Appaiya-Dīkshita constructed the temple. [Aḍai-palam was the birth-place of this great scholar who has left more than 100 works. He was patronized by Chīnna Bomma Nāik, the vassal of Tirumala I of the last Vijayanagara dynasty. See *S. Ind. Inscrns.*, Vol. I, p. 84, and p. 65, on the Virinchipuram and Vēlūr inscriptions. See also *Ep. Ind.*, IV, pp. 269—78. Appaiya-Dīkshita was also patronized by Veṅkaṭa I,—a proof of which is seen in the colophon to his *Kuvalayānanda* (कुवलयानन्द). For his works as a philosopher, grammarian, etc., see *Ep. Rep.*, 1912, p. 89; Dr. Hultzsch's *Rep. Sans. MSS.*, p. xiii; and various notices in Rangācharya's *Des. Catal, Sans. MSS.*

Dēvikāpuram.

152. 351 *of* 1912.—(Tamil.) On the west and south walls of the central shrine in the Brihadāmba temple. Records in Ś. 1399, Hēviḷambi, gift of land to the temple of Tirumala-Uḍaiya-Nāyanār at Dēvakkapuram by Rāyappuḍaiya of Koṇḍapalli and others. [See N. A. *Manual,* II, p. 316.]

153. 352 *of* 1912.—(Tamil.) On the south wall of the first prākara of the same temple. A record of the Vijayanagara king Krishṇadēva-Mahārāya in Ś. 1442, Bahudhānya, Makara, ba. di. 5, Friday, Hasta; corresponding to 21st January, 1519 A.D. The king bears Sāḷuva titles. Registers a lease of certain temple lands to Tirumalai-Nāyaka, one of Kannaḍiya-Nāyakas, living in Marudaraśar-Paḍaivīḍu, by the temple treasurer Īśāna-Śivāchārya of Bhikshā-maṭha at Davakkāpura on the southern bank of Seyyāru, which was a village near Rājagambhīran-malai in Murugamaṅgala-ppaṟṟu, a subdivision of Mēlkunṟa-nāḍu in the district of Paḷagunṟa-kōṭṭam in Jayaṅgoṇḍaśōḷa-maṇḍalam.

154. 353 *of* 1912.—(Tamil.) On the same wall. A record of the Vijayanagara king Krishṇadēva-Mahārāya in Ś. 1441, Bahudhānya Karkaṭaka, śu. di. 13, Tuesday, Aśvini, Siddhayōga. Registers the right of cultivation of temple lands (*uḷavu-kāṇi-yākshi*) granted to a certain Sadāśiva-Nāyaka of Marudaraśar-Paḍai-vīḍu. [The date is a little irregular. Mr. Swamikannu Pillai says that Aśvini and Siddhayōga can occur only on *Friday,* January 7, A.D. 1519.]

155. 354 *of* 1912.—(Tamil.) On the same wall. A record of the Sāḷuva king Immaḍirāyadēva-Mahārāya, son of Naraśiṅgarāya-dēva-Mahārāya (the founder of the usurping line), in Ś. 1429, Raktākshi (wrong) Mīna, ba. di. 10, Friday, Uttiram. Registers a similar right granted to a resident of Dēvakkapuram by the temple trustee, gurukkaḷ, Viśvēśvara-Śivāchārya of Bhikshā-maṭha and others. [*Raktākshi* corresponds to Ś. 1427, and then the date would be Friday, 28th February 1505.] See Nos. 166 and 190.

156. 355 *of* 1912.—(Tamil.) On the same wall. Records in Ś. 1422, Raudri, Karkaṭaka, śu. di. 7, Friday, Attam, corresponding to 3rd July 1500, gift of land in the dēvadāna village of Śembiyamaṅgalam, a house at Dēvakkapuram and food in the temple, to two persons who had to sing in the temple. The grant was made by Tirumalai-Nāyaka and Īśvara-Nāyaka, sons of Eṭṭappa-Nāyaka, for the merit of Narasa-Nāyaka (the founder of the Tuluva dynasty, who died in 1503).

157. 356 *of* 1912.—(Tamil.) On the same wall. A record of the Vijayanagara king Achyutayyadēva-Mahārāya, son of Narasa-Nāyaka-Uḍaiyār in Ś. 1455, Vikriti (wrong), Śinga, su. di. 10, Friday, Uttiram. The king has a long list of *birudas*. Records that Kaḷāttīsura-Nāyaka, son of Tirumalai-Nāyaka of Marudaraśar Paḍaivīḍu, was granted the right of supervision, etc., in the temple and the enjoyment of certain lands at Murugamaṅgalam, from Īśāna Śivāchārya of Bhikshā-maṭha, the trustees and the Kaikkōḷa-mudalis of the Tirumala-Uḍaiya-Nāyinār temple at Dēvakkapuram. [See No. 201 below.]

158. 357 *of* 1912.—(Tamil.) On the west wall of the same prākāra. Records in Ś. 1425, Rudhirōdgarin, gift of land and a house in the village Kailāsa, to a certain Samarapuṅgava-Dīkshita for the merit of king (svāmi) Narasa-Nāyaka (the Tuluva usurper) 'who went to Śivalōka (i.e., died),' by (his subordinates) Tirumalai-Nāyaka and Īśvara-Nāyaka. [The great Vaishṇava writer Mahāchārya had a Samarapuṅgava for his teacher. See *Trien. Cat. Sans. MSS.*, 1910–3, pp. 25 and 1012. Also *Des. Cat. Sans. MSS.*, Vol. X, p. 3642.]

159. 358 *of* 1912.—(Tamil.) On the same wall. A record of the Vijayanagara king Kṛishṇadēva-Mahārāya in Ś. 1441, Bahudhānya, Karkaṭaka, śu. di. 13, Tuesday, Aśvini, Siddhayōga. The king has Saluva titles. Records a gift of revenue, amounting to 33½ *paṇam* to the temple of Tirumala-Uḍaiya-Nāyinār at Dēvasthanam Dēvakkapuram by Harihara-Nāyaka, son of Mallappa Nāyaka of the Kannaḍiya-Nāyakas living at Marudaraśar Paḍaivīḍu for the merit of the king and Tirumalai-Nāyaka. For date see 154 above.

160. 359 *of* 1912.—(Tamil.) On the same wall. Records in Ś. 1418, Durmati, gift of land at Murugamaṅgalam by Tirumalai-Nāyaka and Īśvara-Nāyaka for providing offerings, incense, etc., at festivals.

161. 360 *of* 1912.—(Tamil.) On the same wall. Records in Śubhakrit, that a certain Nāyinappa-Nāyaka provided ghee for the festival of Tiruvādirai in the same temple in order to secure merit for Aḍaippam Mallappa-Nāyaka.

162. 361 *of* 1912.—(Tamil.) On the same wall. A record of the Vijayanagara king Vīrapratāpa Kṛishṇayadēva-Mahārāya in Ś. 1443, Vikrama, Kārtigai, Ēkadaśi, Monday, corresponding to 9th July 1520. Records that Sadāśiva-Nāyaka provided ghee for lamps during the festival of Tirukkārtigai in the same temple, for the merit of chief (svāmi) Tirumalai-Nāyaka.

163. 362 *of* 1912.—(Tamil.) On the north wall of the same prākāra. A record of the Vijayanagara king Kṛishṇayadēva-Mahārāya in Ś. 1444, Vrisha. Records gift of ghee for the same festival by the daughter of the Kannaḍiya chief Dēvappuḍaiyār at Marudaraśar Paḍaivīḍu.

164. 363 *of* 1912.—(Tamil.) On the same wall. A record of the Vijayanagāra king Mahāmaṇḍalēśvara Kṛishṇayadēva-Mahārāya in Ś. 1447, Sarvajit. Records gift of ghee for lamps by Śrīranganāthar, the maṇiakāran (monegar) of *Iḍaitturai*, for the merit of Namaśśivāya-Nāyaka, son of Mallappa-Nāyaka of Marudaraśar-Paḍaivīḍu.

165. 364 *of* 1912.—(Tamil.) On the same wall. A record of the Vijayanagara king Vīrapratāpa Kṛishṇayadēva-Mahārāya in Ś. 1454. The king bears Sāḷuva titles. Records grant of the tax *Paṭṭādai-nūlayam*, at 1½ *paṇam* per annum on each loom, to the temple, for the merit of Kaḷattīśura-Nāyaka.

166. 365 *of* 1912.—(Tamil.) On the same wall. A record of the Vijayanagara king Vīrapratāpa Kṛishṇayadēva-Mahārāya in Ś. 1446, Chitrabhānu, Tai, śu. di. 10, Uttiram, Saturday (=28th March 1523). Records gift of land and a house in the dēvadāna village Sōrappūṇḍi to Vaḍamaḷaiyar, one of the Paṇḍits (vidvan) of Arruvanpāḍi, by Viśvēśvara Śivāchārya of the Bhikshā-maṭha at Dēvakkapuram, the Kaikkōḷa-mudalis and other trustees of the temple. The record is stated to have been engraved on the *kumudappādi* of the temple. [See NA 155 above. Vaḍamalayar was probably the Tamil poet who wrote the *Machchapurāṇa* and *Niḍūrttalapurāṇā*. See *Abhidānachintāmaṇi*, p. 840. Viśvēśvarā might be the Śāktaic and Vira Śaiva author of the *Śyāmārchanataraṅgiṇi* referred to in *Rais. Catal.* II, pp. 288 and 438; but it is doubtful. He ought not to be confounded with the Dharma-śāstraic author of the *Karma vipāka* (see *Des. Cat. San. MSS.*, Vol. II, p. 2626) or the Advaitic writers referred to in NA 190].

167. 366 *of* 1912.—(Tamil.) On the same wall. A record of the Vijayanagara king Vīrapratāpa Kṛishṇayadēva-Mahārāya in Ś. 1444, Vikrama, Kumbha, śu. di. full-moon, Friday, Uttiram, corresponding to 22nd February 1521. Records gift of land and two houses to a certain *Aṭṭavaṇai* Veṅkappa who secured for the temple the village of Śorappūṇḍi as a gift from the king.

168. 367 *of* 1912.—(Tamil.) On the same wall. A record of the Vijayanagara king Vīrapratāpa Kṛishṇayadēva-Mahārāya in Ś. 1452, Sarvadhāri, Kārtigai, śu. di. 10, Uttiram, Saturday (=29th March 1529). Registers that the trustees of the temple granted to a certain Ambalattāḍi the right of cultivating *(ulavu-kāṇi)* the dēvadāna village of Kāmākshi-rāvuttan-taṅgal and fixed 15 *paṇam* and 20 *kalams* of paddy to be paid to the temple every year.

169. 368 *of* 1912.—(Tamil.) On the same wall. A record of the Vijayanagara king Vīrapratāpa Kṛishṇayadēva-Mahārāya in Ś. 1444, Vikrama, Kumbha, śu. di. 10, Saturday, Punarpūśam which corresponded to 16th February 1521. Records gift of the village Uvattūr with its hamlet Tāraipāḍi, to the same temple by a certain Ammaiyappa Nāyinār, as a *tirunāmakkāṇi*. On receiving this, Iśāna-Śivāchārya of the Bhikshā-maṭha and other trustees of the temple made the same donor the lessee of the village and presented a house. See No. 201.

170. 369 *of* 1912.—(Tamil.) On the same wall. A record of the Vijayanagara king Vīrapratāpa Kṛishṇayadēva-Mahārāya in Ś. 1453, Virōdhi, Śittirai, śu. di. 10, Attam. Registers the permanent lease *(ulavu-kāṇiyākshi)* of Dēvarāyan-paṭṭāḍai to a Kannaḍiya-Nāyaka of Gaṅgapuram in Paṅgala-nāḍu.

171. 370 *of* 1912.—(Tamil.) On the same wall. A record of the Vijayanagara king Kṛishṇayadeva-Mahārāya in Ś. 1450, Sarvadhāri, Ani, śu. di. Uttiram, Monday (=22nd June 1528). Records gift of ghee for a lamp.

172. 371 *of* 1912.—(Tamil.) On the same wall. A record of the Vijayanagara king Kṛishṇadēva-Mahārāya in Ś. 1443, Vikrama. Records gift of ghee for a lamp by a lady of Marudaraśar-Paḍaivīḍu.

173. 372 *of* 1912.—(Tamil.) On the same wall. A record of the Vijayanagara king Vīrapratāpa Kṛishṇayadēva-Mahārāya in Ś. 1431, Śukla, Makara (should be Kanni śu. di. 10), Sunday, Tiruvōṇam, corresponding to 23rd September 1509. Records gift of the hamlet Śiṅgayarāvuttan-taṅgal near Kayilāyam as a *Kāṇiyākshi*, to a certain Tiruppāṇi Vasuvana-Uḍaiyār, by Tirumalai Nāyaka, son of Eṭṭappa Nāyaka, and others. The donee was evidently an officer in charge of the works connected with the temple.

174. 373 *of* 1912.—(Tamil.) On the south wall of the second prākāra of the same temple. A record of the Vijayanagara king Achyuṭayyadēva-Mahārāya, son of Vīrapratāpa Narasa-Nāyaka in Ś. 1452, Vikriti, Makara, śu. di. 13, Monday, Pūśam, corresponding to 30th January 1531. Records sale, by the trustees of the Dēvikāpuram temple, of land at Suvarappūṇḍi to a temple of Uḍaiyavar Sadāśivamūrti built by Tirumalai Nāyaka, son of Sadāśiva Nāyaka of Maṛudarasar-Paḍaivīḍu, at Vaḍa-Kayilam which was the *tirunāmakkāṇi* village of Tirumala Uḍaiyār. Maḍapatyam Kaḷattīśura-Nāyaka and Bhikshāmaṭham Īśāna Śivāchārya are mentioned among the trustees.

175. 374 *of* 1912.—(Tamil.) On the same wall. A record of the Vijayanagara king Achyutayyadēva-Mahārāya, son of Vīrapratāpa Narasa-Nāyaka in Ś. 1454, Vikriti (wrong) Paṅguni, śu. di. 11, Monday (=27th February 1531). Registers that certain families of shepherds at Śeṛruppaṭṭu were dedicated to the temple as *tiruviḷakku-kuḍi* by Koṇḍama-Nāyaka, after securing their services with the permission of Kaḷattīśura-Nāyaka who was then governing the Paḍaivīṭṭuśīrmai.

176. 375 *of* 1912.—(Tamil.) On the same wall. A record of the Vijayanagara king Achyutayyadēva-Mahārāya, son of Vīrapratāpa Narasa-Nāyaka in Ś. 1452, Vikriti, Simha, śu. di. 14, Sunday, Tiruvōṇam, corresponding to August 7, A.D. 1530. Registers that the trustees of the temple leased out some lands at Piramanampākkam to Vīramahēsuran Mallikārjuna-Ayyan-maṭha at Śembiya-maṅgalam as *ulavu-kāṇiyākshi*, for maintaining the worship of the god Tirumalauḍaiya-Nāyinār at Vasanta-maṇṭapam.

177. 376 *of* 1912.—(Tamil.) On the same wall. Records in Śarvari Māśi, 14, that Mallappa Nāyaka and Śevvappa Nāyaka appointed certain shepherds to supply ghee for lamps to the same temple in order to secure merit to king Achyutadēva-Mahārāya. [Śevvappa was not improbably the brother-in-law of Achyuta and the founder of the Tanjore dynasty of Nāyakkas.]

178. 377 *of* 1912.—(Tamil.) On the same wall. A record of the Vijayanagara king Vīrapratāpa Achyutayyadēva-Mahārāya in Ś. 1452, Vikriti, Simha (should be *makara, ba* 11), śu. di. 11, Friday, Anusham, corresponding to 13th January 1531. Records gift of land by the residents of Mamanambākkam for the maintenance of worship in the Vasanta-maṇṭapa of god Tirumala Uḍaiyār, for the merit of svāmi Tirumalai-Nāyaka, Immaḍi Tirumalai Nāyaka and Kaḷattīśura-Nāyaka.

179. 378 *of* 1912.—(Tamil.) On the same wall. A damaged record of the Vijayanagara king Sadāśivarāya in Ś. 1471, Saumya. The king receives Sāḷuva titles. Seems to record the supply of ghee for lamps to the same temple.

180. 379 *of* 1912.—(Tamil.) On the same wall. A record of the Vijayanagara king Achyutayyadēva-Mahārāya in Ś. 1457. Records gift of ghee by certain shepherds.

181. 380 *of* 1912.—(Tamil.) On the west wall of the same prākāra. A record of the Vijayanagara king Vīrapratāpa Achyutayyadēva-Mahārāya in Ś. 1455, Hēviḷambi (wrong). Records gift of ghee for lamps.

182. 381 *of* 1912.—(Tamil.) On the same wall. Records in Śubhakrit, Māśi, 17, gift of ghee for lamps by Nayinappa-Nāyaka, agent of Aḍaippam Mallappa-Nāyaka, for the merit of his master.

183. 382 *of* 1912.—(Tamil.) On the north wall of the same prākāra. A damaged and fragmentary record of the Vijayanagara king Vīrapratāpa Achyutayyadēva-Mahārāya in Ś. 1458, Manmatha, Mīna, śu. di. 10, Friday, Tiruvōṇam (= 17th March 1536).

184. 383 *of* 1912.—(Tamil.) On the same wall. A damaged record of the Vijayanagara king Vīrapratāpa Achyutayyadēva-Mahārāya in Ś. 1464, Śubhakrit. Records gift of money for maintaining the festival Uttirattirunāḷ in the same temple by

Nayinappa-Nāyaka, agent of Aḍaippam Mallappa-Nāyaka for the merit of Śevvappa-Nāyaka. [The latter was evidently the founder of the Tanjore Nāik dynasty. See *Tanj. Gazr.*, p. 38.]

185. 384 *of* 1912.—(Tamil.) On the same wall. A record of the Vijayanagara king Vīrapratāpa Achyutayyadēva-Mahārāya in Ś. 1456, Jaya, Kanni, śu. di. 10, Monday. Records gift of money for conducting a festival in the temple certain residents of Śembiyamaṅgalam.

186. 385 *of* 1912.—(Tamil.) On the same wall. A record of the Vijayanagara king Achyutayyadēva-Mahārāya in Ś. 1454, Virōdhi (wrong). Records gift of ghee for a lamp.

187. 386 *of* 1912.—(Tamil.) On the same wall. A record of the Vijayanagara king Achyutadēva-Mahārāya in Ś. 1454, Nandana. Records that Koṇḍama Nāyaka of Śēṟṟuppaṭṭu granted land at Kaṇṇanūr as *ulavukāṇi* and arranged 10 *paṇam* to be paid annually to the temple.

188. 387 *of* 1912.—(Tamil.) On the same wall. A damaged record of the Vijayanagara king Sadāśivadēva-Mahārāya in Ś. 1470, Saumya (wrong), Rishabha, śu. di. full-moon, Monday, Tiruvōṇam. Records gift of some temple land as *kāṇiyākshi* to a private individual.

189. 388 *of* 1912—(Tamil.) On the same wall. A record of the Vijayanagara king Veṅkaṭadēva-Mahārāya, son of Tirumalaidēva Mahārāya in Ś. 1552, Sukla, Tai, 21st day, Monday, Pūśam. Registers that a certain Nayinappa-Nāyaka, son of Kṛishṇappa-Nāyaka, improved a certain land by constructing a tank near it and by digging wells. He made it cultivable and presented the same to the temple. [It is difficult to say who this Veṅkaṭa is. That he cannot be Veṅkaṭa II is clear in the fact that his father is one Tirumalai dēva.]

190. 389 *of* 1912.—(Tamil.) On the east wall of the Naṭarāja shrine in the same temple. A record of the Vijayanagara king Kṛishṇayyadēva Mahārāya in Ś. 1436, Śrīmukha, Karkaṭaka (wrong for Rishabha), śu. di. 10, Friday, Uttiram (= 13th May 1513). Records gift of the village Śembiyamaṅgalam as a *ulavukāṇiyākshi* to Namaśivāya Nāyaka, son of Mallappa-Nāyaka of Marudaraśar Paḍaivīḍu. He was to pay 10 *paṇam* and 10 *kalams* of paddy in the first year, but in the fifth year, 50 *paṇam* and 50 *kalams* of paddy had to be paid. The trustees included Viśvēśvarāchārya of Bhikshā-maṭha. [A Viśvēśvarāchārya is mentioned in Dr. Hultzsch's Rep. Sans. MSS. III, as the author of the *Padavākyārthapañchika*, a commentary on the *Naishadha*; A Viśvēśvara Paṇḍita, the author of a commentary on Śaṅkara's *Vākyavrutti*, is also mentioned. There are also others referred to in No. 166 above. But there is no evidence to prove the identity of any of these.]

191. 390 *of* 1912.—(Tamil.) On the same wall. A damaged record in Ś. 1437, Vibhava (mistake for Bhava), Jyēshṭha, śu. di. 12, Saturday, Viśākha. Seems to record a gift to a Brāhmaṇa by the manager of the temple (kōyil-keḷvi) Viśvēśvara Śivāchārya and Tirumalai-Nāyaka. Refers to Vīra-Naraśiṅgarāya. See Nos. 190 and 166.

192. 391 *of* 1912.—(Tamil.) On the west wall of the kitchen in the same temple. A record of the Vijayanagara king Sadāśiva-dēva-Mahārāya in Ś. 1468, Parābhava, Vrischika, Friday, Tiruvōṇam. Records gift of ghee to the temple by Śūrappa Nāyaka for the merit of Kṛishṇappa-Nāyaka.

193. 392 *of* 1912.—(Tamil.) On the same wall. A damaged record of the Vijayanagara king Achyutadēva-Mahārāya in Ś. 1453, Vikriti.

194. 393 *of* 1912.—(Grantha.) On the second gōpura of the same temple, right of entrance. One Sanskrit verse in praise of Viśvēśvarāchārya. He is stated to have been the foremost devotee of Śrīgirīśvara (i.e., the god on the sacred hill). See Nos. 190 and 166.

195. 394 *of* 1912.—(Tamil.) In the same place. A damaged record of the Vijayanagara king Achyutadēva-Mahārāya in Ś. 1451, Virōdhi. Seems to record a gift by Mallappa Nāyaka, one of the *aḍaippam* servants of the king.

196. 395 *of* 1912.—(Tamil.) In the same place. A record of the Sāluva king Immaḍi Narasimha-Tammayadēva-Mahārāya in Ś. 1426, Raktākshi, Kanni, ba. di. 1, Wednesday, Aśvati (= Wednesday, 25th September 1504). Records gift of land in the village of Śembiyamaṅgalam together with money and houses to a private individual who worshipped in the temples of both the god and the goddess, by Tirumalai-Nāyaka, agent of Narasa-Nāyaka. Mentions Eṭṭappa-Nāyaka, the father of the donor. [Immaḍi Narasimha was the son of Śāluva Naraśinga, the usurper who had to give place to Narasa Nāik.] See No. 254 below.

197. 396 *of* 1912.—(Tamil.) In the same wall. A record of the Śāluva king Immaḍi Narasimharāya-Mahārāya, son of Śāluva-Narasimharāya-Mahārāya in Ś. 1426, Raktākshi, Kumbha, ba, di. 14, Sunday, Tiruvōṇam, Śivarātri (= 2nd February 1505). Records gift of the village Maṇalpākkam *alias* Śōmāśipuram south of Śeyyāru in Kachchūr-nāḍu, a subdivision of Palakunṛa-kōṭṭam in Murugamaṅgalaipaṛṛu, by Samarapuṅgava-Dīkshita, to the temples of the god and the goddess, for oblations. The village was originally granted to him for *agnihōtra* (i.e., keeping the sacred fire) by Tirumalai-Nāyaka. See No. 158 above.

198. 397 *of* 1912.—(Tamil.) In the same wall. A record in Kali 4990, Ś. 1811, Virōdhi and A.D. 1889, November 27. Abhinavapūrnapriya Śrīnivāsa Rao Sahib, Jaghirdar of Ārṇi, piously performed the ashṭabandhana-kumbhābhishēka of Kanakagirīśvara, on this day.

199. 398 *of* 1912.—(Marathi.) On the same gōpura, left of entrance. A record of the Tanjore Mahratha king Tulajarāja Saheb (1763-87), son of Maharaja Saheb Saraphaji in Kshaya Phalguna, ba. di. 10, Monday. Records consecration of the image of the goddess which perhaps had become shaky on its pedestal.

200. 399 *of* 1912.—(Tamil.) In the same place. A damaged record of the Vijayanagara king Śrīraṅgadēva-Mahārāya (i.e., Raṅga II) in Ś. 1499, Īśvara, Kumbha 28 (wrong for 27), ba. di. Sunday, dvitīya, Hasta, corresponding to 22nd February 1578. Registers a gift made to the temple for the merit of Agastyappa-Nāyaka of Vēlūr. Mentions also Bomma-Nāyaka of Vēlūr.

201. 400 *of* 1912.—(Grantha.) In the same place. Records that Īśānaśiva-Yōgīndra, the head of the Gōḷaki-maṭha, obeyed the command of Śiva (i.e., died). [Was he the teacher of the Pāṇḍyan king and writer Varatuṅga? Was he the same as the author of the *Śaivasiddhānta paddhati?* We have no means of answering definitely. He was of course different from his namesake of the Bikshā-maṭha referred to in N.A. 169, etc.]

202. 401 *of* 1912.—(Tamil.) In the same place. A record in Ś. 1401, Viḷambi, Mithuna, śu. di. 7, Monday, Uttirattādi, Śubhayōga and Garajā-karaṇa. Registers that a number of maid-servants (dēvaḍimai) were provided for the temples of Tirumalai-Nāyinār and Periya-Nāchchiyār, by Eṭṭappa-Nāyaka, for the merit of Īśvara Nāyaka.

203. 402 *of* 1912.—(Tamil.) In the same place. An unfinished record of the Sāḷuva king Naraśingaraya-Uḍaiyār (the usurper) in Ś. 1401, Viḷambi, Mithuna, su. di. 7, Monday, Uttirattādi, Śubhayōga, Garajā-karaṇa. "Perhaps Monday, 22nd June, A.D. 1478."

204. 403 *of* 1912.—(Tamil.) On the first gōpura of the same temple. A damaged and unfinished record of the Vijayanagara king Sadāśivadēva-Mahārāya in Ś. 1493, Kshaya (wrong). Seems to register a gift for the merit of Kṛishṇappa Nāyaka and Era-Bomma-Nāyaka and Nalla-Bomma-Nāyaka of Vēlūr.

205. 404 *of* 1912.—(Tamil.) On the same gōpura. Records in Vijaya the levy of taxes on looms for the merit of Liṅgama Nāyaka, while Ēkāmbara-Nāyaka, son of Rāmayappa-Nāyaka, was governing.

206. 405 *of* 1912.—(Tamil.) On the east wall of the Gaṇēśa temple at the fresh water tank in the same village. Records that the temple and the tank were the gift of one of the merchants *(nagarattār)* of the Vaiśiya (i.e., Vaiśya)—Vāṇiyan sect.

207. 406 *of* 1912.—(Tamil.) On the gōpura of the Kanakagirīśvara temple on the hill in the same village. A record in Kali

4990, Ś. 1811, Virōdhi and A.D. 1889, November 27. Copy of No. 397 above.

Mullaṇḍram.

208. 396 *of* 1911.—(Tamil.) On the south wall of the Svayambhunāthēśvara temple. Records in Raudri that the Mahājanās of Prauḍhadēvarāyapuraṁ *alias* Agaram-Mullaṇḍam, including the poet Diṇḍimakavi, assigned house-sites to certain masons in the Kanmāḷatteru. This charter was engraved on the temple of Tāndōnṛīśvaram-Uḍaiyār. [The local chronicle *Vivēkavibhāgapatrika* says that Prauḍhadēva who named the village after himself granted it to eight Brahman families, the Diṇḍimas being one. Mr. Krishna Sastri surmises that this Diṇḍima might be the author of the *Sōmavalliprahasana* and commentary on Śaṅkara's Saundaryalahari (सौन्दर्यलहरि). But as a matter of fact there were a number of Diṇḍimas who figured in the literary world from the eleventh century onward.]

209. 397 *of* 1911.—(Tamil.) On the south wall of the Aruṇāchalēśvara shrine in the same temple. Records in Ś. 1472, Sādhāraṇa, gift of land by a Brāhmaṇa lady to the shrine of Aṇṇāmalainātha built by her, in the temple of Svayambhunātha for the merit of herself and her husband Kumārar-Diṇḍimar Aṇṇāmalainathar.

209-A. On a stone to the east of the south gate. Records that in Krōdhana, Diṇḍimakavi of the village granted to a certain "Rajagocharnum Banda Deva" a house-site. *Ins., S. Dts.*, p. 27, No. 3.

Pūṇḍi.

210. 58 *of* 1900.—(Tamil.) On the west wall of the Jaina temple of Ponniṅātha. A record of Śambuvaraya. Records the building of a Jaina temple called Vīravīra-Jīnālaya and the gift of a village to it.

211. *No.* 25 *of Sewell's List.*—A copper plate grant in five plates recording a double gift by the Vijayanagar sovereign Achyutadēva Rāya in Ś. 1478 (A.D. 1556). The first part bestows the village of Naṅgamaṅgalam, in the district of Chandragiri, in the province of Posturi, on a Rāja whose name is omitted, but who is noted as the son of Sālaka Rājēndra and Tippambika. The second part of the grant bestows the village of Vīrukombu on 54 Brahmans.

212. *No.* 26 *of Sewell's List.*—It records that the Vijayanagara king Achyutadēvarāya, in Ś. 1456 (A.D. 1534), *Jaya*, endowed the temple of Viṭṭhalēśvara (probably the temple of Viṭṭhalasvāmi in Vijayanagar) with the village of Teṅgūru "in the Chandrāchala district (Chandragiri ?), of the province of 'Toṇḍēramaṇḍalam.'

Puttūr near *Arni.*

213. 55 *of* 1900.—(Tamil.) On the south wall of the maṇṭapa in front of the Vidyānathēśvara temple. A record of the Vijayanagara king Vīra-Dēvarāyamahārāya (II), son of Vīra-Vijayārayamahārāya in Ś. 1350 expired, Saumya. Records gift of land.

214. 56 *of* 1900.—(Tamil.) On the north wall of the central shrine in the same temple. A damaged record of the Uḍaiyār king Kampaṇa Uḍaiyār II, son of Vīra-Bokkaṇa Uḍaiyār (I) in Ś. 1292 expired, Sādhāraṇa. Built in. See *Ins. S. Dts.*, p. 26, No. I. The latter says that one Sōmanātha Jīyar was appointed manager of the maṭha and temple.

215. 57 *of* 1900.—(Tamil.) On the north wall of the central shrine in the same temple. A damaged record of the Uḍaiyār king Harihara-Uḍaiyār in Ś. 1299 expired, Piṅgaḷa. Records a gift of land.

215-A. On a stone south of the Mahāmaṇṭapa. Records the gift of one-fifth of the village of Puttūr and two *manais* in Ś. 1340, Subhakrit, by the local people to the local deity. *Ins. S. Dts.*, p. 26, No. 2.

Vellēri (Vellary).

215-B. On a stone in the Sōmēśvara temple. Dated in the third year of Vikramachōḷa. Records that the inhabitants of the village resolved to pay a custom of a "Volapek"(?) of grain for every 100 kuḷis of land to the temple. *Ins. S. Dts.*, p. 27, No. 4.

Vilappakkam.

216. 53 *of* 1900.—(Tamil.) On a slab lying in front of the Nāganāthēśvara temple. A record in the thirty-eighth year of the Chōḷa king Madiraikoṇḍa Parakēsarivarman (Parāntaka I). Records the sinking of a well by the female disciple of Arishṭanēmipiḍarar of Tiruppānmalai (i.e., Pañchapāṇḍavamalai), the preceptor of the local Jains.

217. 54 *of* 1900.—(Tamil.) On a slab lying in front of the Nāganāthēśvara temple. Records an order of Śambuvarāyan.

Vinnamangalam.

218. 21 *of* 1899.—(Tamil.) On the south wall of the central shrine of the Perumāḷ temple. A much damaged record in the seventh year of the Chōḷa king Rājēndra-Chōḷadēva. The historical introduction is identical with that of Parakēsarivarman *alias* Rājēndradēva (1050—63).

219. 22 *of* 1899.—(Tamil.) On the west wall of the same shrine. A much damaged record in the fifth year of the Chōḷa king Rājakēsarivarman *alias* Vīrarājēndradēva.

220. 23 *of* 1899.—(Tamil.) On an erect slab at the north-east corner of the big tank at the same village. A record of the Hoysaḷa king Vīra-Rāmanāthadēva, the date of which is doubtful. Mentions a certain Goppaya-Daṇḍanāyaka and refers to a tank at Vikrama Śōḷa-chaturvēdimaṅgalam. [Vīra Rāmanātha was the son Vīra Sōmēśvara and brother of Vīra Narasimha III, 1254—91. He was the Viceroy of the Southern conquests of the Hoysaḷa dynasty, as is proved by Salem and Trichinopoly epigraphs.]

221. 24 *of* 1899.—(Tamil.) On a Vīrakkal planted in the bed of the same tank. A record in the seventh year of the Chōḷa king Parakēsarivarman. Mentions Viṇṇamaṅgalam.

CHEYYĀR TALUK.

Ālattūr.

A village of this name exists both in the Cheyyār and Tiruvaṇṇāmalai taluks. The former is perhaps the one referred to in the following plates described by Mr. Sewell.

222. *No.* 203 *Sewell's List.*—(Telugu.) Records grant of lands, in Ś. 1501 (A.D. 1579) (see No. 204). The donor and donee are both Nāyuḍus.

223. 204 *of Mr. Sewell's List.*—(Telugu.) Records grant of lands to a Brahman for temple worship by a Nāyuḍu. The year of the grant, as given, is "Ś. 1051, Pramādi;" but these years do not agree, 'and the style of the characters, coupled with other particulars, lead me to think that the entry is a clerical error for "Ś. 1501, Pramādi," which years coincide.'

Atti.

224. 296 *of* 1912.—(Tamil verse.) On the south wall of the Agastīśvara temple. The record eulogises Pallavāṇḍār *alias* Kāḍavarayar who conquered Toṇḍai-maṇḍalam and was the son of Kūḍal-Āḷappirandān *alias* Kāḍavarāyar. [The inscription is important for the information it gives in regard to two kūḍal (Cuddalore) chiefs who claimed Pallava descent and to have conquered Toṇḍamaṇḍalam. The Government Epigraphist argues that the earlier of these whom he calls Kāḍava I should have been a Chōḷa feudatory who defeated an invasion of the Kākatiyas, saved Toṇḍamaṇḍalam, and got the title of 'Protector of Mallai'; that the second (Kāḍava II) was the same as kūḍal-avaniāḷappirandān Kōpperuñjiṅga, the final expeller of the Kākatiyas after a sanguinary battle at Sevūr, the hero who marched as far as Drākshārāma and who declared independence by imprisoning Rājarāja III. See *Ep. Rep.*, 1913, p. 126–7.]

225. 297 *of* 1912.—(Tamil.) On the same wall. A record in the tenth year of the Chōḷa king Tribhuvanachakravartin Rājādhirājādeva (II). Records gift of 32 cows and a bull by Nīrāniṇḍān *alias* Sēdirāyan of Panangudi in Uyyakkoṇḍār-vaḷanāḍu, a district of Śōḷa-maṇḍalam, to the temple of Tiruvagattīśvaram-Uḍaiyār at Atti *alias* Kēraḷāntakanallūr in Perunagarnāḍu, a subdivision of Venkunṛa-kōṭṭam in jayaṅgoṇḍaśōḷamaṇḍalam.

226. 298 *of* 1912.—(Tamil.) On the north wall of the same temple. A record of the Vijayanagara king Vīrapratāpa Kṛishṇadēva-Mahārāya in Ś. 1447, Pārthiva, Mīna, ba. di. 3, Thursday, Chitra, corresponding to 1st March 1526. The king bears Sāḷuva *birudas.* Records that Śōḷīśuramuḍaiyār of Paḍaivīḍu, having secured, tax-free, land at much personal trouble and expense, for the temple of Edirilliśōḷīśuramuḍaiya-Nāyinār at Atti in Atti-paṛṛu adjoining Rājagambhīran-malai of Marudaraśar Paḍaivīḍu in Paḷagunṛa-kōṭṭam, a subdivision of Jayaṅgoṇḍaśōḷa-maṇḍalam, was granted along with other rights the privilege of holding the accountant's place in that temple.

227. 299 *of* 1912.—(Tamil.) On the same wall. A record of the Vijayanagara king Kṛishṇadēva-Mahārāya, 'who took every country,' in Ś. 1448, Vyaya, Mithuna (should be Simha), su. di. 13, Monday Tiruvōṇam corresponding to 20th August, A.D. 1526. Records that the *tirumēnikāval-kāṇiyākshi* (i.e., the right of watching) was granted to Timmu-Nāyaka, son of Pappu Timmu-Nāyaka of Śattirapāḍi in Kalavai-paṛṛu, who recommended Anaiyar-Nāyinār, the *maṭhā-pati* of the temple, to Adaippaṭṭu Vaiyappa-Nāyaka and Pōttu-Nāyaka. On taking this, Anaiyar-Nāyinār got the village of Atti *alias* Krishṇarāyapuram from Kṛishṇadēva Mahārāya while he was encamped on the bank of the Kṛishnavēṇi river, granted as a sarvamānya, to the temple of Uḍaiyavar (i.e., Siva ?) and Perumāḷ of that village. [Uḍaiyavar was not Siva but the Vaishṇava philosopher, Rāmānuja who is generally known by that name among the orthodox. The Government Epigraphist suggests that the king should have been at Kṛishṇavēṇi in order to meet his enemy Vīrarudra Gajapati and come to terms with him. See *Ep. Rep.*, 1908, p. 118, for further reference.]

228. 300 *of* 1912.—(Tamil.) On the east wall of the same temple. In modern characters. Registers in Prabhava that the Paḷḷans had excluded from their (communal) conspiracy the two villages Atti and Āḷappirandān.

229. 301 *of* 1912.—(Tamil.) On a slab set up in the same temple. A record of the Vijayanagara king Kṛishṇadēva-Mahārāya in Ś. 1447, Tāraṇa, Māśi, 25, Monday, Uttirāḍam. The king bears Sāḷuva birudas. Records gift of land to the temple of Edirilliśōḷa-Chōḷīśvaramuḍaiya-Nāyinār at Krishṇarāyapuram *alias* Atti *alias* Kēraḷānta-viṇṇagar. The real date is Saturday (Māśi 24), 18th February 1525, which was Uttirāḍam.

230. 302 *of* 1912.—(Tamil.) On the south wall of the Kariya-Perumāḷ temple in the same village. A record in the eighth year of Tribhuvanachakravartin Vijaya-Gaṇḍagōpāladēva. Records gift of land by the prince (piḷḷaiyār) Rājarāja Śambuvarāyar at Periyanallūr in Kaliyūr-Koṭṭam, to the temple of Ediriliśōḷa-Viṇṇagar-Emberumān, in Atti, a village of Vengunṛa-kōṭṭam, for repairs.

231. 303 *of* 1912.—(Tamil.) On the west wall of the same temple. A record in the eighteenth year of Tribhuvanachakravartin Vijaya-Gaṇḍagōpāladēva. Records gift of three velis of land at Periyanallūr, by Āḷappirandān *alias* Rājarāja Śambuvarāyan to the shrine of Veṇṇaikkadiyaruḷina-Piḷḷai (i.e., Krishṇa) founded by Ammaināchchi *alias* Pālāṟṟil-venṟār, in the temple of Ediriliśōḷa-Vinnagar-Emberumān.

232. 304 *of* 1912.—(Tamil.) On a slab lying in front of the same temple. Records in Durmati that the Mahā-maṇṭapa, the central roof and the well of the temple of Kariya-Perumāḷ at Atti, were the gift of a certain Śennappan.

Kārāṇai.

232-A. 293 *of* 1895.—(Tamil.) On a stone in the temple. A mutilated record of the Uḍaiyār king Vīra Kampaṇa Uḍaiyār (II), son of Vīra . . . Uḍaiyār in K 4472, Ś. 1293, Virōdhikrit.

Kūḷambandal.

233. 413 *of* 1902.—(Tamil.) On the south wall of the maṇṭapa in front of the Śiva temple. A record in the thirty-third year of the Chōḷa king Rājakēsarivarman *alias* Uḍaiyār Rājādhirājadēva (I or II). Records gift of ninety sheep for a lamp.

234. 414 *of* 1902.—(Tamil.) On the north wall of the same maṇṭapa. A record in twenty-second year of the Chōḷa king Parakēsarivarman *alias* Uḍaiyār Rājēndra-Chōḷadēva (I). Records gift of land and gold to 24 dancing girls. Says that the temple was built by the priest Īśānaśiva Paṇḍita. (See *S. Ind. Ins.*, II, No. 9.)

235. 415 *of* 1902.—(Tamil.) On the same wall. An incomplete record of the Chōḷa king Rājādhirāja I (1018—53).

Kuranganimuttam.

(So called because the monkey, the squirrel and the crow worshipped Śiva) was an ancient centre of religious life as it is sung in the *Dēvāram.*

236. 290 *of* 1912.—(Tamil.) On the north wall of the central shrine in the Koyyāmalarīśvara temple. A record in the tenth year of Tribhuvanachakravartin Kōnērimaikoṇḍān. Records gift of land to the temple of Tirukkuraṅgaṇimuttamuḍaiya-Nāyanār at Pallavapuram, a village in Mūvēndur-paṟṟu which was a subdivision of Erikil-nāḍu in Kaliyūr-kōṭṭam. The assessment paid on the land and the taxes realized are enumerated.

237. 291 *of* 1912.—(Tamil.) On the same wall. A record in the twentieth year of the Chōḷa king Kulōttuṅga-Chōḷadēva (III), 'who was pleased to take Madurai (Madura) and the crowned head of the Pāṇḍya.' Records gift of Sattimaṅgalam *alias* Ammainallūr in Erikil-nāḍu, to the temple of Tirukkuranganạimuttam Uḍaiyār at Tirukkuraṅgaṇimuttam in Kaliyūr-kōṭṭam, as a dēvadāna village, by Nīraṇiṅjān Śēdirāyan under orders from Śambuvarāyar.

238. 292 *of* 1912.—(Tamil.) On the south wall of the same shrine. A record in the tenth year of Tribhuvanachakravartin Kōnērmaikoṇḍān. Records gift of five *vēlis* of land for offerings and repairs to the same temple. The land was made rent-free on payment of 25 *pon*. The different items of income are enumerated. The record is signed by Tunjalūruḍaiyān. *Dusi* is mentioned as one of the boundaries of the land.

239. 293 *of* 1912.—(Tamil.) On the west wall of the maṇṭapa in front of the same shrine. A record in the ninth year of the Chōḷa king Kulōttuṅga-Chōḷadēva (III). Records gift of money for a lamp by the residents of Pallavapuram.

240. 294 *of* 1912.—(Tamil.) On a slab set up in front of the same temple. A record of the Vijayanagara king Vīrapratāpa Kṛishṇadēva-Mahārāya in Ś. 1451, Virōdhi, ba. di. 5, Saturday, Uttiraṭṭādi (which should be Pūraṭṭādi). Records gift of the village Pallapuram for maintaining worship (*pūja vritti*) in the temple of Koyyāmalarśūḍuvar at Tirukkuraṅgaṇimuṭṭam of Māvaṇḍūr, in Erikil-nāḍu, for the merit of the king. The date corresponded to Saturday, 26th June, A.D. 1529.

241. 295 *of* 1912.--(Tamil.) On a pillar of the rock-cut cave in the same village (similar to Māmaṇḍūr and Pallāvaram caves). A record in the twenty-fourth year of the Rāshṭrakūṭa king Kaṇṇaradēva (Kṛishṇa III), who took Kachchi (Conjeeveram) and Tanjai (Tanjore).' Records gift of land for providing *śribali* in the temple Kalmaḍai-kāttāḷvār (i.e., the lord who resides in the stone cave), at Pallavapuram in Kāliyūrkōṭṭam, a subdivision of Erikil-nāḍu, by the residents of that village.

Narasamaṅgalam.

242. 260 *of* 1906.—(Sanskrit and Tamil.) On the south wall of the central shrine in the ruined Śiva temple on the hill. A record in the seventh year of the Pāṇḍya king Tribhuvanachakravartin Jaṭāvarman *alias* Sundara-Pāṇḍyadēva I, (1251—61). Begins *samasta* jagadādhāra, etc. An incomplete record. Registers a public sale of the village of Naraśiṅgamaṅgalam in Māvaṇḍūr-nāḍu, a subdivision of Kāḷiyūr-kōṭṭam, a district of Jayaṅgoṇḍa-Chōḷa maṇḍalam.

243. 261 *of* 1906.—(Telugu.) On a stone set up on the bund of the tank in the same village. Records in Ś. 1560, Bahudhānya, the construction of the tank by Veṅkaṭappa-Nāyaka, son of

Chennappa-Nāyaka. It was called Chenna-sāgaram and was provided with a feeding channel from the Pālār. [This Naik is closely associated with the history of Madras. See Col. Love's *Vestiges of Madras*, I, 23, 24, 188 and 347 and II, 328.]

244. 262 *of* 1906.—(Tamil.) On the same stone. A record in Ś. 1560, Bahudhānya. A Tamil copy of No. 243.

245. 263 *of* 1906.—(Grantha.) On another stone in the same place. A record in Jaya. The tank is called Chenna-sāgara and Veṅkaṭappa makes provision for the maintenance of it.

246. 264 *of* 1906.—(Nagari and Sanskrit.) On third stone in the same place. Refers in Ś. 1560, Bahudhānya, to the fact of Veṅkaṭappa-Nāyaka having built the tank.

Tiruppanangāḍu.

247. 233 *of* 1906.—(Tamil.) On the north wall of the Tāḷapurīśvara shrine in the Śiva temple. A record in the twenty-eighth year of the Chōḷa king Rājakēsarivaram *alias* Uḍaiyār śrī Rājādhirājadēva (I or II ?). Records gift of land.

248. 234 *of* 1906.—(Tamil.) On the south wall of the same shrine. A record in the thirty-second year or the Chōḷa king Parakēsarivarman *alias* Uḍaiyār śrī-Rājēndra-Chōḷadēva I, (1011—53). Records sale of land.

249. 235 *of* 1906.—(Tamil.) On the same wall. A record in the forty-fifth year of the Chōḷa king Rājakēsarivarman *alias* Chakravartin śri-Kulōttuṅga-Chōḷadēva (I). Records gift of a lamp. The temple is called Tiruppanaṅgāḍu-Uḍaiyār in Kalumala-nāḍu, a district of Kaliyūr-kōṭṭam, a subdivision of Jayaṅgoṇḍa-Chōḷamaṇḍalam. The donor was a native of Kīḷvēṅgai-nāḍu, a subdivision of Rājarāja-vaḷanāḍu, a district of śōḷamaṇḍalam.

250. 236 *of* 1906.—(Tamil.) On the same wall. A record of the Vijayanagara king Viruppaṇa-Uḍaiyār (Virūpāksha I), son of Vīra-Hariyaṇa-Uḍaiyār (Harihara II) in Ś. 1310 expired, Vibhava. Records gift of land.

251. 237 *of* 1906.—(Tamil.) On the east wall of the shrine. *The length of the measuring rod of the district in which Tiruppanāṅgāḍu was situated is given.* At each end of the inscription is a palmyra tree.

252. 238 *of* 1906.—(Tamil.) On the north wall of the Karipānāthasvāmin shrine in the same temple. An unfinished record. Begins with the *birudas* of some Vijayanagara king whose name is omitted. The inscription records a gift to stone masons.

253. 239 *of* 1906.—(Tamil.) On the same wall. A record of the Vijayanagara king Viruppaṇa-Uḍaiyār (Virūpāksha I), son of Vīra-Ariyaṇa-Uḍaiyār (Harihara II) in Ś. 1313 expired, Prajāpati. Refers to a famine in the Pramōda year.

254. 240 *of* 1906.—(Tamil.) On the west wall of the same shrine. A record of the Vijayanagara king Kṛishṇadēva-Mahārāya, son of Gaṇḍakaṭṭāri Śāḷuva Vanyavēṭṭaikaṇḍaruḷiya Narasanāyakka-Uḍaiyār in Ś. 1432 expired, Pramōda. Mentions Tirumalai-Nāyakkar, son of Eṭṭappa Nāyakkar. See N.A. 196 above.

255. 241 of 1906.—(Tamil.) On the west and south walls of the maṇṭapa in front of the Tāḷapurīśvara shrine in the same temple. A record of the Vijayanagara king Viruppaṇa-Uḍaiyār (Virūpāksha I), son of Ariyaṇa-Uḍaiyār (Harihara II) in Ś. 1303 expired, Dundhubi. The temple is called Āḷuḍaiyār Tiruppanaṅgāvuḍaiya-Nāyanār at Tiruppanaṅgāḍu in Brahmadēśappaṟṟu, a subdivision of Kaḷumalanāḍu in Kaliyūr-kōṭṭam, a district of Jayaṅgoṇḍa-Chōḷamaṇḍalam. Mentions Vāsavanan-tiruvīdi and Aḍaruṅgaḷal Perumāḷ Toṇḍaimānār-manai. Refers to a breach at the sluice of a tank which deprived the villagers of the means of paying the tax called *śūlavari.*

256. 242 *of* 1906.—(Tamil.) On the same walls. Records in Sarvadhārin an agreement between the temple authorities and the weavers.

257. 243 *of* 1906.—(Tamil.) On the south wall of the same maṇṭapa. Refers in Vikārin to the setting up of the images of Dakshiṇāmūrti, Mahāvishṇu, Brahma and Durgā.

258. 244 *of* 1906.—(Tamil.) On the east wall of the maṇṭapa in front of the Kripānāthasvāmin shrine in the same temple. A record in the tenth year of the Chōḷa king Rājakēsarivarman *alias* Tribhuvanachakravartin śrī-Kulōttuṅga-Chōḷadēva. Records gift of 32 cows for a lamp to the temple of Uḍaiyār Tiruppanaṅgāḍuḍaiyār in Kaḷumala-nāḍu, a subdivision of Kāliyūr-kōṭṭam, a district of Jayaṅgoṇḍa-Chōḷamaṇḍalam.

259. 245 *of* 1906.—(Tamil.) On the same wall. A record in the eighteenth year of the Chōḷa king Tribhuvanachakravartin śrī-Rājarājadēva. Records gift of 32 sheep for a lamp by an agent of Śambuvarāyar. [The king is not improbably Rājarāja III, 1216—48. See Nos. 230 and 231 above.]

260. 246 *of* 1906.—(Tamil.) On the same wall. 'Those who fell the living Palmyra tree (shall be subject to punishment inflicted under) the royal order.'

261. 247 *of* 1906.—(Tamil.) On the same wall. Records that some hunters who claimed to belong to the family of Tirukkaṇṇappar made a gift for merit of Śambuvarāya.

262. 248 *of* 1906.—(Tamil.) On the east and north bases of the same maṇṭapa. A record of the Vijayanagara king Kampaṇa-Uḍaiyār II, son of Vīra-Bokkaṇa-Uḍaiyār (i.e., Bukka I) in Ś. 1291 expired, Saumya. Records that three men were made over to the temple under orders from the king to look after the lamps.

263. 249 *of* 1906.—(Tamil.) On the north wall of the same maṇṭapa. A record of the Vijayanagara king Kampaṇa-Uḍaiyār, son of Vīra-Bukkaṇa-Uḍaiyār in Sādhāraṇa (i.e., Ś. 1293). Registers a similar arrangement made by Aḍaippattu Ilakkappar and Ānaikundi Viṭṭappar under orders from the king. See the above inscription.

264. 250 *of* 1906.—(Tamil.) On the same wall. A record of the Vijayanagara king Vīra-Kumāra-Kampaṇa-Uḍaiyār (i.e., Kampaṇa II) in Ś. 1289 expired, Kīlaka. Records that a certain Vijayasimhadēva of the Bōdhāyana-sūtra and the Bhāradvāja-gōtra was appointed temple manager.

265. 251 *of* 1906.—(Tamil.) On the same wall. A record of the Vijayanagara king Viruppaṇa-Uḍaiyar (Virūpāksha I), son of Ariyaṇa-Uḍaiyār (i.e., Harihara II) in Ś. 1303 expired, Dundubhi. Records that the temple authorities sold some of the temple lands in order to repair the breaches of the village tank, because they had no funds and because the lands under it remained uncultivated for a long time.

266. 252 *of* 1906.—(Tamil.) On the same wall. A record of the Vijayanagara king Achyutaiyadēva-Mahārāya in Ś. 1460 expired, Viḷambi. Records gift of land to the temple of Tiruppa-naṅgāvuḍaiya-Nāyinār Anbuḍaiya-Nāyinār for the merit of the king.

267. 253 *of* 1906.—(Tamil.) On the same wall. A record of the Vijayanagara king Vīrapratāpa Achyutayyadēva-Mahārāya in Ś. 1453 expired, Khara. Records that Bhōgayadēva-Mahārāja granted again the *jōḍi* amounting to 50 *pon* for the merit of the king with the permission of Tirumalaiyadēva-Mahārāja.

268. 254 *of* 1906.—(Tamil.) On the inner side of the west wall of the first prākāra of the same temple. A damaged record of the Vijayanagara king Dēvarāya-Uḍaiyār (I), son of Ariyaṇa-Uḍaiyār (Harihara II) in Ś. 1320 expired, Īśvara. Mentions a water channel and the mahāmaṇḍaleśvara Veṅgi-Tribhuvanamalla Sameyadēva, son of Sūryadēva Mahārāja.

Tiruvattūr.

269. 76 *of* 1900.—(Tamil.) On the north wall of the first prākāra of the Vēdapurīśvara temple. A record in the fourth year of the Chōḷa king Tribhuvanachakravartin Rājādhirājadēva. Records gift of a lamp. [See N.A. Manual, Vol. II, p. 309 for the local tradition.]

270. 77 *of* 1900.—(Tamil.) On the north wall of the first prākāra of the same temple. A record in the sixth year of the Chōḷa king Rājakēsarivarman *alias* Tribhuvanachakravartin Kulōttuṅga-Chōḷadēva. Records gift of 16 cows for a lamp, by a man who, while on a hunting excursion, missed his aim and shot a man, the gift being made at the instance of an assembly of the people of the district. Examples of this method of expiation are numerous.

271. 78 *of* 1900.—(Tamil.) On the north wall of the first prākāra of the same temple. A record in the fifth year of the Pāṇḍya king Jaṭāvarman Tribhuvanachakravartin Vīra-Pāṇḍyadēva. Records gift of 64 cows and 2 bulls. [Was this king the same as the Jaṭāvarman Vīra Pāṇḍya who came to the throne in 1253, who conquered Īḻam, Koṅgu and Śōḻamaṇḍalam and who had the anointment of victors at Perumbaṟṟuppuliyūr ?]

272. 79 *of* 1900.—(Tamil.) On the north wall of the first prākāra of the same temple. A record in the eleventh year of the Chōḷa king Tribhuvanachakravartin Kulōttuṅga-Chōḷadēva. Records gift of land for a lamp.

273. 80 *of* 1900.—(Tamil.) On the north wall of the first prākāra of the same temple. An incomplete record in the second year of the Chōḷa king Tribhuvanachakravartin Śrī-Vīrarājēndra Chōḷadēva. Records gift of 90 cows for three lamps.

274. 81 *of* 1900.—(Tamil.) On the north wall of the first prākāra of the same temple. A record in the eighth year of the Chōḷa king Tribhuvanachakravartin Rājādhirājadēva. Records gift of 32 cows for a lamp.

275. 82 *of* 1900.—(Tamil.) On the north wall of the first prākāra of the same temple. Records an order of Madurāntaka Pottappi-Chōḷa, dated in his second year.

276. 83 *of* 1900.—(Tamil.) On the south wall of the same prākāra. A record in the twentieth year of Peruñjiṅgadēva. Records the gift of 32 cows for a lamp by Tiruvēgambamuḍaiyār *alias* Ēkāmbrabhaṭṭa of Kanchikkuri, who describes himself as a Santānika-Śaivāchārya.

277. 84 *of* 1900.—(Tamil.) On the south wall of the same prākāra. An incomplete record in the twenty-first year of the Chōḷa king Tribhuvanachakravartin Rājarājadēva. Records gift of a lamp.

278. 85 *of* 1900.—(Tamil.) On the south wall of the same prākāra. A record in the second year of the Chōḷa king Tribhuvanachakravartin Rājēndra Chōḷadēva. Records gift of 90 sheep for a lamp.

279. 86 *of* 1900.—(Grantha and Sanskrit.) On the south wall of the same prākāra.

280. 87 *of* 1900.—(Tamil.) On the south wall of the same prākāra. A record in the sixth year of the Chōḷa king Parakēsarivarman *alias* Tribhuvanachakravartin Vikrama-Chōḷadēva (1118—35). Records a sale of land under interesting circumstances. A big flood destroyed both the village and the crops and the villagers, on account of their incapacity to pay the taxes, sold 2,000 *kuḻis* of *wet* land for 25 *kāśu* to one Ādittan Uyyavandān (who made it over to the pujāri of the temple). A measuring rod equal to the royal foot which measured the whole world is mentioned, and this might be that of Kulōttuṅga I in whose sixteenth year it was adopted. [See 125 of 1896 at Shiyali and 84 of 1897 at Tirunāgēś-varam in Tanjore district.]

281. 88 *of* 1900.—(Tamil.) On the south wall of the same prākāra. A record in the eighth year of the Chōḷa king Para-kēsarivarman *alias* Tribhuvanachakravartin Vikrama-Chōḷadēva (1118—35). Records sale of 4,250 *kuḻis* of dry land by the same villagers for 20 kāśu. The purchaser was a native of the Chōḷa country and he made it over tax-free to those who had to look after the streets of the Tiruvottūr temple.

282. 89 *of* 1900.—(Tamil.) On the east wall of the same prā-kāra. A record in the sixteenth year of the Chōḷa king Tribhu-vanachakravartin Rājarājadēva. Records gift of a village by Śeṅgēṇi Attimallan Śambuvarāyan *alias* Edirili-Śōḷa-Śambuva-rāyan. [The king was evidently Rājarāja III (1216—48).]

283. 90 *of* 1900.—(Tamil.) On the south wall of the maṇṭapa in front of the central shrine of the same temple. A record in the twentieth year of the Chōḷa king Tribhuvanachakravartin Rāja-rājadēva. Records gift of land for a lamp.

284. 91 *of* 1900.—(Tamil.) On the south wall of the maṇṭapa in front of the central shrine of the same temple. A record in the twentieth year of the Chōḷa king Rājarājadēva. Records gift of land for a flower-garden.

285. 92 *of* 1900.—(Tamil.) On the south wall of the mantapa in front of the central shrine of the same temple. A record in the twenty-second year of the Pāṇḍya king Vīra-Pāṇḍyadēva. Records an order of Kulaśēkhara-Śambuvarāyan.

286. 93 *of* 1900.—(Tamil.) On the south wall of the maṇṭapa in front of the central shrine of the same temple. A record in the thirty-ninth year of the Chōḷa king Tribhuvanachakravartin Tribhuvanavīradēva (Kulōttuṅga III, 1178—1216). Records gift of two gold ornaments.

287. 94 *of* 1900.—(Tamil.) On the south wall of the maṇṭapa in front of the central shrine of the same temple. A record in the thirty-third year of the Chōḷa king Tribhuvanachakravartin Tribhu-vanavīradēva (Kulōttuṅga III) "who took Madura, Īḻam, Karuvūr and the crowned head of the Pāṇḍya." Records gift of land by Śeṅgēṇi Ammaiyappan Aḻagiya-Śōḻan *alias* Edirili-Śōḷa-Śambuva-rāyan. See No. 282 above.

288. 95 *of* 1900.— Tamil.) On the south wall of the maṇṭapa in front of the central shrine of the same temple. A record in the twenty-second year of Peruñjiṅgadēva. Mentions a previous gift made in the seventeenth year of the reign of Śrī-Kulōttuṅga-Chōḷadēva (III) and records a sale of land.

289. 96 *of* 1900.—(Tamil.) On the north wall of the same maṇṭapa. A record in the seventh year of Sakalalōkachakravartin Rājanārāyaṇa-Śambuvarāyan. Records gift of land.

290. 97 *of* 1900.—(Tamil.) On the north wall of the same maṇṭapa. A record in the twelfth year of the Pāṇḍya king Māravarman Tribhuvanachakravartin Sundara-Pāṇḍyadēva. Records gift of land for forty lamps by Vīra-Champanāyan *alias* Śambuvarāyan. Venkayya identifies the Pāṇḍyan with the parricide Sundara, the opponent of Vīra Pāṇḍya (Tīra Pāṇḍya) of the Mussalman historians), who fled to Delhi in 1310. See *Ep. Rep.*, 1900, p. 7, para. 13. Also *Ind. Antiq.*, January 1914.

291. 98 *of* 1900.—(Tamil.) On the north wall of the same maṇṭapa. Records in Krōdhana gift of land to a maṭha called after Kēdārinādar.

292. 99 *of* 1900.—(Tamil.) On the north wall of the same maṇṭapa. A record in the fourth year of Sakalalōkachakravartin Rājanārāyaṇa. Records gift of land.

293. 100 *of* 1900.—(Tamil.) On the north wall of the Chidambarēśvara shrine in the same temple. A mutilated record in the twenty-first year of the Chōḷa king Rājarājakēsarivarman (Rājarāja I). Records a gift of land.

294. 101 *of* 1900.—(Tamil.) On the south wall of the same shrine. A damaged and incomplete record in the twenty-seventh year of the Rāshṭrakūṭa king Kaṇṇaradēva "who took Kachchi and Tanjai" (Kṛishṇa III).

295. 102 *of* 1900.—(Tamil.) On the south wall of the same shrine. A record in the fourteenth year of the Chōḷa king Parakēsarivarman. Records gift of a lamp.

296. 103 *of* 1900.—(Tamil.) On the south wall of the same shrine. Records the building of the Śaṁkaranāraṇa-Īśvarāgaram by Ādittakuttiyar for the merit of his elder brother Śaṁkaranāranār, and the grant of a flower garden thereto by the sabha of Tiruvottūr.

297. 104 *of* 1900.—(Tamil.) On the south wall of the same shrine. A record in the fourteenth year of the Chōḷa king Parakēsarivarman. Records gift of two lamps.

Ukkāl.

The epigraphical name of this place is Bhuvanamāṇikka Vishṇugriham. An inscription of Rājarāja calls the deity *Tiruvāymoḷitēvar* after the prabandhic work of St. Nammāḷvār. In Pallava times the village was evidently called Utkār, Śivachūḷāmani—ch. V.M., Vikramābharaṇa C.M. and Aparājita C. V.M. It was in Pāgur nāḍu, in Kāliyūr kōṭṭam, in Toṇḍamaṇḍalam or Jayaṅkoṇḍachōḷamaṇḍalam.

298. 19 *of* 1893.—(Tamil.) North wall of the shrine in the Perumāḷ temple. A record of the Chōḷa king Kō-Rājakēsarivarman dated in his twenty-third year. Dr. Hultzsch surmises that he might be Aditya I, father of Parāntaka I. Records that a certain Brahmādhirāja deposited 200 kaḷanju with the village assembly for feeding twelve learned Brahmans out of interest. The donor was one of the Āḷumgaṇattār of Uttaramallūr. *S.I.I.*, III, No. I, pp. 2–3.

299. 20 *of* 1893.—(Tamil.) North and west walls of the same shrine. A record of the Chōḷa king Kō-Rājarājakēsarivarman (I), dated in his thirteenth year. Records that a native of the Chōḷa country purchased 550 *kuḻis* of land and gave it to the assembly for supplying four nāḻis of rice daily as interest. Signed on the Sabhā's orders by the *Madhyastan* "*Āirattirunūṟṟuvan*, son of *Nālāyiravan.*" *S.I.I.*, III, No. 2, pp. 4–5.

300. 21 *of* 1893.—(Tamil.) West wall of the same shrine. A record of the Chōḷa king Kō-Rājarāja-Kēsarivarman, dated in his fourteenth year. Records that a native of Chōḷa country bought two pieces of land, one from a private person and the other from the assembly, and deposited it with latter for maintaining a flower garden. *Ibid.*, No. 3, pp. 5–6.

301. 22 *of* 1893.—(Tamil.) West wall of the same shrine. A record of the twenty-ninth year of Chōḷa king Kō-Rājakēsarivarman *alias* Rājarāja (I). Records that a man dug a well near Ukkal, which he named after the king and assigned an allowance of paddy for the men who distributed water in a shed erected near it. *Ibid.*, No. 4, pp. 6—8. The rate of salary is interesting.

302. 23 *of* 1893.—(Tamil.) South wall of the same shrine. A record of the seventeenth year of the Chōḷa king Kō-Rājarāja-Rājakēsarivarman (I). Records supply of rice and oil to the local temple of *Mahāśāsta* (Aiyanār). The tank supervision committee of the Sabhā was entitled to levy a fine of one kaḷanju in favour of the tank-bund from betel-leaf sellers outside the Piḍāri temple. *Ibid.*, No. 6, pp. 9—11.

303. 24 *of* 1893.—(Tamil.) South wall of the same shrine. A record of Kampavarman dated in his tenth year. A certain Śaḍayan made over 400 kāḍi of paddy to the assembly, which was to feed two Brahmans daily for the annual interest of 100 *kāḍi*. *Ibid.*, No. 8, pp. 13–14.

304. 25 *of* 1893.—(Tamil.) South wall of the same shrine. A record of the Rāshṭrakūṭa king Kaṇṇaradēva (Kṛishṇa III), dated in his sixteenth year. Appears to record the purchase of certain lands of the Sabhā by individuals, subject to certain restrictions. *Ibid.*, No. 7, pp. 11—13.

305. 26 *of* 1893.—(Tamil.) South wall of the same shrine. A record of Kampavarma, dated in his fifteenth year, saying that a certain Śaḍayan made over 1,000 *kāḍi* of paddy to the *Sabhā*, which pledged itself to supply 500 *kāḍi* every year to the temple. *S.I.I.*, III, No. 5, pp. 8-9. [So the interest is 50 per cent!]

306. 27 *of* 1893.—(Tamil.) North wall of the same maṇṭapa in the same temple. A record of the Chōḷa king Kō-Parakēsarivarman *alias* Rājēndra-Chōḷadēva (I), dated in his fourth year. Records that the assembly of Ukkāl sold 3,000 kuḷis of land and 5 water levers to a servant of the king who assigned the land for the maintenance of two boats in the village tank. *Ibid.*, No. 10, pp. 15—17.

307. 28 *of* 1893.—(Tamil.) North wall of the maṇṭapa in the same temple. A record of the Chōḷa king Kō-Parakēsarivarman, dated in his sixteenth year. Records grant of land to temple by the assembly at the request of the manager Chakrapāṇi Nambi. *Ibid.*, No. 11, pp. 17-18.

308. 29 *of* 1893.—(Tamil.) North wall of the same maṇṭapa in the same temple. A record of the Chōḷa king Kō-Rājarājakēsarivarman *alias* Rājarājadēva I, dated in his twenty-fourth year. [See *S. Ind. Ins.*, Vol. III, No. 9 and *Mad. Ep. Rep.*, 1897, p. 2. It deals with defaulters of land revenue in villages held by the Brahmans, the Vaikhānasas and Jainas in the Chōḷa, Pāṇḍya and Toṇḍamaṇḍalam countries and authorizes the villagers to confiscate and sell the lands if taxes were unpaid for two full years. The royal secretary and a chief secretary are referred to. For similar documents see Tiruchchirai, Kōnērirājapuram, Tirumālam and other inscriptions.]

309. 30 *of* 1893.—(Tamil.) West wall of the same maṇṭapa. A record of the Chōḷa king Madiraikoṇḍa-Kō-Parakēsarivarman (Parāntaka I), dated in his thirty-seventh year. *Ibid.*, No. 12, pp. 18—20. There is reference to the village committees of general supervision, of tanks, and gardens.

310. 31 *of* 1893.—(Tamil.) South wall of the same maṇṭapa. A record of the Chōḷa king Kō-Rājakēsarivarman, dated in his seventeenth year. *S.I.I.*, III, No. 13, pp. 20-21.

311. 32 *of* 1893.—(Tamil.) South wall of the same maṇṭapa. A record of the Chōḷa king Kō-Parakēsarivarman, dated in his fourth year. *Ibid.*, No. 14, pp. 21-2. [As the king is said to have deprived Vīra Pāṇḍya, Dr. Hultzsch identifies him with Āditya Karikāla II, the elder brother of Rājarāja I.] Records that one Śēnai granted one paṭṭi of land, from the proceeds of which water and fire-pans had to be supplied to a maṇṭapa frequented by Brahmans.

312. 412 *of* 1902.—(Tamil.) On detached stones of the ruined maṇṭapa in front of the Perumāḷ temple. A mutilated record in the twenty-eighth year of the Chōḷa king Tribhuvanachakravartin-Vijayagaṇḍagōpāladēva. Records gift of land.

GUDIYĀTTAM TALUK.

Amuṇḍi (ancient Aimbūṇḍi).

This was in Miyagaraināḍu in Paṅgalanāḍu, a division of Jayaṅkoṇḍaśōḷamaṇḍalam.

313. 62 *of* 1887.—(Grantha and Tamil.) On the southern wall of the Īśvara temple. A record of Kō-Rājakēsarivarman *alias* Chakravartin Kulōttuṅga-Chōḷadēva (I?) *S.I.I.*, Vol. I, No. 130, p. 135.

314. 63 *of* 1887.—(Grantha and Tamil.) A record on the southern wall of the Īśvara temple. Gift of land from the inhabitants of Aimbūṇḍi to the Muppanayīśvara temple. *S.I.I.*, Vol. I, No. 131, pp. 135-36.

315. 64 *of* 1887.—(Grantha and Tamil.) On the southern wall of the Īśvara temple. A record of Tribhuvanachakravartin Kōnērimēnkoṇḍa-Kulōttuṅga-Chōḷadēva (III). Mentions Śeṅgēṇi Ammayappan Vikramachōḷa Śambuvarāyan. *S.I.I.*, Vol. I, No. 132, p. 136.

316. 325 *of* 1901.—(Tamil.) On the west and south walls of the Tritalīśvara temple. A record in the fourteenth year of the Chōḷa king Rājakēsarivarman *alias* Chakravartin Kulōttuṅga-Chōḷadēva.

Arumbarutti.

317. 39 *of* 1887.—(Grantha and Tamil). On a stone. A record of the Vijayanagara king Sadāśivadēva, dated Ś. 1488 (Sunday, Aparap. 12, Kumbha, Akshaya). Gift by Rāmarāja-Tirumalaiyadēva Mahārāja, at the request of Vellore Chinna Bomma Nāik, of the village of Arumbarutti to Jvarakaṇḍēśvara, the Lord of Vellore. See *S.I.I.*, Vol. I, No. 45, pp. 71-72.

Kirmuttugur.

318. 66 *of* 1887.—(Grantha and Tamil.) On stones. A record in the third year of the Pallava king Kō-Vijaya-Narasimhavarman. [Same as No. 325 below.]

319. 67 *of* 1887.—(Grantha and Tamil.) On stones. A record in the eighteenth year of the Pallava king Kō-Vijaya-Narasimhavarman. [Same as No. 324 below.]

320. 68 *of* 1887.—(Grantha and Tamil.) On stones. A record in the twenty-ninth year of the Chōḷa king Madirai-koṇḍa-Parakēsarivarman. [Same as No. 322 below.]

321. 62 *of* 1887.—(Grantha and Tamil.) On stones. A record in the thirty-second year of Madirai-koṇḍa Kō-Parakēsarivarman. [Same as No. 323 below.]

322. 1 *of* 1896.—(Tamil.) On a stone in the same place. A record in the twenty-ninth year of the Chōḷa king Madirai-koṇḍa Parakēsarivarman (i.e., Parāntaka I). Records the death of a warrior who was killed after he had recovered some cattle which the Permānaḍigaḷ (evidently W. Gaṅga king) had seized. See *Ep. Ind.*, IV, 178–79; *S.I.I.*, Vol. I, No. 136, p. 137.

323. 2 *of* 1896.—(Tamil.) On another stone in the same place. A record in the thirty-second year of the Chōla king Madirai-koṇḍa-Ko-Parakēsarivarman (i.e., Parāntaka I). It marks the spot at which an inhabitant of Muttukūr killed a tiger. See *Ep. Ind.*, IV, p. 179; *S.I.I.*, Vol. I, No. 137, p. 137.

324. 3 *of* 1896.—(Tamil.) On another stone in the same place. A record in the eighteenth year of "the Gaṅga-Pallava king" Kō-Vijaya-Narasimhavarman. "The most archaic epigraph of the place." "Below it are figured in bas-relief, an elephant and a goose. As the elephant appears at the top of three inscriptions of the W. Gaṅga dynasty which have been published by Mr. Kittal (*Ind. Antiq.*, VI, p. 101) and as the goose is said to have been the device of the mythical Gaṅga king Koṅkaṇi (*S. Ind. Inscrns.*, II, 387), it may be assumed with some probability that Narasimha-varman belonged to the western Gaṅgas." See also *Ep. Ind.*, IV, pp. 177–78.

325. 119 *of* 1897.—(Tamil.) On a stone in the same place. A record in the third year of Kō-Vijaya-Narasimhavarman. Records the death of a warrior, during a cattle-raid, which had been organized by a certain Śanmadura. The warrior was Atti-mattar Murugan, an inhabitant of Pākkam and a servant of Vali-madura, the chief of Tagaḍūrnāḍu, who ruled over the northern bank of the river in Viṇrunāḍu. See *Ep. Ind.*, IV, pp. 360—62. Also *S.I.I.*, I, No. 135, p. 137.

Koṇḍyāta.

325-A. A C.P. grant of Veṅkaṭa II of the last Vijayanagara dynasty. Records that in Ś. 1558 (A.D. 1636), Dhātri, Ashāḍha, Śu. di. 12, Veṅkaṭa II, while at Penukoṇḍa, granted the village Koṇḍyāta or Gōpāla Śrīpura to Raṅganātha, son of Siṅgarāja, grandson of Lakkarāja, an ornament of Veṅkaṭa's court, who belonged to the Kauśika Gōtra, Āpastamba Sūtra V Yajus-śākhā. [See *Ind. Antiq.*, XIII, 125*ff and Tam. and Sanskt. Inscrns.*, pp. 186—95.]

Malayappattu.

326. 70 *of* 1887.—(Grantha and Tamil.) On a stone in the Vīra temple. A record of the time of the Karnāṭa king Veṅkaṭadēva I in Ś. 1524, Śubhakrit. Gift by Nāṅgama Naik, the son of Bomma Naik, to the Vīra temple (?) at Mariḷiyapaṭṭu. [*S.I.I.*, Vol. I, No. 138, pp. 137–38 and *N.A. Manual*, II, p. 358, and p. 419 where an alleged epigraph of Bommi Nāyuḍu is given to prove that he founded Vellore in Ś. 1320 !]

Śēnūr.

327. 393 *of* 1911.—(Tamil.) On the north wall of the Agastyēśvara temple. A record of the Vijayanagara king Mahāmaṇḍalēśvara Achyutadēva-Mahārāya in Ś. 1461, Vikārin. Records gift of two villages to the temples of Tiruvagattīśuramuḍaiya-Nāyinār and Pachchaivarṇa-Perumāḷ at Śenalūr, for repairs and worship.

328. 394 *of* 1911.—(Tamil.) On the north and west walls of the same temple. A damaged and mutilated record in the twentieth year of the Chōḷa king Rājarāja Rājakēsarivarman I (985—1013). Seems to contain portions of a historical introduction not copied so far and to record a gift of land to the temples of Tiruvagattīśuradēva and Tirumēṟṟaḷidēva, on account of the *drummers* who beat drums during the śrī-bali ceremony. [The introduction mentions the king's destruction of Madurai, his conquest of the haughty kings of Kollam, Kolladēśam and Koḍuṅgōḷūr (Cranganore), and his being waited upon by the *Kaḍalaraśar* or kings of the sea. He had also the epithets Tennaparākraman and Kīrtiparākrama Chōḷa. The Tiruvālaṅgāḍu plates also refer to his conquest of the Pāṇḍya Amarabhujaṅga and the invasion of Paraśurāma's country.]

Tiruvallam.

This place occurs in the *Dēvāram*, and goes back to Pallava times. This is corroborated by the fact that inscription of the Pallava Nandivikramavarman, his Bāṇa contemporary Vikramāditya I and Gaṅga contemporary Prithvīpati I are found. Most of the Chōḷa kings, again have got their epigraphs, with occasional reference to their Gaṅga, Vaiḍumba and Śengēṇi feudatories. Tiruvallam (called also Tīkkāli Vallam or Vāṇapuram) was in Mīyarai nāḍu or Karaivaḷi in Perumbāṇappāḍi, in Paḍuvūrkōṭṭam, in Jayaṅkoṇḍachōḷamaṇḍalam. For the local traditions see *N.A. Manual*, II, p. 356.

329. 75 *of* 1889.—On the west wall of garbhagriha of Bilvanāthēśvara temple. A record in the third year of the Chōḷa king Kō-Parakēsarivarman *alias* Uḍaiyār Rājēndradēva (1050—62). Records that the temple authorities received 25 kaḷanjus from a person who was one of the commissioners of Aimbuni in Karaivaḷi for temple expenses, payment to Dīkshitar, etc. [The interest on 3 *kalanju* is said to be ½ kaḷanju per year. See *S. Ind. Inscrns.*, III, No. 55, pp. 111—3.]

330. 76 *of* 1889.—(Tamil and Grantha.) On a rock, 1 mile north-east of the same place. A record in the sixty-second year of Kō-Vijaya-Nandivikramavarman (the father, according to the Government Epigraphist, of Nripatuṅga and son-in-law of the Rāshṭrakūṭa Amōghavarsha I). Records that a goldsmith granted some land to a temple at Vāṇapuram and Mahābalivāṇarāya confirmed the grant. *S. Ind. Inscrns.*, III, *No.* 42, *pp.* 90—2. According to Prof. Dubreuil the king referred to is Nandivarman Pallavamalla whom he attributes to 717—779 A.D. See his *Pallavas*, *pp.* 74-5.

331. 77 *of* 1889.—On the west wall of *garbhagriha* of Bilvanāthēśvara temple. A record of the Bāṇa king Vāṇa-Vidyādhara-rāja *alias* Vāṇarāyar. Records gift of twenty kaḷanju by the Bāṇa queen (who is said to be the daughter of Kokuni Pratipati, i.e., Prithvīpati I) to the assembly of Tiruvallam for supplying one *uri* of ghee every day for maintenance of a lamp in the temple. *S. Ind. Inscrns.*, III, *No.* 47, *pp.* 98—100.]

332. 78 *of* 1889.—On the west wall of *garbhagriha* in the same temple. A record of the Bāṇa king Vāṇa-Vidyādhara-rāyar *alias* Vāṇarāyar. Similar to the above. The queen's name is here given as Kuṇḍavai. *S. Ind. Inscrns.*, III, *No.* 48, *pp.* 100-1.

333. 79 *of* 1889.—On the west wall of kitchen of the same temple. A record in the third year of Vijaya-Gaṇḍa-Gōpāla-dēva. One Aḷagia Pallavan Edirili Śōḷa Śambuvarāyan (evidently the same as Aḷagia Śōḷan, the feudatory of Rājarāja III) remits 1/16 and 1/5 of the taxes. *S. Ind. Inscrns.*, III, *No.* 63, *p.* 123.

334. 80 *of* 1889.—On the east wall of the maṇṭapa in the same temple. A record in the seventeenth year of Sakalalōkachakravartin "who conquered the goddess of fortune and took the earth."

335. 81 *of* 1889.—On the east wall of maṇṭapa in the same temple. A record in the twenty-third year Kō-Māravarman Tribhuvanachakravartin Vīra-Pāṇḍyadēva.

336. 92 *of* 1889.—On the north wall of the mahāmaṇṭapa in the same temple. A record in the third year of the Chōḷa king Kō-Parakēsarivarman *alias* Rājēndra-Chōḷadēva (I). Records that the assembly of Vānapuram sold 1,000 *kuḻis* of land to the Vaiḍumba Sōmanātha, son of Śaṅkaradēva (son of Tiruvaiyan), which he assigned to Tiruvaiya Īśvara. *S. Ind. Inscrns.*, III, *No.* 53, *pp.* 107—9 and No. 359 below.

337. 190 *of* 1894.—On the south, east and north walls of the same temple. A record in the fourth year of the Chōla king Kō-Parakēsarivarman *alias* Rājēndradēva (1050—63).

338. 298 *of* 1897.—(Tamil.) On a stone built into the floor of the same temple. A record of Bāṇa king Vāṇavidyādhara. Printed in *S. Ind. Inscrns.*, III, *No.* 46. Records gift of twenty kaḷanju of gold by the Bāṇa queen to the assembly to supply daily one *uri* of ghee for a lamp. Fine of five kaḷanju for a day's failure.

339. 299 *of* 1897.—(Tamil.) On the north wall of the Nakulēśvara shrine in the same temple. A record in the fourth year of the Chōḷa king Parakēsarivarman *alias* Rājēndra-Chōḷadēva (I). Printed in *Ibid.*, *No.* 54, *pp.* 109--111. Records that Īrayiravan Pallavaraiyan, an officer of Rājarāja I, built a shrine called

Rājarājeśvara and endowed 2,000 *kulis* of land (which he purchased for 50 kāśu from the assembly of Tiruvallam) for two lamps. *S. Ind. Inscrns.*, III, *No.* 54.

340. 300 *of* 1897.—(Tamil.) On the south wall of the mahā-maṇṭapa. A record in the twenty-third year of the Chōḷa king Kulōttuṅga-Chōḷadēva. Printed in *Ibid., No.* 59. Records the gift of a lamp by a Gaṅga chief, for the benefit of his daughter who was the consort of Vīrachōḷa. Dr. Hultzsch identifies the king with Kulōttuṅga I and Vīrachōḷa with his son, the Viceroy of Veṅgi.

341. 301 *of* 1897.—(Tamil.) On the wall to the north of the tank in the same temple. A record in the eighth year of the Chōḷa king Kulōttuṅga-Chōḷadēva (III). Printed in *Ibid., No.* 63, *pp.* 120–1. Śeṅgēṇi Miṇḍan Attimallan Śambuvarāyan grants the *triśūla kāśu* and *kuṟṟadaṇḍa* to the temple.

342. 302 *of* 1897.—(Tamil.) On the same wall. A record in the eleventh year of the Chōḷa king Kulōttuṅga-Chōḷadēva (III). Gift of the income from the taxes of *vaḍagaṇdam*, *kamugaḍi*, the tax on looms, Ajīvakas and kuṟṟadaṇḍa to the temple of Tīkkāli Vallam. *S. Ind. Inscrns.*, III, *No.* 61, *pp.* 121–2.

343. 303 *of* 1897.—(Tamil.) On the north wall of the mahā-maṇṭapa in the same temple. A record in the thirty-fourth year of the Chōḷa king Kulōttuṅga-Chōḷadēva (III). Records the gift of two lamps by Ariyapiḷḷai, the queen of Amarābharaṇa Śīyagaṅga. See No. 10 of 1893 at Conjeeveram and the note to it. *S. Ind. Inscrns.*, III, *No.* 62, *pp.* 122–3. Śīyagaṅga was the patron of the great Tamil Grammarian Pavaṇandi, the author of the *Nannūl.*

344. 304 *of* 1897.—(Tamil.) On a slab built into the floor of the same temple. A damaged record in the seventeenth year of 'the Gaṅga-Pallava' king Vijaya-Nandivikramavarman.

345. 149 *of* 1898.—(Tamil.) On the south wall of the ruined temple in the midst of the fields to the south of the same place. A record in the fifth year of the Chōḷa king Vikrama-Chōḷa (1118—35). Records a sale of land.

346. 150 *of* 1898.—(Tamil.) On the south wall of the ruined temple in the midst of the fields to the south of the same place. A record in the sixth year of the Chōḷa king Vikrama-Chōḷa (1118—35). Records a sale of land.

347. 1-*a of* 1890.—On the north wall of the mahāmaṇṭapa in the Bilvanāthēśvara temple. A record in the seventeenth year of Kō-Vijaya-Nandivikramavarman, recording the gift of three villages (called by the single name of Viḍēlviḍugu Vikramāditya chaturvedimaṅgalam) at the request of the Bāṇa king Vikramāditya I. The executor was Viḍēlviḍugu kāḍuveṭṭi Tamiḷappērarayan. [See *S. Ind. Inscrns.*, III, *No.* 43, *pp.* 92—4. The inscription furnishes the earliest mention of *Tiruppadiyam.*]

348. 1-*b of* 1890.—On the north wall of mahāmaṇṭapa in the same temple. A record of the Bāṇa king Mahāvali-Vāṇarāja in Ś. 810 (A.D. 888). Records that a Brāhmaṇa of Eṭṭukūr near Kāvēripākkam paid 25 kaḷanju to the villagers of Vannippēḍu in Kāranāḍu for maintaining a lamp on its interest. Fine for failure 5 *kaḷanjus* a day. *S. Ind. Inscrns.*, III, *No.* 44, *pp.* 95-6.

349. 2 *of* 1890.—On the south wall of mahāmaṇṭapa in the same temple.

350. 3 *of* 1890.—(Three Sanskrit verses in grantha alphabet.) On the south wall of the maṇṭapa in front of the Bilvanāthēśvara shriṇe. A record of Vīra-Champa, son of Chōḷabhūpa, in Ś. 1236. Says that the maṇṭapa was constructed by an ascetic named Gñānātman or Gñānamūrti and named after a biruda of the king. A Gñānamurti built also a Śiva shrine called Nāyaka Śivālaya it has been surmised that Vīrachampa was a Nāyaka or lieutenant of an unknown chief. [See *Ep. Ind.*, *Vol.* III, *pp.* ,70 1.]

351. 4 *of* 1890.—On the north wall of mahāmaṇṭapa in the same temple. A record in the fifth year of Chōla king Kō-Parakēsarivarman *alias* Rājēndra-Chōḷadēva (I, 1011—43).

352. 5 *of* 1890.—On the south wall of mahāmaṇṭapa in the same temple. A record in the second year of Ko-Rājakēsarivarman *alias* Uḍaiyār Rājamahēndradēva. A military officer purchased 800 *kuḷis* of land from the Tiruvallam assembly and gave them to temple. The cost was 64 *kāsu* which was equal to 22 *kalanju* and eight *manjāḍi* at the rate of 7 *manjāḍi* for each kāśu. *S. Ind. Inscrns.*, III, No. 56, pp. 113-4.

353. 6 *of* 1890.—On the west wall of the Nakulēśvara shrine. A record in the thirtieth year of Kō-Rājakēsarivarman *alias* Uḍaiyār Rājarājadēva (I).

354. 7 *of* 1890.—On the south wall of mahāmaṇṭapa. A record in the twenty-first year of the Chōḷa king Kō-Parakēsarivarman *alias* Uḍaiyār Rājēndra-Chōḷadēva (I, 1011—53).

355. 8-*a of* 1890.—On the west wall of garbhagriha. A record in the seventh year of the Chōḷa king Kō-Rājarājakēsarivarman (I). Records the setting up of an image of the goddess by a Brāhman and the endowment of a lamp. (1,700 kuḷis of land brought from the assembly of Mandiram in Tunāḍu, i.e., Mēlpādi. *S. Ind. Inscrns.*, III, No. 50, pp. 103-4.)

356. 8-*b of* 1890.—On the west wall of *garbhagriha.* A record in the tenth year of the Chōḷa king Kō-Rājarājakēsarivarman. (985—1013).

357. 9 *of* 1890.—On the base of the verandah round the Bilvanāthēśvara shrine. A record in the twenty-sixth year of Kō-Rājakēsarivarman *alias* Chakravartin Kulōttuṅga-Chōḷadēva (I). Records the gift of a lamp to the temple by a native of Kalavai in Śeṅgunṛanāḍu, a subdivision of Paḷakunṛa kōṭṭam. Refers to the king's conquest over Vikramāditya VI and Jayasimha III. *S. Ind. Inscrns.*, III, 58, pp. 118—20.

358. 10 *of* 1890.—On the south wall of *garbhagriha.* A record in the seventh year of the Chōḷa king Ko-Rājarājakēsarivarman (I). The date has been calculated by Kielhorn to be 26th Sep. 991. (See *Ep. Ind.*, IV, p. 66). The Inscription records the visit of Madhurāntaka Kaṇḍarādittanār to the temple, his performance of the God's Abhishēka with 1,000 jars and inquiry into temple finance. See *S. Ind. Inscrns.*, III, No. 49, pp. 10—3.

359. 11 *of* 1890.—On the north wall of garbhagriha. A record in the sixteenth year of the Chōḷa king Kō-Rājarāja-Rajakēsarivarman (I). Records that the assembly of Vāṇapuram sold 700 *kuḷis* of land to one Śaṅkaradēva (who has the Gaṅga birudas, who granted it to the temple of Tiruvaiya Īśvara named after his father. See *S. Ind. Inscrns.*, Vol. III, No. 51, pp. 104—6. Śaṅkara was evidently the Vaiḍumba chief. See N.A. 336 above).

360. 12 *of* 1890.—On the south wall of *garbhagriha.* A record of Bāṇa king Mahāvali-Vāṇarāyar. Records that a man of Ponpaḍu kūṭṭam (near kacchippēḍu) purchased some land and endowed it for offerings and lamp. The *Sabha* was entrusted with the duty. (40 kaḷanjus = 2 nilams and 1,700 kuḷis). *S. Ind. Inscrns.*, III, No. 45, pp. 96–7.

361. 13 *of* 1890.—On the west wall of mahāmaṇṭapa. A record in the twenty-sixth year of the Chōḷa king Kō-Parakēsarivarman *alias* Uḍaiyār Rājēndra-Chōḷa-dēva (I, 1011—53).

362. 14 *of* 1890.—On the west and south walls of garbhagriha. A record in the twentieth year of the Chōḷa king Kō-Rājarāja-Rājakēsarivarman *alias* Rājarājadēva (I). Records the gift of 90 sheep for a lamp by Nannamārāyar, the son of Vaidumba Tukkarai and ruler of Iṅgaḷḷūr nāḍu in Mahārājapāḍi. An inscription at Miṇḍigal in Kōlār District mentions Mārājavāḍi 7,000 (279 of 1895), the capital of which was Vallūr in Cudappah District. Iṅgaḷḷur has been identified with Iṅganūr near Kāḷahasti. See *S. Ind. Inscrns.*, III, No. 52, pp. 106–7.

363. 15 *of* 1890.—On the north wall of mahāmaṇṭapa. A record in the third year and 200th day of Kō-Parakēsarivarman *alias* Uḍaiyār Ādhirājēndradēva (whom Dr. Hultzsch identifies with the son of Vīrā Rājēndra I and brother-in-law of Vikramāditya VI). Gift of the village revenues of Kukkanūr in Tūy nāḍu and Mandiram by two royal officers to Tiruvallam temple. The inscription iș of great fiscal interest. *Ibid.*, No. 57, pp. 114—8.

364. 16 *of* 1890.—On the south wall of mahāmaṇṭapa. A record in the sixth year of Kō-Rājakēsarivarman *alias* Uḍaiyār Vīrā-Rājēndradēva (I? 1063—70).

365. 17 *of* 1890.—On the south wall of garbhagriha. A record in the thirty-first year of the Chōḷa king Kō-Parakēsarivarman *alias* Uḍaiyār Rājēndra-Chōḷa-dēva (I, 1012—53).

366. 18 *of* 1890.—A record on the south, east and north walls of mahāmaṇṭapa in the same temple.

Udayēndiram.

Corruption of Udayēndiramaṅgalam or Udayachandra-Maṅgalam, named after Udayachandra, the general of Nandivarman Pallavamalla. (717—779, according to Prof. Dubreuil.)

367. 546 *of* 1893.—(Tamil.) On the floor of the Sundararāja-Perumāḷ temple. A fragment of record of the Chōḷa king Ko-Rājakēsarivarman.

367-A. A C.P. grant of Śembiyan Māvalivāṇarāya Prithvīpati II Hastimalla, the Gaṅga-Bāṇa in grantha and Tamil. Records that with the permission of his suzerain Parāntaka I he made the village of Kaḍaikōṭṭūr one with Udayēndiram (in the fifteenth year of Parāntaka). See *Salem Manual,* Vol. II, p. 369 ff. and *S. Ind. Inscrns.*, II, No. 76, pp. 376—90.

368. C.P. grant of the Bāṇa king Vikramāditya II (Sanskrit), recording the gift of the village of Udayēndiramaṅgala to some Brahmans. The plates are incomplete. They give the genealogy of the dynasty from Bali to Vijayabāhu Vikramāditya II, "friend of Kṛishṇarāja." Dr. Kielhorn places the inscription in the middle of the 12th century, and Dr. Hultzsch in the 11th; but it belongs to the 9th. Krishṇa Rāja might be the Rāshṭrakūṭa king Krishṇa II. The inscription has been published in *Ind. Antq.*, Vol. XIII, p. 6 ff. and in *Salem Manual,* Vol. II, p. 388 ff., and in *Ep. Ind.*, Vol. III, 74-9.

369. C.P. of Vīrachōḷa (Grantha). Records that Vīrachōḷa, the feudatory of the Chōḷa Parakēsarivarman, granted, at the instance of his spiritual adviser Nīla, a village named Parakēsari-chaturvēdimaṅgalam to Brāhmans. See *Ind. Antq.*, Vol. IX, p. 47 ff.; *Salem Manual,* Vol. II, p. 365 ff. and *Ep. Ind.*, Vol. III, 79—82.

370. C.P. grant of Nandivarman (I) (Sanskrit). Records that the Pallava king Nandivarman, son of Skandavarman, grandson of Simhavarman and great-grandson of Skandavarman gave the village of Kānchīvāyal and four pieces of forest land in the district of Aḍayāra, to Kuḷaśarmaṇ of the Kauśikagōtra, Taittirīya Śākha and Pravachanasūtra. Issued on the fifth lunar day of the bright half of Viśākha in the first year of his reign. [Kielhorn believes this to be a spurious document imitated in a later period from the Uravapalli grant of Vishṇugōpavarman which is edited by Dr. Fleet in Vol. V, *Ind. Antq.* The fact that the inscription contains a Sanskrit endorsement which is found only in that of Nandivarma Pallavamalla and another in Tamil in the twenty-sixth year of Parāntaka I, does show that the present grant is a copy from earlier originals. See *Ind. Antq.*, Vol. VIII, p. 167 ff.;

Salem Manual II, p. 349 ff.; *Ep. Ind.*, Vol. III, pp. 142—7; also *S.I.I.*, II, No. 74, pp. 361—74, where the sections dealing with Nandivarman's grant of the village of Udayēndram at the request Udayachandra and the combination of this place with Kānchīvayal are dealt with. For a satisfactory settlement of Nandivarman's place in the genealogy and his date see Prof. Dubreuil's *Pallavas*, pp. 24 and 72.

Vēppūr.

371. 20 *of* 1890.—On the north wall of the garbhagriha of the Vasishṭhēśvara temple. A record in the Rākshasa year of Vīra-Bukkaṇa-uḍaiyār.

372. 21 *of* 1890.—On the north wall of the Vighnēśvara shrine in the same temple. A record in the Parābhava year of Vīra, Kambaṇa-uḍaiyār. (Kampaṇa Uḍaiyār II, son of Bukka I ?).

POLUR TALUK.

Kadalādi.

373. *No.* 107, *Sewell's List.*—This is a Vijayanagar grant in five leaves, strung on a ring with a seal bearing the emblems of the boar, sun and moon. The grant, although it states that Narasa had only two sons, distinctly asserts that Kṛishṇa Rāya's successor, Achyutēndra, was younger brother of Kṛishṇa Rāya ("tadanujanma"). The inscription records the grant by Achyuta of the three villages, Kaḍalāḍi, Kūrnatūru, and Māmbākam, which he calls "ornaments of Jayaṁkoṇḍa Chōḷamaṇḍalam," in Ś. 1451, Virōdhi (A.D. 1529).

Kōvilūr (Javadis).

374. 346 *of* 1912.—(Tamil.) On the south wall of the Śiva temple. A record of the Vijayanagara king Vīrapratāpa-Dēvarāya *alias* Mallikārjunarāya, Ś. 1377, Yuva, Karkaṭaka, śu. di. 7, Monday, Sodi (=Monday 21st July 1455). Records gift of the village Gaṇapatimaḍu in Maṅgala-nāḍu near the hill called Rājagambīran-malai to the temple of Tirumūla-Nāyinār, by a certain Timmaya-Nāyaka, for the victory of the king.

375. 347 *of* 1912.—(Tamil.) On the same wall. A record of the Vijayanagara king Dēvarāya-Mahārāya (II) in Ś. 1353, Virōdhikrit, Makara, śu. di. full-moon, Thursday, Pūśam, lunar eclipse (=Thursday, 17th January 1432, lunar eclipse). Records gift of the village Palavarai-paṟṟu near Rājagambhīran to the temple of Tirumūla-Nāyinār in Maṅgala-nāḍu, by Aṇṇāmalainātha, son of Naraśiṅgādēva, chief of Malai-paṟṟu, for the victory of the king.

376. 348 *of* 1912.—(Tamil.) On a slab set up in front of the same temple. Records the death of a certain Villi in a tiger hunt.

Padavēdu.

377. 93 *of* 1887.—(Grantha and Tamil.) On the east and north bases of Ammaiyappēśvara temple. A record of Rājagambhīra Śambuvarāya, who was a contemporary of Tribhuvanachakravartin Rājarājadēva, Ś. 1180, expired. Records a grant to Ammayappēśvara named evidently after a *biruda* of the chief of the family. See *S.I.I.*, Vol. I, No. 78, p. 108.

378. 94 *of* 1887.—(Grantha and Tamil.) On the south base of the same temple. Fragmentary. *S.I.I.*, Vol. I, No. 142, p. 138.

379. 95 *of* 1887.—(Grantha and Tamil.) On the south wall of the same temple. A record of the Vijayanagara king Dēvarāya (II) in Ś. 1356, Pramādi. Gift of 1 *vaḷavu* to the Ammayappa temple. *S.I.I.*, Vol. I, No. 79, p. 109.

380. 96 *of* 1887.—(Grantha and Tamil.) On the south wall of the same temple. A record of the Vijayanagara king Dēvarāya (II), in Ś. 1357. Records the gift of a village. See *S.I.I.*, Vol. I, No. 80, pp. 109–110.

381. 97 *of* 1887.—(Grantha and Tamil.) On the walls of Sōmanāthēśvara temple. A record of the Vijayanagara king Prandha Immaḍi Dēvarāya (II), in Ś. 1371 (expired), on the day of Uttirāḍam, the 13th lunar day of the month of Simha in year Śukla. Mentions the right and left hand castes. Incomplete. See *S.I.I.*, Vol. I, No. 81, pp. 110–111, and *N.A. Manual*, Vol. II, p. 404 (which also gives a long account of the local traditions).

382. 98 *of* 1887.—(Grantha and Tamil.) On the north wall of the same temple. Duplicate of the first four lines of above. *S.I.I.*, Vol. I, No. 143, p. 139.

Tirumalai.

The local rock is called Vaigaimalai and the village at its based Tiruvaigāvūr. See *N.A. Manual*, Vol. II, pp. 405–6.

383. 80 *of* 1887.—(Grantha and Tamil.) On the top of the Tirumalai rock. A record in the twelfth year of the Chōḷa king Kō-Parakēsarivarman, *alias* Uḍaiyār-Rājēndra-Chōḷadēva I (conqueror of Jayasimha). See *S. Ind. Inscrns.*, Vol. I, No. 67, pp. 95—99 and *Ep. Ind.*, Vol. IX, pp. 229—233. The first part of the inscription (quoted in the *Virasōliyam*) describes his conquests. The second part records gift of money for lamp and offerings to a Jain temple on the hill by the wife of a merchant of Malliyūr in Karaivaḷi, a subdivision of Perumbāṇappāḍi. The Jain temple was evidently founded by Kuṇḍavi, the king's aunt, and was in the *pallichchandam* of Vaigāvūr, in Mugaināḍu, in Paṅgalanāḍu, Jayaṅgoṇḍachōḷamaṇḍalam.

384. 81 *of* 1887.—(Grantha and Tamil.) On a buried rock between the Gōpura and the painted cave. A record in the twelfth year of the Chōḷa king Kō-Parakēsarivarman, *alias* Uḍaiyār

Rājēndra-Chōla-dēva (who conquered Jayasimha). Gift of money for two lamps by Chinnavai, evidently a Chōḷa princess and Pallava Queen. See *S.I.I.*, Vol. I, No. 68, pp. 100–101.

385. 82 *of* 1887.—(Grantha and Tamil.) On a buried rock in front of the Gōpura. A record in the twenty-first year of the Chōḷa king Kōrāja-Rājakēsarivarman, *alias* Rājarājadēva I. Records that a certain Guṇavīramunivan built a sluice called after a Jain teacher Gaṇiśēkhara maru porchūriyan, the pure master who is said to have been skilled in the elegant arts (கலைபுரியும,திநிபுணன் வெண்டிமூரான் கணிச்செகரா மரு பொற்சூரியன்). [It is difficult to say who this Guṇavīra Munivar was. Tamil literary traditions speak of (1) Guṇasāgara who composed the *Yāpparuṅgalagārigai* whom the *Abhidhan* attributes to Ś. 300; (2) Guṇabhadra, the teacher of Maṇḍalapurusha, the author of the *Chūḍāmaṇi nigaṇṭu* who was the contemporary of the Rāshtrakūṭa Kṛishṇa III; and (3) Guṇavīra Paṇḍita, the author of *Nēminātham* and *Vachchaṇandimālai*. The last of these was the contemporary of Tribhuvanavīra or Kulōttuṅga III.]

386. 83 *of* 1887.—(Grantha and Tamil.) Inside Gōpura. A record of Rājarājadēva. *S.I.I.*, Vol. I, No. 141, p. 138.

387. 84 *of* 1887.—(Grantha and Tamil.) On the walls of a maṇṭapa at the base of Tirumalai rock. A record in the tenth year of the Pāṇḍya king Kō-Māravarman Tribhuvanachakravartin Vīra-Pāṇḍyadeva. Records that Ambalapperumāḷ, the headman of Pāṇḍaiyūr in Tirumunaippāḍi nāḍu in Rājarājavaḷanāḍu built a sluice for a tank at Vaigai Tirumalai. *S.I.I.*, I, Vol. I, No. 69, p. 101.

388. 85 *of* 1887.—(Grantha and Tamil.) On the walls of a maṇṭapa at the base of Tirumalai rock. A record in the twelfth year of Rājanārāyaṇa Śambuva-rāja, regarding the setting up of a Jaina image (Arhan) by a lady of Ponnūr. *S.I.I.*, 4 I. Vol. I, No. 70, p. 102.

389. 86 *of* 1887.—(Grantha and Tamil.) A record on the walls of a maṇṭapa at the base of Tirumalai rock. Gift of a well for the merit of one Siṟṟinaṅgai by an inhabitant of Aruḷmoḷidēvarpuram. *S.I.I.*, I, Vol. I, No. 71, p. 102.

390. 87 *of* 1887.—(Grantha and Tamil.) On the walls of a maṇṭapa at the base of Tirumalai rock. A record of Ommaṇa Uḍaiyār, son of Kampaṇa Uḍaiyār (II) and grandson of Vīrakampaṇa, in Ś. 1296, expired. The inscription is the receipt for the cost of some land which a certain Vishṇu Kambḷi Nāyaka bought from the villagers of Śambukulapperumāḷagaram or Rājagambhīra Chaturvēdimaṅgalam in Murumaṅgala paṟṟu in Maṇḍaikula nāḍu in Paḷakunṟakōṭṭam in Jayaṅkoṇḍamaṇḍalam. *S.I.I.* I, Vol. I, No. 72, pp. 102–104.

391. 88 *of* 1887.—(Grantha and Tamil.) In a small shrine below the painted cave. Records that one Arishṭanēmi āchārya of

Kaḍaikoṭṭūr, a pupil of Paravādimalla of Tirumalai, caused the image of a Yakshā to be made. *S.I.I.*, Vol. I, No. 73, pp. 104-105.

392. 89 *of* 1887.—(Grantha and Tamil.) Door-way of the painted cave. A record in the twentieth year of Tribhuvanachakravartin Rājarājadēva (III ?). Records gift of lands by Rājagambhīra Śambuvarāyan *alias* Attimallan Śambukula Perumāḷ to an Aṇḍaṅgaḷ Paṅgalarāyar of Vīranpākkam in Tamaṇūr nāḍu. *S.I.I.*, Vol. I, No. 74, p. 105.

393 & 394. 90 *and* 91 *of* 1887.—(Grantha and Tamil.) Doorway of the painted cave. A record of the king Viḍukādaḷagiya Perumāḷ (Vyāmuktaśravaṇōjvala), the Aḍigamān of the Chēra race and Lord of Takaṭa (Tagaḍūr). He was the son of Rājarāja and descendant of Yavanika, king of Kēraḷa or Eḻini, king of Vanji. Records the repair of the images of a Yakshā and Yakshi, the presentation of a gong and the construction of a channel. *S.I.I.*, Vol. I, No. 75, p. 106 and No. 76, p. 107.

395. 92 *of* 1887.—(Grantha and Tamil.) A record on the door-way of the painted cave. See *S.I.I.*, I, No. 77, pp. 107-108. Records the gift of a sluice to the Kaḍappēri tank by one Kariyapperumāḷ Vairādarāyan.

396. 65 *of* 1907.—(Tamil.) On a rock to the left of the painted cave. A record in the nineteenth year of the Rāshṭrakūṭa king Śrī-Kaṇṇaradēva (Kṛishṇa III), "who took Kachchi and Tanjai." Records gift of a lamp to the Yakshā on the Tirumalai at Vaigāvūr by a servant of Gaṅgamādēvi, queen of Kaṇṇaradēva-Pridigaṅgaraiyar. See No. 586 below.

397. 66 *of* 1907.—(Tamil.) In the same place. A record in the fourth year of the Chōḷa king Parakēsarivarman. Records gift of gold for feeding one devotee *(aḍigaḷ)* daily in the paḷḷi on the Tirumalai at Vaigāvūr in Paṅgala-nāḍu, a subdivision of Paḷaguṇrakōṭṭam.

398. 67 *of* 1907.—(Tamil.) On a pillar set up in front of the Śikhāmaṇinātha temple. A damaged record of the Vijayanagara king Pratāpa Immaḍi-Dēvarāya-Mahārāya (II, 1422—47) in Ś. 1373 expired, Prajāpati. The king is said to have witnessed the elephant hunt.

399. 68 *of* 1907.—(Tamil.) On nine detached stones lying in the courtyard of the same temple. Fragments of record in the twenty-second year in which the king's name does not appear.

400. 69 *of* 1907.—(Tamil.) On a boulder in the tank at the same village. A record of the Vijayanagara king Vīrapratāpa Dēvarāya-Mahārāya (II) in Krōdhana. Seems to provide for the removal of silt in certain tanks.

Viralur.

401. 349 *of* 1912.—(Tamil.) On a slab set up near the Pūṅgāvanattamman temple. Refers to a guild of merchants. The record may be of about the time of Rājarāja I.

402. 350 *of* 1912.—(Tamil.) On a slab set up near the Gaṇēśa temple in the same village. An unfinished record of the Vijayanagara king Dēvarāya-Mahārāya (II) in Kīlaka (i.e., Ś. 1351). Records that four hamlets in Śirumuri-Paṅgala-nāḍu were caused to be granted by the king at Vijayanagara, to the temple of Arulālanātha-Nāyanār and Uṇṇāmulai-Nāchchiyar, while Mallappa-Daṇṇāyaka was the Prime-Minister.

TIRUPPATTŪR TALUK.

Tiruppattūr.

403. 248 *of* 1909.—(Tamil.) On the north wall of the central shrine in the Brahmēśvara temple. A record of the Vijayanagara king Vīra-Vijayabhūpatirāya, son of Vīra-Dēvarāya (I) in Ś. 1331, Virōdhi. Built in, in the middle. Records gift of land to the temple of Brahmīśvaramuḍaiya-Nāyanār at Tiruppērūr *alias* Śrī-Mādhava-chaturvēdimaṅgalam in Eyyilnāḍu, a subdivision of Nigarilisōḷa-maṇḍalam.

404. 249 *of* 1909.—(Tamil.) On the same wall. A fragment of record of the Hoysaḷa king Vīra-Vallāladēva (III, 1291—1342) in Ś. 1256, Bhava. See *Mys. Gazr.*, Vol. I, p. 341.

405. 250 *of* 1909.—(Tamil.) On the same wall. A record in the third year of the Hoysala king Viśvanāthadēva (the son of Vira Rāmanātha and grandson of Sōmēśvara) (1233—54). Built in, in the middle. Records that from the year quoted, the dēvadāna villages belonging to the temple of Brahmīśvaramuḍaiya-Nāyanār, were made rent free.

406. 251 *of* 1909.—(Tamil.) On the north wall of the central shrine in the Varadarāja-Perumāḷ temple in the same village. A record of the Vijayanagara king Vīrapratāpa Dēvarāya-Mahārāya (I) in Ś. 1338, Durmukhi. Built in, at the beginning. Mentions a number of divisions (nāḍu) and subdivisions (paṟṟu) belonging to the Mulvāy-rājya and says that the manṟāḍis of these districts were ordered by the king to pay a fee for the grazing of sheep and cows in the forest. The divisions were Tagaḍu nāḍu, Eyilnāḍu, Kalingarai-paṟṟu, Pārūr-paṟṟu, Mukkanūr-paṟṟu, Perumalainādu, Arpūr-paṟṟu, Paiyūr-paṟṟu, Kuḍīvūr-paṟṟu, Tenśīrmaṅgalam-paṟṟu and four others.

407. 252 *of* 1909.—(Tamil.) On four detached stones built into the platform round the flag-staff in front of the same temple. A record of the Chōḷa king Rājarājakēsarivarman *alias* Śrī-Rājarājadēva (I) the date of which is lost. Contains portions of the historical introduction. Mentions Vīranārāyana-chaturvēdimaṅgalam, a brahmadēya in Rājēndraśiṅga-valanāḍu.

408. 253 *of* 1909.—(Tamil.) On a pillar set up in front of the same temple. A record in Prabhava. Gift of lamp by Mādappa-

Daṇṇāyakkar *alias* Vallāladēva, younger brother of the Mahāpradhāna Śingaya-Daṇṇāyakkar, to the temple of Aṇaikātta-Perumāḷ at Mādhava-chaturvēdimaṅgalam.

TIRUVAṆṆĀMALAI TALUK.

Ārappākkam.

409. 38 *of* 1887.—(Grantha and Tamil.) On a stone. A record of the Vijayanagara king Sadāśivadēva, dated Ś. 1488. Records a grant made to the Jvarakaṇḍēśvara temple of Vēllore, at the request of Chinna Bomma Nāyaka, by Mahāmaṇḍ Tirumalaiyadēva Mahārāya (the younger brother of Rāmarāja). See Vilppāka grant of Vēṅkaṭa I for Vēllore chiefs. *S.I.I.*, I, No. 43, pp. 69—71.

Āvūr.

410. Grant of land to the Śiva temple by private parties. *Antiquities*, I, p. 205.

411. In the Śiva temple. A private grant in Ś. 1393 (A.D. 1471), during the reign of Narasimhadēva of Vijayanagar. *Ibid.*, p. 205.

Cheṅgama.

In his *Antiquities* Mr. Sewell mentions five inscriptions in this place.

412. 105 *of* 1900.—(Tamil.) On the north wall of the central shrine of the Rishabhēśvara temple. A record in the thirteenth year of the Chōḷa king Tribhuvanachakravartin Vīrarājēndra-Chōḷadēva. Records gift of land to the temple of Iḍavandurai at Seṅgaimā.

413. 106 *of* 1900.—(Tamil.) On the north wall of the central shrine of the Rishabhēśvara temple. An incomplete and damaged record in Ś. 1180.

414. 107 *of* 1900.—(Tamil.) On the north wall of the central shrine of the Rishabhēśvara temple. Registers a political compact entered into by three chiefs,—between Karikālachōḷa-Āḍaiyūr-nāḍāḷvān and Seṅgēṇi Ammayappan Attimallan or Vikramasōḷa Śambuvarāyan on the one hand and Viḍukādaḷagiaperumāḷ on the other—that they should not fight with each other but help one another in case of attack by others, and form no alliance with certain chiefs among whom Śīyagaṅga was one. See No. 422 below.

415. 108 *of* 1900.—(Tamil.) On the west wall of the same shrine. A record in the seventh year of the Chōḷa king Tribhuvana-chakravartin Vīrarājēndra-Chōḷadēva. Records gift of land.

416. 109 *of* 1900.—(Tamil.) On the south wall of the same shrine. Mentions a certain Āṭkoṇḍān of Kaṇṇanūr. [The Tamil poet Villiputtūrār was patronised by a king Varapati Āṭkoṇḍān but it is extremely doubtful whether the Āṭkoṇḍān of this inscription is the same as he.]

417. 110 *of* 1900.—(Tamil.) On the south wall of the same shrine. A record in the twenty-first year of the Pāṇḍya king Tribhuvanachakravartin Śrīvallabhadēva. Built in.

418. 111 *of* 1900.—(Tamil.) On the south wall of the same shrine. Records verses in praise of a certain Vikki, king of Magada.

419. 112 *of* 1900.—(Tamil.) On the south wall of the same shrine. A record of the Uḍaiyār king Viruppaṇṇa Uḍaiyār, son of Hariyaṇṇa Uḍaiyār (i.e., Harihara II) in Ś. 1318 expired, Dhātri. Records gift of land. [Viruppuṇṇa Uḍaiyār is the second of that name. He is the same as Virūpāksha I.]

420. 113 *of* 1900.—(Tamil.) On the south wall of the same shrine. A record of the Pāṇḍya king Māravarman Tribhuvanachakravartin Parākrama-Pāṇḍyadēva, in his sixth year and Ś. 1262 (A.D. 1340). Built in; records a gift of land. Venkayya suggests that he might have been the successor of Vīra Pāṇḍya, "who became established on the Pāṇḍya kingdom after the flight of Sundara Pāṇḍya to Delhi in A.D. 1310." *Ep. Rep.*, 1900, p. 8, para. 14.

421. 114 *of* 1900.—(Tamil.) On the south wall of the same shrine. A record in the third year of the Chōḷa king Tribhuvanachakravartin Vīrarājēndradēva. Built in; records a gift of land.

422. 115 *of* 1900.—(Tamil.) On the south wall of the same shrine. A record in the twentieth year of the Chōḷa king Tribhuvanachakravartin Kulōttuṅga-Chōḷadēva (III, 1216—48). Registers a political compact between two chiefs, Karikālachōḷa-nāḍāḷvān and Śeṅgēni Ammayappan Attimallan. See No. 414 above. Vidugādaḷagia Perumāḷ is here excluded.

*Tiruvaṇṇamalai.**

423. 469 *of* 1902.—(Tamil.) On the south wall of the central shrine in the Aruṇāchalēśvara temple. A record of the Chōḷa king Parakēsarivarman, who took the head of the Vīra-Pāṇḍya, the date of which is doubtful. Records gift of 96 sheep for a lamp. [The king referred to is probably Parāntaka II Uttama Chōḷa, "the destroyer of Vīra-Pāṇḍya."]

424. 470 *of* 1902.—(Tamil.) On the same wall. A record in the third year of the Chōḷa king Parakēsarivarman. Records gift of gold for a lamp by the Chēra queen Kiḷānaḍigaḷ.

---

* In *Ins. S. Dts.*, pp. 122—25 eleven inscriptions have been given under this heading, I have not thought it worth while to mark the corresponding epigraphs in the text. Two C.P. grants, however, which have not been noted by the Department I have given, under Nos. 548-A and B.

425. 471 *of* 1902.--(Tamil.) On the same wall. A record in the third year of the Chōḷa king Parakēsarivaman, who took the head of Vīra-Pāṇḍya. Records gift of ninety sheep for a lamp. See note to No. 423 above.

426. 472 *of* 1902.—(Tamil.) On the same wall. A record of the Chōla king Parakēsarivarman, the date of which is doubtful. Records gift of ninety sheep for a lamp.

427. 473 *of* 1902.--(Tamil.) On the same wall. A record in the fourth year of the Chōḷa king Parakēsarivarman. Records gift of ninety sheep for a lamp.

428. 474 *of* 1902.—(Tamil.) On the same wall. A damaged record of the Chōḷa king Parakēsarivarman, the date of which is lost.

429. 475 *of* 1902.—(Tamil.) On the same wall. A record of the Rāshṭrakūṭa king Kaṇṇaradēva (Krishna III), the date of which is doubtful. Records gift of twenty cows.

430. 476 *of* 1902.—(Tamil.) On the west wall of the same shrine. A record in the fifteenth year of the Chōḷa king Madirai-koṇḍa Parakēsarivarman (Parāntaka I). Records gift of ninety sheep for a lamp.

431. 477 *of* 1902.—(Tamil.) On the south wall of the first prākāra of the same temple. A record in the nineteenth year of the Chōḷa king Parakēsarivarman *alias* Uḍaiyār Rājēndra-Chōḷadēva (I, 1012–43). Records gift of land for offerings by a servant of the king.

432. 478 *of* 1902.—(Tamil.) On the same wall. A record in the eighteenth year of the Chōḷa king Parakēsarivarman *alias* Uḍaiyār Rājēndra Chōḷa I (1012—43). The inscription opens with the usual historical introduction of Rājēndra Chōḷa I. Records sale of land.

433. 479 *of* 1902.—(Tamil.) On the same wall. A record in the twenty-seventh year of the Chōḷa king Parakēsarivarman *alias* Uḍaiyār Rājēndra Chōḷadēva (I, 1012—43). Records gift of land.

434. 480 *of* 1902.—(Tamil verse.) On the west wall of the same prākāra. A record of the Pallava king Niśśaṅkamalla Sakalabhuvanachakravartin Kōpperuñjiṅga, the protector of Mallai (Māvaliveram). Records gift of ornaments by the king and the erection of buildings by his son. [The latter claims to have driven the "Teluṅgar" to the north to perish. Venkayya thinks it might refer to his fighting against the Kākatiyas who, during the time of Gaṇapati, took possession of Conjeeveram. (*Ind. Antq.*, XXI, p. 197.) Venkayya believed that the victor was one of the princes who took advantage of the subsequent weakness of the Kākatiyas, and was able to go far as Drākshārāmam itself. In his view, the Kopperuñjiṅgas of Conjeeveram, Drākshārāmam and Tripurāntakam were identical.]. See No. 444 below.

435. 481 *of* 1902.—(Tamil.) On the west wall of the same prākāra. A record in the seventh year of the Pāṇḍya king Māravarman *alias* Tribhuvanachakravartin Kulaśēkharadēva. Records gift of 54 cows.

436. 482 *of* 1902.—(Tamil.) On the west wall of the same prākāra. A record in the sixteenth year of the Pāṇḍya king Kōnērimēlkoṇḍān Tribhuvanachakravartin Kulaśēkharadēva. Records gift of 32 cows and one bull by Śrīraṅganāthar *alias* Maḷavachakravartin of Vāraṇāvasi. [Śrīraṅganātha was probably a member of the Yādavarāya line.]

437. 483 *of* 1902.—(Tamil.) On the west wall of the same prākāra. A record of the Vijayanagara king Vira-Virupaṇṇa-Uḍaiyār II (i.e., Virupāksha I), son of Hariyappa-Uḍaiyār (Harihara II) in Ś. 1311, Śukla. Records gift of land. See Nos. 100 and 107.

438. 484 *of* 1902.—(Tamil and Grantha.) On the west wall of the same prākāra. A record in the twentieth year of the Pāṇḍya king Māravarman *alias* Tribhuvanachakravartin Kulaśēkharadēva (I ?). Records gift of 73 cows and 25 calves by Parākrama-Pāṇḍyadēva.

439. 485 *of* 1902.—(Tamil.) On the north wall of the same prākāra. A record in the sixteenth year of the Chōḷa king Tribhuvanachakravartin Rājarājadēva III (1216—48), corresponding to Saturday, 22nd May, 1232. Records gift of land to an image set up by Meykaṇḍadēvan of Tiruveṇṇainallūr. *Ep. Ind.*, Vol. VIII, p. 268. [The inscription gives a clue to the date of Meykaṇḍa, the disciple of Paranjōti Muni and the author of *Śivagnānabōdham*, the chief Bible of Śaiva Siddhānta philosophy. It is thus very important in the history of Tamil literature.]

440. 486 *of* 1902.—(Tamil.) On the same wall. A record in the twenty-sixth year of the Chōḷa king Tribhuvanachakravartin Kulōttuṅga Chōḷadēva. Records rules regarding the sale of house-sites in the temple street.

441. 487 *of* 1902.—(Tamil.) On the north wall of the first prākāra of the Aruṇāchalēśvara temple. A record in the thirty-sixth year of the Pallava king Sakalabhuvanachakravartin Kōpperuñjiṅgadēva (contemporary of Rājarāja III). Records gift of 32 cows and one bull by Kakku-Nāyakadēva, son of Madhusūdanadēva, who was the younger brother of Vijaya-Gaṇḍagōpāladēva. See Nos. 434 and 444.

442. 488 (*a*) *of* 1902.—(Tamil.) On the same wall. A record in the thirty-first year of the Chōḷa king Tribhuvanachakravartin Rājarājadēva (III ? 1216 –48). Records gift of vessels and ornaments by the queen of Sadum-Perumāḷ. See Nos. 434 and 444.

443. 488 (*b*) *of* 1902.—(Tamil.) On the same wall. A record in the ninth year of the Pallava king Sakalabhuvanachakravartin

Kōpperuñjiṅgadēva. Records gift of silver vessels by the same queen. See No. 434.

444. 489 *of* 1902.—(Tamil.) On the same wall. A record in the thirty-first year of the Pallava king Aḷagia Śīyan Sakalabhuvanachakravartin Kōpperuñjiṅgadēva. Records gift of land. From the fact that Mahārāja Simha of Tripurāntakam (Kurnool district) had the same birudas as Peruñjiṅga, and both had the title of Śīya, Venkayya infers that both are identical. See 197, 198 and 202 of 1905 at Tripurāntakam. Also see note to No. 12 above. See No. 434.

445. 490 *of* 1902.—(Tamil.) On the same wall. A record in the twenty-seventh year of the Chōḷa king Tribhuvanachakravartin Rājarājadēva (III ?). Records gift of land by Rājarājadēvan Vānakōvaraiyan for the merit of Ponparippina Perumāḷ. See Nos. 487 and 513.

446. 491 *of* 1902.—(Tamil.) On the same wall. A record in the thirty-second year of the Chōḷa king Tribhuvanachakravartin Rājarājadēva III, corresponding to Friday, February 7th, A.D. 1248. Records gift of 32 cows and 1 bull for a lamp. See *Ep. Ind.*, Vol. VIII, p. 6.

447. 492 *of* 1902.—(Tamil.) A record in the thirty-second year of the Chōḷa king Rājakēsarivarman *alias* Uḍaiyār Rājādhirājadēva. Records gift of gold. [Evidently Rājādhirāja I, 1018—52, is intended, as he alone ruled for more than 32 years.]

448. 493 *of* 1902.—(Tamil.) On the same wall. A record in the twentieth year of Chōḷa king Tribhuvanachakravartin Rājarājadēva (III ?). Records that a number of people joined together to reclaim certain land which had been neglected.

449. 494 *of* 1902.—(Tamil.) On the same wall. A record in the eighteenth year of the Chōḷa king Tribhuvanachakravartin Rājarājadēva (III), corresponding to Sunday, 13th November 1233. Records gift of 120 sheep by the daughter of an officer of Yādavarāyar. *Ep. Ind.*, Vol. VIII, p. 269.

450. 495 *of* 1902.—(Tamil.) On the same wall. A record in the thirtieth year of the Chōḷa king Tribhuvanachakravartin Rājarājadēva (III ?). Records gift of land, 32 cows and 1 bull by Tirukkāḷattidēvan.

451. 496 *of* 1902.—(Tamil.) On the same wall. A record in the fifth year of the Chōḷa king Tribhuvanachakravartin Rājarājadēva (III ?). Records that two persons pledged themselves not to leave the service of prince Pirudi Gaṅgar.

452. 497 *of* 1902.—(Tamil and Grantha.) On the same wall. A record in the twenty-fourth year of the Chōḷa king Tribhuvanachakravartin Rājarājadēva (III ?). Records gift of land by Rājagambhīra Chēdiyarāyan of Kiḷiyur. See No. 489 below.

453. 498 *of* 1902.--(Tamil and Grantha.) On the same wall. A record in the fifth year (i.e., 1250-51) of the Chōḷa king Tribhuvanachakravartin Rājēndra-Chōḷadēva (III). Records gift of land by Simhaṇa-daṇḍanātha for the merit of his uncle Kampaya. [See 501 of 1904 at Vēdāraṇyam in Tanjore district for a probable reference to the same chief.]

454. 499 *of* 1902.—(Tamil.) On the same wall. A record of the Hoysaḷa king Pratāpachakravartin Vīra-Vallāladēva (III) in Ś. 1262, Vikrama. Records gift of land by Vallappadaṇṇāyakar. See No. 482 below.

455. 500 *of* 1902.—(Tamil.) On the same wall. A record in the fifth year of the Pallava king Sakalabhuvanachakravartin Kōpperuñjiṅgadēva. Records gift of land by the king. See Nos. 434 and 444.

456. 501 *of* 1902.—(Tamil.) On the same wall. A record of the Chōḷa king Tribhuvanachakravartin Rājarājadēva (III ?), the date of which is doubtful. Records gift of 32 cows and 1 bull for a lamp.

457. 502 *of* 1902.—(Tamil.) On the same wall. A record in the twenty-fifth year of the Chōḷa king Tribhuvanachakravartin Rājarājadēva (III). Records gift of 32 cows and 1 bull for a lamp.

458. 503 *of* 1902.—(Tamil.) On the same wall. A record in the thirty-second year of the Chōḷa king Tribhuvanachakravartin Rājarājadēva (III), corresponding to Wednesday, April 22, A.D. 1248. Records gift of land by Umai-Aḷvār, queen of Ilakkumadēvar. *Ep. Ind.*, VIII, p. 6. Compare No. 465 below.

459. 504 *of* 1902.--(Tamil.) On the same wall. A record in the thirtieth year of the Chōḷa king Tribhuvanachakravartin Rājarājadēva III. Records gift of 50 cows by Vēṇavuḍaiyān, the younger brother of Śōḷakōn, an officer of Kōpperuñjiṅgan. Compare *Ep. Ind.*, Vol. VIII, p. 272, where it is pointed out that the date corresponded to Sunday, December 17, A.D. 1245.

460. 505 *of* 1902.—(Tamil.) On the same wall. A record in the second year of the Pallava king Sakalabhuvanachakravartin Kōpperuñjiṅgadēva. Records gift of 96 cows and 3 bulls for three lamps by Nīla-Gaṅgaraiyan.

461. 506 *of* 1902.—(Tamil.) On the same wall. A record in the twenty-sixth year of the Chōḷa king Tribhuvanachakravartin Rājarājadēva (III ?). Records gift of land by Tīkkanai Perumāḷ.

462. 507 *of* 1902.—(Tamil verse.) On the same wall. Praises Vānadivākaran Ponparappinān *alias* Magadai-Perumāḷ. See Nos. 487 and 513.

463. 508 *of* 1902.—(Tamil.) On the same wall. A record in the fifteenth year of the Pallava king Sakalabhuvanachakravartin Kōpperuñjiṅgadēva. Records gift of a golden spoon and cup by the queen of Sadum-Perumāḷ. Compare No. 488 (*a*).

464. 509 *of* 1902.—(Grantha and Tamil.) On the same wall. A record of the Hoysaḷa king Pratāpachakravartin Vīra-Vallāḷadēva (III), in Ś. 1262. Records gift of land by Vallappadannāyakkar. Compare No. 472 above.

465. 510 *of* 1902.—(Tamil.) On the same wall. An incomplete record in the thirtieth year of the Chōḷa king Tribhuvanachakravartin Rājarājadēva (III). Records gift of a lamp by Umai-Āḷvār, the queen of Ilakkumadēvar. Compare No. 458 above.

466. 511 *of* 1902.—(Tamil.) On the same wall. A record in the thirty-first year of the Chōḷa king Tribhuvanachakravartin Rājarājadēva. Records gift of 32 cows and one bull for a lamp by the queen of Kaṭṭi-Araśar.

467. 512 *of* 1902.—(Tamil.) On the same wall. A record in the ninth year of the Pallava king Aḷagia Śīyan Sakalabhuvanachakravartin Kōpperuñjiṅgadēva. Records an order of Kōpperuñjiṅgadēvan. See No. 444 above.

468. 513 *of* 1902.—(Tamil.) On the same wall. A record in the fourth year of the Pallava king Sakalabhuvanachakravartin Kōpperuñjiṅgadēva. Records gift of a necklace by Kōpperuñjiṅgadēva. See Nos. 434 and 444.

469. 514 *of* 1902.—(Tamil.) On the same wall. A record of the Pallava king Kōpperuñjiṅgadēva, the date of which is doubtful. Records gift of 48 cows and 2 bulls for one and a half lamp by Kūttāḍuvān *alias* Chēdirāyan. See Nos. 434 and 444.

470. 515 *of* 1902.—(Tamil.) On the same wall. A record in the eighteenth year of the Chōḷa king Tribhuvanachakravartin Rājarājadēva (III ?). Records gift of money.

471. 516 *of* 1902.—(Tamil.) On the same wall. A record in the twenty-seventh year of the Chōḷa king Tribhuvanachakravartin Kulōttuṅga-Chōḷadēva (III), who took Madura, Ceylon, Karuvūr and the crowned head of the Pāṇḍya. Records that several chiefs promised allegiance to the king and to Chēdirāyadēva, apparently the Prime Minister, and not to act against their interests or orders. See No. 455.

472. 517 *of* 1902.—(Tamil.) On the south wall of the Subrahmanya shrine in the same temple. An incomplete record in the twenty-seventh year of the Pallava king Sakalabhuvanachakravartin Kōpperuñjiṅgadēva. Records gift of land. Mentions Nīla-Gaṅgaraiyar. See Nos. 434 and 444.

473. 518 *of* 1902.—(Tamil.) On the same wall. A record in the twenty-seventh year of the Pallava king Aḷagia Śīyan Sakalabhuvanachakravartin Kōpperuñjiṅgadēva. Records that Naṅgai-Āḷvār, queen of Nīla-Gaṅgaraiyar, granted land to an image which she had set up in the temple. See Nos. 434 and 444.

474. 519 *of* 1902.—(Tamil.) On the south wall of the Ekāmranātha shrine in the same temple. A record in the thirteenth year of the Pallava king Sakalabhuvanachakravartin Kōpperuñjiṅgadēva. Records gift of cows for lamps. See Nos. 434 and 444.

475. 520 *of* 1902.—(Tamil.) On the same wall. A record in the fourth year of the Chōḷa king Tribhuvanachakravartin Vijaya-Rājēndra-Chōḷadēva. Records gift of land by Rājādhirāja-Karkaṭa-mārāyan.

476. 521 *of* 1902.—(Tamil.) On the same wall. A record in the twelfth year of the Pallava king Sakalabhuvanachakravartin Kōpperuñjiṅgadēva. Records gift of 32 cows and one bull for a lamp by a merchant.

477. 522 *of* 1902.—(Tamil.) On the west wall of the same shrine. A record in the eleventh year, Chitrabhānu, of the Chōḷa king Tribhuvanavīra-Chōḷadēva. Records gift of land by a queen. [Dr. Kielhorn points out that the king referred to here is not Kulōttuṅga Chōḷa III as the date does not agree; that the only date between 1000 and 1500 A.D. which is equal to the date of the epigraph is Friday, 23rd August 1342, and that we have therefore to infer that there was a king named Tribhuvanavīrachōḷa who began to rule some time between August 31, 1331 and August 23, 1332. See *Ep. Ind.*, Vol. VIII, p. 7-8.]

478. 523 *of* 1902.—(Tamil.) On the south and west walls of the same shrine. A record of the Vijayanagara king Vīra-Sadāśivadēva-Mahārāya in Ś. 1470, Kīlaka. Records gift of land. Mentions Rājanārāyaṇapuram, *alias* Ārkāḍu (the modern Arcot).

479. 524 *of* 1902.—(Tamil.) On the south wall of the same shrine. A record in the twenty-sixth year of the Chōḷa king Tribhuvanachakravartin Kulōttuṅga-Chōḷadēva. Records gift of 16 cows for half a lamp.

480. 525 *of* 1902.—(Tamil.) On the south wall of the Chidambarēśvara shrine in the Aruṇāchalēśvara temple. A record in the fourth year of the Chōḷa king Tribhuvanachakravartin Rājādhirājadēva (?). Records that 52 cows and one bull were given for one and a half lamp by a private person (Nāgan Kailāyan) in order to atone for having accidentally killed another (Śōḷan dēvan) when aiming an arrow at an antelope. [The expiation of grievous hurt was always made in Chōḷa times in this manner. See N.A. 700 below.]

481. 526 *of* 1902.—(Tamil.) On the same wall. A damaged record in the second year of the Chōḷa king Tribhuvanachakravartin Kulōttuṅga-Chōḷadēva. Records gift of gold and land.

482. 527 *of* 1902.—(Tamil.) On the same wall. A record in the fourth year of the Chōḷa king Tribhuvanachakravartin Rājādhirājadēva. Records gift of 32 cows and one bull for a lamp.

483. 528 *of* 1902.—(Tamil.) On the west wall of the same shrine. A damaged record of the Chōḷa king Tribhuvanachakravartin Vīrarājēndra-Chōḷadēva, the date of which is lost. Records gift of a lamp. [*Vira Rājēndra* was the title of the king who ruled from 1063 to 1070 and Kulōttuṅga III. Very probably it is the latter that is referred to here.]

484. 529 *of* 1902.—(Tamil.) On the same wall. A record in the seventh year of the Chōḷa king Tribhuvanachakravartin Rājādhirājadēva. Records gift of 32 cows and one bull for a lamp.

485. 530 *of* 1902.—(Tamil.) On the Kiḷi gōpura in the same temple, right of entrance. A record in the twenty-first year of the Pallava king Kōpperuñjiṅgadēva. Records gift of 32 cows and one bull for a lamp. See Nos. 434 and 444.

486. 531 *of* 1902.—(Tamil.) In the same place. A record in the thirteenth year of the Chōḷa king Tribhuvanachakravartin Kulōttuṅga-Chōḷadēva. Records gift of an ornament by Vīraśēkhara Kāḍavarāyan.

487. 532 *of* 1902.—(Tamil.) In the same place. A record in the twenty-first year of the Chōḷa king Kulōttuṅga-Chōḷadēva (III). Records gift of 96 cows and 3 bulls for 3 lamps by Rājarājadēvan Ponparappinān *alias* Vānakōvaraiyan of Arakalūr. See No. 513 below.

488. 533 *of* 1902.—(Tamil prose and verse.) In the same place. A record in the twenty-first year of the Chōḷa king Kulōttuṅga-Chōḷadēva. Records gift of land by the same person.

489. 534 *of* 1902.—(Tamil.) In the same place. A record in the twenty-fifth year of the Chōḷa king Tribhuvanachakravartin Kulōttuṅga-Chōḷadēva (III). Records gift of land for a lamp by an officer of Rājagambhīra-Chēdiyarāyar. See No. 455 above.

490. 535 *of* 1902.—(Tamil.) In the same place. A record in the fourteenth year of the Chōḷa king Tribhuvanachakravartin Kulōttuṅga-Chōḷadēva. Records gift of ornaments by Kulōttuṅga-Chōḷa-Malaiyakularāyan. [The last-mentioned chief was evidently Chēdiyarāya.]

491. 536 *of* 1902.—(Tamil.) In the same place. A record in the tenth year of the Chōḷa king Tribhuvanachakravartin Kulōttuṅga-Chōḷadēva. Records gift of Malaiyanūr in Tagaḍanāḍu by Rājarājadēvan *alias* Aḍiyamān of Tagaḍur (Dharmāpuri) in Gaṅga-nāḍu. Dr. Venkayya identifies the Chōḷa king with Kulōttuṅga III as "we know from other inscriptions that the son of that Rājarāja was a vassal of the same Chōḷa king." See Nos. 487 and 513.

492. 537 *of* 1902.—(Tamil.) In the same place. A record in the eighteenth year of the Chōḷa king Tribhuvanachakravartin Kulōttuṅga-Chōḷadēva. Records gift of land.

493. 538 *of* 1902.—(Tamil.) In the same place. A record in the twenty-seventh year of the Chōḷa king Tribhuvanachakravartin-Kulōttuṅga-Chōḷadēva III (1178-1216), who took Madura, Ceylon and the crowned head of the Pāṇḍya. Records gift of land by Malaiyan Narasimhavarman *alias* Karikāla-Chōla-Adaiyūrnāḍ-āḷvān.

494. 539 (*a*) *of* 1902.—(Tamil.) In the same place. A record in the twenty-eighth year of the Chōḷa king Kulōttuṅga-Chōḷadēva (III ?). Records gift of land by Malaiyan Vinaivenṟān *alias* Karikāla-Chōḷa-Adaiyūrnāḍ-āḷvān.

495. 539 (*b*) *of* 1902.—(Tamil.) In the same place. A record in the twenty-seventh year of the Chōḷa king Kulōttuṅga-Chōḷadēva (III ?). Records gift of two villages by Nīla-Gaṅgan Kariya-Perumāḷ.

496. 540 *of* 1902.—(Tamil.) In the same place. A record in the fourteenth year of the Chōḷa king Tribhuvanachakravartin Kulōttuṅga-Chōḷadēva. Records gift of 64 cows and 2 bulls for 2 lamps.

497. 541 *of* 1902.—(Tamil.) In the same place. A record in the eighteenth year of the Chōḷa king Tribhuvanachakravartin Kulōttuṅga-Chōḷadēva. Records gift of 32 cows and one bull for a lamp by a chief of Tagaḍūr.

498. 542 *of* 1902.—(Grantha.) In the same place. Records the building of the gōpura by the minister Bhāskara. [We have no evidence to say whether this person was Bhāskara Rāya, the author of the *Vaidika nigaṇṭu*, and *Bhāvanōpanishadprayōgavidhi* or Bhāskara, the author of the *Siddhāntakaumudivilāsa.* His name also reminds us of Bhāskara Irugappa Daṇḍanātha who compiled the *Nānārtharatnamālā* and of the author of the *Sāmarājagāna prayōga.* See Dr. Hultzsch's *Rep. Sans. MSS.*, Vol. III.]

499. 543 *of* 1902.—(Tamil verse.) On the Kiḷi gōpura in the Aruṇāchalēśvara temple, right of entrance. Mentions Magadan Vāṇarpirān.

500. 544 *of* 1902.—(Grantha.) In the same place. Alludes to the gilding of the temple by a Bāṇa chief.

501. 545 *of* 1902.—(Tamil.) In the same place. Records gift of taxes.

502. 540 *of* 1902.—(Tamil.) On the same gopura, left of entrance. A record in the thirteenth year of the Chōḷa king Tribhuvanachakravartin Kulōttuṅga-Chōladēva (III ?). Records gift of land by a chief of Paṅgalanāḍu named Piridivi-Gaṅgan Vaṇṇiya-Mādēvan. See No. 451 for a feudatory of Rājarāja III of this name.

503. 547 *of* 1902.—(Tamil.) In the same place. A record in the twentieth year of the Chōḷa king Tribhuvanachakravartin Kulōttuṅga-Chōḷadēva. Records gift of money by a *guild* of merchants.

504. 548 *of* 1902.—(Tamil.) In the same place. A record in the twenty-ninth year of Chōḷa king Tribhuvanachakravartin Kulōttuṅga-Chōḷadēva. Records gift of land by Śediran Vāṇarāyan.

505. 549 *of* 1902.—(Tamil.) In the same place. A record in the thirtieth year of the Chōḷa king Tribhuvanachakravartin Kulōttuṅga-Chōḷadēva. Records gift of 2 cows for a lamp.

506. 550 *of* 1902.—(Tamil.) In the same place. A record in the fifth year of the Chōḷa king Tribhuvanachakravartin Kulōttuṅga-Chōḷadēva. Records that certain merchants vowed to supply a flag at each of the three annual festivals.

507. 551 *of* 1902.—(Tamil.) In the same place. A record in the nineteenth year of the Chōḷa king Tribhuvanachakravartin Rājarājadēva. Records gift of 32 cows and one bull for a lamp by Edirili-Chōḷa-Śambuvarāyan. See No. 509.

508. 552 *of* 1902.—(Tamil.) In the same place. A record in the second year of the Chōḷa king Vīrarājēndra-Chōḷadēva (I or II ?) Records repairs to a tank.

509. 553 *of* 1902.—(Tamil.) In the same place. A record in the thirteenth year of the Chōḷa king Tribhuvanachakravartin Kulōttuṅga Chōḷadēva. Records gift of 32 cows and one bull for a lamp by Vikrama-Chōḷa Śambuvarāyan. See No. 507.

510. 554 *of* 1902.—(Tamil verse.) In the same place. Praises Ponparappinān *alias* Magadai-Perumāḷ. See Nos. 462, 487 and 513.

511. 555 *of* 1902.—(Tamil.) In the same place. A record in the twenty-seventh year of the Chōḷa king Tribhuvanachakravartin Kulōttuṅga-Chōḷadēva. Records gift of 32 cows and one bull for a lamp.

512. 556 *of* 1902.—(Tamil.) In the same place. A record in the thirty-second year of the Chōḷa king Tribhuvanachakravartin Kulōttuṅga-Chōḷadēva. Records gift of land.

513. 557 *of* 1902.—(Tamil.) In the same place. A record in the thirty-fifth year of the Chōḷa king Tribhuvanaviradēva (Kulōttuṅga III). Records the gilding of the central shrine and the gift of three villages by Rājarājadēvan Ponparappinān *alias* Vanakōvaraiyan of Arkalūr. The date corresponded to Sunday, 2nd June, A.D. 1213. See No. 487 above and *Ep. Ind.*, VIII, p. 4.

514. 558 *of* 1902.—(Tamil.) In the same place. A record in the twenty-seventh year of the Chōḷa king Tribhuvanachakravartin Kulōttuṅga Chōḷadēva (III), who took Madura, Ceylon and the crowned head of the Pāṇḍya. Records gift of land by Chōḷēndrasimha Prithivi-Gaṅgan. See Nos. 451 and 502.

515. 559 *of* 1902.—(Tamil.) In the same place. A record in the twenty-seventh year of the Chōḷa king Tribhuvanachakravartin

Kulōttuṅga-Chōḷadēva. States the purposes for which the proceeds of certain taxes had to be utilised.

516. 560 *of* 1902.—(Tamil.) In the same place. A record in the twenty-fourth year of the Chōḷa king Tribhuvanachakravartin Kulōttuṅga-Chōḷadēva. Records that the temple authorities assigned certain land to two persons in recognition of benefits conferred on the temple.

517. 561 *of* 1902.—(Tamil.) In the same place. A record in the twenty-ninth year of the Chōḷa king Tribhuvanachakravartin Rājarājadēva. Records gift of 24 sheep for a quarter lamp.

518. 562 *of* 1902.—(Tamil.) On the Vallāḷa gōpura in the Aruṇāchalēśvara temple, right of entrance. A record of the Vijayanagara king Ariyaṇṇa Uḍaiyār (i.e., Harihara II) in Ś. 1299, Piṅgaḷa. Records gift of paddy and money for the maintenance of the watchman at the Vīra-Vallāḷa gate. See Mr. Sewell's local list, No. 11 (*Antiquities*, I, p. 207).

519. 563 *of* 1902.—(Tamil.) In the same place. A damaged record of the Vijayanagara king Kṛishṇadēva-Mahārāya in Ś. 1433, Pramōdūta. Records gift of land. [This is apparently Mr. Sewell's No. 12 in the local list where it is said to record an exchange of land between some private parties.]

520. 564 *of* 1902.—(Tamil.) In the same place. A record of the Vijayanagara king Vīra-Vijayabhūpatirāya Uḍaiyār, son of Vīra Dēvarāya (I), in Ś. 1340, Viḷambin. Orders that the Iḍangai and the Valaṅgai castes of Tiruvannāmalai should enjoy the same privileges. See Sewell's local list No. 8 in his *Antiquities*, Vol. I, p. 207.

521. 565 *of* 1902.—(Tamil.) In the same place. A record of the Vijayanagara king Vīra-Vīruppaṇṇa Uḍaiyār (II, i.e., Virupāksha I), son of Ariyappa-Uḍaiyār (Harihara II) in Ś. 1310, Vibhava. Records remission of taxes to the temple.

522. 566 *of* 1902.—(Tamil.) In the same place. A damaged record of the Vijayanagara king Vīrapratāpa-Dēvarāya Mahārāya, the date of which is lost. See Mr. Sewell's local list, No. 7.

523. 567 *of* 1902.—(Tamil.) In the same place. A record of the Vijayanagara king Sadāśivadēva Mahārāya in the Ś. 1489, Prabhava. Records remission of certain taxes in the villages belonging to the temple by order of Achyutappa Nāyaka. [This is evidently No. 9 of Mr. Sewell's local list, which is however doubtful.]

524. 568 *of* 1902.—(Tamil and Grantha.) In the same place. A record of the Vijayanagara king Vīra-Vijayabhūpatirāya-Uḍaiyār, son of Vīra Devarāya Mahārāya (I) in Ś. 1335, Vijaya. Records gift of 32 cows and one bull for a lamp by Annadāta Uḍaiyār, son of the minister Śavuṇḍapp-Uḍaiyār.

525. 569 *of* 1902.—(Tamil and Kanarese.) On the same gōpura, left of entrance. A record of the Vijayanagara king Dēvarāya-Mahārāya (II) in Ś. 1359, Piṅgaḷa. Records gift of land.

526. 570 *of* 1902.—(Tamil.) In the same place. A record of the Vijayanagara king Vīra-Mallikārjunarāya (son of Dēvarāya II) in Ś. 1375, Srīmukha. Records gift of land.

527. 571 *of* 1902.—(Tamil.) In the same place. A record in the twenty-second year of the Pāṇḍya king Tribhuvanachakravartin Srī Vallabhadēva. Records remission of taxes.

528. 572 *of* 1902.—(Tamil.) On the west wall of the second prākāra of the same temple, right of entrance. A record of the Vijayanagara king Viruppaṇṇa-Uḍaiyār (II, i.e., Virūpāksha I), son of Hariyanna-Uḍaiyār (Harihara II) in Ś. 1310, Vibhava. Records that the king's cousin Jammaṇa-Uḍaiyār (son of Kampaṇa II and grandson of Bukka I) granted land to provide for five persons who had to recite the Vēda for the merit of his deceased father Kampaṇa-Uḍaiyār II. [In *S. Ind. Incrns.*, Vol. I, No. 72 Jammaṇa is misread as Ommaṇa. In *Mack. MSS.* (*Ins. S. Dts.*, p. 123, No. 2) the Śaka date is given as 1312.]

529. 573 *of* 1902.—(Tamil.) On the gōpura in the west wall of the third prākāra of the same temple, right of entrance. A record of the Vijayanagara king Jammaṇa-Uḍaiyār, son of Kampaṇa-Uḍaiyār II, son of Vīra-Bokkaṇṇa-Uḍaiyār I, in Ś. 1296 Ānanda. Refers to the same grant. See note to the previous inscription.

530. 574 *of* 1902.—(Tamil.) On a slab set up in front of 1,000-pillared maṇṭapa in the same temple. A record of the Vijayanagara king Kṛishṇadēva-Mahārāya in Ś. 1438, Dhātu. Refers to the king's conquests of Udayagiri, Rauttarāya Mahāpātra, Addaṅki, Vinukoṇḍa, Bellamkoṇḍa, Koṇḍaviḍu, etc., the capture and pardon of Vīrabhadrayya, the son of Pratāparudra of Orissa, Naraharidēva, son of Kumāra Hammīrapātra, Mallu Khan of Rāchūr, etc. To commemorate this he built the Amarēśvara temple at Dharanikōṭa. The inscription records that at Tiruvaṇṇāmalai he built the thousand-pillared maṇṭapa, the tank near the same, the gōpura of eleven storeys, etc. [See the Amarāvati and Śēndamaṅgalam inscriptions. See also *Ins. S. Dts.*, p. 122, No. 1 and *Antiquities*, p. 206, No. 2 in the local list.]

531. On certain copper pots for camphor lamp. Records that Veṅkaṭapati Rāya, "the Prime Minister of Mysore Samastānam" gave in Ś 1668, Akshaya, a pot (4½ bharas in weight) to God Aruṇāchalēśvara. *Ins. S. Dts.*, p. 123, No. 3.

532. A.C.P. in the 'Pareyanad' maṭham. Records that in the reign of Kṛishṇadēva Mahārāya, a certain "Aravalutha modalian" and the inhabitants of the 56 Nāḍus erected a maṭham for the Tambirān of "aleyarum conda", besides the Vimāna of the Amman temple, and gave the village of Melapālayūr (?) as a free gift to the temple for the maintenance of the Tambirāns, besides an allowance of 6 *paṇams* in marriage, rice and cloth. See *M.S.S. Dts.*, p. 123, No. 5.

VELLORE TALUK.

Ambur (Āṇmaiyūr of the inscriptions).

533. 4 *of* 1896.—(Tamil.) On the north wall of the Nāgēśvara shrine. A record of the Vijayanagara king Rājaśekharamahārāya, son of Mallikārjunadēva, in Ś. 1390 expired, Sārvadhārin. Mentions Śāḷuva-Naraśiṅgayadēva (the usurper) and Śennayadēva.

534. 5 *of* 1896.—(Tamil.) On a stone set up near the maṇṭapa in front of the same shrine. A record in the fifteenth year of the Chōḷa king Tribhuvanachākravartin Kulōttuṅga-Chōḷadēva. Records gift to the Nāgēśvara temple at Āṇmaiyūr by the inhabitants of Śittiramēḷi-nāḍu. [For the local legend of the Nāgēśvara temple see *N.A. Manual* II, p. 425.]

535. 6 *of* 1896.—(Tamil.) On the base of the north wall of the same maṇṭapa. A record of the Hoysaḷa king Vīra-Vallāḷadēva (III) in Krōdhana, Ś. 1248. Records gift of land to the Nāgēśvara temple at Āṇmaiyūr.

536. 7 *of* 1896.—(Tamil.) On a stone set up in the Kaṅgareṭṭika Street in the same place. A record in the twenty-sixth year of the Pallava king Kō-Vijaya-Nripatuṅgavikramavarman. [This, as well as the next stone, has a bas-relief representing a warrior, with bow and sword, chauris, lamp, fruits, etc., as he is pierced by arrows. The inscriptions record the death of a son and a nephew of one Akaḷaṅkatturāyar in a cattle-raid of the ruler of Nuḷambapāḍi against Āṇmaiyūr.] See *Ep. Ind.* IV, 180–3.

537. 8 *of* 1896.—(Tamil.) On a stone set up to the right of No. 7. A record in the twenty-sixth year of the Pallava king Kō-Vijaya-Nripatuṅgavikramavarman. [See the previous inscription.] The soldier was the immediate servant of Pirudi Gaṅgaraiyar whom Dr. Hultzsch identifies with the W. Gaṅga Prithvīpati I (son of Śivamāra II, conqueror of Varaguṇa Pāṇḍya and opponent of Amōghavarsha I).

Ariyur (Arugūr).

538. 37 *of* 1887.—(Grantha and Tamil.) On a stone in the same place. A record of the Vijayanagara king Sadāśivadēva in Ś. 1488. See *S.I.I.* I, No. 44, p. 71.

Attiyūr.

539. A. C.P. is given in *Ins. S. Dts.* (in *Mack. MSS.*, p. 27, No. 5) granting the village of Attiyūr as a free gift to Brahmans by Bukka Rāya.

Gaṅganur called Gāṅgēyanallūr in Karaivaḷi Āṇḍināḍu.

The inscriptions of this place are not in their original order and it has therefore been inferred that either the original temple was destroyed and rebuilt or that it was built of stones belonging to another old temple.

540. 16 *of* 1887.—(Grantha and Tamil.) A record in the Gaṅgēśvara temple. Ammayappēśvara Nāyanār is mentioned. Noticed in *S.I.I.*, Vol. I, No. 99, p. 129.

541. 17 *of* 1887.—(Grantha and Tamil.) In the same temple. A record of Sakalalōkachakravartin Rājanārāyaṇa Śambava. *S.I.I.*, Vol. I, No. 1060, p. 129. [This king came to the throne in 1337.]

542 to **546.** 18 *to* 22 *of* 1887.—(Grantha and Tamiḷ.) Fragmentary record in the same temple. *S.I.I.*, Vol. I, Nos. 101–5.

547. 23 *of* 1887.—(Grantha and Tamil.) In the same temple. A record in the forty-first year of Tribhuvanachakravartin Rājarājadēva. This is noticed in *S.I.I.*, Vol. I, No. 106, p. 129.

548. 24 *of* 1887.—(Grantha and Tamil.) On the north wall of Perumāḷ temple. A record of the seventeenth year of Sakalalōkachakravartin Venṟumaṇkoṇḍa Śambuvarāya, the details of the date being Monday, Pūrvapaksha prathamai, Rōhiṇi nakshatra, in Rishabha in *Pramāthi*. Records that one Tiruvēṅgaḍam Uḍaiyān sold to the assembly of Gāṅgēyanallūr or Nīlakaṇṭhachaturvēdimaṅgalam and that of Śri Mallināthachaturvēdimaṅgalam one *kāṇi* of land for 170 பு. (வாசிபடர் விரசமப்பன் குளிகை [பு] ௱௭௰). *S.I.I.*, Vol. I, No. 52, pp. 77–8.

Karaṇipākkam. (Kaḷanipākkam.)

549. 65 *of* 1887.—(Grantha and Tamil.) Front wall of a maṇṭapa. A record of the Karnāṭic king Vīra-Vēṅkaṭapatirāya II in Chitrai 5 of Śrīmukha, Ś. 1556. Records that a Gōvindappa Nāik built a maṇṭapa to serve as a watershed and choultry and endowed lands. *S.I.I.*, Vol. I, No. 133, pp. 136–7.

Mūnjūrpaṭṭu.

550. 25 *of* 1887.—(Grantha and Tamil.) A record inside the Perumāḷ temple.

Nelluvāyi. (Nelvāy.)

551. 26 *of* 1887.—(Grantha and Tamil.) On a pillar in front of Rāmasvāmi Perumāḷ temple. A record of Vīra-Veṅkaṭapatidēva II in Ś. 1557, Yuva. See *S.I.I.*, Vol. I, No. 107, p. 130.

Pallikoṇḍai.

552. 71 *of* 1887.—(Grantha and Tamil.) A record on the wall of Śrī Raṅganāyakā-Perumāḷ temple, dated Ś. 1554 (expired),

Durmati (not consistent). 1554 is evidently mistake for 1544. *S.I.I.*, Vol. I, No. 139, p. 138. [For the local legend and religious importance. See N.A. Manual, p. 424.]

Perumai (Perumugai.)

553. 43 *of* 1887.—(Grantha and Tamil.) On a stone. A record of the Karnāṭa king Raṅgadēva (1578–86). Gift of the village by Krishṇappa Nāik at the request of Chinna Bomma Nāik to the Jvarakaṇḍēsvara shrine at Vellore. Other details same as in Nos. 565 and 563 below. See *S.I.I.*, Vol. I, No. 49, p. 75.

Poygai.

Poygai was called in Chōḷa times Rājēndrachōḷanallūr. It was noted for its Aruḷālaperumāl or Chitrameḻimalai-maṇḍala-Viṇṇagar temple.

554 & 555. 72 *and* 73 *of* 1887.—(Grantha and Tamil.) In the Perumāḷ temple. A record in the twenty-second year of Tribhuvanachakravartin Rājarājadēva (III) in Ś. 1160. Records gift of the village of Kumāramaṅgalam and two others, by a Kēraḷa merchant Ādi Rāma, which he bought from Śeṅgēṅi Vīrasāni Ammayappan Aḻagia Śōḻan Ediriḻi Śambuvarāyan. The taxes and cesses are enumerated. *S.I.I.*, Vol. I, Nos. 59 and 60.

556 & 557. 74 *and* 75 *of* 1887.—(Grantha and Tamil.) In the same temple. A record in the twenty-fourth year of Tribhuvanachakravartin Rājarājadēva (III) in Ś. 1161. Records the gift of the village of Puttūr. *Ibid.*, No. 61. The inscription is of value in enumerating all items of village revenue. These are divided into two heads, viz., *nellāya* (நெல்லாயம்) in kind and *kāśāya* (காசாயம்) in cash. Amidst the former are enumerated. பாடிகாவல், சில்வரி, எடுத்துக்கொட்டி, அரிமுக்கை, etc., and amidst the latter கார்த்திகையரிசி, கார்த்திகைக்காசு, கார்த்திகைப்பச்சை, வேலிப்பயிறு, நீர்நிலக்காசு, தறியிறை, கடையிறை, காலகதப்பாட்டம், தட்டாரப்பாட்டம், ஆசுவக்கடமை, செக்குக்கடமை, எரிபீன்காசு, இநவரி, பட்டோலைக்காசு, etc.: Antarāya; Veṭṭi and other taxes like those on documents, Ajivakas, cloths, oil-mills, washermen.

558. 76 *of* 1887.—(Grantha and Tamil.) A record in the same temple. A duplicate of the above.

559. 77 *of* 1887.—(Grantha and Tamil.) In the same temple. A record in the twenty-eighth year of Rājarājadēva (III) in Ś. 1165 (expired). Records the gift of the village of Attiyūr, bought from the same Śambuvarāya and endowed by the same donor. *Ibid.*, No. 64, pp. 92–3.

Śaduppēri.

560. 27 *of* 1887.—(Grantha and Tamil.) On a stone in the Grāmadēvata temple. A record in the fifty-second year of the

Pallava king Kōvijaya-Nandivikramavarman. Noticed in *S.I.I.*, Vol. I, No. 108, p. 130.

561. 28 *of* 1887.—(Grantha and Tamil.) On an *Aḷavukkal* in the tank. A record of the Choḷa king . . . Kō-Parakēsarivarman. *S.I.I.*, Vol. I, No. 109, p. 130.

562. 40 *of* 1887.—(Grantha and Tamil.) On a stone in the same place. A record of the Vijayanagara king Sadāśivadēva, in Ś. 1488 *Akshaya* (same date as in Ariyūr and Arumbarutti records). Records gift of the village by Tirumalaiya dēva at the request of Chinna Bomma Nāik to the *Jvarakaṇḍēśvara* temple at Vēllore. *S.I.I.*, Vol. I, No. 46, pp. 72-3.

Sampanginellūr.

563. 42 *of* 1887.—(Grantha and Tamil.) On a stone. A record of the Karnāṭa king Raṅgadēva (I). Gift of the village by Krishṇappa Nāik at the request of Chinna Bomma Nāik. Date same as that at Śatuvachchēri. See *S.I.I.*, Vol. I, No. 48, pp. 74-5. See also No. 553 above.

Satyamaṅgalam.

564. A C.P. grant of the Vijayanagara king Dēvarāya (II). (Sanskrit in Nandināgari aphaḷbet) is published in *Ep. Ind.*, Vol. III, pp. 35-41. It records the gift of the agrahāra of Chiṭeyāṭūru (renamed Dēvarāyapuram) in Āṇḍa-nāḍu, a subdivision of Marataganagarapśānta, on Monday, new moon, Āshāḍha, Ś. 1346, Krōdhi, which corresponded, according to Dikshit, to Monday, 26th June, A.D. 1424. The grant was made at the Virūpāksha temple on the banks of the Tuṅgabhadra river. A summary of the epigraph is also given in *Ep. Rep.*, Oct. 1890, p. 2.

Sattuvachchēri.

565. 41 *of* 1887. (Grantha and Tamil.) On a stone. A record of the Karnāṭa king Raṅgadēva (I, 1578-86) in Ś. 1497 (expired). Records grant to the Vellore temple of the village of Sattuvachchēri by his feudatory Kṛishṇappa Nāik at the request of Vellore Chinna Bomma Nāik. [For another inscription of Kṛishṇappa dated Ś. 1500, see *Mys. Inscrns.*, p. 220. The details of the date are Ś. 1497, *Yuva*, Wednesday, Kṛishṇapaksha Trayōdaśi in Makhara. The inscription has been edited in *S.I.I.*, Vol. I, No. 47, pp. 73-4.] See Nos. 553 and 563 above.

Seduvalai.

566. 78 *of* 1887. (Grantha and Tamil.) On a stone. A record of the Vijayanagara king Sadāśivadēva in Ś. 1489, *Prabhava.* Gift to Mārgasahāya, the deity of Viriñchipuram. *S.I.I.*, Vol. I, No. 140, p. 138.

Śekkanūr.

567. 29 *of* 1887. (Grantha and Tamil.) A record on a stone in the same place, saying that the village was granted to the Vēllore temple. *S.I.I.*, Vol. I, No. 50, p. 76.

Śembakkām.

568 to 570. 30—32 *of* 1887.—(Archaic Grantha and Tamil.) On the base of Īśvara temple in the same place. All are fragmentary. The first (on the west base) records some gift by the assembly of Vēlūr alias Paramēśvaramaṅgalam to Ādidāsa Chaṇḍēśvara. The second, which is a similar gift, mentions Śemmaṇpākkam and Rājēndrachōlēśvara, evidently the name of the temple itself. The third (on the south base) begins with the description of the boundaries of some gift. See *S.I.I.*, Vol. I, Nos. 110—2, p. 130.

Śevūr.

571. 33 *of* 1887.—(Grantha and Tamil.) On three stones in the wall of Perumāḷ temple. A record of Dēvarāya II of Vijayanagar. See *S.I.I.*, Vol. I, No. 113,—pp. 130-1.

Śōḷapuram (8 miles south of Vēllore.)

The ancient name of this place was Kāṭṭuttumbūr and it was included in Paṅgalanāḍu in Paḍuvūr kōṭṭam, in Jayaṅkoṇḍachōḷa-maṇḍalam.

572. 421 *of* 1902 *and* 11 *of* 1887.—(Tamil). On the north base of the ruined Śiva temple. A damaged record in the twenty-seventh year of the Chōḷa king Rājarājakēsarivarman alias Rājarājadēva (I). Uyyakkoṇḍān Śōḷapuram is said to have belonged to Mugaināḍu, a subdivision of Paṅgalanāḍu (which included Vēllore, Tirumalai near Pōḷūr, etc.).

573. 422 *of* 1902 *and* 12 *of* 1887.—(Tamil.) On the same base. A record in the thirty-second year of the Chōḷa king Rājakēsari-varman alias Kulōttuṅga-Chōḷadēva I. Records gift of a lamp. Noticed in *S. I. I.*, Vol. I, No. 96. p. 128.

574. 423 *of* 1902.—(Tamil.) On the east base of the same temple. A record of the Chōḷa king Parāntaka I, the date of which is lost. Records gift of land to the Nandikampēśvara temple at Kāṭṭuttumbūr.

575. 424 *of* 1901.—(Tamil.) On the same base. A record in the thirty-first year, the king's name in which is lost. Records gift of land by Prithivī-Gaṅgaraiyan. See note to No. 586.

576. 525 *of* 1902.—(Tamil.) On the south base of the same temple. An incomplete record in the twenty-fourth year of the Chōḷa king Parakēśarivarman alias Chakravartin Kulōttuṅga-Chōladeva.

577. 426 *of* 1902.—(Tamil.) On a slab set up at the Kāḷiyamman temple in the same village. A damaged record. Mentions the wife of 'Prithivī Gaṅgaraiyar.' See note to 586.

578. 427 *of* 1902.—(Grantha.) On the north wall of the Perumāḷ temple in the same village. A fragment of record. Mentions Prithivī-Gaṅgaraśar.

579. 428 *of* 1902.—(Tamil.) On a rock east of the Kaḷḷaṅguṭṭai tank close to the hill in the same village. A record of the Rāshṭrakūṭa king Kaṇṇaradēva in Ś. 871. Published in *Ep. Ind.*, VII, page 194 f. The inscription says that (in year 2 of the reign of Rājāditya, i.e., 948–9) Kaṇṇaradēva killed Rājāditya, and entered Toṇḍamaṇḍalam. On this occasion a pond was constructed for the merit of Kaḷḷinaṅgai, the daughter of the Gaṅga Hastimalla Kaṇṇara Prithvīgaṅgaraiyar, who died at Aruṅgunṟam. See Nos. 586, 592 and 633.

580. 429 *of* 1902 *and* 13 *of* 1887.—(Grantha and Tamil.) On three stones unearthed in the tope opposite to the Śiva temple in the same village. A record in the eighth year of the Gaṅga-Pallava king Vijaya-Kampa, whom Dr. Hultzsch proves to be the son of Vijaya Nandivikramavarman, grandson of Dantivarman and brother of Nripatuṅga. The inscription says that in the eighth year of Vijaya-Kampa king Rājāditya, son Prithivīgaṅgaraiyar, constructed the Īśvara temple on his father's death. [Prithvīgaṅgaraiyar was evidently Prithvīpati II.] See Nos. 586, 592 and 633. *Ep. Ind.*, VII, 192–3.

581. 14 *of* 1887.—(Grantha and Tamil.) On the inner wall of the Perumāḷ temple. A record in the twenty-third year of the Pallava king Kōvijaya. [Kampa] . . . Vikramavarman. Edited in *S. Ind. Inscrns.*, I, pp. 78–9 (No. 53) and *Ep. Ind.*, VII, pp. 193–4 which corrects mistakes in the former edition. The inscription records the building of the temple of Nārāyaṇa, named after the village of Kanakavalli in which some land was granted to it.

582. 15 *of* 1887.—(Grantha and Tamil.) On a stone on the tank-bund. A record of the Karnāṭa king Veṅkaṭappa-Nāyaka in Ś. 1546. *S.I.I.*, I, p. 28, No. 198.

583. 343 *of* 1912.—(Tamil.) On the south base of the ruined Śiva temple. Records in the tenth year of Kulōttuṅga (III) the gift of certain taxes *(silvari)* to the temple of Rājarājēśvaramuḍaiyār at Uyyakkoṇḍān Sōḷapuram, by Seṅgēṇi Ammaiyappan Kaṇṇuḍaiperumāḷ alias Vikrama-Chōḷa Śambuvarāyan.

584. 344 *of* 1912.—(Tamil.) A fragmentary record of the twentieth year of Parakes. Rājēndrachōḷa (I) registering a sale of land (14,000 kuḷis by the *padinārusāṇkol*) to the Mahādēva temple by the local residents.

585. 345 *of* 1912.—(Tamil.) On two detached stones in the same temple. Records gift of land by Kaṇṇaradēva or

Prithivīgaṅgaraiyar, i.e., Prithvīpati II., first subordinate of the Chōḷa Parāntaka I. and then of the Rāshṭrakūṭa Krishṇa III. See No. 586.

586. 346 *of* 1901.—(Tamil.) On the base of the ruined Śiva temple. A record of the Western Gaṅga king Hastimalla (Prithvīpati II.) alias Kaṇṇaradēva-Prithvīgaṅgaraiyar in Ś. 875. Records a gift of ninety sheep for a lamp to a temple of Īśvara and mentions Kāṭṭuttumbūr (i.e., Sōḷapuram). The inscription shows that Prithvīpati became a vassal of the Rāshṭrakūṭa Kṛishṇa III. after Parāntaka I. [See Nos. 579, 592 and 633. The inscription has been edited in *Ep. Ind.*, Vol. VII, pp. 195—7.]

Tellūr.

The name of this village in Vijayanagar times was Teḷḷiyūr or Pukkalappuram and it was included in Vaḍapuri Āṇḍināḍu, in Paṅgalanāḍu in Paḍuvūr kōṭṭam.

587. 34 *of* 1887.—(Grantha and Tamil.) On the base of Īśvara temple. (A record of the Chōḷa king Uḍaiyāṛ Kulōttuṅga, on a stone.) A record of Vīrapratāpa Dēvarāya Mahārāya (II) of Vijayanagara, in Ś. 1353, *Sādhāraṇa* (Monday, pūrvapaksha pañchamī, śravaṇa, in karkaṭaka). Records Nārāṇan and others as servants of the temple. See *S. Ind. Inscrns.*, No. 54, pp. 79-80.

Vellore.

A long description of the local history and antiquities is given in *N.A. Manual, II,* 417—22. Vellore was situated in Paṅgalanāḍu in Paḍuvūr kōṭṭam.

588 to 591. (603—6) 6 to 9 *of* 1887.—(Grantha and Tamil.) Record the perpetual devotion of a certain Chandrapiḷḷai of Kāṭṭēri. See *S. Ind. Inscrns.*, Vol. I, Nos. 91—4, pp. 126—8.

592. 10 *of* 1887.—(Grantha and Tamil.) A record on top of Bāvāji hill of the Pallava king Kaṇṇaradēva (i.e., Krishna III, whose contemporary was the Pallava chief) Tribhuvanadhīra Nuḷamba in his twenty-sixth year. The inscription mentions Vīrachōḷa, i.e., Hastimalla Prithvīpati II, who, as the N.A. 633 shows, was first a feudatory of Parāntaka I and then of Krishṇa III, Nuḷamba was the feudatory of Vīrachōḷa. See *Ep. Ind.*, IV, pp. 81—3 and *S. Ind. Inscrns.*, Vol. I, p. 75.

593. 41 *of* 188.--(Grantha and Tamil.) Stone put up inside the inner gōpura of the temple. Āhavamalla twice mentioned. [Āhavamalla might be the Chāḷukya king who ruled from 1042 to 1068.]

Vēppambaṭṭu.

It was in Āṇḍināḍu in Agapaṛṛu.

594. 35 *of* 1887.—(Grantha and Tamil.) In the Virūpākshēśvara temple. A record of the Vijayanagara king Bukka (II) in

S. 1328 expired, Vijaya (Thursday, *Jyēshtha bahula-amāvāsya*). Records gift of revenue (which is mentioned in *Kulapramāṇas* of pon, *kōvais* and *paṇams*) from two villages to the temple of Virūpāksha at Vēppambaṭṭu. [The inscription is of value in the history of finance, currency and numerical palæography. See *S. Ind. Inscrns.*, Vol. I, No. 55, pp. 80—2.]

595. 36 *of* 1887.—(Grantha and Tamil.) In the same temple. A record of Tirumalai-Nāyaka in Ś. 1443, making a gift to the temple. See *S. Ind. Inscrns.*, Vol. I, No. 114, p. 131.

Vakkaṇāpuram (near Viriñchipuram).

596. 79 *of* 1887.—(Grantha and Tamil.) A record on the walls of the Īśvara temple. Records that a number of people founded the Okkaninṟanāyanār temple and granted to it a maḍaiviḷāgam and 3 vēlis of land. The grant was entrusted to one Kadambavanabhaṭṭa. The villagers bear royal names like Vīraśōḷa Brahmarāyan, Chēdirāyan, Mūvēndirāyan, etc. The record mentions that in other lands a tax of one kalam and 4 *nāḷis* of paddy and a quarter *paṇam* on every 100 kuḷis will be collected. See *S. Ind. Inscrns.*, Vol. I, No. 65, pp. 92—4.

*Viriñjipuram.**

Included in the Paḍavīḍu rājya (known after Paḍavēḍu in Polūr taluk) which was a division of Jayṅkoṇḍa toṇḍamaṇḍalam.

597. 44 *of* 1887.—(Grantha and Tamil.) Inside the front gōpura to the left. A record of the Vijayanagara king Immaḍi Narasimharāya in Ś. 1418, Rākshasa. Mentions Periya Timmaraśu Uḍaiyār and a maṇṭapa built by Eṟṟama Nāyaka at Tiru-Viriñchipuram. See *S. Ind. Inscrns.*, Vol. I, No. 115, p. 131.

598. 45 *of* 1887.—(Grantha and Tamil.) In the same place. A record of the Vijayanagara king Gaṇḍa-kaṭṭāri śāḷuva Dharanīvarāha Narasimharāya in Ś. 1395, Nandana. A gift to vaḷittuṇai Nāyanār, the deity. See *S. Ind. Inscrns.*, Vol. I, No. 116, p. 131.

599. 46 *of* 1887.—(Grantha and Tamil.) In the same place. A record of Sakalalōkachakravartin Rājanārāyaṇa. See *S. Ind. Inscrns.*, Vol. I, No. 117, p. 132.

600. 47 *of* 1887.—(Grantha and Tamil.) In the temple. A record of the Vijayanagara king Achyutadēva in Ś. 1463, Plava. Mentions a certain Kṛishṇama Nāik. See *S. Ind. Inscrns.*, Vol. I, No. 118, p. 132.

---

* It may be pointed out here that the temple of this place is celebrated by *Nāvanitakavi*, the son of Vēdapurīsha Yajvan of the Vādhūlagōtra, who was a native of this place. It is called *Viriñchipurānāthacharita*. See Dr. Hultzsch's *Rep. Sans. MSS.* III, p. VII and No. 2186. See also *N.A. Manual*, II, pp. 425 - 7, for an excellent description of the historical and religious importance of the place.

601. 48 *of* 1887.—(Grantha and Tamil.) Inside the front gōpura to the right. A record of the time of the Vijayanagara king Sāḷuva Narasimhadēva in Ś. 1404 expired, Śubhakrit current—recording gift to the deity by Nāgama Naik. [It is impossible to say definitely whether this Nāgama Nāik was the father of Viśvanātha, the founder of the Nāik dynasty of Madura. See *Ind. Antq.*, Jan. 1914 ff.]

602. 49 *of* 1887.—(Grantha and Tamil.) In the temple. A record of the Vijayanagara king Dēvarāya in Ś. 1347 expired [Wednesday, Anusha, 6th lunar and 3rd solar day, Paṅguni, in Viśvāvasu.] Records that all classes of Brahmans in Paḍaivīḍu Rājya [Kannaḍigas, Tamiḷas, Teluṅgas, Ilāṭas of all gōtras, śūtras and śākhas] met in the presence of God Gōpinātha and settled the sacred law that they should conclude marriage by *kanyādāna* and not after receiving gold, the penalty being excommunication and then punishment by king. See *S. Ind. Inscrns.*, Vol. I, No. 56, pp. 82—4.

603. 50 *of* 1887.—(Grantha and Tamil.) In the temple. A record of the Vijayanagara king Achyutadēva in Ś. 1457 expired, Nandana. Seems to record the gift of a number of kuḷis of land to two Brahmans Timmappaiyan and Śaivādirāyar Vasantarāyaguru. See *S. Ind. Inscrns.*, Vol. I, No. 120, p. 132.

604. 51 *of* 1887.—(Grantha and Tamil.) On the base of the back of the front gōpura, to the right. A record of the Vijayanagara king Kṛishnadēva in Ś. 1435 expired, Śrīmukha current. *S. Ind. Inscrns.*, Vol. I, No. 121, p. 132.

605. 52 *of* 1887.—(Grantha and Tamil.) On the back gōpura of the temple. A record of the Vijayanagara king Kṛishnadēva in Ś. 1432 expired, Pramōdūta. See *S. Ind. Inscrns.*, Vol. I, No. 123, p. 133.

606. 53 *of* 1887.—(Grantha and Tamil.) Inside the back gōpura of the temple. A record of the Vijayanagara king Achyutadēva in Ś. 1454 expired, Nandana. Records gift of the villages of Śiraḷēri, Vīraraśur, etc., by the Kārṇikka Vīrappaiyan of the Gautamānvaya. See *S. Ind. Inscrns.*, Vol. I, No. 123, p. 133.

607. 54 *of* 1887.—(Grantha and Tamil.) On stone built into courtyard floor of the temple. A record of the Pallava king Kōvijaya-Nandivikramavarman, in his ninth year. See *S. Ind. Inscrns.*, Vol. I, No. 124, p. 133.

608. 55 *of* 1887.—(Grantha and Tamil.) In the same place in the temple. A record in the forty-seventh year of the Pallava king Kōvijaya-Nandivikramavarman. See *S. Ind. Inscrns.*, Vol. I, No. 125, p. 133.

609. 56 *of* 1887.—(Grantha and Tamil.) In the same place. A record of the Chōḷa king Kō-Parakēsarivarman *alias* Uḍaiyār

Rājēndradēva (conquered Āhavamalla). Records that the villagers of Gangamārttāṇḍapuram in Miyārināḍu in Adhirājēndravaḷanāḍu Jayaṅkoṇḍa Chḷōa-maṇḍalam gave lands to God Sōmēśvara for flower garden and lamps. See *S. Ind. Inscrns.*, Vol. I, No. 127, pp. 134-5.

610. 57 *of* 1887.—(Grantha and Tamil.) In the temple. A record of the Chōḷa king Madiraikoṇḍa Kō-Parakēsarivarman. (Parāntaka I). See *S. Ind. Inscrns.*, Vol. I, No. 126, p. 133.

611. 58 *of* 1887.—(Grantha and Tamil.) In the temple. A record of Aḷagiya........................Śambuvarāya. See *S. Ind. Inscrns.*, Vol. I, No. 129, p. 135.

612. 59 *of* 1887.—(Grantha and Tamil.) In the temple. A record of Sakalalōkachakravartin Rājanārāyana Śambuvarāya. See *S. Ind. Inscrns.*, Vol. I, No. 128, p. 135.

613. 60 *of* 1887.—(Grantha and Tamil.) In the temple. A record of the king Bommunāyakka in Ś. 1471, *Saumya.* (Thursday, Punarvasu, Pūrvapaksha Saptami of Mēsha), saying that the king, for the merit of Mācha Nāik of Vellore, laid the pavement round the temple. See *S. Ind. Inscrns.*, Vol. I, No. 57, pp. 84-5. *N.A. Manual*, II, p. 427.

614. 61 *of* 1887.—(Grantha and Tamil.) On a stone at the south entrance. A record of the Karnāṭa king Vēṅkaṭapatidēva I, in Ś. 1514 (*Nandana* year, 6th Tai), saying that Periya Eṟṟama Nāik of Punnāṟṟūr granted a house for the location of a *maṭha* to Ānanda Namaśivāya Panḍāram, disciple of Chidambaram Gurunamaśivāyamūrti. See *S. Ind. Inscrns.*, Vol. I, No. 58, pp. 85-6. [The inscription is of literary importance as it gives a clue to the date of Guhainamaśivāya and his disciple Gurunamaśivāya. The latter was the author of *Paramarahasyamālai*, *Chidambara veṇba*, *Aṇṇāmalai veṇba*, etc. For his career see *Abhidānachintāmaṇi*, p. 302. His preceptor, so called from his residence in a *guhai* or cave at Tiruvannāmalai, was the Siddha who wrote the *Aruṇagiriandādi*. See *Ibid.*, p. 288.]

WALAJAPET TALUK.

Ayal (Ayilam).

614-A. *No.* 138, *Sewell's list*—(discovered at Ayal.).—(Nandinagari characters.) Records a grant of the Vijayanagara king. It evidences the bestowal of the village of Dēvarāyapuram, as an agrahāram, by the sovereign Dēvarāya II, in S. 1349 (A.D. 1427), cyclic year Parābhava, on his household priest Narasimhāchārya. The latter divides his village into shares between himself and eight other Brāhmaṇas.

Guḍimāllūr (Kuḍimallūr).

615. 416 *of* 1905.—(Tamil.) On the north wall of the central shrine in the Bhūmīśvara temple. A record in the fourth year of

Sakalalōkachakravartin Rājanārāyaṇa Śambuvarāya. Registers a gift of land to the temple of Kaḍāraṅgoṇḍachōlīśvaramuḍaiya-Nāyinar in Karaivaḷi-Valliyūr, a village of Kalavaippaṛṛu in Paḍuvūr koṭṭam See *N.A. Manual*, II, p. 435.

616. 417 *of* 1905.—(Tamil.) On the same wall. A record of the Vijayanagara king Sadāśivadēvar Mahārāyar in Ś. 1472, Sādhāraṇa. The king bears Śāḷuva birudas. Mentions Kalavaippaṛṛu in Perundimiri-nāḍu, a subdivision of Paḍuvūr-koṭṭam. Records certain arrangements made with regard to the digging of a river channel (āṛṛukkāl). Mentions Kumāra Kṛishṇappa-Nāyaka and Chinna-Bomma-Nāyaka, the chiefs of Vellore.

617. 418 *of* 1905.—(Tamil.) On the same wall. A record in the fourteenth year of the Pāṇḍya king Tirubhuvanachakravartin Vīra Pāṇḍyadēva. Mentions the temple of Kiḍāraṅgoṇḍachōḷīśvaramuḍaiya-Nāyanār at Malliyūr. [The inscription reminds the student of the biruda of the Chōḷa king Rājādhirāja I "who took the head of the Pāṇḍya," who was "the conqueror of Vīra Pāṇḍya of Mallayur." It seems to me that, after conquering Vīra Pāṇḍya, Rājādhirāja should have established the temple in his father's name.]

618. 419 *of* 1905.—(Tamil.) On the same wall. A record in the twelfth year of the Paṇḍya king Māravarman Tribhuvanachakravartin Kulaśēkharadēva [I?]. Built in. Mentions the temple of Kiḍāraṇgoṇḍachōḷīśvaramuḍaiya-Nāyanār at Karaivaḷi-Valliyūr, a village in Kalavaippaṛṛu, a district of Paḍuvūr-kōṭṭam. There is reference also to the right and left hand castes.

619. 420 *of* 1905.—(Tamil.) On the same wall. A record in the seventh year of Sakalalōkachakravartin Rājanārāyaṇa-Śambuvarāya. Registers a remission of taxes in favour of Palataḷi (temple) at Karaivaḷi-Kālppaṛṛu, a village in Kalavaippaṛṛu.

620. 421 *of* 1905.—(Tamil.) On the south wall of the same shrine. Registers in Virōdhikrit, an order of Bommu-Nāyan-Liṅgama-Nāyakar to the weavers of Valliyūr.

621. 422 *of* 1905.—(Tamil.) On the same wall. A record of the Vijayanagara king Ariyaṇa-Uḍaiyār in Dundubhi, i.e., Ś. 1305. *Refers to a fight between the right and left hand castes* which *lasted for four years.* See the inscriptions of Ūṭṭattūr in Trichinopoly district or *Ep. Rep.*, 1913, p. 109, for details about these two caste divisions.

622. 423 *of* 1905.—(Tamil.) On the same wall. A record of the Pāṇḍya king Tribhuvanachakravartin Jaṭāvarman Perumāḷ Sundaṛa-Pāṇḍyadēva, the date of which is lost. Built in at the beginning. Seems to record a gift of land.

623. 424 *of* 1905.—(Tamil.) On the south and east walls of the same shrine. A record in the ninth year of Rājanārāyaṇa-Śambuvarāya Tirumallinādan. Records gift of land.

624. 425 *of* 1905.—(Tamil.) On the same walls. A record in the seventh year of Sakalalōkachakravartin Rājanārāyaṇa-Śambuvarāya. Records that the king remitted taxes payable both in money and in kind on lands whose crops had suffered in Kalavaippaṟṟu (a portion of modern North Arcot). Such lands could not otherwise be taken up for cultivation. This order was to be engraved in the temples at Tiruvallam, Guḍimallūr (in the temple of Mannai-Nāyanār) and Kalavai.

Kaḍappēri.

625. *No.* 82, *Sewell's list.*—(Grantha.) Records a grant by Śrīgirīndra Mahārāja, son of Vijaya Bhūpati and brother of Dēva Rāya II, of a village named Nipataṭāka or Kaḍappēri, re-named Vijayarāyapuram, as free gift, to a number of Brahmans and to two temples in Ś. 1346 [Mr. Sewell gives a wrong reading of the date, namely, Ś. 1425 (A.D. 1503), cyclic year Krōdhi. He also misreads the name of the village and believes that it might be Vijayagōpālapuram in the Kāḷahasti or Vijayapuram in Kārvēṭinagar Zamindari. [The inscription has been edited by Mr. M. Narayanasami Aiyar in *Ep. Ind.*, VIII, pp. 306–17, and the mistakes of Mr. Sewell have been corrected. The inscription says that while Dēvarāya (II) succeeded to the throne of his father, his younger brother Śrīgiribhūpāla went to the country of Maratakapuri and ruled it, and then made a grant of land to Sampatkumāra Paṇḍita and other learned men on Friday, Rēvati Nakshatra, Uttānadvādaśi, Krōdhin, Ś. 1346, which corresponded, according to Kielhorn, to Friday, the 3rd November, A.D. 1424. Sampatkumāra is said to be the son of a very learned doctor named Gōvinda Paṇḍita. Vijayarāmapuram of Mr. Sewell is wrong reading for Vijayarāyapura. Venkayya identifies Maratakapuri with Viriñchipuram, and Mr. Narayanasami Aiyar has identified Nipataṭāka with Kaḍappēri (Walajapet taluk). The inscription refers also to Kalavai, Kāvēripakkam, etc.]

Kalavai.

626. 228 *of* 1901.—(Tamil.) On the south wall of the central shrine in the Tirukkalīśvara temple. A record in the third year of the Chōḷa king Parakēsarivarman *alias* Ādhirājēndradēva. Records sale of land to the temple of Tirukkarīśvara at Ulagaḷanda-Śōḷachaturvēdimaṅgalam.

627. 229 *of* 1901.—(Tamil.) On the west wall of the same shrine. A record in the seventh year of the Chōḷa king Parakēsarivarman *alias* Vikrama-Chōḷadēva (1118–35). Records gift of land. Kalavai is here called Rājanārāyaṇa-chaturvēdimaṅgalam.

628. 230 *of* 1901.—(Tamil.) On the same wall. A record in the seventh year of Rājanārāyaṇa Śambuvarāyan. Records that the king remitted certain taxes on fields, the crops of which had suffered.

629. 231 *of* 1901.—(Tamil.) On the north wall of the same shrine. A record in the fourth year of the Chōḷa king Vikrama-Chōḷadēva. Records gift of land, two lamps and two cows.

630. 232 *of* 1901.—(Tamil.) On the south wall of the maṇṭapa in front of the same shrine, left of entrance. A record in the seventeenth year of the Pāṇḍya king Tribhuvanachakravartin Sundara-Pāṇḍyadēva (I, 1216–35). Begins with *Samasta-jagad-ādhāra*. Records a gift of land to the Tirukkarīśvara temple at Kalavai.

Viravalli (near Lalapet).

630-A. 611 *of* 1904.—(Tamil.) On a rock in the Paḷḷar street. A much damaged record in Ś. 1405 of the Vijayanagara king Mallikārjuna.

Panchapāṇḍavamalai (near Arcot) also called Tiruppānmalai.

See *N. A. Manual*, II, p. 310, for a description of the local Jain antiquities.

631. 10 *of* 1895.—(Tamil.) On a boulder. A record in the fiftieth year of the Pallava king Nandipōttaraśar, saying that the images of a Yakśhi named Ponniyakkiyār and a saint Nāganandin which are preserved to the present day were cut out of the rock by Nāraṇan, the son of Maruttuvar of Pugaḷālaimaṅgalam. See *Ep. Ind.*, Vol. IV, p. 136–7. Yakshas and Yakshis were guardian deities of Jain temples. See *Des. Cat.*, *Sans. MSS.*, XVI, pp. 6367–8, for a work on their method of worship.

632. 19 *of* 1890.—On the rock. A record in the eighth year of the Chōḷa king Kō-Rājarājakēsarivarman (i.e., Rājarāja I). Mentions Tiruppāmalai which mentions Peruntimiri nāḍu, a division of Paḍuvūr-kōṭṭam. Records a gift to the sanctuary on the hill by "a certain Lāṭarāja Vīrachōḷa who seems to have been a vassal of Rājarāja."

*Sholingur.**

633. 9 *of* 1896.—(Grantha and Tamil.) On a boulder near the tank. A record in the ninth year of the Chōḷa king Parāntaka I. The inscription mentions the Gaṅga feudatory Prithvīpati II,

---

* The Chōḷasimhapura of the *Guruparamparas* and Chōḷapuri of the inscriptions. The temple on the local hill, dedicated to Narasimha, is noticed in the *Prabandhas* and so very ancient. The *Guruparamparas* and *Viśvaguṇādarśa* of Veṅkaṭādhvārin also refer to it. The orthodox name of the hill is Gaḍigai or Ghaṭikāchalam. On account of its antiquity and sanctity it has always been a prominent centre of Vaishṇavism, and some of the great leaders of the creed are connected with it. Ādivaṇ Saṭhakōpasvāmi, the founder of the Ahōbilam maṭha had, says the *Satsampradāyamuktavali*, the management of the temple, but it subsequently came into the hands of the influential family of Doḍḍāchārya, a contemporary of Appaiya Dīkshita and Kōṭikanyādānam Tātāchārya and a learned writer on Viśishṭādvaitism. For a short but excellent account of the place see *N.A. Manual*, II, pp. 435–7.

Hastimalla or Vīrachōḷa [see Nos. 592, 579 and 580], lord of the Bāṇas and conqueror of an unnamed enemy in the battle of Vallāḷa. Hastimalla is also called Lord of Parivīpura (Viḷippuram taluk ?) and is said to have executed the gift by Parāntaka I of a paddy field for the upkeep of a tank (evidently the large local tank). See *Ep. Ind.*, Vol. IV, pp. 221—25.

634. 10 *of* 1896.—(Tamil.) On a stone in the north-west corner of the Narasimhasvāmin temple in the same place. First line of the record is lost.

635. 11 *of* 1896.—(Telugu.) On a boulder in the Añjanēya temple on a hill in the same place. A record on the Vijayanagara king Rāmadēvamahārāya of Penugoṇḍa in Ś. 1542 expired, Raudra. Beginning only copied. (Rāma dēva was the claimant who eventually succeeded in the civil war which, as Barrados says, immediately followed the death of Veṅkaṭapati I. See Sewell's *Forg. Empe.* and my *Hist. Naik. King. Madur.*).

Kārikkāl (near Sholingur).

636. 12 *of* 1896.—(Tamil.) On a slab forming the roof of the Ponni-Amman temple. A record in the fifth year of the Chōḷa king Madiraikoṇḍa Kō-Rājakēsarivarman. Dr. Hultzsch identifies him with the son of (Parakēsarivarman ?) Gaṇḍarāditya. *Ep. Ind.*, IV, p. 331. It is doubtful however whether Gaṇḍarāditya was a Parakēsarivarman. [Some of the ruined temples here are traditionally attributed to Narasimha Rāya of Vijayanagar. See *N.A. Manual*, p. 347.]

Puduppāḍi.

637. 426 *of* 1905.—(Tamil.) On the north wall of the central shrine in the Bharadvājēśvara temple. A damaged record in the second year of the Chōḷa king Vikrama-Chōḷadēva (1118—35).

638. 427 *of* 1905.—(Tamil.) On the west wall of the central shrine in the same temple. A damaged record in the sixth year of the Chōḷa king Vikrama-Chōḷadēva (1118—35). Records the gift of a lamp to the temple of Tirukkuraṅguttu-Mahādēvar in Puduppāḍi.

639. 428 *of* 1905.—(Tamil.) On the west and south walls of the same shrine. A record in the third year of the Chōḷa king Parakēsarivarman *alias* Uḍaiyār Śrī-Ādhirājēndradēva [son of Vīra-Rājēndra I, 1063-70]. Built in at the end. Records sale of land by the villagers of Puduppāḍi in the district of Perumbāṇappāḍi to the temple of Tirukkuraṅguttīśvaramuḍaiya-Mahādēvar. The land sold was situated on the bank of the Pālār and had become unfit for cultivation in consequence of a flood in the river, which led to the fields getting silted up with sand.

640. 255 *of* 1906.—(Tamil.) On a stone kept in the Public Works Department bungalow. Contains the words *svasti śri-Iravikulamānikkapperumbaḻḻi* in characters belonging roughly to the eleventh century A.D.

641. 256 *of* 1906.—(Tamil.) On the north and west walls of the central shrine in the Vēdanārāyaṇa-Perumāḷ temple in the same village. Records in Raktākshi, gifts to the temple of Vēdanārāyaṇa-Perumāḷ at Karaivaḷi-Puduppāḍi in Kalavaipaṟṟu.

642. 257 *of* 1906.—(Tamil.) On the south wall of the same shrine. Records in Ś. 1418 expired, Naḷa, gift of land apparently by a Nāyaka.

643. 258 *of* 1906.—(Kanarese.) On the same wall. A record in Raktākshi. A Kanarese version of No. 641.

644. 259 *of* 1906.—(Telugu.) To the left of entrance into the maṇṭapa in front of the same temple. A much damaged record in 1502.

Tiruppārkaḍal.

645. 685 *of* 1904.—(Tamil.) On the south wall of the central shrine in the Kharapurīśvara temple. A record in the sixth year of the Chōḷa king Parakēsarivarman. Built in the middle. Records gift of gold for a lamp. The supervision of this charity was entrusted to *the annual " tank supervision " (committee).*

646. 686 *of* 1904.—(Tamil.) On the same wall. A record in the fifth year of the Chōḷa king Parakēsarivarman. Built in the middle. Records gift of a lamp.

647. 687 *of* 1904.—(Tamil.) On the same wall. A mutilated record in the third year of the Chōḷa king Parakēsarivarman. The temple is called Tirukkarapuram, at Kāviḍippākkam *alias* Amaninārana-chaturvēdimangalam in Paḍuvūr-kōṭṭam.

648. 688 *of* 1904.—(Tamil.) On the same wall. A record in the seventh year of the Chōḷa king Parakēsarivarman. Records a gift of gold. [This and the next two inscriptions mention various village committees besides those for garden and tank supervision, e.g., the great men for supervision of wards, the great men for supervision of the village, " The two hundred," the great men for supervising the *Udāsinas* (translated as ascetics), etc. These together with the learned men and other distinguished men of the village formed the village assembly.]

649. 689 *of* 1904.—(Tamil.) On the west wall in the same shrine. An incomplete record in the fourth year of the Chōḷa king Parakēsarivarman. Records gift of gold for two lamps.

650. 690 *of* 1904.—(Tamil.) On the same wall. A record in the twelfth year of the Chōḷa king Parakēsarivarman. Built in at the end. Records gift of gold for a lamp and for offerings.

651. 691 *of* 1904.—(Tamil.) On the same wall. A damaged record in the seventh year of the Chōḷa king Parakēsarivarman.

652. 692 *of* 1904.—(Tamil.) On the north wall of the central shrine in the same temple. An incomplete record in the third year of Pārthivēndravarman. Records gift of land. [It was in his time evidently that the name Kāviḍipākkam was changed into Kāveripākam.]

653. 693 *of* 1904.—(Tamil.) On the same wall. A record in the twelfth year of the Chōḷa king Madiraikoṇḍa Parakēsarivarman (Parāntaka I, 906—47). Records gift of gold for feeding four Brāhmaṇas. The village is called Kāvaḍippākkam. [The inscription refers to an invasion by the Pāṇḍya and the king of Ceylon. In this it confirms the Udayēndiram plates dated in his 15th year which state that he defeated Rājasimha Pāṇḍya and slew an immense army despatched by the Lord of Laṅka. Venkayya points out that this invasion should have been during the first of two wars against Ceylon. The second was fought in the latter part of the king's reign. See Wijesinhás *Mahāvamśa*, ch. 52, p. 80, quoted in *Ep. Rep.*, 1905, p. 50, and inscriptions 488 and 605 of 1904 at Madura, at Kūram and *Ep. Ind.*, V, p. 43.]

654. 694 *of* 1904.—(Tamil.) On the south wall of the first prākāra of the same temple. A record of the Vijayanagara/Dēvarāya-Mahārāya II (1422—49) " who witnessed the elephant hunt," in S. 1364 expired, Durmati. Records the remission of certain taxes in favour of the temple by the Mahāmaṇḍalēśvara Gaṇḍakaṭṭāri Sāḷuva Tippayadēva-Mahārāja. See No. 663 below.

655. 695 *of* 1904.—(Tamil.) On the same wall. An incomplete record in the thirtieth year of the Chōḷa king Tribhuvanavīradēva (Kulōttuṅga III). The temple is called Tirukkarapuramuḍaiya-Nāyanār at Tiruppārkaḍal.

656. 696 *of* 1904.—(Tamil.) On the north wall of the same prākāra. A damaged record of the Vijayanagara king Vīra-Kampaṇa-Uḍaiyār (II), son or Vīra-Bukkaṇa-Uḍaiyār (I) in Ś. 1294 expired, Paridhāvin.

657. 697 *of* 1904.—(Tamil.) On the east wall of the same prākāra. A record of the Vijayanagara king Ariyaṇṇa-Uḍaiyār (Harihara II), son of Vīra-Bukkaṇa-Uḍaiyār (I) in Ś. 1304 expired, Dundhubi. Records gift of land.

658. 698 *of* 1904.—(Tamil.) On the south wall of the same prākāra. A damaged record in the thirtieth year of the Chōḷa king Tribhuvanachakravartin Kulōttuṅga-Chōḷadēva. Seems to record a gift of land.

659. 699 *of* 1904.—(Tamil.) On the west wall of the same prākāra. A record of Tribhuvanachakravartin Vijaya-Gaṇḍagōpāladeva. Records a gift of land to the temple of Tirukkarapuramuḍaiya Nāyanār at Tiruppārkaḍal. The king is called Madurāntaka-Pottappi-Chōḷa at the end.

660. 700 *of* 1904.—(Tamil.) On the same wall. A record in the sixteenth year of the Pallava king Sakalabhuvanachakravartin-Kōpperuñjiṅgadēva. Mentions Sakkaramūdūr, an independent village *(taniyur)* in Dāmar-kōṭṭam; also Kasirambēḍu-nāḍu in Kāliyur-kōṭṭam.

661. 701 *of* 1904.—(Tamil.) On the east wall of the same prākāra; right of entrance. A damaged and mutilated record of the Vijayanagara king Vīra-Kampaṇā-Uḍaiyār (II), son of Vīra-Bukkana-Uḍaiyār (Bukka I) in Ś. 1291.

662. 702 *of* 1904.—(Tamil.) On the same wall, left of entrance. A record in the fourteenth year of Tribhuvanachakravartin Kōnērinmaikoṇḍān Sundara-Pāṇḍya, "who took every country," i.e., Jaṭāvarman Sundara Pāṇḍya I (1251–64). Records gift of land. The king's order was issued from Kaṇṇanūr. [This place had been the capital of Vīra Somēśvara (1234-at least 1262) and in 1264 it was in the hands of the Pāṇḍyan king.]

663. 703 *of* 1904.—(Tamil.) On the west and south walls of the Raṅganātha Perumāḷ temple in the same village. A record of the Vijayanagara king Dēvarāya-Mahārāya (II), "who witnessed the elephant hunt" in Ś. 1364 expired, Durmati. Records that the Mahāmaṇḍalēśvara Gaṇḍakaṭṭāri Śāluva-Tippayadēva-Mahārāja remitted certain taxes in favour of the temple. See No. 654 above.

Vēlappakkam.

663-A. The Vīlpāka grant of Veṇkaṭapati I. Published in *Ind. Antq.*, II and *Ep. Ind.*, IV, 269-78. Sanskrit and Nandināgari. Records that Veṇkaṭa I of the last Vijayanagara dynasty gave in Vaiśākha Śukla 12, Ś. 1521, Plava (A.D. 1601–2), in the presence of god Veṇkatēśa, the village of Vilapāka to Tiruvēṅgalanātharya, son of Anantabhaṭṭa of Urputtūr and grandson of Sūryadēvārya-bhaṭṭa of the Śrīvatsagōtra, Āpastamba sūtra and Yajus-Śakha. The grant was made at the request of Liṅga, the son of Bomma and grandson of prince Vīrappa Nāik. [These Chiefs are Liṅgama Nāyaka, his father Chinna Bomma Nāyaka and *his* father Virappa Nāyaka of Vellore. Chinna Bomma was the patron of Appaiya Dīkshita. See N.A. 151 above and references given therein.]

WANDIWASH TALUK.

Anaibhōgi.

For the legendary origin of this place see *N. A. Manual*, II, 446.

663-B. A C.P. grant in the village. (Grantha.) Records that Achyuta Rāya granted the two villages of Ānaibhōgi and Vīraguḍi to the Brahman Sūrya Dīkshitar in Ś. 1429, Kāḷayukti. See *Ins., S. Dts.*, p. 150, No. I.

Dēśūr.

664. 244 *of* 1909.—(Tamil poetry.) On the west wall of the Karivaḍa-Īśvara temple. Records in Ś. 1450, Sarvadhāri, the building of a temple for Śeṅgai-Vēlāyudan at Dēśūr.

Kaḷambūr.

665. 245 *of* 1909.—(Tamil.) On a pillar in the Śelliyamman temple. A damaged record in Ś. 982. Records the gift of a lamp to the god Aḷagiyamaṇāḷvār in the temple of Kalikēsariviṇṇagar and mentions the village assembly of Vikkiramaśōḷachaturvēdi-maṅgalam. See note to the next inscription.

666. 246 *of* 1909.—(Tamil.) On a pillar in the Vēṇugōpāla-svāmin temple in the same village. Records in Ś. 892 gift of lamps to the temple of Kalikēsari-Viṇṇagardēvar by the assembly of Kaḷamūr. [Mr. Krishna Sastri surmises that the Pārthivēndra-varman of the Tāyanūr, Madhuramaṅgalam (Chingleput district) and other inscriptions who had the title of Kalikēsari was perhaps the builder of this temple.]

667. 247 *of* 1909.—(Tamil.) On three detached fragments built into the wall of the Kāśiviśvanāthasvāmin temple in the same village. One of the fragments contains a portion of the historical introduction of Parakēsarivarman Rājēndradēva (1050—63). The other two mention a Vishṇu temple and the village of Kaḷamūr *alias* Vikkirama-śōḷa-chaturvēdimaṅgalam in Paṅgala-nāḍu.

Marudāḍu (Maratāḍu).

668. 407 *of* 1912.—(Tamil.) On the south base of the central shrine in the Purandēśvara temple. A record in the twentieth year of the Chōḷa king. Built in. Begins with the historical introduction of Rājēndra-Chōḷa I (*tirumanni vaḷara*, etc.). Records gift of ninety sheep for a lamp to the temple of Peruntirukkōyil-uḍaiya-Mahādēva of Marudāḍu *alias* Vikkirama-śōḷanallūr in Marudāḍu-nāḍu, a subdivision of Venkunṛa-kōṭṭam in Jayaṅgoṇḍaśōḷa-maṇḍalam. Registers also a sale of land for digging a tank.

669. 408 *of* 1912.—(Tamil.) On the west base of the same shrine. A record in the thirty-second year of the Chōḷa king Kulōttuṅga-Chōḷadēva (I) "who abolished the tolls and who ruled the country dispelling darkness." Built in. Records gift of land by purchase from the residents of Marudāḍu, for offerings to the temple of Umāskanda . . . Avanimuḷududai-Nāyaka.

670. 409 *of* 1912.—(Tamil.) On the same base. A record in the fourth year of the Chōḷa king Rājakēsarivarman (i.e., Rājarāja I). Built in in the middle. Records gift of sheep for a lamp to

the temple of Peruntirukkōyil at Marudāḍu in Marudāḍu-nāḍu, a subdivision of Venkunṛa-kōṭṭam.

671. 410 *of* 1912.—(Tamil.) On the north base of the same shrine. A record in the fourteenth year of Sakalalōkachakravartin Rājanārāyaṇan Śambuvarāyar. Records sale of a channel by the residents of Marudāḍu *alias* Vikkiramaśōḷanallūr to the residents of Koṭṭai-ūr in Vaḍavūr-nāḍu, a subdivision of Venkunṛa-kōṭṭam in Jayaṅgoṇḍaśōḷamaṇḍalam.

672. 411 *of* 1912.—(Tamil.) On the same base. A record in the eighth year of the Chōḷa king Rājarājakēsarivarman (i.e., Rājarāja I). Records gift of land for a lamp by the residents of Marudāḍu, to the temple of Peruntirukkōyil-Āḷvār for the merit of a private individual of Māganūr-Puttuṟai who fell in order that Marudāḍu (a village in Marudāḍu-nāḍu of Venkunṛa-kōṭṭam) may not be destroyed (*aḻiyāmai-yanru.*) See *Ep. Rep.*, 1909, p. 120 and *Mys. and Coorg*, pp. 186—8.

673. 412 *of* 1912.—(Tamil.) On the same base. A record in the twelfth year of the Chōḷa king Rājarājakēsarivarman, "who destroyed the ships at Śālai," (i.e., Rājarāja I). Records gift of seventy sheep for a lamp to the same temple by Śeṇbar *alias* Uttamanīli Rājarāja-Aṇukkappallavaraiyan.

674. 413 *of* 1912.—(Tamil.) On the same base. An unfinished record of the Vijayanagara king Vīra-Naraśiṅgadēva-Mahārāya, son of Śāḷuva Naraśiṅgadēva-Mahārāya in Ś. 1429, Kshaya, Paṅguni two, Mīna, śu. di. 5, Attam, Sunday. Contains only the introductory passage and the date. [Diwan Bahadur Swamikannu Pillai says that the date is probably Sunday, 28th March 1506, but *Mīna Paṅguṅi* should be 2 *Mēsha* and *Attam* should be *Rōhiṇi*. The king is evidently Immaḍi Narasimha Tammarāya, the son of the great usurper.]

675. 414 *of* 1912.—(Tamil.) On the same base. Records gift of the village of Vādikkuppam, a hamlet of Marudāḍu, for providing worship in the temple of Peruntirukkōyiluḍaiya-Tambirānār, by Timmarāja, agent of Jagatāpi Errayadēva-Chōḷamahārāja, for the merit of Erramarāja, i.e., perhaps his master Errayadēva-Chōḷamahārāja).

676. 415 *of* 1912.—(Tamil.) On the north wall of the maṇṭapa in front of the same shrine. A record of the Vijayanagara king Achyutadēva-Mahārāya in Vijaya, Tai, 1, Sunday, śu. di. 12, Saṅkramapuṇyakāla (= 28th December 1533). Records gift of the two villages Anṟilēri and Vadikkuppam for the merit of the king's accountant (rāyar-kāraṇikam), Piḷaiporutta-Piḷḷai, during the management of Tiṭṭan, a clerk (Ōlaiyeḷuttu) of the temple.

677. 416 *of* 1912.—(Tamil.) On a slab lying in the same temple. Anṟilēri is stated to be the sarvamānya gift of the temple Peruntirukkōyiluḍaiyār.

678. 417 *of* 1912.—(Tamil.) On a slab lying near the big irrigation tank in the same village. A record in the twelfth year of the 'Gaṅga-Pallava king' Kō-Vijaya-Nripatuṅgavarman. Registers that a certain Koṅgaraiyar Ninṟa-Perumān constructed a bank of stones (*kaliñju*) for the tank of Marudāḍu and had the head of the irrigation channel renovated.

Mēlpādi.

This place, six miles north of Tiruvallam, figures in the Karkāḍ plates of the Rāshṭrakūṭa Krishṇa III as the place of his encampment in 959 and is thus ancient. The inscriptions of Rājarāja I and Rājēndra Chōḷa I in it corroborate the fact. They show that of its two temples the deserted Chōḷēśvara temple, *at first known* as Ariñjigai-Īśvara temple, was built by Rājarāja I, in honour of "the king who died at Āṟṟūr". The name Rājāśrayapuram applied to the village, and the naming of its two streets after Mummuḍichōla, Arumoḷidēva, show also the connexion of the place with Rājarāja. It belonged to Tūynāḍu in Perumbāṇappāḍi in Jayaṅkoṇḍa-chōḷamaṇḍalam. According to tradition its ancient temple was Jain but made Śaivite by the Dēvāram saints. See *N.A. Manual*, II, *p.* 347 for details.

679. 83 *of* 1889.—On the base of garbhagriha of the Chōḷēśvara temple. A record in the twenty-ninth year of the Chōḷa king Ko-Parakēsarivarman *alias* Rājarāja-dēva (II, 1146—78), recording the gift of the hamlet of Pulikkunṟam to the Peruñjigai Īśvara shrine. See *S. Ind. Inscrns.*, Vol. III, No. 16, pp. 24-5.

680. 84 *of* 1889.—On the base of garbhagriha of the Chōḷēśvara temple. A record in the twenty-ninth year of the Chōḷa king Ko-Rājarājakēsarivarman *alias* Rājarājadēva (I). The citizens of Mēṟpādi grant to Ariñjigai-Īśvara temple 5136½ *kulis* of land as tax-free, and the accountant of the 'city' writes it. See *S. Ind. Inscrns.*, Vol. III, pp. 23-4.

681. 85 *of* 1899.—On the north wall of garbhagriha of the same temple. A record in the ninth year of the Chōḷa king Kō-Parakē-sarivarman *alias* Rājēndra-Chōḷa-dēva (I). Some shepherds of the place make a declaration before Lakuḷīśvara Paṇḍita, the head of the maṭha connected with the temple, to supply ghee for a lamp. Hultzsch suggests that the Mēlpāḍi maṭha was a branch of the Lākuḷīśa-Pāśupatas of Kārōhaṇa in Gujerat. *S. Ind. Inscrns.*, Vol. III, No. 18, pp. 27-9.

682. 86 *of* 1889.—On the north wall of garbhagriha of the same temple. A record in the twenty-ninth year of the Chōḷa king Kō-Rājarāja-Rājakēsarivarman *alias* Rājarāja-dēva (I), making the gift of a lamp to the same shrine. *S. Ind. Inscrns.*, Vol. III, No. 17, pp. 26-7.

683. 87 *of* 1889.—On the south wall of garbhagriha of the Sōmanāthēśvara temple (called formerly Chōḷēndrasimhēśvara).

A record in the fourteenth year of the Chōḷa king Mummuḍi-Chōladēva *alias* Kō-Rājarāja-Rājakēsarivarman (I), recording that Īrāyiravan Pallavaraiyan, a well-known officer of Rājarāja I and Rājēndra Chōḷa I, made over 15 kaḻanju of gold to Tiruvallam assembly who in return assigned 1,000 *kulis* of land for the Chōḷēndrasimhēśvara temple. See *S. Ind. Incrns.*, Vol. III, No. 19, pp. 29–30.

684. 88 *of* 1889.—On the south wall of mahāmaṇṭapa in the same temple. A record in the eighth year of Rājarājadēva.

685. 89 *of* 1889.—On the south wall of mahāmaṇṭapa in the Sōmanāthēśvara temple. A record in Plava-samvatsara of Vīra-Kampaṇa-Uḍaiyār.

686. 90 *of* 1889.—On the south wall of mahāmaṇṭapa in the same temple. A record in the sixteenth year of Śamburāyar, " who conquered the goddess of fortune and took the earth."

Neduṅguṇam.

687. 704 *of* 1904.—(Tamil.) On the north wall of the first prākāra of the Rāmachandra-Perumaḷ temple. A record of the Vijayanagara king Vīrapratāpa Vīra-Achyutadēva-Mahārāya in Ś. 1466 expired, Krōdhin. Records gift of land.

688. 705 *of* 1904.—(Tamil.) In the same gōpura of the same temple, right of entrance. Mentions in Rākshasa a certain Śōṇādri-Aiyan, agent of Raghunātha-Nāyakkar-Ayyan (Tanjore Naik). [This and other local inscriptions show that every Tanjore Nāik had agents at Neḍuṅguṇram. Mr. Kuppusami Sastri points out, on the basis of Yagnanārāyaṇa Dīkshita's *Sāhitya-ratnākara*, that the eleven-storeyed gōpura at Tiruvaṇṇāmalai was completed by Chinna Śevvappa Nāik of Tanjore, which is confirmed by two inscriptions there in 1574–5. (*Ep. Rep.*, 1905, p. 61.) It is thus clear that this part of the country was much under the influence of that dynasty.]

689. 706 *of* 1904.—(Tamil.) In the same place. Records in Rākshasi, gift of land to a private individual. Mentions the agent of Raghunātha-Nāyaka referred to in the above epigraph.

690. 707 *of* 1904.—(Tamil.) In the main gōpura of the Rāmachandra-Perumāḷ temple, left of entrance. Śōṇādri-Ayyan is mentioned in Virōdhikrit as the agent of Āriyappa-Ayyan. Records gift of land.

691. 708 *of* 1904.—(Tamil.) On the north wall of the central shrine in the Dīrghāchalēśvara temple in the same village. A record of the Vijayanagara king Kṛishṇadēva-Mahārāyar in Ś. 1454, Sarvajit (wrong). Records gift of land. The cyclic year would correspond to Ś. 1450.

692. 709 *of* 1904.—(Tamil.) On the east wall of the maṇṭapa in front of the same shrine, right of entrance. Records in Vishu, a gift of land by the agent of Achyuta-Vijayarāghava-Nāyakkar-Ayyan. [The last of the Tanjore Nāik dynasty. See *Tanj. Gazr.* p. 40 and my *Hist. of the Nāik dynasty of Madura.*]

693. 710 *of* 1904.—(Tamil.) On the same wall, left of entrance. A record of the Vijayanagara king Vīrapratāpa Vīra-Veṅkaṭapati-dēva-Mahārāya (Veṅkaṭa I, 1586—1615) in Ś. 1518 expired, Durmukhi. Records a gift of money by Achyutappa-Nāyakar-Ayyan for the merit of Dīkshitar-Ayyan. [Achyutappa was the Tanjore Nāik from 1572 to 1614. Dīkshitar was either the celebrated Gōvinda Dīkshita or more probably, Appaiya Dīkshita. For the latter see N.A. 151 *and* N.A. 663 (*a*) *ante.*]

Nerkuṇam.

694. 86 *of* 1908.—(Tamil.) On a slab set up in front of the Silaiyamman temple. A record in the twenty-fourth year of the Chōḷa king Rājakēsarivarman. Records gift of Ērippaṭṭi by Nambiyamallanār, son of Nripatuṅgamaṅgalappērараiyar, for the benefit of the tank at Nerkuṇam in Śiṅgapura-nāḍu.

695. 87 *of* 1908.—(Tamil.) On a slab set up near the big sluice of the tank in the same village. A record of the Vijayanagara king Dēvarāya (II), son of Vijayarāya-Uḍaiyār (Vijaya Rāya I) in Ś. 1352, Sādhāraṇa. Records permission to dig earth in the tank at Nerkuṇam.

Sīyyamaṅgalam.

696. 60 *of* 1900.—(Tamil.) On the north wall of the verandah in front of the Stambhēśvara temple, right of entrance. A record in the fifth year of the Chōḷa king Parakēsarivarman. Records gift of land by an inhabitant of the Pāṇḍya country to the temple of Tirukkaṟṟali-Mahādēvar at Śiyyamaṅgalam in Tennāṟṟūr-nāḍu, a subdivision of Paḷakunṟa-kōṭṭam in Jayaṅkoṇḍa-Sōḷa-maṇḍalam. [The Tirumalai and Tiruvallam inscriptions give the same districts. Tennāṟṟūr is a village in Wandiwash taluk.]

697. 61 *of* 1900.—(Tamil.) On the east wall of the same temple. A record in the twenty-second year of the Chōḷa king Tribhuvanachakravartin Kulōttuṅga-Chōḷadēva. Refers to a hall (*māligai*) built by Kulōttuṅga-Śōḷa-Śambuvarāyan in the Tūṇāṇḍār temple at Śiyyamaṅgalam. [For the description of the temple see *N.A. Manual,* II, p. 445.]

698. 62 *of* 1900.—(Tamil.) On the east wall of the same temple. A record in the twenty-fourth year of the Chōḷa king Tribhuvanachakravartin Kulōttuṅga-Chōḷadēva. Records a gift of land by Kulōttuṅga-Śoḷa-Śambuvarāyan. [Was this "Chembu Rāja," the traditional founder of the place?]

699. 63 *of* 1900.—(Tamil.) On the east wall of the same temple. A record in the sixteenth year of the Chōḷa king

Tribhuvanachakravartin Vikrama-Chōḷadēva (1118--35.) Records gift of the proceeds of certain taxes by Śeṅgēni-Nālāyiravan Ammaiyappan *alias* Rājēndra Śōḷa-Śambuvarāyan. See No. 715.

700. 64 *of* 1900.—(Tamil.) On the east wall of the same temple. A record in the third year of the Chōḷa king Rājakēsarivarman *alias* Tribhuvanachakravartin Kulōttuṅga-Chōḷadēva (I ?). Records gift of sixteen cows for a lamp, by an individual who shot a man by mistake, after the decision to that effect by the governor and people of the district assembled. See N.A. 480 above.

701. 65 *of* 1900.—(Tamil.) On the north wall of the maṇṭapa in front of the same temple. Records in Viśvāvasu a private agreement referring to the temple.

702. 66 *of* 1900.—(Tamil.) On the south wall of the same maṇṭapa. A damaged record of the Chōḷa king Rājakēsarivarman *alias* Tribhuvanachakravartin Kulōttuṅga-Chōḷadēva (I ?) in his ninth year. Records gift of a lamp.

703. 67 *of* 1900.—(A Sanskrit verse in Ārya metre.) On the north wall of the maṇṭapa in front of the central shrine in the same temple, right of entrance. A record of the Pallava king Laḷitāṅkura. Records the building of the shrine called Avanibhājana-Pallavēśvara. See *Ep. Ind.*, Vol. VI, p. 320, where Dr. Hultzsch edits the inscription. *Laḷitāṅkura* is proved by the Vallam inscription to be the title of Mahēndrapōtarāja whom Venkayya identifies with Mahēndravarman I. [Dr Hultzsch therefore infers that he excavated this shrine as he did the Trichinopoly, Vallam and Mahēndravāḍi ones. See *S. Ind. Inscrns.*, I, Nos. 33 and 34; *Ibid.* Vol. II, No. 72; *Ibid.*, Vol. IV, No. 19. Also *Madr. Ep. Rep.*, 1900, p. 5.]

704. 68 *of* 1900.—(Tamil.) On the same wall, left of entrance. A record in the third year of the "Gaṅga-Pallava" king Vijaya-Nandivikramavarman, whom Dr. Hultzsch identifies with the father of Nṛipatuṅga. Records the building of the maṇṭapa in front of the cave temple by a certain Aḍavi, headman of the village of Perumbālaiyūr in Ūṟṟukkāṭṭukkōṭṭam, with the permission of a Gaṅga chief named Nerguṭṭi (who was a vassal of Nandivarman). See *Ep. Ind.*, VI, pp. 320--22.

705. 69 *of* 1900.—(Tamil.) On the rock in the south-east corner of the same temple. A record in the third year of the Chōḷa king Parakēsarivarman (unidentified). Records gift of land, to the temple of Tirukkaṟṟaḷimahādēva of Śiṅgamaṅgalam. Mentions a feudatory named Gaṅgachūḷāmaṇi, Mummuḍichōḷa Śembiyan Śrīgaṅgaraiyar, evidently a local feudatory connected with the Gaṅga chiefs Śaṅkaradēva and Sōmanātha mentioned in the Tiruvallam inscriptions as the contemporaries of Rājarāja I and Rājēndrachōḷa I. *Ep. Rep.*, 1900, p. 9. *S.I.I.*, III, 104 and 107.

706. 70 *of* 1900.—(Tamil.) On the rock in the north-east corner of the same temple. A record in the fourth year of the Chōḷa king Parakēsarivarman, "who took the head of Vīra-Pāṇḍya." Built in at the bottom. [The king was either Āditya II or Parāntaka II Sundarachōḷa.]

Śripurushamaṅgalam.

707. 59 *of* 1900.—(Grantha and Tamil.) On the west wall of the Maṇikaṇṭhēśvara temple. A record of the Pāṇḍya king Tribhuvanachakravartin Sundara-Pāṇḍyadēva. Records the gift of the village of Śrīpurushamaṅgalam to the Brāhmaṇas of Sundara Pāṇḍyachaturvēdimaṅgalam founded by the king to the south of the Aruḷāḷapperumāḷ temple at Conjeeveram. [The king is the same as Jaṭāvarman Sundara Pāṇḍya I, 1251—64, the conqueror of the Kākatīya Gaṇapati, the coverer of the Śrīraṅgam temple with gold and the anointer of heroes at Nellore.]

Tellāru.

708. 71 *of* 1900.—(Tamil.) On the east wall of the Mūlēśvara temple. A record in the sixth year of the Pāṇḍya king Māravarman *alias* Tribhuvanachakravartin Vikrama-Pāṇḍyadēva. Records gift of land. Mentions a certain Vikrama-Pāṇḍya-Mābalivāṇarāyar among the signatories. [It is not improbable that the king was the same as the one who ascended the throne in 1282 and who was the conqueror of the Kākatiya Gaṇapati and Vīragaṇḍagōpāla.] See *N.A. Manual*, II, p. 445 which refers to the local mud fort of Nanda Rāja and Jains.]

Vallam.

[Vallam is derived from Vālmīkam in which Śiva is said to have manifested himself here.]

709. 74 *of* 1900.—(Tamil.) On the south wall of the central shrine of the Śiva temple. A record in the twelfth year of the Pāṇḍya king Tribhuvanachakravartin Sundara-Pāṇḍyadēva. Records gift of five lamps. [The king intended is probably Jaṭāvarman Sundara-Pāṇḍya I, 1251-64.]

710. 75 *of* 1900.—(Tamil.) On the north wall of the same shrine. A record of the Vijayanagara king Naraśiṅgayadēva in Ś. 1391 expired, Virōdhin. Records gift of land. [The king referred to was apparently the usurper Sāḷuva Naraśiṅga.]

Vallimalai (near Tiruvallam).

The following epigraphs show the importance of this place as a Jain centre. The tradition connecting it with Vaḷḷi and God Subrahmaṇya of Tiruttaṇigai is of later origin. See *N.A. Manual*, II, pp. 347-48.

710-A. 91 *of* 1889.—Rock inscription in a *Jaina* cave on the hill· A record of the Gaṅga king, Rājamalla (I), the son of Raṇavikrama, grandson of Śrīpurushā (725—776), and great-grand son of Śivamāra (I, 679—713 circa). Rājamalla was the excavator of the cave.

710-B. 6 *of* 1895.—(Kanarese in Grantha characters.) On the rock. A record of the Gaṅga king Rājamalla. Records the founding of a Jaina shrine. (A better copy of No. 91 of 1889.)

710-C. 7 *of* 1895.—(Kanarese in Grantha characters.) On the same rock. The record of a Bāṇa king. Records the setting up of the image of Dēvasēna, the pupil of Bhavānandin and the spiritual preceptor of the king. [The teacher Bhavānandin who figures here is apparently different from the author of the *Bhavānanda*, a treatise on Nyāya, to whom Dr. Hultzsch refers in his *Rep. Sans., MSS.*, No. 1631.]

710-D. 8 *of* 1895.—(Kanarese.) On the same rock. Records the setting up of a Jaina image, " by the Jaina preceptor Aryanandin." The erection of the image in the above epigraph is also attributed to this saint.

710-E. 9 *of* 1895.—(Kanarese.) On the same rock. A damaged record.

Vaḷuvūr (Vaḷūr).

711. 51 *of* 1908.—(Tamil.) On the south wall of the central shrine in the Brahmapurīśvara temple. A record in the twenty-seventh year of the Chōḷa king Tribhuvanachakravartin Kulōttuṅga-Chōḷadēva III, who was pleased to take Madura and the crowned head of the 'Pāṇḍya'. Records gift of money for six lamps to the temple of Āḷudaiyār-Tiruvayanīśuram-Uḍaiyār at Vaḷugūr in Irumbeḍu-nādu, a district of Venkunṛa-kōṭṭam in Jayaṅgoṇḍa-Chōḷa-maṇḍalam.

712. 52 *of* 1908.—(Tamil.) On the same wall. A damaged record in Kshaya. Records gift of land.

713. 53 *of* 1908.—(Tamil.) On the same wall. An incomplete record of the Vijayanagara king Vīra-Viruppaṇa-Uḍaiyār in Pramōduta. Mentions Śembiyadaraiyar and Ponnaṅgaṭṭi Gāṅgēyar.

714. 54 *of* 1908.—(Tamil.) On the north, west and south walls of the same shrine. A record in the fifth year of Ravivarman *alias* Tribhuvanachakravartin Kulaśēkharadēva. Records the gift of the village of Śāttanūr in Irumbēḍu-nāḍu, a district of Venkunṛa-kkōṭṭam, by the villagers of Chālukkipparṛu to the temple of Tiru-Ayanīśuramuḍaiya-Nāyanār.

715. 55 *of* 1908.—(Tamil.) On the east wall of the manṭapa in front of the same shrine. A record in the twenty-third year of the Chōḷa king Tribhuvanachakravartin Rājarājadēva. Records gift of 22½ kāśu by a devotee for burning 4½ lamps in the temple of Tiruvayanīśvaramuḍaiya-Nāyaṅar at Vaḷugūr. Mentions a certain Kakku-Nāyaka-bhaṭṭāra *alias* Nārppatteṇṇāyira-bhaṭṭa. See No. 699.

716. 56 *of* 1908.—(Tamil.) On the same wall. A record in the seventh year of the Chōḷa king Vīrarājēndradēva. Records gift of paddy to the same temple for offerings at the early morning service (*tiruppaḷḷi-elichchi*) by a native of Ārpākkam in Magaral-nāḍu, a subdivision of Kāḷiyūr-kōṭṭam in Jayaṅgoṇḍa-Chōḷa-maṇḍalam.

717. 57 *of* 1908.—(Tamil.) On the south wall of the same maṇṭapa. A record in the seventeenth year of the Chōḷa king Tribhuvanachakravartin Rājarājadēva (III ?). Records gift of 23 cows and one bull for a lamp by Seṅgēṇi Vīrapperumāḷ *alias* Kulōttuṅga-Chōḷa Śambuvarāya.

718. 58 *of* 1908.—(Tamil.) On the same wall. A record in the seventeenth year of the Chōḷa king Tribhuvanachakravartin Kulōttuṅga-Chōḷadēva. Records gift of taxes in the village of Puravarinallūr for offerings and repairs by Seṅgēṇi Vīrarākkada Sambuvarāya who styles himself a Pallava.

719. 59 *of* 1908.—(Tamil.) On the same wall. A record in the thirty-eighth year of the Chōḷa king Tribhuvanachakravartin Tribhuvanavīradēva (Kulōttuṅga III). Records gift of money for a lamp by Puttulan Periyan Śambuvarāya-Pallavarāyan.

720. 60 *of* 1908.—(Tamil.) On the same wall. A record in the seventeenth year of the Chōḷa king Tribhuvanachakravartin Kulōttuṅga-Chōḷadēva (III ?). Records gift of two lamps by Ammaiyappa Savaka and others.

721. 61 *of* 1908.—(Tamil.) On the west wall of the same maṇṭapa. Refers in Prabhava to an earlier transaction, whereby the two persons mentioned in No. 53 got certain lands as a free gift from the temple. The relinquishment of these lands back to the temple in the year Pramōdhūta (Pramōda) and the receipt of money in return are also recorded.

722. 62 *of* 1908.—(Tamil.) On the north wall of the same maṇṭapa. A record of the Vijayanagara king Bhūpati-Uḍaiyār (1422–3), son of Vīra-Bukkaṇa-Uḍaiyār (II) in Ś. 1332, Vikrita. Purchase of land for the temple by the Sthānattār and the Kaikkōḷar of Vaḷugūr *alias* Kalikaḍindaśōḷanallūr.

723. 63 *of* 1908.—(Tamil.) On the same wall. A damaged record of the Vijayanagara king Śrīgirinātha Uḍaiyār, son of Vīra-Vijaya Bhūpatirāya (1422–3) in Ś. 1348, Viśvāvasu. Mentions Vaḷugūr *alias* Kalikaḍindaśōḷanallūr. See N.A. 625 above.

724. 64 *of* 1908.—(Tamil.) On the south wall of the maṇṭapa in front of the Kāmarasavalli-amman shrine in the same temple. A much damaged record of the Vijayanagara king Sadāśivadēva-Mahārāya in Vibhava. Mentions Kṛishṇappa Nāyakkaraiyan.

725. 65 *of* 1908.—(Tamil.) On the east wall of the prākāra of the same temple. A much damaged record. Seems to fix the taxes on looms, etc., payable by the residents of Vaḷuvūr.

726. 66 *of* 1908.—(Tamil.) On the same wall. A damaged record of the Vijayanagara king Achyutayyadēva Mahārāya, son of Vīrapratāpa-Naraśiṅgadēva, in Ś. 1460, Hēviḷambi. Receives the Śāḷuva titles Mēdinimisāra, Gaṇḍakaṭṭāri and Śāḷuva.

727. 67 *of* 1908.—(Tamil.) On the south wall of the same prākāra. In modern characters. Appears to record in Sarvadhārin a compact (*iśai-yōlai*) entered into by the villagers of Vaḷugūr in connection with an unknown offence committed by a certain Mīnavarayár. Mentions Taṇḍagā-nāḍu.

728. 68 *of* 1908.—(Tamil.) On a slab set up near the sluice of the tank in the same village. A record in the sixth year of the 'Gaṅga-Pallava' king Nripatuṅgappōttaraiyar. Records the construction of the sluice (*tumbu*) by a private person. The village is called Vaḷagūr.

Vēḍal.

729. 69 *of* 1908.—(Tamil.) On the south wall of the central shrine in the Nīlakaṇṭhēśvara temple. A record in the sixteenth year of the Pāṇḍya king Kōnērimēlkoṇḍān Jaṭāvarman Tribhuvanachakravartin Sundara-Pāṇḍyadēva. Records gift of land to the temple of Karaikkaṇḍīśuramuḍaiya-Nāyanār at Viḍāl in Viḍār-paṟṟu *alias* Vikrama-Pāṇḍya-vaḷanāḍu, a district of Venkunṟa-kōṭṭam in Jayaṅgoṇḍa-Chōḷa-maṇḍalam. [It is difficult to identify this king. Jatāvarman Sundara Pāṇḍya I ruled only for thirteen years (1251–64). The exact duration of the second and third kings of that name who ascended the throne in 1270 and 1276 is unknown.]

730. 70 *of* 1908.—(Tamil.) On the same wall. An unfinished record in the twelfth year of the Chōḷa king Kulōttuṅga-Chōladēva.

731. 71 *of* 1908.—(Tamil.) On the same wall. An unfinished record in the fifth year of the Chōḷa king Chakravārtin Rājādhirājadēva (I or II?).

732. 72 *of* 1908.—(Tamil.) On the west wall of the same shrine. An unfinished record in the sixteenth year of the Pāṇḍya king Kōnērimēlkoṇḍān Jaṭāvarman Tribhuvanachakravartin Sundara-Pāṇḍyadēva.

733. 73 *of* 1908.—(Tamil.) On the same wall. A record in the twenty-seventh year of the Chōḷa king Tribhuvanachakravartin Kulōttuṅga-Chōḷadēva. Records gift of the village of Siviri of the inhabitants of Tellāṟṟuppaṟṟu to the temple mentioned in No. 729 above.

734. 74 *of* 1908.—(Tamil.) On the north wall of the central shrine in the same temple. A record in the fifteenth year of

Tribhuvanachakravartin Kōnērimēlkoṇḍān. Records gift of land for offerings and for expenses during the festival of Kōdaṇḍarāmanśandi called after the king.

735. 75 *of* 1908.—(Tamil.) On the east wall of the maṇṭapa in front of the same shrine. A record of the Vijayanagara king Bhūpatirāya Uḍaiyār, son of Vīra Dēvarāya (I) in Ś. 1329, Sarvajit. Records gift of land at Putēri in Ponnūrpaṟṟu in Śiṅgapuranāḍu, a district of Venkunṟa-kōṭṭam in Jayaṅgoṇḍa-Chōḷa-maṇḍalam, by a certain Tuṇaiyirundān Virupparaya kkāṅgayar, for a festival (śandi) named after himself, for offerings and for lamps.

736. 76 *of* 1908.—(Tamil.) On the same wall. A mutilated record of the Vijayanagara king Viruppaṇa-Uḍaiyār (Virūpāksha I), son of Hariyaṇa Uḍaiyār (Harihara II) in Ś. 1314, Āṅgiras. Appears to record a gift of land for a lamp and for daily offerings. Mentions Viḍāl in Ponnūr paṟṟu, a subdivision of Śiṅgapuranāḍu.

737. 77 *of* 1908.—(Tamil.) On the west wall of the same maṇṭapa. A record in the twenty-fifth year of Kulaśēkhara Śambuvarāya. Records gift of land for conducting the festival called Śeyyāṟṟu-venṟàn tirunāḷ.

738. 78 *of* 1908.—(Tamil.) On the north wall of the same maṇṭapa. A record of the Vijayanagara king Kumāra Kampaṇa Uḍaiyār II), son of Bukkaṇa (I) in Sādhārana. Built in at the beginning. Records gift of land for a lāmp, for offerings and repairs.

739. 79 *of* 1908.—(Tamil.) On the same wall. Records in Paridhāvin that Kuñjaramallaraśar made a gift of land at Śirumūr which belonged to the temple.

740. 80 *of* 1908.—(Grantha.) On the gōpura of the same temple. Two verses in praise of the god Śiva called Nīlgrīva (Karaikaṇḍa in Tamil) at Vishapura (which is perhaps the Sanskrit translation of the modern name Veḍāl).

741. 81 *of* 1908.—(Tamil.) Above the entrance into a maṇṭapa in front of a cavern on a hill in the same village. A damaged record in Vijaya. Records the gift of the maṇṭapa which was perhaps intended for a *maṭha.*

742. 82 *of* 1908.—(Tamil.) On a boulder near the natural cave known as Āṇḍār-maḍam on another hill in the same village. A record in the fourteenth year of the Pallava king Nandi. Mentions Vīḍāl and Viḍār-paḷḷi (probably) "the Jaina temple (paḷḷi at Viḍāl."

743. 83 *of* 1908.—(Tamil.) On the same boulder. A damaged record. Mentions Mādēvi Arindamaṅgalam also spelt Mādēvirandamaṅgalam.

744. 84 *of* 1908.—(Tamil.) On a second boulder in front of the same cave. A damaged record in the fourteenth year of the Chōḷa king Rājakēsarivarman. Mentions Kanakavīra-kuratti, a discip le of Guṇakīrttibhaṭārar; also refers to Viḍāl *alias* Mādēvi Arindamangalam in Śiṅgapura-nāḍu. [I have tried in vain to gain information about these. Guṇakīrti reminds us of Guṇavīra; but the identification of these with each other would be one of pure surmise. See N.A. 385 above.]

745. 85 *of* 1908.—(Tamil.) On a pillar of the maṇṭapa in front of the same cave. A damaged and incomplete record in the nineteenth year of the Chōḷa king Madiraikoṇḍa Parakēsarivarman (905–47) Mentions Viṇṇagar Vayiramēghan and a *Kāḷamukha* Dāsapūriyan of the Hārīta gôtra and the Āpastamba-sutra.

Veṅkunṟam Hill.

746. 72 *of* 1900.—(Sanskrit.) On a slab set up at the foot of the hill. Records in Ś. 1619, Īśvara the building of a rest-house near the hill.

747. 73 *of* 1900.—(Tamil.) On a rock on the Veṅkuṟam hill close to the Dhavaḷagirīśvara temple. A record in the sixth year of the Pallava king Nandipōttaraiyan. Records sale of land by the assembly of Veṅkunṟam to a resident of Nelavāyil and includes in the sale "all the paddy . . . all the gold, all the ghee (?) and everything else."

ARCOT SOUTH DISTRICT.

CHIDAMBARAM TALUK.

Chidambaram.

A connected account of Chidambaram based on the inscriptions of its temples is given in *Madr. Ep. Rep.*, 1914, p. 88. It is remarkable that while the history of the place goes to the age of the *Prabandhas* and the *Dēvāram*, i.e., the Pallava times, no records of even the early Chōḷas are to be found in its walls, the earliest being those of Rājēndra Chōḷa I and Kulōttuṅga I. The records of Vikrama-chōḷa then follow and give details of his holy works and the works of his predecessor. The local inscriptions are given in Mackenzie's list in *Ins. S. Dts.*, p. 162—7, in various and scattered notices in *Rais. Catal*, Vol. III and in the original *Mack. MSS.* Owing to the enormous difficulty involved in comparing these and the unprofitable nature of such an examination and comparison, I have not attempted it fully. I have given therefore the departmental list alone, and identifications of six of the sixteen inscriptions in *Ins. S. Dts.* For a full account of the local history, antiquities, etc., see *S. A. Gazr.*, p. 265—74.

1. 115 *of* 1888.—Outside first prākāra, east. Two Sanskrit verses, which praise the victories of Kulōttuṅga-Chōḷa (I) over the five Pāṇḍyas and the Kēraḷas, and which record that he burnt the fort of Kōṭṭāra (near Cape Comorin) and put up a pillar of victory on a peak of the Sahyādri mountains. See *S. Ind. Inscrns.*, Vol. I, p. 168 f. and *Ep. Ind.*, Vol. V, p. 103—4. The king's fame is said to be sung even on the further shore of the ocean by the young women of the Persians (Parsi).

2. 116 *of* 1888.—On the maṇṭapa in front of the east entrance into the first prākāra. Sanskrit fragment.

3. 117 *of* 1888.—Outside first prākāra, north. Dated in the forty-sixth year of Kulōttuṅga-Sōḷa-dēva; mentions Madurāntaki, "the younger sister of our lord." Śiṟṟambalam, here also called Puliyūr, became Chidambaram in Sanskrit, and a different interpretation came to be given to the latter to be "the space of Chit." The other names of the place Puliyūr, Perumbaṟṟappuliyūr and Tillai are mentioned both in the *Prabandhas* and *Dēvāram*. Chidambaram had as many as 14 hamlets as its inscriptions show.

4. 118 *of* 1888.—Outside first prākāra, north. A record of Kō-Rājakēsarivarman, *alias* Uḍaiyār Rājēndra-Śōḷa-dēva I, twenty-fourth year. This is the earliest record in the temple.

5. 119 *of* 1888.—Outside first *prākāra*, north. The inscription records several gifts to the god (Āḷuḍaiyār) of Chidambaram

(Tillai or Tiruchchirrambalam) by Rājarājan-Kuṇḍavai, the daughter of the E. Chāḷukya Rājaraja I (A.D. 1022—63) and younger sister of Tribhuvanachakravartin Kulōttuṅga-Śōḷadēva (I). Further it records, that Rājēndra-Sōḷadēva [II, i.e., Kulōttuṅga I] put up in the wall of a hall in front of the temple a stone, which he had received from the king of Kāmbōja. [A portion of this inscription was published in *Ind. Antq.*, Vol. XXIII, p. 298 and *Ep. Ind.*, Vol. IV, p. 70. It is dated in forty-fourth year of *Jayadhara, a biruda* (according to the *Kaliṅgattupparaṇi*) of Kulōttuṅga I and Kielhorn calculates the details of the date to be Friday, 13th March, A.D. 1114. Also see *Ep. Ind.*, V. p. 105-6.]

6. 120 *of* 1888.—Outside first prākāra, west. Long defaced inscription in Sanskrit verse.

7. 121 *of* 1888.—Inside second prakāra, west, left of entrance. A record of Kō-Parakēsarivarman, *alias* Tribhuvanachakravartin . . . The inscription which is much worn, mentions Ammaṅgai, the daughter of Kulōttuṅga-Sōḷa-dēva.

8. 122 *of* 1888.—Inside second prākāra, west, right of entrance. A record of Kō-Parakēsarivarman, *alias* Tribhuvanachakravartin Vīra-Rājēndradēva, in his fifth year.

9. 123 *of* 1888.—East gōpura. A record of Vikrama-Pāṇḍya.

10. 124 *of* 1888.—West gōpura. A record of Kō-Māravarman Tribhuvanachakravartin Kulaśēkhara-dēva, in his twenty-eighth year. [Most probably the king was Kulaśēkhara I who ruled from 1268 to 1308.]

11. 170 *of* 1892.—(Tamil verse.) Right of entrance to the east gōpura of the Naṭarāja temple. A record of the Pāṇḍya king.

12. 171 *of* 1892.—(Tamil verse.) Right of the entrance to the east gōpura of the Naṭarāja temple. A record of the Pāṇḍya king Sundara-Pāṇḍya (i.e., Jaṭāvarman who ascended the throne in 1251).

13. 172 *of* 1892.—(Tamil verse.) Right of the entrance to the east gōpura of the Naṭarāja temple. A record of the Pāṇḍya king Sundara-Pāṇḍya. See note to (12).

14. 173 *of* 1892.—(Tamil verse.) Right of the entrance to the east gopura of the Naṭarāja temple. A record in modern characters.

15. 174 *of* 1892.—(Tamil.) Left of the entrance to the north gōpura of the same temple. A record of the Vijayanagara king Kṛishṇadēva (1509—30). Records the building of the gōpura.

16. 175 *of* 1892.—Left of the entrance to the north gōpura of the same temple. A record of the Vijayanagara king Krishṇadēva (1509—30). Sanskrit version of No. 15 above.

17. 176 *of* 1892.—(Tamil.) Right of the west entrance to the second prākāra of the same temple. A record of Toṇḍaimān.

Opens with the usual Sanskrit *birudas* of Sundara-Pāṇḍya (1251—64), whose vassal the donor appears to have been.

18. 177 *of* 1892.—(Sanskrit verse.) Right of the west entrance to the second prākāra of the same temple. A record of the Pāṇḍya king Sundara Pāṇḍya (1251—64).

19 to 23. 178 *to* 182 *of* 1892.—(Sanskrit verse.) South wall of the second prākāra of the same temple. A record of the Pāṇḍya king Sundara-Pāṇḍya (1251—64).

24. 183 *of* 1892.—(Sanskrit and Tamil.) West wall of the second prākāra of the same temple. A record of the Pāṇḍya king Sundara-Pāṇḍya (1251—64).

25. 184 *of* 1892.—(Sanskrit verse.) Right of the west entrance to the second prākāra of the same temple. A record of the Pāṇḍya king Sundara-Pāṇḍya (Jaṭāvarman, 1251—64).

26. 455 *of* 1902.—(Tamil.) On the west wall of the second prākāra of the Naṭarāja temple. A record in the thirty-sixth year of the Pallava king Avaniyāḷappirandān Sakalabhuvanachakravartin Kopperuñjiṅgadēva. Records gift of land. [He was the contemporary of Rājarāja III (1216—48) who made himself master of an extensive part of Chōḷa dominions and ruled from 1243 to 1280. See S.A. 329, S.A. 124, etc., for details.]

27. 456 *of* 1902.—(Tamil.) On the same wall. A record in the thirty-sixth year of the Pallava king Sakalabhuvanachakravartin Kopperuñjiṅgadēva. Records an order of Vēṇāḍuḍaiyān, referring to a gift of land. See S.A. 329 and S.A. 32.

28. 457 *of* 1902.—(Tamil.) On the same wall. A record in the ninth year (and eighty-eighth day) of the Chōḷa king Kulōttuṅga-Chōḷa III. Published in *South Ind. Inscr.*, Vol. III, No. 86, p. 210—3. Records a grant of land to temple by a certain Kēraḷarājan, for a flower garden. The inscription gives very minute fractions of *vēlis* and land measures and is thus of value to the historian of land tenure and revenue.

29. 458 *of* 1902.—(Tamil.) On the same wall. A record in the eleventh year (and one hundred and eighteenth day) of the Chōḷa king Kulōttuṅga-Chōḷa III. Published in *Ibid.*, No. 87, p. 213—7. Records the king's sanction of a grant of land to the temple by a certain Vaḷuvarāyan for the maintenance of a flower garden.]

30. 459 *of* 1902.—(Tamil.) On the same wall. A record in the fifth year of the Pallava king Sakalabhuvanachakravartin Kopperuñjiṅgadēva. Records an order of Śōḷakōn of Aragūr or Perumāḷ Piḷḷai, one of the king's chief officers. He was the brother of Vēṇāḍuḍaiyān referred to in S.A. 32.

31. 460 *of* 1902.—(Tamil.) On the same wall. A record in the eighth year of the Pallava king Sakalabhuvanachakravartin Kopperuñjiṅgadēva. Records an order of Sōḷakōn. See S.A. 329

for details about Kōpperuñjiṅga. [In *Ins. S. Dts. (Mack. MSS.)*, p. 163, No. 5, an inscription of this chief in this year granting 1½ *vēlis*, etc., to the Goddess and houses for worshippers, is given but it is doubtful whether it is the same.]

32. 461 *of* 1902—(Tamil.) On the west wall of the second prākāra of the Naṭarāja temple. A record in the thirty-fourth year of the Pallava king Sakalabhuvanachakravartin Kopperuñjiṅgadēva. Records an order of Vēṇāḍuḍaiyān, brother of Śōḷakōn.

33. 462 *of* 1902.—(Tamil.) On the north wall of the same prākāra. A record in the third year of the Pallava king Sakalabhuvanachakravartin Kopperuñjiṅgadēva. Records gift of land. Compare *Ep. Ind.*, Vol. III, page 166.

34. 463 *of* 1902.—(Tamil.) On the same wall. A record in the fifth year of the Pallava king Sakalabhuvanachakravartin Kopperuñjiṅgadēva. Records an order of Śōḷakōn.

35. 464 *of* 1902.—(Tamil.) On the same wall. A record in the fifth year of the Pallava king Sakalabhuvanachakravartin Kopperuñjiṅgadēva. Records an order of Śōḷakōn.

36. 465 *of* 1902.—(Tamil.) On the same wall. A record in the third year of the Pallava king Sakalabhuvanachakravartin Kopperuñjiṅgadēva. Records an order of Śōḷakōn.

37. 466 *of* 1902.—(Tamil.) On the same wall. A record in the third year of the Pallava king Sakalabhuvanachakravartin Kōpperuñjiṅgadēva. Records an order of Śōḷakōn.

38. 467 *of* 1902.—(Tamil.) On the same wall. A record in the sixteenth year of the Pallava king Sakalabhuvanachakravartin Kōpperuñjiṅgadēva. Records an order of Śōḷakōn.

39. 468 *of* 1902.—(Tamil.) On the same wall. A record in the sixteenth year of the Pallava king Sakalabhuvanachakravartin Kōpperuñjiṅgadēva. Records an order of Śōḷakōn.

40. 390 *of* 1903.—(Tamil.) On the east wall of the central shrine in the Tillaiyamman temple. A record in the third year of the Pallava king Sakalabhuvanachakravartin Kōpperuñjiṅgadēva. Records gift of land.

41. 391 *of* 1903.—(Tamil.) On the same wall. A record in the third year of the Pallava king Sakalabhuvanachakravartin Kōpperuñjiṅgadēva. Records sale of land.

42. 392 *of* 1903.—(Tamil.) On the south wall of the same shrine. Records in the third year sale of land. The king's name is not mentioned.

43. 393 *of* 1903.—(Tamil.) On the north wall of the same shrine. A record in the third year of the Pallava king Sakalabhuvanachakravartin Kōpperuñjiṅgadēva. Records sale of land.

44. 394 *of* 1903.—(Tamil.) On the north base of the maṇṭapa in front of the same shrine. A record in the fifth year of the

Pallava king Sakalabhuvanachakravartin Kōpperuñjiṅgadēva. Records sale of land.

45. 395 *of* 1903.—(Tamil.) On the south wall of the same maṇṭapa. Records in the third year sale of land. The king's name is not mentioned.

46. 396 *of* 1903.—(Tamil.) On the same wall. The king's name is not mentioned. Provides in the fourteenth year for the supply of saffron, etc., required for the temple of Tillaivanamuḍaiya-Paramēśuṟi.

47. 397 *of* 1903.—(Tamil.) On the same wall. A record of the Pallava king Sakalabhuvanachakravartin Kōpperuñjiṅgadēva, the date of which is doubtful. Records sale of land.

48. 398 *of* 1903.—(Tamil.) On the north wall of the same maṇṭapa. A record in the fifth year of the Pallava king Sakalabhuvanachakravartin Kōpperuñjiṅgadēva. Records sale of land.

49. 399 *of* 1903.—(Tamil.) On the same wall. A record in the third year of the Pallava king Sakalabhuvanachakravartin Kōpperuñjiṅgadēva. Records sale of land.

50. 400 *of* 1903.—(Tamil.) On the south and east walls of the Bhairava shrine in the same temple. A record of the Pallava king Sakalabhuvanachakravartin Kōpperuñjiṅgadēva, the date of which is doubtful. Records an order of Śōḻakōn.

51. 401 *of* 1903.—(Tamil.) On the north wall of the same shrine. A record in the eighth year (A.D. 1250) of the Pallava king Sakalabhuvanachakravartin Kōpperuñjiṅgadēva. Mentions the temple of Vāraṇavāsi-Mādēvar, and records a sale of land to Śōḻakōnār for building a temple of Piḍāriyar. See N.A. 302.

52. 260 *of* 1913.—(Tamil.) On the south wall of the Bhīmēśvara temple at Śiṅgārattōppu near the same place. A record in the sixth year, Karkaṭaka, first day of the Chōḻa king Tribhuvanachakravartin Vīrarājēndradēva (i.e., Kulōttuṅga III, 1178—1216). Records gift of land at the hamlet of Maṇalūr for two lamps to the temple of Tirukkiḷānjēdi-Mahādēva at Perumbaṟṟappuliyūr, a taniyūr in Rājādhirāja-vaḷanāḍu.

53. 261 *of* 1913.—(Tamil.) On the same wall. A record in the eleventh year, Mēsha, . . . fifth day of the Pallava king Sakalabhuvanachakravartin Kōpperuñjiṅgadēva. Records sale of nine *mās* of land, for 5,000 kāśu to the temple of Nāyanār Tirukkaḷānjēḍi-Uḍaiyār at Paṇṇaṅguḍichchēri *alias* Paramēsarinallūr, a hamlet of Perumbaṟṟappuliyūr. The land sold was a field of the western hamlet of Iḷanāṅgūr *alias* Sudaraśōḻapāṇḍyanallūr which was situated in Gaṅgaikoṇḍaśōḻappērilamai-nāḍu and the sale was witnessed by the assembly of the village. [It is not improbable that Sundaraśōḻapāṇḍyanallūr owed its name to the son of Rājēndrachōḻa I.]

54. 262 *of* 1913.—(Tamil.) On the north wall of the same temple. A record in the second year and one hundred and

twenty-fifth day of the Chōḷa king Parakēsarivarman *alias* Tribhuvanachakravartin Kulōttuṅga-Chōḷadēva (III, 1178—86). Registers an order of the king that, from this date, the assessed lands (*tarampeṟṟa-nilam*) standing in the name of the Subrahmanya-Piḷḷaiyār shrine in the Arumoḷīśvara temple of this village be included with those of the latter, that lands declared to be superior to the eighth class be assessed as per those of the eighth class (*eṭṭām-taram*) and that those below the eighth class be allowed to continue as before and that the site of the temple of Tiruttoṇḍattogai-Īśvaram-Uḍaiyār, its enclosures, premises and the sacred tank, till now included in the account of assessed lands, be removed from that register. The order was executed by the 'land-survey' committee (*nilam-aḷavupaḍi-pperumakkaḷ*) of the village assembly of Perumbaṟṟappuliyūr. Full details of the lands (extent, boundaries, etc.), thus dealt with are recorded. [The inscription is of great value in the history of land revenue assessment. Similar land survey and assessment were made in the time of Rājarāja I and Kulōttuṅga I, e.g., see No. 109 below.]

55. 263 *of* 1913.—(Tamil.) On the same wall. A record in the second year, and one hundred and twenty-first day of the Chōḷa king Tribhuvanachakravartin Rājādhirājadēva *alias* Karikāla-Chōḷadēva. Refers to the order registered in No. 262 (i.e., S.A. 54) and states that it was issued by Villavarāyan at the request of Vaiḍumbarāyan. The document is signed by ten officers of the king of whom the Tirumandira-ōlai-nāyaka was Nārāyaṇa-Mūvēndavēḷān. As these officers occur in the inscriptions of Kulōttuṅga Chōla III, the Government epigraphist surmises that Rājādhirāja Karikāla was another name of his.

56. 264 *of* 1913.—(Tamil.) On the same wall. A record in the seventeenth year, Kanni, twenty-first day of the Chōḷa king Tribhuvanachakravartin Kulōttuṅga-Chōḷadēva III (1178—1216), 'who took Madurai (Madura) and was pleased to take the crowned head of the Pāṇḍya.' Records gift of interest on 1,100 kāśu for maintaining a lamp and a lampstand. It is stipulated that the grant is to be renewed at the end of every five years, after it is produced after each period *before the assembly and the sthānattār.*

57. 265 *of* 1913.—(Tamil.) On the same wall. A damaged record on the Chōḷa king Tribhuvanachakravartin Kulōttuṅga-Chōḷadēva III (1178—1216), 'who was pleased to take Madurai (Madura), Iḷam (Ceylon) and the crowned head of the Pāṇḍya,' in his twentieth year and one hundred and twenty-first day. Seems to record a gift of lamp.

58. 266 *of* 1913.—(Tamil.) On the east wall of the first prākāra, of the Naṭarāja temple, right of entrance. A record in the seventeenth year and two hundred and seventy-second day of the Chōḷa king Tribhuvanachakravartin Rājarājadēva. Records gift of land belonging to the village of Paṇḍūr *alias* Kulōttuṅgaśōḷan Vallam in Rājādhirāja vaḷanāḍu for maintaining the feeding house named Arapperuñjelvi-śōlai at Perumbaṟṟappuliyūr in the west street called Muḍittalaigoṇḍa Perumāḷ-tiruvīdhi.

59. 267 *of* 1913.—(Tamil.) In the same place. A record in the fourth year and two hundred and fiftieth day of the Chōḷa king Tribhuvanachakravartin Rājarājadēva. Records gift of land for the offering called *tiruppāvāḍai* on the day of Pushya in the month of Tai to the god Āḷuḍaiyār. The inscription was ordered to be engraved on the Kulōttuṅga-śōḷan-tirumāḷigai by the Tirumandira-vōlai Rājanārāyaṇa-Mūvēndavēḷān.

60. 268 *of* 1913.—(Tamil.) On the same wall, left of entrance. A record in the third year and ninety-fifth day of the Chōḷa king Parakēsarivarman *alias* Tribhuvanachakravartin Vikrama-Chōḷa-dēva (1118—35). Records gift of land by a native of Tiraimūr in Tiraimu-nāḍu which was a district of Uyyakoṇḍār-vaḷanāḍu at Manārkuḍi-kaṭṭaḷai, a hamlet of Jayaṅgoṇḍaśōḷa-chaturvēdi-maṅgalam in Mērkal-nāḍu, a subdivision of Virudarājabhayaṅkara-vaḷanāḍu, for a flower garden. Also records another gift of land in Pannaṅguḍichchēri *alias* Parakēsarinallūr which was a hamlet of Perumbaṟṟappuliyūr with four tenants (*kuḍi*) for maintaining the garden and for providing the *mantrapushpa* in the temple of Tiruchiṟṟambalam-Uḍaiyār.

61. 269 *of* 1913.—(Tamil.) In the same place. A record in the eighth year and fifty-seventh day of the Pāṇḍya king Māravarman-Tribhuvanachakravartin Vīra-Pāṇḍyadēva. Registers that under the orders of Vikrama-Pāṇḍya Gāṅgēyarāyan some land was set apart for building a quarter to be inhabited exclusively by the weavers (*Śōliya-Śāliyar*) and named Teriyavaraninṟaperumāḷ-puram, on condition that these weavers supplied four new cloths (every year) to the goddess Śivakāmasundari on the day of the *tiruppudiyiḍu* festival and five other small cloths for the shrines of Tirugnānasambandan. See S.A. 71 below, for the identity of the king. The *Śāliyars* are described in Mr. Thurston's *Castes* and *Tribes*, Vol. VI, 276—9.

62. 270 *of* 1913.—(Tamil.) In the same place. A record in the fifth year and two hundred and seventieth day of the Pāṇḍya king Māravarman Tribhuvanachakravartin Vikrama-Pāṇḍyadēva. Built in at the beginning. Registers that, under orders of Gāṅ-gēyarāyan, land was granted for supplying garlands on the occasion of the service called Rājākkaḷnāyan-śandi after the king, and on the day of a festival called *Rājākkaḷnāyanperiyatirunāḷ*. See S.A. 71 below.

63. 271 *of* 1913.—(Tamil.) In the same place. A record of the Vijayanagara king Mahāmaṇḍalēśvara Śrīraṅgarāya (VI) in Ś. 1565, Svabhānu, Paṅguni, 7, Pañchami, Friday and Rēvati, which

Mr. Swamikannu Pillai calculates to be 2nd February, A.D. 1644. (The real month, however, he says, must be Māśi and not Paṅguni.) Records that the king repaired the big maṇṭapa in front of the Tillai Gōvindarājasvāmin shrine in Tiru-Chitrakūḍam, the gōpura of the shrine, the vimānas of the goddesses Puṇḍarīkavalli nāchchiyār and Śūḍikkoḍutta-nāchchiyār and the maṇṭapa in front of Tiruvāḷi-Āḷvān. He is also stated to have made rent-free the five villages Āḍūr, Karuṅguḷi, Kuṟiyāmaṅgalam, Marudāntanallūr and Uḍaiyūr in which the Śrī-Vaishṇavas were permanently living. [See *Ins.*, *S. Dts.*, p. 162, No. 2. For the history of the Gōvindarāja shrine see note to the next inscription. Here it may be noted that the members of the last Vijayanagar dynasty were staunch Vaishṇavites and had the Tātāchāryas for their Gurus.]

64. 272 *of* 1913.—(Tamil.) On the south wall of the same prākāra. A record of the Vijayanagara king Achyutayya-Mahārāya in Ś. 1461, Vishu (wrong) Mithuna, śu. di. 14, Śādhyayōga, Saturday, Anurādha, which corresponded, according to Mr. Swamikannu Pillai, to May 31, A.D. 1539. The king ordered that the image of Tillai-Gōvindarāja-Perumāḷ at Perumbaṟṟappuliyūr in Vaḷudalambaṭṭu-uśāvaḍi, a subdivision of Veṇṇaiyūr-nāḍu in Rājādhirājavaḷanāḍu, might be set up according to the ritual of Vaikhānasasūtra, and granted 500 *pon* which was the income from four villages for the upkeep of daily worship. [The Gōvindarāja shrine has had an eventful history. That it existed in the Pallava period is proved by the fact that the Āḷvārs Kulaśekhara and Tirumaṅgai-mannan refer to it. The next reference is by Māṇikkavāśaga who must be assigned to the middle of the ninth century. See his *Tiruchchiṟṟambalakkōvai*, Stanza 86. Coming to the Chōḷa times we find from the *Kulōttuṅga-Chōḷan-ulā*, the *Rājarājan-ulā* and the *Takkayāgapparaṇi* that Kulōttuṅga II, a bigoted Śaivite, threw the image of Gōvindarāja into the sea. The Vaishṇaviṭe *Guruparamparas*, on the contrary, say that in the time of Rāmānuja the *Chitrakūṭa* at Chidambaram was 'destroyed', the image of Gōvindarāja was removed by the Vaishṇavas to Tirupati, and that Rāmānuja formally solemnised the consecration ceremony. See the *Vaḍag. Gurup.*, 1913, p. 86. It is difficult to say whether the Tamil literary works mentioned above and the *Guruparampara* refer to the same incident. Rāmānuja lived, according to tradition, till 1137 and Kulōttuṅga II ruled as sole monarch from 1135 to 1146 and jointly with his predecessor Vikrama Chōḷa from 1123 to 1135. If the vandalism of Kulōttuṅga II followed his sole assumption of Government, then the removal of the Vishṇu shrine at Chidambaram and the consecration of the new shrine at Lower Tirupati should have been about 1135–6. The next literary reference to the fortunes of the shrine is in the time of Vēdānta Dēśika. The *Guruparampata* says that he took advantage of an internal commotion in Chidambaram to make Goppaṇārya of Gingee to re-establish the image about 1370. See *Vaḍag. Gurup.*, 1913, p. 154. The *Prapannāmritam*, on the other hand, attributes this honour to Mahācharya or Doḍḍācharya of Sholinghur and of Rāma Rāya of "Chandragiri," whom it wrongly supposes to be a king and successor of Kṛishṇadēva Rāya. The present inscription would support the version of the *Prapannāmruta* if Rāma Rāya is taken to be a mistake for Achyuta Rāya. If not, we should have to suppose that after Achyuta Rāya there was another Śaivite attempt to remove the idol and a final restoration of it by Mahācharya late in the sixteenth century. See *Ins., S. Dts.*, p. 162, No. I.

65. 273 *of* 1913.—(Tamil.) On the same wall. A record in the thirty-second year and one hundred and sixtieth day of the Chōḷa king Tribhuvanachakravartin Tribhuvanavīradēva (1178—1216), "who, having taken Madurai (Madura), Īḷam (Ceylon), Karuvūr and the crowned head of the Pāṇḍya, was pleased to perform the anointment of heroes and the anointment of victors." Records that a gift of land for a flower garden called Ponnambalakkūttan, in the village of Kōyilpūṇdi, a hamlet of Perumbaṛṛappuliyūr, was made to the temple of Āḷuḍaiyār by a certain Ponnambalakkūttan *alias* Nandipanman. He also provided for its upkeep by another gift of land made at Śerundimangalam, which was a hamlet of Tyāgavalli chaturvēdimangalam in Mērka-nāḍu. These transactions and gifts were engraved on the walls of the temple by the order of the king's officers at the request of Nandipanman.

66. 274 *of* 1913.—(Tamil.) On the same wall. A record in the fifteenth year and three hundred and sixty-third day of the Pāṇḍya king Jaṭāvarman *alias* Tribhuvanachakravartin Sundara-Pāṇḍyadēva. Records an order of Villavarāyan and other officers of the king that the maintenance of worship and offerings in the temple of Dēvargaḷ-Nāyanār was to be met from certain grants of land made to that temple. [The chief Villavarāyan occurs in S.A. 55 in the reign of Kulōttunga III, 1178—1216. As the Sundara Pāṇḍya referred to is probably the first of that name who ruled from 1251 to 1264, it is probable that the Villavarāyan of this epigraph is a son or successor of his namesake in the other.]

67. 275 *of* 1913.—(Tamil.) On the same wall. An incomplete record in the fourteenth year and one hundred and twenty-fourth day of the Pāṇḍya king Jaṭāvarman *alias* Tribhuvanachakravartin Sundara-Pāṇḍyadēva. Registers another order of Villavarāyan with reference to certain grants of land providing flower garlands to the god and goddess. One of these latter was situated in Vikramaśōḷanallūr (also called *Akkanpaḷḷippaḍai*) near Perumbaṛṛappuḷiyūr and was granted by Svāmidēvar. Still another grant of land, in the hamlet of Kōlam *alias* Śōḷakeraḷadēvanallūr, was made for providing offerings on the occasion when the images were taken on procession to the sea.

68. 276 *of* 1913.—(Tamil.) On the same wall. A record in the sixth year and three hundred and fifty-fifth day of the Pāṇḍya king Māravarman *alias* Tribhuvanachakravartin Vikrama-Pāṇḍya-dēva. Registers an order of Vaṅgattarayan to the temple authorities to engrave on the walls of Vikrama-śōḷan-tirumāḷigai the gift of lands in Paḷḷippaḍai *alias* Vikramaśōḷanallūr, Erukkāṭṭañjēri *alias* Jayaṅgoṇḍaśōḷanallūr and Maṇalūr *alias* Jayaṅgoṇḍaśōḷa-nallūr, for the flower garden Ulagamuḷudumudaiyāḷ-tirunanda-vanam which was so named after the queen. [The Pāṇḍyan king referred to came to throne in A.D. 1282. He boasts of his conquests over the Chōḷas, Vīragaṇḍagōpāla and Gaṇapati of the Kākatīya dynasty.] See S.A. 342 and S.A. 157.

69. 277 *of* 1913.—(Tamil.) On the same wall. A record in the thirteenth year of the Pāṇḍya king Tribhuvanachakravartin-Kōnērinmaikoṇḍān Sundara Pāṇḍyadēva (I? 1251–64). Registers the founding of an agrahāra *named* Vikrama-Pāṇḍya-chaturvēdi-maṅgalam on the western side of Perumbaṟṟappuliyūr and its presentation to 108 learned Brāhmaṇas. For the maintenance of these and of other village accessories (*grāmaparikāra*) the village Rājaśikhāmaṇinallūr *alias* Puḷiyaṅguḍi on the western bank of Ponnēri was acquired and granted, being divided into 147¾ shares (*paṅgu*). [The process of the foundation of a new village is typically illustrated here. For details see *Ep. Rep.*, 1914, p. 92.]

70. 278 *of* 1913.—(Tamil.) On the same wall. A record in the fifth year and 351st day of Tribhuvanachakravartin Kōnērinmai-koṇḍān. Records gift of 116 *vēlis* of land of Āḍūr *alias* Jananātha-nallūr to 108 Brāhmaṇas, to the god Ulagamuḷuduḍaiya-piḷḷaiyār, the maṭha, etc., of Ulagamuḷudumuḍaiya-chaturvēdimaṅgalam, a hamlet on the western side of Perumbaṟṟappuliyūr. The recipients had no tax to pay, but to measure out 4 *kalam* on each *vēli* of land to the temple of Tillai-nāyaka as the donees of Vikrama-Pāṇḍya-chaturvēdimaṅgalam did. [See note to the above.]

71. 279 *of* 1913.—(Tamil.) On the same wall. A record in the fourth year and 192nd day of the Pāṇḍya king Māravarman Tribhuvanachakravartin Vīra-Pāṇḍyadēva. Registers an order of Pallavarāyan to the temple authorities to engrave on the walls of the Kulōttuṅgaśōḷan-tirumāḷigai, a gift of land for offerings to the shrine of Aḷagiya-Tiruchchiṟṟambalamuḍaiyār built by a Brāhman at the hamlet of Kaṟṟaṅguḍi *alias* Pavitramāṇikyanallūr. Mr. Krishna Sastri suggests that this king was the successor of Māravārman Vikrama Pāṇḍya (like whom he had the title *Rājākkaḷ Tambirān*) and identical with that Vīra Pāṇḍva who was the enemy of the Kēraḷa king Ravivarman Kulaśēkhara. See S.A. 61, 87, 112, 120, 143 and 178.

72. 280 *of* 1913.—(Tamil.) On the north wall of the same prākāra. A record in the fourteenth year and 107th day of the

Chōḷa king Tribhuvanachakravartin Rājarājadēva (probably Rājarāja III, 1216–48). Records gift of land at Tirunīṟṟuchchōḷamaṅgalam by a certain Kāḷiṅgarāyan for supplying 500 jack fruits, 5,000 mangoes and 5,000 plantains to the temple of Āḷuḍaiya-Nāyanār. The assembly of that village agreed to make that land rent-free by charging the taxes due on it, to the village. The *tirumandiravōlai* was Neriyuḍaichchōḷa-Mūvēndavēḷān. [See *Ins., S. Dts.* (Mack. MSS.), p. 164, No. 8.]

73. 281 *of* 1913.—(Tamil.) On the same wall. A record in the tenth year and 235th day of the Chōḷa king Tribhuvanachakravartin Rājarājadēva. Built in at the end. Records gift of land by two private individuals for a flower garden. Provision was also made for the servants who looked after the garden. [The Chōḷa king, we may presume, was Rājarāja III, 1216–48.]

74. 282 *of* 1913.—(Tamil.) On the same wall. Records in the third year that under orders of Toṇḍaiman, a land was presented at Midinikkuḍi *alias* Dānavinōdanallūr for a flower garden and made tax-free and the same was engraved on the walls of Vikramaśōḷan-tirumāḷigai.

75. 283 *of* 1913.—(Tamil.) On the same wall. A record in the third year and 115th day of the Chōḷa king Tribhuvanachakravartin Rājarājadēva (III? 1216–48). Records gift of land at Vallam in Veṇṇaiyūr-nāḍu, a subdivision of Rājādhirāja-vaḷanāḍu, for supplying a garland of 130 red lotuses every day. The document registering this grant was engraved under orders of Toṇḍaimān, the *tirumandiravōlai* being Mīnavan Mūvēndavēḷān.

76. 284 *of* 1913.—(Tamil.) On the same wall. A record in the thirty-ninth year and 224th day of the Chōḷa king Tribhuvanachakravartin Tribhuvanavīradēva (1178–1216) "who having taken Madurai (Madura), Īḷam (Ceylon), Karuvūr and the crowned head of the Pāṇḍya, was pleased to perform the anointment of heroes and the anointment of victors." Registers an order of three officers of the king, viz., Toṇḍaimān, Tiruvaiyāruḍaiyān and Madhurāntaka Brahma-Mārāyan, that lands granted by certain Laṅkēśvaran of Kiḷiyūr for providing 200 red lotuses to the temple and for maintaining the people that grew them, was to be engraved on the walls of Vikramaśōḷan-tirumāḷigai. The *tirumandira-ōlai* is stated to be Neriyuḍaichchōḷa Mūvēndavēḷān. Still another gift of land by the same person made for a flower garden in the "thirty-fourth year and fifty-second day" of the king, was also engraved, the old document having "become worn out."

77. 285 *of* 1913.—(Tamil.) On the same wall. A record in the seventeenth year and 197th day of the Chōḷa king Tribhuvanachakravartin Rājarājadēva (III? 1216–48). Records gift of garden land at Kōyilpūṇḍi, a hamlet of Perumbaṟṟappuliyūr, for providing garlands to the shrines of the god and the goddess by a certain

Vāṇādhirājan. The order of the grant was as usual engraved on the walls of the temple.

78. 286 *of* 1913.—(Tamil.) On the same wall. A record in the fifth year and 353rd day of the Pāṇḍya king Māravarman Tribhuvanachakravartin Kulaśēkharadēva (I, 1268–1308). Built in at the end. Records an order of Chēdiyarāyan to engrave on the temple walls a gift of land for providing offerings, etc., in a shrine situated in one of the streets of Perumbaṟṟappuliyūr. [The Chēdirāyan of this inscription could not have been the same as the Piḷḷai Perumāl Chēdirāyan who figures in the life of Kamba.]

79. 287 *of* 1913.—(Tamil.) On the same wall. Registers in the seventh year and 225th day of the king an order of Toṇḍaimān that an arrangement regarding a certain land made in order to provide flowers, coconuts, etc., be engraved on the wall of Vikkiramaśōlan-tirumāḷigai.

80. 288 *of* 1913.—(Tamil.) On the same wall. A record in the ninth year and 200th day of the Pāṇḍya king Sundara-Pāṇḍya-dēva, "who was pleased to take all countries." Records gift of land. Order of Villavadaraiyan approving of certain arrangements about specified temple lands made by the assembly (*mūla parushaiyar*) of Perumbaṟṟappuliyūr. [The king referred to was evidently Jaṭāvarman Sundara Pāṇḍya I, 1251–64.]

81. 289 *of* 1913.—(Tamil.) On the same wall. A record in the seventh year and 252nd day of the Pāṇḍya king Sundara-Pāṇḍyadēva, "who was pleased to take all countries" (1251–64). The first ten lines are engraved over another inscription of Vikrama-Chōḷadēva beginning with the historical introduction பூமாலைமிடைந்து, etc. Order of Toṇḍaimān to the temple authorities remitting certain taxes on lands which had been originally granted for the maintenance of the servants of a flower garden belonging to the temple. The reason for the remission was that the said lands, being close to the sea, had become filled up with sand and overgrown with weeds. Mentions *Virarākshasa-Vēḷaikkārar*. [For an explanation of the *Vēḷir* see *Abhidanachintāmaṇi*, p. 933.]

82. 290 *of* 1913.—(Tamil.) On the same wall. A record in the forty-seventh year of the Chōla king Tribhuvanachakravartin Kulōttuṅga Chōḷadēva I. This is stated to be a copy of an inscription originally engraved on the opposite shrine (Edir-Ambalam). Records gift of land by purchase for supplying garlands of red lotuses to the temple.

83. 291 *of* 1913.—(Tamil.) On the same wall. An unfinished record in the forty-sixth year, Simha, 22nd *tēdi*, of the Chōḷa king Tribhuvanachakravartin Kulōttuṅga-Chōḷadēva. This is evidently also a copy. Refers to the purchase of a *dēvadāna* land by a private individual. (22½ *nilās* for 10 *kaḷanjus*.)

84. 292 *of* 1913.—(Tamil.) On the same wall. Registers an order of Villavarāyan and four other officers assigning the income in paddy from certain lands originally granted for the upkeep of a flower garden, for the maintenance of the servants of the temple and of the flower garden.

85. 293 *of* 1913.—(Tamil.) On the same wall. A record in the eleventh year and fifty-sixth day of the Pāṇḍya king Jaṭāvarman *alias* Tribhuvanachakravartin Sundara-Pāṇḍyadēva (I? 1251—64). An order of the same officer remitting assessments on certain lands granted to the temple for a flower garden. The transactions were engraved on the Vikramaśoḷan-tirumāḷigai.

86. 294 *of* 1913.—(Tamil.) On the same wall. Registers that certain lands granted by Gāṅgēyarāyan were made tax-free and exempted from duties. The car procession was to be maintained and the temple was to receive 100 kāśu as kuḍimai assessment and 6 kalam of paddy as *virabhōga* on each vēli of land.

87. 295 *of* 1913.—(Tamil.) On the same wall. A record in the fourth year and eighteenth day of the Pāṇḍya king Māravarman Tribhuvanachakravartin Vikrama-Pāṇḍyadēva (1282—?). Records an order of Kulaśēkharan Sōḷakōn exempting duties and assessments on lands presented by a certain Chēdiyarāyan for maintaining 36 persons employed in a watershed in the maṇṭapa known as Ānaiyēṟṟukkūḍam, south of the seven-storeyed gōpura, on the east side of Rājakkaḷ-tambirān-tirumāḷigai, 54 persons who prepared offerings for the god, 32 learned Brāhmaṇas, 54 persons who prepared offerings at *Sikali* (i.e., the shrine of goddess?) and lastly the temple supervisors. See S.A. 71.

88. 296 *of* 1913.—(Tamil.) On the north wall of the second prākāra of the same temple. A record in the sixth year of the Pallava king Sakalabhuvanachakravartin Avaniyāḷappirandān *alias* Kōpperuñjiṅgadēva. Registers an order of Śōḷakōn that certain arrangements made by the temple authorities and the village assembly regarding the gift of a flower garden and the maintenance of its servants, may be engraved on the temple.

89. 297 *of* 1913.—(Tamil.) On the same wall. A damaged record in the eighth year of the Pāṇḍya king Jaṭāvarman *alias* Tribhuvanachakravartin Sundara-Pāṇḍyadēva (I? 1251—64). Records an order of Kaḷappāḷarāyar to register, as *tirunāmattukkāṇi*, certain lands granted for conducting festivals and providing offerings in the temple of Tiruchchiṟṟambala Mākāḷi which was founded on the south side of the road by which the god was taken in procession for the sea-bath, and to engrave the same on stone.

90. 298 *of* 1913.—(Tamil.) On the same wall. A record in the thirty-fourth year and forty-fifth day of the Chōḷa king Tribhuvanachakravartin Tribhuvanavīradēva III (1178—1216), "who being pleased to take Madurai (Madura), Karuvūr, Īḷam (Ceylon) and the crowned head of the Pāṇḍya, was pleased to perform the anointment of heroes and the anointment of victors." Registers that at the request of the chiefs Pottappichōḻan and Kārāṇai-Viḻupperaiyan, the original documents pertaining to a gift of land which was made to the temple for a flower garden were preserved in the treasury of the temple and engraved on its walls.

91. 299 *of* 1913.—(Tamil.) On the same wall. A damaged record in the second year and fourteenth day of the Chōḻa king Tribhuvanachakravartin Rājarājadēva (III?). Records gift of land for providing flower garlands to the temple. The grant was ordered to be engraved on the temple walls and the original documents deposited in the temple treasury. The royal Secretary (*tirumandira-ōlai*) was Rājēndraśiṅga-Mūvēndavēḷān.

92. 300 *of* 1913.—(Tamil.) On the same wall. A record in the second year and fourteenth day of the Chōḻa king Tribhuvanachakravartin Rājarājadēva (III?). Records gift of lands for a flower garden and its servants by the donor mentioned in No. 91 above.

93. 301 *of* 1913.—(Tamil.) On the same wall. A record in the thirty-sixth year and one hundredth day of the king. A number of lands which had been granted for a flower garden and were partly enjoyed by the servants of the garden were included at the donor's request in the *tirunāmattukkāṇi* lands of the temple and the fact engraved on the temple walls. The *tirumandira-ōlai* was Neriyuḍaichchōḻa-Mūvēndavēḷān.

94. 302 *of* 1913.—(Tamil.) On the same wall. A record in the twelfth year of the Pallava king Sakalabhuvanachakravartin Avaniyāḷappirandān *alias* Kōpperuñjiṅgadēva. Registers an order of Perumāḷ-Piḷḷai *alias* Śōḻakōn and mentions the gift of land for a flower garden.

95. 303 *of* 1913.—(Tamil.) On the same wall. A record in the third year and fifty-seventh day of the Chōḻa king Tribhuvanachakravartin Rājarājadēva. Mentions the gift of land for a flower garden by Umaiyāḻvi, daughter of Vijayanuḷamban, chief of Nuḷambapāḍi *alias* Nigariliśōḻa-maṇḍalam. She had purchased the land from different people.

96. 304 *of* 1913.—(Tamil.) On the same wall. A record in the seventh year of the Pallava king Sakalabhuvanachakravartin Avaniyāḷappirandān *alias* Kōpperuñjiṅgadēva. Registers an order of Śōḻakōn recording gift of land for a flower garden by a dancing girl.

97. 305 *of* 1913.—(Tamil.) On the same wall. A record in the seventh year of the Pallava king Sakalabhuvanachakravartin Avaniyāḷappirandān *alias* Kōpperuñjiṅgadēva. Registers an order of Sōḻakōn that eight *śandi* oblations like those offered at the shrine of Mūlasthānam-Uḍaiyār in (the temple of) Tiruchchiṟṟambalam, be also offered at the shrine of Dakshiṇāmūrti and that the gift of land made for providing five of these eight *śandis*, be made tax free.

98. 306 *of* 1913.—(Tamil.) On the same wall. A record in the ninth year and eighty-fifth day of the Chōḷa king Tribhuvanachakravartin (Rājarājadēva). Registers an order of the king's officers passed at the request of Gaṅgēyarāyan that certain lands granted to the temple for supplying flowers and maintaining the servants of the flower gardens, were to be made free of *kuḍimai*; that the documents pertaining to the lands in question were to be deposited in the temple treasury *(tirukkaiōṭṭi ?)* and that the transaction was to be engraved on the walls of the temple.

99. 307 *of* 1913.—(Tamil.) On the same wall. A record in the seventeenth year of the Pallava king Sakalabhuvanachakravartin Kōpperuñjiṅgadēva. Registers an order of Sōḷakōn that a gift of land was made for additional offerings in the shrine of Dakshiṇāmūrtidēva (referred to in No. 97 above), and that this land was made a rent-free *tirunāmattukkāṇi* under the command of the king.

100. 308 *of* 1913.—(Tamil.) On the same wall. A record in the eighth year of the Pallava king Sakalabhuvanachakravartin Avaniyāḷappirandān *alias* Kōpperuñjiṅgadēva. Registers an order of Śōḷakōn that the śāliya merchants *(nagara)* were to be provided with land for building their houses on condition that they would supply the necessary cloths for the *pariśattam* of the god and the goddess.

101. 309 *of* 1913.—(Tamil.) On the same wall. A record in the twelfth year and one hundred and twenty-fifth day; and Kumbha, eighth day (in the middle of the record) of the Chōḷa king Tribhuvanachakravartin Kulōttuṅga-Chōḷadēva (III, 1178—1216), "who was pleased to take Madurai (Madura) and the crowned head of the Pāṇḍya." Registers that a certain Ediriliśōḷan *alias* Iruṅgōḷan having founded a temple called Vikramaśōḷīśvaramuḍaiyār at Parakēsarinallūr, a hamlet of Perumbaṟṟappuliyūr, after acquiring the required land from various people and having provided for houses of Brāhmaṇas and temple servants, *the king ordered the assessment on this land to be deducted from the revenue of the village, to be entered in the temple accounts with the original documents preserved in the temple and the whole transaction engraved on the walls of the temple.*

102. 310 *of* 1913.—(Tamil.) On the same wall. A record in the twenty-first year and sixth day of the Chōḷa king Tribhuvanachakravartin Kulōttuṅga-Chōḷadēva (III, 1178—1216), "who was pleased to take Madurai (Madura) and the crowned head of the Pāṇḍya." Registers that a land was granted for a flower garden and another for maintaining its four servants. It was ordered that these lands might be included with other temple lands and that the excess *(maḍakku)* in measurement be deducted from the village accounts. The *tirumandira-ōlai* was Mīnavan-Mūvēnda-vēḷān.

103. 311 *of* 1913.—(Tamil.) On the same wall. A record in the sixteenth year and two hundred and twenty-fourth day of the Chōḷa king Tribhuvanachakravartin Kulōttuṅga-Chōḷadēva (III, 1178—1216), "who was pleased to take Madurai (Madura) and the crowned head of the Pāṇḍya." Records gift of land for a flower garden and its servants. Again the excess of land discovered by comparison with existing village accounts was granted to the temple and the village accountants *(varikkuruśeyvār)* were ordered to correct their figures. The servants of the garden were exempted from certain services usual to *nibandakkārar*. The *tirumandira-ōlai* was Rājanārājayaṇa-Mūvēndavēḷān.

104. 312 *of* 1913.—(Tamil.) On the same wall. A record in the tenth year, Simha, ninth day, of the Pallava king Sakalabhuvanachakravartin Avaniyāḷappirandān *alias* Kōpperuñjiṅgadēva. Registers an order of Perumāḷ-Piḷḷai *alias* Śōḷakōn made for the welfare of the king. Records an exchange of land and refers incidentally to the temple *(Sri-kōil)* of the piḍāri called Tiruchchiṟṟambala Mākāḷi on the south side of the street Vikkiramaśōḷanterku-ttiruvīdhi by which the God was taken on procession to the sea. See S.A. 32.

105. 313 *of* 1913.—(Tamil.) On the same wall. A record in the thirty-fourth year and fifty-second day of the Chōḷa king Tribhuvanachakravartin Tribhuvanavīradēva (Kulōttuṅga III, 1178—1216), 'who having pleased to take Madurai (Madura),Karuvur, Īḷam (Ceylon) and the crowned head of the Pāṇḍya was pleased to perform the anointment of heroes and the anointment of victors.' Records gift of land for a flower garden. It was ordered that the four servants of the garden must supply *iruvāchchi*, *malligai*, and *nandiyāvaṭṭa* flowers to the temple regularly ; when these failed other flowers had to be supplied.

106. 314 *of* 1913.—(Tamil.) On the same wall. A record in the thirty-ninth year of the Chōḷa king Tribhuvanachakravartin Tribhuvanavīradēva (1178—1216), "who having been pleased to take Mudurai (Madura), Karuvūr, Īḷam (Ceylon) and the crowned head of the Pāṇḍya was pleased to perform the anointment of heroes and the anointment of victors." Records gift of land for a flower garden to supply flowers to the temple of the goddess. Refers to a transaction which happened in the thirty-third year of the king.

107. 315 *of* 1913.—(Tamil.) On the same wall. A record in the second year and sixty-ninth day of the Chōḷa king Tribhuvanachakravartin Rājarājadēva (III? 1216—48). Registers that an additional land was granted by a certain Kundan *alias* Laṅkēśvara of Araśūr for the maintenance of a flower garden which had been already granted by himself, for supplying 700 red lotuses to the temple every day. The ten servants and a nāyaka who cultivated the garden were permitted to enjoy the land given them as a kāṇi. The transaction was engraved on the temple walls.

108. 316 *of* 1913.—(Tamil.) On the same wall. A record in the tenth year and three hundred and sixtieth day of the Chōḷa king Tribhuvanachakravartin Rājarājadēva (III? 1216—48). Registers that a flower garden had been founded for the benefit of the temple by a certain Karupparuḍaiyān *alias* Rājādhirājappallavaraiyan at the hamlet of Kōilpūṇḍi surnamed Kshatriyaśikhāmaṇinallūr, that land in three different villages had been granted for the maintenance of the gardeners who had to water the flower plants, pick flowers and supply them to the temple, and that these lands were now included with other temple lands under orders of the King's officers, the transaction being engraved on temple walls and the original documents deposited in the temple treasury.

109. 317 *of* 1913.—(Tamil.) On the same wall. A record in third year and twenty-fourth day of the Chōḷa king Tribhuvanachakravartin Rājarājadēva. Records gift of land for growing red lotuses and for providing food (koṟṟu) and cloth-money to the gardeners who grew them. Refers to the land survey made in the sixteenth year of Śuṅgandavirtta Kulōttuṅgaśōḷadēva (I, 1070—1118) and to the twenty-fifth year of Periyadēvar Tribhuvanavīradēva (Kulōttuṅga III, 1178—86). See No. 54 above.

110. 318 *of* 1913.—(Tamil.) On the same wall. A record in the ninth year of the Pallava king Sakalabhuvanachakravartin Avaniāḷappirandān *alias* Kōpperuñjiṅgadēva. Registers an order of Perumāḷ Piḷḷai *alias* Śōḷakōn, that certain gifts of land for the maintenance of gardeners, be recorded on the temple walls. See No. 104 above.

111. 319 *of* 1913.—(Tamil.) On the same wall. A record in the nineteenth year of the Pallava king Sakalabhuvanachakravartin Avaniāḷappirandān *alias* Kōpperuñjiṅgadēva. Sōḷakōn ordered that a gift of land for a grove of trees be made a rent-free dēvadāna and so registered on the temple walls.

112. 320 *of* 1913.—(Tamil.) On the same wall. A record in the ninth year and one hundred and sixty-sixth day of the Pāṇḍya king Māravarman Tribhuvanachakravartin Vīra-Pāṇḍyadēva. Registers an order of Vīra-Pāṇḍyadēva-Vāṇādhirāyan that a gift of one *tiruvōlai* together with a piece of land for the maintenance of the latter made by a certain Dīpattaraiyan at Śōḷakulavallinallūr, may be deducted from the accounts of Śōḷakulavallinallūr and added to the dēvadāna lands of the temple and that the transaction may be engraved on the temple wall. See S.A. 71.

113. 321 *of* 1913.—(Tamil.) On a pillar of the western entrance into the second prākāra of the same temple; left side. This pillar of the entrance was presented by Perumāḷ Piḷḷai *alias* Sōḷakōnār, one of the chiefs of Avaniāḷappirandān Kōpperuñjiṅga, for the merit of his master. [Mr. Krishna Sastri points out that, according to an inscription at Tripurāntaka (Kurnool District), a certain king Mahārāja Sinha built the eastern gōpuram of this temple and decorated the four sides of it with booty acquired from the four quarters and that this king was evidently Kōpperuñjiṅgadēva.]

114. 322 *of* 1913.—(Tamil.) On a second pillar in the same entrance. Records in Ś. 1422 Raudri, Āvaṇi, fifteenth day, that Tirumalaikoḷundar, the agent of Narasa-Nāyaka, while he was in charge of the temple, enforced that ten cake-offerings and betel leaves, which must be distributed among certain specified individuals for the merit of Narasa Nāyaka, were not to be withheld from them and used otherwise. [For the highly interesting figures in the western gōpura which are illustrative and descriptive of the dancing art in this age, see *Ep. Rep.*, 1914, *pp.* 82–3. Mr. Krishna Sastri quotes from the Bhāratīya-Nāṭya Śāstra to show how scientific these representations are.]

115. 323 *of* 1913.—(Tamil.) At the southern entrance into the first prākāra of the temple; left side. A record of the Vijayanagara king Vīrapratāpa Vīra-Krishṇayadēva-Mahārāya in Ś. 1432, Pramōdūta, Makara, ba. di. Amāvāsya, Monday, Pūrāḍam (= December 10, A.D. 1510). Records gift of three villages with an income 1,400 *rēkai* (gadyāna) for the mahāpūja in the temple of Aḷagiya Tiruchchiṟṟambalamuḍaiya Tambirānār [included in Araśūr-kīlpaṟṟu, a subdivision of Veṇṇaiyūrnāḍu in Rājādhirāja-vaḷanāḍu which was itself a district on the northern bank (of the Coleroon), included in the Province of Bhuvanēkavīran-paṭṭaṇa] and for the maintenance of a feeding house, by a certain śīrmai Appā Piḷḷai.

116. 324 *of* 1913.—(Tamil.) On the door post of a new entrance cut close to the east gōpura of the same temple. Seems as No. 321 (i.e., S.A. 113) above. The pillar evidently belonged to a different part of the temple and has been put in at this entrance by the Nāṭṭukkōṭṭai Cheṭṭis.

117. 325 *of* 1913.—(Tamil.) On the gōpura at the main entrance into the Śivakāmi-Amman shrine in the same temple. Same as S.A. 113.

118. 326 *of* 1913.—(Tamil.) On the east wall of the Mahishāsuramardhani shrine in the same temple. A record in the twelfth year of Pallava king Sakalabhuvanachakravartin Avaniāḷappirandān *alias* Kōpperuñjiṅgadēva. Registers an order of Śōḷakōn that a gift of land made for a flower garden to the shrine of Aṇḍābharaṇadēva be engraved on the wall of the shrine and the original documents connected herewith, be preserved in the temple treasury.

119. 327 *of* 1913.—(Tamil.) On the same wall. A record in the tenth year of the Pallava king Sakalabhuvanachakravartin Avaniālappirandān *alias* Kōpperuñjiṅgadēva. Registers an order of Śōḷakōn that a gift of land made for a flower garden to the shrine of Āṇḍābharaṇadēva be engraved on the wall of the shrine and the original documents connected therewith, be preserved in the temple treasury.

120. 328 *of* 1913.—(Tamil.) On the base of the Nandi-maṇṭapa opposite to the eastern gōpura of the same temple. A record of the Pāṇḍya kiṇg Māravarman Tribhuvanachakravartin Vīra-Pāṇḍyadēva, the date of which is lost. Consists of a number of mutilated and unconnected pieces. Stones out of order. Refers to an arrangement *(vyavasthā)* made by the temple managers. See S.A. 71, for the identification of the king.

121. 329 *of* 1913.—(Tamil.) On the base of the Nandi-maṇṭapa opposite to the southern gōpura of the same temple. Consists of six verses of which five refer to a battle fought evidently at Chidambaram by a certain Munaiyan Vallaiyan Ādittan, chief of Panaiśeyyār, on behalf of the Pāṇḍya (Mīnavan) against the Chōḷa (Vaḷavan). The author of the poetry was Tāynalla-Perumāḷ Munaiyadarayan *alias* Bhuvanēkavīra Toṇḍaimān.

122. 330 *of* 1913.—(Tamil.) On the base of a small shrine in the western prākāra of the same temple. An incomplete record in the sixth year, Simha, 26th day of the Pāṇḍya king Jaṭāvarman *alias* Tribhuvanachakravartin Sundara-Pāṇḍyadēva (I? 1251—64). Contains some detailed account of land measurement.

123. 331 *of* 1913.—(Tamil.) On a slab built into the floor in front of the Gaṇapati shrine in the same temple. An unfinished record in Manmatha, Dhanus. Refers to a gift by purchase of some godowns, by a certain Nāgama-Nāyaka. [Was he the father of Viśvanātha Nāik, the founder of the Nāik dynasty of Madura?]

124. 332 *of* 1913.—(Tamil verse.) On the east gōpura of the same temple; right of entrance. Consists of two verses, the first of which refers to a conquest of the Pāṇḍya king over the Chōḷa, the latter being driven into the forest. The second mentions Kāḍavarkōn and his army melting away before the Pāṇḍya king Sundarattōḷ. [Mr. Krishna Sastri identifies Kāḍavarkōn with Kōpperuñjiṅgadēva and the Pāṇḍya with Jaṭāvarman Sundara Pāṇḍya I.]

125. 333 *of* 1913.—(Tamil verse.) In the same place. A record of the Vijayanagara king Kṛishṇarāya in Ś. 1443, *Vrisha, Kārttika.* (Details not enough for calculation). Records that a certain Maṅgaraśan granted the village of Chidambaranāthapuram to the temple.

126. 334 *of* 1913.—(Tamil.) In the same place. A record of the Vijayanagara king Vīrapratāpa Veṅkaṭadēva-Mahārāya (I) in Ś. 1500, Pārthiva (wrong) Simha, *śu. di.* 10, Monday, Śubhayōga, Svāti. Records gift of four villages to the temple of Chidambarēśvara and Śivakāmasundari-Ammai to provide oblations and sacred bath in early mornings, for the merit of Vaiyappa, Krishṇappa Koṇḍama-Nāyaka. An irregular date. Most probably June 24, A.D. 1577 is intended. See *Ep. Rep.*, 1914, p. 69. See S.A. 131 for an other endowment by the same chief.

127. 335 *of* 1913.—(Tamil.) In the same place. A record of the Vijayanagara king Veṅkaṭadēva-Mahārāya (I) in Ś. 1510 Sarvadhāri, Mārgaḷi, twenty-second day. Records gift of 300 pon for providing 20 (rice) offerings to the god Chidambarēśvara and distributing the same among begging devotees. It is stated that this amount was till then being set apart by the temple for the *ilakkai* and *koṟṟu* of the king and his followers (rājāgaram). "Date can be calculated but not verified."

128. 336 *of* 1913.—(Tamil.) In the same place. Contains three verses that first of which refers to a battle fought on the banks of Veḷḷāru in which a certain Bhuvanēkavīran was victorious. [The last refers to Māravarman Vikrama-Pāṇḍya, who came to the throne in 1283.]

129. 337 *of* 1913.—(Tamil verse.) In the same place. One verse describing the anger of Vikrama Pāṇḍya. [See note to the above inscription.]

130. 338 *of* 1913.—(Tamil verse.) In the same place. One verse in praise of Sundara-Pāṇḍya (Jaṭāvarman I) and his weighing himself against gold. See S.A. 124, 132, 153, etc. See *Ep. Ind.*, III, p. 11 where his covering the Vimāna of the Raṅganātha temple with gold is referred to.

131. 339 *of* 1913.—(Tamil.) In the same place. A record of the Vijayanagara king Veṅkaṭadēva Mahārāya (I) in Ś. 1510, Sarvadhāri, Tai, twenty-second day. Registers that Vaiyappa-Krishṇappa Koṇḍama-Nāyaka ordered that the 30 (rice) offerings for which he had provided 50,000 kalams of paddy in the district of Vīranārāyaṇachchīrmai, be distributed among Śaiva mendicants (*tiruōṭṭuṇāyanār*). "Date can be calculated but not verified." See S.A. 126.

132. 340 *of* 1913.—(Tamil verse.) In the same place. Glorifies the prowess of Sundara-Māran (i.e., Sundara-Pāṇḍya) who annihilated the forces of the Teliṅgas that surrounded him and drove the Bāṇa chief into the forest. [The king was evidently Sundara Pāṇḍya I, Jaṭāvarman whose inscriptions have the introduction *Anaittulahuṅkoṇḍaruḷiya* and who ruled from 1251 to 1264.]

133. 341 *of* 1913.—(Tamil.) In the same place. Mentions Sōḷakulavalli and appears to make provision for singing the *pāmālai* (hymns) of the Nāyanār (Śaiva saints) in the temple of Tirumūlattānamuḍaiyān. Also mentions the village of Kaḷumalam. A record in (date doubtful); Āni, Svāti.

134. 342 *of* 1913.—(Tamil.) In the same place, left of entrance. In modern characters. Registers that Śuppammāḷ, mother of Ayyalammāḷ, who was the wife of Pachchaiyappa-Mudaliyār of Kāñchipuram, repaired this eastern gōpura and founded a Brahman settlement (agrahāra).

135. 343 *of* 1913.—(Grantha.) In niches on the inner walls of the same gōpura. These are labels engraved below images representing women in various dancing postures. The inscriptions are in Sanskrit poetry. For a discussion of these postures as given in the Bhārata-nāṭya Śāstra and illustrations, see *Madr. Ep. Rep.*, 1914, pp. 74—83.

136. 344 *of* 1913.—(Tamil.) On the south gōpura of the same temple; right of entrance. A record of the Śāluva king Vīrapratāpa Tammarāya in Ś. 1425, Rudhirōdgarin, Simha, śu. di. 14, Śravaṇa, Monday (which should be Sunday). Records that a certain Mondukoli Rāmanāyakkar Mallanāyakkar gave the village of Kārikkuḍi, the western hamlet of Perumbaṟṟappuliyūr, for a double garland and offerings to be offered every day. The king receives the usual Vijayanagara titles. The date corresponded to 6th August, A.D. 1503.

137. 345 *of* 1913.—(Tamil verse.) In the same place. A much damaged record. Mentions Por-puliyūr.

138. 346 *of* 1913.—(Tamil.) In the same place. A record of the Vijayanagara king Veṅkaṭadēva-Mahārāya (Veṅkaṭa I, 1586—1614) in Ś. 1510, Sarvadhārin, Mārgaḷi, 22nd day. Same as No. 335 (i.e., S.A. 127) above.

139. 347 *of* 1913.—(Tamil.) In the same place. A record of the Vijayanagara king Veṅkaṭadēva-Mahārāya (Veṅkaṭa I, 1586—1614) in Ś. 1510, Sarvadhārin, Tai, 22nd day. Same as No. 339 (i.e., S.A. 131) above.

140. 348 *of* 1913.—(Tamil.) In the same place. A record of the Vijayanagara king Śrīraṅgadēva-Mahārāya (II) in Ś. 1503 Vrisha, Kumbha, śu. di. 84, Thursday (which should be Tuesday), Śravishṭha (i.e., Dhanishṭha). Records gift of seven villages and of income from pepper trade called *milagu-taragu*, for oblations and festivals in the shrines of the god and goddess, by Vaiyappa Kṛishṇappa-Koṇḍama-Nāyaka. See S.A. 126 and S.A. 131. [I have traced this inscription to *Ins., S. Dts.*, p. 163, No. 4, but here the name of the king is given as Veṅkaṭadēva.]

141. 349 *of* 1913.—(Tamil.) In the same place. A record of the Vijayanagara king Veṅkaṭadēva-Mahārāya (Veṅkaṭa I, 1586—1614) in Ś. 1510, Sarvadhārin, Tai, twenty-second day. Records that the provision made by the chief for twenty offerings to be distributed among the Śaiva mendicants (paradēśi) in the temple, was placed under the *supervision of Namaśśivāya-Uḍaiyār, the "Superintendent of all services* (kaṭṭaḷai)." [The name Namaśśivāya reminds the Tamil literary student of that Guru Namaśśivāya who was the disciple of Guhai Namaśśivāya who devoted himself, at the instance of his teacher, to holy work at Chidambaram, who composed the *Paramarahasyamālai*, the *Chidambaraveṇba*, etc., and who ultimately died at TiruppeRunduṟai. See N.A. 614.

142. 350 *of* 1913.—(Tamil.) In the same place. A record in the fourth year and sixty-seventh day of the Pāṇḍya king Māravarman Tribhuvanachakravartin Vīrakēraḷa *alias* Kulaśēkharadēva. Registers an order of Śēdiyarāyan exempting certain lands granted for a flower garden by a native of Paḷḷikōḍu in Malai-maṇḍalam from paying *kaḍamai* and *kuḍimai* and declaring that these lands might enjoy the privileges of irrigation by channels, percolation and bailing. The king was identical with Ravivarman Kulaśēkhara, the Kēraḷa conqueror. See *Ep. Ind.*, IV, 145; *Ibid.*, Vol. VIII, p. 8. His father Jayasimha had the title Vīrakēraḷa. *Ep. Ind.*, IV, p. 293.

143. 351 *of* 1913.—(Tamil.) On the same gōpura; left of entrance. A record in the fourth year and one hundred and twenty-third day of the Pāṇḍya king Māravarman *alias* Tribhuvanachakravartin Vīra-Pāṇḍyadēva. Registers an order of Śēdiyarāyan that the gift of garden lands made by a certain Villavadaraiyan together with lands provided for the maintenance of eighteen servants of the garden and of the water-shed within it, may be engraved on temple walls. See S.A. 71.

144. 352 *of* 1913.—(Tamil.) On a slab set up near the same gōpura. A damaged record in Ś. 1520, Viḷambin, Āḍi, first day. Provides for some specified repairs to the temple made for the merit of Muttu-Kṛishnappa-Nāyaka, son of Vaiyappa-Kṛishṇappa Koṇḍama-Nāyaka. Also mentions a maṇṭapa on the bank of Kolliḍavāru, built by the same donor. See S.A. 126 and 131.

145. 353 *of* 1913.—(Tamil.) On the west gōpura of the same temple; right of entrance. A record in praise of the Pāṇḍya king (Mīnavan) Vikrama-Pāṇḍya (Māravarman, most probably).

146. 354 *of* 1913.—(Tamil.) In the same place. Three verses describing the glory of king Sundara-Pāṇḍya who conquered the kings of Vēṇāḍu (i.e., Travancore), those of the north (i.e., the Teliṅgas) and those of the Koṅgu (country) and *killed* Gaṇḍagōpāla. [The king is of course Jaṭāvarman Sundara Pāṇḍya I, 1251—64. See S.A. 153.]

147. 355 *of* 1913.—(Tamil.) In the same place. A record of the Vijayanagara king Veṅkaṭadēva-Mahārāya (Veṅkaṭa I, 1586—1614) in Ś. 1510, Sarvadhārin, Mārgaḷi, twenty-second day. Same as No. 335 (i.e., S.A. 127 above).

148. 356 *of* 1913.—(Tamil.) In the same place. A record of the Cochin king Rāmavarma-Mahārāja, of the family of Śēraman Perumāḷ Nāyanār in Ś. 1498, Dhātri, Mārgaḷi, twelfth day. The king is stated to have been born under the asterism Viśākha. Provides for 33 taḷigai (offerings) to be offered to Ānandatāṇḍava-Perumāḷ Nāyanār and distributed among Brāhmaṇas, Mahēśvaras and the temple cooks. [The king referred to was the king of Cochin, one of the successors of Gōdai Varma who came to the throne in 1561 and ruled for an unknown period.]

149. 357 *of* 1913.—(Tamil verse.) In the same place. In praise of the Pāṇḍya king. Mentions Kūḍal (i.e., Madura).

150. 358 *of* 1913.—(Grantha and Tamil.) In the same place. A record of the Vijayanagara king Vīrabhūpatirāya. Registers that 64 cows were granted for maintaining perpetual lamps in the presence of Nrittanātha, by the ministers Chauṇḍarasa and Ādittarasa. [The Government epigraphist points out that if this Chauṇḍarasa is the same as the Vēdic scholar Chauṇḍa-pāchārya, Virabhūpati should be identified with Bukka II in whose time that scholar flourished. *Ep. Rep.*, 1909, p. 115].

151. 359 *of* 1913.—(Tamil.) In the same place. A record of the Vijayanagara king Vīrapratāpa Śrīraṅgadēva-Mahārāya (II) in Ś. 1503, Vrisha, Kumbha, śu. di 14, Thursday (should be Tuesday) Śravishṭha (i.e., Danishṭha). Same as No. 348 (i.e., S.A. 140 above).

152. 360 *of* 1913.—(Tamil.) In the same place. Records in Ś. 1517, Durmukhi, Chaitra, full-moon, Chitra, lunar eclipse gift of a village surnamed Purappēṭṭai, for meeting the expenses of one day during the Aippiśi-Pūram festivities, in honour of the goddess.

153. 361 *of* 1913.—(Tamil verse.) In the same place. The record contains three verses and refers to the fight between Sundara-Pāṇḍya (evidently Jaṭāvarman S.P.) and the Teluṅgas, at Mudugūr in which the dead bodies were strewn up to the banks of the Pērāru. See S.A. 146 which directly refers to the battle.

154. 362 *of* 1913.—(Tamil.) In the same place. A record of the Vijayanagara king Veṅkaṭadēva-Mahārāya I (1586—1614) in Ś. 1510, Sarvadhārin, Tai, twenty-second day. Same as No. 349 above.

155. 363 *of* 1913.—(Tamil verse.) In the same place. Consists of two verses. There is apparently a reference to Sundara-Pāṇḍya's weighing himself against gold and using it for covering the temple. See S.A. 130 above.

156. 364 *of* 1913.—(Tamil verse.) On the same gōpura; left of entrance. A damaged record. Two of the verses are in praise of the Pāṇḍya king (Maran).

157. 365 *of* 1913—(Tamil verse.) In the same place. Three verses extolling Vikrama-Pāṇḍya. The first says that he conquered the king of Vēṇāḍu (i.e., Travancore) at Podiyil. In the second he is addressed as Bhuvanēkavīra and Korkai-kāvala and is stated to have been the enemy of Gaṇapati. The third advises king Vikrama-Pāṇḍya not to go to the north; for there it says is a foe—a woman ruling with a man's name. [The last refers to the celebrated queen Rudramma of the Kākatīya dynasty. See S.A. 68, S.A. 342, etc., for further facts about Vikrama-Pāṇḍya.]

158. 366 *of* 1913.—(Tamil.) In the same place. A record in the twenty-ninth year of the Pāṇḍya king Māravarman Tribhuvana-chakravartin Kulaśēkharadēva (I, 1268—1308). Built in at the bottom. Registers an order of Kaḷiṅgarāyan. Provides for offering to the god Kulōttuṅgaśōḷa-Vināyaka-Piḷḷaiyār who is enshrined on the south side of the seven storeyed gōpura of *Rājāk-kaḷtambirāntirumāḷigai.* Refers to *Ellāndalaiyāna-Perumālśandi.* [*Ellāndalaiyāna* is the epithet of Jaṭāvarman Sundara-Pāṇḍya I, 1251—64.]

159. 367 *of* 1913.—(Tamil.) In the same place. A record of the Vijayanagara king Veṅkaṭadēva-Mahārāya (I, 1586—1614) in Ś. 1510, Sarvadhārin, Tai, twenty-second day. Same as No. 339 above.

160. 368 *of* 1913.—(Grantha.) In niches on the inner walls of the same gōpura. Registers the names of the various dances in Sanskrit, as in No. 343 (i.e., S.A. 135).

161. 369 *of* 1913.—(Tamil.) On a slab set up near the same gōpura. A record of the Vijayanagara king Veṅkaṭadēva-Mahārāya (I) in Ś. 1515, Vijaya, Ādi, first day, Saturday, Jyēshṭha (= 30th June 1593). Registers that for the merit of Vaiyappa-Kṛishṇappa-Koṇḍama-Nāyaka, the districts Dēvamaṇḍalaśīrmai, Vīranārāyaṇachchīrmai, Terku-nāḍu, Vaḍakku-nāḍu, the five villages grouped under Asuvur and all others that had been enjoyed by the temple of Chidambarēśvara from early times, were made tax-free and that a fresh provision was made for a daily offering of 750 *taḷigai.* This was called Koṇḍama-nāyakan kaṭṭaḷai. [I have traced this inscription to *Ins., S. Dts.* (*Mack. MSS.*), p. 167, No. 15.]

162. 370 *of* 1913.—(Tamil.) On the north gōpura of the same temple; right of entrance. A record of the Vijayanagara king Veṅkaṭadēva-Mahārāya (I) in Ś. 1510, Sarvadhārin, Tai, twenty-second day. Same as No. 339 above (i.e., S.A. 131).

163. 371 *of* 1913.—(Tamil.) In the same place. Registers that Vīrapratāpa Kṛishṇadēva-Mahārāya (1509—1530) after having started on a campaign against Simhādri-Pottunūru, planted a pillar of victory there and returning thence, he paid a visit to

Ponnambalam (i.e., Chidambaram), worshipped the god and built the northern gōpura of the temple. See S.A. 233.

164. 372 *of* 1913.—(Tamil.) On the same gōpura; left of entrance. A record of the Vijayanagara king Veṅkaṭadēva-Mahārāya (I, 1586—1614) in Ś. 1510, Sarvadhārin, Mārgaḷi, 22nd day. Same as No. 335 above (i.e., S.A. 127).

165. 373 *of* 1913.—(Tamil.) In the same place. A record of the Vijayanagara king Veṅkaṭadēva-Mahārāya I in Ś. 1510, Sarvadhārin, Tai, 22nd day. Same as 349 above (i.e., S.A. 141).

166. 374 *of* 1913.—(Tamil verse.) In the same place. Registers that three gōpuras were the gifts of kings who wore a crown. This (the northern gōpura) was built by the god himself. The poet evidently means to say that this is the best of the four. We know from S.A. 163 that Kṛishṇarāya built it.

167. 375 *of* 1913.—(Tamil.) On a slab set up near the same gōpura. A record of the Vijayanagara king Veṅkaṭadēva-Mahārāya in Ś. 1515, Vijaya, Āḍi, 1st day, Saturday, Jyēshṭha (30th June 1593). Same as No. 369 above (i.e., S.A. 161).

168. 376 *of* 1913.—(Tamil.) On the north wall of the Karpaga Vināyaka temple, at the western gōpura of the same temple. A record of the Vijayanagara king Vīrapratāpa Dēvarāya-Mahārāya II in Ś. 1349, Plavaṅga, Mīna, śu. di. 5, Sunday, Rōhiṇi (March 21, A.D. 1428). One stone missing in the middle. Registers that the king ordered certain irregularities in temples and temple lands to be set right. A very interesting record which gives a clue to the beneficent rules of Dēvarāya. The inscription says that the king's officers unjustly collected *kāṇikkai*, *Araśupēru*, *Karaṇakkar jōḍi*, *Visēshādāyam* and other taxes from certain villages which were owned by temples and the people of which were tenants (by mortgage, purchase, etc.) of these temples; that the villagers in consequence deserted; that worship in consequence ceased in the temples; and that the king issued an edict of freedom and restoration. See *Ep. Rep.*, 1914, p. 97 and also *Ep. Rep.*, 1908, p. 250.

169. 1 *of* 1915.—(Tamil.) On the north tier of the central shrine in the Gōvindarāja-Perumāḷ temple at Chidambaram. An unfinished record of the Vijayanagara king Achyutadēva-Mahārāya (1530—42) in Ś. 1460, Viḷambi, Paṅguni, 14th day, Monday, Paurṇima, Uttara-Phalguni. Records the reconsecration of Gōvindarājasvāmin at Chitrakūṭa by Achyutarāya. An irregular date. See *Ep. Rep.*, 1915, p. 81. See S.A. 63 and 64.

Erumbūr.

170. 378 *of* 1913.—(Tamil.) On the south base of the central shrine in the Kadambavanēśvara temple. An unfinished record in the sixteenth year of the Chōḷa king Vikrama-Chōḷadēva (1118—35).

Records gift of money for a lamp to the temple of Śiru-Tirukkōyil-Mahādēva at Urumūr *alias* Vikrama-Chōḷa-chaturvēdimaṅgalam, for the merit of Tirumambalamśuṟṟi *alias* Munaiyadaraiyap-Pallavaraiyan, a Chāḷukki of Toṇḍa-maṇḍalam residing at Ānaivāri, the eastern hamlet of Vānavanmādēvi-chaturvēdimaṅgalam in Virudarāja-bhayaṅkara-vaḷanāḍu on the northern bank (of the Coleroon).

171. 379 *of* 1913.—(Tamil.) On the same base. A record in the eighteenth year of the Chōḷa king Madiraikoṇḍa-Parakēsarivarman (Parāntaka I). Records gift of a lamp-stand and of 90 sheep for a lamp, by a certain Kalinīkki Kuṇavan, native of Maruṅgil in Kōnāḍu to the temple of Śiru-Tirukkōyil-Perumānaḍigaḷ, at Urumūr, a dēvadāna in Nalvāyalūr-kūṟṟam on the northern bank (of the Coleroon).

172. 380 *of* 1913.—(Tamil.) On the same base. A record in the twentieth year of the Chōḷa king Tribhuvanachakravartin Rājarājadēva (II ? or III ?). Records gift of money for a lamp, by a native of Urumūr *alias* Vikramachōḷa-chaturvēdimaṅgálam.

173. 381 *of* 1913.—(Tamil.) On the south wall of the same shrine. A record in the twenty-sixth year of the Chōḷa king Madiraikoṇḍa-Parakēsarivarman (i.e., Parāntaka I). Records gift of 90 sheep for a lamp by a lady, to the temple mentioned in S.A. 171 above. The sabhā (assembly) of Urumūr agreed to see the lamp regularly maintained in the temple.

174. 382 *of* 1913.—(Tamil.) On the same wall. A record in the twentieth year of the Chōḷa king Madiraikoṇḍa Parakēsarivarman (905—47). Records gift of a lamp-stand weighing 200 *palams* and of 90 sheep for a lamp to the temple by a resident of the northern suburb of the same village.

175. 383 *of* 1913.—(Tamil.) On the same wall. A record in the tenth year of the Chōḷa king Rājakēsarivarman. Records gift of a lamp-stand and of 90 sheep for a lamp to the temple of Śiru-Tirukkōyil-Mahādēva at Urumūr. The donor was a certain Kurumban Śirugan, native of Villangāṭṭūr in Arumbūr-kūṟṟam, a subdivision of Pāṇḍi-nāḍu.

176. 384 *of* 1913.—(Tamil.) On the same wall. A record in the twenty-eighth year of the Chōḷa king Madiraikoṇḍa Parakēsarivarman (i.e., Parāntaka I). Registers that the central shrine (*śrivimāna*) was built of stone and that the gōpura with the *ashṭaparivāra* was erected by a Iruṅgōḷan Kuṇavan Aparājitan. A gift of 3¼ vēlis of land was also made by the same individual with the permission of king Śōḷaperumanāḍigal Parāntakadēva to the temple of Śiru-Tirukkōyil-Bhaṭāra (the modern Kadambavanēśvara) at Urumūr for *tiruchchennal*, *archanābhōga* and the maintenance of drummers at śrī-bali.

177. 385 *of* 1913.—(Tamil.) On the same wall. A record in the twenty-third year of the Chōḷa king Rājarājakēsarivarman *alias* Rājarājadēva (I). Records gift of 5 *kalañju* of gold by a certain Araiyan Vichchādiran of Urumūr, on receiving which the assembly of Urumūr, a dēvadāna and brahmadēya in Nalvāyalūr-kūṟṟam, a subdivision of Vaḍagarai Rājēndrasimha-vaḷanāḍu, agreed to pay themselves the annual fee usually collected from the drummers of the temple (*uvachchar*) and to have the śrī-bali of the temple properly conducted. [The great poet Kamba belonged to the Uvachchar caste, or rather he was brought up by an Uvachcha.]

178. 386 *of* 1913.—(Tamil.) On the same wall. A damaged record of the Pāṇḍya king Māravarman Tribhuvanachakravartin Vīra-Pāṇḍyadēva in his fifth year, Simha, śu. di. 8, Saturday, Anilam. Registers a sale of land to the temple as a *tirunāmattukkāṇi* of the goddess, by the sabhā of Urumūr *alias* Vikramachōḷa-chaturvēdimaṅgalam. See S.A. 71. Mr. Swamikannu Pillai says that the English equivalent of the date is Saturday, August 18, A.D. 1267.

179. 387 *of* 1913.—(Tamil.) On the west wall of the same shrine. An unfinished record in the seventh year of the Chōḷa king Tribhuvanachakravartin Rājarājadēva. Records gift of 96 sheep for a lamp and of 14 cows for curds and milk, by a native of a place near Poygai-Araśūr to the temple of Tiruvirāmīśvaram-uḍaiya Periyanāyanār at Erumbūr which was also called Urumūr *alias* Vikramachōḷa-chaturvēdimaṅgalam, a brahmadēya in Merkanāḍu, a subdivision of Vaḍagarai Virudarāja-bhayaṅkara-vaḷanāḍu. [The king was very probably Rājarāja III, 1216—48.]

180. 388 *of* 1913.—(Tamil.) On the same wall. An unfinished record in the twenty-third year of the Chōḷa king Rājarājakēsarivarman *alias* Rājarājadēva (I). Records sale of land to the temple by the assembly of Urumūr, a dēvadāna and brahmadēya in Nalvēlūrkūṟṟam, which was a subdivision of Vaḍagarai Rājēndrasimha-vaḷanāḍu. Mentions the taxes *echchōru*, *Vāśalilpandakuḍimai* and *ūriḍu-varippāḍu* from the payment of which the land was evidently exempted by the assembly.

181. 389 *of* 1913.—(Tamil.) On the same wall. A record in the fifth year of the Chōḷa king Parakēsarivarman. Records gift of 90 sheep for a lamp to the temple of Śiru-Tirukkōyil-Bhaṭāra.

182. 390 *of* 1913.—(Tamil.) On the same wall. A record of the Chōḷa king Parakēsarivarman *alias* Tribhuvanachakravartin Kulōttuṅga-Chōḷadēva II in his twelfth year, Vrischika, śu. di. 12, Wednesday, Rēvati (November 8, A.D. 1144). Records gift of land for oblations to the same temple by a certain Tōraṇavallavapperayan, a servant and tenant of Kāḍavarāyan. See S.A. 124.

183. 391 *of* 1913.—(Tamil.) On the north wall of the same shrine. A damaged record in the sixteenth year of the Chōḷa king Parakēsarivarman. Seems to record a gift of gold for a lamp, by a lady.

184. 392 *of* 1913.—(Tamil.) On the north wall of the same shrine. A record in the third year of the Chōḷa king Rājakēsarivarman. Records gift of land for offerings.

185. 393 *of* 1913.—(Tamil.) On the north wall of the same shrine. An unfinished record in the ninth year of the Chōḷa king Parakēsarivarman. Registers that ten kaḻanju of tuḷai-pon were paid to the village assembly for making a certain land which was presented to the temple, tax-free.

186. 394 *of* 1913.—(Tamil.) On the north wall of the same shrine. A record in the ninth year of the Chōḷa king Parakēsarivarman. Records gift of 90 sheep for a lamp.

187. 395 *of* 1913.—(Tamil.) On the north wall of the same shrine. A record in the sixth year of the Chōḷa king Parakēsarivarman *alias* Rājēndra-Chōḷadēva (I, 1011—53). Records gift of land for a lamp and offerings to the temple of Śiru-Tirukkōyil-Mahādēva at Urumūr, a brahmadēya in Nalvāyalūr-kūṟṟam, a subdivision of Vaḍagarai Rājēndraśiṅga-vaḷanāḍu.

188. 396 *of* 1913.—(Tamil.) On the north wall of the same shrine. An incomplete record in the fourth year of the Chōḷa king Parakēsarivarman *alias* Uḍaiyār Srī-Rājēndradēva (1050—63). Refers to a decision *(vyavasthai)* arrived at by the assembly of Vānavanmādēvi-chaturvēdimaṅgalam, a brahmadēya in Mērka-nāḍu, a subdivision of Rājādhirāja-vaḷanāḍu on the occasion when it met in the temple of Vaḷavanmādēvi-Viṇṇagar-Āḻvār. Mentions Vijayaṅgoṇḍaśōḻīśvaram-uḍaiya-kōyil, and the boundaries of certain lands which had been assigned for oblations.

189. 397 *of* 1913.—(Tamil.) On the same wall. A record of the Chōḷa king Rājakēsarivarman *alias* Tribhuvanachakravartin-Rājarājadēva (II) in his seventh year, Makara, śu. di. 8, Saturday, Rēvati. Registers that lands were purchased from the assembly of Urumūr *alias* Vikramachōḷa-chaturvēdimaṅgalam and granted as dēvadāna to the temple of Tiruvirāmīśvaram-uḍaiya-Periya-nāyanār by one Vāsudēvan Periyan *alias* Tiruchchiṟṟambala-Mūvēndavēḷān of Olugarai near Poygai-Araśūr. The taxes *kaḍamai, pāḍikāval*, etc., payable on these lands which amounted to 55 kalams of paddy were agreed to be paid to the temple by the assembly of the village. Refers also to a loan borrowed by the assembly from the temple treasury on account of "bad time" (famine) and scarcity of grain (*akkam*). The amount borrowed was 60 *kāśu* at the rate of interest 2 *tuṇi* and 3 *kuruṇi* of paddy on every *kāśu*.

190. 398 *of* 1913.—(Tamil.) On the same wall. A damaged record in the fourteenth year and 341st day of the Chōḷa king Parakēsarivarman *alias* Rajēndradēva (1012—43). The assembly of the brahmadēya village, Vaḷavanmādēvi-chaturvēdimaṅgalam in Mērka-nāḍu, a subdivision of Vaḍagarai Rājēndrasimha-vaḷanāḍu assembled together in the hall called Tiruvaraṅgadēvan within the temple and in the presence of the "annual supervision committee," agreed to pay in paddy the *śilvari* on certain lands belonging to the temples of Śiru-Tirukkōyil-uḍaiyār, Tiruvēṅgaḍattāḷvār and Tiru-mērkōyil-āḷvār. The income was to be utilized for lamps and offerings.

Lālāpēṭṭai.

191. 377 *of* 1913.—(Tamil.) On a detached fragment built into the waste weir of the Vīrāṇam tank. A record in . . . Sunday, Makha. Contains a portion of the historical introduction of Rājēndra-Chōḷa I (1012—43).

Mannārguḍi. (Kāṭṭumannārkōvil).

[This is the celebrated birth-place of Nāthamuni and Yāmunāchārya.]

191-A. On a stone at the gate of the Vīra-Nārāyaṇa Svāmi temple. Records that the brother of a certain Appā Piḷḷai granted to god Aḷagia Mannār in K. 4442 Āṅgirasa, in the reign of Kṛishṇadēva Rāya 52 Mās. of land in a village. *Ins. S. Dts.*, p. 2, No. 7.

191-B. In the same place. Records that Kṛishṇappa Nāyaka granted to the Rāmānujakūṭa in Ś. 1514, in the reign of Veṅkaṭapati Rāya (I), the villages of Kaṇḍamaṅgalam and Paḷañjanallūr in Gaṅgaikoṇḍa Śīmai. *Ibid.*, p. 2, No. 8.

Śrimushṇam.

The important Vishṇu shrine of the place, generally attributed to the Naik Kings of Tanjore, amidst the fine carvings of which are in fact the figures of Achyutappa and his brothers, is poor in epigraphs. Though not mentioned in the *Prabandhas* it is one of the eight important Svayambhustalas. See *S.A. Gazr.*, pp. 290—92.

192. 145 *of* 1898.—(Tamil.) On the steps leading up to the Vēṇugōpālasvāmin shrine in the Bhūvarāhasvāmin temple. Records in Ś. 1635 expired, Vijaya, the erection of certain buildings by a chief of Uḍaiyārpāḷaiyam.

193. On one of the walls. A Telugu inscription, dated Ś. 1505 (A.D. 1583) recording a private grant to the temple in the reign of Śrī-Raṅgarāya I of Penukoṇḍa (1578—86). See *Antiquities*, I, 213.

194. *No.* 68 *of Sewell's List.*—(Telugu.) Records a grant of five villages for religious purposes by one Śrīnivāsadāsa, in Ś. 1637 (A.D. 1715), Jaya, during the reign of the emperor Farokshir at Delhi, here called Parukūśāha Pāḍuśāhagāru. Śrīnivāsadāsa was patronized by Todar Mull, the Emperor's deputy. [Mr. Sewell is not quite correct in his reading of this epigraph. For a mention of a Todar Mull who might have belonged to the same family see *Trien. Catal. Sans. MSS.*, 1910-3, p. 496.]

Tiruvakkuḷam.

195. 259 *of* 1913.—(Tamil.) On a slab lying near the Paśupatīśvara temple. Records in Ś. 1488 (A.D. 1566), Akshaya, Tai, 15th day, gift of the village of Tiruveshkaḷam to the shrines Chidambarēśvara and Śivakāmasundari Amman of the Tirumūlasthānam temple, by Achutappa-Nāyaka, son of Siru-śevvappa Nāyaka for the merit of Tirumalairājayyan (i.e., the Karnāṭa king Tirumala I). [As Achyutappa came to the throne in 1572, this inscription should have been engraved while his father was king. For the chief events of Śevvappa and Achyutappa see *Tanj. Gazr.*, pp. 38–9.]

CUDDALORE TALUK.

Cuddalore.

The historic importance of Cuddalore begins only after the English purchase of Fort St. David from the Marathas in 1690. The following copper plates do not in reality belong to Cuddalore *Town*, but I mention them here, because they are now either in the Collector's Court of Cuddalore or the Madras Museum and secondly because the exact places are not mentioned. All these have been taken from Mr. Sewell's Lists.

196. *No. 72 of Mr. Sewell's List.*—(Telugu.) A document recording the grant of land by and to private individuals, in Ś. 1672, K. 4851, Pramōdūta (A.D. 1750).

197. *No. 73 of Mr. Sewell's List.*—(Tamil.) A record in Ś. 1447 (A.D. 1525) Ānanda. "It commences with a mythological account of the temple at Chidambaram, and continues to narrate that the '5 caste people and 74 artizans' presented this document to the temple. The document authorizes the payment of certain money by all persons to whom it should be shown, to the holder thereof. The name of the reigning sovereign is given as "Pratividadēva Mahārāya." (Evidently a late forgery.)

198. *No. 74 of Mr. Sewell's List.*—Records a document drawn up by 74 chief priests of the Vaishṇava faith, conferring on a Brāhman certain religious privileges, in Ś. 1460 (A.D. 1538), Viḷambi, during the reign of Achyutadēva Mahārāya of the Vijayanagar dynasty.

199. *No. 75 of Mr. Sewell's List.*—(Tamil.) Records a document, on one side of a large plate, having on its reverse side a large number of mythological figures of both the Saiva and Vaishṇava faiths (Gaṇēśa, the liṅgam, Hanūmān, Narasimha) in high relief and beautifully executed. It states that in Ś. 1518 (A.D. 1596) Hēviḷambi, when Vīra Pratāpa Veṅkaṭapatidēva (I) Mahārāya of the Vijayanagar dynasty was reigning, a Śūdra priest joined with a large number of other Śūdras and made one Kaṇḍiya Dēvar, king of Vriddhāchalam, in the presence of Muttu Kṛishnappa Nāyaka. [Mr. Sewell considers that the latter might be the king of Madura; but it is practically certain that he is the chief referred to in S.A. 144 as the son of Vaiyappa Kṛishṇappa Koṇḍama Nāyaka.]

Cuddalore (Mañjakuppam).

200. 199 *of* 1902.—(Tamil.) On a pillar set up at the southern end of the Pennaiyāru bridge. A record in the ninth year of the Chōḷa king Uḍaiyār Kulōttuṅga-Chōḷadēva. Records gift of eight buffalo cows for a lamp.

201. 200 *of* 1902.—(Tamil.) On a second pillar set up at the same place. A record of the Chōḷa king Parakēsarivarman *alias* Uḍaiyār Rājēndradēva (1050—63), the date of which is doubtful. Records gift of 96 sheep for a lamp.

Cuddalore (Tiruppāpuliyūr).

202. 115 *of* 1902.—(Tamil.) On the south wall of the Pātāḷēśvara shrine. A record in the fourteenth year of the Chōḷa king Rājarāja-Rājakēsarivarman (985—1013). Records gift of 48 sheep for a lamp by a native of Vesālippāḍi.

203. 116 *of* 1902.—(Tamil.) On the same wall. A record in the eighteenth year of the Chōḷa king Madirai-koṇḍa Parakēsarivarman (905—47). Records gift of a garden.

204. 117 *of* 1902.—(Tamil.) On the same wall. A record in the sixth year of the Chōḷa king Chakravartin Vikrama-Chōḷadēva (1118—35). Records gift of money for a lamp.

205. 118 *of* 1902.—(Tamil.) On the same wall. A record in the third year of the Chōḷa king Parakēsarivarman. Records gift of land to five Brāhmaṇas.

206. 119 *of* 1902.—(Tamil.) On the same wall. A record in the third year of the Chōḷa king Rājakēsarivarman *alias* Uḍaiyār Rājamahēndradēva. Records gift of two lamps. The king's fighting with Āhavamalla is mentioned. [He was the immediate predecessor of Vīra Rājēndra I, 1063—70. Āhavamalla was the same as Sōmēśvara I, 1040—1069.]

207. 120 *of* 1902.—(Tamil.) On the same wall. A record in the eighteenth year of the Chōḷa king Madirai-koṇḍa Parakēsarivarman (905—47). Records gift of money for offerings.

208. 121 *of* 1902.—(Tamil.) On the north wall of the same shrine. A record in the thirty-fifth year of the Chōḷa king Rājakēsarivarman *alias* Chakravartin Kulōttuṅga-Chōḷadēva (I ?). Records gift of land.

209. 122 *of* 1902.—(Tamil.) On the same wall. A record in the seventh year of the Chōḷa king Chakravartin Vikrama-Chōḷadēva (1118—35). Records gift of money for a lamp.

210. 123 *of* 1902.—(Tamil.) On the same wall. An incomplete record of the Chōḷa king Parakēsarivarman *alias* Tribhuvanachakravartin Vikrama-Chōḷadēva (1118—35), the date of which is lost.

211. 124 *of* 1902.—(Tamil.) On the same wall. A record of the Chōḷa king Parakēsarivarman *alias* Uḍaiyār Rājēndra-Chōḷadēva (1011—53), the date of which is doubtful. Records sale of land.

212. 125 *of* 1902.—(Tamil.) On the same wall. A fragment of record of the Chōḷa king Parakēsarivarman *alias* Uḍaiyār Rājēndra-Chōḷadēva (1011—53) in his fifth year.

213. 126 *of* 1902.—(Tamil.) On the same wall. A record in the third year of the Chōḷa king Chakravartin Kulōttuṅga-Chōḷadēva. Records gift of money for a lamp.

214. 127 *of* 1902.—(Tamil.) On the same wall. A record in the ninth year of the Chōḷa king Kulōttuṅga-Chōḷadēva. Records gift of a lamp.

215. 128 *of* 1902.—(Tamil.) On the west wall of the same shrine. A record in the forty-ninth year of the Chōḷa king Kulōttuṅga-Chōḷadēva (I, 1070—1118). Partially built in.

216. 129 *of* 1902.—(Tamil verse.) On the same wall. A record in the forty-first year of the Chōḷa king Kulōttuṅga-Chōḷadēva (I, 1070—1118). Records gift of land.

217. 130 *of* 1902.—(Tamil.) On the same wall. A record in the fourth year of the Chōḷa king Rājakēsarivarman. Records gift of sheep for a lamp.

218. 131 *of* 1902.—(Tamil.) On the west wall of the Pātālīśvara shrine. A record of the Chōḷa king Rājēndra-Chōḷa (I, 1011—53), the date of which is lost. Partially built in.

219. 132 *of* 1902.—(Tamil.) On the same wall. A record in the fifth year of the Chōḷa king Rājakēsarivarman *alias* Uḍaiyār Vīrarājēndradēva (evidently the first king of this name). Records gift of a lamp.

220. 133 *of* 1902.—(Tamil.) On the same wall. A record in the fifth year of the Chōḷa king Rājakēsarivarman *alias* Uḍaiyār Vīrarājēndradēva. Records gift of paddy. See the previous inscription.

221. 134 *of* 1902.—(Tamil.) On the south wall of the maṇṭapa, in front of the same shrine. An incomplete record of the Vijayanagara king Vīra-Viruppaṇa in Pramōda. Records gift of land. Mentions the Pushpagiri-maṭha. [This is a branch of the Śaṅkarāchārya maṭha which, according to tradition, came into existence in the time of Vidyāraṇya.]

222. 135 *of* 1902.—(Tamil.) On the base of the verandah of the first prākāra of the same temple. A record of the Pāṇḍya king Perumāḷ Vikrama-Pāṇḍyadēva in his third, fourth and fifth years, i.e., 1285, 1286 and 1287. Records that the king assigned to the temple certain land which had been wrongfully taken possession of by the Brāhmaṇas. Mentions king Peruñjiṅga. See S.A. Nos. 68, 157, etc.

Tirthanagari.

[For the legendary origin of the place. See *S.A. Gazr.*, 317–8.]

223. 155 *of* 1904.—(Tamil verse.) On the south wall of the central shrine in the Śivāṅkurēśvara temple. Mentions Kāḍavarkōn and records a remission of taxes. [The king might be Kōpperuñjiṅga or his father who are called by the Government Epigraphist Kāḍava II and Kāḍava I respectively. See *Ep. Rep.*, 1913, pp. 126–7.]

224. 116 *of* 1904.—(Tamil.) On the west and south walls of the same shrine. A record in the fifteenth year of the Chōḷa king Parakēsarivarman *alias* Tribhuvanachakravartin Kulōttuṅga Chōḷadēva III (1178—1216) who took Madura and the crowned head of the Pāṇḍya. Records gift of land.

225. 117 *of* 1904.—(Tamil.) On the north wall of the same shrine. An incomplete record in the ninth year of the Pallava king Sakalabhuvanachakravartin Kōpperuñjiṅgadēva. Records gift of land. See *Ep. Ind.*, Vol. VII, p. 165.

226. 118 *of* 1904.—(Tamil.) On the south base of the same shrine. An incomplete record in the twenty-first year of the Chōḷa king Tribhuvanachakravartin Kulōttuṅga-Chōḷadēva III "who took Madura, Ceylon and the crowned head of the Pāṇḍya".

227. 119 *of* 1904.—(Tamil.) On the north base of the same shrine. A record in the twenty-second year of the Pallava king Kōpperuñjiṅgadēva. Records gift of taxes to the temple.

228. 120 *of* 1904.—(Grantha.) On the south wall of the maṇṭapa in front of the same shrine. An incomplete record. Contains a number of *birudas*, apparently of some Pāṇḍya king.

229. 121 *of* 1904.—(Tamil.) On the same wall. An incomplete record in the ninth year of the Pāṇḍya king Māravarman Tribhuvanachakravartin Vīra-Pāṇḍyadēva. Records gift of taxes for the celebration of twelve festivals commencing with the festival of Tirunāvukkaraśudēvar. [Appar or Tirunāvukkaraśar was the elder contemporary of Gñānasambanda, and so belonged to the middle of the seventh century. For Vīra Pāṇḍya see S.A. 71. Appar and the three other Śaiva Āchāryas are represented in local carvings. See *S.A. Gazr.*, p. 318.]

230. 122 *of* 1904.—(Tamil.) On the east wall of the same maṇṭapa. An incomplete record in the ninth year of the Pāṇḍya king Maravarman Tribhuvanachakravartin Vīra-Pāṇḍyadēva. Records gift of land. See S.A. 71 for the identification of the king.

231. 123 *of* 1904.—(Tamil.) On the same wall. A record in the sixteenth year of the Pāṇḍya king Tribhuvanachakravartin Kōnērimēlkoṇḍān Sundara-Pāṇḍyadēva. Records gift of land for the festival called Kōdaṇḍarāman-śandi after the king.

232. 124 *of* 1904.—(Tamil.) On the same wall. A record in the fourth year of the Pāṇḍya king Kōnērimēlkoṇḍān Tribhuvana-chakravartin Vikrama-Pāṇḍyadēva. Records gift of land. [For a discussion of the date see *Ep. Ind.*, Vol. VIII, p. 282. Kielhorn would fix it on Sunday, 15th February, 1405. He says that it can be inferred that the king began to rule between January 10 and July 27, A.D. 1401.]

233. 125 *of* 1904.—(Tamil.) On the south base of the same maṇṭapa. A record of the Vijayanagara king Vīrapratāpa Kṛisahṇadēvarāya Mahārāya in Ś. 1439, Īśvara. Built in the middle and in several places. Refers to the king's conquests and mentions a large number of temples which benefited by his remission of 10,000 varāhas. In the same place is a small inscription which calls the maṇṭapa Aiyyan-Ankakkaran-tirumaṇṭapam. See S.A. 163 (at Sēndamaṅgalam).

234. 126 *of* 1904.—(Tamil verse.) On the door post of the gōpura of the first prākāra of the same temple. A complete copy of No. 114.

235. 127 *of* 1904.—(Grantha and Tamil.) On the south wall of Vighnēśvara shrine in the same temple. A mutilated record in the fourteenth year of the Pāṇḍya king Jaṭāvarman Tribhuvanachakravartin Sundara-Pāṇḍyadēva I (1251—64). Begins with *samasta-jagadādhāra*, etc.

235-A. West of Dakshiṇāmūrti shrine. Records that Kōnērinmaikoṇḍān granted in his third year 50 vēlis of land in Kulōttuṅga-chōḷanallūr to the deity. *Ins., S. Dts.*, p. 220, No. 51.

235-B. On the north wall of the Mahāmaṇṭapa. Records that Kōpperuñjiṅgadēva granted in the twentieth year of his reign the village of Śennadanallur. *Ibid.* No. 52.

Tiruchchōpuram.

236. 109 *of* 1904.—(Tamil.) On the south wall of the central shrine in the Maṅgaḷapurīśvara temple. A record in the fourteenth year of the Pāṇḍya king Tribhuvanachakravartin Kōnērimēl-koṇḍān Sundara-Pāṇḍyadēva. Records gift of land for the requirements of a festival called Sundara-Pāṇḍiyan-śandi.

237. 110 *of* 1904.—(Grantha and Tamil.) On the south wall of the same shrine. A record in the seventh year of the Pāṇḍya king Vikrama-Pāṇḍya. Records gift of land. [As the inscription begins with *Samastabhuvanaikavira*, etc., the king should be Māravarman Vikrama-Pāṇḍya who came to the throne in 1283 and whose greatness is evidenced in previous records.]

238. 111 *of* 1904.—(Tamil.) On the east base of the central shrine in the same temple. A record of the Chōḷa king Tribhuvana-chakravartin Rājarājadēva, the date of which is lost. Built in the middle. A portion of the inscription is negative and reads from right to left.

239. 112 *of* 1904.—(Tamil.) On the north base of the same shrine. A record in the third year of the Pāṇḍya king Jaṭāvarman *alias* Tribhuvanachakravartin Vikrama-Pāṇḍyadēva. Records gift of land. [Is this the same as the king referred to in S.A. 232 ?]

240. 113 *of* 1914.—(Tamil.) On stray stones in the roof of the maṇṭapa in front of the same shrine. A mutilated record of the Pāṇḍya king Jaṭāvarman Tribhuvanachakravartin Sundara-Pāṇḍyadēva I the date of which is lost. The donor was a certain Sariputtira-Paṇḍita. Mentions the Śaṅgattār (i.e., perhaps the Buddhist samgha). [The Buddhist Sāriputta who was the contemporary of Gñāna-Sambaṇḍa was of course a much earlier person.]

241. 114 *of* 1904.—(Tamil verse.) On both sides of the entrance into the first prākāra of the same temple. A damaged record. Records that a Toṇḍaimān presented to the Chōḷa king his crown. Records gift of land in Tondaimān nallūr. [Who was this Toṇḍaimān ?]

Tirukanṭhēśvaram.

242. 128 *of* 1904.—(Tamil.) On the east wall of the central shrine in the Naṭanapādēśvara temple. A record in the forty-fourth year of the Chōḷa king Chakravartin Kulōttuṅga-Chōḷadēva. Records gift of money for a lamp. [The king apparently is Kulōttuṅga I who alone had such a long reign. 1070—1118.]

243. 129 *of* 1904.—(Tamil.) On the same wall. A record in the forty-fourth year of the Chōḷa king Chakravartin Kulōttuṅga-Chōḷadēva. Records gift of money for a lamp. See note to the above inscription.

244. 130 *of* 1904.—(Tamil.) On the same wall. A record in the eleventh year of the Chōḷa king Vikrama-Chōḷadēva (1118—35). Records gift of a lamp.

245. 131 *of* 1904.—(Tamil.) On the same wall. A record in the forty-fourth year of the Chōḷa king Chakravartin Kulōttuṅga-Chōḷadēva. Records gift of money for a lamp. See S.A. 242.

246. 132 *of* 1904.—(Tamil.) On the same wall. A record in the forty-fourth year of the Chōḷa king Chakravartin Kulōttuṅga-Chōladēva. Records gift of money for a lamp. See S.A. 242.

247. 133 *of* 1904.—(Tamil.) On the south wall of the same shrine. An incomplete record in the fourteenth year of the Chōḷa king Rājakēsarivarman *alias* Chakaravartin Kulōttuṅga-Chōḷadēva. Records gift of land to provide for the requirements of the shrine of Dakshiṇāmūrti. [The king referred to here might be the same as Kulōttuṅga I, 1070—1118.]

248. 134 *of* 1904.—(Tamil.) On the same wall. A record in the ninth year of the Chōḷa king Parakēsarivarman *alias* Uḍaiyār Rājēndradēva (1050—63). Records gift of gold for a lamp.

249. 135 *of* 1904.—(Tamil verse.) On the same wall. Records gift of gold for a lamp.

250. 136 *of* 1904.—(Tamil.) On the north wall of the same shrine. A record in the forty-eighth year of the Chōḷa king Kulōttuṅga-Chōḷadēva (I, 1070—1118). Records gift of 96 sheep for a lamp.

251. 137 *of* 1904.—(Tamil.) On the same wall. A record in the forty-eighth year of the Chōḷa king Chakravartin Kulōttuṅga-Chōḷadēva (I, 1070—1118). Records gift of money for a lamp.

252. 138 *of* 1904.—(Tamil.) On the same wall. A record in the forty-sixth year of the Chōḷa king Kulōttuṅga-Chōḷadēva (I, 1070—1118). Records gift of money for a lamp.

253. 139 *of* 1904.—(Tamil.) On the same wall. A record in the forty-ninth year of the Chōḷa king Chakravartin Kulōttuṅga-Chōḷadēva (I, 1070—1118). Records gift of two lamps.

254. 140 *of* 1904.—(Tamil.) On the same wall. A record in the forty-fourth year of the Chōḷa king Chakravartin Kulōttuṅga-Chōḷadēva I. Records gift of money for a lamp.

255. 141 *of* 1904.—(Tamil.) On the same wall. A record in the forty-fourth year of the Chōḷa king Chakravartin Kulōttuṅga-Chōḷadēva (I, 1070—1118). Mentions Ādirāyamaṅgalyapuram. Records gift of money for a lamp.

256. 142 *of* 1904.—(Tamil.) On the east base of the same shrine. A record in the forty-ninth year of the Chōḷa king Chakravartin Kulōttuṅga-Chōḷadēva (I, 1070—1118). Records gift of money for a lamp. Two fragments of Kulōttuṅga's inscriptions are also found on this base.

257. 143 *of* 1904.—(Tamil.) On the east and north bases of the same shrine. A record in the twenty-ninth year of the Chōḷa king Kulōttuṅga-Chōḷadēva. Records gift of money for four lamps.

258. 144 *of* 1904.—(Tamil.) On the south base of the same shrine. A record in the forty-second year of the Chōḷa king Chakravartin Kulōttuṅga-Chōḷadēva (I, 1070—1118). Records gift of 50 sheep for a half lamp.

259. 145 *of* 1904.—(Tamil.) On the north base of the same shrine. A mutilated record in the eleventh year of the Chōḷa king Vikrama Chōḷadēva (1118—35).

260. 146 *of* 1904.—(Tamil.) On the same base. A record in the twelfth year of the Chōḷa king Vikrama Chōḷadēva (1118—35). Records gift of money for a lamp.

261. 147 *of* 1904.—(Tamil.) On the same base. A record in the twelfth year of the Chōḷa king Vikrama-Chōḷadēva (1118—35). Records gift of a lamp.

262. 148 *of* 1904.—(Tamil.) On the same base. A record in the thirty-eighth year of the Chōḷa king Kulōttuṅga-Chōḷadēva (I ?). Records gift of money for a lamp.

263. 149 *of* 1904.—(Tamil.) On the south wall of the maṇṭapa in front of the same shrine. A record in the fourth year of Tribhuvanachakravartin Kōnērinmaikoṇḍān. Records a remission of taxes in favour of the temple.

264. 150 *of* 1904.—(Tamil.) On the same wall. A record in the fourteenth year of Tribhuvanachakravartin Kōnērinmaikoṇḍān. Records gift of land from the income of which provision had to be made for offerings, etc., to the image of Kōyil-ponmēynda-Perumāḷ set up at Tiruvayīndirapuram (Tiruvēndipuram) and for celebrating at the temple of Dēvanāyaka-Perumāḷ, a festival called Sundara-Pāṇḍyan-śandi after the king. [Tiruvēndipuram was the birthplace of Vēdānta Dēśika. For his life and labours—see my article in Bo. J.R.A.S., 1915-16, pp. 276—312.]

265. 151 *of* 1904.—(Tamil.) On the same wall. A record in the fourteenth year of the Pāṇḍya king Jaṭāvarman *alias* Tribhuvanachakravartin Sundara Pāṇḍyadēva (I ? 1251—64). Records gift of land for celebrating a festival called Paḷiyilpugaḷāḷan-śandi.

Tirumāṇikuḻi.

This place which is referred to in the *Dēvāram* and in inscriptions as Udavi Tirumāṇikuḻi was included in Rājarājavaḷanāḍu, Mērkā-nāḍu, Vaḍakarai Rājēndrachōḷavaḷanāḍu or Virudarājubhayaṅkara-valanādu. Vishṇu, in his Vāmanāvatāra, is said to have worshipped here with a gem.

266. 148 *of* 1902.—(Tamil.) On the west wall of the Vāmana-purīśvara shrine. A record in the eleventh year of the Chōḷa king Parakēsarivarman *alias* Tribhuvanachakravartin Vikrama-Chōḷa-dēva (1118—35). Records gift of land. Mentions Kulōttuṅga-Chōḷa-dēva. See *Ep. Ind.* VII, pp. 170-1, where Dr. Kielhorn points out that the exact date was Wednesday, 19th December, A.D. 1128.

267. 149 *of* 1902.—(Tamil.) On the north wall of the same shrine. A record of the Chōḷa king Parakēsarivarman *alias* Tribhuvanachakravartin Vikrama-Chōḷadēva (1118—35), the date of which is lost. Partially built in.

268. 150 *of* 1902.—(Tamil.) On the south wall of the maṇṭapa in front of the same shrine. A record in the third year of the Chōḷa king Parakēsarivarman *alias* Tribhuvanachakravartin Vikrama-Chōḷadēva (1118—35). Records gift of land.

269. 151 *of* 1902.—(Tamil.) On the same wall. A record in the fourth year of the Chōḷa king Parakēsarivarman *alias* Tribhuvanachakravartin Vikrama-Chōḷadēva (1118—35). Records gift of money for two lamps.

270. 152 *of* 1902.—(Tamil.) On the same wall. A record in the forty-second year of the Chōḷa king Rājakēsarivarman *alias*

Tribhuvanachakravartin Kulōttuṅga Chōḷadēva. Records sale of land.

271. 153 *of* 1902.—(Tamil.) On the same wall. A record of the Vijayanagara king Dēvarāya II in Ś. 1357, Naḷa. Records gift of land. Engraved over an inscription of Kulōttuṅga III.

272. 154 *of* 1902.—(Tamil.) On the same wall. A record in the thirty-fourth year of the Chōḷa king Kulōttuṅga-Chōḷadēva. Records gift of a lamp.

273. 155 *of* 1902.—(Tamil.) On the same wall. A record in the eighth year of the Chōḷa king Rājakēsarivarman *alias* Tribhuvanachakravartin Kulōttuṅga-Chōḷadēva. Records gift of land. Mentions Vikrama-Chōḷa. (A damaged record.)

274. 156 *of* 1902.—(Tamil.) On the north wall of the same maṇṭapa. A record in the thirty-fifth year of the Chōḷa king Kulōttuṅga-Chōḷadēva. Records gift of two lamps to Sūryadēva and Kshētrapāla (i.e., Bhairava).

275. 157 *of* 1902.—(Tamil.) On the same wall. A record in the third year of the Chōḷa king Tribhuvanachakravartin Kulōttuṅga-Chōḷadēva. Records gift of land.

276. 158 *of* 1902.—(Tamil.) On the same wall. A record in the sixth year of the Chōḷa king Parakēsarivarman *alias* Tribhuvanachakravartin Vikrama-Chōḷadēva (1118—35). Records gift of twelve sheep for a lamp.

277. 159 *of* 1902.—(Tamil.) On the same wall. An incomplete record in the thirteenth year of the Chōḷa king Parakēsarivarman *alias* Tribhuvanachakravartin Vikrama-Chōḷadēva (1118—35).

278. 160 *of* 1902.—(Tamil.) On the same wall. A record in the forty-ninth year of the Chōḷa king Rājakēsarivarman *alias* Tribhuvanachakravartin Kulōttuṅga-Chōḷadēva (I, 1070—1118). Records sale of land.

279. 161 *of* 1902.—(Tamil.) On the east wall of the same maṇṭapa, right of entrance. A record in the nineteenth year of the Chōḷa king Tribhuvanachakravartin Kulōttuṅga-Chōḷadēva III, who took Madura and the crowned head of the Pāṇḍya. Records gift of a golden girdle by an Adiyamān. The date corresponded to Wednesday, 30th April, A.D. 1197. See *Ep. Ind.*, Vol. VII, p. 173.

280. 162 *of* 1902.—(Tamil.) On the same wall. An incomplete record in the fifteenth year of the Chōḷa king Tribhuvanachakravartin Rājarājadēva.

281. 163 *of* 1902.—(Tamil.) On the same wall, left of entrance. A record in the twelfth year of the Chōḷa king Parakēsarivarman *alias* Tribhuvanachakravartin Vikrama-Chōḷadēva (1118—35). Records that the king, while in his palace at Chidambaram, made gift of a land to an image which he had set up at Tirumāṇikuḷi.

282. 164 *of* 1902.—(Tamil.) On the east wall of the prākāra of the same temple, right of entrance. A record in the seventh year of the Chōḷa king Tribhuvanachakravartin Vīrarājēndra-Chōḷa-dēva. Records gift of four cows for a lamp. Dr. Kielhorn points out that if the king referred to is Rājēndra-Chōḷa III, the date is incorrect, but that if he is Kulōttuṅga III, it would be Wednesday, 22nd August, A.D. 1184. See *Ep. Ind.*, Vol. VII, p. 172.

283. 165 *of* 1902.—(Tamil.) On the same wall. A record in the third year of the Chōḷa king Parakēsarivarman *alias* Tribhuvana-chakravartin Kulōttuṅga-Chōḷadēva (III). Records gift of thirty-two cows for a lamp by a native of Kūḍal (Cuddalore). See *Ep. Ind.*, Vol. VII, p. 171, where Kielhorn calculates the date to be the 12th August 1180.

284. 166 of 1902.—(Grantha and Tamil.) On the same wall. A record in the fifth and sixth years of the Pāṇḍyā king Vikrama-Pāṇḍyadēva (?). Records gift of land by the king for offerings on his birthday.

285. 167 *of* 1902.—(Tamil.) On the same wall, left of entrance. A record in the fifth year of the Chōḷa king Tribhuvanachakravartin Rājarājadēva. Records gift of a buffalo cow and her calf by a Paraiyan.

286. 168 *of* 1902.—(Tamil.) On the same wall, left of entrance. A record in the fifth year of Tribhuvanachakravartin Kōnērin-maikoṇḍan. Records gift of land.

287. 169 of 1902.—(Tamil.) On the west wall of the same prākāra. A record in the twenty-first year of the Chōḷa king Tribhuvanachakravartin Kulōttuṅga Chōḷadēva (III), who took Madura, Ceylon and the crowned head of the Pāṇḍya. Records gift of land. The date corresponded to Wednesday, 7th April, A.D. 1199. See *Ep. Ind.*, Vol. VII, p. 174.

288. 170 of 1902.—(Tamil.) On the west wall of the prākāra of the Vāmanapurīśvara temple. A record in the twenty-first year of the Chōḷa king Parakēsarivarman *alias* Tribhuvanachakravartin Kulōttuṅga Chōḷadēva (III), who took Madura, Ceylon and the crowned head of the Pāṇḍya. Records gift of land. See *Ep. Ind.*, Vol. VII, p. 174, where Dr. Kielhorn discusses the date. He corrects *Rishabha* into *Mēsha* and then calculates the date to be Saturday, 10th April, A.D. 1199.

Tiruvaḍi.

289. 28 *of* 1903.—(Tamil.) On the left of the entrance into the Śaranārāyaṇa-Perumāḷ temple. A record in the sixteenth year of the Rāshṭrakūṭa king Kaṇṇaradēva (Krishṇa III). Records gift of 96 sheep for a lamp by a certain Rājāditta-Pallavaraiyar. [The last-mentioned chief had the name Rājāditta evidently from the Chōḷa king who was defeated and slain by Bhūtuga in the battle of Takkōlam. See N.A. 3, 44, 241, etc.

290. 29 *of* 1903.—(Tamil.) On the right of the entrance into the same temple. A record in the fortieth year of the Chōḷa king Rājakēsarivarman *alias* Tribhuvanachakravartin Kulōttuṅga-Chōḷadēva. Records gift of gold for half a lamp. [The king must be Kulōttuṅga I, 1070—1118.]

291. 30 *of* 1903.—(Tamil.) On a pillar of the maṇṭapa in front of the same temple. A record in the seventh year of the Chōḷa king Parakēsarivarman *alias* Tribhuvanachakravartin Vikrama-Chōḷadēva (1118—35). Records gift of land by a merchant. Kielhōrn says that the English equivalent of the date is Thursday, 7th August, A.D. 1124. See *Ep. Ind.*, Vol. VIII, pp. 1-2.

292. 31 *of* 1903.—(Tamil.) On the another pillar of the same maṇṭapa. An incomplete record in the sixth year of the Chōḷa king Parakēsarivarman *alias* Tribhuvanachakravartin Vikrama-Chōḷadēva (1118—35). Records gift of land.

293. 32 *of* 1903.—(Tamil.) On a third pillar of the same maṇṭapa. A record in the fourth year of the Chōḷa king Parakēsarivarman *alias* Tribhuvanachakravartin Vikrama-Chōḷadēva (1118—35). Beginning lost. Records gift of land.

294. 33 *of* 1903.—(Tamil.) On a fourth pillar of the same maṇṭapa. An incomplete record of the Chōḷa king Parakēsarivarman *alias* Rājēndra-Chōḷadēva (1011—43), the date of which is lost.

295. 34 *of* 1903.—(Grantha and Tamil.) On the south wall of the central shrine in the Virattānēśvara temple in the same village. A record of the Kēraḷa king Ravivarma-Mahārāja *alias* Kula-śēkharadēva in his fourth year; Kali 4414; Ś. 1235, corresponding, according to Prof. Kielhorn, to Saturday, December 29th, A.D. 1313. Records that the king had the whole temple washed. [See *Ep. Ind.*, Vol. IV, p. 146 and *Ep. Ind.*, Vol. VIII, pp. 8-9. Dr. Hultzsch points out that in the Aruḷāla Perumāl inscription (see *Ep. Ind.*, Vol. IV., p. 147), the king is said to have stayed at Kāñchi in his fourth year; and the present inscription which is dated in the same year gives the information that it was A.D. 1313.]

296. 35 *of* 1903.—(Tamil.) On the left of the entrance into the same shrine. A record in the sixteenth year of the 'Gaṅga-Pallava' king Nripatuṅga. Records that a chief of Munai repaired the temple and gave gold for a lamp. See *Ep. Ind.*, Vol. VII, p. 196. [Prof. Dubreuil fixes Nripatuṅga's date to be A.D. 854—880.]

297. 36 *of* 1903.—(Tamil.) On the right of the entrance into the same shrine. A record of the Pallava king Nandipōttaraiyar who was victorious at Teḷḷaru. Records gift of gold for a lamp by the king. [This inscription gives a clue to the date of the Poet

Perundēvanār, the author of the Bhāratavenbā, who was patronised by the king who won the battle of Teḷḷāru. This was the same as Nandivarman III, the hero of the Nandikkalambagam.

298. 37 *of* 1903.—(Tamil.) On the northern entrance into the maṇṭapa in front of the central shrine in the same temple. A record in the thirty-second year of the Chōḷa king Rājakēsarivarman *alias* Chakravartin Kulōttuṅga-Chōḷadēva (unidentified). Records gift of 96 sheep for a lamp.

299. 38 *of* 1903.—(Tamil.) In the same place. A record in the thirty-second year of the Chōḷa king Rājakēsarivarman *alias* Chakravartin Kulōttuṅga-Chōḷadēva. Records gift of 192 sheep for two lamps by a merchant.

300. 39 *of* 1903.—(Tamil.) In the same place. An incomplete record in the thirty-first year of the Chōḷa king Rājakēsarivarman *alias* Tribhuvanachakravartin Kulōttuṅga-Chōḷadēva.

301. 40 *of* 1903.—(Tamil.) On the eastern entrance into the same maṇṭapa. Records in the tenth year ; gift of land by Kāḷiṅgaraiyan.

302. 41 *of* 1903.—(Tamil.) On the southern entrance into the same maṇṭapa. A record in the eighth year of the Pāṇḍya king Vīra-Pāṇḍyadēva. Records gift of land. [The king cannot be identified. It might be Māravarman Vīra Pāṇḍya referred to in *S.A.* 71.]

303. 42 *of* 1903.—(Tamil.) On a pillar in the same maṇṭapa. A record in the twenty-third year of the Chōḷa king Parakēsarivarman *alias* Uḍaiyār Rājēndra-Chōḷadēva (I, 1011—53). Beginning lost. Records gift of land.

304. 43 *of* 1903.—(Tamil.) On the north wall of the kitchen in the same temple. A record in the twenty-ninth year of the Chōḷa king Tribhuvanachakravartin Kulōttuṅga-Chōḷadēva (unidentified). Records gift of fifty cows by Kāḍavarāyar. [Was it Kōpperuñjiṅga who had that title ? If so, the king *might* be Kulottuṅga III. See *S.A.* 223 and *N.A.* 224.]

305. 44 *of* 1903.—(Tamil.) On the same wall. A record in the sixteenth year of the Pallava king Sakalabhuvanachakravartin Kōpperuñjiṅgadēva. Records gift of thirty-two cows and one bull for a lamp.

306. 45 *of* 1903.—(Tamil.) On the same wall. A record in the twelfth year of the Chōḷa king Rājakēsarivarman *alias* Tribhuvanachakravartin Kulōttuṅga-Chōḷadēva (I or II ?). Records gift of land by Kulōttuṅga-Chōḷa-Kachchiyarāyan.

307. 46 *of* 1903.—(Tamil.) On the same wall. An incomplete record in the thirteenth year of the Chōḷa king Rājakēsarivarman *alias* Tribhuvanachakravartin Kulōttuṅga-Chōḷadēva. Mentions Kulōttuṅga-Chōḷa-Kāḍavarāyan. See S.A. 304 above.

308. 47 *(a) of* 1903.—(Tamil.) On the west wall of the same kitchen. A record of the Chōḷa king Rājakēsarivarman *alias* Tribhuvanachakravartin Kulōttuṅga-Chōḷadēva, the date of which is lost. Records gift of ninety-six sheep for a lamp.

309. 47 *(b) of* 1903.—(Tamil.) On the same wall. A mutilated record in the eighth year of the Chōḷa king Rājādhirājadēva (II, 1171—86). Mentions Jananātha Kachchiyarāyan.

310. 48 *of* 1903.—(Tamil.) On the same wall. A record in the forty-fourth year of the Chōḷa king Rājakēsarivarman *alias* Chakravartin Kulōttuṅga-Chōḷadēva. Records gift of ninety-six sheep for a lamp.

311. 49 *of* 1903.—(Tamil.) On the south wall of the first prākāra of the same temple. A record in the forty-fourth year of the Chōḷa king Rājakēsarivarman *alias* Tribhuvanachakravartin Kulōttuṅga-Chōḷadēva (I, 1070—1118). Records gift of land to a maṭha of Vāgīsa (i.e., Tirunāvukkaraiyar). The king referred to is evidently Kulōttuṅga I which raises the presumption that the king referred to in the preceding inscriptions is he.

312. 50 *of* 1903.—(Tamil.) On the same wall. A record in the third year of the Pallava king Sakalabhuvanachakravartin Kōpperuñjiṅgadēva. Records gift of thirty-nine cows and one bull for a lamp.

313. 51 *of* 1903.—(Tamil.) On the same wall. A record in the fifth year of Tribhuvanachakravartin Kōnērinmaikoṇḍān. Records gift of land.

314. 52 *of* 1903.—(Tamil.) On the same wall. A record in the third year of the Pāṇḍya king Māravarman *alias* Tribhuvanachakravartin Vikrama-Pāṇḍyadēva (1283—?). Records gift of land. See S.A. 68.

315. 53 *of* 1903.—(Tamil.) On the same wall. A damaged record.

316. 54 of 1903.—(Tamil.) On the same wall. A record in the thirteenth-year of the Chōḷa king Tribhuvanachakravartin Kulōttuṅga-Chōḷadēva. Records gift of ornaments by Kāḍavarāyan. See S.A. 304 and 307.

317. 55 *of* 1903.—(Tamil.) On a pillar of the western side of the verandah close to the same prākāra. A record in the forty-sixth year of the Chōḷa king Rājakēsarivarman *alias* Tribhuvanachakravartin Kulōttuṅga-Chōḷadēva (I, 1070—1118). Beginning lost. Records gift of land.

318. 56 *of* 1903.—(Tamil.) On a slab lying in front of the inner gōpura of the same temple. A record in the third year of the Pallava king Paramēśvara Pōttaraiyar. Records gift of gold. [Was he the Pallava Paramēśvaravarman I or II? We have no evidences to say.]

319. 57 *of* 1903.—(Tamil.) On the same gōpura. A record in the fourteenth year of the Pāṇḍya king Māravarman *alias* Tribhuvanachakravartin Vīra-Pāṇḍyadēva. Records gift of land for two lamps. See *Ep. Ind.*, Vol. VIII, p. 283, where Dr. Kielhorn discusses the date and concludes that it is Saturday, 12th March, 1457, and infers that the king should have begun to reign between 13th March and 28th July 1443.

320. 58 *of* 1903.—(Tamil.) On the same gōpura. A record in the fourth year of the Pāṇḍya king Māravarman *alias* Tribhuvanachakravartin Vikrama-Pāṇḍyadēva. Settles the order in which the dancing girls have to dance before the god. [This is evidently the king who ascended the throne in 1283 and who conquered the Kākatiya and others. See S.A. 68.]

321. 59 *of* 1903.—(Tamil.) On the inner gōpura of the same temple. A record of the Pallava king Sakalabhuvanachakravartin Kopperuñjiṅgadeva. Records gift of land.

322. 60 *of* 1903.—(Tamil.) On a slab lying in the Raṅganātha-Perumāḷ temple in the same village. A damaged record of the Chōḷa king Rājakēsarivarman *alias* Uḍaiyār Rājēndra-Chōḷadēva, (II or Kulōttuṅga I, 1070—1118) the date of which is lost.

Tiruvēndipuram.

323. 136 *of* 1902.—(Tamil.) On the north wall of the maṇṭapa in front of the Dēvanāyaka Perumāḷ shrine. A record in the twenty-third year of the Chōḷa king Tribhuvanachakravartin Kulōttuṅga-Chōḷadeva (I?). Records gift of land at the request of prince (piḷḷaiyār) Vishṇuvardhana Mahārāja (evidently one of the sons of the king who got his name owing to the E. Chāḷukyan connection).

324. 137 *of* 1902.—(Tamil.) On the north wall of the prākāra of the same temple. A record in the tenth year of the Pāṇḍya king Jaṭāvarman *alias* Tribhuvanachakravartin Sundara-Pāṇḍyadēva (III), corresponding to Monday, 23rd July, A.D. 1285. Confirms gifts of land to the temple, which had been made by Sundara-Pāṇḍya I, Vikrama-Pāṇḍya and Vīra-Pāṇḍya. *Ep. Ind.*, Vol. VIII, p. 278–9.

325. 138 *of* 1902.—(Tamil.) On the same wall. A record in the forty-first year of the Chōḷa king Tribhuvanachakravartin Kulōttuṅga-Chōḷadēva (I ?). Records gift of twelve sheep for a lamp.

326. 139 *of* 1902.—(Tamil.) On the same wall. A record in the fiftieth year of the Chōḷa king Chakravartin Kulōttuṅga-Chōḷadēva (I). Records gift of sheep for a lamp.

327. 140 *of* 1902.—(Tamil.) On the same wall. A record in the fifth year of the Chōḷa king Tribhuvanachakravartin

Vikrama-Chōḷadēva [1118–35]. Records gift of money for feeding Vaishṇavas. Refers to a previous gift in the thirty-fifth year of Kulōttuṅga-dēva.

328. 141 *of* 1902.—(Tamil.) On the south wall of the prākāra of the same temple. A record in the sixteenth year of the Pāṇḍya king Māravarman *alias* Tribhuvanachakravartin Sundara-Pāṇḍya-dēva. Records that the temple authorities decided to follow the system of worship practised in all other temples. [It is doubtful whether the king is the first or second of that name.]

329. 142 *of* 1902.—(Tamil.) On the west wall of the prākāra of the same temple. A record in the sixteenth year of the Chōḷa king Tribhuvanachakravartin Rājarājadēva (III 1216–48). This inscription in the Vishṇu temple contains a very interesting account of certain political disturbances which happened in Southern India in the first half of the thirteenth century. It is to the effect that in 1231–2 Peruñjiṅga captured the Chōḷa emperor at Śēndamaṅgalam and that the Hoysaḷa Vīra Narasimha (II) rescued and restored him after a victorious campaign against Peruñjiṅga, obtaining thereby the title of "Establisher of the Chōḷa kingdom." The inscription also states that Parākramabāhu, the king of Ceylon, and an ally of Peruñjiṅga lost his life in the war. As 136 of 1900 distinctly says that in 1229 Peruñjiṅga was a loyal vassal Dr. Hustzsch ascribes the present rising to between 1229 and 1232. Peruñjiṅga regained his power afterwards as No. 38 of 1890 at Conjeeveram says he ascended the throne in 1243. His epigraphs are very numerous in Tamil country, and one is as far as Drākshārama (419 of 1893) which refers to his conquests sung by himself. As for Rājarāja's relations with Narasimha (II) Dr. Hultzsch points out on the basis of the Tirugōkarṇam inscription (410 of 1902) that in 1225 the latter acknowledged the former's sovereignty. See also Ādhamān Kōṭṭai, Salem District. Also *Ep. Ind.*, Vol. VII, pp. 160–70.

330. 143 *of* 1902.—(Tamil.) On the south wall of the prākāra of the same temple. A record in the third year of the Pāṇḍya king Māravarman *alias* Tribhuvanachakravartin Vikrama-Pāṇḍya-dēva. Records sale of land. [Is he the king who ascended the throne in 1283? See S.A. 68.]

331. 144 *of* 1902.—(Tamil.) On the west wall of the Vishva-ksēna shrine in the same temple. A record in the tenth year of the Pāṇḍya king Māravarman *alias* Tribhuvanachakravartin-Vīra-Pāṇḍyadēva. Records gift of land. See the next epigraph.

332. 145 *of* 1902.—(Tamil.) On the same wall. A record in the fifteenth year of the Pāṇḍya king Māravarman *alias* Tribhuvanachakravartin Vīra-Pāṇḍyadēva (apparently the successor of Vikrama Pāṇḍya referred to in S.A. 71).

333. 146 *of* 1902.—(Tamil.) On the western gōpura of the same temple, right of entrance. Records the construction of the gōpura for the merit of Peruñjiṅgadēva.

334. 147 *of* 1902.—(Tamil verse.) In the same place, left of entrance. Refers to a king of Toṇḍai.

335. *C.P.* 18 *of Mr. Sewell's List.*—(Telugu.) Records a grant by Achyuta Rāya in Ś. 1454, K. 4633, Nandana, of the privilege of receiving the holy water and consecrated food after the worship in the temple to one Rāmānujāchāri. [Mr. Sewell says in connection with this place that he is unable to find out where it is, but any ordinary Vaishṇavite will recognize its position near Cuddalore and its importance in the history of Śri-Vaishṇavism, particularly in the time of Vēdānta Dēśika (for whose life and works see my article in *J. Bo. R.A.S.*, 1915-6, pp. 276—312).

Tyāgavalli.

335-A. In the Narttana Gaṇapati shrine in the village. Records that Sundara Pāṇḍya in the fourteenth year of his reign gave 10 *mās* of land to the deity. *Ins. S. Dts.*, p. 206, No. 42.

GINGEE TALUK.

Ālampūṇḍi.

336. The Ālampūṇḍi Plates of Virūpāksha (Granṭha and Tamil). Records that Virūpāksha I, the son of Harihara II, of the first Vijiyanagara dynasty granted on the Pushya Saṅkrānti day of Ś. 1305, Raktākshin, the village of Ālampūṇḍi to certain Brāhmaṇas. [See *Antiquities*, Vol. I, p. 207; *South Arcot Manual*, p. 2; and *Ep. Ind.*, Vol. III, pp. 224—29, where Venkayya edits it.]

Dalavānūr.

337. 48 *of* 1905—(Tamil.) On the south wall of the rock-cut cave right of entrance (cf. upper cave at Trichinopoly). A damaged record.

338. 49 *of* 1905.—(Tamil.) On the pillar at the entrance into the same cave. A damaged record in the fifteenth year of the 'Gaṅga-Pallava' king Vijaya-Nandivikramavarman.

339. 50 *of* 1905.—(Tamil verse.) On one of the pillars inside the same cave. A record of the Pallava king Narēndrapōttaraiyan. Records the excavation of the cave called Śatrumallēśvarālaya. [*In. Ep. Rep.*, 1905, Venkayya points out that this king was Mahēndravarman I, who had the title Śatrumalla, and that the cave should therefore have been excavated in his reign. See *Ep. Ind.*, XII, p. 225.]

340. 51 *of* 1905.—(Sanskrit and Grantha.) On the same pillar; A record of the Pallava king Narēndra *alias* Śatrumalla.

Records the excavation of the cave called Śatrumallēsvarālaya. [See note to the above. On palæographical grounds Venkayya believed this inscription to be earlier than the above. Cf. N.A. 41 to which the present inscription bears a close resemblance in its archaic character when compared with the Trichinopoly and Pallavaram cave epigraphs. See Prof. Dubreuils *Pallavas*, p. 26. For the edition of this inscription, see *Ep. Ind.*, Vol. XII, p. 225.]

341. 52 *of* 1905.—(Tamil.) On the west wall of the central shrine in the Īśvara temple in the same village. A record of Kampaṇa-Uḍaiyār II in Śubhakrit (i.e., Ś. 1285). Records an order of Sāḷuva Maṅgudēva, issued according to a letter from Aṇṇar Goppaṇār. The village is called Talaivanallūr. [Goppaṇa was the celebrated Goppaṇa Uḍaiyār referred to in the *Guruparamparas*, in the *kōyiloḻugu*, as the conqueror of the Mahomedans and restorer of Hindu shrines. See my article on Vedānta Dēśika in *J. Bo. B.R.A.S.*, 1915-6. See also Śrīraṅgam inscription, *Ep. Ind.* VI, 324f.]

342. 53 *of* 1905.—(Grantha and Tamil.) On the south wall of the same shrine. A record of the Pāṇḍya king Vikrama-Pāṇḍya who came to the throne in 1283. Begins *Samasta-bhuvanaikavīra Chandrakula*, etc. The village is called Talaivāynallūr and was a hamlet of Rājarāja-chaturvēdimaṅgalam, a brahmadēya in Panaiyūr-nāḍu. He is said to have been the lord of Madura, the sun to the darkness of the Kēraḷa race, the submarine fire to the ocean of the Chōḷa race and the conqueror of Vīragaṇḍagōpāla and Gaṇapati. See S.A. 68.

343. 54 *of* 1905.—(Sanskrit and Grantha.) On the same wall. A record of the Pāṇḍya king Vikrama-Pāṇḍya, in Ś. 1209. Records the digging of a pond by the king's minister Jayasimha. S.A. 68, 70, etc.

344. 55 *of* 1905.—(Tamil.) On the east wall of the maṇṭapa in front of the temple. A damaged record of the Vijayanagara king Vīrapratāpa Dēvarāya-Mahārāya II in Ś. 1365 expired, Rudhirōdgārin.

Eyil (*Eyyal*).

345. 221 *of* 1906.—(Tamil.) On the north wall of the central shrine in the ruined Śiva temple on the hill. A mutilated record in Pramādin of the Vijayanagara king Vīra-Viruppaṇa-Uḍaiyār (i.e., Virūpāksha I). Records gift of land.

346. 222 *of* 1906.—(Tamil.) On the east wall of the same shrine. Records gift of land.

347. 223 *of* 1906.—(Tamil.) On the same wall. Registers the dedication of two families for maintaining twilight lamps.

348. 224 *of* 1906.—(Tamil.) On the south and east walls of the same shrine. A record in Ānanda of the Vijayanagara king

Jammaṇa-Uḍaiyār, son of Vīra-Kampaṇa-Uḍaiyār II. Records gift of land for a lamp. See S.A. 351 below.

349. 225 *of* 1906.—(Tamil.) On the same wall. Records in Raudri gift of land.

350. 226 *of* 1906.—(Tamil.) On the same walls. Mentions in Raudri the temple of Tirumaḍappērudaiyār. Records gift of land to blacksmiths, carpenters and goldsmiths.

351. 227 *of* 1906.—(Tamil.) On stones lying near the same shrine. An incomplete record in Saumya of the Vijayanagara king Jammaṇa Uḍaiyār, son of Vīra-Kumāra-Kampaṇa-Uḍaiyār II. The temple is called Tirumaḍappēruḍaiya-Nāyinār.

352. 228 *of* 1906.—(Tamil.) On the same stones. A fragmentary record of Sakalalōkachakravartin Rājanārāyaṇa Śambuvarāya, the date of which is lost. [The king came to the throne in 1337.]

353. 229 *of* 1906.—(Tamil.) On the rock to the south of the same temple. A record in the fourth year of the Chōḷa king Tribhuvanachakravartin Kulōttuṅga-Chōladēva. Records gift of money to the shrine of Vināyaka in the temple of Tirumaḍapparai Uḍaiyār at Eyil *alias* Rājēndra-Chōḷanallūr.

354. 230 *of* 1906.—(Tamil.) On a stone set up to the left of the way leading to the same hill. Refers in Plavaṅga to the foundation of a new street at Eyil.

355. 231 *of* 1906.—(Tamil.) On a rock to the south of the same village. A record in the seventh year of the Pāṇḍya king Vikrama Pāṇḍyadēva. Mentions the temple of Tiruvaṇṇāmalai-Uḍaiya-Nāyinār and Eyil. See S.A. 343.

356. 232 *of* 1906.—(Tamil.) On another rock in the same locality. Records in Īśvara gift of land. Mentions Naraśiṅgarāja-Uḍaiyār.

Gingee.

This fine hill-fortress was the seat of an important province in the Vijayanagara period as is plain from a grant of Harihara II dated in A.D. 1383. It remained in the hands of the Rāyas and the Nāiks till about 1645 when it fell into the hands of Bijapūr. Thirty years later it fell into the hands of Śivaji but was captured by the Mughals in 1698 after a celebrated siege of seven years. Its place as capital of the province was taken by Arcot; but thanks to its situation and its strength it figured largely in the Carnatic wars, being taken by the French in 1750 and by the English in 1761. The whole history is ably and succinctly summarised in the *South Arcot Gazetteer*, Garstin's *Manual*, etc. The descriptions of the three fortified hills of the place and of the antiquities therein are ample and show the historic significance of the place. A fine account of Gingee under the Vijayanagar and later rulers is contained in one of the *Mack. M.S.S.*, the *Karnāṭaka Rājas Savistāra charitra*, a summary of which is given in Taylor's Rais, Catal., Vol III. I have given ample reference to the Naik rulers of the place and their activities in my *History of the Naik Kingdom* (*Ind. Antq.* 1915). As for the history of the place under the Maharattas, Mughals and the Nawabs we have got ample materials of which the interesting ballad of Deśing Rāja deserves mention. See Duff's *History of the Mahrattas*, Orme's monumental history, *Madras Journal*, XVI, 348 f, etc. It is curious that the inscriptions of such an important place are so small in number. The department has discovered thus far two, and these are—

357. 57 *of* 1905.—(Persian.) On a slab built into the threshold of the main gate of the fort. Records in Hijra 1125 that the fort was captured by Sā adatu-u-lah Kan, A.D. 1712-3. See *S.A. Gazr., p.* 352.

358. 240 *of* 1904.—(Tamil.) On the south wall of the central shrine in the Veṅkaṭarāmasvāmin temple. A record of the Vijayanagara king Vīrapratāpa-Vīra-Sadāśivadēva-Mahārāya in Ś. 1472, Sādhāraṇa. Records gift of land by the king. The inscription also records a gift by Śūrappa-Nāyakkar for the merit of Sadāśivadēva, and another gift by Aḍappattu Mallappa Nāyakkar for festival.

359. *No.* 70 *of Mr. Sewell's List.*—(Tamil.) Records a document drawn up by Vala (Bala) Veṅkaṭapati Nāyakkan, son (or descendant) of Vala Kṛishṇappa Nāyakkan, Raja of Śenji (Jinji, Ginji), in Ś. 1386 (A.D. 1464), Kaliyuga 4565, Pārthiva, adjudicating on a religious dispute. The name of "Rāma Dēva Mahā Rāya" is mentioned as paramount sovereign.

Mēl-Śēyur (Mēl śevūr.)

360. 209 *of* 1904.—(Tamil.) On the south wall of the central shrine in the Vrishabhapurīśvara temple. A record in the twenty-seventh year of the Chōḷa king Rājakēsarivarman *alias* Uḍaiyār Rājādhirājadēva (I?). Records gift of ninety-six sheep for a lamp.

361. 210 *of* 1904.—(Tamil.) On the same wall. A record in the twenty-sixth year of the Chōḷa king Rājarājakēsarivarman *alias* Rājarājadēva (I, 985--1013). Partly built in.

362. 211 *of* 1904.—(Tamil.) On the west wall of the same shrine. A fragment of record of the Chōḷa king Rājēndra-Chōḷa (I, 1012--53) the date of which is lost.

363. 212 *of* 1904.—(Tamil.) On the north wall of the same shrine. A record in the twenty-third year of the Chōḷa king Rājarājakēsarivarman *alias* Rājarājadēva (I). Registers allotments of paddy to certain temple servants.

364. 213 *of* 1904.—(Tamil.) On the same wall. An incomplete record in the twenty-fourth year of the Chōḷa king Rājarāja-Rājakēsarivarman *alias* Rājarājadēva (I). Records gift of two lamp

365. 214 *of* 1904.—(Tamil.) On the north and west walls of the same shrine. A damaged record in the tenth year of the Chōḷa king Parakēsarivarman *alias* Uḍaiyār Rājēndradēva (1050—63?). Records gift of a lamp.

366. 215 *of* 1904.—(Tamil.) On the south base of the same shrine. A damaged record in the second year of the Chōḷa king Parakēsarivarman. Records gift of a lamp.

367. 216 *of* 1904.—(Tamil.) On the south wall of the maṇṭapa in front of the same shrine. A record in the twenty-second year of the Chōla king Rājarājakēsarivarman *alias* Rājarājadēva (I). Records that an individual belonging to the regiment Jananāthat-teriñjavalaṅgai-vēlaikkārar, set up an image of the goddess Umā-Bhaṭṭāraki. For another division of the Vēḷaikkārar see S.A. 81.

368. 217 *of* 1904.—(Tamil.) On the south base of the same maṇṭapa. A record in the twenty-first year of the Chōla king Madiraikoṇḍa-Parakēsarivarman (905—47). Built in the middle. Records gift of sheep for a lamp.

369. 218 *of* 1904.—(Tamil.) On the same base. A record in the thirty-seventh year of the Chōḷa king Rājakēsarivarman. Mentions Kaṇṇaradēvar (Krishṇa III of the Rāshṭrakūṭa line). (A mutilated record.) See S.A. 289.

370. 219 *of* 1904.—(Tamil.) On the west base of the same maṇṭapa. A record in the forty-fifth year of the Chōḷa king Kulōttuṅga-Chōḷadēva (I?). Records gift of thirty-two cows.

371. 220 *of* 1904.—(Kanarese.) On the same base. A record in Ś. 1392, Vikrita. Built in the middle. Contains the signature Annamarasa at the end.

372. 221 *of* 1904.—(Tamil.) On the north base of the same maṇṭapa. A record in the eighteenth year of the Chōḷa king Rājarāja-Rājakēsarivarman (985—1013). Records that allotments were made for daily requirements.

373. 222 *of* 1904.—(Tamil.) On the east wall of the first prākāra of the same temple. A record in the thirteenth year of the Chōḷa king Rājakēsarivarman *alias* Tribhuvanachakravartiṇ Rājādhirājadēva II (1171—86). Records a gift of land made by Śeṅgēṇi Ammaiyappan Pāṇḍi *alias* Rājarāja Śambuvarāyan. Quotes the fifth year of the king's reign and mentions the donor's grandfather, who claims to have conquered the Pāṇḍya country. See *Ep. Ind.*, Vol. IX, p. 212. Date corresponds to Wednesday, 8th July 1181, in all probability.

374. 223 *of* 1904.—(Tamil.) On the south wall of the same prākāra. A record in the thirteenth year of the Chōḷa king Tribhuvanachakravartin Kulōttuṅga-Chōḷadēva III (1178–1216). Records that two chiefs pledged themselves to be loyal to Śeṅgēṇi Ammaiyappan Rājarāja Śambuvarāyan, "who took the Pāṇḍya country." [Evidently Śeṅgēṇi Ammayappa helped Kulōttuṅga III in a campaign against the Pāṇḍya.]

Śingavaram.

375. 224 *of* 1904.—(Tamil.) On the east wall of the central shrine in the Raṅganātha temple. A damaged record.

376. 225 of 1904.—(Tamil.) On the east base of the maṇṭapa in front of the same shrine. A record in the thirtieth year of the Chōḷa king Rājakēsarivarman *alias* Tribhuvanachakravartin Kulōttuṅga-Chōḷadēva (unidentified). Records gift of thirty-two cows for a lamp.

377. 226 *of* 1904.—(Tamil.) On the same base. A record of the Pāṇḍya king Māravarman Tribhuvanachakravartin Vīra-Pāṇḍyadēva, the date of which is lost. Beginning built in. [Was he the same as the successor of Vikrama Pāṇḍya ?]

378. 227 *of* 1904.—(Tamil.) On the east base of the maṇṭapa in front of the central shrine in the same temple. A record in the seventh year of the Chōḷa king Parakēsarivarman *alias* Uḍaiyār Rājēndradēva (1050—63 ?). Records gift of a lamp by a chief to atone for having stabbed a military officer. See S.A. 393, 570, 580, 594, etc.

379. 228 *of* 1904.—(Tamil.) On the left of the flight of steps leading up to the same shrine. A record in the fourth year of the Pallava king Sakalabhuvanachakravartin Avaniāḷappirandān Kōpperuñjiṅgadēva. Records gift of thirty cows for a lamp. See *Conjeevaram inscriptions. Ep. Ind.*, Vol. VII, p. 165.

380. 229 *of* 1904.—(Tamil.) On the east wall of the central shrine in the ruined Ādivarāha-Perumāḷ temple in the same village. A record of the Vijayanagara king Pratāpa-Dēvarāya-Mahārāya (whom Venkayya considers to be the younger brother of Dēvarāya II) in Paridhāvin. Records that a certain private individual and his family were made over to the temple of Panṛi-Āḻvār to look after the lamps. See 665 of 1904 at Tirumullaivāyil in Chingleput district for the same chief.

381. 230 *of* 1904.—(Tamil.) On the same wall. A record of the Vijayanagara king Pratāpa-Dēvarāya-Mahāraya in Krōdhin. Records a gift similar to that in No. 229. See S.A. 380.

382. 231 *of* 1904.—(Tamil.) On the south base of the same shrine. A record in the thirtieth year of the Pāṇḍya king Māravarman Tribhuvanachakravartin Kulaśēkharadēva I (1268—1308). Records gift of land. See *Ep. Ind.*, Vol. VIII, p. 277, where it is pointed out that the date corresponded to Wednesday, 31st July 1297.

383. 232 *of* 1904. (Tamil.) On the same base. A record of the Vijayanagara king Mallikārjuna-Mahārāya, son of Dēvarāya-

Maharāya II 'who had witnessed the elephant hunt,' in Ś. 1378, Dhātri. Records a gift similar to that of No. 380.

384. 233 *of* 1904.--(Tamil.) On the west base of the same shrine. A record in Kīlaka. Records a gift similar to that of No. 380 above.

385. 234 *of* 1904.—(Tamil.) On the north base of the same shrine. A record of the Vijayanagara king Kumāra-Viruppaṇa-Uḍaiyār (i.e., Virūpāksha I, son of Harihara II) in Kshaya (Ś. 1309). Records a gift similar to that of No. 229. [The name Kumāra has been added to distinguish him from his namesake, the son of Bukka I, who seems to have had nothing to do with the Tamil country.] Virūpāksha, according to the Ālampūṇḍi grant (*Ep. Ind.*, Vol. III, p. 224 ff.) and the Sanskrit drama *Nārāyaṇavilāsa* conquered the Toṇḍira, Chōḷa and Pāṇḍya countries. See S.A. 336.

386. 235 *of* 1904.—(Tamil.) On the same base. A damaged record of the Vijayanagara king Sadāśivadēva-Mahārāya in Ś. 1483, Durmati. The king bears Sāḷuva *birudas*.

387. 236 *of* 1904.—(Telugu.) On the Eḻḻukkuṭṭaippārai in the same village. A private record in Kāḷayukta.

388. 237 *of* 1904.—(Tamil.) On two boulders at the foot of the hill in the same village. Records the foundation of a village called Śrīkaraṇapperuñjēri at the request of an agent of Nīlagaṅgaraiyan Annavanāṭṭaḍigal for providing offerings and for burning lamps in the temple of the Āḻvār at Panṟikunṟu.

389. 238 *of* 1904.—(Tamil.) On a rock in the Tirunātharkunṟu near the same village. Records the *niśidika* of Iḷaiyappaḍārar who fasted for 30 days. The reference is to the Jain habit of religious suicide.

390. 239 *of* 1904.—(Archaic Vaṭṭeḻuttu.) On the same rock. Records the *niśidika* of Chandrānandi-āchārya who fasted for 57 days.

KALLAKURCHI TALUK.

Kallakuruchchi.

390-A. A C.P. grant of "Raṅga (VI)" dated A.D. 1644-5 (Tāraṇa, Phalguni Śu. di 12), recording the grant of this village (surnamed Chinnamaśeṭṭisamudram) in the kingdom of Tiruvāḍi to Koṇḍappa, son of Yellamarāja of the Kavuṇḍinyagōtra, Āpastamba sūtra and Yajuś śākha. It is in Nandinagari character and is of great value in the history of the last Vijayanagara dynasty. See *Ind. Antq.*, Vol. VIII, pp. 153-60 and *Tam. and Sans. Inscrns.*, pp. 196-203.

Tiruvaraṅgam.

391. 66 *of* 1906.—(Tamil.) On the right and left walls of the entrance into the Raṅganātha temple. A record of the

Vijayanagara king Vīrapratāpa Kṛishṇadēva-Mahārāya-Achyutadēva-Mahārāya-Sadāśivadeva-Mahārāya in Ś. 1480 expired, Piṅgaḷa. Records gift of three villages to the Raṅganātha temple at Uttara-Tiruvaraṅgam by the Mahāmaṇḍalēśvara Obaladēva-Mahārāja, son of Kōnēṭayya-Mahārāja and grandson of Rāmarāja-Koṇḍūrājadēva-Mahārāja of the Atrēyagōtra, the Yajus śākha and the Āpastamba sūtra. The villages belonged to Mudiyanū-paṟṟu in Vaḷudilambaṭṭuchchāvaḍi, a subdivision of Korukkaikūṟṟam, a district of Meygunṟa-vaḷanāḍu in Magadai-maṇḍalam granted to the donor by Sadāśivadēva Mahārāya. In the beginning, Mudiyanūrpaṟṟu is said to be on the southern bank of the Peṇṇār river in Tiruvāḍi-rājyam, which belonged to Magadai-maṇḍalam.

TINDIVANAM TALUK.

Giḍaṅgil.

392. 222 *of* 1902.—(Tamil.) On the south wall of the Bhaktaparādhīśvara shrine. A record in the twenty-first year of the Chōḷa king Rājakēsarivarman *alias* Chakravartin Kulōttuṅga Chōḷadēva (I ?). Records gift of sixteen cows for a lamp.

393. 223 *of* 1902.—(Tamil.) On the same wall. A record in the twenty-first year of the Chōḷa king Rājakēsarivarman *alias* Chakravartin Kulōttuṅga-Chōḷadēva. Records gift of forty-five sheep for a lamp by "the father of a boy of six years, who had accidentally killed another boy of seven years with the sickle in cutting wood." See S.A. 378 for a similar example.

394. 224 *of* 1902.—(Tamil.) On the west wall of the same shrine. A record in the thirtieth year of the Chōḷa king Rājakēsarivarman *alias* Chakravartin Kulōttuṅga-Chōḷadēva. Records gift of gold for a lamp and of cows for offerings.

395. 225 *of* 1902.—(Tamil.) On the south wall of the maṇṭapa in front of the same shrine. A record in the tenth year of the Chōḷa king Parakēsarivarman *alias* Tribhuvanachakravartin Vikrama-Chōḷadēva (1118–35). Records gift of gold for four lamps.

396. 226 *of* 1902.—(Tamil.) On the same wall. A record in the third year of the Chōḷa king Parakēsarivarman *alias* Tribhuvanachakaravartin Kulōttuṅga-Chōḷadēva (III). Records sale of land. Mentions the twelfth year of Vikrama-Chōḷadēva. See *Ep. Ind.*, Vol. VII., pp. 171–2. Dr. Kielhorn points out that the date is irregular.

397. 227 *of* 1902.—(Tamil.) On the same wall. A record in the second year of the Chōḷa king Parakēsarivarman *alias* Uḍaiyār Ādhirājēndradēva. This is stated to be a copy of an older inscription. Records gift of land to an image which the donor had set up in the temple. [Ādhirājēndra was the son of Rājakēsarivarman Vīra Rājēndra I, 1063–70.]

398. 228 *of* 1902.—(Tamil.) On the same wall. A record in the eighteenth year of Sakalalōkachakravartin Rājanārāyaṇa-Śambuvarāyan. Records gift of taxes.

399. 229 *of* 1902.—(Tamil.) On the same wall. A record of the Vijayanagara king Vijaya-Bhūpatirāya (1331-44), the date of which is lost. Records gift of land.

Kunimēḍu.

The place is interesting as the site of an early English factory which was established in 1682 and abandoned on the purchase of *Fort St. David* from the Mahrattas in 1698 and the remains of which are still to be seen. (See *Madras Manual*, Vol. III, p. 209 and Garstin's *South Arcot*, p. 407.)

400. 241 *of* 1904.—(Tamil.) On the west base of the ruined Īśvara temple. A damaged record of the Vijayanagara king Vīrapratāpa-Achyutaiyadēva-Mahārāya in Ś. 1455, Nandana. Mentions an agent of Tirumalaidēva-Mahārāja. Records gift of taxes.

401. 242 *of* 1904.—(Tamil.) On the south wall of the maṇṭapa in front of the same temple. A record of the Vijayanagara king Achyutadēva-Mahārāya in Ś. 1451, Vijaya (wrong). Records gift of land. Mentions an agent of Rāmabhaṭṭar.

Olakkūr.

402. 351 *of* 1909.—(Tamil.) On the south wall of the Agastyēśvara temple. A record in the forty-first year of the Chōla king Rājakēsarivarman *alias* Chakravartin Śrī-Kulōttuṅga-Chōḷadēva (I). Records that a private individual paved the floor of the central shrine, set up the *śripādapīṭha* (pedestal) and a *neytāṅgi* (lamp-post), consecrated an image of Vighnēśvara and granted gold for a lamp, to the temple of Tiruvagattīśvaramuḍaiya-Mahādēvar at Uḷakkaiyūr *alias* Rājamahēndranallūr in Oymā-nāḍu *alias* Vijayarājēndra-vaḷanāḍu, which was a subdivision of Jayaṅgoṇḍa-Chōḷamaṇḍalam. [Rājamahēndranallur was evidently founded by Rājamahēndra, the son of Rājēndra (1050-62) and predecessor of Vīra Rājēndra I [1064-70.]

403. 352 *of* 1909.—(Tamil.) On the same wall. A record in the fourth year of Chōḷa king Rājakēsarivarman *alias* Tribhuvanachakravartin Rājādhirājadēva II, 1171-86. Records a hunting accident in expiation of which the party who committed the offence were ordered to give thirty-two cows and one bull to the shrine of Vātāpi-Viṭaṅkar in the temple of Tiruvagattīśuramuḍaiya-Mahādēvar at Ulakkaiūr *alias* Rājamahēndranallūr, by the Brahmans of the village assembly so that "he may escape the possible mischief of the revengeful soul of the victim". See S.A. 378.

404. 353 *of* 1909.—(Tamil.) On the west wall of the same temple. An unfinished record in the fifth year of the Chōḷa king

Rājakēsarivarman *alias* Tribhuvanachakravartin Kulōttuṅga-Chōḷadēva. Refers to a gift of gold, made by Rājēndradēva (evidently Parakesarivarman Rajendra 1050–63), for a stone building to the god Tiruvagattīśuramuḍaiya-Mahādēva at Ulakkaiyūr *alias* Rājamahēndranallūr in Oymānāḍu *alias* Vijayarājēndra-vaḷanāḍu, which was a district of Jayaṅgoṇḍa-Chōḷamaṇḍalam. Rājēndra had placed 100 Kaḷañju of gold in the hands of the residents. The latter completed only the first five Aṅgas of the temple and stopped work. Half the money was still in arrears but "disappeared owing to bad time." Consequently the stone temple originally intended by Rājēndra was never completed. The servants of the temple complained against this conduct of the villagers and on this the latter agreed to supply an image of Sōmaskanda, instead of accomplishing their original bargain.

405. 354 *of* 1909.—(Tamil.) On the north wall of the same temple. A record in Vibhava of the Vijayanagara king Ariyaṇa-Uḍaiyār (i.e., Harihara II). Concessions granted to the Kaikkōḷar (weavers) living in the streets surrounding the temple. These migrated in a body without paying the dues to the temple, as a result of which, it was financially ruined and had to be closed. Subsequently they were persuaded to return and open their looms, paying revised assessments decided upon by the authorities.

406. 355 *of* 1909.—(Tamil.) On the door-post of the entrance into the same temple. A record in the forty-first year of the Chōla king Rājakēsarivarman *alias* Çhakravartin Śrī-Kulōttuṅga Chōḷadēva (I, 1070–1118). Mentions the charities recorded in No. 351 at the end of which this inscription on the door-post, is referred to.

407. 356 *of* 1909.—(Tamil.) On a slab set up in the Brahman street in the same village. In archaic characters, "which may be assigned to the Pallava or the early 'Gaṅga-Pallava' period." Records that the much-worn image at the top of the slab was caused to be cut by the king. The image itself, perhaps, represents Piridiviviḍaṅga-kurati. The inscriptions shows that Jainism was under royal support in the district. Nandivarman cut out, for example, a similar image at Pañchapāṇḍavamalai near Arcot.

408. 357 *of* 1909.—(Tamil.) On a slab (*a virakal*) set up near the village-munsif's chāvaḍi in the same village. Refers to Kampapperumāḷ and to the death of a hero on the occasion when this town was devastated. The occasion of the destruction of the city is not known. Kampapperumāḷ is identified by Mr. Krishna Sastri with Kampavarma of the 'Gaṅga-Pallava dynasty.'

Olindiyāppattu Araśili

409. 194 *of* 1902.—(Tamil.) On the south wall of the Aśvatthēśvara shrine. A record in the sixth year of the Çhōḷa king

Tribhuvanachakravartin Vikrama-Chōḷadēva (1118–35). Records gift of twelve sheep for a lamp.

410. 195 *of* 1902.—(Tamil.) On the east wall of the maṇṭapa in front of the same shrine. A record in the twelfth year of the Chōḷa king Parakēsarivarman *alias* Chakravartin Vikrama-Chōḷadēva (1118—35). Records gift of 96 sheep for a lamp.

411. 196 *of* 1902.—(Tamil.) On the same wall. A record in the fifth year of the Chōḷa king Rājakēsarivarman *alias* Tribhuvanachakravartin Kulōttuṅga-Chōḷadēva. Records gift of 30 cows for a lamp.

412. 197 *of* 1902.—(Tamil.) On the south wall of the same maṇṭapa. A record in the sixteenth year of the Chōḷa king Tribhuvanachakravartin Vikrama-Chōḷadēva (1118—35). Records gift of four cows for a lamp.

413. 198 *of* 1902.—(Tamil.) On the same wall. An incomplete record in the third year of the Chōḷa king Kulōttuṅga Chōḷadēva.

Perumāṇḍūr (evidently a Jain centre in the ancient period).

414. 219 *of* 1902.—(Tamil.) On a pillar of the maṇṭapa in front of the Chandranātha shrine. A record in the fourteenth year of the Chōḷa king Kulōttuṅga-Chōḷadēva (III ?). Records that Rājarāja-Śambuvarāyan granted land to the image of Yakshi. [Chandranātha or Chandraprabhā was the eighth Tīrthaṅkara of the Jains.]

415. 220 *of* 1902.—(Tamil.) On the west wall of the Rishabhanātha shrine in the same village. An incomplete record in the nineteenth year of the 'Gaṅga-Pallava' king Vijaya-Nandivikramavarman. Records gift of paddy. Rishabhanātha was the first Tīrthaṅkara.

416. 221 *of* 1902.—(Tamil.) On the north wall of the same shrine. A record in the fifteenth year of the Chōḷa king Kulōttuṅga-Chōḷadēva (III ?). Records gift of land by Rājarāja-Śambuvarāyar.

Perumukkal (*Permacoil of Orme*).

The place has been connected by tradition with the Rāmāyaṇā and the local hill is called the hermitage of Vālmīki, and the local deity Vālmīśura muḍaiya Mādēvar. The village was formerly called Perumukkil, for the legendary origin of which see *S.A. Gazr.*, p. 366. The isolated rock which rises out of the plain in this village and which has the temple referred to below on its summit, was fortified in the eighteenth century and saw much fighting between the English and the French. The following epigraphs have been recorded. The earliest belongs to Kulōttuṅga I, but the temple was erected in Vikramachōḷa's reign. See 421.

417. 36 *of* 1905.—(Tamil.) On slab set up in a field near the village. A record of the Vijayanagara king Veṅkaṭapatidēva-Mahārāya I in Ś. 1511 expired, Virōdhin. Records gift of land by Veṅkaṭappa-Nāyaka for the merit of Timmakkal at the order of Bommu-Nāyaka, son of Nāgama-Nāyaka. Koṇḍama-Nāyaka, son of Kṛishṇappa-Nāyaka, is also mentioned. See N.A. 204 and 553.

418. 37 *of* 1905.—(Tamil.) On a rock to the right of the way up the hill in the same village. A record in the sixteenth year of the Chōḷa king Rājakēsarivarman *alias* Tribhuvanachakravartin Kulōttuṅga-Chōḷadēva I (1070—1118). Records gift of 30 cows for a lamp to the temple of Tirumalai-Tiruvanmiśvaramuḍaiya-Mādēvar at Perumūkkil. Registers also other gifts made in the forty-third and forty-fifth years.

419. 38 *of* 1905.—(Kanarese.) On a slab to the left of the same way. Records that a certain Lingappa, son of Chikka-Kōnēri-Nāyaka of Paḍaivīḍu built the steps.

420. 39 *of* 1905.—(Tamil.) On the north wall of the central shrine in the Mukhyāchalēśvara temple on the same hill. A record in the fifth year of the Chōḷa king Rājakēsarivarman *alias* Tribhuvanachakravartin Rājādhirājadēva (II, 1171—86.) Records gift of 32 cows for a lamp. Perumukkil is called Gaṅgaikoṇḍa-nallūr.

421. 40 *of* 1905—(Tamil.) On the west wall of the same shrine. A record in the third year of the Chōḷa king Vikrama-Chōḷadēva. Records the building of the temple by Kakku-Nāyakan *alias* Kanakarāyan.

422. 41 *of* 1905.—(Tamil.) On the same wall. A record in the ninth year of the Chōḷa king Tribhuvanachakravartin Vikrama-Chōḷadēva (1118—35). Records gift of the land to the temple of Tiruvānmīga-Iśvaramuḍaiyār.

423. 42 *of* 1905.—(Tamil verse.) On the south wall of the same shrine. Mentions Timmaya-Polaya.

424. 43 *of* 1905.—On the north wall of the maṇṭapa in front of the Mukhyāchalēśvara temple on the hill. A record in the seventh year of the Pāṇḍya king Māravarman *alias* Tribhuvana-chakravartin Vikrama-Pāṇḍyadēva. Records gift of a salt-pan to the temple of Vālmīkīśvaramuḍaiya-Nāyanār. The salt-pan had been enjoyed by the temple for a long time but had lain unused since the time of Pallavan Kōpperuñjiṅgar.

425. 44 *of* 1905.—(Tamil.) On the same wall. A record in the fifth year of the Chōḷa king Rājadhirājadēva (II, 1078—86.) Records gift of 32 sheep for a lamp to the temple of Tiruvāmīśuramuḍaiya-Mahādēvar.

426. 45 *of* 1905.—(Tamil.) On the same wall. A record in the eighth year of the Chōḷa king Parakēsarivarman *alias* Tribhuvanachakravartin Vikrama-Chōḷadēva (1118—35). Records gift of land.

427. 46 *of* 1905.—(Tamil.) On the same wall. A record in the sixteenth year of the Chōḷa king Parakēsarivarman *alias* Tribhuvanachakravartin Rājarājadēva (II, 1146—78). Records gift of 32 cows for a lamp. Perumukkil is called Edirili-Chōḷanallūr.

428. 47 *of* 1905.—(Sanskrit and Grantha.) On the south wall of the same maṇṭapa. Records in Ś. 1090 the gift of a pot by a chief who belonged to the Vrishabha family.

Sandamangalam (Śēndamaṅgalam).

[It was evidently the capital of Kōpperuñjiṅga Dēva. See *S.A. Gazr.*, p. 377.]

429. 68 *of* 1903.—(Tamil.) On the east wall of the maṇṭapa in front of the central shrine in the Āpatsahāyēśvara temple. Records in Saumya gift of land by Jakkaṇa-Uḍaiyār (?).

430. 69 *of* 1903.—(Tamil.) On the same wall. A record in the seventeenth year of the Pallava king Sakalabhuvanachakravartin Kōpperuñjiṅgadēva. Records gift of money for two lamps.

431. 70 *of* 1903.—(Tamil.) On the same wall. A record in the second year of the Pallava king Sakalabhuvanachakravartin Kōpperuñjiṅgadēva. Records gift of 32 cows and one bull for a lamp.

432. 71 *of* 1903.—(Tamil.) On the same wall. A record in the ninth year of the Pallava king Sakalabhuvanachakravartin Kōpperuñjiṅgadēva. Records gift of 32 cows and one bull for a lamp.

433. 72 *of* 1903.—(Tamil.) On the same wall. A record of the Vijayanagara king Vīrapratāpa-Dēvarāya-Mahārāya (II) in Ś. 1352, *Saumya.* Records that the king granted the two villages Kaḷḷakurichchi and Āḍur.

434. 73 *of* 1903.—(Tamil.) On the same wall. Records in the fifth year gift of land for ten lamps.

435. 74 *of* 1903.—(Grantha and Tamil.) On the west wall of the same maṇṭapa. A record of the Vijayanagara king Vīra Kṛishṇadēva-Mahārāya in Ś. 1439, Iśvara. Describes the king's conquests in the north-east and records an order which he issued at Bezvāda. This is a very important epigraph which gives an independent account of Kṛishṇadēva's conquests. See 574 of 1902 at Tiruvaṇṇāmalai, and inscriptions at Amarāvati. The inscription is to the effect that Kṛishṇadēva, while staying in the bank of the Kṛishṇaveṇi between the Anantaśāyin temple at Uṇḍavalli (Guṇṭūr Taluk) and Mallikārjuna temple of Bezvāda, remitted 10,000 gold pieces in favour of the temples between the Gaḍilam and Veḷḷār and from Kōṭṭaikkarai wall to the sea. [This donation is confirmed by 288 of 1903 at Tiruppālatturai, 125 of 1904 at Tīrthanagari and 511 of 1905 at Kaṇṇanūr.]

436. 75 *of* 1903.—(Tamil.) On the same wall. An incomplete record in the fifth year of the Pāṇḍya king Tribhuvanachakravartin Kōnērimēlkoṇḍān Vīra-Pāṇḍyadēva. Records gift of land by the king.

437. 76 *of* 1903.—(Tamil.) On the north wall of the same maṇṭapa. A record in the nineteenth year of the Pallava king Sakalabhuvanachakravartin Kōpperuñjiṅgadēva. Records gift of sixty cows by the king.

438. 77 *of* 1903.—(Tamil.) On the gōpura of the same temple, right of entrance. A record of the Pāṇḍya king Tribhuvana-chakravartin Kōnērimēlkoṇḍān Parākrama Pāṇḍyadēva. Records gift of land.

439. 78 *of* 1903.—(Grantha and Tamil.) In the same place. A record in the fourth year of the Pāṇḍya king Vikrama Pāṇḍyadēva. Records gift of land by the king.

440. 79 *of* 1903.—(Tamil.) On the same gōpura, left of entrance. Records in the seventeenth year gift of land. Mentions Ellāndalaiyāna-Perumāḷ.

441. 80 *of* 1903.—(Tamil.) In the same place. Records in the seventeenth year gift of land. Mentions Ellāndalaiyāna-Perumāḷ.

442. 81 *of* 1903.—(Tamil.) In the same place. A record in the seventeenth year of the Pāṇḍya king Sundara Pāṇḍyadēva. Records that the king granted land to provide for the worship on "the day of Ellāndalaiyāna-Perumāḷ."

Sirṟāmūr (Śittāmūr).

This is the most important Jain centre in the district and the headquarters of the head of all South Indian Jains. See *S.A. Gazr.*, p. 367.

443. 201 *of* 1902.—(Tamil.) On a slab built into the floor close to the well in the Pārśvanātha temple. A record in the seventeenth year of the Chōḷa king Rājakēsarivarman. Records gift of a lamp.

444. 202 *of* 1902.—(Tamil.) On a slab built into the floor of the maṇṭapa in front of the Malainātha shrine in the same village. A record in the tenth year of the Chōḷa king Rājādhirājadēva. Records gift of land.

445. 203 *of* 1902.—(Tamil.) On the base of a boulder at the back of the same shrine. Mentions Kāḍavarkōnpāvai, the queen of a Chōḷa king. [Does Kāḍavarkōn refer to Kōpperuñjiṅgadēva? See N.A. 224 and S.A. 223.]

Tiṇḍivanam.

Tindivanam, like its suburb Giḍangil, was in Oymānāḍu. For a description of the Antiquities of the place see S.A. *Gazr.*, pp. 368—70.

446. 141 *of* 1900.—(Tamil.) On the south wall of the central shrine in the Tintriṇīśvara temple. A record in the tenth year of the Chōḷa king Rājarājakēsarivarman (Rājarāja I). Records gift of land for the maintenance of a musician who was to play on the lute and of a vocalist to accompany the lute (vīṇai). The vīṇai was thus in use in the tenth century. "Of course there is nothing in this to show that the old Dravidian musical instrument Yāḻ had been superseded about this time by the vīṇai." [See Seshagiri Sastri's *Rep. Sans., Tam. MSS.*, 1897, p. 58 and my article on Nāthamuni in *Chris. Coll. Magaz.*, Aug. 1915.]

447. 142 *of* 1900.—(Tamil.) On the west wall of the same shrine. A record in the eighteenth year of the Chōḷa king Rājarāja-Rājakēsarivarman (985—1013). Records gift of land.

448. 143 *of* 1900.—(Tamil.) On the west wall of the same shrine. A record in the fifth year of the Chōḷa king Rājakēsarivarman. Built in in the middle. Records gift of lamps to the temple of Tiruttiṇḍīśvara at Kiḍaṅgil.

449. 144 *of* 1900.--(Tamil.) On the west wall of the same shrine. A record in the eleventh year of the Chōḷa king Rājarājakēsarivarman (Rājarāja I). Records gift of a lamp.

450. 145 *of* 1900.—(Tamil.) On the north wall of the same shrine. A record in the sixteenth year of the Chōḷa king Rājakēsarivarman *alias* Chakravartin Kulōttuṅga-Chōḷadēva (Kulōttuṅga I). Records gift of three lamps.

451. 204 *of* 1902.—(Tamil.) On the south wall of the Tintriṇīśvara shrine. A record in the thirty-ninth year of the Chōḷa king Rājakēsarivarman *alias* Tribhuvanachakravartin Kulōttuṅga Choḷadēva (I). Records gift of thirty cows for a lamp.

452. 205 *of* 1902.—(Tamil.) On the north wall of the same shrine. A record in the fifth year of the Chōḷa king Tribhuvanachakravartin Vikrama-Chōḷadēva (1118—35). Records sale of land.

453. 206 *of* 1902.—(Tamil.) On the same wall. A record in the thirty-ninth year of the king whose name is not mentioned. Records that a certain Kāḍavarāyan lowered the taxes on Giḍaṅgil to three-quarters of the original amount. See S.A. 445.

454. 207 *of* 1902.—(Tamil.) On the south wall of the maṇṭapa in front of the same shrine. A record of the Chōḷa king Rājakēsarivarman *alias* Uḍaiyār Vīrarājēndradēva (I, 1064—70). Built in. Records gift of twelve cows for offerings. *S.I.I.*, Vol. III, pp. 201-2 (No. 83).

455. 208 *of* 1902.—(Tamil.) On the same wall. A record in the fifteenth year of the Chōḷa king Rājarājakēsarivarman. Records gift of ninety sheep for a lamp.

456. 209 *of* 1902.—(Tamil.) On the same wall. A record in the sixteenth year of the Chōḷa king Rājarāja-Rājakēsarivarman (985—1013). Records gift of 180 sheep for two lamps.

457. 210 *of* 1902.—(Tamil verse and prose.) On the same wall. Records the building of the maṇṭapa.

458. 211 *of* 1902.—(Tamil.) On the same wall. A record in the forty-fifth year of the Chōḷa king Kulōttuṅga-Chōḷadēva (I). Records gift of gold for a lamp.

459. 212 *of* 1902.—(Tamil.) On the same wall. A record in the thirty-fifth year of the Chōḷa king Rājakēsarivarman *alias* Chakravartin Kulōttuṅga-Chōḷadēva. Records gift of thirty cows for a lamp.

460. 213 *of* 1902.—(Tamil.) On the same wall. A record in the twenty-eighth year of the Chōḷa king Rājakēsarivarman *alias* Uḍaiyār-Kulōttuṅga-Chōḷadēva. Records gift of ninety sheep for a lamp.

461. 214 *of* 1902.—(Tamil.) On the same wall. A record in the eleventh year of the Chōḷa king Rājarājakēsarivarman (985—1013). Records gift of land.

462. 215 *of* 1902.—(Tamil.) On the same wall. A record in the twenty-eighth year of the Chōḷa king Rājakēsarivarman *alias* Udaiyār Rājādhirājadēva. Records sale of land.

463. 216 *of* 1902.—(Tamil.) On the north wall of the same maṇṭapa. A record in the seventeenth year of the Chōḷa king Rājarāja-Rājakēsarivarman (985—1013). Records that a royal officer made enquiries regarding the affairs of the temple. An incomplete record.

464. 217 *of* 1902.—(Marathi.) On a stone built into the floor of the prākāra of the Lakshmi-Narasimha-Perumāḷ temple in the same village. Records in Ś. 1554, Manmatha (wrong), the construction of buildings in the fort by Khan Alisan-Ambarkhan Saheb (the Killadar of Gingee in 1677 and victim of Sivaji's ambition. See *S.A. Gazr.*, p. 350).

465. 218 *of* 1902.—(Telugu.) On a second stone built into the floor of the same prākāra. A record in Ś. 1554. Manmatha (wrong). A translation of No. 217.

466. 30 *of* 1905.—(Tamil.) On the gōpura of the Tintriṇīśvara temple. A record of the Vijayanagara king Raṅgayadēva-Mahārāya (1578—1586), son of Tirumalaidēva-Mahārāyar, in Ś. 1505 expired, Svabhānu. Records that Vīrappa-Nāyaka, son of Pāppu-Nāyaka of Vēlūr, who was apparently the Governor of Paḍaivīḍu-rājya, and the principal inhabitants and others living in the six countries and eighteen districts ordered that tolls should be levied according to a fixed scale on all the articles brought into the market at Gidaṅgil on Wednesdays and that the proceeds should be spent in repairs of the Tintriṇīśvara temple.

467. 31 *of* 1905.—(Tamil.) On the gōpura of the Tintriṇīśvara temple, left of entrance. A record of the Vijayanagara king Veṅkaṭapatirāya in Ś. 1525 expired, Śōbhakrit. Records that the weavers were ordered to pay a tax, the proceeds of which went to the temple. Mentions Bommu-Nāyaka, agent of Nāgama-Nāyaka.

468. 32 *of* 1905.—(Tamil.) At the entrance into the maṇṭapa of the Lakshminarasimha-Perumāḷ temple in the same village, right side. A record of the Vijayanagara king Gaṇḍakaṭṭāri Śāḷuva Achyutarāya Mahārāya in Ś. 1453 expired, Khara. Built in at the end. Records gift of land. Mentions Mallappa, son of the minister Tipparasar.

469. 33 *of* 1905.—(Tamil.) In the same place, left side. A record of the Vijayanagara king Sadāśivadēva Mahārāya in Ś. 1464 expired, Kīlaka (wrong). Records the gift of a village for the merit of the Mahāmaṇḍalēśvara Rāmarāja Chinna-Timmaiyyadēva Mahārāya. See N.A. 148.

470. 34 *of* 1905.—(Tamil.) On the north wall of the same maṇṭapa. Mentions in Ś. 1439 expired, Īśvara, a certain Perugu Appaḷaiya of the Śrīvatsa gotra.

471. 35 *of* 1905.—(Tamil.) On the south wall of the same maṇṭapa. A record of the Vijayanagara king Vīrapratāpa Kṛishṇarāya-Mahārāya in Ś. 1474 (mistake for 1434) expired, Āṅgirasa. Records gift of land by Tirumalai Nāyaka (the governor of the Tiṇḍivanam śīmai) to Appili of the Śrīvatsa gōtra, son of the minister Mattarasa.

Vayirapuram.

472. 253 *of* 1913.—(Tamil.) On the south base of the Sōmasundarēśvara temple. A record in the fourth year of the Chōḷa king Parakēsarivarman *alias* Rājēndra-Chōḷadēva (I). Records gift of ninety sheep for a lamp by Śāraṇamanri to the temple of Tirunandīśvaram-Uḍaiyār at Vayiramēghapuram *alias* Jananāthapuram in Tirunallūr-nāḍu, a subdivision of Ōymā-nāḍu in Jayaṅgoṇḍaśōḷa-maṇḍalam.

473. 254 *of* 1913.—(Tamil.) On the same base. A record in the ninth year of the Chōḷa king Parakēsarivarman *alias* Rājēndra-Chōḷadēva (I). Records gift of ninety sheep for a lamp to the same temple. Vayiramēghapuram is here called a city (nagaram).

474. 255 *of* 1913.—On the west base of the same temple. A record in the ninth year of the Chōḷa king Parakēśarivarman *alias* Chakravartin Vikrama-Chōḷadēva (1118-35). Records gift of twenty-four sheep for two lamps to the same temple by Peṟṟān Pichchan for the merit of a private individual whom his arrow had killed by accident. See S.A. 378.

475. 256 *of* 1913.—(Tamil.) On the same base. A record in the sixth year of the Chōḷa king Parakēsarivarman *alias* Tribhuvana-chakravartin Vikrama-Chōḷadēva. Records gift of land, exempted from *Śilvari* and *peruvari*, for maintaining various services in the same temple by the residents (*urōm*) of Vayiramēghapuram *alias* Jananāthanallūr, in Tirunallūr-nāḍu, a subdivision of Ōmyā-nāḍu.

476. 257 *of* 1913.—(Tamil.) On the north base of the same temple. A damaged record in the sixth year of the Chōḷa king Tribhuvanachakravartin Vikrama-Chōḷadēva (1158-35). Seems to register a gift of land which was situated in Yeyilūr, a hamlet of Vayiramēghapuram, by the residents (*ūrōm*) of the latter village.

477. 258 *of* 1913.—(Tamil.) On the same base. Records gift of land to the temple of Mūlasthānamuḍaiya-Mahādēva at Vayira-mēghapuram, by the inhabitants (*ūrōm*) of the village.

Tirukkoyilur Taluk.

Āmūr.

478. 307 *of* 1910.—(Tamil.) On a boulder in a field. A record in the tenth year of the Chōḷa king Tribhuvanachakravartin Rāja-rājadēva. Records gift of land by Chēdiyarāya and the headmen of the village to the temple of Tiruvagattīśvaramuḍaiya Mahādēva at Āmūr in Tirumunaippāḍi Mēl-Āṇmūrnāḍu. Registers also a gift of land for a lamp to the same temple by a certain Kulōttuṅga-śōḷa-Kāḍavarāyar.

Aragaṇḍanallūr.

The temple of this place which is noted for its fine gōpura, its elaborate sculptures and some rock-cut remains (consisting of three caves) contains the following epigraphs :—

479. 26 *of* 1905.—(Tamil.) On the south wall of the Aḷagiya-Ponni-Amman temple. A record of the Vijayanagara king Malli-kārjunarāya, son of Vīrapratāpa Dēvarāya-Mahārāya II in Ś. 1378 expired, Dhātri. Records gift of the village of Perichchāli-nallūr, for 200 faṇams, to God Ādichandrēśvara. The inscription is also referred to in *Mack. MSS.* (*Ins. S. Dts.*, p. 141, No. 25).

479-A. On the south side of the Sabhāpati-maṇṭapam. A record of the forty-eighth year of Kulōttuṅgachōḷadēva, granting land to the Iḍaṅgai and Valaṅgai people. See *Ins. S. Dts.*, p. 140, No. 23 and N.A. 520.

479-B. On a stone south of the inner temple and Mahāmaṇṭapa. Records that Perumbāḍikāval village was granted as a free gift to the local Bhaṭṭas by Rājēndrachōḷa chēdirāya in the third year of the reign of Kōpperuñjiṅgadēva. See *Ins. S. Dts.*, p. 140, No. 24.

480. 386 *of* 1902.—(Tamil.) On the south wall of the maṇṭapa in front of the Oppilāmaṇīśvara shrine. A record in the eighth year of the Pāṇḍya king Māravarman *alias* Tribhuvanachakravartin Vikrama-Pāṇḍyadēva. Records gift of taxes. See S.A. 68.

481. 387 *of* 1902.—(Tamil.) On the south wall of the same shrine. A record in the thirty-second year of the Chōḷa king Tribhuvanachakravartin Kulōttuṅga-Chōḷadēva. Records repairs to the temple of Opporuvarumillāda-nāyanār at Tiruvaraiyaṉinallūr by a native of the Pāṇḍya country. [The *Mack. MSS.* mistake the word *Tirukkaṟṟaḷi* for a jewel and give the donor's name as " Andoovanna Pattana Swami ". See *Ins. S. Dts.*, p. 142, No. 26.]

482. 388 *of* 1902.—(Tamil.) On the same wall. A record in the thirty-first year of the Chōḷa king Tribhuvanachakravartin Kulōttuṅga-Chōḷadēva. Records gift of land for three lamps.

483. 389 *of* 1902.—(Tamil.) On the north wall of the same shrine. A record in the twenty-second year of the Chōḷa king Tribhuvanachakravartin Kulōttuṅga-Chōḷadēva. Records gift of land for three lamps.

484. 390 *of* 1902.—(Tamil.) On the same wall. A record in the eleventh year of the Chōḷa king Tribhuvanachakravartin Kulōttuṅga-Chōḷadēva. Records gift of three lamps to the god and of land to an image of the goddess, which the donor had set up himself. *Ins. S. Dts.*, p. 142, No. 29.

485. 391 *of* 1902.—(Tamil.) On the same wall. A record in the eighth year of the Pāṇḍya king Māravarman *alias* Tribhuvanachakravartin Vikrama-Pāṇḍyadēva. Records gift of land. [See *Ins. S. Dts.*, p. 142, No. 30. The *Mack. MSS.* give another record in the second year of the king saying that the village of the Vikrama-Pāṇḍya was granted for the god's festival. See *Ins. S. Dts.*, p. 142, No. 27.]

485-A. On the north side of the Mahāmaṇṭapam. A grant of 1,000 kuḷis of land south of " Authitoomb village " to one " Vanicutapayer " at Tirukōvilūr in the reign of Kōpperuñjiṅgadēvar. *Ibid.*, No. 28. See S.A. 68 above.

485-B. In the same place. Grant of the village of Śembiyan Mahādēviyūr. The king's name is obscure. *Ins. S. Dts.*, p. 143, No. 31.

Elvānāśūr.

The ancient name of this place was Śōḷakēraḷachaturvēdimaṅgalam or Irayanaṟaiyūr. Śōḷakēraḷa is mentioned among the relations of Parakēsarivarman Rājēndradēva (1052—63) for whom he is said to have provided kingdoms and provinces. *S. Ind. Ins.*, Vol. III, No. 26.

486. 128 *of* 1906.—(Tamil.) On the east wall of the first prākāra of the Grāmārdhanāthēśvara temple. A record in the ninth year of the Chōḷa king Kulōttuṅga-Chōḷadēva. Records gift of money for a lamp.

487. 129 *of* 1906.—(Tamil.) On the same wall. A mutilated record in the seventeenth year of the Chōḷa king Parakēsarivarman *alias* Tribhuvanachakravartin Śrī-Rājarājadēva (II) on Sunday, December 2, A.D. 1162. The village is also called Śrī-Śōḷakēraḷa-chaturvēdimaṅgalam. See *Ep. Ind.* IX, 209 10.

488. 130 *of* 1906.—(Tamil.) On the same wall. A record in the seventh year of the Chōḷa king Tribhuvanachakravartin Vīra-rājēndra Chōḷadēva. Records gift of money for a lamp.

489. 131 *of* 1906.—(Tamil.) On the same wall. A mutilated and unfinished record in the eighteenth year of the Chōḷa king Para-kēsarivarman *alias* Tribhuvanachakravartin Śri-Rājarājadēva (II).

490. 132 *of* 1906.—(Tamil.) On the same wall. A record in the eleventh year of the Chōḷa king Tribhuvanachakravartin Kulōttuṅga-Chōḷadēva. Records gift of money for a lamp.

491. 133 *of* 1906.—(Tamil.) On the south wall of the same prākāra. A record in the third year of Uḍaiyār Śrī-Śōḷakēraḷadēva. Records gift of cows and of land by Parāntaka-Yādava Bhīma *alias* Uttamāśōḷa Malāḍuḍaiyār of the Bhārgava gōtra. The village is called Iraiyanaraiyūr, a brahmadēya in Pāṇḍūr-kūṟṟam, a district of Malāḍu *alias* Jananāthavaḷanāḍu.

492. 134 *of* 1906.—(Tamil.) On the same wall. An incom-plete record in the fourteenth year of the Chōḷa king Rājarājadēva. Records gift of money for a lamp. The temple is called Uḍaiyār Ūrbāgaṅgoṇḍaruḷiya-Nāyanār. Refers to Tirumalai (i.e., the hill on which the temple is believed to be built).

493. 135 *of* 1906.—(Tamil.) On the same wall. A record in the thirteenth year of the Chōḷa king Uḍaiyār Śrī-Rājēndra-Chōḷa-dēva (I). Registers an endowment for repairs to be made every ten years from the interest. The temple is called Ūruḍaiya Paramēś-varar.

494. 136 *of* 1906.—(Tamil.) On the same wall. A record in the fifth year of the Pāṇḍya king Māravarman Tribhuvanachakra-vartin Śrīvaladēva (Srīvallabha). Records gift of land for two lamps.

495. 137 *of* 1906.—(Tamil.) On the same wall. A record in the fifteenth year (Monday, March 6, A.D. 1161) of the Chōḷa king Parakēsarivarman *alias* Tribhuvanachakravartin Śrī-Rājarājadēva (II). Records gift of land. See *Ep. Ind.*, Vol. IX, p. 210.

496. 138 *of* 1906.—(Tamil.) On the same wall. A record in the tenth year of the Chōḷa king Tribhuvanachakravartin Rājarāja-dēva (III). Records gift of thirty-two cows for a lamp, by a man who, in the course of a boar chase, shot a person by mistake. See S.A. 378, etc.

497. 139 *of* 1906.—(Tamil.) On the same wall. A record in the tenth year of the Chōḷa king Tribhuvanachakravartin Rājādhirājadēva. Records gift of money for two lamps.

498. 140 *of* 1906.—(Tamil.) On the same wall. A damaged record in the fifteenth year (=Wednesday, April 5, A.D. 1161) of the Chōḷa king Parakēsarivarman *alias* Tribhuvanachakravartin Rājarājadēva (II). Seems to record a gift of land. See *Ep. Ind.*, Vol. IX, No. 209.

499. 141 *of* 1906.—(Tamil.) On the west wall of the same prākāra. A record in the fifth year of the Chōḷa king Parakēsarivarman Śrī-Rājēndra-Chōḷadēva (I). Records gift of land for a flower garden.

500. 142 *of* 1906.—(Grantha and Tamil.) On the same wall. A much damaged record of the Vijayanagara king Kṛishṇarāya in Ś. 1439 expired, Īśvara. A few words traced here and there in the first few lines show that the passage describes the conquests of Kṛishṇarāya.

501. 143 *of* 1906.—(Tamil.) On the north wall of the same prākāra. An incomplete record in the twenty-fourth year of the Chōḷa king Rājarājakēsarivarman *alias* Śrī-Rajarājadēva (I, 985—1013). Records gift of land. The characters are later than the period of Rājarāja I. The same remark applies to the inscriptions of Rājēndra-Chōḷa I found in this temple.

502. 144 *of* 1906.—(Tamil.) On the same wall. A record in the nineteenth year of the Chōḷa king Rājarājadēva. Records gift of money for a lamp.

503. 145 *of* 1906.—(Tamil.) On the same wall. A record in the second year of the Chōḷa king Śrī-Kulōttuṅga-Chōḷadēva. Records gift of money for a lamp.

504. 146 *of* 1906.—(Tamil.) On the same wall. A record in the nineteenth year of the Chōḷa king Rājarājadēva. Records gift of money for a lamp.

505. 147 *of* 1906.—(Tamil.) On the same wall. A record in the second year of the Chōḷa king Śrī-Kulōttuṅga-Chōḷadēva. Records gift of money for a lamp.

506. 148 *of* 1906.—(Tamil.) On the same wall. A record in the tenth year of the Chōḷa king Tribhuvanachakravartin Rājarājadēva (third quarter of the twelfth century ?). Records gift of 32 cows for a lamp, under singular circumstances. A woman who threw a stick at her daughter accidentally hit another girl who died as a result of it on the twentieth day; and the penalty was the provision of the lamp by the husband of the lady. See S.A. 378, 570, 580, etc.

507. 149 *of* 1906.—(Tamil.) On the same wall. A record in the tenth year of the Chōḷa king Rājakēsarivarman *alias* Chakravartin Śrī-Kulōttuṅgadēva. Records gift of land. The temple is called Ūruḍaiya Paramēśvarar.

508. 150 *of* 1906.—(Tamil.) On the same wall. A record of the Chōḷa king Kulōttuṅga-Chōḷadēva, the date of which is lost. Records gift of money for a lamp.

509. 151 *of* 1906.—(Tamil.) On the same wall. A record in the second year of the Chōḷa king Kulōttuṅga-Chōḷadēva. Records gift of a lamp.

510. 152 *of* 1906.—(Tamil.) On the same wall. An unfinished record in the seventh year of the Chōḷa king Tribhuvanachakravartin Śrī-Rājādhirājadēva (I or II?).

511. 153 *of* 1906.—(Tamil.) On the same wall. A record in the twelfth year of the Chōḷa king Rājakēsarivarman *alias* Chakravartin Kulōttuṅga-Chōḷadēva. Records gift of land by a dancing girl of the temple at Jambai.

512. 154 *of* 1906.—(Tamil.) On the west wall of the second prākāra of the same temple. A record in the thirtieth year of the Pallava king Sakalabhuvanachakravartin Peruñjiṅgadēva. Records gift of land. Quotes the second year.

513. 155 *of* 1906.—(Tamil.) On the same wall. Registers that two persons mentioned by name had the hereditary right of serving on the district police (*pādikāval*).

514. 156 *of* 1906.—(Tamil.) On the same wall. Undated. Records the declaration made by a woman before committing *suttee* (sati).

515. 157 *of* 1906.—(Tamil.) On the same wall. A record of the fifth year of the Chōḷa king Rājakēsarivarman *alias* Tribhuvanachakravartin Kulōttuṅga-Chōḷadēva. Records gift of taxes to the temple by Kūḍalūr Araśanārāyaṇan Ēḻiśai Mōgan *alias* Jananātha-Kachchiyarāyan.

516. 158 *of* 1906.—(Tamil.) On the same wall. A record in the sixth year of the Chōḷa king Tribhuvanachakravartin Vīrarājēndra-Chōḷadēva. Records gift of taxes by Kiḷiyūr Malaiyamān Sūriyan Nīrēṟṟān *alias* Rājarāja-Malaiyakularāyan. See *Ep. Ind.*, IX, 213. Also S.A. 590.

517. 159 *of* 1906.—(Tamil.) On the same wall. A record in the thirtieth year of the Pallava king Sakalabhuvanachakravartin Peruñjiṅgadēva. Records gift of land in the village of Māmbaṭṭu by Ponparappina Vānakōvaraiyar. See *Ep. Ind.*, IX, 217.

518. 160 *of* 1906.—(Tamil.) On the north wall of the same prākāra. A record in the seventh year of the Pāṇḍya king Māravarman Tribhuvanachakravartin Vīra-Pāṇḍyadēva. Records gift of land for the daily requirements of the temple among which figure rose-water (*pannir*), musk (*kastūri*), camphor (*karpūram*),

European saffron *(kuṅkumam)* and sandal paste for external application *(mērpūchchu)*.

519. 161 *of* 1906.—(Tamil.) On the east wall of the third prākāra of the same temple. A record of the Vijayanagara king Vijayarāya-Mahārāya in Ś. 1368 expired, Kshaya. A copy of No. 23 of 1905 without the signatures at the end.

520. 162 *of* 1906.—(Tamil.) On the north wall of the same prākāra. A record in Pramādin of the Vijayanagara king Kampaṇa-Uḍaiyār. Records gift of cows. Close to this is another inscription dated in the Śubhakrit year which records the gift of a lamp.

521. 163 *of* 1906.—(Tamil.) On the second gōpura of the same temple, right of entrance. A record in the thirteenth year of the Chōḷa king Parakēsarivarman *alias* Tribhuvanachakravartin Rājarājadēva (II). Records gift of land at the request of Kiḷiyūr Malaiyamān Periya-uḍaiyān Nīṟēṟṟān *alias* Rājarāja-Malaiyakula-rāyan by the king while he was at Āyirattali. See S.A. 524.

522. 164 *of* 1906.—(Tamil.) In the same place. A record in the forty-eighth year of the Chōla king Rājakēsarivarman *alias* Tribhuvanachakravartin Kulōttuṅga-Chōladēva. Records sale by the Sabhā of land which belonged to two absconding accountants, who had incurred debts and left the village without discharging them. [Shows that the accountant was under the control of the Sabhā.]

523. 165 *of* 1906.—(Tamil.) In the same place. An incomplete record in the seventeenth year of the Chōḷa king Vikrama-Chōḷadēva. Records gift of land for daily requirements. Provision is made for the recital of the hymn *Tiruchchāḷal* every Sunday. [The author of the Tiruchchāḷal was Māṇikkavāśaga who, in the opinion of Venkayya, was the contemporary of Varaguṇa Pāṇḍya who ascended the throne in 862. See *Ep. Rep.*, 1907, p. 68.]

524. 166 *of* 1906.—(Tamil.) On the same gōpura, left of entrance. A record in the sixth year of the Chōḷa king Parakēsarivarman *alias* Tribhuvanachakravartin Rājarājadēva (II). Records gift of taxes by Kūḍalūr-Āḷappirandān Mōgan *alias* Rājarāja-Kāḍavarāyan. See S.A. 528.

525. 167 *of* 1906.—(Tamil.) In the same place. A record in the thirty-fifth year of the Chōla king Rājakēsarivarman *alias* Tribhuvanachakravartin Kulōttuṅga-Chōḷadēva (I ?). Records gift of land. The temple is called Ūrbāgaṅgoṇḍaruḷina Mahādēva at Iraivanaraiyūr *alias* Śrī-Śōḷakēraḷa-Chaturvēdimaṅgalam in Paḷūr-kūṟṟam, a district of Milāḍu *alias* Jananātha-vaḷanāḍu.

526. 168 *of* 1906.—(Tamil.) In the same place. A record in the fourth year of the Chōḷa king Parakēsarivarman *alias* Tribhuvanachakravartin Vikrama-Chōḷadēva (1118—35). Records gift of land. The king was at Muḍigoṇḍa-Chōlapuram at the time of making the grant.

527. 169 *of* 1906.—(Tamil.) In the same place. A record in the thirteenth year of the Chōḷa king Parakēsarivarman *alias* Tribhuvanachakravartin Vikrama-Chōladēva (1118—35). Registers the emoluments of the temple priests and the items they had to provide for offerings.

528. 170 *of* 1906.—(Tamil.) In the same place. A record in the sixth year of the Chōḷa king Parakēsarivarman *alias* Tribhuvanachakravartin Rājarājadēva (II). Records the building of the hall *(tirumāḷigai)* by Kūḍal-Āḷappirandān Mōgan *alias* Rājarāja-Kāḍavarāyan Nāludikkumvenṟān. See No. 524 above.

529. 171 *of* 1906.—(Tamil.) In the same place. A record in the twelfth year of the Chōḷa king Trivikrama-Chōḷadēva. Records gift of money for a lamp.

530. 172 *of* 1906.—(Tamil.) In the same place. A mutilated record in the sixth year of the Chōla king Tribhuvanachakravartin Vīrarājēndra-Chōḷadēva. The donor is apparently the same as in S.A. 516 above.

531. 173 *of* 1906.—(Tamil.) On the outer gôpura of the same temple, right of entrance. A damaged record of the Vijayanagara king Śrīraṅgadēva-Mahārāya (1578—86) in Ś. 1504 expired, Chitrabhānu.

532. 174 *of* 1906.—(Tamil.) On the same gōpura, left of entrance. A record of the Vijayanagara king Achyutayyadēva-Mahārāya in Ś. 1457 expired, Manmatha. Records gift of a village by the Mahāmaṇḍalēśvara Chōḷakulatilaka Uraiyūr-puravarādhīśvara Bōgaiyadēva Mahārāja, son of Tippayadēva-Mahārāja, for the merit of the king, under orders from Tirumalaiyadēva-Mahārāja, son of Sālakayyadēva-Mahārāja.

533. 175 *of* 1906.—(Tamil.) In the same place. A record of the Vijayanagara king Achchinda (Achyuta)dēva-Mahārāya in Ś. 1453 expired, Khara. The king is called a Śāḷuva and bears the biruda 'the destroyer of the army of the Tulukkar and Oḍḍiyar.' Mentions Bōgaiyadēva-Mahārāja, son of the Mahāmaṇḍalēśvara Timmayarāja. See the above epigraph.

534. 176 *of* 1906.—(Tamil.) On the slab built into the floor at the entrance into the same temple. A damaged and mutilated record in the seventh year of the Chōla king Rājarājakēsarivarman. Refers to the fifteenth year of Śrī-Uttama Chōḷadēva, described as the son of Śembiyān-Mādēviyār, and mentions two Milāḍu chiefs. As the fifteenth year of Uttama-Chōḷa corresponded to the seventh year of Rājarāja I, Venkayya infers that the former must have ascended the throne in A.D. 977-78.

535. 177 *of* 1906.—(Tamil.) On a rock near the Ottaikuḷam in the same village. A record in the ninth year of the Chōḷa king Parakēsarivarman *alias* Tribhuvanachakravartin. Vikrama-Chōḷadēva (1118—35). Records remission of taxes in favour of seven temples by a Milāḍu chief named Kiḷiyūr Malaiyamān Sūriyan Rāman *alias* Rājēndra-Chōḷa Malaiyakularājan. See S.A. 590.

536. 178 *of* 1906.—(Tamil.) On the same rock. A record in the sixth year of the Chōḷa king Vīrarājēndra-Chōḷadēva. Records gift of land to five temples by Kiḷiyūr Malaiyamān Sūriyadēvan Nīṟṟān *alias* Rājarāja Malaiyakularāyan.

537. 179 *of* 1906.—(Sanskrit and Tamil.) On the same rock. Records gift of gold by a native of the Pāṇḍya country. As the inscription belongs palæographically to the ninth century, Venkayya sees in it an evidence of Pāṇḍya activity against Pallava expansion.

Lōkēśvarapuram.

538. *No.* 67 *of Mr. Sewell's list.*—(Telugu.) Records a grant of the village of Lōkēśvarapuram as an Agrahāram, in Ś. 1666 (A.D. 1744), Kaliyuga 4845, Raktākshi, by Raghunātha Nāyuḍu. His father's and grandfather's names are given, and he is said to belong to the royal family of "Dēvika Rāja." The grant is made by permission of the Divāṇam, or Muhammadan government of Yelavānāsūru.

Pullūrupattu.

539. *No.* 69 *of Mr. Sewell's list.*—(Telugu.) Records a grant of land for religious purposes in Ś. 1664 (A.D. 1742), Kaliyuga 4843, Dundubhi, by the chief people of the village, "belonging to Yelavānāsūru, in the province of Vāligoṇḍapuram," under the Subah of Haiderabad.

Grāmam.

The Śiva temple here was originally known as Śrī-Aṟṟuṭṭaḷ-Mahādēva at Muḍiyūr. It was built by a Kēraḷa general of Rājāditya, the son of Parāntaka I.

540. 180 *of* 1906.—(Tamil.) On the south wall of the central shrine in the Śivalōkanātha temple. A record in the twenty-ninth year of the Chōḷa king Parakēsarivarman. Built in at the beginning. Records gift of a lamp.

541. 181 *of* 1906.—(Tamil.) On the same wall. A record in the third year of the Chōḷa king Tribhuvanachakravartin Rājarājadēva. Built in at the end. The donor is Mōgan Āḷappirandān *alias* Anapāya-Kāḍavarāyan.

542. 182 *of* 1906.—(Tamil.) On the same wall. A record in the twenty-ninth year of Chōḷa king Madiraikoṇḍa Parakēsarivarman (905—47). Records gift of a lamp by a servant of prince Rājāditya. See S.A. 289.

543. 183 *of* 1906.—(Tamil.) On the same wall. A record in the twenty-ninth year of the Chōḷa king Madiraikoṇḍa Parakēsarivarman (905—47). Built in at the end. Records gift of a lamp.

544. 184 *of* 1906.—(Tamil.) On the west wall of the same shrine. A record in the forty-first year of the Chōḷa king Parakēsarivarman (Parāntaka I) who took Madurai (Madura) and Iḻam (Ceylon). Records gift of a lamp.

545. 185 *of* 1906.—(Tamil.) On the same wall. A record in the thirty-fifth year of the Chōḷa king Madiraikoṇḍa Parakēsarivarman (905—47). Records gift of land for two lamps.

546. 186 *of* 1906.—(Tamil.) On the same wall. A record in the thirty-second year of the Chōḷa king Madiraikoṇḍa Parakēsarivarman (905—47). Records gift of land.

547. 187 *of* 1906.—(Tamil.) On the same wall. An incomplete record in the thirty-first year of the Chōḷa king Madiraikoṇḍa Parakēsarivarman (905—47). Records gift of vessels by men who belonged to the army of prince Rājādityadēva. See S.A. 289.

548. 188 *of* 1906.—(Tamil.) On the same wall. A record in the sixteenth year of the Chōḷa king śrī Kulōttuṅga-Chōḷadēva. A few letters are missing at the end of each line. Records gift of a lamp by a person who had by mistake shot a man in hunting. See 378, etc.

549. 189 *of* 1906.—(Tamil.) On the same wall. A record in the tenth year of the Chōḷa king Parakēsarivarman *alias* Uḍaiyār śrī-Rājēndradēva. Records gift of a lamp. The village is called Parāntaka-chaturvēdimaṅgalam in Muḍiyūr-nāḍu in Tirumunaip-pāḍi Nāḍu in Rājēndrachōḷa-valanāḍu.

550. 190 *of* 1906.—(Tamil.) On the north wall of the same shrine. A record in the sixteenth year of the Chōḷa king Parakēsarivarman *alias* Uḍaiyār śrī-Rājēndra-Chōḷadēva (I, 1011—53). The inscription is incomplete. Below it is found a record of the tenth year of Uḍaiyār śrī-Kulōttuṅga-Chōḷadēva without any introduction.

551. 191 *of* 1906.—(Tamil.) On the same wall. A partly mutilated record in the fourth year of Chōḷa king Parakēsarivarman *alias* Uḍaiyār śrī-Rājēndradēva. Records gift of sheep.

552. 192 *of* 1906.—(Tamil.) On the same wall. An unfinished record in the thirty-ninth year of the Chōḷa king Madiraikoṇḍa-Parakēsarivarman (905—47.)

553. 193 *of* 1906.—(Tamil.) On the same wall. A record in the fourth year of the Chōḷa king Rājakēsarivarman *alias* Udaiyâr Rājēndra-Chōḷadēva (1011—53). Records sale of land. The village is called Paranṭaka-chaturvedimaṅgalam. A fragment of the introduction of Rājēndradēva is found at the bottom of the inscription.

554. 194 *of* 1906.—(Tamil.) On the east wall of the maṇṭapa in front of the same shrine. A record of the Vijayanagara-king Vīra-Viruppaṇa-Uḍiyār, son of Harihararāya (II), in Ś. 1317 expired, Yuvan. Registers an order of Śrīmatu-Nañjaṇaṅgaḷ to the authorities of the Pokkiṇaṅguḍuttaruḷiya-Nāyanār temple at Grāmam.

555. 195 *of* 1906.—(Tamil.) On the west wall of the same maṇṭapa. A fragment of record. Mentions Urandai (Uṛaiyūr).

556. 196 *of* 1906.—(Sanskrit and Tamil.) On the south wall of the Śelvāmbika shrine in the same temple. A record in the eighteenth year of the Pāṇḍya king Jaṭāvarman Tribhuvanachakravartin Kōnērinmaikoṇḍān Sundara-Pāṇḍyadēva (I, 1251—61). Begins with the words *samasta jagadādhāra*. The temple is called Uḍaiyār Śrīyāṟṟuttaḷi-Mūlasthānamuḍaiyār Pokkiṇaṅguḍuttaruḷiya-Nāyanār at Grāmam.

557. 197 *of* 1906.—(Tamil.) On the west and south walls of the same shrine. A record in the fifteenth year of the Pāṇḍya king Jaṭāvarman Tribhuvanachakravartin Sundara-Pāṇḍyadēva (I, 1251—61). Recōrds gift of land. Begins *samasta jagadādhāra*, etc. Records that Vīra-Pāṇḍyadēva established a festival called Sundarā Pāṇḍyan-śandi. Mention is also made of the time of Kō-Peruñjiṅga.

558. 198 *of* 1906.—(Sanskirit and Tamil.) On the north and west walls of the same shrine. A record in the nineteenth year of the Pāṇḍya king Tribhuvanachakravartin Kōnērinmaikoṇḍān *alias* Sundara-Pāṇḍyadēva (I, 1251—61). Records gift of land. *Begins samasta jagadādhāra, etc.*

559. 735 *of* 1905.—(Grantha and Tamil.) On the north of the central shrine in the Śivlōkanātha temple. A record of the Chōḷa king Madiraikoṇḍa Parakēsarivarman in Kaliyuga 4044, thirty-sixth year, 147 (7,0) 37th day, Sāturday, Rēvati, Makara. Records that Veḷḷānkumāra, the Kēraḷa general of Prince Rājāditya son of Madhurāntaka, built of stone a Siva temple at Mauḷigrāma (i.e., Muḍiyūr) on the Peṇṇai river. [Dr. Kielhorn infers from this that Parāntaka I began to rule between the 15th January and 25th July, A.D. 907. See *Ep. Ind.* VIII, p. 261.]

560. 736 *of* 1905.—(Tamil.) On the same wall. A record in the fourth year of the Chōḷa king Parakēsarivarman, who took the head of Vīra-Pāṇḍya (i.e., Āditya II). Records gift of a lamp. The temple is called Śrī-Āṟṟutaḷi-Mahādēvar at Triumuḍiyūr in Tirumunaippāḍi.

561. 737 *of* 1905.—(Tamil.) On the west wall of the same shrine. A record in the twenty-fourth year of the Chōḷa king Madiraikoṇḍa-Parakēsarivarman (Parānṭaka I). Records sale of land.

562. 738 *of* 1905.—(Tamil.) On the same wall. A record in the twentieth year of the Rāshṭrakūṭa king Kaṇṇaradēva (Kṛishṇa III). Records gift of sheep for a lamp.

563. 739 *of* 1905.—(Tamil.) On the same wall. A record in the twenty-ninth year of the Chōḷa king Madiraikoṇḍa-Parakēsarivarman (Parāntaka I). Records gift of sheep for a lamp by Veḷḷānkumāran, a native of Nandikarai-Puttūr in Malai-nāḍu and the general of prince Rājāditya. See No. 559 above.

564. 740 *of* 1905.—(Tamil.) On the same wall. A record of the Chōḷa king Madiraikoṇḍa-Parakēsarivarman, the date of which is lost. Records gift of gold for a lamp by a native of Kōṭṭāru.

565. 741 *of* 1905.—(Tamil.) On the south wall of the same shrine. An incomplete record in the third year of the Chōḷa king Uḍaiyār śrī-Rājamahēndradēva.

566. 742 *of* 1905.—(Tamil.) On the same wall. An incomplete record in the twenty-second year of the Rāshṭrakūṭa king Kaṇṇaradēva (III).

567. 743 *of* 1905.—(Tamil.) On the same wall. A record in the twenty-fifth year of the Rāshṭrakūṭa king Kaṇṇaradēva (Krishṇa III). Records a gift by the Vaiḍumba Mahārāja Tiruvaiyan Śrīkaṇṭha. See N.A. 336.

568. 744 *of* 1905.—(Tamil.) On the same wall. A record in the twenty-third year of the Chōḷa king Madiraikoṇḍa Parakēsarivarman. Records gift of ninety sheep for a lamp by the residents of the district of Tirumunaippāḍi.

569. 745 *of* 1905.—(Tamil.) On the same wall. A record in the twenty-ninth year of the Chōḷa king Madiraikoṇḍa Parakēsarivarman. (190—547). Records gift of a lamp by certain servants of prince Rājāditya to the temple of Śrī-Āṟṟuttaḷi-Mahādēvar. Mentions Kuśappāḍi in Muḍiyūr-nāḍu.

Jambai.

This village the antiquity of which is shown by its dolmens and stone circles resembling those at Dēvanūr, Kōṭṭūr, Gaṅgavaram, etc. (see *Ind. Antq.* V, 159 ff.) is also epigraphically rich.

570. 67 *of* 1906.—(Tamil.) On the north wall of the central shrine in the Jambunātha temple. A record in the third year of the Chōḷa king Rājakēsarivarman *alias* Tirubhuvanachakravartin Kulōttuṅga-Chōḷadēva (I ?). Records gift of 64 sheep for two lamps. One Kōvalarāyapēraiyan happened to wound fatally another and the people of the 79 *Nāḍus* met, threw the blame on him and compelled him to endow 64 cows for two lamps. See S.A. 580.

571. 68 *of* 1906.—(Tamil.) On the same wall. A record in the fortieth year of the Chōḷa king Rājakēsarivarman *alias* Tribhuvanachakravartin Kulōttuṅga-Chōḷadēva. Records gift of the village of Kuḷakkuḍi *alias* Vīraśōḷanallūr to the temple of Tiruttāntōnṛi-Īśvaramuḍaiya-Mahādēva at Śaṇbai *alias* Vīrarājēndrapuram on the northern bank of the Peṇṇār in Vānagoppāḍi (*alias*) Rājēndra-vaḷanāḍu. (Seventy-nine *Kaḻanjus* cost.)

572. 69 *of* 1906.—(Tamil.) On the same wall. A record in the thirty-eighth year of the Chōḷa king Tribhuvanachakravartin Kulōttuṅga-Chōḷadēva. Records gift of land for a lamp by a certain Rājarāja-Śiśupāla. See No. 576 below.

573. 70 *of* 1906.—(Tamil.) On the same wall. An unfinished record in the eighth year of the Pāṇḍya king Kōnērinmēlkoṇḍān Tribhuvanachakravartin Sundara-Pāṇḍyadēva. Records gift of the village of Nariyār-ēndal to the temple.

574. 71 *of* 1906.—(Tamil.) On the same wall. A record in the twenty-sixth year of the Chōḷa king Rājarāja-Rājakēsarivarman *alias* Śrī Rājarājadēva I (985—1013). Built in at the beginning. Records sale of land by the assembly of Maruvūr *alias* Vayiramēgha-Chaturvēdimaṅgalam on the southern bank of the river Peṇṇār in Vānakōppāḍi. The village is called Vāḷaiyūr *alias* Nittavinōdapuram.

575. 72 *of* 1906.—(Tamil.) On the north and west walls of the same shrine. A record in the twenty-eighth year of the Chōḷa king Tribhuvanachakravartin Rājarājadēva. Records gift of land by the Mahāmaṇḍalēśvara Kumāra-Padumadēvarasan.

576. 73 *of* 1906.—(Tamil.) On the same wall. A record in the thirty-eighth year of the Chōḷa king Tribhuvanachakravartin Kulōttuṅga-Chōḷadēva. Records gift of land by Śōḷagaṅga-Pallavaraiyan *alias* Piṛavāvenṛān Rājarāja-Siśupālan. See No. 572.

577. 74 *of* 1906.—(Tamil.) On the same walls. A record in the tenth year of the Pāṇḍya king Kōnērinmēlkoṇḍān Tribhuvanachakravartin Kulaśēkharadēva. Records gift of land for celebrating a festival called *Kulaśēkaran-śandi.*

578. 75 *of* 1906.—(Tamil.) On the same wall. A record in the twenty-first year of the Chōḷa king Parakēsarivarman *alias* Uḍaiyār Śrī-Rājēndra-chōḷadēva (1011—43). Records gift of two lamps, one of which was meant for the shrine of Durgā in the temple.

579. 76 *of* 1906.—(Tamil.) On the same walls. A record in the seventeenth year of Tribhuvanachakravartin Kōnērinmaikoṇḍān. Records gift of the village of Śrīpādanallūr which belonged to two residents of Iṛaivanaṛaiyūr in Vaḍagarai Narippaḷḷi-nāḍu, a district of Magadai-maṇḍalam, for celebrating a festival called Bhuvanēkavīran śandi and for repairs.

580. 77 *of* 1906.—(Tamil.) On the west wall of the same shrine. A record in the twenty-eighth year of the Chōḷa king Rājarāja-Rājakēsarivarman *alias* Śrī-Rājarājadēva (I). Records gift of gold (10 kaḷanjus) for a lamp by a merchant of Jambai for the merit of a native of Nāvalūr whom he had stabbed to death for an attempt at the modesty of his concubine. See No. 570 above.

581. 78 *of* 1906.—(Tamil.) On the same wall. A record in the twentieth year of the Chōḷa king Tribhuvanachakravartin Kulōttuṅga-Chōḷadēva. Records gift of land.

582. 79 *of* 1906.—(Tamil.) On the same wall. An incomplete record of the Chōḷa king Rājēndra-Chōḷa I. Most of the historical introduction is preserved. The continuation could not be traced.

583. 80 *of* 1906.—(Tamil.) On the south wall of the same shrine. A record in the third year (A.D. 1054) of the Chōḷa king Parakēsarivarman *alias* Uḍaiyar Śrī-Rājēndradēva. Records gift of 32 kāśu for a lamp. The temple is called Tiruttāntōnṟi-Mādevar at Valaiyūr *alias* Rājēndrapuram. Daily Uḷakku oil. The Uḍaiyān of the place compels a lady to pay a tax (by torture) and she takes poison, and so people from all quarters and nāḍus meet, throw the blame on him and compel him to make the gift. See S.A. 580, 570, etc.

584. 81 *of* 1906.—(Tamil.) On the same wall. A record in the thirty-second year of the Chōḷa king Rājarājakēsarivarman *alias* Uḍaiyār Śrī-Rājādhirājadēva. Partly mutilated and incomplete. Seems to record the gift of a lamp (20 *kāśu*). (Uḷakku oil by *Dēvasahāya marakkāl* a day.).

585. 82 *of* 1906.—(Tamil.) On the same wall. A record in the twenty-fifth year of the Chōḷa king Parakēsarivarman *alias* Uḍaiyār śrī-Rājēndra-Chōḷadēva I (1011—53). Records an agreement among the citizens of the city of Vāḷaiyūr *alias* Nittavinōdapuram on the northern bank of the Peṇṇār river in Vānagoppāḍi *alias* Madurāntaka-vaḷanāḍu, a district of Jayaṅgoṇḍa-Chōla-maṇḍalam.

586. 83 *of* 1906.—(Tamil.) On the same wall. A record in the second year of the Chōḷa king Rājakēsarivarman *alias* Uḍaiyār Śrī-Vīrarājēndradēva. Records gift of 10 kāśu for a lamp.

587. 84 *of* 1906.—(Tamil.) On the same wall. A record in the twenty-fourth year of the Chōḷa king Rājarāja-Rājakēsarivarman *alias* Śrī-Rājarājadēva I (985—1013). Records that the Sabhā of Nerkunṟam *alias* Vayiramēgha-Chaturvēdimaṅgalam gave land in exchange for fields taken up by the bed of their newly constructed tank. [The epigraph shows the Sabha's control over the village lands.]

588. 85 *of* 1906.—(Tamil.) On the same wall. A record in the twelfth year of the Chōḷa king Tribhuvanachakravartin Kulōttuṅga-Chōḷadēva. Records gift of land. Mentions Araṅgam on the southern bank of the Peṇṇār and Āḷavandān Nīrēṟṟa-Perumāḷ *alias* Rājarāja-Śiśupālan. See No. 572 above.

589. 86 *of* 1906.—(Tamil.) On the same wall. An incomplete record in the twenty-sixth year of the Chōḷa king Rājarāja-Rājakēsarivarman *alias* Śrī-Rājarājadēva I (985—1013). Mentions a Bāṇa chief named Maravan Narasimhavarma *alias* Rājarājavānakōvaraiyar. See N.A. 445, 487 and 513.

590. 87 *of* 1906.—(Tamil.) On the same wall. A record in the twenty-fourth year of the Chōḷa king Tribhuvanachakravartin Kulōttuṅga-Chōḷadēva. Records gift of land by a native of Conjeeveram. Mentions Kiḷiyūr Malaiyamān Aḷagiyan Ākaraśūran *alias* Rājagambhīra Chēdiyarāyar. [See N.A. 489 and 452 which shows that this man was a vassal of Rājarāja III also.]

591. 88 *of* 1906.—(Tamil.) On the same wall. A record in Ānanda of the Vijayanagara king Sadāśiva-Mahārāya. Mentions Uṇṇāmulai-Nāyanār.

592. 89 *of* 1906.—(Tamil.) On the same wall. A record of the Vijayanagara king Achyutadēva-Mahārāya in Ś. 1455 expired Jaya. Registers the privileges and duties of the temple superintendent.

593. 90 *of* 1906.—(Tamil.) On the north wall of the maṇṭapa in front of the same shrine. A record in the sixteenth year of the Chōḷa king . . . . . Rājarājadēva. Built in at the beginning. Records gift of land.

594. 91 *of* 1906.—(Tamil.) On the same wall. A record of the Chōḷa king Tribhuvanachakravartin Vikrama-Chōḷadēva, the date of which is lost. Mutilated at the end. A man apparently pushed his wife as a result of which she fell and died. The 1,500 men of the four quarters declared him guilty in their assembly and compelled him to provide for lamps.

595. 92 *of* 1906.—(Tamil.) On the same wall. A record in the ninth year of the Chōḷa king Parakēsarivarman *alias* Tribhuvanachakravartin Vikrama-Chōḷadēva (1118—35). Built in at the beginning. Records gift of 64 cows for two lamps, by a man who in the course of a comparison of martial skill with two Veḷḷāḷas, killed one of them.

596. 93 *of* 1906.—(Tamil.) On the same wall. A record of the Vijayanagara king Vīrapratāpa Virūpākshadēva Mahārāya (II) in Ś. 1395 expired, Nandana. A few syllables are missing in each line from the fourth. Records gift of money.

597. 94 *of* 1906. (Tamil.) On the same wall. An incomplete record of the Vijayanagara king Vīra-Naraśiṅgarāya, son of Śāḷuva Naraśiṅgarāya, in Ś. 1429 expired, Prabhava. Records gift of land by Rāmaya-Śōḷa-Mahārāja, son of the Uraiyūr Chōḷa Pottaya-Śōḷa-Mahārāja of the Solar race and the Kāśyapa-gōtra.

598. 95 *of* 1906.—(Tamil.) On the same wall. A record in the twenty-seventh year of the Chōḷa king Tribhuvanachakravartin

Kulōttuṅga Chōḷadēva. Records an agreement among the vāṇiyar. See N.A. 206.

599. 96 *of* 1906.—(Tamil.) On the west wall of the outer maṇṭapa in the same temple. A record in the sixteenth year of the Pallava king Sakalabhuvanachakravartin Peruñjiṅgadēva, corresponding to Monday, 9th December 1258. Records an agreement among the residents of the country to the north of the river Avinai and to the south of the Peṇṇai. *Ep. Ind.*, Vol. IX, p. 216.

600. 97 *of* 1906.—(Tamil.) On the east wall of the second prākāra of the same temple. A record of the Rāshṭrakūṭa king Kaṇṇaradēva (Krishṇa III), the date of which is lost. Mutilated at the end and incomplete. The temple is called Tānṛōnṛi-Īśvaram at Vaḍagarai-Vāḷaiyūr.

601. 98 *of* 1906.—(Tamil.) On the north wall of the same prākāra. A record in the thirty-third year of the Pāṇḍya king Tribhuvanachakravartin Kulaśēkharadēva. Records gift of land. The temple is called Tiruttāndōnṛi-Āḷuḍaiya-Nāyanār at Śaṇbai *alias* Vīrarājēndraśōḷapuram in Peṇṇai-vaḍagarai Vānagoppāḍi-nāḍu (evidently founded by Vīrarājēndra I, 1064—70).

602. 99 *of* 1906.—(Tamil.) On the wall of the kitchen in the same temple, left of entrance. A record in the fourth year of the Chōḷa king Tribhuvanachakravartin Vijayarājēndradēva. Records the building of the kitchen. [Was the king Rājādhirāja I ?]

603. 100 *of* 1906.—(Tamil.) On the south wall of the Akhilāṇḍēśvari shrine in the same temple. A record in the sixth year of the Chōḷa king Rājakēsarivarman *alias* Uḍaiyār Śrī-Vīrarājēndradēva (1063—1070). Records gift of 500 kuḷis of land to the accountant of Rājēndrapura by the temple authorities to write temple account, among whom figures the mahāvratin Lakuḷīśvara-Paṇḍita as the head of the pūjāris. A namesake of this pūjāri is seen in a Mēlpādi epigraph of Rājēndra Chōḷa I (*S.I.I.*, Vol. III, p. 28) and in Baligāmi epigraph of 1035 (*Ep. Ind.*, Vol. V. p. 227). Perhaps all these were the same. Lakuḷīśvara Paṇḍita was evidently a Kālāmukha. For the history of this sect see Bhandarkar's *Śaivitism, Vaishṇavism, etc.*

604. 101 *of* 1906.—(Tamil.) On the same wall. In modern characters. Records in Khara an endowment to a *maṭha*.

605. 102 *of* 1906.—(Tamil.) On the west wall of the same shrine. A record in the fourteenth year of the Chōḷa king Tribhuvanachakravartin Kulōttuṅga-Chōḷadēva. Records gift of land to the shrine of Tirukkavālīśvaramuḍaiyār at Śaṇbai *alias* Vīrarājēndrapuram on the northern bank of the Peṇṇār in Vānagoppāḍi by Kiḷiyūr Malaiyamān Śēdiyarāyanāyan Ākaraśūran *alias* Rājagambhīra-Chēdiyarāyan. See S.A. 902 and 647, 687, 736, etc.

606. 103 *of* 1906.—(Tamil.) On the same wall. A record of the Vijayanagara king Achutaiyadēva-Mahārāya, son of

Naraśiṅgadēva in Ś. 1554 (for 1454), Nandana. *Refers to the 98 castes included in the iḍaṅgai and valaṅgai.* Registers an agreement apparently among the weavers to contribute to the maintenance of a *maṭha.* See S.A. 728.

607. 104 *of* 1906.—(Tamil.) On the north wall of the same shrine. A record of the Vijayanagara king Sadāśivadēva-Mahārāya, son of Śāḷuva Naraśiṅgadēva-Mahārāya Achyutadēva-Mahārāya in Ś. 1471 expired, Saumya. Records gift of the village of Śuttamalligai for the merit of the king by Aḍappam Śūrappa-Nāyakkaraiyan Kṛishṇama-Nāyakkaraiyan. The village was granted by Rāmappa-Nāyakkar and belonged to Meygunṛada-vaḷanāḍu *alias* Narippaḷḷi-nāḍu in Magadai-maṇḍalam on the southern bank of the Peṇṇār.

608. 105 *of* 1906.—(Tamil.) On the same wall. A mutilated record in the eighth year of the Chōḷa king Tribhuvanachakravartin Vikrama-Chōḷadēva (1118--35). Records gift of land.

609. 106 *of* 1906.—(Tamil.) On the same wall. A record of the Vijayanagara king Achyutaiyadēva-Mahārāya, son of Śāḷuva-Naraśiṅgadēva in Ś. 1552 (for 1452), Nandana. Records gift of the village of Ākkaippāḍi in Meygunṛa-nāḍu *alias* Narippari-nāḍu, a district of Magadai-maṇḍalam on the southern bank of the Peṇṇār, for the merit of the king by Vaiyyappa Nāyakkar. The village granted was in the jurisdiction of Veṅkaṭādri-Nāyaka.

610. 107 *of* 1906.—(Tamil.) On a stone lying on the floor close to the south wall of the same shrine. A fragment of record of the Chōḷa king Madairaikoṇḍa-Parakēsarivarman (905—47), the date of which is lost.

611. 108 *of* 1906.—(Tamil.) On a slab built into the floor at the second entrance into the same temple A damaged record in the twenty-fourth year of the Chōḷa king Madiraikoṇḍa-Parakēsarivarman (905—47). Refers to the building of a maṇṭapa at the city of Valaiyūr by Vīranāraṇiyār, queen of prince Kaṇḍarādittar and daughter of Śōḷamādēviyār.

612. 109 *of* 1906.—(Tamil.) On the slab set up on the left side of the same entrance. A record in the twenty-seventh year of the Chōḷa king Karikāla-Chōḷadēva (unidentified). Refers to the grant in former times of Raṇabhīmamaṅgalam by the Vānakōvaraiyar Vīraparumar.

613. 110 *of* 1906.—(Tamil.) On the south wall of the gōpura at the same entrance. A fragment of record in the twenty-third year of the Rāshṭrakūṭa king Kaṇṇaradēva (Krishṇa III). Seems to record the gift of a lamp.

614. 111 *of* 1906.—(Tamil.) On the gōpura of the same temple, right of entrance. A fragment of record in the thirty-fifth year of the Chōḷa king Madiraikoṇḍa-Parakēsarivarman (905—47). Seems to be an endowment for daily requirements.

615. 112 *of* 1906.—(Tamil.) In the same place. A record in the twenty-sixth year of the Rāshṭrakūṭa king Kaṇṇaradēva (Krishṇa III). Records gift of 96 sheep for a lamp and gold for offerings to the shrine of Sūjya (Sūrya) dēva in the temple of Tiruttānṛōnṛi-Āḷvār at Vāḷaiyūr.

616. 113 *of* 1906.—(Tamil.) In the same place. A record in the fourteenth year of the Pallava king Peruñjiṅgadēva. Records gift of paddy.

617. 114 *of* 1906.—(Tamil.) In the same place. A record in the fourth year of the Chōḷa king Tribhuvanachakravartin Vijaya-rājēndradēva. Records the building of the entrance and of the gōpura by a native of the Chōḷa country, who also built the kitchen according to No. 99 above.

618. 115 *of* 1906.—(Tamil.) In the same place. A mutilated record of the Chōḷa king Madiraikoṇḍa Parakēsarivarman, the date of which is lost.

619. 116 *of* 1906.—(Tamil.) In the same place. A record in the twenty-fourth year of the Rāshṭrakūṭa king Kaṇṇaradēva (Krishṇa III). Records gift of gold for a lamp. This is a fragment which has been pieced together with another found to the left of the entrance.

620. 117 *of* 1906.—(Tamil.) In the same place. An incomplete record in the twenty-fifth year of the Chōḷa king Madiraikoṇḍa-Parakēsarivarman (905—47). Seems to record the gift of a lamp to the shrine of Vīdiviḍaṅgar in the temple of Tānṛōnṛippirān at Peṇṇaivaḍagarai-Vāḷaiyūr. This is a fragment which has been pieced together with another found to the left of the entrance.

621. 118 *of* 1906.—(Tamil.) In the same place. A mutilated record in the twenty-third year of the Rāshṭrakūṭa king Śrī-Kaṇ-ṇaradēva (Krishṇa III). Records gift of a lamp to the temple of Tiruttānṛōnṛi Perumāḷ *alias* Vīdiviḍaṅgadēvar at Vāḷaiyūr on the northern bank of the Peṇṇār in Vānagoppāḍi. Mentions Vēṇāḍu-ḍaiyār.

622. 119 *of* 1906.—(Tamil.) In the same place. A record in the thirteenth year of the Pallava king Sakalabhuvanachakravartin Peruñjiṅgadēva. Records gift of land to the younger brother of a person who cut off his own head in order that a maṇṭapa which was being constructed might be completed. [A remarkable case of self-sacrifice at the altar of superstition. Compare the slaughter of 60 convicts for the construction of an irrigation work in Vijayanagar.]

623. 120 *of* 1906.—(Tamil.) On the same gōpura, left of entrance. A damaged record of the Vijayanagara king Sadāśiva-Mahārāya in Ś. 1485 expired, Pramōda (wrong). Seems to record a gift of land.

624. 121 *of* 1906.—(Tamil.) In the same place. A record of the Chōḷa king Madiraikoṇḍa Parakēsarivarman, the date of which is lost. Records gift of five lamps.

625. 122 *of* 1906.—(Tamil.) In the same place. A record in the eleventh year of the Pallava king Sakalabhuvanachakravartin Peruñjiṅgadēva. Records the exemption from certain taxes of lands in the village of Guṇamaṅgalam on the southern bank of the Pennār.

626. 123 *of* 1906.—(Tamil.) In the same place. A record in the eleventh year of the Pallava king Peruñjiṅgadēva. Records gift of paddy.

627. 124 *of* 1906.—(Tamil.) In the same place. A damaged record in the thirty-third year of the Chōḷa king Madiraikoṇḍa Parakēsarivarman (995-47). Records gift of a lamp.

628. 125 *of* 1906.—(Tamil.) In the same place. A mutilated record in the twenty-eighth year of the Rāshṭrakūṭa king Kaṇṇaradēva (Krishṇa III). Records gift of gold for a lamp.

629. 126 *of* 1906.—(Tamil.) In the same place. A mutilated record of the Rāshṭrakūṭa king Kaṇṇaradēva, the date of which is lost. Records gift of gold for a lamp.

630. 127 *of* 1906.—(Tamil.) On a stone set up at the right of entrance into the same temple. A record of the Vijayanagara king Achyutadēva-Mahārāya, son of Naraśiṅgadēva in Ś. 1452 expired, Nandana. Records the exemption of the temple (lands) from the tax called *Sōmaśūlavari* on the representation of Vaiyyappa-Nāyakkar-Ayyan while Vēlūr Bommu-Nāyaka was the Governor. See N.A. 227.

*Kiḻūr.**

Kīḻūr, near Tirukkōyilūr, famous for its Tiruvīraṭṭānam temple, was situated in Kurukkai Kūṟṟam in Jananātha-vaḷanāḍu and was the capital of the Malayamāns of Malaināḍu or Malāḍu.

631. 230 *of* 1902.—(Tamil.) On the south wall of the Vīraṭṭānēśvara shrine. A record in the eleventh year of the Chōḷa king Rājarājakēsarivarman. Records gift of gold for a lamp.

632. 231 *of* 1902.—(Tamil.) On the south and east walls of the same shrine. A record in the sixteenth year of the Chōḷa king Rājarāja-Rājakēsarivarman. Provides for the supply of temple servants.

633. 232 *of* 1902.—(Tamil.) On the south wall of the same shrine. A record in the thirtieth year of the Rāshṭrakūṭa king Kaṇṇaradēva (Krishṇa III). Records gift of gold for a lamp.

---

* The inscriptions of this place are given in *Ins., S. Dts.,* 134-140 (22 inscriptions). They are fairly detailed, but I have not attempted to identify them with the corresponding records in the above list. Presumably all of them are included in the above.

634. 233 *of* 1902.—(Tamil.) On the same wall. A record in the fifth year of the Chōḷa king Parakēsarivarman *alias* Rājēndra-Chōḷadēva (I, 1011–43). Records gift of ninety sheep for a lamp.

635. 234 *of* 1902.—(Tamil.) On the same wall. A record in the twenty-ninth year of the Chōḷa king Rājarāja-Rājakēsarivarman *alias* Rājarājadēva I (985–1013). Records gift of ninety-five sheep for a lamp.

636. 235 *of* 1902.—(Tamil.) On the same wall. A record of the Rāshṭrakūṭa king Kaṇṇaradēva (Kṛishṇa III), the date of which is lost. Records gift of 20 *kaḻañjus* of gold by a queen of the Vaiḍumba-Mahārāja Tiruvayanar, to the Sabhā of Nenmeli for supplying 20 *kalams* of paddy as interest. See No. 669 below. *Ep. Ind.*, Vol. VII, p. 143.

637. 236 *of* 1902.—(Tamil verse.) On the south, east and north walls of the same shrine. A record in the twenty-seventh year of the Chōḷa king Rājarāja. Records gift of land.

638. 237 *of* 1902.—(Grantha and Tamil.) On the south wall of the same shrine. A damaged record in the fifth year of the Chōḷa king Tribhuvanachakravartin Rājarājadēva.

639. 238 *of* 1902.—(Tamil.) On the north wall of the same shrine. A record in the thirteenth year of the Chōḷa king Rājarājakēsarivarman (985–1013). Records gift of ninety sheep for a lamp.

640. 239 *of* 1902.—(Tamil.) On the same wall. A record in the ninth year of the Chōḷa king Rājarājakēsarivarman (i.e., Rājarāja I). Records gift of gold for a lamp by Amitravalli, the mother of queen Lōkamahādēvi and daughter of Kundaṇan. [The same queen of Rājarāja is mentioned in Tanjore and Tiruvayāru inscriptions. See *S.I.I.* II, 90 and *Ep. Ind.* VII, p. 144.] An Īḷa lamp worth 2 *kāśu* is mentioned.

641. 240 *of* 1902.—(Tamil.) On the north wall of the Vīrattānēśvara shrine in the same place. A record in the fifteenth year of the Chōḷa king Parakēsarivarman. Records gift of land for a lamp.

642. 241 *of* 1902.—(Tamil.) On the same wall. A record in the eighth year of the Chōḷa king Parakēsarivarman *alias* Rājēndra-Chōḷadēva (I, 1011–43). Records gift of ninety-eight cows for offerings.

643. 242 *of* 1902.—(Tamil.) On the same wall. A record in the ninth year of the Chōḷa king Parakēsarivarman *alias* Rājēndra-Chōḷadēva (I, 1011–43). Records gift of gold.

644. 243 *of* 1902.—(Tamil.) On the same wall. A record in the seventeenth year of the Chōḷa king Rājarāja-Rājakēsarivarman (985–1013). Records gift of ninety-six sheep for a lamp.

- **645.** 244 *of* 1902.—(Tamil.) On the same wall. A record in the sixth year of the Chōḷa king Parakēsarivarman *alias* Rājēndra-Chōḷadeva (I, 1011–43). Records sale of land. End built in.

646. 245 *of* 1902.—(Tamil.) On the same wall. An incomplete record in the twenty-first year of the Chōḷa king Parakēsarivarman *alias* Uḍaiyār Rājēndra-Chōḷadēva (I, 1011–43).

647. 246 *of* 1902.—(Tamil.) On the same wall. A record in the sixth year of the Chōḷa king Rājakēsarivarman *alias* Uḍaiyār Kulōttuṅga-Chōḷadēva. Records gift of land by Kiḷiyūr Malaiya-mān Rāja-Chēdiyarāyan.

648. 247 *of* 1902.—(Tamil.) On the same wall. A record in the fourth year of the Chōḷa king Rājakēsarivarman (?) *alias* Uḍaiyār Rājēndra-Chōḷadēva (I, 1011–43). Records gift of thirty-two cows for a lamp by Ādhirājēndra-Kōvalaraiyan.

649. 248 *of* 1902.—(Tamil.) On the same wall. A record in the fourth year of the Chōḷa king Rājakēsarivarman (?) *alias* Uḍaiyār Rājēndra-Chōḷadēva (I, 1011–43). Records gift of ninety-six sheep for a lamp.

650. 249 *of* 1902.—(Tamil.) On the same wall. A record in the second year of the Chōḷa king Parakēsarivarman *alias* Uḍaiyār Rājēndra-Chōḷadēva (I, 1011–43). Records gift of sixteen cows for a lamp.

651. 250 *of* 1902.—(Tamil.) On the same wall. A record in the eighteenth year of the Chōla king Rājarājakēsarivarman (985–1013). Records gift of land.

652. 251 *of* 1902.—(Tamil.) On the same wall. A record in the tenth year of the Chōḷa king Rājarājakēsarivarman *alias* Uḍaiyār Kulōttuṅga-Chōḷadēva. Records gift of 224 cows for seven lamps by a chief of the Malaiyakula.

653. 252 *of* 1902.—(Tamil.) On the same wall. A record in the twenty-ninth year of the Chōḷa king Rājarājakēsarivarma *alias* Rājarājadēva (985–1013). Records gift of 150 cows.

654. 253 *of* 1902.—(Tamil.) On the east wall of the same shrine. A record in the third year of the Chōḷa king Chōḷa-Kēraḷa-dēva. Records gift of ninety-six sheep for a lamp by a merchant.

655. 254 *of* 1902.—(Tamil.) On the same wall. A record in the fourteenth year of the Chōḷa king Rājarāja-Rājakēsarivarman (985–1013). Records gift of ninety-six sheep for a lamp.

656. 255 *of* 1902.—(Tamil.) On the same wall. A record in the sixteenth year of the Chōḷa king Rājarāja-Rājakēsarivarman (I, 985–1913). Records gift of ninety sheep for a lamp.

657. 256 *of* 1902.—(Tamil.) On the same wall. A record in the third year of the Chōḷa king Parakēsarivarman *alias* Uḍaiyār Ādhirājēndradēva. Records gift of thirty-two cows for a lamp.

658. 257 *of* 1902.—(Tamil.) On the same wall. A record in the seventh year of the Chōḷa king Parakēsarivarman *alias* Uḍaiyār Rājēndradēva (1050-62). Records gift of thirty-two cows for a lamp.

659. 258 *of* 1902.—(Tamil.) On the same wall. A record in the sixth year of the Chōḷa king Parakēsarivarman *alias* Uḍaiyār Rājēndradēva. Records sale of land.

660. 259 *of* 1902.—(Tamil.) On the same wall. A record in the seventh year of the Chōḷa king Parakēsarivarman *alias* Uḍaiyār Vīrarājēndradēva. Records gift of thirty-two cows for a lamp. The king was evidently Kullōttuṅga III.

661. 260 *of* 1902.—(Tamil.) On the same wall. A record in the sixth year of the Chōḷa king Parakēsarivarman *alias* Rājēndra-Chōḷadēva (1011-43). Records gift of a golden plate and fly-whisk.

662. 261 *of* 1902.—(Tamil.) On the same wall. A record in the sixth year of the Chōḷa king Parakēsarivarman *alias* Rājēndra-Chōḷadēva (I, 1011-43). Records sale of land.

663. 262 of 1902.—(Tamil.) On the same wall. A record in the fifth year of the Chōḷa king Rājakēsarivarman *alias* Tribhuvanachakravartin Rājādhirājadēva. Records gift of land to four images set up in the temple.

664. 263 *of* 1902.—(Tamil.) On the north wall of the maṇṭapa in front of the same shrine. A record in the sixth year of the Chōḷa king Parakēsarivarman *alias* Rājēndra-Chōḷadēva (I, 1011-43). List of golden articles preserved in the treasury of the temple.

665. 264 *of* 1902.—(Tamil.) On the same wall. A record in the thirty-first year of the Chōḷa king Kulōttuṅga-Chōḷadēva. Records gift of a coconut garden.

666. 265 *of* 1902.—(Tamil.) On the same wall. A record in the fifteenth year of the Chōḷa king Parakēsarivarman. Records gift of land for a lamp.

667. 266 *of* 1902.—(Tamil.) On the same wall. A record in the twenty-third year of the Rāshtrakūṭa king Kaṇṇaradēva. Records gift of 90 sheep.

668. 267 *of* 1902.—(Tamil.) On the north wall of the maṇṭapa in front of the Vīraṭṭānēśvara shrine. A record in the twenty-fourth year of the Rāshṭrakūṭa king Kaṇṇaradēva (Kṛishṇa III). Records gift of 2,304 sheep for 24 lamps by the Vaiḍumba-Maharaja Tiruvayanār. See Nos. 636 and 640 and *Ep. Ind.*, Vol. VII, p. 144.

669. 268 *of* 1902.—(Tamil.) On the same wall. A record in the twenty-first year of the Rāshṭrakūṭa king Kaṇṇaradēva (Kṛishṇa III). Records gift of land by the Vaiḍumba-Mahārāja Śandayan Tiruvayan and his queen Śūttiradēvi. [One of the local Vaiḍumba chiefs was defeated by Parāntaka I. See *S. Ind. Inscrns.*, Vol. II, p. 387. Śaṅkaradēva who was a contemporary of Rājarāja I was evidently the son of this Tiruvayan. See *S. Ind. Inscrns.* Vol. III, pp. 104—6. See also S.A. 72 and *Ep. Ind.*, Vol. VII, pp. 142-3.]

670. 269 *of* 1902.—(Tamil.) On the same wall. A damaged record in the nineteenth year of the Rāshṭrakūṭa king Kaṇṇaradēva (Kṛishṇa III).

671. 270 *of* 1902.—(Tamil.) On the same wall. A record in the twenty-sixth year of the Rāshṭrakūṭa king Kaṇṇaradēva. Records gift of 100 sheep for a lamp.

672. 271 *of* 1902.—(Tamil.) On the same wall. A record in the second year of the Chōḷa king Parakēsarivarman. Records gift of 192 sheep for two lamps by Śembiyan Milāḍuḍaiyār.

673. 272 *of* 1902.—(Tamil.) On the same wall. A record in the tenth year of the Pāṇḍya king Māravarman *alias* Tribhuvana-chakravartin Sundara-Pāṇḍyadēva (I or II ?). Records gift of land.

674. 273 of 1902.—(Tamil.) On the same wall. A record in the fifth year of the Chōḷa king Rājakēsarivarman *alias* Uḍaiyār Vīrarājēndradēva (I, 1064—70). Records gift of forty-eight sheep for a lamp. *S. Ind. Inscrns.*, Vol. III, No. 82, pp. 199-200.

675. 274 *of* 1902.—(Tamil.) On the same wall. Records gift of sheep for a lamp. The date and the name of the king of the record are lost.

676. 275 *of* 1902.—(Tamil.) On the same wall. A record in the third year of the king whose name is not mentioned. Records gift of gold for a lamp.

677. 276 *of* 1902.—(Tamil.) On the same wall. A record in the thirty-first year of the king whose name is lost. Partially built in.

678. 277 *of* 1902.—(Tamil.) On the same wall. A record in the twenty-first year of the "Gaṅga-Pallava king" Vijaya Nripatuṅgavikrama, son and successor of Vijaya Nandivikramavarman (III). Records gift of gold for a lamp, by a servant of Veṭṭuvadaraiyar. The amount was 12 *kaḻañjus.* See *Ep. Ind.*, Vol. VII, pp. 139-40 and *Ins. S. Dts.*, p. 134, No. 4.

679. 278 *of* 1902.—(Tamil.) On the same wall. A record in the seventeenth year of the "Gaṅga-Pallava king" Vijaya-Nandivikrama. Records gift of gold (15 *kaḻañju*) for a lamp by a concubine of Vānakōvaraiyar. The 15 *kaḻañjus* are said to be equal in fineness to the old *kāsu*. The assembly receive the gold and promise to pay 1 *uḻakku* of oil every day as interest. See *Ep. Ind.*, Vol. VII, p. 139 and *Ins. S. Dts.* (Mack. MSS), p. 135, No. 5.

680. 279 *of* 1902.—(Tamil.) On the same wall. A record in the twenty-eighth year of the Chōḷa king Madirai-koṇḍa Parakēsarivarman (i.e., Parāntaka I). Records gift of 100 sheep for a lamp by a daughter of Kayirūr Perumānār or Milāḍuḍaiyār (i.e., chief of Mīlāḍu). See *Ep. Ind.*, Vol. VII, pp. 141–2.

681. 280 *of* 1902.—(Tamil.) On the same wall. A record in the twenty-third year of the Chōḷa king Madirai-koṇḍa-Parakēsarivarman (Parāntaka I). Records gift of 100 sheep for a lamp by 'a soldier' of prince Arikulakēsarin (who is called the king's son in an inscription at Tiruppundurutti near Tanjore and whom Dr. Hultzsch identifies with Ariñjaya, Parāntaka's third son). The donors are called the *Malayāṇa-Oṟṟaichchēvagar* or "the unrivalled warriors of Malayālam". Dr. Hultzsch surmises that it was perhaps a regiment of Nāirs. *Ep. Ind.*, Vol. VII, p. 142.

682. 281 *of* 1902.—(Tamil.) On the same wall. A record in the second year of the Chōḷa king Parakēsarivarman. Records gift of 480 sheep for five lamps.

683. 282 *of* 1902.—(Tamil.) On the west wall of the kitchen in the same temple. A record in the third year of the Chōḷa king Kulōttuṅga-Chōḷadēva. Records gift of land by a merchant to two images set up by him.

684. 283 *of* 1902.—(Tamil.) On the same wall. A record in the thirty-third year of the Chōḷa king Tribhuvanachakravartin Kulōttuṅga-Chōḷadēva. Records that Vānakōvaraiyan assigned certain taxes to the temple.

685. 284 *of* 1902.—(Tamil.) On the same wall. A record in the fifth year of the Chōḷa king Rājakēsarivarman *alias* Tribhuvanachakravartin Kulōttuṅga-Chōḷadēva. Records gift of land.

686. 285 *of* 1902.—(Tamil.) On the same wall. A record in the fourth year of the Chōla king Tribhuvanachakravartin Kulōttuṅga Chōḷadēva. Records the construction of the kitchen by the wife of Vikrama-Chōḷa-Chēdiyarāyan, and mother of Vikrama-Chōḷa-Kōvalarāyan. See S.A. 712.

687. 286 *of* 1902.—(Tamil.) On the same wall. A record in the fifth year of the Chōḷa king Tribhuvanachakravartin Vikrama-Chōḷadēva (1118—35). Records gift of thirty-two cows and one bull for a lamp by Kiḻiyūr-Malaiyamān Vikrama-Chōḷa-Chēdiyarāyan.

688. 287 *of* 1902.—(Tamil.) On the same wall. A record in the eighth year of the Pāṇḍya king Kōnērimēlkoṇḍān Tribhuvanachakravartin Vikrama-Pāṇḍyadēva corresponding to Friday, July 27, A.D. 1408. Records grant of certain taxes to the temple. *Ep. Ind.*, Vol. VIII, p. 281.

689. 288 *of* 1902.—(Tamil.) On the same wall. A record in the second year of the Chōḷa king Tribhuvanachakravartin Rājarājadēva. Records gift of land for eight lamps by Kiḻiyūr Malaiyamān Rājarāja-Chēdiyarāyan. [The details of this inscription are also given in *Ins. S. Dts.*, p. 137, No. 11.]

690. 289 *of* 1902.—(Tamil.) On the right of the entrance into the inner prākāra of the same temple. A record in the eighth year of the Chōḷa king Tribhuvanachakravartin Rājādhirājadēva (I or II?). Records gift of a flower garden.

691. 290 *of* 1902.—(Tamil.) On the left of the entrance into the inner prākāra of the same temple. A record in the tenth year of the Chōḷa king Tribhuvanachakravartin Kulōttuṅga-Chōḷadēva. Records gift of land by Kiḷiyūr-Malaiyamān Kulōttuṅga-Chōḷa-Chēdiyarāyan [i.e., the Chēdirāyan who was the feudatory of Kulōttuṅga Chōḷa.]

692. 291 *of* 1902.—(Tamil.) On the base of the Dakshiṇāmūrti shrine in the same temple. A record in the twentieth year of the Chōḷa king Tribhuvanachakravartin Kulōttuṅga-Chōḷadēva. Records the construction of the shrine by a minister of Magadai-Perumāḷ.

693. 292 *of* 1902.—(Tamil.) On the north wall of the Brihannāyaki shrine in the same village. A record in the twenty-eighth year of the Chōḷa king Tribhuvanachakravartin Kulōttuṅga-Chōḷadēva. Records gift of 130 kāśu for a lamp by a weaver of Tiruppālaippandal.

694. 293 *of* 1902.—(Tamil.) On the same wall. A record in the fifteenth year of the Chōḷa king Tribhuvanachakravartin Kulōttuṅga-Chōḷadēva. Records gift of land.

695. 294 *of* 1902.—(Tamil.) On the south wall of the same shrine. A record in the fourteenth year of the Chōḷa king Tribhuvanachakravartin Rājarājadēva. Records gift of eight cows for a lamp.

696. 295 *of* 1902.—(Tamil.) On a rock in the prākāra of the same temple. A record in the eleventh year of the "Gaṅga-Pallava" king Vijaya-Nandivikramavarman. Records gift of gold for two lamps. A damaged record. See S.A. 678–9 above.

697. 296 *of* 1902.—(Tamil.) On the same rock. A damaged record in the sixteenth year of the "Gaṅga-Pallava" king Vijaya-Nandivikramavarman. Records gift of gold for a lamp. See note to the above epigraph.

698. 297 *of* 1902.—(Tamil.) On the same rock. A damaged record in the eighteenth year of the "Gaṅga-Pallava" king Vijaya-Nripatuṅgavikrama. Records gift of a flower-garden and of gold.

699. 298 *of* 1902.—(Tamil.) On the same rock. A damaged record in the thirteenth year of the Chōḷa king Madirai-koṇḍa Parakēsarivarman (905—47). Records gift of gold.

700. 299 *of* 1902.—(Tamil.) On the same rock. A record in the fifth year of the Chōḷa king Parakēsarivarman. Records gift of 15 Kaḷañjus of gold for a lamp by a queen of Vānakōvaraiyar, Naṅgaikulamāṇikkattār, who was the daughter of Ilāḍaḍigaḷ. See

Ep. Ind., Vol. VII, p. 141 and S.A. 903. The interest on one Kaḷañju per month was one *uri* of oil.

701. 300 *of* 1902.—(Tamil.) On the same rock. A damaged record in the fourth year of the "Gaṅga-Pallava" king Vijaya-Nandivikramavarman. Records gift of gold for a lamp.

702. 301 *of* 1902.—(Tamil.) On the same rock. A damaged record. Records gift of gold for a lamp. Mentions Vānakōvaraiyar.

703. 302 *of* 1902.—(Tamil.) On the same rock. A damaged record in the seventeenth year of the "Gaṅga-Pallava" king Vijaya-Nandivikramavarman. Records gift of gold for a lamp by a concubine of Vānakōvaraizar.

704. 303 *of* 1902.—(Tamil.) On the same rock. A record in the twenty-first year of the "Gaṅga-Pallava" king Vijaya-Nripatuṅgavikramavarman. Records gift of twenty kaḷañjus of gold for a lamp by the same servant of Veṭṭuvadiyarāyar as is mentioned in No. 678 above. See *Ep. Ind.*, Vol. VII, p. 140.

705. 304 *of* 1902.—(Tamil.) On the same rock. A record of the king's name of which is omitted and the date is doubtful. Records gift of gold for a lamp.

706. 305 *of* 1902.—(Tamil.) On the same rock. A record in the third year of the king whose name is omitted. Records gift of gold for a lamp.

707. 306 *of* 1902.—(Tamil.) On the same rock. A record in the fifth year of the Chōḷa king kēsarivarman. Records gift of gold for a lamp.

708. 3 *of* 1905.—(Tamil.) On the south wall of the central shrine in the Vīrattānēśvara temple. A record in the third year of the Chōḷa king Parakēsarivarman *alias* Rājēndra-Chōḷadeva (I). Records gift of ninety-six sheep for a lamp.

709. 4 *of* 1905.—(Tamil.) On the same wall. An incomplete record in the third year of the Chōḷa king Parakēsarivarman *alias* Rājēndra-Chōḷadēva (I, 1011—43).

710. 5 *of* 1905.—(Tamil.) On the same wall. An incomplete record of the Chōḷa king Parakēsarivarman *alias* Rājēndra-Chōḷadēva (I, 1011—43), the date of which is lost.

711. 6 *of* 1905.—(Tamil.) On the same wall. A record in the ninth year of the Chōḷa king Parakēsarivarman *alias* Rājēndra-Chōḷadēva (I, 1011—43). Records gift of one hundred and ninety-two sheep for two lamps.

712. 7 *of* 1905.—(Tamil.) On the same wall. A record in the fifth year of the Chōḷa king Rājakēsarivarman. Records gift of sheep for a lamp. Mentions the queen of Vikrama-Chōḷa-Malāḍuḍaiyār, who was the daughter of the Pāṇḍya king (Pāṇḍyanār). See S.A. 686.

713. 8 *of* 1905.—(Tamil.) On the same wall. A record in the third year of the Chōḷa king Parakēsarivarman *alias* Rājēndra-Chōḷadēva (I, 1011—43). Records gift of ninety-six sheep for a lamp.

714. 9 *of* 1905.—(Tamil.) On the same wall. A record in the twenty-seventh year of the Chōḷa king Rājarājakēsarivarman *alias* Rājarājadēva (I, 985—1013). Records gift of ninety-six sheep for a lamp.

715. 10 *of* 1905.—(Tamil.) On the same wall. A record in the eleventh year of the Chōḷa king Parakēsarivarman *alias* Rājēndra-Chōḷadēvā (I, 1012—43). Records a gift by Irāman Mara-vaḍiyan *alias* Muḍigoṇḍa-Chōḷa-Milāḍuḍaiyān.

716. 11 *of* 1905.—(Tamil.) On the north wall of the same shrine. A record in the sixth year of the Chōḷa king Parakēsari-varman *alias* Rājēndra-Chōḷadēva (I, 1012—53). Records gift of land. An incomplete introduction of Rājarāja I, is engraved between lines twenty-four and twenty-five of this inscription.

717. 12 *of* 1905.—(Tamil.) On the east wall of the same shrine. A record in the fifth year of the Chōḷa king Parakēsari-varman *alias* Uḍaiyār Rājēndradēva. Mentions a certain Śembiyan Chēdivishaya-Mūvēndavēḷān.

718. 13 *of* 1905.—(Tamil.) On the south wall of the maṇṭapa in front of the same shrine. A record in the third year of the Chōḷa king Parakēsarivarman *alias* Rājēndra-Chōḷadēva (I, 1012-53). Records gift of hundred sheep for a lamp by Rāman Mummuḍi-Sōḷar for the merit of his mother Rājaśēkharan-Umainaṅgaiyār, who was the daughter of a certain Munaiyadiyaraiyar and the queen of Paṭṭaḷagan Rāman *alias* Arumoḷidēva-Milāḍuḍaiyār.

719. 14 *of* 1905.—(Tamil.) On the same wall. An incomplete record of the Chōḷa king Rājēndra-Chōḷa I.

720. 15 *of* 1905.—(Tamil.) On the same wall. A record in the twentieth year of the Rāshṭrakūṭa king Kaṇṇaradēva (Krishṇa III). Records gift of gold for a lamp by a native of Vayiramēgha-Chaturvēdimaṅgalam.

721. 16 *of* 1905.—(Tamil.) On the south wall of the maṇṭapa in front of the central shrine in the Vīraṭṭānēśvara temple. A record of the Rāshṭrakūṭa king Kaṇṇaradeva, "who took Kachchi and Tanjai," the date of which is lost. Records a gift by the Vaiḍumba Mahārāja Śrī-Vikramāditya ruling Maḷāḍu, Vānakop-pāḍi, Śiṅgapura-nāḍu and Veṅkunṟakōṭṭam. This Vikramāditya is identified by Venkayya with the Vaiḍumba chief Śandaya-Tiruvayya who was apparently made governor of this region by Kaṇṇara after his victory of Takkōlam. See *Ep. Rep.*, 1907, pp. 78–9.

722. 17 *of* 1905.—(Tamil.) On the same wall. A record in the twenty-eighth year of the Chōla king Rājarājakēsarivarman *alias* Rājarājadēva (I, 985–1013). Records gift of ninety-six sheep.

for a lamp. The temple is called Śrī-Vīrastāna (sthana) muḍaiya-Mahādēva and Tirukkōvalur was in Toṇḍaimaṇḍalam *alias* Jayaṅgoṇḍa-Chōḷamaṇḍalam.

723. 18 *of* 1905.—(Tamil.) On the same wall. An incomplete record of the Chōḷa king Rājakēsarivarman *alias* . . . .

724. 19 *of* 1905.—(Tamil.) On the same wall. A record in the eighth year of the Chōḷa king Rājakēsarivarman *alias* Kulōttuṅga Chōḷadēva. Makes provision for the daily requirements of the temple.

725. 20 *of* 1905.—(Tamil.) On the north wall of the same maṇṭapa. A record in the fourth year of the Chōḷa king Parakēsarivarman *alias* Rājēndra-Chōḷadēva (I, 1012—43). Records a gift made by Pirāntakan Yādava-Bhīman *alias* Uttama-Chōḷa-Malāḍuḍaiyār of the Bhārgavagōtra at the request of a certain Araiyan Malaiyarādittan *alias* Chēdināḍu-Vēḷān of Āviyūr.

726. 21 *of* 1905.—(Tamil.) On the same wall. A record in the second year of the Chōḷa king Parakēsarivarman *alias* Uḍaiyār Rājēndra-Chōḷadēva (I, 1011—43). Records gift of sixteen cows for a lamp.

727. 22 *of* 1905.—(Tamil.) On the west wall of the same maṇṭapa right of entrance. A record in the twentieth year of the Rāshṭrakūṭa king Kaṇṇaradēva (Krishṇa III). Records gift of a lamp by the concubine of śrī-Vikramādittan. See S.A. 721 above.

728. 23 *of* 1905.—(Tamil.) On the north wall of the gōpura in front of the same temple. A record of the Vijayanagra king Vīrapratāpa Vijayarāya-Mahārāya in Ś. 1368 expired, Kshaya. Records an order of the king. Mentions the district called Vaḷudilambaṭṭu-uśāvaḍi. [The Government Epigraphist thinks that, on account of the date, the king referred to should have been Dēvarāya II, an evidence of which is seen in the title " witnesser of the elephant hunt ". The inscription says that the ministers took presents by force from the right and left hand classes at the beginning of each reign; that the discontented ryots in consequence went away to foreign countries; that worship and festivals ceased in temples; the country became full of disease, and many died and that the king therefore prohibited such extortion in future. He had the edict engraved throughout the country. See S.A. 606. The inscription is given in the Mack. MSS. See *Ins. S. Dts.*, p. 140, No. 22.]

729. 24 *of* 1905.—(Tamil.) On a slab detached from the temple and placed near the same gōpura. A record in the eighteenth year of the Rāshṭrakūṭa king Kaṇṇaradēva (Krishṇa III). Records gift of gold.

730. 25 *of* 1905.—(Tamil.) On the same slab. An incomplete record in the eighteenth year of the Rāshṭrakūṭa king Kaṇṇaradēva (Krishṇa III).

Nagar.

731. 303 *of* 1910.—(Tamil.) On the east wall of the maṇṭapa in front of the central shrine in the Nāgavaṇṇa-Perumāḷ temple. A record in the fourth year of the Pāṇḍya king Parākrama-Pāṇḍyadēva (1334) "the lord who cut his way through by his sword." Records gift of the village of Nāḍuḍaiyaperumāḷnallūr, which was split from Kīḻpākkam, by a native of Nagar *alias* Dinachintāmaṇinallūr in Oymā-nāḍu *alias* Vijayarājēndra-vaḷanāḍu to the temple of Nāḍuḍaiya-Perumāḷ in the latter village. It is recorded that 600 *kuḻi* of land in this village belonged to the temples of Tirunāgēśvaramuḍaiya-Nāyanār and Nāḍuḍai-Vināyakappiḷḷaiyār.

732. 304 *of* 1910.—(Tamil.) On the north, west and south bases of the Kailāsanātha temple in the same village. A damaged record of the Vijayanagara king Prauḍhadēvarāya-Mahārāya, "who was pleased to witness the elephant hunt," in Ś. 1378, Dhātri. Mentions the mahāmaṇḍalēśvara Mēdinimisāra Naraśiṅgayadēva-Mahārāja and the temple of Kayilāyamuḍaiyā-Nāyanār. [Mr. Krishna Sastri points out that this Naraśiṅgadēva might be the Śāḷuva usurper, in which case it would be the earliest epigraphical reference to him.]

733. 305 *of* 1910.—(Tamil.) On a slab set up in a street of the same village. A damaged record of the Vijayanagara king Sadāśivadēva-Mahārāya in Ś. 1466, Viśvāvasu. The king bears Śāḷuva titles.

734. 306 *of* 1910.—(Telugu.) On another slab set up in the same place. A much damaged record of the Vijayanagara king Kṛishṇadēva-Mahārāya in Ś. 1449, Vyaya. Seems to record a gift to Brāhmaṇas, one of whom in a suppliant attitude is figured on the stone.

Neyvanai (Terunelveṇṇai.)

735. 370 *of* 1908.—(Tamil.) On the north wall of the central shrine in the Svarnaghaṭēśvara temple. A record in the thirty-sixth year of the Pallava king Sakalabhuvanachakravartin Kōpperuñjiṅgadēva. Records gift of paddy for offerings to the temple of Porkuḍanguḍuttaruḷiya-Nāyanār at Tirunelvanai. Mentions the temple of Tiruvaṇṇāmalaiuḍaiya-Nāyanār and the temple of Tiruvīrattānamuḍaiya-Nāyanār in Tirukkōvalur.

736. 371 *of* 1908.—(Tamil.) On the same wall. A record in the eighth year of the Chōḷa king Vikrama-Chōḷadēva (1118-35). Records gift of land to the god at Tirunelveṇṇai in Kurukkaikūṟṟam, a district in Milāḍu *alias* Jananātha vaḷanāḍu, by Vikkiramaśōḷa-Chchēdiyarāyan of Kiḻiyūr. Mentions Kaḷattūr in Dāmarnāḍu, a subdivision of Tirumunaippāḍi in Rājarāja-vaḷanāḍu.

737. 372 *of* 1908.—(Tamil.) On the north wall of the central shrine in the Svarnaghaṭēśvara temple. Records in Ś. 1384 gift of land for lamps to the temple of Porkuḍaṅguḍuttaruḷiya-Nāyanār at Tirunelvanai in Ādanūrparru, a subdivision of Kurukkai-kūrram in Tirumunaippāḍināḍu, by a native of Paḷampaṭṭiṇam in Paṭṭaṇa-nāḍu, a subdivision of Śembūrkōṭṭam in Jayaṅgoṇḍachōḷa-maṇḍalam.

738. 373 *of* 1908.—(Tamil.) On the same wall. A record in the twelfth year of the Chōḷa king Vikrama-Chōḷadēva (1118–35). Stones out of order. Records gift of land for offerings to various shrines by Malaiyan-Mallan *alias* Rājēndraśōḷa-Malaiyamān of Kiḷiyūr (i.e. the Malayamān who was Rājēndrachōḷa's vassal).

739. 374 *of* 1908.—(Tamil.) On the same wall. A record in the twenty-eighth year of the Chōḷa king Rājakēsarivarman *alias* Tribhuvanachakravartin Kulōttuṅga-Chōḷadēva(I). The end of the inscription is lost. Records gift of lands under the name Śuṅgan-davirttaśōḷanallūr at the request of Porkōyil Toṇḍaimān, a native of Arumbākkam in Jayaṅgoṇḍa-Chōḷa-maṇḍalam.

740. 375 *of* 1908.—(Tamil.) On the same wall. A record in the forty-eighth year of the Chōḷa king Tribhuvanachakravartin Kulōt-tuṅga-Chōḷadēva.(I) Refers to the setting up of the image of Naṭa-rāja (Kūttāḍundēvar) in the temple at Tirunelveṇṇai by Rājēndra-śoḷa-Chēdiyarāyan, a native of Kīḷiyūr which was situated in Tiru-munaippāḍi-nāḍu, a subdivision of Gaṅgaikoṇḍachōḷavaḷanāḍu.

741. 376 *of* 1908.—(Tamil.) On the west wall of the same shrine. A record in the tenth year of the Chōḷa king Rājakēsari-varman *alias* Uḍaiyār śri-Kulōttuṅga-Chōḷadēva. Records gift of 64 cows for two lamps to the temple of Mahādēva at Tirunelveṇṇai for the merit of Rājēndraśōḷa-Malaiyamān. Mentions Dāmar-Kōṭṭam on the southern bank of the Peṇṇai in Tirumunaippāḍi-nāḍu, a subdivision of Rājēndraśōḷa-vaḷanāḍu.

742. 377 *of* 1908.—(Tamil.) On the same wall. A damaged record in the thirty-fourth year of the Chōḷa king Rajakēsari-varman *alias* Chakravartin Kulōttuṅga-Chōḷadēva.

743. 378 *of* 1908.—(Tamil.) On the south wall of the same shrine. A record in the ninth year of the Chōḷa king Para-kēsarivarman *alias* Tribhuvanachakravartin Vikrama-Chōḷadēva. Records gift of ½ lamp.

744. 379 *of* 1908.—(Tamil.) On the same wall. An incomplete record in the ninth year of the Chōḷa king Tribhuvanachakravartin Kulōttuṅga-Chōḷadēva. Records gift of land for offerings to the shrine of the goddess. Milāḍu is stated to be a subdivision of Rājarāja-vaḷanāḍu.

745. 380 *of* 1908.—(Tamil.) On the same wall. A record in the third year of the Chōḷa king Rājakēsarivarman *alias* Tribhu-vanachakravartin Kulōttuṅga-Chōḷadēva. Records gift of land in Panaippākkam under the name Kalikaḍinda-śōḷanallūr at the instance of Śivānandamahāmuni of Tirutturaiyūr (a Śaivite centre of the Naḍu-nāḍu and the birth place of Aruṇandi Śivāchārya, the author of *Śivagñānasiddhiyār*, etc.)

746. 381 *of* 1908.—(Grantha and Tamil.) On the gōpura of the same temple, right and left of entrance. A record of the Vijayanagara king Vīrapratāpa Krishṇadēva-Mahārāya in Ś. 1439, Iśvara. Stones out of order. Refers to the victories of the king in the eastern country and to his remission of taxes in the villages owned by the Vaishṇava and other temples in the Chōḷa-maṇḍala.

Pērangiyūr.

747. 199 *of* 1906.—(Tamil.) On the south wall of the central shrine in the ruined Śiva temple. An incomplete and partially damaged record in the seventeenth year of the Rāshṭrakūta king Śrī-Kaṇṇaradēva, "who took Kachchi and Tañjai." Above this is an unfinished inscription which contains the words Madiraikoṇḍa kō-Parakēsarivarman (905—47).

748. 200 *of* 1906.—(Tamil.) On the same wall. An incomplete record in the seventeenth year of the Chōḷa king Madiraikoṇḍa Parakēsarivarman. Registers a sale of land by the sabhā of Pēringūr.

749. 201 *of* 1906.—(Tamil.) On the same wall. An incomplete record in the thirtieth year of the Chōḷa king Parakēsarivarman *alias* Uḍaiyār Śrī-Rājēndra-Chōḷadēva (I, 1011—53). Records gift of lamps to the temple of Śrī-Mūlasthānamuḍaiya-Mahādēvar at Peringūr, a brahmadēya in Tirumunaippāḍi, a district of Rājēndra-Chōḷavaḷanāḍu.

750. 202 *of* 1906.—(Tamil.) On the same wall. An incomplete and partly damaged record of the Chōḷa king Parakēsarivarman, the date of which is doubtful.

751. 203 *of* 1906.—(Tamil.) On the same wall. A record in the fifth year of the Chōḷa king Parakēsarivarman "who took the head of the Pāṇḍya." Records gift of 96 sheep for a lamp.

752. 204 *of* 1906.—(Tamil.) On the same wall. An unfinished and mutilated record of the Chōḷa king Rājarājakēsarivarman *alias* Śrī-Rājarājadēva(I), the date of which is lost. Records the gift of a lamp.

753. 205 *of* 1906.—(Tamil.) On the same wall. A record in the sixteenth year of the Chōḷa king Kulōttuṅga-Chōḷadēva.

754. 206 *of* 1906.—(Tamil.) On the same wall. A much damaged record. A few words of the historical introduction of Rājarāja I can be made out in the beginning. Seems to record the gift of a lamp.

755. 207 *of* 1906.—(Tamil.) On the same wall. A damaged record in the third year of the Chōḷa king Parakēsarivarman. Records gift of land.

756. 208 *of* 1906.—(Tamil.) On the west wall of the same shrine. A record in the twenty-fourth year (Nov. 6, A. D. 1008) of the Chōḷa king Rāja-Rājarājadēva (I, 985—1013). The inscription seems to have been left unfinished. See *Ep. Ind.* IX, 208 for discussion of date.

757. 209 *of* 1906.—(Tamil.) On the same wall. An incomplete record of the Chōḷa king Rājēndra-Chōḷa I, the date of which is lost. Only a portion of the historical introduction is preserved.

758. 210 *of* 1906.—(Tamil.) On the the same wall. A record in the second year of the Chōḷa king Parakēsarivarman *alias* Śrī-Rājēndra-Chōḷadēva (I, 1011—53.) Records gift of land.

759. 211 *of* 1906.—(Tamil.) On the same wall. A record in the fourth year of the Chōḷa king Rājakēsarivarman. Records gift of land.

760. 212 *of* 1906.—(Tamil.) On the north wall of the same shrine. Beginning built in. A fragment of record containing the concluding portion of two inscriptions.

761. 213 *of* 1906.—(Tamil.) On the same wall. A record of the Chōḷa king Rājakēsarivarman *alias* Uḍaiyār Śrī-Rājādhirājadēva.

762. 214 *of* 1906.—(Tamil.) On the same wall. An incomplete record of the Chōḷa king Rājarājakēsarivarman (Rājarāja I), "who destroyed the ships at Kāndalūr," in his twelfth year. Refers to the *śri-Rudragaṇa-perumakkaḷ* employed in the *śrikārya.*

763. 215 *of* 1906.—(Tamil.) On the same wall. A record of the Chōḷa king Rājēndra Chōḷa I. Only a portion of the historical introduction of the king is preserved.

764. 216 *of* 1906.—(Tamil.) On the same wall. A record of the Chōḷa king Rājakēsarivarman *alias* Uḍaiyār Rājēndra-Chōḷadēva I (1011—43). Records sale of land.

765. 216-A *of* 1906.—(Grantha and Tamil.) On the same wall. A record in the eleventh year of the Chōḷa king Rāja-Rājakēsarivarman "who destroyed the ships at Śālai" (985—1013). Records gift of land.

766. 217 *of* 1906.—(Tamil.) On the same wall. The stones seem to be out of order in this part of the wall.

767. 218 *of* 1906.—(Tamil.) On the north and west walls of the same shrine. A record in the twenty-eighth year of the Chōḷa king Rāja-Rājarājakēsarivarman *alias* Rāja-Rājarājadēva I (985—1013). The continuation of this which seems to be incomplete may be looked for in No. 212 above.

768. 219 *of* 1906.—(Tamil.) On the same walls. A record in the twenty-second year of the Chōḷa king Rāja-Rājarājakēsarivarman *alias* Śrī-Rājarājadēva (985—1013). Records gift of 90 sheep for a lamp.

769. 220 *of* 1906.—(Tamil.) On the same walls. A record in the sixth year of the Chōḷa king Rājakēsarivarman. Records gift of land for a lamp.

Siddhaliṅgamaḍam.

770. 367 *of* 1909.—(Grantha.) On the south wall of the maṇṭapa in front of the central shrine in the Vyāghrapādēśvara temple. Records that a minister of king Rājēndra-Chōḷa (II or Kulōttuṅga I) named Sabhānartaka and surnamed Kāḷiṅgarāja and Mānāvatāra, the ruler of Maṇavil, built a stone temple for Śiva at Siddhaliṅga. The composer of the Sanskrit verse was a certain Aṇḍapiḷḷai-bhaṭṭan. The name Kāḷiṅgarāja figures in Tamil literary legends. See N.A. 37 which refers to a chief of the same name.

771. 368 *of* 1909.—(Tamil.) On the same wall. A record in the sixteenth year of the Chōḷa king Rājakēsarivarman Tribhuvana-chakravartin Kulōttuṅga-Chōḷadēva. Records gift of land to the temple of Tiruppulippagavar at Śiṟṟiṅgūr, a brahmadēya in Kuruk-kai-kūṟṟam which was a subdivision of Malāḍu *alias* Jananātha-vaḷanāḍu. Tiruppulippagavar Muttirattān Gaṅgaikoṇḍān Para-śamaya Āḷvār bought land from one Kāḷidās and gave it away to temple.

772. 369 *of* 1909.—(Grantha.) On the same wall. A record of the Chōḷa king Jayadhara. Records that the ruler of Maṇavil who appears to have borne the surnames Mānāvatāra and Nartaka (i.e., Sabhānartaka), built a vimāna, a prākāra surrounded by areca-palms together with a maṇṭapa, at the agrahara called Siddhaliṅga, for the god Śiva whose feet were worshipped by sage Vyāghrapāda. [The temple was evidently renovated and the older inscriptions rewritten.]

773. 370 *of* 1909.—(Tamil.) On the same wall. A record in the eighteenth year of the Rāshṭrakūṭa king Kaṇṇaradēva (i.e., Kṛishṇa III who took Kachchai and Tañjai). Records a grant of land in the southern hamlet of Koḍiyūr attached to Śiṟṟiṅgūr (i.e., Siddhaliṅga-maḍam), by the assembly of that village, to the dancing woman called Tiruppulippagavar niruttaviṭaṅki and her descendants for dancing before the god during processions.

774. 371 *of* 1909.—(Tamil.) On the same wall. A record in the forty-ninth year of the Chōḷa king Tribhuvanachakravartin Kulōttuṅga Chōḷadēva (I). Records gift of 32 cows (equal to 10 kāśu in money) for a lamp, by a Brāhmaṇa, who "prayed for a son and was blessed with one."

775. 372 *of* 1909.—(Tamil.) On the same wall. A record in the thirteenth year of the Chōḷa king Tribhuvanachakravartin Vikrama-Chōḷadēva (1118—35). Records gift of gold for a lamp by a native of Anattūr Tiruveṇṇainallūr in Kīḷāṇmūr-nāḍu, a subdivision of

Tirumunaippāḍi, to the temple of Tiruppulippagavadēvar at Siṟṟiṅgūr.

776. 373 *of* 1909.—(Tamil.) On the same wall unfinished. A record in the thirteenth year of the Chōḷa king Tribhuvanachakravartin Vikrama-Chōḷadēva (1118—35). Mentions Malāḍu *alias* Jananātha-vaḷanāḍu and Kurukkai-kūṟṟam.

777. 374 *of* 1909.—(Tamil.) On the same wall. A record of the Chōḷa king Parakēsarivarman in his fourth year. Records gift of land for offerings to the temple of Tiruppulippagavadēva by a certain Rājamahēndran Rājēndra-Chōḷa. The Chōḷa king has not been identified.

778. 375 *of* 1909.—(Tamil.) On the same wall. A damaged record in the fifth year of the Rāshṭrakūṭa king Kaṇṇaradēva (Kṛishṇa III), " who took Kachchi (Kanchi) and Tanjai (Tanjore)." Records gift of land for offerings.

779. 376 *of* 1909.—(Tamil.) On the same wall. A record in the twenty-second year of the Chōḷa king Maduraikoṇḍa Parakēsarivarman (i.e., Parāntaka I). Records that the villagers of Marudūr sold to Iraiyankuḍikiḷavan the right of taking water for irrigation to Balippaṭṭi through the sluice of the tank in their village for a specified sum of money. Marudūr is stated to have been situated in Kurukkai-kūṟṟam of Malāḍu.

780. 377 *of* 1909.—(Tamil.) On the same wall. A damaged and unfinished record in the third year of the Chōḷa king Parakēsarivarman. Records a gift of land for a lamp and offerings.

781. 378 *of* 1909.—(Tamil.) On the north wall of the same maṇṭapa. A record in the third year of the Chōḷa king Tribhuvanachakravartin Vikrama-Chōḷadēva (1118—35). Records gift of money for a lamp by Sadiri, the daughter of Tillaināyakan Dēvargaṇḍan Agamuḍaiyan Malaiyan *alias* Rājēndraśōḷa-Chēdirāyan of Periṅgūr in Peringūr-nāḍu, a subdivision of Tirumunaippāḍi in Gaṅgaikoṇḍa Chōḷa-vaḷanāḍu. The lady also presented a lamp-stand and three vessels of bell-metal.

782. 379 *of* 1909.—(Tamil.) On the same wall. A record in the third year of the Chōḷa king Rājakēsarivarman (unidentified). Records gift of a lamp by a certain Śittavaḍavan.

783. 380 *of* 1909.—(Tamil.) On the same wall. A record in the sixth year of the Pāṇḍya king Tribhuvanachakravartin Vikrama-Pāṇḍyadēva. Records gift of land for offerings to the shrine of Āḍavallār in the temple of Tiruppulippagava-Nāyanār by the citizens (nagarattār) of Tirukkōvalur (near Marudūr) *alias* Maduraik-kuvāytta Perumāḷpuram.

784. 381 *of* 1909.—(Tamil.) On the same wall. An unfinished record in the forty-ninth year of the Chōḷa king Rājakēsarivarman *alias* Tribhuvanachakravartin Śrī-Kuḷōttuṅga-Chōḷaḍēva (I).

Records a sale of land by the residents of Śemmarūr in Emappērrūr-nāḍu, a subdivision of Tirumunaippāḍi in Gaṅgai-koṇḍa-Chōḷa-vaḷanaḍu.

785. 382 *of* 1909.—(Tamil.) On the same wall. A record in the forty-ninth year of the Chōḷa king Rājakēsarivarman *alias* Tribhuvanachakravartin Śrī-Kulōttuṅga-Chōḷadēva. Records gift of land for offerings by Pūvan Marudan *alias* Āḻvānaṅkakāra Malaiyamān, a native of Kiḻiyūr in Dāmar-nādu, which was a subdivision of Tirumunaippāḍi.

786. 383 *of* 1909.—(Tamil.) On the same wall. A record in the fourth year of the Chōḷa king Tribhuvanachakravartin Vikrama-Chōḷadēva (1118—35). Records gift of land for offerings by Aḍavaḷḷān Vāsudēvan *alias* Muḍigoṇḍaśōḷa-mūvēndavēḷān of Munnūr *alias* Paṇḍitagōshṭhi-chaturvēdimaṅgalam, in Oymā-nāḍu.

787. 384 *of* 1909.—(Tamil.) On the same wall. A record in the fifth year of the Chōḷa king Parakēsarivarman. Records gift of gold for two lamps. See No. 8 above. The king is unidentifiable.

788. 385 *of* 1909.—(Tamil.) On the same wall. A record in the twenty-fourth year of the Rāshṭrakūṭa king Kaṇṇaradēva (Kṛishṇa III). Records gift of gold to provide a gong and three trumpets to the temple. See Nos. 5 and 9 above.

789. 386 *of* 1909.—(Tamil.) On the east wall of the same maṇtapa. A damaged record in the thirty-first year of the Chōḷa king Rājakēsarivarman *alias* Tribhuvanachakravartin Śrī-Kuḷōttuṅga-Chōḷadēva. Records gift of land for offerings.

790. 387 *of* 1909.—(Tamil.) On the same wall. An incomplete record in the twenty-fifth year of the Chōḷa king Maduraikoṇḍa-Parakēsarivarman (Parāntaka I). Records gift of land for providing music on the three occasions of worship, every day.

791. 388 *of* 1909.—(Tamil.) On the same wall. A record in the thirty-sixth year of the Chōḷa king Tribhuvanachakravartin Kulōttuṅga Chōḷadēva. Records gift of land for offerings to the minor deities in the temple of Tiruppulippagavadēva, by the wife of Malaiyamān Nānūṟṟuvan Malaiyan *alias* Rājēndrachōḷa-Chedirāyan of Kiḻiyūr in Tirumnuaippāḍi. See N.A. 299.

792. 389 *of* 1909.—(Tamil.) On the same wall. An unfinished record in the forty-ninth year of the Chōḷa king Tribhuvana-chakravartin Kulōttuṅga-Chōḷadēva (I).

793. 390 *of* 1909.—(Tamil.) On the same wall. A record in the seventh year of the Chōḷa king Maduraikoṇḍa Parakēsarivarman (i.e., Parāntaka I). Records gift of gold for two lamps.

794. 391 *of* 1909.—(Tamil.) On the same wall. A record in the fourth year of the Chōḷa king Rājarājadēva. Records gift of gold 10 *Kalanjus* for 12 lamps to be burnt during the evening service in the temple.

795. 392 *of* 1909.—(Tamil.) On the same wall. A record in the twenty-eighth year of the Chōḷa king Rājakēsarivarman Rājarājadēva (evidently Rājarāja I). Built in, in the middle. Records gift of gold for lamps and offerings, to the image of Āḍavallār and of land situated below the tank called Rājarājapperēri, for offerings in the main temple. Transcript not full.

796. 393 *of* 1909.—(Tamil.) On the south wall of the verandah round the same shrine. A record in the fourteenth year of the Pāṇḍya king Māravarman Tribhuvanachakravartin Vīra-Pāṇḍyadēva (not identified). Records gift of land for offerings to the shrine of Aḷagiya Tiruchchiṟṟambalam-Uḍaiyār set up in the northern prākāra, by a merchant of Śiṟṟiṅgūr.

797. 394 *of* 1909.—(Tamil.) On the same wall. A record in the tenth year of the Pāṇḍya king Kōnērinmaikoṇḍān Tribhuvanachakravartin Sundara-Pāṇḍyadēva (I ?). Records that certain *Kaikkōḷars* purchased the village of Vilvalam and presented it as a dēvadāna to the temple.

798. 395 *of* 1909.—(Tamil.) On the same wall. A record in the fifteenth year of the Pāṇḍya king Māravarman Tribhuvanachakravartin Vīra-Pāṇḍyadēva (1252—6), equated to 10th December 1267. Records gift of land by purchase to the temple of Tiruppulippagava-Nayanār at Śiṟṟiṅgūr, a brahmadēya in Kurukkai-kūṟṟam, a subdivision of Malāḍu in Rājarājavaḷanāḍu. See *Ep. Ind.* XI, 266 for Mr. Sewell's views and *Ind. Antq.*, 1913, p. 170 for Mr. Swamikannu Pillai's.

799. 396 *of* 1909.—(Tamil.) On the west wall of the same verandah. A record in the twentieth year of Sakalalōkachakravartin Rājanārāyaṇa-Śambuvarāya. Records that the Kaikkōḷars and the mahēśvaras of the temple met at Tiruppuṅgūr and came to a settlement about a temple land which, though free, had yet paid taxes, and had it so entered in the register from the seventeenth year of the king. [*Ep. Ind.* XI, 251. Mr. Sewell discusses the date here and points out that the details given in the inscription (Wednesday, Śravaṇa, Pūrvapaksha-Tritīya of Makara) might correspond to January 2nd, A.D. 1359, but the Nakshatra should be *Dhanishṭa*. As this is the twentieth year Mr. Sewell infers the date of the king's accession to be between January 3rd, A.D. 1339 and March 25th, A.D. 1339.] See N.A. 820 also.

800. 397 *of* 1909.—(Tamil.) On the north wall of the same verandah. A record of the Vijayanagara king Vīra-Dēvarāya Uḍaiyār (I) in Ś. 1329, Sarvajit. Records gift of land in lieu of what was taken up for digging a canal.

801. 398 *of* 1909.—(Tamil.) On the same wall. A damaged record in Ś. 1407, of the Vijayanagara king Virūpākshadēva (I), son of Vīrapratāpa Dēvarāya-Mahārāya (i.e., Dēvarāya II), "who took every country." See Ap. 83.

802. 399 *of* 1909.—(Tamil.) On a stone built into the floor of the same verandah. Appears to record that the whole of this maṇṭapa was the gift of a certain Villavar *alias* Maguḍattiyāgi.

803. 400 *of* 1909.—(Tamil.) On the south wall of the prākāra in the same temple. A record in the ninth year of the Chōḷa king Parakēsarivarman *alias* Tribhuvanachakravartin Kulōttuṅga Chōḷadēva. Records gift of land by Malaiyaman Sūryan Nīrēṟṟan Edirigaṇāyan *alias* Rājarāja-Maḷaiyākularāyan of Kiḷiyūr in Tirumunaippāḍi-nāḍu. See *Ep. Ind.* XI, 245.

804. 401 *of* 1909.—(Tamil.) On the same wall. A record in the fifteenth year of the Chōḷa king Parakēsarivarman *alias* Tribhuvanachakravartin Vikrama-Chōḷadēva (1118—35). Records gift of land to the shrine of the goddess built by Āḷavandai, daughter of Malaiyamān Nānūṟṟuvan Malaiyan *alias* Rājēndraśōḷa-Chēdiyarāyan of Kiḷiyūr and wife of Malaiyamān Rāman Śūriyan *alias* Rājēndraśōḷa-Malaiyakularāyan of the same village, for the merit of her mother. [It is noteworthy that the name Āḷavandāḷ was borne by a princess.]

805. 402 *of* 1909.—(Tamil.) On the same wall. A record in the thirteenth year of the Chōḷa king Parakēsarivarman *alias* Tribhuvanachakravartin Kulōttuṅga-Chōḷadēva (III ?). Records gift of the village of Āḍarpāḍimēyūr *alias* Nallāvūr in Kūḍal, in Rājarājavaḷanāḍu as a dēvadāna to the temple of Tiruppulippagavar, altering the name into Śivapādaśēkharanallūr. Mentions Tribhuvanachakravartin Kōnērinmaikoṇḍān.

806. 403 *of* 1909.—(Tamil.) On the west wall of the same prākāra. A record in the sixth year of the Chōḷa king Tribhuvanachakravartin Vikrama-Chōḷadēva (1118–35). Built in, at the bottom. Records sale of land to the temple.

807. 404 *of* 1909.—(Tamil.) On the same wall. A damaged record in the third year of the Chōḷa king Parakēsarivarman *alias* Tribhuvanachakravartin Kulōttuṅga-Chōḷadēva (II or III?). Mentions Tribhuvanachakravartin Kōnērinmaikoṇḍān and Āḍarpāḍinagaram in Kūḍal. Appears to record a gift of land.

808. 405 *of* 1909.—(Tamil.) On the same wall. A record in the sixth year of the Chōḷa king Tribhuvanachakravartin Vikrama-Chōḷadēva (1118—35). Records sale of land to the temple.

809. 406 *of* 1909.—(Tamil.) On the north wall of the same prākāra. A record in the tenth year of the Chōḷa king Rājakēsarivarman *alias* Tribhuvanachakravartin Kulōttuṅga-Chōḷadēva. Records gift of money for two lamps.

810. 407 *of* 1909.—(Tamil.) On the same wall. A record in the eighth year of the Chōḷa king Tribhuvanachakravartin Rājarājadēva. Records gifts of money by a Brāhmaṇi for offerings, to a shrine of Kshētrapāla-Piḷḷaiyār, built by her in the temple.

811. 408 *of* 1909.—(Tamil.) On the same wall. A record in the sixth year of the Chōḷa king Parakēsarivarman *alias* Tribhuvanachakravartin Vikrama-Chōḷadēva (1118—35). Records gift of land by purchase, for offerings, by the wife of Malaiyamān Tirukkalaimarundān Āḷvānaṅkakāra Malaiyamān.

812. 409 *of* 1909.—(Tamil.) On the east wall of the same prākāra. A record in the seventh year of the Chōḷa king Parakēsarivarman *alias* Tribhuvanachakravartin Rājarājadēva (II). Records gift of land for a flower garden by a native of Maṇaḷūr *alias* Kalyāṇamahādēvi-chaturvēdimaṅgalam, a brahmadēya in Śengunṛa-nāḍu of Vānagoppāḍi on the northern bank of the Peṇṇai (Pennar), in Rājarāja-vaḷanāḍu.

813. 410 *of* 1909.—(Tamil.) On the same wall. A record in the sixth year (Sunday, Hasta, Pūrvapakshaprathamai of Kanyā) of the Pāṇḍya king Māravarman *alias* Tribhuvanachakravartin Vikrama-Pāṇḍyadēva (1283—?). Records gift of land for offerings by the nagarattār of Śiṛṛiṅgūr. Mr. Krishna Sastri at first believed that paleographically this inscription belonged to a period later than the fifteenth century. Mr. Sewell surmised that if he could be taken as the same as Kōnērinmaikoṇḍān Vikrama whose reign began in A.D. 1401, (See *Ep. Ind.*, IX, 228), the date of this inscription would be Monday, September 13th, A.D. 1406. See *Ep. Ind.*, Vol. XI, p. 265. Mr. Krishna Sastri later on revised his opinion and held that paleographically it might be attributed to the thirteenth century, and Mr. Swamikannu Pillai has accordingly calculated the date to be Sunday, August 29, A.D. 1288. See No. 844. Also *Ind. Antq.*, 1915, p. 247, and *Ibid*, 1913, p. 224.

814. 411 *of* 1909.—(Tamil.) On the same wall. A record in the ninteenth year of the Chōḷa king Parakēsarivarman *alias* Tribhuvanachakravartin Rājarājadēva (II, 1146—78). Records gift of land for offerings by Malaiyamān Attimallan Śokkapperumāḷ *alias* Rājagambhīra-Chēdiyarāya of Kiḷiyūr. See S.A. 605. For Śambuvarāyar who had the title Attimallan see N.A. 26 and N.A. 392.

815. 412 *of* 1909.—(Tamil.) On the same wall. Records gift of a bell by a dancing girl.

816. 413 *of* 1909.—(Tamil.) On the same wall. A record in the sixth year of the Chōḷa king Tribhuvanachakravartin Vīrarājēndra-Chōḷadēva. Built in, at the bottom. Mentions Ēḷiśaimōgan *alias* Jananāthakachchiyarāyan, son of Kūḍalūr-Āḷappirandān Araśanārāyaṇan and the village of Vikrama-Chōḷanallūr. Appears to record a gift of taxes collected within the four gates (*Śikhara*) of the temple village.

817. 414 *of* 1909.—(Tamil.) On the same wall. A record in the sixth year of the Chōḷa king Rājakēsarivarman *alias* Tribhuvanachakravartin Vīrarājēndra-Chōḷadēva. Records gift of taxes by Malaiyamān Śokkapperumāḷ Ponparappinān Rājagambhīra-Chēdiyarāyan of Kiḷiyūr.

818. 415 *of* 1909.—(Tamil.) On the same wall. A record in the sixth year of the Chōḷa king Tribhuvanachakravartin Vīrarājēndra Chōḷadēva. Records gift of land for two lamps by a servant of the chief mentioned in No. 817 for the merit of his master.

819. 416 *of* 1909.—(Tamil.) On the same wall. A record in the thirty-fifth year of the Chōḷa king Tribhuvanachakravartin Tribhuvanavīradēva (Kulōttuṅga III). Built in, at the bottom. Records gift of vessels and a lamp stand on behalf of two dancing girls, by a native of Pālaiyūr *alias* Rājanārāyaṇa-chaturvēdimaṅgalam.

820. 417 *of* 1909.—(Tamil.) On the same wall. A record on Monday, day of mūlam, Aparapakshatritīya of Rishabha, in the ninteenth year of the Pallava king Sakalabhuvanachakravartin Kopperuñjiṅgadēva (contemporary of Rājarāja III, 1216—45). Records gift of 32 cows for a lamp by Avaniyāḷappiranda Kōpperuñjiṅgadēvar. See *Ep. Ind.*, XI, 252, where Mr. Sewell points out that the date corresponded to Monday, May 8th, A.D. 1261. An incidental inference is that the king ascended the throne between May 9 and July 30 of A.D. 1243. See S.A. 799.

821. 418 *of* 1909.—(Tamil.) On the same wall. A record in the thirteenth year (March 6, 1283) of the Pāṇḍya king Jaṭāvarman *alias* Tribhuvanachakravartin Sundara-Pāṇḍyadēva (II, 1270-1302). Records that the Śiva-Brāhmaṇas of the temple agreed to provide for offerings in the shrine of Āḷuḍaiya Piḷḷaiyār, from the interest on 2,000 kāśu presented to the temple by Arindavan-Pallavaraiyan in the time of Kōpperuñjiṅgadēva and now placed in their hands. See *Ep. Ind.* XI, 258 and *Ind. Antq.*, 1913, p. 223 for discussions of the date.

822. 419 *of* 1909.—(Tamil.) On the same wall. A record in the tenth year of the Chōḷa king Rājakēsarivarman *alias* Tribhuvanachakravartin Śrī-Kulōttuṅga-Chōḷadēva. Records gift of 64 cows for two lamps on behalf of Śēdiran Malaiyan *alias* Rājēndra-śōḷa-Malaiyamān of Kiḷiyūr on the southern bank of the Peṇṇai (Pennar), in Tirumunaippāḍi, a subdivision of Dāmar-nāḍu, in Rājēndra-vaḷanāḍu.

823. 420 *of* 1909.—(Tamil.) On the same wall. A record in the tenth year of the Chōḷa king Parakēsarivarman (unidentified). Records gift of land for offerings at specified festivals. See No. 777 above.

• **824.** 421 *of* 1909.—(Tamil.) On the same wall. A record in the ninth year of the Chōḷa king Parakēsārivarman (unidentified). Records gift of oil for a lamp. See No. 777 above.

825. 422 *of* 1909.—(Tamil.) On the same wall. A record in the seventh year of the Chōḷa king Parakēsarivarman (unidentified). Records gift of money for two lamps by a female servant of Varagūr-kōṭṭam Uḍaiyān.

826. 423 *of* 1909.—(Tamil.) On the same wall. A record in the seventh year of the Chōḷa king Tribhuvanachakravartin Vikrama Chōḷadēva (1118-35). Built in, at the bottom. Records gift of a lamp by Śōḷan Vichchādiran of Śemmūru.

827. 424 *of* 1909.—(Tamil.) On the same wall. An incomplete record in the eleventh year of the Chōḷa king Tribhuvanachakravartin Rājādhirājadēva. Records the settlement of a dispute concerning water supplied from a specified irrigation canal.

828. 425 *of* 1909.—(Tamil.) On the same wall. Mentions Tiruvaḍigai, Tirutturai, Tiruveṇṇainallūr, Tiruvāmattūr and Tirumudugunṛam in Naḍuvil-maṇḍalam.

829. 426 *of* 1909.—(Tamil.) On the same wall. A record in Śrī-mukha of the Vijayanagara king Krishṇarāya-Mahārāya. Built in, at the bottom. Seems to record a gift of land for a lamp while Taraṇikka-Maṅgarasayya was in charge of the Tiruvāḍirājya.

830. 427 *of* 1909.—(Tamil.) On the same wall. A record in the fourteenth year of the Chōḷa king Rājādhirājadēva. Records gift of a vessel by Kaṇṇan Śūran *alias* Akarasura-Malaiyamān.

831. 428 *of* 1909.—(Tamil.) On a pillar of a maṇṭapa in the same temple. Records gift of the pillar by a dancing girl. Two other pillars in the same place bear the names of their respective donors.

832. 429 *of* 1909.—(Tamil.) On the east wall of the vāhana-maṇṭapa in the same temple. A record in the nineteenth year of the Pāṇḍya king Kōnērinmaikoṇḍān Tribhuvanachakravartin Sundara-Pāṇḍyadēva. Records gift of taxes for a festival established in the king's name, by a certain *aṅgavaidyā* Kūttapperumāḷ.

833. 430 *of* 1909.—(Tamil.) On the south wall of the Nīlaviśālākshiamman shrine in the same temple. A damaged record in the fifteenth year of the king Tribhuvanachakravartin Rājarājadēva. Seems to record a gift of land.

834. 431 *of* 1909.—(Tamil.) On a slab set up in the Brahman street in the same village. In modern characters. Refers in Vibhava to the time of Dēvarāya-Mahārāya, and mentions Vaḷudalampaṭṭuśāvaḍi, Paḍaivīṭṭu-śāvaḍi and Tiruchchirāppaḷḷich-chāvaḍi.

Tāyanūr.

This village (which is noted for its antique dolmens) is epigraphically rich and interesting.

835. 358 *of* 1909.—(Tamil.) On the south wall of the ruined Śiva temple. A damaged record of the Pallava king Sakalabhuvanachakravartin Avaniyāḷappirandān Kopperuñjiṅgadēva (the contemporary of Rājarāja III, 1216—45, whose authority he tried to subvert). The date is lost. Records gift of 4 cows for a lamp to the temple of Tanakkamalai-Āḷuḍaiya-Nāyanār, by a native of Tāyanūr.

836. 359 *of* 1909.—(Tamil.) On a rock near the same temple. A record in the third year of the Chōḷa king Parakēsarivarman "who took the head of the Pāṇḍya." Records gift of 90 sheep for a lamp to the temple of Tanakkamalai-Āḻvār. [Besides 2 other epigraphs of Parakēsarivarman who took the head of the Pāṇḍya and who was either Sundara-Chōḷa or his son Āditya Karikāla II, there are 3 epigraphs of a Pārthivēndravarman who had the same *biruda*. It is an open question whether they were identical.] See note to S.A. 839 below.

837. 360 *of* 1909.—(Tamil.) On the same rock. A record in the fourth year of the Chōḷa king Parakēsarivarman, "who took the head of the Pāṇḍya." Records gift of 80 sheep for a lamp to Tanakkamalai-Āḻvār—the Mahādēva at Tāyanūr which was a village in Śiṅgapura-nāḍu, by a native of Maṇḍaikuḷattūr.

838. 361 *of* 1909.—(Tamil.) On the same rock. A record in the fourth year of the Chōḷa king Parakēsarivarman, "who took the head of the Pāṇḍya." Records gift of 90 sheep for a lamp. Mentions Tirumunaippāḍi.

839. 362 *of* 1909.—(Tamil.) On the same rock. A record in the fifth year of Pārthivēndravarman. Records gift of land on the occasion of a solar eclipse for the *śri-bali-bhōga* in the temple of Tanakkamalai-Mahādēva, at the request made to Nīlagaṅgaraiyan Annavan Nāṭṭaḍigaḷ, by the residents of Tāyanūr in Śiṅgapura-nāṭṭu-Miyvaḷi. For another subordinate of Parthivēndravarman and for the relations between him and the Parakēsarivarman who took the head of Vīra Pāṇḍya see note to N.A. 836 above; also the inscriptions at Madhuramaṅgalam (Chingleput district).

840. 363 *of* 1909.—(Tamil.) On the same rock. A record in the fifth year of Pārthivēndravarman. Records gift of 96 sheep for a lamp by the wife of Mangarangiḷavan Karikkaṇḍan of Tāyanūr. Karikkaṇḍa or Nīlakaṇṭha is referred to in N.A. 729.

841. 364 *of* 1909.—(Tamil.) On a rock in the backyard of a private house in the same village. A record in the fifth year of Pārthivēndravarman. Declares that a certain document which was lost by mistake should not, if found again, be produced as valid.

842. 365 *of* 1909.—(Tamil.) On another rock in the same village. Records in Ś. 1478, Naḷa, that a Śrī Vaishṇava āchārya fixed the standard unit of length (cut on the rock) to be used in measuring lands in three specified villages.

843. 366 *of* 1909.—(Tamil.) On the third rock in a field of the same village. Mentions in Parābhava, Vānadarāyar, the agent of Vīrappa-Nāyakkarayyan (1573—95). [The inscription illustrates the extent of Madura kingdom in the north. For a full discussion of Vīrappa's relations with Vānadarāya see *Ind. Antq.*, May 1916, p. 91.]

*Tirukkōyilūr.**

Tirukkōyilūr is a very ancient religious centre both for the Vaishṇavites and the Śaivites and referred to in the *Prabandhas* as well as *Dēvaram* under the names of Tiruviḍaikaḷi and Tiruvīraṭṭānam. The Trivikramaperumāḷ' and Vīraṭṭānēśvara shrines represent the two faiths. The place figures in the *Guruparampara* as the meeting-place of the earliest Āḷvārs and the birth place of the *Prabandhas* and in the *Periapurāṇa* as the residence of Meypporuṇāyanār. In Chōḷa times it was known as Madurāntakachaturvēdimaṅgalam and included in Kurukkai-kūṟṟam in Milāḍu (district of 2,000 villages, or Jananāthavaḷanāḍu.) See *S.A. Gazr.*, 379-80.

844. 116 *of* 1900.—(Grantha and Tamil.) On the north wall of the first prākāra of the Trivikrama-Perumāḷ temple. A record in the eighth year of the Pāṇḍya king Tribhuvanarājādhirāja Paramēśvara śrī-Vikrama-Pāṇḍyadēva (1283—?). Refers to the king's victory over the Kākatīya king Gaṇapati and records a gift of two lamps. [This inscription is given in *Ins. S. Dts.*, p. 138, No. 14, but the regnal year is wrongly given as the 2nd. It says that 2,608 *kuḷis* of land from the village of Pāṇḍyachaturvēdimaṅgalam was purchased by one Aḷagapperumāḷ and granted to the deity for 2 lamps.] See *Ind. Antq.*, 1913, p. 224 and 1915, p. 247, where it is pointed out that the date is 14th December, A.D. 1291.

845. 117 *of* 1900.—On the north wall of the first prākāra of the Trivikrama-Perumāḷ temple. Records that the agriculturists of Chitramēḷi-periyanāḍu agreed to give annually one *padakku* of paddy for each plough and one *kuruṇi* for each man, to meet the requirements of the temple at Chitramēḷi-Viṇṇagar *alias* Tiruviḍaikkaḷi.

846. 118 *of* 1900.—(Tamil.) On the south wall of the central shrine of the same temple. Records that a chief named Rāman Naraśiṅgan put up a golden pinnacle on the Iḍaikaḷi (temple) at

* It may be pointed out that Tirukkōyilūr was the native place of Ārmugha Svāmigaḷ, the disciple of Guhainamachchivāya of Tiruvaṇṇāmalai and the author of the *Nishthānubhūti* (afterwards commented on by Muttu Krishṇa Brahmam). In *Ins. S. Dts.* (Mack. MSS.), pp. 137—40 ten inscriptions are given in this place. I have identified some of them with the departmental list and given the rest under Nos. 863-A to 863-F.

Kōval (i.e., Tirukkōvalūr). A Tamil poetic version of No. 851 below. See *Ep. Ind.*, Vol. VII, pp. 146–7.

847. 119 *of* 1900.—(Tamil.) On the south wall of the central shrine of the same temple. A record in the third year of the Chōḷa king Rājarājadēva (II). Mentions Narasimhan Kariyaperumāḷ Perianāyan, the grandson of Rāman Naraśiṅgapanman, who had re-built the central shrine of stone. See *Ep. Ind.*, Vol. VII, p. 147.

848. 120 *of* 1900.—(Tamil.) On the south wall of the central shrine of the same temple. Records that the central shrine was re-built for the merit of Naraśiṅgavanmar, lord of Milāḍu. The name of the architect was Śembanguḍaiyān Nārāyaṇa Āditya *alias* Śōḷasundara Mūvēndavēḷān. See *Ep. Ind.*, Vol. VII, p. 147.

849. 121 *of* 1900.—(Tamil.) On the south wall of the central shrine of the same temple. A record in the tenth year of the Chōḷa king Rājakēsarivarman *alias* Uḍaiyār Śrī-Kulōttuṅga-Chōḷadēva. Records gift of two lamps. [See *Ins., S. Dts.* (Mack. MSS.), p. 140, No. 20, for a detailed account of the lands given.]

850. 122 *of* 1900.—(Tamil.) On the south wall of the central shrine of the same temple. A record in the thirty-first year of the Chōḷa king Rājakēsarivarman *alias* Tribhuvanachakravartin-Kulōttuṅga-Chōḷadēva. Records gift of land.

851. 123 *of* 1900.—(Grantha and Tamil.) On the south wall of the central shrine of same temple. A record in the sixth year (i.e., A.D. 1058) of the Chōḷa king Parakēsarivarman *alias* Uḍaiyār śrī-Rājēndradēva (1052—63). Registers the building operations of a chief named Raṇakēsari Rāman *alias* Narasimhavarman, the Lord of Milāḍu (2000) of the Bhārgava lineage. [The inscription mentions Rājēndra's accompanying his elder brother Rājādhirāja in the conquest of Raṭṭapāḍi, his setting up a pillar of victory at Kollāpuram and his alleged victory over Āhavamalla at Koppam.] See *Ep. Ind.*, VII, pp. 145–6, and *Ep. Rep.*, 1900, p. 9, para. 20.

852. 124 *of* 1900.—(Tamil.) On the west and south walls of the same shrine. A record in the seventh year of the Chōḷa king Parakēsarivarman *alias* Tribhuvanachakravartin Kulōttuṅga-Chōḷadēva (II or III ?). Records gift of land.

853. 125 *of* 1900.—(Tamil.) On the west wall of the same shrine. A record in the sixth year of the Chōḷa king Rājakēsarivarman *alias* Uḍaiyār śrī-Kulōttuṅga-Chōḷadēva. The historical introduction which is partially damaged mentions the conquests of the Raṭṭa country. The inscription states that the Sabhā of Tirukkōvalur *alias* śrī-Madurāntaka-chaturvēdimaṅgalam recorded on stone the boundaries of villages granted to the temple of Tiruviḍaikkaḻiāḻvār. A Sanskrit verse in praise of the Trivikrama avatāra is found above this inscription.

854. 126 *of* 1900.—(Tamil.) On the north wall of the same shrine. A record in the third year of the Chōḷa king Śōḷa-Kēraḷa. Records gift of sheep for a lamp and sale of land to a resident of Maṇalūr on the north bank of the Peṇṇār in Vānakoppāḍi *alias* Madurāntakavaḷanāḍu. [The Government Epigraphist surmises that Śōḷa Kēraḷa might be identical with his namesake, the son of Parakēsarivarman Rājēndradēva, mentioned in a Maṇimaṅgalam inscription, in the third quarter of the twelfth century. Koṅgu was called Sōḷakēraḷamaṇḍalam. The inscription provides for the singing of the *Tiruneḍuntāṇḍagam* of Tirumaṅgai Āḷvār whose earliest date is subsequent to Paramēśvaravarman II, the builder of the Paramēśvaraviṇṇagar or Vaikuṇṭha Perumāḷ temple at Conjeeveram.]

855. 127 *of* 1900.—(Tamil.) On the north wall of the central shrine of the Trivikrama-Perumāḷ temple. A record in the third year of the Chōḷa king Śōḷa-Kēraḷadēva. Records sale of land to the temple of Tiruviḍaikkaḷi-āḷvār by the Sabhā of Madurāntaka-chaturvēdimaṅgalam.

856. 128 *of* 1900.—(Tamil.) On the north wall of the central shrine of the Trivikrama-Perumāḷ temple. A record in the twenty-fourth year of the Chōḷa king Parakēsarivarman *alias* Uḍaiyār Rājēndra-Chōḷadēva (I, 1011—53). Records sale of land to the temple of Tiruviḍaikkaḷiāḷvār in Tirukkōvalur *alias* Śrī-Madurāntaka-chaturvēdimaṅgalam.

857. 129 *of* 1900.—(Tamil.) On the north wall of the central shrine of the Trivikrama-Perumāḷ temple. A record in the twenty-third year of the Chōḷa king Rājarājakēsarivarman *alias* Rājarāja-dēva (I, 985—1013). Records sale of land.

858. 130 *of* 1900.—(Tamil.) On the north wall of the central shrine of the Trivikrama-Perumāḷ temple. A record in the thirty-second year of the Chōḷa king Chakravartin Śrī-Kulōttuṅga-Chōḷa-dēva (Kulōttuṅga I). Makes provision for the supply of daily requirements.

859. 131 *of* 1900.—(Tamil.) On the north wall of the central shrine of the Trivikrama-Perumāḷ temple. A much damaged record; mentions Madurāntakadēvar.

860. 307 *of* 1902.—(Tamil.) On the north wall of the prākāra of the Trivikrama temple. A record in the eighteenth year of Tribhuvanachakravartin Kōnērinmaikoṇḍān. Records gift of land.

861. 308 *of* 1902.—(Tamil.) On the same wall. A record in the twenty-sixth year of Sakalabhuvanachakravartin Peruñjiṅga-dēva. Records gift of sixteen cows for a lamp.

862. 1 *of* 1905.—(Tamil.) On the north wall of the central shrine of the Trivikrama-Perumāḷ temple. A record of the Śāḷuva king Gaṇḍakaṭṭāri Śāḷuva Narasimhadēva-Mahārāja in

Ś. 1393 expired, Vikrita. Refers to the outer wall *(tirumadil)* and the gōpura which had collapsed and records that they were repaired by a certain Annamarasa. [The Śāḷuva was evidently the well-known usurper.]

863. 2 *of* 1905.—(Tamil.) On the south wall of the first prākāra of the same temple. A record in the twenty-fourth year of the Chōḷa king Tribhuvanachakravartin Kulōttuṅga-Chōḷadēva (III), "who took Īḷam (Ceylon), Madura, the crowned head of the Pāṇḍya, Kachchi (Conjeeveram) and Karuvūr." Registers an exchange of land. See No. 360 of 1904 at Nārttāmalai in Pudukkōṭṭai State and *S.I.I.*, III, 218. Evidently sometime before 1196 Conjeeveram had been lost and it was now re-taken. See *Ins.*, *S. Dts.* (Mack. MSS.), p. 140, No. 21.

863-A. On the south of the second surrounding wall. Records that Rājarājadēva granted in his tenth year 2½ *vēlis* of land west of Tirukkōyilūr for the God. See *Ins.*, *S. Dts.* (Mack. MSS.), p. 136, No. 13.

863-B. On the western wall of the pagoda. Records that in the reign of Narasa Nāyaka, Narasayyadēva Vīra-Nañja-Pallavarāyan gave in Ś. 1427, 3 kaṟai of land to the deity. *Ibid.*, p. 138, No. 15.

863-C. On a stone near the water-fountain in the temple. Records that in Ś. 1414, Paritāpi, in the reign of Sadāśiva Rāya, Śūrappa Nāyaka granted to God Tirukkōyilūr Āḷvār half a share in 19 villages (enumerated). The date is inconsistent. See *Ibid.*, No. 16. See N.A. 192.

863-D. On the northern wall. Records that Rājēndrachēdirāyan gave 2,400 *kuḻis* of land in Dēvarguḍi for four lamps in the tenth year of the reign of Vikramachōḷa (1118—35). *Ibid.*, No. 17.

863-E. In the north wall. A gift of land in various villages by Rājarājachēdirāyan in the second year of Rājarājadēva. *Ibid.*, No. 18.

863-F. In the same wall. A grant in the fortieth year of the same king, of a "Paroombadi cavel land" in a village for 30 lamps. *Ibid.*, No. 19.

Tirunāmanallūr.

This place is of great importance in the history of Śaivitism. It was the birth-place of Saint Sundaramūrti and the place where king Naraśiṅga Munaiyar, one of the Toṇḍas of Śiva, who was the contemporary of Sundaramūrti, ruled and died. Its name was then Tirunāvalūr and it was included in Mēlūr Nāḍu, a subdivision of Tirumunaippāḍi (which afterwards formed part of Jayaṅkoṇḍachōḷamaṇḍalam). Its Toṇḍīśvara temple was built by king Rājaditya and the Kalinārīśvara temple by Kalinārai. It may be mentioned that Mr. Sewell gives eight inscriptions in this place, but these are vague or undated. The inscription 8 in his list which is said to record a private agreement of the priests with the temple authorities in regard to service is not found in the following list.

864. 325 *of* 1900.—(Tamil.) On the south wall of the Bhaktajanēśvara shrine. A record in the twenty-ninth year of the Chōḷa king Maduraikoṇḍa Parakēsarivarman (905-47). Records gift of 100 sheep for a lamp to the shrine of Agastyēśvara by a physician of prince (piḷḷaiyār) Rājādityadēva. See S.A. 875.

865. 326 *of* 1902.—(Tamil.) On the same wall. A record in the thirty-second year of the Chōḷa king Maduraikoṇḍa-Parakēsarivarman (905—47). Records gift of 100 sheep for a lamp to the temple of Tiruttōṇīśvara *alias* Rājāditya-Īśvara by a servant of prince Rājādityadēva. See S.A. 875.

866. 327 *of* 1902.—(Tamil.) On the same wall. A record in the twenty-ninth year of the Chōḷa king Maduraikoṇḍa-Parakēsarivarman (905—47). Records gift of 100 sheep for a lamp to the same temple by another servant of the same prince.

867. 328 *of* 1902.—(Tamil.) On the same wall. A record in the thirty-second year of the Chōḷa king Maduraikoṇḍa-Parakēsarivarman (905—47). Records gift of 100 sheep for a lamp to the same temple by another servant of the same prince.

868. 329 *of* 1902.—(Tamil.) On the same wall. A record in the thirty-fifth year of the Chōḷa king Maduraikoṇḍa-Parakēsarivarman (905—47). Records gift of 100 sheep for a lamp to the same temple by another servant of the same prince.

869. 330 *of* 1902.—(Tamil.) On the same wall. A record in the thirty-first year of Chōḷa king Maduraikoṇḍa-Parakēsarivarman (905—47). Records gift of 100 sheep for a lamp to the same temple by another servant of the same prince.

870. 331 (*a*) *of* 1902.—(Tamil.) On the same wall. A record in the twenty-ninth year of the Chōḷa king Maduraikoṇḍa-Parakēsarivarman (905—47). Records gift of a diadem.

871. 331 (*b*) *of* 1902.—(Tamil.) On the same wall. A record of the Chōḷa king Maduraikoṇḍa-Parakēsarivarman (905—47), the date of which is lost. Records gift of 100 sheep for a lamp.

872. 332 *of* 1902.—(Tamil.) On the same wall. A record in the thirtieth year of the Chōḷa king Maduraikoṇḍa-Parakēsarivarman (905—47). Records gift of 100 sheep for a lamp.

873. 333 *of* 1902.—(Tamil.) On the same wall. A record in the twenty-ninth year of the Chōḷa king Maduraikoṇḍa-Parakēsarivarman (905—47). Records gift of 100 sheep for a lamp.

874. 334 *of* 1902.—(Tamil.) On the same wall. A record in the thirty-first year of the Chōḷa king Maduraikoṇḍa-Parakēsarivarman (905—47). Records gift of a diadem.

875. 335 *of* 1902.—(Tamil.) On the same wall. A record in the twenty-eighth year of the Chōḷa king Maduraikoṇḍa-Parakēsarivarman (905—47). Says that the temple was founded by prince Rājāditya afterwards killed by the Rāshṭrakūṭa Krishṇa III in 949. The record makes the gift of two lamps by a servant of Kōkkiḻānaḍi, the queen of Parāntaka I and mother of Rājāditya. One gift was 90 sheep for the maintenance of a lamp and the other was an Īḻa lamp which Mr. Krishna Sastri interprets to be a lamp-stand after the fashion of that of Īḻam (or Ceylon) or one made of gold. See *Ep. Ind.*, Vol. VII, pp. 133–34.

876. 336 *of* 1902.—(Tamil.) On the west wall of the same shrine. A record in the thirty-second year of the Chōḷa king Maduraikoṇḍa-Parakēsarivarman (905—47). Records gift of gold for a lamp by an accountant of prince Rājādityadēva.

877. 337 *of* 1902.—(Tamil.) On the west wall of the same shrine. A record in the thirty-fourth year of the Chōḷa king Maduraikoṇḍa-Parakēsarivarman (905—47). Records gift of 100 sheep for a lamp

878. 338 *of* 1902.—(Tamil.) On the same wall. Records in Ś. 876 gift of 100 sheep for a lamp to the temple of Tiruttoṇḍīśvara by a queen of Munaiyadiyaraiyar Kulamāṇikkerumanār. [See No. 896 below. These two inscriptions are interesting for their mentioning the Śaka year. A measure called *mādēvi* (or chief queen) is mentioned. See *Ep. Ind.*, Vol. VII, p. 137.]

879. 339 *of* 1902.—(Tamil.) On the same wall. A record in the thirty-seventh year of the Chōḷa king Maduraikoṇḍa-Parakēsarivarman (905—47). Records gift of gold for a lamp by Āraiyan Śōḻamārāyan.

880. 340 *of* 1902.—(Tamil.) On the north wall of the same shrine. A record in the thirty-sixth year of the Chōḷa king Maduraikoṇḍa-Parakēsarivarman (905—47). Records gift of 90 sheep for a lamp.

881. 341 *of* 1902.—(Tamil.) On the same wall. A record in the thirty-third year of the Chōḷa king Maduraikoṇḍa-Parakēsarivarman (905—47). Records gift of 90 sheep for a lamp.

882. 342 *of* 1902.—(Tamil.) On the same wall. A record in the thirty-eighth year of the Chōḷa king Maduraikoṇḍa-Parakēsarivarman (905—47). Records gift of 90 sheep for a lamp by a merchant.

883. 343 *of* 1902.—(Tamil.) On the same wall. A record in the thirty-third year of the Chōḷa king Maduraikoṇḍa-Parakēsarivarman (905—47). Records gift of 100 sheep for a lamp by a servant of Rājāditya-Malaiyan.

884. 344 *of* 1902.—(Tamil.) On the same wall. A record in the thirty-third year of the Chōḷa king Maduraikoṇḍa-Parakēsarivarman (905—47). Records gift of 60 sheep for offerings.

885. 345 *of* 1902.—(Tamil.) On the same wall. A record in the thirty-third year of the Chōḷa king Maduraikoṇḍa-Parakēsarivarman (905—47). Records gift of 100 sheep for a lamp.

886. 346 *of* 1902.—(Tamil.) On the same wall. A record in the thirty-second year of the Chōḷa king Maduraikoṇḍa-Parakēsarivarman (905—47). Records gift of 100 sheep for a lamp.

887. 347 *of* 1902.—(Tamil.) On the same wall. A record in the twenty-ninth year of the Chōḷa king Maduraikoṇḍa-Parakēsarivarman (905—47). Records gift of 20 sheep for offerings and of two lamps to the shrines of Rājāditya-Īśvara and Agastyēśvara by a servant of Rājādityadēva.

888. 348 *of* 1902.—(Tamil.) On the same wall. A record in the thirty-second year of the Chōḷa king Maduraikoṇḍa-Parakēsarivarman (905—47). Records gift of 100 sheep for a lamp by an accountant of prince Rājādityadēva.

889. 349 *of* 1902.—(Tamil.) On the same wall. An incomplete record in the third year of the Chōḷa king Rājakēsarivarman *alias* Uḍaiyār Rājēndra-Chōḷadēva (I, 1011—53).

890. 350 *of* 1902.—(Tamil.) On the same wall. A record in the forty-first year of the Chōḷa king Chakravartin Kulōttuṅga-Chōḷadēva (I). Records gift of 16 cows for a lamp.

891. 351 *of* 1902.—(Tamil.) On the south wall of the maṇṭapa in front of the same shrine. A record in the thirty-ninth year of the Chōḷa king Maduraikoṇḍa-Parakēsarivarman (905—47). Records gift of a lamp by a servant of prince Rājādityadēva.

892. 352 *of* 1902.—(Tamil.) On the same wall. An incomplete record in the forty-second year of the Chōḷa king Kulōttuṅga-Chōḷadēva (I).

893. 353 *of* 1902.—(Tamil.) On the same wall. A record in the third year of the Chōḷa king Rājakēsarivarman. Records gift of gold.

894. 354 *of* 1902.—(Tamil.) On the same wall. A record in the nineteenth year of the Rāshṭrakūṭa king Kaṇṇaradēva, who took Kachchi and Tanjai (i.e., Krishna III). Records gift of 90 sheep for a lamp.

895. 355 *of* 1902.—(Tamil.) On the same wall. An obliterated record in the third year of the Chōḷa king Ādhirājadēva.

896. 356 *of* 1902.—(Tamil.) On the same wall. Records in Ś. 875 gift of 100 sheep for a lamp to the Tiruttoṇḍīśvara temple by Munaiyadiyarāyan Kulamāṇikkan Rāmadēvan [see S.A. 878 above]. See *Ep. Ind.*, Vol. VII, p. 136.

897. 357 *of* 1902.—(Tamil.) On the same wall. A record in the nineteenth year of the Chōḷa king Rājarāja-Rājakēsarivarman *alias* Rājarājadēva. Records gift of 90 sheep for a lamp.

898. 358 *of* 1902.—(Tamil.) On the same wall. A record in the twenty-fourth year of the Chōḷa king Rājarāja-Rājakēsarivarman *alias* Rājarājadēva (I, 985—1013). Records gift of golden ornaments made in the nineteenth and thirteenth years.

899. 359 *of* 1902.—(Tamil.) On the south wall of the maṇṭapa in front of the same shrine. A record in the tenth year of the Chōḷa king Rājakēsarivarman *alias* Uḍaiyār Kulōttuṅga-Chōḷadēva. Records gift of 128 cows for four lamps. Tirunāmanallūr is here called Tirunāvalur *alias* Rājādittapuram.

900. 360 *of* 1902.—(Tamil.) On the same wall. A record of the Chōḷa king Parakēsarivarman *alias* Rājēndra-Chōḷadēva (I), the date of which is lost. Records gift of a necklace and a bracelet of gold and jewels by a regiment (Vīranārāyaṇa's bowmen) and its commander. See *Ep. Ind.*, Vol. VII, pp. 137-38. Also *S.I.I.*, II, 379 and III, 127.

901. 361 *of* 1902.—(Tamil.) On the same wall. A record in the thirty-seventh year of the Chōḷa king Tribhuvanachakravartin Kulōttuṅga-Chōḷadēva (I ?). Records gift of 32 cows for a lamp.

902. 362 *of* 1902.—(Grantha and Tamil.) On the same wall. A record in the seventeenth year of the Rāshṭrakūṭa king Kaṇṇaradēva (i.e., Krishṇa III), the conqueror of the Chōḷa and Pallava countries. Records gift of gold for a lamp by Narasimhavarman, surnamed Śaktinātha and Siddhavaḍava, the chief of Milāḍu and a member of the line of Śukra and the Malayakula, who ruled over Malaināḍu (miḷāḍu, briefly). Dr. Hultzsch points out that the capital of this nāḍu, according to the *Periapurāṇa* was Tirukkōilūr, that the chiefs of the line claimed connexion with the Chēdi family and used to prefix the name of the reigning Chōḷa king. See *Ep. Ind.*, Vol. XII, p. 135. Also the Kiḷiyūr inscriptions above.

903. 363 *of* 1902.—(Tamil.) On the same wall. A record in the thirty-ninth year of the Chōḷa king Parakēsarivarman who took Madura and Ceylon. Records gift of 100 sheep for a lamp by the elder brother of Mahāḍēvaḍigaḷ, a queen of prince Rājādityadēva, a daughter of Ilāḍarāyar (i.e., the chief of Lāṭa) for the merit of her elder brother Rājādittan Pugaḷvipparagaṇḍa. Dr. Hultzsch points out that the title "chief of Lāṭa" was assumed by a family of local chiefs; that one of these, Vīrachōḷa, was a feudatory of Rājarāja I and that, as he is said to be the son of one Pugaḷvipparagaṇḍa, it is probable that he was the son of Rājāditya's queen's brother. [See *Ep. Ind.*, Vol. VII, p. 134. For Vīrachōḷa see *Ibid.*, Vol. IV, p. 139.]

904. 364 *of* 1902.—(Tamil.) On the same wall. A record in the twenty-eighth year of the Rāshṭrakūṭa king Kaṇṇaradēva. (Krishṇa III). Records gift of a lamp.

30

905. 365 *of* 1902.—(Tamil.) On the same wall. A record in the thirtieth year of the Chōḷa king Kulōttuṅga-Chōḷadēva. Records gift of 48 sheep for a lamp to the Kalinārīśvara temple.

906. 366 *of* 1902.—(Tamil.) On the same wall. A record in the nineteenth year of the Rāshṭrakūṭa king Kaṇṇaradēva, who took Kachchi and Tañjai (Krishṇa III). Records gift of 90 sheep for a lamp.

907. 367 *of* 1902.—(Tamil.) On the same wall. A record in the thirty-ninth year of the Chōḷa king Parakēsarivarman who took Madura and Ceylon (905—47). Records gift of a lamp.

908. 368 *of* 1902.—(Tamil.) On the north wall of the same maṇṭapa. A record in the twenty-first year of the Chōḷa king Rājarājakēsarivarman *alias* Rājarājadēva (I, 985—1013). Records gift of a diadem and a brass pedestal.

909. 369 *of* 1902.—(Tamil.) On the same wall. A record in the third year of the Chōḷa king Parakēsarivarman. Records gift of land by Vikramābharaṇa-Pallavaraiyan, a subordinate of Munaiyadaraiyar Aparājitan Kulamāṇikkerumānār. See No. 878 above.

910. 370 *of* 1902.—(Tamil.) On the same wall. An incomplete record in the eighteenth year of the Chōḷa king Rājarāja-Rājakēsarivarman (985—1013).

911. 371 *of* 1902.—(Tamil and Grantha.) On the same wall. A record in the fourth year of the Chōḷa king Rājakēsarivarman *alias* Uḍaiyār Vīrarājēndradēva (I, 1064—70). Records gift of land by the king to the Tiruttoṇḍīśvara temple at Tirunāvalūr *alias* Rājādittapuram. *S.I.I.*, III, 81, pp. 197—99.

912. 372 *of* 1902.—(Tamil.) On the east wall of the same maṇṭapa. Records the construction of two maṇṭapas and of the east gate by a merchant.

913. 373 *of* 1902.—(Tamil.) On the wall of the prākāra of the same temple, right of entrance. A record in the fifth year of the Chōḷa king Parakēsarivarman *alias* Tribhuvanachakravartin Kulōttuṅga-Chōḷadēva. Records gift of 32 cows for a lamp by a merchant.

914. 374 *of* 1902.—(Tamil.) On the same wall, left of entrance. A record in the seventh year of the Chōḷa king Rājakēsarivarman *alias* Tribhuvanachakravartin Kulōttuṅga-Chōḷadēva. Records gift of metal vessels.

915. 375 *of* 1902.—(Tamil.) On the same wall, left of entrance. An incomplete record in the eighth year of the Chōḷa king Rājakēsarivarman *alias* Tribhuvanachakravartin Rājarājadēva (I ?).

916. 376 *of* 1902.—(Pallava Grantha.) On a sculptured stone recently inserted into the west wall of the *prākāra* of the same temple. Consists of the word Śrī-Kalinārai, which according to S. A. 905 formed part of the name of a shrine which has been recently demolished by the villagers. Dr. Hultzsch concludes from this that the demolished temple of Īśvara was built by a Pallava king named Kalinārai and that a sculptured stone with the figure of a kneeling elephant and a stout person on its *hawda* probably represents him.

917. 377 *of* 1902.—(Tamil.) On a stone at the entrance of the same temple. An obliterated record in the seventeenth year of the Chōḷa king Madiraikoṇḍa Parakēsarivarman (905—47).

918. 378 *of* 1902.—(Tamil.) On the same stone. A record in the twentieth year of the Chōḷa king Madiraikoṇḍa Parakēsarivarman (905—47). Records gift of 45 sheep for a lamp.

919. 379 *of* 1902.—(Tamil.) On a second stone in the same place. A record in the sixteenth year of the Chōḷa king Madiraikoṇḍa Parakēsarivarman (905—47). Records gift of 400 sheep for four lamps.

920. 380 *of* 1902. —(Tamil.) On the same stone. A record in the twentieth year of the Chōḷa king Madiraikoṇḍa Parakēsarivarman (905—47). Records gift of 100 sheep for a lamp.

*Tirunaruṅgoṇḍai.**

The Jain temple referred to in the following inscriptions seems to have been famous in mediaeval history as a stronghold of learning. Kamba, for example, according to tradition, had to get the approval of the local scholars for his *Rāmāyaṇa*.

921. 381 *of* 1902.—(Tamil.) On the base of the verandah round the Chandranātha shrine in the Appandanātha temple. A record in the ninth year of the Chōḷa king Tribhuvanachakravartin Kulōttuṅga-Chōḷadēva. Records gift of taxes to the *Nārpattenṇāyirapperumbaḷḷi* temple by Vīraśēkhara-Kāḍavarāyan. See N.A. 715.

922. 382 *of* 1902.—(Tamil.) In the same place. A record in the third year of Tribhuvanachakravartin Kōnērinmaikoṇḍān. Records gift of land.

923. 383 *of* 1902.—(Tamil.) On the south wall of the store-room in the same temple. A record in the thirteenth year of the Chōḷa king Tribhuvanachakravartin Rājādhirājadēva. Records gift of money for a lamp to the Yakshi in the western temple (Mēlirpaḷḷi). The money was made over to the chief priest Pushpasēnadēva. See N.A. 391, 393-4.

924. 384 *of* 1902.—(Tamil.) On a stone set up at the foot of the hill bearing the same temple. A damaged record in the sixth year of Tribhuvanachakravartin Kōnērinmaikoṇḍān.

---

* The Mack. list of inscriptions given in *Ins.*, *S. Dts.*, pp. 152-4, contains ten epigraphs. Almost all these are different from the inscriptions copied by the Department. I have therefore included them in the list, under Nos 925-A to 925-I.

· **925**. 385 *of* 1902.—(Tamil.) On a rock to the south of the Chandranātha shrine in the same temple. A record in the seventeenth year of the Chōḷa king Rājarāja I. Records gift of land for two lamps. Partially built in. [This is No. 6 in *Ins., S. Dts.*, p. 153. Ten *mās* of land presented.]

925-A. On the back of the inner temple of Pārśvanādhēśvarasvāmi. Records that Vīraśekhara Kāḍavarāyar granted the duties and the hereditary rights of goldsmiths in the village to the God, in the first year of the reign of Kulōttuṅga-Chōḷadēva. *Ins., S. Dts.*, p. 152, No. 1.

925-B. On a stone on the north side of the inner temple. Records that the inhabitants of "Serusatta Nellore" granted ten vēlis of land to the "God Parambulla and Yanadi Mangalamdēvar." *Ibid.*, No. 2.

925-C. On a stone near the tank in the temple. Records that in tenth year of the reign of Vikrama-Chōladēva he granted a portion of land in Tirunarumkoṇḍa, to the Gods Arumoḷidēvar, Nittya Kalyāṇadēvar and "Tirupullidēvar." *Ibid.*, No. 3.

925-D. On a stone on the west of the Kanakamaṇṭapam. Records that "Magalakadēvarāyar" allowed the taxes on the weavers and silversmiths in the village of Tirunarumkoṇḍai and Tarumbadi Koil (?), to the God, in the tenth year of the reign of Rajārājadēva. *Ibid.*, No. 4.

925-E. On the southern wall of the Kanakamaṇṭapam. Records that Kāḍava Rāyar presented forty cows to the God Kachināyakadēvar for the ghee of the lamp, in the fourth year of the reign of Kulōttuṅga-Chōḷadēva. *Ibid.*, No. 5.

925-F. On a stone below the surrounding wall of Nityakalyāṇasvāmi temple. Records that in the seventh year of the reign of Vikramapāṇḍyadēva he granted six *mās* of paddy field in the village of Kuṇḍarattūr besides the taxes on the weavers and other village duties to Appanda Nāyanār. *Ibid.*, No. 7.

925-G. On a stone on the east side of Granary gate on the north side of Chandranāthasvāmi in the temple. Records that the head farmer of Kollūr village granted three *mās* of paddy field in the village of Kuṇḍarattūr to the God Tuppasanadēvar (?), in the tenth year of the reign of Rājarājadēva. *Ibid.*, No. 8.

925-H. On a stone on the west side of a pool. Records that Kucheya Rāyar (Kachchiyarāya) erected a roof in front of the pagoda in the sixth year of the reign of Kopparisingadēvar (i.e., Peruñjiṅga). *Ibid.*, No. 9.

925-I. On a stone below the wall of Nityakalyāṇasvāmi in the temple. Records that in the reign of Vikramapāṇḍyadēva one Vanikuttakadan granted the village of "Gunmatokasi" to the God Appanda Nāyanār. *Ins., S. Dts.*, p. 155, No. 10.

Tirppālappandal.

926. 27 *of* 1905.—(Tamil.) On the south wall of first prākāra of the Madhyasthanāthēśvara temple. A record of the Vijayanagara king Ariyappa-Uḍaiyār (II) in Ś. 1300 expired, Kāḷayukta. Records gift of land to the temple which is here called Tirunāgēśvaramuḍaiyār. Refers to a transaction in former days with Kulaśēkharadēva *alias* Maḷavachchakkravarti.

927. 28 *of* 1905.—(Tamil.) On the same wall. A record in the fourteenth year of the Pāṇḍya king Sundara-Pāṇḍyadēva. Records sale of land.

928. 29 *of* 1905.—(Tamil.) On a rock named Vavvakkuṭṭaimalai near the same village. A damaged record of the Vijayanagara king Kampaṇa-Uḍaiyār, son of Vīra-Bukkaṇa-Uḍaiyār in Ś. 1295 expired, Paridhāvin.

929. 152 *of* 1904.—(Tamil.) On the south base of the central shrine in the Madhyasthanāthēśvara temple. Built in the middle. A record the date of which is lost.

930. 153 *of* 1904.—(Tamil.) On the west base of the same shrine. A record of the Chōḷa king Tribhuvanachakravartin Kulōttuṅga-Chōḷadēva, the date of which is lost. Records gift of money for a lamp.

931. 154 *of* 1904.—(Tamil.) On the north base of the same shrine. An incomplete record in the nineteenth year of the Chōḷa king Tribhuvanachakravartin Kulōttuṅga-Chōḷadēva. Records gift of a door.

932. 155 *of* 1904.—(Tamil.) On the east wall of the maṇṭapa in front of the same shrine. A record in the thirty-seventh year of the Chōḷa king Tribhuvanavīradēva (Kulōttuṅga III). Records gift of land.

933. 156 *of* 1904.—(Tamil.) On the same wall. A record in the eleventh year of Pon-parappina-Perumāḷ. Records the setting up of certain images.

934. 157 *of* 1904.—(Tamil verse.) On the south wall of the same maṇṭapa. An incomplete record. Mentions Magadēśan.

935. 158 *of* 1904.—(Tamil.) On the west wall of the same maṇṭapa. A record in the second year of the Chōḷa king Tribhuvanachakravartin Rājarājadēva. Records gift of money.

936. 159 *of* 1904.—(Tamil.) On the north wall of the same maṇṭapa. A record of the Vijayanagara king Kampaṇa-Uḍaiyār, son of Vīra-Bokkaṇa-Uḍaiyār in Ś. 1291, Saumya. Records gift of land.

937. 160 *of* 1904.—(Tamil.) On the east base of the same maṇṭapa. A mutilated record in the twentieth year of the Chōḷa king Tribhuvanachakravartin Kulōttuṅga-Chōḷadēva.

938. 161 *of* 1904.—(Tamil.) On the south base of the same maṇṭapa. An incomplete record in the twentieth year of the Chōḷa king Kulōttuṅga-Chōḷadēva.

939. 162 *of* 1904.—(Tamil.) On the west base of the same maṇṭapa. A record in the eleventh year of the Chōḷa king Tribhuvanachakravartin Vijayarājēndra-Chōḷadēva. Mentions Aḷagiyachōḷa *alias* Piridigaṅgan *alias* Vaḷandarum-Perumāḷ.

940. 163 *of* 1904.—(Tamil.) On the north base of the same maṇṭapa. A mutilated record of the Vijayanagara king Kampaṇa-Uḍaiyār, son of Vīra-Bokkaṇa-Uḍaiyār in Ś. 1291, Saumya.

941. 164 *of* 1904.—(Tamil.) On the same base. A record in the twenty-first year of the Chōḷa king Tribhuvanachakravartin Kulōttuṅga-Chōḷadēva. Records gift of a musical instrument.

942. 165 *of* 1904.—(Tamil.) On the south wall of the Kanakāmbika shrine in the same temple. An incomplete record in Durmukha.

Tiruveṇṇainallūr.

This place is famous in literary history as the scene of the early life of Kamba, the author of the *Rāmāyaṇa*, and Meykaṇḍadēva, the author of *Śivagnānabōdham*.

943. 309 *of* 1902.—(Tamil.) On the south wall of the Kripāpurīśvara shrine. A record in the sixth year of the Chōḷa king Rājarājakēsarivarman (985—1013). Records gift of ninety sheep for a lamp.

944. 310 *of* 1902.—(Tamil.) On the north wall of the same shrine. A record in the seventh year of the Chōḷa king Tribhuvanachakravartin Vīrarājēndra-Chōḷadēva. Records gift of twelve cows by Rājarāja-Malaiyakularāyan.

945. 311 *of* 1902.—(Tamil.) On the same wall. An incomplete record of Tribhuvanachakravartin Kōnērimēnkoṇḍān.

946. 312 *of* 1902.—(Tamil.) On the south wall of the maṇṭapa in front of the same shrine. A record in the twenty-fifth year of the Chōḷa king Tribhuvanachakravartin Kulōttuṅga-Chōḷadēva III, who was pleased to take Madura and the crowned head of the Pāṇḍya. Records gift of thirty-two cows and one bull for a lamp by Vīraśēkharan *alias* Aḍigaimān of Kūḍalūr.

947. 313 *of* 1902.—(Tamil.) On the south and east walls of the same maṇṭapa. A damaged record in the seventeenth year of the Chōḷa king Tribhuvanachakravartin Kulōttuṅga-Chōḷadēva (III), who was pleased to take Madura and the crowned head of the Pāṇḍya. Records sale of land. Mentions Kāḍavarāyan. See *Ep. Ind.*, Vol. VII, pp. 172-3. The exact date is Thursday, 8th June, A.D. 1195.

948. 314 *of* 1902.—(Tamil.) On the west wall of the same maṇṭapa, left of entrance. A record in the fifth year of the Chōḷa king Tribhuvanachakravartin Rājarājadēva. Records gift of land.

949. 315 *of* 1902.—(Tamil.) On the east wall of the Sabhā in the Kripāpurīśvara temple. A record in the fifteenth year of the Chōḷa king Rajakēsarivarman *alias* Tribhuvanachakravartin Kulōttuṅga-Chōḷadēva II, corresponding to Sunday, 8th May 1148. Records sale of land. See *Ep. Ind.*, Vol. XI, p. 291.

950. 316 *of* 1902.—(Tamil.) On the same wall. An incomplete record in the fifteenth year of the Chōḷa king Tribhuvanachakravartin Kulōttuṅga-Chōḷadēva II. Diwan Bahadur Swamikannu Pillai says that the corresponding date was most probably Monday, 18th August 1147. See *Ep. Ind.*, Vol. XI, p. 290.

951. 317 *of* 1902.—(Tamil.) On the west wall of the same *sabhā*. An incomplete record in the eighth year of the Chōḷa king Parakēsarivarman *alias* Uḍaiyār Rājēndradēva (1050—63). Records gift of land.

952. 318 *of* 1902.—(Tamil.) On the same wall. A record in the sixth year of the Chōḷa king Rājēndradēva. Records gift of land. Partially built in.

953. 319 *of* 1902.—(Tamil.) On the north wall of the same *sabhā*. A record in the ninth year of the Chōḷa king Tribhuvanachakravartin Rājādhirājadēva. Records gift of four cows.

954. 320 *of* 1902.—(Tamil.) On the west wall of the Vaikuṇṭha-Perumāḷ shrine in the same village. A record in the seventh year of Sakalabhuvanachakravartin Peruñjiṅgadēva. Seems to contain a copy of an inscription of the twenty-ninth year of Tribhuvanavīradēva (Kulōttuṇga III) the stones of which had collapsed. The details of the date (Friday, day of Rēvati, aparapaksha-chaturthi of Simha) have been calculated by Kielhorn to be Friday, the 30th July, A.D. 1249. From this and three other dates Kielhorn dates the king's accession to be between 11th February and 30th July of A.D. 1243. [See *Ep. Ind.*, Vol. VII, p. 165.]

955. 321 *of* 1902.—(Tamil.) On the south wall of the maṇṭapa in front of the same shrine. A record in the fourteenth year of the Chōḷa king Tribhuvanachakravartin Rājādhirājadēva. Records gift of money for a lamp. Partially built in.

956. 322 *of* 1902.—(Tamil.) On the same wall. A record in the sixteenth year of the Chōḷa king Tribhuvanachakravartin Rājarājadēva. Records gift of land for a lamp.

957. 323 *of* 1902.—(Tamil.) On the same wall. A record in the fourth year of the Chōḷa king Tribhuvanachakravartin Kulōttuṅga-Chōḷadēva. Records sale of land. Partially built in.

958. 324 *of* 1902.—(Tamil.) On the same wall. A record in the tenth year of the Chōḷa king Tribhuvanachakravartin Kulōttuṅga-Chōḷadēva. Records gift of money for eleven lamps and of four cows for one lamp.

VILLUPURAM TALUK.*

Irumbai.

959. 190 *of* 1902.—(Tamil.) On the south wall of the Mahākālēśvara shrine. A record in the twenty-ninth year of the Chōḷa king Tribhuvanachakravartin Kulōttuṅga-Chōḷadēva III, who took Madura, Ceylon, Karuvūr and the crowned head of the Pāṇḍya. Records gift of land. Partially built in.

960. 191 *of* 1902.—(Tamil.) On the west wall of the same shrine. A record in the second year of the Pāṇḍya king Māravarman *alias* Tribhuvanachakravartin Vikrama-Pāṇḍyadēva. (1283 ?) Records gift of land. Partially built in.

961. 192 *of* 1902.—(Tamil.) On the same wall. A record in the second year of the Pāṇḍya king Māravarman *alias* Tribhuvanachakravartin Vikrama-Pāṇḍyadēva. Mentions Sundara Pāṇḍyadēva.

962. 193 *of* 1902.—(Tamil.) On the east wall of the maṇṭapa in front of the same shrine. A record in the tenth year of Sakalalōkachakravartin Rājanārāyaṇa Śamburāya. Records gift of land.

Koliyanūr.

Dr. Hultzsch believes that neither the Śiva temple nor the ruined Jaina shrine can boast of great age. The village is called Kōliyapuranallūr in the inscriptions.

963. 110 *of* 1897.—(Tamil.) On the east wall of the shrine of the ruined Jaina temple. Records the building of a portion of the temple by a merchant.

964. 111 *of* 1897.—(Tamil.) On the south base of the maṇṭapa in front of the same shrine. Records in Kāḷayukta gift of land. The name of the king is doubtful.

965. 112 *of* 1897.—(Tamil.) Left of entrance into the Valīśvara temple. A much damaged record.

966. 113 *of* 1897.—(Tamil.) At the entrance into the same temple. Records gift of land. The date of the record is indistinct.

---

* In the *Ins.*, *S. Dts.*, p. 144, two inscriptions are given at a place called Chintāmaṇinallūr, which I am not able to identify. Both these belong to the reign of Vikrama Chōḷa. The former grants the revenue of a village to Kulōttuṅga Chōḷēśvara Mahādēva and the latter is damaged.

967. 114 *of* 1897.—(Tamil.) On the south wall of the shrine of the same temple. A record of the Uḍaiyār king Viruppaṇa-Uḍaiyār (I), son of Hariyaṇa-Uḍaiyār (II) in Ś. 1 . . . expired, Vibhava. Records gift of land.

968. 115 *of* 1897.—(Tamil.) On the east wall of the same shrine. A record in the tenth year of Rājanārāyaṇa Śamburāya. Records the building of portions of the temple.

Maṇḍagappaṭṭu.

969. 56 *of* 1905.—(Sanskrit and Grantha.) On a pillar at the right entrance into the maṇṭapa of the rock-cut cave. A record of a Paḷḷava king whose name is lost. Records the excavation of the cave. [Venkayya points out that this cave is smaller than the Trichinopoly and Daḷavānūr caves and also apparently unfinished. With regard to the king who constructed it he surmises, on the ground of analogy, that he must have been Mahēndravarman I. See *Madr. Ep. Rep.*, 1905, p. 47.]

Panamalai.

969-A. In the cave temple near this place.—(Sanskrit). "Consists of one Sanskrit verse, which is identical with the last verse of Rājasimha's large inscription at Kāñchi." (See *S.I.I.*, I, No. 24.) Hence it may be concluded that the cave was excavated by Rājasimha (Narasimhavarman II). See *S.I.I.*, I, No. 31, p. 24.

Panayāvaram.

970. 436 *of* 1903.—(Tamil.) On the west wall of the central shrine in the Nētrōddhārakēśvara temple. A record in the forty-eighth year of the Chōḷa king Rājakēsarivarman *alias* Tribhuvana-chakravartin Kulōttuṅga-Chōḷadēva (I). The passage *viramētuṇai-yāga*, etc., from the inscriptions of Vīrarājēndra I is prefixed to the usual introduction of the king. Records gift of money for a lamp. The temple is called Tiruppanaṅgāḍuḍaiya-Mahādēvar.

971. 437 *of* 1903.—(Tamil.) On the west and north walls of the same shrine. A record in the second year of Tribhuvana-chakravartin Kōnērimēlkoṇḍān. The temple is called Tiruppura-var-Panaṅgāṭṭūr-uḍaiyār Kaṇṇa-manda-Nāyanār. Records gift of land for celebrating a festival called Kōdaṇḍarāman-śandi after the king.

972. 438 *of* 1903.—(Tamil.) On the north wall of the maṇṭapa in front of the same shrine. A record in the third year of the Chōḷa king Parakēsarivarman *alias* Uḍaiyār Ādhirājēndradēva. Built in at the beginning. Records gift of land.

Tiruvakkarai.

973. 166 *of* 1904.—(Tamil.) On the south wall of the central shrine in the Chandramaulīśvara temple. A record in the eighth year of the Chōḷa king Parakēsarivarman *alias* Rājēndra-Chōḷadēva (I, 1011—52). Records gift of sheep for lamps. A grant made in the tenth year is added at the end. The east wall of the first prākāra contains a fragmentary inscription of Ś. 1461, expired Śōbhakrit, dated during the reign of Sadāśiva, son of Vīrapratāpa-Raṅgayadeva, 'who had witnessed the elephant hunt.'

974. 167 *of* 1904.—(Tamil.) On the north wall of the same shrine. A record in the twelfth year of the Chōḷa king Tribhuvanachakravartin Vikrama-Chōḷadēva (1118—35). Records gift of thirty-two cows for a lamp for the merit of a man who died in battle at Māmbākkam.

975. 168 *of* 1904.—(Tamil.) At the southern entrance into the same shrine, right side. A record in the twenty-sixth year of the Chōḷa king Rājakēsarivarman. Records gift of paddy by Pugaḻttuṇai-aḍigaḷ, mother of Viḻuppēraraiyar Ayyākkuṭṭi-aḍigaḷ.

976. 169 *of* 1904.—(Tamil.) At the southern entrance into the same shrine, left side. A record in the nineteenth year of the Chōḷa king Rājakēsarivarman. Records gift of gold by the same donor.

977. 170 *of* 1904.—(Tamil.) At the northern entrance of the first prākāra of the same temple. An incomplete record in the tenth year of the Chōḷa king Parakēsarivarman. Records gift of land.

978. 171 *of* 1904.—(Tamil.) On the east wall of the maṇṭapa in front of the same shrine. A record in the eleventh year of the Chōḷa king Parakēsarivarman *alias* Rājēndra-Chōḷadēva (I, 1011—53). Built in at the bottom.

979. 172 *of* 1904.—(Tamil.) On the east wall of the maṇṭapa in front of the central shrine in the same temple. An incomplete record in the fifth year of the Chōḷa king Parakēsarivarman *alias* Tribhuvanachakravartin Vikrama-Chōḷadēva (1118—35).

980. 173 *of* 1904.—(Tamil.) On the same wall. A damaged and incomplete record in the nineteenth year of the Chōḷa king Parakēsarivarman *alias* Uḍaiyār Rājēndra-Chōḷadēva. (I, 1011—53).

981. 174 *of* 1904.—(Tamil.) On the south wall of the same maṇṭapa. A record in the twenty-ninth year of the Chōḷa king Rājarājakēsarivarman *alias* Rājarājadēva (I, 985—1013.) Records gift of 90 sheep for a lamp.

982. 175 *of* 1904.—(Tamil.) On the same wall. An incomplete record in the forty-fifth year of the Chōḷa king Rājakēsarivarman *alias* Chakravartin Kulōttuṅga-Chōḷadēva (I, 1070—1118). Records gift of land for a lamp.

983. 176 *of* 1904.—(Tamil.) On the same wall. A record in the seventh year of the Chōḷa king Parakēsarivarman *alias* Rājēndra-Chōḷadēva (1011—53). Records gift of 90 sheep for a lamp.

984. 177 *of* 1904.—(Tamil.) On the same wall. A record in the thirty-first year of the Chōḷa king Parakēsarivarman *alias* Uḍaiyār Rājēndra-Chōḷadēva (I, 1011—52), who took the eastern country, the Ganges and Kiḍāram.' Records gift of a musical instrument. Kiḍāram is Burma.

985. 178 *of* 1904.—(Tamil.) On the same wall. A record in the tenth year of the Chōḷa king Kulōttuṅga-Chōḷadēva. Records gift of sheep for a lamp.

986. 179 *of* 1904.—(Tamil.) On the west wall of the maṇṭapa in front of the same shrine. An incomplete record in the seventh year of the Chōḷa king Kulōttuṅga-Chōḷadēva. Refers to an accident in hunting.

987. 180 *of* 1904.—(Tamil.) On the same wall. An incomplete record in the third year of the Chōḷa king Vikrama-Chōḷadēva (1118—35).

988. 181 *of* 1904.—(Grantha and Tamil.) On the same wall. A record in the sixth year of the Pāṇḍya king Vikrama-Pāṇḍyadēva. Begins with *Samastabhuvanaikavira*, etc. Records gift of land for the celebration of a festival called Vikrama-Pāṇḍiyan-śandi after the king. [Vikrama-Pāṇḍya was very probably the king who ascended the throne in 1283.]

989. 182 *of* 1904.—(Tamil.) On the north wall of the same maṇṭapa. An incomplete record in the forty-fourth year of the Chōḷa king Kulōttuṅga-Chōḷadēva (I). Records gift of money for lamps at three temples.

990. 183 *of* 1904.—(Tamil.) On the same wall. A record in the twenty-ninth year of the Chōḷa king Rājakēsarivarman *alias* Tribhuvanachakravartin Kulōttuṅga-Chōḷadēva. Records that two women were appointed as dancing girls in the temple of Tiruvakkarai.

991. 184 *of* 1904.—(Tamil.) On the same wall. A record of the Chōḷa king Tribhuvanachakravartin Rājādhirājadēva, the date of which is lost. Built in. Refers to the twelfth year of Rājarāja I and the third year of Rājādhirājadēva I(?).

992. 185 *of* 1904.—(Tamil.) On the same wall. An incomplete record in the third year of the Chōḷa king Vikrama-Chōḷadēva (1118—35).

993. 186 *of* 1904.—(Tamil.) On the north base of the same maṇṭapa.' An incomplete record of the Chōḷa king Kulōttuṅga-Chōḷadēva (I, 1070—1118), 'who was pleased to abolish tolls', the date of which is lost. Refers to the king as being (encamped) in a tope at Conjeeveram. Records gift of land.

994. 187 *of* 1904.—On the same base. A record in the twenty-eighth year of the Chōḷa king Rājēndra-Chōḷadēva (I, 1011—53). Stones out of order. On the same base is an incomplete introduction of Rājarāja I.

995. 188 *of* 1904.—(Tamil.) On the east wall of the maṇṭapa inside the first prākāra of the same temple. A record in the fourth year of the Pāṇḍya king Vikrama-Pāṇḍyadēva. Records that the maṇṭapa was built by queen Ulagamuḻudumuḍaiyār.

996. 189 *of* 1904.—(Tamil.) On the west and south bases of the samé maṇṭapa. A record of the Vijayanagara king Vīra-Kṛishṇarāya in Ś. 1437, Bhava. Records gift of land to a Śaiva maṭha.

997. 190 *of* 1904.—(Tamil.) On the south wall of the 1,000-pillared maṇṭapa inside the second prākāra of the same temple. A record in the second year of the Chōḷa king Tribhuvanachakravartin Kulōttuṅga-Chōḷadēva (III), "who took Madurai and the crowned head of the Pāṇḍya." Records the building of the maṇṭapa by a certain Ammaiappan Gaṇḍar-śūriyan Śambuvarayan "who took the Pāṇḍya country." See N.A. 720 for an Ammaiyappa.

998. 191 *of* 1904.—(Tamil and Grantha.) On the south base of the 1,000-pillared maṇṭapa inside the second prākāra of the Chandramauḷīśvara temple in the same village. A record of the Pallava king Sakalabhuvanachakravartin Kāḍavan Avaniyāḷappirandān Kōpperuñjiṅgan. Records that the king who bore the surname *Sarvajñakhaḍgamalla* built a sluice for the tank at Olugarai.

999. 192 *of* 1904.—(Tamil.) On the same base. An incomplete record in the sixteenth year of the Chōḷa king Kulōttuṅga-Chōḷadēva. Built in at the beginning.

1000. 193 *of* 1904.—(Tamil.) On the same base. A mutilated record in the sixteenth year of the Chōḷa king Kulōttuṅga-Chōḷadēva. Records gift of 128 cows for four lamps.

1001. 194 *of* 1904.—(Tamil.) On the same base. A record in the sixteenth year of the Chōḷa king Tribhuvanachakravartin Kulōttuṅga-Chōḷadēva. Stones out of order. Records gift of two lampstands by the donor in No. 997 above.

1002. 195 *of* 1904.—(Tamil.) On the right side of the gōpura of the first prākāra of the same temple. A record in the seventh year of the Chōḷa king Tribhuvanachakravartin Rājādhirājadēva (I or II ?). Records the building of the gōpura by the same donor.

1003. 196 *of* 1904.—(Tamil verse.) On the left side of the same gōpura. Records in Ś. 1352 the building of a maṇṭapa and of a gōpura by a certain Gāṅgēyan.

1004. 197 *of* 1904.—(Tamil verse.) In the same place. Refers to the building of the same gōpura and maṇṭapa.

1005. 198 *of* 1904.—(Tamil.) On the east base of the same gōpura, right of entrance. A record of the Śāḷuva king Naraśiṅgadēva in Śōbhakrit (1483–84). Refers to Narasa Nāyaka, an agent of the king (evidently the founder of the Tuluva dynasty) and records the remission of some taxes.

1006. 199 *of* 1904.—(Tamil.) On the west base of the same gōpura, left of entrance. A record in Śōbhakrit. In modern characters.

1007. 200 *of* 1904.—(Tamil.) On the south base of the ruined Śiva shrine within the same temple. An incomplete record in the sixteenth year of the Chōḷa king Rājarāja-Rājakēsarivarman (I, 985—1013). Records a gift to the stone temple of Śivalōka-uḍaiya-Paramasvāmin built by Uḍaiyapirāṭṭiyār Śembiyan-Mādeviyar, queen of Gaṇḍarādittadēvar, who gave birth to Śrī-Uttama-Chōḷa-ḍēva (i.e., Madhurāntaka Uttamachōḷa, the immediate predecessor of Rājarāja I). Records allotments for the various requirements of the temple. For a description of the coins of Madhurāntaka, see Elliot's *Coins in S. India*, Nos. 151 and 154 and *Madr. Ep. Rep.* 1904, p. 11.

1008. 201 *of* 1904.—(Tamil.) On the base of the Varadarāja-Perumaḷ shrine in the same temple. An incomplete record in the twenty-seventh year of the Chōḷa king Rājakēsarivarman *alias* Tribhuvanachakravartin Kulōttuṅga-Chōḷadēva (I ?).

1009. 202 *of* 1904.—(Tamil.) On the west base of the same shrine. A record in the forty-first year of the Chōḷa king Kulōttuṅga Chōḷadēva (I). Records gift of sheep for a lamp.

1010. 203 *of* 1904.—(Tamil.) On the same base. An incomplete record in the forty-first year of the Chōḷa king Kulōttuṅga Chōḷadēva.

1011. 204 *of* 1904.—(Tamil.) On the north base of the same shrine. An incomplete record in the thirtieth year of the Chōḷa king Rājakēsarivarman *alias* Tribhuvanachakravartin Kulōttuṅga-Chōḷadēva.

1012. 205 *of* 1904.—(Grantha and Tamil.) On the west wall of the maṇṭapa in front of the same shrine. An incomplete record in the second year (i.e., 1070–71) of the Chōḷa king Uḍaiyār Ādhirājēndradēva (the immediate predecessor of Kulōttuṅga Chōḷa I). The Sanskrit portion records that the Vimāna, which had been previously built by Kōchchōḷa of bricks, was reconstructed of stone.

1013. 206 *of* 1904.—(Tamil.) On the north base of the same maṇṭapa. An incomplete record of the Chōḷa king Rājakēsarivarman *alias* Tribhuvanachakravartin Kulōttuṅga Chōḷa I.

1014. 207 *of* 1904.—(Tamil.) On the north base of the maṇṭapa in front of the Varadarāja-Perumāḷ shrine. An incomplete record in the eighth year of the Chōḷa king Vikrama-Chōḷadēva (1118—35). Records gift of sheep for a lamp.

1015. 208 *of* 1904.—(Tamil verse.) At the entrance into the same shrine, left side. Records the gift of a door in the twenty-fourth year of an unnamed king.

Tiruvāmattūr.

1016. 402 *of* 1903.—(Tamil.) On the west wall of the central shrine in the Abhirāmēśvara temple. A fragment of record in the twenty-fifth year of the Chōḷa king Rājarājadēva (I).

1017. 403 *of* 1903.—(Tamil.) On the same wall. A record in the third year of the Chōḷa king Parakēsarivarman. Records gift of two lamps by Śembiyan Kattimānaḍigal. Refers also to his building the Tiruchcheṟṟu-maṇṭapam.

1018. 404 *of* 1903.—(Tamil.) A record in the fourth year of the Chōḷa king Parakēsarivarman. Records gift of a lamp by Kaṇḍarādittan *alias*. . . . Mahārājan of Vānagappāḍi.

1019. 405 *of* 1903.—(Tamil.) On the same wall. A record in the third year of the Chōḷa king Rājakēsarivarman. Records gift of sheep for a lamp.

1020. 406 *of* 1903.—(Tamil.) On the north wall of the central shrine in the Abhirāmēśvara temple. A record in the third year of the Chōḷa king Rājakēsarivarman *alias* Uḍaiyār Vīrarājēndradēva. Records gift of gold for a lamp.

1021. 407 *of* 1903.—(Tamil.) On the same wall. A record of the Chōḷa king Parakēsarivarman, the date of which is doubtful. Records gift of a lamp.

1022. 408 *of* 1903.—(Tamil.) On the same wall. A record in the fifteenth year of the Chōḷa king Parakēsarivarman. Records gift of a lamp.

1023. 409 *of* 1903.—(Tamil.) On the south base of the same shrine. A record in the fifteenth year of the Chōḷa king Madiraikoṇḍa-Parakēsarivarman (905—47). Built in at the end. Records gift of 100 sheep for a lamp.

1024. 410 *of* 1903.—(Tamil.) On the same base. A record in the seventeenth year of the Chōḷa king Madiraikoṇḍa Parakēsarivarman (905—47). Built in at the end. Records gift of a lamp.

1025. 411 *of* 1903.—(Tamil.) On the same base. A record in the twenty-ninth year of the Chōḷa king Madiraikoṇḍa Parakēsarivarman. Built in at the end.

1026.—412 *of* 1903.—(Tamil.) On the same base. A record in the thirty-second year of the Chōla king Madiraikoṇḍa Parakēsarivarman. Built in at the end.

1027. 413 *of* 1903.—(Tamil.) On the west base of the same shrine. A record in the sixth year of the Chōḷa king Parakēsarivarman. Built in at the end. Refers to the mason who built the temple.

1028. 414 *of* 1903.—(Tamil.) On the same base. A record in the twenty-sixth year of the Chōḷa king Madiraikoṇḍa Parakēsarivarman (905—47). Built in at the end.

1029. 415 *of* 1903.—(Tamil.) On the same base. A fragment of record of the Chōḷa king Madiraikoṇḍa Parakēsarivarman (905—47), the date of which is lost.

1030. 416 *of* 1903.—(Tamil.) On the north base of the same shrine. A record in the twenty-sixth year of the Chōḷa king Madiraikoṇḍa Parakēsarivarman (905—47). Records gift of a lamp.

1031. 417 *of* 1903.—(Tamil.) On the same base. A record in the sixteenth year of the Chōḷa king Parakēsarivarman. Records gift of gold.

1032. 418 *of* 1903.—(Tamil.) On the same base. A record in the twenty-ninth year of the Chōḷa king Madiraikoṇḍa Parakēsarivarman (905—47). Records gift of gold for a lamp.

1033. 419 *of* 1903.—(Tamil.) On the same base. An incomplete record in the forty-first year of the Chōḷa king Parakēsarivarman, "who took Madirai and Īḷam" (905—47). Records gift of gold for a lamp.

1034. 420 *of* 1903.—(Tamil.) On the same base. A fragment of record of the Chōḷa king Rājēndra-Chōḷa I (1011—53), the date of which is lost. Contains the usual introduction of the king.

1035. 421 *of* 1903.—(Tamil.) On the same base. A fragment of record in the second year of the Chōḷa king Parakēsarivarman *alias* Uḍaiyār Śrī-Rājarājadēva (II ?). The first line of the inscription contains a few words of the introduction of Rājēndradēva and in the second line is the name of the king.

1036. 422 *of* 1903.—(Marathi.) On two slabs built into the floor in front of the entrance into the same shrine. Mentions the temple of Abhirāmēśvara.

1037. 423 *of* 1903.—(Tamil.) On the south wall of the maṇṭapa in front of the same shrine. A record in the tenth year of the Chōḷa king Madiraikoṇḍa Parakēsarivarman (905—47). Records gift of land. Mentions the king's other name Śrī-Parāntaka and an officer of his named Śōḷaśikhāmaṇi-Pallavaraiyan.

1038. 424 *of* 1903.—(Tamil.) On the north wall of the same maṇṭapa. A record in the third year of the Chōḷa king Parakēsarivarman. Records gift of gold for a lamp.

1039. 425 *of* 1903.—(Tamil.) On the south base of the same maṇṭapa. A record in the third year of the Chōḷa king Parakēsarivarman. Records gift of a lamp by Parabūmikan-Mallan *alias*

Gaṇḍarāditta-Pallavaraiyan. [Venkayya identifies the king with Parakēsarivarman Gaṇḍarāditya, the son of Parāntaka (I). Pallavaraiyan evidently took his surname from his suzerain.]

1040. 426 *of* 1903.—(Tamil.) On the same base. A record of the Chōḷa king in Ś. 879. Records gift of a lamp by Parabūmikan Mallan *alias* Gaṇḍarāditta-Pallavaraiyan. See note to the above inscription.

1041. 427 *of* 1903.—(Tamil.) On the same base. A fragment of record of the Chōḷa king Madiraikoṇḍa Parakēsarivarman (905—47), the date of which is doubtful.

1042. 428 *of* 1903.—(Tamil.) On the south wall of the dark maṇṭapa in front of the same shrine. A record in the forty-fifth year of the Chōḷa king Kulōttuṅga-Chōḷadēva (I). Records gift of money for a lamp by an officer of the king.

1043. 429 *of* 1903.—(Tamil.) On the same wall. A record in the third year of the Chōḷa king Parakēsarivarman *alias* Rājēndra-Chōḷadēva I (1011—53). Records gift of 96 sheep for a lamp.

1044. 430 *of* 1903.—(Tamil.) On the same wall. A record in the third year of the Chōḷa king Parakēsarivarman *alias* Rājēndra-Chōḷadēva I (1011—53). Records gift of 1,056 sheep for eleven lamps.

1045. 431 *of* 1903.—(Tamil.) On the north base of the dark maṇṭapa in front of the central shrine in the same temple. A record in the twenty-fourth year of the Chōḷa king Rājakēsarivarman *alias* Rājarājadēva. Built in at the beginning. Records gift of 96 sheep for a lamp.

1046. 432 *of* 1903.—(Tamil.) On the same base. An incomplete record in the thirteenth year of the Chōḷa king Rājarāja-Rājakēsarivarman, "who destroyed the ships at Kāndaḷūr-Śālai" (985—1013).

1047. 433 *of* 1903.—(Tamil.) On the east wall of the first prākāra of the same temple. A record in the second year of the Chōḷa king Rājakēsarivarman *alias* Tribhuvanachakravartin Kulōttuṅga-Chōḷadēva. Records gift of land to a certain Rājarāja-Pichchan and his troupe for singing the *Tiruppadiyam* hymns in the temple. N.A. 134 and 347.

1048. 434 *of* 1903.—(Tamil.) On the south wall of the same prākāra. A record in the fourteenth year (i.e., 1335-6) of Śakalalōkachakravartin Venrumaṇ-koṇḍa-Śambuvarāyar (1322—1337). Refers to the invasion of the Muhammadans and the destruction of the country by them. Venkayya is unable to see what invasion is referred to in this but the Madura chronicles clearly tell us that there was a Mussalman invasion between 1324 and 1327. (See *Ind. Antq.*, Jan. 1914).

1049. 435 *of* 1903.—(Grantha and Tamil.) On the west wall of the same prākāra. A record in the sixth year of the Pāṇḍya king Vikrama-Pāṇḍya. Begins with Samastabhuvanaikavīra-Chandra-kula-maṅgaḷa-pradīpa, etc. Records gift of land for celebrating a festival in honour of the king.

Villupuram.

The ancient name of this place was Jananāthachōlachatur-vēdimaṅgalam and it belonged to Tirumunaippāḍināḍu. It was associated to a certain extent with Jainism, as is proved by the ruins of Jain temples and Jain figures available therein. The following records, however, are purely Hindu.

1050. 116 *of* 1897.—(Tamil.) On the north wall of the shrine in the Kailāsanāthasvāmin temple. A record of the Vijayanagara king Kṛishṇadēva-Mahārāya in Ś. 1439 expired, Īśvara. Records gift of land.

1051. 117 *of* 1897.—(Tamil.) On the same wall. A record of the Vijayanagara king Kṛishṇayyadēva-Chōḷamahārāya in Ś. 1447 expired, Pārthiva. Records gift of land.

1052. 118 *of* 1897.—(Tamil.) On the west wall of the same shrine. A record of the Vijayanagara king Kṛishṇadēva-Mahārāya in Ś. 1449 expired, Tāraṇa (wrong). Records that the Kanmāḷas of Tiruvāḍi-Śīrmai were exempted from taxes. See N.A. 208.

VRIDDHACHALAM TALUK.

Tiṭṭaguḍi.

1053. 5 *of* 1903.—(Tamil.) On the north wall of the maṇṭapa in front of the central shrine in the Vaidyanāthasvāmin temple. A record in the ninth year of the Chōḷa king Tribhuvanachakra-vartin Kulōttuṅga-Chōḷadēva. Records gift of land.

1054. 6 *of* 1903.—(Tamil.) On the same wall. Refers in Śubhakrit to a dispute between two factions in the village which lasted for several years and was settled by the agent of Nāgama-Nāyaka. Compare *South Ind. Inscrns.*, Vol. I, No. 119. See N.A. 601.

1055. 7 *of* 1903.—(Tamil.) On the same wall. Records in Vikārin gifts of land by Bhūpatirāya-Uḍaiyār and Uḍaiyār Malli-dēvarāyar. Tiṭṭaguḍi was also called Vidyāraṇyapuram.

1056. 8 *of* 1903.—(Tamil.) On the same wall. A record of the Vijayanagara king Vīra-Bhūpati-Uḍaiyār, the date of which is lost. Records gift of land. Mentions Mallidēvarāyar and Tiṭṭaguḍi *alias* Vidyāraṇyapuram. A damaged record.

1057. 9 *of* 1903.—(Tamil.) On the south wall of the same maṇṭapa. Records in the forty-second year gift of land by Vaṅgāra-Muttaraiyan.

1058. 10 *of* 1903.—(Tamil.) On the same wall. Records in the fifth year gift of Vāgaiyūr in Magadaimaṇḍalam by Magadēśan Ponparappina-Vānakōvadaraiyan.

1059. 11 *of* 1903.—(Tamil.) On the same wall. A record in the seventh year of the Chōḷa king Tribhuvanachakravartin Vīra-rājēndra Chōḷadēva. Records that Rājarāja Vaṅgāra Muttaraiyan granted an allowance of paddy to an image of the goddess which had been set up by a dancing girl.

1060. 12 *of* 1903.—(Tamil.) On the same wall. A record in the second year of the Pāṇḍya king Tribhuvanachakravartin Kōnērinmaikoṇḍān Kulaśēkharadēva. Records gift of a village in Magadaimaṇḍalam by the king for offerings on his birthday.

1061. 13 *of* 1903.—(Tamil.) On the same wall. A record of the Vijayanagara king Vīra-Kampaṇa-Uḍaiyār (II), son of Vīra-Bokkaṇa-Uḍaiyār (i.e. Bukka I) in Ś. 1295, Paridhāvin. Records gift of land by Sōmayadeṇṇāyakkar.

1062. 14 *of* 1903.—(Tamil.) On the same wall. A record of the Chōḷa king Tribhuvanachakravartin Kulōttuṅga-Chōḷadēva in his third year. Records gift of two villages by Rājarāja-Magadai-nāḍ-āḻvān.

1063. 15 *of* 1903.—(Tamil.) On the same wall. A record in the third year of the Chōḷa king Tribhuvanachakravartin Kulōt-tuṅga-Chōḷadēva. Records gift of cows and money for two lamps by Rājarāja-Magadainād-āḻvān.

1064. 16 *of* 1903.—(Tamil.) On the same wall. A record in the fourteenth year of the Chōḷa king Parakēsarivarman *alias* Tribhuvanachakravartin Rājarājadēva. Records gift of paddy by Rājarāja Vaṅgāra-Muttaraiyan.

1065. 17 *of* 1903.—(Tamil.) On the north wall of the Viśva-nātha shrine in the same temple. A record in the thirteenth year of the Chōḷa king Tribhuvanachakravartin Kulōttuṅga-Chōḷadēva III, who took Madura and the crowned head of the Pāṇḍya. Records gift of ornaments by the wife of a merchant to the image of Vichchēśvara, which had been set up by the same chief.

1066. 18 *of* 1903.—(Tamil.) On the same wall. A record in the eleventh year of the Chōḷa king Tribhuvanachakravartin Kulōttuṅga-Chōḷadēva III, who took Madura and the crowned head of the Pāṇḍya. Records gift of taxes to the same image by the same chief.

1067. 19 *of* 1903.—(Tamil.) On the inner gōpura in the same temple, right of entrance. A record in the twenty-seventh year of the Chōḷa king Tribhuvanachakravartin Rājarājadēva. Records gift of land.

1068. 20 *of* 1903.—(Tamil.) On the same gōpura, left of entrance. A record in the nineteenth year of the Chōḷa king

Tribhuvanachakravartin Rājarājadēva III, corresponding to Wednesday, July 30, 1242. Records gift of land. See *Ep. Ind.*, VIII, p. 271.

1069. 21 *of* 1903.—(Tamil and Grantha.) On the west wall of the Sukhāsīna-Perumāḷ temple in the same village. A record in the fourth year of the Chōḷa king Tribhuvanachakravartin Rājādhirājadēva. Records gift of paddy and money by the inhabitants of Śittiramēḷi-Periyanāḍu.

1070. 22 *of* 1903.—(Tamil.) On the same wall. A record in the ninth year of the Chōḷa king Kulōttuṅga-Chōḷadēva III, who took Madura. Records gift of money for a lamp.

1071. 23 *of* 1903.—(Tamil.) On the north wall of the same temple. A record in the twelfth year of the Chōḷa king Tribhuvanachakravartin Kulōttuṅga-Chōḷadēva III, who took Madura and the crowned head of the Pāṇḍya. Records gift of money by a merchant.

1072. 24 (*a*) *of* 1903.—(Tamil.) On the same wall. A record in the fifth year of the Chōḷa king Tribhuvanachakravartin Kulōttuṅga-Chōḷadēva III, who took Madura and the crowned head of the Pāṇḍya. Records gift of land.

1073. 24 (*b*) *of* 1903.—(Tamil.) On the same wall. A record in the fourth year of the Chōḷa king Tribhuvanachakravartin Kulōttuṅga-Chōḷadēva III, who took Madura and the crowned head of the Pāṇḍya. Records gift of land.

1074. 25 *of* 1903.—(Tamil.) On the south wall of the same temple. A damaged record in the eighth year of the Chōḷa king Kulōttuṅga-Chōḷadēva III, who took Madura.

1075. 26 *of* 1903.—(Tamil.) On the same wall. A record in the fifth year of the Chōḷa king Tribhuvanachakravartin Rājādhirājadēva. Records gift of land by Rājarāja Vaṅgāra-Muttaraiyaṅ.

1076. 27 *of* 1903.—(Tamil.) On the same wall. A record in the thirtieth year of the Chōḷa king Tribhuvanachakravartin Kulōttuṅga-Chōḷadēva III, who took Madura and the crowned head of the Pāṇḍya. Records gift of land.

Toḷudūr.

1077. 399 *of* 1913.—(Tamil.) On the south wall of the Madurāntaka-Chōḷēśvara temple. Refers in the ninth year of the king to an exchange of wet land in Toḷuvūr granted to the temple of Madurāntaka Chōḷīśvaramuḍaiya-Nāyanār, in place of the one at Chandraśēkharanallūr given by Vānakōvaraiyan under the tank called Tirunīṛṛu-Vīramagadaśōḷappēriya-ēri.

1078. 400 *of* 1913.—(Tamil.) On the samē wall. A record in the thirty-second year of the Chōla king Tribhuvanachakravartin Tribhuvanavīradēva (Kulōttuṅga III), who was pleased to take

Madurai (Madura), the crowned head of the Pāṇḍya and Karuvūr. Registers that a certain Śēdiyarāyaveḷḷān, chief of Śembai, built the stone temple and the maṇṭapa for the god Madurāntakēśvara-muḍaiya Nāyanār at Peruntoḷuvūr in Ugaḷūr-kūṟṟam, a subdivision of Vaḍagarai Rājaśiṅga-vaḷanāḍu. He had also presented to the same temple the processional images of the god and goddess.

1079. 401 *of* 1913.—(Tamil.) On a slab lying in the same temple. A fragment of record. Seems to record gifts of land to the temples of Madurāntaka-Īśvaram-Uḍaiyār and Araiśandurai-Nāyanār.

1080. 402 *of* 1913.—(Tamil.) On a conch preserved in the Varadarāja-Perumāḷ temple in the same village. This conch was the gift of Tirunīṟṟu-Virāmagadaśōḷan Tāyilunalla-Perumāḷ, to the temple of Madurānta-Chōḷīśvaram-uḍaiya-Nāyanār at Toḷuvūr.

Vriddhachalam.

In the list of Mackenzie's inscriptions given in *Ins., S. Dts.*, pp. 145—9, there are thirteen inscriptions. Of these three have been identified with three of the departmental list. The other ten have been included.

1081. 132 *of* 1900.—(Tamil.) In the second gōpura of the Vriddhagirīśvara temple, right of entrance. A record in the fourth year of the Pāṇḍya king Tribhuvanachakravartin Kōnērinmai-koṇḍān. Records gift of land to the Brāhmaṇas of Kulaśēkhara-chaturvēdimaṅgalam founded in the name of the king.

1082. 313 *of* 1900.—(Tamil.) On the south wall of the maṇṭapa in front of the central shrine in the same temple. A record in the twenty-eighth year of the Chōḷa king Tribhuvanachakra-vartin Kulōttuṅga-Chōḷadēva. Records gift of 100 cows. See *Ins., S. Dts.*, in Mack. MSS., p. 145, No. I (where the year is, I believe, wrongly given as the twenty-second. It says that the grantor was Rājarāja-Kāḍavarāyan).

1083. 134 *of* 1900.—(Tamil.) On the south wall of the maṇṭapa in front of the central shrine in the same temple. A record in the fifth year of Peruñjiṅgadēva. Records gift of "mango sprouts" made of gold. [The Mack. MSS. also give this inscription. See *Ins., S. Dts.*, p. 144, No. 2. The donor is one "Sambotya Manikayun" (?) and the real donation is 25 kaḻanju of gold for *Tirumaṇṭaḻir* and 5 *kaḻanju* of silver for bracelets.]

1084. 135 *of* 1900.—(Tamil.) On the south wall of the maṇṭapa in front of the central shrine in the same temple. A record in the eighth year of Peruñjiṅgadēva. Records gift of a lamp.

1085. 136 *of* 1900.—(Tamil.) On the south wall of the maṇṭapa in front of the central shrine in the same temple. A record in the fourteenth year of the Chōḷa king Tribhuvanachakravartin

Rājarājadēva (III). Records gift of a lamp by Ediriganāyan Pottappi Chōḷa, one of the bodyguard chiefs of the Pallava king Kopperuñjiṅga. The inscription shows that in 1229 he was still loyal to Rājarāja III. He was to rise against him in 1231. (See S.A. 329.) Dr. Hultzsch says that he re-ascended the throne in 1243, but he who came to the throne in 1243 was another man, his son, in all probability. (See *Ep. Ind.*, Vol. VII, p. 163–4.) This is evidently inscription No. 10 in *Ins., S. Dts.*, p. 149.

1086. 137 *of* 1900.—(Tamil.) On the east wall of the same maṇṭapa, right of entrance. A record in the fifteenth year of the Chōḷa king Rājakēsarivarman *alias* Tribhuvanachakravartin Kulōttuṅga-Chōḷadēva. Records that Āḷappirandān Ēḷisaimōgan *alias* Kulōttuṅga-Śōḷa-Kāḍavarādittan built a maṇṭapa for the mahāsnapaṇa of the god at Tirumudukunṛam in Paruvūr-kūṛṛam, a subdivision of Irungōḷappāḍi in Mērka-Nāḍu, which formed part of Virudarājabhayaṅkara-vaḷanāḍu.

1087. 138 *of* 1900.—(Tamil.) On the south wall of the central shrine in the same temple. A record in the ninth year of the Chōḷa king Parakēsarivarman. Records gift of a lamp.

1088. 139 *of* 1900.—(Tamil.) On the west wall of the same shrine. An incomplete record in the twenty-sixth year of the Chōḷa king Rājakēsarivarman *alias* Rājarājadēva.

1089. 140 *of* 1900.—(Tamil.) On the north wall of the same shrine. A record in the twelfth year of the Chōḷa king Parakēsarivarman. Records gift of a lamp.

1090. On a stone in the southern wall of the Ardhamaṇṭapam. (Tamil.) Records that one Muḍikoṇḍavēḷān granted in the fifteenth year of Kopperuñjiṅgadēva ninty-six goats for supplying quarter measure of ghee daily to God Tirumalaikoṇḍamuḍayār. *Ins., S. Dts.*, p. 146, No. 3.

1091. In the second prākāra wall. A damaged grant of Prauḍhapratāpadēvarāya (Devārāya II) in Ś. 1351, Saumya. *Ibid.*, No. 4.

1092. In the same wall. Records that Śelvappanāyaka granted in Ś. 1155, Nandana, in the reign of Hariharadēva Mahārāya (?) three villages to God Vruddhanātha. *Ibid.*, No. 5.

1093. On the northern wall of the second enclosure. Records that in the reign of Kopperuñjiṅgadēva, Harihara Daṇḍanāyaka and people gave 210 cows to God Tirumalakoṇḍa Uḍaiyār for milk. *Ibid.*, No. 6.

1094. On the inside of the south enclosure wall. Records that Kachchi-Rāyan granted in Ś. 1595, Ānanda, four kalams of grain to the watchmen of the pagoda, in the reign of "Combur Voday" (?). *Ibid.*, No. 7.

1095. On the second north enclosure wall of Paḷaiyamallanāthar temple. Records that Kachchirāya and people granted one *Mā* of land in Vāyalūr to the watchmen of the Vāyalūr village in the twenty-second year of Bukkaṇa Uḍaiyār. *Ins. S. Dts.*, p. 148, No. 8.

1096. On the north wall of the kitchen of the same temple. Records that one Taghavanāyakan (?) gave in the sixteenth year of Kopperuñjiṅga-dēva ninety-six goats to the deity. *Ibid.*, No. 9.

1097. A C.P. in the temple. Records that in the reign of Raṅgappa Maḷavarāyar, the people of Kuḷattūr and Ariyalūr gave to the God the tax of 1 *kāśu* on every bag for each market and two-handfuls of rice in Ariyalūrpēṭa. *Ibid.*, p. 217, No. 44.

1098. A P.G. in the hands of certain temple people. Records that Veṅkaṭarāya Śrīnivāsa Subahdar and the inhabitants of the village granted 50 kuḷis of land to the deity in Ś. 1670, Dhātu. *Ibid.*, p. 217, No. 45.

1099. A P.G. in the hands of the same. Records that Shamsul Dowla (?) Rastam Khan re-established the grants of the former Rājās to the temple. *Ibid.*, p. 218, No. 46.

BELLARY DISTRICT.

ADONI TALUK.

Adoni Fort.

1. On a stone in the fort. Records that Raṅgayya Dhasari (?) Tirumalayya built a battery in the fort in Ś. 1487, Raktākshi. See *Ins., Ced. Dts.*, p. 313, No. 22.

2. On a stone at the bottom of the Murugacheruvu tank in the fort. Records that Rāmarāju Kōnēṭi Timmayyarasalu (?) exempted in Ś. 1645, Śubhakrit, in the reign of Sadāśivarāya, two gate-keepers of the hill-fort from their taxes. *Ibid.*, p. 313, No. 23.

3. On a stone north of the above. Records that Vīra "Hurreyura Gobbodeyurru," son of Vīra Mallirāya, gave one *jukkulā* of land at Mologavallee to "Sunnębova" in Ś. 1299, Piṅgaḷa. *Ibid.*, p. 313, No. 24.

4. On the road of Balakilla fort (Ballekallu ?). (Kanarese and Dēvanāgari.) Records that "Caukanagolada Basava" constructed the above fort. *Ibid.*, p. 314, No. 25.

5. On a stone pillar in the pagoda of Yellamma in the Balakilla (Ballekallu) fort at Adoni. (Kanarese.) Records that Chikka "Dudeudda Harregeya and Basavayya" built the Pagoda of Yellamma in four *aṅkaṇams*. *Ibid.*, 314, No. 26.

6. On the gate of the Adoni fort. (Telugu.) Records that Tirumala Nāyaḍu erected the gate in a certain Raktākshi. *Ibid.*, p. 314, No. 27.

Bhaṭṭarabommalāpuram.

7. On a stone east of the village. Records that Achyutarāya granted Bommalāpuram village in Ś. 1457, Jaya, to Bhaṭṭar (Nāgayyā ?). *Ibid.*, p. 308, No. 6.

8. On a stone in the pagoda of Śambhuliṅgēśvar. (Kanarese.) Records that the queen "Pereyakatala" Dēviyār gave in C.V. 16, in the reign of Tribhuvanamalladēva, some land in Śirugappa village for the festival of Kadhirēśvara. *Ibid.*, No. 7.

9. On a stone in the *Amarēśvara* pagoda. (Kanarese.) A record dated in Ś. 1433, *Prajōtpatti*, of Jakkanāyaka, in the reign of Kṛishṇadēvarāya. *Ibid.*, p. 309, No. 8.

Chinnatumbalam.

10. On a stone in the Pēṭa, north of Basavanakuṭṭa. Records that Pūtadēviar, the queen of Tribhuvanamalladēva, gave to the local Brahmans in C.V. 32, Sarvajit, the tax of 30 pagodas from the revenue land of Tumbalam. *Ins., Ced. Dts.*, p. 307, No. 1.

11. North of the above inscription. (Kanarese.) Records that in the reign of Bhuvanēkamalla, his brother Trilōkyamalla Jayasimha granted in Ś. 990, Kīlaka, nearly 300 muttas of land and four mills to God Svayambu Dakshiṇa-Sōmēśvara for festival. *Ins., Ced. Dts.*, p. 307, No. 2.

12. North of the above inscription. (Kanarese.) A record of the same king. No details given. *Ibid.*, No. 3.

Dayyamdinne.

13. On a stone in the Hanumantarāya pagoda. (Telugu.) Records that in Ś. 1484 Rāmarāja granted the village as free gift to "Pudapadam Bulacharya." *Ibid.*, p. 237, No. 10.

Guruzāla.

14. On a stone near the southern gate of the Rāmēśvara pagoda. (Kanarese.) Records that Daṇḍanāyaka Bhīmarasu granted in year 16, Dundubi, in the reign of Jakadēkamalla, 52 muttas of land for the festival of Rāmēśvaradēva in this village. *Ibid.*, p. 236, No. 8.

15. On the west of the Rāmēśvara pagoda. (Kanarese.) Records that Jaṅgam Jannebhuniah (?) in year 36, Khara, in the reign of Tribhuvanamalla, gave 29 muttas of land for god Rāmēśvara. *Ibid.*, p. 237, No. 9.

Kāggallu.

16. 208 *of* 1913.—(Kanarese.) On a stone in the neighbourhood. Records in Ś. 955, Śrīmukha, *Māgha, śu. di.* 5, Monday, Uttarāyaṇa Saṅkrānti, a gift of land by Udayādityayya, husband of Sigadēvi, to *Uttamarāsipaṇḍita* for the worship of god Mahādēva. He was entitled Jagadēkamalla Noḷamba Pallava Permānaḍi and was ruling at Kampili as his permanent capital *(ikkaviḍu)* and residence. [With regard to the date Diwan Bahadur Swamikannu Pillai says: "In A.D. 1033 Uttarāyaṇa Saṅkrānti fell on Dec. 23·92, Sunday. Monday which was the civil Saṅkrānti was also Māgha *śu.* 1 which came to an end at ·50 next day. As Māgha *śu.* 5 fell on Saturday, December 29·26, the day intended was perhaps Māgha *śu.* which was also the Uttarāyaṇa Saṅkrānti by civil reckoning." *Madr. Ep. Rep.*, 1914, p. 72. For another inscription regarding Udayāditya see the list at Oruvāyi. Udayāditya was called Jagadēkamalla Noḷamba Pallava Permānaḍi evidently after his suzerain Jayasimha II, 1018—42. (Later on Jayasimha III, brother of Vikramāditya VI, had the same title.) See also the inscription at Badanahathi (199 of 1913). It seems that the title Noḷamba Paḷḷava Permānaḍi was given by the W. Chāḷukyan kings after Sōmēśvara I to those chiefs who held sway over Noḷambavāḍi, the hereditary dominion of the Noḷamba Pallavas. [*Ep. Rep.*, 1914, p. 87.]

Kanakaviḍu.

17. On a stone in a local well. Records that Rātchana "Maninikru" gave the village in Subhānu, to the people for occupation. *Ins., Ced. Dts.*, p. 237, No. 11.

Kavutālam.

18. On a stone south of the local Hanumantarāya pagoda.—(Kanarese.) Records that Nadiguru of Adōni gave in Hēviḷambi, an agreement for the population of Kavitāla. *Ibid.*, p. 309, No. 10.

19. On the east wall of the above pagoda. Records that "Sakolu-" (?) Rājayya, the Pradhāni of Achyutarāya, passed an agreement for the population of the village in Ś. 1457, Nandana. *Ibid.*, p. 310, No. 11.

Nandavaram.

20. On a stone pillar of the maṇṭapam near the local Parvatamallikārjuna pagoda. Records that Mallapparasa Daṇḍanāyaka erected the pagoda in 1189, Parābhava, in the reign of the Chāḷukya Sōmēśvaradēva (IV, 1182-9) and gave the fee of a pagoda for a month for the daily worship of deity. *Ibid.*, p. 233, No. 1.

21. On the wall of the Kōṭirāmaliṅga temple.—(Kanarese.) A record of "Nandavarada Dēsāye Hadadara Gouḍa Kulkurnegaḷu" in Chitrabhānu. A damaged grant. *Ibid.*, p. 433, No. 2.

Sultānpūr.

22. *C.P. No.* 116 *of Mr. Sewell's List.*—Records grant of land to the mosque by Masud Khan in Ś. 1586 (A.D. 1664), Pramādīcha.

23. *C.P. No.* 118 *of Mr. Sewell's List.*—A second grant of land to the mosque by the same man, in the same year.

24. *C.P. No.* 130 *of Mr. Sewell's List.*—Records grant of land to the mosque by Masud Khan in Ś. 1586 (A.D. 1664), Pramādīcha.

Tārāpuram.

25. *C.P. No.* 131 *of Mr. Sewell's List.*—Records grant of land to the mosque by Masud Khan in Ś. 1586 (A.D. 1664), *Pramādicha.*

26. *C.P. No.* 133 *of Mr. Sewell's List.*—Records another grant of land to the mosque by Masud Khan in Ś. 1586 (A.D.1664), *Pramādicha.*

ALŪR TALUK.

Chinnahoṭṭūr.

27. 133 *of* 1913.—(Kanarese.) On a stone set up in front of the Channakēśavasvāmin temple. A damaged record, date of which is doubtful. Records the foundation of the temple of Ādikēśavanātha by Pratāpa-Harihararāya (II). On this, the Śrīvaishṇavas of the eighteen nāḍus and others made a gift of five *koḷagas* of land for oblations.

28. 134 *of* 1913.—(Telugu.) On a pillar of the Bhōgēśvarasvāmin temple in the same village. States that this is the inscribed pillar of Narasimha Sarasvati who had the adjuncts *Saptaprathama ḍēvayuga, Śambhutrāya, Śri-Narasimha-varaprasāda, Vēdāntākramita.*

29. 135 *of* 1913.—(Kanarese.) On a slab near a well to the west of the same temple. In archaic characters. Seems to record that the well *(guḷa?)* was dug by a certain Gumasiri Mākaḷa, son of Arjuna.

Chippigiri.

30. In the Chennakēśava temple.—(Kanarese.) A record dated A.D. 1508 recording a grant of lands to the temple by a local chief.

31. In the smaller Veṅkaṭaramaṇa temple. Dated in 1528. Records a grant by king Kṛishṇa Dēva Rāya of Vijayanagar. [*Bellary Gazr.*, I, p. 210.] The place is an important Jain centre and was first fortified by Bijjala Kaḷachūri of the Kaḷachūri dynasty. See *Ibid.*, p. 210. Also Taylor's *Rais. Catal.*, III, 559. East of the village is a *brindāvana* of Vijaya Rāya, a famous Mādhva hymnist.

Hālaharvi.

32. On a slab in front of the Āñjanēya temple, two miles west of the village. Undated. Records "the erection of a choultry by a private party with the consent of Sadāśiva Rāya of Vijayanagar." [*Antiquities*, I, p. 104.]

Gūliam.

33. In the temple of Lakshmī Dēvi in the old village is a pillar with an inscription, dated A.D. 1408, in the reign of Dēva Rāya (I), but "is said to have been brought from Virupāpuram, six miles to the north-east." Vide *Bellary Gazr.*, I, p. 211, for the vicissitudes of the place and for its religious importance.

Harivānam.

34. In front of the enclosure of the Hanūmān temple, on a rock is a Telugu inscription, dated A.D. 1560, which "speaks of Śrīraṅga Rāya Veṅkaṭādri as ruler of the Ādōni pargana and records the grant of Harivānam to Brāhmans as an agrahāram." *Bellary Gazr.*, I, p. 211–2. Veṅkaṭādri is one of the three Āravīti brothers who played such a prominent part in the reign of Sadāśiva Rāya.

Muddanagera (Muddekara?)

35. On a stone north-east of the village. Records that Bhagala . . . Nāik gave some land in Ś. 1440, Vyaya to a Brāhman. *Ins., Ced. Dts.*, p. 238, No. 13.

36. On a stone in the local market. Records that Rāmappanāyaḍu, son of Bhōgappanāyaḍu, gave in S. 1661, Siddhārti, a cowl to the merchants of the place for its population under the condition of demanding no penalties. *Ibid.*, No. 15.

37. On a stone near the above. Records that Lakshmiappa Nāyaḍu and seven other people endorsed the above grant in Ś. 1696, Jaya. *Ibid.*, p. 239, No. 16.

38. On a pillar near the local Chennakēśava pagoda. Records that Rāmappanāyaḍu, son of Bhōgappa, had a pillar erected in the temple and granted in Ś. 1605, Dunmati?, four *munṭas* of land to the architect. *Ibid.*, p. 239, No. 17.

39. On a stone seated near the Vīrabhadra pagoda. Records that the Vīramushṭi Śaivites granted their fees from Muddekara and Timmapuram to God Vīrabhadra in Ś. 1484, Dundubi. *Ibid.*, p. 240, No. 18.

Timmapuram.

40. On a stone in the centre of the village.—(Telugu.) Records that in the reign of Sadāśivarāya in Ś. 1477, Dhātu, the Vipravinōdins gave to God Vēnkaṭādri and Kēśava their fees from the Timmapuram Agrahāram. *Ibid.*, p. 238, No. 14.

BELLARY TALUK.

Āndrahalu.

41. 237 *of* 1913.—(Kanarese.) On a stone in front of the Añjanēya temple. Mahārajādhirāja Vīrapratāpa Haṇḍe Chikamalukapa-Nāyaka records in Ś. 1584, Śubhakrit, Kārttika, śu. di. 15 lunar eclipse, gift of the village of Āndarahalu to a certain Roḍam Śivabasavappa. The record states that the village was originally granted to the king by Alamshanva Sāhēbu for *vajirike* (i.e., for being Vazir). The date, points out Mr. Swamikannu Pillai, is inconsistent, as in Śubhakrit (A.D. 1662-3) there was no lunar eclipse in the lunar month Kārttika. Alamshanva Sāhēbu was evidently Alamghyr Padshah or Emperor Aurangzeb (and not Abdulla Qutb Shah as the Government Epigraphist surmises).

Badanahatti.

42. 199 *of* 1913.—(Kanarese.) On a slab in front of the Vighnēśvara temple. A damaged record, dated in Ś. 949, Prabhava (Vaiśākha śu. di. Thursday) making a gift of land by the Pallava chief

Jagadēkamalla Noḷamba Pallava Permānaḍi. Mentions Ballakuṇḍanāḍu. See No. 1 above.

Old-Bhatrahalli.

43. 198 *of* 1913.—(Kanarese.) On a stone set up in the village. An incomplete and mutilated record. Gives a long list of the titles of a king who belonged to the Sinda family. One of the titles was that he was born of the race of Drishṭīvisha. [" This latter name occurs also in the Vēlūr-pāḷaiyam plates of Vijaya Nandivarman and is there applied to a chief of serpents whom Nandivarman made to dance." (*Ep. Rep.*, 1914, p. 87.) There was a Sinda chief named Udayāditya who was a feudatory of the W. Chāḷukyan Sōmēśvara I and who was different from Udayāditya Jagadēkamalla Noḷamba Pallava Permānaḍi.]

Bailūr.

44. 204 *of* 1913.—(Kanarese.) On a stone set up in the verandah of the Basavēśvara temple. The Western Chāḷukya king Tribhuvanamalla Vikramaditya VI (1076—1126), records in Chāḷukya-Vikrama year 56, Dundubhi (wrong), Āshāḍha ba. di. 10, Sunday, corresponding to June 21, A.D. 1131, gift of land to Dēvarāśi-paṇḍita of Donnayabīḍu for the worship of Mallikārjuna. Mentions the Mahāmaṇḍalēśvara Baḷḷāreya Bīvarasa, a feudatory of the king.

Bellary (General).

45. *C.P. No.* 113 *of Mr. Sewell's List.*—(Telugu.) Records a document purporting to be grant of a village to two Brāhmans in Ś. 1186 (A.D. 1264), Akshaya, when Sadāśivadēva Rāya was ruling at Vijayanagar; the grantor being Anagundi-Rāja, Dēśāyi Krishṇa Rāya. Mr. Sewell considers the grant to be a forgery.

46. *C.P. No.* 114 *of Mr. Sewell's List.*—(Kanarese.) Records a deed of sale of land, dated in Krōdhi only, by two Reḍḍis to two shepherds. The characters are roughly executed and about " two centuries old."

47. *C.P. No.* 115 *of Mr. Sewell's List.*—(Kanarese.) Records a deed of sale of land, dated in Paridhāvi only, by a merchant to a private person. Characters as in 46 above.

48-A. *C.P. No.* 117 *of Mr. Sewell's List.*—Records grant of land to the mosque at Kanamara by Masud Khan in Ś. 1586 (A.D. 1664), Pramādīcha.

48-B. *C.P. No.* 119 *of Mr. Sewell's List.*—Records grant of land to a Reḍḍi by Koṇḍappa Nāyuḍu, son of Appā Nāyuḍu, styled "Rājamānya Rājādhirāja," in Ś. 1642 (A.D. 1720), Vikāri.

49. *C.P. No.* 120 *of Mr. Sewell's List.*—(Kanarese.) A very roughly executed document of a seemingly absurd character, as it narrates the erection of a temple and endowment thereof in Ś. 2001, during the reign of Achyutadēva Rāya of Vijayanagar, in Jaya.

50. *C.P. No.* 121 *of Mr. Sewell's List.*—Records a deed executed in Ś. 1718 (A.D. 1796), between private parties, by which some land is restored to one of their number, in Naḷa.

51. *C.P. No.* 122 *of Mr. Sewell's List.*—Records an agreement executed in Ś. 1729 (A.D. 1807), Akshaya, between private parties, by which some land was restored to one of their number.

51-A. *C.P. No.* 123 *of Mr. Sewell's List.*—(Telugu.) Records grant of the villages, rechristened "Kṛishṇarāyapuram" and Kuṇḍurti, as agrahārams, by Kṛishṇadēva Rāya of Vijayanagar in Ś. 1433 (A.D. 1511), Prajōtpatti. The record is "illegible."

52. *C.P. No.* 124 *of Mr. Sewell's List.*—(Kanarese.) Records grant of the village of Alligrāma to the temples of Vīrabhadra and Chennakēśava in Ś. 1011, Jaya (A.D. 1089), by Rājādhirāja Śrī Bukka Rāya Dēva of Vijayanagar.

53. *C.P. No.* 125 *of Mr. Sewell's List.*—(Telugu.) A document evidencing an agreement between two private individuals of the Gauḍa caste, in Ś. 1719 (A.D. 1797), *Piṅgaḷa*, each to have half the other's village.

54. 127 *of Sewell's List.*—(Kanarese.) Records a deed of sale of two villages, the parties to the deed belonging to the Reḍḍi caste, in Ś. 1670 (A.D. 1748), *Vibhava.*

55. *C.P. No.* 128 *of Mr. Sewell's List.*—(Telugu.) Records grant of the village of Bairehalli to a Brāhman of Śrīśailam by the Vijayanagar Sovereign Śrī Raṅga VI in Ś. 1585 (A.D. 1663), Śōbhakrit. The grant is issued from the village of Vēlāpuri, where the sovereign is said to be sitting on his "jewelled lion throne." Śrī Raṅga had, however, little more than mere nominal power at that time. He was the chief that granted the village of Madras, then called Chennakuppam, to the English in A.D. 1639, his residence being at Chandragiri.

56. *C.P. No.* 129 *of Mr. Sewell's List.*—(Old Grantha characters of "about the tenth century A.D.") Records the grant of a number of plots of land, of which the boundaries are given, to a Vaishṇava temple, but beyond this little can be made out, as the grantor's name, the name of the village, and other important matters all fall in the first corroded plate.

57. *C.P. No.* 134 *of Mr. Sewell's List.*—(Kanarese.) Records a deed of sale of land in *Subhānu*, by a Reḍḍi and two others to two private persons.

58. *C.P. No.* 135 *of Mr. Sewell's List.*—(Kanarese.) A document purporting to be a grant of certain land to two private individuals by Kṛishṇadēva Rāya of Vijayanagar, but the date given is Ś. 1080,

Sōbhakrit (A.D. 1158), which is absurd. [Mr. Sewell, however, is not sure whether it is a forgery or a mere clerical error.]

59. *No.* 132 *of Mr. Sewell's List.*—Records grant of the village of Kṛishṇarāyapuram in the district of Gooty by the sovereign Kṛishṇadēvarāya to a Brāhman named Koṇḍabhaṭṭa in Ś. 1431 (A.D. 1509), *Śukla.* This was in the first year of his reign.

60. *C.P. No.* 2 *of* 1914.—A Nāgari copperplate grant of the Vijayanagara king Virupāksha in Ś. 1389, Sarvajit, Karttika, Śu-di, Utthānadvādaśi. Records gift of land to two Brahmāṇas, one of whom was a doctor and the other a scholar (unnamed) who wrote a work called the *Bhāshyabhūsha.* It records also the gift of the village of Sōmalāpuram, surnamed Virūpākshapuram, to Brāhmans in 60 *vrittis* at the instance of a certain Vīraṇārya. Virūpāksha is said to be the son of Pratāpa or Prauḍhapratāpa (who is not Dēva Rāya II but his younger brother) and Siddalādēvi. See *Ep. Rep.*, 1914, pp. 95–6, for a summary of the plates.

61. *The Kṛishṇāpuram (or Māreḍipalli) plates of Śriraṅga.*—A C.P. grant dated Ś. 1497, Yuva (?), of the reign of Śrīraṅga Rāya (usually styled Srīraṅga II, but in reality the first), the son and successor of Tirumala, the founder of the last Vijayanagara dynasty. It is in Sanskrit, giving details similar to those of the Kūniyūr plates of Veṅkaṭa II, refers to his conquests of the inaccessible Koṇḍavīḍu, Vinukoṇḍa and Udayagiri, and of 84 hill forts in Mahārāshṭra, over Avahaḷurāya and the king of Utkala. The inscription is to the effect that on the twelfth tithi of the bright fortnight of Āshāḍha in Ś. 1497, Yuva, the king granted the village of Māreḍipalli *alias* Kṛishṇāpuram to Aubalabhaṭṭa, son of Varadabhaṭṭa and grandson of Bālēndubhaṭṭa, of the Kāśyapagōtra and Kātyāyana Sūtra. See *Ep. Ind.*, Vol. XI, pp. 326—36, where it is edited by Mr. M. V. Natesa Ayyar.

Bellary.

62. On the east of the Chennakēśava Pagoda in the local fort. (Kanarese.) Records that Basavarasayya fixed the taxes on the weavers of the neighbourhood in Ś. 1457, in the reign of Achyutarāya. See *Ins., Ced. Dts.*, p. 323, No. 52.

63. Near the Hanumantarāya pagoda in the fort. Records that Naḍigūr Dēśāyi Bāba Saheb granted one *vokkala* of land and an allowance of one kāśu for each bag of goods, two kāśu on each loom, 25 betels for each bale and quarter-śēr of oil for daily worship of Hanumanta in Ś. 1578, Dunmuki. *Ibid.*, p. 323, No. 53.

64. South of Mallikārjuna temple. A damaged Kanarese record of Sōvidēvarasu. *Ibid.*, No. 54.

65. On a wooden pillar of the Vīrabhadra pagoda. Records that Haṇḍe Mallaṇṇa, son of Haṇḍe Malakappa Nāyak, erected the pagoda of Vīrabhadra in a certain Krōdhana. *Ibid.*, p. 323, No. 55.

66. On a stone in the Nāganakkēri tank at Bellary. (Kanarese.) Records that Timmaṇa Nāyak granted some land to God Hampi. Virūpāksha in Ś. 1420, Kāḷayukti. *Ins., Ced. Dts.*, p., 324, No. 56.

67. A P.G. in the hands of Śēnappa, astronomer at Bellary. Records that Haṇḍe Hariya Rāmappa Nāyak, son of Hariya Siddhappa Nāyak, Zamindar of Bellary, granted one vokkala of land at Bellary in Ś. 1570, Sarvadhāri, to Chandrabhaṭṭa Jōsya. *Ibid.*, p. 327, No. 70.

68. A P.G. in the hands of the same. Records that Haṇḍe Yeśavanta Haṇḍe Dēvappa Nāyak (Deśāye, Pargana Bellary) granted to one Śrīnivāsabhaṭṭa in Ś. 1619, Īśvara, the duty of a village in Kurugōḍu district. *Ibid.*, p. 327, No. 71.

Chitikinahala.

69. 196 *of* 1913.—(Kanarese.) On a Nandi-stone in front of the Āñjanēya temple. The Vijayanagara king Achyutarāya-Mahārāya registers the gift of the village of Chitikanahala to the temple of Prasanna-Virūpākshadēva of Jentegallu, for the merit of his father Narasana-Nāyaka.

Dammūru.

70. 209 *of* 1913.—(Kanarese.) On the stone pedestal of Vīrabhadrasvāmin. Records in Śaka? Vaiśākha, ba. di. 5, Monday, that this image of Vīrabhadra was set up by Kaṇṇamarasavve, the mother of Pommayiavve, who was the wife of a Mahāmaṇḍalēśvara.

71. 210 *of* 1913.—(Kanarese.) On the rocky floor of the Rāmaliṅgēśvara temple in the same village. A much damaged record of the Western Chāḷukya king Tribhuvanamalla Vikramāditya VI, "ruling at Kalyāṇa," dated Chāḷukya-Vikrama year 31, Vyaya.

Gudadūru.

72. 231 *of* 1913.—(Kanarese.) On a stone in the street. A damaged record dated in Ś. 1589, Parābhava, Māgha, ba. di. 10. Refers to the *talavārike* ("watchman's fee") of Guḍaḍūru, a village in Moke-śīme. "Date can be calculated but cannot be verified."

Guttiganūru.

73. 202 *of* 1913.—(Kanarese.) On a stone lying in front of the Āñjanēya temple. Records in Ś. 1461, Vikārin, Jyēshṭha, ba. di. 5, Friday, corresponding to June 6, A.D. 1639, gift of land by a certain chief named Rāmarasayya to the temple of Mukhya-Prāṇanātha (i.e., Hanūmān) which he had founded on the west side of Yemmegenūru on the road from Kurugōḍu to Vijayanagara for the merit of Hiriya Tirumalarājayya-Mahā-araśu, son of Sāḷakayadēva-Mahā-araśu.

Hirehalu.

74. 214 *of* 1913.—(Kanarese.) On the eastern entrance into the old fort. (See *Bellary Gazr.*, I, 224.) A partly damaged record dated Ś. 1673, Prajōtpatti, Śravaṇa, ba. di. 10. Registers that under orders of a certain chief whose name is not clear on the impression, Sivāji Mallahari-Paṇṭ built the fort at Kire-Hirehaḷu with bastions and gateway. "Date can be calculated but cannot be verified."

Kalkambha (Kallukambham).

75. 64 *of* 1904.—(Kanarese.) On a slab set up near the Kallēś-vara temple. Records in Ś. 949, Prabhava, gift of land. Mentions Jagadēkamalla-Noḷamba-Pallava-Permānaḍi and his capital Vipranārāyaṇa. See No. 16 above.

76. 65 *of* 1904.—(Kanarese.) On a stone close to the chāvaḍi in the same village. A fragment of record, dated in Ś. 952, Pramōda. Jagadēkamalla-Noḷamba-Pallāva-Permānaḍi, is mentioned. See No. 16 above.

77. 66 *of* 1904.—(On a slab lying near a mound.) A damaged record in ancient characters.

78. 67 *of* 1904.—(Kanarese.) On a slab set up in the field called Gōpikalluhoḷa in the same village. Records in Ś. 970, Sarvadhārin, gift of land to the Vishṇu temple at Chiyanapaṭṭi. Trailōkyamalla-Nanni-Nolamba-Pallava-Permanāḍi is mentioned. [See By. 129, for another inscription of the chief's suzerain Trailōkyamalla Sōmēśvara I (1042—68). His reign is one of continual war with Chōḷa kings Rājādhirāja I (1018—53), Rājēndradēva (1052—63) and Virarājēndra I (1064—70). The struggle seems to have been particularly for Noḷambavāḍi 32,000.]

Karekallu.

79. 228 *of* 1913.—(Kanarese.) On a stone near the Vīrabhadra temple. Records in Ś. 1477, Rākshasa, Jyēshṭha, śu. di. 10, gift of land by a private individual to the temple of Prasanna-Kēśava-nātha at Karekallu. "Date can be calculated but cannot be verified."

Karekallu-Virapura.

80. 229 *of* 1913.—(Kanarese.) On a stone in a field. Registers in Ś. 1615, Śrīmukha, Śravaṇa, śu, di. 15, a deed granted by the *Dēśāyis* and *Nāḍukuḷa-karṇis* of Mōke-śīme to a certain Mallikēśāyi, son of Bīramallikēśāyi. The latter was evidently to be permitted to build small bastions *(hude)* on the hillock near Vīrapura. "Date can be calculated but cannot be verified." [Mallikēsāyi = Mallik Shah and Bīrmallikēsāyi = Bīr Mallik Shah.]

Kenchanaguḍḍam.

81. In the southern wall of the temple of Gaṅgādhara. Registers in 1708 that the temple and upper fort were built by Keñchana gauḍa. [For his career and that of his descendants see *Bellary Gazr.*, pp. 226–7. The village was the *brindāvana* of a disciple of the Mādhva saint Rāghavēndrāsvāmi. The latter was evidently the Rāghavēndrayati who wrote a commentary on Vyāsatīrtha's *Tātparyachandrika.* See Dr. Hultzsch's *Rep., Sans. MSS.*, Vol. II, p. 76, No. 1544, and Vol. III, p. 33, No. 2160. A panegyrical work on Rāghavēndra by one Appaṇa is given in No. 1943 of the latter extracts. See *Ibid.*, p. 105.]

Koḷagallu.

82. 234 *of* 1913.—(Kanarese.) On a stone in a street. A record of the reign of the Rāshṭrakūṭa king Akālavarsha Chalakkenallata Krishṇa III. Records in Ś. 888, Raktākshi, Āshaḍha, śu. di. 5, Thursday, corresponding to June 16, A.D. 964, a gift of land at Sūjiṅgallu by a certain Chaṅga-gāvuṇḍa to the ascetic Satyarāśi-Bhaṭāra for maintaining a feeding house in the *maṭha.* The grant was confirmed by Gajadharayya, chief of Svāmi Kārttikēya-tapōvana, ruling at Koḷgalu. See Bhandarkar's *Hist. Dek.*, p. 54–5.

83. 235 *of* 1913.—(Kanarese.) On a stone near a well in the same village. A damaged record of the Western Chāḷukya king Tribhuvanamalla Vikramāditya VI, dated Chāḷukya-Vikrama year 16, Prajāpati, 10, Thursday, which seems to record a grant for a temple, a *maṭha* and vidyādāna. Details of date are said to be not enough for calculation. [This is evidently the inscription referred to in *Ins., Ced. Dts.*, p. 324, No. 58.]

84. 236 *of* 1913.—Nagari (Sanskrit). On a stone in another street of the same village. The Rāshṭrakūṭa king Khoṭṭiga records in Ś. 889, Kshaya, Phalguna, śu. di. 6, Sunday, corresponding, accordingto Mr. Swamikannu Pillai, to Sunday, February 17, A.D. 966, that Krishṇa died in this year and Khoṭṭiga succeeded him. The record is a eulogy of the Kumāra who was installed at Koḷagalagrāma and whose agent was Gadādhara. [For the circumstances under which Khoṭṭiga (Khōṭika) came to the throne, see Bhandarkar's *Hist. Dek.*, p. 54–5.]

85. On a stone in the village. Records that in the reign of Chāḷukyamalla, Juṅgakkavuṇḍa, brother of Appayya Gavuṇḍan, gave to Kēśirājabhaṭṭa for his learning, 30 muṭṭās of land and a garden in year 189 ("of Bhūpāṇḍya"), Raktākshi. *Ibid.*, p. 324, No. 57.

86. Near No. 235. Records in Kanarese a gift in C.V. 51, Hēviḷambi, in the reign of Tribhuvanamalladēva (1075—1126). *Ibid.*, No. 59.

Kōḷūr.

87. 211 *of* 1913.—(Kanarese.) On a stone lying in the Sūryanārāyaṇasvāmin temple. The Western Chāḷukya king Pratāpachakravarti Jagadēkamalla (II, 1139—49 son of Sōmēśvara III), ruling at Kalyāṇa, records in his tenth year, Prabhava, Pushya, śu. di. 2, Thursday, Uttarayāṇa Saṁkramaṇa, that while the Sinda chiefs Immaḍi Bhīma and his younger brother Rāchamalla were ruling the Ballakundenāḍu, a native of Kōḷūru, named Rēvagavuṇḍa, built temples at that village for Śiva, Vishṇu, Āditya (Sun), Vighnēśvara and Bhairava. Gifts of land were made for the worship of these gods by the first of the two Sinda chiefs mentioned already. The date, according to Mr. Swamikannu Pillai, corresponded to Thursday, December 25, A.D. 1147 (but not Uttarāyaṇa Saṅkrānti). For a reference to Rāchamalla see inscription 127 at Sindigere (206 of 1913). Mr. Krishna Sastri draws attention to the fact that the inscription refers to the Kuntala country of 7½ lakhs ('the Raṭṭapāḍi of earlier records') as being first ruled by the Mauryas of the Nandagupta race and then by the Rāshṭrakūṭas before its conquest and rule by the Chāḷukyans. The inscription is referred to in *Ins., Ced. Dts.*, p. 322, No. 50. It does not give these details but adds that 500 Cumbhas, 29 Muttas of land, 4 gardens and 43 mills were granted.

88. On the other side of the above inscription. An incomplete record of Jagadēkamalla Rājamalladēva Gavuṇḍa of Kōḷūr. See *Ins., Ced. Dts.*, p. 322, No. 51. (This is probably the same as the above.)

Kudātani.

For the description of the antiquities of this place see *Madras Journal*, XI, p. 307; *Ibid.*, VII, 130; *J.R.A.S.* VII; *Antiquities*, I, 104 and *Bellary Gazr.*, 227—31.

89. 42 *of* 1904.—(Kanarese.) On a slab set up in front of the central shrine of the Kumārasvāmin temple at Kudātani. The Western Chāḷukya king Tribhuvanamalla (Vikramāditya VI) records in Chāḷukya-Vikrama year 23, Bahudhānya, gift of gold (12 pagodas). [The inscription is referred to in *Ins., Ced. Dts.*, p. 325, No. 60.]

90. 43 *of* 1904.—(Kanarese.) On a slab set up near the platform in front of the same temple. Registers in Ś. 1132, Pramōda, the lands and other property belonging to the temple of Nāgēśa.

91. 44 *of* 1904.—(Sanskrit.) On a slab built into the floor of the same platform. The Rāshṭrakūṭa king Khoṭṭiga refers in Ś. 893, Prajāpati, to the setting up of the image of Skanda by a certain Ghaṇḍādhara. Records gift of land. Incomplete. See By. 84.

92. 45 *of* 1904.—(Kanarese.) On another slab built into the same platform. The Western Chāḷukya king Tribhuvanamalla (Vikramāditya VI) records in Chāḷukya-Vikrama year 24, Pramāthin, lands previously granted to the Bhagavati temple at Koṭṭittōṇe.

93. 46 *of* 1904.—(Kanarese.) On a third slab built into the same platform. A record of the Western Chāḷukya king Jagadēkamalla, dated tenth year, Vibhava. Records gift of land for a feeding house. [This inscription is given in *Ins.*, *Ced. Dts.*, p. 325, No. 61.]

94. 47 *of* 1904.—(Sanskrit and Nagari.) On a fragment of a slab built into the same platform. A mutilated record of the Rāshṭrakūṭa king Nityavarsha (Indra III), who meditated on the feet of Akālavarsha, dated in Ś. 842, Vikrama. Mentions the Chāḷukya Balavarman, father of Daśavarman.

95. 48 *of* 1904.—(Kanarese.) On another fragment built into the same platform. A damaged record dated Ś. 1090, Sarvajit.

96. 49 *of* 1904.—(Kanarese.) On a fragment of a slab built into the west wall of the maṇṭapa in front of the same temple. A record dated in Ś. 903, Vrisha.

97. 50 *of* 1904.—(Kanarese.) On a slab set up in front of the Vīrabhadra temple in the same village. The Western Chāḷukya king Tribhuvanamalla (Vikramāditya VI) records in Chāḷukya-Vikrama year 44, Vikārin, gift of land. [See *Ins.*, *Ced. Dts.*, p. 325, No. 62 where this inscription is given.]

98. 51 *of* 1904.—(Kanarese.) On the pedestal of the Nandi near the shrine of the same temple. The Vijayanagara king Vīrapratāpa-Achyutadēvarāya-Mahārāya records in Ś. 1454, Nandana, gift of land on the occasion of a solar eclipse.

99. 52 *of* 1904.—(Kanarese.) On a slab set up in front of the Bolu-Basava temple. The Hoysaḷa king Vīra-Ballāḷa II records in Ś. 1140, Bahudhānya, the setting up of an image of Telligēśvaradēva and the gift of taxes to it. See By. 117, *Ins.*, *Ced. Dts.*, p. 326, No. 64. [The latter says that the contribution was one *Sōḷiga* of oil for each day by each mill at Kuḍātani.]

100. 53 *of* 1904.—(Kanarese.) On a slab set up at the entrance into the same village. The Rāshṭrakūṭa king Akālavarsha Chalakenallāta (Kṛishṇa III) records in Ś. 870, Kīlaka, the restoration of a gift previously made by a Nāga chief and *by the three hundred mahājanas of Kurumgōḍu.*

101. 54 *of* 1904.—(Kanarese.) On a slab near the Jakkerubhāvi well in the same village. Records in Ś. 971, Virōdhin, gift of land to the temple of Sōmēśvaradēva. [This inscription is also found in Mack. list *Ins.*, *Ced. Dts.*, p. 325, No. 63. It says that the object granted was 129 muttas and 470 *kammas* of land, besides 3 oil mills.]

102. 55 *of* 1904.—(Kanarese.) On a slab built into the floor of the *darga* in the same village. A much damaged record dated in Chāḷukya-Vīkrama year 45, Śārvarin. Records gift of land to the temple of Durgēśvara.

103. On a stone south of the village. (Kanarese.) Records that Vīrappaṇṇa Dēva, alleged to be a descendant of Nārāyaṇapratāpa-chakravarti gave, in Prabhava, some land. See *Ins., Ced. Dts.*, p. 326, No. 65.

Kuntanahalu.

104. 219 *of* 1913.—(Telugu.) On a stone in a field five miles east. A damaged record dated Krōdhi, Phalguna, ba. di. 2. Mentions a Muhammadan chief named Ibhuram Bēku Sāhēbu and seems to register a grant of land.

105. 220 *of* 1913.—(Telugu.) On a stone in another field five miles from the same village. A much damaged record, dated Śubhakrit, Pushya, ba. di. 2. Mentions a certain Muhammadan chief whose name is not clear and records grant of land to a certain Buḍasābi of Beṇṇakallu.

Kurugōḍu.

The history of this important and historic place, as evidenced by chronicles and inscriptions, its antiquities, etc., has been excellently described in *Bellary Gazr.*, I, 231—4.

106. 56 *of* 1904.—(Kanarese.) On a slab set up to the south of the Basavēśvara temple. The Kaḷachūrya king Śaṅkhavarman records in Ś. 1099, Hēmalamba, gifts by Rāchamalla of the Sinda family. [He had been feudatory under Śaṅkama's elder brother and predecessor Rāya Murāri Sōvidēva (1168—78). The *Mack. MSS. Ins., Ced. Dts.*, p. 328, No. 36) say that the gifts were land, flower garden and allowance on goods exported and imported.]

107. 57 *of* 1904.—(Kanarese.) On a rock to the south of the same temple. A record of the Vijayanagara king Vīrapratāpa Kṛishṇarāya Mahārāya. Records in Ś. 1450, Sarvadhārin, gift of land by Kṛishṇarāya Nāyaka, for the merit of the king.

108. 58 *of* 1904.—(Kanarese.) On a slab set up on the north side of the maṇṭapa in front of the Kaḷḷēśvara temple in the same village. The Kaḷachūrya king Rāyamurāri-Sōvidēva (1168-78) records in Ś. 1097, Manmatha, gifts by Rāchamalla and Ajjarasa of Ballare. Mentions Amritāśidēva who followed the Kāḷāmukha doctrine. See By. 106. [This inscription is the same as *Ins., Ced. Dts.*, p. 317, No. 34. The latter gives the details of the grant, e.g., 450 *cumbhas* and 3 *muttas* of land; 2 oil mills; allowance of 2 śōḷigas of goods and 1 *caunee* for each *hon* for exportation and importation; 1,000 betels for each bullock-load of them and 50 for a man's load of them; water pots, buffaloes, bullocks and apes.]

109. 59 *of* 1904.—(Kanarese.) On two faces of a pillar in the bazaar street of the same village. Records in Ś. 1435, Āṅgirasa, that a woman repaired a well in the temple of Santa Mallikārjunadēva and granted land. See *Ins., Ced. Dts.*, p. 319, No. 39.

110. 60 *of* 1904.—(Kanarese.) On the east wall of the shrine of Hanūmat on the Hanūmanta hill in the same village. Nawab Hyder Ali Khan Bahadur records in Ś. 1702, Śārvarin, the building of the temple.

111. 61 *of* 1904.—(Kanarese.) On the Katte-Bhaṇḍa rock north-east of the same hill. In ancient characters. Mentions Kurumgōḍu as a village granted by Śatyāśraya. [The inscription proves that the early Chāḷukyas had territory in the Bellary District. See *Bombay Gazr.*, Vol. I, Part II, pp. 363 and 369, for confirmatory evidences.]

112. 62 *of* 1904.—(Kanarese.) On a broken slab lying in a maṇṭapa in front of the Uṇḍali-Saṅgamaṇa-guḍi in the same village. Dated in the reign of the Vijayanagara king Sadāśiva-Mahārāya. Records in Ś. 1466, Śōbhakrit, a certain Aḷiya-Liṅgarāja renewed the grant of a village previously made by Kṛishṇarāya. During the time of Achyutarāya the village had apparently been resumed through the "mischief of mean-minded men." See *Ins., Ced. Dts.*, p. 319, No. 37.

113. 63 *of* 1904.—(Kanarese.) On the south wall of the ruined temple in the same place. Dated in the reign of the Vijayanagara king Vīrapratāpa-Sadāśivarāya-Mahārāya. Records in Ś. 1467, Viśvāvasu, gift of land (4 *vokkals*) to the Jaina temple by Rāmarājayya, elder brother of Aḷiya-Liṅgarājaya, and grandson of Rāmarāja Oḍeya, for the merit of his father Mallarāja Oḍeya. See *Ins., Ced. Dts.*, p. 319, No. 38.

114. On the south of the Hanumantarāya Pagoda. Records that Rāmarasayya, son of Ayyajeymbarasayya (?) erected the Pagoda of Mukyaprāṇanātha of Yemmaganūr in Ś. 1461, Vikāri, in the road from Kurugōḍu to Vijayanagar and granted 2 *ballas* of land. *Ins., Ced. Dts.*, p. 318, No. 35.

115. See note to No. 118.

Mōka. *

116. 227 *of* 1913.—(Kanarese.) On a stone lying near the Mallēśvara temple. A much damaged record of the Vijayanagara king Vīrapratāpa-Kṛishṇarāya-Mahārāya, dated Ś. 1431, Śukla, Magha, ba. di. 14, Śivarātri. "Date can be calculated but cannot be verified."

---

* The Mackenzie MSS. (*Ins., Ced. Dts.*, p. 311, No. 17) give an inscription in the fort at *Mokya*, which is probably the same as Mōka. It records that Malla Rājayya's Kāryakartā "Cuntajeya Guruva Basitte" granted in Nandana a garden to one Basavaṇṇa Uḍaiyār.

Nalluḍi.

117. 203 *of* 1913.—(Kanarese.) On a hero-stone near the Siddhēśvara temple. In archaic characters, mentions a certain Gummaṇa-Gavuṇḍa.

Oruvāy (Vōravāyi).

118. 68 *of* 1904.—(Kanarese.) On a slab lying on the right side of the entrance into the central shrine of the Benakappa temple. Records in Ānanda, the building of a temple of Vighnēśvara by a private individual, while Immaḍi Rāchamalla of the Sinda family was ruling at Kurugōḍu. The back of the stone registers a gift by Basavaṇa Daṇḍanāyaka, a general of the Hoysala Vīra Ballāḷa II (1181—1207) in the Īśvara samvatsara. See By. 99.

119. 69 *of* 1904.—(Kanarese.) On a slab lying on the left side of the entrance into the same shrine. Dated in the reign of the Western Chālukya king Pratāpachakravartin Jagadēkamalla II (A.D. 1139—49). Records in Ś. 1071, Vibhava, that Lakkheya-Nāyaka, who called himself "the supporter of the kingdom of Immaḍi-Rāchamalla," granted land, after washing the feet of Bhīmarāśi Paṇḍita, a devotee of Kāḷidēva of Oruvāy and a follower of the Lākulāgama. [A stone containing Rāchamalla's inscriptions (No. 253 of Kielhorn's southern list) which is now in the Calcutta museum is considered to have been removed from Kurugōḍu. Here he figures as the feudatory of Sōmēśvara IV. See Nos. 106, 108 and 87 above.

120. 200 *of* 1913.—(Kanarese.) On a mutilated stone lying near the Rāmaliṅgēśvara temple. Dated in the reign of the Western Chāḷukya king Jagadēkamalla I (Jayasimha II, 1018—40) ruling at Pattalakere. Records in Ś. 958, Dhātri, Uttarāyaṇa-Saṅkrānti, the grant of Orvāya to Mādhava Shaḍaṅgavid and two other Brāhmaṇas who had placed the body of Noḷambamahādēvi in the waters of the Ganges, by the subordinate Pallava chief Udayāditya styled the Lord of Conjeeveram. Mentions queen Dēvaladēvi who was a Noḷamba princess and probably daughter of the deceased Noḷamba Mahādēvi. Pattalkere is identified with Dannāyakanakere (Hospet taluk). For another reference to Udayāditya see By. 16. The details of the date are not enough for calculation.

121. 201 *of* 1913.—(Kanarese.) On another stone lying in the same place. A much damaged record of the Western Chāḷukya king Jagadēkamalla I (Jayasimha II), dated Ś. 958, Dhātri, Uttarāyaṇa-Saṁkrānti. This record is a duplicate of the above one. "Details are not enough for calculation."

Rūpanaguḍi.

122. 221 *of* 1913.—(Kanarese). On a rock near the Bailu-Āñjanēya image. Registers in Bahudhānya, Chaitra, śu. di. 1, that this pond *(dône)* and the image of Hanumanta were caused to be made by a certain Malapa, son of Sirumaṇa of Gōvindavāḍi.

123. 222 *of* 1913.—(Telugu.) On a stone near the Pōtalappa-guḍi in the same village. Records in Ś. 1709, Plavaṅga, Vāiśakha, śu. di. 1, Wednesday, corresponding to April 18, A.D. 1787, the building of the temple of Pōtuliṅgasvāmi and of a stone maṇṭapa, by two private individuals.

124. 223 *of* 1913.—(Kanarese.) On a stone near a well in the same village. A fragment of record of the Vijayanagara king Achyutadēva-Mahārāya, date of which is lost. Records gift of land at Yāḷape to the temple of Nārāyaṇadadēva. To the same temple were also granted the *tolls* (*malavisa*) on the grains passing either way through Rūpanaguḍiya-thānya in Yāḷapeyaśīme.

Sañjivarāyanikōṭe.

125. 233 *of* 1913.—(Kanarese.) On a stone in a field. In old characters. Refers to the 8,000 of Būdavāgilu and to the Mahāsāmantādhipati Rājiyaṇṇa Ereyammam. Records gift of land to a temple by Kadamba-Kámarasa and other gāmuṇḍas.

Sindavala.

126. 230 *of* 1913.—(Kanarese.) On a stone set up in the Rāmaliṅgēśvara temple. Dated in the reign of the Western Chāḷukya king Bhūlōkamalla (i.e., Sōmēśvara III, 1126–38), ruling at Kalyāṇapura. Records in his fifth year, Sādhāraṇa, Kārttika, śu. di. 1, Monday, solar eclipse, that under orders of the Mahāpradhāna, Bāṇasuvergaḍe, Mānevergaḍe Śēnādhipati and the Daṇḍanāyaka, Anantapālayya, the Mahāpradhānahergaḍe Bākanayya made a gift of land for worship, repairs, etc., to the temple of Sōmēśvaradēva, built by the residents of Sindavoḷalu in the Sindavāḍi thousand district. [Anantapālaiya was also minister of Vikramāditya VI. Dēwan Bahadur Swamikannu Pillai says that on Sunday, October 5, A.D. 1130, Śukla 1 ended and the eclipse was on the previous day. Neither śu. 1 nor the eclipse was on Monday.]

Sindigeri.

127. 205 *of* 1913.—(Kanarese.) On a stone in front of the Mallēśvara temple. A mutilated record of the Western-Chāḷukya king Jagadēkamalla (II), dated fourth year, Durmati, Bhādrapada, śu. di. 6, Sunday, corresponding to August 10, A.D. 1141. Seems to record a gift of land at Simdamgere for a feeding house. Mentions the teacher Nirvāṇadēva.

128. 206 *of* 1913.—(Kanarese.) On another stone near the same temple. The Western Chāḷukya king Jagadēkamalla (II) records in his fourth year, Durmati, Bhādrapada, śu. di. 6, Sunday, gift of land by a subordinate of the Sinda Mahāmaṇḍalēśvara

Baḷḷārēya Rāchamalladēvaraśa to the teacher Nirvāṇadēva who in his turn appears to have assigned it to the temple of Mallikārjuna at Simdagere for maintaining the Ērkōṭichakravarti *maṭha* and the feeding house. Nirvāṇadēva was the pupil of Kumāradēva, a pupil of Trilōchanadēva, who was in turn pupil of Vāmadeva alias Ērkōṭi-chakravarti, the Kāḷāmukha Achārya of the temple of Svayambhudēva at Muḷugunda. Vāmadēva is said to have been well versed in all Śastras—grammar, logic, literature, drama, medicine, lexicography, rhetoric, śruti, Smriti, Purāṇa, Itihāsa, Mīmāmsa, Nītiśāstra, etc. For an interesting reference to the Kāḷāmukhas see *Ep: Ind.* V, 218.

129. 207 *of* 1913.—(Kanarese.) On a stone near the Basavēśvara temple in the same village. Dated in the reign of the Western Chāḷukya king Trailōkyamalladēva. Records gift of land in the district of Ballakunde 300 by the Vaiḍumba king Mani-Bēṭa-Mahārāja, who was evidently the subordinate of the Pallava chief Trailōkyamalla Irivanoḷamba Naraśiṅgadēva, "the lord of Kānchīpura." [Jayasimha III (C. 1072—9) had the same titles and Mr. Krishna Sastri infers that this "Iriva Noḷamba" was perhaps a prince of the royal family of Jayasimha III.]

Śirivaram.

130. 232 *of* 1913.—(Kanarese.) On a stone in front of the Īśvara temple. Dated in the reign of the Western Chāḷukya king Trailōkyamalla-Āhavamalla (Sōmēśvara I, 1042—68), ruling at Pottalakēre. Records in Ś. 966, *Tārana,* Vaiśākha, śu. di. 5, Thursday corresponding to April 5, A.D. 1044, gift of the village of Kappekallu in Ballekunde 300, to the ascetic Jyēshṭharāśi-Bhaṭāra by the chief Pallarasa, a subordinate of Odeyāditya, for the temple of Mahādēva and for a maṭha. The Brāhmaṇas also got a share in the village. The occasion for the grant was the installation of Trailōkyamalla Nanni-Noḷambādhirāja (i.e., Sōmēśvara I, whose coronation, according to Dr. Fleet, occurred in A.D. 1044-5. See *Dynas. Canar. Dts.*, p. 438.)

Somalāpura.

131. 197 *of* 1913.—(Kanarese.) On a stone set up near a well. The Noḷamba king Kanakarasa, 'lord of Kānchīpura' records in Ś. 953, Pramōda, Āshāḍha ba, di. 10, Sunday, corresponding to June 28, A.D. 1030, gift of land to the temple of Mahādēva at Arakere.

Sômasamudram.

132. 212 *of* 1913.—(Kanarese.) On a stone built into the mud wall in front of the Lakshmīnārāyaṇasvāmin temple. Dated in the reign of the Vijayanagara king Vīrapratāpa Sadāśivadēva-Mahārāya, ruling at Vidyānagara (Vidyānagar). Records in Ś. 1478,

Naḷa, Āshaḍha, śu. di. 11, Thursday, corresponding to June 18, A.D. 1556, gift of land by the Mahājanas of Sōmasamudra in Kurugōḍa-śīme, a subdivision of Muganaḍa veṇṭhēya in Hastināvati-vaḷita, for maintaining a palanquin procession on Ēkādaśi days, in the temple of Lakshmīnārāyaṇa of that village.

133. 213 *of* 1913.—(Kanarese.) On a rock in a field of the same village. A damaged record dated Ś. 1614, Āṅgiras, Chaitra, ba. di. 15, Tuesday, corresponding to April 25, A.D. 1692. Seems to record the construction of a well (gajāgoṇḍa) by the residents of Sōmasamudra.

Tekkalakōṭṭa.

134. In the Amarēśvara temple. Records that the temple was built in 1511 by one Jakka Rāya as an offering to Śiva and in honour of king Kṛishṇadēva Rāya of Vijayanagar. [For a description of the temple, the career of the local saint Kadu Siddhappa and the history of the place as based on a manuscript in the possession of the village headman, see *Bellary Gazr.*, I, 235-6.

Yalpi-Kaggaḷlu.

135. 215 *of* 1913.—(Kanarese.) On a stone in front of the Āñjanēya temple. Dated in the reign of the Vijayanagara king Vīrapratāpa Sadāśivadēva-Mahārāya, ruling at Vidyānagara. Records in Ś. 1485, Rudhirōdgārin, Chaitra, śu. di. 10, gift of land at Kaggallu by Raghunātharājayya, son of Mahāmaṇḍalēśvara Rāmarāja-Tirumalarājayya Mahā-araśu, to the temple of Siddhēśvara at Kēmana-Beḷagallu. "The date can be calculated, but cannot be verified."

Yalpi.

136. 216 *of* 1913.—(Kanarese.) On a stone in front of the Āñjanēya temple. Dated in the reign of the Vijayanagara king Vīrapratāpa Kṛishṇarāya-Mahārāya. Mentions in Ś. 1451, Virōdhi, Māgha, śu. di. 11, that a certain Timmarasa built a choultry and made provision for feeding twelve Brāhmaṇas at Yaḷape which was a *mukhāsā*-village granted to him by Kṛishṇarāya to maintain horses. The charity was made for the merit of king Achyutarāya Mahārāya. "Date can be calculated, but cannot be verified."

137. 217 *of* 1913.—(Kanarese.) On another stone near the same temple. A damaged record of the Vijayanagara king Vīrapratāpa Kṛishṇarāya-Mahārāya, dated Ś. 1431, Śukla, Māgha, ba. di. 14, Śivarātri. Seems to register the remission of marriage-tax in the district Yaḷapi-śīme for the merit of the king, by a favourite chief whose name is lost in the damaged portion of the inscription. "Date can be calculated, but cannot be verified."

138. 218 *of* 1913.—(Kanarese.) On a rock at the same place. Dated in the reign of the Vijayanagara king Vīrapratāpa Sadāśiva-dēva-Mahārāya. Records in Ś. 1465, Śōbhakrit, Phalguna, śu. di. 10, that the Mahāmaṇḍalēśvara Rāmarājayyadēva Mahā-araśu, the agent of the king, remitted the taxes payable by the barbers, in Yaḷappēya-śīme. "Date can be calculated, but cannot be verified."

Yettina-Budehalu.

139. 224 *of* 1913.—(Kanarese.) On a stone in front of the Āñjanēya temple. Mentions in Chāḷukya-Vikrama year 32, Sarvajit, Kārttika, śu. di. 5, Friday, that Sōvarasa Kāvarasa and Duggarāja built a maṇṭapa, probably for the use of travellers, and granted land for its upkeep. Friday is wrong for Tuesday, and the date would then correspond to October 22, A.D. 1107.

140. 225 *of* 1913.—(Kanarese.) On another stone in front of the same temple. An unfinished record of the Vijayanagara king Vīrapratāpa Kṛishṇarāya-Mahārāya, dated Ś. 1445, Bahudhānya (wrong) Śravaṇa, ba. di. 10, "a date which can be calculated, but cannot be verified".

141. 226 *of* 1913.—(Kanarese.) On a stone lying in front of the Basavēśvara temple in the same village. In old characters much damaged. Mentions Sāḷuki Eṛeyamma, whose servant is stated to have split up a stone. Seems to register also a gift of land by *the 8000 of Būdavāgilu.*

Havinahalu-Virapura.

142. 193 *of* 1913.—(Kanarese.) On a stone in front of the Āñjanēya temple. Dated in the reign of the Western Chāḷukya king Trailōkyamalla Āhavamalladēva (i.e., Sōmēśvara I). Records in Ś. 967, Pārthiva, Śravaṇa, ba. di. 5, Monday, corresponding to August 5, A.D. 1045, that Udayāditya Sindarasa "lord of Bhōgavati-pura," and a Sāmanta of Trailōkyamalla Nanni Noḷamba-Pallava Permānaḍidēva, "lord of Kāñchi, the best of cities" who was himself a feudatory of the king and whom Dr. Fleet identifies with Jayasimha III, the third son of Sōmēśvara I (see *Ep. Ind.*, IV, 214 f), conferred on a Pālimayya the right of collecting the tax called *mannēya sāmyada-tēre* at Doṇḍavāṭṭi. See 232 of 1913 at Śirivaram where it is shown that Jayasimha had the title.

143. 194 *of* 1913.—(Kanarese.) On another stone in the same place. A much damaged record of the Vijayanagara king Vīrapratāpa Kṛishṇarāya Mahārāya, dated Ś. 1450, Sarvadhārin, Māgha, śu. di. 6 (a "date which can be calculated but not verified"). Registers the permanent grant of *daśavanda* of the tank at Doṇḍavāṭe to a certain Malesāni, by the people of that village, with the permission of Mudaṇa-Nāyaka who was enjoying that village as a rent-free gift *(umbaḷi).*

144. 195 *of* 1913.—(Kanarese.) On the stone built into the water channel near the same place. The Vijayanagara king Vīrapratāpa Achyutarāya-Mahārāya records in Ś. 1455, Jaya, Vaiśākha, śu. di. 15, gift of the village of Doṇḍavāṭi in Kurugōḍu-śīme to the god Bukkēśvaradēva consecrated by the king in the name and for the merit of Narasaṇa-Nāyaka's mother Bukka-amma. Achyuta's grand-father Īśvara-Nāyaka is also mentioned. "Date can be calculated but not verified."

HADAGALLI TALUK.

Bannigola.

145. 503 *of* 1914.—(Kanarese.) On a mutilated slab lying in front of the Āñjanēya temple (same taluk and district). Mentions in Ś. 1483, Durmati, Vaiśākha, śu. di. 12, Saturday, Bannigoḷa and a gift of 100 *varāhas*.

On the boundary line between *Bannigola* and *Siginahalli*.

146. 504 *of* 1914.—(Kanarese.) On a slab set up on the boundary line. Records in Vikrama, the gift of a rent-free land (mānya) to a certain Sūryarāya on the occasion when he killed Kāchināyakana Timmayya with a hatchet (*koḍali*) and himself died.

Bannikallu.

147. 466 *of* 1914.—(Kanarese.) On a slab set up in a field (same taluk and district). Records in Ś. 1632, Vikrita, Bhādrapada, śu. di. 1, a gift of land to Banaiya by Hatiyammāji of Bāgaḷi.

148. 467 *of* 1914.—(Kanarese.) On a slab lying near the chāvaḍi in the same village. Records in Bahudhānya, Phalguna, śu. di. Pañchami, that the headman, accountant, village watchmen and other people of Banikal made a rent-free grant of land to Niṅkōja, the carpenter of the village temple.

Bannimatti.

149. 469 *of* 1914.—(Kanarese.) On a pillar set up close to the Īśvara temple. Records the death of a hero who was, perhaps, named Chandana. In archaic characters.

Byālahunishi.

150. On a stone near the Vallabhāpuram anicut. Records that it was built in A.D. 1521 by Krishṇadēva Rāya of Vijayanagar. [See *Bellary Gazr.*, I, pp. 91–2.]

Chhatraḍahaḷḷi.

151. 509 *of* 1914.—(Kanarese.) On a column of the stone entrance into a well. Records in Ś. 1465, Śōbhakrit, Kārttika, ba. di. 10, Wednesday, that Yelavaṇṇa of Chhatraḍahaḷḷi built this well and planted an avenue. Also states that his father and brothers, having purchased the right of half *gavuḍike*, constructed a tank and a temple to the north of the village.

152. 510 *of* 1914.—(Kanarese.) On a slab in a field to the north of the same village. Dated in the reign of the Vijayanagara king Vīrapratāpa Sadāśiva-Mahārāya. Records in Ś. 1481, Siddhārthin, Jyēshṭha, ba. di. 7, gift of timber required for baling water to the charity fountain at Chhatradahaḷḷi, by certain residents of the village which belonged to the temple of Mālyavanta Raghunāthadēva. On the same day certain salt manufacturers (uppāra), "the jewels of the Sagara-kula", agreed to give two *ballas* of salt from each salt-pan, to the man who baled out water for the fountain; the smiths too who were worshippers of Kālikādēvi and Kamaṭhēśvara agreed to repair or renew the iron bucket for drawing water and the gavuṇḍas gave a piece of land for the maintenance of the man. "Date can be calculated, but cannot be verified."

Chimnahalli.

153. 518 *of* 1914.—(Kanarese.) On a slab set up in the Āñjanēya temple. Dated in the reign of the Western Chāḷukya king Jagadēkamalla (Jayasimha II). Records in Ś. 953 Śukla Pushya, śu. di. Panchami, Sunday, Uttarāyaṇa Saṁkrānti (which corresponded, according to Mr. Swamikannu Pillai, to January 11, A.D. 1030), that while Jagadēkamalla-Noḷamba-Pallava Kumānaḷi (?) was ruling Kaḍambaḷige 1,000, Kōgaḷi 500, Ballakunde 300, Kuḍiharavi 70, Karavīḍi 30 and five villages in Māsavāḍi-nāḍu, his subordinate Kēṭeya Nāyaka who was ruling at Nelkudure granted land and garden site to the temple of Kalidēva through the teacher Duggarāja-Paṇḍita.

154. 519 *of* 1914.—(Kanarese.) On the same slab. A record of the Yādava king Prauḍhpratāpachakravartin Vīra Mahādēva in his sixth year, Krōdhana, Āshāḍha, ba. di. Amāvāse (new moon), Monday. Gift of Nelkudure by Sōyidēvarasa, a subordinate of the king. Mr. Swamikannu Pillai calculates the date to be Monday, July 13, A.D. 1265.

Dēvagoṇḍanahaḷḷi.

155. 465 *of* 1914.—(Kanarese.) On a pillar set up in front of the Īśvara temple. Records in Ś. 1678, Vyaya, Chaitra, śu. di. 1, that the village of Dēvagoṇḍanahaḷḷi was given as a gift to Rāmaṇṇa-Nāyaka by Mummaḍi Basavappa-Nāyaka of Bāgaḷi. [Mr. Bruce Foote believes that diamond-working should once have been practised here. For his arguments see *Bellary Gazr.*, I, 239–40, based on *memoirs of Geolog. Surv.*, XXV, 87–8.]

Hire-Haḍagaḷi.

The local temple, one of the finest examples of the Chāḷukyan black stone shrines, is described in Rae's *Chaluk. Arch.* and *Bellary Gazr.*, I, 242.

156. 493 *of* 1914.—(Kanarese.) On the pedestal of the Sarasvati image in the Bhīmēśvara-Dēmēśvara temple. The record consists of a praise of the sculptor, whose name is not clear on the impression.

157. 494 *of* 1914.—(Kanarese.) On a slab set up in front of the same temple. A damaged record of the Western Chāḷukya king Vikramāditya (VI) Gaṅgapermāḍidēva, dated in Hēmalambi, Vaiśākha (Punnami) full moon, Sunday, lunar eclipse and Chāḷukya-Vikrama year 32, Sarvajit, Chaitra Amāvāsye (new moon), Monday, solar eclipse and Vishu Samkramaṇa. The king, as a crown prince, was ruling the provinces Gaṅgavāḍi 96,000, Banavāse 12,000 and Noḷambavāḍi 32,000, when the minister Dēmarasa is stated to have consecrated the temple of Dēmēśvara at Posa Vaḍangile which was a village of Brahmans from the time of Janamējaya. About the end of the inscription mention is made of the Hoysaḷa king Vishṇu or Vīra-Vishṇu Tribhuvanamalla (1115—37). [Mr. Swamikannu Pillai says that *Hēmalambi* is wrong as (in 1117) there was no lunar eclipse on Vaiśākha Pūrṇima, which fell moreover on a Wednesday.]

158. 495 *of* 1914.—(Kanarese.) On another slab set up in the same place. A damaged record of the Hoysaḷa king Pratāpa-chakravartin Vishṇuvardhana Vīra-Ballāḷadēva II, dated in Ś. 1133, Prajāpati, Māgha, śu. di. Tadige (Tritīya) (which corresponded, according to Mr. Swamikannu Pillai, to Sunday, Jan. 3, A.D. 1212. (*Śu* 2, however, he points out, is an error for *Śu* 3.) States that the king was ruling the country Nonambavāḍi 32,000, Banavāse 12,000, Huligere 300, the two Beḷuvolas and Māsavāḍi, right up to Heddore,' from his capital Haḷḷavūra *alias* Vijayasamudra. His queen (paṭṭadaraśi) Padumalādēvi is stated to have been ruling at Hosa-Haḍaṅgili. Seems to record a gift of land by the chief Dāvaṇṇa. This king was crowned on Sunday, July 22, A.D. 1173.

159. 496 *of* 1914.—(Kanarese.) On a slab set up near the south wall of the same temple. A damaged record, dated in Ś. 1081, Bahudhānya, Vaiśāka, Paurṇamāse (full moon), lunar eclipse, corresponding to April 15, A.D. 1158. The record begins with a genealogical list of the Western Chāḷukyas and stops with Perma-Jagadēkamalla II (1138—50). It states that the Mahāmaṇḍalēśvara Vīra Pāṇḍyadēva was ruling Kaḍambaḷige 1,000, Ballakuṇḍe 300 and Kōgaḷi 500. His uncle Vikrama Pāṇḍya made a grant of land for the merit of his wife Bāchaladēvi and his daughter Mahādēviyaraśi.

160. 497 *of* 1914.—(Kanarese.) On a slab lying before the Vīrabhadra temple in the same village. A record of the Western Chāḷukya king Tribhuvanamalladēva in Ś. 772, Prajāpati, Pushya, Amāvāsye (new moon), Monday, Vyatipāta, Uttarāyaṇa Saṁkramaṇa (in characters which are very late for the Śaka year quoted, but agree very well with the time of Tribhuvanamalla Vikramāditya VI). Records a gift of land to the temple of Mūlasthānadēva at Hosa-Vaḍaṅgile, by the chief Mahēndra of the Yadu family. Also registers gifts of land at Haḷugi and other places to the temple of Mallikārjunadēva by Maliyaṇṇa on Chaitra, śu. di. Paḍive Prathamā, Monday, in the same year. Mr. Swamikannu Pillai calculates the date to be Monday, January 5, A.D. 851.

161. 498 *of* 1914.—(Kanarese.) On a stone lying in front of Badigēra Vīrabhadrappa's house in the same village. Registers in Ś. 1187, Krōdhana, Chaitra, ba. di. 5, Thursday, that the 120 residents of Hosa-Haḍaṅgile made an arrangement with regard to the house-sites belonging to the temples of Mādhavadēva and Gōpāladēva of Beṇṇevūru.

162. 499 *of* 1914.—(Kanarese.) On the same stone. Records in Ś. 1201, Pramādi, Vaiśākha, śu. di. 15, Monday, Saṁkramaṇa-Vyatipāta, the citizens *(mahājana)* of Hosa-Haḍaṅgili having met together, agreed to give certain lands to the temple of Mādhavadēva of Beṇṇūru.

163. 500 *of* 1914.—(Kanarese.) On a mutilated slab lying in the backyard of Purāṇada Chinnavīrappa's house in the same village. Seems to register in Phalguna, śu. di. Tadige (Tritīya), gift of lands to the temple of Nagarēśvaradēva by the merchants *(nagara)*.

163-A. See p. 320, supplement.

Hālutimmalāpura.

164. 492 *of* 1914.—(Kanarese.) On the slab lying in a canal. Records in Ś. 1634, Nandana Āśvija, śu. di. 5, gift of 10 *khā* of land assessed at 250 varāhas by Hatiyammāji of Bāgaḷi to Baramaya, son of Māriyaṇṇa, in the village of Timmalāpura included in Hamvina (i.e., Hūvina) Haḍagali.

Hampasāgara.

165. 526 *of* 1914.—(Kanarese.) On a slab built into the floor of the chāvaḍi. A damaged record, dated Sarvajit, Pushya, śu. di. 1. Mentions the Nāyaṅkarācharya Bāguḷi Basappa-Nāyaka. [This is evidently the inscription which, according to *Bellary Gazetteer*, is specially cared for by the people. See *ibid.* for a description of the historic choultry and curious religious ceremonies of the place.]

Hōlagondi.

166. 527 *of* 1914.—(Kanarese.) On a slab up in the Baḷḷēśvara temple. The Western Chāḷukya king Tribhuvanamalladēva

Vikramāditya VI records in Chāḷukya-Vikrama year 7, Durmati, Bhādrapada, Amāvāse (new moon), Thursday, solar eclipse, Saṅkrānti Vyatipāta, that the Mahāmaṇḍalēśvara Gaṅgarasa, son of Mahāsāmanta Chāvuṇḍarasa, caused a gift of land to be made by Ēreka-gāvuṇḍa of Poḷalgunde, to the temple of Bāḷēśvara built by his father, through the teacher Kālēśvara-Paṇḍitadēva. The chief Gaṅgarasa who succeeded to the place of his father after the latter's death is stated to have been enjoying Māsavāḍi 140, Poḷalgunde, the *aṅkagadyāna* in the seven and half lakh (country), and the *daśavanda* on the landed property *(Jivita)* of the palace servants *(aramanēya-aṅka)*. [The date seems to be irregular. Mr. Swamikannu Pillai points out that C.V. 7 would be Ś. 1004, i.e., A.D. 1082–3, and *Dundubhi*, not *Durmati*. The full moon was on July 28 and August 25 of 1082, but in no case there was a lunar eclipse.]

167. 528 *of* 1914.—(Kanarese.) On a slab set up in the Sōmēśvara temple in the same village. Mahāmaṇḍalēśvara Vijaya-Pāṇḍyadēva 'ruling Noḷambavāḍi 32,000' records in his fourth year, Sarvadhāri, Phalguna, śu. di. Pañchami, Thursday, Uttarāyaṇa-Saṁkrānti, Vyatipāta, that a certain Mallagāvuṇḍa, chief of Hoḷalgunde, built a temple for Mallinātha and made a gift of land for its upkeep. He was born in the family of Bāliya-kula.

Holal.

See *Bellary Gazr.*, I, 242, for the history of the Anantaśayana image of this place.

168. 470 *of* 1914.—(Kanarese.) On a slab set up at the entrance into the compound of the Vīrabhadra temple. A much-damaged and mutilated record of the Western Chāḷukya king Tribhuvanamalladēva. Registers the praise of the residents of Gaṇḍarāditana-Poḷalayūra.

169. 471 *of* 1914.—(Kanarese.) On another slab set up in the same place. An incomplete record of the Western Chāḷukya king Tribhuvanamalladēva. Records the gift of 100 *kamma* of land in Gauḍagēre to the temple of Kālēśvara by Koylāḷidēva and the 120 residents of Gaṇḍarādityana-Hoḷālu.

170. 472 *of* 1914.—(Kanarese.) On a slab set up near the east wall of the same temple. A damaged record of the Hoysaḷa king Tribhuvanamalla Vīra Ballāḷa II (1192—1220), dated Ś. 1116, Rākshasa. Records a gift of land to Chauḍēya Nāyaka, son of Raṇaraṅga Bhairava Basaveya Nāyaka, who apparently died on the battle field.

171. 473 *of* 1914.—(Kanarese.) On a slab set up in the verandah of the same temple. Records in Ś. 1781, Siddhārthi, Āśvija, śu. di. the building of the Vīrabhadra temple by Gaṅgādharaiyya of Hirē-*matha*.

172. 474 *of* 1914.—(Kanarese.) On a second slab set up in the same place. A damaged record. Seems to record the building of the temples of Kalinātha, Vummaya and Vīrabhadra at Hoḷal, by prādhāni Havaḷi-Nāyaka-Vaḍeya.

173. 475 *of* 1914.—(Kanarese.) On a slab set up near the west wall of the same temple. A damaged record of the Western Chāḷukya king Chāḷukyachakravartin Bhuvanaikamalladēva (Sōmēśvara, II), dated Ś. 996, Ānanda, śu. di. Bidige (Dvitīya), Wednesday, Uttarāyaṇa-Saṁkrānti. Records gift of land to the temple of Gaurēśvara at Gaṇḍarāditya-chaturvēdimaṅgala, by Rudrābharaṇajīya. Mr. Swamikannu Pillai calculates the date to be Wednesday, January 21, A.D. 1075.

174. 476 *of* 1914.—(Kanarese.) On the same slab. The Western Chāḷukya king Jagadēkamalla II (1138—50) records in his fifth year Dundubhi, Āshāḍha, śu. di. 1, Monday, Vyatipāta, Saṁkramaṇa (details not enough for calculation) gift of tolls on three lakhs of arecanuts *(aḍakeyaśuṅka) Vaḍḍarāvuḷa* and *hejjuṅka* to the same temple at Gaṇḍarādityana Hoḷalu, by Vīra Pāṇḍya Aṇuka-Pallavarāya and another who were officers of Vīra-Pāṇḍyadēva.

175. 477 *of* 1914.—(Kanarese.) On the same slab. Records in Chāḷukya-Vikrama year 2, Kāḷayukti, Uttarāyaṇa, gift of one hēṛu of betel leaves by Chaṭṭimayya to the same temple.

176. 478 *of* 1914.—(Kanarese.) On a slab set up in the Gaurīś-vara temple in the same village. Registers in Ś. 1100, Viḷambi, Mārgaśira, śu. di. Pañchami, Thursday, Uttarāyaṇa-Saṁkramaṇa Vyatipāta, the grant of *hejjuṅka* on arecanuts and of certain other tools by Śaṅkara-Daṇḍanāyaka, son of Mādhuvaraśa and a subordinate of Vijaya Pāṇḍya, the lord of Noḷambavāḍi 32,000 in Kuntaḷadēśa, for the daily worship in the temple of Gaurīśvara at Gaṇḍarādityana-Hoḷalu. The latter place was called the best of villages *(grāma-chakravarti)* and the southern Ayyāvoḷe, being the residence of the 500 merchants. Mr. Swamikannu Pillai calculates the date to be Thursday, November 16, A.D. 1178.

177. 479 *of* 1914.—(Kanarese.) On a slab set up near the pond in the same village. The Western Chāḷukya king Pratāpa-chakra-vartin Jagadēkamalladēva II (1138—50) records in his twelfth year Śukla, Vaiśākha, śu. di. Punname, Monday, a *kamma* of garden land for daily worship in the temple of Vāmanēśvara, by the 120 citizens of Gaṇḍarādityana-Hoḷalu, while Sōmidēvarasa was ruling "the twelve villages." The *nakharas* of the village had to protect the charity. Mr. Swamikannu Pillai calculates the date to be Sunday (not Monday), April 24, A.D. 1149.

178. 480 *of* 1914.—(Kanarese.) On the same slab. Records that Vīra-Pāṇḍyadēva, "the Emperor of the Southern region" having visited the temple of Vāmanātha dēva at Gaṇḍarādityana-Hoḷalu, granted tolls on two lakhs of arecanut (aḍakēya-śuṅka) at the request of the Mahāpradhāna Kallimeya-Daṇḍanāyaka.

179. 481 *of* 1914.—(Kanarese.) On a slab set up near the Nandi (bull) called Doḍḍabēvinakaṭṭi-basavaṇṇa in the same village. Records in Raktākshin, Banada, Huṇṇive, that Lakeya-Nāyaka, son of Alampuri Kamaleya-Nāyaka of Uchchaṅgi, killed his enemies and died. Mention is also made of another Lakeya-Nāyaka, son of Nāgeya-Nāyaka.

180. 482 *of* 1914.—(Kanarese.) On the image of Hanūmān in the Hanūmanta temple of the same village. A damaged record dated in Ś ... 40, Phalguna, śu. di. 13. Seems to register the consecration of the image of Hanūmanta at Gaṇḍarādityana-Hoḷalu, the chief of villages (grāma-chakravarti).

181. 483 *of* 1914.—(Kanarese.) On the capital of a pillar in the mukha-maṇṭapa of the Amritēśvara temple in the same village. Records that Bammōja, son of Chōkōja and pupil of Paḍōja of Sōge, who possessed high skill in architecture, made four Śrīkāra-pillars with decorations each costing 20 *gadyānas.*

Hūvinahaḍagalli.

This village, so called from its being "the village of flower boats" in the time of the Vijayanagar emperors, is described in *Bellary Gazr.*, I, 240–1. See Rea's *East. Chaluk. Arch.*, p. 25—7 for a description of its temples.

182. 127 *of* 1913.—(Kanarese.) On a slab near the south wall of the Kaḷḷēśvara temple. The Western Chāḷukya king Tribhuvanamalla Vikramāditya VI records in Ś. 993, Sādhāraṇa, Phalguna, ba. di. 8, Friday, Vyatipāta, corresponding to February 25, A.D. 1071, that while the king was encamped at Gōvindavāḍi "pleased with the victory which he had achieved over Daṇḍanāyaka Biddayya," he granted the village of Koṭigaṅūru in Haḷpoḷa twelve, a subdivision of Kōgaḷi 500, to the temple of Kāḷiḍēva at Pūvinapaḍagili on the request of the *mahājanas* of that village who had gone on a deputation to the king to bless him. Mentions also the Kadamba mahāsāmanta Puṭṭiyaraśa. Biddayya was perhaps one of the king's feudatories who proved a traitor.

183. 128 *of* 1913.—(Kanarese.) On a slab set up at the western entrance into the Kēśavasvāmin temple in the same village. A damaged record of the Western Chāḷukya king Tribhuvanamalla Vikramāditya VI, dated Chāḷukya Vikrama year 15, Pramōda, Aśvayuja, Amāvāse, Sunday, solar eclipse, Uttarāyaṇa-Vyatipāta, corresponding to 24th November, A.D. 1090; Chāḷukya-Vikrama year 17, Aṅgirasa, Vaiśākha, śu. di. 3, Monday, Yugādiparvan, corresponding to April 12, A.D. 1092; Chāḷukya-Vikrama year 50, Viśvāvasu, Banada-Puṇṇami, Monday (See *Ep. Rep.*, 1914, p. 66, for a discussion of this date); and Chāḷukya-Vikrama year 53, Kīlaka,

Kārttika, Paurṇamāsya, Thursday, Krittika, lunar eclipse (November 8, A.D. 1128). The record first mentions that Tribhuvanamalla Pāṇḍyadēva, the lord of Kuḷumbapura, was ruling over Noḷambavāḍi 32,000 and Māsavāḍi one hundred and forty country. Next it gives a eulogistic account of the king's Brahman military officer Ravi-Daṇḍanāyaka, who, it is said, was at the very root of the administration and who conquered the seven Māḷavas. His wife Rebbanabbe or Rebbaladēvi, a native of Pūvina Paḍangili (i.e., Hūvinahaḍagalli) built in that village a temple for Kēśava and made gifts of land for the worship of the god, for feeding Brāhmaṇas and for a flower garden. Other subsidiary grants were also made; viz., (1) a village for conducting repairs to the temple and for worship was granted by king Tribhuvanamalla encamped at Rājāśrayanelevīḍu at the request of Raviyaṇa-Bhaṭṭa (i.e., Raviga-Daṇḍanātha) on the occasion of his making the gift called *Viśvachakra*; and (2) gifts of money and land by several individuals for betel-leaves, sandal, worship oblations, perpetual lamps, Chaitrapūja, etc.

Hyarada.

184. 488 *of* 1914.—(Kanarese.) On a Nandi-pillar lying in a field to the south-east. A damaged record of the Yādava king Bhujabala-Pratāpachakravartin Vīra-Mahādēvarāya (1261—71), dated Ś. 1184. Dundubhi, Chitra, ba. di. Amāvāse (new-moon) Monday, solar eclipse. Seems to provide for the repairs of the temple of Mallikārjuna at Śrīparvata. The date corresponded to April 9, A.D. 1263, but there was, says Mr. Swamikannu Pillai, no solar eclipse on this date.

Kattebennur.

185. 489 *of* 1914.—(Kanarese.) On the slab called "akalakallu" set up in the tank-bed. A damaged record of the Western Chāḷukya king Jagadēkamalla (i.e., Jayasimha II, 1018—42), dated in Krōdhana, Mārgaśira, Tuesday, solar eclipse, corresponding to November 23, A.D. 1025. Mentions a Mahāmaṇḍalēśvara who held the titles Māvanagandhavāraṇa, Raṇadhīra and others.

186. 490 *of* 1914.—(Kanarese.) On a pillar lying in the verandah of the Uduchulavva temple in the same village. A much damaged record of the Western Chāḷukya king Jagadēkamalladēva (Jayasimha II, 1018—42). dated in Ś. 947, Krōdhana. Mentions the Mahāmaṇḍalēśvara Madhu-Marmadēva who was entitled Māvanagaṇdhavāraṇa and Raṇadhīra. Details of date not enough for calculation.

187. 491 *of* 1914.—(Kanarese.) On the base of the column left of entrance into the Āñjanēya temple in the same village. Records in Nandana, Phalguna, śu. di. 5, Monday, that a certain mason named Ālōja brought materials from the ruined temple of

Bhōgēśvara at Koṇḍadakaṭṭi which belonged to a Jaina-basti and built this temple for Hanumappa.

Keñchetinahalli.

188. 512 *of* 1914.—(Kanarese.) On a broken slab lying near a well. Seems to record in Ś. 1466, Krōdhin, Śrāvaṇa, a gift of land to the charity-fountain *(dharma-ēta)* at Keñchiśeṭṭihaḷḷi for the merit of Kṛishṇappa-Nāyaka, son of Bāyappa-Nāyaka.

Kōgaḷi.

The *Bellary Gazetteer* gives an excellent summary of the history of the place as can be gathered from these inscriptions.

189. 520 *of* 1914.—(Kanarese.) On the base of a pillar in the Raṅgamadhya-maṇṭapa of the Jaina-basti. Records gifts of money by different persons for the daily bathing of the images in the temple.

190. 521 *of* 1914.—(Kanarese.) On the pedestal of the smaller Jina-image in the same basti. Registers in Paridhāvi, Chaitra, su. di. Chaturdaśi, Sunday, the construction of the image by a certain Obeyama-Śeṭṭi, a lay pupil of Anantavīryadēva.

191. 522 *of* 1914.—(Kanarese, archaic.) On the pedestal of the chief image in the Vīrabhadra temple in the same village. The Record consists of a verse in the Ārya metre and registers that this image of the Sun-God was made by the grandson of a certain Śivananni.

192. 33 *of* 1904.—(Kanarese.) On a pillar in the basti. The Hoysaḷa king Pratāpachakravartin Vīra Ramanāthadēva (1257—71) records in Yuvan gift of gold to the Jain temple of Chenna-Pārśva at Kōgaḷi. [The inscription shows that Rāmānatha owned an extensive territory not only in Tamil Districts but in Bellary.]

193. 34 *of* 1904.—(Kanarese.) On another pillar in the same basti. The Hoysaḷa king Pratāpachakravartin Vīra Rāmanāthadēva records in Dhātri, gift of gold to the temple of Chenna-Pārśva at Kōgaḷi. See the above epigraph.

194. 35 *of* 1904.—(Kanarese.) On a slab lying in the maṇṭapa in front of the basti. The Western Chāḷukya king Trailōkyamalla (Sōmēśvara I) records gift of land. Mentions Trailōkyamalla-Nanni Noḷamba-Pallava Permānaḍi.

195. 36 *of* 1904.—(Kanarese.) On a slab set up to the east of the same maṇṭapa. The Western Chāḷukya king Āhavamalladēva (I or Taila II) refers in Ś. 914, Nandana, to a victory over the Chōḷa king. Records an agreement made while Ādityavarman of the Kadamba family was governing the Kōgaḷi 500 and the Sundavatti

12.

196. 37 *of* 1904.—(Kanarese.) On another slab set up in the same place. The Western Chāḷukya king Trailōkyamalla (Sōmēśvara I, 1042—68) records in Ś. 977, Manmatha, a gift by the Jaina teacher Indrakīrti. The basti had been built by Durvinīta.

197. 38 *of* 1904.—(Kanarese.) On a slab set up in front of the Kaḷḷēśvara temple in the same village. A damaged record of the Hoysaḷa king Pratāpachakravartin Narasimhadēva, dated fourth year Svabhānu. Records gift of land.

198. 39 *of* 1904.—(Kanarese.) On a slab set up in front of the Vīrabhadrasvāmin temple in the same village. Records in Ś. 1454, Khara, a gift to the image of Vīrabhadra set up by a private individual.

199. 40 *of* 1904.—(Kanarese.) On a vīragal set up in front of the temple of Hanūmat in the same village. A damaged record dated in Ś. 850, Vibhava.

200. 41 *of* 1904.—(Kanarese.) On a *viragal* set up near the chāvaḍi in the same village. A damaged record of the Western Chāḷukya king Trailōkyamalla (Sōmēśvara I), dated in Ś. 969, Sarvajit.

Kotnakallu.

201. 445 *of* 1914.—(Kanarese.) On the slab built into the wall of the Kōṭīśvara temple. A record of the Western Chāḷukya king Chāḷukya-Pratāpachakravartin Jagadēkamalla records in his eleventh year, Vibhava, Pushya, śu. di. 13, Friday, Uttarāyaṇa-Saṁkrānti, Vyatipāta. Gives a genealogical list of the Chāḷukya kings from Taila II. Jagadēkamalla Vīra-Pāṇḍya was the feudatory of Perma-Jagadēkamalla II (1138—50). His maternal uncle was Vikramāditya, the son of Billavarāya. This latter chief granted the village of Koṭṭiganūru to the temple of Kōṭiśaṁkaradēva on the bank of the Tuṅgabhadra river. Another gift to the same temple made in the sixth year, Rudhirōdgarin, is also recorded. In the year Viḷambi Mahāmaṇḍalēśvara Vijaya Pāṇḍya made a grant to the same temple for the merit of his maternal uncle Vikramāditya. The date corresponded to December 24, A.D. 1148.

202. 446 *of* 1914.—(Kanarese.) On the slab built into the wall of the Kōṭīśvara temple. Dated in the reign of the Yādava king Sēvaṇa Mahādēvarāya, "ruling at Dēvagiri". Records in Ś. 1185, Dundubhi, Kārttika, śu. di. 15, Monday, Vyatipāta, Saṁkranti, lunar eclipse, gift of land to the same temple by a certain Madhuvayya of Koṭiganūru through the 500 of Kauravagrāma, a village in Māsavāḍi 140. The date is not quite regular. The week day should be Sunday, and there was no eclipse. The date would then correspond to Sunday, October 29, A.D. 1262.

Magaḷa.

In his *Chaluk. Archi.* (pp. 10—14) Mr. Rea points out that the art reaches the height of its glory in the local temples.

203. 123 *of* 1913.—(Kanarese.) On a slab set up in the Sūrya-nārāyaṇasvāmin temple. A record of the Hoysaḷa king Niśśaṅkapra-tāpa-Chakravartin Vishṇuvardhana-Vīra-Ballāḷa II (C. 1192—1211) with his camp at Hallahara surnamed Vijayasamudra. Supplies in Ś. 1131, Śukla, Śravaṇa, śu. di. Paurṇami, Monday, lunar eclipse, Karkaṭaka-Saṁkramaṇa, Vyatipāta, a genealogy of the Hoysaḷa kings from the founder Sāla down to Vīra-Ballāḷa II and registers that one Sameyada-Garuḍa Marmmarasa of Māgoḷa built a temple for the three gods Śiva, Vishṇu and Sūrya (trikūṭa or trimūrti) and that the king's treasurer, the Brāhmaṇa Siṅgayya and the other Mahājanās of Māmgōḷa, made grants of land. Monday is a mistake for Saturday and the date corresponds to Saturday, 18th July, A.D. 1209.

204. 124 *of* 1913.—(Kanarese.) On a pillar in the same temple. Records in Vikrita, Śravaṇa śu. di. Paurṇami, Monday, that the chief Sameyada-Garuḍa Mammarasa assigned a portion of the rent-free land belonging to the temple of Sōmanāthadēva to Bammōja, the architect of that temple.

205. 125 *of* 1913.—(Kanarese.) On a slab set up in the court-yard of the same temple. A seriously damaged record of the Western Chāḷukya king Tribhuvanamalla Vikramāditya VI, dated Chāḷukya Vikrama year 40, Durmukhī, Pushya, śu. di. Sunday, Uttarāyaṇa-Saṅkrānti. Appears to record a gift of land. (Details of date not enough for calculation.)

206. 126 *of* 1913.—(Kanarese and Sanskrit.) On a slab set up in the Vēṇugōpālasvāmin temple, in the same village. Dated in the reign of the Hoysaḷa king Niśśaṅkapratāpachakravartin Vishṇuvardhana Vīra-Ballāḷadēva II, "Emperor of the south." Supplies in Ś. 1136, Bhāva, Chaitra, śu. di. 11, Thursday, Saṁ-kramaṇa Vyatipāta (corresponding to March 12, A.D. 1215) and Vijaya, Āśvayuja, su. di. 10, Friday, the Hoysaḷa genealogy from Vinayāditya to Vīra-Ballāḷa and records that three private indivi-duals of Māgōḷa consecrated the temple of Śrī-Gōpāla in the middle of that village and that then the Mahājanās of the village, together with the king's representative (*rājādhyaksha*), presented lands and houses for the worship of the god. Also registers grant of money by the *mahāvaḍḍabyavahāri* Vāsudēva-Nāyaka, for a flower garden to the same temple.

Magimavinahalli.

207. 514 *of* 1914.—(Kanarese.) On a slab set up in front of the Vīraṇṇa temple. Records in Ś. 1466, Krōdhin, Magha, śu. di. 15, the foundation of a new village called Chika-Timmapura-agrahāra, for the merit of Tirumalamma, the daughter of Aḷiya-Rāmarāja. She is stated to have been a *maḍavaḷige kumārti*, i.e., a daughter about to be married. The record that follows which is dated in Ś. 1461, Vikārin, Śravaṇa, is one of Rāmayāmātya, who is described as a feudatory of Achyuta.

208. 515 *of* 1914.—(Kanarese.) On another slab set up in the same place. Records in Raudri, Pushya, śu. di. 12, the gift of a salt-pan to uppāra Gōvindaya by the chief residents of Timmāpura-agrahāra.

209. 516 *of* 1914.—(On the Kālamma slab in a field of the same village.) Records that Kāriyappa caused to be made the *giṇḍa-ratna-moga*. (The meaning of this is not clear.)

210. 517 *of* 1914.—(Kanarese.) On a slab set up in the big tank (*hirēkere*) of the same village. Registers in Ś. 1466, Krōdhin, Magha, śu. di. 15, the construction of the tank Kāmasamudra by Bayakara Rāmappayya for the merit of his daughter Kāmamma. The rest of the inscription is identical with No. 514 above and bears the same date, i.e., Ś. 1461, Vikārin, Śrāvaṇa.

Mailār.

The Sōmaliṅgēśvara temple referred to below is evidently the ancient Śiva temple described in the *Bellary Manual* as a centre of pilgrimage, where the singular custom of listening to the prophecy of an inspired child prevails. See *Bellary Gazr.*, I, 243—45.

211. 484 *of* 1914.—(Kanarese.) On a slab set up near the main entrance of the Sōmaliṅgēśvara temple. A slightly damaged record of the Western Chāḷukya king Trailōkyamalladēva (Sōmēśvara I, 1042—68) dated Ś. 968, Vyaya, Phalguna, śu. di. Tadige (Tritīya), Sunday, Uttara-Bhādrapada, Sādhya-yōga. Gift of land, house, stalls, etc., evidently by the chief Kāḷidāsa or Kāḷimayya to the temples of Svayambhudēva and Mūlasthānadēva, through the teacher Chillukāchārya, pupil of Tējōrāśi-Paṇḍita of Maulimaḍu. Records also a gift by Āhavamalla, son of Jagadēkamalla. (i.e., the same king). Mr. Swamikannu Pillai calculates the date to be Sunday, February 1, A.D. 1047.

212. 485 *of* 1914. (Kanarese.) On the lamp-pillar of stone set up in front of the same temple. A damaged record in Śrīmukha, Kārttika, ba. di. 10, Saturday. Seems to register the gift of the pillar.

213. 486 *of* 1914.—(Kanarese.) On the base of a pillar in the Mukha maṇṭapa of the Kallēśvara temple in the same village. Dated in the reign of the Yādava king Bhujabala-Prauḍhapratāpa-chakravartin Vīra-Rāmachandra (1271—1309). Records in Ś. 1205, Chitrabhānu, Jyēshṭha, śu. di. the consecration of the sacred bull Nandikēśvara in front of the god Kalinātha at Goṅgūru, by the chief Jannuva-Nāyaka.

214. 487 *of* 1914.—(Kanarese.) On a memorial stone set up near the Gaṅgimāḷavya temple in the same village. Records in Srīmukha, Bhādrapada, śu. di. 11 that a certain Honnarasa and the liṅga of Mailāra became united, i.e., that the former died.

Morigeri.

215. 441 *of* 1914.—(Kanarese.) On a slab set up in the verandah of the Uddibasavaṇṇa temple. Dated in the reign of the Western Chāḷukya king Trailōkyamalladēva (Sōmēśvara I). Records in Ś. 967, Pārthiva, Kārttika, Puṇṇami, lunar eclipse, that a subordinate of the king was Trailōkyamalla Nanni-Nōḷamba Pallava-Permānaḍigaḷ, who was ruling the districts Ballakunde 300, Kōgaḷi 500, Kadambaḷige 1000, Kuḍiya Haravi 70, and Karividi 30; the five villages and the Noḷambavāḍi 32,000 province. A thousand servants devoted to Noḷambādhirāja, the chief of whom was Daṇḍanāyaka Tikkaṇṇa, were enjoying supreme authority over six villages of which Moriṅgere was one. Tikkaṇṇa gave some land to Sōmēśvara Paṇḍita, pupil of Jñānēśvara Paṇḍita, pupil of Malēyāḷa-Paṇḍita who was the pontiff of Kōgaḷi 500. The record also states that Daṇḍanāyaka Sōvimayya gave a tank and a garden to the temple of Noḷambēśvara after washing the feet of Sōmēśvara-Paṇḍita. Mr. Swamikannu Pillai calculates the date to be Monday, October 28, A.D. 1045.

216. 442 *of* 1914.—(Kanarese.) On the same slab. Dated in the reign of the Eastern Chāḷukya king Vishṇuvardhana Mahārājadhirāja Vijayādityadēva (VII ?). Records in Ś. 987, Krōdhin, Pushya, Puṇṇami, Sunday, Uttarāyaṇa Saṁkrānti, gift of land by the king to the temple of Nolambēśvara at Moringere. The prince is entitled Āhavamallanaṅkakāra. The date, according to Mr. Swamikannu Pillai, corresponded to Sunday, December 26, A.D. 1064 (but Uttarāyaṇa Saṅkrānti fell on the 23rd or 24th).

217. 443 *of* 1914.—(Kanarese.) On another slab set up in the same temple. A record of the Western Chāḷukya king Trailōkyamalla-Āhavamalladēva (Sōmēśvara I), dated in Ś. 967, Pārthiva, Kārttika, Puṇṇami, Thursday, lunar eclipse, Saṅkrānti-Vyatipāta (i.e., the same date as in 176, Thursday being wrong for Monday). Gives a genealogical list of the subordinate Noḷamba chiefs of Pallava descent. Trailōkyamalla Nanni-Noḷamba Pallava-Permanāḍi, ruling over the districts mentioned in No. 215 was the younger brother of Jagadēkamalla-Noḷamba *alias* Immaḍi Nolamba, who was the son of Jagadēkamalla-Noḷamba *alias* Udayāditya, who, again, was the son of Irivabeḍaṅga Noḷamba-Ghaṭeyaṅkakāra. Registers that Tikaṇṇa and other servants established a feeding-house and the temple of Noḷambēśvara at Moriṅgere in order to secure the *parōkshavinēya* of Udayādityadēva, and with the permission of the king, who, having returned from a raid on Śivapa(?)

was camping on his way at Pūvinapaḍaṅgili (i.e., Hūvinahaḍagalli), granted the village Savandiyapāḷa for their upkeep. The same teachers as in No. 441 are mentioned here and are stated to have been followers of Lākuḷīśa and members of *Simhaparshé.* The chief Chaṭṭarasa, Ghaṭṭiyarasa, a subordinate of Sāmanta-Garuḍa and others also made gifts.

218. 444 *of* 1914.—(Kanarese.) On a slab set up near Nāgalakaṭṭa in the same village. Records in Naḷa, Āśvija, śu. di. 5, the restoration of a tank by Nāgapa Liṅgapa, the "*Śyānabhōga*" of Mōrigeri, for the merit of his daughter-Bomova.

Mudunūru.

219. 461 *of* 1914—(Kanarese) (archaic.) On a slab leaning against the temple platform (same taluk and district). A damaged record. Seems to record a gift of land at Mudunūra to a gavuṇḍa. At the beginning of the record is found the name Ghaṅgara Maramma.

220. 462 *of* 1914.—(Kanarese.) On a slab set up in a garden to the north of the same village. Seems to register in Ś. 1634, Nandana, Āśvija, śu. di. 10, a gift of land. Mentions Basapa-Nāyaka and his son.

221. 463 *of* 1914.—(Kanarese.) On a slab set up near the tank to the east of the same village. Records in Ś. 1776, Ānanda, Chaitra, śu. di, 6, Monday, that the twelve village officials (*bāra-balūti*) of Mūdanūru constructed a *maṭha* and agreed to conduct the worship in it.

Nakkarahal.

222. 507 *of* 1914.—(Kanarese.) On a slab set up in front of the Āñjanēya temple. A record of the Vijayanagara king Vīrapratāpa Sadāśivarāya. Mentions in Ś. 1483, Dundubhi Nija-Śravaṇa, śu. di. 10, that a certain Pedapa erected a bund across the canal that passed through the village Nāgarehāḷa. "Date can be calculated but cannot be verified."

223. 508 *of* 1914.—(Kanarese.) On a slab lying to the east of the same village. A record of the Vijayangara king Vīrapratāpa Sadāśiva Mahārāya. Mentions in Ś. 1470, Kīlaka Krishṇapa-Nāyaka, Kōgaḷi-veṇṭhe and Nagarehālu.

Nandihalli.

224. 464 *of* 1914.—(Kanarese.) On a slab set up in a field. The Vijāyanagara king Vīrapratāpa Sadāśivadēva-Mahārāya records gift of the village Voḷalagundi Bhayirāpura surnamed Gōpināthapura in Kōṭūraśīme, to the temples of Bañjēśvara and Gōpinātha at Timmalāpura, an agrahāra established by Rāmapaya. . . . .

Rāmēśvarabanda.

225. 506 *of* 1914.—On a rock in the Tungabhadra river. The record contains the signatures of Śaṅkaranārāyaṇa, Sūrerāya and Krishṇa (Krishṇa).

Raṅgapurām.

226. 121 *of* 1913.—(Kanarese.) On a slab set up at the entrance into the Narasimhasvāmin temple. Dated in the reign of the Western Chāḷukya king Trailōkyamalla (Somēśvara I). Records in Ś. 979, Hēmalamba, Chaitra, śu. di. 8, Thursday, corresponding to March 5, A.D. 1058, a gift of land by the two-hundred mahājanās of Māgoḷa to the temple of Naraśiṅgadēva.

227. 122 *of* 1913.—(Kanarese.) On a second slab set up in the same place. Dated in the reign of the Western Chāḷukya king Tribhuvanamalla Vikramāditya VI. Records in Chāḷukya-Vikrama year 41, Durmukhi Pushya, śu. di. 3, Sunday, Uttarāyaṇa-Saṁkrānti, and the same era, Yuvan, Māgha, śu. di. 5, Sunday, that at the request of the two hundred mahājanās of Māmgoḷa, queen Padmalādēvi who was enjoying that village (as her jāghir) granted some land, free of taxes, to the temple of Naraśiṅgadēva, situated on the south bank of the river Tuṅgabhadra, through her āgent Ghaḷiyamma-Nāyaka, for worship and offerings. Other gifts of land and money are also recorded. The dates are not quite accurate. The first Sunday, says Mr. Swamikannu Pillai, should be Saturday, and the date would then correspond to 9th December A.D. 1116. The second Sunday should be Thursday, and then the date would be January 3, A.D. 1096. Sec *Ep. Rep.*, 1914, p. 66.

Siginahaḷḷi.

228. 505 *of* 1914.—(Kanarese.) On the pedestal of the Gaja-Lakshmi image lying near the chāvaḍi. An incomplete record dated Ś. 1297, Ānanda, Phalguna, śu. di. 8, Monday. Mentions a gauḍa resident of Chiganahaḷḷi.

Śivapāda.

229. 501 *of* 1914.—(Kanarese.) On a slab set up in front of the ruined Āñjanēya temple. A mutilated record of the Western Chāḷukya king Jagadēkamalla Jayasimha II, dated Ś. 963. Seems to register a gift of land to the temple of Siddhēśvara. Mentions the *mahājanas* of Hosā-Vaḍaṅgile and a son of Rāya-Pāṇḍya.

230. 502 *of* 1914.—(Kanarese.) On the base of a pillar in the Mailāra Liṅgapāda shrine in the same village. Registers that Bōmārāśi, the priest of Siddhanātha, appointed Amitarāśi to his place and gave over to him the two villages of the god Siddhēśvara.

Sōgi.

231. 447 *of* 1914.—(Kanarese.) On a pillar of the Mukha maṇṭapa in the Kallēśvara temple (the well-sculptured Śiva temple to which Messrs. Sewell and Rea refer. Records in the sixth year of Hoysaḷa king Pratāpachakravartin Vīra-Narasimhadēva (I) Vyaya, Chaitra, śu. di. 10, Monday, the gift of two *gadyāṇas* from the income in grain in the district of Kōgaḷi-nāḍu in Pāṇḍya-nāḍu, to the temple of Kallināthadēva at Sōgve by Śiripaṇṇa-Maylāradēva, officer of tolls in that district, with the permission of the chief minister (mahāpradhāna) Bommaya-Daṇṇāyaka and others. Two more *gadyānas* were similarly granted by some others with the permission of Boppayya-Daṇṇāyaka, the *officer of the white parasol.* Mr. Swamikannu Pillai considers that the probable date is Sunday, March 13, A.D. 1166, Monday being wrong.

232. 448 *of* 1914.—(Kanarese.) On another pillar in the same place. Records in Śrīmukha, Āśvija ba. di. Ēkādaśi, Thursday, gift of 700 *kamma* of land by the merchant *nānādēśi Maleyāḷa Poṟeyachcha Śeṭṭi,* to the temple of Kalidēva for his own merit and for that of his younger brother Kumārachcha-Śeṭṭi. The land had been acquired by him from Basavi Mūraḍe.

233. 449 *of* 1914.—(Kanarese.) On the third pillar in the same place. The Hoysaḷa king Pratāpachakravartin Vīra Narasimhadēva I records in his sixth year, Vyaya, Chaitra, śu. di. 10, Monday, a gift of money from the grain income of Kōgaḷinādu, in Pāṇḍya-nāḍu by the chiefs mentioned in No. 231, for the daily worship of Sōmanāthadēva at Sōgeya-kōṭe. For the date see No. 231 above.

234. 450 *of* 1914.—(Kanarese.) On a slab set up in front of Dabbaguḍi in the same village. A record of the Western Chāḷukya king Tribhuvanamalladēva (Vikramāditya VI), "ruling at Kalyāṇa," dated in Chāḷukya-Vikrama year 46, Plava, Pushya, śu. di. 5, Sunday, Uttarāyaṇa Saṁkrānti, Vyatipāta. Records that the Mahāmaṇḍalēśvara Tribhuvanamalla-Pāṇḍyadēva was ruling the Noḷambavāḍi 32,000 and the Mahāmaṇḍalēśvara Ghaṭṭiyaraśa was ruling Kōgaḷi 500 evidently as his subordinate. The Brahman Nāgavarmmayya-Nāyaka, the headman of Sōgi, and his brothers Kalimayya Nāyaka and Mahādēvayya Nāyaka being together, made a gift of land, etc., for daily worship to be maintained in the temple of Kēśavadēva which was built by Nāgavarmmayya-Nāyaka. Ghaṭṭiyaraśa was made the guardian of the gift. The corresponding English date, according to Mr. Swamikannu Pillai, is December 16, A.D. 1121, but the week-day ought to be Friday and not Sunday.

235. 451 *of* 1914.—(Kanarese.) On a mutilated slab at the same place. A damaged record of the Western Chāḷukya king Tribhuvanamalladēva (Vikramāditya VI), dated Chāḷukya-Vikrama year 35, śu. di. 13, Sunday. Mentions Nāgavarmmayya-Nāyaka of Sōgi and his younger brother Mahādēva-Nāyaka. See No. 243 for the date.

236. 452 *of* 1914.—(Kanarese.) On a slab set up in the garden (Śriṅgāratōṭa) of the same village. Records in Ś. 1655, Pramādīcha, Bhādrapada, ba. di. 2, a gift of land by Basapa Nāyakarāya of Bāguḷi to his faithful servant Vīrapa of Sōgi.

237. 453 *of* 1914.—(Kanarese.) On a fragment lying before Virappa's house in the same village. The Hoysaḷa king Vishnuvardhana Vīra-Ballāḷa seems to record in Kārttika, ba. di. 5, Thursday, a gift of land to a Jaina Institution.

238. 454 *of* 1914.—(Kanarese.) On the slab set up outside the Kallēśvara temple in the same village. A completely damaged record of the Western Chāḷukya king Jagadēkamalladēva I (Jayasimha II, 1018—45), dated Ś. 960, Bahudhānya. Seems to record a gift of land.

239. 455 *of* 1914.—(Kanarese.) On the back of the same slab. Registers in Ś. 967, Vyaya, Vaiśākha, Huṇṇame (full moon), the praise of Chikka Jēyar, who was evidently a Śaiva (?) teacher. On the date given, this teacher appears to have made a grant of land for the management of a village.

240. 456 *of* 1914.—(Kanarese.) On the back of the same slab. Records the Manneya Ghaṭṭiyarasa of the Kaḍamba family and a servant of Sāmanta-Garuḍa handed over the income of his Manneya to the teacher Mallikārjuna-Bhaṭṭāraka of Sōgi. At the end of the record occurs the date Ś. 971, Virōdhi. It mentions Māraśiṅgayya, the headman of the village.

241. 457 *of* 1914.—(Kanarese.) On a slab set up in the garden of Śāntīśvarasvāmin in the same village. The Vijayanagara king Kṛishṇarāya Mahārāya records in Dhātu, Kārttika, śu. di. 5, that Aruba-Timmaṇa-Nāyaka, the minister (pradhāna) at Kōṭūra, made, for the merit of his master Immaḍi-Basavappavoḍeya, the village of Daṇṇāyakapura for maintaining a water-trough for animals at Sōgi.

242. 458 *of* 1914.—(Kanarese.) On a slab set up in front of a house south of the Kallēśvara temple in the same village. A much damaged record of the Western Chāḷukya king Tribhuvanamalladēva, date of which is lost. Mentions the Mahāmaṇḍalēśvara Barmadēvarasa who was "a venomous serpent to the chiefs of Toṇḍamaṇḍala" and "a thunderbolt to the strong hill-fortresses of Hoysaḷas."

243. 459 *of* 1914.—(Kanarese.) On a second slab set up in the same place. A much damaged record of the Western Chāḷukya king Tribhuvanamalladēva (1076—1126), dated Chāḷukya-Vikrama year 35, Vikrita, Pushya, śu. di., Trayōda śi, Sunday, Uttarāyaṇa Saṁkrānti, Vyatipāta, which corresponded, according to Mr. Swamikannu Pillai, to Sunday, December 25, A.D. 1110.

244. 460 *of* 1914.—(Kanarese.) On a slab built into a wall at the entrance into the Vīrabhadrasvāmin temple in the same village. Records in Kāḷayukti, Mārgaśira, ba. di. 3, Monday, that Gōvindapa Nāyaka, the agent of Kṛishṇapa Nāyaka, granted some privileges to the headman, accountant, and other residents of Sōgi.

Talakallu.

245. 523 *of* 1914.—(Kanarese.) On a slab set up in the Kallēśvara temple. A slightly damaged record of the Western Chāḷukya king Trailōkyamalladēva [Sōmēśvara I *Circa* 1042—68], dated Ś. 947, Nandana, Srahe (?). Trailōkyamalla Noḷamba Pallava Permānaḍidēva, a subordinate of the king was ruling Kōgaḷi 500, Ballakunde 300, and Kaḍambaḷīge 1000. His subordinate was Barmadēva of the phaṇīndra (i.e., serpent) family. He seems to have repaired a tank at Toṇakalu and to have granted land for its maintenance.

246. 524 *of* 1914.—(Kanarese.) On the same slab. Records in Chāḷukya-Vikrama year 37, Durmukhi (wrong), Pushya, śu. di. *Paḍive* (Prathama), Sunday, Uttarāyaṇa-Saṁkrānti, Vyatipāta, a gift of land to the temple of Mūlasthānadēva in the small tank at Toṇali, through the teacher Vāmadēva-Paṇḍita, a pupil of Kalēśvara Paṇḍita of Sōgi. See By. 127 above.

Tāmbarahaḷḷi.

247. 129 *of* 1913.—(Kanarese.) On a rock in the Raṅgappanaguḍḍa hill. Records in Ś. 1575, Vijaya, Jyēshṭha, śu. di. 5, the construction of the utsava-manṭapa for the god Baṇḍeya-Raṅganātha, by the three sons of a certain Sūryarāya of Kennehaḷḷi-Yiṭṭige which was included in Kōṭṭūra-śīme.

248. 130 *of* 1913.—(Kanarese.) On the same rock. A damaged record dated Plava, Bhādrapada, śu. di. 3. . Seems to record a private agreement between a pūjāri of Baṇḍeya Raṅgaiyya and another.

249. 131 *of* 1913.—(Kanarese.) On the same rock. Mentions in Śārvari Pushya, śu. di. 14, that one Sidaiya, son of Ujinivoḍēru, presented perhaps to the same temple gold, women and land, for the merit of his parents.

250. 132 *of* 1913.—(Kanarese.) On the same rock. Records in Pārthiva, Magha, that this deep pond (*gaja-goṇḍa*) was constructed by Sūryarāya, son of Vābarāsaiya, the *sēnābhōga* (*Shanbhogue*) of Yiṭige and a devoted worshipper of Baṇḍe-Raṅganātha.

Timmalāpura.

251. 468 *of* 1914.—(Kanarese.) On a slab built into the platform of the Kallēśvara temple. The Vijayanagara king Vīrapratāpa Sadāśivarāya, "ruling at Vidyānagara," records in

Ś. 1477, Rākshasa, Śravaṇa, śu. di. 5, that Aḷiya Rāmarāja-araśa granted the village of Hakahaṇḍiganūru in the district ruled by Viṭṭhalappa, to a temple. "The date can be calculated but not verified."

Uppināyakanahaḷḷi.

252. 513 *of* 1914.—(Kanarese.) On a pillar set up in front of the Āñjanēya temple. Seems to register grant of tolls for worship in the temple of Hanumantarāya.

Uttaṅgi.

253. 529 *of* 1914.—(Kanarese.) On a slab lying in front of the Śaṅkarēśvara temple in the village. Seems to record the death in battle of a certain Hiriya Somma-Nāyaka who held the titles Chaḷadaṅkarāma and Giridurgamalla. His soṅ Hemmaya-Nāyaka is also mentioned.

254. 530 *of* 1914.—(Kanarese.) On a slab built into the south wall of the same temple. A much-damaged record of the Western Chāḷukya king Jagadēkamalla (c. 1138–50) "ruling at Kalyāṇapura," dated Ś. 1078, Pramāthin (wrong), Akshaya-tritiya Amāvāse (new moon), solar eclipse, Vyatipāta. States that his subordinate Jagadēkamalla Vīra Pāṇḍyadēva was ruling Noḷambavāḍi 32,000 from his capital at Uchchaṅgipura and records gifts to the temples of Basavēśvaradēva and Rāmēśvaradēva at Kuttaṅgi. (An irregular date. Ś. 1078 is apparently incorrect.)

255. 531 *of* 1914.—(Kanarese.) On a mutilated stone lying in a field to the west of the same village. Seems to record in Virōdhi, Aśvija, śu. di. 1, Friday, the death of a certain Mayapa, son of Puṭṭiya Bomma-Gauḍa.

256. 532 *of* 1914.—(Kanarese.) On another slab set up in the same field. Records in Prajāpati, Mārgaśira, śu. di. 5, Friday, the death of Nāgāyi, wife of Bomma-Gavuḍa on this date.

257. 533 *of* 1914.—(Kanarese.) On the third slab set up in the same place. Records in Ś. 1301, Kaḷayukti, Chaitra, śu. di. 5, Thursday, the death of Vāgdēvi, wife of Virūpa-Gavuḍa.

258. 534 *of* 1914.—(Kanarese.) On the fourth slab set up in the same place. Records in Visu (Vrisha), Jyēshṭha, ba. di. 4, Tuesday, the death of Bomma-Gavuḍa, son of Virūpa-Gavuḍa of Uttaṅgi.

Vallabhapuram.

259. "There is a stone anicut here built across the Tuṅgabhadra by Krishṇadēva Rāya in Ś. 1443 (A.D. 1521). Inscriptions on stones at either end record the fact." [Mr. Sewell's *Antiquities*, I, 108, based on the *Journal of Asiatic Society*, Bengal, XIV, 521.]

Varadapuram.

260. 511 *of* 1914.—(Kanarese.) On a stone lying in a field. Records an imprecation that the man who disregards the boundary line of Varadapura, eats dog's flesh.

Yenigi.

261. 525 *of* 1914.—(Kanarese.) On a slab set up in front of the Āñjanēya temple. A record of the Yādava king Prauḍhapratāpa-chakravartin Sēvaṇarāya Kandharadēva (1247—60), "ruling at Dēvagiri," dated in his 12th year, Piṅgaḷa and Ś. 1181, Kāḷayukti, and his 13th year Pushya Amāvāse (new moon), Monday, Uttarāyaṇa Saṁkrānti, solar eclipse, Vyatipāta-yoga. Records that the 120 great men of Pūvina-Paḍaṅgile granted land to the temple of Kusumanāthadēva. See *Ep. Rep.*, 1915, p. 82, for a discussion by Mr. Swamikannu Pillai of the irregular date given in this inscription. See also By. 276 below.

HARPANAHALLI TALUK.

The Harpanahaḷḷi and Hūvinahaḍahalli (Hadagalli) taluks formed the "Kogaḷi 500" of the Western Chāḷukyan and Rāshṭrakuṭa kingdoms.

Bāgaḷi.

See *Bellary Gazr.*, I, 247–8 and Rea's *Chaluk. Archi.*, 6–9 for descriptions of this place.

262. 70 *of* 1904.—(Kanarese.) On a slab set up on the right side of the southern entrance into the central shrine of the Kallēśvara temple. The Western Chāḷukya king Tribhuvanamalla (i.e., Vikramāditya VI) records in Siddhārthin and Hēmalamba, gift of land.

263. 71 *of* 1904.—(Kanarese.) On a slab set up on the left side of the same entrance. The Vijayanagara king Vīrapratāpa Sadāśiva-Mahārāya records in Ś. 1472, Sādhāraṇa, gift of paddy and money to the temple of Kalidēvasvāmin at Balguḷi, while Kṛishṇapa-Nāyaka was governing Kōṭṭūr (included in Kōgaḷi), granted by the king as an *amaramāgāṇe*, and the 32,000 (country). He is suggested to be identical with his namesake mentioned in two inscriptions at Bādāmi and Toḷachgūḍ. (*Ind. Antq.*, X, 64 and 67.)

264. 72 *of* 1904.—(Kanarese.) On a pillar in the maṇṭapa in front of the same shrine. Records in Sarvadhārin a gift by an officer of Vīranaraśiṅgadēva, "who was an architect in establishing the Chōḷa kingdom."

265. 73 *of* 1904.—(Kanarese.) On a slab set up on the west side of the ruined shrine close to the same. Records that Rotta of the Raṭṭa family who had the *biruda* Laṭṭaḷūrapura-Paramēśvara, was governing the Kōgaḷi 500 and the Māsavāḍi 140.

266. 74 *of* 1904.—(Kanarese.) On another slab set up in the same place. The Western Chāḷukya king Tribhuvanamalla (Vikrama VI) records in Chālukya-Vikrama year 37, Nandana, gift of gold for two lamps. Broken.

267. 75 *of* 1904.—(Kanarese.) On the third slab set up in the same place. A record of the Rāshṭrakūṭa king Kaṇṇaradēva (Kṛishna III), dated in Ś. 868, Krōdhin, when Kāṭyēra of the Chāḷukya family was governing the Kōgaḷi 500 and the Masavāḏi 40. [Shows that the Chālukyans occupied a subordinate position under Rāshṭrakūṭa supremacy.]

268. 76 *of* 1904.—(Kanarese.) On the fourth slab set up in the same place. Dated in the reign of the Western Chāḷukya king Tribhuvanamalla (Vikramāditya VI). Records in Chālukya-Vikrama year 47, Śubhakrit, gift of land by a private individual.

269. 77 *of* 1904.—(Kanarese.) On the fifth slab set up in the same place. The Western Chāḷukya king Tribhuvanamalla (1076–1126) records in Chāḷukya-Vikrama year 39, Jaya, gift of land.

270. 78 *of* 1904.—(Kanarese.) On the sixth slab set up in the same place. The Western Chāḷukya king Tribhuvanamalla (1076–1126) records gift of land. The date is lost. On the same stone is another record dated in Ś. 1131, Śukla.

271. 79 *of* 1904.—(Kanarese.) On a slab set up on the north side of the same temple. A mutilated record of the Rāshṭrakūṭa king Nityavarsha Khoṭṭiga dated Ś. 894, Āṅgirasa. Mentions Bhūtuga, the Gaṅga feudatory of the king. Records gift of land. See By. 84 and *Ep. Ind.*, VII, p. 194.

272. 80 *of* 1904.—(Kanarese.) On another slab set up in the same place. The Western Chāḷukya king Trailōkyamalla (c. 1042–68) records in Ś. 978, gift of land. Mutilated. Mentions the Paliyanda 4,000 district.

273. 81 *of* 1904.—(Kanarese.) On the third slab set up in the same place. The Western Chāḷukya king Āhavamalla I (Nūrmaḍi Taila II) records in Ś. 909, Sarvajit, gift of a garden to the image of Ādityadēva, set up by a certain Duggimayya. Mentions Āryavarman who was governing the Kiśukad 70 and the Kōgaḷi 500. [Āhavamalla expelled the Rāshṭrakūṭa Kakka II and re-established his own family.]

274. 82 *of* 1904.—(Kanarese.) On two faces of a pillar in the maṇṭapa in front of the Narasiṁhasvāmin shrine in the same temple. A record dated in Nandana. The same pillar contains another inscription, dated in the Plava samvatsara, which records a grant of land to the temple of Narasiṁhadēva at Viṭṭhalapura.

275. 83 *of* 1904.—(Kanarese.) On another pillar in the same place. Records in Viśvāvasu, gift of land to the temple of Sadāśivadēva by private individuals.

276. 84 *of* 1904.—(Kanarese.) On the third pillar in the same place. The Yādava king Kandhāradēva (c. 1247–60 A.D.) records in his fifth year, Sādhāraṇa, gift of land. [The inscription proves that the Yādavas of Dēvagiri ruled a portion at least of the district. See By. 261 above.]

277. 85 *of* 1904.—(Kanarese.) On a slab set up on the south side of the same temple. The Vijayanagara king Vīrapratāpa Sadāśiva-Mahārāya mentions in Ś. 1472, Sādhāraṇa, Haḍapada Kṛishṇa-Nāyaka who was governing the Kōṭūra-śīma granted by the king. See By. 263 above.

278. 86 *of* 1904.—(Kanarese.) On another slab set up in the same place. A record of the Western Chāḷukya king Tribhuvanamalla (1076–1126). Mentions in Chāḷukya-Vikrama year 4, Siddhārthin, Nigaḷaṅkamalla-Pāṇḍyadēva as ruling the Nonambavāḍi 32,000. Records gift of land. [This is the earliest of the thirteen inscriptions which in this place belong to Vikramāditya VI and it shows that the Bellary District in his reign was under the direct rule ofthe Pāṇḍyas of Uchchaṅgi. Nigaḷaṅkamalla is the earliest of these feudatory chiefs. For his successor Tribhuvanamalla Pāṇḍya see No. 289. They boast of defeating Rājiga Chōḷa (Kulōttuṅga I), the great enemy of their suzerain.]

279. 87 *of* 1904.—(Kanarese.) On the third slab set up in the same place. A record of the Western Chāḷukya king Jagadēkamalla Jayaśiṅgha (II). Mentions in Ś. 940, Kāḷayukti, Udayādityadēva *alias* Jagadēkamalla-Noḷamba-Pallava-Permānaḍi governing the Gaṅgavāḍi 96,000; the Kaḍambaḷige 1,000; the Kōgaḷi 500; a portion of the Masiyavāḍi 140; the Ballakunde 300; and the Kuḍihāra 70 included in the Ededore 2,000. Records gift of land to the Kalidēvasvāmin temple on the occasion of Udayāditya's visit to Pampāpura. [The inscription shows the re-establishment of Chāḷukyan rule in Noḷambapāḍi after the temporary Chōḷa supremacy under Rājarāja I, which lasted from 998 to 1018. See *Ep. Rep.*, 1904, p. 9.]

280. 88 *of* 1904.—(Kanarese.) On the fourth slab set up on the south side of the Kallēśvara temple. The Western Chāḷukya king Jagadēkamalla II records in Chāḷukya-Vikrama year 6(?), Āṅgirasa (wrong), gift of gold to the temples of Kalidēvasvāmin and Narasiṁha. Jagadēkamalla-Vīra-Pāṇḍya is mentioned as a feudatory of the king. See 284, 299 and 300.

281. 89 *of* 1904.—(Kanarese.) On the fifth slab set up on the south side of the Kallēśvara temple. The beginning contains a copy of No. 279. The end, which is mutilated, mentions the tenth year of Pratāpachakravartin Jagadēkamalla, corresponding to the cyclic year Prabhava.

282. 90 *of* 1904.—(Sanskrit and Kanarese.) On the sixth slab set up on the south side of the Kallēśvara temple. The Hoysaḷa king Vīra-Ballāḷa II records in Ś. 1116, Pramāthin, a gift of land. The king's genealogy is given in the beginning. Bāgaḷi is called his capital (*neleviḍu*).

283. 91 *of* 1904.—(Sanskrit.) On the seventh slab set up on the south side of the Kallēśvara temple. A damaged record. Mentions Vijaya-Pāṇḍyadēva.

284. 92 *of* 1904.—(Kanarese.) On the eighth slab set up on the south side of the Kallēśvara temple. The Western Chāḷukya king Pratāpachakravartin Jagadēkamalla II records in his eleventh year, Vibhava, gift of land. Mentions Jagadēkamalla Vīra-Pāṇḍya ruling the Nolambavāḍi, 32,000. See No. 280 above.

285. 93 *of* 1904.—(Kanarese.) On the ninth slab set up on the south side of the Kallēśvara temple. The Western Chāḷukya king Jagadēkamalla Jayasimha (II) records in Ś. 957, Yuvan, gift of gold. See No. 280 above.

286. 94 *of* 1904.—(Kanarese.) On the 10th slab set up on the south side of the Kallēśvara temple. The Western Chāḷukya king Tribhuvanamalla (1076—1126) records in Chāḷukya-Vikrama year 33, Sarvadhārin, gift of gold for a lamp. Mentions Tribhuvanamalla Pāṇḍya ruling the Nolambavāḍi 32,000.

287. 95 *of* 1904.—(Kanarese.) On the eleventh slab set up on the south side of the Kallēśvara temple. The Western Chāḷukya king Tribhuvanamalla (1076—1126) records in Chāḷukya-Vikrama year 32, Sarvajit, gift of taxes for the repair of the big tank at Balguḷi. Mentions the Daṇḍanāyaka Barmarasa.

288. 96 *of* 1904.—(Kanarese.) On the twelfth slab set up on the south side of the Kallēśvara temple. The Western Chāḷukya king Tribhuvanamalla records in Chāḷukya-Vikrama year 28 Svabhānu, gift of taxes for offerings and lamps to the temple of Kalidēvasvāmin.

289. 97 *of* 1904.—(Kanarese.) On the thirteenth slab set up on the south side of the Kallēśvara temple. The Western Chāḷukya king Tribhuvanamalla records in Chāḷukya-Vikrama year 51, Parābhava, gift of a garden to the Kalidēvasvāmin temple. Tribhuvanamalla Pāṇḍya was ruling the Noḷambavāḍi 32,000. The inscription shows that Vikramāditya VI ruled for 51 years. See By. 278

290. 98 *of* 1904.—(Kanarese.) On the fourteenth slab set up on the south side of the Kallēśvara temple. The Western Chāḷukya king Tribhuvanamalla records in Chāḷukya-Vikrama year 39, Jaya, gifts to the Kalidēvasvāmin temple, the big tank and the Brahma-Jīnālaya. The same governor of the Noḷambavāḍi 32,000 and Daṇḍanāyaka Tikkabhaṭṭa are mentioned.

291. 99 *of* 1904.—(Kanarese.) On the fifteenth slab set up on the south side of the Kallēśvara temple. The Western Chāḷukya king Tribhuvanamalla records in Chāḷukya-Vikrama year 46, Plava, gift of taxes in favour of a feeding-house connected with the temple of Kalidēvasvāmin. The Noḷambavāḍi 32,000 was ruled by the same chief. Mentions the Daṇḍanāyaka Sōvarasa.

292. 100 *of* 1904.—(Kanarese.) On the sixteenth slab set up on the south side of the Kallēśvara temple. The Rāshṭrakūṭa king Akālavarsha-Chalakanallata-Kaṇṇaradēva (*Circa* A.D. 945—57) mentions in Ś. 878, Nala, Rottayya as governing the Māsivāḍi 140, the Kōgaḷi 500, and the Kukkanūr 30; and Dhorapayya who calls himself Chāḷukya-Nārāyaṇa.

293. 101 *of* 1904.—(Kanarese.) On the seventeenth slab set up on the south side of the Kallēśvara temple. The Western Chāḷukya king Āhavamalla records in Ś. 913, Khara, the renewal by the king of a grant made by the Rāshṭrakūṭa Kaṇṇaradēva, while Ādityavarmaraśa (evidently successor of Āryavarman) was governing the Kōgaḷi 500. See By. 273 above for Āryavarman and By. 195 which points out that Ādityavarnan was a Kaḍamba.

294. 102 *of* 1904.—(Kanarese.) On a slab set up on the south-west corner of the same temple. A record dated in Ś. 907, Pārthiva. The sculptures at the top of the stone seem to represent a battle.

295. 103 *of* 1904.—(Kanarese.) On another slab set up in the same place. A record of the Western Chāḷukya king Bhuvanaikamalla (Sōmēśvara II, Circa A.D. 1068—75) mentions in Ś. 990, Kīlaka, Trailōkyamalla Noḷamba Pallava-Permāḍi-Jayaśiṅga-dēva (i.e., Sōmēsvara's brother Jayasimha) governor of the Kōgaḷi 500, the Kaḍambaḷige 1,000 and the Ballakunde 300. Records gift of gold for the big tank. Sōmēśvara was also ruler of a part of Mysore. See *Ep. Ind.* IV, p. 214 f. He was defeated by Vīra Rajēndra I and deprived of his dignity as heir-apparent in favour of his younger brother Vikramāditya VI who married a Chōḷa princess.

296. 104 *of* 1904.—(Kanarese.) On a slab set up inside the Male-Mallapa temple, in the same village. Records in Chāḷukya-Vikrama year 33, Sarvadhārin, gift of land to the temple of Nīlēśvara. Tribhuvanamalla-Vīra-Pāṇḍya was governing the Noḷambavāḍi 32,000. A certain Vijaya Pāṇḍya, whose eighth year corresponded to Vikriti, is mentioned at the end.

297. 105 *of* 1904.—(Kanarese.) On a slab set up on the north side of the same temple. The Western Chālukya king Tribhuvanamalla records in Chālukya-Vikrama year 44, Vikārin, gifts to the Nīlēśvara temple. Tribhuvanamalla Pāṇḍya was governing the Noḷambavāḍi 32,000.

298. 106 *of* 1904.—(Kanarese.) On a slab set up at the entrance into the Vīrabhadrasvāmin temple in the same village. A damaged record of the Vijayanagara king Vīrapratāpa Sadāśiva-Mahārāya, dated Ś. 1468, Plavaṅga.

299. 107 *of* 1904.—(Kanarese.) On a slab set up in the maṇṭapa in front of the central shrine of the Sūryanārāyaṇa temple in the same village. The Western Chāḷukya king Pratāpa-Chakravartin Jagadēkamalla II records in Ś. 1082, Vikrama, gift of land to the temple of Lakshmīnārāyaṇa. Vīra Pāṇḍya was governing the Kaḍambaḷige 1,000, the Ballakunde 300 and the Kōgaḷi 500. See No. 280.

300. 108 *of* 1904.—(Kanarese.) On a slab set up in the maṇṭapa in front of the central shrine of the Chennakēśava temple in the same village. A damaged record of the Western Chāḷukya king Jagadēkamalla II, date of which is lost. The lines are numbered on both sides of the inscription. See No. 280 above.

Guḍihaḷḷi.

301. In the temple of Śiva. A record dated Ś. 1449 (A.D 1527) recording a private grant in the reign of Kṛishṇadēva Rāya. [*Antiquities*, I, 109.]

Halavāgalu.

302. In the ancient śiva temple of the fort. Dated in S. 1204 (A.D. 1282). A grant by a private person acting under the orders of the commander-in-chief of Prauḍhapratāpa Chakravarti Rāma-chandranāyaka (1271—1309.) See Rea's *Chaluk, Archi.* pp. 30-1.

Harpanahaḷḷi.

303. C.P. No. 8 of 1912-3. A Sanskrit record of the W. Chāḷukyan king Vikramāditya VI in C.V. era 12, Prabhava (=1087-8) and C.V. 48 (1123-4). Registers grants of the villages of Nirugunda (in Vikkiga 70 in Kōgaḷi 500), Sapava, etc., to certain Brāhmaṇas of the Drāviḍa dēśa and of the village of Ādityapaḷḷi to god Bhīmēśvara of Sapava.

Nilaguṇḍa.

This place, like many others in this district, contains examples of the Chāḷukyan style of architecture.

304. 113 *of* 1913.—(Kanarese.) On a slab set up in the court-yard of the Bhīmēśvara temple. Dated in the reign of the Kaḷa-chūrya king, Tribhuvanamalla Bhujabalachakravartin Bijjaḷadēva. Records in Ś. 1084-85, Chitrabhānu, Pushya, śu. di. 10, Sunday, Uttarāyaṇa-Saṁkrānti, Vyatipāta, that Kalidēvadaṇḍanātha or Kallimayya assigned a portion of the tolls (*Hejjuṅka*, *Vaddaravula* and *Pannaya*) in the districts of Kōgaḷi 500 and Kaḍambaḷike 1,000 for the worship of god Svayambhu-Bhīmēśvara at Niruguṇḍa, with the permission of the Mahāmaṇḍalēśvara Tribhuvanamalla Vīra Pāṇḍyadēva who was ruling over the districts included in the Noḷambavāḍi 32,000 province.

305. 114 *of* 1913.—(Kanarese.) On a second slab in the same place. A damaged record of the Western Chāḷukya king Tribhuvanamalla Vikramāditya VI, ruling at Kalyāṇa, dated Chāḷukya Vikrama year 35, Vikriti, Bhādrapada ba. di. 11, Sunday Uttarāyaṇa-Saṁkrānti (wrong), Vyatipāta, corresponding to September 11, A.D. 1110. Records the gift of one *heru* (bullock-load) of leaves (betel) each month to the temple of Svayambhu-Bhīmeśvara at Nirguṇḍa by the chief minister Daṇḍanāyaka Muddarasa who was in charge of the tolls of Kibbatti.

306. 115 *of* 1913.—(Kanarese.) On a third slab in the same place. A much damaged record of the Western Chāḷukya king Tribhuvanamalla Vikramāditya VI, ruling at Kalyaṇa, dated Chāḷukya Vikrama year 33, Sarvadhārin. Seems to record a gift to the same temple.

307. 116 *of* 1913.—(Kanarese.) On a fourth slab in the same place. A damaged record of the Hoysaḷa king Niśśaṅka-Pratāpachakravartin Naraśiṅgadēva (II), ruling at Dorasamudra, dated Ś. 1145, Svabhānu, Māgha, śu. di. 11, Thursday (wrong for Friday), corresponding to Friday 2nd February A.D. 1224. Records the gift of a village situated east of Māchīyahaḷḷi, for the worship of the god Bhīmēśvara. A subsidiary record at the end of this inscription registers that the Mahāmaṇḍaḷēśvara Bijjarasa Achchutadēva purchased and presented, evidently to the same temple, the village Talavagilahaḷḷi, in the cyclic year Kīlaka, Phalguna śu. di. 13, Sunday.

308. 117 *of* 1913.—(Kanarese.) On a pillar of the same temple. Mentions the Mahāsāmantādhipati Ādipemmaṇa of the Mahābalivaṁśa and the village Nirgguṇḍa.

309. 118 *of* 1913.—(Kanarese.) On a slab set up inside the Muktēśvara temple in the same village. Dated in the reign of the Western Chāḷukya king, Tribhuvanamalla Vikramāditya VI. Records in Chāḷukya-Vikrama year 64 (which is an error for 63) Kāḷayukti, Māgha, śu. di. 5, Sunday (wrong for Saturday), Uttarāyaṇa Saṁkrānti, Vyatipāta corresponding to January 7, A.D. 1139, and Chāḷukya-Vikrama year 61, Naḷa, Māgha, śu. di. 10, Monday (wrong for Sunday), Uttarāyaṇa Saṁkrānti, Vyatipāta, corresponding to January 3, A.D. 1137, that while Tribhuvanamalla Rāya Pāṇḍya, the chief of Kāñchi, the jewel of the Yadu race, the punisher of the Parichchēdins, and the cause of the despair of Rājigachōḷa (i.e., Kulōttuṅga I) was ruling the Noḷambavādi 32,000 and Kaniyakallu 300, the 300 *Mahājanas* of Nirgguṇḍa in Kōgaḷi-nāḍu, the 500 *Bananjigas* and the *Nānādēśis* presented lands and tolls for the worship of Svayambhu Bhīmēśvara situated to the north of the village of Nirgguṇḍa in the "Old ruins" (*haleyahalu*). A similar gift was made in the sixty-first year of the Chāḷukya-Vikrama era, by the gardeners, oil-mongers and others. Still another grant of garden-land was made in the cyclic year Jaya, Pushya, śu. di. 14, Monday, Uttarāyaṇa Saṁkrānti. Vyatipata. Rāya Pāṇḍya was the grandson of Palata Pāṇḍya.

310. 119 *of* 113.—(Kanarese.) On a *viragal* set up in front of the same temple. Records the death of a certain Kallagaṅga, the Mūḷiga of Nīrgguṇḍa on the occasion when Mareyāḷva, son of Chaṇḍiyarasa, fought in Banavāsi-nāḍu to rescue the cows of Nīrgguṇḍa.

311. 120 *of* 1913.—(Kanarese.) On a second *viragal* in the same place. A much-damaged record. Mentions a Pallavarājādhirāja.

312. A C.P. grant of Vikramāditya VI (Sanskrit in Nāgari characters). The inscription records the grant of Nilguṇḍa and two other hamlets to a number of Brahmans by the W. Chāḷukyan king abovementioned in A.D. 1123, in confirmation of a previous grant in 1087. The lords of kingdoms, provinces, village headmen, sheriffs (*Āyuktakas*), commissioners (*Niyuktakas*), etc., are addressed that in C.V. 12 Prabhava, on the thirteenth day of the dark fortnight of Pushya, Saturday, the king gave, on the petition of Palata Pāṇḍya, to 300 Brahmans who came from the Dravidian land, the village of Nīrugunda in the Vikkiga 70, in Kogaḷi 500. The grant was renewed, on the petition of Rāya Pāṇḍya, the grandson of Palata Pāṇḍya (who was moved thererto by Draviḍātya, custodian of the royal office and general superintendent) on C.V. 48, Śōbhakrit, twelfth day of the bright fortnight, Monday, Śravaṇadvādaśi. The first date corresponded, according to Dr. Fleet, to 25th December 1087, and the second to 3rd September A.D. 1123. See *Ep. Ind.* XII, pp. 142—55 where Mr. L. D. Barnett edits the inscription.

HOSPET TALUK.

Ānagundi.

[This village does not belong to the taluk but for convenience sake is included here.]

(*a*) On a stone situated near the Mylār Pagoda at Ānagundi. Records that Rāmarāja Chinnā Timmarāju gave in Ś. 1502, Vikrama, a portion of land with some coconut trees at Ānagundi in free gift for the worship of Mylār Dēvar. *Ins. Ced. Dts.*, p. 420, No. 65.

(*b*) On a stone of a seven headed serpent on the east of the above inscription. Records a grant in the reign of Dēva Rāya (II) in Ś. 1358, Naḷa, of 4 koḷagas of paddy field at Ānagundi in free gift to the God Tiruvēṅgalanātha. *Ins. Ced. Dts.*, p. 420, No. 66.

(*c*) On the south of Ānagundi and near the "Wurregole" shore of Tuṅgabadra river. A record of "Comara Cumpila Bhupala, prince of Cumpeli Desam" in Ś. 1304, Rudhirōdgary.

(*d*) North of the above inscription. Records that in the reign of Sadāśivadēva Mahārāya, in Ś. 1478, Naḷa, a number of boat-people near the Tuṅgabhadra river levied a custom on the working boats. *Ins., Ced. Dts.*, p. 421, No. 68.

Anttāpura.

313. On a stone in the Mallikārjuna pagoda. Records that Viṭhala Rājayya granted a garden with coconut, jack and mango trees for the daily ceremony of Mallikārjuna, in Ś. 1473, Virōdhi, in the reign of Sadāśivadēva Mahārāyalu. *Ins., Ced. Dts.*, p. 421, No. 70.

314. On a stone near the above pagoda. Records that Timmarasiah fixed an allowance of two *paṇams* per month from the tax of "Auvenamuddi" for the lamp ceremony of Mallikārjuna in Ś. 1475, Pramādīcha, in the reign of Sadāśivarāya Mahārāyalu.

Hampe.

The ruins of this historic place have been described in detail in *Bellary Gazetteer* I, 259-78.

315. 1 *of* 1904.—(Sanskrit and Telugu.) On the right side of the south gōpura of the Viṭṭhalasvāmin temple. Records that the Vijayanagara king Achyuta gave in Ś. 1461, Vikārin, the *Ānandanidhi* and made Kubēras of Brāhmaṇas. The left side contains a second copy in Nāgari character. [The same *Nidhi* is referred to in By. 355 and 358, Dg. 24 (*Ep. Carna.* XI) and Hk. 123 (*ibid.*). Rice considers the *Ānandanidhi* to be a bank while Venkayya thinks it might be the name of Achyuta's treasury or a village granted by him to Brahmans. *Ep. Rep.*, 1904, p. 14.

316. 2 *of* 1904.—(Kanarese.) On the right side of the east gōpura of the same temple. A damaged record of the Vijayanagara king Vīrapratāpa Achyutadēva-Mahārāya, dated Ś. 1452, Viḷambin. The Mack. manuscripts say that two donors Heriya Timmappa and his brother Rāgavappa established the *kalaśas* and presented golden plates. *Ins., Ced. Dts.*, p. 414, No. 41.

317. 3 *of* 1904.—(Kanarese.) On the south base of the central shrine in the same temple. Dated in the reign of the Vijayanagara king Achyutarāya-Mahārāya. Records in Ś. 1453, Khara, gift of gold for offerings by the king. [See *Ins., Ced. Dts.*, p. 416, No. 49. The latter says that a Durga temple was erected and the village of Gaurīpuram granted to it.]

318. 4 *of* 1904.—(Kanarese.) On the same base. Dated in the reign of the Vijayanagara king Vīrapratāpa Achyutadēvarāya-Mahārāya. Records in Ś. 1456, Jaya, gift for the merit of the king and of Chikkarāya, [the prince who accompanied him during his visit to Conjeeveram evidently]. See *Ins., Ced. Dts.*, p. 410, No. 25.

319. 5 *of* 1904.—(Kanarese.) On the same base. A record in the reign of the Vijayanagara king Vīrapratāpa Achyutadēvarāya-Mahārāya records in Ś. 1458, Durmukhi, gift of 100 pagodas by a Nāyuḍu for the merit of the king and of Chikkarāya. See *Ins., Ced. Dts.,* p. 410, No. 26.

320. 6 *of* 1904.—(Kanarese.) On the same base. Dated in the reign of the Vijayanagara king Vīrapratāpa-Sadāśivarāya-Mahārāya. Records in Ś. 1465, Śōbhakrit, gift of Naṭṭūr village, land, etc., by Tirumala Tātachārya to God Viṭṭhala. [See *Ins., Ced. Dts.,* p. 410, No. 29.]

321. 7 *of* 1904.—(Kanarese.) On the west base of the same shrine. The Vijayanagara king Vīrapratāpa Sadāśivadēva-Mahārāya records in Ś. 1480, Kāḷayukta, gift of a village. [See *Ins., Ced. Dts.,* p. 411. No. 31.]

322. 8 *of* 1904.—(Kanarese.) On the same base. Dated in the reign of the Vijayanagara king Vīrapratāpa Achyutarāya-Mahārāya. Records in Ś. 1453, Khara, gift by Vēdamārga-pratishṭhāpanāchārya Tāḷavāka Tirumalayya of the Bharadvāja gōtra and Āśvaḷāyana sūtra. [This Tāḷavāka Tirumalayya was a member of the very important Vaishṇava family who figure in Tirupati and Ahobilam. See also *Ins., Ced. Dts.,* p. 411, No. 30.]

323. 9 *of* 1904.—(Kanarese and Sanskrit.) On the north base of the same shrine. A record of the Vijayanagara king Vīrapratāpa Achyutadēvarāya-Mahārāya, dated Ś. 1455, Vijaya. Contains a verse composed by Tirumalammā on the occasion of the gift of *suvarṇamēru* by the king.

324. 10 *of* 1904.—(Kanarese.) On the same base. Dated in the reign of the Vijayanagara king Vīrapratāpa Achyutadēvarāya-Mahārāya. Records in Ś. 1456, Jaya that a private individual set up images of the 12 Āḻvārs and of Tirukkachchi-Nambi. For the career of Tirukkachchi-Nambi see the *Guruparampara. Ins., Ced. Dts.,* p. 412, No. 34.

325. 11 *of* 1904.—(Kanarese.) On the same base. The Vijayanagara king Vīrapratāpa-Sadāśivadēva-Mahārāya records in Ś. 1485, Rudhirōdgārin, gift of land. [See *Ins., Ced. Dts.,* p. 411, No. 32. One Viṭṭhala Dhanamvārulu purchased 12 koḷagas of land at Rāmēśvaram for 60 pagodas and gave it away to God Viṭṭhala.]

326. 12 *of* 1904.—(Kanarese.) On the south base of the maṇṭapa in front of the same shrine. Dated in the reign of the Vijayanagara king Vīrapratāpa-Sadāśivadēvarāya-Mahārāya. Records in Ś. 1466, Krōdhin, gift of two villages by Kōnēṭi-Timmarājā for the benefit of his father Koṇḍarāja. [See *Ins., Ced. Dts.,* p. 408, No. 20, for this inscription.]

327. 13 *of* 1904. (Kanarese.) On the north base of the same maṇṭapa. A record of the Vijayanagara king Vīrapratāpa-Sadāśivadēva-Mahārāya. Records in Ś. 1476, Ānanda, the erection of a maṇṭapa for the swinging festival by Udayagiri Timmarāja, son of Kōnēṭaya and grandson of Ārivīṭi-Rāmarāja-Koṇḍayadēva. [*Ins., Ced. Dts.*, p. 412, No. 36. The village of Tirumalapuram worth 600 pagodas in revenue given.]

328. 14 *of* 1904.—(Kanarese.) On the same base. Dated in the reign of the Vijayanagara king Vīrapratāpa-Sadāśivadēva-Mahārāya. Records in Ś. 1476, Ānanda, gift of gold. Mentions Musalimaḍuvu-Vīrapparāja-Timmarājayya. The gift was made with the consent of Aḷiya Rāmappayyadēva-mahā-araśu. [This is the same as *Ins., Ced. Dts.*, p. 414, No. 33.]

329. 15 *of* 1904.—(Telugu.) On the north wall of the maṇṭapa in front of the deserted shrine to the west of the same temple. A record of the Vijayanagara king Vīrapratāpa—Sadāśivadēva-Mahārāya. Records in Ś. 1483, Raudri, gift of a garden to the shrine of Tirumaṅgai-Āḷvār by Śrīraṅgaraja, son of Kurucheṭi-Obularāja. [See *Ins., Ced. Dts.*, p. 415, No. 46, where this inscription is given.]

330. 16 *of* 1904.--(Kanarese.) On the left side of the north gōpura of the Achyutarāyasvāmin temple in the same village. A record of the Vijayanagara king Vīrapratāpa-Achyutadēva-Mahārāya. Records in Ś. 1456, Jaya, gift of the village of Achyutarāyapuram to the shrine of Tiruvēṅgalanātha, built by Hiriya-Tirumalarāja-Oḍeya, son of Lakkarāja-Oḍeya. [This inscription is given in *Ins., Ced. Dts.*, p. 407, No. 19.]

331. On the north and south faces of a stone tablet set up in front of a maṇṭapa in the Siva temple at Pampāpati. (Sanskrit and Kanarese.) Records the gift of the village of Siṅganāyakanahaḷḷi to the Virūpāksha shrine and the building of the Raṅgamaṇṭapa there. The date of the grant is Ś. 1430 (expired), Śukla, Māgha Śu. 14, on the day of the king Kṛishṇadēva Rāya's coronation festivities. [See *Asiatic Researches*, Vol. XX, pp. 25 and 39; *Ind. Antq.* V, 73 f; Inscrns. in *Dharwar and Mysore*, 1866, No. 32; *Pāḷi, Sans. and old Kanar Inscrns.* 878, No. 116 and above all *Ep. Ind.*, Vol. I, pp. 361-71. The inscription is very important as it furnishes the date of Kṛishṇadēva Rāya's coronation. It is also interesting for its mention of the chief religious centres of the period, the rituals of the coronation, etc. It is given in *Ins., Ced. Dts.*, p. 402, No. 4, and Kielhorn's *S. List*, No. 502.

332. In the Pagoda of Durgā north of the Virūpākshēśvar temple at Hampi. Records that the son of Immaḍi Rājamalla, Prince of Kuntaladēśam, ruling at "Curagode Chowdayah", granted a portion of land at Hampi for the daily ceremony of Virūpākshēśvar, in Ś. 1121. *Ins., Ced. Dts.*, p. 402, No. 6.

333. On a stone near the south gate of Virūpakshēśvar Pagoda. A record in the reign of Sōmēśvara Dēvarasu in Ś. 1159, Dunmukhi, giving the rules for the daily supply of articles to the pagōda and the payment of 181 pagodas yearly to Virūpāksha-dēva. *Ins., Ced. Dts.*, No. 7.

334. On a stone opposite to the above inscription. Records a grant of 24 grounds of land at Ahōbalam village to Virūpāksha-dēva, in Ś. 1351, Saumya, in the reign of Harihara Rāyalu. *Ibid.*, No. 8.

335. On a stone pillar in the pagoda of Prasanna Virūpāksha on the Hill Hēmakuṇṭaparvatam. Records that Viracompili Dēva Śinga Nāyaka and Puramaya Nāyaka erected a pagoda of Īśvar on the Hēmakuṇṭaparvatam and seated there a liṅgam, in Saumya. *Ins., Ced. Dts.*, p. 404, No. 9.

336. (Kanarese.) On the stone round the Viṭṭhaḷasvāmi pagoda. Records that one Śrīnivāsāchārya gave in Ś. 1486, Raktākshi, in the reign of Sadāśivarāya, the village of Mukkundi agrahāram to God Viṭṭhaladēva. *Ins., Ced. Dts.*, p. 406, No. 17.

337. On the gate stone of the Viṭṭhaladēva temple. Records that in Ś. 1435, Śrīmukha, Kṛishṇadēva and his two queens erected the gōpuram and presented one gold plate worth 991 pagodas, besides 25 silver lamps, 200 cows and 4 villages, to Viṭṭhaladēva for worship. *Ins., Ced. Dts.*, p. 408, No. 21 and p. 413, No. 38.

338. West of the above inscription. Records that in the same date Kṛishṇadēva gave the village of Liṅgapuram in Tekkalakōṭa and other gifts to the deity. *Ibid.*, p. 408, No. 22.

339. West of the above inscription. A gift of the same king in Pramādi, the objects of the grant being Dēvasamudra, and four other villages in Rāyadrug taluk. *Ibid.*, p. 408, No. 23.

340. On a stone west of Viṭṭhaladēva pagoda. Records that in Vyaya, Kṛishṇadēvarāya granted Bhadraśeṭṭihaḷḷi, Śayaṇapuram, etc., and the taxes on boats of the Tuṅgabhadra. *Ibid.*, p. 409, No. 24.

341. On a stone west of the above inscription. A record of Achyutarāya in Ś. 1458, Dunmukhi. *Ibid.*, p. 410, No. 27.

342. On the east side of the above inscription. A record of Sadāśivarāya dated in Ś. 1455, Jaya, granting the tax of 300 pagodas in his own village and some other lands at Samudram, Anantapuram, etc., by Musalamaḍugu Veṅkaṭarāju Timmarāju. *Ibid.*, p. 412, No. 55.

343. On the south wall of the Viṭṭhala Īśvara pagoda, Records that Kōnēṭi Koṇḍarāju gave in Ś. 1483, Dunmati, ten kolagas of land at Rāmasāgaram in Kampḷi district. *Ibid.*, p. 413, No. 37.

344. On a stone in the 100-pillared maṇṭapam. Records that Kṛishṇadēvarāya erected it in Ś. 1438, Dhātu. *Ibid.*, p. 413, No. 39.

345. On the west of the above inscription. (Tamil and Grantha.) Same date and information. *Ibid.*, No. 40.

346. In the main gate of the Viṭṭhala temple. Records that in Ś. 1457, Manmatha, Chikka Timmapa granted 200 pagodas for daily offerings in the temple. *Ins., Ced. Dts.*, p. 414, No. 42.

347. In front of the Viṭṭhala pagoda near the gōpuram. Records that Śrīraṅgayya, son of Rāmarājakōnēṭayya, measured the streets of the pagoda of Bhāshyakāra (i.e., Rāmānuja 1017—1137) in the reign of Sadāśivarāya. *Ibid.*, No. 43.

348. On a stone in the pagoda of the Āḻvārs west of the Viṭṭhalasvāmi temple. Records that Ahōbalarāja, son of Rāmarāja Kōnētirāja, erected the pagoda and Raṅgamaṇṭapam in Ś. 1478, Naḷa, purchased three villages from one Tirumalabhaṭṭa and granted them for the Tirumaṅgaiyāḻvār festival. *Ibid.*, p. 415, No. 45.

349. In the pagoda of Rāmachandrasvāmi. Records that in Ś. 1435, Śrīmukha, Kṛishṇadēvarāya granted Vanakuṇṭa and five other villages to God Rāmachandra's annual festival. *Ibid.*, p. 415, No. 47.

350. South of the above inscription. Records that Timmarāju built in Ś. 1442, Vikrama, in the reign of Kṛishṇadēva, a maṇṭapam in the Rāma temple and granted one kuṇṭa of land. *Ibid.*, p. 416, No. 48.

Hospet.

An excellent account of this place, as based on inscriptions, chronicles, etc., is given in *Bellary Gaztr.*, Vol. I, pp. 278—81.

351. 23 *of* 1904.—(Kanarese.) On two pillars, in a maṇṭapa on the way to Jambunātha temple. Records a gift in Ś. 1471, Saumya, in the reign of Sadāśivarāya, to a Hanumān temple on the Jambukēśvara hill.

352. In the mosque to the east of the bazaar street. A Hindustani inscription dated H. 1200 (A.D. 1785-86) by Gaffur Khan, Subehdar of Hospet under Tippu.

Kallirāmpur.

353. On the wall of the Āñjanēya temple. A record dated Ś. 1600, in the reign of Veṅkaṭapatirāya. *Antiquities*, Vol. I, p. 305.

Kamalāpuram.

354. 545 *of* 1893.—(Sanskrit and Kanarese.) On two fragments of a sculptured piece of black granite discovered by Mr. Sewell north-west of the Mahānavami-Dibbe. The Sanskrit portion of the record refers three times to the death of an ascetic named Māladhāridēva.

Kamalāpur.

355. 17 *of* 1904.—(Sanskrit and Telugu.) On the left side of the north gōpura of the Chikka-Hude temple. A record of the

Vijayanagara king Achyuta dated in Ś. 1461, Vikārin. (Duplicate of No. 315 above.)

356. 18 *of* 1904.—(Kanarese.) On the maṇṭapa in the field called Papajāgalūra-hōḷa near the same village. Dated in the reign of the Vijayanagara king Vīrapratāpadēvarāya-Mahārāya II. Records in Siddhārthin (i.e., Ś. 1362) the building of a well by Ahamudakhāna (Ahmad Khan), a servant of the king. The inscription is interesting for the mention of a Mussalman servant of the Rāya. For Dēvarāya's sympathetic policy towards the Mahomedans see *Forg. Empe.*

357. 19 *of* 1904.—(Telugu.) On a slab set up in the field called Murugudigaḍḍe in the same village. Refers in Ś. 1453, Khara, to the temple of Tiruveṅgalanātha.

358. 20 *of* 1904.—(Sanskrit and Telugu.) On the left side of the east gōpura of the Paṭṭābhirāmasvāmin temple in the same village. A record of the Vijayanagara king Achyuta, dated Ś. 1461, Vikārin. The right side contains another copy in Nāgari characters. See By 315 and 355.

359. 21 *of* 1904.—(Kanarese.) On a rock near the Kalaśapura Āñjanēya temple on the Hospet-Kampili road. A damaged record of the Vijayanagara king Vīrapratāpadēvarāya-Mahārāya, dated in Ś. 1356, Pramādin. Records that Śāluva Śaṁkharaśa built the temple.

360. 22 *of* 1904.—(Kanarese.) On a rock east of the Travellers' Bungalow at Kamalāpur, on the Bellary road. The Vijayanagara king Vīrapratāpa Achyutarāya-Mahārāya records in Ś. 1453, Khara, gift of land.

Kampli.

An important and historic place. A Chāḷukyan capital in 1064, the scene of a battle between the Chōḷas and Chāḷukyas (see *Ind. Antq.*, Vol. XIX, p. 340), one of the strongholds of the chiefs of Ānagundi (*Forg. Empe.*, p. 17), an outpost of Vijayanagar, a seat of later polygars, it has had a continuous history. See *Bellary Gaztr.*, I, p. 283.

361. 27 *of* 1904.—(Kanarese.) On a slab set up to the east of the Pampāpati temple. The Vijayanagara king Vīrapratāpa Sadāśivadēva-Mahārāya, records in Ś. 1474, Paridhāvin, gift of land to the Hampādēvi shrine in the Virūpāksha temple. See *Ins., Ced. Dts.*, p. 401, No. 1.

362. On the south-west of Kampli in front of the Sōmēśvar pagoda. Records that Rāmarāju Koṇḍarāju Mahārāju, seated the Sōmēśvar Liṅgam at Kampli, granted a portion of land for the divine service of God Sōmēśvara, in Ś. 1483, Dunmati, in the reign of Sadāśivarāya. *Ins., Ced. Dts.*, p. 401, No. 2.

363. On a stone in the pagoda of Hanumantarāya. Records that Veṅkaṭapati Dēva Mahārāyalu established certain regulations to the merchants of the place in Ś. 1612, Pramōdūta. *Ins., Ced. Dts.*, p. 402, No. 3.

363-A. *C.P.* 13 *of* 1905.—Dated in S. 1447 (A.D. 1525–6) in the reign of Kṛishṇadēvarāya. It records the grant of a village to the Mādhva teacher Vyāsa Tīrtha who "commented on all the Śāstras" and who was a disciple of Brahmaṇya Tīrtha. "The village was originally named Beṭṭakoṇḍa, but was re-named Vyāsa-samudram after the donee and Kṛishṇarāyapura after the donor. Clubbed with this village was Kaṇḍukūru (in the Madanapalle taluka) close to which is the big tank called Vyāsa-samudram." Mr. Sewell's *Antiquities*, Vol. I, p. 132. The same Mādhva teacher figures as the donee in an inscription of Kṛishṇadēva at Tirumala (No. 74 of 1889). Prof. Aufrecht says that he was the founder of the Vyāsarāya maṭha and lived about 1339 (*Catalogus Catal.*, p. 619). The date is of course wrong. Vyāsa Tīrtha was the author of the *Tātparyachandrika*, the *Chandrikā*, etc., the former of which has been commented on by Rāghavēndra Tīrtha and the latter criticized by Rāmasubbā-Śāstri of Tiruviśanallūr. For a reference to Vyāsa Tīrtha's part in the religious activities of Kṛishṇadēvarāya's court and his relation with his contemporary Vallabhāchārya see Gada's *Sampradāyadipikā* and Muraḷīdharadāsa's *Śrivallabhāchāryacharitra*, quoted in Seshagiri Sastri's *Rep. San. Tam. MSS.*, 1896–7, pp. 16 and 24.

Kṛishṇāpuram.

364. On a stone in front of the Raṅgamaṇṭapam in the local temple. Records that Kṛishṇadēvarāya, on his arrival at Kṛishṇāpuram from Udayagiri in Ś. 1435, Bhava (= 16th February 1515), established the image of Bālakṛishṇa at Kṛishṇāpuram and granted six villages in free gift for the festivals, besides the tax on Kṛishṇāpuram and jewels of precious stones and gold and silver vessels. [See *Ins., Ced. Dts.*, p. 404, No. 10; *Asia. Res.*, Vol. XX, p. 30; Kielhorn's *Southern List*, No. 505.]

365. On a stone in the local Āñjanēya temple. The same record as the above. *Ibid.*, No. 11. Kielhorn's *Southern List*, No. 506.

366. On a stone near the "Caralla" Narasiṁhaswāmi temple. Records that Kṛishṇadēva Rāya established in Ś. 1451, Virōdhi, the image of Lakshmi Nṛisiṁha at Kṛishṇāpuram and granted to the deity "Vunganore and Bellachinta" villages. *Ibid.*, No. 12. [This inscription has been edited in *Asiastic Researches*, XX, 29 f. and *Ep. Ind.*, I, 398—402. The date actually corresponded to 23rd April A.D. 1529. See also Kielhorn's *Southern List*, No. 513.]

367. On a stone south-west of the above pagoda near a channel. Records that Gōpinātha Dīkshitar, son of Virūpāksha Bhaṭṭa, established in Ś. 1445, *Tārana*, the Raghunāthasvāmi image and granted some allowance for worship. *Ins., Ced. Dts.*, p. 405, No. 13.

368. On a stone near the pagoda of Mallikārjuna. Records that Bokkasam Yellamma erected the temple on the banks of the lake of Vijayanagaram, seated the image of Mallikārjuna, purchased a garden for 40 pagodas and granted it to Mallikārjuna, in Ś. 1483, Raudri, in the reign of Sadāśivarāya. *Ins., Ced. Dts.*, p. 405, No. 14.

369. On the stone lying in the pagoda of Vidyāraṇyalu between the limits of Rāmapuram and Kṛishnāpuram. Records that Daḷavāy Jaṅgamiah granted a stock of the grains for the daily and annual ceremonies and presented some jewels and silver furniture to the temple of Tiruvēṅgalanāthasvāmi, in Ś. 1467, Viśvāvasu, in the reign of Sadāśivarāya. *Ibid.*, p. 406, No. 15.

370. Near the pagoda of Vīrabhadra. Records that Daḷavāy Jaṅgamiah seated a figure Muda Vīraṇa near the channel of the Kṛishṇāpuram Peṭṭa and presented golden jewels and silver furniture, to Muduvīraṇa, in Ś. 1467, Viśvāvasu, in the reign of Sadāśiva-Rāya. *Ibid.*, p. 406, No. 16.

371. On a stone on the Hill of Kṛishṇāpuram. Records that Lakshmīdhara Daṇḍanāyak erected a temple in the cave of the Mālayaparvatam Hill near Pampāpuram and seated there Gaṇēśa, presented jewels and furniture, etc., and granted ten *kolagas* of the paddy field below the tank of the above village in free gift to Gaṇēśa, in Ś. 1332, Virōdhi, in the reign of Dēvāraya I, son of Hariharra Rāyalu (II). *Ibid.*, p. 407, No. 18.

Malpaṅguḍi (Malapannanagudi).

372. 25 *of* 1904.—(Kanarese.) On a slab lying in front of the temple. Dated in the reign of the Vijayanagara king Vīrapratāpa-Dēvarāya-Mahārāya (I). Records in Ś. 1333, Khara, the establishment of a watershed by a private individual. [This is evidently the inscription referred to by Mr. Sewell under date Ś. 1332.]

372-A. 26 *of* 1904.—(Kanarese.) On a stone beam over the steps of the *Śūlebhāvi* well in the same village. Mentions in Pārthiva, a certain Triyambakayya.

Nāgenahaḷḷi.

373. In the Raṅganātha pagoda. On a stone at Nāgenahaḷḷi Fort. Records that Raṅganātha Dīkshatulu built the temple of Śiva and Vishṇu at Nāgasamudram and placed therein the images of Nāgēśvara and Nāgasvāmi and granted the village to the gods, in Ś. 1438, Dhātu, in the reign of Kṛishṇadēva Mahārāya. *Ins., Ced. Dts.*, p. 421, No. 69.

Nimbāpur.

For some noteworthy geological features of the place around which legends have gathered, see *Antiquities*, I, 105.

374. 24 *of* 1904.—(Sanskrit and Kanarese.) On a rock near the Kapilāśrama. A record of the Vijayanagara king Vīrapratāpa-Immaḍi-Prauḍhadēvarāya-Mahārāya, dated in Ś. 1372, Pramōda. In Nāgari characters.

Rāmpuram.

375. In the village. Records that Chinna Veṅkaṭapati Rāyalu granted the village of Rāmpuram in the district of Hosūr in free gift for the worship of the God Virūpāksha Dēva during his reign, in Ś. 1620, Pramādi. *Ins., Ced. Dts.*, p. 418, No. 58.

376. On the east of Hanūmanta pagoda in the village. Records that Tirumalarayya, son of Śrīraṅgarāja, granted 11½ *Koḷagas* of paddy field at Kalaśapuram for the worship of the God Viśvēśvar, in Ś. 1478, Naḷa, in the reign of Sadāśivarāya. *Ibid.*, p. 418, No. 59.

377. Near the above pagoda. Records that Dēvarāya seated the image of Hanumanta Dēva and granted a portion of land at Kalaśapuram to Hanumantadēva during his reign in Ś. 1356, Pramādīcha. *Ibid.*, p. 419, No. 60.

378. On the north-east of the above inscription. Records that Achyuta Mahārāya granted twelve *koḷagas* of paddy field at Kalaśapuram in gift to Kākali Veṅkaṭa Dīkshatalu during his reign in Ś. 1448, Vyaya, *Ibid.*, p. 419, No. 61.

Śaṅkalāpuram.

379. 398 *of* 1896.—(Sanskrit and Kanarese.) On a slab near Hospet. The Vijayanagara king Krishṇarāya records, on Tuesday, the 6th tithi of the dark fortnight of the *nija* Bhādrapada in Ś. 1435, Śrīmukha, gift of the village of Śaṅkalāpuram to the temple of Kōṭa-Vināyaka. [Mr. Sewell gives an inscription of Ś. 1467 in the Vīrabhadra temple, but considers it wrong as it is attributed to the reign of Krishṇadēva Rāya. The present inscription is edited by Dr. Hultzsch in *Ep. Ind.*, Vol. IV, 266–9. The corresponding date is Tuesday, the 20th September A.D. 1513. It is Kielhorn's *Southern List*, No. 504.]

Timmalāpuram.

380-A. to D. Contains vestiges of three fortified walls, within which stands the temple of Gōpāl Kṛishṇa. "An inscription near the entrance is said to state that it was built in A.D. 1539 by Baikāra Rāmappayya (apparently some local chief) to celebrate the birth of his eldest son. Three or four hundred yards from it, also within the inner wall of the fort, is another large temple with another high gōpuram which contains three images and a liṅgam. It is deserted. An inscription in front of it says it was built by the same Rāmappayya mentioned above. Between the innermost and middle walls of the fort is a ruined temple to Vīrabhadra. Near it is a well, and an inscription states that this also was constructed by the same Rāmappayya. Besides smaller ruined buildings, this middle wall also encloses a dilapidated temple to Mallikārjuna which again, according to an inscription in front of it, was erected by the same Rāmappayya." The style of these temples is the same as that of Hampe. Mr. W. Francis believes that the place should once have been one of considerable importance, but deserted on account of its unhealthiness. See *Bellary Gazr.*, I, 285.

Veṅkaṭapuram.

381. Opposite to the Veṅkaṭapuram fort. A damaged record in the reign of Vīra Narasimhadēva in Ś. 1380, Īśvara. *Ins., Ced. Dts.*, p. 419, No. 63.

382. On the east of the above inscription. Records that Chandragiri Dēvarasayya exempted certain taxes in the Jantakulla Māgāṇi in favour of temples and Brahmins in Ś. 1466, Krōdhana, in the reign of Sadāśivadēva Mahārāya. *Ibid.*, p. 420, No. 64.

Vijayanagar.

383. 16 *of* 1889.—(Kanarese.) A record of Achyutarāya, dated Ś. 1469, Śārvari. *Ins., Ced. Dts.*, p. 417, No. 51.

384. 17 *of* 1889.—(Sanskrit.) On a lamp pillar in front of the Ganagitti temple. A record of Harihara (II), son of Bukka I, dated Ś. 1307, Krōdhana, Phalguna, Kṛishṇapaksha dvitīya, Friday (= Feb. 16, A.D. 1386), saying that Iruga, the son of Daṇḍanāyaka Chaicha, one of Harihara's ministers, caused a temple (Chaityālaya) of Kuṇḍu Jinanātha to be built at Vijayanagara which belonged to Kuntaḷa Vishaya in Karnāṭa country. (This is the earliest inscription in the local list. See *S.I.I.*, Vol. I, No. 152, pp. 155-160. Irugappa was the author of the Sanskṛit Nighaṇṭu *Nānārtharatnamālā*. नानार्थ रत्नमाला. A Jain teacher Simhanandin and his apostolic pedigree is given in the inscription.) *Ins. Ced. Dts.*, p. 416, No. 50; *Ind. Antq.*, Vol. XXIII, p. 126, No. 77; and Kielhorn's *Southern List*, No. 469.

385. 18 *of* 1889.—No details given.

386. 19 *of* 1889.—(Telugu.) A record of Sadāśiva Rāya, dated Ś. 1467, Viśvāvasu.

387. 20 *of* 1889.—(Kanarese.) An inscription of Kṛishṇadēvarāya.

388. 21 *of* 1889.—(Kanarese.) A record of Timmarāja, son of Chikka Timmayyadēva, dated Ś. 1443, Vikrama.

389. 22 *of* 1889.—(Kanarese.) A record of "Annāḷadēvi," dated in Durmukhi.

390. 23 *of* 1889.—In the temple of Rāmachandradēva. A Sanskṛit epigraph of king Dēvarāya.

391. 24 *of* 1889.—(Kanarese.) A record of Kṛishṇadēvarāya, dated Ś. 1435, Śrīmukha. *Ins., Ced. Dts.*, p. 413, No. 38.

392 & 393. 25 *and* 26 *of* 1889.—(Sanskṛit and Kanarese.) A record of Kṛishṇadēvarāya, dated in Ś. 1435 expired, Bhava, saying that he placed a figure of Kṛishṇa which he had brought from a victorious campaign against Udayagiri or Udayādri, in a maṇṭapa in front of the Kṛishṇa temple. See No. 419 for a later copy of No. 25.

394. 27 *of* 1889.—A Sanskṛit record of Ś. 1461, Vikārin.

395. 28 *of* 1889.—No details given.

396. 29 *of* 1889.—A Sanskṛit and Kanarese record of Kṛishṇarāya, dated Ś. 1430 expired, Śukla. The large Śiva temple which is now called Pampāpati was formerly called Virūpākshadēva. *S.I.I.*, I, No. 153, p. 162, and Kielhorn's *Southern List*, No. 490.

397. 30 *of* 1889.—Same details as the above.

398. 31 *of* 1889.—No details given.

399. 32 *of* 1889.—(On a stone near a ruined pagoda.) A Sanskṛit record of Dēvarāya II, dated Ś. 1348, Parābhava, *S.I.I.*, Vol. I, No. 153, pp. 160–167. Records the building of a Chaityālaya to Pārśvanātha in the Pansupari street. [The inscription is also given in *Ins., Ced. Dts.*, p. 418, No. 56.

400. 33 *of* 1889.—(Kanarese.) An inscription of Achyutarāya, dated Ś. 1455, Nandana.

401. 34 *of* 1889.—A Kanarese record of Kṛishṇarāya, dated Ś. 1451, Virōdhin.

402. 35 *of* 1889.—A Kanarese record of Sadāśivarāya, dated Ś. 1467, Viśvāvasu. [This inscription is given in *Ins., Ced. Dts.*, p. 417, No. 55, as situated in the west wall of a Chikka . . . temple. It records the building of a maṇṭapam in the Yādavasvāmi temple by Timmarāja for the salvation of his parents.]

403 to 407. 36 *to* 40 *of* 1889.—No details given.

408. 41 *of* 1889.—(Sanskrit and Kanarese.) In a gateway near Kudderukulu. An inscription of Achyutarāya.

409. 42 *of* 1889.—In the Jain Basti south of Hampi. (No details given.)

410. 43 *of* 1889.—A Kanarese epigraph of Sadāśivarāya, dated Ś. 1486, Raktākshin.

411. 44 *of* 1889.—A Kanarese record of Kṛishṇadēva, dated Ś 1435, Śrīmukha. *Ins., Ced. Dts.*, p. 415, No. 47.

412. 45 *of* 1889.—No details given.

413. 46 *of* 1889.—(Kanarese.) Inscription of Sadāśiva, in Ś. 1483, Dunmati. *Ins., Ced. Dts.*, p. 413, No. 37.

414. 47 *of* 1889.—A Telugu record of Raṅgayyadēva, son of Rāmarāja. No date is given.

415. 48 *of* 1889.—A Kanarese record of Kṛishṇarāya, dated Ś. 1435, Śrīmukha.

416. 49 *of* 1889.—Same details as in the above.

417. 50 *of* 1889.—A Telugu record of Sadāśiva, dated Ś. 1483, Raudri.

418. 51 *of* 1889.—A Telugu record of Sadāśivarāya, dated in Ś. 1478, Naḷa. *Ins., Ced. Dts.*, p. 415, No. 45.

419. 498 *of* 1907.—(Sanskrit and Kanarese.) On a slab set up in the Kṛishṇasvāmin temple. A record of the Vijayanagara king Vīrapratāpa Vīra Kṛishṇarāya-Mahārāya, dated Ś. 1435 expired, Bhava. Fresh copy of No. 25 of 1889.

420. 499 *of* 1907.—(Kanarese.) On a broken slab built into the floor of the Chaṇḍikēśvara temple in the same village. A record of the Vijayanagara king Vīrapratāpa Vīra-Sadāśivadēva-Mahārāya, dated Ś. 1467, Viśvāvasu. Fresh copy of No. 35 of 1889.

421. 500 *of* 1907.—(Kanarese.) On a broken slab in the underground temple. The Vijayanagara king Vīrapratāpa Vīra-Kṛishṇarāya Mahārāya records in Ś. 1435, Śrīmukha, gift of land to the temple of Prasanna Virūpāksha on the "occasion of our coronation."

422. 501 *of* 1907.—(Kanarese.) On a rock near the Jaina temple in the same village. Mentions in Īśvara, Bukkayave, the queen *(ardhāṅgalakshmi)* of Vīra-Harihararāya (Harihara II).

423. On the vicinity of Raghunāthasvāmi temple in the Penukoṇḍa gate. Records that Timmarāja gave in Śārvari, Ś. 1463, some land to God Raghunātha whose image Achyutarāya set up. *Ins., Ced. Dts.*, p. 417, No. 51.

424. On a stone west of the above. Records that in Khara, Ś. 1453, in the regin of Achutarāya, Narasimhanāyaka gave 12 Koḷagas of land at Kamalāpuram. *Ibid.*, p. 416, No. 52.

425. North of the "Umburjung Daraga". Records that Kṛishṇadēvarāya gave in Ś. 1444, Chitrabhānu, some land to Tiruveṅgalanātha. *Ibid.*, p. 417, No. 53.

426. North of the above. Records that in Ś. 1465, Śubhakrit, Sadāśivarāya granted a garden to Vulukoṇḍa Veṅkaṭēśvara. *Ibid.*, p. 417, No. 54.

KUDLIGI TALUK.

Ambali.

427. 28 *of* 1904.—(Kanarese.) On a slab set up in front of the Kallēśvara temple (See *Bellary Gazr.*, I, 287–8). Dated in the reign of the Western Chāḷukya king Tribhuvanamalla (Vikramāditya VI). Records in Chālukya-Vikrama year 30, Pārthiva, gift of taxes by Kēśirāja and Kalimarasa for the repairs of the big tank at Ammele.

428. 29 *of* 1904.—(Kanarese.) On another slab set up in the same place. Dated in the reign of the Western Chāḷukya king Tribhuvanamalla (Vikramāditya VI). Records in Ś. 1004, and Chāḷukya Vikrama year 7, Dundubhi, the grant of the village to a Brāhmaṇa by the Gaṅga king Durvinīta. Contains a genealogy of the Chāḷukya king. Records also gift of land to the temple of Kalidēvasvāmin.

429. 30 *of* 1904.—(Kanarese.) On the maṇṭapa in front of the same temple. Records in Paridhāvin, gift of land by Jagadala-Pāṇḍya of the Kadamba family.

430. 31 *of* 1904.—(Kanarese.) On a slab set up in front of the Āñjaneya temple in the same village. The Western Chāḷukya king Pratāpachakravartin Jagadēkamalla II (1138–50) records in Ś. 1065, Rudirōdgarin, gift of land for the requirements of the temple of Narasimha, built by Jñānaprakāśabhaṭṭārakadēva.

431. 32 *of* 1904.—(Kanarese.) On a vīragal near a well in the same village. Records the death of a hero named Būtuga.

Hyalya.

432. Near a māṇṭapa in the old Śiva temple. Said to record a grant to the temple by "Sōmēśvara Rājēśvara, son of Mallinātha."

Kōṭṭūru.

433. "In the north wall of the house of Virūpāksha Śastri's house in the fort is a stone with an inscription, dated Ś. 1469 (A.D. 1547), in the reign of Sadāśiva of Vijayanagar." (*Antiquities*, I, 110.) Mr. Sewell also mentions a Kanarese inscription, "the purport of which is unknown" in the bazaar street opposite the gate of the Śiva temple. For the religious importance of the place, its Liṅgayet and Jain associations, see *Bellary Gazetteer*, I, 290–1. The latter moreover notes the existence of four inscriptions not yet examined.

Saṅgamēśvara.

434. "West of this village, near a well, is an inscription in Kanarese on a stone bearing the 'figure of a man.' It is dated Ś. 1654 (A.D. 1732), and records a grant by a private person." (*Antiquities*, I, 110.)

Śiranāyakanihaḷḷi.

435. "A furlong north of the village is a stone inscription, dated Ś. 1640 (A.D. 1718), recording a private grant to the temple." (*Antiquities*, I, 110.)

RĀYADRUG TALUK.

This taluk is rich in inscriptions and copper plates. Mr. Sewell mentions as many as seventy-six villages possessing them; but definite details of the inscriptions of four places only are given by him. The Epigraphical Department has till 1915 surveyed Rāyadrug, and all these are here given.

Bhūpasamudra.

436. On a stone east of the village. Dated Ś. 1478 (A.D. 1556.) States that the above name was given to the village, which was formerly called Kriyāśaktipura.

437. On a stone in the village, recording the erection of a pillar in front of the Āñjanēya temple by a private person in Ś. 1470 (A.D. 1548).

Bidarakoṇṭa.

438-A to C. Besides an "illegible" inscription "on a stone at a tank." Mr. Sewell mentions four, one on a stone in a field recording a private donation to a temple, a second on a sandy heap on the village boundary; and two on a stone in a field, undated and recording a grant to a temple by Naraśiṅga Rāvu Rāma Rāvudēvāra in the time of Bāba Saheb. (*Antiquities* I, p. 111.)

Harēsamudra.

439. On a stone near the hamlet of Sakkarepalle. Records a private grant to the temple in Ś. 1476 (A.D. 1654). Mr. Sewell also mentions two inscribed stones in the jungle.

Raṅgasamudram.

440 to 444. Mr. Sewell mentions five inscriptions in this place —one close to the Āñjanēya temple, dated Ś. 1648 (A.D. 1726) and recording a private grant and four others (private grants), dated Ś. 1648, Ś. 1651, Ś. 1680 and Ś. 1681. No other details given.

Pulukuṇṭa.

445. On the stone seated near the Sōmēśvar Pagoda. Records that Niś-śaṅkamalla Parākrama Rāya granted in Ś. 1049, Plavaṅga, one *Kaṇḍuga* of land as free gift for the divine worship of the God Sōmēśvaradēva. *Ins., Ced. Dts.*, p. 234, No. 4.

446. On a stone near the pagoda of Sōmēśvaradēva. Records that Aḍapam Viśvanāth Nāyaḍu fixed a fee (*Tirukāṇika*) to the God Sōmēśvaradēva, in Ś. 1451, Sarvadhāri, in the reign of Kṛishṇadēva Mahārāya. *Ins., Ced. Dts.*, p. 235, No. 5.

447. On the wall of the pagoda of Kēśavasvāmi. Records that Nāyanigāru built in Ś. 1464, Śubhakrit, the pagoda of the God, and granted two tūms of sowing land for the daily worship and sacred food of the God Chennakēśavasvāmi, in the reign of Achyutadēva-Mahārāya. *Ins., Ced. Dts.*, p. 235, No. 6.

448. On a stone in the centre of the village. Records that Sadāśivadēva Mahārāya and Aḷiya Rāmayyadēva Mahārāja exempted the taxes of the barbers of the village, in Ś. 1466, Krōdhana. *Ins., Ced. Dts.*, p. 236, No. 7.

Rāyadrug.

449. 102 *of* 1913.—(Telugu.) On a stone built into the gōpura of the Rāmasvāmin temple. A record of Veṅkaṭapati Nāyaka, grandson of Daḷavāyi Veṅkaṭapati Nāyaka of the Achyuta gōtra, ruling on the throne at Rāyadurgapaṭṭaṇam. Records in Ś. 1648, Parābhava, Mārgaśira, śu. di. 2, Monday, the consecration of the image of Paṭṭābhirāmasvāmi and the building of the temple, gōpura, prākāra, etc., by a certain Narasimhayya of Kuṇḍurpi, under the orders of the king. " Details of date not enough for calculation."

450. 103 *of* 1913.—(Telugu.) On a second stone built into the same gōpura. A record of Timmappa-Nāyaka, grandson of Daḷavāyi-Timmappa-Nāyaka of the same gōtra, ruling at Rāyadurgapaṭṭaṇa. Records in Ś. 1686, Tāraṇa, Phalguna, śu. di. 15, lunar eclipse, gift of the village Mūvulakuṇṭa surnamed Rāma-pura in the Kalyāṇagiri-hobaḷi, to the same temple, for daily offerings and worship. [This or the previous inscription is No. 3 of Mr. Sewell's list. The latter says that the image of the deity was originally at Penukoṇḍa, but that Musari Konēṭi Nāyaka removed it to Kundarpi (Dharmavaram taluk) whence it was removed thither in the reign of Pedda Kōnēti Nāyaka and consecrated. The details of date not enough for calculation.]

451. 104 *of* 1913.—(Telugu.) On the central shrine of the Mādhavarāyasvāmin temple in the same village. Dated in the reign of the Vijayanagara king Vīrapratāpa Sadāśiva Mahārāya ruling at Vidyānagara. Records in Ś. 1478, Naḷa, Jyēshṭha, śu. di. 15, Mahā-Vaiśāka Paurṇami-puṇya-kāla, that the Mahāmaṇḍalēśvara Rāmarāja Viṭṭhalarāja-Tirumaḷayyadēva-Mahārāja remitted taxes on agrahāras in the Rāyadurgaśīma which was enjoyed by him as Nāyaṅkara, for the merit of his father Viṭṭhalarāja. [This is evidently inscription 2 of Mr. Sewell's list. " Details of date not enough for calculation."

452. 105 *of* 1913.—(Telugu.) On a slab set up in front of the same temple. Dated in the reign of the Vijayanagara king Vīrapratāpa Vīra Sadāśiva-Mahārāya, ruling at Vidyānagara. Records in Ś. 1478, Naḷa Kārttika, ba. di. 30, solar eclipse, that Mahāmaṇḍalēśvara Krishnamarāja of the Aravīṭi family granted the village of Bagināyanipalle *alias* Mādhavarāyapura to the temple of Mādhavēśvara at Rāyagiri, for the merit of his father

Viṭṭhalarāja. [Inscription 1 of Mr. Sewell. "Details of date not enough for calculation."]

453. 106 *of* 1913.—(Kanarese.) On the dhvajastambha of the same temple. Records in Krōdhana, Kārttika, śu. di. 12, the gift of this pillar (garuḍa-kambha) by a native of Kalidēvanahaḷḷi to the temple of Mādhavadēva of Rāyadurga.

454. 107 *of* 1913.—(Telugu.) On a rock of the hill, in the same village. Records that in Vishu, Māgha, śu. di. 5, a certain goldsmith named Śēshādri raised a maṇṭapa in memory of his brother Prasannayya.

455. 108 *of* 1913.—(Telugu.) On a boulder by the side of an image of Āñjanēya in the same village. Records that in Paridhāvi, Vaiśākha, śu. di. 5, a certain Mallayya of Ratnagiri caused this Āñjanēya image to be cut.

456. 109 *of* 1913.—(Kanarese.) On the pedestal of the Rasa Siddha images in the same village. Records in Pramāthi, Māgha, śu. di. 1, Monday, that a *niśidhi* was constructed on this day. In eight different sections of the stone are given the names of eight persons whom perhaps the images represent. Some of these were Chandrabhūti of the Mūlasaṅgha and Chandrēndra, Bādayya and Timmaṇṇa of the Āpanīya (i.e., Yāpanīya)-saṅgha. [This is Mr. Sewell's "illegible" inscription 4.] For Rasa Siddha's story see *Bellary Gazetteer*, pp. 300–1.

457. 110 *of* 1913.—(Kanarese.) On the dhvajastambha of the Jambukēśvarasvāmin temple, in the same village. Records in Ś. 1595, Pramādhin, Jyēshṭha, śu. di. 12, that Jakkappa, son of Timmarasayya, the *śānubhōga* of Rāyadurga, presented a well and a lamp pillar to the temple of Jambhunāthadēva of that village. [Mr. Sewell refers to this inscription, but gives a wrong reading of it.]

458. 111 *of* 1913.—Kanarese (Sanskrit.) On the pedestal of a Jaina image kept in the taluk office of the same village. A damaged record of the Vijayanagara king Harihara (I), dated Ś.1277, Manmatha, Mārgaśira, Purṇima. Records that a Jaina merchant named Bhōgarāja consecrated the image of Santānānta Jīnēśvara. The merchant is stated to have been a pupil of Māghanandivratin, the disciple of Amarakīrti Āchārya of Kundakundānvaya, Sārasvata-gachchha, Balātkāragaṇa and Mūla-sangha. [For a description of the local Jaina images see *Bellary Gazetteer*, I, 301. "Date can be calculated but cannot be verified."]

459. 112 *of* 1913.—(Kanarese.) On a slab set up under a margosa tree, to the east of the same village. Records in Ś. 1534, Paridhāvin, Vaiśākha, śu. di. 15, lunar eclipse, gift of the village Viṭṭhalapura by Tammarāya, son of the Mahā Nāyakāchārya Buṭṭuka Eṛapa-Nāyaka of Rāyadurga, for the worship of the Īśvarasthāna of his mother Pennavva-Nākti (i.e., Nāyakitti).

460. *C. P. No. 7 of* 1912–13. A Sanskrit record of the Vijayanagara king Kṛishṇadēva Rāya in Ś. 1446, Tāraṇa, Vaiśākha, śu. ḍi. 15. Records gift of the village of Peyalabaṇḍa *alias* Kṛishṇarāyapura to a certain Nrisimhādhvarin.

Rāyadurgam.

461. *C. P. No. 126 of Mr. Sewell's List.*—(Kanarese.) Records a declaring the settlement of a boundary dispute, in Ś. 1709 (A.D. 1787), Plavaṅga, between the towns of Rāyadurgam, and Molakalamūru in the Maisūr territories. Both these towns possess important hill fortresses.

Tāllakēra.

462 to **469.** In his *Antiquities* Mr. Sewell gives eight inscriptions in this village. These are—

(1) On a stone near the edge of a tank. Records its construction by a private person in Ś. 1281.
(2) Near a well in a Reḍḍi's land. Grant of lands for the sinking of the well in Ś. 1649.
(3) In the temple of Vīrabhadra. Undated. Grant of land for a private party by two local chiefs.
(4) Near the temple of Hanumantarāya in the hamlet of Jaṅgamayyapaḷḷi. No details given.
(5) In a field. Undated. A private grant to the temple.
(6) In the hamlet of Mallēla. No details.
(7) On a stone north of a clump of trees in the hamlet of Kanahalapalli. No details.
(8) Near the weavers' houses in the principal village. No details.

Vyaparala. (Vēparālla.)

470. *C. P. No. 112 of Mr. Sewell's List.*—(Kanarese.) Records a document evidencing a sale of land in Ś. 1574 (A.D. 652), Nandana, by the village authorities of Vyāparāla to a private person, apparently a local chief from the title Śrīmat prefixed to his name.

SIRUGUPPA TALUK.

Balakundi.

470-A. On a stone pillar in the village. A damaged record of a grant to "Kyata" Dēvar by Śrīdarāyar, son of "Mapirnuya" in Ś. 930, Kīlaka. *Ins., Ced. Dts.*, p. 310, No. 14.

471. On a stone west of the village. Records that the inhabitants of four villages including Balakundi granted in Ś. 939, Piṅgaḷa, an allowance of 1,000 Gadyāṇas or Pagodas for the divine service, in the reign of Jagadēkamalla (I, 1018—42), *Ibid.*, p. 371, No. 15.

472. Near the Hanumantarāya Pagoda. Records that Vipravinōdi Mantramūrti Ayyapa Vasuvayya and Gōvindayya, granted their annual allowance to Hanumantadēvar, in Ś. 1482, Raudri, in the reign of Sadāśivarāya. *Ins., Ced. Dts.*, p. 371, No. 16.

Hāvinahālu.

473. On a stone in the village. A grant of the village Gundiganūr in the Kurugōḍu district in free gift, in the reign of Sadāśivarāya in Ś. 1465, Śubhakrit, for the festival of God Virūpāksha. *Ins., Ced. Dts.*, p. 320, No. 43.

474. On the other side of the above inscription. Records that Nāgappa, son of Apparasa, granted eight *Koḷagas* of paddy field at Gundiganūr, in his own land in free gift to Allapa, in Ś. 1465, Śubhakrit, in the reign of Sadāśivarāya. *Ins., Ced. Dts.*, p. 321, No. 44.

Konchigiri.

475. On the stone near the Pagoda of Kalledēva. Records that Suyadēva of Bhōghavatipuram granted 30 *muttas* of land in free gift, in the forty-fifth year, Śarvari, of Tribhuvanamalla. (Vikramāditya VI ?.) *Ins., Ced. Dts.*, p. 321, No. 46.

476. On the west of the above inscription. A damaged record in the reign of Pratāpa Chakravarti Jagadēkamalla (II, 1138—50), grandson of Tribhuvanamalla at Kalyāṇapuram, of a grant by Rājamalladēva prince of Bhōghavatipuram. *Ibid.*, p. 321, No. 47.

Sirigeri.

477. On the south of Sirigeri field. A damaged record in Ś. 1519, Hēviḷambi, in the reign of Haṇḍe Hanuma Nāik at Bellary. *Ins., Ced. Dts.*, p. 321, No. 45.

Śiruguppa.

478. In front of the fort. Records that Bhīmāji Viśvanāth, in Kāḷayukti, "fortified" a bastion and 2 chāvaḍies at the fort of Śiruguppa. *Ins., Ced. Dts.*, p. 310, No. 13.

479. On a stone near a well. Records that Daḷapati Rāyaḍu, in Ś. 1549, Prabhava, fortified a battery, dug the well of "Sebhu Dēvar Bhāvi," in the reign of Abdul Mahommed. *Ibid.*, p. 315, No. 28.

Sandur State.

The history of this interesting state is given in detail in *Bellary Gazr.*, Vol. I, pp. 309—15. It is based on Munro's *Letter to the Board*, 1802; Duff's *Mahrattas*, a family chronicle and British records. Newbold has given an account of the Mahratta family and "the valley of Sondur" in the *Madras Journal*, Vol. VIII, 128 ff. See also

Kelsall's *Dt. Manual*, 241—59. The following epigraphs have been taken from the *District Gazetteer* and Mr. Sewell's *Antiquities.*

Kumāraswāmi Temple.

480 & 481. "A Śāsanam states that the temple was founded in Ś. 641 (A.D. 719). There is an inscription here dated Ś. 1137 (A.D. 1215)." (*Antiquities*, I, 108.) The first of these is mentioned by Newbold and alleged to be a Hale Kannaḍa plate granted by "a king of the Marale dynasty named Bijala Naicanu." Mr. Francis points out that no such king is known to history and no definite pronouncement is possible about it. With regard to the second, i.e., the inscription of 1215, it is not referred to anywhere else. But Mr. Francis draws attention to an inscription in a detached stone inside the central shrine which says "that in 1205 A.D., a feudatory of the Hoysaḷa king Vīra Ballāḷa II (1191—1212 A.D.) directed the revival of an endowment to the temple which had been made in the time of the Rāshṭrakūṭa king Kṛishṇa III (940—56), but had been discontinued." (*Bellary Gazr.*, I, 321.) For the description of the legends and caves of the temple, its sati stones and festivals see *Ibid*, 322-3. The *Baji Rao Stone* is a singular memorial of a political episode. The *Gazr.* mentions some inscriptions on the sati stones and the Navulasvāmi Kumārasvāmi temple. These are yet to be examined.

Sandur.

482. "In the office of the Agent of the Rāja, at Sandūr, is a copper plate document evidencing the grant of land in *inām* to village carpenters, and the building of villages by a Narapati king." His name is given in the copy sent me, as "Krishṇa Rāja, and the date as Ś. 1210 (A.D. 1288). There is probably an error somewhere." (*Antiquities*, I, 108.)

SUPPLEMENT.

163-A. A C.P. grant in Prākrit of the eighth year (Saṁva 8, vāsa 6, diva 5), of the Pallava king Dharma-Mahārāja Śivaskanda-varman, issued from Kāñchīpura. The king confirms a gift made by his father Bappadēva. The record mentions *Sātāhanirattha* (Bellary District) as forming part of the Pallava kingdom and so shows that the Pallavas ruled over an empire which extended so far to the west. It is one of the earliest Pallava records available. See *Ep. Ind.*, Vol. I, pp. 2—5; where its importance for determining the age of the early Pallavas on palœographical grounds is given.

CHINGLEPUT DISTRICT.

GENERAL.

The following copper plates mentioned by Mr. Sewell in his *Antiquities*, Vol. II, have not been properly located by him. He simply says that they were obtained for examination from the District Court, Chingleput. As the particular villages are not mentioned, I have given them under the heading " general."

1. *C.P. No.* 13 *of Mr. Sewell's List.*—(Modern Grantha.) Records a grant in Ś. 1008 (A.D. 1086), Kaliyuga 4187, *Nandana*. The grant purports to have been executed by one Vīra Śaṅguḍaiyān of the Chōḷa country. [The dates are inconsistent. Evidently a forgery. Edited in *Tam. and Sanskt. Inscrns.*, p. 145. It refers to the establishment of a village near the five Peṇṇais named Mantappēḍu on the site of an agrahāra destroyed by the Rāya and the authority to enjoy one-eighth of it by a person on payment of 250 pons. The inscription refers to the measuring rod of 64 feet, to the privileges of smiths, vaṇṇiyars, weavers and fishermen. Written by one Narasimhāchāri. It ends with the words *Yekkōl Appāji.*]

2. *C.P. No.* 14 *of Mr. Sewell's List.*—In all respects similar to the above, of which it is apparently a duplicate. Edited in *Tam. and Sanskt. Inscrns.*, pp. 146–47. Like the above it records the building of the village on the site of the one ruined by the Rāya and the purchase of some share in it by the same person.

3. *C.P. No.* 15 *of Mr. Sewell's List.*—(Modern Telugu with a Persian seal.) Records grant in Ś. 1008 (A.D. 1086), Kaliyuga 4187, *Nandana*. The grantor's name is omitted, but it states that he constructed the village of Mannavēḍu, near Arni, " after having divided the city of the Rāyalu and dug a reservoir in the Agrahāram " of a Brahman. On the reverse is a mantram in Grantha characters.

4. *C.P. No.* 16 *of Mr. Sewell's List.*—(Tamil.) Records grant by a Mussulman chief, styled *Mahā rāśa rāśa māniya rāya śri Rirāyaśi Kuppa Chandu Sāyapu avergaḷ*, otherwise Kutb Chand Saheb, in *Pramādicha*, of certain lands, fees, exemption from taxation, and liberty to ride in a palanquin, to Śivandapāda Śeṭṭiyār, of the village, as a reward for faithful service, in the village of Arikōshaṭṭi puduppēṭṭai. Five *kāṇis* of land were given for the maintenance of the palanquin, besides exemption from the taxes on ploughing, the right to collect one measure for every bag of grains that came to the village for sale and one *śēr* for every bag of provisions, etc. See *Tam. and Sanskt. Inscrns.*, pp. 158–59.

4-A. *C.P. No.* 17 *of Mr. Sewell's List.*—Records a grant by a chief (who is given a number of titles some of which are Vijayanagara ones) in Ś. 1488 (A.D. 1566), Prabhava, the second lunar day, Paṅguni

12, Wednesday, Rōhiṇi, to one Tambuśeṭṭi as a reward for the discovery of a theft in the palace. The record says that the thieves were Tambu's relations, that he paid 2,000 pons for their release and that he was given by the Rāya the privilege of collecting a handful for his food from all kinds of grain which came to the market and fourteen villages surrounding the village of Pālaiyanam. (Pālaiyanūr in Madhurāntakam Taluk?.) See *Tam. and Sanskt. Inscrns.*, pp. 156—58.

5. *C.P. No.* 21 *of Mr. Sewell's List.*—(Now in the Madras Museum.) Records grant by a "Vallabha Mahārāja" in Ś. 1377 (A.D. 1455), year *Bhava*, of certain lands and ceremonial privileges in some temples to one Vaṇṇiyappa Śinna Piḷḷai, minister (*Tantri*) of Śiṅgeri Śaṅkarāchāriyār, the chief of the priests of the temple at Siṅgēri. The deed was executed in the presence of Śaṅkarāchāriyār and bears his Narasimha seal. It is in very corrupt and modern Tamil, and edited in *Tam. and Sanskt. Inscrns.*, pp. 152—54.

6. *C.P. No.* 101 *of Mr. Sewell's List.*—(Grantha and Tamil.) It records the dedication of certain lands to a Śiva temple in the village of Nittapinoki Nallūr (Nitya-vinōdinallūr?) issued by Tappunatta Mumma Nayanār, in the fourteenth year of the reign of "Kōpirirājakēsarivarmā." No date given. The seal on the ring joining the plates has a *triśulam* between two *Nandis.*

7. *C.P. No.* 139 *of Mr. Sewell's List.*—(Madras Museum Plate No. 1.) (Tamil in Grantha characters.) Records a grant, similar to 1, 2 and 3 above. Records a grant in K. 4190, Ś. 1011, Manmatha, Chitrai 22, by "the most powerful" chief Vīraśaṅguḍaiyān. The object of the grant was some land in Aḷakkayyar said to be in Kāñchīmaṇḍalam. See *Tam. and Sanskt. Inscrns.*, pp. 137—39.

The plate contains certain diagrams to show the divisions of the land granted.

8. *C.P. No.* 140 *of Mr. Sewell's List.*—(Madras Museum Plate No. 2.) Records grant of lands. This is similar to No. 4 in its characters, and in its wordings. Edited in *Tam. and Sanskt. Inscrns.*, p. 140.

9. *C.P. No.* 142 *of Mr. Sewell's List.*—(Telugu.) Records on one side some mantrams with a Telugu seal, and on the other a representation of a tree, a cow, two human figures, and some other animals.

10. *C.P. No.* 143 *of Mr. Sewell's List.*—(Museum Plate No. 5.) Another plate of the same series as No. 1 slightly different in character. See *Tam. and Sanskt. Inscrns.*, p. 142.

11. *C.P. No.* 144 *of Mr. Sewell's List.*—(Madras Museum Plate No. 6.) This is in every respect identical with No. 1. Edited in *Tam. and Sanskt. Inscrns.*, pp. 143-44.

12. *C.P. No.* 145 *of Mr. Sewell's List.*—(Madras Museum Plate No. 7.) (Tamil.) Records a sale-deed by which the followers *(janaṅgaḷ, uḷḷattār)* of Muttiyappa Nāyakka, of the village of Krishṇa-ōḍai,

sold some lands to a merchant of Arṇi, in Ś. 1351 (A.D. 1429), Kaliyuga 4519, *Vikāri*, during the reign of "Vīraśiṅga Rāya Tēva Mahārāya" over the Toṇḍamaṇḍalam. Edited in *Tam. and Sanskt. Inscrns.*, pp. 150—52.

13. *C.P. No.* 148 *of Mr. Sewell's List.*—(Madras Museum Plate No. 10.) (Tamil.) Records a sale-deed by the followers of Muttiyappa Nāyakka of the same village, who sold during the reign of Vīraśiṅga Rāya, some lands to another merchant in Ś. 1349 (A.D. 1427), Kaliyuga 4517, *Plava*. The cost of 1,925 kuḷis (by the 32 span-rod) is given as 125 Pulicat pagodas. See *Tam. and Sanskt. Inscrns.*, pp. 148—50, for a detailed edition of this inscription.

14. *C.P. No.* 147 *of Mr. Sewell's List.*—(Telugu.) Records a grant of land in Ś. 1011 (A.D. 1089), Kaliyuga 4190, *Manmatha*. On the reverse is a mantram in Grantha characters, surrounded with Telugu letters, and a design with Vaishṇava emblems of a very modern type.

15. *C.P. No.* 149 *of Mr. Sewell's List.*—Word for word the same as No. 1 above.

16. *C.P. No.* 178 *of Mr. Sewell's List.*—This is exact fac-simile of the inscriptions Nos. 1 and 2 above.

CHINGLEPUT TALUK.

Chingleput.

[See *Antiquities*, Vol. I, p. 188, for a history and antiquities of the place.]

17. 294 *of* 1895.—On a stone in the Madras Museum from Chingleput. A Tamil inscription of Vīra Veṅkaṭapati Rāya (I), dated Ś. 1530 (expd.) *Saumya*. Damaged.

18. 295 *of* 1895.—On a stone in the same place. (Tamil.) Records a grant of land to a Vaishṇava temple in the time of Nīlagaṅgaraiyan.

19. 296 *of* 1895.—(Vaṭṭaḷuttu.) In the same place. Mutilated.

20. 297 *of* 1895.—(Tamil.) In the same place. A record of the fifth year of Tribhuvanachakravartin Vīra Rājēndra Chōḷadēva (II), recording a gift of land by Nīlagaṅgaraiyan.

21. 298 *of* 1895.—(Persian.) In the same place. Dated A.H. 104.

22. 299 *of* 1895.—(Tamil.) In the same place. A much damaged record of Achyutadēva Mahārāya (1530—42).

23. 39 *of* 1911.—On a slab built into the steps of the Sub-Collector's office, Chingleput. A Dutch record of A.D. 1749, mentioning the laying of the foundation of a fort (perhaps Orange of Sadras, according to Dr. Vogel), planned by C. P. Keller. See Tirukkaḷukkunṛam inscriptions where the latter's name is found. See *Ep. Rep.*, 1911, p. 93.

24. 29 *of* 1912.—On a slab in the District Judge's bungalow at Chingleput. A Dutch record which Mr. Cotton believes to be the epitaph on a Dutch tombstone brought from Sadras. It reads: "man's life is as a flower that fades."

Idaiyanpadal (near Śāḷuvankuppam).

[See *Antiquities*, Vol. I, pp. 189–90.]

25. 56 *of* 1890.—On a rock to the north of the caves at Śāḷuvankuppam, near Mahābalipuram. Gives the name Atiraṇachaṇḍapallavēśvaragriham to the temple. *S.I.I.* I, No. 23, and *Ep. Ind.*, X, p. 14.

26. 57 *of* 1890.—On another rock close to the preceding. A record of Tribhuvanavīradēva (Kulōttuṅga III?), dated in his twenty-seventh year.

27 & 28. 534 *and* 535 *of* 1907.—(Sanskrit.) On the right and left walls of the rock-cut maṇṭapa near Śāḷuvankuppam. They record the erection of the Atiraṇachaṇḍēśvara shrine by Atyantakāma. [Rājasimha of Kāñchi or Narasimhavarman II. See *South Ind. Inscrns.*, Vol. I, Nos. 21 and 22, and *Ep. Ind.*, X, pp. 12—14, Nos. 23 and 24.

Irugunṟappaḷḷi.

29. 617 *of* 1904.—(Tamil.) On a slab lying in a garden. Records in Durmati a gift for the merit of Velikōṭi Śiṅgama Nāyakkar-Ayyan. In modern characters. [The chief was evidently a member of the Veṅkaṭagiri family. See *Antiquities*, II, pp. 240—43 for the genealogy of these chiefs.]

Kaḷattūr.

A centre of the Kāḷāmukha sect of Śaivitism. Gōmaṭham Śailarāśi Paṇḍita and Gñānarāśi Paṇḍita were, for example, owners of this and Tiruvānakkōyil temples. As Mālār-Kaḷandai it is also famous in literary history as the native place of Poet Pugaḷēndi, the author of the *Naḷaveṇbā*.]

30. 332 *of* 1911.—(Tamil.) On the south wall of the central shrine in the Munkuḍumīśvara temple. The Pāṇḍya king Jaṭāvarman (unidentifiable) seems to record in his eighth year a gift of land. Mentions Gaṅgaikoṇḍaśōḷa-chaturvēdimaṅgalam, which was perhaps another name of Kaḷattūr. Stones missing.

31. 333 *of* 1911.—(Tamil.) On the same wall. A record of the Chōḷa king Tribhuvanachakravartin Rājarājadēva. Records in his thirteenth year, gift of money for a lamp by a merchant who was a resident of Māḍavīdipperunderu at Tiru-Mayilārpil in Puliyūr-kōṭṭam to the temple of Peruntirukkōyil-Mahādēva at Kaḷattūr, a village in Kaḷattūr-kōṭṭam which was a subdivision of Jayaṅgoṇḍaśōḷamaṇḍalam.

32. 334 *of* 1911.—(Tamil.) On the same wall. Records in the eighth year of the Chōḷa king Tribhuvanachakravartin Rājarājadēva that Aravindavalli, a dēvaraḍiyāḷ of Tiruvoṟṟiyūr, set up in the same temple an image of Chaṇḍēśvara and presented money for a lamp. Also, the merchant mentioned in No. 333 gave a lamp stand.

33. 335 *of* 1911.—(Tamil.) On the same wall. A record of the Chōḷa king Tribhuvanachakravartin Kulōttuṅga-Chōḷadēva (III ?). Records in his fifth year gift of land in the village of Śiru-Taṇḍaḷam by one of the *parikkirattu-peṇḍugaḷ* of Vaḷudalai-Māmbākkam in Vallanāḍu, a subdivision of Dāmar-kōṭṭam, to the temple of Āvuḍaiya-Nāyanār at Kalattūr.

34. 336 *of* 1911.—(Tamil.) On the same wall. Records in the fifteenth year of the Chōḷa king Tribhuvanachakravartin Rājarājadēva gift of money for lamps by two dancing girls.

35. 337 *of* 1911.—(Tamil.) On the same wall. Records in the fifteenth year of the Chōḷa king Tribhuvanachakravartin Rājarājadēva gift of a lamp by a Vāṇiyan.

36. 338 *of* 1911.—(Tamil.) On the same wall. Records in the thirteenth year of the Chōḷa king Tribhuvanachakravartin Kulōttuṅga-Chōḷadeva, " who was pleased to take Madurai (Madura) and the crowned head of the Pāṇḍya " (i.e., Kulōttuṅga III, 1178—1216), gift of land by certain dancing girls of the temple. Mentions Kaḷattūr *alias* Gaṅgaikoṇḍaśōḷa-chaturvēdimaṅgalam.

37. 339 *of* 1911.—(Tamil.) On the west wall of the same shrine. Records in the fifteenth year of the Chōḷa king Tribhuvanachakravartin Vikrama-Chōḷadēva (1118—35) gift of two lamps to the temple of Peruntirukkōyil-Mahādēva at Kaḷattūr by a Brāhmaṇa resident of that village.

38. 340 *of* 1911.—(Tamil.) On the same wall. Records in the fifth year of the Chōḷa king Tribhuvanachakravartin Kulōttuṅga-Chōḷadēva gift of money for two lamps.

39. 341 *of* 1911.—(Tamil.) On the same wall. Records in the twenty-third year of the Chōḷa king Tribhuvanachakravartin Kulōttuṅga-Chōḷadēva, " who was pleased to take Madurai (Madura) and the crowned head of the Paṇḍya " (i.e., Kulōttuṅga III, 1178—1216), gift of three lamps.

40. 342 *of* 1911.—(Tamil.) On the same wall. Records in the fourteenth year of the Pāṇḍya king Māravarman Tribhuvanachakravartin Sundara Pāṇḍyadēva gift of land for offerings to the same temple by Kakkunāyakkan, one of the Kaikkōḷars of the temple. Mentions Gaṅgaikoṇḍaśōḷa-chaturvēdi-maṅgalam. [The king was in all probability Māravarman Sundara Pāṇḍya II " who took every country," who came to the throne in 1238-9 and ruled till about 1251. For the exploits for a chief named Kakku Nāyaka see N.A. 441.]

41. 343 *of* 1911.—(Tamil.) On the north wall of the same shrine. Records in the fourteenth year of the Pāṇḍya king Māravarman Tribhuvanachakravartin Sundara-Pāṇḍyadēva gift of land for offerings by Aḷuḍaiyanāyaka, another Kaikkōḷa of the same temple. See note to the above.

42. 344 *of* 1911.—(Tamil.) On the same wall. Records in the fourteenth year of the Pāṇḍya king Māravarman Tribhuvanachakravartin Sundara-Pāṇḍyadēva gift of land for offerings by Mallandai, a third Kaikkōḷa of the same temple. The donors in Nos. 40 and 41 were his brothers.

43. 345 *of* 1911.—(Tamil.) On the same wall. Records in the thirteenth year of the Chōḷa king Tribhuvanachakravartin Kulōttuṅga-Chōḷadeva (III), "who was pleased to take Madurai (Madura) and the crowned head of the Pāṇḍya," gift of land by two sisters who were the dancing girls *(dēvaraḍiyār)* of the temple. Registers that one of these set up the image of Kshētrapāla in the temple. Mentions Pālipākkam, a hamlet of Kaḷattūr.

44. 346 *of* 1911.—(Tamil.) On the same wall. Records in the twelfth year of the Chōḷa king Tribhuvanachakravartin Kōnērinmaikoṇḍān an order of his to the chief Toṇḍaimān, on the two hundred and ninety-third day of the year, to grant certain lands in and around Kaḷattūr clubbed together under the name of Kulōttuṅgaśōḷan Tiruttoṇḍattogainallūr as a *dēvadāna* to the temple of Peruntirukkōyiluḍaiya Mahādēva for the *tirumaḍaiviḷāgam* and a flower garden. Anapāya Mūvēndavēḷān is stated to have been the royal secretary *(tirumandira-ōlai)*. As *Anapāya* is proved by a Tiruvārūr inscription (269 of 1901) to be a title of Kulōttuṅga II, it is plain that the Kulōttuṅga of this inscription is Kulōttuṅga II, a conclusion which palæography confirms. See Tiruvānakkōyil and Tiruvārūr inscriptions.

45. 347 *of* 1911.—(Tamil.) On the same wall. Records in the twelfth year of the Chōḷa king Tribhuvanachakravartin Kulōttuṅga-Chōḷadēva (III), "who was pleased to take Madura and the crowned head of the Pāṇḍya," gift of land by a dancing girl (dēvaraḍiyāḷ) of the temple.

46. 348 *of* 1911.—(Tamil.) On the same wall. Records in the thirteenth year of the Chōḷa king Tribhuvanachakravartin Kulōttuṅga-Chōḷadēva (III), "who was pleased to take Madurai (Madura) and the crowned head of the Pāṇḍya," gift of 1,153 kuḷi of land by another girl of the same temple. Mentions Ottippākkam, a hamlet of Kaḷattūr.

47. 349 *of* 1911.—(Tamil.) On a slab built into the floor of the Mukha-maṇṭapa in the same temple. A record of the Pallava king Nandivarma-Mahārāja. Mentions in his fourteenth year Kaḷattūr-kōṭṭam and a certain Paramēśvara. [It is not known which of the Nandivarmans is referred to.]

48. 350 *of* 1911.—(Tamil.) Round the Amman shrine in the same temple. Records in Prabhava gift of the village of Kalppattu in Kaḷattūr-śīmai to the temple of Peruntirukkōyiluḍaiya-Nāyinār for the merit of Vīra-Naraśiṅgarāyar, by a certain Vīrappa-Nāyaka, son of Vīmarāyi-rāvuttar.

49. 351 *of* 1911.—(Tamil.) In the same place. Records in the fifteenth year of Tribhuvanachakravartin Vijayagaṇḍagōpāladēva (1250—83) that a certain Aruḷāḷapperumāḷ *alias* Rājarāja-Viḷuppa-raiyan constructed the shrine of the goddess and presented lands to it for the merit of his mother.

* *Māvalivaram (Mahābalipuram).*

For an excellent account of the local architectural works and a valuable bibliography on the same see *Antiquities* I, 189—91. The place is well-known in Vaishṇavite history as the birthplace of one of the three first Āḷvars and referred to both in the *Dēvāram* and *Nālāyirprabandha.*

50. 1 *of* 1887. Inside shore temple. Records that in the ninth year of Vīra Rājēndrachōḷa (I or II ?) the Mahāsabha of Śiridavūr or Narasimhamaṅgalam gave 2,000 kuḷis of land to the Lord of Tiruk-kaḍalmalli. See *S.I. Inscrns.*, Vol. I, No. 42, pp. 68–9.

51. 2 *of* 1887. On the south base of the shore temple. A record of the twenty-fifth year of Kō-Rājakēsarivarman Rājarāja (I), giving very interesting details of a contract amongst the villagers for the division of land among them and the dues of the land-less. *S.I. Inscrns.*, No. 40, pp. 63—6.

52. 3 *of* 1887. On the north base of the shore temple. A record of the twenty-sixth year of Rājarāja I. Mentions the three shrines of Rājasimha Pallavēśvaradēva, Kshatriyasimha Pallavēśvaradēva and Paḷḷikoṇḍār. [Tirumaṅgai Āḷvār refers to the existence side by side of Śiva and Vishṇu.]

53. 4 *of* 1887. Inside Gaṅgaikoṇḍa Maṇṭapam. No details.

54. 5 *of* 1887. Front wall of the Varāhasvāmi temple. No details.

55. 54 *of* 1890. On a rock-cut niche into the left of the Varāhasvāmin temple. A record of the Chōḷa king Kō-Parakēsarivarman *alias* Uḍaiyār Rājēndradēva (1050—62), dated in his ninth year.

---

* The inscriptions collected by Colonel Mackenzie in this place are enumerated and summarized in *Ins., S. Dts.*, p. 187, Nos. 13—18 and *Rais. Catal*, III, pp. 333—4. I have given them under No. 81-A to 81-F. It is not improbable that a few are repetitions of the epigraphs copied by the Department. The original Mack. MS. is No. 845 (No. 50, C. M. 1019), section 6. I have inquired in the Oriental Manuscripts Library for it and been informed that it is missing.

56. 55 *of* 1890. On a stone near the tank at Pavaḷakkāran sattram (or chāvaḍi). A record of the Vijayanagara king Achyutadēva, dated in Ś. 1457 expired, Manmatha. [Sir Walter Elliot has misread this inscription as that of Vikramadēva, dated Ś. 1157.]

57. 310 *of* 1901. On the east wall of the Gaṅgaikoṇḍa maṇṭapa. (Tamil.) A record of the fourteenth year of Tribhuvanachakravartin Kulottuṅgachōḷadēva. Mentions Āmūrnāḍu in Āmūrkōṭṭam in Jayaṅkoṇḍachōḷa maṇḍalam.

58 to 74. 512 *to* 528 *of* 1907.—(Archaic script.) Inscriptions on the Dharmarājaratha. See *South Ind. Ins.*, Vol. I, Nos. 1 to 17, where Dr. Hultzsch edits these. They consist of a string of titles of the Pallava king Narasimhavarman II. [Burnell mistook the titles to be those of a deity. Dr. Hultzsch identifies Atyantakāma with Paramēśvaravarman I, but Mr. Krishna Sastri with Narasimhavarman II. See *Ep. Rep.*, 1913, p. 89.

75. 529 *of* 1907.—On the third storey of the same *ratha*, west. The *ratha* is called Atyantakāma-Pallavēśvara-griham. [Owing to his identification of Atyantakāma with Paramēśvaravarman I and Rājasimha with his predecessor, Hultzsch believes that the son appropriated to himself the Dharmarāja-ratha which his father had excavated; but the excavator was probably Paramēsvara's son Narasimhavarman II and he was himself Atyantakāma.

76. 530 *of* 1907.—On a pillar of the rock-cut maṇṭapa south-west of the "Gōpis' churn" in the same village. Consists of the biruda Vāmāṅkuśa.

77. 531 *of* 1907.—In the Gaṇēśa temple in the same village. The alphabet of this and the next is attributed by Burnell on palœographical grounds to about A.D. 700. It differs from the alphabet of 58—74 in being extremely florid. See *South Ind. Ins.*, Vol. I, No. 18.

78. 532 *of* 1907.—In the Dharmarāja maṇṭapa in the same village. The inscription says that the Gaṇēśa shrine and this maṇṭapa were made by Atyantakāma (i.e., Narasimhavarman II). See *South Ind. Ins.*, Vol. I, No. 19.

79. 533 *of* 1907.—In the Rāmānuja maṇṭapa in the same village. This inscription consists of the last verse of the above two inscriptions and seems to have been a third inscription of Atyantakāma. See *South Ind. Ins.*, Vol. I, No. 20.

80. 566 *of* 1912.—(Pallava-grantha.) On the plinths of two balipīṭhas recently excavated in the courtyard of the shore temple. A damaged record of the Pallava king Narasimhavarman II who had the titles of Rājasimha and Atyantakāma. Registers four Sanskrit verses in praise of the king.

81-A. On a stone in the temple of Varāhasvāmi. Records gift of land by the people of Chennapuram in the ninth year of . . . Varma. *Ins., S. Dts.*, p. 187, No. 13.

81-B. On a stone in the temple of Sthalaśayana-Perumāḷ temple. Records grant of 1,000 kuḷis to the God in the twentieth year of the reign of Ko-Parakēsarivarman. *Ins.*, *S. Dts.*, p. 187, No. 14.

81-C. On the north wall of the same temple. Records that Daḷavāy Tirumalanāyaka granted the village of Kunnattūr to Sthalaśayana-Perumāḷ in Bahudhānya, in the reign of Śrī-Raṅgarāya. *Ibid.* No. 15.

81-D. Below the above. Records grant of land in Chedirāyanellore to the God and Śrī-Vaishṇava Brahmins in the reign of . . . Varma Raṅgarāja. *Ibid.*; p. 188, No. 16.

81-E. On the south side of the temple. Records gift of twelve māḍas to the priests for a lamp by Ādinārāyaṇa in the reign of Tribhuvanachakravarti. *Ibid.*, p. 189, No. 17.

81-F. Below the above. Records that in the reign of "Soomukaharayen" in Svabhānu, the people of Mahābalipuram and twelve other villages declared, the lands of Sthalaśayana-Perumāḷ to be rent-free. *Ibid.* No. 18.

Nandivanam.

82. 255 *of* 1910.—(Grantha.) On a slab set up in the Gaṇēśa temple. Records gift of a perpetual lamp to . . . at Nandipura by a certain Śekkiḷan Kuṭṭēra. [Sēkkiḷān is a sub-caste of the Veḷḷāḷa community. The great author of the Periapurāṇa, for instance was a member of the Śekkiḷa community.]

Nerumbūr.

83. 271 *of* 1912.—(Tamil.) On the west base of the Tiruvālīśvara temple. A damaged record of the Vijayanagara king Kampaṇa-Uḍaiyār (II), dated Plavaṅga, Mīna, śu. di. 10, Monday, Śōdi (wrong for Rēvati), corresponding to Monday, 24th May 1367. Seems to record gift of lands for offerings to the temple of Tiruvanīśuramuḍaiya-Nāyanār by Varāhapiḷḷai, son of Chakravarti Kāḷiṅgarāyan.

84. 272 *of* 1912.—(Tamil.) On the same base. The Vijayanagara king Gajavēṭṭaikara Dēvarāya (i.e., II, 1422—49), fixes in Ś. 1358 (A.D. 1436–7), Naḷa, Tai Saṁkramaṇa, that two *paṇams* were to be paid as *paṭṭāḍai-nūlāyam* on each loom of the Kaikkōḷar living in the *tirumaḍaiviḷāgam* of the temple of Tiruvanīśuramuḍaiya-Nāyanār at Nerumūr in Kaḷattūr-paṟṟu.

85. 273 *of* 1912.—(Tamil.) On the same base. Sakalalōkachakravartin Rājanārāyaṇan Śambuvarāyar records in his ninth year (i.e., A.D. 1346), gift of land for offerings and other services, to the temple of Tiruvāymīśuramuḍaiya-Nāyanār at Nerumūr.

86. 274 *of* 1912.—(Tamil.) On a pillar of the maṇṭapa within the same temple. Records the gift of the pillar by Kaṇṇāramudaiya Pallavarāyan of Ilaṭṭūr.

87. 275 *of* 1912.—(Tamil.) On the threshold of the entrance into the same temple. A mutilated record of the Chōḷa king Rājarāja-Rājakēsarivarman (Rājarāja I), date of which is lost. Contains a portion of the historical introduction beginning with *tirumagaḷ pōla*. Seems to record a gift of land for lamps and offerings to a temple at Nerumūr.

88. 276 *of* 1912.—(Tamil.) On a slab set up in the street of the same village. Sakalalōkachakravartin Rājanārāyaṇan Śambuvarāyar fixes in his seventh year (i.e., 1344 A.D.), the rate of *kaḍamai* and *vāśalvari* to be paid by the Kaikkōḷar living in the premises of the temple of Tiruvanīśuramuḍaiya-Nāyanār.

Taiyūr.

88-A. On a stone in the local temple. Records that Tīttārappiḷḷai (son of Appaiya), granted in Ś. 1458, Dunmuki, in the reign of Achyutadēvarāya, the village of Koṇḍanallūr for the worship of God Tirumurugēśvara-Uḍaiyār. *Ins., S. Dts.*, p. 185, No. 5, and *Rais. Catal., III*, p. 343.

Tirukkachchūr.

89. 261 *of* 1909.—(Tamil.) On the north wall of the central shrine in the Kachchapēśvara temple. Dated in the eighth year of the Chōḷa king Tribhuvanachakravartin Rājādhirājadēva (II, 1178--86). Records that the oil-mongers of Kāñchi and its suburbs and those of the twenty-four *nagaras* met in the temple of Tirukkāṭṭupaḷḷiyuḍaiya-Nāyanār, at Kāñchi-mānagaram and decided that the usual tax on oil mills in the temple premises, together with a specified quantity of oil and a fee of one *kāśu* per oil-mill, be paid to the temple for offerings and lamps. This they declared to be their *Jātidharma*. [The assembly seems to have diverted the tax from Government to temple thus enhancing its own burden.]

90. 262 *of* 1909.—(Tamil.) On the same wall. Records in the fifteenth year of the Chōḷa king Tribhuvanachakravartin Rājarājadēva (III ?), gift of land for a lamp to the temple of Tiruvālakōyiluḍaiya-Nāyanār at Tirukkachchūr in Śeṅgunṟa-nāḍu, a subdivision of Kaḷattūr kōṭṭam in Jayaṅgoṇḍa-chōḷamaṇḍalam.

91. 263 *of* 1909.—(Tamil.) On the same wall. Records gift of bell-metal vessels to the same temple by a private individual.

92. 264 *of* 1909.—(Tamil.) On the same wall. Records in the fourteenth year of the Chōḷa king Tribhuvanachakravartin Rājarājadēva gift of money for a lamp to the same temple. Tirukkachchūr was known also by its surname Nittavinōdanallūr. [See *Ep. Ind.*, XI, 248, where Mr. Sewell points out from the chronological details of the epigraph that the date is December 18th, A.D. 1229.]

93. 265 *of* 1909.—(Tamil.) On the west wall of the same shrine. Records in the third year of the Chōḷa king Rajakēsarivarman *alias* Tribhuvanachakravartin Kulōttuṅgachōḷadēva gift of land for a lamp.

94. 266 *of* 1909.—(Tamil.) On the same wall. An unfinished record of the forty-sixth year of Chōḷa king Kulōttuṅga-Chōḷadēva (I). Records gift of ninety sheep for a lamp. Mentions Velimānāḍu in Uṟṟukkāṭṭu-kōṭṭam, a subdivision of Jayaṅgoṇḍa-Chōḷamaṇḍalām.

95. 267 *of* 1909.—(Tamil.) On the north wall of the same shrine. Records in the seventh year of the Chōḷa king Rājakēsarivarman Tribhuvanachakravartin Kulōttuṅgachōḷadēva gift of land for a lamp by a native of Tirukōvalur in Naḍuvil-nāḍu.

96. 268 *of* 1909.—(Tamil.) On the same wall. Records in the thirteenth year of Rājanārāyaṇan Śambuvarāyar gift of land by a Jīyar (priest) of Pushpagiri whose name, perhaps, was Śaṁkaraśiva. See *Ep. Ind.*, XI, 250–1, where Mr. Sewell points out that the details of the date (Sunday, Krittika, Aparapaksha dvitīya, tulā) are irregular both for A.D. 1349 and 1350, which should have been his thirteenth year as the Kāñchi and Śevilimēḍu inscriptions show that he came to the throne in 1337.

97. 269 *of* 1909.—(Tamil.) On the same wall. Records in the fifth year of the Chōḷa king Rājakēsarivarman *alias* Uḍaiyār śrī-Kulōttuṅgachōḷadēva gift of ninety sheep for a lamp by a certain Tiruvaraṅgadēvan *alias* Virudarājabhayaṅkarachchōḷiyaraiyan.

98. 270 *of* 1909.—(Tamil.) On the south wall of the maṇṭapa in front of the same shrine. Records in the third year of the Chōḷa king Tribhuvanachakravartin Rājarājadēva III gift of money for two lamps. [See *Ep. Ind.*, XI, 248, where Mr. Sewell discusses the details of the date and finds them to be irregular.]

99. 271 *of* 1909.—(Tamil.) On the same wall. Records in the tenth year of the Chōḷa king Tribhuvanachakravartin Kulōttuṅgachōḷadēva (III), "who was pleased to take Madurai (Madura) and the crowned head of the Pāṇḍya," gift of money for a lamp by the wife of Pañchanadivāṇan *alias* Rājarāja-Nīlagaṅgaraiyan. See No. 103.

100. 272 *of* 1909.—(Tamil.) On the same wall. Records in the fourteenth year of the Chōḷa king Tribhuvanachakravartin Rājarājadēva (III ?) gift of money for a lamp by a native of Piḷḷaippākkam *alias* Kaitavakaitavanallūr in Māgaṇūr-nāḍu, a subdivision of Śeṅgāṭṭu kōṭṭam in Jayaṅgoṇḍachōḷamaṇḍalam.

101. 273 *of* 1909.—(Tamil.) On the same wall. Records in the twelfth year of the Chōḷa king Tribhuvanachakravartin Rājarājadēva gift of vessels to the same temple.

102. 274 *of* 1909.—(Tamil.) On the same wall. A record of the Chōḷa king Kulōttuṅgachōḷadēva (III, 1178—1216). Refers in

his thirty-seventh year to the failure of crops in the tenth year and the consequent troubles as regards payment of taxes. An incomplete record.

103. 275 *of* 1909.—(Tamil.) On the same wall. An inscription of the Chōḷa king Tribhuvanachakravartin Kulōttuṅgachōḷadēva (III), "who was pleased to take Madurai (Madura), Īḻam (Ceylon), and the crowned head of the Pāṇḍya." Records in his thirteenth year, gift of thirty-two cows and one bull for a lamp, Kulōttuṅgaśōḷa - Kaṇṇappan Ādināyan Pañchanadivāṇan *alias* by Rājarāja Nīlagaṅgaraiyan of Tiruchchuram in Kulōttuṅga-Chōḷa Vaḷanāḍu, a subdivision of Puliyūr-kōṭṭam in Jayaṅgoṇḍa-Chōḷamaṇḍalam.

104. 276 *of* 1909.—(Tamil.) On the same wall. Records in the twentieth year of the Chōḷa king Tribhuvanachakravartin Kulōttuṅga-Chōḷadēva (III), "who was pleased to take Madurai (Madura) and the crowned head of the Pāṇḍya," gift of land for a lamp.

105. 277 *of* 1902.—(Tamil.) On the same wall. Records in the eighteenth year of Tribhuvanachakravartin Rājarājadēva (III ?) gift of money for a lamp by a native of Piḷḷaippākkam *alias* Kaitava Kaitavanallūr in Māgaṇūr-nāḍu, a subdivision of Seṅgāṭṭu-kōṭṭam in Jayaṅgoṇḍa-chōḷamaṇḍalam.

106. 278 *of* 1909.—(Tamil.) On the north wall of the same maṇṭapa. Records gift of a lamp. Built in at the beginning. In continuation of this is engraved a fragmentary record of Kulōttuṅgachōḷadēva (III).

107. 279 *of* 1909.—(Tamil.) On the same wall. Refers in the thirty-seventh year of the Chōḷa king Kulōttuṅgachōḷadēva (III) to the troubles mentioned in No. 102 and records that a private individual of Ōymā-nāḍu provided for offerings in the temple. [The residents of Tirukkachchūr borrowed from him 15 *kāśus* and allowed him towards interest a piece of land which was the common property of the village, besides paying the tax due to Government on that land. It shows that the assembly was responsible for the revenue even in bad times.]

108. 280 *of* 1909.—(Tamil.) On the same wall. The Chōḷa king Kulōttuṅga-Chōḷadēva records in his forty-fifth year gift of three cows for a lamp.

109. 281 *of* 1909.—(Tamil.) On the same wall. Records in the twenty-second year of the Chōḷa king Tribhuvanachakravartin Kulōttuṅga-Chōladēva (III) "who was pleased to take Madurai (Madura) and the crowned head of the Pāṇḍya," gift of thirty-two cows and one bull for a lamp by a certain Mullaippāḍi-Tiruchchura Kaṇṇappan whose titles are identically the same as those of Kulōttuṅgaśōḷa Kaṇṇappan mentioned in No. 103.

110. 282 *of* 1909.—(Tamil.) On the same wall. An unfinished record of the Chōḷa king Tribhuvanachakravartin Kulōttuṅgachōḷadēva (III), *alias* Tribhuvanavīradēva, "who being pleased to take Madurai (Madura), Īḷam (Ceylon), Karuvūr and the crowned head of the Pāṇḍya, was pleased to perform the anointment of heroes and victors", in his fortieth year. Mentions an order (*ōlai*) of a certain Irunandivarman.

111. 283 *of* 1909.—(Tamil.) On the same wall. Records in the thirty-sixth year of Tribhuvanachakravartin Kōnērinmaikoṇḍān gift of land for offerings to the same temple in the village of Śeṅgunṟam *alias* Arumoḷidēvanallūr and in another which was situated in Valla-nāḍu. Arumoḷidēvanallūr was apparently named after Śekkiḷār, the author of the *Periapurāṇa* who was a native of Kunṟattūr.

112. 284 *of* 1909.—(Tamil.) On the same wall. Records in the thirty-seventh year of the Chōḷa king Tribhuvanachakravartin Tribhuvanavīradēva (Kulōttuṅga Chōḷa III) gift of money for a lamp by a native of Iṟaiyūr in Kunṟa-nāḍu, a subdivision of Ūṟṟukkāṭṭu-kōṭṭam in Jayaṅgoṇḍa Chōḷamaṇḍalam.

113. 285 *of* 1909.—(Tamil.) On the same wall. Records in the twenty-eighth year of the Chōḷa king Tribhuvanachakravartin Kulōttuṅgachōḷadēva (III), "who was pleased to take Madurai (Madura), Īḷam (Ceylon) and the crowned head of the Pāṇḍya," gift of thirty-six sheep for three lamps.

114. 286 *of* 1909.—(Tamil.) On the same wall. Records in the twenty-second year of Tribhuvanachakravartin Kōnērinmaikoṇḍān gift of lands in three villages, viz., Pārippākkam, Arumbākkam and Māttūr which belonged to Māṅgāḍu-nāḍu, a subdivision of Puliyūr-kōṭṭam *alias* Kulōttuṅga-chōḷa-vaḷanāḍu, in Jayaṅgoṇḍa-Chōḷamaṇḍalam. These lands were to be looked after by the servants of the temple of Tiruvaiyār-Uḍaiyār at Kūttanbākkam in Māṅgāḍu-nāḍu.

115. 287 *of* 1909.—(Tamil.) On the same wall. Records in the twenty-third year of the Chōḷa king Tribhuvanachakravartin Kulōttuṅgachōḷadēva (III) "who was pleased to take Madurai (Madura), and the crowned head of the Pāṇḍya" gift of money for two lamps. One of the donors was a native of Vēlūr in Damanūr-nāḍu, a subdivision of Ūṟṟukkāṭṭu-kōṭṭam.

116. 288 *of* 1909.—(Tamil.) On the same wall. Records in the fourth year of the Chōḷa king Tribhuvanachakravartin Kulōttuṅgachōḷadēva gift of 4 *kāśu* for two lamps by a native of Uḷalūr *alias* Rājarājanallūr in Kaḷattūr-nāḍu, a subdivision of Kaḷattūr-kōṭṭam in Jayaṅgoṇḍachōḷamaṇḍalam.

117. 289 *of* 1909.—(Tamil.) On the same wall. Records in the fifth year of the Chōḷa king Tribhuvanachakravartin Kulōttuṅga-Chōḷadēva gift of 4 *kāśu* for two lamps.

118. 290 *of* 1909.—(Tamil.) On the same wall. Records in the thirty-fifth year of the Chōḷa king Tribhuvanachakravartin Kulōttuṅga-Chōḷadēva (III) *alias* Tribhuvanavīradēva, "who having taken Madurai (Madura), Īḻam (Ceylon), Karuvūr and the crowned head of the Pāṇḍya, was pleased to perform the anointment of heroes and victors (i.e., Kulōttuṅga III, 1186—1216)", gift of a village of 67 *vēlis* of land by one Nandivarman, as an auxiliary endowment to the temple of Tiruvālakkōyil-Uḍaiyār at Tirukkachchūr. Mentions Maḍaiyārpuḷḷiyam in Vallanāḍu. The dēvadāna lands had been dwindling, the daily worship and repairs neglected, and hence this donation.

119. 291 *of* 1909.—(Tamil.) On the same wall. A mutilated record of the Chōḷa king Tribhuvanachakravartin . . . Madurai (Madura) and the crowned head of the Pāṇḍya (evidently Kulōttuṅga III), date of which is lost. Records gift of 3,000 new *kāśu* for lamps.

120. 292 *of* 1909.—(Tamil.) On the same wall. An incomplete record of the Chōḷa king Kulōttuṅga Chōḷadēva, dated twenty-fifth year. Seems to record a gift of lamp.

121. 293 *of* 1909.—(Tamil.) On the same wall. Records in the twenty-second year of the Chōḷa king Tribhuvanachakravartin Kulōttuṅga Chōḷadēva gift of thirty-two cows and one bull for a lamp.

122. 294 *of* 1909.—(Tamil.) On the same wall. A damaged record of the Chōḷa king Tribhuvanachakravartin Rājarājadēva, dated in his sixth year. Seems to record a gift of land.

123. 295 *of* 1909.—(Tamil.) On the east wall of the same maṇṭapa. A record of the Chōḷa king Tribhuvanachakravartin Kulōttuṅga-Chōḷadēva (III) "who was pleased to take Madurai (Madura), Karuvūr, and the crowned head of the Pāṇḍya". The residents of the village of Śeṅgunṟam who saw that there was no facility for the irrigation of the lands in Ambarpākkam *alias* Iraṇḍidutyāginallūr which was a hamlet of Śeṅgunṟam and a dēvadāna of the temple, excavated, at the expense of the temple, a tank in their own holding, put up a sluice to it, and agreed to irrigate the lands of both villages from it. [It seems that the cost of excavation fell to the temple, while the land to the residents. Hence both profit by the transaction.]

124. 296 *of* 1909.—(Tamil.) On the same wall. Records in the seventeenth year of the Chōḷa king Tribhuvanachakravartin Rājarājadēva gift of money for a lamp by a native of Mūlaṅguḍi in Uyyakkoṇḍavaḷanāḍu, a district of Chōḷa-maṇḍalam.

125. 297 *of* 1909.—(Tamil.) On the same wall. Records in the fifteenth year of the Chōḷa king Tribhuvanachakravartin Kulōttuṅga-Chōḷadēva (III), "who was pleased to take Madurai

(Madura) and the crowned head of the Pāṇḍya," gift of 2 old *kāśu* for a lamp.

126. 298 *of* 1909.—(Tamil.) On the same wall. Records in the thirty-third year of the Chōḷa king Tribhuvanachakravartin Tribhuvanavīradēvā, "who having taken Madurai (Madura), Īḷam (Ceylon), Karuvūr and the crowned head of the Pāṇḍya, was pleased to perform the anointment heroes and victors" (i.e., Kulōttuṅga III), gift of money for a lamp by a native of Iraiyūr in Kunṟa-naḍu, a subdivision of Ūṟṟukkaṭṭu-kōttam in Jayaṅgoṇḍa-Chōḷa-maṇḍalam.

127. 299 *of* 1909.—(Tamil.) On the same wall. Records in the twenty-ninth year of the Chōḷa king Tribhuvanachakravartin Kulōttuṅga-Chōḷadēva (III) "who was pleased to take Madurai (Madura), Īḷam (Ceylon) and the crowned head of the Pāṇḍya," gift of 4 old *kāśu* for two lamps by a native of Vēlūr in the district of Dāmanūr-nāḍu.

128. 300 *of* 1909.—(Tamil.) On the south wall of the outer prākāra of the same temple. A record of the Pāṇḍya king Jaṭā-varman *alias* Tribhuvanachakravartin Sundara-Pāṇḍyadēva (II? 1276—90); fixes the taxes in his fourteenth year, to be paid by traders, weavers and oil-mongers, to the king and to the temple. These were six *paṇams* per year on each shop-keeper, on each loom of the Kaikkōḷar, on each loom of the Śāliyar and on each oil monger.

129. 301 *of* 1909.—(Tamil.) On the same wall. Records that Poyyāmoḻimaṅgalam was the proprietary village (*kāṇi*) of a certain Perunambi, a descendent of Śāttanār who, among the learned assembly (Kaḍigai) of that village, was entitled *Muttamiḻāchārya* and was well-versed in the Tamil language. The Government Epigraphist suggests that "we may have to find in this a possible reference to Śāttanār, the author of the ancient work *Maṇimēgalai*." [The name Poyyāmoḻimaṅgalam also suggests the Tamil poet Poyyāmoḻippulavar, who was a native of Uṟaiyūr (130) in Śeṅ-gaṭṭukkōṭṭam. For his life see *Abhidānachintāmaṇi*, p. 741-42.]

130. 302 *of* 1909.—(Tamil.) On the same wall. Records in the fourteenth year of the Paṇḍya king Jaṭāvarman *alias* Tri-bhuvanachakravartin Sundara-Pāṇḍyadēva gift of thirty cows and one bull for a lamp by a native of Māṇanallūr *alias* Vīraśōḷa-chatur-vēdimaṅgalam in Śembūr-kōṭṭam, a subdivision of Jayaṅgoṇḍa-Chōḷa-maṇḍalam. [See *Ep. Ind.*, Vol. XI, p. 259, where Mr. Sewell points out that the details of date would suit Jaṭāvarman S.P. II (1276-90). Mr. Sewell infers from this epigraph that the king's accession day should have been subsequent to July 3, A.D. 1276.]

131. 303 *of* 1909.—(Tamil.) On the same wall. Records in the seventh year of the Pāṇḍya king Jaṭāvarman *alias* Tribhuvana-chakravartin Sundara-Pāṇḍyadēva gift of one buffalo for a lamp.

[See *Ep. Ind.*, Vol. XI, pp. 254-5, where Mr. Sewell says that it is a very irregular date, which cannot belong either to the first or second king of this name.]

132. 304 *of* 1909.—(Tamil.) On the same wall. A record of the Pāṇḍya king Jaṭāvarman *alias* Tribhuvanachakravartin Sundara-Pāṇḍyadēva in his eighth year. Mentions the temple of Dēvarādhīśuramuḍaiya-Nāyanār and the village of Maṇarkuḍi which was a dēvadana of the Tirukkachchūr temple.

133. 305 *of* 1909.—(Tamil.) On the same wall. Records in the eighth year of the Pāṇḍya king Jaṭāvarman *alias* Tribhuvanachakravartin Sundara-Pāṇḍyadēva (I) gift by a temple dancing girl, of a lamp and a brass image carrying it. [See *Ep. Ind.*, Vol. XI, p. 256, where Mr. Sewell fixes the date as Monday, May 27, A.D. 1258.]

134. 306 *of* 1909.—(Tamil.) On the same wall. Records in the second year of the Pāṇḍya king Tribhuvanachakravartin . . . Pāṇḍyadēva gift of land at Perumbēḍu in Māgaṇūr-nāḍu, a subdivision of Śeṅgāttu-kōṭṭam, by two private individuals of Dharmāpuram in Śurattūr nāḍu, a subdivision of Puliyūr-kōttam in Jayaṅgoṇḍa-Chōḷamaṇḍalam. Mentions Pañchanadivāṇan Aruṇagiripperumāḷ Nīlagaṅgaraiyan. See No. 103 above.

135. 307 *of* 1909.—(Tamil.) On the west wall of the same prākāra. A record of the reign of the Pāṇḍya king Māravarman Tribhuvanachakravartin Vīra-Pāṇḍyadēva. Fixes the rates at which certain taxes had to be collected on cattle (*Āṭṭiṟaippāṭṭam*) in (the district of) Iraṇḍāyiravēlipaṟṟu. One of the signatories was Sundara-Pāṇḍya-Kaṇḍiyadēvan. The scale of taxes "exempted the calves and the young ones of sheep and goats, but imposed one *paṇam* per year on each head of ten cows, on each herd of five buffaloes and on each herd of fifty sheep." See S.A. 178 for the probable identity of the king.]

136. 308 *of* 1909.—(Tamil.) On the same wall. Records in the seventeenth year of the Pāṇḍya king Jatāvarman *alias* Tribhuvanachakravartin Sundara-Pāṇḍyadēva (II) gift of three cows for a lamp by a merchant of Madhurāntaka-chaturvēdimaṅgalam, while the king was residing in the street Bhuvanamuḷudupperunderuvu of that village. [See *Ep. Ind.*, Vol. XI, p. 259, where Mr. Sewell discusses the details of the date and decides that it should be Monday, August 25, A.D. 1292.]

137. 309 *of* 1909.—(Tamil.) On the same wall. Records in the nineteenth year of the Pāṇḍya king Māravarman Tribhuvanachakravartin Sundara-Pāṇḍyadēva gift of taxes collected in the village of Nāriyanpākkam which belonged to Iraṇḍāyiravēli-paṟṟu, to the *maṭha* of Mudaliyār Perumāḷ-Tādar of that village. [Tādan reminds the literary student of the rival of Kamba who criticised his *Mummaṇikkōvai* and who got from the admiring Chōḷa the village of Kūvam in Toṇḍamaṇḍalam.]

138. 310 *of* 1909.—(Tamil.) On the same wall. Records in the tenth year of the Pāṇḍya king Jatāvarman *alias* Tribhuvanachakravartin Sundara-Pāṇḍyadēva (II, ? 1276—90) gift of two *vēli* of land in Iraṇḍāyiravēlipaṟṟu north of (Tirukkachūr) to two worshippers in the temple of Tiruvēgambamuḍaiya-Nāyanār at Kāñchīpuram (Conjeeveram).

139. 311 *of* 1909.—(Tamil.) On the north wall of the same prākāra. Records in the twenty-eighth year of Tribhuvanachakravartin *alias* Vijayagaṇḍagōpāladēva the sale of land mentioned in No. 134 situated in Oḍḍaṅgāḍu, a hamlet of Perumbēḍu, by the residents of the latter village, to a native of Dharmāpuram.

140. 312 *of* 1909.—(Tamil.) On the same wall. A record of the Vijayanagara king Viruppaṇa-Uḍaiyār (Virūpāksha I), son of Ariyaṇa-Uḍaiyār (Harihara II) in Dundubhi. Records that two families *(kuḍi)* were dedicated for the hereditary service of the temple, viz., to look after its lamps, and declared by the villagers to be free from all assessments.

141. 313 *of* 1909.—(Tamil.) On the same wall. The Vijayanagara king Vīra-Viruppaṇa-Uḍaiyār (Virūpāksha I) records in Raktākshin, dedication of two other families for the same purpose and for carrying the god in procession.

142. 314 *of* 1909.—(Tamil.) On the same wall. Records in the fifteenth year of the Pāṇḍya king Jaṭāvarman *alias* Tribhuvanachakravartin Sundara-Pāṇḍyadēva (II) the renewal of a contract by the Śiva Brāhmaṇas, to burn a lamp in the temple. Quotes the twentieth year of Kulōttuṅga-Chōḷadeva (II), the thirty-eighth year of Tribhuvanavīradēva (i.e., Kulōttuṅga III), the fifteenth year of Rājarājadēva (III), the seventeenth year of Rājarājadēva and the seventh year of Sundara-Pāṇḍyadēva (I ?).

143. 315 *of* 1909.—(Tamil.) On the same wall. A record of the Pāṇḍya king Jaṭāvarman *alias* Tribhuvanachakravartin Sundara-Pāṇḍyadēva, dated in his thirteenth year (Wednesday, Aśvini, Pūrvapaksha-pañchami of Kumbha). Records a gift to the temple of Tirukkachchūr. Refers to the confiscation of the property of some rebellious and misbehaved people at Uttippākkam. Mr. Kṛishṇa Sastri identifies this king with Jaṭāvarman Sundara Pāṇḍya II, but Mr. Sewell points out in *Ep. Ind.*, Vol. XI, p. 256, that the dates are satisfactory neither for the first nor the second king of that name. The date works out correctly for Sundara Pāṇḍya III, who, according to Mr. Swamikannu Pillai, came to the throne in March 1294. The present date corresponds regularly to 8th February, A.D. 1306. The inscription is very interesting, for the insight it gives into the method of criminal administration of those days.

43

A number of Brāhmans of the village of Uttippākkam (and certain Veḷḷāḷas) gave up their caste duties, took up the profession of highway men, wore weapons, "murdered the Brāhmans, cut off their ears, insulted the Brāhman ladies, committed robbery, destroyed cattle, and sold them," to the distress and dismay of the people. The offenders were beaten, fined, deprived of their homes and kept under surveillance (?), but they did not mend. The people complained to Pottappi Rāyar who was in charge of the country and he sent a chief named Vaḷḷuvanāḍāḷvān Iruṅgōḷar at the head of a band of Malayāḷa soldiers. Many criminals succeeded in escaping to the hills and even in rescuing some who were caught. The king ordered the confiscation and sale of their lands to temples and charitable institutions; but of the proceeds the major portion was paid into the treasury in lieu of the fines, and the rest presented to the temple as a permanent charity in the name of the criminals.

144. 316 *of* 1909.—(Tamil.) On a detached stone built into the south wall of the maṇṭapa in front of the Añjanākshi-amman shrine in the same temple. A fragmentary record of the Chōḷa king Tribhuvanachakravartin Tribhuvanachōḷadēva "who took Madurai (Madura), Īḷam (Ceylon), Karuvūr and the crowned head of the Pāṇḍya and was pleased to perform the anointment of heroes and victors" (i.e., Kulōttuṅga III), date of which is lost. Refers to the setting up of an image of the Śaiva saint Tirunāvukkaraśudēva (i.e., Appar).

145. 317 *of* 1909.—(Tamil.) On another detached stone built into the same wall. A fragment of a record of the Pāṇḍya king Sundara-Pāṇḍyadēva, "who was pleased to take every country." [The identity of the king affords a problem. See, however, note to 147.]

146. 318 *of* 1909.—(Tamil.) On the south and east walls of the Marundīśvara temple in the same village. The Sāḷuva king Naraśiṅgarāya records in Ś. 1406, Saumya, that a new village designated Marundakkunādayapuram was founded on the hill at Tirukkachchūr for the merit of the king by Nāgamanāyaka who was the foremost of his servants *(mudarppāvāḍai)*, and that the Kaikkōḷar and others occupying that village were to pay a certain tax (i.e., ¼ paṇam per month on each loom). [Was Nāgama the father of Viśvanātha Nāik of Madura? Naraśiṅga, it should be noted, does not recognize a suzerain.]

147. 319 *of* 1909.—(Tamil.) On the north wall of the Vighnēśvara shrine near the tank, in the same village. Records in the eighth year of the Pāṇḍya king Jaṭāvarman *alias* Tribhuvanachakravartin Sundara-Pāṇḍyadēva (I, ? 1251—64) "who was pleased to take every country," gift of land in Brahmakuḷattūr *alias* Veṭṭaikāraṅkuḷattūr in Ūṟṟukkāṭṭu-kōṭṭam, to the temple of Nārpatteṇṇāyira-Viṇṇagar Emberumān at Tirukkachchūr. [See *Ep. Ind.*, XI, 255, where Mr. Sewell points out that the date is irregular, and suits neither Jaṭāvarman Sundara Pāṇḍya I or II.]

*Tirukkaḻukkunṟam.**

[This is the celebrated Pakshitīrtha, mentioned in the Dēvāram and known in Chōḷa times as Ulagaḷandaśōḷapuram in Kaḷattūr-nāḍu in Kaḷattūr-Kōṭṭam. See *Antiquities*, I, 191 and *Ind. Antq.*, X, 198.]

148. 167 *of* 1894.—(Tamil.) On the wall of the strong room of the Vēdagirīśvara temple. A record of the Chōḷa king Kō-Rāja-kēsarivarman (a predecessor of Parāntaka I), dated in his twenty-seventh year, renewing a grant made by the Pallava kings Skandaśishya and Vātapikoṇḍa Narasimhavarman. [See *Madras Christian College Magazine* for October 1890, and *Ep. Ind.*, III, 277—80. Mr. Venkayya identifies Narasimha with Narasimhavarman I, the contemporary of Gñānasambanda and Śiruttoṇḍa.]

149. 168 *of* 1894.—(Tamil.) On the same wall. A record of the Chōḷa king Madiraikoṇḍa Kō-Parakēsarivarman (i.e., Parāntaka I) in his thirteenth year. Records gift of a lamp by Neḍumāl Śāttan Śennipperayan of Karaikkāṭṭūr in Āmūr-kōṭṭam and his mother. See *Ep. Ind.*, III, 280-1.

150. 169 *of* 1894.—(Tamil.) On the same wall. A record of the Rāshṭrakūṭa king Kaṇṇaradēva (Krishṇa III), dated in his seventeenth year. Published by Venkayya in the *Madras Christian College Magazine* for April 1892, and *Ep. Ind.*, III, pp. 282—6. Records gift of lamp by a native of Kārai.

151. 170 *of* 1894.—(Tamil.) On the same wall. A record of the Rāshṭrakūta king Kaṇṇaradēva, dated in his nineteenth year. Records that a Śāttan of Kārai built a hall in the shrine and provided for water, fire, etc., besides one paṭṭi of land which he had purchased from Īśāna Śiva or Nakkaḍi Bhaṭṭa. The money was deposited with the local Sabhā.

152. 171 *of* 1894.—(Tamil.) On the same wall. A record of the Chōḷa king Kō-Parakēsarivariman *alias* Rājēndra-Chōḷadēva (I, 1012—43) in his sixteenth year. Gift of a lamp.

153. 172 *of* 1894.—(Tamil.) On the same wall. Records in the twenty-sixth year of the Chōḷa king Kō-Rājakēsarivarman *alias* Rājadhi-rājadēva gift of land. [The king was very probably Rājādhirāja I who ruled from 1018 to 1052.]

154. 173 *of* 1894.—(Tamil.) On the same wall. Records in the fifth year of the Chōḷa king Kō-Parakēsarivarman *alias* Rājēndra-dēva (1052—63) gift of land.

* The inscriptions collected by Mackenzie have been given in *Ins., S. Dts.*, pp. 168—77, Nos 1 -27 and *Rais. Catal.*, III, 341-2. I have traced thirteen of them to the corresponding ones above. The remaining fourteen I have given under Nos. 193—193-N.

155. 174 *of* 1894.—(Tamil.) On the same wall. Records in the fourteenth year of the Chōḷa king Rājakēsarivarman *alias* Kulōttuṅgachōḷadēva (1070—1118) gift of 90 ewes for a lamp. See *S.I.I.*, III, No. 69, pp. 143—8.

156. 175 *of* 1894.—(Tamil.) On the same wall. Records in the seventh year of the Chōḷa king Kō-Rājakēsarivarman *alias* Vīra-Rājendradēva (I, ? 1063—70) gift of a lamp.

157. 176 *of* 1894.—(Tamil.) On the same wall. Records in the third year of the Chōḷa king Vikrama-Chōḷadēva (1118—35) gift of a lamp.

158. 177 *of* 1894.—(Tamil.) On the east wall of the second prākāra of the same temple, right of entrance. A damaged record of the Vīra-Dēvarāya-Uḍaiyār, dated Vikriti.

159. 178 *of* 1894.—(Tamil.) On the same wall. Records in the third year of Rājanārāyaṇa Śamburāya (i.e., A.D. 1340) gift of a lamp.

160. 179 *of* 1894.—(Tamil.) On the south wall of the prākāra. A record of the Chōḷa king Kō-Rājakēsarivarman *alias* Kulōttuṅga-Chōḷadēva (I), dated in his forty-second year. Records that an inhabitant of Rājarājapuram made over 10 *kāśu* to temple authorities who purchased, with this some land for maintaining a *maṭha* of Naminandi Aḍaigaḷ and one of the 63 devotees of Śiva). *S.I.I.*, III, No. 75, pp. 164—8. Also *Ins.*, *S. Dts.*, p. 169, No. 6 and *Ind. Antq.*, Vol. XXI, p. 281-ff.]

161. 180 *of* 1894.—(Tamil.) On the same wall. Records in the twenty-third year of the Chōḷa king Kō-Rājakēsarivarman *alias* Kulōttuṅga-Chōḷadēva a copy of a former copper-plate recording the boundaries of Tirukkaḻukkunṟam. [This inscription is given in *Ins.*, *S. Dts.*, p. 170, No. 8, but the year is given as 33.]

162. 181 *of* 1894.—(Tamil.) On the same wall. Kō-Perunjiṅgadēva records in his twenty-first year, gift of a lamp. See *Ep. Ind.*, VII, 165. The date corresponded, according to Kielhorn, to Saturday, the 10th February, A.D. 1274.

163. 182 *of* 1894.—(Tamil.) On the same wall. A record of Tribhuvanavīradēva (i.e., Kulōttuṅga III, 1178—1216) in his thirty-seventh year relating gift of a lamp.

164. 183 *of* 1894.—(Tamil.) On the west wall of the same prākāra. An incomplete record of the Chōḷa king Kō-Parakēsarivarman *alias* Rājadhirājadēva (II ?), dated in his ninth year. Records gift of a lamp.

165. 184 *of* 1894.—(Tamil.) On the same wall. Gift of land by Kōnērinmaikoṇḍān in his thirty-fourth year, for repairs of the temple.

166. 185 *of* 1894.—(Tamil.) On the inside of the east wall of the third prākāra of the same temple, right of entrance. A damaged record of Kampaṇa-Uḍaiyār (II ?), son of Vīra (Bukka I ?), dated Ānanda. [This is evidently Inscription No. 22, in *Ins.*, *S. Dts.*, p. 174, No. 22. It says that the property of the deity stolen by a man was restored at the expense of his own, worth 750 *paṇams.*]

167. 186 *of* 1894.—(Tamil.) On the west wall of the Tripurasundari shrine in the same temple. Records in the ninth year of the Pāṇḍya king Kō-Jaṭāvarman *alias* Sundara-Pāṇḍyadēva (I, 1251--64), gift of a lamp. See *Ep. Ind.*, VI, 307, where Kielhorn points out that the exact date is Sunday, 15th June A.D. 1259. [See *Ins.*, *S. Dts.*, p. 173, No. 19, where the regnal year is misread as I.]

168. 187 *of* 1894.--(Tamil.) On the same wall. Records in the ninth year of the Pāṇḍya king Kō-Jaṭāvarman *alias* Sundara-Pāṇḍyadēva (1251—64) gift of gold. *Ind. Antq.*, XXI, 343. [See the Śrīraṅgam and Tiruppukkuḷi inscriptions; *Ind. Antq.* XXII, p. 221; and *Ep. Ind.*, VI, p. 307, where Kielhorn gives the date as Tuesday, 29th April 1259.] See also *Ins.*, *S. Dts.*, p. 173, No. 20.

169. 188 *of* 1894.--(Tamil.) On both sides of the entrance into the second prākāra of the same temple. Records in the ninth year of the Pāṇḍya king Sundara Pāṇḍyadēva the setting up of a liṅga by a chief of Aḍigai and gift of 67½ *paṇams.* [See *Ins.*, *S. Dts.*, p. 174, No. 21, where this inscription is given.]

170. 189 *of* 1894. -(Tamil.) On the south wall of the Bhaktavatsala temple on the hill. A much damaged record of the Pāṇḍya king Sundara Pāṇḍya.

171. 57 *of* 1909.—(Tamil.) On the north wall of the kitchen in the Bhaktavatsalēśvara temple, left of entrance. The Vijayanagara king Vīrapratāpa Bukkarāya II records in Ś. 1328, Vyaya, gift of land for repairs and for the festival called Bukkarāyaṇ-śandi (named after the king), to the temple of Tirukkaḻukkunṟamuḍaiya Nāyinār. See *Ins.*, *S. Dts.*, p. 171, No. 10.

172. 58 *of* 1909.—(Tamil.) In the same place. Dated in the reign of the Vijayanagara king Pratāpa Bukkarāya (II). Records in Ś. 1328, Vyaya, gift of land to the temple of Tirumalai Āḻuḍaiya Nāyanar, by the people of Āyiravēlippaṟṟu. See *Ins.*, *S. Dts.*, p. 171, No. 11, where this inscription is given.]

173. 59 *of* 1909.—(Tamil.) In the same place. A damaged record of the Pāṇḍya king Jaṭāvarman *alias* Tribhuvanachakravartin Vīra-Pāṇḍyadēva, dated thirteenth year. Records gift of a village for the festival called Kāḷiṅgarāyan-śandi to the same temple by the inhabitants of Kaḷattūr-paṟṟu. Tirukkaḻukkunṟam was a village in Kaḷattūrkōṭṭam in Jayaṅgoṇḍachōḷa-maṇḍalam. Mentions Kappalūr *alias* Ulagaḷandaśōḷanallūr in Muttūrukkūṟṟam in Pāṇḍi-maṇḍalam. [The king came to the throne in 1253 and so the year of the inscription was A.D. 1266. I have traced this inscription in the Mack. MSS. See *Ins.*, *S. Dts.*, p. 172, No. 13.]

174. 60 *of* 1909.—(Tamil.) In the same place. A damaged record of the Vijayanagara king Vīrapratāpa Dēvarāya, dated in Ś. 1320, Paridhāvi. [This inscription is given in the Mack. MSS. It is said to record the grant of Vaṅgalappākkam to Tirukkaḷukkunṛa Nāyanār. See *Ins.*, *S. Dts.*, p. 171, No. 12.]

175. 61 *of* 1909.—(Tamil.) On the same wall, right of entrance. Records in the tenth year of Sakalalōkachakravartin Rājanārāyaṇa Śambuvarāya (i.e., A.D. 1347) gift of land, by purchase, to the temple of Tirukkaḷukkunṛamuḍaiya-Nāyanār. Mentions Pudup-paṭṭiṇam *alias* Śōḷamārttāṇḍanallūr in Mondūr-nāḍu, a subdivision of Āmūrkōṭṭam, a district of Jayaṅgoṇḍachōḷa-maṇḍalam. [See *Ins.*, *S. Dts.*, p. 172, No. 16. It says that the village was worth 350 *paṇams*.]

176. 62 *of* 1909.—(Tamil.) In the same place. Records in the seventh year of the Pāṇḍya king Māravarman *alias* Tribhuvanachakravartin Vikrama-Pāṇḍyadēva gift of cows for a lamp to the shrine of Shaṇmukha-Piḷḷaiyār by a native of Vānavanmādēvi-chaturvēdimaṅgalam in Āmūrkōṭṭam. [Is this king identical with that Māravarman Vikrama Pāṇḍya who came to the throne in 1282 and who was the victor over Viragaṇḍa Gōpāla and Gaṇapati of the Kākatīya dynasty ?]

177. 63 *of* 1909.—(Tamil.) In the same place. Records in the reign of the Vijayanagara king Vīra-Vijaya-Bhūpatirāya (Bukka III), in Vijaya, gift of taxes for a festival by Nāgēśvaramuḍaiyān Villavarāyan who was the agent of the king. See *Ins.*, *S. Dts.*, p. 172, No. 14.

178. 64 *of* 1909.—(Tamil.) In the same place. Records in the reign of the Vijayanagara king Bhūpatirāya, in Ś. 1330, gift of 32 cows for a lamp by a native of Nerkulam, at the rate of ¼ measure of ghee daily for a lamp. See *Ins.*, *S. Dts.*, p. 172, No. 15 also. [Bhūpati was son of Bukka II.]

179. 65 *of* 1909.—(Tamil.) At the top of the second pillar from the right in the upper verandah of the Orukāl maṇṭapa, on the hill. A damaged record. Mentions Kaḷattūr Kōṭṭam, Mūlatānāṭṭu Perumānaḍigaḷ and Vātāpikoṇḍa Naraśiṅgapōttaraśa (i.e., Narasimhavaram I, the conqueror of Vatāpi).

180 to 188. 66 *to* 73 *of* 1909.—(English.) On the eight pillars of the upper and lower verandah in the same maṇṭapa. Records in seventeenth century A.D. signatures of Dutch officers.

189. 74 *of* 1909.—(English.) On the walls of the same maṇṭapa. Records in seventeenth century A.D. signatures of Dutch officers.

190. 75 *of* 1909.—(English.) At the entrance into one of the temple kitchens on the same hill. Records signatures of Dutch officers of the nineteenth century.

191. 329 (*a*) *to* (*m*) *of* 1911.—(Roman characters.) On the wall at the entrance into the birds' kitchen, on the hill. The following names (read tentatively) are engraved:—(*a*) A.D. Kiergr $\frac{A}{m}$ $\frac{1}{d}$ 1666; (*b*) C. J. Keys, Price, ...Gyfford; (*c*)............H. C. Rabel, 89 Alack, L. Gray,.........Anne; (*d*) H. Dubon 1749; (*e*) .... vkerck; (*f*) T. Campic............; (*g*) D. V. A. S.; (*h*) J. A. Van Braam Nederld Commisss XX Febry MDCCCXIII, C/40 I.S. Peelman; (*i*) N. D. Jong Heere 1749; (*j*) 85 T. Poughion, 35; (*k*) P. E. Van Hogendrop, A. Vandenbroek; (See Cotton's *Tombs*, p. 187, No. 1006). A.M.E., L. Brachi-1793, M. Dormx, Wed. L. Aag............ C.W. Cantervisscher 179............; (*l*) W. Van Somesen..............; P. St. Paul, C. J. Kevsersg, 1750, C. P. Keller'; (*m*) Lucas, L. Hemsinck......... $\frac{8}{m}$ $\frac{18}{d}$ 1662. [The last was either the chief at Sadraspatam from A.D. 1666 to 1686 or an engineer of that name who died in 1661. See *Ep. Rep.*, 1912, p. 92, for details.]

192. 330 *of* 1911.—(Roman characters.) On the wall of the temple kitchen on the same hill. Perhaps damaged at the right end. Registers the names:—W. Silves, H. Stee............5.

193. 331 *of* 1911.—(Roman characters.) On the west wall of a ruined maṇṭapa in the north main street of the same village. "Geo: Dawson lived in this Choy. Fm. 18 October to 9 December 1769." Dawson was a Madras civilian. Entered the Company's service in 1751. Member of Madras Council, 1768. Chief of Cuddalore, 1769. Returned to England, 1776. See *Ep. Rep.*, 1912, p. 92.

193-A. On the south wall of the gate in the temple of Bhaktavatsalasvāmi. Records that one Toṇḍamāna Rāyan purchased the village "Echencaurana" for 250 golden *paṇams* and granted it to the God in Vibhava. *Ins., Ced. Dts.*, p. 158, No. 1.

193-B. In the same place. Records that one Nārāyaṇadēva and another gave in the reign of Virupaṇṇa Uḍaiyār the village of Vampaṭṭu (?) for 1,360 *paṇams*. *Ibid.*, No. 2.

193-C. On the south wall of the gate of Bhaktavatsala temple. Records that in the same reign, in Vibhava, 53 *vēlis* of land in a village were sold for 1,560 *paṇams*. *Ibid.*, No. 3.

193-D. In the same place. Records that Vīra Kampaṇa Uḍaiyār levied on the local weavers a tax of 70 *paṇams* per annum, to be paid to the deity. *Ibid.*, No. 4.

193-E. In the same place. Records that in the reign of Vīra Bukkaṇa-Uḍaiyār, in Naḷa, certain allowances were made to the deity. *Ibid.*, No. 5.

193-F. On the southern surrounding wall. Records that Tillaimūvāyiranambi and his brother Rāmabhaṭṭa purchased four *patakam* of land for 100 *kāśus* and granted it to the God Tirukkaḻukkunṟa Nāyanār in the twenty-fifth year of Kulōttuṅgachōḷa. *Ibid.*, No. 7.

193-G. In the same place in the same wall. Records that in the same year of the same king one Kanakarāya granted 90 sheep for ghee at the rate of ¼ measure daily. *Ins., Ced. Dts.*, p. 158, No. 9.

193-H. On the eastern wall of the gate of the kitchen in the Bhaktavatsala shrine. Records in the reign of Dēvarāya the sale of 3¾ *karai* of land at Kottappākkam for 820 *paṇams* and its endowment to the deity. *Ibid.*, p. 173, No. 17.

193-J. On the northern prākāra wall. Records that Tiruveṇkaṭṭu-Uḍaiyān granted 550 *kuḻis* of land to the deity in the twenty-first year of Tribhuvanavīradēva (Kulōttuṅga III). *Ibid.*, p. 173, No. 18.

193-K. On a stone in the tank of Śaṅkha-tīrtham. Records that Kulōttuṅga-Chōḷadēva granted in his third year 32 *vēlis* of land in the village of Kulōttuṅgachōḷa-Nellōre. *Ibid.*, p. 175, No. 23.

193-L. In the prākāra of the pagoda on the top of the hill. Records that a certain chief erected the maṇṭapam in front of the Vēdagirīsvāmi temple. *Ibid.*, p. 175, No. 24.

193-M. On the south wall of the inner temple. Records the presentation of a jewel to the God by a private person. *Ibid.*, p. 176, No. 25.

193-N. On a gate step of the Vināyaka temple in the southern wall of Vēdagirīśvara temple. Records that one Sūryadēva of Pūvinūr village erected the steps to ascend the hill and the pagoda of Vināyaka. *Ibid.*, p. 176, No. 26.

193-P. On the western wall of the maṇṭapam of the Amman shrine. Records the gift of the village of Amaranputtūr for the Āvaṇi festival by the inhabitants of a village to God Ādichandrēśvara. *Ibid.*, p. 177, No. 27.

*Tiruppōrūr.**

194. *76 of* 1909.—(Pallava-Grantha.) On two pillars in maṇṭapa in front of the Dēvayāna-amman shrine in the Kandasvāmin temple. Records the birudas of the Pallava king Rājasimha (Narasimhavarman II).

194-A. On a surrounding wall of the Goddess in the Subramaṇya temple. Records that in the reign of Kō-Parakēsarivarman it was ordered that the people of Chaturvēdimaṅgalam should pay to the temple one *kalam* of grain, ¾ measure of oil and four measures of rice per day and to give the rest of the rent in charity for twelve Brahmans. *Ins., S. Dts.*, p. 184, No. 1.

194-B. On the downstair of above. Records that Goppaṇarāya (?) gave 1,000 *kuḻis* of land to God Subramaṇya. *Ibid.*, No. 2.

* The Mackenzie Inscriptions of this place have been summarised in *Ins., S. Dts.*, p. 184-f and *Rais. Catal.*, III, p. 343. They have been included in the text under Nos. 194-A—194-D.

194-C. Below the above inscription. Records that Vijayagaṇḍagōpāla gave in the fifteenth year of his reign some cows to Subramaṇya. *Ins., S. Dts.*, p. 184, No. 3.

194-D. Below the above inscription. Records that Vikramachōḷa (1118—35) gave some land to the same deity in the village of Panaippākkam. *Ibid.* No. 4.

*Tiruvaḍandai.**

One of the 108 sacred places of Vaishṇavism mentioned in the Prabandhas. Its antiquity is further proved by its epigraphs of the time previous to that of Rājarāja I, — of Rājakēsarivarmans, Parakēsarivarmans, Pārthivēndravarman, the Rāshṭrakūṭa (Kṛishṇa III), etc. In the time of the Pāṇḍya kings it was called Asurakulakālanallūr.

195. 258 *of* 1910.—(Tamil.) On the south wall of the central shrine in the Varāha-Perumāḷ temple. A record of the Chōḷa king Rājakēsarivarman *alias* Uḍaiyār śrī-Vijayarājēndradēva (Rājādhirāja I, 1018—1052) in his thirty-fifth year, relating gift of the village of Tiruvaḍandai to the God of the village. The village is stated to have belonged to Paḍuvūr-nāḍu, a subdivision of Kalyāṇapuraṅgoṇḍaśōḷa-kōṭṭam in Jayaṅgoṇḍachōḷa-maṇḍalam. Mentions a number (70) of officers in the king's service. [The name of the Kōṭṭam shows that the king was the conqueror Kalyāṇapura. The Kōnērirājapuram inscriptions also give this and other *birudas*. The inscription says that the income from the tax on oilmills (Śekkiṟai), viniyōga, looms (தறியிறை), on smiths (தட்டாரப்பாட்டம்), etc., was to be utilized in the celebration of festivals on the day of Pūrvaphalguni, the king's constellation.

196. 259 *of* 1910.—(Tamil.) On the same wall. An unfinished record of the Chōḷa king Rājakēsarivarman *alias* Uḍaiyār śrī-Vīrarājēndradēva (I ? 1063—70), dated in his sixth year. Mentions the residents of Kōmaḷam (Covelong) *alias* Vīraśōḷapaṭṭiṇam in Paḍuvūr-nāḍu, a subdivision of Āmūr-kōṭṭam.

197. 260 *of* 1910.—(Tamil.) On the same wall. Records in the twenty-ninth year of the Chōḷa king Rājakēśarivarman (Rājarāja I) that the residents of Taiyūr in Kumiḻi-nāḍu, a subdivision of Āmūr-kōṭṭam, received 15 *kaḻañju* of gold from a merchant of Koḍungālūr (Cranganore) in Malaināḍu, and agreed to pay interest in paddy 24 kalams, 2 tūṇis, 1 padakku nānāḻi every year (details of feeding interesting) to the temple of Āḻvār at Tiruviḍavandai in order to feed 30 Brāhmaṇas.

198. 261 *of* 1910.—(Tamil.) On the same wall. Records in the eighth year of the Chōḷa king Rājakēsarivarman (Rājarāja I)

---

* The *Mack. MSS.* (*Ins., S. Dts.*, pp. 185-6, Nos 8-12 and *Rais. Catal.*, III, p. 343) give in five inscriptions in this village, and they seem to be included in the above.

gift of money by a merchant of Mayilarppil (Mylāpore), in Puliyūr-kōṭṭam, to the shrine of the goddess (Bhaṭṭāraki) in the temple of Āḷvār Varāhadēva at Tiruviḍavandai, from the interest on which oil was supplied to feed a perpetual lamp, by the assembly and the residents of Tiruviḍavandai.

199. 262 *of* 1910.—(Tamil.) On the same wall. Dated in the third year of the Chōḷa king Rājakēsarivarman. Records gift of 15 *kaḷanju* of gold (*Urukkuchchemmaipon*) by a merchant of Ālaiyur in Śōṇāḍu, from the interest on which the residents of Māḍambākkam *alias* Anuttiramaṅgalam, in Neḍuṅgunṟa-nāḍu of Puliyūr-kōṭṭam, agreed to supply oil (one *uḷakku* every day) for a perpetual lamp to burn in the temple at Tiruviḍavandai. [The penalty was 8¼ *kāṇam* for failure. This had to be paid to the Council of Justice (*Dharmaśāsana*), besides one *manjāḍi* of gold to the king.]

200. 263 *of* 1910.—(Tamil.) On the north base of the same shrine. Dated in the fourth year of the Chōḷa king Rājakēsarivarman. Records gift of 20 *kaḷañju* of gold (*tuḷainiṟaipon*) by a merchant of Purushōttamamaṅgalam in Vaḷḷuva-nāḍu, a district of Malai-nāḍu, for a perpetual lamp to be burnt in the temple of Varāhadēva, from the oil supplied as interest on the amount by the residents of Paḍuvūr in Paḍuvūr-nāḍu, a district of Āmūr-kōṭṭam. [The penalty for failure was a fine of 4¼ *kāṇam*.]

201. 264 *of* 1910.—(Tamil.) On the same base. Records in the eighth year of Rājamārāyar "who took the head of the Vīra-Pāṇḍya," gift of the image of Maṇavāḷapperumāḷ to the temple of Varāhasvāmin by two Brāhmaṇa residents of Talaiśayanapuram *alias* Taiyūr; and also of gold for offerings by the same two individuals. [Rajamārayar, says Mr. Krishna Sastri, was evidently the same as Pārthivēndravarman, the feudatory of Parāntaka I. The Talaśayana temple of Taiyūr was of course different from that of Māvalivaram. *Ins., S. Dts.*, p. 186, No. 11.]

202. 265 *of* 1910.—(Tamil.) On the same base. Records in the eighth year of Pārthivēndrādivarman gift of 93 sheep for a lamp to the temple of Varāhadēva at Tiruviḍavandai by a resident of Talaiśayanapuram *alias* Taiyūr. See *Ins., S. Dts.*, p. 187, No. 12.

203. 266 *of* 1910.—(Tamil.) On the same base. Records in the ninth year of the Chōḷa king Rājakēsarivarman gift of 48 sheep for a half-lamp to the same temple.

204. 267 *of* 1910.—(Tamil.) On the same base. Records in the nineteenth year of the Chōḷa king Rājakēsarivarman *alias* Uḍaiyār Śrī-Rājarājadēva (I) gift of 30 *kaḷañju* of gold by a merchant of Tiruvoṟṟiyūr in Puḷarkōṭṭam, to the same temple. The residents of Taiyūr, on receiving this amount, agreed to pay as interest 90 *nāḷis* of oil and 20 *kalams* of paddy by *Kachchipāḍu-ninṟān marakāl*, to the assembly of Tiruviḍavandai for burning a lamp in the temple and feeding 35 Brāhmaṇas after Paṅguni uttira dvajārōhaṇa.

205. 268 *of* 1910.—(Tamil.) On the same base. Records in the fourth year of the Chōḷa king Parakēsarivarman gift of 30 *kaḻanju* of gold by a native of Vaḍagarai Innambar in Śōṇāḍu. The money was received by the residents of Tiruviḍavandai who agreed to burn a perpetual lamp in the temple of Maṇavāḷap-perumāḷ, for which they had to give 90 *nāḻis* of oil as the interest on the 30 *kaḻanjus*. The stipulation was definitely made that it was to be in kind alone and that irregularity in supply meant a daily fine of 4¼ *kāṇam* to the council of justice and one *manjāḍi* to the king. The inscription also tells us that the worship in the temple was controlled and regulated by a committee called *Unnāḻigaivāriyam*.

206. 269 *of* 1910.—(Tamil.) On the same base. Records in the sixth year of Parakēsari Vēndirādivarman gift of 12 *kaḻanju* of gold for a lamp by a native of Taiyūr. [The king was perhaps the same as the Pārthivēndravarman who took the head of Vīra Pāṇḍya and whose inscriptions are found in North Arcot, South Arcot and Chingleput districts.]

207. 270 *of* 1910.—(Tamil.) On the same base. Records in the twentieth year of the Rāshṭrakūṭa king Kaṇṇaradēva, "who took kachchi and Tañjai," gift of land for a lamp to the temple of Varāhadēva, where the wife of a certain Ālattūḷān Raṇakēsari of Paḍuvūr had set up an image.

208. 271 *of* 1910.—(Tamil.) On the north wall of the same shrine. An unfinished historical introduction of Vīrarājēndradēva I (1063--70) commencing with the words *tiruvaḷar*.

209. 272 *of* 1910.—(Tamil.) On the same wall. Records in the twenty-seventh year of the Chōḷa king Rājakēsarivarman *alias* Rājarājadēva (I) gift of land for offerings to the same temple by the residents of Taiyūr *alias* Rājakēsarinallūr in Kumiḻi-nāḍu, a subdivision of Āmūr-kōṭṭam, which was a district of Jayaṅgoṇḍachōḷa-maṇḍalam.

210. 273 *of* 1910.—(Tamil.) On the same wall. Records in the nineteenth year of the Chōḷa king Rājakēsarivarman (Rājarāja I) gift of 16⅛ *kaḻanju* of gold by a merchant of Kaḍarpārpaḷḷi in Malai-nāḍu for feeding 12 Brāhmaṇas in the same temple for 30 days in the month of Kumbha. [The detailed cost of feeding 12 Brāhmanas a day is given. The inscription is also given in *Ins. S. Dts.*, p. 186, No. 9.

211. 274 *of* 1910.—(Tamil.) On the west base of the same shrine. Records in the seventeenth year of the Chōḷa king Rājakēsarivarman (Rājarāja I) dedication of 12 families (*kuḍis*) of *Paṭṭinavas* (fishermen) for conducting a seven-day festival called Rājarājadēvar-tirunāḷ which fell on the nakshatra *Śatabhishaj* in the month of Āvaṇi, evidently the king's constellation. The 12 families were to pay a tax of ¾ *kaḷanju* per head earned by them "either by weaving or by venturing on the sea (to fish ?)." The orders were signed by the overseers of the district (*Nāḍukaṇkātchi* and the *nāḍuvagai*.)

212. 275 *of* 1910.—(Tamil.) On the same base. Records in the second year of the Chōḷa king Rājakēsarivarman *alias* Uḍaiyār Śrī-Rājamahēndradēva gift of 90 sheep for a lamp by a native of Śirudavūr.

213. 276 *of* 1910.—(Tamil.) On the south wall of the maṇṭapa in front of the same shrine. An unfinished record of the Pāṇḍya king Jaṭāvarman Tribhuvanachakravartin Vīra-Pāṇḍyadēva, (who came to the throne in 1253), dated in his thirteenth year. Records gift of land at Karaivaḷi Nenmali by the inhabitants of Āyiravēli-paṟṟu, to the shrine of the goddess in the temple of Varāha-Nāyanār at Asurakulakālanallūr *alias* Tiruviḍavanda, for maintaining a worship established there by a native of Nerkunṟam in Mēlūr-nāḍu which was a subdivision of Kulōttuṅgaśōḷa-vaḷanāḍu.

214. 277 *of* 1910.—(Tamil.) On the same wall. Dated in the tenth year of the Paṇḍya king Māravarman Tribhuvanachakravartin Vīra Pāṇḍyadēva (unidentifiable). Records purchase of land by the temple trustees (*tānattār*), in a public auction, "under moral pressure." "Neither the residents nor the assembly of the village were prepared to bid for the land which a temple woman was forced to sell by public auction in order to pay a fine imposed on her by Kaḷiṅgarāyar, probably a minister of the king, and hence the temple had to purchase it.

215. 278 *of* 1910.—(Tamil.) On the same wall. Records in the twenty-seventh year of the Chōḷa king Rājakēsarivarman *alias* Chakravartin Śrī-Kulōttuṅga-Chōḷadēva (I ?) gift of money for offerings by a Brāhmaṇa lady of Śirudavūr.

216. 279 *of* 1910.—(Tamil.) On the same wall. A fragment of record of the Pāṇḍya king Tribhuvanachakravartin Kulaśēkharadēva, dated in his twentieth year. Records gift of land to the shrine of the goddess.

217. 280 *of* 1910.—(Tamil.) On the same wall. Records in the fifth year of the Chōḷa king Vikrama-Chōḷadēva (1118—35) gift of 9 *dramma* (i.e., *drachma* which was thus current in the twelfth century) for a lamp, by a resident of Satyāśrayakulakāla-chaturvēdimaṅgalam in Kaḷattūr-kōṭṭam, named evidently after Vikrama-Chōḷa's victory over the West Chāḷukyan Satyāśraya.

218. 281 *of* 1910.—(Tamil.) On the same wall. Records in the forty-fifth year of the Chōḷa king Rājakēsarivarman *alias* Chakravartin Śrī-Kulōttuṅga-Chōḷadēva (I) gift of paddy by a native of Tirumaṅgalam, a village in Puḷal-nāḍu which was a subdivision of Puḷār-kōṭṭam *alias* Rājēndraśōḷa-vaḷanāḍu, for feeding 50 Brāhmaṇas in the Vaishṇava maṭh *Kalichchiṅgan-maḍam*, erected by the residents of Tiruviḍavandai.

219. 282 *of* 1910.—(Tamil.) On the same wall. A fragment of record of the Chōḷa king Parakēsarivarman *alias* Chakravartin Vikrama-Chōḷadēva (1118–35), date of which is lost. Seems to record a gift by a Brāhmaṇa lady. Mentions Śembūr-kōṭṭam.

220. 283 *of* 1910.—(Tamil.) On the north wall of the same maṇṭapa. Records in the forty-third year of the Chōḷa king Rājakēsarivarman *alias* Chakravartin śrī-Kulōttuṅga-Chōḷadēva (I) gift of paddy for feeding 12 itinerant *(apūrvi)* Brāhmaṇas, by a native of Vāmanamaṅgai in Tiruvaḷundūr-nādu, a subdivision of Rājanārāyaṇa-vaḷanāḍu, which was a district of Chōḷamaṇḍalam.

Tiruvadisulam.

221. 335 *of* 1908.—(Tamil.) On the north wall of the central shrine in the Jñānapurīśvara temple. A record of the Chōḷa king Kulōttuṅga-Chōḷadēva relating in his sixteenth year, gift of twelve sheep for a lāmp to the temple of Āḷudaiyār Tiruviḍaichchuramuḍaiya Nāyanār in Vallanāḍu, a subdivision of Kaḷattūr-kōṭṭam in Jayaṅgoṇḍa-Chōḷamaṇḍalam.

222. 336 *of* 1908.—(Tamil.) On the same wall. A record of Kōnērinmaikoṇḍān in his fifth year relating gift of the two villages of Perundenbākkam in Vaḷḷa-nāḍu, a subdivision of Kaḷattūr-kōṭṭam and Mēl Perundenbākkam in Āmūr-kōṭṭam.

223. 337 *of* 1908.—(Tamil.) On the west wall of the same shrine. Dated in the reign of the Vijayanagara king Vīrapratāpa, Achyutadēva Mahārāya, "who was pleased to witness the elephant hunt." Records in Ś. 1455, Nandana, gift of money for offerings and lamps to the temple of Nāḍu-vāriyum-Tambirānār at Tiruviḍaichchuram by the mahāmaṇḍalēśvara Kumāra-Jalakarāja Tirumalayadēva Mahārāya, for the merit of the king. Mentions Śeṅgaḷunīrpaṭṭu-śīrmai (i.e.), the Chingleput country.

224. 338 *of* 1908.—(Tamil.) On the west and south walls of the same shrine. A record of the Chōḷa king Parakēsarivarman *alias* Tribhuvanachakravartin Vikrama-Chōḷadēva (1118–35) relating gift of land for two lamps.

225. 339 *of* 1908.—(Tamil.) On the south wall of the same shrine. Records in the tenth year of the Chōḷa king Vikrama-Chōḷadēva (1118–35) gift of 12 sheep for a lamp by a native of Pulipākkam. Mentions Paḷḷapuram in Puliyūr-kōṭṭam.

226. 340 *of* 1908.—(Tamil.) On the same wall. Records in the forty-seventh year of the Chōḷa king Rājakēsarivarman *alias* Tribhuvanachakravartin Kulōttuṅga-Chōḷadēva (I) a grant of land in the village of Tiruviḍaichchuram to the temple of Tiruviḍaichchuram Uḍaiyār, by a native of Kaḷattūr. Mentions Vallam *alias*

Jayaṅgoṇḍaśōḷanallūr in Vallanāḍu. Begins with the historical introduction *pugaḷ-śūḻnda puviyil*, etc.

227. 341 *of* 1908.—(Tamil.) On the same wall. Records in the fourth year of the Chōḷa Chakravartin Kulōttuṅga Chōḷadēva (I, 1070—1118) gift of land.

228. 342 *of* 1908.—(Tamil.) On the east wall of the same shrine. A record of the Pallava king Peruñjiṅgadēva in his fourteenth year relating gift of three cows for a lamp. Mentions Piḷḷaiyār Nīlagaṅgaraiyar. Built in at the beginning.

229. 343 *of* 1908.—(Tamil.) On the same wall. A record of the Vijayanagara king Viruppaṇa Uḍaiyār in Pramōda relating gift of three cows for a lamp. Mentions Piḷḷaiyār Nīlagaṅgaraiyar; also the districts Kaḷattūrpaṟṟu, Tirukkaḻukkunṟappaṟṟu and Āyiravēlippaṟṟu. Built in at the beginning.

230. 344 *of* 1908.—(Tamil.) On the east wall of the maṇṭapa in front of the same shrine. A record of the Vijayanagara king Bukkaṇa Uḍaiyār, son of . . . Uḍaiyār in Vikrama relating gift of a lamp. Some slabs on the right side of the inscription appear to have been removed and replaced by others. Mentions Iraṇḍāyiravēlippaṟṟu in Kaḷattūr-kōṭṭam.

231. 345 *of* 1908.—(Tamil.) On the west wall of the same maṇṭapa. A much damaged record of the Vijayanagara king Kumāra Vijaya-Uḍaiyār, son of Vīra Dēvarāya (I), dated Jaya. Seems to record a gift of land.

232. 346 *of* 1908.—(Tamil.) On the east wall of the Gōvardanāmbāḷ shrine in the same village. Records that a native of Perundaṇḍālam built a shrine and set up the image of the goddess Tirukkāmakkōṭṭamuḍaiya-Periyanāchchiyār in the temple of Tiruviḍaichchuramuḍaiya-Nāyaṉār.

233. 347 *of* 1908.—(Tamil.) On the west wall of the same shrine. An unfinished record of Tirubhuvanachakravartin Vijayagaṇḍagōpāladēva, dated fourth year. Seems to record the gift of a lamp to the shrine of the same goddess.

Uḷalūr.

234. 17 *of* 1899.—(Tamil.) On a slab. Dated in the time of the Pallava king Nandipōttaraiyar. Records a granṭ by the villagers of Uḷalūr. Nandipōttaraiyar was Nandivarman Pallavamalla, the opponent of the Western Chāḷukyan king Vikramāditya II. See *S.I. Inscrns.* I, p. 145. This Nandipōttaraiyar is different from the conqueror of his enemies at Teḷḷāru, who was the hero of the Tamil poem *Nandikkalambagam* and the patron of the poet Perundēvanār, the author of the *Bhārata veṇba* who refers to him in his invocatory verses of the Uttiyōgaparva. The invocatory verses prefixed to the Tamil works *Puranānūru*, *Aganānūru*, *Naṟṟuṇai*,

Kaṛundogai and *Aiṅgurunūru* are believed to have been composed by the same Perundēvanār and so these anthologies must have been compiled in the time of the same king.

Unamañjēri.

234-A. A C.P. grant (Sanskrit language in Nandināgari script) of Achyuta Rāya of Vijayanagar, dated Ś. 1462 (expired), Sārvari, the twelfth of the bright half of Kārttika corresponding, according to Dr. Kielhorn, to the 12th October A.D. 1540. Records that the king granted the village of Uhinai or Achyutarāyēndrapuram in the Śeṅkaḷanīrpaṭṭu-śīma of the Kumuḷi-nāḍu in Raṇḍāyiramahāvaḷipaṭṭu of Amūr-kōṭṭam in Paḍavīḍu Rājya, in Jayaṅkoṇḍachōḷamaṇḍalam, at the request of his minister Virūpāksha Nāik, to a number of Brahmans. The gōtras, vēdaśākhas, etc., of the latter are given, together with their parentage, their *vrittis* or shares, etc. See *Ep. Ind.*, III, 147—58, where Dr. Kielhorn edits the plate.

Uragaḍam.

235. 248 *of* 1913.—(Tamil.) On the south base of the Kōdaṇḍarāmasvāmin temple. Records in Vrisha, Paṅguni, fourth day, gift of thirty *paṇam*, for the celebration of a festival in the temple of Raghunātha-Perumāḷ in the month of Āvaṇi, by Achchama, (wife of) Pattaṅgi Appaiyaṅgār.

236. 249 *of* 1913.—(Tamil.) On the same base. Records in Chitrabhānu, Āvaṇi, twenty-fourth day, gift of land and money (400 *paṇam*) by Āchāḷ, wife of Agari Aṇṇaṅgār, to the temple of Chakravartitirumuganār at agaram Uragaḍam *alias* Śrī-Parāṅkuśapuram.

237. 250 *of* 1913.—(Tamil.) On the north base of the same temple. Records in Śrīmukha, Vaigāśi, twenty-eighth day, gift of land by a certain Nallarāyan, son of Karambacheṭṭu Varadarāśan, to Raghunātha-Perumāḷ at the same village, for conducting the Srī-Rāmanavami festival.

238. 251 *of* 1913.—(Tamil.) On a rock to the south of the Vaḍamallīśvara temple, in the same village. A much damaged record of the Chōḷa king Rājakēsarivarman, dated in his seventh year.

239. 252 *of* 1913.—(Tamil.) On a rock to the west of the same temple. A damaged record of the Chōḷa king Parakēsarivarman *alias* Rājēndra-Chōḷadēva (I), dated in his fourth year. Records gift of sheep for a lamp by a certain Kāttan Kampanāḷi to the temple of Tiruvaḍamalaiāḷvār at Uragaḍam *alias* Pallavamalla-Chaturvēdimaṅgalam (named evidently after Nandivarman II, Pallavamalla), a village in Kaḷattūr-nāḍu, which was a subdivision of Kaḷattūr-kōṭṭam, a district of Jayaṅgoṇḍaśōḷamaṇḍalam.

Urattūr.

240. 256 *of* 1910.—(Tamil.) On the base of the Agastyēśvara temple. A record of the Vijayanagara king Vīrapratāpa Achyutayyadēva Mahārāya in Ś. 1451, Vikriti, relating gift of the village of Panaittaṅgal, a hamlet of Urattūr in . . . a subdivision of Iraṇḍāyiravēlipaṟṟu *alias* Seṅgāṭṭu-kōṭṭam in Jayaṅgoṇḍachōḻa-maṇḍalam, to the temple of Tiruvagattīśuramuḍaiya-Tambirānār, for the merit of Śellappar *alias* Vīra-Naraśiṅgarāyanāyaka Śāḷuva-Daṇṇāyakkar. Vīra-Naraśiṅga has been identified with Nuniz's Salavanaque who 'held very large territory bordering on Ceylon. The *Achyutarāyābhyudaya* gives the name Chellappa to the Chōḷa feudatory who was the cause of Achyuta's campaign of 1532. See my article in *Ind. Antq.*, 1914.

241. 257 *of* 1910.—(Telugu.) On a slab set up in the same temple. Records in Ś. 1735, and Kali 4914, Śrīmukha, that maṇṭapas, gōpuras, gardens, images, etc., were built in the Śiva and Vishṇu temples at Urattūr, by a certain Avanigaḍḍala Paṭṭābhirāmuḍu.

Vallam.

242. 185 *of* 1892.—(Tamil.) On two pillars in the cave temple. A record of the Pallava king Mahēndra Pōtarāja *alias* Guṇabhara. See *S.I.I.*, II, No. 72. Venkayya believes that Guṇabhara (in the form of Guṇadhara) is referred to as the patron of Appar in the *Periapurāṇa* and as Appar was an elder contemporary of Gñānasambanda who lived in the time of Narasimhavarman I, he infers that Guṇabhara was Narasimha's father Mahēndravarman I. Appar and Sambanda were thus the respective contemporaries of the father and son Mahēndravarman I and Narasimhavarman I. See *Ep. Ind.*, III, p. 278. Mahēndravarman was also excavator of the Trichinopoly and other rock-cut temples.

243. 186 *of* 1892.—(Tamil.) On a pillar in the same temple. A record of Sakalabhuvanachakravartin Kōpperuñjiṅgadēva in his fourteenth year relating gift of a lamp to the temple of Vasantēśvara, at Vallam in Vallanāḍu, a subdivision of Kaḷattūr- kōṭṭam.

Vaḷuvadūr.

244. 326 *of* 1911.—(Tamil.) On the south wall of the central shrine in the Agnīśvara temple. Records in the thirteenth year of the Pāṇḍya king Jaṭāvarman *alias* Tribhuvanachakravartin Sundara-Pāṇḍyadēva that eleven lamps were burnt by Brāhmaṇas who had borrowed small amounts of money from the treasury, in the temple of Tiruvagnīśvaramuḍaiya Nāyanār at Vaivaḷudūr.

245. 327 *of* 1911.—(Tamil.) On the west wall of the same shrine. Records gift of money for six lamps to the same temple.

246. 328 *of* 1911.—(Tamil.) On a stone set up at Mūnṟukallu-mōḍu near the same village. Mentions Tirukkaḷukkunṟam in Kaḷattūr-kōṭṭam, a subdivision of Jayaṅgoṇḍachōḷamaṇḍalam, and perhaps also the temple of Tirumalai-Āḷuḍaiyasvāmin of that village.

Vēdanārāyaṇapuram.

247. 618 *of* 1904.—(Tamil.) On the slopes of the hill. Mentions in Kīlaka a certain Daḷavāy-Nāyakkar. In modern characters.

CONJEEVERAM TALUK.

Ārpākkam.

248. 20 *of* 1899.—(Tamil.) On the south wall of the central shrine in the Tiruvālīśvara temple. A record of the Chōḷa king Parakēsarivarman *alias* Tribhuvanachakravartin Rājādhirājadēva, dated in his fifth year. [The inscription is very important as it confirms the Sinhalese expedition against the Pāṇḍya country in the twelfth century. "It sets forth that the army of Ceylon having taken possession of the Pāṇḍyan country, drove away king Kulaśēkhara, who was then in Madura and then began (?) to fight in battle with the feudatories of the great king Śrī-Rājādhirājadēva;" that the danger of the spreading of the war into the districts of Toṇḍi and Pāśi struck terror into the hearts of the people of the Chōḷa country; that Edirili-Śōḷa-Śambuvarāyan went near the sacred feet of "Svāmidēvar" and requested him to avoid the calamity by prayers, oblations and worship; and that, as the result of his worship of Śiva for 28 days, the Sinhalese generals Jayadratha Daṇḍanāyaka, Laṅkāpuri Daṇḍanāyaka, etc., fled. Śambuvarāyan in gratitude gave the village of Arpākkam to the Svāmi who, in his turn, distributed the income from the village among his relations. The Svāmi was Umāpati dēva *alias* Jñāna-Śiva dēva, a native of Dakshiṇa Lāṭa in Gauḍa-dēśa. Venkayyah believes that the Edirili-Sōḷa-Śambuvarāyan mentioned here must have been an ancestor of Aḷagia Śōḷan of the Poygai inscriptions of Rājarāja III (See *S.I.I.*, Vol. I, 86 ff); that his solicitude for success arose from the fact that his son Pallavarāya was the Chōḷa general and that he was a devotee of Śiva and the Brāhmaṇas whose enemies the invaders were, as is seen in their removal of the sacred door and treasure of the Rāmēśvaram temple. Venkayyah compares the account of this inscription with the Sinhalese chronicle and points out that the invasion should be attributed to the third quarter of the twelfth century. See *Madr. Ep. Rep.*, 1899, pp. 8—13. For the continuation of the war under Kulōttuṅga III see inscription 3 of 1899 (Ālaṅguḍi, in Tanjore District), and 1 of 1899 (Tirukkoḷḷambūdūr).]

Conjeeveram.

The history of Conjeeveram can hardly be attempted here. See *Antiquities*, I, pp. 176–77, and bibliography given therein. For political, religious and literary history of the land it is unequalled in interest. The inscriptions of this place collected by Colonel Mackenzie have been enumerated and summarised by Rev. Taylor in his *Rais. Catal.*, III, pp. 329—41, and number 140 (three however belonging to Śrīperumbudūr). I have not endeavoured to compare this list with the departmental list. The original Mack. MS. containing them (No. 845, old Nos. 50 C.M. 1019) is missing. Another list, made by Sir Walter Elliot, is given in *Antiquities* I, pp. 178—87, and contains 283 epigraphs. I have not thought it necessary to examine them as the departmental list is not yet complete and so a proper comparison is impossible at this stage.

249. 1 *of* 1888.—(Sanskrit.) Round Rājasimhēśvara shrine in the Kailāsanātha temple. A record of Rājasimha (Narasimhavarman II) its builder. See *S.I.I.*, I, No. 24, pp. 12—14.

250. 2 *of* 1888.—(Sanskrit.) Inside prākāra of the Rājasimhēśvara shrine in the Kailāsanātha temple, first to third tiers. A record of Rājasimha; in Pallava characters. See *S.I.I.*, Vol. I, No. 25, pp. 14—21. The record gives a string of titles of the king (Narasimhavarman II).

251. 3 *of* 1888.—(Sanskrit.) Inside prākāra of Rājasimhēśvara shrine in the Kailāsanātha temple, fourth tier. A record of the same king. See *S.I.I.*, Vol. I, No. 26, pp. 21—22.

252. 4 *of* 1888.—(Sanskrit.) Round Mahēndravarmēśvara shrine in the Kailāsanātha temple. A record of Mahēndra, son of Rājasimha. See *S.I.I.*, Vol. I, No. 27, pp. 22—23. The record is to the effect that Mahēndravarman built a shrine in his own name near that of Rājasimhēśvara.

253. 5 *of* 1888.—(Sanskrit.) First niche to the right of front entrance. A record in Pallava characters, saying that it is the temple of Nityavinītēśvara. See *S.I.I.*, Vol. I, No. 28, p. 23.

254. 6 *of* 1888.—(3 Sanskrit verses.) Third niche to the right of front entrance. A record of Raṅgapatāka (queen of Narasimha vishṇu) in Pallava characters. [*Ibid*, No. 29, pp. 23—24.]

255. 7 *of* 1888.—(Sanskrit.) Fifth niche to the right of front entrance. A record in Pallava characters, of a queen. [*Ibid*, No. 30, p. 24.]

256. 8 *of* 1888.—(Kanarese.) On the back of a pillar in the maṇṭapa in front of Rājasimhēśvara shrine in the Kailāsanātha temple in the same place. A record of the W. Chāḷukyan Vikramāditya (II). Records that, after his conquest of Conjeeveram, Vikramāditya Satyāśraya did not confiscate the property of the Rājasimhēśvara temple, but returned it. See *Ep. Ind.*, III, pp. 359—60.

257. 9 *of* 1888.—(Tamil and Grantha.) Inside Rājasimhēśvara shrine in the Kailāsanātha temple. A record of Madiraikoṇḍa Kō-Parakēsarivarman. Seems to record an agreement of the people of two *Śēris* of Conjeeveram. *S.I.I.*, I, No. 145, pp. 139—40.

258. 10 *of* 1888.—(Tamil and Grantha.) Inside Rājasimhēś-vara shrine in the Kailāsanātha temple. A record of Kō-Rāja-kēsarivarman. Records an agreement made by the Sabhā of some village to furnish daily one *uḻakkū* of oil for a lamp as interest for fifteen kaḻañjus of gold deposited with it. *S.I.I.*, I, No. 147, pp. 140—41.

259. 11 *of* 1888.—(Tamil and Grantha.) Inside Rājasimhēś-vara shrine in the Kailāsanātha temple. A fragment of record in Śanskrit. Dānārṇavanripa mentioned.

260. 12 *of* 1888.—(Tamil and Grantha.) Inside mahāmaṇṭapa of Rājasimhēśvara shrine in the Kailāsanātha temple.

261 & 262. 13 *and* 14 *of* 1888.—(Sanskrit.) Inside mahā-maṇṭapa of Rājasimhēśvara shrine in the Kailāsanātha temple. A fragment of record.

263. 15 *of* 1888.—(Sanskrit.) Inside mahāmaṇṭapa of Rāja-simhēśvara shrine in the Kailāsanātha temple. A fragmentary record. Chōḻa-Trinētra mentioned.

264. 16 *of* 1888.—(Tamil and Grantha.) Inside mahāmaṇṭapa of Rājasimhēśvara shrine in the Kailāsanātha temple. A record in the fifteenth year of Kō-Parakēsarivarman. Contains an agreement made by the inhabitants of some village to pay for a lamp (one uḻakku per day and 7 *nāḻis* and 1 *uri* per mensem) as interest for a sum of money deposited with it by the temple authorities. *S.I.I.*, I, No. 148, pp. 141—42.

265. 17 *of* 1888.—(Tamil and Grantha.) Inside mahāmaṇṭapa of Rājasimhēśvara shrine in the Kailāsanātha temple. A record of Kō-Parakēsarivarman.

266. 18 *of* 1888.—(Tamil and Grantha.) Inside mahāmaṇṭapa of Rājasimhēśvara shrine in the Kailāsanātha temple. A record in the twelfth year of Korāja-Rājakēsarivarman (I), saying that the sabhā of a village pledged itself to supply annually 140 *kāḍies* of paddy as interest for the sum of 33 kaḻanjus deposited with it, to the temple treasurers. The penalty for failure was a fine of ¼ pon daily. *S.I.I.*, I, No. 146, p. 140.

267. 19 *of* 1888.—(Sanskrit.) Inside mahāmaṇṭapa of Rāja-simhēśvara shrine in the Kailāsanātha temple. A fragmentary record.

268. 20 *of* 1888.—(Tamil and Grantha.) Inside mahāmaṇṭapa of Rājasimhēśvara shrine in the Kailāsanātha temple. A record in the third year of Kō-Rājakēsarivarman. The villagers of Maṇalūr pledge themselves to furnish oil for a lamp from the interest of 18 kaḻañjus, 3 mañjāḍis and 1 kuṉṟi of gold deposited with them by the temple treasury. The interest was 1 uḻakku of oil every day. *S.I.I.*, I, No. 84, pp. 115—16.

269. 21 *of* 1888.—(Tamil and Grantha.) At the entrance into the mahāmaṇṭapa of Rājasimhēśvara shrine in the Kailāsanātha temple. Fragment of a record.

270. 22 *of* 1888.—(Tamil and Grantha.) Round the base of the maṇṭapa in front of Rājasimhēśvara shrine in the Kailāsanātha temple. A record in the fourth year of Kō-Parakēsarivarman. Records that the villagers of Kallaḍupūr pledged themselves to furnish every year 90 kāḍis of paddy as interest for 20 kaḻañjus of gold deposited with them by Ādidāsa Chaṇḍēśvara at Tiruvottūr. *S.I.I.*, I, No. 85, pp. 1161—17.

271 & 272. 23 *and* 24 *of* 1888.—(Tamil and Grantha.) Pillars in the maṇṭapa in front of Rājasimhēśvara shrine. A record in the fifteenth year of Madiraikoṇḍa Kō-Parakēsarivarman (Parāntaka I). Record that a certain Chaṇḍaparākrama vīra gave 270 sheep for three lamps to the Rājasimhēśvara shrine. *S.I.I.*, I, Nos. 82 and 83, pp. 112—15. Certain *Mannāḍi* families undertake to provide the daily ghees.

273. 25 *of* 1888.—(Tamil and Grantha.) Pillars in the maṇṭapa in front of the Rājasimhēśvara shrine in the Kailāsanātha temple. A record in the twenty-sixth year of Tribhuvanachakravartin Rājarājadeva. Records that some person pledged himself to supply daily one āḻākku of ghee for five lamps. *S.I.I.*, I, No. 150, p. 143.

274. 26 *of* 1888.—(Tamil and Grantha.) Pillars in the maṇṭapa in front of Rājasimhēśvara shrine in the Kailāsanātha temple. A fragment of record.

275 & 276. 27 *and* 28 *of* 1888.—(Tamil and Grantha.) On the Pillars in the maṇṭapa in front of Rājasimhēśvara shrine in the Kailāsanātha temple. Records of Kampaṇa Uḍaiyār II in S. 1286 (expired), Viśvāvasu. The first records that in the time of Kulōttuṅga Chōḻa, the Rājasimhēśvara temple had been closed, its landed property sold and its environs transferred to a neighbouring shrine, and that Koppaṇaṅgal, the minister of Kampaṇa, reopened the temple and restored its property. See *S.I.I.*, I, 80, 86, pp. 117—18. The second records that with the sanction of Koppaṇaṅgaḻ, the temple authorities sold some houses in the northern row of the Sannadhi street to certain Mudalis at the price of 150 *paṇas*. See *S.I.I.*, I, No. 87, pp. 120—23.

277. 29 *of* 1888.—(Tamil and Grantha.) Pillars in the maṇṭapa in front of the Rājasimhēśvara shrine in the Kailāsanātha temple. A record in Kīlaka (Ś 1291) of Vīra-Kampaṇa-Uḍaiyār. Records that, with the sanction of Koppaṇaṅgaḻ, the temple authorities gave a maṭha near the temple and some land to a certain Gaṅgaiyar of Tirumudukuṉṟam (Vriddhāchalam ?). *S.I.I.*, I, No. 88, pp. 123—25.

278. 30 *of* 1888.—(Tamil and Grantha.) Window of the same maṇṭapa. No details.

279. 31 *of* 1888.—(Tamil and Grantha.) North wall of the same maṇṭapa. No details.

280. 32 *of* 1888.—(Sanskrit.) Round garbhagriha of the Vaikuṇṭha-Perumāḷ temple. A fragmentary record.

281. 33 *of* 1888.—(Sanskrit and Tamil.) Round garbhagriha of Vaikuṇṭha-Perumāḷ temple. Fragment of a record.

282. 34 *of* 1888.—(Tamil and Grantha.) Round garbhagriha of Vaikuṇṭha-Perumāḷ temple. A record in the seventeenth year of some mahārāja, whose name is lost. The inscription afterwards mentions Dantivarma-mahārāja. [Paramēśvaravarman II was the builder of this temple. See No. 285.]

283. 35 *of* 1888.—(Tamil and Grantha.) Round garbhagriha of Vaikuṇṭha-Perumaḷ temple. A record in the forty-sixth year of Kō-Rājakēśarivarmaṉ *alias* Chakravartin Kulōttuṅga Chōḷa-dēva (I).

284. 36 *of* 1888.—(Tamil and Grantha.) Round garbhagriha of Vaikuṇṭha-Perumāḷ temple. A record in the forty-eighth year of Ko-Rājakēsarivarman *alias* Chakravartin Kulōttuṅga Chōḷa-dēva (I).

285. 37 *of* 1888.—(Tamil and Grantha.) Inside verandah round the garbhagriha of Vaikuṇṭha-Perumāḷ temple. Hiraṇya-varma-mahārāja mentioned. For a description of the sculptures in this place and the light they throw on Pallava history see *Ep. Rep.*, 1906, pp. 62—3. Venkayya believed that they represent the events which took place at the death of Paramēśvaravarman II and the choice of Nandivarman Pallavamalla, the son of Hiraṇyavarman, as king by the people.

286. 38 *of* 1888.—(Sanskrit.) First cave from north, south wall of the temple at Māmaṇḍūr near the same place. All but illegible. See p. 381 and supplement to this district.

287. 39 *of* 1888.—(Tamil and Grantha.) Second cave from north, north wall. A record in the sixteenth year of Kō-Rājarāja-Rājakēsarivarman (I).

288. 40 *of* 1888.—(Tamil and Grantha.) Second cave from north, south wall. A record in the fifth year of Kō-Parakēsarivarman.

289. 228 *of* 1910.—(Tamil.) On the south base of the Jvarahareś-vara temple. Records in the twentieth year of Tribhuvanachakra-vartin Vijaya-Gaṇḍagōpāladēva gift of tax on looms to the temple of Śuravaṭṭāramuḍaiya Nāyanār in the city (nagaram) of Kāñchī-puram in Eyirkōṭṭam, a district of Jayaṅgoṇḍachōḷa-maṇḍalam, by the Pallava chief Tripurāśar-Nallasittarasan of Ambalūr.

290. 229 *of* 1910.—(Tamil.) On the north base of the same temple. Dated in the fifth year of the Chōḷa king Tribhuvana-chakravartin Vikrama-Chōḷadēva (1118—35). Records gift of land by Sundara-Śoḷa-vēḷār, a native of Vishāru (*alias* Kulivallanallūr) in

Virpēḍu-nāḍu, a subdivision of Kāliyūr kōṭṭam which was a district of Jayaṅgoṇḍachōḷa-maṇḍalam, to the Śuravaṭṭālamuḍaiya-Nayanar. Sundarachōḷa built a maṇṭapam and the king inspected it.

291. 230 *of* 1910.—(Tamil.) On the same base. The Vijayanagara king Kampaṇa-Uḍaiyār (II) records in Kīlaka (i.e., Ś. 1291) gift of the privilege of supervision in the temple of Śuravaḍinda Nāyanār, to a certain Aḷagiyatiruchchiṟṟambalamuḍaiyār, son of Bhuvanaikabāhudēvar.

292. 11 *of* 1895.—(Kanarese.) On a pillar in the Kailāsanātha temple. A record of the Western Chāḷukya king Vikramāditya II. Kielhorn's *Southern List* No. 43. Published in the *Epigraphia Indica*, Vol. III, page 359 f.

293. 12 *of* 1895.—(Tamil.) On a stone built into the verandah round the *garbhagriha* of the Ulagaḷanda-Perumāḷ temple, in the same place. A record of the Pallava king Teḷḷāṟṟeṟinda Nandipōttaraiyar (III), dated in his eighteenth year. Published by Mr. Venkayya in the *Madras Christian College Magazine,* Vol. VIII, page 98 ff.

294. 1 *of* 1893.—(Tamil.) South wall of the Śmaśānēśvara shrine in the Ekāmranātha temple. A record of the Chōḷa king Kō-Rājakēsarivarman *alias* Kulōttuṅga-Chōḷadēva (I), dated in his sixth year.

295. 2 *of* 1893.—(Tamil.) North wall of the second prākāra of the same temple. A record of the Kākatīya king Gaṇapati, dated Ś. 1172 expired.

296. 3 *of* 1892.—(Telugu.) North wall of the second prākāra of the same temple. A record of the Vijayanagara king Sadāṣivadeva, dated Ś. 1472, Saumya.

297. 4 *of* 1893.—(Tamil.) West wall of the second prākāra of the same temple. A record of the Chōḷa king Tribhuvanachakravartin Rājarājadēva, dated in his fifteenth year.

298. 5 (*a*) *of* 1893.—(Tamil.) West wall of the second prākāra of the same temple. A record of the Chōḷa king Tribhuvanachakravartin Rājarājadēva, dated in his nineteenth year.

299. 5 (*b*) *of* 1893.—(Tamil.) West wall of the second prākāra of the same temple. A record of the Chōḷa king Kō-Rājakēsarivarman *alias* Kulōttuṅga-Chōḷadēva, dated in his second year.

300. 6 *of* 1893.—(Tamil.) West wall of the second prākāra of the same temple. A record of the seventeenth year, of the Chōḷa king Tribhuvanachakravartin Rājarājadēva (III). Mentions Gaṇḍā-Gōpāla. See *Ep. Ind.*, VI, 282, where the date is pointed out to be Tuesday, 18th January, A.D. 1233.

301. 7 (*a*) *of* 1893.—(Tamil.) West wall of the second prākāra of the same temple. A record of the Chōḷa king Kō-Parakēsarivarman *alias* Rājādhirājadēva (?), dated in his second year.

302. 7 (*b*) *of* 1893.—(Tamil.) West wall of the second prākāra of the same temple. A record of the Chōḷa king Rājarājadēva, dated in his nineteenth year.

303. 7 (*c*) *of* 1893.—(Tamil.) West wall of the second prākāra of the same temple. A record of the Chōḷa king Tribhuvanachakravartin Rājādhirājadēva (II ?), dated in his eighth year.

304. 8 *of* 1893.—(Tamil.) West wall of the second prākāra of the same temple. A record of the Chōḷa king Rājarājadēva, dated in his second year.

305. 9 *of* 1893.—(Tamil.) South wall of the second prākāra of the same temple. A record of the Chōḷa king Kō-Parakēsarivarman *alias* Rājarājadēva (II), dated in his fifteenth year, corresponding to Thursday, 12th January, A.D. 1161. *Ep. Ind.*, VIII, 3.

306. 10 *of* 1893.—(Tamil.) North wall of the second prākāra of the same temple. A record of the Chōḷa king Tribhuvanachakravartin Kulōttuṅgachōḷadēva (III), dated in his twenty-seventh year. *Ep. Ind.*, VI, 251.

307. 11 *of* 1893.—(Tamil.) West wall of the second prākāra of the same temple. A record of the Chōḷa king Kō-Rājakēsarivarman *alias* Kulōttuṅga-Chōḷadēva, dated in his second year.

308. 12 *of* 1893.—(Tamil.) East wall of the Naṭarāja shrine in the same temple. A record of the Vijayanagara king Bukkarāya (II), dated Ś. 1328 expired, Vyaya.

309. 13 *of* 1893.—(Sanskrit fragment.) In the gōpura of the 1,000 pillared maṇṭapa in the same temple.

310. 14 *of* 1893.—(Tamil.) West, south and east walls of the Muktīśvara temple. A record of the Pallava king Nandivarman, dated in his twenty-eighth year.

311. 15 *of* 1893.—(Tamil.) North wall of the same temple. An incomplete record of the Chōḷa king Ko-Parakēsarivarman *alias* Rājēndra-Chōḷadēva (I), dated in his eighteenth year.

312. 16 *of* 1893.—(Tamil.) North and west walls of the same temple. An obliterated record of the Vijayanagara king Tirumaladēva (1566—77.)

313. 17 *of* 1893.—(Tamil.) North wall of the Pāṇḍava Perumāḷ temple (the Tiruppāḍagam of the *Nālāyiraprabandha*). A record of the Chōḷa king Kō-Rājakēsarivarman *alias* Kulōttuṅga-Chōḷadēva (I), dated in his fifth year. Records that a merchant provided the temple with a flower garden and purchased from the village of Ōriravirukkai some land for the benefit of the gardeners. *S.I.I.*, III, No. 68, pp. 140—3. The cost of 2,000 kuḷis (tax-free) was 11 Kaḷañjus equal in fineness to the *Madhurāntaka mādai* and the assembly could not levy in consequence *Vēlikkāśu*, *Nirailai*, *Śilvari*, *Śōrumaṭṭu*, etc.

314. 18 *of* 1893.—(Tamil.) South wall of the same temple. A record of the Chōḷa king Kō-Rājakēsarivarman *alias* Kulōttuṅga-Chōḷadēva (I) dated in his thirty-ninth year. Records gift of two kaḷañju and two *mañjāḍi* by a merchant to the Pūjāris who were to supply two nāḷis of curds daily. *Ibid.* No. 74, pp. 163—4.

315. 33 *of* 1893.—(Tamil.) Base of the west wall of the "rock" in the Aruḷāḷa-Perumāḷ temple. A record of the ninth year of the Chōḷa king Kō-Parakēsarivarman *alias* Vikrama-Chōḷadēva. Records the gift of 780 *kalams* of paddy out of the interest of which worship during thirteen days of *Jyēshṭha*, the alleged constellation of Pūdattāḷvār and Poygai Āḷvārs, was to be held every year. [The inscription is of great literary and religious value as it refers to the worship of the Āḷvārs and the *Iyarpā* of the *Nālāyiraprabandha*. It however differs, in assigning a single star to both the Āḷvārs, from the *Guruparamparaṣ*. The inscription gives also the prices of the articles to be bought. See *S.I.I.*, III, No. 80, p. 186—90.]

316. 34 *of* 1893.—(Sanskrit in Kanarese characters.) Base of the west wall of the "rock" in the Aruḷāḷa-Perumāḷ temple. Records in the reign of Chōḷa-Tikka I (son of Manma Siddhi), in Ś. 1157 gift of cows by the minister Tripurāntaka.

317. 35 *of* 1893.—(Sanskrit.) Base of the north wall of the same. A record of Tammu-siddhi, dated Ś. 1127. Records the erection of portions of the temple. Informs that the king was crowned at the city of Nellore. Gives the genealogy of the line. See *Ep. Rep.*, 1893, p. 5 and *Ep. Ind.*, Vol. VII, 152—5.

318. 36 *of* 1893.—(Tamil.) Base of the north wall of the same. A record of the Chōḷa king Tribhuvanachakravartin Kulōttuṅga-Chōḷadēva, dated in his twenty-seventh year.

319. 37 *of* 1893.—(Tamil.) Base of the east wall of the same. A record of the Gaṇḍa-Gōpāla.

320. 38 *of* 1893.—(Tamil.) Left entrance to the Narasimha shrine in the same temple. A record of the Chōḷa king Tribhuvanachakravartin Kulōttuṅga-Chōḷadēva, dated in his sixteenth year.

321. 39 *of* 1893.—(Tamil.) Base of the verandah round the "rock" in the same temple, east. Tribhuvanachakravartin Gaṇḍa-Gōpāladēva mentions in his seventeenth year a feudatory, Nala-Siddha of Kāñchi.

322. 40 *of* 1893.—(Tamil.) South side of the same. A record of Tribhuvanachakravartin Kōnērinmaikoṇḍān. Refers to the coins of Kōdaṇḍarāman and Koliyugarāman. For descriptions of these see *Madras Journal*, 1887—8.

323. 41 *of* 1893.—(Sanskrit and Tamil.) South side of the same. A record of Tribhuvanachakravartin Gaṇḍa-Gōpāladēva, dated in his twenty-second year. [The name Nīlagaṅga appears in connection with this chief. He was the contemporary of Kulōttuṅga III, who ascended the throne in 1177-8 as the inscriptions at Maṇimaṅgalam (21 of 1896) and Maḍhurāntakam (131 of 1896) show.]

324. 42 *of* 1893.—(Tamil.) South side of the same. A record of Tribhuvanachakravartin Kōnērinmaikoṇḍān, dated in his twenty-first year. Only beginning copied. See No. 322 above which it resembles in its numismatic interest.

325. 43 *of* 1893.—(Grantha and Tamil.) West side of the same. A record of the Kākatīya king Pratāparudra, dated Ś. 1238, expired, Naḷa. Partially built in. See *Ep. Ind.*, VII, 128-32, where Dr. Hultzsch edits the inscription. It says that Muppiḍi Nāyaka, the general of Pratāparudra, came to Kāñchi, and installed a certain Mānavīra as Governor and granted the revenues of two villages to the Aruḷāḷapperumāḷ temple, which amounted to 1002 *Gaṇḍa Gōpālamāḍai*. The dates of the two grants were Friday, 11th June A.D. 1316 and Wednesday, 16th June A.D. 1316. The inscription is of interest as showing that Pratāparudra (whose inscriptions are found as far as Jambukēśvaram) was in possession of Kāñchi soon after it had been in the hands of Ravivarman of Kērala. Dr. Hultzsch therefore believes that Muppiḍi Nāyaka perhaps drove him away and installed Mānavīra, evidently a member of the later Chōḷas denoted by Gaṇḍagōpāla, Nallasiddhi, etc., as his feudatory. See *Ep. Ind.*, VII, 128-132.

326. 44 *of* 1893.—(Tamil.) West wall of the second prākāra of the same temple. A record of Tribhuvanachakravartin Gaṇḍa-Gōpāladēva.

327. 45 *of* 1893.—(Sanskrit.) West wall of the second prākāra of the same temple.

328. 46 *of* 1893.—(Tamil.) North wall of the second prākāra of the same temple. A record of Alluntikamahārāja Gaṇḍa-Gōpāladēva, dated in his seventh year.

329. 47 *of* 1893.—(Tamil.) North wall of the second prākāra of the same temple. Mentions Tribhuvanachakravartin Gaṇḍa-Gōpāladēva and records a grant by Brahma-Śeṭṭi, a minister of Gaṇapati (Kākatīya, evidently).

330. 48 *of* 1893.—(Tamil.) North wall of the second prākāra of the same temple. A record of the Chōḷa king Tribhuvana-chakravartin Rājādhirājadēva (II ?) in his fourteenth year. Mentions a Gaṅga chief, Āhavamallaraśan.

331. 49 *of* 1893.—(Tamil.) In the gōpura near the Abhishēka maṇṭapa in the same temple, left of entrance. A record of the Choḷa king Ko-Rājakēsarivarman *alias* Kulōttuṅga-Chōḷadēva (I), dated in his forty-third year.

332. 50 *of* 1893.—(Sanskrit.) In the same gōpura right of entrance. Addressed to the Vedic scholar Sāyaṇa. Mentions his mother Śrimāyi, his father Māyaṇa, his elder brother (Mādhava), his younger brother the poet Bhōganātha and his preceptor Śrīkaṇṭhanātha. The inscription is thus of great value.

333. 51 *of* 1893.—(Sanskrit.) In the outermost gōpura of the same temple, right of entrance. A record of the Chōḷa king Champa, son of Vīra Chōḷa, dated Ś. 1236, presenting a new car to the temple. See *Ep. Ind.*, III, 71–2. See No. 3 of 1890 at Tiruvallam in North Arcot District.

334. 52 *of* 1893.—(Sanskrit.) In the outermost gōpura of the same temple, right of the entrance. A record of the Pāṇḍya king Sundra-Pāṇḍya (Jaṭāvarman) who ascended the throne in 1251.

335. 53 *of* 1893.—(Sanskrit.) On the same gōpura, left of entrance. Tikka (I ?) boasts of victories over various kings. See No. 316.

336. 54 *of* 1893.—(Tamil.) West and north walls of the Śmaśānēśvara shrine in the Ēkāmranātha temple. A record of the Chōḷa king Kō-Rājakēsarivarman *alias* Rājādhirājadēva I, dated in his twenty-seventh year. Only historical introduction copied. One Māran Tēvaḍigaḷ deposits five *kaḻañjus* in temple treasury for offerings. The interest on this (at the rate of one *kā* two *tu* for each *kaḻañju*) is eight *kā*. [The account of expenditure and prices given.]

337. 22 *of* 1890.—South base of the Anēkataṅgāpādam temple. Records in the thirty-fourth year of Kulōttuṅga (I) grants of two vēlis of land to the temple of Anāiyapaḍaṅga. The land granted was at Conjeeveram itself, north of the temple of Tirukkaṟṟaḷi Mahādēva (i.e., Rājasimhēśvara or Kailāsanātha). See *S.I.I.*, II, No. 78, pp. 392–3.

338. 23 *of* 1890.—North base of the same. Seems to be dated in Naḷa. Records that the authorities of the Anēkataṅgā temple assigned 1,400 kuḻis of land to certain Kaikkōḷars connected with the temple.

339. 24 *of* 1890.—West base of the same. A record of Kulōttuṅga-Chōḷadēva (I), dated in his twentieth year, saying that he granted three *vēlis* of land at Tāmar (i.e., Dāmal) or Nittavinōdanallūr in Tāmar-nāḍu, a subdivision of Tāmar-kōṭṭam, to the Mahādēva of the Anēkataṅgāpādam temple. See *S.I.I.*, Vol. II, No. 77, pp. 390–2.

340. 25 *of* 1890.—West and south walls of the Sabhānāyaka shrine in the Ēkāmbaranātha temple. A record of the Pāṇḍya king Bhuvanēkavīra *alias* Samarakōlāhala, dated Ś. 1391 (expired), Virōdhi. Records that he granted to the temples of Ēkāmbaranātha and Kāmākshi two villages in the Pāṇḍya country named after himself. For his coins see Elliot's *Coins of S. Ind.*, Plate III, No. 138, and *Ep. Rep.*, 1890, p. 2.

341. 26 *of* 1890.—(Sanskrit verse.) North wall of the second prākāra of the same temple. A record of the Kākatīya king Gaṇapati, dated Ś. 1172, Saumya year. Mentions Rudradēva and Mahādēva also, and the gift of a village by his minister Sāmanta Bhōja. See *Ind. Antq.*, XXI, 197 ff., where Dr. Hultzsch has published it.

342. 27 *of* 1890.—(Sanskrit verse.) North wall of the second prākāra of the same temple. A record of Tribhuvanachakravartin Vijaya-Gaṇḍa-Gōpāladēva, dated Ś. 1187, sixteenth regnal year. So he ascended the throne in Ś. 1172 (A.D. 1250). See also 350 and 351.

343. 28 *of* 1890.—South wall of the Nāyar Maṇṭapa in the Ēkāmranātha temple. A record of Kampaṇa-uḍaiyār, dated Ānanda year.

344. 29 *of* 1890.—Right of the entrance into the inner prākāra of the Kāmākshi temple. A record of the Vijayanagara king Harihara II, dated Ś. 1315, expired, Śrīmukha year.

345. 30 *of* 1890.—Left of the front entrance into the Ulagaḷanda-Perumāḷ temple. A record of Sakalalōkachakravartin Rājanārāyaṇa Śāmbuvarāya, dated Ś. 1268, expired, Vyaya, ninth regnal year. So he ascended throne in Ś. 1259, (A.D. 1337).

346. 31 *of* 1890.—Right of the entrance into the east wall of the second prākāra of the Aruḷāla-Perumāḷ temple. A record of Hariyaṇa Uḍaiyār II, dated Ś. 1300, expired, Krōdhana year.

347. 32 *of* 1890.—Left of the entrance into the same temple. A record of the Vīra-Hariyaṇa-Uḍaiyār II, dated Ś. 1300, expired, Kāḷayukti year.

348. 33 *of* 1890.—Right of the entrance into the Tāyār Sannadhi at the same temple. A record of Vīra-Kampaṇa-Uḍaiyār, dated Ś. 1288, expired, Parābhava year.

349. 34 *of* 1890.—(Sanskrit verse.) East wall of the so-called rock (*malai*) in the same temple. A record of the Kēraḷa king Jayasimha and his son Ravivarman. The latter, called also Kulaśēkhara Saṅgrāmadhīra, was born in Ś. 1188, and married a Pāṇḍya princess. At the age of 33 he ascended the throne of Kēraḷa. He then conquered Vīra Pāṇḍya and was crowned at Madura in his forty-sixth year (i.e., Ś. 1234). He was the Lord of Kūpaka and Kollam. See *Ep. Ind.*, IV, 145-8.

350. 35 *of* 1890.—South wall of the "rock" in the same temple. A record of Tribhuvanachakravartin Vijaya-Gaṇḍagōpāladēva, dated Ś. 1187, sixteenth regnal year.

351. 36 *of* 1890.—South wall of the "rock" in the same temple. A record of Tribhuvanachakravartin Vijaya-Gaṇḍa-Gōpāladēva, dated Ś. 1187, fifteenth regnal year.

352. 37 *of* 1890.—Left of the entrance into the first prākāra of the same temple. A record of the Vijayanagara king Mallikārjunadēva, dated Ś. 1387, expired, Pārthiva year.

353. 38 *of* 1890.—East wall of the Abhishēka Maṇṭapa at the same temple. A record of Sakalabhuvanachakravartin Kō-Peruñjiṅgadēva, dated Ś. 1182, expired, eighteenth regnal year. So he ascended the throne in Ś. 1165 (A.D. 1243). He must have been the predecessor of Vijaya Gaṇḍagōpāla referred to in Nos. 342, 350 and 351. The exact date of the present inscription, according to Kielhorn, is Sunday, 31st Oct., A.D. 1260. *Ep. Ind.*, VII, p. 164.

354. 39 *of* 1890.—South wall of the Abhishēka-Maṇṭapa at the same temple. A record of the Vijayanagara king Virūpākshadēva, dated Ś. 1392, expired, Vikriti year.

355. 49 *of* 1900.—On the south wall of the first prākāra of the Kāmākshi temple. (Tamil.) A record of Achyuta Rāya of Vijayanagar, dated Ś. 1456 (A.D. 1534), Vijaya. Refers to his conquest and records the grant of eight villages to the temple.

356. 50 *of* 1900.—On the south wall of the second prākāra of the Arulāḷaperumāḷ temple. A record of Achyuta Rāya of Vijayanagar, dated Ś. 1454 (A.D. 1632), expired, Nandana. Refers to his conquests and records the gift of jewels and seventeen villages to the temple.

357. 51 *of* 1900.—On the same place. A record of the same king in the same date. Records gift of a jewelled couch, discus, etc., to the king (1050-62).

358. 416 *of* 1902.—On the north wall of the central shrine in the Tirukkāliśvara temple at Vēppaṅguḷam near Conjeeveram. (Tamil.) Records a gift of land in the sixth year of Parakēsarivarman Uḍaiyār Rājēndradēva (1050–62.)

359. 417 *of* 1902.—(Tamil.) On the south, west and north walls of the same shrine. A record of the twenty-eighth year of Rājakēsarivarman Uḍaiyār Rājādhirājadēva (I ?).

360. 418 *of* 1902.—(Tamil.) On the same walls. A record of the third year of Parakēsarivarman Ādhirājēndradēva. Partly built in.

361. 419 *of* 1902.—(Tamil.) In the same place. A record of the sixteenth year of Parakēsarivarman Rājēndrachōḷadēva (1011–43) providing for a supply of paddy by a number of villages in payment of interest on gold borrowed from the temple.

362. 420 *of* 1902.—(Tamil.) On the east wall of the same shrine. Records gift of 90 sheep for a lamp in the sixth year of Parakēsarivarman Rājēndrachōḷadēva (1011–43).

363. 1 *of* 1906.—On the south wall of Śakkēśvara temple. (Tamil.) Records a sale of land in the fifteenth year of the Chōḷa king Parakēsarivarman.

364. 2 *of* 1906.—On a stone built into the floor at the entrance into the Śmaśānēśvara shrine in the Ēkāmbaranātha temple. Mutilated *inscription* of the first (fifth) year of Parakēsarivarman *alias* Uttama Chōḷadēva.

365. 3 *of* 1906.—On the same stone. Mutilated. Mentions queen Vīranāraṇi(yār). Date lost. By the same king.

366. 4 *of* 1906.—On the big gōpura in the same temple. Unfinished. Refers to *Iḍaṅgaivari.* Dated in Ś. 1378, Dhātri, in the reign of the Vijayanagara king Vīrā-Mallikārjunadēva-Mahārāya.

367. *C.P. No.* 146 *of Mr. Sewell's List* (*and Madras Museum plate No.* 8) (Tamil.) Records a document declaring the settlement of a dispute about some lands, between some men of the Mudaliyār caste. It is dated in Ś. 1456 (A.D. 1534), Kaliyuga 4434, *Nandana.* [Date inconsistent.] See *Tamil and Sanscrit Inscrns.*, pp. 154–6, where it has been edited.

368. A C.P. grant of Kō-Parakēsarivarman Uttama Chōḷadēva in the sixteenth year of his reign, at the request of a minister of his confirming the contents of the stone inscriptions which refer to the dues to be paid to the temple of Vishṇu at Kachchippēḍu. See Nos. 264, 266, 268, 270 for instance. For Uttama Chōḷa's coins, see Elliot's *Coins of South India*, Nos. 151 and 154. For the description of the present plates see *Ep. Rep.*, 1891, pp. 4–5.

369. A C.P. dated Ś. 1646 (referred to by Taylor in his *Rais. Catal.*, III, p. 340). Commemorates a gift of thirteen villages in free tenure, through Rāmānujāchariar.

370. Among the copper plates of Conjeeveram there are a number of forged ones. One of these (No. 6, Appendix A, *Madr. Ep. Rep.*, 1910) is deposited in the Madras Museum and consists of a single plate. Mr. Krishna Sastri believes that it is "one of a series of forgeries compiled by the Iḍaṅgai faction in its zeal to justify its preference over the *Valangai*, in matters social. The dates given, viz., Ś. 1098 and K. 4421, do not correspond. Nevertheless the story related of how the car procession of Kāmākshi Amman at Conjeeveram was successfully managed by the Iḍaṅgai Kammāḷans in spite of the obstacles thrown in its way by their opponents of the Valaṅgai section and how in this matter the Kambaḷattāns from Malabar helped the former by their ingenuity in exorcism, has its own interest to the ethnologist." (*Madr. Ep. Rep.* 1910, p. 11.)

371. Another forged grant of the same character dealing with the voluntary levying of a fee by the *Añju-Pañchalattār* (i.e., the five Kammāḷars) among themselves. This is also dated in Ś. 1098, K. 4421. (*Ibid.*)

Dāmal.

372. 139 *of* 1896.—(Tamil.) On the west wall of the shrine of the Śiva temple. Dated in the reign of the Vijayanagara king

Tirumalaiyadēva, son of Krishṇadēva. Records in Ś. 1446 expired, Tāraṇa, gift of land to the Panṛiśvara temple at Tamar.

Eḍayarpākkam.

373. 251 *of* 1910.—(Tamil.) On the north base of the Śiva temple. Dated in the reign of the Chōḷa king Tribhuvanachakravartin Kulōttuṅga-Chōḷadēva. Records in his thirty-eighth year a gift of two lamps to the temple of Tiruppaḍakkāḍuḍaiyār in Puriśai-nāḍu, a subdivision of Maṇavir-kōṭṭam in Jayaṅgoṇḍa-chōḷamaṇḍalam. Built in at the bottom.

374. 252 *of* 1910.—(Tamil.) On the same base. Dated in the thirty-eighth year of the Chōḷa king Rājakēsarivarman *alias* Chakravartin Śrī-Kulōttuṅga-Chōḷadēva (I ?). Records gift of 95 sheep for a lamp to the temple of Tiruppaḍakkāḍuḍaiya Mahādēva at Puriśai in Puriśai-nāḍu, a subdivision of Maṇavir-kōṭṭam in Jayaṅgoṇḍa-chōḷamaṇḍalam.

375. 253 *of* 1910.—(Tamil.) On the south base of the same temple. Dated in the eleventh year of the Chōḷa king Tribhuvanachakravartin Rājādhirājadēva (II). Records that at the request of the temple trustees the villagers had to take away one *vēli* of land originally granted to the temple for a lamp and give a number of cows in exchange. The land was at Puriśai (a dēvadāna village of Tiruppaḍakkāḍuḍaiyār), and granted by a Brāhmaṇa lady of Iḍaiyāṟṟuppākkam *alias* Rājavidyādhara-chaturvēdimaṅgalam. Built in at the bottom. The reason for the transaction was that the land was in the corner of the village and had no irrigational facilities and so none would cultivate it. The land thus became village property.

376. 254 *of* 1910.—(Tamil.) On the same base. A damaged record of the Chōḷa king Rājakēsarivarman *alias* Chakravartin Śrī-Kulōttuṅga-Chōḷadēva (I ?), dated in his twelfth year. Records sale of land by the residents of Puriśai to the temple of Tiruppaḍakkāḍuḍaiyār of Iḍaiyāṟṟuppākkam *alias* Rājavidyādhara-chaturvēdimaṅgalam, for the maintenance of a lamp, for the sum of 30 *kāśus* which a Brahman lady had left in the hands of the shepherds of Iḍayarpākkam. These shepherds had refused to measure oil for ¾ lamp for 30 *kāśus*. Hence this sale and endowment to the temple. [Though mentioned in the *Dēvāram* this place has not got ancient epigraphs and this is probably due to the removal of them by later repairers.]

Iḷambayaṅgōṭṭur (Elamayan Kōṭṭūr).

377. 231 *of* 1910.—(Tamil.) On the south base of the temple of Dēvanāyakasvāmin. Records in the twelfth year of the Chōḷa king Rājādhirājadēva (II, 1178--86) that the stone temple was built by the paṇḍāri Śivacharaṇālayan *alias* Śivapādaśēkhara-Mūvēndavēḷān.

378. 232 *of* 1910.—(Tamil.) On the same base. Records in the thirteenth year of the Pāṇḍya king Kōnērimēlkoṇḍān Tribhuvanachakravartin Jaṭāvarman Sundara-Pāṇḍyadēva gift of money for a lamp to the temple at Iḷambayaṅgōṭṭūr in Kāṉṟūr-nāḍu, a subdivision of Maṇavir-kōṭṭam in Jayaṅgoṇḍa-chōḷamaṇḍalam, by a native of Vallam in Puliyūr-kōṭṭam *alias* Kulōttuṅgachōḷa-vaḷanāḍu.

379. 233 *of* 1910.—(Tamil.) On the same base. Records in the fourth year of Tribhuvanachakravartin Vīra-Gaṇḍagōpāladēva gift of land at Kaliyanallūr in Tiruvēlūr-nāḍu to the same temple, by Madurāntaka-Pottappichchōḷan Vīra-Gaṇḍagōpālan.

380. 234 *of* 1910.—(Tamil.) On the west base of the same temple. An unfinished record of the Chōḷa king Tribhuvanachakravartin Tribhuvanavīradēva (Kulōttuṅga III), " who was pleased to perform the anointment of heroes and the anointment of victors," dated in his thirty-eighth year. Refers to a former gift of land by Śeṅgēṇi Ammaiyappan Vanniyanāyan Śambuvarājan, to the temple of Iḷambayaṅgōṭṭūruḍaiya Nāyanār at Kōṭṭūr *alias* Śōḷavichchādira-chaturvēdimaṅgalam in Kāṉṟūr-nāḍu. See *Ep. Rep.*, 1900.

381. 235 *of* 1910.—(Tamil.) On the north base of the same temple. Records in the thirty-fourth year of the Chōḷa king Tribhuvanachakravartin Tribhuvanavīradēva (Kulōttuṅga III) " who, having taken Madurai (Madura) and the crowned head of the Pāṇḍya, was pleased to perform the anointment of heroes and the anointment of victors," gift of money for a lamp, by a temple woman.

382. 236 *of* 1910.—(Tamil.) On the same base. Records in the nineteenth year of Tribhuvanachakravartin Vīra-Gaṇḍagōpāladēva gift of five cows for a lamp by Kulōttuṅgaśōḷa-Chchambuvarāyan *alias* Aḷagiya-śōḷan, to the same temple. This was in Tamaṇur-nāḍu, a subdivision of Uṟṟukkāṭṭukōṭṭam, in Jayaṅkoṇḍa-chōḷamaṇḍalam.

Kāvantaṇḍāḷam.

383. 203 *of* 1901.—(Tamil.) On the south wall of the central shrine in the Chōḷēśvara temple. Records in the twenty-sixth year of the Chōḷa king Tribhuvanachakravartin Kulōttuṅga-Chōḷadēva III a sale of land.

384. 204 *of* 1901.—(Tamil.) On the same wall. Records in the fifth year of the Chōḷa king Vikrama-Chōḷadēva a sale of land.

385. 205 *of* 1901.—(Tamil.) On the west wall of the same shrine. Dated in the reign of the Chōḷa king Vikrama Chōḷadēva. Records a sale of land.

386. 206 *of* 1901.—(Tamil.) On the south wall of the Lakshmīnārāyaṇa temple in the same village. An incomplete record of the Chōḷa king Rājakēsarivarman *alias* Rājēndra-Chōḷadēva II (Kulōttuṅga-Chōḷa I), dated in his fourth year. See *Ep. Ind.*, VII, 1-2, where Kielhorn fixes the date on Thursday, 7th November 1073. Also *S.I.I.*, III, No. 77, pp. 172-3.

387. 207 *of* 1901.—(Tamil.) On the same wall. Records in the fourteenth year of the so-called Gaṅga-Pallava king Kampavarman gift of land by Mānasarpa, an inhabitant of Kulanūr in Vēṅgai-nāḍu to the Vishṇu temple which he had built at Kāvantaṇḍāḷam. Dr. Hultzsch identifies Kulanūr with Kūḷam or Kolanu, modern Ellore. *S.I.I.*, III, p. 172.

388. 208 *of* 1901.—(Tamil.) On the same wall. Provides in the eighteenth year of the "Gaṅga-Pallava" king Kampavarman for the celebration of certain festivals at the Mānasarpa-Vishṇugriha.

389. 209 *of* 1901.—(Grantha.) On the west wall of the same temple. Records that Mānasarpa built the Vishṇu temple.

390. 210 *of* 1901.—(Grantha and Tamil.) On the north and west walls of the same temple. An incomplete record of the Chōḷa king Parakēsarivarman *alias* Rājēndra-Chōḷadēva (I), dated in his fourth year. Records a gift of land to the temple of Rājēndra-Chōḷa Īśvara called after the king.

391. 211 *of* 1901.—(Tamil.) On the north wall of the same temple. An incomplete record of the Chōḷa king Parakēsarivarman, dated in his fifteenth year.

Kūram.

This place was in the Manyavāntara Rāshtra of Nīrveḷūr, a division of Uṟṟukkāṭṭukkōṭṭam and its Śiva temple represents the ancient Vidyāvinīta-Pallava-Paramēśvara temple, built, as is proved by an inscription discovered by Prof. Dubreuil, during the time of Paramēśvaravarman I. In the history of South Indian Vaishṇavism it is famous as the birth-place of Kūrattāḻvān, the faithful companion and disciple of Rāmānuja (1017--1137).

392. 32 *of* 1900.—(Tamil.) On the north wall of the Kēśavaperumāḷ temple. Records in the twelfth year of the Chōḷa king Rājarājakēsarivarman (Rājarāja I) gift of land by the Sabhā of Kūram to a temple of Subrahmaṇya.

393. 33 *of* 1900.—(Tamil.) On the north wall of the Kēśavaperumāḷ temple. Records in the seventeenth year of the so-called Gaṅga-Pallava king Vijaya-Nripatuṅgavikramavarman a sale of land. Prof. Dubreuil attributes the king to A.D. 854—880.

394. 34 *of* 1900.—(Tamil.) On the south wall of the same temple. A record of the Chōḷa king Madirai-koṇḍa Parakēsarivarman (Parāntaka I), dated in his fortieth year. Built in. See *Ep. Ind.*, VII.

395. 35 *of* 1900.—(Tamil.) On the south wall of the same temple. A much damaged record of the so-called Gaṅga-Pallava king Vijaya-Dantivikramavarman (*C* 779—830), dated in his twelfth year.

396. 36 *of* 1900.—(Tamil.) On a pillar in the Śiva temple at the same village. An obliterated record. Mentions Kūram.

397. 37 *of* 1900.—(Tamil.) On another pillar in the same temple. A much damaged record of the so-called Gaṅga-Pallava king Nripatuṅga, dated in his twenty-first year.

398. 38 *of* 1900.—(Tamil.) On a third pillar in the same temple. A damaged record of the Pallava king Nandivarma Mahārāja. Records a gift of land.

399. 39 *of* 1900.—(Tamil.) On a fourth pillar in the same temple. Records in the twenty-seventh year of the Chōḷa king Rājakēsarivarmaṇ gift of a lamp.

400. A. C.P. grant (Sanskrit and Tamil) of the Pallava king Paramēśvaravarman I, son of Mahēndravarman II and grandson of Narasimhavarman I, the conqueror of Vātāpi. Records that the king gave the village of Paramēśvaramaṅgalam in Panmānāḍu in Maṇayirkōṭṭam, to the Śiva temple at Kūram. [Refers to Paramēśvaravarman's "conquest" of the W. Chāḷukyan Vikramāditya (I). For the latter's version, see *Ind. Antq.*, VI, p. 77. For a summary of the present epigraph, see *Ep. Rep.*, 1888, pp. 3-4; Kielhorn's *Southern List*, No. 628; and for a detailed edition of it. *S.I.I.*, I, No. 150, pp. 144-155. Dr. Hultzsch identifies Maṇayil (*Maṇ-eyil* or mud fort) with Eyil in South Arcot District. Prof. Deubreuil believes this temple to be the most ancient monument in South India built of stones placed one above another. See his *Pallavas*, p. 45.]

Maduramaṅgalam.

This place figures in the *Guruparampara* as the birth-place of Embār or Gōvindabhaṭṭa, the cousin and according to the Prabandhic school, the successor of Rāmānuja. The Vaiśhṇava tradition implies that Embār was the first to receive the title of *Uḷḷaṅgai koṇarnda Nāyanār* and that he built a Śiva temple in his name. But inscription 401 shows that the name existed two centuries earlier.

401. 320 *of* 1909.—(Tamil.) On a stone built into the west wall of the Uḷḷaṅgaikuḷunda-Nāyanār temple. Records in the 9th year of Pārthivendrādhipativarman gift of 90 sheep for a lamp by Ulōka-Mahārāyar to the temple of Ulōkamahārāya-Tiruchchiṟṟambalattāḷvār at Maḷalaimaṅgalam in Maṇayirkōṭṭam. [Venkayya believed that Pārthivēndravarman was a contemporary of Parakēsarivarman Āditya karikāla II as both had the title "who took the head of Vīra Pāṇḍya." Mr. Krishna Sastri however points out that the title was first assumed by Sundara Chōḷa,

Āditya's father. See Tāyanur and Kaḷamūr inscriptions. (North Arcot District.)

402. 321 *of* 1909.—(Tamil.) On a stone built into the floor of the maṇṭapa in front of the Vaikuṇṭha-Perumāḷ temple in the same village. A damaged record of Pārthivendrādhipativarman, dated in his ninth year. Mentions Ulōka-Mahārāyar. See note to 401.

Māgaral.

403. 215 *of* 1901.—(Tamil.) On the south wall of the central shrine in the Tirumālīśvara temple. Records in the eleventh year of the Chōḷa king Parakēsarivarman *alias* Tribhuvanachakravartin Kulōttuṅga-Chōḷadēva (II ?) gift of land to the Agastyēśvara temple at Māgaral in Māgaral-nāḍu, a subdivision of Eyir-kōṭṭam.

404. 216 *of* 1901.—(Tamil.) On the west wall of the same shrine. Records in the seventh year of the Pāṇḍya king Tribhuvanachakravartin Sundara-Pāṇḍyadēva (I, 1251—64), a gift of land. Begins with *Samasta-jagad-ādhāra.*

405. 217 *of* 1901.—(Tamil.) On the north, west and south walls of the same shrine. Records in the fifth year of the Chōḷa king Tribhuvanachakravartin Rājarājadēva (III) sale of land by the Sabhā of Ukkal *alias* Vikramābharaṇa-chaturvēdimaṅgalam. The date corresponded to Wednesday, 19th August, A.D. 1220. See *Ep. Ind.*, Vol. VII, p. 75.

406. 218 *of* 1901.—(Tamil.) On the east wall of the maṇṭapa in front of the Tirumālīśvara temple. Records in the seventh year of the Pāṇḍya king Jaṭāvarman *alias* Sundara-Pāṇḍyadēva (I, 1251—64) "who conquered every country" that a private person opened out streets and colonized the environs of the Agastyēśvara temple.

407. 219 *of* 1901.—(Tamil.) On the south wall of the same maṇṭapa. An incomplete record of the Chōḷa king Parakēsarivarman *alias* Tribhuvanachakravartin Rājarājadēva (II, 1146—78) dated in his tenth year. Records gift of land for a lamp.

408. 220 *of* 1901.—(Tamil.) On the north wall of the same maṇṭapa. Records that the Chōḷa king Tribhuvanachakravartin Tribhuvanavīradēva (Kulōttuṅga III) in his thirty-second year, restored at the request of a certain Nandivarman certain land which had previously belonged to the Agastyēśvara temple.

409. 221 *of* 1901.—(Tamil.) On the south wall of the maṇṭapa in front of the central shrine in the Vaikuṇṭhaperumāḷ temple at the same village. Records in the twenty-eighth year of the Chōḷa king Tribhuvanachakravartin Rājarājadēva (III ?) gift of a lamp to the temple of Tirumērkōyil-Vīṟṟirunda-Perumāḷ.

410. 222 *of* 1901.—(Tamil.) On the same wall. Records in the twenty-eighth year of the Chōḷa king Tribhuvanachakravartin Rājarājadēva (III ?) gift of two lamps to the same temple.

411. 223 *of* 1901.—(Tamil.) On the same wall. Records in the twenty-eighth year of the Chōḷa king Tribhuvanachakravartin Rājarājadēva (III ?) gift of a lamp to the same temple.

412. 224 *of* 1901.—(Tamil.) On the same wall. Records in the twenty-third year of the Chōḷa king Tribhuvanachakravartin Rājarājadēva (III ?) the building of the central shrine, the Ardhamaṇṭapa, another maṇṭapa, a flight of steps, and the śrīpīṭha.

413. 225 *of* 1901.—(Tamil verse.) Above the entrance of the Tāyār-Sannadhi in the same temple. Records in the sixth year of the Chōḷa king Rājarāja the building of the shrine.

Perambākkam.

414. 277 *of* 1912.—(Tamil.) On a slab set up in a field. A much damaged record, dated in Nandana, Tai. Mentions an agent of Vaiyappa-Nāyaka.

Śevallimēḍu.

415. 40 *of* 1900.—(Tamil.) On the north wall of the Kailāsanātha temple. Records in the second year of the Chōḷa king Rājakēsarivarman *alias* Tribhuvanachakravartin Kulōttuṅga-Chōḷadēva gift of a lamp.

416. 41 *of* 1900.—(Tamil.) On the north wall of the Kailāsanātha temple. Records in the second year of the Chōḷa king Tribhuvanachakravartin Kulōttuṅga-Chōḷadēva gift of a lamp.

417. 42 *of* 1900.—(Tamil.) On the north wall of the Kailāsanatha temple. Records in the ninth year of Sakalalōkachakravartin Rājaṇārāyaṇa Sambuvarāya, Ś. 1268, Vijaya, gift of land by Tiruvēṅgaḍamuḍaiyān Kaḷiṅgarāyan.

418. 43 *of* 1900.—(Grantha and Sanskrit.) On the west wall of the same temple. A record of the sixteenth year of the Chōḷa king Vikrama-Chōḷa (who is called Akaḷaṅka), recording gift of land by three persons. [See *Ep. Ind.*, Vol. II, pp. 227—30, and 279, where Dr. Kielhorn discusses the details of the date and concludes that it should be Monday, 5th May, A.D. 1124.]

419. 44 *of* 1900.—(Tamil.) On the west wall of the same temple. An incomplete record of the Chōḷa king Tribhuvanachakravartin Kulōttuṅga-Chōḷadēva, dated in his tenth year. Records a gift of land.

420. 45 *of* 1900.—(Tamil.) On the south wall of the same temple. A record of the seventh year of Sakalalōkachkravartin Rājanārāyaṇa Śambuvaraiyan. Records grant of land for the upkeep of a water-shed and a garden (tōppu).

421. 46 *of* 1900.—(Tamil.) On the south wall of the same temple. Records in the eighteenth year of Sakalalōkachakravartin Venru-maṇ-koṇḍa Śambuvarāyan, gift of land for maintaining a water-shed and a garden.

422. 47 *of* 1900.—(Tamil.) On the south wall of the maṇṭapa in front of the Lakshmīnarasimha temple. The Vijayanagara king Achyutarāya records in Ś. 1456 expired, Manmatha, a grant of land for the maintenance of a Brāhmaṇa who had to recite the Vēdas in the Obalēśvara temple at Ōbachchi-amman-samudram. The grant was made by the king on the bank of the Krishṇavēṇi for the merit of his mother Ōbāchchi-amman (Obāmbika of the copper plates).

423. 48 *of* 1900.—(Tamil.) On the south wall of the maṇṭapa in front of the Lakshmīnarasimha temple. A damaged record of the Vijayanagara king Achyutarāya, dated in Ś. 1462 expired, Śārvarin. Mentions the Obalēśvara temple at Ōbāchchi-amman-samudram. Built in.

Śivankūḍal.

424. 278 *of* 1912.—(Tamil.) On the south wall of the central shrine in the Śivakkoḻundīśvara temple. A mutilated record of the Chōḻa king Tribhuvanachakravartin Kulōttuṅga-Chōḻadēva I, dated in the twenty-fifth year. Records sale of land by the assembly of Śivankūḍal to the temple of Śivakkoḻundāṇḍār (of that village).

425. 279 *of* 1912.—(Tamil.) On the same wall. A record of the fifth year of Chōḻa king Rājakēsarivarman Kulōttuṅga-Chōḻadēva I. A number of inscribed slabs fixed into the wall in disorder and containing portions of the historical introduction beginning with *pugaḻ-śūḻnda-puṇari.*

426. 280 *of* 1912.—(Tamil.) On the same wall. Seems to record in the twenty-eighth year of Kulōttuṅga-Chōḻadēva a sale of land by the assembly of Śivankūḍal.

427. 281 *of* 1912.—(Tamil.) On the same wall. A fragment of record of the Chōḻa king Rājakēsarivarman *alias* Tribhuvana-chakravartin Kulōttuṅga-Chōḻadēva I, dated in his forty-ninth year.

428. 282 *of* 1912.—(Tamil.) On the west wall of the same shrine. A fragment of record of the Chōḻa king Rājakēsarivarman *alias* Chakravartin Kulōttuṅga-Chōḻadēva I, dated in his fiftieth year. Records sale of land for providing a lamp to the temple of Śivakkoḻundāṇḍār at Śivankūḍal by the assembly of Maḻalai-maṅgalam which was a brahmadēya village in Jayaṅgoṇḍaśōḻa-maṇḍalam.

429. 283 *of* 1912.—(Tamil.) On the same wall. A record of the Chōḻa king Tribhuvanachakravartin Vikrama-Chōḻadēva. Records in his tenth year, gift of land by purchase, for providing two lamps to the temple of Mahādēva called Śivakkoḻundāṇḍār at Śivankūḍal.

430. 284 *of* 1912.—(Tamil.) On the north wall of the same shrine. A mutilated record of the Chōḻa king Kulōttuṅga-Chōḻadēva I, dated in his fifth year. Records sale of land by the assembly of Śivankūḍal to the same temple. Begins with the introduction *pugaḷ śūḷnda puṇari.*

431. 285 *of* 1912.—(Tamil.) On the same wall. The Chōḷa king Tribhuvanachakravartin Vikrama-Chōḷadēva (1118—35) records in his tenth year, sale of land to the temple for conducting a festival of seven days beginning with Āni-Uttiraṭṭādi, the asterism under which the king was born.

432. 286 *of* 1912.—(Tamil.) On the same wall. Records in the eleventh year of the Chōḷa king Tribhuvanachakravartin Vikrama-Chōḷadēva a sale of land by the assembly of Maḷalaimaṅgalam, a brahmadēya in Kānṟūr-nāḍu, which was a subdivision of Maṇayir-kōṭṭam.

433. 287 *of* 1912.—(Tamil.) On the south wall of the maṇṭapa in front of the same shrine. Records in the twenty-fifth year of Tribhuvanachakravartin Vijaya-Gaṇḍagōpāladēva gift of land by purchase, to the shrine of the goddess Marakatavalli-Nāchchiyār in the temple of Śivakkoḷunduḍaiya-Nāyanār at Śivankūḍal in Nirvēlur-nāḍu, a subdivision of Ūṟṟukkāṭṭu-kōṭṭam in Jayaṅgoṇḍaśōḷa-maṇḍalam, by a native of Pūndāḷaikkuḍi in Virudarāyabhayaṅkaravaḷanāḍu which was a district of Sōḷa-maṇḍalam.

434. 288 *of* 1912.—(Tamil.) On the east wall of the same maṇṭapa. Dated in the reign of the Vijayanagara king Vīrapratapa Vīra-Achyutayyadēva-Mahārāya. Records in Ś. 1455, Vijaya, Mēsha, śu. di. 12 Uttiram, Monday, corresponding to 6th April 1533, gift of the village Obalarasanallūr, a hamlet of Śivankūḍal in Māppēḍu-śīrmai, a subdivision of Nīrvēlūr-nāḍu in Ūṟṟukkāṭṭu-kōṭṭam of Chandragiri-rājya in Jayaṅgoṇḍaśōḷa-maṇḍalam, by Ellappa-Nāyaka, son of Śeṭṭiyappa-Nāyaka, to the same temple for oblations and worship.

435. 289 *of* 1912.—(Tamil.) On a pillar lying in the same temple. Records in the third year of the Chōḷa king Parakēsarivarman *alias* Rājēndra Chōḷadēva I that the assembly of Śivakūḍal in Nīrvēlūr-nāḍu in Ūṟṟukkāṭṭu-kōṭṭam, a district of Jayaṅgoṇḍaśōḷa-maṇḍalam, received money from a private person and declared certain lands below the tank Brahmādhirāyapputtēri rent-free in order to provide for offerings and lamps in the temple of Mahādēva of this village.

Tennēri.

436. On a stone in the tank-bund. (Tamil.) Records that the tank was dug by Tātāchārya. *Antiquities,* I, p. 188.

437. 190 *of* 1901.—(Tamil.) On the east wall of the maṇṭapa in front of the Āpatsahāyēśvara temple. Records in the twenty-third year of the Chōḷa king Tribhuvanachakravartin Kulōttuṅga-Chōḷadēva III, gift of two cows for a lamp.

438. 191 *of* 1901.—(Tamil.) On the south wall of the same maṇṭapa. Records in the fourteenth year of the Pāṇḍya king Jaṭāvarman *alias* Sundara-Pāṇḍyadēva gift of land.

439. 192 *of* 1901.—(Tamil.) On the same wall. Records in the eleventh year of the Pāṇḍya king Jaṭāvarman *alias* Sundara-Pāṇḍyadēva (I, 1251—64), "who was pleased to conquer every country" gift of land to the Anantēśvara temple at Tiraiyanūr.

440. 193 *of* 1901.—(Tamil.) On the south wall of the central shrine in the same temple. Records in the thirteenth year of the Chōḷa king Tribhuvanachakravartin Rājādhirājadēva (II, 1178-86), "who took Īḻam and Madurai," gift of land by a merchant from Pūndamali (Poonamallee) to the image of the goddess Tirup-paḷḷiarai-Nāchchiyār set up by him.

441. 194 *of* 1901.—(Tamil.) On the same wall. Records in the thirty-third year of the Chōḷa king Tribhuvanachakravartin Kulōttuṅga Chōḷadēva the appointment of an āchārya to perform worship at the temple.

442. 195 *of* 1901.—(Tamil.) On the same wall. Records in the thirty-sixth year of the Chōḷa king Rājakēsarivarman *alias* Kulōttuṅga-Chōḷadēva I, gift of a lamp.

443. 196 *of* 1901.—(Tamil.) On the north wall of the same shrine. A record of the Chōḷa king Parakēsarivarman *alias* Tribhuvanachakravartin Kulōttuṅga-Chōḷadēva (II, 1123-46). Records in his fifth year gift of land to the temple of Anantēśvara at Tiraiyanēri in Tyāgavallivaḷanāḍu, a subdivision of Ūṟṟukkāṭṭu-kōṭṭam. The king bore the surname Tirunīṟṟu-Chōḷa.

444. 197 *of* 1901.—(Tamil.) On the same wall. A record of the Chōḷa king Rājakēsarivarman *alias* Kulōttuṅga-Chōḷadēva I. Records in his forty-first year sale of land.

445. 198 *of* 1901.—(Tamil.) On the south wall of the Kaṇḍa-līśvara temple in the same village. Dated in the reign of the Chōḷa king Rājakēsarivarman *alias* Vīrarājēndradēva (I ?) gift of a lamp to the shrine of Āḍavallār in the Uttama-Chōḷa-Īśvara temple.

446. 199 *of* 1901.—(Tamil.) On the same wall. A record of the Chōḷa king Rājarājakēsarivarman I. Mentions in his eleventh year, Madurāntakadēva *alias* Uttama-Chōḷadēva, and records a gift of vessels to the same temple.

447. 200 *of* 1901.—(Tamil.) On the north wall of the same temple. A mutilated record of the Chōḷa king Rājarāja Rājakē-sarivarman *alias* Rājarājadēva I, date of which is lost. 154th day.

448. 201 *of* 1901.—(Tamil.) On the same wall. Records in the seventeenth year of the Chōḷa king Rājarāja-Rājakēsarivarman I gift of a lamp to the temple of Uttama-Chōḷa-Īśvara.

449. 202 *of* 1901.—(Tamil.) On the same wall. A damaged record of the Chōḷa king Rājarājakēsarivarman I, dated in his twelfth year. Mentions Uttama-Chōḷa-chaturvēdimaṅgalam. Its Sabhā met at the temple Tirumuṟṟam and made a *vyavastā*.

Tirupparuttikkunṟu.

450. 40 *of* 1890.—North wall of the store room in the Jaina temple. A record of Rājarājadēva, dated in his twentieth year.

451. 41 *of* 1890.—(Tamil and Grantha.) Base of the same wall. A record of Irugappa, son of Daṇḍanātha Vaichaya, dated Dundubhi year (Ś. 1305). Records that Irugappa made to the temple a grant for the benefit of Bukkarāja (II), the son of Harihara II. Dr. Hultzsch points out that the chief is the same as the Iruga, son of Chaicha, who built the Jain temple at Vijayanagar in Ś. 1307. See *S.I.I.*, I, p. 156. For the present epigraph see *Ep. Ind.*, VII, 115-6. According to Dr. Kielhorn the details of the date do not work out correctly. See *Ep. Ind.*, VI, 329.

452. 42 *of* 1890.—(Grantha.) On the roof of the maṇṭapa in front of the shrine in the same temple. A record in Prabhava year (1387-8). Records that the maṇṭapa was built by the same General Irugappa at the instance of his preceptor Pushpasēna. See *Ep. Ind.*, VII, p. 116.

453. 43 *of* 1890.—On the base of the verandah in front of the same shrine. A record of Tribhuvanachakravartin Kulōttuṅga-Chōḷadēva, dated in his twenty-first year.

454. 44 *of* 1890.—West wall of the Śāntimaṇṭapa in the same temple. A record of Rājarājadēva, dated in his eighteenth year.

455. 45 *of* 1890.—Right of the entrance into the same temple. A record of Vijayanagara king Krishṇadēva, dated in Ś. 1440 expired, Bahudhānya year.

456. 188 *of* 1901.—(Tamil.) On the base of the verandah in front of the Jaina temple of Trailōkyanātha. A record of the Vijayanagara king Kṛishṇarāya ; records in Dhātri gift of a village by the king to the temple.

457. 189 *of* 1901.—(Tamil verse.) On a stone built into the platform in the same temple.

Tirupputkkuḷi

458. 18 *of* 1899.—(Tamil.) On the east wall of the central shrine of the Vijayarāghavaperumāḷ temple, right of entrance. The Uḍaiyār king Kampaṇa-Uḍaiyār, son of Bukkaṇa-Uḍaiyār, records in Ś. 1287, expired, Viśvāvasu, gift of a jewel to the God Vijayarāghavaperumāḷ at Tirupputkuḷi.

459. 19 *of* 1899.—(Grantha and Tamil.) On the east base of the maṇṭapa in front of the central shrine of the same temple. The Pāṇḍya king Sundara Pāṇḍya records the building of the maṇṭapa. [The king is said to have conquered all countries and covered the temple of Śrīraṅgam with gold, and so he has been identified with Sundara Pāṇḍya I (1251-64) referred to in the

Raṅganātha inscription and the *Kōyiloḷugu*. The maṇṭapa was built for the merit of Kulaśēkhara who was evidently his predecessor. It is doubtful whether he was his father as the Muhammadan historians say or his brother as the *Mahāvamśa* says. See *Ep. Rep.*, 1899, p. 16.]

460. 52 *of* 1900.—(Tamil.) On the north wall of the first prākāra of the Vijayarāghavaperumāḷ temple. Records in the eighth year of the Pāṇḍya king Śaḍagōpavarman *alias* Tribhuvanachakravartin Vikrama-Pāṇḍyadēva, the gift of the village of Paḍuvūr *alias* Vīrachampanallūr in Paḍuvūr-kōṭṭam by Vīra-Champa. Venkayya suggests that the king Vikrama Pāṇḍya should have been a contemporary of the parricide Sundara Pāṇḍya (who fled to Delhi in 1310) and of Vīra Champa. See N.A. 290 (N. Arcot) at Tiruvottūr.

Ūttukkāḍu.

461. 345 *of* 1906.—(Tamil.) On the south wall of the ruined Perumāḷ temple. A record of the so-called Gaṅga Pallava king Vijaya-Kampavarman in his twenty-fifth year. Gift of three lamps.

462. 346 *of* 1906.—(Tamil.) On a pillar of the maṇṭapa in front of the same temple. A record of the Chōḷa king Rājakēsarivarman in his seventeenth year. Records gift of land.

463. 347 *of* 1906.—(Tamil.) On a stone set up near the tank bund in the same village. A record of the thirty-second year of the Chōḷa king Madirai-koṇḍa Parakēsarivarman (Parāntaka I) regarding the construction of the tank.

464. 348 *of* 1906.—(Tamil.) On the same stone. First two lines in Telugu characters and the rest in Tamil. The latter seems to refer to the cutting of a man's head, represented in the sculpture on the same stone.

465. 349 *of* 1906.—(Telugu.) On the right side of the steps leading to the same tank. Records in Ś. 1598, Naḷa, that a certain Pēṭa-Gaṅgareḍḍi whose ancestry is given, repaired the tank, built the margin of stones and two flights of steps.

466. 350 *of* 1906.—(Tamil.) On a stone set up in a field near the same village. Records in Prajāpati gift of land. A tiger is engraved at the top of the inscription.

467. 351 *of* 1906.—(Tamil.) On a stone set up near the Kaṇṇar-maṇṭapam in the same village. Records in Hēmalamba gift of land for a flower garden.

MADURĀNTAKAM TALUK.

Achcharapākkam.

468. 233 *of* 1901.—(Tamil.) On the north wall of the gōpura of the Akshēśvara temple, right of entrance. Dated in the reign of the Vijayanagara king Kṛishṇarāya. Records in Ś. 1450,

Virōdhin, a gift by Vīra-Narasimharāya-Nāyakar for the merit of the king on the occasion of a lunar eclipse.

469. 234 *of* 1901.—(Tamil.) On the east wall of the maṇṭapa in front of the same temple, right of entrance. An incomplete record of the Chōḷa king Tribhuvanachakravartin Kulōttuṅga-Chōḷadēva (III), the date of which is lost. Mentions Ammaiyappan Śambuvarāyan.

470. 235 *of* 1901.—(Tamil.) On the same wall. Records in the reign of Tribhuvanachakravartin Kōnērinmaikoṇḍān gift of land to an image set up by Āṭkoṇḍanāyakan *alias* Śēdiyarāyan.

471. 236 *of* 1901.—(Tamil.) On the same wall, left of entrance. Records in the third year of the Chōḷa king Tribhuvanachakravartin Rājarājadēva gift of sheep for a lamp.

472. 237 *of* 1901.—(Tamil.) On the same wall left of entrance. Records in the thirty-fifth year of the Chōḷa king Tribhuvanachakravartin Tribhuvanavīradēva (Kulōttuṅga III) gift of gold for a lamp.

473. 238 *of* 1901.—(Tamil.) On the south wall of the same maṇṭapa. Records in the fifth year of the Pāṇḍya king Māravarman *alias* Tribhuvanachakravartin Vikrama-Pāṇḍyadēva "who conquered every country," gift of land. The king was evidently the same as the Māravarman Vikrama Pāṇḍya who came to the throne in 1282 and who conquered Vīra Gaṇḍagōpāla and Kākatīya Gaṇapati.

474. 239 *of* 1901.—(Tamil.) On the same wall. A record of the Chōḷa king Tribhuvanachakravartin Kulōttuṅga-Chōḷadēva (III). Records in his twelfth year, gift of jewels by Śeṅgēṇi Ammaiyappan "who took the Pāṇḍya country."

475. 240 *of* 1901.—(Tamil.) On the same wall. Records in the fifteenth year of the Chōḷa king Tribhuvanachakravartin Kulōttuṅga-Chōḷadēva (III ?) that Attimallan Kulōttuṅga Chōḷa Śambuvarāyan granted the proceeds of certain taxes to the temple.

476. 241 *of* 1901.—(Tamil.) On the same wall. A record of the Chōḷa king Tribhuvanachakravartin Rājarājadēva (III ?). Records in his third year, gift of ten buffalo cows for a lamp to the temple of Ātchikoṇḍaruḷiyadēva.

477. 242 *of* 1901.—(Tamil.) On the same wall. A record of the Pāṇḍya king Tribhuvanachakravartin Vikrama-Pāṇḍyadēva. Records in his third year gift of land to the same temple. See No. 473.

478. 243 *of* 1901.—(Tamil.) On the same wall. Records in the seventh year (Kārttika, Aparapaksha, Sunday, Aśvini) of the Pāṇḍya king Tribhuvanachakravartin Vīra-Pāṇḍyadēva gift of land to the same temple. See *Ep. Ind.*, VII, 11, where Dr. Kielhorn argues that the intended date was probably 13th July A.D. 1259.

479. 244 *of* 1901.—(Tamil.) On the west wall of the same maṇṭapa. Records in the eighteenth year of the Chōḷa king

Parakēsarivarman *alias* Tribhuvanachakravartin Rājarājadēva II, grant of the proceeds of a tax by Rājanārāyaṇa Śambuvarāya of the Śeṅgeṇgaḷ family.

480. 245 *of* 1901.—(Tamil.) On the same wall. Records in the fourth year of the Pāṇḍya king Jaṭāvarman *alias* Tribhuvana-chakravartin Vikrama-Pāṇḍyadēva gift of land. (See No. 473).

481. 246 *of* 1901.—(Tamil.) On the north wall of the same maṇṭapa. Records in the third year of the Chōḷa king Rājakēsari-varman *alias* Tribhuvanachakravartin Kulōttuṅga-Chōḷadēva that the king clubbed several villages together into one, called it Kali-kaḍinda-Śōḷan Śattanūr and granted it to the temple. The village belonged to Oymānāḍu *alias* Vijayarājēndra-vaḷanāḍu.

482. 247 *of* 1901.—(Tamil.) On the same wall. Records in the fifth year of the Chōḷa king Rājakēsarivarman *alias* Tri-bhuvanachakravartin Kulōttuṅga-Chōḷadēva gift of land. Men-tions the image of Kulōttuṅga-Chōḷadēva, which was set up in the same temple, and Ōymānāḍu *alias* Vijayarājēndravaḷanāḍu.

483. 248 *of* 1901.—(Tamil.) On the same wall. The Chōḷa king Rājakēsarivarman *alias* Tribhuvanachakravartin Kulōttuṅga-Chōḷadēva records in his ninth year, gift of sheep for a lamp.

484. 249 *of* 1901.—(Tamil.) On the same wall. Records in the sixth year of the Pāṇḍya king Māravarman Tribhuvanachakra-vartin, gift of land.

485. 250 *of* 1901.—(Tamil.) On the south wall of the central shrine in the Akshēśvara temple. A record of Vijayanagara king Kampaṇa-Uḍaiyār II, son of Vīra-Bokkaṇa-Uḍaiyār I, recording in Ś. 1283, Plava, gift of land to a *maṭha* at Kāñchipuram. Mentions the minister Sōmappar and Koppaṇṇar (Goppaṇa Rāya ?).

486. 251 *of* 1901.—(Tamil.) On the same wall. A damaged record of the Pāṇḍya king Māravarman *alias* Tribhuvanachakra-vartin Vikrama-Pāṇḍyadēva, dated in his third year (A.D. 1285?). Records gift of land.

487. 252 *of* 1901.—(Tamil.) On the same wall. The Pāṇḍya king Jaṭāvarman *alias* Tribhuvanachakravartin Sundara-Pāṇḍya-dēva II (1276—90) records in his fifteenth year, gift of land. The actual date is Monday, 28th August 1290. See *Ep. Ind.*, VIII, p. 280. After Mr. Swamikannu Pillai's researches this king has to be called Sundara Pāṇḍya III.

488. 253 *of* 1901.—(Tamil.) On the west wall of the same shrine. The Chola king Rājakēsarivarman *alias* Vīrarājēndradēva (I, 1063—70) records in his fifth year, gift of paddy and of the proceeds of taxes.

489. 254 *of* 1901.—(Tamil.) On the north wall of the same shrine. An incomplete record of the Chōḷa king Rājakēsarivar man *alias* Kulōttuṅga-Chōḷadēva I, dated in his forty-second year.

490. 255 *of* 1901.—(Tamil.) On the same wall. A record of the Vijayanagara king Vīra-Bukkaṇa-Uḍaiyār (I) recording in Ś. 1298, Naḷa, gift of land.

491. 256 *of* 1901.—(Tamil.) On the same wall. Records in the forty-ninth year of the Chōḷa king Rājakēsarivarman *alias* Kulōttuṅga-Chōḷadēva (I) gift of sheep for a lamp.

492. 257 *of* 1901.—(Tamil.) On the same wall. Records in the sixth year of the Chōḷa king Parakēsarivarman *alias* Vikrama-Chōḷadēva (1118—35) gift of a lamp.

493. 258 *of* 1901.—(Tamil.) On the same wall. Records in the seventh year of the Chōḷa king Parakēsarivarman *alias* Vikrama-Chōḷadēva (1118—35) gift of a lamp.

494. 259 *of* 1901.—(Tamil.) On the north wall of another shrine in the same temple. Records in the forty-third year of the Chōḷa king Rājakēsarivarman *alias* Kulōttuṅga-Chōḷadēva I (1070—1118) gift of sheep for a lamp.

495. 260 *of* 1901.—(Tamil.) On the west wall of the same shrine. An incomplete record of the Chōḷa king Sakalalōka-chakravartin Rājanārāyaṇan Śamburāyan, dated in his eighteenth year (A.D. 1355).

496. 261 *of* 1901.—(Tamil.) On the south wall of the same shrine. Records in the third year of the Chōḷa king Parakēsarivarman *alias* Rājēndra-Chōḷadēva I (1011—43) gift of sheep for a lamp.

Kadambarkōyil.

497. 226 *of* 1901.—(Tamil.) On the north, west and south walls of the central shrine in the Kadambanāthēśvara temple. A mutilated record of the Chōḷa king Rājakēsarivarman *alias* Vīra-rājēndradēva (1064—70), the date of which is lost. Records gift of land.

Kadapperi near *Madurāntakam.*

498. 129 *of* 1896.—(Tamil.) On the outer side of the east wall of the second prākāra of the Śvētanārāyaṇēśvara temple, right of entrance. The Chōḷa king Kō-Rājakēsarivarman *alias* Rājādhi-rājadēva (1018—52) records gift of money, on a date which is lost. (Śvētāraṇya is in Tamil Tiruveṇkāḍu.)

499. 130 *of* 1896.—(Tamil.) In the same place. A much worn out record of Tribhuvanachakravartin Tribhuvanavīradēva (Kulōttuṅga III) "who was pleased to take Madurai and the crowned head of the Pāṇḍya", dated in his thirty-seventh year.

500. 131 *of* 1896.—(Tamil.) In the same place. Recordsin the sixteenth year of the Chōḷa king Tribhuvanachakravartin Kulōttuṅga-Chōḷadēva gift of a lamp. See *Ep. Ind.*, IV, 265.

501. 132 *of* 1896.—(Tamil.) On the same wall, left of entrance. Records in the ninth year of the Chōḷa king Kō-Parakēsarivarman *alias* Rājarājadēva (II 1146—78) gift of land.

502. 133 *of* 1896.—(Tamil.) On the inner side of the south wall of the same prākāra. The Vijayanagara king Prauḍha-Dēvarāya records in Ś. 1370 expired, the gift of the village of Karunguḻi to the temple. [Karunguḻi was the birth place of the famous Rāmaliṅgapillai, a saint who lived early in the nineteenth century and who wrote the *Tiruvaruṭpā.*]

503. 134 *of* 1896.—(Tamil.) On the inner side of the east of the same prākāra. Records in the fortieth year of the Pāṇḍya king Kō-Māravarman *alias* Kulaśēkharadēva I (1268—1308) gift of land to two images. See *Ep. Ind.*, VI, 300, where it is pointed out that the exact date is Saturday, 24th February 1308.

504. 135 *of* 1896.—(Tamil.) On the east wall of the shrine in the same temple right of entrance. Records in the twenty-ninth year of the Chōḻa king Kō-Rājakēsarivarman *alias* Kulōttuṅga-Chōḻadēva (I ?) gift of a lamp.

505. 136 *of* 1896.—(Tamil.) On the same wall, left of entrance. Records in the thirty-fifth year of the Chōḻa king Kō-Rājakēsarivarman *alias* Kulōttuṅgā-Chōḻadēva (I ?) gift of a lamp.

506. 137 *of* 1896.—(Tamil.) On the south wall of the same shrine. Records in the sixth year of the Chōḻa king Kulōttuṅgadēva the pledging of certain land.

507. 138 *of* 1896.—(Tamil.) On the north, west and south walls of the same shrine. Records in the fifteenth year of the Chōla king Kō-Rājakēsarivarman *alias* Kulōttuṅga-Chōḻadēva gift of land. [The temple was built by a military officer of the king.]

508. 262 *of* 1901.—(Tamil.) On the west wall of the central shrine in the Kōdaṇḍarāma-Perumāḷ temple at Madurāntakam. Records in the third year of the Chōḻa king Rājakēsarivarman *alias* Tribhuvanachakravartin Kulōttuṅga-Chōḻadēva gift of an arecanut garden for maintaining two lamps.

509. 263 *of* 1901.—(Tamil.) On the north wall of the same shrine. Records in the ninth year of the Chōḻa king Parakēsarivarman *alias* Tribhuvanachakravartin Vikrama-Chōḻadēva gift of money. Contains also the first few words of another inscription of the eleventh year of the king's reign.

Madurāntakam.

510. *C.P. No.* 141 *of Mr. Sewell's List.*—(Modern Telugu.) Records gift of certain lands to the temple of Chandraśēkhara by one Periya Namaśivāya Nāyanār, in Ś. 482 (A.D. 560). The date is of course absurd. "The language of the deed, though mostly Telugu, has an admixture of modern Tamil terms. There are a number of figures of weapons, etc., at the top and bottom, including a matchlock with bayonet."

Māmaṇḍūr.

See Cg. Nos. 286—8, where the local inscriptions have been placed by oversight and also supplement to this district.

511. 612 *of* 1904.—(Tamil.) On the north base of the Maṇḍūkanāthēśvara temple. A mutilated record of the Chōḷa king Rājarāja I, date of which is lost. Contains a portion of the historical introduction. Records gift of 90 sheep for a lamp.

Neḍumāram.

512. 270 *of* 1912.—(Telugu.) On a slab built into the roof of the Ādikēśava-Perumāḷ temple. The back side and the top of the slab are built in. The inscription is in modern characters and registers the construction of a temple for Chennakēśava, west of the village Nemḍambaram, by a certain Lakshmayya, for the merit of Chennakēśava-Nāyanivāru.

Neyyaḍipākkam.

513. 212 *of* 1901.—(Tamil.) On the right of the entrance into the Piridigaṅgēśvara temple. Records in the third year of the Chōḷa king Tribhuvanachakravartin Vīrarājēndra-Chōḷadēva gift of two lamps. The temple is called Pirudigaṅgavuḍaiyār and the village Neyyaruppākkam in Toḍupaḷuvūr-nāḍu, a subdivision of Kāliyūr-kōṭṭam.

514. 213 *of* 1901.--(Tamil.) On the east wall of the maṇṭapa in front of the Marundīśvara temple. The Uḍaiyār king Śayaṇa Uḍaiyār (son of Kampa I?) records in his sixteenth year gift of land to the Marundīśvara temple.

515. 214 *of* 1901.—(Tamil.) On the south wall of the central shrine of the same temple. The Uḍaiyār king Sayaṇa Uḍaiyār records in his sixteenth year gift of land. The village is called Neyyaḍarpākkam.

Paramēśvaramaṅgalam.

516. 257 *of* 1912.—(Tamil.) On the slab near a Gaṇēśa image outside the Kailāsanātha temple. Records in the sixteenth year of the "Gaṅga-Pallava" king Nripatuṅgavarman (*circa* 850–80), gift of gold (11 *kaḻanju*) for offerings to the god Mahādēva in the temple of Śailēśvara, at Paramēśvaramaṅgalam. The money was deposited on interest in the hands of the *Gaṇapperumakkaḷ* of Śailēśvara by Nandi-Niraimati, son of Maṇṇaikuḍi-maṟamaḍakki Viḷupperaraiyan. Engraved by Śatturuśiṅgapperundachchan. [Mr. Krishna Sastri points out that Maṇṇaikuḍi was the place where Udayachandra, the General of Nandivarman II (*circa* 712–79), defeated the Pāṇḍyan king and surmises that an ancestor of Viḷupperaraiyan should have taken part in it, thus obtaining a hereditary title. The *Gaṇapperumakkaḷ* should have been, like the *Āḷumgaṇattār*, the direct managers of the village affairs. A similar term is *Amritagaṇattār*. See Tiruvoṟṟiyūr inscriptions. Maṇṇaikuḍi has been identified with Maṇṇi near Kumbhakōṇam.

517. 258 *of* 1912.—(Tamil.) On the back side of the same slab. Records in the fifteenth year the consecration of the image of Gaṇapati-Bhaṭārar and the construction of a temple for the same at Śailēśvara, by a Brāhmaṇa lady who provided forty *kāḍi* of paddy for lamps and worship. The record is evidently connected with No. 516.

518. 259 *of* 1912.—(Tamil.) On a slab set up near the Vaikuṇṭha-Perumāḷ temple in the same village. A much damaged record of the Vijayanagara king Kṛishṇadēva-Mahārāya, dated in Ś. 1444, Chitrabhānu, Makara, śu. di. 10, Monday, Tiruvōṇam (29th September, A.D. 1522). Mentions the Mahāmaṇḍalēśvara Mēdinimiśāra Gaṇḍakaṭṭāri Śāḷuva Nāgayyadēva Maha-araśa.

Perumber.

This place, like Achcharapākkam and Madurāntakam, was included in the Kaḷattūr-kōṭṭam. It is also called Tribhuvananallūr and a hamlet of Madhurāntaka-chaturvēdimaṅgalam.

519. 264 *of* 1901.—(Tamil.) On the west wall of the maṇṭapa, in front of the Tāndōnrīśvara temple. Records in the eleventh year of the Chōḷa king Rājakēsarivarman *alias* Kulōttuṅga-Chōḷadēva I gift of land. The assembly of Madurāntakam remits the taxes (*antarāya and magamai*) on it. Signed by citizens in different *chēris* of the city, named after Chōḷa kings. The tax on 32 *paḍāgas* is nearly 12 *kaḻanjūs*. *S.I.I.*, III, No. 78, pp. 173–8.

520. 265 *of* 1901.—(Tamil.) On the east wall of the same maṇṭapa. A record of Rājarājadēva II in his eighteenth year; records gift of four cows for a lamp in the temple of Śrīkaraṇīśvara at Perumbērur.

521. 266 *of* 1901.—(Tamil.) On the same wall. Dated in the reign of the Chōḷa king Rājakēsarivarman *alias* Vīrarājēndradēva (I, 1064—70); records in his seventh year gift of land (after its being reclaimed) by the assembly of Mādhurāntaka-chaturvēdimaṅgalam to the temple. *S.I.I.*, III, No. 84, pp. 202–4.

522. 267 *of* 1901.—(Tamil.) On the same wall. Dated in the reign of the Chōḷa king Parakēsarivarman *alias* Tribhuvanachakravartin Rājarājadēva II. Records in his eighteenth year gift of land for a lamp by a native of Tagaḍūr.

523. 268 *of* 1901.—(Tamil.) On the same wall of the same maṇṭapa. Records in the ninth year of the Chōḷa king Parakēsarivarman *alias* Kulōttuṅga-Chōḷadēva II gift of ten cows for a lamp.

Pulipparakoyil.

524. 293 *of* 1910.—(Tamil.) On the south wall of the central shrine in the Vyāgrapādēśvara temple. Dated in the reign of the Vijayanagara king Vīra-Bukkaṇa-Uḍaiyar (II, 1399--1406), in

Svabhānu (i.e., Ś. 1326). Records the gift of certain taxes on the residentsliving in the *tirumaḍaiviḷāgam* of the temple of Tiruppulippagava-Nāyanar. The resident Śeṭṭis, Kaikkōḷars and Vāṇiyas were to pay two *paṇams* per year on each individual and two *paṇams* on each loom. Mr. Krishna Sastri believes that these apparently covered all the taxes payable by them, viz., *Paṭṭāḍainūlāyam, āṭṭaisammādam, periyasammādam, kaiyērpu, māḍavritti, daṇṇāyakanmagamai*, etc.

525. 294 *of* 1910.—(Tamil.) On the north wall of the same shrine. Dated in the reign of the Vijayanagara king Vīra Vijayabhūpatirāja Uḍaiyār (son of Dēvarāya I), in *Hēmalamba* (i.e., Ś. 1340). Records that the trustees of the temple, after consulting the revenue authorities of the Chandragiriśālā, granted a remission of six *paṇams* which they had used to take in excess from the Kaikkōḷars living in its *tirumaḍaiviḷāgam*, as *vāśalpaṇam* ; but collected as before three *paṇams* from each family (?) of Kachchavaḍa Vāṇiyar, three *paṇams* from each family of *Śenpaḍayar*, 40 *paṇams* on cloths and four towards *Kārttigaikāṇikkai*.

526. 295 *of* 1910.—(Tamil.) On the south wall of the maṇṭapa in front of the same temple. Dated in the reign of the Vijayanagara king Vīrapratāpa Prauḍhadēvarāya Mahārāya (1449–65) in Ś. 1374, Āṅgirasa. Records gift of the village Kaṇakkanpaṭṭu *alias* Śēd'rāya-nallūr, to the temple of Tiruppulippagava-Nāyanar at Paṭṭūr, the northern hamlet of Madhurāntaka-chaturvēdimaṅgalam in Kaḷattūr-kōṭṭam, a district of Jayaṅgoṇḍachōḷamaṇḍalam, by Dēvappagaḷ, son of Mahāpradhāna Annadāta-Daṇṇāyaka, for the health of the king.

527. 296 *of* 1910.—(Tamil.) On the north wall of the same maṇṭapa. A damaged record of the Pāṇḍya king Māravarman Tribhuvanachakravartin Sundara-Pāṇḍyadēva (not identified), dated in his twelfth year. Mentions a number of chiefs Amarakōn, Vēṇuvuḍaiyān, Pallavamārāyan, Adiyamān, Nandipanman, etc., apparently vassals of the king. Seems to register certain privileges agreed to by the Mahēśvarās, Sthānattārs, priests and the Kaikkōḷars of the temple, in the presence of a certain Kaṇḍiyadēvar. [The privileges were that " their daughters' children and sons' sons were to be allowed freedom of action in the temple and in the village, and were to receive betel-leaves (as a token of honour) in the *Tiruvōlakkam*," etc.]

528. 297 *of* 1910.—(Tamil.) On the same wall. A damaged record of the Vijayanagara king Vīra-Bukkaṇa-Uḍaiyār (II), dated Ś. 1327, Pārthiva. Mentions Agaram Vaḷudippākkam, the northern hamlet of Madhurāntaka-chaturvēdimaṅgalam.

529. 298 *of* 1910.—(Tamil.) On the east wall of the same maṇṭapa. Ṣakalalōkachakravartin Rājanārāyaṇa Śambuvarāya (1337–60) records in his sixth year, gift of taxes payable within the four limits of the tirumaḍaiviḷāgam, for the worship in the temple of Tiruppulippagava-Nāyanār. The taxes are the *tarikkadamai* on looms, *pērkkadamai* (on individuals), payable by the Kaikkōḷars, Śāliyars and Vāṇiyars.

530. 299 *of* 1910.—(Tamil.) On the same wall. A record of the Vijayanagara king Viruppa (i.e., Viruppaṇa) Uḍaiyār, (i.e. Virūpāksha I), son of Ariyaṇa Uḍaiyār (Harihara II); mentions in Ś. 1319, Īśvara, Madhurāntaka-chaturvēdimangalam in Kaḷattūr-kōṭṭam.

531. 300 *of* 1910.—(Tamil.) On the same wall. Records in Kāḷayukta gift of two looms in favour of a shrine of Ilaiya Nāyanār, in the street to the west of the temple of Pulippagavar, under the orders of the Mangappa-Uḍaiyār.

532. 301 *of* 1910.—(Tamil.) On the slab set up in the same temple. Records gift of land in the village of Abhimāna-vātāpinal-lūr to the temple of Tiruveṇgāḍuḍaiya-Nāyanār in Madhurāntaka-chaturvēdimangalam. Mentions also the temple of Tiruppulippa-gavar at Paṭṭūr.

533. 302 *of* 1910.—(Tamil.) On a slab set up in a street of the same village. Records in Sāruvadi (Śārvari) gift of taxes collected from the residents of the southern street in Pulippara-kōyil, for the health of Naraśingarāja Uḍaiyār, by a certain Timmarāja-Uḍaiyār.

Śeyyūr.

534. 430 *of* 1902.—(Tamil.) On the north wall of the central shrine in the Valmīkanātha temple. Records in the fifth year of the Chōḷa king Rājakēsarivarman *alias* Uḍaiyār Vīrarājēndradēva (I?) gift of land by a military officer

535. 431 *of* 1902.—(Tamil.) On the same wall. A damaged record of the Chōḷa king Rājakēsarivarman *alias* Tribhuvanachak-ravartin Kulōttunga-Chōḷadēva, date of which is lost. Records gift of thirty cows for a lamp.

536. 432 *of* 1902.—(Tamil.) On the west wall of the same shrine. Records in the ninth year of the Chōḷa king Vikrama-Chōḷadēva (1118—35) gift of a lamp.

537. 433 *of* 1902.—(Tamil.) On the same wall. Records in the third year of the Chōḷa king Vikrama-Chōḷadēva gift of land for a lamp.

538. 434 *of* 1902.—(Tamil.) On the south wall of the same shrine. Records in the third year of the Chōḷa king Vikrama-Chōḷadēva gift of 96 sheep for two lamps.

539. 435 *of* 1902.—(Tamil.) On the same wall. A record of the Chōḷa king Kulōttunga-Chōḷadēva I, dated in his forty-seventh year.

540. 436 *of* 1902.—(Tamil.) On the same wall. Records in the fourth year of the Chōḷa king Rājarājadēva gift of twelve sheep for a lamp.

541. 437 *of* 1902.—(Tamil.) On the same wall. An epigraph of the Chōḷa king Kulōttuṅga-Chōḷadēva (I) recording in his forty-ninth year gift of money for a lamp.

542. 438 *of* 1902.—(Tamil.) On the south wall of the maṇṭapa in front of the same shrine. An epigraph of the Chōḷa king Vikrama-Chōḷadēva (1118—35) recording in his eighth year gift of ninety sheep for a lamp.

543. 439 *of* 1902.—(Tamil.) On the same wall. An epigraph of the Chōḷa king Tribhuvanachakravartin Rājarājadēva recording in his ninth year gift of a salt pan.

544. 440 *of* 1902.—(Tamil.) On the same wall. A damaged record of the Chōḷa king Tribhuvanachakravartin Rājādhirājadēva, dated in his eighth year.

545. 441 *of* 1902.—(Tamil.) On the north wall of the same maṇṭapa. An epigraph of the Chōḷa king Rājarājadēva recording in his fifth year gift of money for offerings to Piḷḷaiyār for thirty-two days of the year.

546. 442 *of* 1902.—(Tamil.) On the same wall. An epigraph of the Chōḷa king Kulōttuṅga-Chōḷadēva recording in his twelfth year gift of a lamp.

547. 443 *of* 1902.—(Tamil.) On the same wall. An epigraph of the Chōḷa king Rājādhirājadēva recording in his sixth year the setting up of an image of Kēdāradēva.

548. 444 *of* 1902.—(Tamil.) On the same wall. An epigraph of the Chōḷa king Rājakēsarivarman *alias* Tribhuvanachakravartin Kulōttuṅga-Chōḷadēva which records in his fourth year gift of land as śrīdhana to the goddess.

549. 445 *of* 1902.—(Tamil.) On the same wall. An epigraph of the Chōḷa king Kulōttuṅga-Chōḷadēva which records in his fourth year gift of salt-pans.

550. 446 *of* 1902.—(Tamil.) On the south wall of the maṇṭapa in front of the Kailāsanātha temple in the same village. An epigraph of the Chōḷa king Vikrama-Chōḷadēva which records in his eighth year gift of twelve sheep for a lamp.

551. 447 *of* 1902.—(Tamil.) On the same wall. An epigraph of the Chōḷa king Kulōttuṅga-Chōḷadēva which records in his forty-fourth year gift of twelve sheep for a lamp.

552. 448 *of* 1902.—(Tamil.) On the same wall. Records in the forty-fifth year of the Chōḷa king Kulōttuṅga-Chōḷadēva (I) gift of twelve sheep for a lamp.

553. 449 *of* 1902.—(Tamil.) On the north wall of the same maṇṭapa. Dated in the reign of the Chōḷa king Tribhuvanachakravartin Kulōttuṅga-Chōḷadēva (III) who took Madura, the crowned head of the Pāṇḍya, Ceylon, and Karuvūr. Records in his twenty-third and twenty-sixth years gift of money for two lamps.

554. 450 *of* 1902.—(Tamil.) On the east wall of the same maṇṭapa. Records in the tenth year of the Chōḷa king Rājādhirājadēva gift of money.

555. 451 *of* 1902.—(Tamil.) On the same wall. An incomplete record of the Chōḷa king Kulōttuṅga-Chōḷadēva (I), dated in his forty-eighth year.

556. 452 *of* 1902.—(Tamil.) On the same wall. Records in the fifth year of the Chōḷa king Rājādhirājadēva gift of money for three festivals.

557. 453 *of* 1902.—(Tamil.) On the same wall. Records in the fifth year of the Chōḷa king Rājarājadēva gift of twelve sheep for a lamp and of money for a festival.

558. 454 *of* 1902.—(Tamil.) On the west wall of the central shrine in the same temple. A record of the Chōḷa king Rājādhirājadēva recording gift of money for two festivals. The date is doubtful.

Tiruppulivānam.

559. 43 *of* 1898.—(Tamil.) On the west wall of the Vyāghrapādēśvara temple. A record of the Chōḷa king Tribhuvanachakravartin Kulōttuṅga-Chōḷadēva III, in his eighteenth year. Gift of cows for a lamp, by a person who killed another by mistake.

560. 44 *of* 1898.—(Tamil.) On the west wall of the same temple. Records in the ninth year of the Chōḷa king Rājakēsarivarman *alias* Kulōttuṅga-Chōḷadēva (I ?) gift of cows for a lamp.

561. 45 *of* 1898.—(Tamil.) On the same wall. A record of the Chōḷa king Rājakēsarivarman *alias* Kulōttuṅga-Chōḷadēva (I ?), dated in his twenty-fifth year. End built in.

Tiruvānakkoyil.

Like Kaḷattūr this place was a centre of Kāḷāmukha activity.

562. 284 *of* 1910.—(Tamil.) On the north wall of the central shrine in the Tiruvālīśvara temple. An unfinished record of the Pāṇḍya king Jaṭāvarman *alias* Tribhuvanachakravartin Sundara-Pāṇḍyadēva (I, 1251—64), "who was pleased to take all countries," dated in his fourteenth year. Seems to register sale of house-sites to the weavers and dancing girls of the temple of Tiruvālakkōyiluḍaiya-Nāyanār at Vittūr, the northern hamlet of Madhurāntakachaturvēdimaṅgalam, a *taniyūr* in Jayaṅgoṇḍachōḷa-maṇḍalam.

563. 285 *of* 1910.—(Tamil.) On the same wall. Records in the thirteenth year of Rājanārāyaṇa Śambuvarāya a gift of land at Vittūr, the northern hamlet of Madhurāntaka-chaturvēdimaṅgalam, a village in Kaḷattūr-kōṭṭam.

564. 286 *of* 1910.—(Tamil.) On the south wall of the same shrine. Records in the twelfth year of Rājanārāyaṇa Śambuvarāya (1337—60) gift of taxes collected within the *maḍaviḷāga* of the temple of Tiruvālakkōyiluḍaiya-Nāyanār at Vittūr, for festivals, worship, etc., in the same temple. The taxes were collected from the Śeṭṭis, Kaikkōḷars, Kaṟṟivaḍavāṇigar, Śekkuvāṇigar and Dēvanāyaṅgār.

565. 287 *of* 1910.—(Tamil.) On the same wall. Records in the nineteenth year of Sakalalōkachakravartin Rājanārāyaṇa gift of three *vēli* of land for conducting worship in the temple. [The lands were old Dēvadāna lands, but had gone out of possession to the detriment of worship in temple. Rājanārāyaṇa evidently restored the state of things as before the Mussalman invasions.]

566. 288 *of* 1910.—(Tamil.) On the same wall. Records in Vishu (Vrisha) that Tiruvēṅgaḍanāthar granted the fields called *nāchchan māniyam* to the temple of Tiruvāliyappan, for the merit of Vīrappanāyakkar-Ayyan.

567. 289 *of* 1910.—(Tamil.) On the same wall. Records in Bahudhānya, gift of houses, lands and certain privileges to the dancing girls whom a certain Varadarāja had newly appointed for service in the temple, which had been in difficulty owing to lack of maid-servants.

568. 290 *of* 1910.—(Tamil.) On the same wall. A record of the Pāṇḍya king Jaṭāvarman *alias* Tribhuvanachakravartin Sundara-Pāṇḍyadēva; records in his fourteenth year gift of six cows for two lamps by a certain Pushpagiri-jīyar. See No. 562 above.

569. 291 *of* 1910.—(Tamil.) On the west wall of the maṇṭapa in front of the same shrine. Records in Vikāri that a certain Timmarāśayya of Nāraṇapura built this (maṇṭapa) for the merit of Malaiyappaiyan.

570. 292 *of* 1910.—(Tamil.) On the same wall. Records in Vikāri gift of a house and land for a dancing girl who took up service in the temple of Tiruvālakkōyiluḍaiya-Tambirānār, for the merit of Timmarāśayyan, son of Rāmarāśayyan of Nāraṇapura.

571. 352 *of* 1911.—(Tamil.) On the south wall of the central shrine in the Tiruvālīśvara temple. Records in the fifteenth year of the Chōḷa king Tribhuvanachakravartin Rājarājadēva gift of a lamp to the temple of Tiruvālakkōyiluḍaiya-Mahādēva at Kaḷattūr in Kaḷattūr-kōṭṭam, a subdivision of Jayaṅgoṇḍachōḷa-maṇḍalam, by Paraśivan Taḷuvakkuḷaindān Āḷuḍaiyān, a native of Kuvalai in

Veṅkunṛa-kōṭṭam. Mentions the Kāḷāmukha priests Gōmaḍattu Jñānarāśi-Paṇḍita and Śailarāśi-Paṇḍita.

572. 353 *of* 1911.—(Tamil.) On the same wall. A record of the Vijayanagara king Tribhuvanachakravartin Viruppaṇa-Uḍaiyar (Virūpāksha I), son of Vīra-Ariyaṇa-Uḍaiyār (and therefore brother of Bukka II). Records in Ś. 1320 gift of land in the hamlet of Uttamasōḷaviḷāgam to the temple of Tiruvālakkoyiluḍaiya-Nāyanār at Kaḷattūr, by Vēṇavuḍaiyān, one of the Kaikkōḷa Mudalis of the temple. It is stated that Uttamaśōḷaviḷāgam was originally granted to the temple by Vīra-Kampaṇa-Uḍaiyār for worship and repairs. Mentions Pūṇḍarīkan Rājēndraśōḷa-Tamiḷadaraiyan Āṭkoṇḍān Maṇḍalapurushan.

573. 354 *of* 1911.—(Tamil.) On the same wall. A record of Rājanārāyaṇa Śambuvarāyar, recording in his third year gift of fifteen cows to the same temple by Mallinādan Rājanārāyaṇa Śambuvarāyan.

574. 355 *of* 1911.—(Tamil.) On the same wall. Dated in the reign of the Chōḷa king Tribhuvanachakravartin Rājarājadēva. Records in his fourth year gift of a lamp to the temple of Tiruvālakkōyiluḍaiya-Mahādēva, by the merchant of Tiru-Mayilappil in Puliyūr-kōṭṭam mentioned in Nos. 333 and 334 of 1911.

575. 356 *of* 1911.—(Tamil.) On the same wall. Dated in the reign of the Vijayanagara king Bukkaṇa Uḍaiyār (i.e., Bukka II), son of Vīra-Arirāya (i.e., Harihara II). Records in Tāraṇa (Ś. 1326) purchase of land at Puduppākkam by Vēṇavuḍaiyān, one of the Kaikkōḷa-Mudalis of the temple, perhaps for re-presentation to it.

576. 357 *of* 1911.—(Tamil.) On the same wall. Belongs to the reign of the Chōḷa king Tribhuvanachakravartin Kulōttuṅga-Chōḷadēva (III), "who was pleased to take Madurai (Madura) and the crowned head of the Pāṇḍya." Records in his twenty-seventh year gift of four cows for a lamp by a native of Āṟṟūr in Ūṟṟukkāṭṭu-kōṭṭam. Mentions the two Kāḷamukha priests referred to in No. 571 above.

577. 358 *of* 1911.—(Tamil.) On the same wall. Dated in the reign of the Chōḷa king Vikrama-Chōḷadēva (1118—35). Records in his tenth year gift of land at Śiru-Taṇḍālam to the god Chandraśēkhara at Tiruvālakkōyil by a number of people, one of whom was a native of Koḍuvūr (in Paṭṭiṇa-nāḍu, a subdivision of Śembūr-kōṭṭam) and another of Paṭṭiṇam.

578. 359 *of* 1911.—(Tamil.) On the west wall of the same shrine. Dated in the reign of the Chōḷa king Tribhuvanachakravartin Kōnērimēlkoṇḍān (Kulōttuṅga II ?). Records in his twelfth year an order of the king on the two hundred and ninety-third day of the year, to present certain lands in the village of Arumbākkam, a subdivision of Uḷalūr *alias* Rājarājanallūr in Kaḷattūr-kōṭṭam, clubbed together under the new name Anapāyanallūr, for maintaining worship in the temple of Tiruvālakōyiluḍaiya-Mahādēva. The royal secretary was Anapāya-Mūvēndavēḷān as in No. 346 of 1911 at Kaḷattūr. See also No. 582 below.

579. 360 *of* 1911.—(Tamil.) On the north wall of the same shrine. Records in the ninth year of the Chōḷa king Vikrama-Chōḷadēva (1118—35) gift of a lamp. Mentions Gōmaḍattu Śailarāśi-Paṇḍita. See Nos. 571 and 576 above.

580. 361 *of* 1911.—(Tamil.) On the same wall. Dated in the third year of Sakalalōkachakravartin Rājanārāyaṇa Śambuvarāya. Records in his third year gift of fifteen cows for half a lamp by one of the Kaikōḷar belonging to the temple of Tiruvālakōyiluḍaiya Nāyaṅār. Mentions the measure *Rājakēsari-nāḷi.*

581. 362 *of* 1911.—(Tamil.) On the same wall. Records in the tenth year of Rājanārāyaṇa Śambuvarāya that the residents of Kaḷattūr-paṟṟu gave Nariyanśēri *alias* Puṇḍarīkanallūr, a hamlet of Kaḷattūr, to the Kaikkōḷa mentioned in No. 580, as a sarvamānya grant.

582. 363 *of* 1911.—(Tamil.) On the same wall. The Chōḷa king Tribhuvanachakravartin Kōnērinmaikoṇḍān (Kulōttuṅga II) records in his twelfth year an order to the chief Toṇḍaimān on the two hundred and ninety-third day of the year to grant some lands in the village of Nenmali in Valla-nāḍu, clubbed together under the new name Kulōttuṅgaśōḷan Tirunīṟṟuchchōḷanallūr for maintaining worship in the temple. The royal secretary was Anapāya Mūvēndavēḷān as in Nos. 346 and 359. [According to Tamil literary tradition Toṇḍaimān was the title given by Kulōttuṅga II to the brother of Śekkiḷār, the author of the Periapurāṇa.]

583. 364 *of* 1911.—(Tamil.) On the west wall of the same shrine. Sakalalōkachakravartin Rājanārāyaṇa Śambuvarāya records in his twelfth year that the *tirumaḍaiviḷāgam* and the surrounding lands were given as a sarvamānya grant to the sthānattār of the temple, for maintaining worship and repairs.

584. 365 *of* 1911.—(Tamil.) On the same wall. A damaged record of the Chōḷa king Tribhuvanachakravartin Rājarājadēva (III ?), dated in his twenty-sixth year. Records gift of land by a certain Karikālaśōḷa-Tamiḷadaraiyan for burning a lamp on the hill north of the temple of Tiruvālakōyiluḍaiya-Nāyanār.

Tiruvāṇḍavar.

585. 613 *of* 1904.—(Tamil.) On the south wall of the maṇṭapa in front of the central shrine of the Tiruvāṇḍanāthēśvara temple. A fragment of record of Rājanārāyaṇa Śambuvarāya, dated in his eighth year.

586. 614 *of* 1904.—(Tamil.) On the same wall. A fragment of record of the Chōḷa king Tribhuvanachakravartin Vikrama-Chōḷadēva, date of which is lost. Records gift of a lamp.

587. 615 *of* 1904.—(Tamil.) On a slab set up in the same place. A fragment of record of the Vijayanagara king Achyuta, dated Durmukha (i.e., Ś. 1459). The king bears Śāḷuva *birudas*. The village is called Tiruvāṇḍavāru. In the same village is a modern inscription, dated in Vikāri.

588. 616 *of* 1904.—(Tamil.) On a slab set up in a field to the east of the same village. Dated in the reign of the Vijayanagara king Vīrapratāpa Vīra-Rāmadēva-Mahārāya (1620—30). Records in Ś. 1547, expired, Krōdhana, gift of land by a Nāyaka.

Uttaramallūr.

589. 1 *of* 1898.—(Tamil.) On the west wall of the Vaikuṇṭha Perumāḷ temple. A record of the Chōḷa king Madirai-koṇḍa Parakēsarivarman, dated in his fourteenth year. Contains a letter from the king to the villagers regarding disqualifications for appointments. [The inscription is one of the most valuable documents in South Indian constitutional history. It throws a flood of light on the committee system of village government, the method of village administration by the assembly, the qualifications for membership, etc. See *Ep. Rep.*, 1899, pp. 24—27, where the inscription is fully summarised.]

590. 2 *of* 1898.—(Tamil.) On the same wall. A record of the Chōḷa king Madirai-koṇḍa Parakēsarivarman, dated in his twelfth year. Contents similar to those of No. 589. [This epigraph is of the same nature and value as the previous one, but earlier and a little less elaborate. See *Ep. Rep.*, 1899, pp. 27-8. This was amended by the later regulation given above.]

591. 3 *of* 1898.—(Tamil.) On the same wall. Records in the eighth year of the so-called Gaṅga-Pallava king Vijaya-Kampavarman gift of land to the temple of Mahādēva in the neighbouring village of Puliyūr.

592. 4 *of* 1898.—(Tamil.) On the same wall. Records in the tenth year of the Chōḷa king Parakēsarivarman gift of land to the temple of Mahādēva in the neighbouring village of Tiṭṭattūr.

593. 5 *of* 1898.—(Tamil.) On the same wall. Records in the eighth year of the Gaṅga-Pallava king Vijaya-Kampavikramavarman gift of land to Mahāvishṇu.

594. 6 *of* 1898.—(Tamil.) On the same wall. Records in the eighth year of the so-called Gaṅga-Pallava king Vijaya-Kampavikramavarman gift of land to Mahāvishṇu.

595. 7 *of* 1898.—(Tamil.) On the same wall. Records in the ninth year of the so-called Gaṅga-Pallava king Vijaya-Kampavarman a sale of land. Incomplete.

596. 8 *of* 1898.—(Tamil.) On the same wall. Records in the fifteenth year of the Chōla king Madirai-koṇḍa Parakēsarivarman

(Parāntaka I) gift of land to the temples of Tiruppulivalam and Tulāvārattaḷi.

597. 9 *of* 1898.—(Tamil.) On the same wall. Records in the sixteenth year the Chōḷa king Madirai-koṇḍa Parakēsarivarman (Parāntaka I) gift of land for offerings and lamps.

598. 10 *of* 1898.—(Tamil.) On the same wall. Records gift of gold in the reign of the Chōḷa king Parakēsarivarman for a lamp to a temple of Mahādēva, date of which is lost.

599. 11 *of* 1898.—(Tamil.) On the same wall. A damaged record of the "Gaṅga-Pallava" king Vijaya-Kampavikramavarman, dated in his tenth year.

600. 12 *of* 1898.—(Tamil.) On the same wall. Records in the fifteenth year of the Chōḷa king Madirai-koṇḍa Parakēsarivarman (Parāntaka I) rules regarding the exchange of gold.

601. 13 *of* 1898.—(Tamil.) On the same wall. Records in the third year of Pārthivēndrādhipativarman gift of land.

602. 14 *of* 1898.—(Tamil.) On the same wall. Records in the fifteenth year of the Chōḷa king Parakēsarivarman gift of land.

603. 15 *of* 1898.—(Tamil.) On the north wall of the same temple. Records in the third year of Pārthivēndrādhipativarman gift of land.

604. 16 *of* 1898.—(Tamil.) On the same wall. Records in the third year of Pārthivēndrādhipativarman gift of land.

605. 17 *of* 1898.—(Tamil.) On the same wall. Records in the third year of Pārthivēndrādhipativarman gift of land.

606. 18 *of* 1898.—(Tamil.) On the same wall. Records in the third year of Pārthivēndrādhipativarman gift of land *for the support of ṭeachers of grammar.*

607. 19 *of* 1898.—(Tamil.) On the same wall. Records in the third year of Pārthivēndrādhipativarman gift of land to the temple at Tiruppulivalam.

608. 20 *of* 1898.—(Tamil.) On the same wall. Records in the sixteenth year of Pārthivēndrādhipativarman gift of land.

609. 21 *of* 1898.—(Tamil.) On the same wall. Records in the third year of Pārthivēndrādhipativarman gift of land to the temple at Tirumāliruñjōḷai.

610. 22 *of* 1898.—(Tamil.) On the same wall. Records in the third year of Pārthivēndrādhipativarman gift of land to Durga-Bhaṭṭāraki.

611. 23 *of* 1898.—(Tamil.) On the same wall. Records in the third year of Pārthivēndrādhipativarman gift of land to a temple of Śēṭṭai.

612. 24 *of* 1898.—(Tamil.) On the same wall. Records in the fourth year of Pārthivēndrādhipativarman gift of land.

613. 25 *of* 1898.—(Tamil.) On the same wall. Records in the third year of Pārthivēndrādhipativarman gift of land to a temple of Mahādēva.

614. 26 *of* 1898.—(Tamil.) On the same wall. Records in the third year of Pārthivēndrādhipativarman gift of land to the Vishṇu temple at Śōmanēri.

615. 27 *of* 1898.—(Tamil.) On the same wall. Records in the fourth year of Pārthivēndrādhipativarman gift of land to Gaṇapati.

616. 28 *of* 1898.—(Tamil.) On the same wall. Records in the fifth year of Pārthivēndrādhipativarman gift of land to the temple at Tiruvunniyūr.

617. 29 *of* 1898.—(Tamil.) On the same wall. Records in the fourth year of the Chōḷa king Parakēsarivarman *alias* Rājēndra-Chōḷadēva (I, 1011—43) gift of land.

618. 30 *of* 1898.—(Tamil.) On the same wall. Records in the fourth year of the Chōḷa king Parakēsarivarman *alias* Rājēndra-Chōḷadēva (I, 1011—43) gift of land to the temple at Tiruppuli-valam.

619. 31 *of* 1898.—(Tamil.) On the same wall. A damaged record of the so-called Gaṅga-Pallava king Vijaya-Kampavarman, dated in his fifteenth year.

620. 32 *of* 1898.—(Tamil.) On the same wall. Records in the eleventh year of Pārthivēndrādhipativarman gift of land by a queen.

621. 33 *of* 1898.—(Tamil.) On the same wall. Records in the fourth year of the Chōḷa king Parakēsarivarman *alias* Rājēndra-Chōḷadēva gift of land.

622. 34 *of* 1898.—(Tamil.) On the same wall. Records in the sixteenth year of the Chōḷa king Parakēsarivarman gift of land.

623. 35 *of* 1898.—(Tamil.) On the same wall. Records in the fourteenth year of the Chōḷa king Parakēsarivarman gift of land.

624. 36 *of* 1898.—(Tamil.) On the same wall. Records in the fifth year of Pārthivēndrādhipativarman gift of land.

625. 37 *of* 1898.—(Tamil.) On the same wall. Records in the sixth year of Pārthivēndrādhipativarman gift of land.

626. 38 *of* 1898.—(Tamil.) On the east wall of the same temple. Records in the third year of Pārthivēndrādhipativarman gift of land.

627. 39 *of* 1898.—(Tamil.) On the same wall. Records gift of land for a *maṭha* for learned Brāhmaṇas. Beginning built in.

628. 40 *of* 1898.—(Tamil.) On the same wall. Records in the eighth year of the Chōla king Rājakēsarivarman gift of land for feeding Brāhmaṇas.

629. 41 *of* 1898.—(Tamil.) On the same wall. Records in the twenty-third year of the Rāshṭrakūṭa king Kaṇṇaradēva III, "who conquered Kachchi and Tañjai" allotment of revenue to the temple.

630. 42 *of* 1898.—(Tamil.) On the north wall of the same temple. Records in the fifteenth year of the "Gaṅga-Pallava" king Vijaya-Kampavarman gift of gold. End built in.

631. 49 *of* 1898.—(Tamil.) On the south wall of the Sundara-varada Perumāḷ temple. Records in the twelfth year of Pārthivēndrādhipativarman gift of land by a queen to the Vishṇu temple built by Koṅgaraiyar.

632. 50 *of* 1898.—(Grantha.) On the same wall. Two verses in praise of the architect.

633. 51 *of* 1898.—(Tamil.) On the north wall of the same temple. A record of "the Gaṅga-Pallava king" Vijaya Danti-vikramavarman, dated in his tenth year. Only the first few words are preserved.

634. 52 *of* 1898.—(Tamil.) On the same wall. Records in the thirteenth year of Pārthivēndrādhipativarman gift of sheep for two lamps to the temple of Koṅgaraiya by the same queen as in No. 631.

635. 53 *of* 1898.—(Tamil.) On the north wall of the Subrah-maṇya temple. Records in the fourth year of the Chōḷa king Para-kēsarivarman *alias* Rājēndra-Chōḷadēva (I, 1011—43) the hereditary appointment of a Pūjāri.

636. 54 *of* 1898.—(Tamil.) On the west and south walls of the same temple. A record of the Chōla king Rājarāja-Rājakēsarivar-man I recording in his seventeenth year gift of sheep for a lamp by different people.

637. 55 *of* 1898.—(Tamil.) On the south wall of the temple. Records in the fourth year of Pārthivēndrādhipativarman gift of land.

638. 56 *of* 1898.—(Tamil.) On the north wall of the Kailāsa-nātha temple. Records in the third year of the Chōḷa king Para-kēsarivarman *alias* Rājēndra-Chōḷadēva (I, 1011—43) gift of land.

639. 57 *of* 1898.—(Tamil.) On the east and north walls of the Koḷambesvara temple. Records in the ninth year of the Chōḷa king Rājakēsarivarman *alias* Kulōttuṅga-Chōḷadēva (I, 1070—1118) gift of money for a lamp.

640. 58 *of* 1898.—(Tamil.) On the south wall of the Mādari-Amman temple. Records in the twenty-fourth year of the Chōḷa king Madirai-koṇḍa Parakēsarivarman (Parāntaka I) gift of gold for a lamp.

641. 59 *of* 1898.—(Tamil.) On the west wall of the same temple. Records in the third year of Pārthivēndrādhipativarman gift of land.

642. 60 *of* 1898.—(Tamil.) On the same wall. Records in the third year of Pārthivēndrādhipativarman gift of land.

643. 61 *of* 1898.—(Tamil.) On the south wall of the Vaikuṇṭha-Perumāḷ temple. Records in the twenty-first year of the "Gaṅga-Pallava" king Dantivikramavarman a resolution of the village assembly.

644. 62 *of* 1898.—(Tamil.) On the same wall. Records in the eighth year of the Chōḷa king Rājakēsarivarman a resolution of the village assembly.

645. 63 *of* 1898.—(Tamil.) On the same wall. Records in the sixteenth year of the "Gaṅga-Pallava" king Nripatuṅgavarman gift of gold for a lamp to the temple of Mahādēva at Trippulivalam

646. 64 *of* 1898.—(Tamil.) On the same wall. Records in the sixth year of the "Gaṅga Pallava" king Vijaya-Kampavarman gift of land to the Vishṇu temple of Gōvardhana.

647. 65 *of* 1898.—(Tamil.) On the same wall. A record of the "Gaṅga-Pallava" king Vijaya-Kampavarman, dated in his eighteenth year. End built in.

648. 66 *of* 1898.—(Tamil.) On the same wall. A damaged record of the Chōḷa king Rājakēsarivarman *alias* Kulōttuṅga-Chōḷadēva (I, 1070—1118), dated in his twenty-first year.

649. 67 *of* 1898.—(Tamil.) On the same wall. A damaged record of the Chōḷa king Tribhuvanachakravartin Tribhuvanavīradēva (Kulōttuṅga III, 1178—1216), dated in his thirty-seventh year, Mithuna, Apara 9, Sunday, Hasta (= 7th June A.D. 1215). *Ep. Ind.*, V, 199.

650. 68 *of* 1898.—(Tamil.) On the same wall. A record of the Chōḷa king Parakēsarivarman *alias* Vikrama-Chōḷadēva (1118—35) in his fifteenth year. Sale of land.

651. 69 *of* 1898.—(Tamil.) On the same wall. Records in the twelfth year of Pārthivēndrādhipativarman gift of land.

652. 70 *of* 1898.—(Tamil.) On the same wall. Records gift of cows for a lamp. In archaic characters.

653. 71 *of* 1898.—(Tamil.) On the same wall. Records gift of land.

654. 72 *of* 1898.—(Tamil.) On the same wall. Records in the twenty-fourth year of the "Gaṅga-Pallava" king Nandivarman gift of land.

655. 73 *of* 1898.—(Tamil.) On the same wall. Records in the third year of Pārthivēndrādhipativarman gift of land.

656. 74 *of* 1898.—(Tamil.) On the same wall. Records in the ninth year of the Pallava king Danti-Pōttaraṣar gift of gold for digging a tank.

657. 75 *of* 1898.—(Tamil.) On the same wall. Records in the twenty-sixth year of the Chōḷa king Rājakēsarivarman gift of gold for a water-shed.

658. 76 *of* 1898.—(Tamil.) On the same wall. A record of the Chōḷa king Tribhuvanachakravartin Kulōttuṅga-Chōḷadēva III in his twenty-sixth year. Gift of land.

659. 77 *of* 1898.—(Tamil.) On the same wall. A record of the Rāshṭrakūṭa king Kaṇṇaradēva (Krishṇa III), "who conquered Kachchi and Tañjai," in his twenty-fifth year. A resolution of the village assembly, regarding fines.

660. 78 *of* 1898.—(Tamil.) On the same wall. Records in the third year of the Chōḷa king . . . Kēsarivarman gift of gold for a lamp to the temple of Mahādēva at Trippulivalam.

661. 79 *of* 1898.—(Tamil.) On the same wall. An incomplete record of Pārthivēndrādhipativarman, dated in his seventh year.

662. 80 *of* 1898.—(Tamil.) On the same wall. A record of the "Gaṅga-Pallava" king Dantivarman recording in his seventh year a sale of land.

663. 81 *of* 1898.—(Tamil.) On the east wall of the same temple. The fragment of a record of the "Gaṅga-Pallava" king Nripatuṅgavarman, dated in his twenty-fifth year.

664. 82 *of* 1898.—(Tamil.) On the same wall. The fragment of a record of the "Gaṅga-Pallava" king Vijaya-Nripatuṅgavikramavarman, date of which is lost.

665. 83 *of* 1898.—(Tamil.) On the same wall. A record of the "Gaṅga-Pallava" king Vijaya-Nripatuṅgavikramavarman in his twenty-sixth year. Sale of land.

666. 84 *of* 1898.—(Tamil.) On the west wall of the same temple. A record of the "Gaṅga-Pallava king" Vijaya-Kampavarman in his twenty-first year. Gift of gold for repairing a tank.

667. 85 *of* 1898.—(Tamil.) On the south-east wall of the same temple. A record of the "Gaṅga-Pallava" king Vijaya-Kampavikramavarman in his eighth year. Sale of land.

668. 86 *of* 1898.—(Tamil.) On the same wall. A record of the "Gaṅga-Pallava" king Kampa-Perumān in his twenty-third year. Allotment of gold and paddy.

669. 87 *of* 1898.—(Tamil.) On the same wall. A record of the Chōḷa king Madirai-Koṇḍa Parakēsarivarman (Parāntaka I, 906—47) in his fourteenth year. Gift of gold for a lamp to the temple of Mahādēva at Trippulivalam.

670. 88 *of* 1898.—(Tamil.) On the same wall. A record of Pārthivēndrādhipativarman, dated in his second year. Partially built in.

671. 89 *of* 1898.—(Tamil.) On the same wall. A record of the Rashṭrakūṭa king Kaṇṇaradēva, "who conquered Kachchi and Tañjai" in his eighteenth year. Gift of gold for a lamp.

672. 90 *of* 1898.—(Tamil.) On the same wall. A damaged record of the "Gaṅga-Pallava" king Vijaya-Kampavarman, dated in his fifteenth year.

673. 91 *of* 1898.—(Tamil.) On a stone lying near the Iraṭṭai-taḷigai-Īśvara temple. An incomplete record of the Chōḷa king Rājakēsarivarman, dated in his seventeenth year.

674. 92 *of* 1898.—(Tamil.) On another stone lying near the same temple. Records in the fourth year of the Chōḷa king Parakēsarivarman *alias* Rājēndra Chōḷadēva (I, 1011—43) gift of land. Fragment.

PONNERI TALUK.

Kāṭṭūr.

675. 249 *of* 1912.—(Tamil.) On a pillar of the maṇṭapa in front of the central shrine in the Tiruvaḷḷīśvara temple. Dated in reign of the Chōḷa king Tribhuvanachakravartin Kulōttuṅga-Chōḷadēva III. Records in his twentieth year, gift of cows for a lamp, by a lady to the temple of Tiruvaḷḷīśuram-Uḍaiyār at Kāṭṭūr.

676. 250 *of* 1912.—(Tamil.) On the second pillar of the same maṇṭapa. Dated in the reign of the Chōḷa king Tribuvanachakravartin Rājarājadēva III. Records in his fourteenth year gift of 90 sheep for a lamp by a shepherd, to the temple of Tiruvaḷḷīśura-muḍaiya Mahādēva at Kāṭṭūr *alias* Rājēndraśōḷa-nallūr near Perumbēḍu in Paiyūr-kōṭṭam, a district of Jayaṅgoṇḍaśōḷa-maṇḍalam.

677. 251 *of* 1912.—(Tamil.) On the third pillar in the same place. A damaged record of the Chōḷa king Tribhuvanachakravartin Kulōttuṅga Chōḷaḍēva III, dated in his twentieth year. Records gift of land for a lamp to the temple of Tiruvaḷḷīchchuram-Uḍaiyār at Kāṭṭūr *alias* Rājēndraśōḷanallūr, which the donor had purchased from the residents of Kaḍarpākkam.

678. 252 *of* 1912.—(Tamil.) On a slab set up in the same temple. Records in the ninth year of Pārthivēndrādhipativarman a sale of land as *taṇṇippaṭṭi* by the residents of Kāṭṭūr in Paiyūr-kōṭṭam to Paṭṭaiyanār, the *mēnāyaka* of Perundaram, who built the temple of this village.

679. 253 *of* 1912.—(Tamil.) On the same slab. Dated in the reign of the Chōḷa king Rājarājakēsarivarman (985—1013) "who destroyed the ships at Kāndaḷūr Śālai." Records in his tenth year gift of 45 sheep for a half lamp to the temple of Tiruvaḷḷi-śurattu-Mahādēva at Kāṭṭūr in Paiyūr-kōṭṭam, by a resident of the village.

680. 254 *of* 1912.—(Tamil.) In the same place. A damaged record of the Chōḷa king Rājarājakēsarivarman (985—1013) "who destroyed the ships at Kāndaḷūr-Śāḷai, dated in his eleventh year." Seems to record a gift of twenty-three sheep and a gold lamp, to the same temple.

681. 255 *of* 1912.—(Tamil.) In the same place. Belongs to the reign of the Chōḷa king Rājarājakēśarivarman (985—1013), "who destroyed the ships at Kāndaḷūr Śāḷai." Records in his eleventh year sale of land by the residents of Kāṭṭūr in Paiyūr-kōṭṭam to a certain Nakkanālai Nakkan of Villippākkam, which belonged to Iruṅganūr Kūvam in Maṇayir-kūṟṟam, a subdivision of Maṇayir-kōṭṭam. No details of prices given.

682. 256 *of* 1912.—(Grantha and Tamil.) On a slab lying in the Vīṟṟirunda-Perumāḷ temple in the same village. In characters of about the eleventh century A.D. Registers that the community of merchants (*nānādēśi*) at Mayilarppil, declared Ayyapuḷal-Kāṭṭūr, to be a *virapaṭṭaṇa* and laid down certain rules of conduct to be followed by the members of the *Vāḷañjikā* sect residing in that village. [A very interesting record which eulogises the gild, refers to 500 *Viraśāsanas*, glorifying their deeds, etc. See *Madr. Ep. Rep.*, 1912-13, pp. 99-100 for details. See also *Inscrns.* 342 of 1912 at Basinikoṇḍa, 349 of 1912 at Vīralūr, *Ep. Carna.*, Vol. VII (Sk. 118. and *Ep. Ind.*, VII, p. 97.]

Māḍambākkam.

683. 318 *of* 1911.—(Tamil.) On the south wall of the central shrine in the Dhēnupurīśvara temple. An epigraph of the Chōḷa king Tribhuvanachakravartin Vīrarājēndra Chōḷadēva (not identified) recording in his tenth year gift of twenty *vēli* of land north of Māḍambākkam *alias* Ulaguyyavandaśōḷa-chaturvēdimaṅgalam, a village in Neḍuṅguṇṟanāḍu which belonged to Puliyūr-kōṭṭam *alias* Kulōttuṅgaśōḷa-vaḷanāḍu, a subdivision of Jayaṅgoṇḍachōḷa-maṇḍalam, to the temple of Śiṟṟēri-Āḷuḍaiya-Nāyanār, under orders of Pañchanadivāṇan Nīlagaṅgaraiyan, a contemporary of Kōpperuñjiṅgadēva. See N.A. 473.

684. 319 *of* 1911.—(Tamil.) On the same wall. Dated in the reign of the Vijayanagara king Vīraśrī Kumāra-Dēvarāya (II). Records in Prabhava (Ś. 1348) that eight house-sites of the sthānattār, being lost to them, fresh sites were provided for, in the street of the Kaikkōḷar. Mentions Śiṟṟēri-Āḷuḍaiya-Nāyanār at Māḍanpākkam *alias* Ulaguyyavandaśōḷa-chaturvēdimaṅgalam in Neḍuṅguṇṟa-nāḍu, a district of Ārāyiravēli-paṟṟu, a subdivision of Puliyūr-kōṭṭam *alias* Kulōttuṅgaśōḷa-vaḷanāḍu, in Jayaṅgoṇḍachōḷa-maṇḍalam.

685. 320 *of* 1911.—(Tamil.) On the same wall. An incomplete and damaged record of the Vijayanagara king Vīrapratāpa Sadāśiva-Mahārāya "who took every country," date of which is lost.

686. 321 *of* 1911.—(Tamil.) On the same wall. A record of the Chōḷa king Tribhuvanachakravartin Rājarājadēva recording in his second year gift of two cows for providing curds to the temple of Śiṟṟēri-Uḍaiya-Nāyanār at Māḍambākkam *alias* Ulaguyyavandaśōḷa-chaturvēdimaṅgalam.

687. 322 *of* 1911.—(Tamil.) On the west wall of the same shrine. A record of the Pāṇḍya king Jaṭāvarman *alias* Tribhuvanachakravartin Sundara Pāṇḍyadēva (III? 1276—90); quotes in his tenth year, the fifteenth year of Peruñjiṅgadēva and records a gift of land to maintain lamps, offerings and festivals in the temple of Śiṟṟēri-Āḷuḍaiya-Nāyanār.

688. 323 *of* 1911.—(Tamil.) On the north wall of the same shrine. Dated in the reign of the Chōḷa king Tribhuvanachakravartin Vīrarājēndrachōḷadēva (not identified). Records in his thirty-sixth year gift of the village of Maduraippākkam in Neḍuṅguṉṟa-nāḍu, a subdivision of Puliyūr-kōṭṭam in Jayaṅgoṇḍachōḷamaṇḍalam, to the same temple, by order of Aruṇagiri Perumāḷ Nīlagaṅgaraiyan. See No. 683 above.

689. 324 *of* 1911.—(Tamil.) On the south wall of the verandah round the same shrine. A record of the Vijayanagara king Vīra-Kampaṇa-Uḍaiyār (II), son of Bukkaṇa-Uḍaiyar (i.e., Bukka I) in *Ānanda* (Ś. 1296), relating gift of the village of Māḍanpākkam to the temple by a certain Viṭṭappar with the permission of the king. The inscription is of great interest as it enumerates the various dues and obligations to which the tenants were subjected. These were the *purakkalanaiyār pērkaḍamai* (which Mr. Kṛishṇa Sastri interprets as the obligations of the people who live outside the village), fees on cotton looms, caste obligations, fees of oil-mills, *vilvari, vāśalvari, uḷugalvari, nallerumai, narpaśu, kārttigaippachchai, tiruppudiyidu,* "the share *(mērvai)* of grain from each harvest granted to village watchmen, market-fees (*śandaimudal*)," the *āśuvaḍimakkaḷpēr*, the *veṭṭivari*, etc. All these were to be paid to the temple for worship and repair instead of to the Government.

690. 325 *of* 1911.—(Tamil.) On the north wall of the same verandah. A damaged record of the Pāṇḍya king Jaṭāvarman *alias* Tribhuvanachakravartin Sundara-Pāṇḍyadēva, dated in his fifteenth year. Records sale of houses in the *tirumaḍaiviḷāgam* to temple servants. It is not known which of the Sundara Pāṇḍyas is referred to.

Nāgalāpuram.

691. 619 *of* 1904.—(Kanarese.) On the south, east and north walls of the central shrine in the Vēdanārāyaṇasvāmin temple. A record of the Vijayanagara king Vīrapratāpa Vīra-Kṛishṇarāya. The gift of certain villages. (The date is doubtful.)

692. 620 *of* 1904.—(Tamil.) On the north wall of the Vēdavallittāyār shrine in the same temple. Dated in the reign of the

Vijayanagara king Śrīraṅgadēva-Mahārāya records in Pramāthin the grant of certain privileges to the *Pañchalattār* (i.e., the five artisan communities).

693. 621 *of* 1904.—(Sanskrit and Grantha.) On the north, west and the south walls of the same shrine. An epigraph of the Vijayanagara king Kṛishṇadēva-Mahārāya. Records in Ś. 1436, Bhava, gift of land.

694. 622 *of* 1904. On the west wall of the maṇṭapa in front of the same shrine. A damaged record.

695. 623 *of* 1904.—(Tamil.) On the north wall of the same maṇṭapa. Dated in the reign of the Vijayanagara king Vīraprātāpa-Kṛishṇadēva Mahārāya. Seems to record in Ś. 1442 expired, Vikrama, an agreement among certain merchants.

696. 624 *of* 1904.—(Tamil.) On the same wall. A record of the Vijayanagara king Vīrapratāpa Kṛishṇadēva-Mahārāya, in Ś. 1442 expired, Vikrama. Mentions a number of kōṭṭams and nāḍus.

697. 625 *of* 1904.—(Sanskrit and Grantha.) At the entrance into the second gōpura of the same temple, right side. The Vijayanagara king Kṛishṇarāya-Mahārāya records gift of two villages.

698. 626 *of* 1904.—(Kanarese.) In the same place, left side. The Vijayanagara king Vīrapratāpa Kṛishṇarāya-Mahārāya records in Sarvadhārin (i.e., Ś. 1451), gift of land.

699. 627 *of* 1904.—(Sanskrit and Grantha.) On the left and right sides of the second gōpura of the Vēdanārāyaṇasvāmin temple. A record of the Vijayanagara king Kṛishṇarāya relating in Ś. 1445, Svabhānu, gift of land. One of the objects of the grant was the recitation of the Sanskrit Vēdās and the Drāviḍa-Vēda (the Prabandha) and the exposition of Vēdānta. [The temple is said to have been built at the command of the deity conveyed in a dream to a certain Haridāsa. See next inscription.]

700. 628 *of* 1904.—(Tamil.) At the entrance into the north gōpura of the same temple. A record of the Vijayanagara king Kṛishṇadēva-Mahārāya in Ś. 1445 expired, Svabhānu. Refers to the origin of the temple and says that it was built at the command of Emberumān (i.e., Vishṇu) who appeared in a dream to a private individual, Haridāsa. [Refers also to a visit which the king paid to Aragaṇḍapuram (i.e., Nāgalāpuram) on his way to Kumbakōṇam for the Mahāmakha festival, just after his return from the campaign in the north.]

701. 628-*A of* 1904.—(Tamil.) In the same place. Dated in the reign of the Vijayanagara king Kṛishṇadēva-Mahārāya. Records in Ś. 1445 expired, Svabhānu, gift of land.

702. 629 *of* 1904.—(Tamil.) On the east wall of the outer prākāra of the same temple. A damaged record of the Vijayanagara king Kṛishṇadēva-Mahārāya, the date of which is indistinct,

703. *C.P. No.* 12 *of* 1905.—A record of Kṛishṇadēva Rāya, dated in Ś. 1445, making grant of several villages to the temple of Nīlamāṇikyadēva (i.e., Vēdanārāyaṇaperumāḷ) and to Haridāsa mentioned in No. 700 above. To the latter was entrusted the entire management of the temple.

Nallūr.

703-A. The Nallūr grant of Harihara II. A C.P. grant in Sanskrit verse and Nandināgarī character, recording the gift of the village (which was in Mēguṇa-vaḷanāḍu or Nalatūripāḷem Śīma in Paiyūr-Kōṭṭam) to Brāhmans by Harihara II in Ś. 1321, Pramādhin, Kārttika, lunar eclipse, corresponding, according to Dīkshit, to Wednesday, 15th October A.D. 1399. See *Ep. Ind.*, III, 113—26.

Naraśiṅgapuram.

704. 237 *of* 1910.—(Tamil in Telugu characters mixed with Tamil ones.) On the south wall of the central shrine in the Narasimha-Perumāḷ temple. A record of the Vijayanagara king Vīrapratāpa Achyutayyadēva-Mahārāya, dated Ś. 1456, Jaya. [A fresh copy of No. 17 of 1896, noticed on page 4 of the *Annual Report on Epigraphy* for 1895-96, paragraph 12.] It assigns an allowance of money, food, etc., to certain Brāhmans for the recitation of the Vēdas to the merit of the king's father Narasa Nāyaka, in whose name the village was founded.

705. 238 *of* 1910.—(Tamil.) On the same wall. Belongs to the reign of the Vijayanagara king Vīrapratāpa Achyutayyadēva-Mahārāya. Records in Ś. 1455, Vijaya, gift of the village of Periya-Puḷiyāvi surnamed Narasimhapuram to Brāhmaṇas, for the merit of the king by an agent of his named Tīttāra-pillai, on the occasion of the consecration of the image of Lakshminarasimha-mūrti.

706. 239 *of* 1910.—(Tamil.) On the same wall. Belongs to the reign of the Vijayanagara king Vīrapratāpa Achyutayyadēva-Mahārāya. Records in Ś. 1457, Manmatha, gift of land to Śrī-Vaishṇavas by the same chief for the merit of Periyasvāmi Narasa Nāyaka on the occasion of the consecration of Prahlādapurandara —the name given to the image carried in processions in the Lakshmīnarasimha-Perumāḷ temple—at Kūvam Tyāgasamudra-nallūr surnamed Narasanāyakapuram in Kunṛūr-nāḍu, a subdivision of Teṅkarai Maṇavil-kōṭṭam in Chandragiri-rājya, which belonged to Jayaṅgoṇḍachōḷa-maṇḍalam. [Kūvam Tyāgasamudram was named after Vīranārayāna Śambuvarāya (1331—83), a contemporary of the Iraṭṭayar, Kaḷamēgha, etc., who celebrated his generosity to poets by calling his city Tyāgasamudram.]

707. 240 *of* 1910.—(Tamil.) On the same wall. Dated in the reign of the Vijayanagara king Vīrapratāpa Achyutayyadēva-Mahārāya. Records in Ś. 1456, Jaya, gift of land and a house for the merit of Periyasvāmi Narasa-Nāyaka in the presence of Viṭṭhalēśvara on the banks of the Tuṅgabhadra river, to each of two Vaishṇava Brāhmaṇas who recited a *purāṇam* (*Bhaktisañjivini*) in the same temple.

708. 241 *of* 1910.—(Tamil.) On the same wall. Records gift of land to a Brāhmaṇa on the occasion of the consecration of Lakshmīnarasimhamūrti.

709. 242 *of* 1910.—(Tamil.) On the north wall of the same shrine. Dated in the reign of the Vijayanagara king Vīrapratāpa Achyutadēva-Mahārāya. Records in Ś. 1455, Vijaya, gift of a house and some special privileges by Tīttāra-piḷḷai of Kāñchipuram to the watchman in the temple of Lakshmīnarasimhamūrti.

710. 243 *of* 1910.—(Tamil.) On the same wall. A damaged record of the Vijayanagara king Vīrapratāpa Vīra-Veṅkaṭapatidēva (I) Mahārāya, dated Ś. 1530, Saumya. Mentions Gobbūri Obarāja and the gift of sixty-five gold pieces called *Veṅkaṭarāya-varāhans* and seems to regulate the festivals and the daily services in the temple of Aḷagiyaśiṅgar at Kūvam Tyāgasamudranallūr *alias* Narasimhapuram. [For the description of the *Veṅkaṭarāya-varāhans* see *Ind. Antq.*, XX, 207 ff. The Obarāja of this inscription is evidently the brother-in-law of Veṅkaṭa I, mentioned by Barrados. See *Forg. Empe.*, p. 222-33; see also No. 707 above.]

711. 244 *of* 1910.—(Tamil.) On the south wall of the Nāchchiyār shrine in the same temple. Records in the thirty-fifth year of the Chōḷa king Rājakēsarivarman *alias* Chakravartin śrī-Kulōttuṅga-Chōḷadēva (I? 1070—1118) the consecration of a shrine (apparently for Rāma, Sīta and Lakshmaṇa) in the temple of Madurāntaka-Viṇṇagar in Madurāntakanallūr which was a village in Kānṟūr-nāḍu, a subdivision of Maṇayir-kōṭṭam, and a gift to it, of oil for two lamps, by the inhabitants of Kaḍāraṅgoṇḍaśōḷapuram in Paśali-nāḍu of the same kōṭṭam.

712. 245 *of* 1910.—(Tamil.) On the same wall. Registers the consecration of the same shrine by a certain Vāṇiyan Paṇṇanāndāḷi Śūrai *alias* Śīrāmadūta of Kiḍāraṅgoṇḍaśōḷapuram, with the help of its residents, and provides for offerings and lamps. Kiḍāraṅgoṇḍaśōḷapuram must have been called after Rājēndrachōḷa I whose conquests included Kaṭāha or Kaḍāra (i.e., Lower Burma). See N.A. 615, 617 and 618.

713. 246 *of* 1910.—(Tamil.) On the west wall of the same shrine. Records a sale of land to Vāsudēvan Rājasundaran, a resident of Iruṅganūr, apparently by the assembly of Madurāntakanallūr. Mentions Iḷambiyaṅgōṭṭūr,

714. 247 *of* 1910.—(Tamil.) On the north wall of the same shrine. An unfinished record. Contains portions of the historical introduction of Kulōttuṅga I, beginning with the words *pugaḻmādu.*

715. 248 *of* 1910.—(Tamil.) On the same wall. An unfinished record of the Chōḷa king Parakēsarivarman *alias* Chakravartin Vikrama-Chōḷadēva (1118—35), dated in his seventh year. Seems to register a sale of land by the assembly of Kōṭṭūr *alias* Śōḷavichchādira-chatur-vēdimaṅgalam in Kānṟūr-nāḍu, a subdivision of Maṇayir-kōṭṭam in Jayaṅgoṇḍachōḷa-maṇḍalam. Mentions also Madurāntakanallūr in the same kōṭṭam.

716. 249 *of* 1910.—(Tamil.) On the same wall. Records in the thirty-fourth year of the Chōḷa king Rājakēsarivarman *alias* Chakravartin śrī-Kulōttuṅga-Chōḷadēva (I?) gift of land by the inhabitants of Madurāntakanallūr to the god, goddess and Iḷaiyāḻvār (i.e., Lakshmaṇa), in the temple of Madurāntaka-Viṇṇagar-Āḻvār.

717. 250 *of* 1910.—(Tamil.) On a slab set up in front of the main gōpura of the same temple. Dated in Ś. 1467 in the reign of the Vijayanagara king Vīrapratāpa Sadāśivadēva-Mahārāya. Records in Ś. 1467, *Viśvāvasu,* remission of taxes in the village of Kūvam Narasanāyakkarpuram, by a certain Śaṅkaranāyaka Liṅganāyaka for the merit of Śinna-Timmayyadēva-Mahārāja, son of Rāmarāja-Timmaya and brother of Rāmarāja Timmarāja Viṭṭhala, the general of Sadāśiva Rāya and cousin brother of Aḷiya Rāma Rāya. Prince Chinna Timma is mentioned in the Telugu poem *Bālabhāgavatamu* of Dōsur Kōnērikavi as the brother of Viṭṭhala. Chinna Timma was evidently governor of Chandragiri Rājya of which Naraśingapuram was a part.

Nattam.

718. 260 *of* 1912.—(Tamil.) On the south wall of the Śeṇbagēśvara temple. A fragment of record of the Chōḷa king Tribhuvanachakravartin Rājarājadēva III, date of which is lost. Records a gift of land apparently by the assembly of Paramēśvaramaṅgalam *alias* Śōḷakulatilaka-chaturvēdimaṅgalam.

719. 261 *of* 1912.—(Tamil.) On the same wall. A mutilated record of the Chōḷa king Parakēsarivarman *alias* Rājēndra-Chōḷadēva (I, 1011—43), dated in his ninth year. Records gift of 90 sheep for a lamp and of one lamp stand.

720. 262 *of* 1912.—(Grantha and Tamil.) On the west and north walls of the same temple. A mutilated record of the Chōḷa king Parakēsarivarman *alias* Rājēndra-Chōḷadēva I (1011—43), dated in his third year. Mentions Paramēśvaramaṅgalam *alias* Nigarili-śōḷachaturvēdimaṅgalam, the assembly of *samvatsara-vāriyam* (i.e., the annual supervision committee) which consisted of twelve men which formed part of the *mahā sabha* and which was elected in the month of *Tulā* every year. The committee performing the duties connected with that village, met in the hall called Rājēndraśōḷan-chatuśśāli, and Kañjaran Aiyyan Sūryan was the settlement officer (*vagai-śeyginṟa*) of the district. See No. 727 below. These confirm the Uttaramallūr inscriptions about the village assembly and subordinate committees.]

721. 263 *of* 1912.—(Tamil.) On the same walls. A mutilated record of the Chōḷa king Parakēsarivarman *alias* Rājēndra-Chōḷa-dēva I (1011—43), dated in his sixth year. Records gift of land for supplying the paddy required for offerings in the temple at Paramēśvaramaṅgalam *alias* Nigariliśōḷa-chaturvēdimaṅgalam in Śembūr-kōṭṭam which was a district of Jayaṅgoṇḍaśōḷa-maṇḍalam. Mentions the assembly of that village which included twelve members of the *samvatsara-vāriyam*. Salary in paddy of temple servants given.

722. 264 *of* 1912.—(Tamil.) On a stone built into a wall of the maṇṭapa of the same temple. A fragment of record of the Chōḷa king Tribhuvanachakravartin Kulōttuṅga-Chōḷadēva I, date of which is lost. Seems to record a sale of land.

723. 265 *of* 1912.—(Tamil.) On another stone in the same place. A fragment of record of the Chōḷa king Rājarājadēva III, dated in his third year. Records gift of a lamp to the temple at Paramēśvaramaṅgalam *alias* Śōḷakulatilaka-chaturvēdimaṅgalam.

724. 266 *of* 1912.—(Tamil.) On a third stone in the same place A fragment of record of Tribhuvanachakravartin Kōnērin-maikoṇḍān, date of which is lost. Mentions Perumanṟattāḷvār of Paḷampaṭṭiṇam (old town).

725. 267 *of* 1912.—(Tamil.) On a slab built into the roof, above the Subrahmaṇya image, in the same temple. A much-damaged record of the Vijayanagara king Vīra-Kampaṇa-Uḍaiyār (II), son of Vīra-Bukkaṇa-Uḍaiyār (I), dated Ānanda. Seems to fix the levying of certain taxes.

726. 268 *of* 1912.—(Tamil.) On a pillar lying in front of the same temple. Records that this flower garden was the gift of Padaiyādān Mādan *alias* Kulōttuṅgaśōḷa-Gāṅgēyarāyan. See N.A. 548 and S.A. 61, 62, 86 and 98.

727. 269 *of* 1912.—(Tamil.) On another pillar in the same place. Fragment. Refers to queen Dantipirāṭṭiyār and to a certain Vīrakōśamaṅgalamuḍaiyār Uḍaiyapirāṭṭiyār who caused all the waste lands in the village of the temple maḍaippaḷḷi pura to be cultivated and the income used for festivals on the winter and summer solstices, eclipses, Aippaśi-vishu, Śittirai-vishu, and Māśi-Magam, for the welfare of Dantipirāṭṭiyār and Rājēndra-Chōḷadēva. The *Urvāriyam* seems to have been, according to Mr. Krishna Sastri, the committee whose function was to see the lands of the village properly cultivated and to collect the produce.

Rāmagiri.

728. 630 *of* 1904.—(Tamil.) On the south wall of the central shrine of the Vālīśvara temple. Records in the eleventh year of the Chōḷa king Tribhuvanachakravartin Kulōttuṅga-Chōḷadēva gift of 32 cows for a lamp.

729. 631 *of* 1904.—(Tamil.) On the same wall. Records gift of 61 cows for 2 lamps. The name of the king and the date of the record are lost.

730. 632 *of* 1904.—(Tamil.) On the same wall. An incomplete record of the Chōḷa king Tribhuvanachakravartin Kulōttuṅga-Chōḷadēva, dated in his fifteenth year. Records gift of money for a lamp by Vīrarājēndra Vīranuḷamba-Duraiyaraiśan, lord of Kāñchipuram.

731. 633 *of* 1904.—(Tamil.) On the same wall. Records in the fifth year of the Chōḷa king Tribhuvanachakravartin Rājarāja-dēva (III?) a gift by Vīra-Narasimhadēva *alias* Yādavarāya.

732. 634 *of* 1904.—(Tamil.) On the same wall. A damaged record of Kembana-Uḍaiyār (Kampaṇa-Uḍaiyār) in Ānanda.

733. 635 *of* 1904.—(Tamil.) On the west wall of the same shrine. A record of the Chōḷa king Tribhuvanachakravartin Rājādhirājadēva relating gift of 3 lamps (the date is lost). Built in the middle and incomplete.

734. 636 *of* 1904.—(Grantha and Tamil.) On the north wall of the same shrine. An incomplete record. Mentions a chief with a string of *birudas* in Sanskṛit from which we learn that he was a devotee of the Kāḷahasti and Tirupati temples and that he was the ruler of Veṅgi.

735. 637 *of* 1904.—(Tamil.) On the same wall. Records in Ś. 1338 expired, Naḷa (wrong) gifts by a chief.

736. 638 *of* 1904.—(Tamil.) On the same wall. The Chōḷa king Tribhuvanachakravartin Rājarājadēva records in his tenth year, gift of 32 cows for a lamp. The village was situated in Ninṟavūrnāḍu, a district of Kunṟavattana-kōttam, a subdivision of Jayaṅgoṇḍa-Chōḷamaṇḍalam.

737. 639 *of* 1904.—(Tamil.) On the same wall. An incomplete record of Kampaṇa-Uḍaiyār, dated Viśvāvasu. The temple is called after Tiruvālīśuramuḍaiya-Nāyinār.

738. 640 *of* 1904.—(Grantha and Tamil.) On the east wall of the maṇṭapa in front of the same shrine. Dated in the reign of the Chōḷa king Tribhuvanachakravartin Kulōttuṅga-Chōḷadēva (III). Records a gift by *Śaśikula-Chāḷuki Tani-ninṟu-venṟa* Vīra-Naraśiṅga-dēva *alias* Yādavarāya, who is mentioned with a string of birudas in Sanskṛit. The date of the record is indistinct. See N.A. 58.

739. 641 *of* 1904.—(Tamil.) On a pillar of the same maṇṭapa. Vīra-Kampaṇa-Uḍaiyār records in Sādhāraṇa gift of the pillar.

740. 642 *of* 1904.—(Tamil.) On the west wall of the prākāra of the Vālīśvara temple. Records in Dundubhi a gift of land by Bukkarāya-Uḍaiyār to a certain maṭhādhipati who is called *Satyadarśanigaḷ*. The temple is called Tirukkārikkarai.

741. 643 *of* 1904.—(Tamil.) On the west wall of the Bhairava shrine in the same temple. A record of the Vijayanagara king Vīra-Harihararāya in Pramāthin. The temple is called Tirukkāri-kaṟai-uḍaiya-Nāyanār at Naḍuvumalai in Ninṟaiyūr-nāḍu, a district of Kunṟavattana-kōṭṭam which was a subdivision of Jayaṅgoṇḍa-Chōḷamaṇḍalam.

742. 644 *of* 1904.—(Tamil.) On the same wall. A record of the Chōḷa king Tribhuvanachakravartin Vīrarājēndra-Chōḷadēva in his sixth year. The temple is called Tirukkārikaṟaippiḷḷaiyār in Naḍuvilmalai Ninṟaiyūr-nāḍu, described as in No. 741.

743. 645 *of* 1904.—(Tamil.) On the same wall. A record of the Chōḷa king Tribhuvanachakravartin Rājarājadēva in his twenty-sixth year. Gift of money for a lamp.

744. 646 *of* 1904.—(Tamil.) On the same wall. An epigraph of the Chōḷa king Tribhuvanachakravartin Rājarājadēva (III ?) recording in his sixteenth year, gift of 32 cows for lamp to the temple of Tirukkārikaṟai-uḍaiyār in Ninṟaiyūr-nāḍu, a district of Kunṟavattana-kōṭṭam, a subdivision of Jayaṅgoṇḍa-Chōḷamaṇḍalam.

745. 647 *of* 1904.—(Tamil.) On the same wall. An inscription of the Chōḷa king Tribhuvanachakravartin Rājarājadēva recording in his ninth year gift of money for a lamp.

746. 648 *of* 1904.—(Tamil.) On the same wall. An incomplete record of Yādavarāya, dated in his thirty-sixth year. Records gift of land.

747. 649 *of* 1904.—(Tamil.) On the same wall. An incomplete record of Tribhuvanachakravartin Aḷḷuntikkaraiśan *alias* Gaṇḍa-gōpāla, dated in his fourth year. See S.A. 146. Evidently he was different from Vīragaṇḍagōpāla, the contemporary of Vikrama Pāṇḍya who is mentioned in N.A. 708, S.A. 68 and S.A. 342.

748. 650 *of* 1904.—(Tamil.) On the north wall of the same shrine. An incomplete record of the Chōḷa king Tribhuvanachakravartin Kulōttuṅga-Chōḷadēva, dated in his twenty-sixth year.

749. 651 *of* 1904.—(Tamil.) On the north and west walls of the same shrine. A record of the Chōḷa king Tribhuvanachakravartin Vīrarājēndra-Chōḷadēva recording in his sixth year, gift of ninety-six sheep. Built in in the middle.

750. 652 *of* 1904.—(Tamil.) On the east wall of the same shrine. A fragmentary record of the Chōḷa king Kulōttuṅga I containing a portion of the historical introduction.

751. 653 *of* 1904.—(Tamil.) On the same wall. An epigraph of the Chōḷa king Tribhuvanachakravartin Rājarājadēva recording in his twenty-seventh year gift of money for a lamp.

752. 654 *of* 1904.—(Tamil.) On the same wall. An incomplete record of Tribhuvanachakravartin Vīra-Narasimhadēva-Yādavarāja, dated in his thirty-sixth year.

753. 655 *of* 1904.—(Tamil.) On the same wall. A record of the Chōḷa king Tribhuvanachakravartin Rājarājadēva(III ?) recording in his twenty-fifth year gift of money for a lamp to the temple of Tirukkārikaraippiḷḷaiyār.

754. 656 *of* 1904.—(Tamil.) On the same wall. The Chōḷa king Tribhuvanachakravartin Rājarājadēva III records in his twenty-ninth year, corresponding to 26th June 1245, gift of sixteen *māḍai* for a lamp. "The date shows that the reign of Rājarāja III could not have commenced before approximately the 27th June 1216 A.D." *Ep. Ind.*, VIII, 271–72.

755. 657 *of* 1904.—(Tamil.) On the same wall. Records an order of Madurāntaka-Pottappi-Chōḷa.

756. 658 *of* 1904.—(Tamil.) On the same wall. Dated in the reign of the Chōḷa king Tribhuvanachakravartin Rājarājadēva(III ?). Records in his tenth year gift of thirty-two cows for a lamp.

757. 659 *of* 1904.—(Tamil.) On the same wall of the maṇṭapa in front of the Bhairava shrine in the Vālīśvara temple. Records in the third year of Tribhuvanachakravartin Vīra-Gaṇḍagōpaladēva gift of sixteen buffalo-cows for a lamp. Mentions Rājāśraya-Śaśikula Chāḷukki Vīra-Narasimhadēva *alias* Yādavarāya. See Cg. 738 and 747 above.

758. 660 *of* 1904.—(Tamil.) On the back of the stone bull through the mouth of which water flows into the tank within the same temple. Records the setting up of the bull by a carpenter. In ancient character.

759. 661 *of* 1904.—(Tamil.) At the entrance into the ruined gōpura at the same temple. A mutilated record of the Vijayanagara king Virūpāksharāya (II, 1465—86), son of Gajavēṭṭai-Pratāpa Dēvarāya (II), dated in Śārvarin. The Śaka date is not preserved in full. Damaged.

Satyavēḍu.

760. 31 *of* 1912.—(Tamil.) On a stone lying in the courtyard of the Mātaṅgēśvara temple. Records in the fourth year of the "Gaṅga-Pallava" king Aparājitavarman gift of the village of Tuṟaiyūr with its income (consisting of *ponnu* and *puravu*) for worship in the temple of Mahādēva at Mātaṅganpaḷḷi in Tēkkūr-nāḍu, a subdivision of Paiyyūr-Iḷaṅgōṭṭam, by Kumarandai Kurumbarādittan *alias* Kāḍupaṭṭi Pēraraiyan of Śēra-nāḍu. [Kurumbarādittan or the son among the Kurumbas denotes a Pallava.]

761. 32 *of* 1912.—(Tamil.) On a stone in the Ardha-maṇṭapa of the same temple. Records in the fifth year of the "Gaṅga-Pallava" king Aparājitavarman gift of 100 sheep for a lamp, to the same temple by Poṟṟinaṅgai, wife of the chief mentioned in No. 760. Mentions the measure called *viḍēlviḍugu*, named after the Pallava king who had that title (i.e., Nandivarman III). See N.A. 347.

762. 33 *of* 1912.—(Telugu.) On stones built into a well in front of the same temple. Records in Ś. 1608, *Akshaya*, gift of a well and a garden by Kṛishṇareḍḍi of Dēśūru whose ancestor, Peda-Kṛishṇareḍḍi, is stated to have been the disciple of Tirumalai-Tōḷappāchārya, to have belonged to the Paṇṭakula and to the Madurāntaka-gōtra. [Tirumalai Tōḷappāchārya was the teacher of Maṭḷa Ananta, the author of *Kākusthaviyayamu*, who is proved both by Viresaliṅgam Pantulu and Mr. Krishna Sastri to have lived about 1565. See *Ep. Rep.*, 1912, p. 88. Pedda Krishṇa Reḍḍi therefore should have lived then.]

763. 34 *of* 1912.—Sanskrit (Telugu.) On the same stones. A record of the Nawab Qutb Shahi Abulu Hasanu (Abu Hasan 1672—88) of Gōlkoṇḍa. Refers in Ś. 1608, Akshaya, to the construction of the same wall by Pedakṛishṇavibhu (i.e., Kṛishṇareḍḍi).

Śivapuram.

764. 18 *of* 1896.—(Tamil.) On the east wall of the Śiva temple, left of entrance. The Chōḷa king Kō-Parakēsarivarman *alias* Rājēndra-Chōḷadēva (I, 1012—43) records in his eighth year, gift of two lamps to the temple of Rājārajēśvara. [Dr. Hultzsch believes that this temple, like that at Tanjore, should have been founded by Rājarāja I.]

Tiruveḷavāyil.

765. 247 *of* 1912.—(Tamil.) On the entrance into the central shrine in the Veḷavāyilēśvara temple. A much damaged record of Pārthivēndrādhivarman, dated in his eleventh year. Seems to provide for the burning of a lamp in this maṇṭapa by two merchants. Mentions Puḷal-kōṭṭam.

766. 248 *of* 1912.—(Tamil.) On a slab in the same temple. A mutilated record of the Chōḷa king Rājēndra-Chōḷa I, date of which is lost. Records gift of land for offerings to the god Rishabhavāhanadēva, in the temple of Svāmīśvaram-Uḍaiyār at Tiruvaḷḷaivāyil, by the residents of Tattamuñji, Attimaṇichchēri, Kāṭṭūr *alias* Rājēndraśōḷapuram, and Tiruvaḷḷaivāyil.

SAIDAPET TALUK

Kunnattūr.

This was the birth place of Śēkkiḻār, the author of the *Peria Purāṇa*, but no inscription concerning him is available here.

767. 255 *of* 1909.—(Tamil.) On a slab set up near the Perumālkōyil tank. An incomplete and damaged record of the Vijayanagara king Vīrapratāpa Śrīraṅgadēva Mahārāya, dated Ś. 1501, Bahudhānya. Records gift of land at Kunṟattūr to the temple of Talaśayana-Perumāḷ at Kaḍalmallai for the merit of the king's brother Veṅkaṭapatidēva-Mahārāja (i.e., Veṅkaṭa I) by the general Gobbūri Tirumalai Nāyakkar. Kunnattūr was situated in Perumbākka-śīrmai which belonged to Tirukkaḷukkunṟa-paṟṟu in Mugandur-nāḍu, a subdivision of Āmūr-kōṭṭam, a district of Paḍaivīḍu-rājya in Jayaṅgoṇḍa-chōḷamaṇḍalam. [The donor is identified by Mr. Krishna Sastri with the general who made a grant of two villages to the Triplicane temple in A.D. 1584—85. See *Kūvam* and *Triplicane* inscriptions. *Ep. Rep.*, 1904, p. 25.]

768. 256 *of* 1909.—(Tamil.) On a slab set up in the Nādanandēśvara temple at Manamai, a hamlet of the same village. A damaged record of the Chōḷa king Tribhuvanachakravartin Kulōttuṅga-Chōḷadēva (III, 1178—1216) "who was pleased to take Madurai (Madura) and the crowned head of the Pāṇḍya," dated twenty-fourth year. Records gift of three cows for a lamp to the temple of Tiruvagattīśvara-Uḍaiyār at Manamai *alias* Jananāthanallūr, a village in Āmūr-nāḍu which was a subdivision of Āmūr-kōṭṭam in Jayaṅgoṇḍa-chōḷamaṇḍalam.

769. 257 *of* 1909.—(Tamil.) On a slab built into the floor at the entrance into the Īśvara temple in the same hamlet. An incomplete record of the Chōḷa king Kulōttuṅga-Chōḷadēva, dated sixth year. Refers to a hunting accident. [Gives an insight into the method of administration of criminal justice. Two persons go out on a hunting expedition and the arrow of one aimed at the game hits and kills the other. As the record is mutilated we are not able to say how the matter was decided; but the usual expiation was to provide for a perpetual lamp for the merit of the deceased.]

770. 258 *of* 1909.—(Tamil.) On two detached fragments built into the shrine of the same temple. One of the stones mentions Sundara-Pāṇḍyadēva (not identified) and the other the thirteenth year of, perhaps, the same king. The first also refers to the Vishṇu temple called Śendāmaraikkaṇṇa-Viṇṇagar.

771. 259 *of* 1909.—(Tamil.) On the south wall of the shrine of the goddess in the same temple. Dated in the reign of the Pāṇḍya king Tribhuvanachakravartin Sundara-Pāṇḍyadēva. Records gift of two cows for a lamp by a lady of Uttaranmērūr, named Dēvargaḷammai, who was a member of the *Nyāyattār* or committee of justice at Uttaranmērūr temple mentioned in No. 768. The date is doubtful. [Mr. Krishna Sastri identifies the king with Jaṭāvarman Sundara-Pāṇḍya II 1276—90, and rightly draws attention to the fact that a woman was a member of the committee.]

772. 260 *of* 1909.—(Tamil.) On the west wall of the same shrine. Records in the seventh year of the Pāṇḍya king Jaṭāvarman *alias* Tribhuvanachakravartin Sundara-Pāṇḍyadēva gift of lamp to the same temple. See note to the above epigraph.

Little Mount (near Madras).

772-A. 93 *of* 1898.—(Armenian). On a stone set up at the foot of the steps leading to the Church. A cross is carved out above the inscription, a copy which was submitted to Professor Hubschmann at Strassburg. He first deciphered it. The record is dated in year 1112 (of the Armenian patriarch Moses), i.e., A.D. 1663 and is an epitaph of an Armenian merchant named Khōja David, son of Khōja Margarē. [See *Ep. Ind.*, Vol. VI, p. 89.]

Māṅgāḍu.

773. 348 *of* 1908.—(Tamil.) On the south wall of the central shrine in the Vaḷḷīśvara temple. Records in the twenty-third year of the Chōḷa king Tribhuvanachakravartin Rājarājadēva (III ?) gift of money for a lamp by a certain Śittavaṭadēvan Gaṇḍarādittan. Mentions Māṅgāḍu *alias* Aḻagiyaśōḻanallūr in Puliyūr-Kōṭṭam. Built in at the beginning. A Śittavaḍavan is mentioned in S.A. 782.

774. 349 *of* 1908.—(Tamil.) On the same wall. Records in the sixteenth year of the Chōḷa king Tribhuvanachakravartin Rājarājadēva (III ?) gift of money for a lamp to the temple of Tiruveḷḷikīḻmēya-Nāyanar at Māṅgāḍu *alias* Aḻagiyaśōḻanallūr in Puliyūr-Kōṭṭam.

775. 350 *of* 1908.—(Tamil.) On the same wall. Seems to register a gift of land in the reign of the Vijayanagara prince Pratāpadēvarāya. Built in at the end. Mr. Krishna Sastri surmises that the chief referred to must be the younger brother of Dēvarāya II.

776. 351 *of* 1908.—(Tamil.) On a slab built into the floor of the same shrine. Records in the third year of the "Gaṅga-Pallava" king Vijaya-Aparājitavarman gift of gold for a lamp and offerings to the temple of Tiruvellikīḻ-Mahādēva at Māṅgāḍu by a native of Kachchippēḍu. [It is doubtful whether Aparājita was identical with Nripatuṅga or his successor.]

777. 352 *of* 1908.—(Tamil.) On another slab built into the same floor. An incomplete record of the "Gaṅga-Pallava" king Vijaya-Nandivikramavarman, dated seventeenth year. Mentions a native of Kunṟattūr and the temple of Tiruveḷḷikīḻuḍaiya.

778. 353 *of* 1908.—(Tamil.) On the north wall of the central shrine in the Kāmākshi-amman temple. Dated in the time of the Vijayanagara king Pratāpadēvarāya. Records in Parābhava gift of land to the temple of Āvuḍaiya-Nāchchiyār in Māṅgāḍu *alias* Aḻagiyaśōḻanallūr, in Māṅgāḍu-nāḍu, a subdivision of Puliyūr-

Kōṭṭam *alias* Kulōttuṅgaśōḷa-vaḷanāḍu in Jayaṅgoṇḍachōḷa-maṇḍalam. Mentions Dēvaraya Uḍaiyār. See No. 775 for the identity of the chief.

779. 354 *of* 1908.—(Tamil.) On the west wall of the same shrine. Records in the reign of the Vijayanagara chief Pratāpadēvarāya an agreement among the villagers of Māṅgāḍu prohibiting the sale of lands to outsiders or even the gift of them as a dowry. [The inscription affords a unique example of the attempt at the preservation of the corporate unity of the village.] [See No. 775 above.]

780. 355 *of* 1908.—(Tamil.) On the south wall of the same shrine. Records in the reign of the Vijayanagara king Vīrapratāpa Dēvarāya Mahārāya, (II, 1422—49), in Plava, sale of land to the temple of maṇṇaippuru Āvuḍai Nāchchiyār in Māṅgāḍu. Puliyūr-Kōṭṭam was otherwise named Kulōttuṅga-śōḷavaḷanāḍu. *Plava* corresponded to A.D. 1421-2.

781. 356 *of* 1908.—(Tamil.) On the gōpura of the same temple, right of entrance. A damaged record in Ānanda. Records gift for the merit of Daḷavāy Śeñjama-Nāyakkan. Mentions Pūndaimalai śīrmai.

782. 357 *of* 1908.—(Tamil.) On a slab built into the floor in the same gōpura. A fragment of record of the Chōḷa king Parakēsarivarman, dated fifteenth year. Records gift of a lamp. Māṅgāḍu is stated to have been situated in Puliyūr-Kōṭṭam.

783. 358 *of* 1908.—(Tamil.) On two stones built into the floor of the court-yard in the same temple. Dated in the fifth year of the Pāṇḍya king Tribhuvanachakravartin Kōnērinmaikoṇḍān Sundara Pāṇḍyadēva I (1251—64) "who was pleased to take every country". Records gift of land as a *Paḷḷichchandam* to a paḷḷi whose name is not quite distinct.

784. 359 *of* 1908.—(Tamil.) On the east wall of the first prākāra of the same temple. A damaged record in Virōdhin. Appears to record an agreement among the residents of Māṅgāḍu. Mentions Achchutappa-Nāyaka. See N.A. 523 and 693.

785. 360 *of* 1908.—(Tamil.) On the same wall. A much-damaged record of the Vijayanagara king Vīrapratāpa Vīra-Veṅkaṭayyadēva-Mahārāya (I 1586—1614), dated Ś. 1508, Vyaya.

786. 361 *of* 1908.—(Tamil.) On a pillar in the Māri-amman temple in the same village. Dated in the reign of the Vijayanagara king Kṛishṇadēva Mahārāya (1509—30). Registers in Bhāva, a gift of land to the temple of Parama-Nāyanār at Māṅgāḍu for the merit of Vīra-Naraśiṅgarāya-Nāyakkar who appears to have been also called Śellappa. [The Nāik was evidently the Śāluva chief whose rebellious behaviour was the cause of Achyuta Rāya's southern campaign in 1532. See my *Hist. Naik King.* in *Ind. Antq.*, September 1914, for details.]

Maṇimaṅgalam.

This place (Ratnāgrahāra in Sanskrit) was the site of one of the battles between the Pallava Narasimhavarman I and the Western Chāḷukyan Puḷakēśin II. Later on it figures in the endowments of almost every Chōḷa king. It had then the successive names of Lōkamahādēvi-chaturvēdimaṅgalam, Rājachūḷāmaṇi-Chaturvēdimaṅgalam, Grāmaśikhāmaṇi-Chaturvēdimaṅgalam and was first in Māganūr-nāḍu in Śeṅgāṭṭu-Kōṭṭam in Jayaṅgoṇḍachōḷamaṇḍalam, but later on in Kunṟattūr nāḍu, a district of Puliyūr-Kōṭṭam in Kulōttuṅga-chōḷa vaḷanāḍu. It had three temples referred to below :—

787. 2 *of* 1892.—(Tamil.) North wall of the maṇṭapa in front of the Rājagōpāla-Perumāḷ temple. A record of the fifth year of the Chōḷa king Ko-Rājakēsarivarman Vīra Rājēndra I. The epigraph gives an interesting account of the king's war with the Chāḷukyans, Veṅgi, etc. It records gift of 4,450 *kūḷis* of land by Sēnāpati Jayaṅgoṇḍachōḷa Brahmādhirāja. [See *S.I.I.* III, No. 30, pp. 64—71.]

788. 3 *of* 1892.—(Tamil.) East side of the outer wall of the second prākāra of the Rājagōpāla-Perumāḷ temple. A record of the Chōḷa king Kō-Parakēsarivarman *alias* Rājēndradēva, dated in his fourth year. A very important inscription detailing all the king's achievements against Āhavamalla (Sōmēśvara I), Ceylon, etc. [See *S.I.I.*, Vol. III, No. 29, pp. 58—64.]

789. 4 *of* 1892.—(Tamil.) South wall of the maṇṭapa in front of the Rājagōpāla-Perumāḷ temple, first inscription. A record of the Chōḷa king Tribhuvanachakravartin Kulōttuṅga-Chōḷadēva, dated in his forty-eighth year. One Vīravalli Tiruvaraṅga Uḍaiyān Sahasran purchases land and assigns produce to temple. [See *S.I.I.* III, No. 32, pp. 74-75.]

790. 5 *of* 1892.—(Tamil.) South wall of the maṇṭapa in front of the Rājagōpāla-Perumāḷ temple, second inscription. A record of the twelfth year of the Chōḷa king Tribhuvanachakravartin Kulōttuṅga-Chōḷadēva (III), recording that a military officer purchased 600 *kūḷis* of land and assigned them to temple. [See *Ep. Ind.*, IV, p. 220, where Kielhorn calculates the date to be Monday, 4th December A.D. 1189. See *S.I.I.* III, No. 36, pp. 82-83.]

791. 6 *of* 1892.—(Tamil.) North and west walls of the garbhagriha of the Rājagōpāla-Perumāḷ temple. A record of the twenty-ninth year of Chōḷa king Kō-Rājakēsarivarman *alias* Jayaṅgoṇḍachōḷa Rājādhirājadēva (1018—53), "who destroyed the palace of the Chāḷukyan king in the city of Kampili. This is a very important epigraph which gives all the details of Rājādhirāja's achievements. It records that the villagers made over 2,000 *kūḷis* of land to the temple for 100 *kāśu*. According to Kielhorn the date corresponded to Wednesday, 3rd December A.D. 1046. [See *S.I.I.* III, No. 28, pp. 51--58.]

792. 7 *of* 1892.—(Sanskrit and Tamil.) South wall of the garbhagriha of the Rājagōpāla-Perumāḷ temple. A record of the Chōḷa king Kō-Rājakēsarivarman, dated in his sixth year, in which a person purchased 4,000 *kūḻis* from the local people and gave it to Vishṇu temple. [*S.I.I.* III, No. 27, pp. 50-51.]

793. 19 *of* 1896.—(Tamil.) On the east wall of the Dharmēś-vara temple. Records in the eighteenth year of the Chōḷa king Tribhuvanachakravartin Rājarājadēva gift of two *Kaḻañjus* lamps. [*S.I.I.* III, No. 41, pp. 87-88.]

794. 20 *of* 1896.—(Tamil.) On the east wall of the maṇṭapa in front of the Rājagōpāla-Perumāḷ temple. Records in the eighteenth year of the Chōḷa king Tribhuvanachakravartin Rāja-rājadēva (III ?) the building of the steps leading to the maṇṭapa, by two brothers. [*S.I.I.* III, No. 39, pp. 85-86.]

795. 21 *of* 1896. -(Tamil.) On the same wall. A record of the Chōḷa king Tribhuvanachakravartin Kulōttuṅga-Chōḷadēva (III), "who took Madurai and the crowned head of the Pāṇḍya." Records in his twenty-eighth year, gift of $7\frac{1}{10}$ old *kāśu* out of the interest of which four lamps were to be maintained in the Krishṇa temple. [See *S.I.I.* III, No. 37, p. 84.]

796. 22 *of* 1896.—(Tamil.) On the south wall of the same maṇṭapa. An incomplete record of the Pāṇḍya king Kō-Jaṭāvarman *alias* Sundara-Pāṇḍya, dated in his fifteenth year. [See Cg. 781 above for the probable identity of the king.]

797. 23 *of* 1896.—(Tamil.) On the west wall of the same maṇṭapa. A record of the forty-eighth year of the Chōḷa king Kō-Rājakēsarivarman *alias* Kulōttuṅga-Chōḷa (I). Records the gift of 1,050 *kūḻis* of land by a private person to the temple for the expenses of the new moon procession days. The land had been purchased by him from several persons. The date, according to Kielhorn, was Friday, the 25th January 1118. [See *Ep. Ind.*, IV, p. 263 and *S.I.I.* III, No. 31, pp. 71-73.]

798. 24 *of* 1896.--(Tamil.) On the same wall. A record of the Chōḷa king Kō-Parakēsarivarman *alias* Vikrama-Chōḷadēva (1118--35). Records in his fourth year, the purchase of some land from the villagers and gift of it to temple. [See *S.I.I.* III, No. 33, pp. 75—77.] For offerings after the God's bath.

799. 25 *of* 1896.—(Tamil.) On the same wall. A record of the eighth year of Chōḷa king Tribhuvanachakravartin Kulōttuṅga-Chōḷadēva (II). Quotes an inscription of the thirteenth year of Vikramachōḷadēva. Records gift by the village Mahāsabha of two pieces of land (previously purchased from Sāhaṇi Mādhava Bhaṭṭa, etc.), to the temple. [*S.I.I.* III, No. 34, pp. 77-78.]

800. 26 *of* 1896.—(Grantha and Tamil.) On the outside of the east wall of the second prākāra of the same temple. Records in the eighteenth year of the Chōḷa king Tribhuvanachakravartin Rājarājadēva (III), gift of two lamps by Vādhūla Śrī Kṛishṇasūri वाधूलगात्रार्णवपूर्णचन्द्रः, निधिरागमानां. to Śrīrāma Bhaṭṭa and his brother Vīṟṟunda Bhaṭṭa, priests in the temple of Mannanār. [See *S.I.I.*, III, No. 40, pp. 86—87.]

801. 27 *of* 1896.—(Tamil.) On the same wall. A record of the Chōḷa king Rājarājadēva (III ?) in his thirteenth year; gift of money for two lamps. *S.I.I.*, III, No. 38, p. 85.

802. 28 *of* 1896.—(Tamil.) On the same wall. An incomplete record of the Chōḷa king Rājarājadēva, dated in his tenth year.

803. 29 *of* 1896.—(Tamil.) On the same wall. Records in the eighth year of the Chōḷa king Kō-Parakēsarivarman *alias* Rājarājadēva (II), gift of land by the Sabhā of Maṇimaṅgalam to the temple. The land had been purchased from Sāhiṇi Mādhava Bhaṭṭan. One Araṭṭamukki dāsan is called the overseer of the Śrī Vaishṇavas. [See *S.I.I.*, III, No. 35, pp. 79—82.]

804. 274 *of* 1897.—(Tamil.) In the maṇṭapa in the Rājagōpāla-Perumāḷ temple. A damaged record of the Vijayanagara king Dēvarāya (II), dated in Ś. 1357, Rākshasa.

805. 275 *of* 1897.—(Tamil.) On the south wall of the shrine in the same temple. Records in Rudhirōdgārin assignment of a number of shares to the temple.

806. 276 *of* 1897.—(Tamil.) On the north wall of the same shrine. Records in the twentieth year of the Chōḷa king Tribhuvanachakravartin Kulōttuṅga-Chōḷadēva (III) gift of four lamps. See *Ep. Ind.*, V, 199, where the details of the date are discussed and proved to be irregular.

807. 277 *of* 1897.—(Tamil.) On the south wall of the Dharmēśvara temple. A mutilated record of the Pāṇḍya king Jaṭāvarman *alias* Sundara-Pāṇḍyadēva (I or II ?), dated in his fourteenth year.

808. 278 *of* 1897.—(Tamil.) On the east wall of the same temple. Contains an order regarding temple revenue from Nīlagaṅgaraiyan. See No. 683 above.

809. 279 *of* 1897.—(Tamil.) On the same wall. Contains a similar order from Madhurāntaka-Pottappi-Chōḷa *alias* Gaṇḍagōpāla, the father of Nīlagaṅgaraiyar. See Cg. 683 above.

810. 280 *of* 1897.—(Tamil.) On the south wall of the same temple. A record dated in Rudhirōdgārin. Resembles No. 275.

811. 281 *of* 1897.—(Tamil.) On the same wall. A record of Tribhuvanachakravartin Nāyanār Śrīraṅganāthar *alias* Yādavarāyar, dated in his seventeenth year. See N.A. 58, 436 and 449.

812. 282 *of* 1897.—(Tamil.) On the north wall of the same temple. A record of the Chōḷa king Tribhuvanachakravartin

Kulōttuṅga-Chōḷadēva (III) in his twenty-ninth year (mīna, Pūrva 7, Wednesday, mrigasīrsha, corresponding to 7th March, A.D. 1207. Gift of two lamps. See *Ep. Ind.*, V, 198–9.

813. 283 *of* 1897.—(Tamil.) On a pillar in front of the Vaikuṇṭha Perumāḷ temple. A record containing a portion of the usual introduction of the inscriptions of Rājēndra-Chōḷa I.

814. 284 *of* 1897.—(Tamil.) On the west wall of the same temple. Records in Krōdhana gift of land.

815. 285 *of* 1897.—(Tamil.) On the south wall of the same temple. Records in the thirty-ninth year of the Pāṇḍya king Māravarman *alias* Kulaśēkharadēva (I, ? 1268—1308) that prince Nīlagaṅgaraiyar granted a garden of palm trees for the merit of his father.

816. 286 *of* 1897.—(Tamil.) On the same wall. A record of the Pāṇḍya king Jaṭāvarman *alias* Sundara-Pāṇḍyadēva (II ? 1276—90) mentions in his eleventh year a certain Vāṇarāyadēvar.

817. 287 *of* 1897.—(Tamil.) On the same wall. A record dated in Rudhirōdgarin. Resembles Nos. 805 and 810.

818. 288 *of* 1897.—(Tamil.) On the north wall of the same temple. An incomplete record of the Vijayanagara king Dēvarāya, the date of which is lost.

819. 289 *of* 1897.—(Tamil.) On six stones built into the walls of the same temple. Records in the fifteenth year of the Chōḷa king Rājarāja I gift of land (800 *kuḻis*) to Tiruvāyappāḍi-Śrī-Kṛishṇa-Perumāḷ, by the village assembly which met at water-shed. See *Ep. Ind.*, V, 197.

820. 290 *of* 1897.—(Tamil.) On three stones in the same place. Records in the twenty-second year (Rishabha, Pūrva 10, Thursday, Hasta) of the Chōḷa king Rājarāja-Rājadēva (I, 985—1013) gift of land (800 *kuḻis*) to Tiruvāyappāḍi-Śrī-Kṛishṇa-Perumāḷ, by the village assembly met at water-shed. *Ep. Ind.*, V, 197, where the date is discussed and decided in favour of 27th April, A.D. 999.

821. 291 *of* 1897.—(Tamil.) On a stone in the same place. The Chōḷa king Kulōttuṅga-Chōḷadēva records gift of land to Tiruvāyappāḍi-Aḻvār, date of which is doubtful.

822. 292 *of* 1897.—(Tamil.) On two stones in the same place. Records in the fifth year of the Chōḷa king Rājakēsarivarman gift of sheep for a lamp to Tiruvāyappāḍi-Srī-Kṛishṇa-Perumāḷ.

823. 293 *of* 1897.—(Tamil.) On the south wall of the Kailaśanātha temple. A record dated in Rudhirōdgarin. Resembles Nos. 805, 810 and 817.

824. 294 *of* 1897.—(Tamil.) On the same wall. A record of the Vijayanagara king Achyutadēva; mentions in Ś. 1449 Vyaya, a Mahāmaṇḍalēśvara Sindaiyadēva.

825. 295 *of* 1897.—(Tamil.) On the north and west walls of the same temple. A record of the Vijayanagara king Achyutadēva; mentions in Ś. 1452, Virōdhin a Mahāmaṇḍalēśvara-Sindaiyadēva.

826. 296 *of* 1897.—(Tamil.) On two stones built into the inner walls of the same temple. A fragment of the record of the Chōḷa king Rājarāja-Rājakēsarivarman (I, 985—1013), dated in his fifteenth year.

827. 297 *of* 1897.—(Tamil.) On a stone in the same place. A record of the Chōḷa king Vikrama-Chōḷadēva (1118—35) in his fifth year; gift of land.

Pāḍi.

This place known as Tiruvalidāyam in the Dēvāram has no records of antiquity except a few of Pārthivēndravarman and Rājarāja I. This is due perhaps to the vandalism of later day repairers.

828. 214 *of* 1910.—(Tamil.) On the south wall of the maṇṭapa in front of the central shrine in the Tiruvallīśvara temple. A record of Tribhuvanachakravartin . . . dēva in his sixteenth year saying that a Brāhmaṇa of Tiruveṇgāḍu set up the god Aḷagiya-tiruchchiṟṟambalam-Uḍaiya-Nāyanār in the enclosure of the temple of Tiruvallidāyam-Uḍaiya-Nāyanār at Tiruvallidāyam in Ambattūrnāḍu, a subdivision of Puḷar-kōṭṭam *alias* Vikramachōḷa-vaḷanāḍu, in Jayaṅgoṇḍa-chōḷamaṇḍalam and provided for offerings. Mentions the grain measure *Tirujñānasambanda-nāḻi.*

829. 215 *of* 1910.—(Tamil.) On the same wall. Dated in the reign of the Vijayanagara king Dēvarāya (II, 1422—49). Records in Ś. 1350, Plavaṅga, gift of the tax (*iḍangai vari*) payable by the *Paḷḷis* of the village of Pāḍi, to the same temple and that by the community of *Iḍaṅgai* classes and the *Vaṉṉiyars* living in the village surrounding Chandragiri. See S.A. 728 for the *Iḍaṅgais* and Cg. 1 for the *Vaṉṉiyars.*

830. 216 *of* 1910.—(Tamil.) On the same wall. Records in the twenty-eighth year of the Chōḷa king Tribhuvanachakravartin Rājarājadēva (III ?) gift of money for offerings to the shrine of Kshētrapāla-piḷḷaiyār, built in the same temple by a resident of Pāḍi.

831. 217 *of* 1910.—(Tamil.) On the same wall. Records in the third year of Tribhuvanachakravartin Vijaya-Gaṇḍagōpāladēva that a dancing girl of the Tiruvēgambam-Uḍaiya-Nāyanār temple at Kāñchi consecrated the image of the Goddess Tiruvīdināchchiyār in the temple at Tiruvallidāyam and presented both to the God and the Goddess a number of jewels and vessels.

832. 218 *of* 1910.—(Tamil.) On the same wall. Records in the ninth year of the Chōḷa king Tribhuvanachakravartin Rājarājadēva (III) (A.D. 1225) that the temple of Tiruvallidāyamuḍaiya-Nāyanār was situated in . . . chintāmaṇipura, a suburb of Tiruvallidāyam and that two gardens and two houses were given by Śāḷukki Nāraṇan-Yādavarāyan (evidently of the same family as Vīra Narasimha Yādavarāya and Śrīraṅganātha Yādavarāya). See No. 811 above.

833. 219 *of* 1910.—(Tamil.) On the south wall of the central shrine in the same temple. Records in the eighth year of the Chōḷa king Tribhuvanachakravartin Rājarājadēva (III ?) gift of money for a lamp by a certain Śilambaṇindān Yādavarāyan of Paramēśuramaṅgalam in Śembūr-kōṭṭam. See No. 811 above.

834. 220 *of* 1910.—(Tamil.) On the west and south walls of the same shrine. Dated in the reign of the Vijayanagara king Vīrapratāpa Virūpākshadēva Mahārāya; records in Ś. 1548, Nandana (wrong) gift of land for maintaining lamps in the temple, by the *mahājanas* of Pāḍi Tiruvallidāyam, in the name of the Śāḷuva chief Gaṇḍakaṭhāri Bommayyadēva Mahārāja. Mentions Rājāśraya-Chaturvēdimaṅgalam *alias* Agaram Kūrattūr.

835. 221 of 1910.—(Tamil.) On the north and west walls of the same shrine. Dated in Dhātri (Ś. 1319), during the reign of the Vijayanagara king Vīra-Hariharāya (II). Records an order of Mallappa Uḍaiyār, evidently the pradhāni, fixing the taxes payable by the eighteen professional castes (*paṭṭāḍāi*) of Pāḍi-Tiruvaḷḷidāyam, to the temple of Tiruvaḷḷidāyamuḍaiya Nāyanār, viz., *Paṭṭāḍaiāyam, Paṭṭāḍainūlāyam, māḍaviraṭṭi, Śammādam, Śekku*, etc.

836. 222 *of* 1910.—(Tamil.) On the west wall of the same shrine. Madurāntaka Pottappichchōḷa records in his thirty-third year gift of the village of Tiruvallidāyam for the repair of the temple and the feeding of the Mahēśvaras therein. The inscription ends with the signature of Gaṇḍa-gōpāla. The title Madhurāntaka Pottappi chōḷa was assumed by (1) Vīragaṇḍa-gōpāla and (2) Vijayagaṇḍa-gōpāla, a feudatory of Kōpperuñjiṅga. Mr. Kṛishṇa Sastri believes that (1) was the contemporary of (2) and that he was identical with his Telugu namesake of the family to which Tammasiddhi of the Tiruvoṟṟiyūr and Conjeeveram inscriptions belonged. See N.A. 659 and 441.

837. 223 *of* 1910.—(Tamil.) On the north wall of the maṇṭapa in front of the same shrine. Records in the tenth year of the Chōḷa king Tribhuvanachakravartin Rājarājadēva (III ?) gift of land by purchase, for two lamps.

838. 224 *of* 1910.—(Tamil.) On the same wall. Dated in the reign of the Vijayanagara king Dēvarāya-Mahārāya (I); records in Vikāri (i.e., Ś. 1342) sale of the village Nuḷappiyāṟṟu-Maṇañjēri *alias* Nyāyaparipālanpēṭṭai, to the same temple.

839. 225 *of* 1910.—(Tamil.) On a slab lying in the court-yard of the same temple. Records in the sixth year of Pārthivēndravarman sale of land for a lamp to the temple of Mahādēva at Tiruvalidāyil in Tuḍamuni-nāḍu, a subdivision of Puliyūr-kōṭṭam, by the assembly of Kūrattūr *alias* Parāntaka-chaturvēdimaṅgalam in Ambattūrērikiḷ-nāḍu, a subdivision of Puḷal-kōṭṭam.

840. 226 *of* 1910.—(Tamil.) On the same slab. Records in the tenth year of the Chōḷa king Rājarāja Rājakēsarivarman (995—1013) gift of ninety sheep for a lamp to the temple of Mahādēva at Tiruvalidāyam in Tuḍamuniyūr-naḍu, a subdivision of Puliyūr-kōṭṭam.

841. 227 *of* 1910.—(Tamil.) On the same wall. A damaged record of the Chōḷa king Rājarājakēsarivarman *alias* Rājarājadēva (I), dated in his second year. Records gift of paddy for offerings to a shrine built by a certain Śeṅgaṅkiḷān Tiruvēlikaḷibhaṭṭan in the temple of Mahādēva at Tiruvālidāyil, in Tuḍamuni-nadu.

Pallavaram.

842. 369 *of* 1908.—(Pallava Grantha.) In the rock-out cave (now used as a place of worship by the Muhammadans). Contains the *birudas* of the Pallava king Mahēndravarman I.

843. 55 *of* 1909.—(Telugu verse.) On a slab set up near a well in the village of Old Pallavaram. Records that Śēku Mūsāmiyā, son of Śēku Alavaddīnu, founded a street at Pallavaram and the garden Ibhurāmu-bāg named after Said-Ibhurānemusāhēbu.

844. 56 *of* 1909.—(Tamil.) On the same slab. Records in Pramāthin that the villagers of Pallapuram *alias* Avubalamāsamudram sold a piece of land for a well to Śēku Mūsāmiyā, son of Śēku Alāvaddīn. The slab bears small epigraphs in Arabic on the top of each of the two faces and of the two sides.

844-A. On a stone discovered here by Major Taylor and deposited in the Madras Museum. A grant of land to the temple at Ālattūr in Puliyūrkōṭṭam in the fifteenth year of Rājarāja I. *Antiquities* I, 325.

Poonamallee.

845. 31 *of* 1911.—(Tamil.) On the south base of the Perumāḷ temple. An incomplete record of the Pāṇḍya king Jaṭāvaram *alias* Vikrama-Pāṇḍyadēva (c. 1285), dated in his fifth year. Records gift of land for worship, to the temple of Piḷḷaikovil (modern Perumāḷ temple) in the Brāhmaṇa quarter *(agaram)* of Kumugāṇippākkam in Māṅgāḍu-nāḍu, a subdivision of Puliyūr-kōṭṭam which was a district of Jayaṅgoṇḍachōḷamaṇḍalam.

846. 32 *of* 1911.—(Tamil.) On the same wall. Records in the twenty-fourth year of Vijaya-Gaṇḍagōpāladēva gift of a cow for a lamp by a native of Śemmambākkam, to the temple of Piḷḷai.

847. 33 *of* 1911.—(Tamil.) On the same base. Records in his thirty-first year, gift of agaram Śērapāṇḍya-chaturvēdimaṅgalam (Poonamallee) which was split up from Kaliyugarāmanallūr as a sarvamānya grant to the assembly of that village. The figure of a fish surmounted by an *aṅkuśa* is depicted on the right margin of the record. [See note to the next inscription.]

848. 34 *of* 1911.—[Grantha (verse).] On the same base. Records that the Chēra king who conquered Sundara Pāṇḍya granted the village Chērapāṇḍya-chaturvēdimaṅgalam for the enjoyment of the Brāhmaṇas. [Mr. Krishna Sastri identifies this Sundara Pāṇḍya with Jaṭāvarman Sundara Pāṇḍya II (1276—90) and his Chēra conqueror with Ravivarman Kulaśēkhara. The name Chērapāṇḍya-chaturvēdimaṅgalam and the surmounting of the Pāṇḍya fish with the Chēra *aṅkuśa,* shows distinctly the conquest. See *Ep. Rep.* 1911, p. 79.]

Sōmaṅgalam.

This village belonged to Māganūr-nāḍu in Śeṅgāṭṭu kōṭṭam and was called Rājaśikhāmaṇi-Chaturvēdimaṅgalam.

849. 182 *of* 1901.—(Tamil.) On the north, west and south walls of the Saundararāja-Perumāḷ temple (ancient Chitrakūṭa). A record of the Chōḷa king Rājakēsarivarman *alias* Rājēndra-Chōḷadēva II (Kulōttuṅga I) in his third year; gift of land. *S.I.I.,* Vol. III, No. 67, pp. 139–40.

850. 183 *of* 1901.—(Tamil.) On the east wall of the maṇṭapa in front of the Sōmanāthēśvara temple at the same village. A record of the Chōḷa king Tribhuvanachakravartin Kulōttuṅga-Chōḷadēva III. Refers in his fourteenth year (Makara, Pūrva I, Pushya, Thursday, January 2, A.D. 1192), to heavy rains and consequent breach of the tank bund in the twelfth and thirteenth years of the king's reign and provides for the annual repair of the tank. See *Ep. Ind.*, Vol. VII, p. 6.

851. 184 *of* 1901.—(Tamil.) On the same wall. An epigraph of the Chōḷa king Tribhuvanachakravartin Rājādhirājadēva recording in his eleventh year, gift of a lamp.

852. 185 *of* 1901.—(Tamil.) On the same wall. An inscription of the Chōḷa king Tribhuvanachakravartin Kulōttuṅga-Chōḷadēva III recording in his twenty-eighth year, gift of money for a lamp.

853. 186 *of* 1901.—(Tamil.) On the same wall. Records in the thirty-first year of the Chōḷa king Tribhuvanachakravartin Tribhuvanavīradēva (Kulōttuṅga III) gift of money for a lamp.

854. 187 *of* 1901.—(Tamil.) On the same wall. Records in the seventh year of the Chōḷa king Tribhuvanachakravartin Rājarājadēva gift of five cows. Mentions Nīla-Gaṅgaraiyan.

St. Thomas' Mount.

855. 289 *of* 1895.—(Pahlavi.) Round the cross in the Church. It has been attributed to the ninth century and reads: "He whom the suffering of the selfsame Messiah, the forgiving and upraising, has saved, is offering the plea whose origin was the agony of this." Compare *Indian Antiquary*, Vol. III, p. 308 ff. *Ep. Ind.*, Vol. IV, p. 174 f. where Dr. E. W. West edits it.

Śriperumbūdūr.

856. A C.P. grant (presented by the local Dharmakartā to the Department) of Achyuta Rāya of Vijayanagar, dated in Ś. 1460, Viḷambin (A.D. 1538) saying that, while at the temple of Viṭṭhalēśvara at Vijayanagara, he gave the village of Āranēri *alias* Raghunāthapuram, to a Vāmana Yajvan, son of Kṛishṇa Yajvan. The village was in Pāṭavīṭu Rājyam, Kuṇṇa-nāḍu, Ūttukkāḍu-pattu and Śeṅgāṭṭukkōṭṭam. [The record is in Sanskrit verse and Tamil, both written in the Nāgari character (which is unique in case of Tamil)]. See *Ep. Rep.* 1890, p. 3.

856-A. A C.P. in the temple of Śrī Rāmānuja (Sanskrit and Grantham). Records that Sadāśiva Rāya granted in Ś. 1478, Naḷa, a number of villages to the temple. [More than twenty-eight have been enumerated.] The inscription is given in the Mack. collections (*Ins., S. Dts.*, p. 158, No. I.)

Tirumaḻiśai.

(Celebrated in the history of Śrī Vaishṇavism as the birth place of Tirumaḻiśai Āḻvār.)

857. 1 *of* 1911.—(Tamil.) On the south wall of the Jagannātha Perumāḷ temple. Records in the twenty-sixth year of Vijayagaṇḍagōpāladēva gift of land by Pañchanadivāṇan Tiruvaṇṇāmalai-Perumāḷ Laṅkēśvaradēva (a feudatory of his) to the temple of Tirumaḻiśai in Māṅgāḍunāḍu, a subdivision of Puliyūrkōṭṭam in Jayaṅgoṇḍachōḷa-maṇḍalam. *See* No. 836 above. A Laṅkēśvara of Kiḻiyūr who was a vassal of Kulōttuṅga III is given in S.A. 76 and another of Araśūr who was a vassal of Rājarāja III in S.A. 107.

858. 2 *of* 1911.—(Tamil.) On the same wall. Dated in the reign of the Chōḷa king Tribhuvanachakravartin Vīrarājēndra-Chōḷadēva (Kulōttuṅga III, 1186—1216); records in his sixteenth year gift of 1650 *kuḻi* of land by prince (piḷḷaiyār) Kulōttuṅga-śōḷa-Kaṇṇappan Nallanāyanār Pañchanadivāṇan Nīlagaṅgaraiyan, to the temple of Tirumaḻiśai-Aḻvār at Tirumaḻiśai *alias* Pukkaturai-vallava-chaturvēdimaṅgalam in Mēn-Māṅgāḍu-nāḍu. Mr. Krishna Sastri believes that the donor was apparently a different, an earlier man than his namesake and subordinate of Vijayagaṇḍa-gōpāla. See Cg. 836 above.

859. 3 *of* 1911.—(Tamil.) On the same wall. Records an order of Nīlagaṅgan to the *tānattār* of the temple of Tirumaḻiśa Emberumān and registers a grant of land to the temple of Jagannātha at Pañchanadivāṇa-chaturvēdimaṅgalam. See the above epigraph.

860. 4 *of* 1911.—(Tamil.) On the same wall. Records in the thirtieth year of Tribhuvanachakravartin Vijayagaṇḍa-gōpāladēva gift of land to the temple of Tirumaḻiśai Emberumān by Pañchanādivāṇa Aruṇagirī-Perumāḷ Nīlagaṅgaraiyan. Mentions also the temples of Agattīśuram-Uḍaiyār and Subramaṇya-Piḷḷaiyār in the suburbs of Tirumaḻiśai.

861. 5 *of* 1911.—(Tamil.) On the same wall. Records in his twenty-fourth year an order of Nīlagaṅgaraiyan of the gift of the tax *(ponvari māḍai)* in the hamlet of Arayappākkiḻāñchēri, to the temple of Tirumaḻiśai Āḻvār.

862. 6 *of* 1911.—(Tamil verse.) On the same wall. Records in thirtieth year gift of land to the temple under the orders of the same chief.

863. 7 *of* 1911.—(Tamil.) On the base of the same wall. Dated in the reign of the Vijayanagara king Ariyaṇa-Uḍaiyār (Harihara II). Records in Śukla (i.e., Ś. 1312) sale of land to the temple of Jagannātha of Tirumaḻiśai-Viṇṇagar at Tirumaḻiśai *alias* Pukkaturaivalla-chaturvēdimaṅgalam. Built in at the right end.

864. 8 *of* 1911.—(Tamil.) On the same base. Records in the sixteenth year Tribhuvanachakravartin Vijaya-Gaṇḍa-gōpāladēva gift of three lamps to the temple of Tirumaḻiśai Emberumān at Tirumaḻiśai in Māṅgāḍu-nāḍu, a subdivision of Puliyūr-kōṭṭam *alias* Kulōttuṅgaśōḻa-vaḷanāḍu in Jayaṅgoṇḍachōḻamaṇḍalam.

865. 9 *of* 1911.—(Tamil.) On the same base. An unfinished record of the Vijayanagara king Vīrapratāpa-Dēvarāya-Virūpāksharāya, dated Khara (i.e., Ś. 1394). Mentions Iraṇḍāyiravēlipaṟṟu in Jayaṅgoṇḍachōḻa-maṇḍalam.

866. 10 *of* 1911.—(Tamil.) On the south and west base of the same temple. Dated in the reign of the Vijayanagara king Harihara (Ariyaṇa)-Uḍaiyār II; records in Śukla (i.e., Ś. 1312) sale of land to the temple of Jagannātha, by the assembly of Tirumaḻiśai *alias* Pukkaturaivalla-chaturvēdimaṅgalam.

867. 11 *of* 1911.—(Tamil.) On the same bases. An unfinished record dated in his sixth year. Records an order of Nīlagaṅgan and registers gift of taxes on certain lands to the same temple. Mentions the streets Pālaṟṟuvenṟāntiruvīdi and Ponparppinān-tiruvīdi (at Tirumaḻiśai).

868. 12 *of* 1911.—(Tamil.) On the north base of the same temple. Dated in the reign of the Vijayanagara king Ariyaṇa-Uḍaiyār (Harihara II); records in Śukla (i.e., Ś. 1312) gift of the houses in Ponparappinān-tiruvīdi to the temple, in memory of a certain Tirukkaikkōn Venṟumālaiyiṭṭān.

869. 13 *of* 1911.—(Tamil.) On the same base. Records in the nineteenth year of the Pallava king Sakalabhuvanachakravartin Peruñjiṅgadēva gift of four houses. Built in at the beginning. [As his accession was between 11th February and 30th July A.D. 1243, the present inscription should be attributed to A.D. 1261.]

870. 14 *of* 1911.—(Tamil.) On the north wall of the same temple. Dated in the reign of Vijayagaṇḍa-gōpāladēva; records an order of Nīlagaṅgaraiyan giving the lands in the village of Vaḷattuvaḷviṭṭanallūr, the eastern hamlet of Tirumaḻiśai, to the temples of Nirvaṇṇa Perumāḷ at Tirunīrmalai and of Tirumaḻiśai Emberumān.

871. 15 *of* 1911.—(Tamil.) On a pillar in the maṇṭapa in front of the central shrine of the Uttaṇḍēśvara temple in the same village. A record of the Chōḷa king Tribhuvanachakravartin Rājarājadēva; records in his fifteenth year gift of money for a lamp to the temple of Agattīśuramuḍaiya-Nāyanār at agaram Tirumaḻiśai *alias* Pukkatuṟaivala-chaturvēdimaṅgalam.

872. 16 *of* 1911.—(Tamil.) On another pillar in the same maṇṭapa. Records gift of money for the Tiruvēṭṭai-festival by Śittiramēḻi *alias* Kūttan, a goldsmith of Tirumaḻiśai.

873. 17 *of* 1911.—(Tamil.) On the third pillar in the same place. Records in the twelfth year of the Chōḷa king Rājarājadēva gift of three cows for a lamp.

874. 18 *of* 1911.—(Tamil.) On the same pillar. A record of the Chōḷa king Tribhuvanachakravartin Rājādhirājadēva in his sixth year gift of three cows for a lamp. Mentions Śemmambākkam in Puliyūr kōṭṭam, a subdivision of Jayaṅgoṇḍa-chōḷamaṇḍalam.

875. 19 *of* 1911.—(Tamil.) On the fourth pillar in the same place. Dated in the reign of the Chōḷa king Kulōttuṅga-Chōḷadēva (I); records in his forty-fifth year gift of 10,000 *kuḻi* of land to the temple of Agattīśvaramuḍaiya-Mahādēva at agaram Śērakulavalli-chaturvēdimaṅgalam by the Nagarattār of Uyyakkoṇḍaśōḻapuram in Māṅgāḍu-nāḍu, a subdivision of Kulōttuṅgaśōḻa-vaḷanāḍu.

876. 20 *of* 1911.—(Tamil.) On the north base of the same shrine. A damaged record of the Vijayanagara king (Ariya)ṇa Uḍaiyār (Harihara II), dated Śukla (i.e., Ś. 1312). Seems to record a gift to the temple of Ottāṇḍār. Built in and completed. See next epigraph.

877. 21 *of* 1911.—(Tamil.) On the same base. A fragment of the record of the Vijayanagara king Ariyaṇa-Uḍaiyār (Harihara II), dated Śukla. Mentions the temple of Ottāṇḍār and refers to the street called *Nārpatteṇṇāyira-perunderuvu* in agaram Tirumaḻiśai. See N.A., 715 and S.A., 921.

878. 22 *of* 1911.—(Tamil.) On the same base. An incomplete record of the Vijayanagara king Rāmarāja-Veṅkaṭapatirāyadēva-Mahārāya, dated in Jaya (i.e., Ś. 1517 or 1577). Mentions Dinakara-Piḷḷaiyavargaḷ, agent to Achyutappanāyakar-Ayyan and the god Ottāṇḍīśura-Tambirānār in the temple of Tirumaḷisai-Uḍaiyār. [The king could neither be Veṅkaṭa I whose father was Tirumala and grandfather Raṅga nor Veṅkaṭa II owing to chronological difficulties. For Achyutappa Nāyakar see N.A., 693.]

879. 23 *of* 1911.—(Tamil.) On the same base. An incomplete record of the Vijayanagara king Achutadēva-Mahārāya, dated Ś. 14... ?, Vikāri. Mentions the Kaikkōḷar community of Tirumaḷiśai.

880. 24 *of* 1911.—(Tamil.) On the south base of the same shrine. An incomplete record of the Vijayanagara king Ariyaṇa Uḍaiyār (Harihara II), dated Krōdhana (i.e., Ś. 1308). Mentions the temple of Ottāṇḍīśura Nāyanār at Tirumaḷiśai.

881. 25 *of* 1911.—(Tamil.) On the same base. A record of the Chōḷa king Vīrarājēndra-Chōḷadēva (Kulōttuṅga III, 1178—1216). Records in his tenth year, gift of four cows for two lamps to the temple of Agattīśuramuḍaiya-Nāyanār at agaram Tirumaḷiśai.

Tirumullaivāyil.

882. 662 *of* 1904.—(Tamil.) On the south wall of the central shrine in the Maśilāmaṇīśvara temple. Records in thirtieth year, an order of Madurāntaka-Pottapi-Chōḷa making over the proceeds of certain taxes to the temple for celebrating a festival called Vijayagaṇḍagōpālan-śandi. See Cy. 836 above.

883. 663 *of* 1904.—(Tamil.) On the same wall. An incomplete record of the Chōḷa king Tribhuvanachakravartin Kulōttuṅga-Chōḷadēva (III), who took Madura and the crowned head of the Pāṇḍya, dated in his twenty-fourth year.

884. 664 *of* 1904.—(Tamil.) On the same wall. A record of the Vijayanagara king Harihararāya (II) in Svabhānu (i.e., Ś. 1326), gift of land.

885. 665 *of* 1904.—(Tamil.) On the same wall. Records in the time of the Vijayanagara king Pratāpa-Dēvarāya ("the younger brother of Dēvārāya II"), in Krōdhin (i.e., 1347), a gift of land. See S.A., 380.

886. 666 *of* 1904.—(Tamil.) On the same wall. Records in the tenth year of the Pāṇḍya king Jaṭāvarman Tribhuvanachakravartin Sundara-Pāṇḍyadēva (III ?) gift of the proceeds of certain taxes by the inhabitants of Puḷarkōṭṭam and Īkkāṭṭu-kōṭṭam in favour of the temple at Tirumullaivāyil in Kānappērūr nāḍu, a district of Puḷarkōṭṭam which was a subdivision of Jayaṅgoṇḍa-Chōḷamaṇḍalam. See Cy. 910 below.

887. 667 *of* 1904.—(Tamil.) On the same wall. Records in the twenty-first year of the Chōḷa king Tribhuvanachakravartin Kulōttuṅga-Chōḷadēva (III), who took Madura and the crowned head of the Pāṇḍya, gift of 24 new *Bhujabala-māḍai* for two lamps.

888. 668 *of* 1904.—(Tamil.) On the same wall. A record of the Vijayanagara king Vīrapratāpa-Bukkarāya (II), in Pārthiva (i.e., Ś. 1328), gift of land.

889. 669 *of* 1904.—(Tamil.) On the west wall of the same shrine. Dated in the reign of the Chōḷa king Parakēsarivarman *alias* Uttama-Chōḷadēva; records in his fourteenth year, gift of land by Śembiyan Mādēviyār, queen of Gaṇḍarāditta-Perumāḷ, and daughter of Maḷavarāyar. The land was purchased from the villagers of Ambattūr in Ambattūr-nādu, a district of Puḷar-kōṭṭam. In comparatively modern characters.

890. 670 *of* 1904.—(Tamil.) On the same wall. Dated in the reign of the Pāṇḍya king Jaṭāvarman *alias* Tribhuvanachakravartin Sundara-Pāṇḍyadēva (III? 1276—90). Records in his eighteenth year, an agreement among the inhabitants of Puḷarkōṭṭam *alias* Vikrama-Chōḷavaḷanāḍu in Jayaṅgoṇḍa-Chōḷamaṇḍalam.

891. 671 *of* 1904.—(Tamil.) On the same wall. Records in the reign of the Vijayanagara king Harihara in Vikrama (i.e., Ś. 1323) gift of temple vessels.

892. 672 *of* 1904.—(Tamil.) On the north wall of the same shrine. Records in his fourth year, an order of Madurāntaka-Pottapi Chōḷa; signed by Gaṇḍagōpāla. See No. 836 above.

893. 673 *of* 1904.—(Tamil.) On the north wall of the central shrine in the Māśilāmaṇīśvara temple. Records in the thirty-ninth year of the Chōḷa king Tribhuvanachakravartin Tribhuvanavīradēva (Kulōttuṅga III), gift of land.

894. 674 *of* 1904.—(Tamil.) On the same wall. Records in the sixteenth year of the Chōḷa king Tribhuvanachakravartin Rājarājadēva (III?) gift of land. The village of Kolippaḍāgai *alias* Kulōttuṅga Chōḷa-chaturvēdimaṅgalam in Kānappērūr-nāḍu, a district of Puḷarkōṭṭam is mentioned.

895. 675 *of* 1904.—(Tamil.) On the same wall. Belongs to the reign of the Vijayanagara king Vīrapratāpa Hariyarāya-Mahārāya (i.e., Harihara II). Records in Prabhava (i.e., Ś. 1310) gift of land.

896. 676 *of* 1904.—(Tamil.) On a slab built into the floor of the maṇṭapa in front of the same shrine. An incomplete record of Pārthivēndravarman, dated in his fifth year. Mentions the village of Kalikēsari-chaturvēdimaṅgalam.

897. 677 *of* 1904.—(Tamil.) On a pillar within the same maṇṭapa. Records in the third year of the Chōḷa king Parakēsarivarman *alias* Rājēndra-Chōḷadēva (I), the building of the maṇṭapa.

898. 678 *of* 1904.—(Tamil.) On a second pillar in the same place. Records in the seventh year of the Chōḷa king Parakēsarivarman *alias* Rājēndra-Chōḷadēva (I, 1011—43) gift of land for a lamp.

899. 679 *of* 1904.—(Tamil.) At the entrance into the same maṇṭapa, right side. A mutilated record of the Vijayanagara king Vīrapratāpa Dēvarāya-Mahārāya, date of which is lost. Seems to record the remission of certain taxes in favour of a number of temples.

900. 680 *of* 1904.—(Tamil.) In the same place, left side. Dated in the reign of the Vijayanagara king Vīrapratāpa Mallikārjunadēva-Mahārāya. Records in Prajāpati (i.e., Ś. 1374), gift of land by the villagers of Kolippaḍāgai *alias* Kulōttuṅga-Chōḷa-chaturvēdimaṅgalam.

901. 681 *of* 1904.—(Tamil.) On the east wall of the first prākāra of the same temple, right of entrance. Records in the third year of the Chōḷa king Parakēsarivarman *alias* Rājēndra-Chōḷadēva (I, 1011—43) gift of ninety sheep for a lamp.

902. 682 *of* 1904.—(Tamil.) On a pillar built into the same prākāra. An incomplete record of the Chōḷa king Parakēsarivarman *alias* Rājēndra-Chōḷadēva (I, 1011—43) dated in his third year. Records a gift of jewels.

903. 683 *of* 1904.—(Tamil.) On a slab built into the floor of the maṇṭapa in front of the Latāmadhyāmbā shrine in the same temple. Pārthivēndrādhipativarman records in his thirteenth year gift of ninety sheep for a lamp.

904. 684 *of* 1904.—(Tamil.) On a pillar lying at the southern entrance into the same maṇṭapa. Records in the third year of the Chōḷa king Parakēsarivarman *alias* Rājēndra-Chōḷadēva (I, 1011—43), gift of land.

Tirunirmalai.

Of the two temples of Raṅganātha in this place the one on the hill was perhaps the earlier one sung by Pūdattāḷvār and Tirumaṅgai Āḷvār.

905. 532 *of* 1912.—(Tamil.) On the east wall of the Nirvaṇṇar shrine in the Raṅganātha-Perumāḷ temple. A damaged record of the Chōḷa king Tribhuvanachakravartin Rājarājadēva III, date of which is lost. Records gift of money (*paḷaṅ-kāśu*) for a lamp.

906. 533 *of* 1912.—(Tamil.) On the same wall. Dated in the reign of the Chōḷa king Tribhuvanachakravartin Rājarājadēva III. Records in his seventh year, Tulā, 26, ba. di. 2, Kārttigai, Sunday (= Sunday, 23rd October, 1222), gift of money for a lamp to the temple of Tirunīrmalai Emberumān, at Tirunīrmalai in Śūrattūr-nāḍu of Puliyūr-kōṭṭam, a subdivision of Jayaṅgoṇḍaśōḷamaṇḍalam, by Kaikaiyarāyan Thiruvagattīśuramuḍaiyān of Malayambākkam in Māṅgāḍu-nāḍu of the same division.

907. 534 *of* 1912.—(Tamil.) On the same wall. A record of the Chōḷa king Tribhuvanachakravartin Rājarājadēva III in his sixteenth year and fortieth day, relating gift of land for maintaining a service called Tiruvāḷiparappinān-śandi (i.e., festival of the man who spread Śri Vaishṇavism) in the temple of Tirunīrmalai-Emberumān by a certain Madurāntaka Pottappichōḷan Gaṇḍa-gōpālan (a subordinate of the king Vīra Narasimha Yādava Rāya). See No. 836 above.

908. 535 *of* 1912.—(Tamil.) On the same wall. Dated in the reign of the Chōḷa king Tribhuvanachakravartin Rājarājadēva III; records in his sixth year, Mīna, Monday, Urohaṇi, corresponding to 21st March, 1222, gift of two lamps to the same temple by Tiruchchūr-Kaṇṇappan Abayampukkān Nīlagaṅgaraiyan Kaḍak-kan-Śōḷagaṅgadēvan.

909. 536 *of* 1912.—(Tamil.) On the east and north walls of the same shrine. Records in the twenty-sixth year of Tribhuvana-chakravartin Vijaya-Gaṇḍagōpāladēva gift of 1,460 kuḷis of land at Kōvūr in Maṅgāḍu-nāḍu, to the same temple, by a certain Tiru-nalluḷān Tirunaṭṭaperumān Tyāgamēgan of Maduraivāyil in Pērūr-nāḍu, a subdivision of Puliyūr-kōṭṭam *alias* Kulōttuṅgaśōḷa-vaḷanāḍu in Jayaṅgoṇḍaśōḷamaṇḍalam.

910. 537 *of* 1912.—(Tamil.) On the north wall of the same shrine. Dated in the reign of the Pāṇḍya king Jaṭāvarman *alias* Tribhuvanachakravartin Sundara Pāṇḍyadēva III (1276—90). Records in his seventeenth year, Mīna (which ought to be *simha*), śu. di. 5, Wednesday, Tiruvōṇam, corresponding to July 30, A.D. 1292, gift of six vēlis of land and of taxes collected from the puṛakkaḷanai-kuḍimakkaḷ living near the temple, by a certain Aruṇagiripperumāḷ *alias* Nīlagaṅgaraiyan.

911. 538 *of* 1912.—(Tamil.) On the same wall. An unfinished record of the Pāṇḍya king Jaṭāvarman *alias* Sundara-Pāṇḍyadēva (III, ? 1276—90), dated in his eleventh year.

912. 539 *of* 1912.—(Tamil.) On the west and south walls of the same shrine. Records in the thirtieth year of the Chōḷa king Kulōttuṅga-Chōḷadēva III, gift of money for a lamp. One of the tiers below this bears writing which is also continued on a corre-sponding tier of the south wall. This latter begins abruptly with the description of the land granted.

913. 540 *of* 1912.—(Tamil.) On the south wall of the same shrine. Dated in the reign of the Chōḷa king Tribhuvanachakra-vartin Vīrarājēndrachōḷadēva (i.e., Kulōttuṅga-Chōḷa III). Records in his twelfth year, Mēsha, śu. di. 13, Monday, Punarpūśam, gift of money *(māḍai)* for a lamp to the temple of Tirunīrmalai-Emberu-mān, by a native of Pulippākkam *alias* Śīlachintāmaṇi-chaturvēdi-maṅgalam, in Amūr-kōṭṭam.

914. 541 *of* 1912.—(Tamil.) On the same wall. A record of the Chōḷa king Tribhuvanachakravartin Vīrarājēndrachōḷadēva (i.e., Kulōttuṅga Chōḷa III). Gift of money for a lamp; date lost.

915. 542 *of* 1912.—(Tamil.) On the same wall. Dated in the reign of the Chōḷa king Tribhuvanachakravartin Vīrarājēndra-Chōḷadēva (i.e., Kulōttuṅga-Chōḷa III). Records in his fourth year, Makara, śu. di. 10, Monday, Aviṭṭam, gift of a lamp to Nirvaṇṇan of Tirunīrmalai by an oil-monger of Pūvirundamalai nagaram (Poonamallee).

916. 543 *of* 1912.—(Tamil.) On the same wall. Records in the sixth year of the Chōḷa king Tribhuvanachakravartin Rājarāja-dēva III gift of money for a lamp.

917. 544 *of* 1912.—(Tamil.) On the same wall. A record of the Chōḷa king Tribhuvanachakravartin Rājarājadēva III, in his sixteenth year, Dhanus, śu. di. 5, Sunday, Aviṭṭam (= Sunday 30th November, 1231). Gift of money for a lamp.

918. 545 *of* 1912.—(Tamil.) On the same wall. A damaged record of the Chōḷa king Tribhuvanachakravartin Vīrarājēndra-Chōḷadēva (i.e., Kulōttuṅga-Chōḷa III), dated in his fourth year (ninth year), Mīna, śu. di. 12, Sunday, Magam, corresponding to 26th March 1187. Records gift of two lamps to the shrine of Nirvaṇṇan of Tirunīrmalai.

919. 546 *of* 1912.—(Tamil.) On the same wall. A damaged record of the Chōḷa king Tribhuvanachakravartin Vīrarājēndra-Chōḷadēva (i.e., Kulōttuṅga-Chōḷa III), dated in his thirty-fourth year of Mēsha, śu. di. 5, Wednesday, Mrigaśīrsha. Records gift of money for a lamp by a certain Kaliyugameyyan *alias* Nandipan-man, one of the *agambaḍi-mudalis* of Nāyanār Śōḷagaṅgadēva, to the temple of Nirvaṇṇa Perumāḷ at Tirunīrmalai in Śurattūr-nāḍu, a subdivision of Puliyūr-kōṭṭam *alias* Kulōttuṅgaśōḷa-vaḷanāḍu, in Jayaṅgoṇḍaśōḷa-maṇḍalam.

920. 547 *of* 1912.—(Tamil.) On the same wall. A damaged record of Tribhuvanachakravartin Vijaya-Gaṇḍagōpāladēva, dated in his twenty-fourth year, Vrischika, ba. di. 5, Wednesday, Pūśam (= Wednesday, 1st November, 1273). Records gift of money for a lamp. Mentions Vallamerindān Pañchanadivāṇan. See Cg. 836 above.

921. 548 *of* 1912.—(Tamil.) On the same wall. A damaged record of the Chōḷa king Tribhuvanachakravartin Vīrarājēndra-Chōḷadēva (i.e., Kulōttuṅga-Chōḷa III), dated in his tenth year, Makara, śu. di. 5, Monday, Tiruvōṇam. Records gift of a lamp by a native of Nelmali in Paḍuvūr-nāḍu, a district of Āmūrkōṭṭam, to the same temple.

922. 549 *of* 1912.—(Tamil.) On the same wall. Dated in the reign of the Chōḷa king Tribhuvanachakravartin Rājarājadēva III. Records in Dhanus, śu. di. 5, Sunday, Aviṭṭam, gift of money for a lamp by Īḷappaḍaivenṟān, one of the *agambaḍiyar* of prince piḷḷaiyār) Śōḷagaṅgadēva. The regnal year is lost.

923. 550 *of* 1912.—(Tamil.) On the same wall. Dated in the reign of the Chōḷa king Tribhuvanachakravartin Rājarājadēva III; records in his fourteenth year, Rishabha, śu. di. 10, Wednesday, Attam (= 22nd May, A.D. 1230), gift of money for a lamp by Paṭṭāladēvan-Paḷḷikoṇḍān, a native of Peruṅganal-Vaṭṭambākkam.

924. 551 *of* 1912.—(Tamil.) On the same wall. Dated in the reign of the Chōḷa king Tribhuvanachakravartin Vīrarājēndra-chōḷadēva (i.e., Kulōttuṅga Chōḷa III). Records in his second year, Simha, śu. di. 2, Friday, Attam, gift of thirty-two cows for a lamp.

925. 552 *of* 1912.—(Tamil.) On the same wall. A damaged record of the Chōḷa king Tribhuvanachakravartin Vīrarājēndra-Chōḷadēva (i.e., Kulōttuṅga-Chōḷa III), dated in his sixth year, Tulā 23, śu. di. 13, Wednesday, Rēvati, corresponding to 30th October, 1183. Records gift of one *Gaṇḍagōpālaṉ-pudu-maḍai* for a lamp, by a native of Nandanapākkam. [Mr. Swamikannu Pillai points out that *Tulā* is wrong for *Vrischikā* and *Wednesday* for *Sunday.*]

926. 553 *of* 1912.—(Tamil.) On the same wall. A portion of the historical introduction of Vikrama-Chōḷa commencing with *pūmālai-miḍaindu*, etc., is preserved.

927. 554 *of* 1912.—(Tamil.) On the north wall of the Chakra-varti-Tirumagan shrine in the same temple. Dated in the reign of the Pāṇḍya king Tribhuvanachakravartin Sundara-Pāṇḍyadēva (III? 1276—90). Provides in his sixteenth year, for services and festivals in the temple of Pammanakka Nāyanār, by a merchant of Pammal. See Cg. 910 above.

928. 555 *of* 1912.—(Tamil.) On the west wall of the same shrine. Dated in the reign of the Pāṇḍya king Māravarman Tribhuvanachakravartin Kulaśēkharadēva I (1268—1308). Records in his thirty-seventh year, Karkaṭaka, śu. di. 5, Wednesday, Uttiram, corresponding to the 8th July 1304, gift of the village Vaḍakkupaṭṭu surnamed Kumāragōpālanallūr to the temple of Pammanakka-Nāyanār at Pammal in Śurattūr-nāḍu, a district of Puliyūr-kōṭṭam *alias* Kulōttuṅgaśōḷa-valanāḍu which was a sub-division of Jayaṅgoṇḍaśōḷa-maṇḍalam, by Pañchanadivāṇan Tiru-vēgamban *alias* Nīlagaṅgan, in order to celebrate a festival on the day of the asterism Hasta of the month of Paṅguni, in which he was born. The village was purchased from the residents of Perum-bākkam *alias* Rājarājanallūr in Kālpāy-nāḍu of the same division.

929. 556 *of* 1912.—(Tamil.) On the south wall. An incom-plete record of the Chōḷa king Tribhuvanachakravartin Vīra-rājēndra-Chōḷadēva (i.e., Kulōttuṅga-Chōḷa III), dated in his thirty-fourth year Rishabha, śu. di. 3, Wednesday, Punarpūśam. Records gift for another festival in the same temple by Pañcha-nadivāṇan Nallanāyan *alias* Sōḷagaṅgadēvan. With regard to the date Mr. Swamikannu Pillai says that the regnal year may be thirty-second or thirty-ninth, i.e., 1210 or 1217.

930. 557 *of* 1912.—(Tamil.) On the south wall. Dated in the reign of the Chōḷa king Tribhuvanachakravartin Vīrarājēndra-Chōladēva (i.e., Kulōttuṅga Chōḷa III). Records in his thirty-third year, Karkaṭaka, śu. di. 10, Rōhaṇi, corresponding to Saturday, 17th July 1210, gift of land to the temple of Pammalnakka-Nāyanār by Pañchanadivāṇa-Nīlagaṅgaraiyan Nallanāyan *alias* Sōḷagaṅgadēvan at Aṇaikkaraichchēri *alias* Sōḷagaṅgadēvanallūr. This Nilagaṅga was evidently a later chief than the one mentioned in Cg. 858.

931. 558 *of* 1912.—(Tamil.) On the south wall. An unfinished record of the Chōḷa king Tribhuvanachakravartin Vīrarājēndra-Chōḷadēva (i.e., Kulōttuṅga III), dated in his thirty-fourth year, Rishabha, śu. di. 3, Wednesday, Punarpūśam.

932. 559 *of* 1912.—(Tamil.) On two detached slabs fixed into the main gōpura of the same temple, left of entrance. Fragments. Record apparently a gift of land in Taṇṇiyālattūr, by Pañchanadivāṇa Nīlagaṅgarāiyan to a Śiva temple at Paḷḷippaḍai-Agaram. Mentions the terms *pādi kāval* and *ūr-kāval.*

933. 560 *of* 1912.—(Tamil.) On the west wall of the Nrisimha-svāmin shrine in the Raṅganātha-Perumāḷ temple on the hill, in the same village. Belongs to the reign of the Chōḷa king Tribhuvanachakravartin Vīrarājēndra-Chōḷadēva (Kulōttuṅga III). Records in his third year Simha, śu. di. 10, Monday, Aviṭṭam, gift of one *Gaṇḍagōpālan maḍai* for a lamp to the temple of Śiṅgapperumāḷ at Tirunīrmalai, by an oil-monger named Āyiravaṇṇan Aḷkoṇḍavilli *alias* Tirukkachchinambidāsan of Pūvirundamallinagaram. Tirukkachchi Nambi was a contemporary and teacher of Rāmānuja and the adoption of his name shows the growing influence of Śri Vaishṇavism. For an account of the famous Tirukkachchi Nambi (who was also a native of Pūvirundamalli) see Sūḍāmaṇippulavar's *Vaiśyapurāṇam*, p. 115—22, and the *Guruparamparas.*

934. 561 *of* 1912.—(Tamil.) On the south wall of the same shrine. A damaged record of the Chōḷa king Tribhuvanachakravartin Rājarājadēva III, dated in his twenty-third year, Mithuna, ba. di. 10, Sunday, Aśvati, corresponding to 29th May 1239. Records gift of one *Gaṇḍagōpālan-pudu-māḍai* for a lamp to the same temple by a native of Peruṅganal Vaṭṭambākkam.

935. 562 *of* 1912.—(Tamil.) On the south wall of the same shrine. A damaged record of the Chōḷa king Tribhuvanachakravartin Rājarājadēva III, dated in his nineteenth year, Mēsha, śu. di. 12, Monday, Tiruvōṇam. Seems to record a gift of one *Gaṇḍagōpālan-maḍai* for a lamp.

936. 563 *of* 1912.—(Tamil.) On the south wall of the same shrine. Dated in the reign of the Chōḷa king Tribhuvanachakravartin Rājarājadēva III. Records in his fourteenth year Rishabha, śu. di. 10, Thursday, Attam (= 23rd May 1230), gift of money for a lamp by a native of Peruṅganal Vaṭṭambākkam.

937. 564 *of* 1912.—(Tamil.) On the north wall of the *yāgāśāla* in the same temple. A much damaged record of the Vijayanagara king Vīra-Veṅkaṭarāya (I, 1586--1614), dated Śārvari (= A.D. 1600–01). Mentions that while Tātāchārya was managing *(pārupatya)* some grants were made in favour of the temple of Aḷagiyaśiṅga at Tirunīrmalai. [Tātāchārya was the preceptor of Veṅkaṭa I. See S. A. 63 and next epigraph.]

938. 565 *of* 1912.—(Tamil.) On the south wall of the same *yāgaśāla.* A damaged record, dated Śārvari (= A.D. 1600–01). Mentions Tātāchārya. He was the famous *Kōṭikanyādānam* Tātāchārya who crowned Veṅkaṭa I. The Conjeeveram inscriptions say that he was in charge of the temples there. The present record shows that he was supervising other Vaishṇava temples. It may be mentioned that he was the adopted son of *Pañchamatabhañjanam Tātāchārya.* The teacher's life forms the theme of a *Kāvya* called *Lakshmikumārōdayam*, recently published at Kumbakōnam.

Tiruśūlam near Pallāvaram.

939. 311 *of* 1901.—(Tamil.) On the west wall of the Dharmapurīśvara temple. Records in the thirty-seventh year of the Chōḷa king Tribhuvanavīradēva (Kulōttuṅga III) gifts by the merchants of the city of Pūndamalli *alias* Uyyakkoṇḍān-Śōḷapuram.

940. 312 *of* 1901.—(Tamil.) On the north wall of the same temple. Dated in the reign of the Chōḷa king Śuṅgandavirtta-Kulōttuṅga-Chōḷadēva *alias* Tribhuvanachakravartin Kōnērinmaikoṇḍān (I, 1070—1118). Records in his thirty-ninth year that he granted to the temple the village of Munnalūr, changing its name, after his own title, into Tirunīṟṟuchchōḷanallūr.

941. 313 *of* 1901.—(Tamil.) On the same wall. Dated in the reign of the Chōḷa king Tribhuvanachakravartin Kulōttuṅga-Chōḷadēva (III), who took Madura, Ceylon, Karuvūr and the crowned head of the Pāṇḍya. Records in his thirty-first year gift of 10 buffalo cows for a lamp by Śittiramēḷi-Malaiyarāyan.

942. 314 *of* 1901.—(Tamil.) On the west wall of the same temple. A record of the Chōḷa king Parakēsarivarman *alias* Tribhuvanachakravartin Vikrama-Chōḷadēva (1118—35) in his ninth year, sale of land.

943. 315 *of* 1901.—(Tamil.) On the south wall of the same temple. Dated in the reign of the Chōḷa king Rājakēsarivarman *alias* Uḍaiyār Rājēndra-Chōḷadēva (Kulōttuṅga I?) in his third year; gift of paddy for offerings.

944. 316 *of* 1901.—(Tamil.) On the same wall. A record of the Chōḷa king Kulōttuṅga-Chōḷa I. Sale of land, the date lost. Partially built in.

945. 317 *of* 1901.—(Tamil.) On the same wall. Dated in the reign of the Chōḷa king Rājakēsarivarman *alias* Chakravartin Kulōttuṅga-Chōḷadēva (I). Records in his thirty-eighth year, gift of 24 sheep for 2 lamps.

946. 318 *of* 1901.—(Tamil.) On the same wall. Dated in the reign of the Chōḷa king Chakravartin Vikrama-Chōḷadēva (1118—35). Records in his fourteenth year, sale of land.

947. 319 *of* 1901.—(Tamil.) On the same wall. Records in the fourth year of the Chōḷa king Tribhuvanachakravartin Rājādhirājadēva gift of 3 cows for a lamp.

948. 320 *of* 1901.—(Tamil.) On the same wall. Records in the sixteenth year of the Chōḷa king Tribhuvanachakravartin Rājarājadēva gift of sheep for lamps. Incomplete.

949. 321 *of* 1901.—(Tamil.) On the same wall. Dated in the reign of the Chōḷa king Tribhuvanachakravartin Rājādhirājadēva (I or II ?). Records in his fourth year, gift of 31 cows and 1 bull for a lamp by Rājarāja Malayarāyan.

950. 322 *of* 1901.—(Tamil.) On the same wall. Records in the sixth year of the Chōḷa king Rājakēsarivarman (?) *alias* Chakravartin Vikrama-Chōḷadēva (1118—35) gift of 12 sheep for a lamp by a Brāhmaṇi.

951. 323 *of* 1901.—(Tamil.) On the same wall. Records in the thirty-eighth year of the Pāṇḍya king Māravarman *alias* Tribhuvanachakravartin Kulaśēkharadēva (I) gift of 32 cows for a lamp. Damaged.

952. 324 *of* 1901.—(Tamil.) On the same wall. An incomplete record of the Chōḷa king Parakēsarivarman *alias* Tribhuvanachakravartin Vikrama-Chōḷadēva (1118—35), date of which is lost. Partially built in.

Tiruvāmūr.

953. 77 *of* 1909.—(Tamil.) On the west wall of the Tripurasundari-amman shrine in the Vēdapurīśvara temple. Records in the fourteenth year of the Chōḷa king Parakēsarivarman *alias* Uḍaiyār Śrī-Rājēndra-Chōḷadēva (I, 1011—43), gift of sheep for a lamp to the temple of Mahādēva at Tiruvāṇmiyūr, a dēvadāna in Kōṭṭūrnāḍu, a subdivision of Puḷiyūr-kōṭṭam in Jayaṅgoṇḍachōḷamaṇḍalam.

954. 78 *of* 1909.—(Tamil.) On the same wall. A damaged record of the Chōḷa king Rājakēsarivarman *alias* Uḍaiyār Śrī-Rājādhirājadēva (I, 1018—52), dated twenty-seventh year. Records gift of land to the same temple.

955. 79 *of* 1909.—(Tamil.) On the east wall of the same shrine. An incomplete record of the Chōḷa king Uḍaiyār Śrī-Rājēndra Chōḷadēva (I or II ?), dated thirty-third year.

956. 80 *of* 1909.—(Tamil.) On the same wall. A record of the eleventh year of the Chōḷa king Parakēsarivarman *alias* Uḍaiyār Śrī-Rājēndradēva (1050—63). Mentions the Śiva-Brāhmaṇas of Tiruvāṇmiyūr.

957. 81 *of* 1909.—(Tamil.) On the same wall. A record of the sixth year of the Chōḷa king Parakēsarivarman *alias* Rājēndra-chōḷadēva (I, 1011—43) gift of money for a garland.

958. 82 *of* 1909.—(Tamil.) On the same wall. An incomplete record of the Chōḷa king Parakēsarivarman *alias* Uḍaiyār Śri-Rājēndrachōḷadēva (I, 1011—43). Records gift of money and paddy for offerings.

959. 83 *of* 1909.—(Tamil.) On the base of the same shrine. Dated in the reign of the Chōḷa king Parakēsarivarman *alias* Rājēndra-Chōḷadēva (I, 1011—43). Seems to record in his ninth year a similar grant.

*Tiruvoṟṟiyūr.**

The great religious and historical importance of this place, together with its temple, maṭhas, pavilions, maṇṭapams, etc., is described in detail by Mr. Krishna Sastri in *Ep. Rep.*, 1912, p. 68, and *ibid.*, 1913, p. 86.

960. 366 *of* 1911.—(Tamil.) On the east wall of the second prākāra in the Ādhipurīśvara temple. Records in the thirty-first year of the Chōḷa king Tribhuvanachakravartin Tribhuvanavīradēva, 'who having been pleased to take Madurai (Madura), Īḷam (Ceylon), Karuvūr, and the crowned head of the Pāṇḍya, was pleased to perform the anointment of heroes' (i.e., Kulōttuṅga III, 1178—1216) gift of a cow, a bull and a calf, for a lamp to the temple of Tiruvoṟṟiyūruḍaiya-Nāyanār by a devotee in the Kuḷandaiyāṇḍār-maḍam at Kuḷattūr in Veṅkunṟa kōṭṭam. [See *Ins., S. Dts.*, p. 105, No. 6, where this inscription is given.]

961. 367 *of* 1911.—(Tamil.) On the same wall dated in the reign of the Vijayanagara king Vīrapratāpa-Dēvarāya (II). Records in Krōdhin (Ś. 1346) gift of a salt-pan in the village of Maṇali in Puḷal-nāḍu as a dēvadāna to the temple of Tiruvoṟṟiyūruḍaiya-Nāyanār at Tiruvoṟṟiyūr in Puḷar-kōṭṭam, a subdivision of Jayaṅgoṇḍachōḷamaṇḍalam, by the residents of that village. Mentions the salt-pan called Paḍampakkanāyakappēraḷam. [Puḷal-nāḍu and Puḷal-kōṭṭam were evidently named after the village Puḷal near Madras on the road to Nellore. The deity was so called

---

* About 24 inscriptions of this place collected by Mackenzie have been given in *Ins., S. Dts.*, pp. 104—110.

because he is on an anthill covered by a metallic protector. The inscription is given in *Ins., S. Dts.*, p. 105, No. 8.]

962. 368 *of* 1911.—(Tamil.) On the same wall. Dated in the reign of the Chōḷa king Parakēsarivarman *alias* Tribhuvanachakravartin Kulōttuṅgachōḷadēva (III), 'who was pleased to take Madurai (Madura) and the crowned head of the Pāṇḍya,' in the nineteenth year. Says that the king was present at the Rājarājan tirumaṇṭapam to see the Āni-festival in the temple of Tiruvoṟṟiyūr-Uḍaiyār. The dēvadāna village Ādanpākkam in Śūrattūr-nāḍu, a subdivision of Puliyūr kōṭṭam *alias* Kulōttuṅgaśōḷa-vaḷanāḍu being reported by the chief of the maṭha, the sthānattār, the temple supervisor, manager, chief accountant and tenants of the villages to be lying waste for want of tenants, the king ordered that it might be leased out to certain persons specified in the inscription.

963. 369 *of* 1911.—(Tamil.) On the same wall. Dated in the reign of the Chōḷa king Parakēsarivarman *alias* Tribhuvanachakravartin Rājarājadēva (II). Records in his seventeenth year gift of 12 buffaloes for a lamp by Ariyan Tiruchchiṟṟambalamuḍaiyān Paduman *alias* Kaṭṭimān of Kāsmīrapura to the temple of Tiruvoṟṟiyūr-Uḍaiyār at Tiruvoṟṟiyūr in Puḷar-kōttam, a subdivision of Vikramaśōḷa-Vaḷanāḍu in Jayaṅgoṇḍa-chōḷa-maṇḍalam. Mentions the king's queen Mukkōkkiḷānaḍigaḷ.

964. 370 *of* 1911.—(Grantha and Tamil.) On the same wall. Records in thirteenth year of king Tribhuvanachakravartin Rājarājadēva gift of 32 cows and a bull for a lamp by a certain Tiruvēṅkaṭacharaṇālayan, the headman of Nuḷappiyāṟu in Ambattūrnāḍu.

965. 371 *of* 1911.—(Grantha and Tamil.) On the same wall. A record of the ninth year of king Rājakēsarivarman *alias* Tribhuvanachakravartin Rājādhirājadēva (II, 1172—86). Records that the king was present on the occasion of Paṅguni Uttiram festival in the temple of Paḍambakka-Nāyakadēva when in the same place were also present Chaturānana-Paṇḍita who owned a *maṭha* in the temple and Vāgīśvara-Paṇḍita, who expounded the Sōmasiddhānta (i.e., the doctrine of the Kāpālika Śaivas), the kōyil Nāyaka, the Srīkārya and others hearing the *purāṇa* of Āḷuḍaiyanambi. The Dēvadāna village Vaḍugapperumbākkam being reported to be lying waste (for want of tenants?), the king ordered it to be leased out to a certain Amudaṅgiḷavan Pēriyan Śōman. The inscription is interrupted by a wall in the middle. [Vāgiśvara Paṇḍita was different from Vākkānandamuni who, according to Tamil literary tradition, lived in the time of Kulōttuṅga III and at whose instance the *Veṇbāppāṭṭiyal* was composed by Guṇavīra Paṇḍita. He was the author of the *Gñānāmrutam*, on *pati*, *paśu* and *pāśa*.]

966. 372 *of* 1911.—(Tamil.) On a slab built into the floor, at the entrance into the same prākāra. A damaged record of the "Gaṅga-Pallava" king Vijaya Kampavarman (son of Nandivarman

III and brother of Nripatuṅga), dated in his nineteenth year. Registers a gift of land by Nirañjana-guravar of Tiruvoṟṟiyūr to the temple of Nirañjadēśvarattu-Mahādēva which he had constructed at that village. It is stated that the assembly of Maṇali sold the land to Nirañjanaguravar. Mentions one of the signatories whose name was Peruntalaikkāvaḍi Tiruvoṟṟiyūrān.

967. 98 *of* 1912.—(Tamil.) On the south wall of the central shrine in the Ādhipurīśvara temple. Records in the third year of the Chōḷa king Tribhuvanachakravartin Rājādhirājadēva (II) gift of ninety sheep for a lamp to the temple of Tirvoṟṟiyūr-Uḍaiyār by Vaḷḷaikiḷān Mâdavan Paḍambakka-Nâyakan *alias* Tiruchchiṟṟambala-Mūvēndavēḷān, a native of Kaḍarpākkam.

968. 99 *of* 1912.—(Tamil.) On the same wall. Dated in the reign of the Chōḷa king Tribhuvanachakravartin Rājarājadēva (III). Records in his twenty-seventh year Dhanus, ba. di. 2, Wednesday, Punarpūśam (Wed., 10th Decr. 1243) gift of 32 cows, a bull and a lamp-stand by a native of Ānāṅgūr in Panaiyūr-nāḍu, a subdivision of Naḍuvu-nāḍu *alias* Rājarājavaḷanāḍu. The donor was evidently residing at Koṉṟūr Villipākkam, which was a subdivision of Ambattūr-nāḍu in the district of Puḷal-kōṭṭam *alias* Vikkiramaśōḷa-vaḷanāḍu in Jayaṅgoṇḍaśōḷa-maṇḍalam.

969. 100 *of* 1912.—(Tamil.) On the same wall. Dated in the reign of the Chōḷa king Tribhuvanachakravartin Rājādhirājadēva (II). Records in the tenth year of his reign gift of 12 buffaloes for a lamp by Kaliyan Taṇḍai-Tirunaṭṭapperumāḷ *alias* Vikkiramaśōḷa-Paḍuvūrnāḍāḷvān, to the same temple. He is stated to have been the officer in charge of the *tiruvellaikkāval* (the precincts) of the temple at Tiruvoṟṟiyur.

970, 101 *of* 1912.—(Tamil.) On the same wall. A record of Chōḷa king Tribhuvanachakravartin Rājādhirājadēva (II), in his fourth year, registering gift of 32 cows for a perpetual lamp by one of the servants of the temple doing the duty called *kālumpiḍārum.*

971. 102 *of* 1912.—(Tamil.) On the same wall. Dated in the reign of the Chōḷa king Rājakēsarivarman *alias* Uḍaiyār śri-Rājādhirājadēva (I). Records in his twenty-eighth year and 134th day a sale of land by certain members of the assembly of Maṇali *alias* Śiṅgavishṇu-Chaturvēdimaṅgalam, a dēvadāna village of the temple of Tiruvoṟṟiyūr Uḍaiyār to the military officer (*Daṇḍanāyakam*) Parāntakamārāyan *alias* Rājādhirāja-Nīlgaṅgaraiyar, a resident of Śattimaṅgalam in Innambar-nāḍu which was a subdivision of Rājendraśiṅga-vaḷanāḍu, a district of Śōḷa-maṇḍalam. [For the various meanings of *Perundanam* and *Śirudanam* see *Ep. Rep.*, 1913, p. 97.]

972. 103 *of* 1912.—(Tamil.) On the same wall. A record of the Chōḷa king Rājakēsarivarman *alias* Uḍaiyār śrī-Rājādhirājadēva (I). Records in his twenty-sixth year an enquiry into temple affairs by the officers (*adhikāri*) Vaḷavan Mūvēndavēḷār and Vikkirama Śiṅga-Mūvēndavēḷār, (*Perundanam Daṇḍanāyakam*) held in the maṇṭapa of the temple called Maṇṇaikoṇḍa-śōḷan. The inscription says that certain lands which had been lying waste were improved and cultivated at the instance of the officers. It incidentally mentions that 14,648 kuḷis (7⅛ Velis) had to pay tax (or temple share) at the rate of 28 kalams of paddy by *Arumoḻitēvan marakkāl.* (So total 199 *Kalams*, 1 *tū*, 1 *pa*). Again 10,752 *kuḻis* (5 Vēḷis and 2¼ mās) had to pay at the rate of 19 *kalams* a *Veli.* (Total 102 *ka, lku*, 4 *na*). Prices of articles are given.

973. 104 *of* 1912.—(Tamil.) On the same wall. A record of the Chōḷa king Parakēsarivarman *alias* Uḍaiyār śrī-Rājēndra-Chōḷadēva (I, 1012—43). Records in his thirty-first year gift of 150 *kāśu* by Chaturānana-Paṇḍita of Tiruvoṟṟiyūr for bathing the god Mahādēva of that place with clarified butter on the birthday festival of the king which fell on the nakshatra Tiruvādirai in the month of Mārgaḷi. See No. 965 above for a later Chaturānana Pandita and No. 1050 for an earlier. It is evident that *Chaturānana* is a general title rather than an individual name. Kamba, it may be noted, refers in one of his stray verses to the maṭha.

974. 105 *of* 1912.—(Tamil.) On the same wall. A damaged record of the Chōḷa king Parakēsarivarman *alias* Uḍaiyār śrī-Rājēndra Chōḷadēva (I), dated in his thirty-second year.

975. 106 *of* 1912.—(Tamil.) On the west wall of the same shrine. A record of the Chōḷa king Tribhuvanachakravartin Rājarājadēva (III). Records in his thirteenth year, Karkaṭaka 9th day, Wednesday, Makha and dvitīya, corresponding to July 5, A.D. 1228, gift of ninety ewes, a ram and a lamp-stand by Śambuvarāyan Aḷagiyaśīyan, son of Śambuvarāyan Pallavāṇḍār.

976. 107 *of* 1912.—(Tamil.) On the same wall. An unfinished record of the Chōḷa king Tribhuvanachakravartin Rājādhirājadēva (I ?) dated in his sixth year. Records gift of 32 cows for a lamp by a certain Periyanāyan *alias* Māṇikkavāśagan, one of the devotees doing service in the temple of Tiruvoṟṟiyūr-Uḍaiyār.

977. 108 *of* 1912—(Tamil.) On the same wall. A record of the Chōḷa king Tribhuvanachakravartin Vīrarājēndrachōḷadēva (Kulōttuṅga III). Records in his ninth year, Karkaṭaka (which should be eighth year, Mēsha) śu. di. 13, Friday, Rēvati, corresponding to 19th April, A.D. 1185, gift of 300 cows called *Aśaṅgādagaṇḍan-surabhi* for providing *pañchagavya*, to the temple of Tiruvoṟṟiyūr Uḍaiya Nāyanār, by Kulōttuṅgaśōḷa Paiyūrnāḍāḷvān-Vaḷaiyamaḷagiyan Oṟṟi-araśan.

978. 109 *of* 1912.—(Tamil.) On the same wall. A record of the Chōḷa king Tribhuvanachakravartin Rājarājadēva (III). Records in his eighth year, gift of money for offerings to the god Karāṇai Viṭaṅkadēva, on the day of Tiruvādirai in the month of Mārgaḷi, by a native of Paḷuvūr in Dāmar-kōṭṭam, a subdivision of Jayaṅgoṇḍaśōḷa-maṇḍalam. The money was deposited with the inhabitants of Igaṇaiyūr, a dēvadāna village of the temple. [Mr Krishna Sastri infers that the place might have been called Kārāṇai after the well-known home of Lakuḷīśa.]

979. 110 *of* 1912.—(Tamil.) On the same wall. A record of the Pāṇḍya king Jaṭāvarman *alias* Tribhuvanachakravartin Sundara Pāṇḍyadēva III (1276–90). Records in his thirteenth year Simha, ba. di. 3, Friday, Uttiraṭṭādi, corresponding to August 5, A.D. 1289, an agreement by which the residents of Puḷar-kōṭṭam granted the *pon-vari* collected both in the northern and southern divisions of Tiruvoṟṟiyūr for maintaining the *Vyākhyāna-maṇṭapa* (the hall where discussions were held) and conducting repairs in the temple. The inscription shows that provision was made for *Vyākhyāna* or expoundation of doctrines. See No. 1071 below.

980. 111 *of* 1912.—(Tamil.) On the same wall. A record of the Chōḷa king Rājakēsarivarman *alias* Chakravartin Kulōttuṅga-Chōḷadēva (I). Records in his eighteenth year gift of 90 sheep for a lamp by Śōḷanśōruḍaiyāḷ *alias* Kāḍavan-Mahādēvi, queen of Chakravartin Kulōttuṅga-Chōḷadēva to the temple of Tiruvoṟṟiyūr Uḍaiyār. [This queen has not been mentioned in any other inscriptions hitherto collected.]

981. 112 *of* 1912.—(Tamil.) On the same wall. An unfinished record of the Chōḷa king Rājakēsarivarman *alias* Tribhuvanachakravartin Kulōttuṅga-Chōḷadēva (I), dated in his thirty-seventh year. Records sale of land for conducting certain festivals in the temple, to the assembly of Maṇali *alias* Śiṅgavishṇu-chaturvēdimaṅgalam by Paḷḷikoṇḍān Rāmadēvanar *alias* Irumaḍiśōḷa Muvēndavēḷār, a native of Śiṟṟāmūr in Vēṇḍāḷai Vēlūr kūṟṟam, a subdivision of Rājēndraśōḷa-vaḷanāḍu in Śōḷa-maṇḍalam.

982. 113 *of* 1912.—(Tamil.) On the same wall. A record of the Chōḷa king Tribhuvanachakravartin Rājarājadēva III, providing in his twenty-first year for a flower garland and offerings by Oṟṟi-araśan, son of Paiyūrnāḍāḷvān Vaḷaiyam-aḷagiyan, who is evidently identical with the donor mentioned in No. 977 above.

983. 114 *of* 1912.—(Tamil.) On the same wall. Dated in the reign of the Chōḷa king Tribhuvanachakravartin Kulōttuṅga-Chōḷadēva; records in his eleventh year, gift of twelve buffaloes for a lamp and a lamp-stand shaped like himself to Tiruvoṟṟiyūr-Uḍaiyār by Tiruvaraṅgam Uḍaiyān *alias* Danmaparipālan Rājādhirāja Malaiyarāyan, son of Munaiyadaraiyan *alias* Kulōttuṅgaśōḷa-Malaiyarāyan of Naḍuvilmalai Tiruneḍumpirai in Perumūr-nāḍu, a subdivision of Maṇavil-kōṭṭam. Records also the gift of twelve buffaloes for a lamp, a silver lamp-stand and a silver bugle *(kāḷam)* to the goddess Āḷudaiya Nāchchiyār. The lamp-stands were called *Danmaparipālam* after the donor.

984. 115 *of* 1912.—(Tamil.) On the same wall. Dated in the reign of the Chōḷa king Tribhuvanachakravartin Rājarājadēva (III). Records in his twenty-sixth year, Tulā, twenty-third day, ba. di. 14, Aśvati, Sunday (= twentieth October, 1241), gift of thirty-two cows, a bull and a lamp-stand of two flats, by a resident of Vēlūr which was a dēvadāna village of the temple.

985. 116 *of* 1912.—(Tamil.) On the same wall. Belongs to the reign of the Chōḷa king Tribhuvanachakravartin Rājarājadēva III. Records in his third year, gift of thirty-two cows for a lamp by one of the worshippers (*dēvakarmin*) of the temple, named Sūryadēvan *alias* Vyākaraṇadāna-Bhaṭṭa.

986. 117 *of* 1912.—(Tamil.) On the north wall of the same shrine. Dated in the reign of Tribhuvanachakravartin Vijaya-Gaṇḍagōpāladēva in his tenth year, Kanni, ba. di. Saturday 5, Pūśam (= 13th September 1259). Records gift of ninety ewes and two rams for a lamp, by Perumāḷ Nāchchi, senior queen of prince (piḷḷaiyār) Pañchanadivāṇan Nīlagaṅgaraiyar.

987. 118 *of* 1912.—(Tamil.) On the same wall. A record of the Chōḷa king Rājakēsarivarman *alias* Tribhuvanachakravartin Kulōttuṅga-Chōḷadēva (I); records in his twenty-third year gift of ninety sheep for a lamp to the temple of Tiruvoṟṟiyūr-Uḍaiyār by Śeyyan Oṟṟikoṇḍān, son of Oṟṟiśeyyan *alias* Śōḷavallava-Mūvēnda-vēḷān, a native of Iḷanagar in Puraṅgarambai-nāḍu, a district of Śōḷa-maṇḍalam.

988. 119 *of* 1912.—(Tamil.) On the same wall. Dated in the reign of the Chōḷa king Rājakēsarivarman *alias* Chakravartin Kulōttuṅga-Chōḷadēva (I). Records in his thirtieth year gift of ninety sheep for a lamp by Mūvāmudalā Jñānamūrti Paṇḍitan *alias* Madurāntaka Brahmādhirājan of Vatsa-gōtra, a native of Nālūr and the commandant of forces (sēnāpati) of Chakravartin Kulōttuṅga-Chōḷadēva. [The same Brahman military officer is mentioned in No. 990.]

989. 120 *of* 1912.—(Tamil.) On the same wall. Dated in the reign of Tribhuvanachakravartin Tribhuvanavīradēva, "who was pleased to perform the anointment of heroes and the anointment of victors" (i.e., Kulōttuṅga-Chōḷa III); records in his twenty-sixth year, gift of the village Kuḷappākkam *alias* Śivapādaśēkharanallūr in Puliyūr-kōṭṭam *alias* Kuḷōttuṅgaśōḷa-vaḷanāḍu and of gold ornaments to the God Vyākaraṇadāna Perumāḷ and his consort at the request of a certain female mendicant called Tiruvoṟṟiyūr-ammai. The king is here referred to as Ulaguyya-Nāyanār. [God *Vyākaraṇadānaperumāḷ* is evidently so called because Śiva is said to have produced the first fourteen aphorisms of Pānini from his kettle-drum.]

990. 121 *of* 1912.—(Grantha.) On the same wall. A record of the Chōḷa king Jayadhara (i.e., Kulōttuṅga I); records in his thirtieth year, gift of a lamp to the God Śiva at Ādhipura by Jñānamūrti *alias* Madhurāntaka, perhaps identical with the military officer mentioned in No. 988 above. Published in *Ep. Ind.*, Vol. V, p. 106, but here Jñānamūrti is said to have been the father or preceptor of the donor.

991. 122 *of* 1912.—(Tamil.) On the same wall. Dated in the reign of the Chōḷa king Tribhuvanachakravartin Rājarājadēva (III). Records in his nineteenth year, Simha, su. di. 3, Uttiraṭṭādi (wrong for Uttiram), Sunday, corresponding to July 30, A.D. 1234, gift of five women and their descendants for husking paddy in the temple by Vāyalūrkiḻavan Tiruvēgambam-Uḍaiya Sendāmaraikkaṇṇan *alias* Senninallūr in Pērūr nāḍu, a subdivision of Puliyūr-kōṭṭam *alias* Kulōttuṅgaśōḻa-vaḷanāḍu which was a district of Jayaṅgoṇḍaśōḻa-maṇḍalam.

992. 123 *of* 1912.—(Tamil.) On the same wall. A record of the Chōḷa king Rājakēsarivarman *alias* Tribhuvanachakravartin Rājarājadēva (II). Records in his twenty-seventh year (A.D. 1172) gift of ninety-six cows for three lamps by Kulōttuṅgaśōḻa-mahīpāla, son of Āṟṟūr-nāḍāḻvān, a native of Eyilnūrnilai Āmūr *alias* Chōḻēndraśiṅganallūrpaḷḷi in Paiyyūrkōṭṭam, a subdivision of Vikkiramaśōḻavaḷanāḍu in Jayaṅgoṇḍaśōḻamaṇḍalam.

993. 124 *of* 1912.—(Tamil.) On the same wall. Dated in the reign of the Chōḷa king Rājakēsarivarman *alias* Chakravartin Kulōttuṅga-Chōḷadēva (I). Records in his thirty-seventh year gift of a lamp and ninety sheep by a native of the Chōḷa country named Araiyan Rājēndraśōḻan *alias* Rājaśēkhara-Mūvēndavēḷān.

994. 125 *of* 1912.—(Tamil.) On the same wall. An unfinished record of the Chōḷa king Parakēsarivarman *alias* Tribhuvanachakravartin Ulaguyyavanda Perumāḷ (i.e., Kulottunga III), dated in his third year. Refers to a certain Pugaḻvāṇaiyan of Karuviḷi in Miḻalai-kūṟṟam in Pāṇḍi-nāḍu, who received from the king, while the latter was encamped at that place, the chiefship of Ponmāṟu in Kālavāynāḍu, a subdivision of Puliyūr-kōṭṭam in Jayaṅgoṇḍaśōḻamaṇḍalam, which was a division of Toṇḍaimaṇḍalam. [The inscription refers to *Rājadrōhins* at Ponmāṟu and the appointment of a man of the south so far in the north is significant.]

995. 126 *of* 1912.—(Grantha.) On the south base of the same shrine. Records that the vimāna (i.e., the central shrine) was built by the architect Ravi *alias* Vīra-Chōḷa at the bidding of Chaturānana, the pupil of Nirañjana Guravar, and under the auspices of Rājēndra Chōḷa I (1012—43), son of Rājarāja. The inscription is of a high technical value as many architectural terms are given. See Cg. 965 and 973 above for reference to Chaturānana Paṇḍita.

996. 127 *of* 1912.—(Tamil.) On the same base. Dated in the reign of the Chōḷa king Uḍaiyār Śrī-Rājādhirājadēva (I). Records in his third year sale of land (2,308 *kuḻis*), irrigational facilities and house-sites for tenants; 120 *kuḻis* also sold by the residents of Vēshshārupāḍi to the Brāhmaṇa lady, Āriyavammai, wife of Prabhākara Bhaṭṭa of Mērkaḷāpura in Ārya-dēśa (northern country?), for the purpose of feeding the Mahēśvaras in *Rājēndraśōḻan* which was evidently a *maṭha* built by her in the temple. See No. 1001.

997. 128 *of* 1912.—(Tamil.) On the west base of the same shrine. A record of the Chōḷa king Vīrarājēndradēva I (1063-70). Records that some waste land of the temple (60 *vēḻis*) in Śiṅga-vishṇu-chaturvēdimaṅgalam was reclaimed by the order of the king and being named Vīrarājēndraviḷāgam after the king, its produce was utilized for services in the temple, including the recital of Māṇikkavāśagaś *Tiruvembāvai*, the Dēvāram *Tiruppadiyams* and maintenance of priests, dancing masters and girls.

998. 129 *of* 1912.—(Tamil.) On the same base. A record of the Chōḷa king Rājakēsarivarman *alias* Uḍaiyār Śrī-Rājādhirāja-dēva I (1018—52). Records in his thirty-eighth year sale of land by the assembly of Kuraṭṭūr in Ambattūr-nāḍu, a subdivision of Puḻar-kōṭṭam, for conducting the daily services in the temple of Tiruvoṟṟiyūr Uḍaiyār-Kārāṇai-Viṭaṅkadēvar. Tiruvallivāyal is stated to have been a village in Tuḍamuni-nāḍu, a subdivision of Puliyūr-kōṭṭam. Typical document of sale.

999. 130 *of* 1912.—(Tamil.) On the same base. Dated in the reign of the Chōḷa king Rājakēsarivarman *alias* Kulōttuṅga-Chōḷadēva (I). Registers in his seventh year and 290th day that Kuḷamuḷār Ēran Kūttanūr *alias* Rājarāja-Mūvēndavēḷār, an officer, (adhikari) of the king held an enquiry into temple affairs in the maṇṭapa called *Rājarājan* (within the temple) and assigned some money for the service called *Virarājēndrantiruppaḷḷieḻuchchi.*

1000. 131 *of* 1912.—(Tamil.) On the west and south bases of the same shrine. A record of the Chōḷa king Rājakēsarivarman *alias* Uḍaiyār Śrī-Rājēndra-Chōḷadēva (Kulōttuṅga Chōḷadēva I). Records in his second year, gift of 12 *vēlis* of land purchased for 240 *kāśus* by the military officer (sēnāpati) Rājarājan Paranri-parākshasanār *alias* Vīraśōḷa-Iḷaṅgōvēḷār, in order to conduct the service called *Tiruchchāndādal* of the god Kārāṇai Viṭaṅkadēvar. Partly published in *S.I.I.*, Vol. III, p. 132. See No. 978 above. [The income from the 12 *vēlis* is said to be 576 *kalams* worth 144 *kāśu*. The price of one vēli = 20 *kaśu*, i.e., 100 *kuḻis* cost 1 kāśu. The measurement is by the 16-span-rod. Amongst the dues *(antarāya* and *kuḍimai)* payable are mentioned *pūppon pañchavāram, vēlikkāśu, nirvilai, veṭṭi, muṭṭaiyāḷ, echchōru* and *kuṟṟunel.*]

1001. 132 *of* 1912.—(Tamil.) On the same bases. A record of the Chōḷa king Rājakēsarivarman *alias* Uḍaiyār Śrī-Rājādhirāja-dēva (I). Records in his thirty-first year, a sale of land by the assembly of the brahmadēya villages of Sundaraśōḷa-chaturvēdimaṅgalam and Vānavanmahādevi-chaturvēdimaṅgalam. It was purchased by Nāgalavvaichchāni *alias* Āriyammai, wife of Prabhākara Bhaṭṭa, a resident of Mēgalāpuram in the Ārya-dēśa and a devotee of the temple of Tiruvoṟṟiyūruḍaiya Mahādēva. The purchased land was given to the *maṭha* called *Rājēndraśōḻan* which was built by that lady. Records also other sales of land to the same lady and for the same purpose, by the residents of Ennūr in Nāvalūr-nāḍu, which was a subdivision of Puḻarkōṭṭam and by the merchants (*nagarattār*) of Tiruvoṟṟiyūr in the years thirty-one and twenty-seven of the same reign, respectively. See No. 996 above.

1002. 133 *of* 1912.—(Tamil.) On the north base of the same shrine. A record of the Chōḷa king Rājakēsarivarman *alias* Uḍaiyār Śrī-Rājēndra Chōḷadēva (Kulōttuṅga-Chōḷadēva I). Records in his third year, sale of land by the residents of Ennūr in Nāval-nāḍu, a subdivision of Puḻar-kōṭṭam for midday services in the temple and for feeding a Brāhmaṇa learned in the Vēdas and a Śivayōgin, the money being paid by the officer Ādittan Tarparamporuḷar *alias* Madurāntaka Mūvēndavēḷār, a native of Aridāyamaṅgalam in Muḍichchōnāḍu, which was a subdivision of Kalyāṇapuraṅgoṇḍaśōḷa-vaḷanāḍu (evidently named after Rājādhirāja I, 1018—52). [The income from the land is said to be 35 *kalams* per *vēli*,—a poor return. Three ways of irrigation are authorized, viz., by damming the river, by hand-*piccotas* and by baskets.]

1003. 134 *of* 1912.—(Tamil.) On the same base. An unfinished record of the Vijayanagara king Vīrapratāpa-Dēva-Mahārāya-Kṛishṇadēva-Mahārāya, dated Ś. 1448, Bhava (wrong) Kārttika, sixth day, Thursday, ba. di.

1004. 135 *of* 1912.—(Tamil.) On the same base. A record of the Chōḷa king Rājakēsarivarman *alias* Uḍaiyār Śrī-Vīrarājēndradēva; records in his fourth year, sale of land by the residents of Eḻinuḷai, a village in Paiyyūr-kōṭṭam, a subdivision of Jayaṅgoṇḍaśōḷa-maṇḍalam, for the Rājēndraśōḷa-maṭham. The price money for the land was paid by Tiruvaraṅgadēvan *alias* Mummuḍiśōḷa Brahmamārāyan, a native of Vīranārāyaṇa-chaturvēdimaṅgalam which was a taniyūr in Rājēndraśiṅga-vaḷanāḍu of Śōḷamaṇḍalam.

1005. 136 *of* 1912.—(Tamil.) On the same base. A record of the Chōḷa king Rājakēsarivarman *alias* Uḍaiyār Śrī-Vīrarajēndradēva. Records in his second year, apportionment of money paid by the weaver (śāliya) merchants residing in the quarter called *Jayaśiṅgakulakālaperunderu* in Tiruvoṟṟiyūr, for special services to be offered in the temple on the day of Āślēsha on which the king was born, as settled by the officer Jayaśiṅgakulakāla-Viḻupparaiyar of Kurugāḍi in Kiḻār-kūṟṟam, a subdivision of Nittavinōda-vaḷanāḍu in Śōḷa-maṇḍalam. *Vakkāṇikkum-maṇṭapa* mentioned.

Jayaśiṅgakulakāla was an epithet of Vīrarājēndra as he was the opponent of the Western Chālukyan king Jayasimha III.

1006. 137 *of* 1912.—(Tamil.) On the same base. A record of the Chōḷa king Rājakēsarivarman *alias* Uḍaiyār śrī-Rājādhirāja-dēva (I 1018–53). Records in his twenty-eighth year, gift of money for special offerings on the day following the festival of Paṅguni-Uttiram. The assembly of Kāvanūr *alias* Kamalanārāyaṇa-chaturvēdimaṅgalam received the amount (i.e., 30 *kāśu*) and agreed to pay as interest 75 kalams of paddy every year for the expenses of that day. A good idea of temple establishment and salaries of temple servants and prices is given. [The *Tiruttoṇḍattogai*, the original nucleus of the *Periapurāṇa*, composed by Sundaramūrti is referred to in the inscription, as well as the images of the sixty-three saints.]

1007. 138 *of* 1912.—(Tamil.) On a pillar of the verandah round the same shrine. A record of the Chōḷa king Parakēsarivarman *alias* Uḍaiyār śrī-Rājēndra-Chōḷadēva (I). Records in his thirtieth year gift of 90 sheep for a lamp by a Gaṅgaikoṇḍaśōḷan *alias* Uttamaśōḷamārāyan of Tiruvārūr in Tiruvārūr-kūṟṟam, which was a subdivision of Kshatriya-śikhāmaṇi-vaḷanāḍu, for the merit of a certain Gaṇavadi Iḍumban *alias* Tannaimunivar-peṇḍirgaṇḍa Viśaiyarāyan who stabbed himself and died in order to relieve the distress of the donor. The record incidentally registers also another gift of 90 sheep for a lamp by Nimbaladēvi, wife of Indaḷadēva of Talaigrāma in Virāṭa-dēśa (i.e., Hangal in Dharwar). For another emigrant see N.A. 672 and Cg. 1024, p. 120, below. Also *Mysore and Coorg*, pp. 186—8 ; *Ep. Rep.*, 1908-9.

1008. 139 *of* 1912.—(Tamil.) On the second pillar in the same place. A record of the Chōḷa king Parakēsarivarman *alias* Uḍaiyār śrī-Rājēndra-Chōḷadēva (I). Records in his twenty-ninth year gift of money deposited on interest in paddy with the inhabitants of Igaṇaiyūr, for providing offerings every year on the festival of the first crop (pudiyīḍu ?), and made by Nakkan Kōdai *alias* Kānchīpura-naṅgai, a maid-servant (*magaḷ*) of Tiruvēgambam-uḍaiya-Mahādēva of the city (*nagaram*) of Kānchīpuram, in Eyir-kōṭṭam, a subdivision of Jayaṅgoṇḍaśōḷa-maṇḍalam.

1009. 140 *of* 1912.—(Tamil.) On the third pillar in the same place. A record of the Chōḷa Parakēsarivarman *alias* Uḍaiyār śrī-Rājēndra-Chōḷadēva (I 1012—43). Records in his twenty-ninth year gift of money (*tuḷai-niṟai pon* and *Madurāntakadēvanmāḍai*) for celebrating the festival of Mārgaḷi-Tiruvādirai and for feeding three Brāhmaṇas learned in the Vēdas. The money was borrowed on interest in paddy by the merchants (nagarattār) of Tiruvoṟṟiyūr and by the residents of Mañjiyan kāraṇai, a village in Karigaippērūr nāḍu, a subdivision of Puḷar-kōṭṭam, the interest on paddy being 90 kalams. [The interest on one kaḷañju (துளைநிறை பொன்) was 2 *kalams* of paddy per annum by the *Rājakēsarimarakkāl*; and the interest on one *Madhurāntakadēvan māḍai* was also 2 *kalams*. The latter therefore, says Mr. Krishṇa Sastri, should have weighed one *kaḷañju* of gold.]

1010. 141 *of* 1912.—(Tamil.) On the fourth pillar in the same place. A record of Parakēsarivarman *alias* Uḍaiyār Śrī-Rājēndra-Chōḷadēva (I). Records in his twenty-ninth year gift of money (*Rāja rājan kāśu*) for feeding a Brāhmaṇa, by Kūttan Gaṇavadi, the military officer of Gaṅgaikoṇḍān *alias* Uttamaśōḷa-Mārāyan who was also styled *Śirudanam-Perudanam-Mārāyan*. The money was received by the merchants of Tiruvoṟṟiyūr on interest to be paid in paddy. Mentions also Āriyammai and her money gift. [The *Rājarājankāśu*, points out Mr. Krishna Sastri, should have been in weight and value half of *Madhurāntaka dēva māḍai* as the interest on it was one-half of that on the latter.]

1011. 142 *of* 1912.—(Tamil.) On the fifth pillar in the same place. A record of the Chōḷa king Rājakēsarivarman *alias* Uḍaiyār Śrī-Rājādhirājadēva (I). Records in his twenty-seventh year gift of money by the members of the assembly of Maṇali *alias* Śiṅgavishṇu-chaturvēdi-maṅgalam. (Was this derived from the Pallava king Simhavishṇu ?) The money was deposited on interest in paddy with the revenue accountant (*puravuvaritiṇai-kaḷattu-kaṇakkan*) of Śiruvappēḍu, *alias* Mummuḍi-śōḷanallūr, for conducting the festival of Māśi-Magam.

1012. 143 *of* 1912.—(Tamil.) On the sixth pillar in the same place. A record of the Chōḷa king Parakēsarivarman *alias* Uḍaiyār Śrī-Rājēndradēva. Records in his third year gift of 90 sheep for a lamp by Vēḷāḷa Madurāntakan *alias* Taṇḍanāyakan Rājādhirāja-Iḷaṅgovēḷān of Naḍār, a village in Tiraimūr-nāḍu which was a subdivision of Uyyakoṇḍān-vaḷanāḍu in Śōḷa-maṇḍalam.

1013. 144 *of* 1912.—(Tamil.) On the seventh pillar in the same place. A record of the Chōḷa king Rājakēsarivarman *alias* Uḍaiyār Śrī-Rājādhirājadēva (I), dated in his twenty-seventh year. The inscription stops with the introduction of the king beginning with *tingaḷēr taru*, etc.

1014. 145 *of* 1912. (Tamil.) On the eighth pillar in the same place. A record of the Chōḷa king Rājakēsarivarman *alias* Kulōttuṅga-Chōḷadēva (I). Records in his tenth year, gift of 12 milch cows for *pañchagavya* and lamps, by Āchchān Tiruchchiṟṟambalamuḍaiyān *alias* Gurukularājar of Ponpaṟṟi in Miḷalai-kūṟṟam, a district of Rājarāja-Pāṇḍināḍu.

1015. 146 *of* 1912.—(Tamil.) On the ninth pillar in the same place. Dated in the reign of the Chōḷa king Parakēsarivarman *alias* Uḍaiyār Śrī-Rājēndra-Chōḷadēva (I 1012—45). Records in his twenty-sixth year that the officer Rājēndraśiṅga Mūvēndavēḷār enquired into temple affairs in the hall called *Vakkāṇikkum-maṇṭapam* and fixed the details of service to be maintained from *kuṟṟadaṇdam* and 'excess paddy' collected from the servants of the temple and the tenants of the *dēvadāna* villages. [The articles to be purchased are enumerated and the prices given.]

1016. 147 *of* 1912.—(Tamil.) On the tenth pillar in the same place. A record of the Chōḷa king Rājakēsarivarman *alias* Uḍaiyār śrī-Rājādhirājadēva (I). Records in his thirty-first year, gift of 90 sheep for a perpetual lamp to the temple of Tiruvoṟṟiyūr-uḍaiya-Mahādēva by Chaturan-Chaturi, wife of Nāgan Peraṅgāḍan and a dancing girl (*devaraḍiyāḷ*) of the temple. [Mr. Krishna Sastri surmises from this that regular marriage and conjugal life existed among this community in those days.]

1017. 148 *of* 1912.—(Tamil.) On the eleventh pillar in the same place. A record of the Chōḷa king Rājakēsarivarman *alias* Uḍaiyār śrī-Rājādhirājadēva (I). Records in his twenty-ninth year, gift of paddy for offerings by certain Perumān Madurāntakan *alias* Rājēndraśōḷa-Veṅgaṉāṭṭaraiyan, for maintaining which he purchased land in Āmūr *alias* Chōḷēndraśiṅganallūr in Paiyyūr-kōṭṭam. [The interest on 10 *kalams* of paddy for a year is 1 *kuruṇi* of *patteṭṭukkuttal* (பத்தெட்டுக்குத்தல்) rice.

1018. 149 *of* 1912.—(Tamil.) On the twelfth pillar in the same place. A record of the Chōḷa king Rājakēsarivarman *alias* Uḍaiyār śrī-Vijayarājēndradēva (Rājādhirājadēva I). Records in his thirty-third year, gift of 92 sheep for a lamp by a certain Sundaraśoḷa-Pāṇḍya Viḻupparaiyan who was a servant of the temple (*paṇimagan*) and a resident of Kāñchīpura in Eyil-nāḍu, a subdivision of Eyir-kōṭṭam.

1019. 150 *of* 1912.—(Tamil.) On the thirteenth pillar in the same place. A record of the Chōḷa king Parakēsarivarman *alias* Uḍaiyār śrī-Rājēndradēva (1050—62), dated in his sixth year. Contains only the historical introduction beginning with *tirumaruviyaśeṅgōl*, etc., and the date.

1020. 151 *of* 1912.—(Tamil.) On the fourteenth pillar in the same place. A damaged record of the Chōḷa king Rājakēsarivarman *alias* Uḍaiyār śrī-Rājādhirājadēva (I), dated in his twenty-second year. Records gift of money for providing every day, a bundle of grass for a cow and for other services. Ten *kāśus* invested for interest of 4¼ *kaśus* every year for feeding Brāhmaṇas.

1021. 152 *of* 1912.—(Tamil.) On the fifteenth pillar in the same place. A damaged record of the Chōḷa king Parakēsarivarman *alias* Uḍaiyār śrī-Rājēndradēva (1050—62), dated in his eighth year. Records gift of 90 sheep for a lamp by a native of Tirukkāna-Pērūr in Tirukkāna-Pērūr-Nāḍu, which was a subdivision of Rājarāja-Pāṇḍināḍu.

1022. 153 *of* 1912.—(Tamil.) On the sixteenth pillar in the same place. A record of the Chōḷa king Parakēsarivarman *alias* Uḍaiyār śrī-Rājēndra-Chōḷadēva (I). Records in his twenty-sixth year a sale of land (24 ½ *paṭṭis*) by the residents of the dēvadāna village Igaṇaiyūr to Śāttan Irāmadēviyār who is called the *aṇukkiyār* (maid servant?) of the king. The purpose of the sale was to maintain twelve *dēvaraḍiyār* in the temple to serve the goddess Gauri.

1023. 154 *of* 1912.—(Tamil.) On the seventeenth pillar in the same place. A record of the Chōḷa king Rājakēsarivarman *alias* Kulōttuṅga-Chōḷadēva (I). Records in his seventh year and two hundred and ninetieth day sale of land by the residents of Igaṇaiyūr Śīrāḷan Gaṇḍarādittan *alias* Irumuḍiśōḷa Viḷupparaiyan of Koṟṟamaṅgalam in Tirunaṟaiyūr-nāḍu, a subdivision of Kshatriyaśikhāmaṇi-vaḷanāḍu which was a district of śōḷa-maṇḍalam for maintaining a water-shed in the quarter called Śaṅkarappāḍi *alias* Rājarājapperunderu at Tiruvoṟṟiyūr. [A tax called *Kālaḷavupāṭṭam* is mentioned. It is surmised that it was imposed on the measurers of grain in temple granaries. But this is doubtful.]

1024. 155 *of* 1912.—(Tamil.) On the eighteenth pillar in the same place. Dated in the reign of Rājēndra-Chōḷadēva (I). Records in his thirtieth year a sale of land (4,000 *kuḷis*) for maintaining a flower garden and supplying garlands to Nāgaḷabbaisāni *alias* Āriyavammai, wife of Prabhākara-Bhaṭṭa of Mērkalāpuram in the Ārya-dēśa. The land belonged to the villages of Ādambākkam and Savaṇṇa in Śurattūr-nāḍu, a subdivision of Puliyūr-kōṭṭam: [The lands purchased included house-sites for tenants and it was specified that the tenants were not to pay any kind of *iṟai* or *kuḍimai* such as *Veṭṭi, amañji, kuṟṟunel*, etc. The measuring rod of 16 spans *(padinaṟu śāṇkōl)* is mentioned. See 1007 above.]

1025. 156 *of* 1912.—(Tamil.) On the nineteenth pillar in the same place. A record of the Chōḷa king Parakēsarivarman *alias* Uḍaiyār śrī-Rājēndra-Chōḷadēva (I). Records in his thirtieth year sale of land (2,000 *kuḷis* by *padināru śāṇkōl* for 8 *Madhurāntaka-māḍais*) by the assembly of Maṇali *alias* Simha-vishṇu-chaturvēdimaṅgalam to a native of Parittikkuḍi in Nenmali-nāḍu, a subdivision of Arumoḷidēva-vaḷanāḍu, which was a district of Śōḷa-maṇḍalam, for presenting it to the temple. So one *Madurāntakadēvanmāḍai* was the cost of 250 kuḷis of land. The *māḍai* must have been issued, says Mr. Krishna Sastri, either by Rājēndrachōḷa I or Uttamachōḷa Madhurāntaka (970—85), the immediate predecessor of Rājarāja I. For the value of the *māḍai* see 1009 and 1010 above.

1026. 157 *of* 1912.—(Tamil.) On the west wall of the same verandah. A record of the Chōḷa king Parakēsarivarman *alias* Tribhuvanachakravartin Rājarājadēva (II). Records in his sixth years gift of 32 cows for a lamp by a native of Munaippāḍi-nāḍu in Naḍuvil-nāḍu.

1027. 158 *of* 1912.—(Tamil.) On a slab built into the floor of the same verandah. Records in fourth year of the "Gaṅga-Pallava" king Kō-Vijaya-Aparājitavarman gift of *ūrkkarchemmai*-gold for a lamp to the god Tiruvoṟṟiyūr Mahādēva by Amatti *alias* Kurumbakōḷali, a concubine (bhōgi) of Vairamēghan *alias* Vāṇakōvaraiyar, son of Perunaṅgai. The amount (30 kaḷanju) was placed in the hands of the assembly of Ādambākkam, a hamlet of Tiruvoṟṟiyūr, and the *Amritagaṇa* committee, on interest at 3 *mañjāḍi* per *kaḷañju*, every year. [Vairamēghan had the title Vānakōvaraiyan as he was probably in charge of the feudatory Bāṇa kingdom. The inscription is of value in mentioning the rate of interest in the 9th century to be 3 *manjāḍis* on 1 *kaḷañju* (i.e., 20 *manjāḍis*) and so 15 per cent.]

1028. 159 *of* 1912.—(Grantha and Tamil.) On the second slab in the same place. Records in the eighth year of the "Gaṅga Pallava king" Kō-Vijaya-Aparājitavarman Pōttaraiyar gift of 60 kaḷañju of *ūrkkarchemmai*-gold for offerings and a lamp, by Paitāṅgi kaṇḍan, chief of Kāṭṭūr in Vaḍagarai Innambar-nāḍu, a district of Śōḷa-nāḍu.

1029. 160 *of* 1912.—(Grantha and Tamil.) On a third slab in the same place. A damaged record of the Chōḷa king Madirai-koṇḍa Parakēsarivarman (Parāntaka I), dated in his thirty-fourth year. Records gift of a lamp to the temple of Tiruvoṟṟiyūr-Mahādēva by Māran Paramēśvaran *alias* Śembiyan Śōḷiyavarāyan of Śirukuḷattūr in Poyyiṟ-kūṟṟam, a subdivision of Teṅkarai-nāḍu which was a district of Śōḷa-nāḍu. [Refers to a military officer of the king who defeated Śītpuli, destroyed Nellore, and on his return from there made the grant. See No. 1105 below. The inscription is very important as proving Parāntaka's conquest beyond Toṇḍai.

1030. 161 *of* 1912.—(Tamil.) On the fourth slab in the same place. A record of "the Gaṅga-Pallava" king Kō-Vijaya-Aparājitavarman; records in his fourth year gift of gold (30 *kaḷañju*) for a lamp to the same temple by Śappakkan *alias* Pātradāni who was a concubine (bhōgi ?) of Vairamēghan *alias* Vāṇakōvaraiyar, son of Śāmi-Akkan. Mentions the assembly of Ādambākkam, a suburb of Tiruvoṟṟiyūr and the Amritagaṇa (committee). A portion of the slab at the bottom is apparently cut off. Mr. Kṛishṇa Sastri believes that this Śāmi-Akkan is the same as Perunaṅgai in No. 1027 above. He further surmises that Vairamēghan was perhaps the son of Aparājita and called Vāṇakōvaraiyar as he was probably in charge of the Bāṇa kingdom.

1031. 162 *of* 1912.—(Tamil.) On the fifth slab in the same place. A record of the "Gaṅga-Pallava" king Kō-Vijaya-Nripa-tuṅgavarman; records in his eighteenth year gift of gold for offerings by Paliyapilli, one of the queens of Vidēlvidugu-Pallavaraiyar of Umbaḷa-nāḍu. A portion of the slab at the bottom is apparently cut off. See No. 1057 for the Chōḷa feudatory of the same name.

1032. 163 *of* 1912. (Tamil.) On the sixth slab in the same place. A record of the " Gaṅga-Pallava king " Kō-Vijaya-Aparājitavarman ; records in his seventh year, gift of gold (30 *kaḷañju*) for a lamp by the queen Mahādēvi-Aḍigaḷ to the temple of Tiruvoṟṟiyūr-Mahādēva. The assembly of Ādambākkam, a suburb of Tiruvoṟṟiyūr in Puliyūr-kōṭṭam, and the Amritagaṇa (committee) received the gold on interest.

1033. 164 *of* 1912.—(Grantha and Tamil.) On the seventh slab in the same place. A damaged record of the Chōḷa king Madiraikoṇḍa Parakēsarivarman (Parāntaka I), dated in his thirtieth year. Records gift of gold for two lamps by Kōdaṇḍarāmar, eldest son of the Chōḷa king Parakēsarivarman [Kōdaṇḍarāman was identical with Rājāditya]. A portion of the gold seems to have been borrowed on interest in the thirty-fifth year of the king, by the residents of Veḷḷivāyil, a village in Puḷal-ērikkīḻ-nāḍu. See 318 and 347 of 1904 at Kuḍumiyāmalai and 203 of 1903 at Toṇḍamanāḍu near Kāḷahasti.

1034. 165 *of* 1912.—(Tamil.) On the eighth slab in the same place. A damaged record of the Chōḷa king Parakēsarivarman, *probably* Parāntaka I, dated in his seventh year. Records gift of gold for a lamp by Kāraṇai Viḻupparaiyar Arivāḷan Puttan. The assembly of Maṇali in charge of Tiruvoṟṟiyur received the amount on interest.

1035. 166 *of* 1912.—(Tamil.) On the ninth slab in the same place. A damaged record of the Chōḷa king Uttama-Chōḷadēva Parakēsarivarman (son of Gaṇḍarāditya, 970—86), dated in his fifteenth year. Records gift of an image of Śrībalidēva, eight bugles, (*kāḷa*) and 24 fly-whisks with gold handles, by the king. The inscription refers to *Śenniyeṟippaḍai* or the army which was victorious at Śenni. See 1114 below.

1036. 167 *of* 1912.—(Grantha and Tamil.) On the tenth slab in the same place. Records in the twenty-seventh year of the Chōḷa king Madiraikoṇḍa Parakēsarivarman gift of 90 sheep for a lamp by Dēvan Kēsari *alias* Kuñjaramalla-Pallavaraiyan, a resident of Perumpaṇṟūr in Vēḷār-nāḍu, a subdivision of Śōḷa-nāḍu. The inscription shows that Parāntaka had the title Kuñjaramalla.]

1037. 168 *of* 1912.—(Grantha and Tamil.) On the eleventh slab in the same place. A damaged record of the Chōḷa king Madiraikoṇḍa Parakēsarivarman (Parāntaka I), dated in his thirty-fifth year. Records gift of gold (50 *kaḷañju*) for feeding two *Mahāvratis* every day, by Ilāḍaippēraraiyan *alias* Śōḷaśikhāmaṇi-Pallavaraiyan. Śōḷaśikhāmaṇi was a title of Parāntaka I.

1038. 169 *of* 1912.—(Grantha and Tamil.) A record of the Chōḷa king Madiraikoṇḍa Parakēsarivarman (Parāntaka I). Records in his twenty-ninth year gift of gold for a lamp by Iravi Nīli, daughter of Vijayarāgha(va)dēva, the Chēra king. The amount was apparently invested on a field at Tiruvoṟṟiyur which yielded the annual interest of 4½ *kaḻañju*. [The inscription shows the friendly relation of Parāntaka with the Chēras

1039. 170 *of* 1912.—(Grantha and Tamil.) On the same slab. Records in the thirtieth year of Madiraikoṇḍa Parakēsarivarman gift of gold for a lamp by Arindigai perumānār, son of Chōḷa-Perumānaḍigaḷ (i.e., Parāntaka I), to the god Śiva at Ādhigrāma.

1040. 171 *of* 1912.—(Tamil.) On the thirteenth slab built into the floor of the same verandah. A much damaged record, the date and the name of the king are doubtful. Seems to record a gift of gold which was received on interest by the assembly of Ādambākkam, a suburb of Tiruvoṟṟiyūr, and the *Amritagaṇa* (committee).

1041. 172 *of* 1912.—(Tamil.) On the fourteenth slab in the same place. A fragment record of the Chōḷa king Rājarājakēsarivarman (Rājarāja I), dated in his seventeenth year. Seems to record a gift of gold for feeding a Brāhmaṇa.

1042. 173 *of* 1912.—(Tamil.) On the fifteenth slab in the same place. A fragment of record of the Chōḷa king Madiraikoṇḍa Parakēsarivarman, dated in his twentieth year. Mentions the wife of Kēraḷa Kurumban(?) *alias* Parakēsari-Mūvēndavēḷar, of Vaḷudivāḷmaṅgalam in Tirukkānappēr-kūṟṟam in Munai-Pāṇḍināḍu.

1043. 174 *of* 1912.—(Tamil.) On the sixteenth slab in the same place. Records in the reign of the "Gaṅga-Pallava-king" Kō-Vijaya Kampavarman gift of twenty-seven *kaḻañju* of gold for offerings by Pūdi Arindigai, wife of Viḍēlviḍugu Iḷaṅgōvēḷār of Koḍumbāḷūr in Kō-nāḍu. The money was placed in the hands of the residents of Vaikkāṭṭūr, (a suburb) of Tiruvoṟṟiyūr, on interest at 3 *mañjāḍi* per *kaḻañju*, per annum. See 1057 below.

1044. 175 *of* 1912.—(Tamil.) On the seventeenth slab in the same place. A damaged record of the Chōḷa king Parakēsarivarman (probably) Parāntaka I, dated in his seventh year. Seems to record a sale of land which was situated in Igaṇaiyūr, a village of Tiruvoṟṟiyūr.

1045. 176 *of* 1912.—(Tamil.) On the eighteenth slab in the same place. Records in the twenty-fourth year of the Chōḷa king Parakēsarivarman (probably) Parāntaka I, gift of gold for a lamp by Śembiyan Mūvēndavēḷān *alias* Śāttan Ulagan, chief of Vaṇḍāḷañjēri in Tirunaraiyūr-nāḍu of Śōḷa-nāḍu. The money was deposited for interest with the residents of Kuḷumaṇippākkam near Māṅgāḍu in Puliyūr-kōṭṭam.

1046. 177 *of* 1912.—(Grantha and Tamil.) On the nineteenth slab in the same place. Dated in the reign of the Rāshṭrakūṭa king Kaṇṇaradēva (Kṛishṇa III), 'who took Kachchi and Tañjai. Records in his eighteenth year, gift of gold (30 kaḻanju) for a lamp by Naraśiṅgayyan, son of Lakshmaṇaiyyan, a merchant in the camp (*kaṭaka*) of the Vallabha (i.e., Rāshṭrakūṭa) king. The merchant was a native of Mānyakhēṭa. The gold was deposited with the residents of Śeṟṟuppēḍu (modern Chetput) in Tuḍarmuniyūr-nāḍu, a district of Puliyūr-kōṭṭam. The inscription is of interest in showing that peaceful men followed the Rāshṭrakūṭa army of invasion to the south thereby introducing the Kanarese people in that region.

1047. 178 *of* 1912.—(Tamil.) On the same slab. Records in the nineteenth year of the Rāshṭrakūṭa king Kaṇṇaradēva, 'who took Kachchi and Tañjai' gift of ninety sheep for a lamp and one Īḻa-lamp-stand by Tatpurushabhaṭāra of Kaḻakkuḍi.

1048. 179 *of* 1912.—(Tamil.) On the same slab. Records in the twenty-second year of the Rāshṭrakūṭa king Kaṇṇaradēva, 'who took Kachchi and Tañjai' gift of gold for a lamp by the mother of the Vallabha king Kaṇṇaradēva. The gold was deposited on permanent interest (நிலைபொலியூட்டு) of 15 per cent with the assembly of Kurattūr *alias* Parāntaka-chaturvēdimaṅgalam in Ambattūr-ērikīḻ-nāḍu, a subdivision of Puḻar-kōṭṭam.

1049. 180 *of* 1912.—(Tamil verse.) On the eighteenth slab built into the floor of the same verandah. Records in the twelfth year of the "Gaṅga-Pallava king" Aparājita (the upper portion of the stone is missing) gift of land by purchase from the residents of Igaṇaimūdūr, for offerings to a shrine called Śōḻamāl-Īśvara in the temple at Oṟṟimūdūr (i.e., Tiruvoṟṟiyūr). The donor's name is lost. [The relation between the "Gaṅga-Pallava" line with the Chōḻa is evidenced by the inscription.]

1050. 181 *of* 1912.—(Grantha and Tamil.) On the twenty-first slab in the same place. A record of the Rāshṭrakūṭa king Kaṇṇaradēva (Krishṇa III), 'who took kachchi and Tañjai' Records in his twentieth year, gift of money (100 *nishkas* of pure gold) by Chaturānana-Paṇḍita, the pupil of Nīrañjanaguru, for providing *bali* in the temple at Tiruvoṟṟiyūr. The Grantha portion gives an interesting account of the early career of Chaturānana. It says that he was a native of Kēraḻa and a favourite of the Rāshṭrakūṭa king Vallabha, that he went over to the Chōḻa country, became a friend of Rājāditya and at his death in the hands of the Rashṭrakūṭa king, blamed himself for not dying with him, became a Sanyāsin, being initiated by Nīrañjanaguru, and came to Tiruvoṟṟiyūr. Mr. Krishna Sastri surmises that he was a spy. For the prevalence of certain Kēraḻa customs in the temple see *Ep. Rep.*, 1913.

1051. 182 *of* 1912.—(Tamil.) On a slab built into the floor of the same shrine. Records in the twenty-ninth year of the Chōḷa king Madiraikoṇḍa Parakēsarivarman gift of gold for feeding a learned Brāhmaṇa by a native of Eṭṭiyārkurichchi in Pāṇḍināḍu, who had accepted service in the temple.

1052. 183 *of* 1912.—(Tamil.) On a slab built into the floor of the maṇṭapa in front of the same shrine. Appears to record in Bahudhānya an order of Muttambi Mudaliyār who was the minister of Hajarat Dāvadu-Khan, authorising a certain Ulli-Vēṅkaṭēśa-Śeṭṭiyār to conduct the charities connected with the temple. [Daud Khan was Nawab of the Karnatik from 1703-10. Veṅkaṭa Cheṭṭi was not improbably the merchant who rented Tiruvoṟṟiyūr and four other villages granted by Daud Khan to the Company in 1708. See *Vestiges of Madras*, II, pp. 21-2.]

1053. 184 *of* 1912.—(Grantha and Tamil.) On a second slab in the same place. Records in the twenty-sixth year of the Chōḷa king Madiraikoṇḍa Parakēsarivarman gift of ninety sheep for a lamp and one Īḷa-lamp-stand, by a native of Śōḷa-nāḍu.

1054. 185 *of* 1912.—(Tamil.) On a third slab in the same place. A much damaged record. Seems to register a sale of land as *bhaṭṭavritti* by a certain Mūrtiperumānār.

1055. 186 *of* 1912.—(Tamil.) On the fourth slab in the same place. Records in his twenty-first year gift of two Īḷa—lamp-stands, 360 sheep for maintaining two perpetual lamps and a *chauri* with a gold handle, by Mūvēnda Pallavaraiyan *alias* Āditta Piḍāran, son of Vīra-Nāraṇa-Pallavaraiyan *alias* Aruṇmoḷi, who was a native of Kūgūr in Vaḍa-Panaṅgāḍu, a subdivision of Mīkūṟṟu in Śōḷa-nāḍu.

1056. 187 *of* 1912.—(Tamil.) On the same slab. A much damaged record of the Chōḷa king Madiraikoṇḍa Parakēsarivarman (Parāntaka I, 905—47), dated in his twenty-sixth year. Mentions a quarter of Tiruvoṟṟiyūr called Śūraśūḷāmaṇipperunderu. [*Sūḷāmaṇi* reminds one of the celebrated Jain work of that name by Tōlāmoḷittēva. It has been suggested that it was written in the reign of the Pāṇḍya king Jayanta, son of Māravarman *Avanichūlāmaṇi* and grandson of Kaḍuṅgōn (about A.D. 620). *Tamil studies*, p. 219.]

1057. 188 *of* 1912.—(Tamil.) On the fifth slab in the same place. A damaged record of the "Gaṅga-Pallava king" Kō-Vijaya-Kampavikramavarman, dated in his ninth year. Records gift of gold for lamps by Kañjaran Amarnīdi *alias* Pallavadiyaraiyar, a native of Kañjanūr in Indalūr-nāḍu, which was a subdivision of Śōḷa-nāḍu. See No. 1043. [Amarnīdi was evidently named after the Śaivite saint of that name for whose career see *Periyapurāṇa*, 1905 edition, p. 129-132.]

1058. 189 *of* 1912.—(Tamil.) On the sixth slab in the same place. A damaged record of the "Gaṅga-Pallava" king Kampavarman, dated in his sixth year. Records gift of gold for a lamp by Vēmban Kuṇuṅgan-Amman of Iraiyanśēri residing at Mayilappil (i.e., Mylapore). The amount was deposited for interest with the assembly of Maṇali (which was a village) of Tiruvoṟṟiyūr.

1059. 190 *of* 1912.—(Tamil.) On the same slab. Records in the sixth year of the "Gaṅga Pallava" king Kō-Vijaya-Aparājitavikrama-Pōttaraiyar gift of gold for two lamps by the community of Mahēśvaras. The same assembly took possession of the amount.

1060. 191 *of* 1912.—(Tamil.) On the south wall of the first prākāra of the same temple. Registers in twenty-first year an order (*ōlai*) of Madurāntaka Pottappichōḻan. (Unfinished.)

1061. 192 *of* 1912.—(Tamil.) On the same wall. Records in the fourth year of the Chōḻa king Rājakēsarivarman *alias* Tribhuvanachakravartin Kulōttuṅga-Chōḻadēva (II), sale of 8,593¾ *kuḻi* of land, by the assembly of Punnaivāyil *alias* Rājanārāyaṇa chaturvēdimaṅgalam in Vikkiramaśōḻa vaḷanāḍu, a district of Jayaṅgoṇḍaśōḻa-maṇḍalam, to certain private individuals who made a gift of it to the temple of Uḍaiyār Tiruvoṟṟiyūrār, for maintaining 28 perpetual lamps.

1062. 193 *of* 1912.—(Tamil.) On the same wall. An unfinished historical introduction of the Chōḻa king Parakēsarivarman *alias* Rājarājadēva II (1146—78), beginning with *pūmaruviyapoḻil-ēḻum.*

1063. 194 *of* 1912.—(Tamil.) On the same wall. A record of the time of Sakalalōkachakravartin Rājanārāyaṇa Śambuvaraya. Seems to record a gift of land for offerings by a certain Aḻagaiyarāyan Vīṟṟirunda-Perumāḷ Kuḻandai-Piḷḷai to the temple of Tiruvoṟṟiyūr-uḍaiya Nāyanār.

1064. 195 *of* 1912.—(Tamil.) On the same wall. Records that in the time of the Vijayanagara king Kampaṇa-Uḍaiyār II, son of Bokkaṇa (Bukka I), in Sādhāraṇa, the temple authorities assembled in the *Vyākaraṇadāna* hall under the leadership of the officer (adhikāri) Tuṇaiyirunda-nambi Koṅgarāyar and settled the order of precedence to be followed during services in the temple, by Ishabattaḷiyilār and Dēvaraḍiyār. See *Ep. Rep.*, 1913, p. 118, for very interesting details about the temple servants, their disputes for privileges and the decisions of the trustees and Nāṭṭārs thereon.

1065. 196 *of* 1912.—(Tamil.) On the west wall of the same prākāra. Dated in the reign of the Vijayanagara king Ariyarāya (i.e., Harihara II). Seems to record in Dundubhi, Kanni, śu. di Paurṇai, Monday, Uttiraṭṭādi, corresponding to 22nd September 1382, a procedure similar to that mentioned in No. 1064.

1066. 197 *of* 1912.—(Tamil.) On the same wall. Records in the thirty-second year of the Chōḷa king Tribhuvanachakravartin Tribhuvanavīradēva "who took Madurai (Madura), Īḷam (Ceylon), Karuvūr and the crowned head of the Pāṇḍya and who was pleased to perform the anointment of heroes and the anointment of victors" (i.e., Kulōttuṅga III), sale of land to a certain Uḍaiyapiḷḷai *alias* Pāṇḍaraṅgan Vairāgi of Madurāntaka-Chaturvēdimaṅgalam, by the assembly of Punnaivāyil *alias* Rājanārāyaṇa-chaturvēdimaṅgalam in Puḷal-nāḍu, a district of Puḷar-kōṭṭam *alias* Vikkiramaśōḷa-valanāḍu in Jayaṅgoṇḍaśōḷa-maṇḍalam. The land was assigned to maintain a flower garden for the temple and to provide for offerings on certain festive occasions.

1067. 198 *of* 1912.—(Tamil.) On the same wall. Records in the twenty-second year of the Chōḷa king Tribhuvanachakravartin Rājarājadēva III an order of Madhurāntaka Pottappi-Chōḷa. Records also gift of Uḷarūr *alias* Śembiyan Karuppūr in Kōṭṭūr-nāḍu, a subdivision of Puliyūr-kōṭṭam, as a dēvadāna village to the temple, by a certain Karuppuḷār Perumāṇḍi-Nāyakkar.

1068. 199 *of* 1912.—(Tamil.) On the same wall. Records in the seventh year of the Chōḷa king Tribhuvanachakravartin Rājarājadēva III an order of Vīra-Naraśiṅga *alias* Yādavarāyan. The king declared that Tiruvoṟṟiyūr and the other villages of the temple which had originally been rent-free (*iṟaṅgal*) were to be taxed, the collections, however, being made payable into the treasury of the temple. They were, in other words, placed in the *niṅgal* list. The taxes enumerated are *Veṭṭi, puḍavaimudal, Tiraik-kāśu, āśuvigaḷ-kāśu, kuḍikāśu, inavarikāśu, kārttigai kāsu, Vēlich-chinnam, veṭṭikkāśu, Śirupāḍikkāval, Kaṅkāṇi* fees, *Kuṟṟadaṇḍam, paṭṭi daṇḍam*, and fees on uvachchars, weavers, oil mongers, dyers, salt-pans, etc. For Vīra Narasimha Yādavarāya, see No. 1096 below and Tirumalai inscriptions (Chittoor District).

1069. 200 *of* 1912.—(Tamil.) On the same wall. Dated in the reign of the Chōḷa king Rājakēsarivarman *alias* Chakravartin Kulōttuṅga-Chōḷadēva I. Records in his forty-ninth year, gift of a portion of Pavanambākkam near Araiśūr in Paiyyūr-kōṭṭam renamed Eḷuttarivarṇallūr, for feeding fifty devotees in *Kulōttuṅga-śōḷan maḍam*, situated within the temple of Tiruvoṟṟiyūr Uḍaiyār. The order was issued at the instance of the king while he was in his palace at Gaṅgaikoṇḍa-śōḷapuram.

1070. 201 *of* 1912.—(Tamil.) On the same wall. A record of the Chōḷa king Tribhuvanachakravartin Kōnērinmaikoṇḍān (Kulōttuṅga III). Records in his thirty-eighth year and two hundred and thirty-ninth day gift 80 *vēlis* of land at Kuḷattūr *alias* Kulōttuṅgaśōḷan Kāvanūr detached from Punnaivāyil *alias* Rājanārāyaṇachaturvēdimaṅgalam by Durgaiyāṇḍi-Nāyakkan, agent of Sittaraiśan, for the maintenance of the Vyākaraṇadāna-Vyākhyāna-maṇṭapa built by himself in the temple of Tiruvoṟṟiyūr. The officer Vānadarāyar and the tirumandira-ōlai, Neriyuḍaichchōḷa-Mūvēndavēḷān, are also mentioned. The land was free of tax (including *Antarāyappaṭṭam*).

1071. 202 *of* 1912.—(Tamil.) On the same wall. A record of the Chōḷa king Tribhuvanachakravartin Tribhuvanavīradēva, "who was pleased to perform the anointment of heroes and the anointment of victors" (Kulōttuṅga III). Records in his thirty-fifth year, Simha, śu. di. 12, Friday, Uttiraṭṭādi (= Friday, 10th August 1212), the circumstances under which the grant recorded in No. 1070 was made. [The inscription refers to the levying of *ponvari* on land at ¼ *māḍai* per *vēli* (without the usual exemption of waste land) and to the compulsion of the assembly of Puṇṇavāyal to bear the responsibility of collecting the whole. As they would not, they were arrested and liberated after the sale of 80 *vēlis* for 200 *kāśu* to clear the arrears. The inscription also refers to the *vyākarṇa-maṇṭapa*, its teachers and pupils.]

1072. 203 *of* 1912.—(Tamil.) On the north wall of the same prākāra. A record of Sakalalōkachakravartin Rājanārāyaṇan Śambuvarāyar in his seventh year, Śiṅga, ba. di. 2, Thursday, Punarpūśam, that certain lands and house-sites were confiscated to the temple, the owners having dishonestly misappropriated such of the temple treasures buried underground as had escaped the Muhammadans (Tulukkar) who had, before this, occupied the country. The reference is the invasion of 1327. See *Ind. Antq*., 1914, p. 4.

1073. 204 *of* 1912.—(Tamil.) On the same wall. Records in Piṅgaḷa an order of the temple trustees *(tānattār)* assigning the quarter called Nārppatteṇṇāyirapperunderu for *the exclusive dwelling of sculptors and other artisans.* See N.A. 715, S.A. 921 and Cg. 147.

1074. 205 *of* 1912.—(Tamil.) On the same wall. Dated in the reign of the Vijayanagara king Ariyaṇa-Uḍaiyār (Harihara II). Records in Raudri, Kanni, śu. di. 12, Tuesday (which should be Wednesday), Aviṭṭam, gift of ½ *karai* of land in the village of Pāḍiāḍumperumāḷnallur, to the temple of Tiruvoṟṟiyūr-uḍaiya-Nāyanār for maintaining certain festivals and the Aṅgarāyan-maṭam by Aṅgarāyar Mudaliār and others of Puḷal *alias* Rāja-sundarinallūr. The date corresponds to 12th September 1380.

1075. 206 *of* 1912.—(Grantha and Tamil.) On the same wall. A record of the Chōḷa king Tribhuvanachakravartin Rājādhirāja-dēva II. Records in his ninth year, that gifts of lamps and cows made in the previous years but not engraved on stone, were now so recorded by the temple accountant Tiruvoṟṟiyūr-uḍaiyān Uravākkinān (*maitrikara,* in Sanskrit) at the instance of the *maṭhapati* Chaturānana-Paṇḍita. See No. 1050 above.

1076. 207 *of* 1912.—(Tamil.) On the same wall. Records in the twelfth year of Sakalalōkachakravartin Rājanārāyaṇan Śambuvarāyar, Pūraṭṭādi, first day, gift of land at Kāḍuvankōṭṭam with the order of Tikkama-Nāyaka declaring the land tax-free, for offerings and festivals, by Vāgīśuradēva-Mudaliyār of *Kiḷai-maṭham*, while he was on his death bed. The purchase of this land is stated to have been engraved on the stone wall of the Tirumūlattānamuḍaiya-Nāyanār temple at Puḷal. A portion of the land was also assigned to Aḷagiya-Tiruchchiṟṟambalamuḍaiyār who was to succeed Vāgīśa as the head of that *maṭha.* This Vāgīśa was of course different from him who is mentioned in No. 965 above.

1077. 208 *of* 1912.—(Tamil.) On the same wall. An unfinished record of the Vijayanagara king Kampaṇa Uḍaiyar (II), dated Ś. 1290, Kīlaka, Kumbha, śu. di. 14, Sunday, Aśvati, corresponding to 11th February, 1369. Records that the order of precedence in service to be followed by Īshabattaḷiyilār and Dēvaraḍiyār as settled in the fifth year of Rājanārāyaṇa Śāmbuvarāyar by the Mudaliār of Mēlai-maṭham in Perumbaṟṟappuliyūr, being found not to be satisfactory, Kāmarasa-Viṭṭappa of Anaigundi inquired into temple affairs and instituted necessary changes. [Gives an example of the interference of • central government in temple affairs.]

1078. 209 *of* 1912.—(Tamil.) On the same wall. A record of the Chōḷa king Tribhuvanachakravartin Kōnērinmaikoṇḍān (i.e., Kulōttuṅga III) in his twenty-seventh year and sixty-ninth day. Records gift of land for maintaining a special service called *Tribhuvanavīran-śandi.* The land (100 vēlis) was situated in Kuḷappākkam *alias* Śivapādaśēkharanallūr, a village in Puliyūrkōṭṭam *alias* Kulōttuṅgaśōḷavaḷanāḍu and was granted rent-free on the Chitra-Vishu day of the twenty-sixth year. The royal secretary *(tiru-mandira-ōlai)* was Mīnavan Mūvēndavēḷān. The document is signed by eight officers.

1079. 210 *of* 1912.—(Tamil.) On the same wall. The Vijayanagara king Kampaṇa Uḍaiyār records in Plavaṅga, Kambha, ba. di. 3, Wednesday (mistake), Attam, corresponding to Monday, 7th February 1368, sale of a house to the temple of Tiruvoṟṟiyūr-uḍaiya-Nāyanār at Tiruvoṟṟiyūr, which was a *niṅgal* village.

1080. 211 *of* 1912.—(Tamil.) On the same wall. The Chōḷa king Tribhuvanachakravartin Rājarājadēva III records in his nineteenth year and forty-third day, Simha, śu. di., an order on the occasion while he heard a temple *Padiyilār* sing in the *agamārga* style in the Rājarājan tirumaṇṭapam on the night of the eighth day of the Āvaṇi-ttirunāḷ. It was to detach sixty vēlis of land which had been purchased by a native of Vēḷshāṛu, from Maṇali *alias* Śiṅga-Vishṇu-chaturvēdi- maṅgalam and to call it Uravākkinanallūr as suggested by the temple trustees. See No. 1011 above.

1081. 212 *of* 1912.—(Tamil.) On the same wall. Rājanārāyaṇa-Śambuvarāyar refers in his fifth year to the settlement of the due order of precedence in temple service as between the Īshabattaḷiyilar, the Dēvaraḍiyār, and the Padiyilār who had become either extinct or reduced after the former settlement during the office of Pottapparāyar *alias* Vāṇaraiyar in the reign of Perumāḷ Sundara Pāṇḍyadēva (i.e., Jaṭāvarman I, 1251—64), "who took every country". The inscription enumerates in detail their duties. See *Ep. Rep.*, 1913, p. 127-8.

1082. 213 *of* 1912.—(Tamil.) On the same wall. Dated in the reign of the Vijayanagara king Sayaṇa-Uḍaiyār; records in his seventh year, Vijaya, sale of land (2 *karai*) in the village Nāyappākkam *alias* Paḍiāḍum-Perumāḷnallūr for maintaining certain festivals in the temple, by some residents of Puḷal *alias* Rājasundarinallūr (see also No. 1074 above). The God is called Mudaliyār-Pāḍi-Āḍuvār.

1083. 214 *of* 1912.—(Tamil.) On the same wall. A record of the Chōḷa king Tribhuvanachakravartin Rājarājadēva III. Records in his fourth year, Dhanus, ba. di. Wednesday, Śōdi and ēkādaśi (=Wednesday, 4th December 1219), gift of 17 buffaloes and one lampstand of three flats, by the chief of Paramēśvaramaṅgalam *alias* Sōḷakulatilaka-chaturvēdimaṅgalam in Śembūr-kōṭṭam, a district of Jayaṅgoṇḍaśōḷa-maṇḍalam.

1084. 215 *of* 1912.—(Tamil.) On the same wall. Registers a sale of two houses by the temple, to Mudaliyār Vāgīśuradēva of Kīḷai-maḍam at Tiruvārur. See No. 1076 above.

1085. 216 *of* 1912.—(Tamil.) On the south wall of the Kāḷi shrine inside the same temple. Records in the sixth year of the Chōḷa king Tribhuvanachakravartin Vīrarājēndra Chōḷadēva (Kulōttuṅga III), gift of money by Aḷagan Jñānasambandan, a native of Paḷuvūr in Dāmar-kōṭṭam, for maintaining the festival called *Uttirāyaṇa-śirappu* in the temple. The money was deposited with three residents of Vēḷśāṛu.

1086. 217 *of* 1912.—(Tamil.) On the base of the stone pedestal of the Naṭarāja image in the Naṭarāja shrine of the same temple. Records that this pedestal *Virarājēndran* was caused to be built by Śivalōkanādan of Tiruveṇkāḍu.

1087. 218 *of* 1912.—(Tamil.) On a slab built into the floor of the same shrine. A damaged record of the Chōḷa king Rājarāja-Rājakēsarivarman *alias* Rājarājadēva I, dated in his nineteenth year. Seems to register sale of houses belonging to the temple.

1088. 219 *of* 1912.—(Tamil.) On the east, north, and west bases of the same shrine. A record of the Chōḷa king Parakēsarivarman *alias* Uḍaiyār śri-Ādhirājēndradēva. Records in his third year a sale of land, by the assembly of Sundaraśōḷa-chaturvēdimaṅgalam in Puḷal-nāḍu, a district of Jayaṅgoṇḍaśōḷa-maṇḍalam to the temple of Tiruvoṟṟiyūr-Uḍaiyār. Beginning and end built in.

1089. 220 *of* 1912.—(Tamil.) On the same base. A record of the Chōḷa king Rājakēsarivarman *alias* Uḍaiyār śri-Rājādhirājadēva (I). Records in his twenty-eighth year sale of land for offerings in the temple of Kārāṇai Viṭaṅkadēva at Tiruvoṟṟiyūr, by the assemblies of Sundaraśōḷa-chaturvēdimaṅgalam and Vānavanmādēvi-chaturvēdimaṅgalam. Beginning and end built in.

1090. 221 *of* 1912.—(Tamil.) On the same base. A record of the Chōḷa king Rājakēsarivarman *alias* Kulōttuṅga-Chōḷadēva I. Records in his tenth year gift of 30 *kalams* of paddy for offerings, to the shrine of Kumārasvāmidēva, under orders from the officers Sundaraśōḷa-Mūvēndavēḷār and Gurukularājar. Beginning and end built in. [Some lands originally enjoyed by the *Taḷiyilār* are said to have been resumed and others given instead.]

1091. 222 *of* 1912.—(Tamil.) On the same base. Dated in the reign of the Chōḷa king Rājakēsarivarman *alias* Uḍaiyār śrī-Rājēndra-Chōḷadēva (Kulōttuṅga I). Records sale of land to the temple by the assemblies of the two villages mentioned in No. 1089 above. Beginning and end built in.

1092. 223 *of* 1912.—(Tamil.) On the east wall of the maṇṭapa in front of the same shrine. Records in Śubhakrit, Paṅguni, twenty-ninth day, assignment of servants and a lamp to the temple of Tiruvoṟṟiyūr-uḍaiyār-Tambirānār, for the merit of Sadāśivarāya, by Sarvarasa-Koṇḍamarasayya.

1093. 224 *of* 1912.—(Tamil.) On the same wall. Dated in the reign of the Vijayanagara king Dēvarāya-Mahārāya (II). Records in Virōdhi, Āḍi, second day, gift of paddy for offerings by a certain Aḷagiya-Tiruchchiṟṟambalamuḍaiyān Nallanāyanār of Pullūr.

1094. 225 *of* 1912.—(Tamil.) On the same wall. Dated in the reign of the Vijayanagara king Kumāra Bukkaṇa Uḍaiyār. Records in Kshaya, Kumba, śu. di. 14, Friday, Pūśam, gift of land by a dancing girl named *Ainnūṟṟuttalaikkōli*, for a special service which was to be named after herself.

1095. 226 *of* 1912.—(Tamil.) On the same wall. A record of the Vijayanagara king Vīrapratāpa Dēvarāya-Mahārāya (II). Records in Plavaṅga an order (*rāyasam*) of the king to the effect that some lands which had originally been in the hands of the tenants and servants of the temple of Tiruvoṟṟiyūr in Chandragiri-rājya and which had been taken away from them by a new system of lease introduced by Government, be redeemed and restored at the State cost; and that the taxes of *jōḍi*, *mugampārvai*, *aṅgaśālai*, *Śambaḍam*, *viśēshādāyam*, *ariśi-kāṇam*, *Nallerudu*, *Narpaśu*, *Veṭṭi* and *Kaṭṭāyam* be henceforth collected by the Mahēśvaras.

1096. 227 *of* 1912.—(Tamil.) On the south base of the Subrahmaṇya shrine in the same temple. Records in the ninth year of the Chōḷa king Tribhuvanachakravartin Rājarājadēva III, an order of Vīra-Narasiṃhadēvan *alias* Yādavarāyan and the gift of the village Periya-Mullaivāyil in Nāyaṟu-nāḍu, a subdivision of Puḷalkōṭṭam, for offerings to the god Vīra-Narasimhēśvaramuḍaiya-Nāyanār, set up by him in the verandah round the central shrine of the temple.

1097. 228 *of* 1912.—(Tamil.) On the north base of the Gaurīśvara shrine in the same temple. Records in the fifth year of the Chōḷa king Rājakēsarivarman *alias* Uḍaiyār śri-Vīrarājēndradēva (I, 1063—70), sale of land to the temple of Tiruvoṟṟiyūruḍaiya Paḍambakkanāyakkar by the assemblies of Sundaraśōḷa-chaturvēdimaṅgalam and Vānavanmādēvi-chaturvēdimaṅgalam. Another document which was drawn up in the sixth year of the king is recorded in continuation. It consists also of a sale of land by the assembly of Śiṅgavishṇuchaturvēdimaṅgalam for a garden (named Vīrarājēndran-tirunandavanam) founded by Paśupati Tiruvaraṅgadēvan *alias* Rājēndra Mūvēndavēḷār of Maṇakkuḍi in Iḍaiyan-nāḍu, a subdivision of Vīrarājēndra vaḷanāḍu in Jayaṅgoṇḍa-śōḷa-maṇḍalam.

1098. 229 *of* 1912.—(Tamil.) On the same base. Records in the twenty-eighth year of Chakravartin Kulōttuṅga Chōḷadēva I, sale of land to certain mendicants *(tapasya)* of the temple, by the assembly of Punnaivāyil *alias* Rājanārāyaṇa-chaturvēdimaṅgalam. Beginning lost.

1099. 230 *of* 1912.—(Tamil.) On the west base of the same shrine. A record of the Chōḷa king Rājakēsarivarman *alias* Kulōttuṅga-Chōḷadēva I; records in his tenth year, gift of 90 sheep for a lamp by a native of Anaṅgur in Panaiyūr-nāḍu, a subdivision of Rājēndraśōḷa-vaḷanāḍu.

1100. 231 *of* 1912.—(Tamil.) On the south base of the same shrine. Records in the twelfth year of a Chōḷa king gift of a lamp by the same individual. End built in. Begins with the historical introduction *tirumagaḷ jayamagaḷ*, etc.

1101. 232 *of* 1912.—(Tamil.) On the same base. Records in the fifth year of the Chōḷa king Rājakēsarivarman *alias* Uḍaiyār śrī-Vīrarājēndradēva (I, 1063--70) that this stone temple was constructed for Paḍambakkanāyakkadēva, by the chief mentioned in No. 1097 above. The term *Paḍambakka* connects the place with the local tradition; but the Government Epigraphist points out that the present image of Gauḷīśvara therein is not improbably that of Lakuḷīśa himself.

1102. 233 *of* 1912.—(Tamil verse.) On the same base. A record evidently in praise of Kulōttuṅga-Chōḷa I.

1103. 234 *of* 1912.—(Tamil.) On a pillar of the kitchen in the same temple. Records gift of gold (30 *kaḻañju*) for a lamp to the temple of Tiruvoṟṟiyūr-Mahādēva. The amount was placed in the hands of the residents of Kaṇḍalūr in Paiyyūr-kōṭṭam, a dēvadāna village of Tiruvoṟṟiyūr. Beginning lost.

1104. 235 *of* 1912.—(Tamil.) On a second pillar of the same kitchen. A record of the Chōḷa king Rājakēsarivarman *alias* Mummuḍi-Chōḷadēva Rājarāja I. Records in his third year, gift of a gold necklace *(paḷḷittoṅgal)* called *Rājarājan*, a shell-like cup of gold *(Ōṭṭuvaṭṭil)* called *Mummudiśōḻan* and a gold door for the *mēvāśi*, called *Rājarājan*, by a certain Guṇaśīlan of Muḷḷikkuṟumbu in Uraiyūr-kūṟṟam of the Chōḷa country, for the merit of Aḍigaḷ Nīrāḍi, chief of Ūṟṟukkāḍu, a village in Āvūr-kūṟṟam of Śōṇāḍu, who was in charge of the temple affairs (*śri-kārya*) of the god Tiruvoṟṟiyūr-Āḷvār.

1105. 236 *of* 1912.—(Grantha and Tamil.) On a broken pillar lying near the same. The Grantha portion mentions a military officer of Śirukuḷattūr who was victorious at Nellore and was desirous of making a gift to the temple of Śiva at Ādhigrāma. The Tamil portion refers to land which, not being tax-free before, was made tax-free in the thirty-eighth year of Chakravartin (Parāntaka I) and given to the same god; vide No. 1029 above. Chīṭpuli was probably the E. Chāḷukyan Bhīma II or some feudatory of his.

1106. 237 *of* 1912.—(Tamil.) On a pillar lying near the shrine of the goddess in the same temple. Records gift of this door-way called Ellāndalaiyāna-Perumāḷ-tiruvāśal, for the merit of Perumāḷ Sundara-Pāṇḍyadēva, by Ēnāḍi Mērkuḍaiyān Periyanāyan *alias* Pottappirāyan. [The Government Epigraphist identifies the king with Jaṭāvarman Sundara Pāṇḍya I (1251--64).]

1107. 238 *of* 1912.—(Tamil.) On the Gōpura of the same temple; right of entrance. Dated in the reign of Tribhuvanachakravartin Vijayagaṇḍagōpāladēva. Records in his fifteenth year, Makara, śu. di. Monday, Śōdi, (= 2nd September, 1264), gift of land for feeding Mahēśvaras in the *Tirujñānasambanda-maṭha* at Tiruvoṟṟiyūr, a village of Puḻar-kōṭṭam *alias* Vikkiramaśōḻa-vaḷanāḍu in Jayaṅgoṇḍaśōḻamaṇḍalam by a merchant of Tirunāvalūr, who purchased it from a certain Paḍuvūrnāḍāḷvān of Kaṭṭuppākkam in Eḻumūr-Tuḍarmuḍi-nāḍu, a district of the same kōṭṭam.

1108. 239 *of* 1912.—(Tamil.) In the same place. A record of Tribhuvanachakravartin Vijayagaṇḍagōpāladēva in his third year, Rishabha, śu. di. 5, Anusham. Records gift of land at Peruṅgarai in Paiyyūr-kōṭṭam, to the *maṭha* of Nandikēśvara *alias* Ariyavratam-koṇḍa Mudaliyār and his pupils, by a certain Kiḍārattaraiyan.

1109. 240 *of* 1912.—(Tamil.) In the same place. A damaged record of the Vijayanagara king Savaṇa-Uḍaiyār (I), dated in his ninth year (i.e., A.D. 1357). Mentions that some of the *agambadiyār*, serving under the chief of Paḍuvūr (viz., Kāḷiṅgarāyan, Śēdiyarāyan, Ādittan, etc.), lived in the village and served as *kāval* for a long time, neglected their duty for reasons unexplained and caused much loss to the people (and so had to be punished).

1110. 241 *of* 1912.—(Tamil.) On the same gōpura, left of entrance. Records in the second year, an order of Madurāntaka Pottappichōḷan. Remission of certain taxes payable by the shepherds in consideration of five perpetual lamps maintained by them in the temple of Tiruvoṟṟiyūruḍaiya Nāyanār. The document bears the signature of Mānavijaya.

1111. 242 *of* 1912.—(Tamil.) In the same place. A record of Tribhuvanachakravartin Śrīraṅganātha Yādavarāyar. Records in his sixteenth year Khara, Rishabha, ba di. 14, Tuesday, Urōhaṇi, gift for a special service in the temple, called Kāḷiyūrkiḷavanśandi by a resident of Śēṟṟuppēḍu (Chetpat), in Eḷumūr-Tuḍarmuninādu which was a subdivision of Puḷar-kōṭṭam *alias* Vikkirama-śōḷa-vaḷanāḍu in Jayaṅgoṇḍaśōḷa-maṇḍalam, of land situated in Kāḍuvankōṭṭam *alias* Aḷiyavradamkoṇḍaviḷagam, which was detached from Śēlaivāśal in Puḷal-nāḍu and formed part of the western boundary of Tiruvoṟṟiyūr.

1112. 243 *of* 1912.—(Tamil.) In the same place. A record of Tribhuvanachakravartin Vijaya-Gaṇḍagōpāladēva in his twenty-first year, Simba su. di. 5, Wednesday, Śōdi, corresponding to 12th August 1271. Gift of eight cows for a quarter lamp, by a resident of Tiruvoṟṟiyūr.

1113. 244 *of* 1912.—(Tamil.) In the same place. The Śāḷuva king Naraśiṅgayadēva records in Chitrabhānu, Tai, 10, gift of the taxes *śekkāyam* and *magamai* for maintaining a lamp and conducting repairs in the temple of Tiruvoṟṟiyūruḍaiya-Nāyanār with the permission of Īśura-Nāyakkar who was the agent of the king. (He was evidently the father of Narasa Nāyaka).

1114. 245 *of* 1912.—(Tamil.) On a pillar lying to the south of the tank in front of the same temple. The Chōḷa king Uttama-Chōḷadēva (1970—86) *alias* Parakēsarivarman records in his sixteenth year, gift of 868 kaḷañju of (*tuḷai-niṟai*) gold for a plate (*kuḷit-taṭṭu*) and of 40 kaḷañju for offerings, to the temple of Tiruvoṟṟiyūr-Āḷvār, by Nandisaran *alias* Parakēsari-Viḷupparaiyan of Eḷinūr in Puraṅgarambai-nāḍu, a district of Śōṇāḍu, who was the officer managing the temple affairs at the time. See 1035 above.

1115. 246 *of* 1912.—(Tamil.) On a pillar lying to the south of the same temple. A record of the Chōḷa king Madiraikoṇḍa Rājakēsarivarman (whom Mr. Krishna Sastri identifies with Gaṇḍarāditya). Records in his fifth year, gift of 90 sheep for a lamp by Kaḍuttalai Nāgamayyan, son of Śiṅgamayyan of Kalēśi

Perundaram who had accompanied Uḍaiyār Uttamaśōḻadēva (Gaṇḍarāditya's son) to the temple of Tiruvoṟṟiyūr-Mahādēva.

1116. 104 *of* 1892.—(Sanskrit.) East wall of the second prākāra of the Ādhipurīśvara temple, right of entrance. A record of the Chōḻa king Tammu-Siddhi, dated 1129. The inscription gives the genealogy of Tammu Siddhi's line and mentions Karikāl Chōḻa, Madhurāntaka Pottappi Chōḻa, etc. See *Ep. Ind.*, VII, 148—52.

1117. 105 *of* 1892.—(Sanskrit.) South wall of the first prākāra of the Ādhipurīśvara temple. A record of the Chōḻa king Rājēndra, the son of Rājarāja.

1118. 106 *of* 1892.—(Tamil.) West and south walls of the first prākāra of the Ādhipurīśvara temple. A record of the Chōḻa king Ko-Rājakēsarivarman *alias* Rājēndra-Chōḻadēva II (i.e., Kulōttuṅga I), dated in his second year. A general grants 240 *kāśu* which the temple authorities employ in purchasing land from 5 villages. [*S.I.I.*, III, No. 64, pp. 132—4.]

1119. 107 *of* 1892.—(Tamil.) South wall of the first prākāra of the Ādhipurīśvara temple. Records in the thirty-first year of the Chōḻa king Kō-Rājakēsarivarman *alias* Rājādhirājadēva gift of land by Ariyammai who purchased the land from the Sabhā.

1120. 108 *of* 1892.—(Tamil.) West wall of the first prākāra of the Ādhipurīśvara temple. A record of Tribhuvanachakravartin Rājādhirājadēva, dated in his sixth year.

1121. 109 *of* 1892.—(Sanskrit.) North wall of the first prākāra of the Ādhipurīśvara temple. A gift of lamp by one Madhurāntaka in the thirtieth year of Jayadhara (i.e., Kulōttuṅgachōḻa I). See *Ep. Ind.*, V, p. 106. It is said to have been made for the merit of the "illustrious Gñānamūrti."

1122. 110 *of* 1892.—(Tamil.) North wall of the first prākāra of the Ādhipurīśvara temple. A record of the Chōḻa king Tribhuvana-chakravartin Rājarājadēva, dated in his eleventh year. See *Ep. Ind.* VI, p. 283.

1123. 399 *of* 1896.—(Tamil.) On the south wall of the central shrine of the Ādhipurīśvara temple. A record of the Chōḻa king Kō-Parakēsarivarman *alias* Rājēndra-Chōḻadēva (I, 1011—43), dated in his thirty-first year. Opens with the same historical introduction as the Tanjore inscription of the nineteenth year Chaturānana Paṇḍita of *Tirunārāyaṇa maṭha* at Tiruvoṟṟiyur deposits 150 *kāśus* in the temple treasury for neyyāḍi during Mārgaḻi Tiruvādirai. See *S.I.I.*, II, No. 20.

1124. 400 *of* 1896.—(Tamil.) On the west wall of the same shrine. Records in the thirteenth year of the Pāṇḍya king Kō-Jaṭāvarman *alias* Sundara-Pāṇḍyadēva (III, 1276—90) gift of land. See *Ep. Ind.*, VI, 310–1, where Dr. Kielhorn points out that the exact date is Friday, 5th August 1289.

1125. 401 *of* 1896.—(Tamil.) On the same wall. A record of the Chōḷa king Kō-Rājakēsarivarman *alias* Kulōttuṅga-Chōḷadēva, dated in his seventh year. End built in.

1126. 402 *of* 1896.—(Tamil.) On a stone built into the floor of the north wall of the first prākāra of the same temple. The Chōḷa king Kō-Parakēsarivārman records in his seventh year gift of gold for a lamp.

1127. 403 *of* 1896.—(Grantha and Tamil.) On the east wall of the second prākāra of the same temple, left of entrance. A record of the Chōḷa king Kō-Rājakēsarivarman *alias* Rājādhirājadēva, dated in his ninth year. Built in in the middle.

1128. 404 *of* 1896.—(Tamil.) On the same wall. A record of the Chōḷa king Kō-Parakēsarivarman *alias* Kulōttuṅga-Chōladēva III "who took Madurai and the crowned head of the Pāṇḍya," dated in his nineteenth year. Built in in the middle.

1129. 405 *of* 1896.—(Grantha and Tamil.) On the north wall of the same prākāra. Records in the ninth year of the Chōḷa king Tribhuvanachakravartin Rājādhirājadēva (II ?) gift of cows for a lamp.

Vallam.

1129-A. On the gate of the Dēvanāyakaperumāḷ temple at Vallam. Records that in the fifth year of the reign of Rājēndra-chōḷa he fixed the duty of supplying daily one measure of oil for lamp upon the local oil-mongers. Ins. S. Dts., p. 181, No. 12.

Veḷachchēri.

1130. 302 *of* 1911.—(Tamil.) On the north wall of the central shrine in the Daṇḍīśvara temple. Records in the sixth year of the Chōḷa king Parakēsarivarman *alias* Rājēndra-Chōḷadeva (I) gift of 90 sheep for a lamp to the temple of Tirudaṇḍēśuramuḍaiya-Mahādēva at Veḷichchēri, a brahmadēya in Puliyūr-kōṭṭam which was a subdivision of Jayaṅgoṇḍachōḷamaṇḍalam by a Brāhmaṇa lady, the wife of one of the managing members *(āḷuṅgaṇạttār)* of the village.

1131. 303 *of* 1911.—(Tamil.) On the same wall. Records in the twenty-fifth year of the Chōḷa king Tribhuvanachakravartin Kulōttuṅga-Chōḷadēva (III) who was pleased to take Madurai (Madura) and the crowned head of the Pāṇḍya, gift of land by Śēdirayādēva to the *maṭha* of Tirunāvukkaraśu at Tiruvānmiyūr in Kulōttuṅgaśōḷa vaḷanāḍu, a subdivision of Jayaṅgoṇḍachōḷa-maṇḍalam. The land granted was situated at Veḷichchēri *alias* Jīnachintāmaṇi-chaturvēdi-maṅgalam.

1132. 304 *of* 1911.—(Tamil.) On the same wall. A record of the Chōḷa king Rājarājakēsari Mummuḍi-Chōḷa (Rājarāja I). Records in his tenth year gift of land for offerings and lamps to the temple of Taramaṇi-Mahādēva in the hamlet of Veḷichchēri in Kōṭṭūr-nāḍu, a subdivision of Puliyūr-kōṭṭam. Mentions Amudan Pichchan *alias* Śembian Kīḻanāṭṭukkōn, a native of Vaigūrchchēri in Kiḻārkūṟṟam which was district of Śōṇāḍu (i.e, the Chōḷa country). See Tirumalpuram inscriptions which show that the king had the title Mummuḍichōḷa in his fourth year.

1133. 305 *of* 1911.—(Tamil.) On the north, west and south walls of the same shrine. A record of the Chōḷa king Parakēsarivarman *alias* Rājēndra-Chōḷadēva (I). Records in his tenth year that the assembly of Veḷichchēri, a brahmadēya in Kōṭṭūr-nāḍu of Puliyur-kōṭṭam, sold 1,500 *kuli* of land to the temple of Tiruttaṇḍīśuramuḍaiya-Mahādēva and receiving 13 *kāśu,* made the land tax-free. Records also that 23 *kāśu* were presented for a lamp by a Brāhmaṇa lady of that village. Built in at the beginning.

1134. 306 *of* 1911.—(Tamil.) On the west wall of the same shrine. Dated in the seventh year of the Chōḷa king Madiraikoṇḍa Rājakēsarivarman (evidently Gaṇḍarāditya, son of Parāntaka I). Records that two persons of Ārkkāṭṭu-kūṟṟam in Śōṇāḍu, purchased land from the assembly of Veḷichchēri in Puliyūr-kōṭṭam and presented it to the temple of Tiruttaṇḍīśvarattu Mahādēva for burning a lamp therein and for providing offerings to a shrine of Gaṇapati built by themselves in that temple.

1135. 307 *of* 1911.—(Tamil.) On the same wall. A record of the Chōḷa king Tribhuvanachakravartin Rājarājadēva. Records in his seventh year gift of money for two lamps by the *kāraṇattān* of Vēḷichchēri *alias* Jīnachintāmaṇi-chaturvēdimaṅgalam in Kōṭṭūr-nāḍu which was a subdivision of Puliyūr-kōṭṭam *alias* Kulōttuṅga-śōḷa-vaḷanāḍu in Jayaṅgoṇḍachōḷamaṇḍalam, to the temple of Tirudaṇḍīśvaramuḍaiya-Nāyanār.

1136. 308 *of* 1911.—(Tamil.) On the same wall. A record of the Chōḷa king Parakēsarivarman *alias* Rājēndra-Chōḷadēva (I). Records in his third year gift of 90 sheep for a lamp by Pattaṅgi Kaḷakumāra kramavittan, one of the managing members in the village of Veḷichchēri, a brahmadēya in Kōṭṭūr-nāḍu which was a subdivision of Puliyūr kōṭṭam in Jayaṅgoṇḍachōḷamaṇḍalam, to the temple of Tiruttaṇḍīśvaradēva.

1137. 309 *of* 1911.—(Tamil.) On the same wall. A record of the Chōḷa king Parakēsarivarman *alias* Rājēndra-Chōḷadēva (I). Records in his third year gift of 90 sheep for a lamp to the same temple. Mentions a native of Āṟṟūr, one of the villages in Vēśalippāḍi.

1138. 310 *of* 1911.—(Tamil.) On the same wall. A record of the Chōḷa king Tribhuvanachakravartin Kulōttuṅga-Chōḷadēva (III), "who was pleased to take Madurai (Madura) and the crowned head of the Pāṇḍya." Records in his twenty-fifth year gift of money for two lamps.

1139. 311 *of* 1911.—(Tamil.) On the west and south walls of the same shrine. A damaged record of the Chōḷa king Parakēsarivarman *alias* Rājēndra-Chōḷadēva (I), dated in his sixth year. Sale of land which was held by the non-Brahmans of Veḷichchēri, to the temple, with the permission of the king.

1140. 312 *of* 1911.—(Tamil.) On the south wall of the same shrine. A record of the Chōḷa king Rājakēsarivarman in his ninth year. Gift of ninety sheep for a lamp to the god Tirukkaṟṟaḷi-Mahādēva in the temple of Tirruttaṇḍīśvaram at Veḷichchēri, by one of the managing members of that village.

1141. 313 *of* 1911.—(Tamil.) On the same wall. A record of the Chōḷa king Tribhuvanachakravartin Rājarājadēva in his twenty-second year. Gift of money for a lamp to the image of Nāyanār-Tiruchchiṟṟambalamuḍaiyār, set up in the temple of Tiruttaṇḍīśvaramuḍaiyār-Nāyanār, by a native of Veḷichchēri *alias* Jīnachintāmaṇichaturvēdimaṅgalam.

1142. 314 *of* 1911.—(Tamil.) On the same wall. A record of the Pallava king Peṙñjiṅgadēva, in his eighteenth year. Gift of money for a lamp to the same temple at Veḷichcheri *alias* Jīnachintāmaṇichaturvēdimaṅgalam, by a native of Kīranguḍi in Chōḷamaṇḍalam.

1143. 315 *of* 1911.—(Tamil.) On the same wall. Records in the fifth year of the Chōḷa king Maduraikoṇḍa Rājakēsarivarman gift of ninety sheep for a lamp to the temple of Tirudaṇḍīśvaradēva at Veḷichchēri in Kōttūr-nāḍu of Puliyūr-kōṭṭam, by one of the managing members of the village. For the probable identity of the king see No. 1134 above.

1144. 316 *of* 1911.—(Tamil.) On the south wall of the Śelliyamman temple in the same village. Records in the tenth year of Pārthivēndrādhipativarmaṅ gift of land for offerings to the temple of *Saptamātrikkaḷ*, by Tiruvetpūruḍaiyān Ḍēvaḍigaḷ, a native of Tiruvetpūr in Malla-nāḍu a subdivision of Śōḷa-nāḍu.

1145. 317 *of* 1911.—(Tamil.) On the same wall. An incomplete record of the Chōḷa king Parakēsarivarman, dated in his fourth year. Records gift of land for a lamp and offerings to the temple of Kāḷa-Bhaṭāri at Veḷichchēri in Puliyūr-kōṭṭam by the assembly of that village.

TIRUVALLŪR TALUK.

Kachchuri.

1146. A C.P. grant of Veṅkaṭapati I (1586—1614) of the last Vijayanagara dynasty, dated on the twelfth day of the bright half of Āshāḍha in Ś. 1526 (A.D. 1604), Krōdhin, saying that the king gave a number of Brahmans the village of Kachchūri *alias* Veṅgalāmbapuram (together with some hamlets), in the Chandragirirājyam,

Ikkāṭṭukōṭṭam (i.e., Ikkāḍ in Tiruvaḷḷoor Taluk) in Kachchināḍu and Nārāyaṇavanam division. See *Ep. Rep.*, Oct. 1890, p. 3.

Kuvam.

1147. 328 *of* 1909.—(Tamil.) On the south wall of the central shrine in the Tripurāntakēśvara temple. A record of Tribhuvanachakravartin Vijayagaṇḍagōpāladēva. Records in his fifth year gift of money for a lamp. Mentions Kūvam *alias* Tyāgasamudranallūr (well known in Tamil literary traditions.)

1148. 323 of 1909.—(Tamil.) On the same wall. A record of the Chōḷa king Tribhuvanachakravartin Rājarājadēva; mentions the temple of Tiruvirkōlamuḍaiya-Nāyānar. Built in in the middle.

1149. 324 *of* 1909.—(Tamil.) On the same wall. An unfinished record of the Chōḷa king Rājakēsarivarman Tribhuvanachakravartin Kulōttuṅgachōḷadēva (I?). Contains the historical introduction beginning with *pūmēvu.*

1150. 325 *of* 1909.—(Tamil.) On the same wall. A record of the Chōḷa king Rājakēsarivarman *alias* Chakravartin Śrī-Kulōttuṅga. Chōḷadēva. Records gift of land. Quotes the twentieth year of the king. Built in, in the middle.

1151. 326 *of* 1909.—Tamil (prose and verse). On the west wall of the same shrine. Records in the forty-second year of the Chōḷa king Rājakēsarivarman *alias* Chakravartin Srī-Kulōttuṅga-Chōḷadēva gift of paddy and fishing taxes (*minpāṭṭam*) for the repair of the tank Tirubuvanamādēvipperēri at Kūvam *alias* Madhurāntakanallūr in Kānṟūrnāḍu, a subdivision of Maṇavir-kōṭṭam in Jayaṅgoṇḍa-chōḷa-maṇḍalam.

1152. 327 *of* 1909.—(Tamil.) On the same wall. Veṅkaṭapatirāya of Ānaigoṇḍi records in Bahudhānya, gift of land in Tribhuvanamādēviviḷāgam near Kūvam, to a temple the name of which is doubtful. In modern characters.

1153. 328 *of* 1909.—(Tamil.) On the north and west walls of the same shrine. A record of the Chōḷa king Parakēsarivarman *alias* Uḍaiyār Śrī-Rājēndradēva (1052—63); records in his fifth year sale of land by the assembly of Kōṭṭūr *alias* Chōḷa-vidyādhara-chaturvēdimaṅgalam to a person for 160 *kaśus* through which a feeder channel from the Tribhuvanamādēvipperiyēri at Kūvam *alias* Madhurāntakanallūr, was to pass.

1154. 329 *of* 1909.—(Tamil.) On the north wall of the same shrine. A record of the Chōḷa king Parakēsarivarman *alias* Tribhuvanachakravartin Kulōttuṅga-Chōḷadēva (III). Records in his eighth year gift of money for a lamp by a certain Kurumudi Śiṅgan Gōvindan *alias* Vānavan Mūvēndavēḷān, to the temple of Tiruvirkōlam-Uḍaiyār at Kūvam *alias* Tyāgasamudranallūr.

1155. 330 *of* 1909.—(Tamil.) On the same wall. A record of the Chōḷa king Rājakēsarivarman *alias* Chakravartin Srī-Kulōttuṅga-Chōḷadēva (I) in his forty-eighth year, recording gift of land for offerings to the shrine of Vrishabhavāhanadēva in the same temple.

1156. 331 *of* 1909.—(Tamil.) On the south wall of maṇṭapa in front of the same shrine. Records in the twenty-fourth year of Tribhuvanachakravartin Vijayagaṇḍa-gōpāladēva gift of a lamp to the temple of Tiruvirkōlam-Uḍaiyār at Kūvam *alias* Tyāgasamudra-nallūr.

1157. 332 *of* 1909.—(Tamil.) On the same wall. Mahāmaṇḍa-lēśvara-Gobbūri Obarājayyadēva-Mahārāja, provides in Ś. 1532, Sādhāraṇa, for special worship in the Mārgaḷi month, in the temple of Tiruvirkōḷīśvara. Mr. Krishna Sastri identifies the donor with his namesake of the Triplicane inscriptions and with Oba Rāya, the brother-in-law of Veṅkaṭa I, mentioned by Barrados. See *Forg. Empe.*, p. 231.

1158. 333 *of* 1909.—(Tamil.) On the same wall. Records in the sixteenth year, of Tribhuvanachakravartin Vijayagaṇḍagōpāla-dēva, gift of thirty *old kāśu* for a perpetual lamp.

1159. 334 *of* 1909.—(Tamil.) On the same wall. Records in the reign of the Chōḷa king Tribhuvanachakravartin Vīrarājendra-Chōḷadēva gift of money for a lamp by a native of Kōṭṭūr in Ambar-nāḍu, a subdivision of Chōḷamaṇḍalam. Built in, in the end.

1160. 335 *of* 1909.—(Tamil.) On the same wall. A record of Tribhuvanachakravartin Vīragaṇḍagōpāladēva; records in his fifth year gift of a lamp.

1161. 336 *of* 1909.—(Tamil.) On the same wall. Records in the fifteenth year of the Chōḷa king Tribhuvanachakravartin Kulōttuṅga-Chōḷadēva gift of twenty *kāśu* for a lamp by Kachchika-damban Taḻuvakkuḻaindān Uyyavandān *alias* Śembiyan Viḻup-paraiyan, a native of Paḻaiyanūr in Paḻaiyanūr-nāḍu, in Maṇavir-kōṭṭam.

1162. 337 *of* 1909.—(Tamil.) On the same wall. A record of the twenty-seventh year of Tribhuvanachakravartin Kōnērinmai-koṇḍān. Gift of land for festival called Kulaśēkharan-śandhi after the name of the king.

1163. 338 *of* 1909.—(Tamil.) On the same wall. Dated in the twentieth year of the Chōḷa king Rājakēsarivarman *alias* Chakra-vartin Śrī-Kulōttuṅga Chōḷadēva (i.e., 1070—1118). Records in his twentieth year sale of land to a certain Akkalibhaṭṭan in the second year of Uḍaiyār Śrī-Vīrarājēndradēva (1063—70), by the assemblies of four villages, viz., Madhurāntakanallūr in Kānṟūr-nāḍu, a subdivision of Maṇayir-kōṭṭam, Naraśiṅgamaṅgalam and two others, all of which claimed the land. This land was presented to the temple by the purchaser in the twentieth year of Chakra-vartin Kulottuṅga-Chōḷadēva. [The inscription is interesting as it discloses a clash of jurisdictions and a skilful way in which it was overcome.]

1164. 339 *of* 1909.—(Tamil.) On the same wall. Records in the twenty-eighth year of Tribhuvanachakravartin Vijayagaṇḍagōpāladēva gift of ten *paṇam* for a lamp by a native of Vaigāvūr in Ūṟṟukkāṭṭukōṭṭam.

1165. 340 *of* 1909.—(Tamil.) On the north wall of the same maṇṭapa. Built in, at the beginning. Gift of land for a garden, a lamp and offerings.

1166. 341 *of* 1909.—(Tamil.) On the same wall. Records in twenty-eighth year (of Vijayagaṇḍagōpāla?) gift of money for a lamp. Built in, at the beginning.

1167. 342 *of* 1909.—(Tamil.) On the east wall of the same maṇṭapa. A record of the Vijaynagara king Bukkarāya (II), son of Harihararāya (II). Records in Kali, 4488, Prabhava, gift of land by Prince Obaladēva-Mahārāja, the son of Bukka (II), in Tribhuvana mādēviviḷagam and in Kūvam *alias* Tyāgasamudranallūr, both of which belonged to Kāñchīpuramrājya.

1168. 343 *of* 1909.—(Tamil.) On the same wall. Records in the seventh year of the Chōḷa king Tribhuvanachakravartin Rājādhirājadēva (II). Gift of money for a lamp.

1169. 344 *of* 1909.—(Tamil.) On the same wall. Records in the sixteenth year of Sakalalōkachakravartin Rājanārāyaṇa Tirumallinātha Śambuvarāya. Gift of land for a lamp, in Tribhuvanamādēviviḷagam. Built in, at the end. See Cg. 706.

1170. 345 *of* 1909.—(Tamil.) On the same wall. A record of the Chōḷa king Tribhuvanachakravartin Kulōttuṅga-Chōḷadēva; records in his third year, gift of money for a lamp, by a native of Tiruvīḷimiḷalai.

1171. 346 *of* 1909.—(Tamil.) On the same wall. A damaged and incomplete record of the Chōḷa king Tribhuvanachakravartin Rājarājadēva, dated in his second year. Seems to provide for festivals and processions.

1172. 347 *of* 1909.—(Tamil.) On a slab set up near the temple kitchen. Records in Bahudhānya, gift of a "fund" of Rs. 80 for the sacred bath of the god by a certain Araśappa Mudaliyār. In modern characters.

1173. 348 *of* 1909.—(Telugu.) On a slab set up in a grove of trees near the same village. A mutilated record. Records gift of the grove planted by Timmanāyanivārū who was then in possession of Kūvam, for the merit of Timmappa-Nāyuḍu.

1174. 349 *of* 1909.—(Tamil.) On a slab set up in another grove of trees near the same village. Records in A.D. 1855, Ānanda, gift of the grove for maintaining a lamp in the temple of Tripurāntasvāmi.

1175. 350 *of* 1909.—(Telugu.) On a slab set up near the temple tank in the same village. Dated in the reign of Kuḍupu Sāhu of Golakomdda (Golconda) in Ś. 1592, Virōdhikrit (wrong). Records that Timmanāyanivāru (a feudatory of his) planted a grove of trees at Kūvam for the merit of Timmappa-Nāyuḍu and presented it to the temple of Tervikkōlēśvarasvāmi. See Aminabad inscription (Guṇṭūr district).

1176. 30 *of* 1912.—(Tamil.) On four slabs recently removed from a maṇṭapa and placed in the court-yard of the Tripurāntakēśvara temple. Records in Ś. 1536, Rākshasa, that it provides for the Friday worship of the goddess Payyaravalgul-Ammai, by two agents of Immaḍi-Sennama-Nāyakkar and the residents of Kūvam.

Tiruppāśūr.

According to inscriptions Tiruppāśūr belonged to Kākkaḷūr nāḍu in Īkkāṭṭukkōṭṭam named respectively after the two villages of Kākkaḷur and Īkkāḍu in Tiruvaḷḷūr taluk. The *Mack. MSS.* give a number of inscriptions in this place and I have included them in the following list:—

1177. 406 *of* 1896.—(Grantha and Tamil.) On the west wall of the central shrine of the Vāchīśvara temple. Records in the thirty-sixth year of the Chōḷa king Tribhuvanachakravartin Tribhuvanavīradēva gift of gold for a lamp by Vīranarasimhadēva *alias* Yādavarāya, a feudatory of Kulōttuṅga III and then of Rājarāja III. The present inscription mentions the gold coin of the Hoysaḷa dynasty *Bhujabalamāḍai.*

1178. 407 *of* 1896.—(Grantha.) On the north wall of the same shrine. The Chōḷa king Tammusiddhi records in Ś. 1129 (A.D. 1207) grant of the village of Kaivaṇḍūr near Tiruppāśūr to the temple. *Ep. Ind.*, VII, 126—8 where this is translated.

1179. On the northern wall of the Nāyanār temple. Records that Kāḷahasti Cheṭṭiār gave in Ś. 1454, in the reign of Achyutadēva to God Kāḷahastīśvara, whose image he established, 250 paṇams. *Ins., S. Dts.*, p. 118, No. 24.

1180. On the north pial of the temple. Records that in the tenth year of Rājarājadēva 47 *kāśu* were given to the Paṭṭamār for worship. *Ibid.*, No. 25.

1181. On the north wall of the Mahāmaṇṭapa. Records that a vassal chief of Rājarājadēva granted in his twenty-first year 32 cows for lamp and one bullock for drum to the temple. *Ibid.*, No. 26.

1182. On the back wall of the inner temple. Records that in the thirty-third year of Kulōttuṅgachōḷa the daughter of a Nārpattennāyiravan gave 30 *kāśu* for a jewel and two measures of rice daily. *Ibid.*, No. 27.

1183. On the pial near the west wall of the inner temple. Records that Kāḷiṅgarāya gave in the reign of Kulōttuṅgachōḷa 36 *kāśus* to the people of Dhāsyapuram (?) for six lamps and 42 *kāśus* to the priests of Tiruppāśur for four lamps. *Ins., S. Dts.*, No. 28.

1184. On the north pial of the inner temple. Records in the fourth year of Vīra-Rājēndrachōḷa gift of 9 *Kaḻañju* pons for ear-ring and 10 *Kaḻañju* pons for necklace to Panamalanāchchiār. *Ibid.*, No. 29.

1185. On the northern wall of the Brahma temple. Records a gift in the thirteenth year of Rājarājadēva of 10 gold *kāśus* for lamp. *Ibid.*, No. 30.

1186. On the southern wall of the same temple. Records that in K. 4473, Paritāpi, in the reign of Vīra-Kampaṇa Uḍaiyār a chief purchased a garden and granted it to the temple. *Ibid.*, No. 31.

1187. On the surrounding wall of the same temple. Records in the reign of Kulōttuṅgachōḷa gift of 5½ *Kaḻañju* of gold to the Sthānattār for a jewel to the Goddess. *Ibid.*, No. 32.

1188. On the northern surrounding wall of Tiruppāśur Uḍaiya Nāyanār. Records gift of three gold *kāśus* for a lamp in the tenth year of Kulōttuṅgachōḷa. *Ibid*, No.. 33.

1189. On the north pial of the inner temple. Records gift of five villages in the thirtieth year of Rājaśēkhara Pāṇḍyan to the deity. *Ibid.*, p. 1211, No. 34.

1190. On the eastern wall of the same. Records that Aryappa Daṇḍanāyaka gave away the duties and extra emoluments of the merchants to the temple in Ś. 1349, Plavaṅga, in the reign of Vīrapratāpadēva Mahārāya (II). *Ibid.*, No. 35. [Was the donor identical with the king's uncle Harihara III ?]

1191. On the western wall of the Gōpuram. Records that Kaṇḍappa Aiyar, prime minister of Amin (?) Raṅgappaiyar raised the rent of the village of Perumbākkam. *Ibid.*, No. 36.

1192. On the south Prākāra wall of the same temple. Records that the people of Nārāyaṇachaturvēdimaṅgalam gave some land to the deity. *Ibid.*, No. 37.

Tiruvaḷḷūr.

1193. On a stone south of the Vimānam of the Vīra-Rāghava temple. Records that in the fifth year of the reign of Kulōttuṅgachōḷa one Tiruvēṅkaṭadēvan gave to God Vīra-Rāghava one thousand *kuḻis* of land in "Talacaurecheri" for Makara Saṅkramaṇa festival. *Ins., S. Dts.*, p. 111, No. 1.

1194. In the inner eastern wall of the Vāhana-Maṇṭapam. Records that Vīra-Rāghava Śaṭhakōpa-Jeer presented to the God 133 pons for a festival on its mortgage interest, in Ś. 1552, Prajōtpatti, in the reign of Vīra-Veṅkaṭarāya (II). *Ibid.*, No. 2. The Jeer was evidently the thirteenth of the Ahobalam line who, according to the

Satsampradāyamuktāvali (1914 edn., p. 65–8), presided over the maṭha from 1630 to 1675.]

1195. On the northern surrounding wall. Records that Raghunātha Nāyakar gave in Ś. 1543, Durmati, in the reign of Rāmadēva Mahā-Rāya (1620–30) some land north of Tiruvaḷḷur. *Ins., S. Dts.*, p. 112, No. 3.

1196. On the western wall. Records that Tuppākki Krishṇanāyaka gave in Ś 1516, Manmatha, in the reign of Narasimhadēva nine shares of land out of 100 in Chinnamāmbāsamudram to the deity. *Ibid.*, No. 4.

1197. On the surrounding north wall near Garuḍa in the temple. Records that Kṛishṇappa Nāyaka settled in Ś. 1595, Vijaya, the dispute of *Saḷipavada* (?). *Ibid.*, No. 5.

1198. On the eastern wall near the Terucottanambi in the temple. Records that Aḷagappaśeṭṭi granted 2,800 *kuḷis* of land in Auvaremputti and 300 *kuḷis* of land in the village of Kākaḷūr, and erected a maṇṭapam to the God Vīra-Rāghavasvāmi, in Ś. 1542, Raudri, in the reign of Vira-Veṅkaṭapati Rāyadēva Mahārāyar (II ?). *Ibid.*, p. 113, No. 6.

1199. On the southern wall near Kanakavalli Goddess in the temple. Records that Raghupatiaiyar granted one of the share of the land in Śikkamayapuram village and a share of land in Vīra-Rāghavapuram to the God, in Ś. 1553, Āṅgirasa, in the reign of Vīra-Veṅkaṭarāyadēva Mahārāya II. *Ibid.*, No. 7.

1200. On the western wall of the inner temple Raṅgamaṇṭapam of the temple. Records that the Paṇḍārattār of the Vīra-Rāghava Pagoda granted village as free gift to the God and Brahmans in equal shares, in Manmatha. *Ibid.*, No. 8.

1201. On the south wall of the temple. Records that Prapirāja (?) granted half share of a Brahman Aghrahāram situated on the north of "Tirapasore" to the God Vīra-Rāghavaperumāḷ, in Ś. 1580, Viḷambi, in the reign of Śrī-Raṅgarāyadēva Mahārāya VI. *Ibid.*, p. 113, No. 9.

1202. On the northern and western inner wall of the "Paruyagusamalla" Maṇṭapam in the temple. Records that Narasimha Śaṭhagōpa-Jeer granted the village of Vangatsore as free gift for the offering of food to the God Vīra-Rāghavaperumāḷ, in Ś. 1559, Prabhava, in the reign of Vīra-Veṅkaṭapatirāya Dēva Mahārāya. *Ibid.*, p. 114, No. 10. See No. 1194 above, for an apparent inconsistency.

1203. On the south of Garuḍa figure in the temple. Records that Anantāḷvār placed the stones round the temple of Vīra-Rāghavasvāmi in Ś. 1481, Siddhārti. *Ibid.*, No. 11.

1204. On the southern surrounding wall of the temple. A record of Sadāśivadēva Mahārāya, in Ś. 1487, Krōdhana. *Ibid.*, No. 12.

1205. On a stone in the inner temple of Kanakavalli. Records that Pāpu Timmayyadēva Mahārāja granted the village Puttaharam as free gift for the inn of Tirunattānam, in Ś. 1487, Viśvāvasu, in the reign of Sadāśivadēva Mahārāyar. *Ins., S. Dts.*, p. 115, No. 13.

1206. On a stone on the surrounding inner temple of Kanakavalli Nāchchiyār in the village. Records that Bala-Majappayyadēva Mahārāja granted Rāvuttanallūr village as free gift to the God, in Ś. 1471, Saumya, in the reign of Sadāśivadēva Mahārāya. *Ins., S. Dts.*, No. 14.

1207. On a stone on the western inner wall of Raṅga-Maṇṭapam in the temple. A damaged grant to the God Tiruvaḷḷur Appan by Rāmachandradēva in Śubhakrit. *Ibid.*, No. 15.

1208. On a stone on the western inner wall of Raṅgamaṇṭapam of the temple. A grant by Madurāntaka chōḷa for Vāyasavutsavam and offering of food, etc., to the God and Sthānattār. *Ibid.*, No. 16.

1209. On a stone on the eastern inner wall of Vāhanamaṇṭapam of the temple. A record in Ś. 1552, Prajōtpatti. *Ibid.*, No. 17.

1210. On a stone on the western wall of the temple of Sēnamudaliyār. A record in Ś. 1552. *Ibid.*, No. 18.

1211. On a stone on the north side of wall of the spire gate in the temple of Vīra-Rāghavasvāmi. A damaged record of Raghunātha Nāyakar and Vīra-Rāghava Nāyakar, in Ś. 1542, Raudri, in the reign of Vīra-Rāmadēva Mahārāyalu (1620—30). *Ibid.*, p. 117, No. 19.

1212. On a stone on the south side of the gate of Gōpuram of the temple. A damaged grant in Ś. 1523. *Ibid.*, No. 20.

1213. In the same place. A damaged record of a grant by Vīra-Veṅkaṭarāya (II 1630–40) in Ś. 1555, Durmukki. *Ibid.*, No. 21.

1214. On a stone in the northern side of the gate. Records that in Ś. 1527, Prabhava, Vīra-Veṅkaṭadēva (II) granted land at Vīra-Rāghavapuram to the same deity. *Ibid.*, No. 22.

1215. On a stone in the western wall of the southern Prākāra. A record of Vīra-Veṅkaṭapati in Ś. 1555, Śrīmukha. *Ibid.*, No. 23.

1216. On the western wall of the Amman temple. Records that Kōnērinmaikoṇḍān granted 19 vēli of Nañjai and 11½ vēli of Puñjai lands in the village of "Calcandanatha village" to the goddess. See *Ins., S. Dts.*, p. 185, No. 7.

Vellāttukkōṭṭai (Vellutercota).

1218. On a stone in the Chōḷēśvara temple. Records that one Bharata-Pāṇḍya levied a duty of two *kāśu* on each bag of grain and four *kāśu* on each bag of salt to be paid by the local people to God Ādichandrēśvara, in the twelfth year of his reign. *Ins., S. Dts.*, p. 178, No. 1

1219. Below the above. Records that in the eighteenth year of Rāmanāthadēva the Sthānattār made some grant. Damaged. *Ins., S. Dts.*, p. 178, No. 2.

1220. Below the above. Records that in the twenty-fifth year of the reign of Pāṇḍyadēva the inhabitants of Vallam granted some *kuḷis* of land to the Brahman Pallavanāyaka Bhaṭṭa. *Ibid.*, No. 3.

1221. Below the above. Records that in the reign of Kōnērinmaikoṇḍān the local people granted to Chōḷēśvara and Goddess some land. *Ibid.*, No. 4.

1222. Below the above. Records that in the eighth year of Rāmanāthadēva the local people gave some land in Vallam to God Ādichandrēśvara. *Ibid.*, No. 5.

1223. Below the above. Records that Kōnērinmaikoṇḍān granted in his ninth year forty *vēlis* of land in Nattakkāṭṭūr to Karikālachōḷēśvara. *Ibid.*, No. 6.

1224. Below the above. A gift of land west of Māṅguḍi to the God and Goddess. *Ibid.*, No. 7.

1225. Below the above. Records that Kulaśēkharadēva granted in his twelfth year 23 *vēlis* of land west of Māṅguḍi to the same deity. *Ibid*). No. 8.

1226. Below the above. A gift of the people of Vallam for the annual festival of the deity in Āḍi. *Ibid.*, No. 9.

1227. On the downstair of the above. Records that in the reign of Sundarapāṇḍya the people of "Yarevorenad" undertook to perform the ten days' festival of Karikālachōḷēśvara, in the eighteenth year of the king. *Ibid.* p. 180, No. 10.

1228. Below the above. Records that in the eighth year of the reign of Rāmanātha the oilmongers of Vallam undertook to supply ¾ measure of oil per day for lamp to God Ādichandrēśvara. *Ibid.*, No. 11.

Vāyalūr.

1229. 362 *of* 1908.—(Tamil.) On the north wall of the central shrine in the Vyāghrapurīśvara temple. Records in Ś. 1247, Krōdhana, gift of land for offerings to the temple of Tiruppilavāyaluḍaiya-Nāyanār by Tarusi Timmaraśar, son of Rāyatariśi Bommayadēva Mahārāya who was a mahāmaṇḍalēśvara and bore the title Tribhuvanakkaṭṭāri.

1230. 363 *of* 1908.—(Tamil.) On the west and south walls of the same shrine. Records in the eighth year of the Pāṇḍya king Jaṭāvarman *alias* Tribhuvanachakravartin Sundara-Pāṇḍyadēva (I, 1251–64) who was pleased to take every country, an agreement among the villagers of Vāyalūr that they would neither purchase nor mortgage the lands belonging to the temple of Tiruppilavāyiluḍaiya-Nāyanār and three others.

1231. 364 *of* 1908.—(Tamil.) On the south wall of the same shrine. A record of the Vijayanagara king Viruppaṇa-Uḍaiyār (Virūpāksha I), son of Ariyaṇa-Uḍaiyār (Harihara II), son of Vīra-Bukkaṇa-Uḍaiyār (I) in Rudhirōdgārin. Records that the weavers at Vāyalūr *alias* Jananāthanallūr in Paṭṭiṇa-nāḍu, a subdivision of Śembūr-kōṭṭam in Jayaṅgoṇḍachōḷa-maṇḍalam, were taxed three *paṇam* on each loom.

1232. 365 *of* 1908.—(Tamil.) On a portion of the east wall of a partially demolished maṇṭapa in the same temple. A much-damaged record of the Vijayanagara king Dēvarāya Uḍaiyār (II), son of Vīra-Vijayarāya-Uḍaiyār, dated Kīlaka. Seems to register a gift of land in the village of Ārambākkam in Tirukkaḷukkunṟap-paṟṟu. Mentions Jananāthanallūr *alias* Vāyalūr in Ponnūrnāḍu.

1233. 366 *of* 1908.—(Tamil.) On a slab built into the floor in the gōpura of the same temple. Records in the twelfth year of the Chōḷa king Rājarājakēsarivarman (I) "who destroyed the ships at Śālai," gift of land for a lamp to the temple of Mahādēva. Mentions Mōndūr-nāḍu, a subdivision of Āmūrkōṭṭam.

1234. 367 *of* 1908.—(Tamil.) On some detached stones built into the same gōpura. A record of the Rāshṭrakūṭa king Kaṇṇara-dēva (Krishṇa III) "who took Kachchi (Conjeeveram) and Tañjai (Tanjavur)." Seems to record in his twenty-second year a sale of land.

1235. 368 *of* 1908.—(Pallava-Grantha.) On a pillar in the same gōpura. A record of the Pallava king Rājasimha; gives a long list of the kings of the Pallava dynasty who preceded Rājasimha (Narasimhavarman II). The record is of the greatest value in the construction of the Pallava genealogy. See Prof. Dubreuil's *Pallavas*, pp. 18–20.

Supplement.

286. 38 *of* 1888.—(See p. 357.) In his *Pallavas* published in 1917, Prof. Dubreuil has deciphered part of this epigraph. It seems to be a panegyric on the literary and musical talents of Mahēndra-varman I. He points out that the cave was, to judge from its architectural features, excavated in the time of Mahēndravarman I and that this is confirmed by the expression *Mattavilāsādipadam-prahasana* found in the inscription. Mattavilāsa was a title of Mahēndravarman and a *prahasana* in Sanskrit bearing this name has been discovered by Pandit Ganapati Sastri of Travancore. The present epigraph is surmised by Prof. Dubreuil to refer to *Svaras* and *Varṇas*, and he believes that the Kuḍumiyāmalai inscription on music was perhaps due to the same king. See his *Pallavas*, pp. 37–9, and *Ep. Ind.*, XII, pp. 226–37.

CHITTOOR DISTRICT

CHANDRAGIRI TALUK.

Chandragiri.

This important and historic place was founded, according to tradition, by a Yādava king named Immaḍi Narasimha in A.D. 1000, but epigraphical finds in it belong only to the later periods of S. Ind. history. One of its inscriptions mentions seventy-four temples in it most of which seem to have been destroyed by the Muhammadans. For a brief description of the ruins of the place, Hindu and Jain, *See Ep. Rep.*, 1904, p. 5. A number of inscriptions, it will be seen, are in Tamil. In the Vijayanagar period it was in Vaikuṇṭhavaḷanāḍu, a subdivision of Tiruvēṅgaḍakkōṭṭam.

1. 243 *of* 1904.—(Tamil.) On the east wall of the central shrine in the ruined temple near the palace. Mentions in Ś. 1383, Khara (wrong), the temple of Sōmēśvaramuḍaiya Nāyinār.

2. 244 *of* 1904.—(Tamil.) On another shrine in the same temple. A damaged record of the Vijayanagara king Vīrapratāpa-Vīra-Achyutayadēva-Mahārāya in Ś. 1459, Hēviḷambi. Records a gift by Achyutarāya-Nāyaka, governor of Gingee.

3. 245 *of* 1904.—(Tamil.) On the south wall of the maṇṭapa in front of the temple called Maṇḍu-Giḍḍaṅgi in the same village. Records in Vikrama, gifts to the temples of Virūpāksha-Nāyinār and Kāḷikādēvi at Chandragiri.

4. 246 *of* 1904.—(Tamil.) On the east wall of the Kōdaṇḍarāmasvāmin temple in the same village. A record of the Vijayanagara king Vīrapratāpa-Vīra-Sadāśivadēva-Mahārāya in Ś. 1469, Plavaṅga. Mentions the temple of Raghunātha. Records a gift of land for the merit of the king and of Rāmarājayya.

Tiruchchānūr.

(Popularly known as Chiratānūr.) Earlier inscriptions call it Tiruchchoginūr and later ones Tiruchchuganūr, a fact which made Venkayya surmise that the connection of the place with Śuka is a later myth. Venkayya believes that an ancient temple of the place which was recently destroyed was called Iḷangōyil; that it was "apparently built as an accompaniment of the temple at Tirupati" and that the deity of the latter was therefore originally Śiva. Every link in this argument however is open to question.

5. 259 *of* 1904.—(Tamil.) On a detached stone lying in the temple. A fragment of record of the Chōḷa king Madiraikoṇḍa

Parakēsarivarman (Parāntaka I), the date of which is lost. Mentions Nāmmāḷvāraḍigaḷ and Putūruḍaiyān, the king's officers. The inscription is of singular value as it *proves* that Nammāḷvār was already a well-known saint about A.D. 910.

6. 260 *of* 1904.—(Tamil.) On the west base of the vāhana maṇṭapa in front of the temple. A record in the twenty-ninth year of the Chōḷa king Madiraikoṇḍa-Parakēsarivarman (Parāntaka I). Records gift of a lamp apparently by a native of Koduṅgōḷūr in Malai-nāḍu (i.e., Cranganore in Cochin). The village is called Tiruchchōgunūr twice. See Cg. 197.

7. 261 *of* 1904.—(Tamil.) On a detached stone lying outside the prākāra of the same temple. A fragment of record of the Chōḷa king Parakēsarivarman *alias* Rājēndra-Chōḷadēva (I, 1011—43), the date of which is lost.

8. 262 *of* 1904.—(Tamil.) On a detached stone built into the floor at the entrance into the same temple. A record in the fifty-first year of "the Gaṅga-Pallava king" Vijaya-Dantivikramarāja. Records gift of a lamp by Ulaga-Perumānār to the shrine of Tiruviḷangōil-Perumānaḍigaḷ in Tiruchchoginūr in Kuḍavūrnāḍu, a subdivision of Tiruvēṅgaḍa-kōṭṭam.

9. 263 *of* 1904.—(Tamil.) On a detached stone built into the outer prākāra of the same temple. A fragmentary record of the thirty-second year of the Chōḷa king Madiraikoṇḍa-Parakēsarivarman (905—47).

Tirumalai (Tirupati).

9-A. 53 *of* 1889.—(Telugu.) Second prākāra, south wall. A record of Krishṇarāya in Ś. 1436, expired, Bhava. Mentions Kṛishṇarāya's attack on Pratāparudra Gajapati, his pursuing him as far as Koṇḍavīḍu and his capture of Udayagiri.

9-B. 54 *of* 1889.—(Kanarese.) Second prākāra, south wall. A record of Kṛishṇarāya in Ś. 1436, expired, Bhava.

9-C. 55 *of* 1889.—(Tamil.) Second prākāra, south wall. A record of Kṛishṇarāya in Ś. 1436, expired, Bhava.

9-D. 56 *of* 1889.—(Kanarese.) Second prākāra, east wall, left of entrance. A record of Kṛishṇarāya in Ś. 1436, Bhava.

9-E. 57 *of* 1889.—(Tamil.) Second prākāra, east wall, left of entrance. A record of Timmarāja, son of Mallayadēva in Ś. 1403, expired, Plava.

9-F. 58 *of* 1889.—(Tamil.) Second prākāra, east wall, left of entrance. A record in the eighth year of Tribhuvanachakravartin Tiruvēṅgaḍaṇātha Yādavarāya.

9-G. 59 *of* 1889.—(Tamil and Grantha.) Second prākāra, east wall, right of entrance. A record of Narasimhadēva in Ś. 1397, expired, Manmatha.

9-H. 60 *of* 1889.—(Tamil.) First prākāra, north wall. A record of Ahōbalarāja Kampayadēva-mahārāja in Ś. 1381, expired, Bahudhānya.

9-I. 61 *of* 1889.—(Tamil.) First prākāra, north wall. A record in the sixteenth year of Kō-Vīra-Rājarājavīrēndravarman. Dr. Hultzsch calls this and the next three inscriptions as the most curious in the collection and considers them to be modern and faulty copies of Chōḷa inscriptions made in the time of Vīra Narasimhadēva who rebuilt the temple. The temple thus was in existence even in the days of Rājarāja and Rajēndrachōḷa. *Ep. Rep.*, Apr. 1889, p. 1.

9-J. 62 *of* 1889.—(Tamil.) First prākāra, north wall. A record in the fourteenth year of Kō-Paratra-Mahēndravarman (?).

9-K. 63 *of* 1889.—(Tamil.) First prākāra, north wall. A record in the fourteenth year of Kō-Paratravarman (?).

9-L. 64 *of* 1889—(Tamil.) First prākāra, north wall. A record in the seventh year of Kō-Parakēsarivarman *alias* Rājēndra-Śōḻadēva (I, 1011—43).

9-M. 65 *of* 1889.—(Telugu.) First prākāra, north wall. A record of Kṛishṇarāya in Ś. 1434, expired, Āṅgirasa. Gift by Chimnāji Amma, queen of Kṛishṇarāya.

9-N. 66 *of* 1889.—(Telugu.) First prākāra, north wall. A record of Kṛishṇarāya in Ś. 1434, expired, Āṅgirasa. Gift by Tirumalamma, the queen of Kṛishṇarāya. See By. 323.

9-O. 67 *of* 1889.—(Tamil.) First prākāra, west wall. A record of Narasimharāja-Uḍaiyār in Ś. 1393, expired, Khara.

9-P. 68 *of* 1889.—(Tamil and Grantha.) A record in the first prākāra, south wall. No details given.

9-Q. 69 *of* 1889.—(Tamil.) First prākāra, south wall. A record of Narasimharāja-Uḍaiyār in Ś. 1384, expired, Chitrabhānu.

9-R. 70 *of* 1889.—(Tamil and Grantha.) Left of entrance into the first prākāra. A record of Tribhuvanachakravartin Sundara-Pāṇḍyadēva.

9-S. 71 *of* 1889.—(Tamil.) Left of entrance into the first prākāra. A record of Tribhuvanachakravartin Srī-Vīra-Narasimhadēvā Yādavarāya.

9-T. 72 *of* 1889.—(Tamil.) Right of entrance into the first prākāra, inside. A record in the second year of Sundara-Pāṇḍyadēva.

9-U. 73 *of* 1889.—(Grantha.) Right of entrance into the first prākāra, outside. No details given.

9-V. 74 *of* 1889.—(Tamil.) On a stone in front of a house in the north main street. A record of Kṛishṇarāya in Ś. 1445, expired, Svabhānu. [The Mādhva teacher Vyasatīrtha, the founder of the

Vyāsarāya Maṭha, figures here. Vyāsa Tīrtha was the disciple of Brahmaṇya Tīrtha and author of the *Chandrikā*, the *Nyāyāmritam*, the *Tarkatāṇḍava*, the *Bhēdōjjivana*, etc. His birth place was Bennūr in Mysore and his *brindāvana* is one of the nine Brindāvanas of Mādhva teachers in Anagundi estate. His disciple was the celebrated Vijayēndratīrtha, the contemporary and rival of Appaiya Dīkshita. See By. 363-A for other details.]

10. 249 *of* 1904.—(Tamil.) On the south wall of the first prākāra of the Veṅkaṭēśa-Perumāḷ temple. A record of the Śāluva king Timmarājadēva-Mahārāja-Uḍaiyār, son of Guṇḍurāja-Uḍaiyār in Ś. 1385, Subhānu. Records gift of the merit of Naraśiṅgarāja-Uḍaiyār.

11. 250 *of* 1904.—(Tamil.) On the same wall. A record of the Śāḷuva king Naraśiṅgayyadēva-Mahārāja-Uḍaiyār (the usurper), son of Guṇḍayyadēva-Mahārāja-Uḍaiyār in Ś. 1389, Sarvajit. Records gift of five villages to the temple.

12. 251 *of* 1904.—(Tamil and Telugu.) On the west wall of the same prākāra. A record of the Śāḷuva chief Parvatarāja, son of Sāḷuvarāja in Ś. 1387, Pārthiva. Records gift for offerings.

13. 252 *of* 1904.—(Tamil and Telugu.) On the north wall of the same prākāra. A record of the Sāḷuva chief Sirrumallaiyadēva-Mahārāja, son of Malagaṅgayadēva-Mahārāja, in Ś. 1372, Pramōda. Records gift of 1,200 *paṇam*. These chiefs belonged evidently to a collateral line of the Sāḷuvas. So also perhaps the chief mentioned in No. 15 below.

14. 253 *of* 1904.—(Tamil.) On the same wall. A record of the Śāḷuva king Naraśiṅgadēva-Mahārāja (the usurper), son of Guṇḍayadēva-Mahārāja in Ś. 1378, Dhātri. Records gift of the village of Alipuram in Vaikuṇḍa-Vaḷanāḍu (a subdivision of Chandragiri-rājya).

15. 254 *of* 1904.—(Tamil.) On the same wall. A record of the Śāḷuva king Erra-Kampayadēva-Mahārāja in Ś. 1368, Kshaya. Records gift of 1,000 *paṇam*. See note to No. 13 above.

16. 255 *of* 1904.—(Tamil.) On the same wall. A record of Tammayyadēva-Mahārāja, son of the Mahāmaṇḍalēśvara Hōsabirudaragaṇḍa-Kaṇṭamarāja-Vallapparayar in Ś. 1389, Sarvajit. Refers to the digging of a channel at the village of Maniyakkōnpaṭṭu. At the end of the inscription the king is said to have belonged to the family of Pina-Mādhavavarman of Bezvāḍa of the solar race. [A certain Tammarāya, grandson of Mādhavavarman and son of Kaṇṭamarāju Valabhayya is referred to in 208 and 209 of 1892 at Udayagiri, Nellore district.]

17. 256 *of* 1904.—(Tamil.) On a stone built into the floor of the first circuit of the same temple. Fragment of a record of a Chōḷa king.

18. 257 *of* 1904.—(Tamil.) On a slab set up in the western street in the same village. A record of Śiru-Tirumalai-rāja in Plava. Records sale of land.

19. 258 *of* 1904.—(Tamil.) On a slab set up in a garden near the Āḷvārcheruvu tank in the same village. Records in Ś. 1326, Tāraṇa, the building of the Lakshmi-Narasimha-maṇṭapa and the laying out of a flower garden.

19-A. 711 *of* 1904.—(Tamil.) On the south wall of the first circuit (called Mukkōṭi-ēkādaśi-pradakshiṇa) in the Vēṅkaṭēśa-Perumāḷ temple in the same place. A fragmentary record of Tribhuvanachakravartin Vijaya-Gaṇḍagōpāladēva, the date of which is lost. Records gift of money for a lamp. Another fragment belonging to the same king is built into the west wall.

19-B. 712 *of* 1904.—(Grantha and Tamil.) On the same wall. A fragment of record of the Pāṇḍya king Jaṭāvarman Sundara-Pāṇḍya (I ?), the date of which is lost. Contains a portion of the Sanskrit introduction published in *Ind. Antq.*, Vol. XXI, p. 121.

19-C. 713 *of* 1904.—(Tamil.) On the north wall of the same circuit. A fragment of record of the Chōḷa king Kulōttuṅga I. Contains a small portion of the introduction. On the west wall is another fragment in which the name Uḍaiyār Srī-Vīrarājēndra-dēva (I ?) occurs.

19-D. 714 *of* 1904.—(Tamil.) On the same wall. A fragment of record of Yādavarāja Vīra-Naraśiṅgadēva, the date of which is indistinct. Mentions Nellūr *alias* Vikramasimhapura.

20. 567 *of* 1912.—(Tamil.) On a tier of the south wall of the central shrine in the Śrīnivāsa-Perumāḷ temple. Records in Ś. 1453, Khara, Mīna, śu. di. 5, Thursday, Aśvati, gift of money (3,000 *paṇam*) for offerings, to the temple of Tiruvēṅgaḍam-Uḍaiyān. Refers also to an earlier grant by Kṛishṇarāya-Mahārāya. [For a description of the statues of Kṛishṇa Rāya and his queens Chinnā Dēvi and Tirumalādēvi, and Veṅkaṭa I, see *Ep. Rep.*, 1904, pp. 5-6.]

21. 568 *of* 1912.—(Telugu.) On one hundred and fifty plates of copper preserved in the Tallapākamvāri-koṭṭu within the first circuit of the same temple. Register songs of various Rāgas and Tāḷas composed in praise of Vēṅkaṭēśa, by a member of the Taḷḷapākam family.

CHITTOOR TALUK.

Kānippākkam.

22. 57 *of* 1907.—(Tamil.) On the east wall of the central shrine in the Maṇikaṇṭhēśvara temple. A record of the Chōḷa king Vīrarājēndra-Chōḷadēva (II, i.e., Kulōttuṅga III, 1178—86 in Ś. 1108 and in his eighth year. Built in in the middle. Records gift of a lamp by Iḷaraiyan Sagararasan Śīyagaṅgan. [Śiyagaṅga was the patron of the Tamil Grammarian Pavaṇandi, the author of the *Nannūl*. See No. 64 below and N.A. 343.]

23. 58 *of* 1907.—(Tamil.) On the south wall of the same shrine. A record in the nineteenth year of the Pāṇḍya king Sundara-Pāṇḍyadeva. Records gift of land by the people of Tuynāḍu. Refers to the shrines of Pārthivīśvara and Maṇivaṇīśvara at Kāvanippākkam.

24. 59 *of* 1907.—(Tamil.) On the same wall. Remission of taxes by Śiraimīṭṭa-Perumāḷ *alias* Śīyagaṅgar. The temple is called Maṇivaṇḍīśvaramuḍaiyār at Kāvaṇippākkam.

25. 60 *of* 1907.—(Tamil.) On the north wall of the same shrine. An incomplete record of the Chōḷa king Kulōttuṅga-Chōḷadēva (III), in Ś. 1102 and in his twelfth year. Mentions Śūranāyakan *alias* Śīyagaṅgan of the Gaṅga family who was the lord of Kuvalālapura.

Kaṭṭamachchi near *Chittoor.*

26. 61 *of* 1907.—(Tamil.) On a rock in the garden known as Navābu-tōpu. A record in the thirty-first year of the Chōḷa king Madiraikoṇḍa Parakēsarivarman (Parāntaka I). Records sale of land by the villagers of Kīḷaikkaṭṭamachchi in Tuynāḍu.

Gōpālapuram.

27. 248 *of* 1904.—(Telugu.) On a stone near an image of Āñjanēya. A damaged record.

Maṅgāpuram.

28. 247 *of* 1904.—(Telugu.) At the entrance into the central shrine of the Kalyāṇa-Veṅkaṭēśvara temple. Refers in Ś. 1462, Śārvarin, to the setting up of images of certain Vaishṇava Āḷvārs and āchāryas at Alamēlumaṅgāpuram.

Mogili.

29. 587 *of* 1906.—(Tamil.) On a slab set up within the Mogilīśvara temple. A record in the sixth year of the Chōḷa king Rājarājadēva. The temple is called Tirumāṇiyūral-Nāyanār at Muḷibil.

30. 588 *of* 1906.—(Tamil.) On a slab set up in the courtyard of the same temple. A damaged record of the Vijayanagara king Vīra-Harihararāya.

Pūtaḷapaṭṭu.

31. 53 *of* 1907.—(Tamil.) On the north wall of the maṇṭapa in the Śiva temple. A record of the Vijayanagara king Vīrapratāpa Kṛishṇayyadēva-Mahārāya in Ś. 1438 expired, Īśvara. The temple seems to be called Bhīmēśvaramuḍaiya-Nāyinār and the village Puttalaippaṭṭu; Paḷuvūr-kōṭṭam in Toṇḍai-maṇḍalam is also mentioned.

32. 54 *of* 1907.—(Tamil.) On the south wall of the central shrine in the Varadarāja-Perumāḷ temple in the same village. A damaged record of the Vijayanagara king Vīra-Sadāśivadēva-Mahārāya, in Ś. 1471 expired, Saumya.

33. 55 *of* 1907.—(Tamil.) On the same wall. A mutilated record of the Vijayanagara king Vīra-Sadāśivadēva Mahārāya in Ś. 1467 expired, Viśvāvasu. The village is called Pūtaḷaippaṭṭu.

34. 56 *of* 1907.—(Tamil.) On the south wall of the first prākāra of the same temple. A fragmentary record, much damaged.

Raṅgampēṭṭai.

35. 63 *of* 1907.—(Tamil.) On a stone lying in a field near the place. A damaged record of the Vijayanagara king Vīra-Sadāśivadēva-Mahārāya in Ś. 1490 expired, Prabhava. Mentions Vēlūr Nalla-Bommu Nāyaka. See N.A. 204.

Tēnēpaḷḷi.

36. 64 *of* 1907.—(Tamil.) On the south wall of the Dakshiṇāmūrti shrine in the ruined Śiva temple. A damaged record of the Vijayanagara king Vīrapratāpa-Achyutayyadēva-Mahārāya in Ś. 1462 expired, Śārvari. Mentions the shrine of Mallikārjuna at Tēniyappaḷḷi.

Timmareḍḍipaḷḷi.

37. 62 *of* 1907.—(Telugu.) On a stone set up on the bund of the tank. Mentions in Khara the mahāmaṇḍalēśvara Tirumala-rājayya.

KĀḶAHASTI TALUK.

Guḍimallam.

38. 204 *of* 1903.—(Tamil.) On the south wall of the central shrine in the Paraśurāmēśvara temple. A record in the fifteenth year of the Chōḷa king Rājarājadēva. Mentions the temple of Paraśurāmīśuramuḍaiya-Nāyanār. [The Rājarāja of this and the following epigraphs is evidently the third of that name.]

39. 205 *of* 1903.—(Tamil.) On the same wall. A record in the fifteenth year of the Chōḷa king Rājarājadēva. Records gift of gold for a lamp.

40. 206 *of* 1903.—(Tamil.) On the west wall of the central shrine in the Paraśurāmēśvara temple. A record in the fifteenth year of the Chōḷa king Rājarājadēva. Records gift of gold and paddy.

41. 207 *of* 1903.—(Tamil.) On the same wall. A record in the thirteenth year of the Chōḷa king Tribhuvanachakravartin Rājarājadēva. Records gift of gold for a lamp.

42. 208 *of* 1903.—(Tamil.) On the same wall. A record in the twenty-seventh year of the Chōḷa king Tribhuvanachakravartin Rājarājadēva. Records gift of gold for a lamp.

43. 209 *of* 1903.—(Tamil.) On the north wall of the same shrine. A record in the fifteenth year of the Chōḷa king Rājarājadēva. Records gift of gold for a lamp.

44. 210 *of* 1903.—(Tamil.) On the south base of the same shrine. A record in the ninth year of the Chōḷa king Tribhuvanachakravartin Rājarājadēva. Records gift of land by Chāḷukya-Nārāyaṇa-Yādavarāya *alias* Ghaṭṭiyadēva. See Nos. 101, 102, 111 and 120.

45. 211 *of* 1903.—(Tamil.) On the same base. A record in the fifth year of the Chōḷa king Tribhuvanachakravartin Rājarājadēva (III). Records gift of land.

46. 212 *of* 1903.—(Tamil.) On the west base of the same shrine. A record in the ninth year of the Chōḷa king Parakēsarivarman *alias* Chakravartin Vikrama-Chōḷadēva (1118—35). Records the building of the temple for the merit of Nāraṇadēva *alias* Kulōttuṅga-Chōḷa-Karupparuḍaiyān by his son.

47. 213 *of* 1903.—(Tamil.) On the north base of the same shrine. An incomplete record in the eighth year of the Chōḷa king Vikrama-Chōḷadēva (1118—35). Refers to the setting up of an image of Chaṇḍēśvara.

48. 214 *of* 1903.—(Tamil.) On the south wall of the maṇṭapa in front of the same shrine. A record in the nineteenth year of the Chōḷa king Rājarājadēva. Records gift of cows for a lamp. Records that a certain Karkaṭarāya built a well for the sacred bath.

49. 215 *of* 1903.—(Tamil.) On the west wall of the same maṇṭapa. Records in Ś. 1208, an order of Vīra-Narasimhadēva that two tanks shall be fed by a certain channel. [This chief is apparently not the same as Vīra Narasimha Yādava Rāya. He seems to be two generations later.]

50. 216 *of* 1903.—(Tamil.) On the north wall of the same maṇṭapa. A record in the twentieth year of the Chōḷa king Rājarājadēva. Records gift of gold for two lamps.

51. 217 *of* 1903.—(Tamil.) On the same wall. A record of the Chōḷa king Rājarājadēva, the date of which is doubtful. Records gift of gold for a lamp.

52. 218 *of* 1903.—(Tamil.) On the south base of the same maṇṭapa. A record in the tenth year of the Chōḷa king Tribhuvanachakravartin Rājarājadēva (III?). Records gift of a lamp.

53. 219 *of* 1903.—(Tamil.) On the same base. A record in the fourteenth year of the Chōḷa king Rājarājadēva (III?). Records gift of a lamp by an officer of Yādavarāya. See No. 44 above.

54. 220 *of* 1903.—(Tamil.) On the north base of the same maṇṭapa. A record in the second year of the Chōḷa king Rājarāja-dēva (III ?). Records gift of land.

55. 221 *of* 1903.—(Tamil.) On the same base. A record in the sixteenth year of the Chōḷa king Tribhuvanachakravartin Rāja-rājadēva (III). Records gift of a lamp by Aḍigaímān, an officer of Yādavarāya. [For an Aḍigaimān of Kūḍalūr in the reign of Kulōttuṅga III, see S.A. 946. They were probably the same.]

56. 222 *of* 1903.—(Tamil.) On a slab set up in front of the same shrine. A record in the fourth year of the Chōḷa king Rajakēsarivarman. Records a gift of land for offerings, etc., to an image set up by Madurāntakan Gaṇḍarāditta̱r [i.e., evidently Gaṇḍarāditta, son of Madurāntaka. Venkayya believes that the Tiruvallam inscription (*S.I.I.*, III, No. 49) might refer to the same chief].

57. 223 *of* 1903.—(Tamil.) On a stone lying in front of the entrance into the same shrine. A record of the Bāṇa king Vijayā-ditya Mahābali-Bāṇarāya, son of Bāṇa Vidyādhara and Mahādevi Aḍigaḷ in Ś. 820. Records gift of gold (30 kaḷanju) for a lamp and for offerings. The assembly received the amount, undertaking to pay interest. See *Ep. Ind.*, Vol. XI, pp. 227–8. [Vijayāditya's reign ended with his conquest by Parāntaka I, 905—47.]

58. 224 *of* 1903.—(Tamil.) On six detached stones lying in front of the same shrine. A record of the Bāṇa king Vijayāditya Bāṇarāya in Ś. 827. Records gift of gold (20 *kaḷañju*) for a lamp, by Kaḍigai Tāḷi, the headman of Vīramaṅgalam. The interest on this gold was 4 *kaḷañjus* annually at the rate of 4 *Man-jāḍis* for each *kaḷañju*. This would purchase 180 *Nāḻis* of ghee at the rate of 45 for a kaḷañju. This was to be given by the assembly which received the money at the rate of 1 *uṛi* per day. See *Ep. Ind.*, Vol. XI, pp. 228–9. See also note to the previous epigraph.

59. 225 *of* 1903.—(Tamil.) On the same stones. A damaged record in the thirty-second year of the Chōḷa king Madiraikoṇḍa-Parakēsarivarman (Parāntaka I).

60. 226 *of* 1903.—(Tamil.) On a stone set up near the well in the same temple. A record in the forty-ninth year of the "Gaṅga-Pallava" king Vijaya-Dantivikramavarman. Records gift of land while Vijayāditya-Mahāvali-Bāṇarāya was ruling the earth, by the kiḻār (headman) of Kaliyamaṅgalam, one of the members of the village committee, for digging pits in this and depositing the silt on certain local bund. See *Ep. Ind.*, Vol. XI, pp. 225–6. Also Ct. 8 above where it is shown that Dantivarman ruled for fifty-one years. [The Vijayāditya here mentioned is the grandfather of his name-sake in the previous two epigraphs.]

61. 227 *of* 1903.—(Tamil.) On the same stone. A damaged record of the Chōḷa king Rājarājadēva, the date of which is doubtful.

62. 228 *of* 1903.—(Tamil.) On a stone lying near the same well. A mutilated record in the twenty-fourth year of "the Gaṅga-Pallava" king Nripatuṅga (grandson of Dantivarman referred to in No. 60). Records a grant made while Vāṇavidyādhara Mahābali-Vāṇarāyar who was governing the country to the west of the Telugu road. See Tiruvállam inscription *S.I.I.*, III, No. 42 and *Ep. Ind.*, Vol. XI, pp. 226–7.

63. 229 *of* 1903.—(Tamil.) On a second stone lying near the well in the Paraśurāmēśvara temple in the same village. A record in the twenty-third year of the Pallava king Nandipōttaraiyar. Records a gift of land made while Vikramāditya-Māvalivāṇarāyar was governing the country to the west of the Telugu road, by Muḷḷūr Kiḻār, one of the members of the committee administering the village. The land was purchased by the donor from another member of the same committee. The assembly ordered certain oil mills to be established here for regularly supplying oil to the lamp. See *Ep. Ind.*, Vol. XI, pp. 224–225, where Venkayya edits the inscription. [He points out that, according to Mr. Gopinatha Rao, the Vikramāditya of this epigraph is the same as the contemporary of Nandivarman III, but that this is palæographically unsound.]

Kāḷahasti.

In the time of Rājarāja I it came to be called Mummuḍichchōḷa-puram, which it retained till the middle of the sixteenth century. The local temple existed in his reign while it was renovated by Kulōttuṅga III. The legends and antiquities of the place are summarised in *Ep. Rep.*, 1893, p. 2.

64. 195 *of* 1892.—(Tamil.) On the east wall of the second prākāra of the Kāḷahastīśvara temple. A record in the third year of the Chōḷa king Tribhuvanachakravartin Kulōttuṅga-Chōḷadēva (III). Records a grant by a daughter of the Gaṅga king Śīyagaṅga of Kuvalālapura (Kolar). See N.A. 343 where this chief is called Amarābharaṇa. The inscription is of value in literary history as Pavaṇandi, the author of *Nannūl*, was in this chief's court. See No. 22 above.

65. 196 *of* 1892.—(Tamil.) On the east wall of the second prākāra of the same temple. A record in the tenth year of the Chōḷa king Rājarājadēva (III). Records gift by a queen of Yādava-rāya.

66. 197 *of* 1892.—(Tamil.) On the east wall of the second prākāra of the same temple. A record in the fifteenth year of the Chōḷa king Chakravartin Kulōttuṅga-Chōḷadēva (III). Records gift by Vīra-Rākshasa-Yādavarāja.

67. 198 *of* 1892.—(Tamil.) On the north wall of the second prākāra of the same temple. A record in the nineteenth year of the Chōḷa Tribhuvanachakravartin Kulōttuṅga-Chōḷadēva (III).

Records gift by a queen of Madhurāntaka-Pottappi-Chōḷa. [Was he Errasiddha, the son of Bēṭa I or Vijaya Gaṇḍagōpāla, as N.A. 659 says?]

68. 199 *of* 1892.—(Tamil.) On the wall of the kitchen of the same temple. A record in the twenty-eighth year of the Chōḷa king Rājarājadēva. Records gift by Kāmarasan, a descendant of the Pallava race.

69. 200 *of* 1892.—(Tamil.) On the wall of the kitchen of the same temple. A record in the eighth year of the Chōḷa king Rājarājadēva (III). Records gift by Vīra-Narasimhadēva *alias* Yādavarāya.

70. 201 *of* 1892.—(Sanskrit.) On a stone in front of the Maṇikaṇṭhēśvara temple in the same place. A record of the Kākatiya king Gaṇapati. Endowment for offerings by his minister Sāmanta Bhōja. See *Ind. Antq.*, XXI, p. 197, where Dr. Hultzsch edits a Conjeeveram inscription referring to this officer. See Cg. 341.

71. 202 *of* 1892.—(Sanskrit.) Right of the entrance to the gōpura of the same temple. Appears to allude to the devotee Kaṇṇappa.

72. 276 *of* 1904.—(Tamil.) On the east wall of the central shrine in the Kāḷahastīśvara temple in the same place. A record in the twelfth year of the Chōḷa king Parakēsarivarman *alias* Rājēndra-Chōḷadēva (I). Records gift of money.

73. 277 *of* 1904.—(Tamil.) On the same wall. A record of the Chōḷā king Parakēsarivarman *alias* Uḍaiyār śrī-Rājēndra Chōḷa (I), the date of which is lost. Records gift of a lamp.

74. 278 *of* 1904.—(Tamil.) On the same wall. An incomplete record of the Chōḷa king Rājakēsarivarman *alias* Uḍaiyār śrī-Rājādhirājadēva. Stops with the name of the king.

75. 279 *of* 1904.—(Tamil.) On the same wall. An incomplete and damaged record of the Chōḷa king Parakēsarivarman *alias* Uḍaiyār śrī-Rājēndra-Chōḷadēva (I, 1011—43), in his twenty-first year.

76. 280 *of* 1904.—(Tamil.) On the same wall. A record in the eighteenth year of the Chōḷa king Parakēsarivarman *alias* Uḍaiyār śri-Rājēndra-Chōḷadēva (I, 1011—43). Records gift of 32 cows for a lamp. Mentions Paiyyūr-Iḷaṅgōṭṭam and its subdivision Vēṅgaḷanāḍu.

77. 281 *of* 1904.—(Tamil.) On the same wall. A record of the Chōḷa king Parakēsarivarman *alias* Uḍaiyār śrī-Rājēndra-Chōḷadēva (I, 1011—43), the date of which is damaged. Records a gift of gold.

78. 282 *of* 1904.—(Tamil.) On the south wall of the same shrine. A record in the second year of Chōḷa king Rājakēsarivarman *alias* Uḍaiyār śrī-Vīrarājēndradēva (I). Records gift of 96 sheep for a lamp.

79. 283 *of* 1904.—(Tamil.) On the same wall. A record in the twenty-eighth year of the Chōḷa king Rājakēsarivarman *alias* Uḍaiyār śrī-Rājādhirājadēva (I, 1018—52). Records gift of two lamps. Mentions the king's conquest of Vīra-Pāṇḍya, the Chēra king and Ceylon.

80. 284 *of* 1904.—(Grantha and Tamil.) On the same wall. An incomplete record of the Chōḷa king Rājarājakēsarivarman *alias* śrī-Rājarājadēva (I, 985—1013) in his twenty-seventh year. Records gift of a diadem.

81. 285 *of* 1904.—(Tamil.) On the same wall. A record in the fourth year of the Chōḷa king Parakēsarivarman *alias* śrī-Rājēndra-Chōḷadēva (I, 1011—43). Records gift of gold.

82. 286 *of* 1904.—(Tamil.) On the same wall. A record in the fourth year of the Chōḷa king Parakēsarivarman *alias* śrī-Rājēndra-Chōḷadēva (I, 1011—43). Records gift of 96 sheep for a lamp in order to secure merit for a soldier who was killed in a private quarrel.

83. 287 *of* 1904.—(Tamil.) On the same wall. An incomplete record of the Chōḷa king Parakēsarivarman *alias* Uḍaiyār śrī-Rājēndra-Chōḷadēva (I).

84. 288 *of* 1904.—(Tamil.) On the north wall of the same shrine. A record in the eighteenth year of the Chōḷa king Parakēsarivarman *alias* Uḍaiyār śri-Rājēndra-Chōḷadēva (I, 1011—43). Records gift of 96 sheep for a lamp.

85. 289 *of* 1904.—(Tamil.) On the same wall. A record in the twenty-fourth year of the Chōḷa king Parakēsarivarman *alias* śrī-Rājēndra-Chōḷadēva. Records gift of a gold diadem by the king and of 30 cows for a lamp by a private individual.

86. 290 *of* 1904.—(Tamil.) On the same wall. A record in the twelfth year of the Chōḷa king Parakēsarivarman *alias* śrī-Rājēndra-Chōḷadēva. Records gift of cows and gold.

87. 291 *of* 1904.—(Tamil.) On the same wall. A record in the twelfth year of the Chōḷa king Parakēsarivarman *alias* Rājēndra-Chōḷadēva (I, 1011—43). Records gift (1) of gold for celebrating the festival of the Krittikā-dīpa and (2) of 90 sheep by a chief of Miḷāḍu called Gaṅgaikoṇḍa Chōḷa-Miḷāḍuḍaiyān.

88. 292 *of* 1904.—(Tamil.) On the same wall. An incomplete record in the twenty-first year of the Chōḷa king Parakēsarivarman *alias* Uḍaiyār śrī-Rājēndra-Chōḷadēva (I).

89. 293 *of* 1904.—(Grantha and Tamil.) On the north, east and south bases of the same shrine. A record of the Chōḷa king Rājakēsarivarman *alias* śrī-Rājarājadēva I (985 -1013), the date of which is not mentioned. The inscription seems to stop abruptly with the name of the king. In what looks like a continuation of it a gift of 32 cows is recorded.

90. 294 *of* 1904.—(Tamil.) On the same bases. An incomplete record in the sixteenth year of the Chōḷa king Rājarāja-Rājakēsarivarman (Rājarāja I, 985—1013).

91. 295 *of* 1904.—(Tamil.) On the north, east and south bases of the central shrine in the same temple. A damaged record in the twenty-third year of the Chōḷa king Parakēsarivarman *alias* Uḍaiyār śrī-Rājēndra-Chōḷadēva (I, 1011—48).

92. 296 *of* 1904.—(Tamil.) On the same bases. A record in the twenty-second year of the Chōḷa king Parakēsarivarman *alias* Uḍaiyār śrī-Rājēndra-Chōḷadēva (I, 1012—43). Records gift of a lamp.

93. 297 *of* 1904.—(Tamil.) On the same bases. A record in the twenty-third year of the Chōḷa king Parakēsarivarman *alias* śrī-Rājēndra-Chōḷadēva (I, 1011—43). Records gift of gold.

94. 298 *of* 1904.—(Tamil.) On the same bases. A record in the twenty-fourth year of the Chōḷa king Rājarājakēsarivarman (Rājarāja I). Records gift of gold to the shrine of Maṇikeṅgai-Mādēvar. [The inscription shows that the shrine existed in the time of Rājarāja I though "the present building . . . came into existence in the reign of Kulōttuṅga III."]

95. 299 *of* 1904.—(Grantha and Tamil.) On the same bases. An incomplete record in the twenty-seventh year of the Chōḷa king Rājarājakēsarivarman *alias* Rājarājadēva (I). Seems to enforce payment of arrears of interest due from certain endowments.

96. 300 *of* 1904.—(Tamil.) On the caves of the same shrine. A much damaged record of the Chōḷa king Parakēsarivarman *alias* Uḍaiyar śrī-Rājēndra-Chōḷadēva (I, 1011—43), the date of which is lost.

97. 301 *of* 1904.—(Tamil.) On the north wall of the shrine immediately to the south of the first prākāra of the same temple. A much-damaged record of the Vijayanagara king Vīrapratāpa Vīra-Sadāśivadēva-Mahārāya in Ś. 1489, expired, Prabhava.

98. 302 *of* 1904.—(Tamil.) On the same wall. A damaged record of the Vijayanagara king Vīrapratāpa Vīra-Sadāśivadēva-Mahārāya in Ś. 1491, expired, Śukla. Kāḷahasti (so spelt here) is called Mummuḍi-Sōḷapuram.

99. 303 *of* 1904.—(Tamil.) On one of several stray stones placed in the verandah of the shrine of the goddess in the same temple. An incomplete record in the thirty-second year of the Chōla king Tribhuvanachakravartin Kulōttuṅga-Chōḷadēva (I or III ?).

100. 92 *of* 1903.—(Tamil.) On the south wall of the second prākāra of the Kāḷahastīśvara temple. A record of the Vijayanagara king Vīra-Sadāśivadēva-Mahārāya in Ś. 1469, Plavaṅga. Records gift of money by a Kaṇakkuppiḷḷai.

101. 93 *of* 1903.—(Tamil.) On the same wall. A record in the thirty-first year of the Chōḷa king Tribhuvanachakravartin Kulōttuṅga-Chōḷadēva (III ?). Records gift of land by Yādavarāya (most probably Vīra Narasimha. See N.A. 58). Incomplete.

102. 94 *of* 1903.—(Tamil.) On the same wall. A record in the seventh year of the Chōḷa king Tribhuvanachakravartin Vīrarājēndra-Chōḷadēva (II, Kulōttuṅga III). Records gift of land by Narasimha Tirukkāḷattidēva *alias* Yādavarāya. See N.A. 58. [The present epigraph shows that Yādavarāya and Tirukkāḷatti were identical.]

103. 95 *of* 1903.—(Grantha and Tamil.) On the same wall. Records gift of a salt pan by Yādavarāya Tirukkāḷattidēva Mahārāja. See note to the above epigraph.

104. 96 *of* 1903.—(Tamil.) On the same wall. A record in the fourteenth year of the Chōḷa king Tribhuvanachakravartin Kulōttuṅga-Chōḷadēva (III). Records gift of 96 sheep and one ram for a lamp.

105. 166 *of* 1903.—(Tamil.) On the east wall of the record room in the Kāḷahastīśvara temple. An incomplete record in the twenty-first year of the Chōḷa king Tribhuvanachakravartin Rājarājadēva (III ?). Records gift of 32 cows for a lamp.

106. 167 *of* 1903.—(Tamil.) On the same wall. A record in the eleventh year of the Chōḷa king Tribhuvanachakravartin Rājarājadēva (III ?). Records gift of money for a lamp.

107. 168 *of* 1903.—(Tamil.) On the same wall. A record in the seventeenth year of the Chōḷa king Rājarājadēva (III ?). Records gift of 32 cows for a lamp by a certain Vīmarasar.

108. 169 *of* 1903.—(Tamil.) On the same wall. A record in the sixteenth year of the Chōḷa king Rājarājadēva (III ?). Records gift of 96 sheep for a lamp.

109. 170 *of* 1903.—(Tamil.) On the same wall. A record in the twentieth year of the Chōḷa king Tribhuvanachakravartin Rājarājadēva (III ?). Records gift of gold for a lamp.

110. 171 *of* 1903.—(Tamil.) On the same wall. A record in the ninth year of the Chōḷa king Tribhuvanachakravartin Rājarājadēva (III ?). Records gift of money for a lamp.

111. 172 *of* 1903.—(Tamil.) On the same wall. A damaged record in the fifteenth year of the Chōḷa king Rājarājadēva (III). Mentions Śaśikula-Chāḷukki Vīra-Naraśiṅgadēva (evidently the same as Yādavarāya). See N.A. 449 and No. 120 below.

112. 173 *of* 1903.—(Tamil.) On the east wall of the record room in the same temple. A record in the fourth year of Tribhuvanachakravartin Vijayagaṇḍagōpāladēva (1250—83). Records gift of land. See N.A. 10, N.A. 441, Cg. 49, Cg. 342 and Cg. 353.

113. 174 *of* 1903.—(Tamil.) On a pillar set up close to the same wall. Records in Ś. 1289, Plavaṅga, that a chief named Vaḷḷi-araśar who calls himself Lord of Ayōdhyāpura killed 150 tigers. He has great titles, but he was evidently a local chief who took advantage of the unsettled condition of the times to establish a petty chiefdom of his own.

114. 175 *of* 1903.—(Tamil.) On the east wall of the Mrityuñja-yēśvara shrine in the same village, and in the same temple. A record in the seventeenth year of the Chōḷa king Kulōttuṅga-Chōḷa-dēva. Records gift of money for a lamp.

115. 176 *of* 1903.—(Tamil.) On the same wall. A damaged record in the fourteenth year of the Chōḷa king Kulōttuṅga-Chōḷadēva.

116. 177 *of* 1903.—(Tamil.) On the same wall. A record of the Vijayanagara king Vīrapratāpa-Kṛishṇarāya in Ś. 1450, Sarva-dhārin. Records gift of money and paddy; also contains the beginning of an inscription of the sixteenth year of Tribhuvana-chakravartin Kulōttuṅga-Chōḷadēva (III ?).

117. 178 *of* 1903.—(Tamil.) On the south wall of the same shrine. A record in the nineteenth year of the Chōḷa king Tribhu-vanachakravartin Kulōttuṅga-Chōḷadēva (III ?). Records gift of gold for two lamps.

118. 179 *of* 1903.—(Tamil.) On the same wall. A record in the tenth year of the Chōḷa king Rājarājadēva (III ?). Records gift of money for a lamp.

119. 180 *of* 1903.—(Tamil.) On the north wall of the same shrine. A damaged record of the Vijayanagara king Vīra-Sadā-śivadēva in Ś. 1467, Viśvāvasu. Tirukkāḷatti bore the surname Mummuḍi-Sōḷapuram.

120. 181 *of* 1903.—(Tamil.) On the same wall. A record in the tenth year of the Chōḷa king Rājarājadēva. Records gift of 96 sheep for a lamp by the queen of Śaśikula-Chāḷukki Tirukkāḷatti-dēva *alias* Yādavarāya. See No. 111 above.

121. 182 *of* 1903.—(Tamil.) On the same wall. A record in the tenth year of the Chōḷa king Rājarājadēva (III). Records gift of money for a lamp. Mentions Śaśikula Chāḷukki Vīra-Naraśiṅga-dēva *alias* Yādavarāya. See No. 111 above.

122. 183 *of* 1903.—(Tamil.) On the south base of the same shrine. A record in the eighth year of the Chōḷa king Rājarāja-dēva (III). Records a gift by Śaśikula Chāḷukki Tani-ninṟu-venṟa Vīra-Naraśiṅgadēva *alias* Yādavarāya. See N.A. 449.

123. 184 *of* 1903.—(Tamil.) On the same base. A fragment of record.

124. 185 *of* 1903.—(Tamil.) On the south and east bases of the same shrine. An incomplete record in Ś. 1292, Sādhāraṇa. Records gift of land for a flower-garden and a water-shed.

125. 186 *of* 1903.—(Tamil.) On the same bases. A record of the Vijayanagara king Sadāśivadēva in Ś. 1475, Pramādin. Built in at the beginning. Records gift of money.

126. 187 *of* 1903.—(Tamil.) On the north base of the same shrine. A record of the Vijayanagara king Vīrapratāpa-Vīra-Krishṇayadēva in Ś. 1432, Pramōda. Built in at the end.

127. 188 *of* 1903.—(Tamil.) On the east and north bases of the same shrine. A record of the Vīraśrī-Savaṇa-Uḍaiyār in his fifteenth year, Śubhakrit. Records gift of 32 cows for a lamp. [The chief should be the first of this name, i.e., the son of Kampa (I). Śubhakrit corresponded to A.D. 1362.]

128. 189 *of* 1903.—(Tamil and Grantha.) On the west wall of the first prākāra of the same temple, right of entrance. A record in the sixth year of the Chōḷa king Rājarājadēva. Mentions Ghaṭṭi-dēva-Mahārāja with a number of Sanskrit *birudas*. See No. 44.

129. 190 *of* 1903.—(Tamil and Grantha.) On the same wall. Mentions in Ś. 1304, Dundubhi, Mallappa-Uḍaiyār, son of Vīra-Māchappa-Uḍaiyār, with a number of *birudas* in Grantha characters. [Was he the prime minister of Dēvarāya (II) referred to in N.A. 402? He seems to be too early for such an identification.]

130. 191 *of* 1903.—(Tamil.) On the same wall. A record in the fifteenth year of the Chōḷa king Tribhuvanachakravartin Rājarājadēva (III). Records gift of 96 sheep for a lamp. Mentions Śaśikula-Chaḷukki Tirukkāḷattidēva *alias* Yādavarāya. See No. 111 above.

131. 192 *of* 1903.—(Tamil.) On the west wall of the first prākāra of the Kāḷahastīśvara temple, right of entrance. A record of the Vijayanagar king Vīrapratāpa-Harihararāya (II, 1377—1402), in Ś. 1323, Vrisha. Records a gift by a guru named Pūrṇagiri, disciple of Amarēndragiri. [I have not succeeded in getting information about these. Pūrṇagiri is evidently not the same as Pūrṇānanda, the author of the yōgic treatise *Shaḍchakranirūpaṇa*. See Hultzsch's *Sans. MSS.*, I, No. 273*b*. Can Amarēndragiri be the same as Amarēndra Sarasvati whose disciple's disciple Gīrvāṇēndra composed the Tantric treatise *Prapañcha sārasaṅgraha*? See Prof. Rangacharya's *Des. Cat. Sans. MSS.*, Vol. XV, pp. 5734—7.]

132. 193 *of* 1903.—(Tamil.) On the same wall. A record of the Vijayanagar king Vīrapratāpa-Dēvarāya II in Ś. 1357. Beginning built in. Appears to record a gift by Chikkaraśar, son of Mādi-araśar Ayyalu-Peggaḍaiyar.

133. 194 *of* 1903.—(Tamil.) On the same wall. Records in Ś. 1292, Sādhāraṇa, that a certain private individual who had no heirs bequeathed his eight cows to the temple. An incomplete record.

134. 195 *of* 1903.—(Tamil.) On the same wall. A fragment of record. Mentions the daughter of Vīra-Naraśiṅgadēva *alias* Yādavarāya and the son of Madhurāntaka-Pottappi-Chōḷa Manumasittarasar. See N.A. 58 and No. 111 above.

135. 196 *of* 1903.—(Telugu.) On the west wall of the second prākāra of the same temple. A record of the Vijayanagara king Vīrapratāpa-Vīra-Kṛishṇadēva Mahārāya in Ś. 1438, Dhātri. Refers to the king's conquests, his visit to Kāḷahasti and to his building the 100-pillared maṇṭapa and the big gōpura. [See N.A. 530 of the same date at Tiruvaṇṇāmalai which gives the same information.]

136. 197 *of* 1903.—(Tamil.) On the east base of the central shrine in the Maṇikaṇṭhēśvara temple in the same village. A record in the eleventh year of the Chōḷa king Tribhuvanachakravartin-Vīrarājēndra-Chōḷadēva. Records the building of the temple, the maṇṭapa and a flight of steps. The temple was called Tirumaṇi-kkeṅgaiyuḍaiya-Nāyanār. [Venkayya identifies the king with Kulōttuṅga Chōḷa III (1178—1216).

137. 198 *of* 1903.—(Tamil.) On the north wall of the maṇṭapa in front of the same shrine. Records in Ś. 1242, Raudri, a private agreement.

138. 199 *of* 1903.—(Tamil.) On the same wall. A record in Ś. 1242, Raudra. Quotes the seventh year of Rājagaṇḍagōpaladēva. (He cannot be identical with Vijaya Gaṇḍagōpāla).

139. 200 *of* 1903.—(Tamil.) On the south base of the shrine of the goddess in the same temple. A record in the eighth year of the Chōla king Rājarājadēva (III). Records a gift by Śaśikula-Chālukki Tani-ninṟu-venṟa Vīra-Naraśiṅgadēva *alias* Yādavarāya to the god Mallikārjuna set up in the temple of Māṇikkeṅgaiuḍaiya-Nāyanār by the donor himself. See No. 111 above.

140. 201 *of* 1903.—(Tamil.) On the Vishṇu shrine in the same temple. A record in the seventh year of Tribhuvanachakravartin Aḷḷuntirukkāḷadēva *alias* Gaṇḍagōpāla. Records gift of gold for a lamp to the temple of Tirumānikkengai-uḍaiya-Nāyanār. See No. 112 above.

141. 202 *of* 1903.—(Tamil.) On the gōpura of the same temple, left of entrance. A record in the seventh year of Tribhuvanachakravartin Vijayagaṇḍagōpāladēva (1250—83). Records gift of land to the temple of Māṇikkeṅgai-uḍaiya-Nāyanār by Nallasittarasar, son of Bhīmarasar of Tyāgasamudrappēṭṭai. [It is difficult to identify this Nallasiddha. He was apparently the contemporary of his namesake who was the son of Manmakshmā vallabha, the patron of Tikkaṇa Sōmayāji, who lived about A.D. 1250.]

142. 203 *of* 1903.—(Tamil.) On the Brahmaliṅga to the south-east of the same temple. An incomplete record in the fourth year of the Chōḷa king Tribhuvanachakravartin Kulōttuṅga-Chōḷadēva (III ?)

143. *C.P. No.* 22 *of* 1910-1.—A Sanskṛit record of "Raṅga VI" of the last Vijayanagara dynasty, dated in the same year as his Kaḷḷakursi grant, registering the donation of the village of Kāsaram and of a tank for the midday sacred bath and offerings of Kāḷahastiśvara and for maintaining a feeding institute. The donation was made at the request of a certain Veṅkaṭa, son of Kāri Channa and grandson of Pedda Veṅkaṭa (Veṅkaṭa II ?).

Toṇḍamanād near *Kāḷahasti.*

144. 230 *of* 1903.—(Tamil.) On the base of the central shrine in the Kōdaṇḍarāmēśvara temple. A record in the thirty-fourth year of the Chōḷa king Maduraikoṇḍa Parakēsarivarman. Records gift of gold for feeding 1,000 Brāhmaṇas on certain festivals. Mentions the temple of Kōdaṇḍarāmēśvara *alias* Ādityēśvara and a certain Vāgīśvara-Paṇḍitabhaṭṭāra. [From the two names of the shrine Venkayya infers that Kōdaṇḍarāma must have been either Rājāditya or Gaṇḍarāditya, the sons of Parāntaka I. Later research has proved that it was Rājāditya.] See Cg. 965 for a later Vāgīśvara Paṇḍita.

145. 231 *of* 1903.—(Tamil.) On the south base of the Vīṟṟirunda-Perumāḷ temple in the same village. An incomplete and damaged record in Ś. 1165.

146. 232 *of* 1903.—(Tamil.) On the west base of the same temple. A record in the fifth year of the Chōḷa king Rājarājadēva. Records that Ghaṭṭidēva *alias* Yādavarāja granted the village of Kiḍāraṅgoṇḍa-Śōḷapuram (named after Rājēndrachōḷa I). See No. 102 above.

147. 233 *of* 1903.—(Grantha and Tamil.) On a slab set up on the bank of the tank in the same village. A record of Tikkaya-dēvamahāraja in Ś. 1187, Krōdhana. Records the building of the tank sluice by the king. [Was Tikkaya the same as Tikka II, the son of Tikkaṇa Sōmayāji's patron ?]

MADANAPALLE TALUK.

Ālēṭipalle.

148. 439 *of* 1914.—(Kanarese, archaic.) On the slab called Kattivīrappabanda. A record of the Vaiḍumba king Vaiḍumba Mahārāja, approximately in the ninth century A.D. Records that a certain Śrī-Kanki, son of Vīra-satti, the servant of Vaiḍumba Mahārāja, led the army in the battle of Tiruvala and fell. The hero is entitled the supporter of the throne of Erega, the right arm of the Mahārāja and the bee at the lotus foot of Kimudēva. [Was

Erega the father of Rāchamalla I who was deposed by the Rāshṭrakūṭa Krishṇa III and killed by Bhūtuga II?]

Badikāyalapalle.

149. 440 *of* 1914.—(Telugu.) On a rock to the west of the Peddacheruvu tank. Records in Krōdhana, Āśvija, ba. di. 10, that Kadupanāyani Raghunāyakulu Nāyanigāru of Krottapāḷem granted rent-free ten *tums* of wet land for the maintenance of the Veṅkaṭappa Nāyani tank.

Basinikoṇḍa.

150. 342 *of* 1912.—(Tamil.) On two slabs lying in a field. A record in the thirty-second year of the Chōḷa king Rājakēsarivarman *alias* Uḍaiyār śrī-Rājādhirājadēva (I). One of the slabs is mutilated. Registers that the 1,500 merchants of the four quarters including *nāḍu, nagara* and *nānādēśi,* met at Śīrāvaḷḷi in Mūgaināḍu, a subdivision of Pūraṇi-Mārāyapāḍi of Jayaṅgoṇḍa-śōḷamaṇḍalam and resolved to convert the village Sīrāvaḷḷi into a Nānādēśīya-Dasamāḍi-Erivīrapaṭṭaṇa and to grant certain privileges to the residents of that village. It was made a Vīraśāsana. [The inscription is of great interest to the economic historian, as it shows that the organization of the gild did not only exist, but had a wide influence over allied communities in different parts of India. See N.A. 401 and Cg. 682.

Chinna-Tippāsamudram.

151. 374 *of* 1904.—(Telugu.) On a slab set up in a grove called Polimēratōpu. In ancient characters. Records the death of a hero.

152. 375 *of* 1904.—(Telugu.) On another slab set up in the same place. In ancient characters. Records the death of a hero.

Chippili.

153. 298 *of* 1905.—(Kanarese.) On a slab set up in a field of the village, close to the Chippili-Vēmpalle road. Vaiḍumba-Mahārāja (Manuja-Trinētra) records that a hero lost his life in rescuing cows. [Was the chief the same as Gaṇḍa Trinētra who fought the battle of Soremati?]

154. 299 *of* 1905.—(Kanarese.) On another slab set up in the same place. A record of Puṇyakumāra; records that, while the king was ruling Chirppuli, a hero named Paraśurāman fell in battle. See Cd. 455 for the possible identity of the king.

155. 300 *of* 1905.—(Telugu.) On the third slab set up in the same place. A record of Vaiḍumba-Mahārāja; mentions Chirppuli. Records that a certain hero fell in a cattle raid. See No. 153 above.

156. 301 *of* 1905.—(Kanarese.) On a slab set up in a field north of the same village. Records a gift by Śrī-Malladēvan. Mentions Bāṇarasan and Chirppuli.

Kammapalle.

157. 297 *of* 1905.—(Telugu.) On a slab set up in a field north of the village, near Madanapalle. Dated in the reign of the Vijayanagaram king Vīrapratāpa Kṛishṇadēva-Mahārāya ; records in Ś. 1446, Svabhānu, gift of land near the big canal *(peda-kālva)* of Madunapalli or Madunapalya.

Koṭṭakōṭa.

158. 438 *of* 1914.—(Persian.) On a slab built into the south wall of the Jumma Masjid. A damaged and illegible record. Records that the mosque was dedicated to God and Prophet on the twentieth Rabi-ul-Awal 900 A.H.

Madanapalle.

159. 287 *of* 1905.—(Telugu.) On a slab set up and worshipped in the Pōturāju temple. A damaged record. In archaic characters. Mentions *pannaya* in line 4.

160. 288 *of* 1905.—(Telugu.) On a slab set up near the Śiva temple west of the same village. Records that a hero named Chandrāditya fought for cows and died.

161. 289 *of* 1905.—(Telugu.) On another slab set up in the same place. A damaged record.

162. 290 *of* 1905.—(Telugu.) On a third slab set up in the same place. A much damaged record of Vaiḍumba-Irigaya Mahārāja. Appears to record the death of a hero.

163. 291 *of* 1905.—(Telugu.) On a slab lying at the same place. Records that a hero fought for cows and died.

164. 292 *of* 1905.—(Telugu.) On a slab set up in a field at Basinikoṇḍa near Madanapalle. Records that a hero of Loṅkuḷa died in a combat at Mudumaḍuvu.

165. 293 *of* 1905.—(Telugu.) On another slab set up in the same place. Records that Śrīgaṅga, chief of Loṅkuḷa, fell in the combat mentioned in No. 164.

166. 294 *of* 1905.—(Telugu.) On a broken slab lying in the same place. Records that another hero (name not completely preserved) who is called Vikrama-Rāman also fought and fell in the same combat. Mentions Loṅkuḷa.

167. 295 *of* 1905.—(Kanarese.) On a slab set up in a field west of the same village. Records that while Vaiḍumba-Mahāraja (Gaṇḍa-Trinētra) and Bāṇarasa captured Soramati in the face of the Noḷamba and Daḍiga-Rāchamalla, a hero fell in the battle which ensued. [The Bāṇarasa was evidently Vijayāditya conquered by Parāntaka I (905—47) or his father. He was apparently an ally of the Vaiḍumba Gaṇḍa Trinētra and an enemy of Noḷamba (Mahēndrādhirāja ?.]

168. 296 *of* 1905.—(Kanarese.) On another slab set up in the same place. A record of Vaiḍumba-Mahārāja (Gaṇḍa-Trinētra); mentions Bāṇarasa, Daḍiga-Rāchamalla and Maydaḍi. Records the death in battle of a certain Manujarādēva. See note to the above epigraph.

168-A. *C.P. No.* 1 *of* 1913.—A grant of the Vijayanagara king Tirumala I in Ś. 1493, Prajāpati, Māgha, śu. di. 12, in Sanskṛit. Records the grant of Penunguḷūru to Brahmans at the request of Tirumal Rāja, one of the chiefs of the Maṭla family.

168-B. *C.P. No.* 9 *of* 1913.—A record of the Vijayanagara king Krishṇadēva Rāya in Ś. 1498, Dhātri, Māgha, ba. di. 10. Registers that certain men paid their homage to the king with 50 varāhas and received offices and service ināms in the village of Lōmaḍa. The *mēras* and other income due to them mentioned. [The date is wrong as Krishṇadēva died in 1530.]

168-C. *C.P. No.* 10 *of* 1913.—The record of one Yara Timma Rāja, Governor of Ghanḍikōṭa and "brother-in-law of Mahādēvarāya ruling at Vijayanagar" dated in Śārvari, Vaiśākha, *śu. di.* 15. [Registers that two Reḍḍis came from the seaside (district) with their cattle and children to the village Rāvulakollu and got permission to construct a village near the hill. The record defines the boundaries and the service *inams.* The Government Epigraphist believes that the Vijayanagar king might be Tirumala I.]

168-D. *C.P. No.* 11 *of* 1913.—A record dated in Ś. 1508, Vyaya, Vaiśākha, *śu. di.* 15, Monday, lunar eclipse. Records that one Anuguṇḍa Veṅgalappa settled a dispute between the *agrahārikas* and the *karaṇams* of the village of Avuḍūru, in regard to the distribution of service inam lands.

168-E. *C.P. No.* 12 *of* 1913.—A record of Ś. 1633, *Virōdhi,* vaiśākha, *śu. di.* 10. Records that on the occasion of a car festival at Conjeeveram it was found that something was wrong with the divine glory of the images and that as one Kanumanūru Raṅgachārlu put things right by his magical skill, he was privileged by the chiefs present including Harsadu Aṇavardikānu Sāyappū (i.e.), Hazrat Anvarud-in Khan Sahib ?), to collect certain specified annuities from different classes of people in the 56 countries.

168-F. *C.P. No.* 13 *of* 1913.—A Telugu record dated Ś. 1464, Krōdhana (wrong), Bhādrapada *śu. di.* 10, Thursday. Professes to settle certain disputes between the Baḍugalavāru and Palnāṭe Vīralu in the matter of paraphernalia in public processions. The Judges evidently were the Śaivas, Vaishṇavas and great men of Conjeeveram.

168-G. *C.P.* No. 14 *of* 1913.—A record in Telugu, dated Ś. 1283, Jaya (wrong), Mārgaśira *ba. di.* 10. Records the boundaries of the village of Kasunūru or Tiruvēṅgalanallūr in Guṭṭi Rājya and the details of the *mēra, mirāś* and other service *ināms* granted to village servants.

Mallela.

169. 437 *of* 1914.—(Kanarese archaic.) On a slab near Yarram Reḍḍi's house. A record of Bīra-Mahāraja, ruling over Pulvēri-nāḍu. Records that while Tōḍaṅkan was governing Mallyal (Mallēla), a native of Kottanūru fell in a cattle feud (?), after destroying Nekkuṇḍi.

Pedda-Tippāsamudram.

170. 533 *of* 1906.—(Telugu.) On a slab set up near the ruined Śiva temple in the Yēnugarāti-maḍi field. A record of the Vaiḍumba king Kaṇḍa-Trinētra-Vaiḍumba-Mahāraja; records that Prabhuchelvuṇḍu distinguished himself in the battle of Sōre-mati between the king and Noḷamba, and fell. [Kaṇḍa was the last independent chief of the line conquered by Parāntaka I (905—47). Kaṇḍa's Noḷamba enemy was either Mahēndrādhirāja or his son Aiyappa. See Ct. 167 above for other details.]

171. 534 *of* 1906.—(Kanarese.) On a slab lying in the same place. A record of the thirty-fifth year of the Chōḷa king Para-kēsarivarman *alias* Uḍaiyār Vijaya-Rājēndra-Chōḷadeva, dated in 981, Hemalamba (A.D. 1057). He is said to have gained victories over Vīra Pāṇḍya and the Chēra king, conquered Ceylon and Ṛaṭṭapāḍi and planted a pillar of victory at Kalyāṇapuram. Venkayya therefore identifies the king with Parakēsarivarman Rājēndra-dēva (1050—62), but he never reigned for 35 years. So the date, he concludes, should be a mistake.

172. 535 *of* 1906.—(Telugu.) On a slab found in the same place. A fragment in archaic characters. Seems to record the death of a hero; mentions Maḍambūr.

173. 536 *of* 1906.—(Telugu.) On a slab lying in a field in the hamlet of Pullagaṇṭivāripaḷḷe, near the same village. A record of the Vaiḍumba king Kalige-Trinētra; mentions the eldest son of Vīra Mahārāju. See Ct. 170 above.

174. 537 *of* 1906.—(Tamil.) In a maṇṭapa close to No. 173. A record of the Chōḷa king Ādirājēndradēva (son of Vīra Rājēndra I, 1063—1070). Mentions in his third year Koyyakuṟai-nāḍu *alias* Mēlai Māṟāpāḍi in Iraṭṭapāḍi-koṇḍa-chōḷamaṇḍalam. Refers to a Cheṭṭi who died for his village.

PALMANĒR TALUK.

Daṇḍapalle.

174-A. *C.P.* No. 6 *of* 1912–13.—A record (unique in the case of Vijaya) in Sanskrit and Kanarese of the Vijayanagara king

Vijayabhūpati in Ś. 1332, Vikriti, Bhādrapada, śu. di. 11, Monday, Śravaṇa. Records that he founded near Daṇḍapalle in Hulināḍu (Pulināḍu), a village called Kriyāśaktipura and presented it to a certain Kṛishṇa Paṇḍita who made a gift of it to Brāhmaṇas. The king's spiritual teacher Kāśīvilāsa Kriyāśakti Dēśika is mentioned. Kriyāśakti was also the teacher of Bukka I, Harihara II and the minister Mādhava (not Vidyāraṇya), and made the early Vijayanagar emperors adherents of devotional Śaivitism as distinct from Advaitism. The seal of Tryambaka at the end of the epigraph also shows this. Mentions the king's mother Dēmāmbika, daughter of Nūka Bhūpāla of the solar race, i.e., the Reḍḍi chief Nūka Nūṅka who was the husband of Anna Vēma's sister Vēmasāni.

Kaḷakattūr.

175. 306 *of* 1912.—(Kanarese.) On a slab set up in a field. A record of the Noḷamba (Pallava) king Noḷambādiyarasa. Refers to the death of a hero, the raising of a monument on his tomb and the gift of a *Kalnāḍu.* Under the orders of his Gaṅga suzerain Permāḍi, Noḷambādhirāja (Mehēndra or his father) led a successful expedition against Taḷakāḍu, in the course of which he despatched two of his subordinate chiefs, Kāḍuveṭṭi and Maḍura, against Puḷināḍu. The latter captured the town of Permāvi and burnt it. This roused the indignation of the Bāṇa king Vijayāditya Vīrachūṭāmaṇi Prabhumēru who dispersed the enemy's forces and killed many chiefs in the conflict. It was on this occasion that the hero, mentioned in the present record, fell and was immortalized. The Noḷamba's invasion of Pulināḍu is confirmed by Ct. 255, Ct. 243 and Ct. 196.

176. 307 *of* 1912.—(Kanarese.) On a rock in a field in the same village. A damaged record. In archaic characters.

Kiḻapaṭla.

177. 308 *of* 1912.—(Telugu.) On the north wall of the central shrine in the Kōnēṭirāyasvāmin temple. A much damaged record of the Vijayanagara king Śrīraṅgadēva-Mahārāya, ruling at Penugoṇḍa, the date of which is doubtful.

Kūrmāyi.

178. 309 *of* 1912.—(Tamil.) On the east wall of the maṇṭapa in front of the central shrine in the Varadarāja-Perumāḷ temple. A record of the Vijayanagara king Kampaṇa-Uḍaiyār (II), son of Vīra-Bukkaṇa-Uḍaiyār (I) in Kaliyuga 4452 (mistake for 4462), and Ś. 1283, Plava, Pūraṭṭādi, Kanni, śu. di. 7, Tuesday, Mūlam, corresponding to 7th September 1361. Records gift of tolls for providing (daily), a flower-garland and a lamp to the temple of Edirkoṇḍa-Perumāḷ at Kurumāvi (a village) in Puli-nāḍu, under orders from the mahāpradhāni Sōmappa-Uḍaiyār and the treasurer Viṭṭappayyan. See S.A. 1061.

179. 310 *of* 1912.—(Telugu.) On the east wall of the central shrine in the same temple, left of entrance. A record of the Vijayanagara king Vīrapratāpa-Sadāśivadēva-Mahārāya in Ś. 1482, Siddhārthi, Vaiśākha, śu. di. 2, Monday (which should be Sunday), corresponding to Sunday, 9th April 1559. Records gift of land for *archanavritti*, i.e., the maintenance of worship, in the temple of Varadarāja at Kurumāvi in Puli-nāḍu, a district of Chittūri-rājya to a private individual.

PUNGANŪRU TALUK.

Agastyakoṇḍa Hill.

180. 556 *of* 1906.—(Tamil.) On four tiers of the south, east and north walls of the Agastyēśvar temple. A record in the twenty-ninth year of the Chōḷa king Rājakēsarivarman *alias* Chakravartin śrī-Kulōttuṅga-Chōḷadēva (I). Records gift of a village to the temple of Tiruvagattīśvaramuḍaiya Mahādēva at Koyaṟṟūr *alias* Uttamaśōḷapuram in Puli-nāḍu, a subdivision of Perumbāṇappāḍi in Jayaṅgoṇḍa-Chōḷamaṇḍalam.

181. 557 *of* 1906.—(Tamil.) On the north wall of the same temple. Records in Kīlaka gift of land to a drummer *(uvachchan)*.

182. 558 *of* 1906.—(Kanarese.) On the west wall of the same temple. Records in Ś. 1298, Ānanda, gift of lamps, cows, vessels and land to the temple of Agastināthadēva.

183. 559 *of* 1906.—(Tamil.) On the base of the same wall. A record in the fourteenth year of the Chōḷa king Tribhuvanachakravartin-Vīrarājēndra-Chōḷadēva (Kulōttuṅga III ?). Records that the queen of Uttama-Chōḷa-Gaṅga *alias* Śelvagaṅga set up and consecrated an image of Tirunāvukkaraśudēva. See Cg. 144 and Ct. 190 below.

184. 560 *of* 1906.—(Telugu.) On the base of the west and south walls of the same temple. Mentions in Ś. 1577, Manmatha, Immaḍi-Chikarāvu Timmaya-Gaunivāru. See No. 191 below.

185. 561 *of* 1906.—(Tamil.) On the south wall of the maṇṭapa in front of the central shrine of the same temple. A record of the Gaṅga king Śelvagaṅga, son of Uttamachōḷa-Gaṅga Padumidēva in Ś. 1251. The second figure of the date is doubtful. Records gift of an ornament by Śīpatināyan, son of the king. [This chief was evidently different from him who is mentioned in No. 183 above. He is perhaps the same as the Padumi Sēyan Uttama. Śōḷagaṅga and Gaṅga Perumāḷ, son of Padimadēva Uttama-Śōḷa Gaṅga referred to in Kl. 242 and Kl. 244. *Ep. Carna.*, Vol. X, Part II, p. 43.]

186. 562 *of* 1906.—(Tamil.) On the base of the same wall, right of entrance, first tier. An incomplete record of Uttama-chōḷa-Gaṅgan *alias* Vīra-gaṅgan Veṭṭum-Amarābharaṇan. Records gift of land in Naṅgili. For epigraphs of the same chief see Ct. 235 and *Ep. Carna.*, X, p. XIII. *Amarābharana* was also the title of Sīyagaṅga, the patron of Pavaṇandi.

187. 563 *of* 1906.—(Tamil.) On the same base; second, third and fourth tiers. A record in the nineteenth year of the Chōḷa king Rājarājadēva (III). Records gift of two cows for a lamp by Śūra-Nāyakar *alias* Śīyagaṅgar. See note to the above epigraph.

188. 564 *of* 1906.—(Tamil.) On the base of the Dakshiṇā-mūrti-maṇṭapa in the same temple, first and second tiers. Records gift of land by Vaḍugapiḷḷai *alias* Toṇḍamān.

189. 565 *of* 1906.—(Tamil verse.) On the same base. Built in in the middle. Mentions Aḍigēśan.

190. 566 *of* 1906.—(Tamil.) On the boulder called Durga-guṇḍu on the same hill. A damaged record of Uttamachōḷa Gaṅga *alias* Śelvagaṅga. At the bottom of this is another damaged inscription which mentions no king. See Ct. 183 above.

Āvulapalle.

191. 340 *of* 1912.—(Telugu.) On a slab set up in the Śrīni-vāsamūrti temple. A damaged record in Saumya. Records gift of a dēvadāna to the temple of Prasanna-Vēṅkaṭēśvara at Āvula-palle, by Chikkarāya Timmayagavunigāru of Sugatūru. See No. 184 above.

192. 341 *of* 1912.—(Telugu.) On a slab set up at the tank bund in the same village. A damaged record in Saumya. Records gift by Vīrayagaunivāru of Ānēkallu, to the temples of Prasanna-Vēṅkaṭēśvara and Mallikārjuna at Āvulapalle. Mentions Sugatūri Chikkarāya Timmayagavuṇigāru. See No. 184.

Bhimagānipalle.

193. 320 *of* 1912.—(Telugu.) On a slab set up in the north prā-kāra of the Bhīmēśvara temple. Records in Ś. 1725, Rudhirōd-gārin, gift of land at Bhīmapuram near Moḍugalapalle to the temple of Bhīmēśvara, by Sugatūri-Mummaḍi-Chikkarāya who constructed the temple and the pond near it. He is also stated to have repaired the village tank.

Budidipalle.

194. 569 *of* 1906.—(Kanarese.) On a slab set up in the fields behind the ruined village. A record of the Bāṇa king Mahāvali-Bāṇarasa Vikramāditya Bāṇakandarpa Jayamēru. Mentions Miniki. [He was the father of Vijayāditya Bāṇarāya conquered by the Chōḷa Parāntaka I, pp. 905—47.]

195. 570 *of* 1906.—(Kanarese.) On another slab set up in the same place. A record of the Bāṇa king Māvali-Vāṇarasar. Mentions Miniki and records the death of a hero.

196. 571 *of* 1906.—(Kanarese.) On a third slab set up in the same place. A record of the Bāṇa king Mahāvali-Vāṇarasa Bāṇa-Vidyādhara. Mentions Miniki and refers to the raid of the army of Noḷamba on Puli-nāḍu. Mr. Krishna Sastri identified the Noḷamba who instituted this raid with the Noḷamba Mahēndrādhirāja. See the Dharmāpuri inscriptions, *Ep. Ind.*, Vol. X, pp. 54–70. See also Ap. 127, Ap. 63 and Ct. 175.

Chalamangala.

197. 312 *of* 1912.—(Telugu.) On a slab set up in a field. A damaged record in Ś. 1265, Svabhānu. Mentions the Mahāsāmantādhipati Raṁgappa-Nāyaka.

198. 313 *of* 1912.—(Kanarese.) On a *viragal* set up in the backyard of a house in the same village. A much damaged record of the Bāṇa king Mahāvalī Bāṇarasa, the date of which is doubtful. See No. 194 above.

199. 314 *of* 1912.—(Tamil.) On the north base of the Sōmēś-vara temple in the same village. A fragment of record of the Chōḷa king. Contains a portion of the introduction of Rājēndra-dēva (1050—62) which refers to his setting up of a pillar of victory at Kollāpuram. Mentions Paraśurāmīśvaram-Uḍaiyār at Vippiram-bēḍu in Śilaināḍu, a subdivision of Tiruvēṅgaḍakōṭṭam. Vippi-rambēḍu is the ancient name of modern Guḍimallam near Rēṇiguṇṭa.

Edapañjāni.

200. 586 *of* 1906.—(Tamil.) On the base of the verandah in front of the Kāśiviśvēśvara temple. A fragment of record of the Chōḷa king Parakēsarivarman Rājēndradēva (1050—62), the date of which is lost. Stones out of order. A few words of the historical introduction of the king are preserved. Mentions Karkaḍūr in Puli-nāḍu, a subdivision of Perumbāṇappāḍi in Jayaṅgoṇḍa-Chōḷa-maṇḍalam.

Embāḍi.

201. 578 *of* 1906.—(Kanarese.) On a *viragal* set up in the village. In archaic characters. Records the death of a gavuṇḍa on the occasion of the capture of the town of Uppunelli.

202. 579 *of* 1906.—(Kanarese.) On another *viragal* set up in the same place. Records the death of a hero on the same occasion.

203. 580 *of* 1906.—(Kanarese.) On the third *viragal* set up in the same place. A record in Ś. 887. While Vajjaḷadēva was ruling Puli-nāḍu, during the reign of Śrī-Ballaha, the capture of

Uppunelli occurred. Perhaps this is the date of the other local inscriptions. It falls in the reign of Kṛishṇa III. It is not known who this Vajjaḷa was. The Government Epigraphist suggests that it might be one of the two *Vajjaḍas* of the Silahāras of Koṅkaṇa; but there is no evidence of their connection with this part of the country.]

204. 581 *of* 1906.—(Kanarese.) On the fourth *viragal* set up in the same place. Records the death of a gavuṇḍa during the capture of Uppunelli.

205. 582 *of* 1906.—(Kanarese.) On the fifth *viragal* set up in the same place. A native of Toṇḍa-nāṇḍu died during the capture of Uppunelli.

206. 583 *of* 1906.—(Kanarese.) On the sixth *viragal* set up in the same place. Records the death of a merchant on the same occasion.

207. 584 *of* 1906.—(Kanarese.) On a *viragal* lying by the side of a private house in the same village. A damaged record of the Bāṇa king Māvali-Vāṇarasa. See Ct. 194 above.

208. 585 *of* 1906.—(Tamil.) On a slab lying in front of a private house in the same village. A record in the fifth year of the Chōḷa king Parakēsarivarman *alias* Uḍaiyār śri-Rājēndra-Chōḷadeva (I). The order issued by the king in the fifth year was registered in the twenty-third year.

Guttapalle.

209. 311 *of* 1912.—(Tamil.) On a slab set up in a field. Records in the seventh year the death of a hero at Madanapalle when Śelvagaṅgamārāyan, after capturing his enemy in Mārāyappāḍi, was bringing back the cattle. See Ct. 185 above.

Karshaṇapalle.

210. 321 *of* 1912.—(Tamil.) On the east and north bases of the maṇṭapa in front of the central shrine in the Arkēśvara temple. A record in the thirty-sixth year of the Chōḷa king Rājakēsarivarman *alias* Uḍaiyār śrī-Rājādhirājadēva (I). Records gift of tax on oil mills, to provide a lamp in the temple of Aṅgakkāṛa-Īśvaram Uḍaiyār at Muttukūr *alias* Erivīrappaṭṭaṇam (a mile off Karshaṇapalle) in Puli-nāḍu (the region proper of the Bāṇas and Vaiḍumbas) which was a subdivision of Tyāgābharaṇa-vaḷanāḍu in Jayaṅgoṇḍaśōḷa-maṇḍalam, by Śōḷakulakāraṇa-Mūvēndavēḷān who was the revenue officer in charge of the district, for the prosperity of the emperor.

211. 322 *of* 1912.—(Tamil.) On a pillar of the porch of the same maṇṭapa. Records the construction of the steps *(sōpāna)* by certain *āśāris (karumān).*

212. 323 *of* 1912.—(Kanarese.) On a slab built into the Nandimaṇṭapa of the same temple. A fragment of record of the Baṇa king Baṇarasa. See No. 194 above.

213. 324 *of* 1912.—(Tamil.) On a slab set up in the same temple. A record of the Vijayanagara king Vijayarāya-Uḍaiyār (1409—22) ruling at Mulvāyil in Ś. 1332, Vikrita, Chaitra, śu. di. 5, Thursday lunar eclipse (= Thursday 21st March 1409). Records gift of a portion of income accruing to the royal treasury from certain lands at Muttakkūru, in favour of the temple of Aṅgakkarīśvaramuḍaiya-Nāyinār at that village which belonged to Vaḍa-Puli-nāḍu, a subdivision of Nigariliśōḷa-maṇḍalam, by the chief Sammaṭṭi Vīra-Ōbaḷadēva Chōḷamahārāja. [" The Sammaṭṭi family to which the chief Ōbaḷadēva belonged, may be the same as Sammēta whose members Lakkayadēva Mahārāja and Bommayadēva Mahārāja are known to have been the dependants of Dēvarāya II and to have borne the title *Antembaragaṇḍa*." *Ep. Rep.*, 1913, p. 119, para. 53.

214. 325 *of* 1912.—(Kanarese.) •On another slab set up in the same temple. A record of the Noḷamba (Pallava) king Vīramahēndra-Noḷambādhirājadēva. States that the king returned from Chōḷa-nāḍu, entered Noḷambavāḍi and camped at Kolāla in Gaṅgaru-śāsira (district). On this occasion he raised Kīrtigavuṇḍa to the position of Noḷambagavuṇḍa of Puli-nāḍu and gave him as a *koḍage* grant the village Kiriya-Belagatūru (in that district). [The inscription gives a genealogy of the line from Dilīpa Iriva Noḷamba up to Vīramahēndra, six generations in all. Evidently Vīra Mahēndra helped the Rāshṭrakūṭa Kṛishṇa III in his invasion of the Chōḷa country.]

215. 326 *of* 1912.—(Kanarese.) On a third slab set up in the same temple. A record of the Western Gaṅga king Priduvīpati (evidently the same as the chief referred to in Nos. 223 and 226 below), the younger brother of Durvinīta. Records that Śivarāsibhaṭāra, son of Gaṭṭada-bhaṭāra set up the minor images in the temple and presented three stone oil-mills to it. [The Government Epigraphist points out the probable significance of the early Gaṅga title being assumed by a prince of the Gaṅga-Bāṇa line, but how it is yet to be ascertained.]

216. 327 *of* 1912.—(Kanarese.) On a slab set up in a field in the same village. A record of the Bāṇa king Mahāvali Bāṇarasar, whom Venkayya identified with Vikramāditya I of Udayēndram plates. Refers to the death of a hero at Kutilāla, on the occasion when Ballaha (Rāshṭrakūṭa Gōvinda III) took up arms against Kāḍuveṭṭi for exacting tribute. The hero was a servant of Bāṇarasa Vijayitta (i.e., Vikramāditya's son Vijayāditya II Vīrachūḷāmaṇi Prabhumēru), who was ruling Gaṅgaru-śāsira. [The

Bāṇas were evidently in temporary occupation of the Gaṅgaru-śāsira country which was purely a Gaṅga land and governed by the Noḷamba potentates. It is not improbable that the Bāṇa occupation was in retaliation of the Noḷamba invasion of Pulināḍu under the orders of Gōvinda III.]

217. 328 *of* 1912.—(Kanarese.) On the same slab. Seems to record the death of a Gaṅga king Prithuvīpatiyarasa (I ?).

218. 329 *of* 1912.—(Kanarese.) On another slab set up in the same place. A record of the Chōḷa king Rājēndra-Chōḷa (I). Records the death of a private individual of Muttukūru.

219. 330 *of* 1912.—(Kanarese.) On the same slab. Mentions the death of a hero at Muttukūru and the grant of land to him below the southern tank, as *koḍagē.*

220. 331 *of* 1912.—(Kanarese.) On a third slab set up in the same place. The top portion of the slab is lost. Records that the *gāmuṇḍas* of Muttukūru presented some wet land to the son of a deceased hero.

221. 332 *of* 1912.—(Kanarese.) On the south slab in the same place. A record of the Bāṇa Śembiyan Mahābali Bāṇarasa. Records that while Vikkiyanna, son of Prithvīpati (II), was governing the Puli-nāḍu sixty district, a quarrel arose between him and Pallava-Dhavaḷa, in which he and a hero died. The latter's brother Kuṇḍiga raised this monumental stone in memory of the dead hero. [Chembiyan Mahābalirāya was a title bestowed on the Gaṅga feudatory Prithvīpati II Hastimalla by the Chōḷa Parāntaka I who presented the Bāṇa kingdom to him in A.D. 915–6. See *Ep. Ind.*, XI, p. 238.]

222. 333 *of* 1912.—(Kanarese.) On the fifth slab in the same place. Mentions Avabbe, the queen of Prithuvayya.

223. 334 *of* 1912.—(Kanarese.) On the sixth slab in the same place. A record of the Western Gaṅga king Prithvīpati. Mentions a servant of the king named Chāmuṇḍa. See No. 215 above.

224. 335 *of* 1912.—(Kanarese.) On the seventh slab set up in the same place. A much damaged record of the Bāṇa king Mahābali Bāṇarasa (Vikramāditya I ?).

225. 336 *of* 1912.—(Kanarese.) On the eighth slab set up in the same place. Mentions Muttukūru and the death of a hero in a cattle raid.

226. 337 *of* 1912.—(Kanarese.) On the ninth slab set in the same place. A record of the Western Gaṅga king Priduvayya. Mentions the Pāṇḍya and the Chōḷa king and the death of a hero. [The battle here referred to was evidently the one in which Prithvīpati I died for his friend, the "Gaṅga-Pallava" Aparājita in the battle of Śrīpurāmbiyam near Kumbakōnam. The Pāṇḍya referred to was Varaguṇa. See No. 302 below.]

227. 338 *of* 1912.—(Kanarese.) On the tenth slab set up in the same place. A damaged record. Seems to mention the chief "Bāgigayyamaindembam Baṅkarasa" and the death (?) of one of his servants.

Laḍḍigam.

This is ancient Koyaṟṟūr. The local temple was built by a feudatory of Kulōttuṅga I named Iruṅgōḷa and so the deity was named after him.

228. 544 *of* 1906.—(Tamil verse.) On the gōpura of the Nīlakaṇṭhēśvara temple, right of entrance. In praise of the sword of Aḍigan, i.e., Aḍiyamān Viḍugādaḷagiya Perumāḷ, whose name and emblems are engraved below the inscription.

229. 545 *of* 1906.—(Tamil verse.) In the same place; left of entrance. In praise of Adigēśan, i.e., Tagaḍūr Adiyamān Viḍugādaḷagiya Perumāḷ, whose names and emblems are engraved below the inscription.

230. 546 *of* 1906.—(Tamil.) On the south wall of the prākāra of the same temple. An unfinished record in the ninth year of the Chōḷa king Vikrama-Chōḷadēva (1118—35). Mentions the temple of Irungōḷīśvaramuḍaiya-Mahādēvar at Koyaṟṟūr *alias* Uttama-Chōḷapuram. [Venkayya points out that one of the places conquered by the Hoysaḷa king Vishṇuvardhana, Kōyatūr, which has been hitherto identified with Coimbatore, might in reality refer to this place.]

231. 547 *of* 1906.—(Grantha and Tamil verse.) On the north wall of the same prākāra. In praise of the Kēraḷa king Adhikēndra Vyāmuktaśravaṇōjjvala. The Tamil verses refer to his engraving the bow on the wall of Iruṅgōḷīśvara temple. The inscription has the Chēra bow and other emblems on each side of it.

232. 548 *of* 1906.—(Tamil.) On the south wall of the same shrine in the temple, right of entrance. Records gift of money for three lamps to the temple of Iruṅgōḷīśvaramuḍaiya-Mahādēvar at Koyaṟṟūr *alias* Uttama-Chōḷapuram.

233. 549 *of* 1906.—(Tamil.) In the same place. A record in the fourteenth year of Uttamachōḷa-Gaṅga *alias* Śeṇbagāchchipati-Nāyanār. Records gift to the temple of Iruṅgōḷīśvaramuḍaiya Nāyanār at Koyaṟṟūr.

234. 550 *of* 1906.—(Tamil.) In the same place. An unfinished record in the twentieth year of the Chōḷa king Kulōttuṅga-Chōḷadēva. Records gift of 96 sheep for a lamp to the same temple.

235. 551 *of* 1906.—(Tamil.) On the same wall, left of entrance. A record in the ninth year of the Chōḷa king Rājarājadēva (III). Records gift of money for the merit of Uttamachōḷa-Gaṅga Veṭṭum Amarābaraṇan Akaḷaṅka-Śīyagaṅga *alias* Sittaviḍadēva. The temple is called Iruṅgōḷīśvaramuḍaiya Nāyanār at Koyaṟṟūr *alias* Uttama-Chōḷapuram in Vaḍa-Puli-nāḍu, a subdivision of Perumbāṇappāḍi in Jayaṅgoṇḍa-Chōḷa-maṇḍalam. See Ct. 186 above.

236. 552 *of* 1906.--(Tamil verse.) On the east wall of the same shrine. In praise of Viḍugādaḷagiyan of Ten-Tagaḍai, whose enemies were the Kāḍava, the Māgada and the Gaṅga.

237. 553 *of* 1906.—(Tamil.) On the south, east, north and west walls of the same shrine. A record in the sixteenth year of the Chōḷa king Rājakēsarivarman *alias* Chakravartin śrī-Kulōttuṅga Chōḷadēva (I). Records gift of the village of Mādamaṅgalam in Pulināḍu, a district of Raṭṭapāḍikoṇḍa-Chōḷa-maṇḍalam (calling it Gaṅgaikoṇḍa-Chōḷanallūr) to the temple of Iruṅgōḷīśvaramuḍaiya Mahādēvar built at Koyaṟṟūr *alias* Uttamaśōḷapuram in the same nāḍu by Āḍavalān Gaṅgaikoṇḍa-Chōḷa *alias* Iruṅgōḷan. Many officers mentioned and also the village taxes exempted.

Minikibanda near Miniki.

238. 568 *of* 1906.—(Grantha and Tamil.) On the rock. A record in the thirty-ninth year of the Chōḷa king Kulottuṅga I. The Sanskrit portion mentions the Gaṅga family and Konkuṇivarman. The introduction belongs to Kulottuṅga I, whose name is not mentioned. But the name Rajakēsarivarman and the title Chakravartin occur at the end of the introduction. The date here noted is incidentally mentioned. Records the construction of a channel to the tank at Uppanelli in Mudukurukki in Vaḍa-Pulināḍu, a subdivision of Perumbāṇappāḍi in Nigarili-Chōḷamaṇḍalam. The channel was improved by the son of the chief who built it.

Nekkuṇḍi near Mittapalli.

239. 567 *of* 1906.—(Tamil.) On a boulder in the fields. A record of Uttamachōḷa Gaṅga-Śelvagaṅga. Records gift of land in the village of Nerkkuṇḍi to the temple of Tiruvagattīśvaramuḍaiya-Nāyanār. See No. 183 above.

Mudugalapalle.

240. 315 *of* 1912.—(Kanarese.) On a *viragal* set up in a field. A mutilated record. Seems to mention Mahārājavāḍi.

241. 316 *of* 1912.—(Kanarese.) On another *viragal* in the same place. Refers to a cattle raid and the death of a hero.

242. 317 *of* 1912.—(Kanarese.) On a slab set up to the west of the same village. A damaged record. Refers to a certain Sāmantavallava, son of Dōsiyarasa.

243. 318 *of* 1912.—(Kanarese.) On another slab set up in the same place. A mutilated record. Refers to the raid on Puli-nāḍu by the Noḷamba king, under orders of Koṅguṇiaraśar and to the capture of Koyaṟṟūr. On this occasion the servant of a brother of

Dōsiyarasa, the chief of that country, fought and fell. [The Konguṇiaraśar referred to is the Gaṅga king Permānaḍi, and the Noḷamba is Noḷambādhirāja. See Ct. 255 and Ct. 176.]

244. 319 *of* 1912.—(Kanarese.) On a third slab set up in the same place. A mutilated record. Mentions Koyaṟṟūr and a certain Indragāni.

Mugavāḍi.

245. 572 *of* 1906.—(Kanarese.) On a slab set up in front of the Pūṇḍīśvara temple. A record of the Vijayanagara king Vīra-Bukkarāya (II) in Ś. 1323, Pārthiva. Registers an order of Jommanna Oḍeya and mentions Dēvarāya-Oḍeya.

246. 573 *of* 1906.—(Tamil.) On another slab set up in the same place. A damaged record in the third year of the Chōḷa king Parakēsarivarman *alias* Uḍaiyar Śrī-Ādhirajēndradēva (son of Vīra Rājēndra I who ruled from 1064 to 1070). Records gift of land. The village Mukkaivāḍi was situated in Puli-nāḍu, a sub-division of Perumbāṇappāḍi in Paḍuvūr-kōṭṭam, a district of Jayaṅgoṇḍa-Chōḷamaṇḍalam.

247. 574 *of* 1906.—(Tamil.) On a stone forming the roof of a small shrine in the courtyard of the same temple. A fragment of record of the Chōḷa king Parakēsarivarman Rajēndradēva (1050—63), the date of which is lost. Contains the beginning of the historical introduction of the king.

Nelapalli.

248. 242 *of* 1913.—(Kanarese.) On a rock in a field. A record of the Noḷamba Pallava king Iriva-Noḷamba (II) Ghaṭēyaṅkakāra Pallavāditya. Registers that while the king was encamped at Ve(nv)ūruponne in Parevināḍu he conferred the title of *Mummaḍi-gavare* Pallavāditya Noḷambaśeṭṭi on a *Bāḷigāra* merchant of Kōyatūru and presenting him with royal insignia gave for his perpetual enjoyment as *koḍage* the village of Koḷatūru in Puli-nāḍu, converting it into a mercantile town (*vaiśyadatti* nagara) named Pallavādityapura. [The king was the grandson of Vīramahēndra of Ct. 214. The paraphernalia included a horse, an umbrella-bearer, a throne, *addaṅgi*, etc.]

249. 243 *of* 1913.—(Kanarese.) On the same rock. In the same old characters as No. 242. Refers to the 48,000 of the mercantile community, to Mummaḍi Gavaṟeśeṭṭi of Kāñchīpura and to his younger brother Sundarachōḷa-Dharmaśeṭṭi.

250. 244 *of* 1913.—(Tamil.) On a hero-slab in a field of the same village. Registers that in a face-to-face tiger hunt arranged by Śrīkaṇṭhayyan, son of Māvaḷivaṇa-Vichchādirar *alias* Puḷalam-maraiyar, a certain Indappan pierced a tiger and died with it. [Was the king identical with Bāṇa-Vidyādhara Mahābali Vikramāditya I?]

Pudupaṭla.

251. 554 *of* 1906.—On a slab set up in the village. In archaic characters, consists of the description of a king. Appears to be a fragment of a Bāṇa inscription.

252. 555 *of* 1906.—(Kanarese.) On a pillar set up in front of the Chaṇḍēśvari temple in the same village. A damaged and mutilated record of the Bāṇa king Mahābali-Bāṇarasa. In archaic characters. Appears to record a case of suttee. See note to 250.

Puṅganūru.

253. 540 *of* 1906.—(Tamil.) On a broken slab lying on the tank-bund, west of the fort. A damaged record in the third year of the Chōḷa king Rājakēsarivarman *alias* Uḍaiyār Śrī-Rājēndra-Chōḷadēva (II, i.e., Kulōttuṅga I?). Mentions the tank called Rājēndraśōḷapperiyēri at Puṅganūr *alias* Vaḷavanārāyaṇa-chaturvēdimaṅgalam in Pulināḍu, a district of Raṭṭapāḍikoṇḍa-Chōḷa-maṇḍalam.

254. 541 *of* 1906.—(Grantha and Tamil.) On a slab set up in the court-yard of the Sōmēśvarasvāmin temple in the same village. A record in the fourth year of the Chōḷa king Rājakēsarivarman *alias* Uḍaiyār Śrī-Vīra-rājēndradēva (Vīra-Rājēndra I, 1064—70). The inscription opens with the *birudas* of the king. Mentions the Tirukkōḷīśvaram-uḍaiya-Mahādēvar at Puṅganūr *alias* Vaḷava-nārāyaṇa-chaturvēdimaṅgalam in Puli-nāḍu of Perumbāṇappāḍi, a subdivision of Paḍuvūr-kōṭṭam in Jayaṅgoṇḍa-Chōḷa-maṇḍalam. A chief presents 4,200 *kuḻis* of land, and the assembly receives the paddy and maintains worship and expenses according to scales detailed.

255. 542 *of* 1906.—(Kanarese.) On a slab set up outside the same temple. A record of the Bāṇa king Mahāvali-Vāṇaraśar Vijayādityan *Vīra-chūḷāmaṇi* Prabhumēru (evidently the father of Vikramāditya II Vijayabāhu, and the victim of the Chōḷa Parāntaka's ambition). The king was ruling the Vaḍugavaḷi 12,000 and Maṇṇe 200. Refers to the raid on Koyaṭūr by Kāḍu-veṭṭi-Muttaraśan. [See Ct. 243 and Ct. 175 for further information regarding the Noḷamba invasion of Pulināḍu under Kāḍuveṭṭi.]

256. 543 *of* 1906.—(Kanarese.) On a slab set up in a field in front of the village of Chadaḷḷa, close to the Puṅganūr Chadum road. A record of the Bāṇa king Mahavali-Bāṇarasa. Refers to the battle of Sōremati where the Bāṇa opposed the Noḷamba, Rāchamalla and Mayindāḍi on behalf of the Permānaḍi (i.e., the Gaṅga-king). Mentions Mādhavarasa of Kaṅganūra. [Rācha-malla was evidently Satyavākya Koṅguṇivarma Permānaḍi Rājamalla whose final date is A.D. 971. See *Ep. Ind.,* Vol. VI, p. 59.]

Somala.

257. 339 *of* 1912.—(Telugu.) On a slab set up in a field. Records in Tāraṇa gift of Ñelapalle to a private individual, by another private individual.

Yāṭavākili.

258. 575 *of* 1906.—(Tamil.) On the base of the Chandramauḷīśvara temple. A record in the twenty-second year of the Chōḷa king Parakēsarivarman *alias* Uḍaiyār śrī-Rājēndra-Chōḷadēva (I). Records gift of land to the temple of Irugīśvaramuḍaiya-Mahādēvar built by a Veḷḷāḷa at Eṭṭāvāykkāl in Puli-nāḍu, a subdivision of Perambāṇappāḍi in Jayaṅgoṇḍa-Chōḷamaṇḍalam.

259. 576 *of* 1906.—(Tamil.) On the walls of the same temple. A record in the twenty-ninth year, Viśvāsi (Viśvāvasu), of the Chōḷa king Rājarāja-Chōḷadēva. The temple is called Irugīśvara-muḍaiya Nāyanār at Eṭṭāravākkāl in Vaḍa-Puli-nāḍu, a subdivision of Perumbāṇappāḍi in Jayaṅgoṇḍa-Chōḷa-Maṇḍalam.

260. 577 *of* 1906.—(Tamil.) On the slab set up in the courtyard of the Chennakēśavasvāmin temple in the same village. A record of the Vijayanagara king Kampaṇa-Uḍaiyār in Jaya. Records gift of the village of Eṭṭavāykkāl in Puli-nāḍu.

PUTTŪR TALUK.

Kārvēṭinagar.

261. 392 *of* 1911.—(Tamil.) On detached slabs round the central shrine in the Vēṇugōpāla-perumāḷ temple. A record in the eleventh year of the Chōḷa king Tribhuvanachakravartin Rājarājadēva (III). The fragments appear to have included this and two other records of the same king and of the same date and to have registered gifts of land to the Śiva temples at Nārāyaṇapuram in Vaṭṭiya-nāḍu, a subdivision of Kunṟavattana-kōṭṭam. Some of the temples mentioned are Avimuktīśvaramuḍaiya-Nāyanār, Lakkīśvaramuḍaiya-Nāyanār and Akkaśālīśvaramuḍaiya-Nāyanār. Mention a certain Vīra-Naraśiṅgadēvan *alias* Yādavarāyan. Also a fragment is found of an unnamed Sāḷuva king. See No. 102 above.

Kempulapāḷaiyam.

262. 383 *of* 1911.—(Tamil.) On the base of the central shrine in the Agastyēśvara temple. A record in the fifteenth year of the Chōḷa king Tribhuvanachakravartin Rājarājadēva (III?). Records gift of two *māḍai* for a lamp to the temple of Tiruvagattīśura-muḍaiya Nāyanār at Nārāyaṇapuram in Vaṭṭiya-nāḍu, a subdivision of Kunṟavattana-kōṭṭam in Jayaṅgoṇḍachōḷa-maṇḍalam by Rājanārāyaṇa Mūvēndavēḷān, a native of Pirāṭṭi-Kuḷattūr in Dāmar-nāḍu, a subdivision of Dāmar-kōṭṭam.

263. 384 *of* 1911.—(Telugu.) On the beams of the maṇṭapa in the Ammanāchi-Amman temple in the same village. Registers in Ś. 1669, Prabhava, that Mahāmaṇḍalēśvara Śēshāchalapatirāju-dēva-Mahārāja, son of Rāmarāja and grandson of Guṇḍoli Kṛishṇamarāja, of the Kāśyapa-gōtra, repaired the Sabhāmaṇṭapa of the temple of Ammanāchchamma (called Āmnāyākshi in Sanskrit) at Nārāyaṇapuram, the northern entrance to Kāñchipīṭha.

Nārāyaṇavanam.

264. 373 *of* 1911.—(Tamil.) On the north, west and south walls of the central shrine in the Kalyāṇa-Vēṅkaṭēśa-Perumāḷ temple. A record of the Vijayanagara king Vīrapratāpa Vīra-Achyutarāya Mahārāya in Ś. 1463, Plava. Records that a certain Viruppaṇṇa founded a town called Vēṅkaṭādrisamudram on the borders of Nārāyaṇapuram and constructed there the temple of Vēṅkaṭādri-Perumāḷ for the merit of Vēṅkaṭādrirāya-Mahārāya. To this temple he gave for offerings, with the permission of the king, some complete villages and shares in others. [Mr. Krishna Sastri surmises that the Vēṅkaṭādri mentioned here might be the son of Achyuta Rāya who, after the demise of Achyuta, was for a short time on the throne and who was supported by the Sālaka chiefs as against the Āravīti brothers who supported Sadāśiva.]

265. 374 *of* 1911.—(Tamil.) On the west and south walls of the same shrine. Registers in Krōdhin an oral agreement (*vāk-patram*) among three private individuals.

266. 375 *of* 1911.—(Tamil.) On a slab fixed into the floor of the maṇṭapa in front of the same shrine. A record of the Chōḷa king Rājarājakēsarivarman (Rājarāja I), the date of which is lost. Registers that Vikkiyaṇṇan Pugaḷvipparagaṇḍan of the Chāḷukki family and two others, the chiefs of Vaṭṭiya-nāḍu in Kunṟavattaṇa-kōṭṭam, gave certain privileges to the Veḷḷaḷas of that district. [Pugaḷvipparagaṇḍan was a title borne by some Lāḍa chiefs and by the Bāṇa king Vijayāditya II. Chāḷukki must also have been a family of feudatories.]

267. 376 *of* 1911.—(Telugu.) On the inner gōpura of the same temple. Records in Ś. 1545, Dundubhi, gift of a village for offerings and festivals to the temple of Kalyāṇa-Veṅkaṭēśvara-svāmin of Nārāyaṇapura, by the Mahāmaṇḍalēśvara Tirumalarāja, son of Śrīraṅgarāja and grandson of Kaṭṭāri-Sāḷuva-Mahārāja of the Kāśyapa-gōtra and the Āpastamba-sūtra.

268. 377 *of* 1911.—(Telugu.) On the outer gōpura of the same temple. A record of the Vijayanagara king Vīrapratāpa-Vīra-Veṅkaṭadēva Mahārāya (Veṅkaṭa II), ruling at Penugoṇḍa, in S. 1544, Raudri. Built in at the left end. Records gift of tolls by common consent, to the temple of Kalyāṇa Veṅkaṭēśvara, by the mercantile community, of Ayyavōḷe headed by Prithiviśeṭṭi

Rāyanimaṇtri-Bhāskara, while Śāḷuva Makarāja Tirumalarājayya dēva was ruling the country [i.e., the Śāḷuva chief of Kārvēṭinagar who rose to prominence at this time and who had the Śāḷuva emblem of the boar with the dagger. Bhāskara is even now the title of the Brahman Guru of the *Kōmaṭis*. According to tradition Rāyanimantri lived in the time of Krishṇadēva, but the present inscription shows that he was later. The Government Epigraphist draws attention to Guruzada Śrīrāmamūrti's *Rāyani-bhāskara charitramu* wherein it is stated that Prithvīśeṭṭi received a *firman* from Alamghyr Padshah. It is not possible to reconcile this with the above events. See *Ep. Rep.*, 1912, pp. 83–4, for some popular traditions about it.]

269. 378 *of* 1911.—(Tamil.) On two detached slabs built into the floor of the Vāhana-maṇṭapa in the same temple. A record in the seventeenth year of the Chōḷa king Tribhuvanachakravartin Rājarājadēva. Records gift of tolls by common consent to the temple of Kavarīśvaramuḍaiya-Nāyanār at Nārāyaṇapuram in Tiruvēṅgaḍa-kōṭṭam, by the mercantile community.

270. 379 *of* 1911.—(Tamil.) On two other detached slabs built into the same floor. A record in the eighth year of the Pāṇḍya king Sundara-Pāṇḍyadēva (Jaṭāvarman I,? 1251–64) "who took every country." Records gift of twenty pack bullocks to the temple of Kavarīśvaram-Uḍaiyār, by a certain Periyapiḷḷai *alias* Rāja-nārāyaṇa-Śērakōn, one of the subordinates of Yādavarāya. See No. 111 above.

271. 380 *of* 1911.—(Tamil.) On two detached slabs built into the maṇṭapa opposite the main entrance into the same temple. A record of the Chōḷa king Tribhuvanachakravartin Rājarājadēva the date of which is lost. Seems to record the gift of the village Pondaipākkam in Śey-nāḍu for repairs and other requirements, to the temple of Kavarīśvaramuḍaiya-Nāyanār.

272. 381 *of* 1911.—(Tamil.) On the west wall of the central shrine in the Parāśarēśvara temple in the same village. A record of the Vijayanagara king Vīrapratāpa Vīra-Sadāśivadēva-Mahārāya in Ś. 1473, Paridhāvin. Records gift of 40 *paṇam* for offerings to the temple of Ambaliṅgamuḍaiya Nāyanār at Nārāyaṇapuram in Tiruvattiyūrnāḍu, a subdivision of Kunṟavarttana kōṭṭam in Jayaṅgoṇḍa-chōḷa-maṇḍalam, by a *Kammāḷa* of that village.

273. 382 *of* 1911.—(Telugu.) On a slab built into the floor of the court-yard in the same temple. Records in Pramādīcha (Pramādin) gift of the village of Yippatoṅgali to the priests of Kāḷahasti on the occasion of the *kumbhābhishēka* (i.e., the renovation) of the temple of Agastīśvara (also called Parāśārēśvara), by Kaṭṭāri-sāḷva Makārāja-Bommarājudēva-Mahārāju. [Perhaps also a grandson of Makārāja. See Mr. Sewell's *Antiquities*, II, 184–5, and Cox's *N. A. Manual*, p. 222, for details about the history of Kārvēṭinagar.]

Sattravāḍa.

274. 387 *of* 1911.—(Tamil.) On a slab set up in front of the Dēśa-Vināyaka temple. A record in the eighteenth year of Yādavarāyar Śrīranganāthar. The residents of Tiraṇi-nāḍu in Neḍu-nāḍu and others gave to a certain Mēḷittēvan, the village of Tiraṇi as a *rudirappaṭṭi*. This he presented to the Dēśa-Vināyaka temple at Sattirappāḍi and *prohibited the sects of Saṅkētisamayakkārar and Vīra-koḍiyar from entering it.*

275. 388 *of* 1911.—(Tamil.) On a slab set up by the side of a well in the same village. A record of the Śāḷuva king Śelva (Śāḷuva) Tippadēva-Mahārāja, son of Śāḷuva Tippayadēva-Mahārāja in Dundubhi (= Ś. 1364). Records a charter granted to the Śēṇiyans by Daḷavāy Śrīraṅga-Rāvuttar. [Evidently this Śāḷuva Tippa was the brother of the Śāḷuva Goppa, the son of Śāḷuva Tippa, referred to in Tekal inscriptions, Mysore.]

276. 389 *of* 1911.—(Tamil.) On the east wall of the manṭapa in front of the central shrine of the Chidambarēśvara temple in the same village. A record of the Vijayanagara king Vīrapratāpa Dēvarāya-Mahārāya (II) in Ś. 1349, Plavaṅga. Built in at the bottom. Mentions the Śāḷva and Vaishṇava shrines of Chandragiri-rājya, viz., Kāñchīpuram, Tirukkāḷatti, Tiruvoṟṟiyūr, Tiruvālaṅgāḍu, Tiruppālaivanam and others. Refers to the *vibhūti-kāṇikkai* collected in the temple of Aḷagiya Tiruchchiṟṟambalamuḍaiya Nāyanār at Śattirappāḍi in Maṅgaḷūr-nāḍu, a subdivision of Kunṟavattana-kōṭṭam in Jayaṅgoṇḍachōḷa-maṇḍalam and to certain royal orders *(rāyasam)* issued to Ariyappa-Daṇṇāyaka Bhikshāvritti-Ayyagaḷ and Dēvarāya-Uḍaiyār of Chandragiri.

277. 390 *of* 1911.—(Tamil.) On the west and north walls of the Varadarāja Perumāḷ temple in the same village. A much damaged record of the Vijayanagara king Vīrapratāpa Vīra-Achyutayya-dēva-Mahārāya in Ś. 1459, Hēviḷambi. Mentions Maṅgaḷūr-nāḍu, a subdivision of Nārāyaṇapurappaṟṟu in Kunṟavattaṇa-kōṭṭam of Jayaṅgoṇḍachōḷa-maṇḍalam.

278. 391 *of* 1911.—(Tamil.) On a slab set up in the main street in the same village. Registers that Gaṇḍaraguḷi Māraya-Nāyakkar, son of Mahāpradhani Sōmaya-Daṇṇayaka, gave to the temple of Aḷagiya-Tiruchchiṟṟambalamuḍaiya-Nāyanār, a piece of land with the right to take water from the tank of Vasavanappanēri.

Yōgi-Mallāvaram.

279. 264 *of* 1904.—(Tamil.) On the south wall of the Parāśarēśvara temple. A much damaged record in the forty-first year of the Chōḷa king Rājakēsarivarman *alias* Chakravartin Kulōttuṅga-Chōḷadēva (I).

280. 265 *of* 1904.—(Tamil.) On the west and south walls of the same temple. A record in the twenty-fourth year of the Chōḷa king Rājakēsarivarman *alias* Chakravartin Kulōttuṅga-Chōḷadēva (I?). Records gift of a lamp to the temple of Tippalādrīśvaramuḍaiya-Mahādēva at Tiruchchuganūr in Kuḍavūr-nāḍu, a subdivision of Tiruvēṅgaḍa-kōṭṭam in Rājēndra-Śōḷamaṇḍalam.

281. 266 *of* 1904.—(Grantha and Tamil.) On the west wall of the same temple. A record of the Chōḷa king Vīrarājēndra-Chōḷadēva, the date of which is lost. Records gift of two lamps.

282. 267 *of* 1904.—(Grantha and Tamil.) On the same wall. A record in the sixteenth year of the Chōḷa king Vikrama-Chōḷadēva (1118—35). Records gift of land.

283. 268 *of* 1904.—(Tamil.) On the north wall of the same temple. A record in the ninth year of the Chōḷa king Tribhuvanachakravartin Rājarājadēva (II or III?). Records gift of gold.

284. 269 *of* 1904.—(Tamil.) On the same wall. A record in the ninth year of the Chōḷa king Tribhuvanachakravartin Rājarājadēva. Quotes the twenty-third year of Rājakēsarivarman *alias* Rājarājadēva.

285. 270 *of* 1904.—(Tamil.) On the same wall. A record in the thirty-sixth year of the Chōḷa king Rājakēsarivarman *alias* Chakravartin Kulōttuṅga-Chōḷadēva (I). Records gift of land.

286. 271 *of* 1904.—(Tamil.) On the north and west bases of the same temple. A record in the sixth year of the Chōḷa king Tribhuvanachakravartin Rājarājadēva (III). Records gift of land. Refers to a battle between Vīra-Naraśiṅgadēva *alias* Yādavarāya and Kāḍavarāya at Uratti.

287. 272 *of* 1904.—(Tamil.) On a pillar built into the wall of a maṇṭapa in the south-east corner of the same temple. A fragment of record.

288. 273 *of* 1904.—(Grantha and Tamil.) On four detached stones lying in front of the same temple. A mutilated record of the Chōḷa king Chakravartin Vīrarājēndradēva(I) in Ś. 991, Saumya, in his seventh year. Mentions the temple of Piplādrīśvaramuḍaiya-Mahādēvar. [The inscription shows that Vīra Rājēndra came to the throne in 1063-4.]

289. 274 *of* 1904.—(Tamil.) On the east wall of the Kalyāṇa-maṇṭapa in front of the same temple. An incomplete record. Refers to the setting up of an image of Gaṇapati by a private individual.

290. 275 *of* 1904.—(Tamil.) On the south wall of the same maṇṭapa. A record in the fourteenth year of the Chōḷa king Tribhuvanachakravartin Rājarājadēva (III). Records gift of land for the merit of Vīra-Naraśiṅgadēva-Yādavarāya. See Ct. 111 above.

TIRUTTANI TALUK.

Arungulam.

291. On a large stone north-west of the village. Records the grant of the village as *inām* in Ś. 1477 (A.D. 1555) during the reign of Sadāśiva Rāya of Vijayanagar.

292. On a stone. An "unintelligible" epigraph said to have great power in curing cattle disease. *Antiquities*, I, p. 156.

Kārumbēḍu.

293. 385 *of* 1911.—(Telugu.) On a slab in the kitchen of the Nāgādhīśvarasvāmin temple. Records in Ś. 1752, Vikriti, that Tiruveṅgalāmbā, the queen of a prince of the family of Kaṭṭāri Śāḷuva Mākarāja, built a shrine for Sōmasundarēśvara and Mīnākshi, in the temple of Nāgādhīśvara situated on the bank of the river Kuśasthali. The chief belonged to the Kārvēṭinagar line.

294. 386 *of* 1911.—(Telugu.) On a slab built into the wall of the Utsava-maṇṭapa in the same temple. A record in Ś. 1692, Vikriti. States that the maṇṭapa was built by Tirumalakoṇḍama, wife of Bopparāju-Veṅkaṭanarasimharāja and daughter of the Mahāmaṇḍalēśvara Vellāṇti Kēśavarāja. The name of the village is given as Kadirapura on the bank of the Kuśasthali river.

Santāna Vēṇugōpālapuram.

295. On a wall of the prākāra of the Vishṇu temple. An epigraph of Ś. 1678 (A.D. 1756) recording a grant by the Zamindar.

Tiruttani.

296. 429 *of* 1905.—(Tamil.) On the north wall of the central shrine in the Vīrattānēśvara temple. A mutilated record. Registers a sale of land to a private individual for feeding pilgrims going to and returning from Śrīvēṅgaḍam, i.e., Upper-Tirupati.

297. 430 *of* 1905.—(Tamil.) On the north, west and south walls of the same shrine. A record in the twenty-eighth year of the Chōḷa king Rājakēsarivarman *alias* Rājarājadēva (I). Records sale of land by the assembly of Jananātha-chaturvēdimaṅgalam in Mēnmalai Taṇiyal-nāḍu (a district) of Jayaṅgoṇḍa-Chōḷamaṇḍalam to a private individual for feeding pilgrims going to and returning from Śrīvēṅkaḍam.

298. 431 *of* 1905.—(Tamil.) On the west wall of the same shrine. A record in the eleventh year of the Chōḷa king Vikrama-Chōḷadēva (1118—35). Records gift of 12 sheep for a lamp to burn at the temple of Tiruvīrattānam-Uḍaiyār.

299. 432 *of* 1905.—(Tamil.) On the same wall. A record in the fourth year of the Chōḷa king Rājakēsarivarman. Provides for a lamp. Mentions the village of Tiruttaṇiyal in Kunṟavattaṇa-kōṭṭam. The "*annual committee*" of the village had to supervise the endowment.

300. 433 *of* 1905.—(Tamil verse.) On the south wall of the same shrine. Records that a certain Nambi-Appi built the temple at Tiruttaṇiyal of granite. The verse (veṇbā) is said to have been composed by a king, whose name is, however, not given.

301. 434 *of* 1905.—(Tamil.) On the same wall. A record in the nineteenth year of the Chōḷa king Parakēsarivarman *alias* Śrī-Rājēndra-Chōḷadēva (I, 1011—43). Records gift of 30 cows for a lamp. The temple is called Tiruvīrattānam-uḍaiya-Mahādēvar in Tiruttaṇiyal.

302. 435 *of* 1905.—(Tamil.) On the same wall. A record in the eighteenth year of "the Gaṅga-Pallava king" Vijaya-Aparājitavikramavarman. Records gift of 1,000 *kuḷi* of land by Nambi-Appi to the temple of Tiruvīrattānam at Tiruttaṇiyal. [See *Ep. Rep.*, 1906, p. 65, where Venkayya argues that Aparājita should have been the son of Nripatuṅga and that it was to help him that his Gaṅga feudatory Prithvīpati I met Varaguṇa Pāṇḍya in battle at Tiruppirāmbiam. Venkayya further points out that it was this Aparājita who was conquered by Āditya I of the imperial Chōḷa line.]

303. 436 *of* 1905.—(Tamil.) On the east and north walls of the maṇṭapa in front of the same shrine. A much-damaged record in the tenth year of the Chōḷa king Parakēsarivarman *alias* Śrī-Rājēndra-Chōḷadēva (I, 1011—43).

304. 437 *of* 1905.—(Tamil.) On the same walls. A mutilated record. Seems to mention the temple on the hill dedicated to the god Subramaṇya; records the gift of 90 sheep.

305. 438 *of* 1905.—(Tamil.) On a stone set up at the entrance into the same temple. A record in the sixteenth year of the Chōḷa king Parakēsarivarman. Registers a sale of land by the assembly of Tiruttaṇiyal, a village in Kunṟavarttana-kōṭṭam. Mentions Śiruvēlūr in Teṅkarai-Iḷaiyūr-nāḍu, a district of Veśālippāḍi.

306. 439 *of* 1905.—(Tamil.) On a stone set up close to the garbhagriha of the Subramaṇya temple in the same village. A record in the thirty-second year of the Chōḷa king Maduraikoṇḍa Parakēsarivarman (Parāntaka I). Built in at the bottom. Records gift of land apparently by a certain Parakēsari-Muttaraiyan to the temple of Subramaṇya-Piḷḷaiyār, who was pleased to stand on the hill at Tiruttaṇiyal near Aguvūr, the eastern hamlet of Peruṅgāñji in Ogavala-nāḍu, a district of Mēlūr-kōṭṭam, which formed part of Jayaṅgoṇḍa-Chōḷamaṇḍalam. The characters of the inscription are comparatively modern.

307. 440 *of* 1905.—(Tamil.) On the south wall of the central shrine in the Ārumugasvāmin temple in the same village. A much damaged record of the Vijayanagara king Vīra-Kampaṇa-Uḍaiyār in Viśvāvasu (i.e., Ś. 1288).

308. 441 *of* 1905.—(Tamil.) On a stone built into the floor of the antarāla-maṇṭapa of the same temple. A damaged record of the Chōḷa king Madirai-koṇḍa Parakēsarivarman (Parāntaka I), the date of which is indistinct.

309. 442 *of* 1905.—(Telugu.) On the east wall of the first prākāra of the same temple. The prākāra was apparently built by the mahāmaṇḍalēśvara Tiruvēṅgalanātharājadēva-Chōḷa-Mahārāju of Vellāṇḍu.

310. 443 *of* 1905.—(Tamil.) On the north wall of the central shrine in the Vijayarāghava-Perumāḷ temple in the same village. A record of the Vijayanagara king Vīrapratāpa Sadāśivadēva-Mahārāya in Ś. 1471, Saumya. Records gift of a village by the mahāmaṇḍalēśvara Rāmarāja-Chinna-Timmayadēva-Mahārāya. The village is called Tiruttaṇi in Taṇigaināḍu, a district of Kuṉṟa-varttana-kōṭṭam.

311. 444 *of* 1905.—(Tamil.) On the north, west and south walls of the central shrine and maṇṭapa of the same temple. A record in the 31st year of the Chōḷa king Rājakēsarivarman *alias* Rājādhirāja I. Historical introduction is similar to No. 221 of 1894.

312. 445 *of* 1905.—(Tamil.) On the west and south walls of the central shrine in the Vijayarāghava-Perumāl temple. A record of the Chōḷa king Parakēsarivarman *alias* Uḍaiyār Śrī-Rājēndra-Chōḷadēva (I, 1011—43), the date of which is lost. Beginning missing. Records sale of land to the temple called Tiruvananda-puram by the assembly of Jananātha-chaturvēdimaṅgalam in Mēnmalai-Taṇiya-nāḍu.

313. 446 *of* 1905.—(Tamil.) On the west wall of the same shrine. A fragment containing a portion of the introduction of Rājēndra-Chōḷa I.

314. 447 *of* 1905.—(Sanskrit in Telugu.) On the south wall of the same shrine. Records that a certain Nārāyaṇarāja built the temple. He claims to be fourth in descent from Karikāla-Chōḷa; See Mr. Sewell's antiquities, Vol. I, p. 158 f, where a list of Kārvēti-nagar chiefs is given. The chiefs of the present epigraph closely resemble them. See also *Ep. Rep.*, 1906, p. 86, para. 61.

315. 448 *of* 1905.—(Telugu.) On the same wall. This contains a Telugu translation of No. 447.

316. 449 *of* 1905.—(Tamil.) On the same wall. A record in the thirty-fourth year of the Chōḷa king Madiraikoṇḍa Parakēsari-varman (i.e., Parāntaka I). Records a gift of land by the assembly of Tiruttaṇiyal in Kuṉṟavattana-kōṭṭam to the temple of Tiruva-nandapuram.

317. 450 *of* 1905.—(Sanskrit and Telugu.) On the south wall of the maṇṭapa in front of the same shrine. Records that a certain Bommarāja, whose genealogy is given at considerable length and who was a descendant of Nārāyaṇarāja of No. 314 above, renewed grants made by his ancestors.

318. 451 *of* 1905.—(Tamil.) On the same wall. An incomplete record of the Vijayanagara king Vīrapratāpa Sadāśivadēva-Mahārāya in Ś. 1486, Raktākshin. The king boasts of having looted Ceylon.

Tiruvālaṅgāḍu.

In the Dēvāram this place is called Ālaṅgāḍu near Paḻaiyanūr. The inscriptions also mention it and include the place under Paḻaiyanūr-nāḍu in Mēlmalai division of Jayaṅkoṇḍachōḻamaṇḍalam. It is sung by the three Dēvāram hymners and by Kāraikkālammaiyār (who is said to be constantly worshipping the God here) in her two *Mūtta-Tiruppadiyaṃs.*

319. 14 *of* 1896.—(Tamil.) On the east wall of the second prākāra of the Vaṭāraṇyēśvara temple, right of entrance. A record in the second year of the Chōla king Ko-Rājakēsarivarman *alias* Rājēndra-Chōḻadeva (II or Kulōttuṅga-Chōḻa I). [Records the settlement of 25 families of Śaṅkarappāḍi at Tiruvālaṅgāḍu and their duty of looking after 15 lamps of the temple. See *S.I.I.*, III, No. 65, pp. 134-6.]

320. 15 *of* 1896.—(Grantha and Tamil.) On the south wall of the Naṭarāja shrine in the same temple, left of entrance. A record in the eighteenth year of the Pallava king Madhusūdanadēva, son of Tripurāntakadēva. Records gift of land. The king bears the title Vijaya-Gaṇḍagōpāla.

321. 16 *of* 1896.—(Tamil.) On the west wall of the same shrine. A record in the ninth year of the Chōḻa king Kō-Parakēsarivarman *alias* Tribhuvanachakravartin Parāntakadēva, "a later Chōḻa king who bore the name of his ancestor Parāntaka."

322. 408 *of* 1896.—(Grantha.) On the east wall of the Naṭarāja shrine in the Vaṭāraṇyēśvara temple in the same place. A record of the Chōḻa king Tammusiddhi in Ś. 1129. Records gift of the revenues due to the king in the villages belonging to the temple to the Lord of Vaṭāṭavi. See *Ep. Ind.*, VII, p. 119 ff, where Dr. Luders edits it.

323. 452 *of* 1905.—(Tamil.) On the east wall of the first prākāra of the Naṭarājasvāmin shrine in the same temple. A fragment of record of the Chōḻa king Tribhuvanachakravartin Kulōttuṅga-Chōḻadēva (III, 1178—1216) "who took Madura and the crowned head of the Pāṇḍya." Mentions Manumasitti Araiyar. [Manmasiddhi was evidently the elder brother of Tammusiddhi of the previous epigraph.]

324. 453 *of* 1905.—(Tamil.) On the same wall. A record in the fifth year of the Chōḻa king Vikrama-Chōḻadēva (1118—35) records gift of twelve sheep for a lamp by a native of Ūrrukkāḍu *alias* Aḷagiyaśōḷanallūr in Ūrrukkāṭṭu-kōṭṭam.

325. 454 *of* 1905.—(Tamil.) On the same wall. An incomplete record of the Vijayanagara king Vīrapratāpa Pratāpa-Dēvarāya-Mahārāya in Ś. 1357, Rākshasa. Records sale of land. The temple is called Tiruvālaṅgāḍuḍaiya-Nāyanār at Paḷaiyanūr in Mēlmalai-Paḷaiyanūr-nāḍu, a subdivision of Vaḍagarai-Maṇavīr kōṭṭam. [The Government Epigraphist identifies the king with Srīgiri, the younger brother of Dēvarāya II who is mentioned as the ruler of Marataka-nagara in 1424—5 in the Madras Museum Plates of Dēvarāya II, and also the Satyamaṅgalam plates. He further believes that he was the assassin referred to by Abdur Razzak. For Abdur Razzak's story see *Forg. Empe.*, p. 73-4.

326. 455 *of* 1905.—(Tamil.) On the same wall. An unfinished record of the Chōḷa king Rājakēsarivarman *alias* Chakravartin Vikrama-Chōḷadēva (1118—35) in his seventh year. Introduction begins with the words *pūmādu puṇara.* Registers a public sale of land by the villagers of Polipākkam in Naḍuvumalai Perumūr-nāḍu to a merchant of Tirumayilāppil in Puliyūr-kōṭṭam. Refers to a survey of the country (*ulagaḷavu*). See No. 329 below.

327. 456 *of* 1905.—(Tamil.) On the same wall. A record in the twenty-third year of the Chōḷa king Tribhuvanachakravartin Kulōttuṅga-Chōḷadēva (III, 1178—1216) "who was pleased to take Madura, Iḷam (Ceylon) and the crowned head of the Pāṇḍya." Records sale of the village of Muduvūr in Naḍuvinmalai Erumūr-nāḍu.

328. 457 *of* 1905.—(Tamil.) On the same wall. An incomplete record of the Pāṇḍya king Jaṭāvarman Tribhuvanachakravartin Sundara-Pāṇḍyadēva (I ?), the date of which is not clear.

329. 458 *of* 1905.—(Tamil.) On the same wall. An unfinished record in the sixth year of the Chōḷa king Rājakēsarivarman *alias* Chakravartin Vikrama-Chōḷadēva. Introduction begins with the words *pūmadu puṇara.* Registers a public sale of land by the villagers of Valaikuḷam *alias* Nittavinōda-chaturvēdimaṅgalam in Mēlmalai-Vēlūr-nāḍu to a native of Kaḷḷikkuḍi *alias* Purōvari-nallūr in Puṛappaṛalai-nāḍu, (a district) of Rājarāja-Pāṇḍi-nāḍu. [Vikrama Chōḷa is generally Parakēsarivarman and the adoption of the title Rājakēsari is anomalous.]

330. 459 *of* 1905.—(Tamil.) On the same wall. A record in the sixth year of Tribhuvanachakravartin Kōnērinmaikoṇḍān. Records gift of land in the village of Maṇavil in Maṇavil-nāḍu, a subdivision of Maṇavir-kōṭṭam.

331. 460 *of* 1905.—(Tamil.) On the same wall. A record in the eleventh year of "the Gaṅga-Pallava king" Nripatuṅgadēva. Records that queen Kāḍavanmādēviyār made a gift of 108 *kaḷañju* of gold to the temple at Tiruvālaṅgāḍu in Paḷaiyanūr-nāḍu. Mentions Perumalaiyūr, a brahmadēya in Kākkaḷūr-nāḍu, a subdivision of Īkkāṭṭu-kōṭṭam.

332. 461 *of* 1905.—(Tamil.) On the same rock. A record in the fifteenth year of the 'Gaṅga-Pallava king' Nripatuṅgadēva. Records gift of gold for two lamps. Mentions the village of Pulvēlūr in Eyirkōṭṭam; also the measure *Pirudimāṇikkam*. This and the previous epigraph are engraved in comparatively modern characters of about the twelfth century. They may be copies of old inscriptions though no statement to that effect is made.

333. 462 *of* 1905.—(Tamil.) On the east wall of the first prākāra of the Naṭarājasvāmin shrine in the same temple. Records in the twenty-sixth year gift of the proceeds of certain taxes to the temple at Tiruvālaṅgāḍu for maintaining perpetual lamps. The document is signed by Tikkarasan. See No. 335 which shows that the probable king was Vijayagaṇḍagōpāla.

334. 463 *of* 1905.—(Tamil.) On the same wall. A record in the eighth year of the Chōḷa king Tribhuvanachakravartin Rājarājadēva (III?). Records gift of sixteen cows for a lamp.

335. 464 *of* 1905.—(Tamil.) On the same wall. A record in the twenty-ninth year of Tribhuvanachakravartin Vijayagaṇḍagōpāladēva. Records gift of land by Tikkaraśar Viśaiyadēvan described as belonging to "Tyāgasamudra-paṭṭaigaḷ."

336. 465 *of* 1905.—(Tamil.) On the same wall. A record in the twelfth year of the Chōḷa king Rājakēsarivarman *alias* Tribhuvanachakravartin Rājādhirājadēva (II). Partly built in. Introduction begins with the words *kaḍal śūḻnda parmadar*. Refers to the war of Pāṇḍya succession in which the Sinhalese generals Laṅkāpura-Daṇḍanātha and Jayadratha Daṇḍanātha took part. It "seems to describe the part played in the war by a traitor named Śri Vallabha." See Cg. 248.

337. 466 *of* 1905.—(Tamil.) On the same wall. A record in the eleventh year of the Chōḷa king Tribhuvanachakravartin Kōnērinmaikoṇḍan Rājādhirāja (II). Records gift of land in the village of Kōṭṭūr *alias* Chōḷavidyādhara-chaturvēdimaṅgalam in Kānṛūr-nāḍu, a subdivision of Maṇavir-kōṭṭam. The temple at Kōṭṭūr is referred to as Iḷambayaṅgōṭṭūruḍaiyār. Reference is also made to the Revenue Survey in the sixteenth year of the reign of Śuṅgandavirtta Kulōttuṅga-Chōḷa I.

338. 467 *of* 1905.—(Tamil.) On the same wall. A record in the sixth year of the Chōḷa king Parakēsarivarman *alias* Tribhuvanachakravartin Vikrama-Chōḷadēva (1118—34). Records sale of land by the assembly of Perumūr *alias* Rājanārāyaṇa-Chaturvēdimaṅgalam in Perumūr-nāḍu.

339. 468 *of* 1905.—(Tamil.) On the north wall of the same prākāra. Records that the enclosing hall was constructed by

Ammaiyappan Paḷiyañji Pallavaraiyan. The alphabet shows that he probably belonged to the thirteenth century. [Ammaiyappan was the title or name of a feudatory of Kulōttuṅga III.]

340. 469 *of* 1905.—(Tamil.) On the same wall. A record in the tenth year of the Chōḷa king Tribhuvanachakravartin Rājadhirājadēva (II?). Records gift of gold for two lamps to the shrine of the goddess Periyanāchchiyar of Tirukkāmakkōṭṭam in the Tiruvālaṅgāḍu temple.

341. 470 *of* 1905.—(Tamil.) On the same wall. A record of the Vijayanagara king Mallikārjunadēva-Mahārāya, son of Dēva-Mahārāya II in Ś. 1373, Pramōda. Records gift of four lamps for the merit of the king.

342. 471 *of* 1905.—(Tamil.) On the same wall. A record of Vijayanagara king Mallikārjunarāya, son of Dēvarāya-Mahārāya (II) in Ś. 1372, Śukla. Records gift of a lamp for the merit of the king.

343. 472 *of* 1905.—(Tamil.) On the same wall. A record of the Vijayanagara king Kampaṇa-Uḍaiyār in Ānanda. Records gift of land.

344. 473 *of* 1905.—(Tamil.) On the same wall. A record of the Vijayanagara king Krishṇarāya in Vikrama. Records the remission of some tax at Śakkiranallūr. Mentions *Amaram* Timmarasaiyaṅgār.

345. 474 *of* 1905.—(Tamil.) On the same wall. A record in the thirteenth year of the Chōḷa king Rājakēsarivarman *alias* Tribhuvanachakravartin Rājādirājadēva II, "who was pleased to take Madura and Ceylon" [a title due to his victory over the Sinhalese ally of a Pāṇḍyan candidate.] Introduction begins with the words *kaḍal śūḻndu parmadar.* Records gift of three lamps by Paḷaiyanūruḍaiyān Vēdavanamamuḍaiyān Ammaiyappan Pallavaraiyan. For Rājādhirāja's part in the Sinhalese war see Cg. 248.

346. 475 *of* 1905.—(Tamil.) On the same wall. A mutilated record. Records sale of land.

347. 476 *of* 1905.—(Tamil.) On the same wall. A record of the Vijayanagara king Vīra-pratāpa-Sadāśivadēva-Mahārāya in Ś. 1484, Rudhirōdgārin. Registers an endowment for the celebration of a festival. Mentions the Vēdamārga-pratishṭhāpanāchārya-Dharmaśivāchārya. [Dr. Hultzsch mentions a Dharmarājādhvari or Dīkshita who wrote the *Vēdāntaparibhāshā* and a Dharmasūri who wrote the *Dattaratnākara* and the drama *Narakadhvamsavyāyōga.* These however are evidently not identical with the teacher mentioned in this epigraph. See No. 368 below.]

348. 477 *of* 1905.—(Tamil.) On the same wall. A record in the thirty-second year of the Chōḷa king Tribhuvanachakravartin Kulōttuṅga Chōḷadēva (III?). Records gift of 70 kāśu for offerings

Mentions two villages: (1) Vaḷḷuvanpākkam in Oḷugaiyur-nāḍu, a subdivision of Paḍuvir-kōṭṭam and (2) Perumūr *alias* Rājanārāyaṇa-chaturvēdimaṅgalam in Naḍuvinmalai-Perumūr-nāḍu.

349. 478 *of* 1905.—(Tamil.) On the south wall of the same prākāra. A record in the twenty-first year of the Chōḷa king Rājarājadēva (III). Records gift of four cows for a lamp.

350. 479 *of* 1905.—(Tamil.) On the same wall. A record of the Vijayanagara king Vīrapratāya-Dēvarāya-Mahārāya (II) in Ś. 1349, Plavaṅga. Built in at the beginning. Tiruvālaṅgāḍu is said to be situated in the Chandragiri-rājyam. Mentions Ariyappa Daṇṇāyakkar and Bhikshāvritti Aiyagaḷ.

351. 480 *of* 1905.—(Tamil). On the same wall. Records in Nandana a gift for the merit of Mallaṇa-Uḍaiyār by Gopparāśar-Mādi-araśar.

352. 481 *of* 1905.—(Tamil.) On the same wall. An incomplete record in the twelfth year of the Chōḷa king Tribhuvanachakravartin Rājarājadēva. Registers a sale of land by the villagers of Paḷaiyanūr in Paḷaiyanūr-nāḍu, a dēvadāna granted to the Tiruvālaṅgāḍu temple in Maṇavir-kōṭṭam. [The *Tiruttoṇḍar-purāṇa* closely connects the two places by the story of Paḷaiyanūr Nīli and the Veḷḷāḷas who died in consequence of their being the security for her murdered husband. See *Abhidānakōśam*, pp. 409—10.]

353. 482 *of* 1905.—(Tamil.) On the same wall. A record in the thirty-second year of the Chōḷa king Tribhuvanachakravartin Tribhuvanavīradēva (i.e., Kulōttuṅga III) "who was pleased to take Madurai and the crowned head of the Pāṇḍya and who was pleased to perform the anointment of heroes and the anointment of victors." Records gift of a lamp to the temple of Tiruvaraṅgil-Aṇḍamuṛanimirndaruḷina-Nāyanār at Tiruvālaṅgāḍu in Tirup-paḷaiyanūr-nāḍu, a subdivision of Maṇavir-kōṭṭam. The donor was Aṛaṇilaiviśāgan Trailōkyamallan Vatsarājan of Arumbākkam in Illattūr nāḍu, a subdivision of Kunṛavattana-kōṭṭam, who rendered the *Bhārata* into elegant Tamil and followed the path of Śiva (i.e., the Śaiva creed). [Venkayya points out that this translation of the *Mahābhārata* is extinct unlike those of Perundēvanār whom he attributes to the ninth century, Villiputtūrār and Nallāppaḷḷai.]

354. 483 *of* 1905.—(Tamil.) On the third gōpura of the same temple an incomplete and damaged record of the Chōḷa king Parakēsarivarman *alias* Uḍaiyār śrī-Rājēndra-Chōḷadēva (I, 1011—43), the date of which is indistinct. Contains only the historical introduction.

355. 484 *of* 1905.—(Tamil.) In the same place. A record in the forty-sixth year of the Chōḷa king Rājakēsarivarman *alias* Chakravartin Kulōttuṅga-Chōḷadēva (I). Records sale of land to the temple at Tiruvālaṅgāḍu in Naḍuvilmalai by the assembly of Rājanarāyāṇa-chaturvēdimaṅgalam in Naḍuvil-malai Perumūr-nāḍu.

356. 485 *of* 1905.—(Tamil.) In the same place. A record in the thirty-first year of the Chōḷa king Rājakēsarivarman *alias* Uḍaiyār śrī-Rājādhirājadēva (I ?) Records sale of land by the assembly of Siṅgaḷāntaka-chaturvēdimaṅgalam in Naḍuvinmala Perumūr-nāḍu.

357. 486 *of* 1905.—(Tamil.) In the same place. A record in the twenty-eighth year of the Chōḷa king Rājakēsarivarman *alias* Uḍaiyār śrī-Rājādhirājadēva (I ?) Records sale of land by the assembly of Nittavinōda śaruppēdimaṅgalam in Mēnmalai-Mēlūr-nāḍu.

358. 487 *of* 1905.—(Tamil.) In the same place. A record in the thirteenth year of the Chōḷa king srī-Rājādhirājadēva. Records sale of land.

359. 488 *of* 1905.—(Tamil.) In the same place. A record in the twenty-eighth year of the Chōḷa king Rājakēsarivarman *alias* Uḍaiyār śrī-Rājādhirājadēva (I ?) Records sale of land.

360. 489 *of* 1905.—(Tamil.) In the same place. A mutilated record of the Chōḷa king Rajakēsarivarman *alias* Uḍaiyār . . .

361. 490 *of* 1905.—(Tamil.) On the same gopura, left of entrance. A mutilated record in the twenty-eighth year of the Chōḷa king Rājakēsarivarman *alias* Uḍaiyār śrī-Rājādhirājadēva (I ?).

362. 491 *of* 1905.—(Tamil.) In the same place. A mutilated record of the Chōḷa king Rājakēsarivarman *alias* Rājādhirājadēva (I ?). Contains a portion of the king's historical introduction.

363. 492 *of* 1905.—(Tamil.) In the same place. A damaged record of the Chōḷa king Rājakēsarivarman *alias* Uḍaiyār śrī-Rājādhirājadēva (I ?), the date of which is lost.

364. 493 *of* 1905.—(Tamil.) In the same place. A mutilated record in the twenty-seventh year of the Chōḷa king Uḍaiyar Śrī-Rājēndra-Chōḷadēva (II ?). Records an order of Rājēndraśiṅga Mūvēndavēlān.

365. 494 *of* 1905.—(Tamil.) In the same place. An incomplete record of the Chōḷa king Rājākēsarivarman *alias* Rājādhirājadēva, the date of which is damaged.

366. 495 *of* 1905.—(Tamil.) In the same place. A record in the twenty-eighth year of the Chōḷa king Rājākēsarivarman *alias* Uḍaiyār srī-Rājādhirājadēva (I ?). Records sale of land.

367. 496 *of* 1905.—(Tamil.) In the same place. A damaged record of the Chōḷa king Rājakēsarivarman *alias* Uḍaiyār śrī-Rājādhirājadēva (I ?).

368. 497 *of* 1905.—(Tamil.) On the west wall of the Bhramarāḷakāmba shrine in the same temple. A record of the Vijayanagara king Vīrapratāpa Tirumalaiyadēva-Mahārāya in Ś. 1493, Prajāpati. Mentions the Śaiva teacher Anantaśivāchārya, his pupil Ponnambala Dharmasivāchārya and the latter's pupil Immaḍi-Dharmaśivāchārya. The goddess is called Vaṇḍārkuḷal-Nāchchiyār. The king referred to is Tirumala I of the last Vijayanagara dynasty. For his literary importance see *Ep. Rep.*, 1898-9, paragraph 13. See also No. 347 above.

369. 498 *of* 1905.—(Tamil.) On the dhvajastambha in the same temple. A record of the Śāḷuva king Śāḷuva Tippaiyadēva-Mahārāja in Ś. 1363, Durmati. Records the setting up of a bronze dhvajastambha.

370. A C.P. grant of Rājēndrachōḷa I (compared only to the Ānaimaṅgalam grant or the large Leyden grant in the Leyden University Museum in Holland.) It is in 31 plates, the first ten plates being in Sanskrit and Grantha character and the rest in Tamil. It is a record of the sixth year of Rājēndrachōḷa I (1011—1043 at least) and registers the grant of the village of Paḷaiyanūr to the Śiva temple at Tiruvāliṅgāḍu. [The Sanskrit portion contains reference to the conquest of Kaṭāha or Kaḍāram which took place only after the fifteenth year of the king while the Tamil portion describes only the conquests up to sixth year. So the former is a later addition, which is corroborted by the separate numbering of the two parts. The inscription is of unique value in regard to Chōḷa history and has been summarized in detail in *Ep. Rep.*, 1906, pp. 66—69. The invasions of the Gangetic region, Burma, etc., are referred to in detail.

VĀYALPĀD TALUK.

Devulapalli.

371. A C.P. grant of Immaḍi Narasimha, edited by Mr. J. Ramayya Pantulu in *Ep. Ind.*, Vol. VII, p. 74 ff. It is in Sanskrit verse and in the Dēvanāgari script of the Vijayanagar type,—the last word *Śri-Ramachandra* being in Telugu characters. It records that Immaḍi Narasimha, son of Nrisimharāya, gave the village of Dēvalapalle in Mārjavāḍa Śima of the Penugoṇḍa-Mahārājya to a Brahman, on Ś. 1427, Bhādrapāda Full-moon, Sunday lunar eclipse, corresponding to 25th August A.D. 1504. [The inscription is of value in throwing light on the two kings of the Śāḷuva dynasty Naraśingarāya and his son Immaḍi Narasimha and Mr. Ramayya Pantulu has fixed the position of these in relation to their Tuluva successors Narasa Nāik and Vīra Narasimha.]

COIMBATORE DISTRICT.

AVANĀŚI TALUK.

Avanāśi.

The ancient name of this place, as evidenced by the *Dēvāram* and inscriptions (see Nos. 12 and 20 below), seems to have been Tirupukkuḷiyūr.

1. 170 *of* 1909.—(Tamil.) On the south wall of the central shrine in the temple of Avanāśīśvara. A damaged record in the twenty-first year of Vīrarājēndradēva. Records gift of money for offerings to a shrine of Kshētrapāla by Vīrapperumāḷ Ediriladān, who is called one of the Piḷḷais of the king. [The king was the most prominent of the Koṅgu line under Chōḷa titles. He ruled from *Circa.* 1207 to *Circa.* 1252.]

2. 171 *of* 1909.—(Tamil.) On the same wall. An incomplete record in the fifteenth year of Rājakēsarivarman *alias* Tribhuvana-chakravartin Vīrarājēndradēva. Records gift of 32 lamps by a certain Avināśi *alias* Śīkāḷiyān and also of money for feeding mendicants, by Āṟṟūruḍaiyān Tiruppurāmbiyamuḍaiyān, a merchant of Ēraḷapuram. See *Mack. MSS. Ins., S. Dts.*, p. 6, No. 5 and the note to the above epigraph.

3. 172 *of* 1909.—(Tamil.) On the same wall. A record in the fourth year of Tribhuvanachakravartin Kulōttuṅga-Chōḷadēva. Records gift of money for a lamp by Marudan Malaiyan *alias* Kulōttuṅgaśōḷa-Vikramādittadēvan, one of the feudatories (sāmanta) of the king.

4. 173 *of* 1909.—(Tamil.) On the same wall. An incomplete record in the fifteenth year of Kulōttuṅga-Chōḷadēva. Records gift of money for a lamp to the temple of Avināśiyāṇḍār.

5. 174 *of* 1909.—(Tamil.) On the north wall of the same shrine A record in the seventeenth year of Vīrarājēndradēva. A portion of the stone is lost. Records gift of money for offerings. See Cb. 2 above.

6. 175 *of* 1909.—(Tamil.) On the same wall. A record of Kōnērinmaikoṇḍān. Records gift of the village of Pāppārpūṇḍi *alias* Vīrarājēndranallūr in Vaḍaparisāra-nāḍu, to the temple of Avināśiyāḷuḍaiyār. *Ins., S. Dts.*, p. 9, No. 17 or 18.

7. 176 *of* 1909.—(Tamil.) On the same wall. An incomplete record in the fourth year of Vīra-Chōḷadēva. Seems to record the gift of certain taxes to the temple of Avināśi-Āḷuḍaiyār.

8. 177 *of* 1909.—(Tamil.) On a pillar of the maṇṭapa in front of the same shrine. Records in Plavaṅga that the maṇṭapa was

built by a certain Vānadarāyavaḍamalaiyappar. Another pillar close to this mentions the same person.

9. 178 *of* 1909.—(Tamil.) On a pillar of the verandah round the same shrine. A damaged record in the twenty-ninth year of Tribhuvanachakravartin Vīrarājēndradēva. Seems to record a gift of land by Marudan Mudali *alias* Vaṇika-chakravartin, a merchant of Mūttan *alias* Amarabhuyaṅgaranallūr in Perunāḍu. See Cb. 2 above.

10. 179 *of* 1909.—(Tamil.) On another pillar of the same verandah. A record in the second year of Tribhuvanachakravartin Vīra-Chōḷadēva. Records gift of money for a pillar of the maṇṭapa of the sacred bull (Rishabadēva) in the same temple.

11. 180 *of* 1909.—(Tamil.) On the south wall of the Brihatkaruṇāmbika shrine in the same temple. A damaged record in the thirty-second year of the Pāṇḍya king Sundara-Pāṇḍyadēva. Seems to record a gift of money and mentions Māḍakkuḷakīḻ-Madurai in Pāṇḍi-maṇḍalam. [The last fact seems to show that the king intended was Māravarman Sundara Pāṇḍya I, 1216—35, but he did not rule for such a long time.]

12. 181 *of* 1909.—(Tamil.) On the west wall of the same shrine. A damaged record in the thirty-first year of Sundara-Pāṇḍyadēva. Records gift of money for paddy to a shrine of Sundara-Nāyanār set up by the king on the tank-bund at Pukkuḷiyūr, by a merchant of Araṇaiyūr *alias* Śivallapuram in Kīḻvaḷi-nāḍu, a subdivision of Pāṇḍi-maṇḍalam. Mentions also Kañjappaḷḷi *alias* Kulōttuṅgaśōḷa-chaturvēdimaṅgalam. [In *Ins., S. Dts.*, p. 9, No. 15, the date of this inscription is given as the twenty-first year.]

13. 182 *of* 1909.—(Tamil.) On the same wall. An incomplete record in Prabhava. An order from Chaṇḍīśvara to the *tēvaraḍiyār* in the temple of Avināśiyāḷuḍaiya-Nāyanār.

14. 183 *of* 1909.—(Tamil.) On the north wall of the same shrine. A damaged record in the seventh year of Vīra-Pāṇḍyadēva. Mentions the street Vikkiramasōḷan-tiruvīdi. [Was it Rājakēsarivarman Tribhuvanachakravartin referred to Cb. 196 and 197 ? He ruled from 1265 to *Circa.* 1281.]

15. 184 *of* 1909.—(Tamil.) On the south wall of the maṇṭapa in front of the same shrine. A record in the ninth year of Rājakēsarivarman *alias* Tribhuvanachakravartin Vīrapāṇḍyadēva. Records that the inhabitants of the two districts of Veḷḷa-nāḍu and Pūluva-nāḍu in Vaḍaparisāra-nāḍu settled that four families *(kuḍi)* in the village of Śevūr *alias* Śembiyankiḻānaḍinallūr, a dēvadāna of the temple, were to be freed from certain obligations, perhaps in favour of the temple. See note to No. 14 and *Ins., S. Dts. (Mack. MSS.)*, p. 5, No. 4.

16. 185 *of* 1909.—(Tamil.) On the same wall. A record in the eighth year of Vīra-Pāṇḍyadēva. Mentions the taxes payable by

the temple tenants in the dēvadāna village of Śevūr *alias* Śembiyan-kiḷānaḍinallūr. See Cb. 196.

17. 186 *of* 1909.—(Tamil.) On the same wall. A record in the second year of Rājakēsari Kōnērinmaikoṇḍān (Vīra Pāṇḍya ?). Records gift of the village of Vanavāsi *alias* Vīra-Śōḷanallūr in Kīṭpānāḍu to the shrine of Peruṅgaruṇaichchelviyār, the goddess in the temple of Avināśiyāḷuḍaiyār. The gift was made on the occasion of the king's coronation (abhishēka). See *Ins.*, *S. Dts.*, in *Mack. MSS.*, p. 4, No. 1.

18. 187 *of* 1909.—(Tamil.) On the same wall. A record in the fourteenth year of Vīra-Pāṇḍyadēva. Records gift of paddy by the villagers of Pāppārpūṇḍi *alias* Vīrarājēndranallūr, to the shrine of Sundara-Nāyanār at Tenpaḷḷi. See *Mack. MSS.*, *Ins.*, *S. Dts.*, p. 5, No. 3. [For the probable identity of Vīra Pāṇḍya see Cb. 14 above.]

19. 188 *of* 1909.—(Tamil.) On the same wall. An incomplete record in Pramōdūta. Records that two artisans (āśāri) were appointed to attend to the ten kinds of repairs (*daśa-kriyai*) on receiving from the temple the endowment called *tachchāchāriyak-kāni.*

20. 189 *of* 1909.—(Tamil.) On the same wall. A record of the Hoysaḷa king Vīra-Vallāḷadēva (III, 1292—1341) in Ś. 1204, Dundubhi (wrong). Records gift of the village of Tenpaḷḷi-nattam *alias* Sitakaragaṇḍanallūr by a feudatory of the king named Mādappa-Daṇṇāyaka, son of Perumāḷ-Daṇṇāyaka of the race of Maṭigolayakula, for a festival called Immaḍi Rāguttarāyan-śandi, in the temple of Avināśiyāḷuḍaiya-Nāyanār at Tiruppukkoḷiyūr. [Perumāḷ Nāyakar was the founder of Daṇāyakankōṭṭai in the time of Narasimha III. For the great power which the chiefs of the place had in the days of the Hoysaḷa decline see *Ep. Rep.*, 1906–07, pp. 49—51 Vīra Ballāḷa III was crowned on Thursday, 31st January, A.D. 1292.

21. 190 *of* 1909.—(Tamil.) On the same wall. Records in Dundubhi gift of money for a lamp by a native of Palatoḷu in Kuruppunāḍu.

22. 191 *of* 1909.—(Tamil.) On the same wall. A record in the twelfth year of Tribhuvanachakravartin Kulōttuṅga-Chōḷa-dēva. Records gift of the tax *kuḍikānam* by the villagers of Veḷḷanūr in Vaḍaparisāra-nāḍu, to the shrine of the goddess Peruṅgaruṇaich-chelviyār. The *Mack. MSS.* say (see *Ins.*, *S. Dts.*, p. 8, No. 12) that the gift was 12 measures of grain every year. [A Koṅgu king named Kulōttuṅga is referred to in an inscription of Vikramachōḷa 1255–63 of 555 of 1905.]

23. 192 *of* 1909.—(Tamil.) On the same wall. A record in the twenty-eighth year of Tribhuvanachakravartin Vīrarājēndradēva

66

(A.D. 1207—52). Records gift of money for oil, by prince Nachchinārkiniyar *alias* Kaṇḍiyadēvar, son of king Ulaguḍaiya-Perumāḷ Vīrarājēndradēva, for bathing the god and the goddess on Saturdays. [The king's name reminds us of the Tamil commentator Nachchinārkkiniyar whom Professor Seshagiri Sastri assigns to the eleventh century. *Mack. MSS.* (*Ins., S. Dts.*, p. 8, No. 13).]

24. 193 *of* 1909.—(Tamil.) On the same wall. A record of Kōnērimēlkoṇḍān. Records gift of a village in Vaḍaparisāranāḍu, to the temple of Avināśiyāḷuḍaiyār.

25. 194 *of* 1909.—(Tamil.) On the same wall. Records in Dundubhi gift of money for a lamp by a native of Aḍavūr in Kuruppunāḍu.

26. 195 *of* 1909.—(Tamil.) On the same wall. An incomplete record in the fifth year of the Pāṇḍya king . . . *alias* Tribhuvanachakravartin Kulaśēkharadēva (I or II?). Records gift of money for a lamp.

27. 196 *of* 1909.—(Tamil.) On the same wall. An incomplete record of Tribhuvanachakravartin Kōnērinmaikoṇḍān. Records gift of the village Valaippāḍi in Nallūrkkānāḍu for the festival Avanivēndarāmanśandi named after the king in the temple of Avināśiyāḷuḍaiya-Nāyanār in Śevvūr-nāḍu. *Ins., S. Dts.*, p. 8, No. 14.

28. 197 *of* 1909.—(Tamil.) On the north wall of the same maṇṭapa. A record in the fifth year of the Pāṇḍya king Māravarman *alias* Tribhuvanachakravartin Kulaśēkharadēva (I or II?). Records gift of money for a lamp by a native of Araṅgur in kīḷkarai-Pūndurai-nāḍu.

29. 198 *of* 1909.—(Tamil.) On a slab set up near the Kalyāṇamaṇṭapa in the same temple. A record of Vīra-Nañjarāya-Uḍaiyār in Ś. 1419, Piṅgaḷa. Records that a merchant (Śeṭṭi) of Emmarkkāl in Tenkaḍambai-nāḍu (Terkaṇāmbi) provided for the mid-day offerings to the god at Avināśi which was reputed to be the southern Benares (dakshiṇa-Vārāṇasi). For the reference in the *Mack. MSS.*, see next inscription. This is No. 11.

30. 199 *of* 1909.—(Tamil.) On another slab set up near the same maṇṭapa. A record of Vīra-Chikkarāya-Uḍaiyār, son of Vīra-Nañjarāya-Uḍaiyār (the Ummattūr chief who held the Turkoṇāmbi district), in Ś. 1430, Vibhava. Records that a merchant of the same village in Tinaikkaṇāmbai-nāḍu (Terkaṇāmbi) provided for offerings in the same temple. Rice mentions a slightly different genealogy of the chiefs of the line. [This is probably *Ins.* 10 in p. 7 of *Ins., S. Dts.* See *Ep. Carna.* IV, Introdn., p. 27, for the different version.]

31. 200 *of* 1909.—(Tamil.) On the third slab set up in the same place. A record of Mahāmaṇḍalēśvara Vīra-Nañjarāya Uḍaiyār in Ś. 1421, Siddhārthin. Records gift of land (3 *Salagas*) by the king's minister Onnakkan Seṭṭiyār of Emmarkāl in Tinaikkaṇāmbi-nāḍu. A detailed version of this is in *Ins., S. Dts.*, p. 7, No. 9. It says that 15 pons and a plantation of 1,000 coconut trees were given. [Nañjarāya was in charge of Terkaṇāmbi and large part of Coimbatore district at the time of Tuḷuva usurpation.]

32. 201 *of* 1909.—(Kanarese.) On a slab set up in front of the gōpura of the same temple. A record of Krishṇarāja-Voḍeya (1734--65) of Mahisūru ruling at Śrīraṅgapaṭṭaṇa in Ś. 1678, and Kali 4857, Dhātri. Records that the various parts of the temple of Avināśi were repaired by a certain Śaṅkarayya and that a liṅga called Saṁkarēśvara was set up in the south-east corner of the temple. [Saṅkarayya is called a *gurikāra* (officer ?) at Coimbatore and subordinate of Daḷavāi Dēvarājayya, the king's agent and the real ruler of Mysore till the advent of Haidar Ali. See *Ins., S. Dts.*, p. 6, No. 6.]

33. On a stone north-east of the place in a puñjai land. Records that Siṅgaṇa Uḍaiyār granted in Ś. 1460, Nandana, in the reign of Achyuta Rāya (1530—42) to god Avanāśiliṅgam's treasury, half (a vēli of) land and dug a tank, called Śellaṅga Samudram *Ibid.*, p. 9, No. 16.

34. On a stone in the Nartana-maṇṭapa. Records that Kōnērinmaikoṇḍan granted to the deity some land in the village of Kalmaḍai grāmam. *Ibid.*, p. 9, No. 18.

35. In the hands of the local karṇam. Records that Guru Karimallayya, the Prime Minister of Chikkadēva Rāya Uḍaiyar (1672—1704) granted in Ś. 1617, Yuva, to the local god and goddess, the fees of 14 *paṇams* on some bags and 12 paṇams on some other bags of goods. *Ibid.*, p. 10, No. 19.

Kāramaḍai.

36. In the hands of Ramasastri and Mahādeva (in the time of Mackenzie). Records that Ś. 1479, Īśvara, Dēvarājarasa, Daḷavāi to Krishṇarāja Uḍaiyār, granted the village of Bhūsarapaḷḷam (?) to Brahmans. *Ins., S. Dts.*, p. 32, No. 11.

Karuvalur.

37. On the southern wall of the inner temple of Karuṇākarapperumāḷ. Records the grant of land in the village to the God in the reign of Kōnērinmaikoṇḍān. *Ins., S. Dts.*, p. 47, No. 20.

Kunnattūr.

38. On a stone in the southern wall of the Lakshmi Nārāyaṇasvāmi temple. Records the grant of the village to the God by a Kōnērinmaikoṇḍān. *Ins., S. Dts.*, p. 30, No. 5.

39. On the banks of the Kuruchchikuḷam tank, north of the village. A record of Vīrachikka Uḍaiyār in Paritāpi. Gift of the tank and land to the God Kundram Uḍaiyār of Kunnattūr. *Ins., S. Dts.*, p. 30, No. 6.

Naḍuvachchēri.

40. On the western wall of Vināyaka temple in the Kōdēśvara temple. Records that Kōnērinmaikoṇḍān granted the village of Kōḍi-Tennūr (?) as free gift to God Pūmburādīśvara Uḍaiyār. *Ins., S. Dts.*, p. 10, No. 20.

41. On a stone west of the Garuḍa maṇṭapa. A grant of land to the God Kōdēśvara. *Ibid.*, No. 21.

42. On the south side of a maṇṭapa in the same shrine. Records that the inhabitants of "moondrapondee" gave, in the reign of Kulōttuṅga Chōḷa dēva, some grant (mutilated in the original) to Kōdaprāṭṭi-tavamuḍaiyār. *Ibid.*, p. 11, No. 22.

Puduppāḷaiyam.

43. On a stone east of the village. (Kanarese and Telugu.) Records in Raktākshi the gift of 40¾ land in the village of Mānoor to a Brahman Rāmalinga Śāstri. *Ins., S. Dts.*, p. 54, No. 12.

Śēvūr (*Chevvūr*).

44. At the back of the Mahāmaṇṭapam in the temple of Veṅkaṭaramaṇasvāmi. Records grant of land (i.e., *vēli*) in Ś. 1233, to God Aḷagapperumāḷ by Vīraṇapperumāḷ (?) and Aḷagappiḷḷai in the reign of Vīra Ballāḷadēva III. *Ins., Ś. Dts.*, p. 42, No. 1.

45. On the back side of the Vimānam. Records in the twentieth year of Sundara Pāṇḍya (Māravarman I ? 1216—35) the repair of the temple by the people. *Ibid.*, No. 2.

46. On the north side of the Mahāmaṇṭapam. Records gift of a garden in Ś. 1244, to Gaṇapati by Yerumañjaya Daṇṇāyakar in the reign of Vīra-Ballāḷa (III, 1292—1341). *Ibid.*, No. 3.

47. On the southern wall of the Vimānam. Records the grant of the village of Kariyampāḍu to the God and Śrī-Vaishṇavas in the fifteenth year of Vīra-Pāṇḍya. [Was it the Koṅgu king who ruled from 1265 to 1281 ? See Cb. 14 above.] *Ibid.*, No. 4.

48. On the south side of the Aḷvār Maṇṭapa. Records gift of land by the people of Vaḍa-Parisāranāḍu to Āḷvār in the twentieth year of Sundara Pāṇḍya (Māravarman I ? 1216–36). *Ibid.*, No. 5.

49. On the north wall of the Ardha-Maṇṭapam. Records a gift by the people of Veḷḷāḷanāḍu and another to God in the fourteenth year of Vīra Pāṇḍya. *Ibid.*, No. 6. See note to 47 above.

50. On the west of the Vimānam. Records performing of Maṇavāḷaperumāḷ festival by people in the ninteenth year of Vīra Pāṇḍya. *Ibid.*, No. 7. See No. 47 above.

51. On the south side of the Ardha-Maṇṭapam. Sale of dry field in the twenty-seventh year of Sundara Pāṇḍya (unidentifiable as no Sundara Paṇḍya who ruled for such a long time is known). *Ins., S. Dts.*, p. 42, No. 8.

52. On the west side of the same. Records sale of a garden for 300 paṇams in the reign of Sundara Pāṇḍya 'Seruvennandan (?)'. *Ibid.*, No. 9.

53. On the west side of the Vimānam. A damaged grant in Ś. 1256, in the reign of Vīra-Ballāḷa (III, 1292—1341). *Ibid.*, No. 10.

54. On the south side of the Mahāmaṇṭapam in the temple. Records that Vīra Maṅgirāja exempted in Śukla, the taxes on the weaver looms of Paroolnāḍu, Vīrachōḷavaḷanāḍu and Oḍuvaṅgalanāḍu. *Ibid.*, p. 45, No. 11.

55. On the west side of the above. Grant of land by Vīrachōḷa Īśvaradēva in Svabhānu, to God Tirukapālēśvaramuḍaiyār. *Ibid.*, p. 45, No. 12. [Was the king the same as Rājādhirāja Vīrachōḷa who is referred to in 593 of 1905 ?]

56. On the west side of the above. A damaged record of the fourteenth year of Vīra-Rājēndradēva. (Koṅgu king ? 1207—52.) *Ibid.*, No. 13.

57. In the same place. A record of the same king, granting some land. *Ibid.*, No. 14.

58. On the back side of Vaḷḷīśvarasvāmi temple. A damaged grant of the twentieth year of Vīra-Rājēndra. *Ibid.*, No. 15. See note to No. 55.

59. On the corner of the Ardha-Maṇṭapam. A damaged grant of Mummuḍichōḷa in the reign of Kulōttuṅgachōḷa (second year). *Ibid.*, p. 46, No. 16. See Cb. 22 above.

60. South of the above. A grant of the village of 'Kuladīpanallūr' by Kōnērinmaikoṇḍān to God Kapālēśvara. *Ibid.*, No. 17.

61. On the south side of the Mahāmaṇṭapam in the same temple. Grant of five pons for lamp in the twentieth year of Vīra-Rājēndradēvan by Āryavalli. *Ibid.*, No. 18. See No. 56.

62. On the southern wall of the Nartana-maṇṭapam in Vaḷḷīśvara temple. Grant of twenty-five pons to God Kapālēśvara for a lamp by Chōḷakkavuṇḍan in the reign of Vīra-Nañjarāyan. *Ibid.*, No. 19.

63. On one of the three stones north of the village in the temple of Mukkōṇiśvara between the shrines of the God and Goddess. Records that two chiefs granted a garden and some land to God Mukkuṇīśvara in Ś. 1447, Pārthiva, in the reign of Kṛishṇadēva Rāya (1509—30). *Ibid.*, p. 49, No. 27.

BHAVĀNI TALUK.

Aṇḍiyūr.

64. On a stone west of Dakshiṇāmūrti temple. A damaged record of the reign of Vīra Pāṇḍya Dēva. See Cb. 14. *Ins., S. Dts.*, p. 31, No. 7.

65. On a stone west of the Tāndōnrīśvarasvāmi temple. Dated in the reign of Vīra Ballāḷa Dēva (III ?). Records that a stone tub was carved by one "Auputtu Cattan" for throwing the flower offerings in. *Ins., S. Dts.*, p. 31, No. 8.

66. On a stone on the north side of Īśvara temple. Records that a chief granted forty paṇams to the temple in the sixth year of the reign of Sundara Pāṇḍya Dēva (unidentified). *Ibid.*, No. 9.

67. On a stone on the western side of the same temple. Records that the same chief presented a lamp to God Āṇḍīśvaramuḍaiyār in the thirtieth year of the reign of Sundara Pāṇḍya Dēva. *Ibid.*, No. 10. See note to Cb. 51.

Bhavānikūḍal.

67-A. On a stone in front of the maṇṭapam of Ponnāramauḷiamman in the local Īśvara temple. Records that it was erected in a certain Pārthiva by "Emmucuttee" Mudaliar and another. *Ins. Ś. Dts.*, No. 1. [Is *Emmucuttee* the same as Immaḍi Gheṭṭi ?]

68. On the first surrounding wall of the same temple. Records that Daḷavāi Dēvarāya of Krishṇarāja Uḍaiyār (1734—65) erected a maṇṭapam. *Ibid.* No. 2. See No. 32 above.

69. In the mahāmaṇṭapam. Records that one "Emmadecutti" Mudaliār erected various parts of the temple. *Ibid.* See No. 67-A.

70. On a stone in front of the Umāmahēśvara shrine. Records that Nārāyaṇa Kavuṇḍan erected the Ardhamaṇṭapam and the *Vimāna* in year Vijaya.

Oricheri (Varucheri).

71. On a stone in the local temple. Records that Prauḍha Dēva Rāja granted the village as a free gift in Ś. 1200 Pramādi to Tirumalai Nallānchakravarti and Govindarāja chakravarti. *Ins., S. Dts.*, p. 3, No. 6.

Varadanallūr (Vattanallore).

72. On a stone in the hands of one Rāma Ayyangar. Records that Pratāpadēva Mahārāya granted the village and erected an agrahāram to Allāla Bhaṭṭa and nine other Brahmans. *Ins., S. Dts.*, p. 2, No. 5.

COIMBATORE TALUK.

General.

73. *C.P. No.* 187 *of Mr. Sewell's List.*—(Tamil and Grantha.) Records a grant by Raghunāthadēva Mahārāja, son of Śrī Veṅkaṭadēva Mahārāja of Uraiyūr, agent of Viśvanātha Nāyakka Vīrappa Nāyakka of Madura (1609—23) and feudatory of Vīra Rāmadēva (1620—30) then ruling at Penukoṇḍa. The date of the grant is much injured, but it seems to be Ś. 1542 (A.D. 1620), Ś. 1541 having expired, Kāḷayukti.

Komārapāḷayam.

74. On the back side of the inner temple of Subrahmaṇya. Records that in Ś. 1598, Naḷa, in the reign of Chikka Dēva (1672—1704), one Raṅganātha Śeṭṭi and another erected two maṇṭapams and granted one *Salagai* of paddy land. *Ins., S. Dts.*, p. 4, No. 2.

Pērūr.

See Mr. Sewell's *Antiquities,* I, 217 where this place is noticed and with references to Buchanan and Fergusson. Three inscriptions only are mentioned by him. Of these the first two are included in this list. The third is alleged to be an inscription of Kōnērimaikoṇḍān Sundara Pāṇḍya who is unidentifiable. The temple is said to have been built by Aḷakādri Nāiḍu, a brother-in-law of Tirumal Nāik (1623—59).

75. 547 *of* 1893.—(Tamil.) On a stone built into the floor of the maṇṭapa at the southern entrance to the central shrine of the Gōshṭhīśvara temple. A fragment in very archaic characters.

76. 548 *of* 1893.—(Sanskrit and Tamil.) On the north wall of the maṇṭapa in front of the same shrine. A record of the Hoysaḷa king Vīra-Vallāḷadēva (III, 1292—1341) in Ś. 1245, expired, Rudhirōdgārin.

77. 549 *of* 1893.—(Tamil.) On the north wall of the same shrine, first tier. A record in the twenty-fourth year of Vikrama-Chōḷadēva. [Was he a Chōḷa or Koṅgu-Chōḷa ?] Records gift of a lamp.

78. 550 *of* 1893.—(Tamil.) In the same tier. A record in the twenty-seventh year of Vikrama-Chōḷadēva. Records gift of rice. Referred to in Antiquities, I, 217.

79. 551 *of* 1893.—(Tamil.) In the same tier. A record in the twelfth year of Vikrama-Chōḷadēva. [The Chōḷa king of this name ruled only for seventeen years from 1118 to 1135. Was this the Koṅgu king who ruled from 1004 to 1045 ? See Cb. 190.] Records gift of paddy.

80. 552 *of* 1893.—(Tamil.) In the same tier. A record in the second year of Karikāla-Chōḷadēva. Records gift of land. Karikāl was evidently a Koṅgu-Chōḷa.

81. 553 *of* 1893.—(Tamil.) On the same wall, second tier. A record in the second year of Kō-Rājarāja-Karikāla Chōḷadēva. Records gift of a lamp. See No. 80.

82. 554 *of* 1893.—(Tamil.) On the same wall, third tier. A record in the second year of Karikāla-Chōḷadēva. Records gift of a lamp. See No. 80.

83. 555 *of* 1893.—(Tamil.) In the same tier. A record in the fifteenth year of Vīra-Chōḷadēva (Parāntaka I or Koṅgu-Chōḷa ?). Records gift of paddy.

84. 556 *of* 1893.—(Tamil.) On the same wall, fifth tier. An incomplete record in the third year of Kōnērimaikoṇḍān.

85. 557 *of* 1893.—(Tamil.) On the same wall, sixth tier. A record in the second year of Karikāla-Chōḷadēva. Records gift of a lamp. See No. 80 above.

86. 558 *of* 1893.—(Tamil.) In the same tier. An incomplete record in the thirty-seventh year of Atirājarāja . . . jadēva.

87. 559 *of* 1893.—(Tamil.) On a stone built into the same wall. A record in Kaliyuga 4734.

88. 560 *of* 1893.—(Tamil.) On the west wall of the same shrine, first tier. A record in the seventeenth year of the Chōḷa (?) king Vikrama-Chōḷadēva (1118– 35). Records gift of a lamp.

89. 561 *of* 1893.—(Tamil.) In the same tier. A record in the sixteenth year of Vīra-Rājēndradēva. Records gift of a lamp by a merchant from the Pāṇḍya country. [The king was evidently the Koṅgu-Chōḷa who ruled from 1207 to 1252?]

90. 562 *of* 1893.—(Tamil.) On the south wall of the same shrine, first tier. A record in the fifteenth year of Kōnērimēl-koṇḍān. Confers certain rights on the artisans of the southern Koṅgu country.

91. 563 *of* 1893.—(Tamil.) In the same tier. A record in the twelfth year of Karikāla-Chōḷadēva. Records gift of a lamp by a palanquin bearer.

92. 564 *of* 1893.—(Tamil.) In the same tier. A record in the eleventh year of Karikāla-Chōḷadēva. Records gift of a lotus pond. See No. 80 above.

93. 565 *of* 1893.—(Tamil.) In the same tier. A record of Kōn-ērimaikoṇḍān. Records gift of land.

94. 566 *of* 1893.—(Tamil.) On the south wall of the maṇṭapa in front of the same shrine, left of entrance. An obliterated record of the Hoysaḷa king Vīra-Vallāḷadēva.

95. 567 *of* 1893.—(Tamil.) In the same place. A record in the sixteenth year of king Vīra-Pāṇḍyadēva. Records gift of paddy. See note to Cb. 47.

96. 568 *of* 1893.—(Tamil.) In the same place. A record in the fourth year of the Pāṇḍya king Kō-Māravarman *alias* Vīra-Pāṇḍ-yadēva.

97. 569 *of* 1893.—(Tamil.) On the same wall, right of entrance. A record of the Hoysaḷa king Vīra-Vallāḷadēva. Built in. Records gift of paddy by a native of the Pāṇḍya country.

98. 570 *of* 1893.—(Vaṭṭeḷuttu.) On the inner side of the north wall of the outer prākāra of the same temple. A record in the third year of Ko-Atiśaya-Chōḷa Vīra-Nārāyaṇadēva (Parāntaka I?).

99. In the north-west corner of the garbhagriham. A record dated K. 4734 (A.D. 1633) making a private grant of lands to the temple.

Veḷḷalūr.

100. 141 *of* 1910.—(Tamil.) On the south wall of the maṇṭapa in front of the Varadarāja-Perumāḷ temple. A record of the Hoysaḷa king Vīra-Vallāḷadēva (III), in Chitrabhānu. Records gift of land to the temple of Tiruvulagaḷanda-Perumāḷ, by the assembly of Vaḷḷalūr in Pērūr-nāḍu. Mentions the grain measure *tiruvā-naikkāl.*

101. 142 *of* 1910.—(Tamil.) On the east entrance into the maṇṭapa in front of the central shrine in the Tēnīśvara temple in the same village; right side. A record in the eighteenth year of Tribhuvanachakravartin Vikrama-Chōḷadēva. Records that certain classes residing in Annadāna-śivapuri *alias* Veḷḷalūr in Pērūr-nāḍu provided for worship in the temple of Avināśi-Āḷuḍai-yār at Tiruppukkōḷiyūr. [The king was apparently the Koṅgu-Chōḷa who came to the throne in 1005.]

102. 143 *of* 1910.—(Tamil.) On the same entrance; left side. A record in the seventeenth year of Vīra-Chōḷadēva Koṅgu king. Records gift of the door-post for the merit of a certain Kōvan-Araśan.

103. 144 *of* 1910.—(Tamil.) On the south entrance into the same maṇṭapa. A record in the fourth year of Rājarājadēva. Records gift of money for a lamp by a merchant of Manaipambaḍi in Vāyaṛaikkal-nāḍu, to the god of Tennūrpāḍi.

104. 145 *of* 1910.—(Tamil.) On a pillar in the same maṇṭapa. A record in the fourteenth year of Vikrama-Chōḷadēva. Records gift of the pillar by a private individual. The king was evidently the Koṅgu chief who ruled from 1004 to 1045.

105. 146 *of* 1910.—(Tamil.) On another pillar in the same place. An incomplete record in the ninth year of Vikrama-Chōḷadēva. See note to the above epigraph.

106. 147 *of* 1910.—(Tamil of about the ninth century A.D.) On the third pillar in the same place. A record in the eleventh year of the Chēra king Kōkkaṇḍan Vīranārāyaṇa, 'the sovereign jewel of the Chandrādityakula.' Records gift of the stone pillar to the maṇṭapa of Nakkanār at Veḷilūr-Tennūr, by a private individual. [The kings Kōkkaṇḍa or Kaṇṭha and Ravi mentioned in this inscription, says Mr. Krishna Sastri, may be identical with the two kings of the same name at Nāmakkal. (See *Ep. Ind.*, III, 79—82.) All these Chēra kings apparently claimed to be the descendants of both the sun and moon (Chandrādityas). The title *Viranārāyaṇa*

67

was not improbably assumed by the chiefs as they were feudatories of Vīra Nārāyaṇa or Parāntaka I, 905—47.]

107. 148 *of* 1910.—(Tamil.) On the fourth pillar in the same place. A record in the twenty-fourth year of the Chēra king Kōkkaṇḍan Ravi, 'the sovereign jewel of the Chandrādityakula.' Records gift of the stone pillar to the same maṇṭapa, by another private individual. [See Tillaisthānam inscriptions (Tanjore district) where we get evidences which seem to prove that Kōkkaṇḍan of this and previous inscription was the contemporary of Varaguṇa Pāṇḍya and Āditya-Chōḷa, the father of Parāntaka I.]

108. 149 *of* 1910.—(Tamil.) On the fifth pillar in the same place. A record in the third year of Vikrama-Chōḷadēva (Koṅgu-Chōla). Records gift of money for twenty lamps by a native of Kaṇṇaṅguḍi in Tañjāvūr-kūṟṟam, a district of Pāṇḍikulāśani-vaḷanāḍu, which was a subdivision of Chōḷa-maṇḍalam, to the temple of Tēnūr-Āṇḍār at Vaḷḷalūr.

DHARAPURAM TALUK.

Dhārāpuram.

109. On the north wall of maṇṭapam in the temple of Uttama Rāghavaperumāḷ temple in Dhārāpuram Fort. Records that in K. 4488, Prabhava, Śrīnātha (?) Dēvarāja Uḍaiyār (a chief of Ariyappa Uḍaiyār) re-established the maṇṭapam and past endowments. *Ins., S. Dts.*, p. 197, No. 16.

Koriñjivāḍi near *Dhārāpuram.**

110. 580 *of* 1893.—(Tamil.) On the doorway of the shrine of the Śokkanātha temple. A record in the twenty-fifth year of Kō-Rājakēsarivarman *alias* Sundara-Pāṇḍyadēva (unidentified). Records gift of two pillars.

111. 581 *of* 1893.—(Tamil.) On the north wall of the same shrine. A record of the Vijayanagara king Mahārāya Dēvarāya II, son of Vīra-Vijayarāya, in Ś. 1363 expired, Durmukhi (mistake for Durmati). Records gift of land. [I have traced this inscription to *Ins., S. Dts.* (Mack. MSS.), p. 117, No. 19. Curiously enough it mentions the year correctly.]

112. 582 *of* 1893.—(Tamil.) On the same wall. A record of the Pāṇḍya king Kōnērinmaikoṇḍān Vīra-Pāṇḍyadēva. Records gift of land. [*Ins., S. Dts.*, p. 197, No. 18. It attributes the inscription to the thirtieth year of the reign and records grant of three *mās* and one *kāṇi* of land. The king has not been identified.]

---

* The inscriptions of this place collected by Mackenzie are listed in *Ins., S. Dts.*, pp. 197—8, Nos. 17—21. All these are in the departmental list, except an inscription of Kōnērinmai-koṇḍān in his thirtieth year granting six *mās* of land. (No. 19.)

113. 583 *of* 1893.—(Tamil.) On the south wall of the same shrine. A record in Raudri of Mahārāya-Dēvarāya-Uḍaiyār. Records gift of land. [As Raudri corresponds to 1440 and as there is no *Raudri* year possible in Dēvarāya I's reign, it follows that the king intended here is Dēvarāya II.]

114. 584 *of* 1893.—(Tamil.) On the north wall of the shrine of Mīnākshi-Amman in the same temple. A record in the fourth year of Kōnērinmaikoṇḍān. Records gift of land. [This might be *Ins., S. Dts.*, p. 198, No. 20, but doubtful.]

115. 585 *of* 1893.—(Tamil.) On the west and south walls of the same shrine. A record of Kōnērinmaikoṇḍān. Records gift of land (13½ mās). *Ibid.*, p. 198, No. 21.

Bōlumāmpaṭṭi.

116. 150 *of* 1910.—(Tamil.) At the entrance into the central shrine in the Nāgēśvara temple. A record in the twenty-seventh year of Vīrarājēndradēva. Records that a private individual a resident of Adirādarājan-tirumaḍaiviḷāgam, set up these two door-posts in the temple of Tirunāgīchchuram-Uḍaiyar. [Mr. Krishṇa Sastri points out that the name Adirādarājan Tirumaḍaiviḷāgam reminds the old Chēra rule. Was the king the same as the Koṅgu chief who ruled from 1207 to 1252?]

117. 151 *of* 1910.—(Tamil.) On the south wall of the same shrine. A record in the third year of Rājarājadēva. Records gift of land for offerings to the temple of Tirunāgīśvaram-Uḍaiyār at Muṭṭam *alias* Amarabhujaṅgaranallūr. Mentions Uttamaśīli vāykkāl.

118. 152 *of* 1910.—(Tamil.) On the same wall. A record in the third year of Rājarājadēva. Records gift of land to the servants of the same temple, for providing offerings.

119. 153 *of* 1910.—(Tamil.) On the west wall of the same shrine. An incomplete record in the seventeenth year of Vikrama-Chōḷa-dēva. Mentions the same temple.

120. 154 *of* 1910.—(Tamil.) On the north wall of the same shrine. An incomplete record in the twenty-seventh year of Rāja-kēsarivarman *alias* Tribhuvanachakravartin Vīrarājēndradēva (1207—52). Seems to register gifts of land made by the early Chēra kings Adirādarājadēva and Rājarājadēva, to the temples at Muṭṭam surnamed (apparently in the period of the Chēra rule). Ravivarma-chaturvēdimaṅgalam and Amarabhujaṅgaranallūr. Mentions Kōḷūr *alias* Arumoḷidēva-chaturvēdimaṅgalam and Rājarājanallūr.

121. 155 *of* 1910.—(Tamil.) On the wall of the maṇṭapa in front of the Nāgēśvari shrine in the same temple. A record in the thirty-second year of the Koṅgu-Chōḷa Vikrama-Chōḷadēva (1005—45). Built in at the beginning and stones out of order.

Records gift of money for offerings to the shrine of Kōṭidēvar in the temple of Tirunāgīchcharam-Uḍaiyār. Ravivarma-chaturvēdimaṅgalam and Amarabhujaṅgaranallūr are both mentioned as the surnames of Muṭṭam.

122. 156 *of* 1910.—(Tamil.) On the west wall of the Veṅkaṭēśvara Perumāḷ temple in the same village. Records gift of money for a lamp to the temple of Kulaśēkhara-Viṇṇagar-Emberumān.

123. 157 *of* 1910.—(Tamil.) On the same wall. Records gift of money for a lamp to the same temple.

Kāṅgyam.

123-A. On a stone in the temple of Agastyēśvara. Records that in K. 4633, Ānanda (?), in the reign of Bālayyadēva Rāja, the people of two villages gave a piece of land to the deity. *Ins., S. Dts.*, p. 35, No. 20.

Kurukkaipāḷayam.

123-B. A C.P. in the hands of Īśānaśivāchārya, Superintendent of the local maṭha. Records in Ś. 4452 a grant of land to God Tirumala vali nāthasvāmi and Gñānaśiva Svāmiyār. *Ins., S. Dts.*, p. 40, No. 41.

Muttūr.

124. 158 *of* 1910.—(Tamil.) On the south wall of the central shrine in the Chōḷēśvara temple. A record in the seventh year of Kulōttuṅga-Chōḷadēva. Records gift of money for a lamp by a merchant of Kāṅgayam to the temple of Kulōttuṅgaśōḷīśvaram-Uḍaiyār at Muttūr. See Cb. 250 which reveals the existence of a Koṅgu-Chōḷa who ruled from 1145 to 1163 at least.

125. 159 *of* 1910.—(Tamil.) On the same wall. An incomplete record in the fifth year of Vīrarājēndradēva (? 1207—52). Records the gift of money for a lamp by a merchant.

126. 160 *of* 1910.—(Tamil.) On the same wall. An incomplete record in the seventh year of Kulōttuṅga-Chōḷadēva. Seems to record a gift to the temple of Kulōttuṅgaśōḷīśvaram Uḍaiyār at Muttūr in Kāṅgaya-nāḍu. See note to 124.

127. 161 *of* 1910.—(Tamil.) On the same wall. A damaged record in the sixth year of Kōnērinmaikoṇḍān. Registers an order to Pāparāja of Muttūr that he should provide for offerings in the temple of Kulōttuṅgaśōḷīśuram-Uḍaiyār, out of the tax he had to pay to the king.

128. 162 *of* 1910.—(Tamil.) On the west wall of the same shrine. A damaged record in the eighth year of Kulōttuṅga-Chōḷadēva. On the left margin are engraved the syllables Rājakēsari Mentions Muttūr in Kāṅgayanāḍu. See No. 124 above.

129. 163 *of* 1910.—(Tamil.) On the same wall. An incomplete record in the eighth year of Rājakēsari Tribhuvanachakravartin

Kulōttuṅga-Chōḷadēva. Records that some residents of Muttūr borrowed money from the same temple. See No. 124 above.

130. 164 *of* 1910.—(Tamil.) On the north wall of the same temple. A record in the fourth year of Vīrarājēndradēva (Koṅgu chief ?, 1207—52). Records gift of a lamp, by a lady, to the same temple. Mentions Kottanūr in Tenkarai-nāḍu.

131. 165 *of* 1910.—(Tamil.) On the same wall. A record in the fourth year of Vīrarājēndradēva (Koṅgu chief ?, 1207—52). Records gift of money for a lamp to the shrine of Periyanāchchiyār at Muttūr by the son of Uttamaśōḻappallavaraiyan, one of the Kuvālanvaḷavar of Muttūr.

132. 166 *of* 1910.—(Tamil.) On the same wall. A damaged record in the twentieth year of Vīrarājēndradēva (1207—52 ?). Records gift of money for offerings to the temple of Kulōttuṅga-śōḻīchcharam Uḍaiyār at Muttūr.

Paḷaiyakōṭṭai.

132-A. A C.P. in the hands of Śakkarai Kavuṇḍan recording that in K. 4346 Prabha(va), in the reign of Virupākshārāya, his minister Nañjana Uḍaiyār appointed one Aḷaga Uttama Kavuṇḍan (?) of Kāriyūr as the manager of the twenty-four Nāḍs for his heroic exploits against the "Koṅgarayer." *Ins., S. Dts.*, p. 40, No. 42. [The date and the name of the king seem to throw suspicion on the genuineness of the record.]

Parañjērvali.

133. 556 *of* 1908.—(Tamil.) On two pillars lying in the Vīranārāyaṇa Perumāḷ temple. A damaged record in the ninth year of Rājādhirāja-Vīranārāyaṇa-Vīra-Chōḷa. Seems to record a gift of land. [*Ins., S. Dts.*, p. 28, No. 2, which says that the gift was a tank with some land. The king might be the same as Parāntaka I or more probably the Koṅgu-Chōḷa who ruled from 1118 onward.]

134. 557 *of* 1908.—(Tamil.) On a slab lying in the same temple. In modern characters. Records in Viḷambi, gift of money for a lamp to the temple of Vīranārāyaṇa at Parañjērpaḷḷi.

135. 558 *of* 1908.—(Tamil.) On a broken pillar lying in the Madhyapurīśvara temple in the same village. A mutilated record in the fifth year of the Chōḷa king Vikrama-Chōḷadēva (1118—35).

136. 559 *of* 1908.—(Tamil.) On a slab set up near the well in the same temple. A record in the fifth year of the Chōḷa king Vikrama-Chōḷadēva (1118—35). Records gift of money for offerings to the temple of Naṭṭūramarndār in Paranśērpaḷḷi in Kāṅgayanāḍu.

137. 560 *of* 1908.—(Tamil.) On the second slab set up in the same temple. A record in the first year of the Chōḷa king Rāja-Vikrama-Chōḷadēva. Probably a copy of an older record in modern characters. Records gift of village and a tank to the temple of Naṭṭūramarnda-Nāyanār at Parañjērpaḷḷi in Kāṅgēya-nāḍu. [A mutilated version of this is in *Ins., S. Dts.*, p. 28, No. 1, where Vikrama Chōḷa is called "Vīrāmāpondiyadēvur."]

Veḷḷiyaraśal.

138. 619 *of* 1905.—(Tamil.) On the west wall of the central shrine in the Māndīśvara temple. A record in the sixteenth year of Vīrarājēndradēva (1207—52). The village is called Vaḷḷierichchal in Kāṅgēya-nāḍu and the temple Māndānīśvaram Uḍaiyār. Mentions also Rājakēsaripuram.

139. 620 *of* 1905.—(Vaṭṭeḷuttu.) On a stone built into the south wall or the maṇṭapa in front of the same shrine. A fragment of record. Mentions Tiruppāṇḍikkoḍumuḍi.

140. 621 *of* 1905.—(Vaṭṭeḷuttu.) On a second stone built into the same wall. A fragment of record in the thirty-third year of the king whose name is mutilated. Mentions a native of Āmūr.

ERODE TALUK.

Erode.

141. 12 *of* 1891.—(Tamil.) South wall of the Ārdrakapālēśvara temple. A record of the fourth year of Kō-Rājakēsarivarman *alias* Ravikōdai *alias* Kōkkalimūkkan.

142. 13 *of* 1891.—(Tamil.) In the same place. A record of the Vijayanagar sovereign Vīra Veṅkaṭapatirāya I, dated Ś. 1510 (expired), Sarvadhāri.

143. 14 *of* 1891.—(Tamil.) On the west and south walls of the same temple. A record of the Hoysaḷa king Vīra Vallāḷadēva (III, 1292—1340), dated Ś. 1262 (expd.), Vikrama.

144. 15 *of* 1891.—(Tamil.) In the same place. A record of the twenty-second year of Kō-Ravikōdai.

145. 16 *of* 1891.—(Tamil.) On the west wall of the Raṅganāthasvāmi temple. A record of Kō-Rājakēsarivarman *alias* Vīra Pāṇḍyadēva in his tenth year. [The inscription is unique as an example of a Pāṇḍyan king wearing a Chōḷa title. He was evidently the Koṅgu ruler from 1255 to 1281. See Cb. 196 and 197. Also 150 of 1905 at Venjamākūḍalur, Trichinopoly Dt.]

146. 17 *of* 1891.—(Tamil.) On the east wall of the same temple. A record of Ś. 1449 (expd.), Pramōdūta (inconsistent). Mentions Chikkarāya.

147. 167 *of* 1910.—(Tamil.) On the door posts of the entrance into the central shrine in the Raghunāthasvāmin temple. A record in the fifteenth year of the Chōḷa king Madiraikoṇḍa-Parakēsarivarman (905—47). In characters much later than the time of Madiraikoṇḍa Parāntaka I. Records that the people of Eḷugaraittiruvāyappāḍi-nāḍu agreed to pay certain taxes for the worship of

Veṇṇaikkūtta Nāyanār (i.e., Raghunātha) in the temple of Paḷḷigoṇḍāḷvār at Īrōḍu. "The fee is specified as follows:—½ *paṇam* on each tenant (*kuḍi*); ⅛ *paṇam* from the bridegroom and ⅛ from the bride in each marriage ceremony; and 1 *kunṛi* and 1 *manjāḍi* of gold as *śuḍugāṭṭuppāṭṭam*."

148. 168 *of* 1910.—(Tamil.) On the south wall of the maṇṭapa in front of the central shrine in the Ārdrakapālēśvara temple in the same village. A record of Vīrarāya-Tāvakka-Māraiyanāyaka-Uḍaiyār in Ś. 1426, Rudhirōdgārin. Records gift of land for repairs and festivals to the temple of Toṇḍīśvaramuḍaiya-Mahādēva at Īrōḍu in Kāñchittuṇḍam, a subdivision of Mēlkarai Pūndurai-nāḍu.

149. 169 *of* 1910.—(Tamil.) On the same wall. A damaged record of the Vijayanagara king Parvata-Rāhuttar in Ś. 1432, Prajōtpatti. Records gift of money (Dēvarāyapon) for offerings to the temple of Toṇḍayappar or Toṇḍīśvaramuḍaiya-Tambirānār at Īrōḍu in Kāñchittuṇḍam, a subdivision of Mēlakaṛai-nāḍu which was a district of Koṅgu-maṇḍalam. The donor was a *gavuṇḍan*, one of the *Okkaḷmakkaḷu* (cultivators) of Ummattur-śīrmai. [Mr. Krishna Sastri suggests that Parvata Rāhuttar might have been a prince of the royal family placed by Kṛishṇa Rāya in charge of the newly conquered Ummattūr country or one of the rebellious chiefs whom he had to punish. For the *Dēvarāyapon* or pagoda see *Ind. Antq.*, XX, p. 302.]

150. 170 *of* 1910.—(Kanarese.) At the entrance into the same maṇṭapa right of the Dvārapālaka image. A damaged record of the Maisūr king Kaṇṭhīrava Narasarāja-Vaḍeru (1638—59), in Manmatha. Mentions Daḷavāyi Hampayya and Madhura. See *Mys. Gazr.*, I, p. 364. The incription shows the triumph of Mysore arms over Madura in the reign of Tirumal Nāik. See *Ind. Antq.*

151. On the south wall of the Mahāmaṇṭapam in the temple of Toṇḍēśvara. Records in the reign of Vīrarāyā grant of two mās of land by Savakkamārāya ? Nāyakar to the deity by himself. *Ins., S. Dts.*, p. 89, No. 10.

152. On the east of the front Maṇṭapam. Grant by Parvatarāya of the village of Ummattūr in Ś. 1333, Prajōtpatti. *Ibid.*, p. 90, No. 11. The date is inconsistent and should be Ś. 1433. See No. 149 above.

153. In the same place. A gift of land by Āhiyappa Gōvinda. *Ibid.*, No. 12.

154. On the western wall. Records a grant of land by one "Kokale Mookur" in the fourth year to God Toṇḍēśvara. *Ibid.*, No. 13.

155. On the west of the inner temple. Records in Ś. 1262, in the reign of Vīra Ballāḷadēva (III, 1292—1340) gift of the village of Pendulore by the people of Pūnduṛaināḍu. *Ibid.*, No. 14.

156. On the south of the Mahāmaṇṭapam. Records that the people of Pūnduṟaināḍu gave in Sarvadhāri, in the reign of Vīra Veṅkaṭapatirāya 102, *vēḷis* of land to the deities Toṇḍēśvara, Paḷḷikoṇḍa Perumāḷ, etc. *Ins., S. Dts.*, p. 89, No. 15. [If Sarvadhāri is taken to be year 1588, the emperor referred to should be Veṅkaṭa I, 1586—1614.]

157. On the west of the inner temple. Records grant of land in Ahiyūr to God Toṇḍēśvara in the twenty-second year Tiruvunda "Tadur." *Ibid.*, No. 16.

158. On the west side of the inner temple. Records in Ś. 1449, in the reign of Vīraśēkhara Rāya, that the people of Pūnduraināḍu granted a village near Chāttanūr to Gods Paḷḷikoṇḍa and Toṇḍēśvara. *Ibid.*, p. 92, No. 17.

159. On the west side of the inner temple. Records in the twentieth year of Vīra-Pāṇḍya (1265—81) gift of a village by the people of Pūnduṟaināḍu. *Ibid.*, No. 18.

160. On a stone at the gate of the Perumāḷ temple. A record of the gift of land by Periyakoṇḍappan and Chinnakoṇḍappan to the God and Goddess. *Ibid.*, No. 19.

161. On the southern wall of the Vināyaka Maṇṭapa. Records the grant of the village of Yerukka Kadalayanur? to God Gōdaprāṭṭitavamuḍaiyār by Kōnērinmaikoṇḍān. *Ibid.*, p. 93, No. 20.

162. On the south side of the Vināyaka temple. Records the grant of the "Auchoo" to the God for worship and food offering in the twenty-ninth year of Vīra-Rājēndrachōḷa (Koṅgu chief?). *Ibid.*, No. 21.

Kavaṭṭampāḷaiyam.

163. 601 *of* 1905.—(Tamil.) On a slab set up at the tank near the village. A damaged record of Tribhuvanachakravartin Kōnērinmaikoṇḍān. Mentions Kūḍūr.

Sarkār-Periyapāḷaiyam.

164. 304 *of* 1908.—(Tamil.) On the north wall of the Sugrīvēśvara-temple. A record in the twenty-second year of the Pāṇḍya king Sundara-Pāṇḍyadēva. Provides for the maintenance and supervision of an irrigation tank at Sūralūr *alias* Sundara-Pāṇḍya-nallūr in Vūyaraikkā-nāḍu which belonged to the temple of Kurakkuttali-Āḷuḍaiya-Nāyanār.

165. 305 *of* 1908.—(Tamil.) On the same wall. A record in the eighth year of the Pāṇḍya king Tribhuvanachakravartin Kōnērinmaikoṇḍān Vīra-Pāṇḍyadēva. Records gift of land for the requirements of a festival named after the king, in the temple of Kurakkuttali-Āḷuḍaiya-Nāyanār, the lord of Mugandanūr in the Vīra-Śōḷa-Vaḷanāḍu. Mentions Valuppūṟṟakkū-nāḍu. See No. 145 above.

166. 306 *of* 1908.—(Tamil.) On the same wall. A record in the third year of the Pāṇḍya king Sundara-Pāṇḍyadēva. Records gift of money for a lamp to the shrine of Vaḍuga-Piḷḷaiyār in the temple of Kurakkattali-Āḷuḍaiyār Nāyanār, the lord of Mugandanūr in Vīraśōḷa-vaḷanāḍu, by a certain śeṭṭi surnamed Śēramān-Tōḷan of Paḷinallūr.

167. 307 *of* 1908.—(Tamil.) On the same wall. A record in the fourth year of the Pāṇḍya king Sundara-Pāṇḍyadēva. Records gift of land.

168. 308 *of* 1908.—(Tamil.) On the same wall. A damaged record of Tribhuvanachakravartin Kōnērinmaikoṇḍān. Mentions Tirukkurakkuttaḷi-Uḍaiyār.

169. 309 *of* 1908.—(Tamil.) On the same wall. A record in the thirteenth year of Tribhuvanachakravartin Kōnērinmaikoṇḍān Vīrarājēndradēva (1207—36). Records gift of land to Appan Vīrarājēndra-śōḷachakravartin, one of the priests of the temple of Āḷuḍaiya-Nāyanār at Maṇṇiyūr in Vaḍa-pariśāra-nāḍu. Mentions also the temple of Kurakkuttali Āḷuḍaiya-Nāyanār, the lord of Mugandanūr in Vīraśōḷa-Vaḷanāḍu.

170. 310 *of* 1908.—(Tamil.) On the west wall of the same temple. A record in the twenty-seventh year of the Pāṇḍya king Tribhuvanachakravartin Kōnērinmaikoṇḍān Sundara-Pāṇḍyadēva. Records gift of land tō the same individual.

171. 311 *of* 1908.—(Tamil.) On the same wall. A record of the Pāṇḍya king Tribhuvanachakravartin Kōnērinmaikoṇḍān Sundara-Pāṇḍyadēva, the date of which is lost. Records gift of land for offerings and repairs. Mentions Tenkarai-Chchūralūr.

172. 312 *of* 1908—(Tamil.) On the same wall. A record in the twenty-fourth year of the Pāṇḍya king Tribhuvanachakravartin Kōnērinmaikoṇḍān Sundara-Pāṇḍyadēva. Record gift of land in Tenkarai-Chchūralūr.

173. 313 *of* 1908.—(Tamil.) On the south wall of the Sugrīvēśvara temple. A record in the 22nd year of the Pāṇḍya king Sundara-Pāṇḍyadēva. Refers to Śūralūr *alias* Sundara-Pāṇḍyanallūr which was a gift by Sundara-Pāṇḍya to the temple of Kurakkuttali-Nāyinār. Mentions *also* Sīdakkaṛchi in Vayāraikkānāḍu.

174. 314 *of* 1908.—(Tamil.) On the same wall. A record in the twenty-fourth year of the Pāṇḍya king Tribhuvanachakravartin Kōnērinmaikoṇḍān Sundara-Pāṇḍyadēva. Records gift of land for offerings.

175. 315 *of* 1908.—(Tamil.) On a pillar set up in the courtyard of the same temple. A record of Ummattūr king Mahāmaṇḍalēśvara Vīra-Nañjarāya-Uḍaiyār in Ś. 1421, Siddhārthin. Records gift of land by a merchant (śeṭṭi) to the temple of Kurakkuttaḷi-

68

Tambirānār, the lord of Mugandanūr in Kailāsanivāsa-chaturvēdimaṅgalam. Mentions the *Kavuṇḍas* of Vaḍaparisāra-nāḍu. See Nos. 30 and 31 above.

176. 316 *of* 1908.—(Tamil.) On the west wall of the Varada. rāja-Perumāḷ temple in the same village. Mentions in Nandana the temple of Perumāḷ Varadaraśar at Mugundanūr.

177. 317 *of* 1908.—(Tamil.) On the west and south walls of the same temple. A record in the fourteenth year of Tribhuvana-chakravartin Kōnērinmaikoṇḍān. A damaged record. Mentions Vikramaśōḷachaturvēdimaṅgalam and the temple of Vikrama-Chōḷa Vīṇṇagarāḷvār named after the king.

Tiṅgaḷūr.

178. 602 *of* 1905.—(Tamil.) On the north wall of the central shrine in the Chandramauḷīśvara temple. A record of the Hoysaḷa king Vīra-Sōmēśvara (son of Vīra Narasimha II and father of Vīra Narasimha III and Vīra Rāmanātha), in Subhānu (i.e., Ś. 1146). Built in at the end.

179. 603 *of* 1905.—(Tamil.) On the south base of the same shrine. A record in the twentieth year of the Koṅgu-Chōḷa king Rājakēsarivarman *alias* Tribhuvanachakravartin Vīrarājēndra-dēva (1207—52). Records that a native of Vijayamaṅgalam made some repairs to the temple of Chandrapura-Uḍaiyār at Tiṅgaḷūr.

180. 604 *of* 1905.—(Tamil.) On the south and east bases of the same shrine. A record of Kōnērinmaikoṇḍān. Built in at the beginning. Records gift of a tank (kuḷam) for celebrating a festival called Kulōttuṅga-Śōḷanśandi.

181. 605 *of* 1905.—(Grantha and Tamil.) On the east and north bases of the same shrine. A record of the Koṅgu-Chōḷa (?) Kōnerinmaikoṇḍān Kulōttuṅga-Chōḷa. Records gift of the village of Tēraiyūr *alias* Kulōttuṅga-Chōḷanallūr in Kuruppu-nāḍu to the temple of Chandrapurīśvaramuḍaiyār at Tiṅgaḷūr in the same nāḍu.

182. 606 *of* 1905.—(Tamil.) On the north wall of the maṇṭapa in front of the same shrine. A record in the fourth year of the Chōḷa king Vikrama-Chōḷadēva (1118—35). Registers a letter from Akaḷaṅkanāḍāḷvān.

183. 607 *of* 1905.—(Tamil.) On the south wall of the same maṇṭapa. A damaged record in the thirty-fifth year of the Koṅgu-Chōḷa king Rājakēsarivarman *alias* Tribhuvanachakravartin Vīra-rājēndradēva (1207—52).

184. 608 *of* 1905.—(Tamil.) On the west wall of the same maṇṭapa left of entrance. A record in the thirteenth year of the Koṅgu Chōḷa king Vikrama-Chōḷadēva. Records gift of a lamp.

185. 609 *of* 1905.—(Tamil.) In the same place. A damaged record in the forty-first year of Vīrarājēndradēva. Records gift of a lamp.

186. 610 *of* 1905.—(Tamil.) On a pillar of the same maṇṭapa. A record in Ś. 1197, second year of the Chōḷa king Parakēsarivarman *alias* Tribhuvanachakravartin Vikrama-Chōḷadēva (1118—35). A portion of the inscription has to be read upwards from the bottom.

187. 611 *of* 1905.—(Tamil.) On another pillar of the same maṇṭapa. A record in the third year of the Pāṇḍya king Vīra-Pāṇḍyadēva. Records that a private individual set up a *balipīṭha.*

188. 612 *of* 1905.—(Tamil.) On a third pillar of the same maṇṭapa. A record in the fourth year of the Chōḷa king Vikrama Chōḷadēva (1118—35). Records the setting up of an image by a native of Sundara-Pāṇḍyapuram in the Pāṇḍya country.

189. 613 *of* 1905.—(Tamil.) On a fourth pillar of the same maṇṭapa. A record in the forty-first year of the Chōḷa king Vīrarājēndradēva. Records the gift of four rows of pillars.

190. 614 *of* 1905.—(Tamil.) On the door post of the kitchen in the Pushpanātha (Jaina) temple in the same village. A record in S. 967, fortieth year of the Koṅgu-Chōḷa king Vikrama Chōḷadēva (A.D. 1004—45). Records the building of the mukhamaṇṭapa of the temple which is called *Śandiravasadi.* The king has the epithet Kōnāṭṭān. [The inscription is referred to in *Mack. MSS.** See *Ins., S. Dts.*, p. 100, No. 12.]

191. 615 *of* 1905.—(Tamil.) On the south wall of the central shrine in the Aḷagiyarāja Perumāḷ temple in the same village. A record in the third year of the Koṅgu-Pāṇḍya king Tribhuvanachakravartin Kōnērinmaikoṇḍān Vīra-Pāṇḍyadēva (1265—81). Records gift of land to the temple of Sundara-Pāṇḍya-Viṇṇagar-Emberumān at Tiṅgaḷūr.

192. 616 *of* 1905.—(Tamil.) On the same wall. A record in the fourteenth year of Rājakēsarivarman *alias* Tribhuvanachakravartin Vīra-Paṇḍyadēva (1265—81). Records gift of land.

193. 617 *of* 1905.—(Tamil.) On the west wall of the same shrine. A record in the twenty-third year of the Pāṇḍya king Jaṭāvarman *alias* Tribhuvanachakravartin Sundara-Pāṇḍyadēva (I or II ?). Records gift of money (23 faṇams acc. to *Mack. MSS.*) for two lamps. Mentions Tirupputtūr in Kēraḷaśiṅga-vaḷanāḍu, a subdivision of Pāṇḍi-maṇḍalam. See *Ins., S. Dts.*, p. 98, No. 6. It is not known whether the king referred to is he who came to the throne in 1251, 1271 or 1276.

194. 618 *of* 1905.—(Tamil.) On the north wall of the central shrine in the Aḷagiyarāja-Perumāḷ temple. A record in the

---

* The *Mack. MSS.* also refer to two other inscriptions here, one of which is damaged, and refers to "Munivetadoornooperar." The other is a record of Vira Ballāla granting the village of "Auricanellore" to the God "Parumbam Nāyanār." See *Ins., S. Dts.*, p. 100, Nos. 13 and 14.

eighteenth year of king Rājakēsarivarman *alias* Tribhuvanachakravartin Vīra-Pāṇḍyadēva (1265—81). Registers an endowment for offerings by the villagers of Taunri *alias* Vikrama-Śōḷapuram. The sign for *aydam* is used in this inscription in the word *abkam* in line 4. [The inscription is given in *Ins.*, *S. Dts.*, p. 98, No. 7. It says that one measure of rice and some oil were endowed.]

Vengambūr (" Vangumpoor ").

195. On a stone in the local temple of Īśvara. Records that in the second year of Vīra-Pāṇḍyadēva, Sundara-Pāṇḍya Naraśingadēva granted the village as free gift to God Vīrajayaṅkoṇḍēśvara Uḍaiyār. See *Ins.*, *S. Dts.*, in *Mack. MSS.*, p. 89, No. 9.

Vijayamaṅgalam.

196. 544 *of* 1905.—(Tamil.) On the south base of the central shrine in the Kariyamāṇikka-Perumāl ṭemple. A damaged record of Rājakēsarivarman *alias* Tribhuvanachakravartin Vīra-Pāṇḍyadēva in Ś. 1202, in his fifteenth year. Records gift of money for a lamp. Mentions Vīra-Chōḷa-chaturvēdimaṅgalam. The temple is called Tirumērkōyil Śittiramēḷi Viṇṇagar-Nāyanār Karumāṇikkāḷvār at Viśaiyamaṅgalam in Kuruppu-nāḍu. [The inscription shows that this king came to the throne in 1265.]

197. 545 *of* 1905.—(Tamil.) On the same base. A damaged record of Rājakēsarivarman *alias* Tribhuvanachakravartin Vīra-Pāṇḍyadēva in Ś. 1202. Regnal year lost. Records gift of a flower garden and of a lamp. See note to the above epigraph.

198. 546 *of* 1905.—(Tamil.) On the north base of the same shrine. A record in the tenth year of Rājakēsarivarman *alias* Tribhuvanachakravartin Vīrarājēndradēva (apparently the Koṅgu-Chōḷa, 1207—36). Records a gift for offerings. The temple is called Tirumērkōyil Śittiramēḷi-Viṇṇagarāḷvār at Viśaiyamaṅgalam in Kuruppunāḍu. The gift is placed under the protection of *the ninety-nine belonging to the left hand caste.*

199. 547 *of* 1905.—(Tamil.) On the north base of the central shrine in the Kariyamāṇikka-Perumāḷ temple. A record in the twelfth year of the Páṇḍya king Tribhuvanachakravartin Vīra-Pāṇḍyadēva. Records a gift for a lamp. The temple is called Śittiramēḷi-Viṇṇagar-Emberumān Karumāṇikkāḷvār at Viśaya-maṅgalam. [See Cb. 196 above for the probable identity of the king.]

200. 548 *of* 1905.—(Tamil.) On the east wall of the maṇṭapa in front of the same shrine, right of entrance. A record in the twenty-third year of the Paṇḍya king Jaṭāvarman *alias* Tribhuvanachakravartin Sundara-Pāṇḍyadēva (I? 1251—64). Built in at the end. Records gift of a lamp. See Cb. 193.

201. 549 *of* 1905.—(Tamil.) In the same place. A record in the twenty-eighth year of the Pāṇḍya king Jaṭāvarman *alias* Tribhuvanachakravartin Sundara-Pāṇḍyadēva (I ?, 1251—64). Built in at the end. Records gift of a lamp. See Cb. 193.

202. 550 *of* 1905.—(Tamil.) On the same wall, left of entrance. A record in the seventeenth year of the Pāṇḍya king Jaṭāvarman *alias* Tribhuvanachakravartin Sundara-Pāṇḍyadēva (I ?, 1251—64). Built in at the beginning. Records the gift of a lamp. See Cb. 193.

203. 551 *of* 1905.—(Tamil.) In the same place. A damaged record in the twenty-fourth year of the Pāṇḍya king Jaṭāvarman *alias* Tribhuvanachakravartin Sundara-Pāṇḍyadēva (I, 1251—64 ?). Built in at the beginning. Records gift of a lamp.

204. 552 *of* 1905.—(Tamil.) On the south base of the same maṇṭapa. A record of the Hoysaḷa king Vīra-Vallāḷadēva (III) in Ś. 1249, Prabhava. Records gift of land by the residents of Kuruppunāḍu for the prosperity of the king and of the country. [This and other inscriptions of Vīra-Ballāḷa show that even after the Musalman conquest he maintained his rule in Koṅgu country.]

205. 553 *of* 1905.—(Tamil.) On the same base. A record in the second year of the Pāṇḍya king Jaṭāvarman *alias* Tribhuvanachakravartin Sundara-Pāṇḍyadēva (I ?, 1251–64). Records gift of a lamp.

206. 554 *of* 1905.—(Tamil.) On the north base of the same maṇṭapa. A record in the seventeenth year of Rājakēsarivarman *alias* Tribhuvanachakravartin Vīra-Pāṇḍyadēva (1265—81). Records gift of a lamp. Mentions Kaṅgaya-nāḍu.

207. 555 *of* 1905.—(Tamil.) On a pillar lying near the south prākāra of the same temple. A record in Ś. 1179, second year of Vikrama-Chōḷadēva. Records gift of a door post. [The inscription shows that there was a Koṅgu-Choḷa named Vikrama who came to the throne in 1256. See Cb. 230 below, wherefrom it is certain that he ruled till 1263 at least.]

208. 556 *of* 1905.—(Tamil.) On the north wall of the central shrine in the Nāgēśvarasvāmin temple in the same village. A damaged record in the fifth year of the Koṅgu-Chōḷa king Rājakēsarivarman *alias* Tribhuvanachakravartin Vīrarājēndradēva. Mentions Ugayppāḍi, Rājarājapuram and the temple of Tirunāgīśvara.

209. 557 *of* 1905.—(Tamil.) On the same wall. A record in the forty-second year of Vīrarājēndradēva (1207—52). Records gift of a lamp.

210. 558 *of* 1905.—(Tamil.) On the same wall. A record in the forty-first year of Vīrarājēndradēva. Records gift of a lamp. Mentions Piḍāriyūr. See No. 208.

211. 559 *of* 1905.—(Tamil.) On the east wall of the same shrine. A damaged record in the thirtieth year of Vīrarājēndradēva. Records gift of a lamp. See No. 208.

212. 560 *of* 1905.—(Tamil.) On the same wall. A record in the forty-first year of Vīrarājēndradēva. Records gift of a lamp.

213. 561 *of* 1905.—(Tamil.) On the south wall of the same shrine. A record in the thirteenth year of the Koṅgu-Chōḷa king Rājakēsarivarman *alias* Tribhuvanachakravartin Vīrarājēndradēva. Built in at the end. See No. 208.

214. 562 *of* 1905.—(Tamil.) On the same wall. A record in the thirtieth year of Vīrarājēndradēva. Records gift of a lamp.

215. 563 *of* 1905.—(Tamil.) On the same wall. A record in the twentieth year of Vīrarājēndradēva. Records gift of a gold ornament for the goddess and a lamp. Mentions Viśaiyamaṅgalam and Pūvāṇiya-nāḍu.

216. 564 *of* 1905.—(Tamil.) On the north wall of the maṇṭapa in front of the same shrine. A record in the third year of Vīra-Pāṇḍyadēva. Records gift of a lamp by a merchant. See Cb. 196.

217. 565 *of* 1905.—(Tamil.) On the same wall. A damaged record of Sundara-Pāṇḍyadēva. Mentions the temple of Vikrama-Chōḷīśvaramuḍaiyār at Vijayamaṅgalam. See Cb. 196.

218. 566 *of* 1905.—(Tamil.) On the same wall. A record in the fifth year of Vīra-Pāṇḍyadēva. Records gift of a lamp. See Cb. 196.

219. 567 *of* 1905.—(Tamil.) On the same wall. A record in the third year of Vīra-Pāṇḍyadēva. Records gift of a lamp. The village is called Viśaiyamaṅgalam. See Cb. 196.

220. 568 *of* 1905.—(Tamil.) On the same wall. A record in the fourth year of the Chōḷa (?) king Tribhuvanavīradēva (Kulōttuṅga III). Records gift of money for offerings. Mentions Kāṅgayam in Kāṅgayanāḍu.

221. 569 *of* 1905.—(Tamil.) On the same wall. A record in Ś. 1202, fifteenth year of king Tribhuvanachakravartin Kōnērimaikoṇḍān Vīra-Pāṇḍyadēva. Records that the king re-named a ruined tank (at Vāgaipputtūr) Vīra-Pāṇḍyappērēri and granted all lands irrigated by it free of taxes to the villagers, who had to make provision for offerings to the goddess apparently from the produce of the land.

222. 570 *of* 1905.—(Tamil.) On the east wall of the same maṇṭapa. A record in the fourth year of king Vikrama-Chōḷadēva. Records gift of a lamp. For the probable identity of the king see Nos. 207 and 230.

223. 571 *of* 1905.—(Tamil.) On the same wall. A record in the thirteenth year of king Vikrama-Chōḷadēva. Records gift of a lamp.

224. 572 *of* 1905.—(Tamil.) On the same wall. A record in the fourth year of Tribhuvanavīradēva. Records gift of two lamps. See No. 220 above.

225. 573 *of* 1905.—(Tamil.) On the south wall of the same maṇṭapa. An unfinished record in Ś. 1022, ... year of Abhimāna Rājādhirāja. [Records gift of a lamp. The record shows the existence of a Koṅgu-Chōḷa chief named Rājādhirāja. See next epigraph.]

226. 574 *of* 1905.—(Tamil.) On the same wall. A damaged record of . . . . Śōḷa-Rājādhirāja in Ś. 1022, Regnal year lost. Records a gift for offerings to the temple of Tiru-nāgēśvaram-Uḍaiyār. See the previous inscription.

227. 575 *of* 1905.—(Tamil.) On the same wall. A damaged record in the nineteenth year of Vīra-Pāṇḍyadēva. See Cb. 196.

228. 576 *of* 1905.—(Tamil.) On the same wall. A damaged record of the Chōḷa king Rājādhirāja, the date of which is lost. Mentions Uttama-Chōḷachaturvēdimaṅgalam, in Vīra-Chōḷa-vaḷa-nāḍu. See Cb. 225.

229. 577 *of* 1905.—(Tamil.) On the same wall. A record in the eighth year of Kulōttuṅga Chōḷadēva. Records the setting up of the image of the goddess and an endowment for offerings and for two lamps.

230. 578 *of* 1905.—(Tamil.) On the same wall. A record in Ś. 1185, seventh year of Vikrama-Chōḷadēva. Refers to the repairs of the maṇṭapa and registers copies made of the inscriptions found on the walls (two of Kulōttuṅga and five of Vīrarājēndra). The same Vikrama Chōḷa is referred to in Cb. No. 207 above.

231. 579 *of* 1905.—(Tamil.) On the same wall. A record in the thirteenth year of Kulōttuṅga-Chōḷadēva. Records a gift by a sāmanta named Kulōttuṅga-Chōḷa-Vikramādityadēva. See Cb. 190 for the probable identity of the king.

232. 580 *of* 1905.—(Tamil.) On the same wall. A record in the third year of king Vīrarājēndradēva. Records gift of a lamp.

233. 581 *of* 1905.—(Tamil.) On the same wall. A record in the eighth year of a Chōḷa king whose name is lost. Records gift of a lamp.

234. 582 *of* 1905.—(Tamil.) On the west wall of the same maṇṭapa right of entrance. A record in the third year of Tri-bhuvanachakravartin Kōnērimaikoṇḍān Tribhuvanavīradēva. (Kulōttuṅga III, ? 1178–1216) "Parakēsari" is engraved at the beginning of the inscriptions. Registers an order addressed to the pūjāris and temple managers of a number of districts and towns.

235. 583 *of* 1905.—(Tamil.) In the same place. A record in the eleventh year of Vikrama-Chōḷadēva. Records gift of a lamp. See Cb. 190.

236. 584 *of* 1905.—(Tamil.) On the same wall, left of entrance. A record in the fourteenth year of Rājakēsarivarman *alias* Tribhuvanachakravartin Vīrarājēndradēva (1207–52). Registers an order for offerings and for 90 lamps on the day of Śivarātri.

237. 585 *of* 1905.—(Tamil.) On the north wall of the shrine of the goddess in the same temple. Registers an order regarding the division of the income in all temples of Kuruppunāḍu.

238. 586 *of* 1905.—(Tamil.) On the north wall of the shrine of the goddess in the Nāgēśvarasvāmin temple. A record in the ninth year of Vīra-Pāṇḍyadēva. Records gift of a lamp. The goddess is called Tirukkāmakkōṭṭattāvaḍi-nāchchiyār. See Cb. 196.

239. 587 *of* 1905.—(Tamil.) On the south wall of the same shrine. A record in the twelfth year of Vīra-Pāṇḍyadēva. Records gift of a lamp. See Cb. 196.

240. 588 *of* 1905.—(Tamil.) On the same wall. A record in Dundubhi (i.e., Ś. 1245) of the Hoysaḷa king Vīra-Vallāḷadēva (III). Records gift of the village of Āmūr *alias* Rāhuttarāyanallūr.

241. 589 *of* 1905.—(Tamil.) On the north wall of the maṇṭapa in front of the same shrine. A record in the twenty-seventh year of the Pāṇḍya king Sundara- Pāṇḍyādēva. Records gift of money for a lamp. The goddess is called Tirukkāmakkōṭṭattāḷuḍaiya nāchchiyār.

242. 590 *of* 1905.—(Tamil.) On the same wall. Registers in Ś. 1265, Subhānu, an agreement of the *villagers to adopt heaped measures.*

243. 591 *of* 1905.—(Tamil.) On the south wall of the same maṇṭapa. A record in the twenty-seventh year of the Pāṇḍya king Sundara-Pāṇḍyadēva. Records gift of money for a lamp by the villagers. The money was obtained by selling the paddy belonging to the shrine of the goddess.

244. 592 *of* 1905.—(Tamil.) On a stone built into the western wall of the first prākāra of the same temple. A damaged record in Ś. 1022, ... year of . . . . . . Rājādhirājadēva. Seems to register a gift of land. See Cb. 225 where the same king is referred to.

245. 593 *of* 1905.—(Tamil.) On a slab set up near the same prākāra. A record in Ś. 1044, fifth year of Rājādhirāja Vīra-Chōḷadēva. Records gift of land. Mentions Kaṅgaya-nāḍu, the temple of Nangaīnīli at Tennūr near Vijayamaṅgalam and Ugāppāḍi. [The inscription throws light on another Koṅgu-chōḷa king of this name. He was apparently ruler from A.D. 1117 to 1123 at least.]

246. 594 *of* 1905.—(Tamil.) On a stone built into the west wall of the Sōmēśvara temple in the same village. A damaged record in the third year of Vīrarājēndradēva.

247. 595 *of* 1905.—(Tamil.) On the north wall of the same temple. A record in the twenty-eighth year of the Pāṇḍya king Sundara-Pāṇḍyadēva. Mutilated and stones out of order. Records the gift of a lamp to the temple of Attāṇīśvaram-Uḍaiyār.

248. 596 *of* 1905.—(Tamil.) On the east wall of the central shrine in the Chandranātha (Jaina) temple in the same village. A damaged record of the Vijayanagara king Vīra-Harihara-rāya-Uḍaiyār (III), son of Vīra-Dēvarāya-Uḍaiyār (Devarāya I), in Ś. 1334, Nandana. Records gift of land.

249. 597 *of* 1905.—(Grantha and Tamil.) On the east face of a pillar of the maṇṭapa in front of the same shrine. The stone (commemorating the) *niśidika* of Pullappa, younger sister of Chāmuṇḍarāja, who, the Government Epigraphist surmises, might be the same as the minister of the two Gaṅga kings Mārasimha II and Rāchamalla II, who set up the Jaina colossus at Śravaṇa Belgola. (*Ep. Ind.*, VII, p. 108 f.).

250. 598 *of* 1905.—(Tamil.) On the north and west faces of the same pillar. A record of the Koṅgu-Chōḷa king Rājakēsarivarman *alias* Tribhuvanachakravartin Kulōttuṅga-Chōḷadēva in Ś. 1085, and in his fourteenth year. Records gift of land for offerings to the Vīraśaṅghātapperumbaḷḷi at Vijayamaṅgalam. [The record reveals the existence of a Koṅgu-Chōḷa chief who came to the throne in A.D. 1149 and ruled till 1163 at least.]

251. 599 *of* 1905.—(Tamil.) On the door post of the eastern entrance into the same maṇṭapa, right side. A fragment of record. Registers an endowment for the requirements of certain festivals.

252. 600 *of* 1905.—(Tamil.) In the same place, left side. A mutilated record in Ś. 1189, forty-sixth year (of whom ?). Records gift of the door-post.

GŌBICHETTIPĀLAIYAM TALUK.

Āyalūr.

253. On a stone marked with conch and discus. Records the grant in Pramādi, of the village of Āyalūr to God Trivikrama Viṇṇaharam Perumāḷ of Elattūr. *Ins., S. Dts.*, p. 49, No. 26.

Danayakankōṭṭai.

254. 436 *of* 1906.—(Tamil.) On the west wall of the central shrine in the ruined Śiva temple in the fort. A record in Ś. 1270, expired, Virōdhin. The temple is called Tāndōnrīśuramuḍaiyār at Turavalūr *alias* Nīlagiri-sādāraṇan-kōṭṭai in Oḍuvaṅganāḍu, a district of Koṅgu-maṇḍalam.

255. 437 *of* 1906.—(Tamil.) On the south wall of the maṇṭapa in front of the same shrine. A record of the Hoysaḷa king Vīra-Vallāḷadēva (III, 1292-1341) in Ś. 1260, expired, Pramāthin. Records gift of two villages to the temple of Tāndōnṛīśvaramuḍaiya-Nāyanār at Turavalūr *alias* Nīlagirisādhāraṇan-kōṭṭai by Mādappan Śiṅgaya-Daṇṇāyakkar. One of them had been granted in Ś. 1258, expired, Īśvara.

256. 438 *of* 1906.—(Tamil.) On the same wall. Specifies in Ś. 1269, expired, Sarvajit, the names of the dancing girls who had to serve in the temple of Tāndōndṛīśvaramuḍaiyār at Turavalūr *alias* Nīlagiri-sādhāraṇan-kōṭṭai in Oḍuvaṅga-nāḍu, a district of Koṅgu-maṇḍalam.

257. 439 *of* 1906.—(Tamil.) On the same wall. Registers in Virōdhin an order of the god Chaṇḍēśvara. The place is called Turavalūr *alias* Nīlagiri-sādhāraṇan-kōṭṭai in Oḍuvakka-nāḍu, a district of Koṅgu-maṇḍalam.

258. 440 *of* 1906.—(Tamil.) On the north wall of the same maṇṭapa. Records in Sarvajit that the Mahāpradhāna Immaḍi-Rāhuttarāya Śiṅgaiya-Daṇṇāyaka granted *to the temple the proceeds of certain taxes on weavers and a ferry boat.*

259. 441 *of* 1906.—(Tamil.) On the same wall. A record of Vīra-Nañjarāya-Uḍaiyār in Ś. 1419, expired, Piṅgaḷa. Records gift of money for offerings.

260. 442 *of* 1906.—(Tamil.) On the same wall. Mentions in Vyaya the mahāpradhāna Immaḍi-Rāhuttarāya Śiṅgaya-Daṇṇāyaka. Records that the *Vaiśyavāṇiya-nagarattār* agreed to contribute a fixed amount for the benefit of the temple on certain articles of merchandise such as female cloths, pepper, arecanuts, thread, salt, grains and horses. The temple is called Tāndōnṛīśvara-muḍaiyār at Tiruvalūr *alias* Sitakaragaṇḍan-kōṭṭai in Oḍuvaṅga-nāḍu. [The record affords one of the examples of voluntary co-operation among people for common purposes.]

261. 443 *of* 1906.—(Grantha.) On the east wall of the maṇṭapa in front of the Vishṇu temple in the same village. Refers to the boar incarnation of Vishṇu.

262. 444 *of* 1906.—(Grantha and Tamil.) On the south and east walls of the same maṇṭapa. An incomplete record of the Hoysaḷa king Vīra-Vallāḷadēva (III, 1292—1341) in Ś. 1245, expired, Rudhirōdgārin. Records gift of land by the residents of Ēḷugarai-nāḍu for the requirements of the temple of Mādhava-Perumāḷ.

263. 445 *of* 1906.—(Tamil.) On one of the pillars of the maṇṭapa in front of the Vīrabhadrasvāmin temple in the same village. In modern characters. Mentions in Krōdhana the Vīrabhadrasvāmin temple.

264. 446 *of* 1906.—(Kaṇarese.) On the dhvajastambha of the same temple. Records in Ś. 1669, expired, Prabhava, the setting up of the *dipada vrishabhastambha.*

Elattur.

265. On the back of the inner temple of Chōḷēśvarasvāmi. Records the grant of Vaḍakkuḷam tank in the village by the local people in Siddhārti, in the fourteenth year of Kōnērinmaikoṇḍān. *Ins., S. Dts.*, p. 48, No. 23.

266. On a stone in the Tiruvikramanārāyaṇasvāmi temple. Records grant of some dry land to the God by Dāmōdara Nambi. *Ibid.*, No. 24.

267. On a conch and discus-marked stone north of the above temple. Records grant of a garden in the village to the deity in Bahudhānya in the reign of Vīra-Ballāḷadēva. *Ibid.*, No. 25.

Kanakaṃpāḷaiyam.

This village which is referred to in the following copper-plate grant is probably the village of that name in the Gōbicheṭṭipāḷaiyam taluk.

268. *C.P. No.* 83 *of Mr. Sewell's List.*—Records an agreement by the heads of the Kauṇḍan caste, in the village, in the matter of social and religious customs, executed in Ś. 1120, Kaliyuga 4299, Prabhava, in the reign of "Śrī Vīra Nāgappa Raṅga Raṅgayyavāru" (no royal titles given), over the Karnāṭadēśa.

Kanakanipālaiyam.

269. *C.P. No.* 29 *of Mr. Sewell's List.* Records a deed by which, in Ś. 1504 (A.D. 1582), *Vrisha*, Tirumalanāyakka of Madura, "King of Karnāṭa dēśa" made Ṭimma Kauṇḍan the spiritual head of his caste in twenty-four divisions of the "Koṅganāḍu." [Mr. Sewell considers the document to be spurious on the ground that Tirumal Nāik really began to rule only in A.D. 1623. The record is of interest in throwing light on the social arrangements of the age.]

Kuduvoy.

270. On a stone in the temple of Nayēśvara temple. Records that Chennayan, son of Paḷḷikoṇḍān, erected the Mahāmaṇṭapam in K. 4825 (?), Śubhakrit. *Ins., S. Dts.*, p. 199, No. 24.

271. On a stone in the same temple. Records a grant in the fourth year of Vīra Pāṇḍyadēva (unidentified). Damaged. *Ibid.*, p. 199, No. 25.

272. On the south of the Mahāmaṇṭapam, in the temple of Periyaperumāḷ. Records that the local inhabitants gave some land in Ś. 1411, Sādhāraṇa, for Brahmans, in the reign of Vīra . . . Rāyar. *Ibid.*, p. 200, No. 26.

273. In the same place. Records that the inhabitants of Puṅganūrnāḍu repaired the temple and gave some land in the reign of Viranandarāyar. *Ibid.*, No. 27.

Kugalūr.

274. 469 *of* 1913.—(Tamil.) On the north and east walls of the Madhyapurīśvara temple. A mutilated record in the third year and tenth day of the Kongu (?)-Chōḷa king Parakēsari Tribhuvana-chakravartin Kōnōinmakoṇḍān Tribhuvanavīradēva. Stones out of order. An imperfect copy of Cb. 293 below (Annual Report for 1911, p. 77, paragraph 37). [The record reveals the existence of a Kongu-Chōḷa who had the same titles as Kulōttunga III.]

275. 470 *of* 1913.—(Tamil.) On the east wall of the same temple. A damaged and incomplete record in the second year of Kongu (?) Paṇḍya king Sundara-Paṇḍyadēva. Seems to record a gift of land for a lamp by Naṭṭugamiṇḍan Nāṭṭūr-Āṇḍān and other inhabitants of Kūvalūr in Kānchikkūval-nāḍu.

276. 471 *of* 1913.—(Tamil.) Above the entrance into the same temple. A record of the Hoysaḷa king Vīra-Vallāḷadēva (III) in Pramōdūta (i.e., Pramōda = A.D. 1330–31) Tai. Records gift of money for a lamp by a certain Śokkan Nāṭṭūrān of Kūvalūr in Kāñchikkūval-nāḍu to the temple of Nāṭṭūr Āṇḍār of that place.

277. 472 *of* 1913.—(Tamil.) In the same place. A record in the twenty-sixth year of Kongu (?) Pāṇḍya Sundara-Paṇḍyadēva. Built in at the right end.

*Nambiyūr.**

278. 202 *of* 1909.—(Tamil.) On the south wall of the Tāntōn-ṛīśvara temple. An incomplete record in the eleventh year of Vīra-Pāṇḍyadēva. Records gift of a lamp to the temple of Tāntōn-ṛīśvaram-Uḍaiyār by a native of Nambi-Pērūr.

279. 203 *of* 1909.—(Tamil.) On the same wall. An incomplete record in the eleventh year of . . . Pāṇḍyadēva. Records gift of a lamp to the temple of Tāntōnṛīśvaram-Uḍaiyār by a native of Nambi-Pērūr.

280. 204 *of* 1909.—(Tamil.) On the same wall. An incomplete record in the eleventh year of Vīra-Pāṇḍyadēva. Records gift of lamps by a native of Nambi-Pērūr in Vaḍaparisāra-nāḍu to the temple of Tāntōnṛīśvaram-Uḍaiyār.

281. 205 *of* 1909.—(Tamil.) On the east wall of the same temple; left of entrance. A damaged and incomplete record in the eleventh year of Vīra-Pāṇḍyadēva. Records gift of a lamp to the same temple by a native of Nambi-Pērūr.

282. 206 *of* 1909.—(Tamil.) On the north wall of the same temple. A record in the fourteenth year of Vīra-Pāṇḍyadēva. Records gift of money for a lamp by a native of Pattali in

---

* The *Mack. MSS.* (*Ins., S. Dts.*, p. 47, Nos. 21-2) give two inscriptions of which one is the same as No. 218. The other has been included above as 285.

Kāṅgayanādu to the temple of Tāntōnṛīśvaram-Uḍaiyār at Nambi-Pērūr. *Ins., S. Dts.*, p. 47, No. 21.

283. 207 *of* 1909.—(Tamil.) On the same wall. A record in the eleventh year of . . . Pāṇḍyadēva. Records gift of money for a lamp.

284. 208 *of* 1909.—(Tamil.) On two broken pieces of a slab set up in Pudūr, a hamlet of the same place. A fragment of record in Īśvara (A.D. 1517–18) of Mahāmaṇḍalēśvara Vīra-Nañjaṇṇa-Uḍaiyār, a later prince of the Ummattūr line. [This chief is evidently the same as Nañjarāja Uḍaiyār (1512—40) mentioned by Rice as the son of Immaḍi Dēpaṇṇa Uḍaiyār. He is of course later than his namesake of Cb. 31. See *Ep. Carna.*, Vol. IV, p. 27.]

285. On a trident-marked stone at Santamēḍu bazaar north of Nambiyūr. Records that one Koottaghayan (?) and Mukkūttan allowed the taxes of the market to God Tānṛōnṛīśvara. *Ins., S. Dts.*, p. 47, No. 22.

Pāriyūr.

286. 182 *of* 1910.—(Tamil.) On the east wall of the maṇṭapa in front of the central shrine in the Amaraphaṇīśvara temple. A much damaged record in the eleventh year of Vīra-Pāṇḍyadēva. Records a gift to the shrine of the goddess in the temple of Amaraviṭaṅka Perumāḷ at Pāriyūr in Kāñchikūva-nāḍu. See *Ins., S. Dts.*, p. 7, No. 8.

287. 183 *of* 1910. (Tamil.) On the base of the same wall. An incomplete and damaged record of Vīra-Pāṇḍyadēva in his eleventh year. Seems to record a gift of land in the villages of Kāvaḷūr and Vayyilpaṭṭi. [This is probably the inscription referred to in *Mack. MSS. Ins., S. Dts.*, p. 7, No. 7.]

288. An inscription of Vīra-Pāṇḍya dated in his second year and recording a gift of ten paṇams for a lamp. *Ins., S. Dts.*, p. 17, No. 41.

289. 184 *of* 1910.—(Tamil.) On the east, north and west bases of the same maṇṭapa. A record in Prabhava of the Hoysaḷa king Bhujabalavīra-Vallāḷadēva (III). Records gift of money for a lamp to the temple of Amaraviṭaṅka-Perumāḷ. See *Ins., S. Dts.*, p. 17, No. 40, where the year is given as *Prabhava.*

290. 185 *of* 1910.—(Tamil.) On the east and north bases of the same maṇṭapa. A record in the third year of Tribhuvanachakravartin Kōnērimaikoṇḍān Tribhuvanavīradēva a powerful king who had the same titles as Kulōttuṅga III (date uncertain). The inscription commences with the syllables śrī-Parakēsari. Refers to an order of the king remitting the tax *Vottachu* on a number of Śaiva temples in the Vaḍa-Koṅgu country. [The inscriptions is very important as it enumerates the twenty Nāḍus of the northern Koṅgu country and as it gives us an idea of the state in relation to temple finance. See *Ep. Rep.*, 1911, p. 77–78 for details. The inscription is referred to in *Ins., S. Dts.*, p. 17, No. 39.]

291. 186 *of* 1910.—(Tamil.) On the north wall of the same maṇṭapa. A slightly damaged record in the fifteenth year of Tribhuvanachakravartin Kōnērimaikoṇḍān. Registers certain privileges granted to the *Kanmāḷars* of Kāñchikkūval-nāḍu. See Karuvūr.

292. 187 *of* 1910.—(Tamil.) On the west wall of the same māṇṭapa. A record in the fourth year of Tribhuvanachakravartin Kōnērinmaikoṇḍān. Records gift of the tank Araiyarkuḷam which was a dēvadāna of the temple of Amaraviṭaṅka-Perumāḷ to the *sthānattār* of that temple in order to maintain a festival established there in the name of the king. See *Ibid.*, p. 18, No. 42.

293. 188 *of* 1910.—(Tamil.) On the same wall. A record of Tribhuvanachakravartin Kōnērimanikoṇḍān. Transfer of the dēvadāna tank to the tenants of Pāriyūr on permanent tenure on their agreeing to pay one-third of the produce to the temple to meet the requirements of the festival established in the name of the king.

294. 189 *of* 1910.—(Tamil.) On the south wall of the same maṇṭapa. A record in the twentieth year of Sundara-Pāṇḍyadēva. Records gift of money for a lamp by a native of Pāriyūr.

295. 190 *of* 1910.—(Tamil.) On the door posts of the western entrance into the same maṇṭapa ; left side. A record in the third year of Tribhuvanavīradēva. Records gift of the door post by Muḍigoṇḍa-Sāhaṇi, nephew of Mallaya-Sāhaṇi, a native of Māmbaḷḷi, in Pōsala-nāḍu. [May be a record of the king mentioned in Cb. 293 above.]

296. 191 *of* 1910.—(Tamil.) In the same place, right side. A record in the third year of Tribhuvanavīradēva (Kulōttunga III?). Records gift of the door post by Ponna-Panaiyan, one of the Panaiya-veṭṭuvar of Pāriyūr.

297. 192 *of* 1910.—(Tamil.) On the base round the Nandi-maṇṭapa in the courtyard of the same temple. Records in Kaliyuga Ś. 4966, Raktākshi (i.e., A.D. 1864–65), the building of the maṇṭapa by certain Veḷḷāḷa-gavuṇḍans of Nanjēgavuṇḍan-pāḷaiyam.

Perundalayūr.

298. In the local Śiva temple. An 'illegible' record of the twenty-third year of Sundara Pāṇḍya dēva. *Antiquities*, II, p. 216.

299. (Kanarese.) A C.P. in the temple, recording gift of lands by Kṛishṇarāja Uḍaiyār of Mysore. *Ibid.*

Satyamangalam.

300. 209 *of* 1909.—(Tamil.) On the east and north walls of the temple of Āṇḍavarkōyil on the Davaḷagiri hill. A record of Vīrapratāpa-Chikkadēvarāja (1672—1704), ruling a Maisur in Ś. 1598, Naḷa. Records that the king built a temple for Kumārasvāmi on the Dhavaḷagiri hill which was known as the Dūrvāsa-kshētra and was situated near the confluence of the rivers Chintāmaṇi and Bhavāni at Satyamaṅgalam in Oḍuvaṅga-nāḍu.

301. 171 *of* 1910.—(Tamil.) On the basement of the Mīnâkshi-Sundarēśvara temple. A record in the fourth year of Kulōttuṅga-Chōḷadēva. Stones out of order and damaged. Mentions Tiṅgaḷūr in Kuruppanāḍu.

302. 172 *of* 1910.—(Tamil.) In the same place. A record in the twentv-fourth yeār of . . . ndradēva. Stones out of order. Records gift of money for offerings to the temple of Kailāyamuḍaiyār by one of the *Veḷḷāḷanpiḷḷān* residents of Kulappāḷūr in Kuruppu-nāḍu.

303. A C.P. in the hands of "Voommamach Eswara" Sastri, son of Mahādēva Aiyan. A sale of land by Kṛishṇa Rāja Uḍaiyār in Ś. 1682, Vikrama. Says that the villages of Guddanāyakanpāḷayam, Tirumalai Śeṭṭippāḷayam, etc., were given for 7,920 pagodas to Rāmāvadhāni and two other Brahmans. See *Ins., S. Dts.*, p. 102, No. I.

304. A C.P. in the hands of 'Yagya' Śāstri, son of Subbā Dīkshitar. Records that the village of Gōpālasamudram was sold by Kṛishṇa Rāja Uḍaiyār to two Brahmans (Subbā Śāstri and Rāmā Śāstri) for 1110 pagodas. *Ibid.*, No. 2.

305. A C.P. in the hands of Śrīnivāsāchārya, son of Kuppāchārya. The sale of Lavagumpāḷayam (?) by the same king to Kuppāchārya in Ś. 1684. *Ibid.*, No. 3.

306. On a stone in the Mahādēva temple south of Bastapāḷayam on the north of the Bhavāni river. A grant of land in the village of "Comaree" by Dēva Rāja Uḍaiyār in Ś. 1591, *Saumya. Ibid.*, No. 4. Evidently the same inscription is mentioned in No. 308.

307. A C.P. in the local Śiva temple, recording a grant by Krishṇa Rāja Uḍaiyār of Maisūr. *Antiquities*, II, 216.

Seṅgalarai. Śivayapāḷaiyam (near Satyamaṅgalam).

308. 181 *of* 1910.—(Kanarese.) On a stone set up on the way to the Bhavāni river. A record of the Maisūr king Vīrapratāpa Dēvarāja-Voḍeya (Doḍḍadēva Rāja, 1659—72), son of Dēvarāja-Voḍeya, in Ś. 1591, Saumya. Mentions Satyamaṅgala in Uḍuvaṅkanāḍu and registers the gift of Bestarapāḷaya surnamed Komārapura to the temple of Kumārasvāmin on the Dhavaḷagiri hill in

Dhūrvāsakshētra at the confluence of the rivers Chintāmaṇi and Bhavāni. [This temple is the modern Āṇḍavarkōvil on the Dhavaḷagiri hill near Satyamaṅgalam, which is referred to in Cb. 300 above.]

Vinnappaḷḷi.

309. On a stone east of the agrahāram. Records that in Ś. 1593, Virōdhikrit, Dēva Rāja Uḍaiyār (Doḍḍa dēva ?, 1659—72) divided the village into 64 shares and granted it to 64 Brahmans. The epigraph is in Kanarese. See *Ins., S. Dts.*, p. 29, No. 4.

KOLLEGAL TALUK.

Eraganahalli.

310. 175 *of* 1910.—(Kanarese.) On a slab lying near a well. A record of the Vijayanagara king Vīrapratāpa Achyutarāya-Mahārāya in Ś. 1454, Nandana. Mentions Nañjaluguḍa (the modern Nanjanguḍ, see *Mys. Gazr.*, II, 287-8) and registers the apportionment of land at Eraganahalli between the feeding houses of Jaṁgamas and Brāhmaṇas, probably instituted at Nañjanguḍ.

311. 176 *of* 1910.—(Kanarese.) On another slab set up in the same place. A much damaged record of the Vijayanagara king Vīrapratāpa Achyutarāya-mahārāya in Ś. 1462, Vikāri.

312. 177 *of* 1910.—(Kanarese.) On a slab lying near the pond west of the same village. A much damaged record in Ś. 1316, Bhava.

313. 178 *of* 1910.—(Kanarese.) On a slab set up near the same pond. A much damaged record of the Vijayanagara king Vīrapratāpa Achyutarāya-Mahārāya in Ś. 1454, Nandana.

314. 179 *of* 1910.—(Kanarese.) On three sections of a *viragal* near the pipul-tree west of the same village. A record of the Vijayanagara king Mahāmaṇḍalēśvara Vīra-Hariyappāḍeya (Harihara II), in Ś. 1308, Kshaya. Registers that a Gauḍa of Eraganahalli killed certain robbers with his axe and fell in the affray.

315. 180 *of* 1910.—(Kanarese.) On a slab set up close to the same pipul tree. Registers in Paridhāvi a settlement between the Gauḍās of Ummattūr and the Kuruba-Gauḍās of Haḍināḍu-śīme.

Koḍuvēli.

316. 173 *of* 1910.—(Tamil.) On a pillar lying near the Bhavāni anicut. A record in the ninth year of Vīrarājēndradēva. Records gift of money for a lamp to the temple of Tirumunai-Āḷuḍaiyār, by a native of Teṅkarai-Koḍuvēḷi in Vaḍaparisāranāḍu.

317. 174 *of* 1910.—(Tamil.) On a slab lying near the same anicut. A damaged record in the thirteenth year of Vīrarājēndradēva (Koṅgu-Chōḷa ?). Mentions the same temple and village.

Koḷḷēgāl.

Originally known by the name of Koḷḷāgara and from Chōḷa times onward, as Tribhuvanamādēvi-chaturvēdimaṅgalam, this place was included (in Vijayanagara times), in the Śivasamudra-sthala in Haḍināḍu Śīma.

318. 13 *of* 1910.—(Tamil.) On the south wall of the Lakshmīnārāyaṇasvāmin temple. A record of the Hoysaḷa king Pratāpa-chakravartin Vīra-Vallāḷadēva in Raudra. Mentions Koṅgiṇikirai (tank) and records a gift of land to the temple of Vīṟṟirunda-Perumāḷ at Koḷḷagar *alias* Tribhuvanamādēvi-chaturvēdimaṅgalam. Refers also to the temple of Muḍigoṇḍīśvaram-Uḍaiyār at Muḍigoṇḍaśōḷapuram.

319. 14 *of* 1910.—(Tamil.) On the west wall of the same temple. A damaged record in Śōbhakrit. Records gift of money for a lamp to the same temple. The village is called Koḷḷagar *alias* Tribhuvanamahādēvi-chaturvēdimaṅgalam.

320. 15 *of* 1910.—(Kanarese.) On a slab set up in front of the entrance into the same temple. A record of the Vijayanagara king Vīrapratāpa Sadāśiva-Mahārāya in Ś. 1491, Śukla. Records gift of the village of Koḷagala which belonged to Śivanasamudrada-sthala in Haḍināḍu-śīmē, to a certain Rāmarāja-Nāyaka, by Rāmarājayyadēva-Mahā-araśu (Rāma III), son of Mahāmaṇḍalēśvara Rāmarāju-Tirumalarājayya. [Inscriptions of Rāmarāja Tirumala-rājayya (Tirumala I) are seen in N.A. 317, By. 134 and By. 137.]

321. 16 *of* 1910.—(Tamil.) On a slab built into the steps in the same place. A record of the Hoysaḷa king Pratāpa-chakravartin Vīra-Naraśiṅgadēva in Tāraṇa. Records gift of land to the temple of Vaṇḍuvarai-Perumāḷ. The village is called Koḷḷagar *alias* Tribhuvanamahādēvi-chaturvēdimaṅgalam as in No. 14.

322. 17 *of* 1910.—(Tamil.) On a third slab lying in the same place. Refers to the merchants of Ayyapoḷil and records a gift to the temple of Maṇalīśvaramuḍaiya Mahādēva, by the residents of Koḷḷagar *alias* Tribhuvanamādēvi-chaturvēdimaṅgalam in Paḍināḍu. [Ayyapoḷil is evidently the same as Ayyavoḷe, for a reference to which see By. 176.]

323. A C.P. grant in the possession of the local karṇam. "It records a gift of land to his ancestors by Kṛishṇarāja Uḍaiyār (1734—66) of Maisūr in Ś. 1682 (A.D. 1760)."

Kunthur.

324. 21 *of* 1910.—(Kanarese.) On a slab set up to the east of the Basavēśvara temple. Haḍināḍu-śīme was under the rule of the Mahāmaṇḍalēśvara Nandiyāla Nāriyaparājayya. Records in Ś. 1467, Krōdhi, a gift to the Mahānandīśara-maṭha at Kuntūru.

325. 22 *of* 1910.—(Kanarese.) On another slab in the same place. A damaged record of the Vijayanagara king Vīra-Achyuta-Mahārāya in Ś. 1452, Virōdhi. Refers to the king's *bhujabala* *pradhāna* Rāmabhaṭlayya. [See Ap. 141 and 142 for two very interesting records of Rāmabhaṭlu.]

326. 23 *of* 1910.—(Kanarese.) On the third slab set up in the same place. A record of the Ummattūr king Vīra-Yimmaḍi-Chikarāya-Voḍeya, son of Vīra-Nañjarāya-Voḍeya, in Ś. 1434, Āṅgira. Records gift of taxes in the village of Kuntūru in Haḍi-nāḍu for providing food and clothing to fifty Voḍeyārs of the *Śivāchāra* sect, who were connected with the Śalūra-Śāntadēvara-Simhāsana. See Cb. 30 above.

327. 24 *of* 1910.—(Kanarese.) On two slabs lying in front of the Mahāliṅgēśvara temple in the same village. A record of the Western Gaṅga king Nītimārga-Permānaḍigaḷ. Records a gift of land to a temple of Mahādēva at Kundattūru, by Parabbeyarasi who was ruling Kundattūru. [See Kielhorn's *Southern List*, p. 6, for Nītimārga's place in W. Gaṅga genealogy. He can be assigned to about A.D. 850.]

Modalli.

328. 245 *of* 1913.—(Kanarese.) On a stone in front of the Nandimaṇṭapa of the Doḍḍapādēśvara temple. A record of the Vijayanagara king Achyutarāya-Mahārāya in Ś. 1456, Jaya, Phalguna, śu. di. 5, Sunday (February 7, A.D. 1535, but Monday). Registers that Mādappayya, the agent of Rāmappayya, "who was bearing the burden of the kingdom with the king" restored the villages and lands belonging to the temple of Mallikārjuna at old Moḍahalli in Haḍināḍu-śīme, and remitted certain taxes in its favour.

329. 246 *of* 1913.—(Kanarese.) On another stone in the same place. A damaged record of the Vijayanagara king Kampaṇa-Oḍeya (II), son of Vīra-Bukkaṇṇa Oḍeya I in Ś. 1290, Parābhava, Chaitra, *ba. di.* 10. Refers to the temple of Mallināthadēva at Modēhalli and seems to register a gift of tolls. "Date can be calculated but not verified."

330. 247 *of* 1913.—(Kanarese.) On a stone set up in a field of the same village. A record of the Vijayanagara king Vīra-Harihara-Mahārāya (II) in Ś 1313, Prajōtpatti, Phalguna, śu. ḍi. 15, Tuesday. Records gift of land to certain specified Brāhmaṇas in the village of Mōdahalli surnamed Kamparājapura. Refers to a previous gift by Hiriya-Kamparāya. The two verses in the end are written in Grantha characters. [Mr. Swamikannu Pillai points out that the week-day should be Saturday and not Tuesday.]

Muḍigoṇḍam.

Called evidently after Muḍigoṇḍa or Rājēndrachōḷa I, it was in former times an important commercial centre and hence known as Dēśi-Uyyakkoṇḍapaṭṭaṇa, while the local Vaishṇavite deity worshipped chiefly by the merchants, is called Dēśipperumāḷ. Evidently in later days Vaishṇavism declined and Liṅgayatism became the creed of these merchants. The terms *Nagara* and *Dēśi* which even today mark the different sections occur in these inscriptions. A third section is that of the *Vīrakoḍiyar*. Muḍigoṇḍam was also formerly a Jain centre. (See No. 339.)

331. 2 *of* 1910.—(Tamil.) On the south wall of the Lakshmī-Nārāyaṇasvāmin temple. An unfinished record of the Hoysaḷa king Vishṇuvardhana (1115—1141). Mentions a long list of *birudas* of the king.

332. 3 *of* 1910.—(Tamil.) On the same wall. A record in Rudhirōdgari of the Hoysaḷa king Vīra-Vallāḷadēva (II, 1173—1220). Mentions Muḍigoṇḍaśōḷapuram *alias* Dēśi Uyyakoṇḍa-paṭṭaṇa and records that the merchants of the eighteen towns (north of the Kāvēri river) including Talaikkāḍu *alias* Rājarāja-pura and those of the eighteen towns south of the same river including Muḍigoṇḍachōḷapuram, made grants to the temple of Nārāyaṇa-Perumāḷ also called "Dēśi-Perumāḷ." The year evidently corresponded to A.D. 1203.

333. 4 *of* 1910.—(Tamil.) On the same wall. A record in Hēmalambi (A.D. 1237?) of the Hoysaḷa king Sōmēśvaradēva (A.D. 1253-54). Records gift of land for festivals in the same temple.

334. 5 *of* 1910.—(Tamil.) On the same wall. An unfinished record of the Hoysaḷa king Vīra-Vallāḷadēva (II, 1173—1220) in Ś. 1111, Saumya. Provides for offerings in the temple of Dēśi-Perumāḷ at Muḍigoṇḍaśōḷapuram *alias* Dēśi-Uyyakoṇḍaśōḷapaṭṭa-ṇam in Pāḍi-nāḍu, a subdivision of Gaṅgaikoṇḍaśōḷa-vaḷanāḍu of Muḍigoṇḍaśōḷamaṇḍalam.

335. 6 *of* 1910.—(Tamil.) On the west wall of the same temple. A record in Viḷambi (probably A.D. 1238) of the Hoysaḷa king Vīra-Sōmēśvaradēva (1253-54). Mentions Koḷḷagar and records gift of land to the same temple.

336. 7 *of* 1910.—(Tamil.) On the north wall of the same temple. A record in Sādhāraṇa of the Hoysaḷa king Pratāpacha-kravartin Vīra-Sōmēśvaradēva. Records gift of an areca garden to the same temple by the mahājanās of Durgaiyār-agaram. See above epigraph.

337. 8 *of* 1910.—(Tamil.) On the west wall of the Muḍigoṇ-ḍēśvara temple in the same village. Records gift of money for a lamp to the temple of Muḍigoṇḍachōḷīśvaram-Uḍaiyār. On the other walls of this temple are fragments of Tamil inscriptions which are not connected with one another and do not form a complete record. Some of the fragments refer to the Chōla king Vikrama-Chōḷa, others to the merchants of Muḍigoṇḍachōḷapuram and the rest to gifts of lamps.

338. 9 *of* 1910.—(Tamil.) On a slab set up in front of the Muḷḷāchamma temple in the same village. A record in Sādhāraṇa of the Hoysaḷa king Bhujabala Vīragaṅga Vīra-Vallāḷa. Records gift of land to the temple of Muḷnāchchi by Dāsaya Nāyaka, son of Agattiyāṇḍi-Nāyakkar who was the commander (sēnāpati) of the *Valaṅgai* force (வலங்கைச்சேனை) of the king. Mentions Ālakka-miṇḍan. The king referred to is Vīra Vallāḷa II (1173—1220). The reference to the *valaṅgai* forces is noteworthy.

339. 10 *of* 1910.—(Kanarese.) On a slab built into the steps in the southern side of the tank in the same village. A mutilated record in Ś. 1031. Records gift of a village in Haḍi-nāḍu to the temple of Nakhara-Jīnālaya at Muḍigoṇḍachōḷapura, dedicated to Chandraprabhāsvāmi, for repairs and worship.

340. 11 *of* 1910.—(Tamil.) On a slab built into the steps on the west side of the same tank. A mutilated record in Piṅgaḷa (A.D. 1257, most probably) of the Hoysaḷa king Pratāpachakravartin Vīra-Naraśiṅgadēva (III, 1254—92?). Mentions Muḍigoṇḍa-śōḷapura *alias* Dēśi-Uyyakkoṇḍaśōḷapaṭṭaṇa.

341. 12 *of* 1910.—(Tamil.) On a slab built into the floor of the Śiva temple in the same village. A mutilated record of the Hoysaḷa king Vishṇuvardhana (1115—41). An incomplete and damaged record. Contains a list of the king's conquests.

Siddayyanapura.

342. 1 *of* 1910.—(Kanarese.) On a slab set up on the tank bund. A mutilated record of a Western Gaṅga king. Mentions Koḷḷagara and records a gift of 6 *gadyānas* for a lamp, to a temple of Āditya. [The record shows that the term *gadyāna* was current even in such an early period as that of the Gaṅgas.]

Śiṅganallūr.

343. 18 *of* 1910.—(Kanarese.) On a slab set up in the court-yard of the Basavēśvara temple. A record of the Vijayanagara king Harihararāya (II), son of Vīra-Bukkaṇa-Oḍeya (I), in Ś. 1319, Īśvara. Refers to the 500 merchants of Ayyavoḷe and records a gift by these, at Śiṅgananallūru for feeding the members of their community. See Cb. 322 above.

344. 19 *of* 1910.—(Kanarese.) On another slab set up in the same place. A record of the Vijayanagara king Vīra-Dēvarāya-Mahārāya (I), son of Harihara-Mahārāya (II), in Kali 4522 (wrong) and Ś. 1330, Sarvadhāri. Some of the *birudas* of the king are new. Mentions the Mahāpradhāna Nāgamanāyaka-Oḍeya.

345. 20 *of* 1910.—(Kanarese.) On a slab lying outside the same temple. A damaged record of Śrīraṅgarāya in Ś. 1581 (A.D. 1659), Vikāri. Mentions a certain Dēvarāja-Voḍeya and Śiṅgananallūru.

346. A C.P. in the hands of "Madakara" Nārāyaṇaiyar in the village. Records that a certain Karikālchōḷa erected the village of Śiṅgamāpuram in K. 1469 Plavaṅga and granted it to Gōvinda Dāsar's son. See *Ins., S. Dts.*, p. 221, No. 55. [The inscription looks suspicious, e.g., the name of the king and the Kali date.]

347. A C.P. grant in the hands of the local people. Records that in Ś. 1469, Plavaṅga, Sadāśiva Rāya granted the village of Gōvinda-Vāmapuram to the Brahman (Govinda Dāsa?) *Ibid.*, p. 221, No. 56.

Śivasamudram.

348. 356 *of* 1901.—(Kanarese.) On a slab set up in the Vīrabhadra temple. A record of the Vijayanagara king Veṅkaṭapatirāya (I) in Ś. 1526, Krōdhin. Records gift of land by Tirumalarāja Nāyaka. [Was the latter the Viceroy of Śrīraṅgapaṭṭaṇam?]

349. 357 *of* 1901.—(Kanarese and Tamil.) On a slab built into the roof of the verandah of the Māriyamman temple at the same village. Records in Ś. 1743, Vishu, and A.D. 1821, a gift of land to Rāmasvāmi-Mudaliyār. See *Antiquities* I, 215, and *Madras Journal*, I, 83, for an excellent account of the traditions of the place and the work of the Mudaliyār. See also *Buchanan*, I, 406 f.

PALLADAM TALUK.

Avānaśippāḷaiyam.

350. In the Śiva temple in the hamlet of Koḍuvāy. A record of K. 4835 (A.D. 1734).

351. In the Vishṇu temple of the same place. An epigraph dated in Ś. 1411 (A.D. 1489) recording an agreement by private people for the performance of temple service.

Nāraṇāpuram.

352-A-B. Two copper plates recording grants to the Aṅgāla-Paramēśvari temple of this village came to the notice of the Department in 1909–10. They were found in the possession of a convict in the Coimbatore Jail. The first of these (No. I, Appendix A, *Madr. Ep. Rep.*, 1910) "which is written on five copper plates held together by an iron ring, states that in Ś. 1719, Piṅgaḷa (=A.D. 1797) the Śeṭṭis of Pallaḍa-grāman in Varāka-nāḍu, a subdivision of Koṅgumaṇḍalam, whose community was distinguished by 24 different castes," made a gift to the temple of Aṅgāla-Paramēśvari. The introduction refers to the Vijayanagara kings and the Nāiks of Madura. The second grant is "a single plate which begins with a list of *birudas* of the Vijayanagara kings Prauḍha-dēva Mahārāya, Kṛishṇarāya and others; then speaks of the Nāyakās of Madura, Viśvanātha and Tirumala; then of the Sultans of Mysore, *viz.*, Hyder and Tippu, and then, coming down to the rule of the

'Kumpini' (Honourable the East India Company) rulers; it mentions Mahārāya Shediri Āraḍiśudurai (Mr. T. B. Hurdis) in whose time, i.e., in Ś. 1722, Raudri (= A.D. 1800), the Gavuṇḍans of Nāraṇāpuram became scattered on account of an epidemic brought on by the goddess Aṅgāla-Paramēśvari of that village. Consequently the worship in the temple suffered and the Gavuṇḍans met together and decided to levy a tax on their community and conduct the worship of the goddess as before." (*Madr. Ep. Rep.*, 1910, p. 10.)

Paṭṭaṇam.

353. 210 *of* 1909.—(Tamil.) On a slab set up in the village. A record of Mahāmaṇḍalēśvara Vira-Nañjana-Uḍaiyār in Piravava (Prabhava) [A.D. 1507–8]. Records that this village was originally called Maḍukkōḍu in the district of Vāyiraikkā-nāḍu (?) and being in a ruined condition for a long time, was rebuilt by six merchants (*nānādēśi*) under the name Śrīnāthapaṭṭaṇa. [Vīra-Nañjana Uḍaiyār was most probably an Ummattūr chief and identical with his namesake of Cb. 284.]

Periyapāḷayam.

354. On the west of the inner temple of Varadarājasvāmi. Records that in Ś. 1667 Vikrama, Kōnērinmaikoṇḍan established an agrahāram and granted it to twenty-four Brahmans. The village is called Chōḷa-chaturvēdimaṅgalam. See *Ins., S. Dts.*, p. 98, No. 8.

Śāmaḷāpuram.

355. On a stone in the possession of a Brahman. Records that in the second year of the reign of Rājarājadēva Karikāl Chōḷa the village of Sāmaḷāpuram was granted to seven Brahmans. One of these is called Bhāratam Bhaṭṭa. See *Ins., S. Dts.*, p. 94, No. 1.

Perumānellūr.

356. On a stone in the Uttamachōḷēśvara temple. (Tamil.) Records that in the tenth year of Sundara Pāṇḍya, some land was given by Piṛai-śūḍumperumān to the deity for a flower garden. *Ins., S. Dts.*, p. 14, No. 30.

357. On the north of the inner temple. Records the restoration of the same grant in the nineteenth year of the same king. *Ibid.*, p. 14, No. 31.

358. Below the above inscription. Records that Ponnambalakkūttan granted, in the fifteenth year of Vīra Pāṇḍya Dēva, 15 paṇams for God Chatrapada Piḷḷayar for annual supply of dress. *Ibid.*, No. 32.

359. Above the same. Records that in the first year of Vīra Pāṇḍya Dēva, one Śerupiḷḷayan presented to God Uttamachōḷēśvaramuḍaiyār one *pañchāla-achchu* for a lamp. *Ibid.*, No. 33.

360. Above the same. Undated. The inhabitants of "Paroompalaundayoor" purchased a tank for the deities in the reign of Vīra Pāṇḍya Dēva. *Ins.*, *S. Dts.*, p. 15, No. 34.

361. West of south gate of the Ardhamaṇṭapam. (Tamil.) Records that in the eighth year of Sundara Pāṇḍya Dēva the people of the village of "Amachoyunkara" Chaturvēdamaṅgaḷam granted 50 kalams of paddy per year for the God's worship and food. *Ibid.*, p. 15, No. 35.

362. Above the same. Records that a chief gave in the fourth year of Vira Rājēndra Dēva one *pañchāla-achchu* to the God for a lamp. *Ibid.*, p. 16, No. 36.

363. On the north of the temple of Uttamaliṅgar. The gift of village by Kōnērinmaikoṇḍan to the people of "Paroomapalempulivoor" *Perumani Perumānallur* (?) *Ibid.*, No. 37.

364. On the east of the Uttamachōḷeśvarasvāmi temple vimāna. Records that Ponnambalakūttan re-established the chatrapala Piḷḷaiyār, erected a pagoda and gave 50 varāhas in the hands of one Āḷkoṇḍān, in the seventh year of the reign of Vīra Paṇḍya Dēva, for worship. *Ibid.*, p. 16, No. 38.

Tirumuruganpūṇḍi.

365. 571 *of* 1893.—(Tamil.) On the south wall of the maṇṭapa in front of the shrine of the Muruganātha temple. A record in the fortieth year of Vīra-Rājēndradēva (Koṅgu-Chōḷa, 1207–52?). Records gift of a lamp.

366. 572 *of* 1893.[1]—(Tamil.) In the same tier. A record of Kōnērimaikoṇḍān. Records gift of paddy. [*Mack. MSS.* say that a village was transferred to the deity for worship and one hundred and sixty *kalams* were given every year. *Ins.*, *S. Dts.*, p. 12, No. 25.]

367. 573 *of* 1893.—(Tamil.) On the same wall, third tier. A record in the eighth year of Kulōttuṅga-Chōḷadēva (Chōḷa or Koṅgu-Chōḷa?). Records gift of a lamp.

368. 574 *of* 1893.—(Tamil.) On the same wall, fourth tier. A record in the eighth year of Kulōttuṅga-Chōḷadēva. Records gift of a lamp. [It is uncertain whether the king was Chōḷa or Koṅgu-Chōḷa.]

369. 575 *of* 1893.—(Tamil.) On the south wall of the same shrine in the same temple. A record in the fourteenth year of Vikrama-Chōḷadēva (Koṅgu Chōḷa?). Records gift of land for a flower garden.

370. 576 *of* 1893.—(Tamil.) On the east wall of the same shrine. Records in Pārthiva gift of paddy by a native of the

---

[1] *Mack. MSS.* give two other inscriptions of Kōnērinmai-Koṇḍān here, recording gift of land to the deity. *Ins.*, *S. Dts.*, p. 13, Nos. 26 and 28.

Pāṇḍya country. [The *Ins., S. Dts.*, gives a different version of this epigraph. It records that the king gave in his third year four kalams and two *tuṇi* of grain to a Brahman. See *Ins., S. Dts.*, p. 13, No. 27.]

371. 577 *of* 1893.—(Tamil.) On the north wall of the same shrine. A record in the eleventh year of Vikrama-Chōḷadēva. Records gift of paddy. [*Ins., S. Dts.*, p. 13, No. 29, gives a mutilated version of this.]

372. 578 *of* 1893.—(Tamil.) On a stone to the north of the same temple. A record of the Mahāmaṇḍalēśvara Vīra-Nañjayarāya-Uḍaiyār in Ś. 1421, expired, Siddhārthin. Records gift of land by a merchant. See Cb. 31 above.

373. 579 *of* 1893.—(Tamil.) On another stone in the same place. A record of Vīra Nañjarāya-Uḍaiyār in Ś. 1419, expired, Piṅgaḷa. Records gift of gold by a merchant. See Cb. 31.

374. A C.P. in the hands of a local Sthānika. Records that in 225, Chitrabhānu, in the reign of Tirumal Nāik, his Guru Raghunātha Paṇḍit and the people of the neighbouring villages granted to Subrahmaṅya Paṇḍit, the priest of the temple, a piece of land and the contribution of one *paṇam* per house every year, and two paṇams for a marriage. *Ibid.*, p. 12, No. 24.

POLLACHI TALUK.

Anaimalai.

375. C.P. No. 171 *of Mr. Sewell's List.*—A record in the possession of Ponnayya Kurukkaḷ, a priest of the Śiva temple at Anaimalai. Records grant by Mādayya, "agent of the Maisūr Rajas," at Coimbatore, of land to certain Brahmans, in Ś. 1685 (A.D. 1763), Kaliyuga 4864, Subhānu, during the reign of Kṛishṇa Rāja Uḍaiyār (1734—66) at Śrīraṅgapaṭṭaṇam.

376. C.P. No. 172 *of Mr. Sewell's List.*—Records grant of lands to the Śiva temple in the same place, by the same Mādayya, in the same reign, and in the same year.

377. C.P. No. 173 *of Mr. Sewell's List.*—Records grant of lands to a choultry on the road from Ānaimalai to Calicut, by the same Mādayya, in the same reign, and in the same year.

378. "On a stone a little to the north of the village is an inscription, dated Ś. 1692 (A.D. 1770)." [*Antiquities*, I, 221.]

Mailampaṭṭi.

379. In the hands of Śēshaiya, son of Subbaiya. Records that "Nundina" Uḍaiyar, the Prime Minister of Vīravasanta Rāya, gave in Ś. 1509, thirty *vēli* of dry field as a free gift to Rāmachandra Bhaṭṭa. See *Ins., S. Dts.*, 101, No. I.

UDAMALPET TALUK.

Kadattūr (" Cradaootoore ").

380. On a stone on the south side of the Arjunēśvara temple. Records that Vīrachōḷa Tribhuvanaliṅga dēvar granted some land to the deity in Kannaḍiputtūr. See *Ins., S. Dts.*, p. 66, No. 8.

381. In the same wall. The same king granted in his fifteenth year some gold to Tirumaruda Uḍaiyār and Āḷuḍaiya Nāchchiyār. *Ibid.*, No. 7.

Kannaḍiputtūr.

382. 211 *of* 1909.—(Tamil.) On the south wall of the Kailāśanātha temple. A record in the seventeenth year of Vīra-Chōḷadēva. Records gift of land for offerings, to the shrine of the goddess by a certain Śingam Śōḷan *alias* Anuttirappallavaraiyan. See Cb. 133.

383. 212 *of* 1909.—(Tamil.) On the same wall. A record in the second year of Vīra-Nārāyaṇadēva. Records gift of money for lamps to two temples at Kannaḍiputtūr in Karaivaḷi-nāḍu. [The king might be Parāntaka I]. See also Cb. 106 and 107.

384. 213 *of* 1909.—(Tamil.) On the same wall. A damaged record of Vikrama-Chōḷadēva, the date of which is lost. Records gift of money. [The king might be any of the Koṅgu-Chōḷas of this name who came to the throne in 1004, 1255 and 1273.]

385. 214 *of* 1909.—(Tamil.) On the same wall. A record in the tenth year of Vīra-Nārāyaṇadēva. Records gift of money for a lamp by the general (sēnāpati) VīraśōḷaKulaśēkharavarman, to the temple of Tiruvanantīśvaram-Uḍaiyār. See No. 383.

386. 215 *of* 1909.—(Tamil.) On the west wall of the same temple. A damaged record of Tribhuvanachakravartin Vīra-Nārāyaṇadēva, the date of which is lost. Records gift of money for two lamps. See No. 383.

387. 216 *of* 1909.—(Tamil.) On the same wall. An incomplete record of Vīrarājēndradēva (the Koṅgu-Chōḷa, ? 1207–52) the date of which is lost. Mentions Vīrarājēndra-Anuttirappallavaraiyan and a shrine of Dakshiṇāmūrti.

388. 217 *of* 1909.—(Tamil.) On the same wall. An incomplete record in the eighteenth year of Tribhuvanachakravartin Vīrarājēndradēva (1207–52 ?). Records a gift to a shrine of Vināyaka in the temple of Tiruvanantīśvaram-Uḍaiyār by one of the king's generals whose name, however, is lost.

389. 218 *of* 1909.—(Tamil.) On the door post of the entrance into the same temple. A damaged record in the seventeenth year of Vīrachōḷadēva. Records gift of paddy to the temple of Tiru-Anandīśuram-Uḍaiyār by the residents of Kannaḍiputtūr. See Cb. 133.

390. 219 *of* 1909.—(Tamil.) On the door post of the entrance into the Tirunandikēśvara temple in the same village. A record in the twentieth year of Vikrama-Chōḷadēva (1004—45 ?). Records gift of money for offerings to the same temple.

391. 220 *of* 1909.—(Tamil.) On the west wall of the Kaliyuga-Varadarāja-Perumāḷ temple in the same village. A record in the third year of Tribhuvanachakravartin Kōnērinmaikoṇḍān. Records that a piece of land which was situated at Śōḷamādēvinallūr and was originally granted by Sundara-Pāṇḍya to the temple of Śokka-nārayāṇa-Perumāḷ at Kannaḍiputtūr *alias* Vīrapāṇḍya-chaturvēdi-maṅgalam in Karaivaḷi-nāḍu, was confirmed by the King. See Cb. 196 and 197.

392. 221 *of* 1909.—(Tamil.) On the east wall of the Śelva-Vināyaka temple in the same village. A fragment of record of Vīrarājēndradēva (1207—36 ?). Records gift of money to a temple, whose name is lost on the stone.

393. *C.P. No.* 190 *of Sewell's List.*—(Telugu.) Records grant of land to a Brahman in Ś. 1577, Manmatha, by Tirumal Nāik of Madura, in the reign of Śri Raṅga Rāya of Vijayanagar. [The record shows that even after the final downfall of the Chandragiri dynasty, theoretical allegiance was paid to "Vijayanagar."]

394. A C.P. in the hands of Lakshmaṇaiyar, son of Veṅkaṭaiyar in the village. Records that in Ś. 1587, Viśvāvasu, in the reign of Śrīraṅgadēva Mahārāya, Viśvanātha Nāyaka-Chokkanātha Nāyaka, one Vīra Nāyaka granted 15 *mās* of land in Kāniyūr village to the local people. See *Ins., S. Dts.* (*Mack. MSS.*), p. 224, No. 66. Chokkanātha ruled from 1660 to 1680. See *Ind. Antq.*, 1916.

395. In the hands of the same. Records that Raghunātha Dēva Mahārāya gave the village of "Balargapore" to the people, in Ś. 1541, in the reign of Vīra Rāmadēva Mahārāya (i.e., Rāma IV, 1620-30). *Ibid.*, p. 225, No. 67.

Kāniyūr.

396. *C.P. No.* 186 *of Mr. Sewell's List.*—(Tamil and Grantha.) Records a grant of land in the village, ten miles south-west of Uḍamalpet, to some Brāhmans of the neighbouring village of Koḷumam, in Ś. 1587, Viśvāvasu (A.D. 1665), by Chokkanātha Nāyakka of Madura (1560-80), in the reign of Śrī Raṅgadēva Mahārāya. See Nos. 393 and 394.

397. *C.P. No.* 189 *of Mr. Sewell's List.*—Records grant of lands in Puttūr and Kāniyūr villages in Ś. 1682, Vikrama (A.D. 1760), by Chikka-Kṛishṇa-Rāja (1734-66) of the Maisūr dynasty.

Kāraittoṛu (Kāraittoḷuvu of Udamalpet ?).

398. *C.P. No.* 152 *of Mr. Sewell's List.*—(Tamil.) Records a deed by which, in Kaliyuga 4419, Piṅgaḷa (A.D. 1318), certain lands were presented by the villagers to their village priest for temple service.

The document states that the grant was made while "Mallikārjuna Rāya, Vīradēva Rāya, Virūpāksha Rāya, and Prauḍhadēva Mahārāya" were ruling the world. The document is not genuine.

Koḷumu.

·399. "On the back of the Vimānam" in the Chōḷēśvarasvāmi temple. Rāja Kaṇḍiya Dēvar gave, in the eleventh year of Vīrachōḷa a village as free gift, to the deity. See *Ins.*, *S. Dts.*, in *Mack. MSS.*, p. 64, No. 2.

400. On a stone north of the Vimāna in the same temple. Records that in the twenty-first year of Vīrachōḷa, Rājarāja Aṇukkappallavaraiyan granted lands in a number of villages to the God. *Ibid.*, No. 3.

401. On a stone in the Kanakasabhā-maṇṭapam. Records that in Ś. 1625, Svabhānu, Śunkaya Tennāyakar (?), feudatory (?) of Vīra Sōmēśvara Dēva granted the village of Kiḷ-Kallāpuram or Śrī Mādhava chaturvēdimaṅgalam as free gift to the people. *Ibid.*, No. 4.

402. On a stone in the same maṇṭapa. Records that in Ś. 1627, in the reign of "Pratapa Chacravurty Nayakur" the inhabitants re-established the above village. [Evidently Kiḷ-Kallāpuram was Koḷumu.] *Ibid.*, No. 5.

Komāraliṅgam.

This place was known as Kumāraṅgabhīma-chaturvēdimaṅgalam and Paradārasahōdara-chaturvēdimaṅgalam evidently after the Daṇa-yakan kōṭṭai chiefs who had the biruda *Paradārasahōdara.*

403. 106 *of* 1909.—(Tamil.) On the west wall of the Kāśi-Viśvanātha temple. A record in the twentieth year of Tribhuvanachakravartin Vīrarājēndradēva (A.D. 1207-*circa* 1252) who was pleased to rule the two Koṅgus together. Beginning lost. Records gift of money by Śōḷan Laṅkēśvaradēva to the temple of Tiruvālanduṟai Uḍaiyār at Tiruvālanduṟai in Karaivaḷināḍu, for the decoration *(mēlpūchchu)* of the idol.

404. 107 *of* 1909.—(Tamil.) On the south wall of the Vēṅkaṭēśvara-Perumāḷ temple in the same village. An unfinished record in the nineteenth year of Vīrarājēndradēva (1207-*circa* 1252). Records gift of land by a resident of Iraṭṭaiyanpāḍi in Vaigāvināḍu to a monk of the Tirunīriṭṭāntirumaḍam near the temple of Muttirattīśiram Uḍaiyār at Koḷumam in Karaivaḷi-nāḍu.

405. 108 *of* 1909.—(Tamil.) On the north wall of the same temple. A fragment of record of Rājakēsarivarman *alias* Tribhuvanachakravartin, the date of which is doubtful. Mentions Koḷumam in Karaivaḷi-nāḍu and the channel Adhirādarāja-Vāykkāl.

406. 109 *of* 1909.—(Tamil.) On the same wall. A fragment of record in the twelfth year of Rājarāja Karikāla-Chōḷadēva. Mentions the same nāḍu and the same village.

407. 110 *of* 1909.—(Tamil.) On the same wall. A damaged record of Rājarāja Karikāla-Chōḷadēva, the date of which is lost. Records gift of gold for a lamp.

408. 111 *of* 1909.—(Tamil.) On the same wall. A fragment of record of Tribhuvanachakravartin Vīranārāyaṇadēva, the date of which is lost. The second line contains the beginning of a record of Vīrarajēndradēva. (1207-*circa* 1252).

409. 112 *of* 1909.—(Tamil.) On the same wall. A fragment of record in the second year of Vikrama-Chōḷadēva. Mentions Pāṇḍimaṇḍalam. [It is not known which of the Koṅgu Chōḷa Vikramas is referred to here.]

410. 113 *of* 1909.—(Tamil.) On the same wall. A fragment of record of Vīrarājēndradēva (1207–36 ?), the date of which is lost. Mentions Vaigāvi-nāḍu.

411. 114 *of* 1909.—(Tamil.) On the same wall. A record in the twenty-first year of Kōnērinmaikoṇḍān. Stones out of order. Records gift of rice for offerings to a shrine of Gaṇapati built at Koḷumam for the merit of the king.

412. 115 *of* 1909.—(Tamil.) On the same wall. A fragment of record in the tenth year of (Koṅgu-Chōḷa ?) Vīrarājēndradēva. (Damaged.) Mentions a *maṭha* in the quarter called Adirādarājan-Tirumaḍaiviḷāgam and the village Kannaḍiputtūr.

413. 116 *of* 1909.—(Tamil.) On the *balipīṭha* of the same temple. A fragment of record in the twenty-third year of Vīrarājēndradēva (1207–52). Mentions the temple of Adiya-Śōḷīśaram-Uḍaiyār.

414. 117 *of* 1909.—(Tamil.) In the same place. A fragment of record of Vīrarājēndradēva (1207—36), the date of which is lost. Seems to record a gift of money.

415. 118 *of* 1909.—(Tamil.) On the north base of the Karivaradarāja Perumāḷ temple in the same village. A record in the third year of Tribhuvanachakravartin Parakēsarivarman Kōnērinmaikoṇḍān. Records gift of land to the servants of the temple of Aḷagar Tirumalai in Pāṇḍimaṇḍalam, by a certain Nārāyaṇan Āḷavandi *alias* Brahma-Pallavaraiyan of Vīranārāyaṇa-chaturvēdimaṅgalam, a brahmadēya in Vīrakēraḷa-vaḷanāḍu. [The king referred to might be the one who ruled from 1207–1252, but he is usually called a Rājakēsarivarman and not Parakēsarivarman.]

416. 119 *of* 1909.—(Tamil.) On the same base. A record in the twentieth year of Parakēsarivarman *alias* Tribhuvanachakravartin Vīra-Chōḷadēva. Records gift of land to the temple of

Kariyāpirān by Kurāṅgāṭṭu Śrī-Krishṇan of Kumaraṅgabhīma-chaturvēdimaṅgalam (a Brahmadēya in Karaivaḷi nāḍu), for burning sixteen lamps in the temple. See Cb. 133.

417. 120 *of* 1909.—(Tamil.) On the same base. A damaged record in the twentieth year of Parakēsarivarman *alias* Tribhuvanachakravartin Vīra-Chōḷadēva. Refers to flower gardens enjoyed by the temple. See Cb. 133.

418. 121 *of* 1909.—(Tamil.) On the same base. A damaged record in the third year of Rājakēsarivarman *alias* Tribhuvanachakravartin Vīranārāyaṇadēva. Records gift of land for offerings by a Sōmayājin surnamed Vīraśōḷa-Brahmēndra to the temple of Kariyapirān, "just as he had obtained it from Perumāḷ Vīrachōḷadēva." The latter was evidently identical with the 'Vīrachōḷa Kulaśēkhara referred to in 214 of 1909 at Kannaḍiputtūr. He was "perhaps different from Vīrachōḷa, the ruler of the two Koṅgus."

419. 122 *of* 1909.—(Tamil.) On the same base. A damaged record of Kōnērinmaikoṇḍān, the date of which is lost. Built in at the end. Records an order (*ōlai*) of the king to the residents of Koḷumam and mentions the village Kumaraṅgabhīma-chaturvēdimaṅgalam in Karaivaḷi-nāḍu.

420. 123 *of* 1909.—(Tamil.) On the same base. A damaged and incomplete record of Kōnērinmaikoṇḍān, the date of which is lost. Records gift of paddy for offerings to the temple of Karumāṇikka-Āḷvār.

421. 124 *of* 1909.—(Tamil.) On the same base. A much damaged record of Kōnērinmaikoṇḍān, the date of which is lost. Mentions Jayaṅgoṇḍaśōḷa-chaturvēdimaṅgalam and contains the beginning of two inscriptions of a certain Parakēsarivarman.

422. 125 *of* 1909.—(Tamil.) On the same base. A damaged record in the nineteenth year, the king's name being lost. Records gift of land to a private individual. [Seems to refer to a gift of Vīrachōḷa similar to those of his at Saṅgrāmanallūr. See Nos. 436 and 437 below.]

423. 126 *of* 1909.—(Tamil.) On the west and south bases of the same temple. A record in the twenty-second year of Rājakēsari Kōnērinmaikoṇḍān (Vīrarājēndradēva 1207–1252). Records gift of paddy for offerings to the shrine of Śiṅgapperumāḷ in the temple of Kariyapirān. Mentions the three districts of Vaigāvināḍu, Karaivaḷi-nāḍu and Vīrakēraḷa vaḷanāḍu.

424. 127 *of* 1909.—(Tamil.) On the same base. A record in the twentieth year of Rājakēsarivarman *alias* Tribhuvanachakravartin Vīrarājēndradēva (1207–1252). Records gift of land to the same shrine.

425. 128 *of* 1909.—(Grantha and Tamil.) On the south base of the same temple. A record of Rājakēsari Kōnērinmaikoṇḍān

Vīrarājēndradēva (A.D. 1207—C. 1236). Records gift of land for maintaining a flower-garden, to the temple of Emberumān Vēdanāyaka-Perumāḷ at Tirunārāyaṇapuram.

426. 129 *of* 1909.—(Tamil.) On the same base. A record of Kōnērmaikoṇḍān (probably Vīra Rājēndra, 1207—52). Records an order to the Śrī-Vaishṇavās of Tiruvaraṅgam in Śōḷa-maṇḍalam and registers a gift of land to the temple of Aḷagiyamaṇavāḷa-Perumāḷ. Mentions Kōvanputtūr (Coimbatore) *alias* Vīrakēraḷa-nallūr in Pērūr-nāḍu. For the legendary origin of Kōvanputtūr based on the *Tamil MS. Chōḷapūrvapaṭṭayam*, see *Journal of S. Ind. Assocn.*, 1914.

427. 130 *of* 1909.—(Tamil.) On the same base. An unfinished record of Kōnērinmaikoṇḍān. Records gift of land for maintaining a flower-garden for the benefit of the shrine of Vēdanāyaka-Perumāḷ. Mentions the temple of Adhirādarāja-Iśvaram-Uḍaiyār.

428. 131 *of* 1909.—(Tamil.) On the south wall of the same temple. A record in the twenty-second year of Parakēsarivarman *alias* Tribhuvanachakravartin Vikrama-Chōḷadēva (Koṅgu Chōḷa, 1005—45 ?). Records gift of money for offerings by Dēvan Śilamban *alias* Tribhuvanagaṅgadēva, a feudatory (sāmanta) of the king, to the temple of Kariyapirān at Kumaraṅgabhīma-chaturvēdimaṅgalam, a brahmadēya in Karaivaḷi-nāḍu.

429. 132 *of* 1909.—(Tamil.) On the same wall. A record of the Vijayanagara king Vīrapratāpa Harihararāya-Uḍaiyār (III), in Ś. 1332, Khara. Records gift of lands to the temples of Kariyapirān at Kumaraṅgabhīma (Paradārasahōdara)-chaturvēdimaṅgalam and Kumaraṅgabhīmēśvaramuḍaiyār at Mēlai-Kannaḍipputtūr.

430. 133 *of* 1909.—(Tamil.) On the west wall of the same temple. A record in the seventeenth year of Tribhuvanachakravartin Kōnērinmaikoṇḍān. Records gift of land distributed over several villages, to the same temple. [One of these villages Amarabhujaṅganallūr was apparently founded by the early Kēraḷa king Vīrakēraḷa Amarabhujaṅgavarman.]

431. 134 *of* 1909.—(Tamil.) On the north wall of the same temple. A record in the twenty-seventh year of Vikrama-Chōḷadēva. Records gift of paddy for offerings. See Cb. 428 above.

432. 135 *of* 1909.—(Grantha and Tamil.) On the same wall. A record in the twenty-fifth year and Ś. 1153 of Tribhuvanachakravartin Kōnērinmaikoṇḍān Vīrarājēndradēva (1207—52). Records gift of land for offerings to the ten Āḷvārs in the temple of Aḷagar at Tirumāliruñjōlai in Kīḷ-Iraṇiyamuṭṭa-nāḍu, a subdivision of Pāṇḍi-maṇḍalam. The land was situated in the village of Ulaguḍaiyapirāṭṭi-chaturvēdimaṅgalam in Rājarāja-vaḷanāḍu which was split up from Karaivaḷi-nāḍu. [Iraṇiyamuṭṭa was the native district of the Tamil poet Peruṅ-Kauśikanār. Mr. Krishna

Sastri suggests that Ulagudaiyapiratti-chaturvēdimaṅgalam was probably named after a queen of Vīra Rājēndra who was known as Ulagapperumāḷ. See Cb. 23 above.

433. *C.P. No.* 185 *of Mr. Sewell's List.*—An early but undated grant of a Punnāḍ Rāja, named Ravidatta, during a solar eclipse. Records grant of several villages "in the Punnāḍ country" to Brahmans, himself residing at the city of Kīttipura. Punnāḍ is the extreme south of Maisūr.

434. *C.P. No.* 188 *of Mr. Sewell's List.*—(Telugu.) Records grant of lands in Komāralingam, ten miles south-east of Uḍamalpēt, in Ś. 1589, Plavaṅga (A.D. 1667), by Chokkanātha Nāyakka of Madura, in the reign of Śrī-Raṅgadēva Rāya, to a Brāhman (named Sōmayājēśvarlu). This is a record where the Telugu language is rendered in Grantha characters. [This grant is given also in *Ins., S. Dts.*, p. 64, No. I. The object granted is the village of Rāmasamudram included in Komāraliṅgam.]

Kuḍimaṅgalam.

435. In the old Śiva temple. A record of Ś. 1450 (A.D. 1528).

Saṅgrāmanallūr.

436. 136 *of* 1909.—(Tamil.) On the south wall of the central shrine in the Chōḷeśvara temple. A record in the forty-fifth year of Rājakēsarivarman *alias* Tribhuvanachakravartin Vīrarājēndradēva (1207—52). Records gift of land for offerings to the shrine of Nittaninṟāḍuvār (built by a certain Kachchiyarāyan) in the temple of Vira-Chōḷīśvaram-Uḍaiyār at Kuḷumam in Karaivaḷināḍu. [The temple was apparently founded by Vīra Chōḷadēva who came to the throne about 1118. Kachchiyarāyan figures, in the legends of the *Chōḷapūrvapaṭṭayam.*]

437. 137 *of* 1909.—(Tamil.) On the same wall. A record of Kōnērmaikoṇḍan Vīrachōḷa (evidently referred to in the above epigraph). Records that the king caused a liṅga to be set up, and a temple to be built on the occasion of a solar eclipse which happened to fall on the day of his *janmanakshatra* and called it Vīra Chōḷīsvara. It was consecrated by a certain Kaṇṇabhaṭṭan who was appointed manager of the temple.

438. 138 *of* 1909.—(Tamil.) On the same wall. A record in the twenty-third year of Kōnērinmaikoṇḍān. Records gift of land and certain privileges to the architect who built the temple mentioned in the above epigraph.

439. 139 *of* 1909.—(Tamil.) On the same wall. A damaged record in the twenty-first year of Vīra-Chōḷadēva. Records a gift of land and mentions among its boundaries the road Śēranaimēnkoṇḍa-Śōḷan-peruvaḷi.

440. 140 *of* 1909.—(Tamil.) On the west wall of the same shrine. An incomplete record in the fifteenth year of Rājakēsarivarman *alias* Tribhuvanachakravartin Vīra-Pāṇḍyadēva (1265—81). Records gift by the citizens (nagarattār) of two specified villages in the district of Tuvarāpati-nāḍu and in that of Uraiyūr-kūṟṟam in Rājagambhīra-vaḷanāḍu, a subdivision of Chōḷamaṇḍalam.

441. 141 *of* 1909.—(Tamil.) On the same wall. A damaged record in the twentieth year of Vīra-Chōḷadēva (1118—23?). Records gift of land in the village of Vīranārāyaṇa-chaturvēdimaṅgalam in Vīrakēraḷa-vaḷanāḍu. See No. 444 where either this or another Vīrachōḷa is mentioned.

442. 142 *of* 1909.—(Tamil.) On the same wall. A record in the twenty-first year of Vīra-Chōḷadēva (1118—23 ?). Records gift of paddy for a lamp by a certain Śirināyakan *alias* Vīraśōḷa-Nuḷamban.

443. 143 *of* 1909.—(Tamil and Grantha.) On the same wall. An incomplete record of Tribhuvanachakravartin Kōnērinmaikoṇḍān Vīrarājēndradēva (A.D. 1207—1252). Records gift of the village Iraṭṭaiyanpāḍi in Vaigāvi-nāḍu to a number of temples situated in Karaivaḷi-nāḍu. Refers to an invasion of the king in which Karaivaḷi-nāḍu was devastated and damage done to the temples in it. It was as in expiation of these damages that he gave for their renovation the village of Raṭṭiyambāḍi. See No. 467 below.

444. 144 *of* 1909.—(Tamil.) On the same wall. A record in the twenty-first year of Parakēsarivarman *alias* Tribhuvanachakravartin Vīra-Chōḷadēva, " who ruled the two Koṅgus together." Records gift of land for offerings by Gandarādichchanśeṭṭi *alias* Adirādarājakkaṇḍiyadēva, a feudatory (sāmanta) of the king. Was he the king who came to the throne in 1118?

445. 145 *of* 1909.—(Tamil.) On the north wall of the same shrine. A much damaged record of Tribhuvanachakravartin Kōnērinmaikoṇḍān. Appears to record a gift of land. Mentions the village of Kallāpuram *alias* Vikramachōḷanallūr in Karaivaḷi-nāḍu.

446. 146 *of* 1909.—(Tamil.) On the same wall. A record in the third-year of Vikrama-Chōḷadēva. Built in, at the beginning and incomplete. Mentions Ōḍatturai. [It is difficult to say which of the three Koṅgu-Chōlas of this name is referred to here.]

447. 147 *of* 1909.—(Tamil.) On the same wall. A record in the twenty-third year of Tribhuvanachakravartin Vikrama-Chōḷadēva. Records gift of land at Kīranūr in Pongalūrkkā-nāḍu to the temple of Vīrachōḷīśvaram-Uḍaiyār at Koḷumam in Karaivaḷināḍu, by Pāṇḍiyan *alias* Vikkiramaśōḷa-Iruṅgōḷan who was an expert in playing on the *yāḻ*. See note to the above epigraph. For the reference to *yāḻ* see S.A. 446.]

448. 148 *of* 1909.—(Tamil.) On the same wall. An incomplete record in the twenty-fifth year of Tribhuvanachakravartin Kōnērinmaikoṇḍān. Records gift of paddy for supplying food to three ascetics (tapasiyar) of the *Tiruttoṇḍattogaiyānmaḍam* (i.e., St. Sundara) in the quarter known as Vīraśōḻantirumaḍaiviḷāgam at Koḻumam.

449. 149 *of* 1909.—(Tamil.) On the same wall. A damaged and incomplete record in the seventeenth year of Tribhuvanachakravartin Kōnērinmaikoṇḍān. Records gift of land to a private person whose surname was Kaṇḍan Adiyan, in the village of Kallāpuram *alias* Vīraśōḻanallūr.

450. 150 *of* 1909.—(Tamil.) On the same wall. A record in the twenty-first year of Parakēsarivarman *alias* Tribhuvanachakravartin Vīra-Chōḻadēva, "who ruled the two Koṅgus together." Records gift of land for offerings to the temple of Vīra-śōḻa-Īśvaram-Uḍaiyār set up by the king for his merit at Koḻumam in Karaivaḻi-nāḍu. Another incomplete record on the same wall, of Vīra-Chōḻa, "who ruled the two Koṅgus together" refers to the founding of the temple and attempts to give a list of the lands presented to it on the occasion. Still another record gives the twenty-third year of, apparently, the same king and mentions Vīraśōḻan-tirumaḍaiviḷāgam.

451. 151 *of* 1909.—(Tamil.) On the south base of the maṇṭapa in front of the same shrine. A record in the thirteenth year of Kōnērinmaikoṇḍān. Stones out of order. Records gift of paddy to a shrine of Perumpiḷḷai-Āḻvār in the same temple.

452. 152 *of* 1909.—(Tamil.) On the same base. A record in the sixteenth year of Kōnērimēlkoṇḍān. Records gift of land in the village of Umāparamēśvarinallūr in Kāvāḍikka-nāḍu, to the shrine of the goddess in the same temple.

453. 153 *of* 1909.—(Tamil.) On the same base. A record in the eighth year of Vīra-Nārāyaṇadēva. Records a sale of land by public auction and mentions Kēraḷakēsarinallūr in Karaivaḻi-nāḍu. See Cb. 106.

454. 154 *of* 1909.—(Tamil.) On the north wall of the same maṇṭapa. A record of Kōnērimaikoṇḍān. [It records an order of the king that an enquiry should be made by the temple trustees as to the inhabitants living within the temple premises *(maḍaviḷāgam)* who had not paid the taxes *daṇḍa kūṟṟam* and *Manṟupāḍu*; that these collections from defaulters should be paid into the temple treasury, that the king's officer should not enter into those premises, that cesses, assessments, etc., payable to the royal treasury were remitted, and that the property of the temple servants who had no heirs living in temple premises should go to the temple.]

455. 155 *of* 1909.—(Tamil.) On the same wall. A record of Kōnērimēnkoṇḍān. Records gift of paddy.

456. 156 *of* 1909.—(Tamil.) On the same wall. A damaged record of Kōnērinmēnkoṇḍān (Vīraśōḷadēva). Seems to record a gift of land by a daughter of Vīraśōḷadēva, "who ruled the two Koṅgus together," to the shrine of Nittaninṟāḍuvār, in the same temple. See No. 444 above.

457. 157 *of* 1909.—(Tamil.) On the same wall. A record of Kōnērinmaikoṇḍān. Records gift of the village of Dēvanpādi *alias* Vīranārāyaṇanallūr in Kāvāḍikkanāḍu, to the shrine of Tribhuvanasundara which was set up for the merit of the king's uncle *(māmaḍi)*. Two other grants of land by the same king (i.e., Vīra-nārāyaṇa) are recorded : One for the god Tribhuvanasundara and His consort and another for the shrine of Dakshiṇāmūrti. Mentions Onbadukaṛai-nāḍu and Tiruvālanduṛai *alias* Kēraḷa-kēsarinallūr. [The inscription fixes the fiscal relation between the king and the temple trustees.]

458. 158 *of* 1909.—(Tamil.) On the base of the maṇṭapa in front of the Naṭarāja shrine in the same temple. Some of the stones are out of order. Records in Ś. 1267, Pārthiva, gift of land by Ketaya-Daṇḍanāyaka (son of Mādappa Daṇḍanāyaka), to the mahājanās of Mādhava-chaturvēdimaṅgalam (evidently named after his father) and Tennavadarāya-chaturvēdimaṅgalam for the 'victory and increase' (Vijayābhyudaya) of his younger brother Śiṅgaya Daṇḍanāyaka. [Kētaya, like Śiṅgaya, was the son of Mādappa Daṇāyaka referred to in Cb. 20.]

459. 159 *of* 1909.—(Tamil.) On the same base. Records in Ś. 1265, Subhānu, gift of the two villages mentioned in No. 158 by Kētaya-Daṇḍanāyakan, son of Mādhava. Mentions Kaṇṇappan Tennavadaraiyan of Seḷuvanūr and Oṭṭaikkumiṇḍān. See Cb. 469 below.

460. 160 *of* 1909.—(Tamil.) On a slab built into the floor in front of the same maṇṭapa. A fragment of record in the tenth year of Vīra-Nārāyaṇadēva. Mentions Pāṇḍi-manḍalam. See Cb. 106.

461. 161 *of* 1909.—(Tamil.) On the second slab in the same place. A fragment of record in the thirty-seventh year of Sundara-Pāṇḍyadēva. Seems to record gift of paddy.

462. 162 *of* 1909.—(Tamil.) On the third slab in the same place. Mentions in Sarvajit a certain Vīdiviṭaṅkanāyinār who imposed a fresh tax on the hereditary trustees (sthānattār) of the Aḷagiyā-Tiruchchiṟṟambalam-Uḍaiyān temple. [Mr. Krishna Sastri believes that this refers to the invasion mentioned in No. 443 above.]

463. 163 *of* 1909.—(Tamil.) On the south wall of the Agnīś-vara shrine in the same temple. A record in the twenty-ninth year of Tribhuvanachakravartin Kōnērinmaikoṇḍān. Records gift of land to those who recited the *Mahābhārata* at the village of Tiruvālanduṟai *alias* Vikramaśōḷa-chaturvēdimaṅgalam in Karaivaḷināḍu.

464. 164 *of* 1909.—(Tamil.) On the north wall of the same shrine. A record in the twenty-ninth year of Tribhuvanachakravartin Kōnērinmaikoṇḍān. Records gift of land for offerings to the shrine of a liṅga called Śokkanār, set up by Tilla-Nāyaka within the temple of Vīrachōḷīśvaramuḍaiya-Nāyanār at Koḷumam. The land was situated in Ulaguḍaipirāṭṭi-chaturvēdimaṅgalam in Karaivaḷi-nāḍu.

465. 165 *of* 1909.—(Tamil.) On the same wall. A record in the twenty-ninth year of Tribhuvanachakravartin Kōnērinmaikoṇḍān. Refers to the gift mentioned in the above epigraph.

466. 166 *of* 1909.—(Tamil.) On a slab set up in front of the central shrine in the same temple. Records in Viḷambi gift of six villages by a Nāyaka to the shrine of Nittiyappar.

467. 167 *of* 1909.—(Tamil.) On the door post of the gōpura of the same temple. States that the soldiers must protect the gōpura, the temple and its premises.

468. 168 *of* 1909.—(Tamil.) On a slab built into the floor of the Varadarāja-Perumāḷ temple in the same village. Records the gift of the stone.

469. 169 *of* 1909.—(Tamil.) On a rock at Kōvilturai in the same village. A damaged record in Siddhārthi of Mahāmaṇḍalēśvara Vīra Savaṇa-Udaiyār (son of Bukka I ?). Mentions the Mahājanās of Agaramputtūr *alias* Mādhava-chaturvēdimaṅgalam which was split up from Tenmūr Oṭṭaikkumiṇḍān in Karaivaḷināḍu. [See No. 459 above. Mr. Krishna Sastri surmises, on the basis of the connection of this village with the chiefs who claimed control over the Nilgiris and who had the title of Nīlagirisādhāraṇan, that Nīlagiri was even in those days called *Oṭṭaikkumiṇḍān* or Ootacamund.]

Śōḷamādēvi.

470. 222 *of* 1909.—(Tamil.) On the south wall of the Kulaśēkharasvāmin temple. A record in the twenty-seventh year of Vikrama-Chōḷadēva (1005—45). Records gift of land by a private individual to the temple of Kulaśēkhara-Īśvaramuḍaiyār at Śōḷanmādēvinallūr in Karaivaḷi-nāḍu.

471. 223 *of* 1909.—(Tamil.) On the same wall. A damaged record in the fifteenth year of Vīrarājēndradēva (1207—52). Records gift of land to the same temple. Mentions among the boundaries of the land the temple of Koṅgaviṭaṅka-Īśvaram-Uḍaiyār at Kaḍaṟṟūr.

472. 224 *of* 1909.—(Tamil.) On the same wall. A record in the eighth year of Vikrama-Chōḷadēva. Records gift of the row of slabs *(paṭṭi)* on which the inscription is engraved, by an ascetic of the *mēlaimaṭha*.

473. 225 *of* 1909.—(Tamil.) On the same wall. A record of Vīra-Chōḷadēva. Records gift of money for worship in the same temple by two individuals, one of whom was called Śōḷan Araiyan *alias* Vīraśōḷa-Vaṇigaiyarāyan.

474. 226 *of* 1909.—(Tamil.) On the same wall. A record in the twenty-first year of Vīra-Chōḷadēva. Records gift of money by two Veḷḷāḷa ladies to the same temple.

475. 227 *of* 1909.—(Tamil.) On the north wall of the same temple. A record of Vīra-Chōḷadēva, the date of which is lost. Records gift of land to the shrine of the goddess.

476. 228 *of* 1909.—(Tamil.) On the same wall. A damaged record of Vīra-Chōḷadēva, the date of which is lost. Appears to record a gift to the same shrine.

477. 229 *of* 1909.—(Tamil.) On the same wall. A record in the twenty-first year of Vīra-Chōḷadēva. Records gift of land for offerings, to the shrine of Kshētrapālappiḷḷaiyār, in the same temple.

478. 230 *of* 1909.—(Tamil.) On the same wall. The record gives a list of the lands belonging to the temple.

479. 231 *of* 1909.—(Tamil.) On the same wall. A record in the twentieth year of Vīra-Chōḷadēva. Records gift of land.

480. 232 *of* 1909.—(Tamil.) On the same wall. A record of Tribhuvanachakravartin Kōnērimēlkoṇḍān. Records sale of land belonging to the *manrāḍu* of Kāḍavarāyan, who became a traitor (drōhi) to the king, in favour of the temple servants. [This was perhaps the usual way in which treason in villages was dealt with in those days.]

481. 233 *of* 1909.—(Tamil.) On the same wall. A damaged record in the thirtieth year of Vīrarājēndradēva (I, 207—52). Appears to record a gift of land.

482. 234 *of* 1909.—(Tamil.) On the same wall. A record in the twenty-ninth year of Tribhuvanachakravartin Vīrarājēndra-dēva (1207—52). Records gift of land to the *maṭha* on the western side of the temple of Kulaśēkharēśvaram-Uḍaiyar.

483. 235 *of* 1909.—(Tamil.) On the same wall. A record in the twenty-first year of Tribhuvanachakravartin Vikrama-Chōḷa-dēva (1005—45). Records gift of paddy in lieu of money utilized for the repairs of a maṇṭapa in the temple.

484. 236 *of* 1909.—(Tamil.) On the east wall of the same temple; right of entrance. A record in the twelfth year of Para-kēsarivarman *alias* Tribhuvanachakravartin Vikrama-Chōḷadēva

(1005—45 ?). Records gift of a garden to the *matha* on the eastern side of the temple for maintaining lamps.

485. 237 *of* 1909.—(Tamil.) On a pillar within the same temple. A record in the twenty-second year of Vikrama-Chōḷa-dēva (1005-45). Records gift of the pillar by a certain Mōḍan Tirunaṭṭa-Perumāḷ.

486. 238 *of* 1909.—(Tamil.) On another pillar in the same place. A record in the twenty-first year of Tribhuvanachakra-vartin Vikrama-Chōḷadēva (1005—45 ?). Records gift of the pillar.

487. 239 *of* 1909.—(Tamil.) On the third pillar in the same place. A record in the twentieth year of Vikrama-Chōḷadēva (1005—45 ?). Records gift of the pillar.

488. 240 *of* 1909.—(Tamil.) On the door post of the eastern entrance into the same temple. A record in the twentieth year of Tribhuvanachakravartin Vikrama-Chōḷadēva (1005—45 ?). Records gift of the two door posts and two step stones by a woman, for the merit of a certain Adiyaśōḷan Araiśan *alias* Maṇigaiyarāyan.

489. 241 *of* 1909.—(Tamil.) On the door post of the southern entrance into the same temple. A record in the twentieth year of Tribhuvanachakravartin Vikrama-Chōḷadēva (1005—45 ?). Records gift of the two door posts and two step stones.

490. 242 *of* 1909.—(Tamil.) On the door post of the entrance into the Tambrāṭṭiyamman temple in the same village. A record in the twenty-fourth year of Parakēsarivarman *alias* Vikrama-Chōḷadēva (1005—45 ?). Records gift of money for the Śivarātri festival to be conducted in the temple of Rājarāja-Īśvaram-Uḍaiyar at Kaḍappāḍi *alias* Vīraśōḷapuram. The coins presented were marked with *śri-yakki*, 'the glorious yakshi.'

491. 243 *of* 1909.—(Tamil.) On a stone built into the wall of the same temple. A record in the third year of Vikrama-Chōḷa-dēva. Records gift of money for a lamp by a native of Kannaḍi-puttūr. The name of the temple which was to benefit by the gift, is lost. [The king might be any of those who came to the throne in 1005, 1255 or 1273.]

Supplementary note.

433. This copper plate grant has been edited by Dr. Fleet in *Ind. Antq.*, XVIII, 362–9. He incidentally discusses the topography of the Punnāḍ district and criticises Mr. Rice.

CUDDAPAH DISTRICT.

BADVEL TALUK.

Katteragunḍla.

1. On a stone near the Chennakēśava pagoda. Records that Veṅgalayya granted in Ś. 1448, Paritāpi, in the reign of Kṛishṇadēvarāya, the duties of the different goods that passed by Chennāvaram, and Chavūr, in the district of Gaṇḍikōṭa to God Chennakēśava for festival. (*Ins., Ced. Dts.*, p. 515, No. 1.) It is also referred to by Mr. Sewell in his *Antiquities*, I, p. 126.

2. Near the above. Records that a person granted in Ś. 1448, Pārthiva, in the reign of Kṛishṇadēvarāya, two puṭṭis of his own share in the village to the same deity. *Ibid.*, p. 515, No. 2, and Mr. Sewell's local list, No. 3.

3. On the surrounding wall of the pagoda. Records that Yellamarasayya granted in Ś. 1452, Virōdhi, the village of Hosalapāḍu for the festival of the deity. (*Ins., Ced. Dts.*, p. 515, No. 3.) Mr. Sewell wrongly attributes this to "the reign of Vīrapratāpa Mahādēvarāya." See *Antiquities*, local list, No. 2.

4. On a stone west of the village, Records that Nanda Timmarāja exempted the rent of a village with the permission of Sadāśivarāya in Ś. 1469, Parābhava. *Ins., Ced. Dts.*, p. 515, No. 4, and Mr. Sewell's local list, No. 4.

5. A P.G. in charge of Bommacharaṇareḍḍi in the village. Records that the karṇams of the district appointed one Chennayya as the chief of the people of Katteragunḍla as a reward for his discovery of its limit in Ś. 1479, Manmatha, in the reign of Śrīraṅgarāya. *Ibid.*, p. 517, No. 8. [There was no *king* of this name in that year.]

6. In charge of the same Reḍḍi. Records that the karṇams of the district granted some land in the village to Bommapedda Ayyala Reḍḍi in Parābhava in the reign of Prauḍhadēvarāya. *Ibid.*, p. 517, No. 9.

Kōḍūru.

7. On a stone in the pagoda of Durga. (Telugu.) Records in Ś. 1475, Paritāpi, in the reign of Sadāśivarāya, an allowance of contribution from the pilgrims for the annual festival of the deity. *Ins., Ced. Dts.*, p. 517, No. 7. The village is called Pedda Kōḍūru.

8. On the gate of Chennakēśava pagoda. (Telugu.) Records in Ś. 1469, Prabhava, that Nandyāl Timmarāya, a feudatory of Sadāśivarāya, granted the rent of a village for meeting the expense of a ceremonial. *Ibid.*, p. 517, No. 10.

9. On a stone in the same temple. (Telugu.) Records that the same chief remitted the tax on barbers, drummers and pipers of the pagoda. *Ins., Ced. Dts.*, p. 517, No. 11.

9-A. On a stone in the Bhairava temple of the same village. A record dated in Ś. 1319, Dhātu, regarding the establishment of the temple on the hill in the reign of Vīra-Dēvarāya (I) who must have been a mere prince then. *Ibid.*, p. 517, No. 12.

Palugurāḷḷapalle.

10. In the temple of Durgā. Dated in Ś. 1475 (A.D. 1552). A grant in the reign of Sadāśiva Rāya of Vijayanagar. *Antiquities*, I, 126.

11. On the top of a hill near the Bhairava temple. Dated Ś. 1318 (A.D. 1396). Records repairs to the temple in the reign of Śrī Vīra-Dēva Rāya at Udayagiri by Lakkadēva Mahārāja. *Ibid.* [See *Cuddapah Gazr.*, I, 233–34, for the rise of a local *maṭha* here.]

Pōrumāmilla.

12. 91 *of* 1913.—(Sanskrit.) On two slabs set up in front of the ruined Bhairava temple near the local tank. A record of Bhāskara *alias* Bhavadūra, son of Bukka I, of Vijayanagar, dated K. 4470, Ś. 1291, Saumya, Kārtika, Śukla 14, Thursday. The tank is one of the two largest ones in the district. The other is at Badvel. See *Cuddapah Gazr.*, pp. 226—30, for a detailed analysis of the epigraph. It gives a beautiful account of the rules and regulations, the technical details of tank construction. [Bhāskara is hitherto unknown. *Bhavadura* is considered by the Government epigraphist to be the Sanskṛit form of the Hindusthani *Bahadur*.] Records that Bhāskara's minister Anantarājan (called Anantarasa in 339 of 1901 at Penukoṇḍa) constructed the tank at Pōrumāmilla which exists to-day.

13. In the Lakshmīkāntasvāmi temple. Dated Ś. 1477 (A.D. 1555). Commemorates a grant to a private person in the reign of Sadāśiva Rāya of Vijayanagar by Varadarājayya dēva Mahārāja, son of Raṅga Rāja, and grandson of Nandyāla Varadarāja.

Tellapāḍu.

14. On a stone in the village (Telugu.) Records that in Ś. 1432, Peddōbala Nāyaḍu, subordinate of Sadāśivarāya, granted nine *tūms* of land to repair the sluice of the local tank. See *Ins., Ced. Dts.*, p. 516, No. 5. [A *tūm* is ⅛ *puṭṭi* in some parts of Cuddapah and one-twentieth in other parts. It is a grain measure and evidently land capable of being sowed with 9 *tūms* is meant here.]

15. On the other side of the same stone. A record of the same chief in the same year. A gift of land on the establishment of the image of Bhairava to the survey stone-cutter. *Ibid.*, p. 516, No. 6.

Varikuṇṭa.

16. An inscription in the temple of Rāmasvāmi, dated Ś. 1525 (A.D. 1603), recording a grant to a private party by Hanuma Rājayyadēva Mahārāja in the reign of Veṅkaṭapati (I, 1586—1614) at Chandragiri.

CUDDAPAH TALUK.

Ambāvaram.

17. On a stone near the temple of Aṅkālamma. (Telugu.) A damaged grant in Ś. 1669, Prabhava, wrongly attributed to the reign of Sadāśivarāya. *Ins., Ced. Dts.*, p. 348, No. 48.

17-A. In the pagoda of Chennakēśava. (Telugu.) A record of Sadāśivarāya, dated in Ś. 1477, Rākshasa. Records grant of an allowance from the village to the deity by Tirumalayya (evidently of Nandyāla).

Chennūru.

18. On a stone in the pagoda of Nāgēśvara. (Sanskrit and Telugu.) Dated in Ś. 1236, Pramādīcha. Records the grant of the village to the Brahmans by a son of Pratāparudra of the Kākatīya dynasty. *Ins., Ced. Dts.*, p. 354, No. 69. [The king ruled till A.D. 1323.]

19. In the same place. (Sanskrit.) A record of Kṛishṇadēvarāya in Ś. 1444, Vishu. Records that Śiṅgabhūpāla rebuilt the Nāgēśvara pagoda, dug a tank, and gave some land. *Ibid.*, No. 70. [The epigraph shows that in the Vijayanagar period it was the capital of an administrative unit consisting of several villages in Ghaṇḍikōṭa Śīma of Udayagiri province.]

Chinnadāsaripalle.

20. On a stone near the pagoda of Ōbaladēva. (Telugu.) Records that in Ś. 1292, Sādhāraṇa, in the reign of Vīra Bukkarāya (I), Maṅgayyadēva Mahārāja built a village and granted it as a free gift for the God Ahōbalēśvara. *Ins., Ced. Dts.*, p. 335, No. 10. Also *Cuddapah Gazr.*, p. 185.

20-A. On a stone north of the same. (Telugu.) A record of Achyutadēvarāya in Vijaya, regarding an allowance in the district of Gaṇḍikōṭa by Bācharasu. *Ibid.*, p. 355, No. 11. *Cuddapah Gazr.*, p. 186.

Chinamāsapalle (Chinnamāchupalle).

21. 330 *of* 1905.—(Kanarese.) On a slab lying in front of the Āñjanēya temple. Dated in the reign of the Vijayanagara king Vīrapratāpa Kṛishṇarāya-Mahārāya. Records in Ś. 1436, Bhava, gift of the village of Chikamamchupaḷḷi in the Chenūri-śīme, which was included in the district of Muḷiki-nāṭi-śīme, to the temple of

Channakēśavadēva at Pushpagiri. [The inscription is also given in *Ins., Ced. Dts.*, p. 356, No. 72.] See No. 19 above.

Chintakommadinne.

22. On a stone in the Janārdanasvāmi temple. (Telugu.) Records that in Ś. 1498, Naḷa, Ellappa Nāyaḍu, feudatory of Sadāśivarāya, granted to the God some land in the village. *Ins., Ced. Dts.*, p. 331, No. 2. Referred to also in *Cuddapah Gazr.*, p. 186.

23. On a stone near the Dvajastambha. (Telugu.) Records that Śāḷuva Narasappayya gave in Ś. 1453, Khara, in the reign of Achyutadēvarāya, some allowance in the village to a person. *Ibid.*, p. 32, No. 3.

24. On a stone near the pagoda of Gaṅgamma. (Telugu.) Records that "Hazarat Durbundage Dēvanaḷavāru" granted in Ś. 1669, Prabhava, three *Kuṇṭas* of *Daśavantam* for the yearly repair of the tank to the Reḍḍis, Kāpus, Kammas and farmers of the place. *Ibid.*, p. 332, No. 4. See also *Cuddapah Gazr.*, p. 186.

Chintalapattūru.

25. 318 *of* 1905.—(Telugu.) On a slab built into the outer wall of the ruined temple of Indranāthasvāmin, near Pushpagiri. Records that in the reign of the Vijayanagara king Vīrapratāpa Sadāśivadēva-Mahārāya, in Ś. 1469, Plavaṅga, Aḷiya Rāmayya-dēva-Mahārāja remitted the tax on barbers in the Karnāṭaka country, and the mahāmaṇḍalēśvara Timmayyadēva of Nandyāla did the same for the whole of Ghaṇḍikōṭaśīma and for three villages belonging to the Indranātha temple.

26. 319 *of* 1905.—(Telugu.) On a pillar lying at the entrance into the same temple. Records in Vibhava a gift by Mahā-maṇḍalēśvara Murārikēśavadēva Mahārāja and Sōmidēvarāja who were "lords of Kalukada, the best of towns," to the temple of Indrēśvara at Pushpagiri. [The Kaḷachūri king Sōmēśvara, also called Sōvi dēva and Rāyamurāri, ruled from 1167 to 1175.]

27. 320 *of* 1905.—(Telugu.) On the same pillar. Records gift of land by the Mahāmaṇḍalēśvara Āhavamalladēva to the temple of Indrēśvaradēva. An imprecatory verse engraved in Grantha characters is found at the end. [Was the king the Kalachūri king who ruled from 1180 to 1183?]

28. 321 *of* 1905.—(Kanarese.) On a slab set up in the court-yard of the same temple. A record of the Pallava king Mahā-maṇḍalēśvara-Chiddanadēva-Mahārāja in Ś. 1104 (A.D. 1182), Śubhakrit, recording gift of land in the village of Kōḍūru in Muḷiki-nāḍu to the temple of Indrēśvaradēva at Pañchanati-tīrtha. [His birudas resemble those of Tripurāntakadēva Madhusūdana in Ct. 320 and Nallasiddharasa in Cg. 321. The latter were the feudatories of Vijayagaṇḍagōpāla.]

29. 322 *of* 1905.—(Telugu.) On the north wall of the central shrine in the same temple. Records in Ś. 1217, Manmatha, a private agreement.

30. 323 *of* 1905.—(Grantha and Tamil.) On the four corner slabs built into the inside of the dome of the antarāḷa-maṇṭapa in the same temple. A damaged record. Mentions the Gōḷagi-maṭha. See N.A. 201.

31. 324 *of* 1905.—(Telugu.) On a pillar in the same maṇṭapa. Records in Ś. 1182, Raudri, a transfer of rights by three priests of the Indrēśvara temple. Mentions the temples of Kamalaśaṁkara, Vaijanātha, Rudrapāda, Durgādēvi, Pushpēśvara and Mallinātha-dēva.

Cuddapah.

For an excellent historical notice of the place see *Cuddapah Gazr.*, pp. 178—80.

32. On a stone in the Veṅkaṭēśvara pagoda. (Telugu.) Records that in Ś. 1439, Īśvara, that Timmarasa, the minister of Kṛishṇadēvarāya, granted the Cuddapah village to God Tiruvēṅ-galanātha for daily ceremonies. *Ins., Ced. Dts.*, p. 350, No. 53. [Timmarasa was the well-known Śāḷuva Appāji.]

33. On a stone east of the above. (Telugu.) Records that in Ś. 1484, Dundubhi, a feudatory of Sadāśivarāya erected a stone maṇṭapa and planted a garden near it. *Ibid.*, No. 55.

34. On the south wall of the Raṅga-maṇṭapa. (Telugu.) Records that in Ś. 1460, Hēviḷambi, that Tātareḍḍi and Nāgareḍḍi granted six *tūms* of land to Vasanta. *Ibid.*, No. 55.

35. On the wall west of the above. (Telugu.) Records that in Ś. 1474, Virōdhikrit, Nandyāla Aubalēśvara Mahārāya granted some land to God Ahōbalēśvara. *Ibid.*, No. 56.

36. On a stone near the above. (Telugu.) Records that in Piṅgaḷa, Ś. 1483, Nandyāl Aubalarāja, feudatory of Sadāśiva, granted some land to God Tiruvēṅgalanātha. *Ibid.*, No. 57.

37. On a wall in the Tiruvēṅgalanātha pagoda. (Telugu.) Records that in Ś. 1620, Pramādi, "Asana Nayaken," son of Śūrappa, presented a crown to the deity. *Ibid.*, p. 352, No. 58.

38. On the eastern wall of the above inscription. (Telugu.) Records that in Ś. 1473, Pramādi, Aubalarāja, feudatory of Sadāśiva, granted half *kuṇḍa* of dry field in Cuddapah to the deity. *Ibid.*, No. 59.

39. On the wall of the pagoda. (Telugu.) A grant by the same chief in the same year to the same deity. *Ibid.*, No. 60.

40. On the steps of the Bugga-kālva at Cuddapah. (Telugu.) Records that in Ś. 1639, Hēviḷambi, Kṛishṇājipantulu built the steps. *Ibid.*, No. 61.

41. On a stone in the temple. (Telugu.) A grant of Dēvarāya (II) in Ś. 1364, Dundubhi. *Ins., Ced. Dts.*, p. 352, No. 62.

42. On the banks of the Cuddapah tank. (Telugu.) A grant in Ś. 1220, Viḷambi to Siddhanāthasvāmi by a chief who had the title of Gaṇḍapeṇḍara. *Ibid.*, No. 63.

43. On a stone near the local tank. (Telugu.) Records that in Ś. 1227, Krōdhi, one Tripurāntaka granted to Siddhanāthasvāmi one *kuṇṭa* of wet field. *Ibid.*, No. 64.

44. On a stone in the pagoda of Hanūmanta. (Telugu.) Records that in Ś. 1439, Īśvara, Kṛishṇadēvamahārāya's minister Śāḷuva Timmarasa made a gift to the deity of Siddhāvaṭṭam. *Ibid.*, No. 67.

45. On the mosque west of Cuddapah. (Telugu.) Records that in H. 1130, in the reign of Faraksir, "Mayanubdulnābi Khan, Subhedar of Cuddapah," built the mosque. [This chief was the celebrated founder of the Cuddapah Nawab dynasty. For his exploits see *Cuddapah Gazr.*, pp. 180 and 41. He died about 1730.]

46. A paper grant in the mosque of Abdul Nabi. (Telugu.) Records that the merchants of different countries fixed a fee to be paid to the mosque in Ś. 1599, Piṅgaḷa. *Ibid.*, p. 360, No. 83. [The date appears to be too late as Abdul Nabi became governor in 1714. See *Cuddapah Gazr.*, p. 41.]

47. A paper grant in the same place. (Telugu.) Records that in Ś. 1626, Chitrabhānu, that the Reḍḍis and Karṇams of Nāgarājupaḷḷe granted, by order of Abdul Khān Saheb, four *tūms* of ground to "Sakha-Abdul Latteeba." *Ibid.*, No. 84.

48. A paper grant in the same place. (Telugu.) Records, that "Bapujuhersa Tarufdar" granted, by order of Nabab Bhakdumedal Khan two *tūms* of ground to Dasu Mahommed. *Ibid.*, No. 85.

49. A paper grant in the same place. (Telugu.) Records a grant by the same man to Siddhi Mahomed, the *Khāji* of Cuddapah. *Ibid.*, No. 86.

50. A paper grant in the same place. (Telugu.) Records that in "36 of the Sun year," Merugamahummud of Hyderabad fixed some fees in the market of Cuddapah for the illumination of the local mosque. *Ibid.*, No. 87.

Gōṭūru.

51. On a stone in the pagoda of Bhairavēśvara. (Kanarese.) Records in Ś. 1440, Bahudhānya, gift of some land to Mummuḍi Reḍḍi, in Gōṭūru. *Ins., Ced. Dts.*, p. 358, No. 77.

52. On a stone near the same. (Kanarese.) Records in Ś. 1319, Īśvara, that Gaṅgadēva Mahārāja gave to the architect Bommayya

Bhaṭṭu one-fourth *kunṭa* of wet land for constructing the Bhairavēśvara temple. *Ins., Ced. Dts.*, p. 358, No. 78. [*Kunṭa* is said to denote an excavation of a cubit in depth in width in some parts of the district. But it is not used in that sense here. *Cuddapah Gazr.*, p. 117.]

53. On a stone in the same pagoda. (Kanarese.) A record of Ahōbhala Dēvachōḷa Mahārāja, son of Apratimalla Gaṇapatichōḷa Mahārāja in Ś. 1342, Plava. Gift of seventeen *tūms* of land to God Bhairavadēva. *Ibid.*, p. 79.

54. On a stone south of the above. (Kanarese.) Records that the Karṇam and people of Gōṭūr elected in Ś. 1588, Parābhava, a temple of Omalamma and granted land. *Ibid.*, p. 359, No. 80.

Gurrampāḍu.

55. On a stone in the Chennakēśava pagoda. (Kanarese.) Records that in Ś. 1453, Khara, Tirumalayya, a feudatory of Achyutarāya, gave the village as free gift to the God. *Ins., Ced. Dts.*, p. 357, No. 74.

56. On a stone near the above. (Kanarese.) Records in Ś. 1500, Bahudhānya, gift of land to Veṅkaṭa Sōmayāji by Tirumalayyadēva Mahārāja in the reign of Śrīraṅgadēva Mahārāja. *Ibid.*, No. 75.

57. On a stone near the above. (Kanarese.) Tirumala Nāyaḍu gives to the God in Ś. 1316, Bhava, some land in the village. *Ibid.*, No. 76.

Komārunipalli.

58. A Telugu copper-plate in the hands of "Cavalekanlu at Cammapulla." Records that in Ś. 1479, Kaḷayukti, in the reign of Sadāśivarāya and Gutti Tirumalayya, the fourteen villagers of Uṭukūru district gave lands and fees at three *paṇams* for a marriage in these villages to Lakkanāyaḍu, son of "Marakathirappa" Nāyaḍu. *Ins., Ced. Dts.*, p. 334, No. 8.

Kopparti (*Rāmachandrapuram*).

59. Upon the sluice of the tank. (Telugu.) Records that Garuḍamitta Gummaṇa Ayyavāru, in Ś. 1588, Parābhava, dug a tank and built a sluice in Kṛishṇarāyapuram Agrahāram. *Ins., Ced. Dts.*, p. 338, No. 17.

Koppolu.

60. On a stone in the village. (Telugu.) Records that in Ś. 1466, Krōdhi, Nandyāl Timmayya, feudatory of Sadāśivarāya, gave the dues of the village to learned men. *Ins., Ced. Dts.*, p. 109, No. 53.

61. On a stone near the house of a Fakir. (Telugu.) Records that in Ś. 1476, in the reign of Sadāśivarāya, the *Viramushṭi* people granted a tax of one pagoda per year to God Śēshēśvara. *Ibid.*, No. 54.

62. A Telugu record dated in 1429, Akshaya, wherein Immuḍi Rāya Dēvarāya (II) granted the dues of the village to the local God. *Ins., Ced. Dts.*, p. 109, No. 55.

Koṭlūru.

63. On a stone on the bank of the river. (Telugu.) Records that Gaṅga Sāhiṇi, prince of Kākatiyapuram, made some gift to the attendants of Pushpagiri temple in Ś. 1196, Piṅgaḷa. Gaṇga Sāhiṇi was the celebrated General of Queen Rudrammā of Warangal (1257—1295). *Ibid.*, p. 344, No. 38.

Lēbāka.

64. On a stone in the pagoda of Rāmasvāmi. (Telugu.) Records grant of land in Ś. 1226, Krōdhi, in the reign of Tripuradēvarāya to the God of Lēbāka. *Ibid.*, p. 110, No. 57.

65. On a stone near the Sōmēśvara pagoda. (Telugu.) Records in Ś. 1539, Piṅgaḷa, gift of two *tūms* of land to the Goddess of Kamalāpuram. *Ibid.*, p. 110, No. 58.

66. On a stone in front of the Pātāḷēśvara pagoda. (Kanarese.) A record of a Palnāḍ chief. No details. *Ibid.*, No. 59.

67. On a stone in the pagoda of Sōmēśvara. (Telugu.) Records that in the reign of Sadāśivarāya, in Ś. 1475, Pramādīcha, a partition of villages was made between two cousins. *Ibid.*, p. 111, No. 60.

Moyillakālva.

68. On a stone in the Tiruvēṅgalanātha pagoda. (Telugu.) Records that Rāyasam Veṅkaṭappa gave, in the reign of Achyutadēva Mahārāya, in Ś. 1458, Dunmati, some land to God Tiruvēṅgalanātha. *Ibid.*, p. 337, No. 15.

69. On a stone above the previous record. (Telugu.) A record of Veṅkaṭappa Guru saying that in Śubhakrit he placed an image of Lakshmi in the above temple and gave one *puṭṭi* of land. *Ibid.*, No. 16.

Pendlimarri.

70. On a stone in the Vīrabhadra pagoda. (Telugu.) Records that, in the reign of Sadāśiva Mahārāya, in Ś. 1469, Prābhava, Nandyal Timmayya Rāja exempted the tax of the local barbers. *Ins., Ced. Dts.*, p. 334, No. 9. [The author of the *Cuddapah Gazetteer* draws attention to the fact that this was ruled by a Kaṭhāri Maṅgayya in Ś. 1292, in the reign of Bukka I. See No. 20 above.]

Pushpagiri.

This place is highly sacred both for the Vaishṇavites who call it *Tirumala-Madhya-Ahōbilam* (midway between Tirupati and

Ahōbilam) and for the Śaivites who call it *madhya-Kailāsam* midway between Benares or Uttara Kailāsam and Chidambaṛam or Dakshiṇa Kailāsam. For the legends regarding its origin see *Cuddapah Gazr.*, pp. 183—84. The place became the centre of one of the four Śaiva maṭhas *Āmarttaka, Raṇabhadra, Gōḷaki* and *Pushpagiri.*

71. 302 *of* 1905.—(Telugu.) On a slab set up at the southern gōpura of the Vaidyanāthasvāmin temple, right of entrance. Dated in the reign of the Vijayanagara king Vīrapratāpa Achyutadēva Mahārāya. Records in Ś. 1462, Śārvarin, a gift by the general Timmaraśayya, son of Sōmarasayya of Chandragiri. The former was in charge of the Ghaṇḍikōṭa-śīma, to which Pushpagiri belonged. [The inscription is given in *Ins., Ced. Dts.*, p. 339, No. 20.]

72. 303 *of* 1905.—(Telugu.) On another slab set up in the same place. A record of the Vijayanagara king Vīrapratāpa Achyutadēva-Mahārāya. Records in Ś. 1463, Plava, a gift by the same chief and mentions Aghōraśivāchārya. See also *Ins., Ced. Dts.*, p. 339, No. 20. [A teacher of this name figures in the history of Śaiva-Siddhāntism as the author of one of the eighteen *Paddatis* and the commentator of *Mrigēndrāgama* ; but he is said to have been born and died at Chidambaṛam. It is *his Paddati* and that of Vāmadēva that are the most widely current.

73. 304 *of* 1905.—(Sanskrit in Telugu.) On a pillar within the Trikuttēśvara shrine in the court-yard of the same temple. A record dated in Ś. 1176, Ānanda. The north, east and south faces of the pillar, respectively, record (1) that Kavalāyi, the wife of Gaṇḍapeṇḍara Gaṅga-sēnāpati of the Kāyastha family, founded the shrine of Kamalēśvara after her own name; (2) that Hāchālamba, the daughter of king Allugi, " lord of the town of Morata " founded the shrine of Hachalēśvara after her own name; (3) that the Pallava king Khaṇḍeraya of the solar race established the shrine called Pallavēśvara and that thus the name Trikūṭa was given to the group formed by the three shrines. The same Sanskrit verses are repeated on two other pillars in Nāgari and Grantha characters. [See *Ins., Ced. Dts.*, p. 339, No. 22, where the details are given in marvellous accuracy.]

74. 305 *of* 1905.—(Telugu.) On a slab set up near the south wall of the central shrine in the same temple. A record dated in Ś. 1769, Kīlaka. Mentions two Śaiva teachers.

75. 306 *of* 1905.—(Kanarese.) On a slab lying south of the Śiva shrine near the Durgā temple in the same village on the bank of the Pennēru river. A record of the Raṭṭa king Kṛishṇa Kannehaḍadēva (evidently Krishṇa III), saying that on his visit to Jōti he gave twelve *mattas* of land to the temples at Pushpagiri including those of Nāgeśvarā and Pushpēśvara. Those who ruled over Muḷiki-nāṇḍu in Honnavāḍi were required to respect this charity.

76. 307 *of* 1905.—(Telugu.) On the base of the antarāḷa-maṇṭapa of the Chennakēśavasvāmin temple in the same village. Records in Ś. 1423, Durmati, that Aghōraśivāchārya plastered the Śikhara of the temple. Vide *Ins., Ced. Dts.*, p. 341, No. 26, which gives the date Ś. 1422. See No. 72 above.

77. 308 *of* 1905.—(Telugu.) On the base of the antarāḷa-maṇṭapa of the Chennakēśavasvāmin temple in the same village. Records in Ś. 1442, Pramāthin, gift of taxes by a number of rope-dancers to the temple of Channakēśava. Vide *Ins., Ced. Dts.*, p. 341, No. 27.

78. 309 *of* 1905.—(Kanarese.) On a pillar within the same maṇṭapa. Dated in the reign of the Vijayanagara king Vīra-pratāpa Kṛishṇarāya-Mahārāya. Records in Ś. 1436, Bhava, gift of the village of Chinamāmchupaḷḷi in the Chernūra-śīma, which was included in Muḷikināṇḍu, to the temple of Channakēśāvadēva. Vide *Ins., Ced. Dts.*, p. 341, No. 28.

79. 310 *of* 1905.—(Telugu.) On a beam of the same maṇṭapa. Records in Ś. 1358, Naḷa, that a certain Kampayya repaired portions of the temple. See *Ins., Ced. Dts.*, p. 342, No. 30. The latter says that the donor was the son of "Lakaya Dēva Mahārāja."

80. 311 *of* 1905.—(Telugu.) On the beam over the entrance into the central shrine of the same temple. A damaged record dated in Ś. 1513, Khara. Mentions Mahāmaṇḍalēśvara Veṅkaṭā-drirājayyadēva-Mahārāju. See *Ins., Ced. Dts.*, p. 342, No. 31.

81. 312 *of* 1905.—(Telugu.) On a pillar in the antarāḷa-maṇṭapa of the Santāna Mallēśvara temple in the same village. Records in Ś. 1337, Manmatha, a sale of land.

82. 313 *of* 1905.—(Telugu.) On another pillar in the same maṇṭapa. Records in Ś. 1216, Jaya, a private agreement. Five temples of Pushpagiri are here mentioned, viz., Vejanātha (i.e., Vaidyanātha), Kamalaśaṁkara, Durgādevi, Rudrapādamu Rāmēś-vara. See *Ins., Ced. Dts.*, p. 342, No. 32.

83. 314 *of* 1905.—(Telugu.) On a pillar at the entrance into the Umāmahēśvara shrine in the same temple. Records in Ś. 1220 Śārvarin (wrong) sale of land by the priests of the temples of Mallināthadēva, Sōmanāthadēva and Channakēśavadēva on the hill. See *Ins., Ced. Dts.*, p. 344, No. 36, which seems to give this epigraph.

84. 315 *of* 1905.—(Telugu.) On a slab set up at the entrance into the north outer wall of the same temple. Dated in the reign of the Vijayanagara king Vīrapratāpa Sadāśivadēva-Mahārāya. Records in Ś. 1481, Siddhārthin, gift of land by Kōnēṭi-Tiru-vēṅgalanāthayya, son of Pedda-Tirumalayya and grandson of

Tāḷapāka Annamayya, to the temple of Channarāya. See *Ins., Ced. Dts.*, p. 340, No. 25, for another summary of this inscription.

85. 316 *of* 1905.—(Kanarese.) On a broken slab lying on the steps leading to the river from the eastern gōpura of the same temple. Trailōkyamalla-Mallidēva-Mahārāya records in Ś. 1061, Siddhārthi, the consecration of the god Kēśavadēva on the southern side of the Rudrapāda temple. The king was ruling from his capital at Vallūru. See next epigraph.

86. 317 *of* 1905.—(Tamil.) On the same slab. Records in Ś. 1061, Siddhārthi, in the reign of Trailōkyamalla Mallidēva-Mahārāja, a grant of land by an officer of the king. [The king was evidently the same as the greatest of the Konidena branch of the Telugu-chōḍas who ruled from 1137 to 1148.]

87. On a stone situated on the bank of the river. (Telugu.) Records that in Ś. 1447, Pramādi, "Raguliah Tippa Rāja Kavali Dēvarāya" granted to God Chennakēśava Vidyānātha 1,000 gold *māḍas*. (*Ins., Ced. Dts.*, p. 340, No. 23.)

88. On a stone close to the above. (Telugu.) Records that in Ś. 1464, Vikāri, in the reign of Achyutadēvarāya. Peddagōvindaayya and others made a grant to the God. *Ibid.*, p. 340, No. 24.

89. On a stone north of the Vidyānāth Pagoda. (Telugu.) Records that one Lakshmīdēva Daṇḍanāyaka built a village called Lakshmīpuram and granted it to Vidyānāthasvāmi. *Ibid.*, p. 341, No. 29.

90. On the south pillar of the maṇṭapam of Chennakēśavasvāmi. (Telugu.) Records in 1332, Manmatha, a sale of land. *Ibid.*, p. 343, No. 33.

91. On the eastern pillar of the Chennakēśava maṇṭapam. Records in Ś. 1337, Vishu, a sale of land. *Ibid.*, p. 343, No. 34.

92. On the northern pillar of the same. (Telugu.) Records in Ś. 1235, Pramāthi, a sale of land. *Ibid.*, p. 342, No. 35.

93. A C.P. in the local maṭha. (Sanskrit in Dēvanagari.) Records that in Ś. 1467, Prabhava, Sadāśivarāya granted the village of Pudūr to God Sachchidānanda. *Ins., Ced. Dts.*, p. 361, No. 88.

94. In the same place. (Telugu.) Records that a Karṇam gave in Ś. 1624, Chitrabhānu, a village to Narasimha Bhārati for lights and distribution of food to the people in the maṭha. *Ibid.*, p. 363, No. 89. [In his *Rep. Sans. Tam. MSS.*, Vol. II, Prof. Seshagiri Sastri gives a number of Narasimha Bhāratis who were later than Vidyāraṇya in the Śriṅgēri maṭha; but there is no evidence to connect the Bhārati of this epigraph with any of them.]

95. In the same place. A Kanarese record dated Ś. 1636, Vijaya, recording that Huṇḍa Prasannappa Nāyaka paid thirty pagodas yearly for feeding the inmates of the maṭha. *Ibid* No. 90.

96. In the same place. Records that in Ś. 1637, Manmatha, some land was given to Vidyāśaṅkara Bhārati by Haṇḍe Hanumappa Nāyakar. *Ins., Ced. Dts.*, p. 363, No. 91. See Prof. Seshagiri Sastri's *Rep., Sans. Tam. MSS.*, 1896–97, p. 11.

97. In charge of the Maṭha. A Kanarese grant in Kīlaka of thirty pagodas annually by Haṇḍe Rāmappa Nāyak. *Ins., Ced. Dts.*, p. 363, No. 92. See By. 67.

98. In the same place. A Telugu grant in Ś. 1653, Raudri, of two *muṇṭas* of land in a village by the Reḍḍis and Karṇams of the place. *Ibid.*, No. 93.

99. In charge of the Maṭha. (Kanarese.) Records in Ś. 1664, Dundubhi, the gift to Nrisimhabhārati of an annual allowance of Rs. 100. *Ibid.*, No. 94. See No. 94 above.

100. In the same place. (Telugu.) Records that "Dhulipala Achunnah" granted in Ś. 1645, Śōbhakrit, the village of Vīrarāmāpuram to the Maṭha.

101. In the same place. (Telugu.) Records grant in Ś. 1652, Sādhāraṇa, of the village of Punduṅgi to the Maṭha by Pedda Narasimha Nāyaḍu. *Ibid.*, No. 96.

102. In the same place. (Telugu.) Records that in Ś. 1684, Chitrabānu, Bāla Veṅkaṭa Reḍḍi gave the village of Gollapalle for Śrōtriyam rent of thirty pagodas. *Ibid.*, No. 97.

103. In the same place. (Telugu.) Records that in Ś. 1686, Tāraṇa, Rāja Rām Rāju Vīrabhadra Rao granted a village in the district of Mācherla to the Maṭha. *Ibid.*, No. 98.

104. In the same place. (Telugu.) Records that in Ś 1694, Nandana, Rāmappa Nāyaḍu gave the village of Gollapalle in the subdivision of Puppore to the Maṭha. *Ibid.*, No. 99.

105. In the same place. (Telugu.) Records that in Ś. 1175, Sivarāmbāva Gorpad issued a precept to the Reḍḍis and Karṇams of Puppūr to continue the above villages as usual. *Ibid.*, No. 100.

106. In the same place. (Telugu.) A record of F. 1209, in which Nārāyaṇ Rao, Amīl of "Secondurgud," ordered the Reḍḍis and Karṇams of Puppalūr to continue the above gift. *Ibid.*, No. 101.

107. In the same place. A Kanarese record, dated Ś. 1694, Nandana, to the effect that Siddarāmappa granted twelve pagodas every year from Siddammāpēṭa. *Ibid.*, No. 102. See By. 67.

108. In charge of the Maṭha. A Telugu record, dated Ś. 1695. Vijaya, recording that Kumāra Rāmappa Nāyani gave the village of Kammavārupalle to the Maṭha. *Ibid.*, p. 366, No. 103.

109. In the same place. (Kanarese.) Records that in Ś. 1695, Vijaya Mallappa Nāyani gave a village. *Ibid.*, No. 104.

110. In the same place. (Kanarese.) Records in the same year the grant of a village by Chimanāji Rao. *Ibid.*, No. 105.

111. In the same place. (Kanarese.) Records in H. 1194 the grant of the village of Koṇḍareḍḍipāḷam for a Śrōtriyam rent of fifty pagodas by Nawab Walaja. *Ins., Ced. Dts.*, No. 106.

112. In the same place. (Telugu.) Records that one Prabhākara Nāyaḍu gave in Ś. 1700, Viḷambi, the village of Viśvanāthapuram in the district of Mārella. *Ibid.*, No. 107.

113. In the same place. (Telugu.) Records that a Veṅkaṭādri Nāyuḍu gave in Ś. 1710, Pḷavaṅga, a village. *Ibid.*, No. 108.

114. In the same place. (Telugu.) Records in F. 1200, the regrant of the above village by the committee of Guṇṭur. *Ibid.*, No. 109.

115. In the same place. (Telugu.) Records in Ś. 1710, the gift of the village of Sattipalle in the Vinukoṇḍa district by Guṇḍarāyaḍu. *Ibid.*, No. 110.

116. In the same place. (Telugu.) The continuation of the above gift by the Committee of Guṇṭur in F. 1200. *Ibid.*, No. 111.

117. In the same place. (Telugu.) Rāja Vēṅkaṭēśvara Rao Masumdār, granted the village of Reṭṭappāḷam in Ś. 1715, Pramādīcha. *Ibid.*, No. 112.

118. In the same place. (Telugu.) Raja Nārāyaṇ Rao, Masumdār, gave in the same year the village of "Nuzallapulla," in the subdivision of "Nadallah." *Ibid.*, No. 113.

119. In the same place. (Telugu.) Gift of the village of Liṅgamguṇṭa in Ś. 1712, Sādhāraṇa, by Veṅkaṭaguṇḍa Rāyaḍu. *Ibid.*, No. 114.

120. In the same place. (Telugu.) Gift of the village of Pattapāḍu in the district of the "Five Mahals" by Kumāra Yāchamanāyaḍu in Ś. 1724, Dundubhi. *Ibid.*, No. 115. [The chief was the ruler of Veṅkaṭagiri from 1776 to 1804. He sided with the English against Haidar Ali.]

121. In the same place. (Telugu.) Records in Ś. 1726, Raktākshi, that Rāja Dāmarla Kumāra Veṅkaṭappa Nāyaḍu gave some land in Māmbākkam for feeding the people of the Maṭha. *Ibid.*, p. 368, No. 116. [This was the Kāḷahasti chief who slew in battle the brother of Nawab Mahomed Ali Khan. See *Vestiges of Madras*, p. 24.]

Puṭlampaḷḷi.

122. On a stone in the pagoda of Dhanakuṇḍamma in the south-east of the village. (Telugu.) Records that one Pedda Timmarasayya Gāru granted the village of Yāpaguṇṭa to the gods Bhairavēśvara and Ishṭakāmēśvara of Siddhāvaṭṭam. See *Ins., Ced. Dts.*, p. 331, No. 1.

Rudraiyāgāripalli.

123. On a stone south of the village. (Telugu.) Records in Ś. 1446, Tāraṇa, that Timmayyadēva Mahārāya, a feudatory of Kṛishṇadēva Rāya, granted a village for the expenses of the daily festivals of God Tiruvēṅgalanātha. *Ins., Ced. Dts.*, p. 333, No. 7.

Tādigoṭla.

124. On a stone in the village. (Telugu.) In Ś. 1193, Prajōtpatti, Brahmarākshasa Gaṇḍara Tripurāntakadēva Mahārāya granted a village near Chennūr to Brahmans. *Ibid.*, p. 355, No. 68.

Tollagaṅganapalli ("*Tallagumpulla*").

125. On a stone in the village. A Kanarese record, dated in Ś. 1685, Svabhānu. Tippa Reḍḍi of "Duggumpulla" built a stone well at "Tollogunganapulla." *Ibid.*, p. 356, No. 73.

Tuḍumulaḍinne.

126. On a stone near the Chenna Kēśava temple. (Sanskrit.) A record in Ś. 1455, Virōdhi, in the reign of Achyuta Rāya. *Ibid.*, p. 338, No. 19.

JAMMALAMADUGU TALUK.

Balapanagūḍūru.

127. On a stone in the temple east of the village. (Telugu.) One Sōmalarāju Timmarāju grants to the deity two *muṇṭas* of ground for a flower garden. See *Ins., Ced. Dts.*, p. 96, No. 155.

Bhimaguṇḍam.

128. On a stone near the Chenna Kēśava pagoda. A Telugu grant in Sarvadhāri recording that Gaṇḍikōṭa Rāja granted eight *muṇṭas* of land for the sculptor Kāśiliṅga Bhaṭṭu who carved the image of Chenna-Kēśava. *Ibid.*, p. 90, No. 126.

129. On a stone near the water pandal in the village. (Telugu.) One Nārāyaṇa, son of Tirumala Rāja of "Bhojanapullah," gave in Ś. 1479, Piṅgaḷa, in the reign of Sadāśiva Rāya, two *tūms* and six *muṇṭas* of land to Brahmans for the maintenance of the watershed. *Ibid.*, p. 90, No. 127.

130. On a stone north of the village. (Telugu.) Records that in Ś. 1477, Rākshasa, in the reign of Sadāśiva Rāya, certain Vipravinōdins granted their dues from Achyutarāyapuram to the deity. *Ibid.*, No. 128.

Bhūtamāpuram (*Bhūtapuri ?*).

131. On a stone near the hall at Bhūtapuri village. (Telugu.) Records that in Ś. 1461, Vikāri, Pedda Gōvindayya and three other Vipravinōdins granted this village to the God Chenna-Kēśava. *Ibid.*, p. 68, No. 33.

Bondalakunṭa.

132. On a stone near a well. A Telugu record of Bomma Nāyaḍu, son of Lakki Nāyaḍu, in Ś. 1433, Pramōdūta, in the reign of Kṛishṇa-dēva Rāya. Endows 5 *tūms* of land for the diggers of the well. See *Ins.*, *Ced. Dts.*, p. 6, No. 3.

133. On a stone in front of Chenna-Kēśava pagoda. A Telugu grant of Śiṅgayya Rāja, son of Chinna Timma Rāja, in Ś. 1466, Krōdhi, in the reign of Achyuta Rāya. Grant of 4½ *tūms* of land to the God. *Ibid.*, No. 4.

134. In the front pillar of the Hanumanta Rāya pagoda. (Telugu.) The same donor (as in the above) gave in Ś. 1467, Viśvāvasu, a piece of land to one Chittrāju Anantarāya. *Ibid.*, No. 5.

135. On a stone near the Vīrabhadra temple. (Telugu.) Records in Ś. 1480, Kāḷayukti, that Vīramushṭi Vīrayya and Nañjayya presented the income of Vīramushṭi people to Vīrabhadra. *Ibid.*, No. 6.

136. On a stone east of the village. (Telugu.) Records that Nandyāla Timma Rāja, feudatory of Śadāśiva Rāya, remitted the tax on local barbers in Ś. 1496, Plavaṅga. *Ibid.*, p. 7, No. 7.

137. On a stone in a paddy field. (Telugu.) A gift of 5 *tūms* by the same chief in Piṅgaḷa to one Kēśirāju Chinnappa. *Ibid.*, No. 8.

138. On a stone in front of the Chenna-Kēśava pagoda. (Telugu.) A grant of land to the deity in Ś. 1503, Vishu. Mentions Pemmasāni Timmayya Nāyaḍu and Tippa Reḍḍi. *Ibid.*, No. 9.

Bukkapaṭṇam.

139. On a stone south of the village. (Telugu.) Records that in the reign of Dēva Mahārāya, in Ś. 1353, Sādhāraṇa, all castes of people gave to Gods Vīrabhadra and Nārāyaṇadēva at Bukkapaṭṇam, besides 2 *kunṭas* of dry field and a garden, a fee from every individual from ½ to ¼ *Śuṅkam* on the three classes of marriage at Bukkapaṭṇam. *Ins.*, *Ced. Dts.*, p. 76, No. 69.

140. On a stone near Bukkapaṭṇam limits. (Telugu.) One "Coolapagarājā, son of Vijayadēvuḍu," gave the village of "Coodupi Cuntah to Balyamanaudha of Coducoonta." *Ibid.*, No. 70.

141. On a stone near a local canal. (Telugu.) Records in Ś. 1451 Virōdhi, that the inhabitants of Bukkapaṭṇam fixed the duties of 2 *kāśu* for each *bala* (bag ?) of cotton, 2 kāśu for that of pepper, 2 for jaggery and 2 per grain bag. *Ibid.*, No. 71.

142. On a stone in the Vīrabhadra pagoda. (Telugu.) Records that in Ś. 1471, Saumya, in the reign of Sadāśiva Rāya, the

Viramushti people gave to God Rāmalinga of Podatūr (Proddatur ?) the 3 pagodas they received from the Brahmans of Narasimhapuram agrahāram. *Ibid.*, No. 72.

143. On a stone in the Chennakēśava temple east of the village. (Telugu.) Records that in Ś. 1468, Parābhava, in the reign of Sadāśiva Rāya, the jugglers gave away the allowance they had been receiving from the Brahmans of Vīra-Naraśingapuram agrahāram to Gods Tiruvēngalanātha and Chenna-kēśava of Narasimhapuram. *Ibid.*, No. 73.

Chāmalūru.

144. On a stone near the temple. (Telugu.) Records that the Vipravinōdi Brahmans gave away, in the reign of Sadāśiva Rāya, the annual fees they had been receiving from the Brahmans of Chāmalūr to God Chenna-Kēśava. *Ins., Ced. Dts.*, p. 75, No. 65.

Chinna Muḍiyam.

145. On a stone in the street. (Telugu.) Records that in Ś. 1480, Kāḷayukti, Rāmarājayya Pīmmarāju Gāru, a feudatory of Sadāśiva Rāya, exempted the barbers of the village from taxes. *Ibid.*, p. 96, No. 154.

Choutapalli.

146. On a stone in front of the Narā-Nārāyaṇasvāmi pagoda. (Telugu.) Records that Mummuḍi Nāyaḍu, counsellor of Nandyāla Kṛishṇama Rāyalu, exempted in Ś. 1484, Dundubhi, the duties of weavers of the village so that they could build houses and reside there. *Ibid.*, p. 83, No. 97.

147. On a stone at the gate of the pagoda of Narasimhasvāmi. (Telugu.) Records that Śrinivāsāchārya, son of Kṛishṇamāchārya of Tirumala Bukkapaṭṇam, repaired in year Vikāri, the temple with wooden beams. *Ibid.*, p. 83, No. 98.

Dānavulapāḍu.

148. 331 *of* 1905.—(Sanskrit in Kānarese.) On a pedestal in front of the Jaina image in the ruined Jaina temple recently discovered. A record of the Rāshṭrakūṭa king Nityavarsha. Records that the king caused the pedestal to be made for the bathing ceremoney of a Jaina saint named Śānti. [Nityavarsha was the same as Indra IV, brother of Kṛishṇa III.]

149. 332 *of* 1905.–(Kanarese.) On a slab set up in the same locality. Records the *niśidhi* of a merchant of Penugoṇḍe, whose preceptor was the Jaina teacher Kanakakīrtidēva. [See N.A. 385 and 744 for references to the latter and the note thereon.]

150. 333 *of* 1905.—(Kanarese poetry and Sanskrit.) On a pillar set up in the same place. A record of the time of the Rāshṭrakūṭa king Indra III (915—17), named Indra IV in *Antiquities*, II,

p. 233. It records a praśasti of the daṇḍanāyaka Śrīvijaya, who belonged to the Balikula and bore the title *Anupamakavi.* The inscription was written (i.e., composed) by his accountant Guṇavarman. [Poet Kavīśvara in his *Kavirājamārga* quotes a Śri Vijaya several times. But Dr. Fleet has shown (*Ind. Antq.*, XXXIII, 270) that Kavīśvara was patronised by Nripatuṅga Amōghavarsha I (814—78); so the Śri Vijaya referred to in *kavirājamārga* was evidently an earlier man than the one referred to in the present epigraph. See *Ep. Rep.*, 1906, p. 80. Also *Ep. Ind.*, X, pp. 147—53.]

151. 334 *of* 1905.—(Kanarese.) On an other pillar set up in the same place. Records the *niśidhi* of a Vaiśya woman from Penugoṇḍa. For examples of *niśidhi* see S.A. 389 and By. 456.

152. 335 *of* 1905.—(Kanarese.) On the third pillar set up in the same place. Records the *niśidhi* of a Jaina teacher. Mentions Kurmāri.

153. 336 *of* 1909.—(Sanskrit and Telugu.) On the fifth pillar set up in the same place. A damaged record dated in Ś. 1319, Īśvara. Seems to be the *niśidhi* of a merchant.

154. 337 *of* 1905.—On a broken pillar lying in the same place. A fragment of record. Mentions Kurumāri Raṭṭaguḷḷa.

155. 338 *of* 1905.—On the sixth pillar set up in the same place. Records the *niśidhi* of a merchant from Penugoṇḍe and of his wife.

155-A. 339 *of* 1905.—(Kanarese.) On a mutilated slab lying on the bank of the river Penneru. A fragment of record of the Chāḷukya king Vijayāditya. Mentions Bhūpāditya.

155-B. 340 *of* 1905.—(Telugu.) On a slab lying in the bed of the same river. In archaic characters. A damaged record. The date and name of the king are perhaps on the other side of the huge stone.

155-C. 341 *of* 1905.—(Telugu.) On a broken pillar lying on the bank of the same river. A mutilated and damaged record of Kapyana, son of . . . la-Mahārāja. Mentions Kuṟumaṟi.

Dēvaguḍi.

156. 342 *of* 1905.—(Telugu.) On a slab set up on the north side of the central shrine in the Talakāntamma temple. The Vijayanagara king Kṛishṇarāya records in Ś. 1437, Dhātri, a *daśavanda* gift for the merit of the king and of Sālva-Gōvindaraja-Voḍiyalu (Uḍaya). See Ap. 205 for another epigraph of this chief.

157. 343 *of* 1905.—(Telugu.) On another slab set up in the same place. A damaged record of the Vijayanagara king Kṛishṇarāya, dated Ś. 1440, Bahudhānya. Records another *daśavanda* gift for the merit of the same two persons. The village is called Dēviguḍi.

158. 344 *of* 1905.—(Telugu.) On a pillar in the mukha-maṇṭapa of the same temple. A damaged record, dated Ś. 1202, Vikrama.

159. 345 *of* 1905.—(Telugu.) On a pillar set up in the court-yard of the same temple. Dated in the reign of the Vijayanagara king Vīrapratāpa Dēvarāya-Mahārāya (II), son of Harihārāya II, in Ś. 1328, Vyaya. Records gift of land at Dānavulapāḍu to the temple of Taḷakaṇṭadēvi by the king after his coronation. The order was carried out by Nāgappa-Daṇṇāyaka.

160. 346 *of* 1905.—(Kanarese.) On a *vīragal* set up in the same place. Records in Śukla, that Mahāmaṇḍalēśvara Bhīmarasa met Chandra-Daṇḍanāyaka of Kaṭaka near Kuṛumaṛi, killed two of his horses and a cavalier together with his charger, and himself fell. The hero was a devotee of Taḍalakaṭidēvi.

161. 347 *of* 1905.—(Kanarese.) On another viragal set up in the same place. A record of the Western Chāḷukya king Jagadē-kamalla (II, 1138—49) dated in his thirteenth year, Śukla, saying that a subordinate of the Mahāmaṇḍalēśvara Bhīmarasa of Kuṛumaṛi fell in a fight with Mādhuvarasa, the brother-in-law of Chandra Daṇḍanāyaka of Kaṭāka, referred to in the above epigraph.

162. 348 *of* 1905.—(Telugu.) On a slab set up close to the main gōpura of the same temple. Dated in the reign of the Vijayanagara king Vīrapratāpa Sadāśivadēva-Mahārāya, in Ś. 1468, Prābhava. Records a gift by Mahāmaṇḍalēśvara Koṇḍrāju-Chikka Timmayadēva Māhāraju. See By. 326.

Dombara-Nandyāla.

163. 353 *of* 1905.—(Telugu.) On a slaḅ built into the east wall of the central shrine in the Chennakēśavasvāmin temple. An epi-graph of the Vijayanagara king Vīrapratāpa-Kṛishṇadēva-Mahā-rāya. Records in Ś. 1443, Vrisha, gift by three chiefs of the taxes payable at the village of Nandēla (which belonged to the district), of Rēnāḍu in the Ghaṇḍikōṭa-śīma, for a perpetual lamp in the temple of Chennakēśavadēva. The grant was made on the occasion of the consecration of the temple. *Ins., Ced. Dts.*, p. 64, No. 17.

Ghaṇḍikōṭa.

[For an excellent historical account of the place see *Cuddapah Gazr.*, p. 191—4.]

164. 485 *of* 1906.—(Telugu.) On the south wall of the prākāra of the ruined Raṅganāyaka temple. Dated in the reign of the Vijayanagara king Vīra-Sadāśivadēva-Mahārāya. Records in Ś. 1497, Piṅgaḷa, gift of land to the temple of Raghunāyakalu at Ghaṇḍikōṭa, by Mahāmaṇḍalēśvara China-Avubalēśvaradēva-Mahārāju, son of Avubalēśvaradēva Mahārāju and grandson of

Avubalarājayadēva Mahārāju of Nandyāḷa. See *Ins.*, *Ced. Dts.*, p. 61, No. 3.

165. 486 *of* 1906.—(Telugu.) On the same wall. Dated in the reign of the Vijayanagara king Vīrapratāpa Vīra-Sadāśivadēva-Mahārāya. Records in Ś. 1467, Viśvāvasu, gift of village by Nandyāla Timmayadēva Mahārāju, grandson of Nandyāla Avubalēśvaradēva Mahārāju to the temple of Raghunāthadēva on the Ghaṇḍikōṭa-durga. *Ibid.*, p. 61, No. 4.

166. 487 *of* 1906.—(Telugu.) On the north wall of the same prākāra. Records in Bhava, gift to the Raghunāyaka temple at Ghaṇḍikōṭa by a merchant (Kōmaṭi).

167. 488 *of* 1906.—(Telugu.) On the east face of a slab set up in a field near the Kaṅgiṇimahāl, in the same village. Records in Bahudhānya, remission of taxes in favour of the fishermen living in the new street at Kammadurgam by Mahāmaṇḍalēśvara Narasimharājayyadēva Mahārāju of Nandyāla. See *Mack. MSS.*, *Ins.*, *Ced. Dts.*, p. 61, No. 5.

168. 489 *of* 1906.—(Telugu.) On a boulder near the Nagadhari, outside the fort, in the same village. Records in Ānanda, gift of two gardens to the temple of Channarāya at Nāgadhāri by Kṛishṇappa-Timmarāju-Nāgarāju-Veṅkaṭrāju-Koṇḍrāju of Arāvīṭi for the merit of Raṅgapatirāju.

169. 490 *of* 1906.—(Persian.) On a boulder near the waterfall in the garden called Parebagh on the bank of the Penneru river, at the foot of the Ghaṇḍikōṭa hill.

170. On a stone on the south of Mādhavasvāmi pagoda. (Telugu.) Records that in Ś. 1478, Naḷa, in the reign of Sadāśiva Rāyulu, Nandyāla Timmarāju gave allowances in different villages for the worship of Aṅkālamma. *Ins.*, *Ced. Dts.*, p. 62, No. 6.

171. On a stone near the east gate of the above. A Telugu record of Nandyāla Ahōbala Mahārāja in Manmatha, exempting the taxes of the washers. *Ibid.*, No. 7.

172. On a stone on the bank of Pināki river. (Telugu.) Records that in Ś. 1245, Dundubhi, Gaṅgareḍḍigāru granted a flower garden for the worship of the Goddess. *Ibid.*, No. 8.

173. On a stone behind the above. (Telugu.) Jaghapati "Cuṅchirajoo and Vayadava Chodavarajoo" granted in Krōdhana 3½ *kuṇṭas* of dry field for betel-nuts. *Ibid.*, No. 9.

174. On a stone near the pagoda of Yāgaussuṇda Narasimhasvāmi. (Sanskrit.) Records that in Ś. 1297, Rākshasa, Bukkarāyalu (I) re-established the God Yōgānanda Narasimhasvāmi and erected a pagoda. *Ibid.*, No. 11.

175. On a stone on the west of the pagoda. (Telugu.) Records that Chinnamanāyani Gāru, son of Annamanāyanigāru erected a pagoda of Āḷvārs in Plavaṅga. *Ibid.*, No. 12.

176. On a stone near the mosque in a garden. (Persian.) Records that in H. 1102 "Sahusan Daravashu" erected a mosque. *Ibid.*, No. 13. The chief was probably an officer or one of the successors of Meer Jumla, the first Nawab of the place under Golconda rule. See *Cuddapah Gazetteer*, p. 193.

177. On a stone in the garden of Dareep bagh on the south of Pinãki river. (Persian). Records that in H. 1178, Syed Miah, Subadar of Cuddapah, erected a water-sluice near the bank of the river. *Ins., Ced. Dts.*, p. 64, No. 14. [Miah might have been one of the two sons of the Nawab Abdul Nabi Khan.]

Gaṅgãpuram.

178. On a stone in the dam of the local lake. (Telugu.) Records that the lake was dug in the time of Krishṇadēva Rãya in Ś. 1432, Pramōdūta. See *Ins., Ced. Dts.*, p. 82, No. 93.

Garisalũru.

179. On a stone in the ruined temple north-east of the village. (Telugu.) Records that Narasabhūpãluḍu gave in Ś. 1453, Khara, in the reign of Achyuta Rãya, twelve *muṇṭas* of dry land in the village to the Chenna Kēśava temple, besides building the *Mukha-maṇṭapa*. *Ibid.*, p. 86, No. 110.

Gorigenũru.

180. On a stone near the hill-fort. (Telugu.) Records that in Ś. 1682, Vikrama, during the management of Veṅkaṭa Reḍḍi at Jammalamuḍugu that the Reḍḍis of the village built the hill-fort. *Ibid.*, p. 93, No. 140.

Guṇḍḷakuṇṭa.

181. On a stone in the Chennakēśava pagoda. (Telugu.) Records that Pãpa Timmarãja gave in Ś. 1473, Virōdhi, in the reign of Sadãśiva Rãya, two *kuṇṭas* of dry land in the *Hora* village to a Brahman Chennamiah. *Ibid.*, p. 95, No. 147.

182. On a stone south-east of the above. (Telugu.) Grant of their annual allowances by the Vipravōḍins in Ś. 1473, Paritãpi, to God Chenna-Kēśava. *Ibid.*, No. 148.

183. On a stone near a local well. (Telugu.) Records that in Ś. 1581, Vikãri, "Vibharam Sultan, the Prime Minister of Kaunavaji Coli Saheb," gave to Chinna Guruvayya some land for excavating a well. *Ibid.*, p. 95, No. 149.

184. On a stone in the Chennakēśava pagoda. (Telugu.) Records that Rãmarãja Timma Rãja exempted in Ś. 1480, Kãḷa-yukti, in the reign of Sadãśiva Rãya, the local barbers from taxation. *Ibid.*, No. 150.

185. On a stone in the same pagoda. An effaced Telugu grant of Sadāśiva Rāya in Ś. 1489, Prabhava.

Jammalamaḍugu.

The following records are taken from the *Mack. MSS., Ins., Ced. Dts.*, pp. 17—61. Most of them, I regret to say, are mere paper grants and so do not come under *epigraphs.* But having listed and numbered them, I have not thought it necessary to remove them. Almost all these are in Mahratti and Persian.

186. In charge of Buddu Khan. (Mahratti.) Records that in Ś. 1193, Mir Saheb issued an order to the Amil of Jammalamaḍugu, to pay monthly 3½ pagodas for the mosque of Abdul Syed Khan *Ins., Ced. Dts.*, p. 17, No. 1. See next record.

187. In charge of Buddu (Bade ?) Khan. (Mahratti.) Records that Tippu Sultan issued a precept in H. 1196, to Timma Reḍḍi of Jammalamaḍugu to pay monthly 3½ pagodas for the mosques of Abdul Syed Khan. *Ibid.*, No. 2. [Abdul Syed Khaṉ was the first and last Nawab of Jammalamaḍugu, to whom the town and surrounding territory were granted as a jaghir by Tippu. See *Cuddapah Gazetteer*, pp. 188-89.

188. In charge of Buddu Khan. (Telugu.) Records that in H. 1114, Bahadur Khan issued an order to the Amil to pay daily a gold *paṇam* to the God Veṅkaṭēśvarasvāmi. *Ibid.*, No. 3.

189. Records in Telugu and Persian that in H. 1205, "Baramahal Rāja Tajopunt" issued an order to the Amil Dēśapāṇḍya-Dēśamuk to pay daily a gold *paṇam* to the God Veṅkaṭēśvarasvāmi. *Ins., Ced. Dts.*, p. 18, No. 4.

190. Records in Mahratti and Persian that in H. 1210, Amin Saheb issued an order to the Amil to pay daily two annas for the mosque. *Ibid.*, No. 5.

191. Records in Mahratti and Persian that in H. 1210, Amin Saheb issued an order to the Amil of Jammalamaḍugu to pay four annas daily for the mosque. *Ibid.*, No. 6.

192. Records that in H. 1251, Sayud Hamid Khan ordered a Shaikdar to pay two annas daily to Fakir Rahiman. *Ibid.*, No. 7.

193. Mahomed Sayud orders in H. 1167, the payment of two annas daily from the duties of the place to the same Fakir. *Ibid.*, No. 8.

194. A similar grant of the same officer in H. 1176. *Ibid.*, No. 9.

195. A grant by the same chief in H. 1171, to various holy people. *Ibid.*, No. 10.

196. An order of Abdul Halim Khan to Veṅkaṭa Mustājur in H. 1171, to pay four pagodas to Fakir. *Ibid.*, No. 11.

197. An order of the same Nawab in H. 1176, to pay four annas daily to Abdur Rahiman. *Ibid.*, No. 12.

198. An order of Nawab Masum Khan in H. 1176, to Veṅka Mustājur for payment of two annas to the same Fakir. *Ins., Ced. Dts.*, p. 18, No. 13.

199. An order of the same chief in H. 1169, to the Amil of Jammalamaḍugu to pay four annas daily to the same Fakir. *Ibid.*, No. 14.

200. An order of Amin Saheb in H. 1210, for payment of two annas. *Ibid.*, No. 15.

201. In charge of Nāgambhaṭ and another. An order of Amin Saheb in H. 1185, to the Amil for payment of half *paṇam* to Śēshabhāṭṭa. *Ibid.*, No. 16.

202. A record of Mahomed Amin Khan in H. 1210, issuing a similar order of payment to Śēshabhaṭ. *Ibid.*, No. 17.

The rest of the records of this place are given, for the sake of convenience, in the form of a tabular statement.

Granter.	To whom granted.	Date.	Amount.
203. Bāramahal Rāja Tajopunt.	Śobabhaṭ ...	H. 1205.	Half *paṇam* by Amil. *Ibid.* 18.
204. Do.	Do. ...	H. 1205.	One-third *paṇam*. *Ibid.* 19.
205. Bālaveṅkaṭa Reḍḍi. (Telugu.)	Three persons ...	...	Four *tūms* of land. *Ibid.* 20.
206. Mahajid Khan. (Mahratti.)	Mirza Y-Nallaudin.	H. 1117.	Half *paṇam* daily. *Ibid.* 21.
207. Do.	Mosque ...	H 1179.	Appointing Jayamalluḍīn for the mosque.
208. Bālaveṅkaṭa Reḍḍi.	Josrama Fakir...	H. 1182.	One gold paṇam by ninety villages during Moharrum.
209. Kṛishṇāji Veṅkāji Gāru. (Telugu.)	Do. ...	H. 1887.	Similar to the above.
210. Do.	Do. ...	H. 1188.	Do. (Telugu.)
211. Amil Kāmappa ...	Do. ...	H. 1191.	Do.
212. Amil Rāyalu Veṅkāji.	Do. ...	H. 1196.	Do.
213. Kṛishṇāji Amil ...	Do. ...	H. 1196.	Do.
214. Obala Reḍḍi ...	Do. ...	H. 1197.	Do.
215. Narasu Veṅkāji Amil.	Do. ...	H. 1195.	Do.
216. Vali Mahomed Amil.	Do. ...	H. 1196.	Do.
217. Gulam Mahomed Amil of Ghaṇḍikōṭa.	Do. ...	H. 1217.	Do.
218. Kōnēri Rao Amil ...	Do. ...	H. 1206.	Do.
219. Nārāyaṇ Rao Amil...	Do. ...	H. 1206.	Do.
220. Krishṇāji Kōdaṇḍ ...	Do. .	H. 1201.	One paṇam for each village to be paid by Reḍḍies and Karṇams of Muḍiyam, Pālore and Ghaṇḍikōṭa.
221. Chadupu Nārāyaṇ Reḍḍi.	Do. ...	Virōdhikrit.	Do.
222. Dilawer Dowla ...	Do. ...	H. 1207.	Do.
223. Koṇḍa Reḍḍi ...	...	H. 1203.	Do.
224. Veṇkatareḍḍi ...	...	H. 1208.	Do.
225. Mahomed Amin Khan Bahadur.	...	H. 1210.	Do.

Granter.	To whom granted.	Date.	Amount.
226. "Jaligani Kṛishṇappa".	...	...	One paṇam for each village to be paid by Reḍḍies and Karṇams of Mudiyam, Pālore and Ghaṇḍikōṭa.
227. "Mukkamulla Veṅkata Reḍḍi."	...	...	Do.
228. Amil Veṅkāji ...	...	H. 1211.	Do.
229. Amil Mirza Khan ...	...	H. 1212.	Do.
230. Chundolall	...	H. 1209.	Do.
231. Mukkumulla Veṇkata Reḍḍi.	...	H. 1214.	Do.
232. Hari Rao of Kilicla-paṭṭi.	...	H. 1214.	Do.
233. Ahmedshah Padshah.	Mosque of Sumshud Khan.	(Telugu and Persian.)	Two annas daily and puṭṭi and 12 *tūms* of land
234. The Reḍḍies and Karṇams of Danavulapāṭi.	Kristṇappa ...	Ś. 1687, Telugu.	Eight kuṇṭas of land for seventy pagodas in the village of Danavulapāḍu.
235. Kalim . Khan Mayana.	Kristṇamma ...	H. 1180.	Do. (Mahratti).
236. Bālaveṅkaṭa Reḍḍi.	Rāmakristṇam Pantulu Telugu.	Ś. 1687.	Allowed to inhabit the above village and enjoy it.
237. Veṇkāji and Kṛishṇāji.	Do.	H. 1188.	Do.
238. The Reḍḍies and Karṇams of Dêvaguḍi.	Rāyalu Pantulu.	Ś. 1697.	Two puṭṭies and two tūms of wet and dry land in Māramāpore village.
239. Fakir Mahommed Amil of Ghaṇḍikoṭa.	Vengia	1198.	One kuṇṭa and ten tūms of dry field, one and a half Kuṇṭas and eleven tūms of wet field in the Pada (Pedda) Dandalore village.
240. Do.	Do.	Do.	Do.
241. Nawab Naḍnam Khan.	Do.	17 of Rajub.	Do.
242. Do.	Do.	1198.	Do.
243. Nawab Khadayagani Saheb.	Do.	Do.	Do.
244. Nawab Naknam Khan.	Do.	1090	Do.
245. Nawab Khadayagini Saheb.	Do.	Do.	Do.
246. Syed Davud Khan	Do	Do.	Three kuṇtas of land in the village of Pedda-Daṇdlore.
247. Nawab Khadayagini.	Do.	1070	A Cowle to Venkiah to enjoy the above land for the labour of digging a tank.
248. Venkāji and Kṛishṇāji.	Do.	F. 114	An order to the Reḍḍies and Karṇams of Padadandlore, to restore the kānams to the different persons.
249. Do. ...	Do.	1198	Three kuṇtas and six tūms.
250. Syed Abdul Rasul ...	Do.	Khara.	An order to repair the tank with the rent of his land.
251. Guzzala Vobala Reḍḍi.	Do.	1216	An order to inspect the work of the tank, executed by Sobayya.

	Granter.	To whom granted.	Date.	Amount.
252.	Nawab Rahim Khan.	Vengia	H. 1185.	A precept to the Dēśamuk and Dēśa Pāṇḍu to continue the village of Tuguṭla-Pulla to Raffee Saheb.
253.	Sakulli Mahommed.	Do.	H. 1196.	Do.
254.	Raja Tajapunt Bahdur.	(Mahratti) ...	H. 1215.	Do.
255.	Do.	(Telugu) ...	H. 1210.	Do.
256.	Nawab Rustum Dowlah.	Do. ...	H. 1207.	Do.
257.	Nawab Reḍḍi ...	...	T. 1219.	Do.
258.	Canogovi Visaji Bhāskara. (In the possession of Kāmanūr Agrahāram Brahmans.)	Inhabitants of "Luchmanbapuram" (Lakshmāmbapuram).	...	Three kuṇṭas of land in Kāmanūr and Godiganore villages in nineteen shares.
259.	The Reḍḍies and Karṇams of Sidhigapulla. (In the possession of Sidigapulla Brahmans.)	Sōmayājulu (?)	...	A portion of land in the village of "Sidhigapulla".
260.	Bālavenkaṭa Reddi.	...	F. 1171.	Do.
261.	Reḍḍies and Karṇams of Palore. (In charge of Achyuta Narasim.)	Achunta (?) Vamamna.	S. 1689.	Five kuṇṭas of lands in the village of Gōpālapuram for twenty-five pagodas.
262.	Do.	Do.	Do.	One kuṇṭa of dry field in the village of Palore
263.	"Mahomed Shah Padushah; Cavidulla Khan Killadar".	Daughter of Mahommed Shah Fakir.	1156 Sun (Persian and Telugu).	Five tūms of land in the pass of Ghaṇḍikōṭa.
264.	Mahomed Shah; Cavidulla Khan, Killedār Gaṇḍikōṭa.	Badurudin, son of Shaik Mahomed.	26 Zuloos (Persian and Telugu).	A garden of Śankasalum.
265.	Sha Alam Mureed; Mahomed Zafur Killadar.	Daughter of Shaik Mahommed.	38 Do.	Five tūms of land in the pass of "Divarconah".
266.	Alam Padusha Gazi, Nabi Khan Killadar.	Salil Durusha ...	1119.	Five tūms of land in the "Abyabed".
267.	In the reign of Alamgir Padshā, Mahomed Nabi Khan.	Shaik Mahommed.	1135.	Garden of Śunkasāri (Sunkasāla ?)
268.	In the reign Shah Alum Padsha; Mahomed Nabi Khan Killadar of Gaṇḍikōṭa.	Mustafur Durvasha.	F. 1117.	Five tūms of dry land in the village of "Yatore and Badadore."
269.	In the reign Alangir Padshā; Zulfikar Khan.	Kalif Mustafur...	1109.	A village.
270.	Alim Khan	Hussain Beg Khaṭla.	1184.	A village. (It is in Mahratti and Persian.)
271.	Tippu Sultan ...	... ..	H. 1199.	A precept to continue above.
272.	Raja Ullikhan ...	Hussain Beg ...	H. 1193.	Do.

Granter.	To whom granted.	Date.	Amount.
273. Sayud Nahajeb ...	......	H. 1191.	Order to Rahim to discontinue receipt of two pagodas from the renter for manufacturing powder
274. Shah Alum; Nabi Khan.	Kalim Khalim...	40 ?	Fifteen tūms of land in Yeṭṭore, etc. (Telugu and Persian.)
275. Do.	Kalim Nāik ...	1133 Sun	Lands in various villages. (Telugu and Persian.)
276. Do.	......	1233 Sun	Appointed Sakhu David as Khaji.
277. Zulfikhar Khan ..	Moha Sinhaji .	1109 Sun	Order to pay daily one rupee from Jammalamudugu District.
278. Mahommed Shah; Yannudkhan.	A Khaji ..	1132.	A similar order from 'Ullela Purgana.' (Jillela ?)
279. Mayana Abdul Fati Khan.	Do. ..	1134.	Do.
280. Hamadut Nabi Mayana; Halim Khan.	Khaji Mahommed Fazul.	1177.	A similar order to Rājappāḷam District.
281. Mahommed Nabi ...	Do.	1186 Sun	Four tūms of land.
282. Nawab Hammed-ul-Nabi.	Do.	H. 1186	Order to Dēśmuk and Dēsapaṇḍyas of Jammalamaḍugu to grant four tūms of land and daily ¼ seer of oil.
283. Sadāśivarāya; Timmappa-Nāidu	A deity (Ganga ?) (A C. P. in Telugu.)	Ś. 1468, Parābhava.	Levied a tax on the Bōyas, viz., one paṇam during marriage, one muṇṭa of rice per 100 betels and cloth on occasions.
284. Tirumaladēva Mahārāya. (Telugu C.P.)	Chinnama Cheṭṭi (?)	Ś 1487 Rudhirōtgāri.	Four tūms in Padattūr for digging a canal. (Proḍḍattur ?)
285. Reddies and Karṇams of Kōṭalapulla. P. G. (Telugu.)	Sarvadhāri ? ...	Ś. 1593 Kara.	Four tūms of land for building fort and village.
286. Vāmāji Padshah ...	Shaha Ulla in Telugu and Persian.	H 1174	The village of Dharapulla for mosque of Shaha Ulli, in Gaṇḍikōṭa District.
287. Alangir; Azuf Khan.	Mahommed Durvaha in Telugu and Persian.	47 Z.	Twenty *Begas* in Dombara-Nandyala for the mosque at Rājupāḷam.
288. Alangir Pādsha; Azuf Khan.	......	49 Z.	Do.
289. Mahomed Shah; Kavidilla Khan, Killadar of Gaṇḍikōṭa.	Mahomed Durvaha. Mahratta and Telugu.	H, 1164.	Eight muṇṭas of land in the same village.
290. Abdul Khader Khan; Mayana.	Rashun Khan ...	1136 Sun	Quarter land at Diguvapaṭam village.
291. Kavidilla Khan ...	(Telugu and Persian.)	1156 Sun	Above continued.
292. Do. ...	Do.	Do.	A garden in the same village.
293. Ananta Pantulu ...	Kōnēri ? Venkaṭādri Bhaṭ.	Ś. 1602 Raudri Telugu.	Village of Nolamitalapalle for Śrōtriyam rent of 10 pagodas.
294. Narasa Kēsava, Tarifdar of Gaṇḍikōṭa.	Akkala Somajulu-(?)	Ś. 1623 Vishu.	Land for garden in the village of Kumbaladinne.

	Granter.	To whom granted.	Date.	Amount.
295.	Srīnivāsa Tarif-dar...	Akkala Sōmayājulu (?)	S. 1618, Dhātu.	Grant of above village for Srōtriyam rent of 80 pagodas
296.	Narasakēsava Tarif-dar.	Do.	1620 Bahu-dhānya	Same as above.
297.	Rāmaṇṇa	Do.	..	Villages of Bhūdamāpuram and Kumbāla-dinne.
298.	In the reign of Thanisha ; Narasakēsava Tarifdar.	Alkana (Akkaṇṇa ?) Sōmayājulu.	1633	One kuṇṭa and 15 tūms of land in Bolumāpuram.
299.	Do.	Do.	1633	Village of Bhūtamāpuram for 201 pagodas or Śrotriyam.
300.	Nawab Abdul Musum Khan ; Bālavēnkaṭa Reḍḍi?	Kāsi Bhaṭ and Rāma Bhaṭ	...	One kuṇṭa land at Kumbala-dinne.
301.	Do.	Aiyavārulu Sāstrulu.	1684, Chitra-bhānu.	Two kuṇṭas in Mādhava-puram.
302.	Acharasu Rangā-chārlu ? (In charge of Śrīnivāsachari.)	Kṛishṇamā-chārlu.	1615, Śrīmukhi.	Fifteen tūms of land in Yāpūr.
303.	Do.	Do.	Do.	Six tūms of land in Guṇḍā-varam.
304.	Do.	Do.	Do.	Ten tūms at Yāpūr.
305.	Do.	Do	Do.	Village of Aiyavāṛi voola? for 5 pagodas' Śrōtriyam rent.
306	Sankaradi Narasu, Amildār.	A Reḍḍi (Canu and Basi Reḍḍi ?).	1661, Sidhārthi.	Land in "Vodirata".
307.	The people of Jammalamadugu.	Do.	Do.	Continued the above.

Kāllutla.

308. On a stone near a wall north-west of the village. Records in Telugu that in Ś. 1425 Svabhānu, Tippa Rāju granted 10 *tums* and 2 muṇṭas of dry field for raising a *pacota* for the well to provide water for bullocks. *Ins., Ced. Dts.*, p. 90, No. 129.

Kosinēpalli.

309. 408 *of* 1904.—(Telugu.) On three faces of a pillar lying near the thrashing floor. A record of a Chōḷa-Mahārāju who is said to have belonged to the Solar race, the Kāśyapa gōtra and the family of Karikāla, and who ruled over Renāṇḍu. [The king was most probably identical with Mahēndravikramavarman's father, Puṇyakumāra of the Cuddappah-Chōḷa line. See Nos. 453 and 455.]

310. 409 *of* 1904.—(Telugu.) On a slab lying in the same place. Records in Siddhārthin, a private gift. *Ins., Ced. Dts.*, p. 7, No. 11. A Śrōtriyam is purchased and then given away as a private gift.

311. 410 *of* 1904.—(Telugu.) On a slab set up opposite to the Āñjanēya temple in the same village. A record of Vijayanagara king Vīrapratāpa Sadāśivadēva-Mahārāya in Ś. 1476, Ānanda. Records that Kosanēpalle belonged to the Chernuri-śīma and was also called Harihararāyapura. See *Ins., Ced. Dts.*, p. 7, No. 10. The latter says that the grant was made for the festival of Tiruvēṅgalanātha.

Mādhavapuram.

312. On a stone in the Hanumanta pagoda. (Telugu.) Records that one Haridāsa Rāju gave some land to one Veṅkaṭarāyulu. *Ins., Ced. Dts.*, p. 68, No. 34.

Mailavaram.

313. On a pillar in the temple. (Telugu.) Records that in a certain Virōdhikrit, Rāmarāja Rāmayyagāru erected the Bōgha-Maṇṭapam. *Ibid.*, p. 64, No. 15.

314. On a stone near the same. (Telugu.) Records that Malla Timmuḍu Cheṭṭi, son of Peppiśeṭṭi, gave some land in Plava. *Ibid.*, No. 16.

Moraguḍi.

315. On a stone in the ruined Chennakēśava pagoda. (Telugu.) Records that the Vipravinōdins granted to the deity the duties they had been receiving from Viṭṭhala Agrahāra on the Saṅkrānti day. *Ibid.*, p. 64, No. 18.

Mucchumarṛi.

316. On a stone in the Mādhavarāya pagoda. (Telugu.) Records that in Ś. 1454, Achutarāya granted the village to the deity. *Ibid.*, p. 81, No. 91.

317. On a stone in a field. (Telugu.) Records that Immaḍi Dēvarāja (II, 1422—49), granted in Ś. 1362, Raudri, some land to Gods Raṅganātha and Gōpinātha for flower garden. *Ibid.*, p. 82, No. 92.

Muddanūr.

318. 405 *of* 1904.—(Telugu.) On a slab set up in a field by the side of the road from Chilamkūru. A record of Chōḷa Mahārāju. The king is described as in No. 309 above. Śirumbūru is mentioned. Records gift of land and an oil-mill to Ādityabhaṭāra. See No. 309, above.

319. 406 *of* 1904.—(Telugu.) On a slab lying in the courtyard of the Śiva temple. A record of Chōḷa Mahārājulu. The slab is broken at the bottom and bears at the top a tiger with a twisted tail. Mentions Chilkanūru (vide Chilamkūru.) See No. 309 above.

320. 407 *of* 1904.—(Telugu.) On a slab lying on the compound wall of the same temple. Records in Ś. 1565, Vishu, gift of a pillar by a Reḍḍi to the Chennakēśava Perumāḷ temple at Muddanūru. The cyclic year quoted corresponds to Ś. 1564 current.

Nagamaladinne (Namala Dinnah).

321. On a stone in the village. (Telugu.) Records that in the reign of Achyuta Rāya, Ś. 1439, Īśvara, the learned Brahmans of the village paid the taxes for the deity for conducting a festival. *Ins., Ced. Dts.*, p. 86, No. 111.

322. On a stone south of the above. (Telugu.) Records that Rāmarāja Timmarāja exempted the local barbers from taxes in Ś. 1480, Kaḷayukti, in the reign of Sadāśivarāya. *Ibid.*, p. 86, No. 112. See Cg. 717, By. 451, etc., for Timmarāja. He was evidently the same as Viṭṭala.

323. On a stone north of the above. (Telugu.) Records that in the reign of Veṅkaṭapaṭi I, in Ś. 1533, Virōdhi, Jallaraṅgapati Rāju and the local inhabitants granted some land to one Tirumalaiya for casting an image of Chennakēśava. *Ibid.*, p. 87, No. 113.

324. On a stone near the water pandal. (Telugu.) Records that in Ś. 1466, in the reign of Sadāśivarāya, Chinna Timmarāju gave the village as a free gift to Brahmans. *Ibid.*, p. 87, No. 114, See S.A. 469 for Chinna Tumma.

Nallapalli.

325. On a stone south west of the village. (Telugu.) Records that in Ś. 1478, Naḷa, in the reign of Sadāśivarāya the Vīramushṭi people granted away their allowance in the village to God Viśvēśvara. *Ibid.*, p. 7, No. 12.

326. On a stone on the south-west of Chennakēśava pagoda, (Telugu.) Records that in the reign of Sadāśivarāyalu, in Ś. 1478, Naḷa, Vipravinōdi Vīramushṭi Vīrappa granted the allowances they had been receiving from the village to God Viśvēśvara. *Ibid.*, p. 8, No. 13.

327. On a stone in the compound wall of the Chennakēśava pagoda. (Telugu.) Records that in the reign of Sadāśivarāyalu, in Ś. 1476, Ānanda, Vipravinōdi Siddhayya granted the allowance due from the agrahāram Brahmans for the festival of Chennakēśava Perumāḷ. *Ibid.*, No. 14.

328. On a stone on the south. (Telugu.) Records that "Cullapa ?" Ōbayya granted a license for 8 years to the farmers of the village to pay 3 paṇams for each *tūm*. *Ibid.*, No. 15.

329. On the western wall of the pagoda. (Telugu.) Records that in Ś. 1545, Prabhava, Gorive Reḍḍi raised the Garuḍastambham. *Ibid.*, No. 16.

330. On the bottom of the pillar in the pagoda Aiyavayya. (Telugu). Records in that in Ś. 1455, Vijaya, Malla Reḍḍi, son of

Nallapalle Malla Reḍḍi, erected a Garuḍastambham in front of Hanumanta Rāya. *Ins., Ced. Dts.*, No. 17.

331. On the south of the pagoda. (Telugu.) Records that in the reign of Sadāśivarāyalu in Ś. 1469, Plavaṅga, Nandyāla Timmarāja remitted the barbers' taxes. *Ibid.*, No. 18.

332. On the wall of a garden. (Telugu.) A record in Ś. 1350, Pramādīcha, that Appayarāju, son of Rācharāju, made a gift to Aiyagāru. (The grant is effaced in the original.) *Ibid.*, p. 9, No. 19.

333. On the stone wall of the Varadarāja pagoda. (Telugu.) Records that in the reign of Sadāśivarāyalu, in Ś. 1466, Krōdhi, Nandyāla Timmarāja remitted the taxes, etc., to Dūdala Varadarāja. *Ibid.*, No. 20.

334. On the stone pavement in the Dūdala Varadarāja pagoda. (Telugu.) Records that the merchant of Chinta-guṇṭa regranted certain fees at the monthly rate of one *paṇam* for every bale of the piece goods, drugs, etc., 2 *kāśus* for the grain-bag in Ś. 1625, Svabhānu, for the lamp ceremony of God Varadarāja. *Ibid.*, No. 21.

335. On the west of the above. (Telugu.) Records that Paṭṭikoṇḍa Varadarāja dug a large tank in the village of Dūdalapalle in Krōdhi. *Ibid.*, No. 22.

336. Near a well in the pagoda. (Telugu.) A record of Mallikārjuna Rāya (1447—65) in Ś. 1387, Pārthiva. *Ibid.*, p. 9, No. 23.

337. On a stone south of the Īśvara pagoda. (Telugu.) Records that in Ś. 1438, Bahudhānya, one Bairasu gave some land to Malla Reḍḍi and Basava Reḍḍi. *Ibid.*, No. 24.

Obalāpuram.

338. On a stone on the northern boundary of the village. (Telugu.) Records in Ś. 1476, Rākshasa, in the reign of Sadāśivarāya the measuring of the limits between Vijaya Bukkarāyapuram and Brāhmaṇapaḷḷi. *Ibid.*, p. 84, No. 101.

339. On a stone in the local hill. (Telugu.) Records that Nārāyaṇa Reḍḍi, son of Sarivi Reḍḍi, built the steps to the hill, in Krōdhana. *Ibid.*, No. 102.

340. On a stone near the ruined tank. (Telugu.) Records that in Ś. 1624, Chitrabhānu, Veṅkaṭa Bhāghavatulu dug a well. *Ibid.*, p. 84, No. 103.

Pālūru.

341. On a stone in the Chennakēśava temple. (Telugu.) Records that Rāma Reḍḍi, son of Pedda Reḍḍi, made a grant to the deity in Ś. 1690, Virōdhi. *Ibid.*, p. 88, No. 120.

342. On a stone in the Śiva temple. (Telugu.) Records that Rāma Reḍḍi and others erected the temple in Ś. 1646, Krōdhi. *Ibid.*, No. 121.

343. On a stone in the same. Records that in Ś. 1692, Khara, Śingarayya, Karṇam of the village, built the Kalyāṇa-maṇṭapam. *Ins., Ced. Dts.*, p. 88, No. 122.

344. On a stone near the Kamalamma well. (Telugu.) Records that in the reign of Golconda Sultan Abdul Saheb Nakanam Khan dug a well in the village in Ś. 1568, Vyaya. *Ibid.*, p. 89, No. 123. See *Cuddapah Gazr.*, p. 179.

345. On a stone in the Chennakēśava Pagoda. (Telugu.) Records that Timma Reḍḍi and Nañja Reḍḍi built the Mukha-maṇṭapa. *Ibid.*, No. 124.

346. On a stone in the temple of Agastyēśvara. (Telugu.) Records that in the reign of Kṛishṇadēvarāya, in Ś. 1432, Pramōdūta, Kasavulla Bōjayya of Pālūr got from Naravulla Tippa-nāyaḍu some land as mānyam for repairing the temple. *Ibid.*, No. 125.

Peddamuḍiyam.

Mr. Jayanti Rāmayya Pantulu has identified this place with Muḍivēmu which is celebrated in the E. Chāḷukyan grants as the birth place of Vishṇuvardhana, the progenitor of the Chāḷukyan lines. See *Cuddapah Gazr.*, p. 189–90.

347. 349 *of* 1905.—(Telugu.) On a slab set up in the court-yard of the Vīrabhadrēśvara temple. Dated in the reign of the Vijayanagara king Vīrapratāpa Sadāśivadēva-Mahārāya. Records in Ś. 1473, Virōdhakrit, gift of the tax called *viramushṭipannu* pay-able by the *Tammaḷas* and others of Muḍiyam, or Brahmala-Muḍiyam also called Trilōchanapuram, to the Sōmēśvara temple at the place. The village was situated in Ranataśīma, a subdivision of Ghaṇḍikōṭarājya.

348. 350 *of* 1905.—(Sanskrit and Kanarese.) On a huge slab set up to the west of the Śiva temple. Belongs to the reign of the Western Chāḷukya king Tribhuvanamalladēva (Vikramāditya VI). Records in Ś. 1046, Krōdhin, Chāḷukya-Vikrama year 49 (A.D. 1124), gift of Muḍivēma, "the big agrahāra" and "the emperor of villages, which has been in existence for four ages" to the one hundred and eight *mahājanas* of that place by the ruler of the Reṇāḍu seventy district, who was a subordinate of Mahāmaṇḍalēśvara Atyaṇa-Chōḷa-Mahārāja. [As this chief had the same titles as those of the Cuddapah Chōḷa line, the Government Epigraphist believes that it should have been a later offshoot of it. See *Ep. Ind.*, XI, p. 3442, footnote 2.]

349. 351 *of* 1905.—(Telugu.) On a broken slab lying near No. 350. In archaic characters. Mentions the "one hundred and eight" (residents of Peddamuḍiyam).

350. 352 *of* 1905.—(Telugu.) On a slab set up in the same place. A damaged record of Chōḷa-Mahārāja, dated Śaka (year lost). The king was born of the solar race, the Kāśyapa-gōtra and the Karikāla family. At the top of the inscription a standing tiger with its mouth open is engraved. See No. 309 above.

Pedda Daṇḍluru.

351. On a stone in the north wall of the local fort. (Telugu.) Records that in Ś. 1684, Chitrabhānu, Sayud Abdul Rasud and his wife erected the fort at Parallapalli. *Ins., Ced. Dts.*, p. 92, No. 139.

Ponnatōṭa.

352. On a stone in the Chennakēśava temple. (Telugu.) Records that in Ś. 1496, Bhava, in the reign of Śrīraṅgarāya Nandyāla Narasimha-rāju granted to Bhōga Nayarappa (Nāriy-appa ?) some land in the village. *Ibid.*, p. 61, No. 1.

Rēgaḍīpaḷḷi.

353. On a stone in a field south of the village. (Telugu.) Records that in Ś. 1433, Prajōtpatti, Naraśiṅgarāju, son of Nandyāla Ōbalarāja, granted to Śiṅgarāchārya and Anantāchārya, sons of Veṅgalāchārya of Yadolla, 4½ *kuṇṭas* of land in the village of Podatore (Proḍḍatur ?). *Ibid.*, p. 76, No. 68.

Timmāpuram (Timmalāpuram).

354. In charge of the local Śrōtriyamdār. (Telugu.) Records that in Ś. 1623, Vishu, the Reḍḍis and Karṇams of Panlizuvi (evidently, Penuzuvvi) granted 15 pagodas and some land to Sadā-śiva bhaṭ and Haribhaṭ. *Ibid.*, p. 53, No. 131.

355. In the hand of Narasimhāchārlu. (Telugu.) Records that in Ś. 1696 Jaya, Kṛishṇāji and Vēṅkāji granted Māchumaṛṛi village for 181 pagodas to Narasimha Śāstrulu. *Ibid.*, No. 132.

356. With the same. The communication of the same order to the Reḍḍis and Karṇams of the village by the donors. *Ibid.*, p. 53, No. 133.

357. A record of Amil Ōbala Reḍḍi in Fasli 1194, issuing an order to the same to continue the above. *Ibid.*, No. 134.

358. In charge of Śrīnivāsāchārlu. An order of "Khunore Narasimma" to Kaṇḍukūr Kōnappa to repair a canal. *Ibid.*, p. 53, No. 135.

359. A Telugu and Persian record ordering, in 1137, Śrīnivāsā-chārlu to return and reside at Koṇḍapuram. *Ibid.*, No. 136.

360. Records (in Telugu) gift by Veṅkāji Tirumal, Amil of Jammalamaḍugu, in Ś. 1673, of Koṇḍapuram as a Śrōtriyaṃ for 50 pagodas. *Ibid.*, No. 137.

361. In the hands of the same. (Mahratti.) Continuation of the above in 1699, by Kañchanapaḷḷi Rāmachandra Rāmāji, Amil of Jammalamuḍugu. *Ibid.*, No. 138.

362. A Mahratti and Persian grant of the village of Vohannapeṭṭa (?) for 70 pagodas Śrōtriyam to Daṇḍapāṇi Raghunāthāchārylu by Mahomed Khan in the reign of Alanghir. *Ins., Ced. Dts.*, No. 139.

363. An order in Mahratti and Persian of Tāsi Khan in H. 1152, to continue the above. *Ibid.*, No. 141.

364. A record of Tippu Sultan (in Mahratti) in Ś 1216, Kīlaka, ordering Asuf Mahomed to continue the villages of Ōbalapēṭṭa and Koppōlu to Raṅgāchārlu and Sumati Śrīnivāsāchārlu together with other allowances. *Ibid.*, No. 141.

365. A record in Mahratti and Persian of Nawab Ibrahim Khan dated H. 1142, ordering the Amil of Jammaḷamuḍugu to continue Śrōtriyam village to one Raghunāthāchāryalu. *Ibid.*, No. 142.

366. An order (in Mahratti and Persian) of Mayana Bade Saheb in H. 1157, to Veṅka "Shaikdar" Carcoon to continue the above. *Ibid.*, No. 143.

367. A record of Ibrahim Khan (in Mahratti) in 1196, to continue the above to Raṅgāchārya. *Ibid.*, No. 144.

368. A similar order of Nawab Masud Khan in H. 1215, to Dēśmuk and Dēśapāṇḍya to continue the Śrōtriyam. *Ibid.*, No. 145.

369. A Telugu record of Narasakēśava, Tarif-dar, granting Ōbammāpēṭṭa to Tātāchārya as Śrōtriyam for 100 pagodas in Ś. 1631, Virōdhi. *Ibid.*, No. 146. For the Tātāchāryas see S.A. 63 and Cg. 436.

370. A Telugu order by the same officer to continue the same. *Ibid.*, No. 147.

371. A gift of the village of Guṇḍlūr for 100 pagodas to Kandāḍa Varadāchārya by Veṅkaṭaro Hanumāji in Ś. 1646, Krōdhi. *Ibid.*, No. 148. [The Kandāḍais, like the Tātāchāryas, were a celebrated Śrī Vaishṇava family.]

372. A Telugu-Persian order of the same officer to continue the above. *Ibid.*, No. 149.

373. Same as above. *Ibid.*, No. 150. (Telugu.)

374. An order of the same officer in Telugu granting the above village to Tātāchārya to 1124, for 70 pagodas. *Ibid.*, No. 150. See No. 369 above.

375. Same as above. *Ibid.*, No. 152. (Mahratti.)

376. A Telugu record of Mahomed Nabi, Havuldar of Jammalamuḍugu, dated Ś. 1664, Siddhārthi, granting the above Śrōtriyam for 100 pagodas to Raṅgāchārya, son of Tātāchārya. *Ibid.*, No. 153.

377. An order of Mir Saheb to the Amil of Ghaṇḍikōṭa to continue the above Śrōtriyam, but for 105 pagodas. *Ibid.*, No. 154.

378. An order in Persian and Telugu of Ōbala Reḍḍi, Amil of Jammalamuḍugu, in F. 1193, granting the above Śrōtriyam to Kēśavāchārya for 120 pagodas. *Ibid.*, No. 155.

379. A Telugu record of Rāyalu Pantulu in Ś. 1642, Śārvari, granting three kuṇṭas of land for 20 pagodas in the village of Vastavēmula, to the learned Brahman Veṅkaṭaśāstrulu. *Ins., Ced. Dts.*, No. 156.

380. A Telugu record of Narasakēśava Pantulu of Jammalamuḍugu, dated Ś. 1627, Vyaya, granting three *tūms* of land in the above village to Karṇam Śēshāchalam. *Ibid.*, No. 157.

Uppalūru.

381. On a stone in the Hanumanta pagoda. (Telugu.) Records that in Ś. 1445, Śōbhana, Ōbalanāyuḍu gave eight *tums* of land to a sculptor Banda-Bhaṭṭa for carving an image of Hanūmanta. *Ibid.*, p. 87, No. 115.

Velpuchērla.

382. On a stone in front of Aṅkālamma temple. (Telugu.) Records that one Guṇḍurti Pāpayya granted three villages to the Goddess in Ś. 1468, Viśvāvasu, in the reign of Sadāśivarāya. *Ibid.*, p. 9, No. 25.

Veṅkayakālva (Vanakalva).

383. On a stone in a field in the north. (Telugu.) Records that Ellama Nāyuḍu, son of Nayanamma, gave some land in Ś. 1417, Raktākshi. *Ibid.*, p. 80, No. 85.

384. On a stone near the Mādhava pagoda. (Telugu.) Dated in Ś. 1468, Parābhava, in the reign of Sadāśivarāya. Records that the Vipravinōdins gave away the annual allowance they had been receiving from a village to the deity. *Ibid.*, p. 80, No. 86.

385. On a stone near the pagoda of the Goddess. (Telugu.) A similar gift of the Vīramushṭi people in Ś. 1468. *Ibid.*, p. 81, No. 87.

386. On a stone in a garden. (Telugu.) A record of Nandyāla Timmarāja in Ś. 1469, Plavaṅga, in the reign of Sadāśivarāya. Damaged. *Ibid.*, p. 81, No. 88.

Vēparāla.

[All records of this place except 387 and 389 are in Telugu. Those two are in Mahratti.]

387. In charge of the Agrahāram. A Mahratti record dated H. 1180, recording grant of four kuṇṭas of land to Cānareḍḍi and Basa Reḍḍi by Nawab Hamed-ul-Nabi. *Ibid.*, p. 50, No. 123.

388. In charge of the same. Akkarāsu Bānōji Pantulu orders the grant of a village to Boṇḍi Lilasahi (?) in 1193 Sun. *Ibid.*, No. 124.

389. With the same. Mazud Hamed-ul-Nabi orders the managers of Koppa and Timmalāpuram to continue the Śrōtriyam for 20 pagodas to Śrīnivāsachāri. *Ibid.*, No. 126.

390. A Mahratti order of Tippu Sultan in H. 1200, to the Amil of Jammalamuḍugu. *Ins., Ced. Dts.*, p. 50, No. 126.

391. An order of Amīl Koṇḍareḍḍi in F. 1201, to the Reḍḍis and Karṇams of Pālūr. No details. *Ibid.*, No. 127.

392. Narasimhadēva Mahārāja granted to one Pedda Appaḷāchārya in Ś. 1330, Sarvajit, the villages of Tāḷḷapoḍḍatūr, Guṇḍalur, etc. *Ibid.*, No. 128.

393. Kañchapaḷḷi Raṅgaṇṇa Pantulu appointed in Ś. 1590, Kaḷayukti, Pedda Appaḷāchārya as the manager of the above. *Ibid.*, No. 129.

394. Pemmasāni Timmanāyuḍu appointed in Ś. 1566, Tāraṇa, one Bukkapatṇam Tātāchārya to be the head of all *samayāchāram* of Gaṇḍikōṭa district. He was to receive the *Gurusēvā*, to be present at *Harisēva*, and punish people who swerved from the right path. *Ibid.*, p. 52, No. 130. The record is interesting for giving an insight into the manner in which the Tātāchāryas became powerful.

Yerraguḍi.

395. On a stone in the Āñjanēya pagoda. (Telugu.) Records that Nandyāla Narapparāja, son of Naraśiṅgarāja, granted Yerraguḍi in Ś. 1470, Kīlaka, to God Ahōbalēśvara. *Ins., Ced. Dts.*, p. 75, No. 63.

396. On a stone near the canal north-east of the village. (Telugu.) Records that an inhabitant of Jammaladinnē gave Veṅkayya in Prabhava 12 muṇṭas of dry field in the village. *Ibid.*, No. 64.

Yenumalachintala.

397. On a stone in the Āñjanēya temple. Records that in Ś. 1474, Saumya, in the reign of Saḍāśivarāya, Chinna Timmanāyuḍu, son of Pemmasāmi Nāyuḍu, granted this village to God Tiruvēṅgalanātha of Tāḍpatri. *Ibid.*, p. 79, No. 81.

398. On a stone near the temple west of the village. (Telugu.) Records that in Ś. 1466, Krōdhi, in the reign of Sadāśivarāya, Aḷiya Rāma-rāya exempted the duties of the local barbers. *Ibid.*, No. 82.

399. In front of the above. (Telugu.) Records that in Ś. 1432, Pramōdūta, Timmarasa, the prime-minister of Kṛishṇadēvarāya, granted the *marriage fees* collected from the different tribes of Gaṇḍikōṭa, Penugoṇḍa, Chandragiri, etc., to the deity. *Ibid.*, p. 80, No. 83.

400. In a field east of the village. (Telugu.) Records that in the reign of Śāḷuva Mummuḍi Narasimharāyalu, in Ś. 1420, Kaḷayukti, Rāma-rāya granted two *māḍas*, a garden, etc., to a man of Siddāvaṭṭam. *Ibid.*, p. 80, No. 84. The chief was evidently the son and the successor of the Sāḷuva usurper Naraśiṅga.

KAMALAPURAM TALUK.

Animēla.

This place formed originally part of the territory of the Vaiḍumbas.

401. Near the ancient temple of Saṅgamēśvara. A record dated Ś. 1465 (A.D. 1543) recording a grant by a Vijayanagar king.

402-A—B. In the same place. Two other epigraphs dated Ś. 1400 and Ś. 1500.

402-C. In the Chennakēśavasvāmi temple. A grant of Maṭla Kumāra Ananta in Ś. 1566. See *Cuddapah Gazr.*, p. 207.

Chadiperāla.

403. On a stone in the avenue of the village. (Telugu.) Records that Champa Reḍḍi, son of Vīra Reḍḍi, purchased some lands in Ś. 1353, Saumya, and presented it to God Agastyēśvara. *Ins., Ced. Dts.*, p. 116, No. 95. See also No. 429 below.

Chilamkūru.

404. 395 *of* 1904.—(Kanarese.) On two faces of a pillar set up in a field. A record of Trailōkyamalla Mallidēva Mahārāja in Chāḷukya-Vikrama year 56, Paridhāvin, recording the building of a tank at Chirmakūru. The king was ruling over the Muḷiki three hundred district. *Ins., Ced. Dts.*, p. 392, No. 89 (which however gives the wrong date of C.V. 5 and not 56). [The chief mentioned here was apparently the feudatory of Jayasimha III, 1072—77.]

405. 396 *of* 1904.—(Telugu.) On a broken pillar lying in another field adjoining the above. Mentions Chōḷa-Mahādēvulu. See 309 above.

406. 397 *of* 1904.—(Telugu.) On a slab set up behind the image of Hanumat in the Āñjanēya temple in the same village. Records in Ś. 1364, Durmati, the setting up of the image of Hanumantadēva, by one Gummaṇa, son of "Jakkavajjalu." See *Ins., Ced. Dts.*, p. 390, No. 84.

407. 398 *of* 1904.—(Telugu.) On two faces of a pillar set up near the dvajastambha of the same temple. Records in Ś. 1598, Naḷa, that the Reḍḍis of Chilumakūru set up a lamp-pillar in the shrine of Sañjīvarāya (i.e., Hanūmat). *Ins., Ced. Dts.*, p. 391, No. 86.

408. 399 *of* 1904.—(Telugu.) On two faces of a pillar set up close to the south wall of the same temple. Dated in the reign of the Vijayanagara king Vīrapratāpa Kaṭhāri Śāḷuva Vīra-Sadāśivarāyadēva-Mahārāya. Records in Ś. 1469, Parābhava, remission of taxes on barbers in three specified districts (*Śima*) under orders of Rāmarājayya. See *Ibid.*, p. 390, No. 83.

409. 400 *of* 1904.—(Telugu.) On three faces of a pillar lying in front of the Agastyēśvara temple in the same village. A record of the Chōḷa king Vikramāditya-Chōḷa-Mahārājulu; mentions the queen Eḷañchōḷa Mahādēvi, Uttamāditya-Sāmantaka and the village of Chirubūru (perhaps the modern Chilamkūru). Two other faces of the pillar mention Vallava-Raṭṭaguḍi and Chaḷki-Raṭṭaguḍi. [This king is not improbably the same as the one referred to in No. 309 above. The king had the titles of *Muditaśilākshara* (one who delighted in stone scripts), *Navarāma*, etc.—evidently after the model of the Pallava king Mahēndravarman I. For an elaborate note on the *Pallava-Raṭṭaguḍi* see *Ep. Ind.*, Vol. XI, p. 343.]

410. 401 *of* 1904.—(Telugu.) On three faces of a pillar lying in the verandah in front of the same temple. Bandaya, son of Harirarāchaparu, son of Vallava-Saḷki and Chirubūru are mentioned. A damaged record. *Vallava Saḷki* evidently indicates a combination of Chāḷukyan and Pallava or Rāshṭrakūṭa lines.

411. 402 *of* 1904.—(Telugu.) On a slab lying in the same verandah. Records in Ś. 1431, Śukla, the construction of a tank to the west of Mutyāla Chilmukūru by the chief Chōḍapparāju-Kāḷayya (son of Chōḍapparāju) for the merit of his parents. See *Ins., Ced. Dts.*, p. 392, No. 88.

412. 403 *of* 1904.—(Telugu.) On another slab lying in the verandah in front of the Agastyēśvara temple. Records gift of land by the eldest son of Vikramāditya Bempaṇādhirāja. [He was not improbably the same as the one referred to in No. 453 below.]

413. 404 *of* 1904.—(Telugu.) On a pillar lying in the courtyard of the same temple. Dated in the reign of the Vijayanagara king Harihararāya (II), son of Vīra-Bukkarāya (I). Records in Ś. 1304, Dundubhi, a gift of land made while the Mahāmaṇḍalēśvara Vīradēvarāya Oḍeya, the king's son (later on Dēvarāya I), was governing Udayagiri. Chirumakūru is stated to have been a village in Muḷiki-nāḍu. [From this and similar inscriptions concerning Kampaṇa Uḍaiyār and Virūpaṇṇa Uḍaiyār, the Government Epigraphist infers that "the Vijayanagar princes sent out as rulers of provinces assumed the title Oḍeya or Uḍaiyār (in Tamil), which belonged to them originally as Hoysaḷa feudatories, while the higher title Mahārāja or Mahārāyaw as reserved for the reigning sovereign." *Ep. Rep.*, 1905, p. 58. The present inscription is also given in *Ins., Ced. Dts.*, p. 390, No. 81.

414. On a stone in the village. (Telugu.) Records that in Ś. 1475, Paritāpi, Chinnarāju and Koṇḍarāju granted to a Bōye some land for digging a water channel in the village. *Ibid.*, p. 391, No. 85.

415. In a pillar in the Hanumantarāya pagoda.—(Telugu.) Records that in Ś. 1670, Akshaya, one Chinnappa Reḍḍi erected a maṇṭapa and granted some land. *Ibid.*, No. 87.

416. In a field east of the village. (Telugu.) A record of Sadāśivarāya in Ś. 1466, Krōdhi. *Ins., Ced. Dts.*, p. 392, No. 90.

Gaṅgāvaram.

[The following records taken from *Mack. MSS.* are in Telugu.]

417. On a stone in the pagoda of the village. Records that in Ś. 1179, Piṅgaḷa, in the reign of Gaṅgapatirāyalu, the people granted the village to the local God. *Ins., Dts.*, p. 114, No. 82.

418. In the same place. Records that in Ś. 1666, Akshaya, Yerrama Reḍḍi, son of Timma Reḍḍi, established an image and granted lands at Amīrpuram. *Ibid.*, No. 83.

419. In the same place. The Reḍḍis and Karṇams of Mīrāpuram granted land to God Rāmaliṅga in Ś. 1666, Akshaya. *Ibid.*, No. 84.

420. On a stone in the compound wall of Agastyēśvara. Records that one Chandraśēkhara gave in Ś. 1446, Vijaya, four *puṭṭis* of land to the God. *Ibid.*, p. 115, No. 85.

421. South of the above. A record of a Vīraśaiva in Ś. 1471, Sādhāraṇa, granting the allowance of the Vīramushṭi people to the deity. *Ibid.*, No. 86.

422. On a third stone. Records that in Ś. 1464, Śubhakrit, in the reign of Achyutarāya, one Mallaya granted to the deity the different duties of the Ghaṇḍikōṭa Śīma. *Ibid.*, No. 87.

423. On a fourth stone. A gift of 50 *māḍas* in the same year by two Reḍḍis. *Ibid.*, No. 88.

424. On a stone in the pagoda of Agastyēśvara. Records that Nāga Reḍḍi and other jugglers granted away in Ś. 1515, Khara, in the reign of Veṅkaṭapatirāya (I, 1586—1614), the allowance which they had been receiving for "the bamboo play" to God Agastyēśvara of Chaḍipirāla. *Ibid.*, No. 89.

425. A damaged record of Ś. 1439, Vibhava, mentioning Vīra-Narasimmarāya and Dōchirāju and Gōvindarāju. *Ibid.*, No. 90.

426. On a stone in the front of Aṅkālamma pagoda. Records that Nandyāla Chinna Ōbalarāju gave some land in Ś. 1430, Piṅgaḷa, to God Channakēśava of Bāshapuram. *Ibid.*, No. 91.

427. A record of Ś. 1442, Vikrama, mentioning a grant of ten tūms in Chāḍupalli to the same God by one Gōvindarājulu Uḍayalu, and his feudatory Kaṇṇayya, son of Narasayya. *Ibid.*, No. 92.

428. In the Vēṇugōpāla pagoda. Records that one Kattaman Śiṅgarāju Chōḍamahārāja repaired the canal of the tank in Ś. 1501, Bahudhānya, in the reign of Dēvamahārāya. *Ibid.*, No. 93.

429. In the same temple. Records that Nandyāla Chinna Ōbalarāya gave in Ś. 1474, 10 tūms of land in Chāḍipaḷḷi to God Vēṇugōpālasvāmi of Chaḍipirāla. *Ibid.*, No. 94.

Gollapalli.

430. On a stone in the ruined pagoda. (Telugu.) Records that Timmarājayya Mahārāja gave to one Tirumalayya of the village, 13 tūms of land in Ś. 1461, Raudri, in the reign of Sadāśivarāya. *Ins., Ced. Dts.*, p. 116, No. 98.

Kalamaḷḷa.

431. 376 *of* 1904.—(Telugu.) On two faces of a slab set up close to the east wall of the Āñjanēya shrine in the Channakēśava temple. A damaged record of the Vijayanagara king Vīrapratāpa Sadāśivadēva-Mahārāya, dated Ś. 1479, Piṅgaḷa. Records gift by Rāchirāju (son of Mādhavarāju Apparāju) to the Channakēśava temple at Kalumaḷa. See *Ins., Ced. Dts.*, p. 389, No. 79.

432. 377 *of* 1904.—(Telugu.) On a second slab set up in the same place. Dated in the reign of the Vijayanagara king Vīrapratāpa Vīra Veṅkaṭapatirāya (I). Records in Ś. 1515, Vijaya, gift of taxes to the temple of Channakēśava-Perumāḷ at Kalumaḷa by the agent of Mahāmaṇḍalēśvara Nandīla Aubhalrājayyadēva-Mahārāju. Penugoṇḍa is mentioned as the king's residence. [*Ins., Ced. Dts.*, p. 389, No. 76.]

433. 378 *of* 1904.—(Sanskrit and Telugu.) On another face of the same slab. In archaic characters. Mentions Rēvaśarman of the Bhāradvāja-gōtra.

434. 379 *of* 1904.—(Telugu.) On a slab set up at the entrance into the same temple, left side. An incomplete record of the Vijayanagara king Vīrapratāpa Sadāśivadēva-Mahārāya, dated Ś. 1472, Sādhāraṇa. Records gift to the Channakēśava temple at Kalumaḷa, by the Vipravinōdins. *Ibid.*, p. 389, No. 78.

435. 380 *of* 1904.—(Telugu.) On two faces of a broken pillar lying in the courtyard of the same temple. In archaic characters. Mentions Dhanañjayeṇḍu, ruler of Rēnāṇḍu. [He was evidently the same as Dhanañjayavarman, the third son of Nandivarman of the Cuddapah Chōḷa line. See No. 455 below. Also *Ep. Carna.*, XII, p. 7.]

436. 381 *of* 1904.—(Telugu.) On two faces of a pillar lying outside the prākāra of the Channakēśava temple. Dated in the reign of the Vijayanagara king Vīrapratāpa Kaṭhāri Śāḷuva Vīra Sadāśivarāyadēva-Mahārāya. Records in Ś. 1469, Parābhava, remission of taxes on barbers at Kalumaḷḷa situated in the Pulivindala-śīma, by Mahāmaṇḍalēśvara Tirumalayyadēva Mahārāja of Yeraguḍi with the permission of Rāmarājayya. Mentions Kandanavōlu. See *Ins., Ced. Dts.*, p. 390, No. 80.

437. 382 *of* 1904.—(Telugu.) On a slab set up outside the same prākāra. Records in Kīlaka, a grant by Mahāmaṇḍalēśvara Karnāṭa Raghunātharājadēva Mahārāja. [See *Ins., Ced. Dts.*,

p. 389, No. 77. Grant of an annual allowance of 3½ pagodas at Kalamalla.] See By. 134.

Kamalāpuram.

438. On a stone in the Channakēśava pagoda .(Telugu.) Records that one Mallanāyaḍu gave in Ś. 1473, Virōdhikrit, in the reign of Sadāśivarāya, some land to a barber named Pūmala Chinnayya for the use of musicians. *Ins., Ced. Dts.*, p. 99, No. 9. [The inscription shows that the barber was also musician, a combination not rare even now.]

439. A Telugu record of Gulla Nāgappa Nāyaḍu in Ś. 1444, Pramādi, in the reign of Kṛishṇadēvarāya, granting four tūms of land for a water pandal. *Ibid.*, No. 10.

Kōḍūru.

The following inscriptions which are in Telugu have been taken from *Mack. MSS.*

440. On a stone in the local pagoda. Records that Nandyāla Timmayyadēva granted to God Channakēśava some land in Nandapāḍu in Ś. 1478, Naḷa, in the reign of Sadāśivarāya. *Ibid.*, p. 98, No. 1.

441. On a stone in the Vighnēśvara pagoda. A damaged gift of the same chief in Ś. 1469, Plavaṅga. *Ibid.*, No. 2.

442. To the east of the above. A grant of the same chief in Ś. 1475, Pramādi, to one Chōḷama Reḍḍi of Kōḍūr. *Ibid.*, No. 3.

443. On a stone near the Āñjanēya pagoda. Gift of the village of Kōḍūr to God Channakēśava by the same chief in Ś. 1470, Kīlaka. *Ibid.*, No. 4.

444. On a side of the above. A grant of the same chief in Ś. 1474, Saumya, to one Basavayya. *Ibid.*, No. 5.

445. On a stone north of the above. A record in the reign of Sadāśivarāya dated in Ś. 1170 (1470?), Śubhakrit, damaged. *Ibid.*, No. 6.

446. On the south of the Āñjanēya pagoda. Records that Dommarivāḷu granted the local allowances on jugglers to the deity in Ś. 1456, in the reign of Achyutarāya. *Ibid.*, No. 7.

447. On a stone near the Chennakēśava pagoda. A damaged grant of Nandyāla Narasyyadēva to Channakēśava in Ś. 1466, Viśvāvasu. *Ibid.*, No. 8.

Kommaḍḍi.

448. On a stone in the village. A damaged Telugu grant to the learned people of Vupuṭūr in Ś. 1534, Paritāpi, in the reign of Veṅkaṭapatirāya (I, 1586—1614) by Nāgappanāyaḍu. *Ins., Ced. Dts.*, p. 105, No. 30.

Lingāla.

449. On a stone in the Vīrabhadra Pagoda (Telugu.) Records that Vīrareḍḍi, son of Śiṅganalla Reḍḍi, granted in Ś. 1721, Kāḷa yukti, a lamp-stand to God Vīrabhadra. *Ins., Ced. Dts.*, p. 106, No. 37.

450. On a stone in the Channakēśava temple. (Telugu.) Records that Nandyāla Timmarāja remitted the tax on the local barbers and jugglers in Ś. 1469, Parābhava, in the reign of Sadāśivarāya. *Ibid.*, No. 36.

Malepāḍu.

451. 391 *of* 1904.—(Telugu.) On a slab lying behind the Gōpālakṛishṇa temple. A record of the Rāshṭrakūṭa king Nityavarsha. Mentions a certain Vallavarāju. See No. 148 above.

452. 392 *of* 1904.—(Telugu.) In archaic characters. On two faces of a pillar lying in front of the same temple. Erikal-Munyarāju records a gift of land.

453. 393 *of* 1904.—(Telugu.) On two faces of a pillar lying near a well west of the same village. King Chōḷa-Mahārājādhirāja Vikramāditya Satyāditunru (Satyadityuṇḍū), son of Śaktikomāra Vikramāditya, who was ruling the Siddhi (i.e., Siddhout thousand) and the Rēnāṇḍu seven thousand (district) made a gift of land to a certain Rēvaśarman of the Kāśyapa-gōtra. Mentions Chirumbūru. The inscription has to be read from the bottom. Rēvaśarman is mentioned in No. 433 above, but he is there said to have belonged to the Bhāradvāja gōtra. [The king is not mentioned in No. 455 and so his position is unknown.]

454. 394 *of* 1904.—(Telugu.) On the beam of the verandah of the Śiva temple east of the same village. A damaged record. In archaic characters.

455. A copper plate grant discovered in this village by Mr. Jayanti Ramayya Pantulu is noticed in *Madr. Ep. Rep.*, 1905, p. 48 and edited by Mr. Krishna Sastri in *Ep. Ind.*, XI, pp. 337—46. The plate records the gift of some land in the village of Biripāṟu on the southern bank of the river Suprayōga in the Hiraṇyāshṭra district by Pōrmukharāma Purushaśārdūla Puṇyakumāra who had also the titles of Mārdavachitta and Madanavilāsa. (He was the son of Chōḷa Mahārāja, grandson of Dhanañjayavarman and great-grandson of Nandivarman of Kāśyapa gōtra, solar line and Karikāla-chōḷa's family, who was the founder of the dynasty.) It is very important as it furnishes the earliest Telugu record from the Cuddapah district and brings to light a dynasty of Chōḷa kings in Pallava territory in the eighth century. The names of some of the monarchs and their titles show the Chōḷa and Pallava combination. Mr. Venkayya believed the crest on the plate to be a *tiger*, but Mr. Krishna Sastri considers it to be a lion. The latter comes incidently to the conclusion that Karikāl Chōḷa "must have flourished in the end of the fifth century A.D." The opinion has been given that the Chōḷa region which Hiouen Tsang has referred to might be the region ruled by these early Chōḷas. Rice gives certain Chōḷas in the Ālvāḍi 600, in Maddagiri taluk, Tumkur district, in the eighth century; and these perhaps were also connected with the Chōḷas of Cuddapah. See *Ep. Carna.*, XII, Introdn., p. 7 and *Ep. Ind.*, XI, p. 341.

Niḍujuvvi.

456. South of the Chennakēśava pagoda. A Telegu record of Vijaya Bukkarāya, dated in Ś. 1299, Kāḷayukti. Damaged. *Ins., Ced. Dts.*, p. 392, No. 91.

457. In front of the Vighnēśvara pagoda. A Telugu record of Rāmarāja Timmarājayyadēva in Ś. 1466, Viśvāvasu, granting 5 tūms of land for a choultry to Jappabōyaṇṇa. *Ibid.*, p. 393, No. 92, and *Antiquities*, p. 125.

458. On the west of the Īśvara pagoda. (Telugu.) Records that the same chief exempted the Karṇams of Niḍujuvvi from their taxes in Ś. 1470, Kīlaka. *Ibid.*, No. 93.

459. On a stone north of the pagoda. (Telugu.) Records that the Tambalavāṇḍlu sold their land in the village for 100 *māḍas* in Ś. 1308, Krōdhana. *Ibid.*, No. 94.

460. In the Chaṇḍēśvara temple. A Telugu private record dated Ś. 1128. See *Antiquities*, p. 125.

Pālagiri.

[All the inscriptions of this place are in Telugu and have been taken from *Mack. MSS.*]

461. On a stone in front of Īśvara Pagoda. Records that in Ś. ...97 Durmukhi, in the reign of Kanada(?) Vaidumba Mahārāju. Bhīma Mahārāju re-established the Pagoda of Sammatētvar. *Ins., Ced. Dts.*, p. 11, No. 35. [See *Cuddapah Gazr.*, p. 205, where it is shown that this is a record of a Vaidumba chief and also refers to Rashtrakuṭa Krishṇa III. It is dated A.D. 1056.]

462. On a stone in front of Chennakēśavasvāmi God. Records a grant of 5 Kuṇṭas and 4 tūms of land for a garden and offering of food to the God Chennakēśava, in Ś. 1426, Krōdhana, in the reign of Sāḷuva Naraśiṅga Rāyulu by Kāmarasu Timmayya. *Ibid.*, No. 36. [Was it Immaḍi Narasimha ?]

463. On a stone on the eastern gate of Saṅgamēśvar on the bank of Pāpāgni. Records that in the reign of Sadāśivarāya, in Ś. 1465, Śōbhakrit, Guruviah Dēva Chōḍa Mahādēva Rāyalu granted the villages of Animala in Ghaṇḍikōṭa, Dēnipāḷam in the Doraguṇṭaśīma, etc. *Ibid.*, No. 37.

464. On a stone on the bank of the Pāpāgni river. Records that in Ś. 1453, Khara, the Vīramushṭi people granted quarter paṇam for each bag of goods that passed through foot-paths in Polivāṇḍala, Chintaguṇṭa and other places. *Ins., Ced. Dts.*, p. 11, No. 38.

465. On a stone out of the eastern gate. Records that Gaṅgādhara Chōḷamahārāya granted land to the deities in Ś. 1515, Nandana, in the reign of Veṅkaṭapatirāya (I, 1586—1614). *Ibid.*, p. 12, No. 39.

Paṇḍillapaḷḷi.

466. On a stone in the pagoda of Prasanna Vēṅkaṭēśa. (Telugu.) Records that Rāyasam Ayyamanarasayya erected the Pagoda of Kēśava and granted some lands to the musicians in Ś. 1447, Sarvadhāri, in the reign of Kṛishṇadēvarāya (1509—30). *Ins., Ced. Dts.*, p. 116, No. 99. See Ap. 131 and Ap. 138.

467. On a stone south of the village. (Telugu.) Records that a feudatory of Sadāśivarāya (1542—65) granted 7 *puṭṭis* and 13½ *tūms* of land in Ś. 1476, Ānanda, to the learned Brahmans of the place. *Ibid.*, No. 100.

Peddampāḍu.

All the records of this place have been taken from *Mack.* MSS. and are in Telugu.

468. On a stone in the village. Records a grant in Ś. 1222, Śārvari, of the village Śērapuram (?) to God Agastyēśvara in the reign of Ambadēva Mahārāju. *Ins., Ced. Dts.*, p. 100, No. 11.

469. A record in Ś. 1484, Dundubhi, by Raghunātharāju in the reign of Sadāśivarāya (1542—65). *Ibid.*, No. 12.

470. On a stone in front of the Agastyēśvara pagoda. Records that in Ś. 1357, Ānanda, Nāgamarāju, son of Mallamarāju, established the idol of Veerabhadrēśvar. *Ibid.*, No. 13.

471. On a stone in the pagoda of Agastyēśvara. Records that in Ś. 1358, Rākshasa, Nāgarāju raised a pillar in the pagoda of Agastyēśvara. *Ibid.*, No. 14.

472. On a stone in front of Gōpāladēvasvāmi pagoda. Records that in the reign of Sadāśivarāya, in Ś. 1470, Kīlaka, Bukkarāju Timmarāju restored the former lands to the karṇams of the village. *Ibid.*, No. 15.

473. On a stone near the Garuḍasthambam pillar in the pagoda. Records that in Ś. 1635, Vijaya, Timmareḍḍi, son of Yella Reḍḍi, cast the gold and silver images of Madanagōpālasvāmi and raised the Dvajasthambham pillar and some lamp-stands to the God Madanagōpālasvāmi. *Ibid.*, No. 16.

474. Records that in Ś. 1573, Plava, in the reign of Vīraveṅkaṭapatidēva Mahārāyalu, Timmanāyaḍu cultivated the lands giving a *cowl* to the inhabitants of the village. *Ibid.*, No. 17.

475. On a stone in the pagoda of Chennakēśavasvāmi. Records that in the reign of Achyutadēvarāyalu, in Ś. 1457, Mummuḍi

Tusakuppa (?) Pāpanāyaḍu granted half puṭṭi of land in a grove on the east of the village to Chennakēśavasvāmi. *Ins., Ced. Dts.*, No. 18, p. 102.

476. On the door frame of Chennarāyasvāmi. Records that in Ś. 1459, Hēviḷambi, Vallabayya, son of Kṛishṇamarāju, constructed a door-frame to the pagoda of Channarāyasvāmi. *Ibid.*, p. 102, No. 19.

Podadūrti.

477. On a stone lying in a field of Veṅkaṭapuram. (Telugu.) Records that Kṛishṇadēvarāya granted some land in Giḍḍalore to a private person in Ś. 1455, Śrīmukha. *Ins., Ced. Dts.*, p. 108, No. 47.

Poḷladūrti.

All the epigraphs of the place are in Telugu and taken from *Mack. MSS.*

478. On a stone in the pagoda. Records that in Ś. 1435, Śrīmukha, Rācharāju granted some land in the village to God Chennakēśava. *Ins., Ced. Dts.*, p. 111, No. 63.

479. On another stone. Records that in Ś. 1454, Nandana, in the reign of Achutarāya, Kuṇḍurti Tirumalayya granted the village of Poḷḷadūrti as free gift to its learned Brahmans. *Ibid.*, p. 111, No. 64.

480. Near the above. Records that Nandyāla Timmayya built the village in Ś. 1468, Parābhava, in the reign of Sadāśiva, and granted it to God Chennakēśava. *Ibid.*, p. 112, No. 65.

481. On a stone in the Agastyēśvara temple. Records that Mallanāyaḍu granted some land in the village to Agastyēśvara in Ś. 1447, Paritāpi, in the reign of Kṛishṇadēvarāya. *Ibid.*, No. 66.

482. On a stone in the pagoda of Mūlasthānēśvara. Records that Rāmarāja Śiṅgarāja Tirumalarāja granted some lands in Nandana, in the reign of Achutarāya. *Ibid.*, No. 67.

Rāmachandrapuram.

483. C.P. in the hands of Rāmachandrapuram Brahmans. (Telugu.) Records that in Ś. 1636, Vijaya, Kañchanapaḷḷi Rāmachandrapantulu built in the reign of Maṭḷa Anantarāju the village, and granted it in favourable rent to seven Brahmans. The rent was fixed at five *aparanji chakrams*. *Ins., Ced. Dts.*, p. 264, No. 82, and p. 284, No. 143 (two copies).

Veludūrti.

484. On a stone in the pagoda. (Telugu.) Records that in the reign of Sadāśivarāya, in Ś. 1479, Naḷa, Aubala-rājayya seated the metal images in the village and granted twelve pagodas for offering food to Chennakēśava Perumāḷ. *Ins., Ced. Dts.*, p. 103, No. 25.

485. On a stone east of the Chennakēśavasvámi. (Telugu.) Records that in the reign of Sadāśivarāya, in Ś. 1472, Saumya, Immaḍi-Basavanāyaḍu continued the fifteen tūms of dry field to the God Tripurāntaka. *Ins., Ced. Dts.*, p. 104, No. 26.

PRODDATUR TALUK.

Annalūru.

486. On a stone near the pagoda of Īśvara in the ruined village. (Telugu.) Records that in Ś. 1183, Durmati, "Junnugu Dēva Mahārāja" seated the form of Bheemaya-liṅgam and granted this village for divine service. *Ins., Ced. Dts.*, p. 369, No. 3.

Arakaṭavēmula.

487. On a stone situated in the pagoda of Gōpālasvāmi. (Telugu.) Records that in the reign of Sadāśivarāya, in Ś. 1472, Sādhāraṇa, Chinna Aubalarāja, son of Nandyāla Pedda Aubalarāja, erected a pagoda at Arakaṭa-vēmula Agrahāram, placed there the image of Gōpāla-Kṛishṇa Dēva and granted hamlets of the above agrahāram and an allowance of 31½ pagodas on the tax of Ghaṇḍikōṭa Durgam, to the God Gōpāla-Kṛishṇadēva. *Ins., Ced. Dts.*, p. 378, No. 34.

488. On a stone pillar Garuḍasthambam in the above pagoda. (Telugu.) Records that in the reign of Kṛishṇadēva Rāyalu, in Ś. 1446, Sarvajit, certain jugglers granted their allowance of the village of Arakaṭavēmula or Bhairavasamudram Agrahāram in the Ghaṇḍikōṭa district to Gōpālakṛishṇadēva and Hanumanta Rāya. *Ibid.*, p. 378, No. 35.

489. 474 *of* 1906.—(Telugu.) On two faces of a pillar set up in the courtyard of the Vishṇu temple. The western Chāḷukya king Śrīvallabha-Mahārājādhirāja records a gift to a certain Vinnaśarman. Pērbāṇa-vamśa and Būpāditya are mentioned.

490. 475 *of* 1906.—(Telugu.) On a slab lying in the same courtyard. Mentions in Kshaya, Kāmarasugāru-Timmayya and Brāhmala Muḍiyam, the ancient name of Peddamuḍiyam in the Jammalamaḍugu taluka; also Nandyāla in Rēṇāṇḍu. According to the *Mack. MSS.* (*Ins. Ced. Dts.*, p. 379, No. 6), Kāmarasa dug the tank of Bhairavasamudram in the village.

491. 476 *of* 1906.—(Telugu.) On a mutilated slab lying in front of the Bhairava temple in the same village. Records in Ś. 1431, Śukla, gift of land (one of the forty-two Vrittis of the village) by the *mahājanas* of Chavuḍūru to Peda Timmarasayya, son of Kāmarasu, perhaps identical with the person mentioned in the above epigraph. [The inscription is also given in *Mack. MSS.* See *Ins., Ced. Dts.*, p. 379, No. 37.]

Bollāvaram.

492. In the Vēṇugōpalasvāmi temple. An undated inscription recording the grant of a village to the temple by " Pāpa Timmayyadēva Mahārāja, son of Rāma Rāja Timma Rāja " in the reign of Sadāśivadēva at Vijayanagar. *Antiquities*, I, p. 124.

493. On a stone in front of the pagoda of Gōpinātha. (Telugu.) Records that in the reign of Sadāśivarāya, in Ś. 1465, Śubhakrit, Pāpatimmarāja (son of Rāmarāju Timmarāju) granted his own shares of the taxes of Bolāvaram-peṭṭa in Gūḍalūre district to the daily-ceremony of Gōpinātha. *Ins., Ced. Dts.*, p. 383, No. 53.

494. On a stone north of the above. (Telugu.) Records that in Ś. 1470, Kīlaka, Parvatayya, son of Makkam Aḍugula Rudrayya, granted the taxes of the inhabitants of Bollāvaram to Gōpinātha. *Ibid.*, p. 383, No. 54.

Chauḍūru.

495. 483 *of* 1906.—(Kanarese.) On a slab lying in the Bhīmēśvara temple. A damaged record of the Telugu Chōḍa king Bhujabalavīra-Nalasiddanadēva-Chōḷamahārāja, dated Ś. 1114, Paridhāvin. Mentions Śālūru. The king boasts of having levied tribute from Kāñchi. His capital was Vallūrupura, evidently the same as Vallūru, eight miles north-west of Cuddapah. It was the capital of Mahārājapāḍi 7000. *Ep. Rep.*, 1907, p. 89, para. 70. See *Ins., Ced. Dts.*, p. 371, No. 5, where this inscription is given.

496. 484 *of* 1906.—(Telugu.) On a pillar lying near the Māriyamma temple in the same village. A mutilated record. In archaic characters. Mentions the king's *birudas*, viz., Mahārājadhirāja, Paramēśvara and Bhaṭāra.

Chinna Guruvalūru.

497. On a stone south of the village. (Telugu.) Records that in Ś. 1458, *Durmukhi*, in the reign of Achyuta Dēva Rāya, Aḍappam Śūrappa Nāyaḍu gave to God Vidyānātha of Pushpagiri five *tūms* of dry field between the villages of Chinna Guruvalūru and Miḍatūru in " Coyala-cunta " district. *Ins., Ced. Dts.*, p. 386, No. 64.

Dāsaripaḷḷi.

498. On a stone in the village. (Telugu.) Records that the village was granted to God Tiruvēṅgalanātha by Parvata Rāya in Ś. 1437, Yuva, in the reign of Kṛishṇadēva Rāya. *Ibid.*, p. 372, No. 12.

Duvvūru.

Besides the lithic inscription given below, the Mack. MSS. (See *Ins., Ced. Dts.*, pp. 395—98) give one stone epigraph and seven paper grants in this 'District', and I have included them. All these are in Telugu.

499. 470 *of* 1906.—(Telugu.) On a slab set up in the courtyard of the Kōdaṇḍarāmasvāmin temple in the old village. Records in Ś. 1531, Saumya, contributions by merchants at a fixed rate (1/8 per bag of cotton and 1/16 of salt, etc.) on articles of merchandise for the benefit of the temple of Kōdaṇḍa-Raghunāthasvāmin at Duvvūru. [Referred to by Mr. Sewell in his *Antiquities*, I, 125, and given in Mack. List, *Ins., Ced. Dts.*, p. 375, No. 25.

500. A paper grant recording the gift, by " Calore Nallappa " Reḍḍi, of the village of Gōpālapuram as Śrōtriyam for 22 pagodas to one Appāji in year Īśvara for looking after a pagoda and digging a tank. *Ins., Ced. Dts.*, p. 395, No. 100.

501. A paper grant continuing the above by the Reḍḍis and Karṇams in Ś. 1696, Manmatha. *Ibid.*, No. 101.

502. A paper grant continuing the above and granted to Appāji in 1704, Śubhakrit, by Gani Beg, Amil of Duvvūr. *Ibid.*, No. 102.

503. A paper grant reducing the rent of the above, in 1713, Virōdhikrit, by Kumāra Kṛishṇa Reḍḍi. *Ibid.*, No. 103.

504. A paper grant in the possession of "Darbha Veṅkaṭabhaṭṭu." Records in Ś. 1671, Śukla, the gift of four *puṭṭis* of land in Sattepaḷḷe by the Reḍḍis and Karṇams to Veṅkaṭa Sōmayājulu. *Ibid.*, No. 104.

505. A paper grant in the possession of the same. Śaṅkarāji Narasa, Sarkār of Duvūr pergana, continues the above it the same year. *Ibid.*, No. 105.

506. A paper grant of Muhammad Sahib, dated in Ś. 1674, Āṅgirasa, granting the above land for 80 pagodas for the purpose of building a village named Śaṅkarapuram and establishing a college of Vēdas and Śāstras. *Ibid.*, No. 106.

507. A paper grant of the same chief to the Reḍḍis and Karṇams of Sattepaḷḷe-Śaṅkarāpuram continuing the above. *Ibid.*, No. 107.

508. On a stone at the foot of the hill east of Duvūr. Records that three kuṇṭas of field were given to God Tiruvēṅgalanātha by Malla Nāyaḍu and Narapa Nāyaḍu in Ś. 1419, Piṅgaḷa, in the reign of Narasiṁha Rāyalu. *Ibid.*, p. 77, No. 74.

Gōpāvaram.

509. 479 *of* 1906.—(Telugu.) On two faces of a slab set up in the middle of the village. Dated in the reign of the Vijayanagara king Vīrapratāpa Achyutadēvarāya-Mahārāya. Records in Ś. 1455, Vijaya, gift of land (five tūms of dry field, etc.) to the temple of Hanumat at Gōpāvaram by Jagatiba (Jaganobbagaṇḍa) Kāñchirāju Raṅgayyadēva-Chōḍamahārājulu. Mentions Mahāmaṇḍalēśvara Sālakarājayya-Tirumalayyadēva-Mahārājulu; see No. 174 of 1906. The inscription is also given in *Ins., Ced. Dts.*,

p. 381, No. 44. Sālakarāja was the emperor's chief general and led the campaign of 1532 in South India. See By. 19. Ap. 10.

510. 480 *of* 1906.—(Telugu.) On a mutilated stone set up in the same place. A fragment of record. Mentions Kandāḷa Dēvarājācharya of the Vādhūla-gōtra and his son. The former receives the title Vēdamārga-pratishṭhāpanāchārya. Dēvarāja belonged to the celebrated family of the Kandāḷās whose head Mudaliyāṇḍān was a trusted follower of Rāmānujāchārya.

511. 481 *of* 1906.—(Telugu.) On another mutilated slab set up in the same place. Dated in the reign of the Vijayanagara king Sadāśivadēvarāya Mahārāya. Records in Ś. 1464, Śubhakrit, a gift of land by Appaṅgāru, son of the āchārya mentioned in No. 480 above. [The inscription is also given in Mack. List. *Ins., Ced. Dts.*, p. 381, No. 45, where it is mentioned that the grant was made to one Nārāyaṇayya, son of Bhōjanapaḷḷi Raṅgayya.]

Guḍipāḍu.

512. On a stone in the Chennakēśava temple. (Telugu.) Records that in the reign of Veṅkaṭapati Rāya (1, 1586—1614), in Ś.1524, Rāyaṇamantri Bhāskarayya gave the God Chennakēśava a fee of 1 *kāśu* per every bullock-load of salt, 2 *kāśus* for one of cotton and ½ *kāśu* for other goods in the Gaṇḍikōṭa district. *Ins., Ced. Dts.*, p. 385, No. 59. See Ct. 268.

513. On a stone near a local well. (Telugu.) One Chinna Bhaṭṭa digs a well and endows two muṇṭas of land for a flower garden in a certain Naḷa. *Ibid.*, No. 60.

Iḍamaḍaka (Verumuḍḍaka).

514. On a stone north-east of the village. (Sanskrit and Telugu.) Records that Mallabhūpa, son of Rāchaṇa, dug a tank called Anantasamudram in Ś. 1338, Jaya, in the reign of Vijaya Dēva Rāya. *Ibid.*, p. 371, No. 7.

515. On a stone near the Vīrabhadra pagoda. (Telugu.) Grant of a tax by Chinna Timma Rāja and Koṇḍarāja to the deity in Ś. 1471, Saumya, in the reign of Sadāśiva Rāya. *Ibid.*, No. 8.

516. On a stone near the Hanumanta pagoda. (Telugu.) Records that Goppayya Dēva, son of Pinnayya Dēva, granted Jillēlla in free gift to God Ahōbala Naraśimha in Ś. 1381, Pramādi, in the reign of Mallikārjuna Rāya, son of Prauḍha Dēva Rāya (II). *Ibid.*, No. 9.

Jillēlla.

517. 471 *of* 1906.—(Telugu.) On a slab set up near a water-course by the side of the road in the village. A record of the time of the Vijayanagara king Vīrapratāpa Sadāśivadēva Mahārāya. Records in Ś. 1471, Saumya, gift of the proceeds of certain taxes collected in the village of Jillēlla to the temple of Vīrabhadradēva at Jillēlla by the Mahāmaṇḍalēśvara China-Timmarāja Koṇḍayadēva Mahārāju of the Ātrēya gōtra, Āpastamba-sūtra and the Yajuśśākhā.

518. On a stone north of the village near the Hanumanta temple. (Telugu.) Records that Vēligōṭe Kṛishṇamanāyanagāru remitted the former tax of three *māḍais* in Sarvayukti. *Ins., Ced. Dts.*, p. 430, No. 31.

519. On the east of the above. The same chief gives a similar exemption from the lands of God Chennakēśava. *Ibid.*, No. 32.

520. East of the above. (Telugu.) Records that in Ś. 1477, Rākshasa, Vipravinōdi Mantramūrti and other jugglers give to the deity their own allowance at Jillēlla. *Ibid.*, No. 33.

Jonnavaram.

521. On a stone near the Hanumantarāya pagoda. (Telugu.) Records a grant of Tripurānṭakarāya at Duvūr in Ś. 1194, Prajōtpatti. *Ibid.*, p. 369, No. 2.

Kallūr.

522. On a stone in the Agastyēśvara pagoda. Records that Vīramushṭi Liṅgayya granted to the deity the local allowance of three māḍais in Ś. 1511, in the reign of Veṅkaṭapatirāya I (1586—1614). *Ibid.*, p. 388, No. 70.

523. On a stone north of the pagoda. A Telugu record of Dēvarāya exempting the *Pañchalavāru* or artificers from tax. *Ibid.*, p. 388, No. 71.

524. On a stone at the gate of the pagoda. (Telugu.) Records that Nārāyaṇagāru gave some land for repairing a canal to the Reḍḍis and Karṇams of Kuchupalla in Ś. 1452, in the reign of Achyutarāya. *Ibid.*, No. 72.

Kāmanūru.

525. 469 *of* 1906.—(Telugu.) On a stone unearthed in the bed of the stream. The record mentions Chākalaguṇḍu. In archaic characters.

526. On a stone near the Gōpālasvāmi pagoda. (Telugu.) Records that the merchants of different places granted their allowance in Muḷikināḍ and Rēṇāḍ districts in Ś. 1458, Durmukhi. *Ibid.*, p. 385, No. 61.

Kānagūḍūru.

The following epigraphs which have been taken from *Mack. MSS.* are in Telugu.

527. On a stone west of the village. Records that Pinnamarāja, son of Rāmarāja Basavarāja, gave some land in the village for a watershed in Ś. 1448, Vyaya, in the reign of Kṛishṇadēvarāya. *Ins., Ced. Dts.*, p. 376, No. 26.

528. On a stone in the Chennakēśava pagoda. Records that Gaṅgarasayya, son of Muchikunta Kommarāju, gave some land in Koṟṟappāḍu village to two Nāyaḍus in Ś. 1439, Īśvara, in the reign of Kṛishṇadēvarāya. *Ibid.*, No. 27.

529. On a stone at the gate of the above temple. Records that in Ś. 1449, Sarvajit, the Dommaravāṇḍlu of Koṟṟapāḍ granted their local allowance to the God in Ś. 1449, Sarvajit. *Ibid.*, No. 28.

530. On a stone in a wall of the pagoda. Records that Gaṅgarasayya, son of Muchukunta Kommarāju, built the pagoda. *Ibid.*, p. 376, No. 28.

Koṟṟapāḍu.

531. 477 *of* 1906.—(Telugu.) On a pillar set up in the courtyard of the Chennakēśavasvāmin temple.—A record of the Vijayanagara king Kṛishṇadēva-Mahārāya in Ś. 1449, Sarvajit, Koṟṟapāḍu belonged to the Ghaṇḍikōṭa-śīma.

532. 478 *of* 1906.—(Telugu.) On two faces of a slab lying in the same courtyard. A much damaged record of the Vijayanagara king Vīrapratāpa Kṛishṇadēva-Mahārāya, date of which is lost. Mentions Sāḷuva-Komāra-Timmarasa-Ayyavāru.

Kottapalli.

533. On a stone near the Pōtarāju temple. (Telugu). Records that in Ś. 1445, Svabhānu, in the reign of Kṛishṇadēvarāya, some land was granted to the deity by 'Vassatirtha Sripada-Uḍayalu?' (Vyāsatīrtha?) See *Ins., Ced. Dts.*, p. 382, No. 50.

534. East of the above. (Telugu.) Records that Kāñchi Pāparāju gave some land to the Reḍḍis of Kottapalli in Ś. 1507, Tāraṇa, in the reign of Śrīraṅgarāya (1578—86) of Penukoṇḍa. *Ibid.*, No. 51.

535. On a stone west of the Hanumantarāya pagoda. (Telugu.) Records that Jillēlla Raṅgapatirāju granted land to the Reḍḍis in Ś. 1530, Plavaṅga, in the reign of Veṅkaṭapatirāya of Penukoṇḍa. *Ibid.*, No. 52.

Māchanapalle.

536. Near a well west of the village. An "illegible" epigraph.

Maḍūru.

Three records of this place which are in Telugu have been taken fram *Mack. MSS.*

537. On a stone in the village. Records that Chinna Timmarāja, son of Pedda-koṇḍarāja, gave the village to the Rāmānuja-Kūṭam at Ahōbalam in Ś. 1466, Krōdhi, in the reign of Sadāśivarāya. *Ibid.*, p. 387, No. 66.

538. On a stone in the street. Records that Kōnēṭi Chinna Timmarāju gave the same grant in the same year. *Ibid.*, No. 67.

539. On a stone east of the village. Records that Simha-Bhaṭlu, son of 'Śurutta Aubalabaṭṭu, gave eight tūms of land at Ammāvaram agrahāram to Rāmayya, son of "Pullapotenene" in Ś. 1477, Rākshasa, in the reign of Sadāśivarāya. *Ins., Ced. Dts.*, p. 387, No. 68.

Maidukūru.

540. On a stone in the street. (Telugu.) Records that Gaṅgasāni gave 68 shares in the village to Brahmans in Ś. 1181, Siddhārti, in the reign of Gaṇapati. *Ibid.*, p. 369, No. 4.

Nandyelampēṭa.

541. Near the Vīrabhadra pagoda. (Telugu.) Records that the merchants of the place gave a monetary contribution during each marriage to God and Goddess of the place in Ś. 1666. *Ibid.*, p. 374, No. 18.

542. On a stone east of the above. (Telugu.) The Reḍḍis, Karṇams and merchants of the place give a similar grant in Ś. 1667, Krōdhana. *Ibid.*, No. 19.

543. On a stone near the pagoda.—(Telugu.) Records "Jalakunti" Appayya and Śūrappa Rāmaṇṇa granted annually 2½ paṇams from the local taxes to the deity in Ś. 1664, Dundubhi. *Ibid.*, No. 20.

544. On a stone near the Tiruvēṅgalanātha pagoda. (Telugu.) Gift of a village to the God by Kṛishṇadēvarāya. *Ibid.*, No. 20.

Nerravāda.

545. On a stone in the village. (Telugu.) Records that Vīrappaṇṇa granted the "Nervadi" village to the God Kāḷahastīśvar in Ś. 1458, Durmukhi, in the reign of Achyutarāya. *Ibid.*, p. 386, No. 65.

Paidēla.

546. On a stone near the Īśvara pagoda. (Telugu.) Records that the jugglers granted their local allowance to God Rāmēśvara Rāmayya. *Ibid.*, p. 376, No. 30.

Parlapāḍu.

547. On a stone in the village. (Telugu.) Grant of the village to Ahōbalēśvara by Chinna Timmarāju, son of Rāmarāju, in Ś. 1467, Viśvāvasu, in the reign of Sadāśivarāya. *Ibid.*, p. 379, No. 38.

548. A C.P. in the hand of the local karṇam. (Sanskrit and Nāgari.) Records that Veṅkaṭapatirāya (I) gave to Veṅkatasōmayājulu in Ś. 1511, Virōdhi, the village of Veṅkaṭarāyasamudram or Rāmachandrapuram in Awk śīma. *Ibid.*, p. 388, No. 73.

Peddaśeṭṭipallc.

549. 482 *of* 1906.—(Telugu.) On a slab lying in the courtyard of the Chennakēśavasvāmin temple. Records in Ś. 1480,

Kaḷayukta, gift of land to the temple of Channakēśava-Perumāḷ at Seṭṭipaḷḷe by Mahāmaṇḍalēśvara Rāmarāju Rāyanarāju Koṇḍayya-dēva-Mahārāju. Aḷiya-Rāmarājayyavāru is also mentioned.

Proddatūru.

550. 466 *of* 1906.—(Telugu.) On four faces of a pillar set up near Mallāreḍḍi's house. A partially damaged record of the Chōḷa king Chōḷamahārājulu of the solar race, the Kāśyapa gōtra and the family of Karikāla. The king was ruling the Rēnāṇḍu seven thousand (country). Records gift of land. See Nos. 409 and 455.

551. 467 *of* 1906.—(Telugu.) On a slab built into the wall of another house near No. 486. A fragment of record of the Vijayanagara king Dēvarāya-Oḍaya I, dated Ś. 1331, Virōdhin.

552. 468 *of* 1906.—(Telugu.) On a stone set up close to the image of Āñjanēya near the market at the same village. A damaged record, dated Ś. 1329, Sarvajit. Seems to record that the image of Hanumat was set up by a Reḍḍi and some land was given. [The Mack. List, *Ins.*, *Ced. Dts.*, p. 382, No. 47, gives this inscription. It says the donor is Timma Reḍḍi, son of Achummulla Reḍḍi.]

553. A P.G. in the hand of the weaver Akkaṇa. Records in Ś. 1622, Vikrama, a grant of land to one Chuñchi and exemption from the tax on the weaver loom. *Ins.*, *Ced. Dts.*, p. 306, No. 203.

554. P.G. in the hands of Veṅkaṭaśāstri. (Telugu.) Records that the inhabitants of the place granted in Ś. 1708, Prabhava, seven and a half *tūms* of land for a favourable rent of 10 pagodas to Kṛishṇa Bhaṭṭa. *Ibid.*, No. 204.

555. A C.P. in the hands of the same. (Telugu.) Records that Maṭḷa Tiruvēṅgalanātha and Anantarāja gave some land in Pichappādu to Poli Reḍḍi and Pāpa Reḍḍi in Ś. 1708, Prabhava. *Ibid.*, No. 205.

556. On a stone in the pagoda. (Telugu.) Records that Chinna Timmarāju gave some lands to the local karṇams in Ś. 1471, Kīlaka, in the reign of Sadāśivarāya. *Ibid.*, p. 381, No. 43.

557. On a stone south-east of the fort. (Telugu.) Records that in Ś. 1676, Śrīmukha, Veṅkaṭareḍḍi dug and built a tank to the deity. *Ibid.*, No. 46.

558. On a stone in the Agastyēśvara pagoda. (Telugu.) Records that Vīrappa, son of Mindagūḍala Tripurāntaka, erected the inner part of the temple in Ś. 1666, Raktākshi. *Ibid.*, No. 48.

Rāmēśvaram.

559. 383 *of* 1904.—(Sanskrit and Kanarese.) On four faces of a pillar set up in the courtyard of the Rāmaliṅgēśvara temple. The Rāshṭrakūṭa king Kṛishṇa III (Duradaṅkakāra) records gift of land and taxes to the temple of Rāmēśvara. The king's general is said to have taken Kāñchi from "the knavish Dramiḍas."

560. 384 *of* 1904.—(Telugu.) On two faces of another pillar set up in the same place. A record of the time of the Chōḷa king Pōrmukharāma Puṇyakumāra Prithvivallabha Chōḷa-Mahārāju. Records gift of land to the Vasantēśvara (temple) at Tārumunru by Vasanti-Pōri Chōḷa-Mahādēvi, in the fields of Vīripariti-Mārpiḍugu. Raṭṭaguḍlu was the *ajñāpti*. See No. 455 above.

561. 385 *of* 1904.—(Kanarese.) On two faces of a third pillar set up in the same place. Dated in the reign of the Vijayanagara king Vīrapratāpa Kṛishṇarāya-Mahārāya. Records in Ś. 1436, expired, Bhava, gift of the village of Payindale in the Chernūraśīma to the temple of Rāmayyadēva at Rāmēśvara which belonged to the district of Ghaṇḍikōṭa-śīme. See *Ins., Ced. Dts.*, p. 394, No. 97.

562. 386 *of* 1904.—(Telugu.) On a slab set up in the same place. Narasanāyaniṅgāru records in Ś. 1420, Kāḷayukta, gift of land at Rāmēśvaram Podatūru to the temple of Rāmayyaliṅga at Rāmēśvara, a village in Muḷikināḍu. The Śāḷuva Immaḍi-Narasimharāya (the son of the usurper Naraśiṅga) is also mentioned. [See *Ins., Ced. Dts.*, p. 393, No. 96, for this inscription. It mentions a measure called *Dareguda pramāṇam.*]

563. 387 *of* 1904.—(Sanskrit and Telugu.) On another slab set up in the same place. The Vijayanagara king Kṛishṇadēva Mahārāya records in Ś. 1432, Pramōda, a remission of the marriage tax payable by the brides and bridegrooms of all castes in the many divisions which constituted the Vijayanagara Empire. The order of the king was carried out by Sāluva-Timmappayya, Gōvindayya and Adapi-Nāyaniṅgāru. The Leyden grant also refers to the *Kaṇṇāḷakkāṇam* and shows that it prevailed as early as the eleventh century.

564. 388 *of* 1904.—(Telugu.) On two faces of the Nandi pillar in front of the shrine of the goddess in the same temple. Records in Ś. 1472, Sādhāraṇa, that a Vīra-Śaiva guru made a gift to the temple of Mukti-Rāmēśvara.

565. 389 *of* 1904.—(Telugu.) On a slab set up in a maṇṭapa in front of the same temple. Records in Ś. 1430, Vibhava, gift of the various customs of the village by Śāḷuva-Gōvindarāja for the merit of the king, Vīra-Narasimharāya, his own father Rāchirāja and Śāḷuva Timmayya. The donor built the prākāra wall and a maṇṭapa of the temple. See *Ins., Ced. Dts.*, p. 393, No. 95.

566. 390 *of* 1904.—(Telugu.) On a pillar in the Navagraha-maṇṭapa behind the Mūlasthānēśvara temple at Rāmēśvaram. An incomplete record dated Ś. 1596, Ānanda. Mentions the Reḍḍis and Karṇams of Rāmēśvaram. [The *Ins., Ced. Dts.*, p. 380, No. 42, says that it records a grant of the land by the inhabitants of

Ramēśvaraṁ village to an architect who built the Bōghamaṇṭapam.]

567. On a stone in front of the Raṅgamaṇṭapam. (Telugu.) Records that Guṇḍlūru Chinnayya granted to the deity in a certain Pramādīcha, the tax of three weaver-looms and three shops of his own and the tax of "*Pinjari-Stāvaram, Eḍugastāvaram, Kanakastāvaram*, etc." at the village. *Ins., Ced. Dts.*, p. 379, No. 39.

568. On a stone near the Dvajastambham. (Telugu.) Records that Timmarāja remitted the tax on the barbers in different villages in Ś. 1469, Plavaṅga, in the reign of Sadāśivarāya. *Ibid.*, No. 40.

569. On a stone in the main gōpuram of Vīrabhadra. (Telugu.) Records that certain people granted an allowance of thirteen paṇams, etc., to Goddess Aṅkālamma in Ś. 1452, Sarvadhāri, in the reign of Kṛishṇadēvarāya. *Ibid.*, p. 384, No. 56.

570. On a stone near a local well. (Telugu.) Records that Rāvanūr Veṅkaṭaśāstri dug the well in a certain Krōdhi. *Ibid.*, No. 57.

571. On a stone in the village. (Telugu.) The Brahmans granted eighteen puṭṭis of land for the local God in Ś. 1437, Yuva, in the time of Kṛishṇadēva Rāya. The village also seems to have called "Prauḍhadēvarāyapuram." *Ibid.*, p. 385, No. 58.

572. On a stone in front of the above pagoda. (Telugu.) Records that the local people granted one and a half kuṇṭa of dry field to a carpenter for erecting the spire and room in the pagoda in Ś. 1598, Naḷa. *Ibid.*, No. 41.

573. On a stone north of the Raṅga maṇṭapam. (Telugu.) Records that "Nausu-guddum Rāmayyadēvuḍu" bought a flower garden from the temple in Ś. 1281, Vikāri, and gave it as a free gift. *Ibid.*, p. 394, No. 98.

574. On a wall of the Rāmēśvara pagoda. (Telugu.) Records that the Dharmakartas disposed of their lands to a person. *Ibid.*, No. 99.

Sarvireḍḍipaḷḷi.

575. On a stone east of the village. (Telugu.) Records that Tirumaladēvamma, the queen of Kṛishṇadēvarāya granted to Raghunātha of the "Putmum Vyasula Maṭṭum" the village of Kāvalūr in free gift. *Ins., Ced. Dts.*, p. 387, No. 69.

Śivapuram.

576. On a stone in the Īśvara temple. (Telugu.) Records that Bukkarāju and Chintamarāju granted the village to God Tiruvēṅgalanātha of Parinepāḍ in Ś. 1461, Vikāri, in the reign of Achyutarāya. *Ibid.*, p. 375, No. 24.

Tāḷḷamārapuram.

577. On a stone in front of the Āñjanēya pagoda. Records that some jugglers granted to God Rāmaliṅga their local allowance of forty paṇams in Ś. 1445, Chitrabhānu, in the reign of Kṛishṇa Rāya. *Ibid.*, p. 384, No. 55.

578. 472 *of* 1906.—(Telugu.) On a slab set up in front of the Madanagōpāla temple. Dated in the reign of the Vijayanagara king Vīrapratāpa Sadāśivadēva-Mahārāya. Appears to record the remission of certain taxes on barbers by Mahāmaṇḍalēśvara Rāmarājayyadēva-Mahārāju. Dated Ś. 1469, Plavaṅga.

579. 473 *of* 1906.—(Telugu.) On another slab set up in the same place. Records in Ś. 1656, Pramāthin, gift of a *garuḍastambha* pillar to the temple of Śrī-Madanagōpāla-svāmin of Taṅgatūru.

Taṅgatūru.

580. On a stone near the pagoda of the Kumudvati river east of the village. (Old Kanarese.) Records that in the reign of Bhujabala Vīranārāyaṇa Āhavamalladēva the temple of Mūlasthāna Pāpavināśadēva was established in Ś. 1013, Prajōtpatti. The record is in the Halakanaḍa language. See *Ins., Ced. Dts.*, p. 369, No. 1.

Tondaladinne.

581. On a stone in the Hanumanta pagoda. (Telugu.) Records that Chinna Timmarāju, son of Koṇḍa Rāju, gave the village to God Ahōbala Narasimha in Ś. 1469, Plavaṅga, in the reign of Sadāśivārāya. *Ins., Ced. Dts.*, p. 372, No. 11.

Timmulappāḍu (Timmapāḍu ?).

582. On a stone west of the village. (Telugu.) Records that Narasapantulu, Tarifdār, granted one and half a kuṇṭas of dry land to a Brahman named Sadāśivabhaṭ in Ś. 1623, Vishu, for excavating a well and building the village of Poliḍūḍi. *Ibid.*, p. 81, No. 89.

Upparapalle.

583. 325 *of* 1905.—(Telugu.) On a white marble slab set up by the side of the Cuddapah-Pushpagiri road close to the ruined Śiva temple called Mobhudēvalam. A record of the Vaiḍumba-Mahārāja (Bhuvana-Trinētra) in Ś. 894. Records the coronation of the king. [His relation to other Vaiḍumbas is not known.]

584. 326 *of* 1905.—(Sanskrit and Telugu.) On a huge pillar lying in front of the same temple. Dated in the reign of the Vijayanagara king Vīrapratāpa Kṛishṇadēvarāya Mahārāya in Ś. 1446, Tāraṇa. Records that Peda Śiṅgama-Nāyaniṅgāru of the Jupalli family rebuilt the Nāganātha (or Nāgēśvara) temple of stone, dug a tank near it and granted land to the temple. A long genealogy of the chief is given at the beginning. He was ruling over the Chernūri-śīma and the Potḷa-dūrti-śīma districts *(sthala)* included in Muḷiki-nāḍu, a subdivision of the Ghaṇḍikōṭa-śīma, which formed part of the Udayagiri-rājya.

585. 327 *of* 1905.—(Grantha and Tamil.) On a pillar of the maṇṭapa in front of the ruined Śiva temple called Mobhudēvaḷam. Records in Ś. 1181, Siddhārthin, the building of the maṇṭapa for the stone bull by a private individual. The village is called *Udakāśayagrāma*, which is evidently a translation of the Telugu *Cheruvuru*, now known as Chernūru.

586. 328 *of* 1905.—(Sanskrit and Telugu.) On a broken slab lying in the same maṇṭapa. A fragmentary record of the Kākatīya king Pratāpa Rudradēva Mahārāja (1295—1323), dated Ś. 1236, Pramādhin. A subordinate of the king claims to have reduced the fort of Ghaṇḍikōṭa. A damaged record.

587. 329 *of* 1905.—(Sanskrit and Telugu.) On another similar piece lying in the same maṇṭapa. A fragment of record of the Kākatīya king Pratāpa Rudradēva Mahārāja (1295—1323). Refers to the king having appointed Goṅkaya Reḍḍi, a servant of his son Juttaya, to the governorship of Ghaṇḍikōṭa and Muḷiki-nāṇḍu districts.

Vanipeṇṭa.

[The following records taken from *Mack. MSS.* are all in Telugu.]

588. On a stone near the Chennarāya pagoda. Records that Vīrama-Nāyaḍu granted some land to the deity in Ś. 1408, Prabhava, in the reign of Śāḷuva Narasimmarāya (the usurper). *Ins., Ced. Dts.*, p. 372, No. 13.

589. On the north wall of the above pagoda. Records that the managers of the temple gave some land to a stone-cutter and iron-smith, in Ś. 1441, Pramādi, in the reign of Kṛishṇadēvarāya. *Ibid.*, No. 14.

590. On the eastern wall of the above. Records that Rāyasam Gaṅgarasu, son of Muchuguṇṭa Kommarasu, gave some land below the tank to the people in Ś. 1443, Vishu, in the reign of Kṛishṇadēvarāya, for repairing the tank. *Ibid.*, No. 15.

591. North of the above. Records that Veṅkaṭayya and his brother Appayya disposed of their land to God Chennakēśava in Śukḷa 1491, in the reign of Sadāśivarāya for 170 pagodas. *Ibid.*, No. 16.

592. On a wall of the above pagoda. Records that certain Vipra-vinōdins granted their local allowances of two villages to God Chennakēśava in Ś. 1475, Pramādīcha, in the reign of Sadāśivarāya. *Ibid.*, No. 17.

Vellala.

593. On a stone in the local Bhīmēśvara pagoda. (Telugu.) Records that Chinna Vīraṇṇa Nāyuḍu, son of Kaṇḍanavōli Kāñchiśeṭṭi, granted 12 *tūms* of land in the village to the deity in Ś. 1447, Pārthiva, in the reign of Kṛishṇadēvarāya. *Ins., Ced. Dts.*, p. 377, No. 31.

594. On a stone in front of the Āñjanēya pagoda. (Telugu.) Records that Gaṅgayya Rāja and Chinna Timmarāja, son of Aubalarāja, gave 36 *puṭṭis* and 16 *tūms* of land to the Gods and Brahmans of the village in Ś. 1467, Viśvāvasu, in the reign of Sadāśivarāya. *Ibid.*, No. 32.

595. On a stone in the Āñjanēya pagoda. (Telugu.) Records that Chinna Timmarāja granted to the Karṇam exemption from tax in Ś. 1479, Piṅgaḷa, in the reign of Sadāśivarāya. *Ibid.*, No. 33.

PULIVENDLA TALUK.

Kommanūtala.

596. A forged C.P. grant dated Ś. 856, *Jaya*, relating the local story of seven Kōmaṭi brothers who offered their heads to God Veṅkaṭēśa for miraculously finding some wells of fresh water on a bare rock. The merchants of Vijayanagar and Adavēni (Adoni) countries built a temple on the spot in their memory and made endowments.

Mōpūr.

597. 496 *of* 1906.—(Telugu and Sanskrit.) On slab lying behind the western gōpura of the Bhairavēśvara temple at Mōpūr. A record of the Vijayanagara king Vīrapratāpa Kumāra-Dēvarāya Mahārāya (Dēva Rāya II), son of Vīra-Vijaya-Bukkarāya-Mahārāya (III); records in Ś. 1347, Viśvāvasu, the building of the gōpura of Mōpūr Bhairavadēva by Tirumalarāya, a servant of the king. Incomplete.

598. 497 *of* 1906.—(Telugu.) In archaic characters. On a stone lying near No. 597. Records gift of land by Śri-Mallirāju.

599. 498 *of* 1906.—(Telugu.) On a slab set up in front of the central shrine in the same temple. Dated in the reign of the Vijayanagara king Vīrapratāpa Vīra-Sadāśivadēva Mahārāya. Records in Ś. 1466, Krōdhin, remission of certain taxes in the villages belonging to temples and Brāhmaṇas of the Ghaṇḍikōṭa-śīma by the mahāmaṇḍalēśvara Timmayadēva-Mahārāju, son of Naraśiṅgayadēva-Mahārāja and grandson of Avubhaladēva-Mahārāja of Nandyāla.

600. 499 *of* 1906.—(Telugu.) On another slab set up in the same place. A record of the Vijayanagara king Vīrapratāpa-Vīra-Achyutarāya Mahārāya in Ś. 1452, Vikrita. Gift to the temple of 235 *varāhas*, payable every year in the villages belonging to the temple of Bhairavēśvara at Mōpūru. The donor was Ayyaparasugāru, son of Rāyasam Koṇḍamarasayyagāru.

601. 500 *of* 1906.—(Telugu.) On a slab lying near the Vībhūti-maṇṭapa in the same temple. Dated in the reign of the Vijayanagara king Vīraśrī-Savaṇṇa-Oḍaya, "lord of the Eastern Ocean." Records in Ś. 1275, Vijaya, gift of a village by the king for the merit of his father Kampaṇa-Oḍaya (I) and his mother Mengadēvi-ammā. [The chief ought not to be confounded with his namesake, the son of Bukka II.]

602. 501 *of* 1906.—(Telugu.) On a slab built into the main drain in the same temple. A damaged record, the date and the name of the king of which are lost. Remission of taxes for the merit of Vīra-Narasimharāya and Śāḷuva-Timmayya.

603. 502 *of* 1906.—(Telugu.) On a slab built into the floor at the entrance into the central shrine of the same temple. An unfinished record dated in Dundubhi. Appears to be a gift by an officer of the mahāmaṇḍalēśvara Nandēla Timmarājayyadēva-Mahārāju to the Bhairavēśvara temple at Mōpūru.

604. 503 *of* 1906.—(Telugu.) On the wall at the entrance into the maṇṭapa in front of the same shrine, left side. A record of the Vijayanagara king Vīraśrī-Savaṇa-Oḍaya (I), "lord of the Eastern Ocean," ruling at Udayagiri-paṭṭaṇa. Records in Ś. 1273, Nandana, gift of land to Bhairavadēva of Mōpūru by the king for the merit of his father Kamparāju and his mother Meṅgadēvi-ammā.

605. 504 *of* 1906.—(Telugu.) In the same place. A much damaged record of the Vijayanagara king Vīraśrī-Savaṇa-Oḍaya (I), dated Ś. 1283, Śubhakrit.

606. 505 *of* 1906.—(Telugu.) In the same place, right side. Records in Ś. 1295, Pramādin, a transaction concerning temple priests.

607. 506 *of* 1906.—(Telugu.) On the right and left door posts of the entrance into the same maṇṭapa. Records in Ś. 1231, Sauvume (Saumya), the gift of the door post by the mahāmaṇḍalēśvara Bhrammidēva Chōḷa-Mahārāja, grandson of Bhōgaladēvi and Bhrammidēva. The chief calls himself "the worshipper of the divine and glorious lotus feet of the god Bhōganāthadēva of Pāmiḍi." [These chiefs formed one of the numerous Telugu chōḍa dynasties of later times.]

608. 507 *of* 1906.—(Telugu.) On a vīragal set up in the courtyard of the same temple. Records in Ś. 1233, Sādhāraṇa, the death of Ahubalanātha, son of the mahāmaṇḍalēśvara Chāḷukya-Nārāyaṇa, Veṅgi-Tribhuvanamalla, lord of the town of Ayōdhya, worshipper of the feet of Allāḷanātha, Pōtarāju Pemmayadēva Mahārāju. The hero had gone on an expedition to the Mārajavāḍi country and died at Dhārātīrtha.

609. 508 *of* 1906.—(Telugu.) On the base of the central shrine in the same temple. A damaged record in Yuvan. Appears to record transfers of rights in temple service and its emoluments.

610. 509 *of* 1906.—(Telugu.) On the same base. A damaged record dated in Ś. 1292, Sādhāraṇa. Appears to record transfers of rights in temple service and its emoluments.

611. 509-*A of* 1906.—(Telugu.) On the same base. A damaged record, dated Ś. 1238, Rākshasa. Another inscription is found close to this, but its date is doubtful.

612. 510 *of* 1906.--(Telugu.) On the same base. A record, dated in Ś. 1823, Vrisha. Built in at the end.

613. 511 *of* 1906.—(Telugu.) On the same base. A record, dated in Ś. 1268, Sarvajit. Built in at the end.

614. 512 *of* 1906.—(Telugu.) On the same base. A record, dated in Ś. 1296, Ānanda. Built in at the end.

615. 513 *of* 1906.—(Telugu.) On the same base. A record, dated in Ś. 1384, Chitrabhānu. Built in at the end.

Muttukūru.

616. 514 *of* 1906.—(Telugu.) On a slab built into the platform in front of the Chennakēśavasvāmin temple. Records in the reign of the Vijayanagara king Sadāśivadēva-Mahārāya in Ś. 1469, Parābhava, remission of taxes on barbers in the Ghaṇḍikōṭaśīma made originally by Rāmarājayya. Subsequently these as well as a few others were remitted by a local chief at Muttukūru, which belonged to the temple of Tiruvēṅgalanātha.

617. 515 *of* 1906.—(Telugu in archaic characters.) On a pillar set up in the courtyard of the same temple. Mentions Muttukūru and seems to record the death of a hero.

618. 516 *of* 1906.—(Telugu.) On a pillar set up at the entrance into the courtyard of the same temple. Dated in the reign of the Sāḷuva king Immaḍi-Naraśiṅgadēva-Mahārāya, son of Śāḷuva-Naraśiṅgadēva-Mahārāya (the usurper): Records in Ś. 1415, Pramādin, gift of taxes payable in the village of Muttukūru in favour of the temple of Chennakēśvaradēva by a servant of Narasanāyiniṅgāru who was a subordinate of the king. The village Muttukūru was situated to the south-east of the Bhairava-kshētra on the Mōhanāchala hill in the Mukti-nāḍu country. [Narasa was evidently the founder of the Tuḷuva dynasty after overthrowing his master Immaḍi Narasimha.]

619. 517 *of* 1906.—(Telugu.) On the door post of the entrance into the central shrine of the same temple. Records in the reign of the king Chōḷamahārājulu gift of land to a certain Pīmana (Bhīmaṇa)-goravalu by Bhikkirāju. The king was ruling the Rēnāṇḍu seven thousand (country).

620. 518 *of* 1906.—(Telugu.) On a pillar lying in front of the Śiva temple in the same village. A much damaged record. In archaic characters.

Nallacheruvupalle.

621. 495 *of* 1906.—(Telugu.) On a pillar lying near the well called Kaṭṭubhāvi on the way to the Mōpūr temple from Nallacheruvupalle. A damaged record. In archaic characters. Mentions Eḷa-Chōḷa-Mahārāju and Mutturāju. [Mr. Sewell says that the temple was enlarged and beautified by the Vijayanagar sovereign in Ś. 1466 (A.D. 1544). Eḷachōḷa figures among the ancestors of a Chōḷa chief named Śrīkanṭha in a C. P. in the Madras Museum. See *Ep. Ind.*, V, p. 123, footnote. It is not known whether he was a Cuddapah Chōḷa and if so what his relation was to the Bastar Chōḷas of the eleventh century or the Chōḷas of Niḍugal and Hēmāvati, to whom Rice refers.]

622. On the south stone pillar of the Mukha-Maṇṭapam of the Bhairavēśvara temple. (Telugu.) Records that Vīra Kampaṇa Uḍaiyār, in Ś. 1165 (?), Pārthiva, granted the villages of Alavalapati (Alavalapāḍu?) and Goṭṭūru to God Bhairavēśvara. *Ins., Ced. Dts.*, p. 10, No. 32. (Both these villages are in Pulivenḍla taluk.)

623. On a pillar of the same. (Telugu.) Records an exemption of tax of the local temple by Ayyapparasa in Ś. 1452, Vikriti, in the reign of Achyutarāya. *Ibid.*, No. 33.

624. In the same.—(Telugu.) Records a similar exemption in different villages in Ś. 1466, Krōdhi, by Nandyāla Timmarāja, son of Naraśiṅgarāja, in the reign of Sadāśivarāya. *Ibid.*, No. 34.

Pārṇapalle.

625. 60 *of* 1912.—(Telugu.) On a rock close to the bank of the river. Registers in Ś. 1318, Dhātri, that an irrigation channel was blocked up and that it was restored under the orders of Mallappa-Voḍaya, son of Irugapa-Daṇṇāyaka. [Irugappa was evidently the Jain minister of Bukka II and author referred to in By. 384 and Cg. 451. Mr. Sewell mentions an inscription in this place dated Ś. 1398 in the reign of Prauḍhadēva, but Mr. Krishna Sastri believes it to be a mistake of the one copied.]

Pernapāḍu.

626. On a stone near the Bhairava pagoda. (Telugu.) Records that in the reign of Dēvarāya (II), in Ś. 1330, Kīlaka, Pinnayyadēva Mahārāja established the God Bhairava, dug a well, planted a garden of various trees, and granted three *tūms* of land in the village. *Ins., Ced. Dts.*, p. 375, No. 22.

Pulivendla.

627. 491 *of* 1906.—(Telugu.) On a slab set up at the entrance into the Raṅganāthasvāmin temple. Dated in the reign of the Vijayanagara king Vīrapratāpa Kṛishṇarāya-Mahārāya. Records in S. 1431, Śukla, the gift of a village by Narasayyadēva-Mahārāju of the Vasishṭhagōtra, and the Sūrya-vamśa, who was a descendant of Mādhavavarman of Bezvāḍa. It belonged to Pulivindala-sthala in the Muḷikināṭi-śīma, a subdivision of the Ghaṇḍikōṭa-śīma, a district of the Udayagiri-rājya. See Kn. 81.

628. 492 *of* 1906.—(Telugu.) On two faces of a slab lying at the entrance into the Āñjanēyasvāmin temple in the same village. Dated in the reign of the Vijayanagara king Vīrapratāpa Achyutadēva-Mahārāya. Records in Ś. 1457, Manmatha, a charter granted to the merchants, Reḍḍis, Karṇams, etc., of Pulivindala-śīma, by Yellappa-Nāyaniṅgāru of the Tuluva (country) who was the agent of Timmarāju-Sālakayya-dēva-Mahārāju.

629. 493 *of* 1906.—(Telugu.) On three faces of a pillar set up at the entrance into the Śiva temple in the same village. Records in Nandana gift of land by the Mahāmaṇḍalēśvara Jatāpi Kāñchayyadēva-Mahārāju.

630. 494 *of* 1906.—(Telugu.) On a slab lying near Gōvinda Rao's house in the same village. Hajarati Mahammad Jāphara Sāpēbu (evidently a local chief), records in Ś. 1613, Prajāpati, gift of charter to the merchants *(Komaṭis)* and oil-mongers of Pulivindhula who had deserted the town as they had been forced to supply provisions on credit to the authorities *(divānam)*.

Śuṅkēsula.

631. On a stone in the Narasimhasvāmi pagoda in the fort. (Telugu.) Records that a village was granted to the deity in Ś. 1264, Chitrabhānu, in the reign of Prauḍha Uḍaiyalu at Awk-śīma. *Ins., Ced. Dts.*, p. 91, No. 130. [This village gave its name to Nrisimha Kavi, the author of *Kavikarṇarasāyana* and *māndhātai charitra.*

Tonḍuru.

[The following epigraphs which are in Telugu have been taken from *Mack. MSS.*]

632. On a stone south of the village. Records the grant of the allowance of Valamore to God Chennakēśava by the jugglers in Ś. 1467, Viśvāvasu, in the reign of Sadāśivarāya. *Ibid.*, p. 10, No. 26.

633. On a stone near the Gōpālasvāmi temple. Records that Naraśiṅgarāju granted six tūms of land in the village in Ś. 1476, Ānanda, in the reign of Sadāśivarāya. *Ibid.*, No. 27.

634. On a stone below the above. Records that Cheṭṭi Anantarāju Raṅgarāju granted five tūms of dry field to one Koṇḍarāsu, in a Saumya. *Ibid.*, No. 28.

635. On a stone in front of the Āñjanēya pagoda. Records that Gobbūri Narasarāju granted to two sculptors two tūms of land in Ś. 1478, Naḷa, for carving the Hanumanṭa image. *Ins., Ced. Dts.*, p. 10, No. 29.

636. On a stone in front of the Chennakēśava pagoda. Records that in the same reign Sumati Raṅgarāju granted to the deity the duties of Āvalūr-pēṭa in Ś. 1466, Krōdhi. *Ibid.*, No. 30.

637. On a stone in a side of the spire. Records the erection of the spire in Ś. 1347, Viśvāvasu, by Tirumalarāja in the reign of Vīrapratāpadēvarāya (II). *Ibid.*, No. 31.

Ulimella.

638. 519 *of* 1906.—(Telugu.) On a slab set up in front of the Chennakēśavasvāmin temple. A mutilated record of the Vijayanagara king Vīrapratāpa Dēvarāya-Mahārāya, dated in Parābhava. Mentions the temple of Chennakēśava-Perumāḷ at Ulimila (Ulimella).

Vēmpaḷḷi.

639. On a stone in front of the mosque. (Telugu and Persian.) Records that "Naknama Khan" erected it in 1590, 'Plavaṅga.' *Ins., Ced. Dts.*, p. 12, No. 41.

640. A Telugu C.P. in the hands of Hanumakoṇḍa Veṅgalayya. A record of Ś. 1508, Vyaya, regranting a former land to one Lōkarāju, etc. (Not clear.) *Ibid.*, No. 42.

641. A Telugu C.P. in the hands of Tirumala Tātāchārya. Records the gift of Pālūru (Pulivenḍla taluk) in Ś. 1566, Tāraṇa, to Kumāra Tātāchārlu by Pammasāni Timmanāyaḍu. *Ibid.*, No. 43. See Cg. 937.

PULLAMPET TALUK.

Akipāḍu.

642. On a stone south of the village. A Telugu record dated in Ś. 1356, Ānanda. Mentions Gajapati Kāñchirāju and Pushparāju in the reign of Dēvarāya (II). *Ins., Ced. Dts.*, p. 246, No. 20.

Anantarasupēṭa (Kumāra Anantarasupeta) ?.

643. A P.G. in the hands of Śeṭṭipaḷḷi Pāpabhaṭṭu in the place. (Telugu.) Records the grant of the village at a favourable rent of 12 pagodas to Kṛishṇam Bhaṭlu by Rāmadās Timmarasu, Tarifdār. *Ins., Ced. Dts.*, p. 304, No. 196.

Anantarasupuram.

644. A C.P. in Sanskriṭ in the hands of Kumāra Anantapuram Brahmans. Records that Maṭla Kumāra Anantarāsu and his brother Veṅkaṭa-rāmarāsu built the village in Ś. 1619, Īśvara, and granted it as free gift to eighteen Brahmans. *Ins., Ced. Dts.*, p. 286, No. 144.

Anantasamudram.

645. On a rock stone south of the village. (Telugu.) Records that in a Paritāpi, the 24 tribes of Dommaras granted the annual allowance of 20 *paṇams* due to them from Dāsarapaḷḷi to God Kamparāya of that place. *Ins., Ced. Dts.*, p. 281, No. 130.

Attirāla.

This is the ancient Tiruvaṛatturai of Mēlpākanādu, a subdivision of Ādhirājēndrachōḷamaṇḍala. The following epigraphs show that the Paraśurāmēśvara shrine was earlier than Rājarāja III and improved by the Sāhiṇi family of Gaṅgaya and Ambadēva.

646. 398 *of* 1911.—(Tamil.) On the inner prākāra wall of the Paraśurāmēśvara temple. A record of the sixteenth year of the Chōḷa king Tṛibhuvanachakravartin Rājarājadēva III. Records gift of 1 māḍai for a lamp to the temple of Tiruvirāmīśvaradēva at Tiruvaṛatturai in Mēr-Pākkainādu, a subdivision of Ādhirājēndra-chōḷa-maṇḍalam, by a native of Nenpākkai.

647. 399 *of* 1911.—(Tamil.) On the outer prākāra wall of the same temple. Records in Ś. 1212, Vikrita, gift of 12 *māḍais* for lamps by the wife of Ponungaṇṭi Vāsireḍḍi, to the temple of Paraśurāmīśvaramuḍaiya-Nāyanār at Tiruvaṛatturai in Pottappināḍu, a subdivision of Mēr-Pākkai-nāḍu in Ādhirājēndra-maṇḍalam.

648. 400 *of* 1911.—(Tamil.) On the same wall. Records in Ś. 1205, Pārthiva (wrong), gift of two *māḍais* for providing a flower garland to the same temple (here called Tiruvirāmīśura-muḍaiya-Nāyanār).

649. 401 *of* 1911.—(Tamil.) On the same wall. Records in Ś. 1200, Bahudhānya, gift of 12 *māḍais* for a lamp to the shrine of Vairava-piḷḷaiyār at Tiruvaṛatturai by a native of Puḍōli.

650. 402 *of* 1911.—(Tamil.) On the same wall. A record in Ś. 1209, Sarvajit, providing for the supply of 1 *nāḷi* of curds every day to the temples of Tiruvirāmīśuramuḍaiya-Nāyanār, and Vairava-piḷḷaiyār, for the merit of the chief who was ruling the Pottappi-nāḍu.

651. 403 *of* 1911.—(Tamil.) On the same wall. Records in Ś. 1202, Vikrama, gift of 15 *māḍais* for lamps and garlands to the temple of Paraśurāmīśvaramuḍaiya-Nāyanār, by a native of Maṇ-dappaḷḷi.

652. 404 *of* 1911.—(Tamil.) On a slab set up at the ruined main entrance into the same temple. Records in Ś. 1194, Āṅgirasa, an agreement by the residents of the Pottappi-nāḍu district who had met in the maṇṭapa called Chitramēḷi to raise one *māḍai* from each village in order to construct an embankment on the side of the river and to prevent any injury from floods to the temple of Paraśurāmīśvaramuḍaiya-Nāyanār.

653. 405 *of* 1911.—(Telugu.) On another slab set up in the same place. An unfinished record of the Sāḷuva king Naraśiṅgayyadēva-Mahārāja, dated Ś. 1399, Hēmalambi. Registers that Annamarasayya (evidently an officer of his) came to Araturēvulu, enquired into the affairs of the Kritrīśvara, Paraśurāmēśvara and the Bhairava temples and seeing that the income had been stopped in the interval, restored the temple lands at Prōli, for the merit of king Naraśiṅgayyadēva Mahārāja. [The Mack. List, *Ins., Ced. Dts.*, p. 248, No. 26, gives the same inscription. It says that the restored lands amounted to 166 kuṇṭas. The Śāḷuva referred to was the celebrated usurper.]

654. 406 *of* 1911.—(Telugu.) On a third slab lying broken in the same place. A damaged record of Ambadēva-Mahārāja, ruling at Vallūri-paṭṭaṇa, dated Ś. 1209, Sarvajit (A.D. 1287). Mentions among others, the districts of Gaṇḍikōṭa, Reṇāḍu, Yeruva, Pottapi-nāṇḍu and Muḷiki-nāṇḍu and the temple of Paraśurāmēśvara at Araturēvula-mahāsthāna. Refers to a number of tanks, canals and villages founded and called after either the name of the king or one of his *birudas*. There is reference to repairs made in the temple by his ancestor Gaṅga Sāhini, the feudatory of king Gaṇapati about A.D. 1250. [The Mack. List, *Ins., Ced. Dts.*, p. 247, No. 25, gives this inscription.]

655. In Attiralla village. A Telugu record of Dēvamahārāja granting a piece of land to Gods Bhairava and Rāmanātha in Ś. 1198, Dhātu. *Ibid.*, p. 247, No. 25.

656. A Telugu C.P. in the hand of Pāpagāru, manager of the temple. Records that the Reḍḍis, Karṇams and Brahmans of the Pottapi-ṇāṇḍu fixed a grant of a *Patika* for each *Ghattivarāha* of the revenue of the village to Trātēśvarasvāmi, in Ś. 1609, Vibhava, in the reign of Veṅkaṭa Rāmarāzudēva Chōḍa Mahārāja. *Ins., Ced. Dts.*, p. 261, No. 72, and p. 283, No. 135. [The chief referred to is, of course, a member of the Maṭḷa family mentioned in previous epigraphs.]

657. A C.P. in Telugu in the hands of the manager of the temple. Records that the karṇams and people of the Pulugūru-nāṇḍu fixed a contribution of one *patika* for each *Ghaṭṭivarāha* from the revenue of the village to the God Guddaṇḍarasvāmi, in Ś. 1609, Vibhava, in the reign of Muttu Vēṅkaṭarāmarāsu. *Ibid.*, p. 261, No. 73 or p. 283, No. 136.

Bommāvaram.

658. Near the pagoda of Hanumantarāya. (Telugu.) Records that Guravarāju and Chinnaśuṅga exempted the local barbers from all the usual taxes, in Ś. 1480, Kāḷayukti, in the reign of Sadāśivarāya. *Ins., Ced. Dts.*, p. 258, No. 61.

659. On the bank of the Bommāvaram. (Telugu.) Records that Misaragaṇḍa Kaṭhāri Sāḷuva Mallarāja gave some land below the tank to God Bōghēśvara in Ś. 1363, Durmati, *Ins.*, *Ced. Dts.*, p. 258, No. 62. A copy of it is No. 74 in p. 262 and No. 137 in p. 283.

659-A. Near the pagoda of Yellamma. (Telugu.) Records that Muttukumāra Anantarāja's *Mudrakartā*, Basavayya, gave 10 kuṇṭas of land to Pāppaṇṇa in Ś. 1557, Bhava. *Ibid.*, No. 63.

660. On a stone near the Hanumantarāya pagoda. (Telugu.) Records that Rāmanāyaḍu Tāsari Pāpanāyaḍu granted to Hanumanta the various fines collected from Bommāvaram and other villages in the year Śrīmukha with the permission of Pedda Ōbalanāyaḍu. *Ibid.*, p. 282, No. 133.

Chinna Ōrampāḍu.

661. On a wall of the Vīrabhadra pagoda. (Telugu.) Records that Chella Naramareḍḍi erected the inner pagoda in Ś. 1558. *Ibid.*, p. 281, No. 128.

Chiyyavaram.

662. In the south ward of Chiyyavaram. (Telugu.) Records that Kaṭhāri Śāḷuva Yerra Kamparāja granted the village as free gift in Ś. 1327, Pārthiva, for the annual festival of God Tiruveṅgalanātha. *Ibid.*, p. 258, No. 60.

Yerraguṇṭlakōṭa.

663. A cadjan grant in the village. (Telugu.) Records that Veṅkatarāmarāja Dēva Chōḍa Mahārāja made a grant of land to Subbā Bhaṭṭa in Ś. 1605, Raktākshi. *Ibid.*, p. 272, No. 101. A copy of this is No. 150 in p. 288.

Gaṅgarāsupuram.

664. In a stone on the street of the village. (Telugu.) Records that Malladēva Chōḍa Mahārāja established the village for learned Brahmans in Ś. 1389. *Ibid.*, p. 257, No. 58.

Guṇḍḷūru.

665. 617 *of* 1907.—(Telugu.) On a slab set up in the Lakshmīnārāyaṇasvāmin temple. A mutilated record of the Vijayanagara king Vīrapratāpa Dēvarāya Mahārāya, date of which is lost. Records a gift while Rāyadēva Mahārāju, son of the *antyembaragaṇḍa* Sammeṭa Lakkayadēva-Mahārāju, was governing Guṇḍḷūru in Pottapi-nāṇḍu. [Is this the same as *Ins.*, *Ced. Dts.*, p. 247, No. 22 ?].

666. 618 *of* 1907.—(Grantha and Tamil.) On another slab set up in the same place. A damaged record of Gaṇḍapeṇḍara

Ambadēva-Mahārāja, dated Ś. 1213, Khara. Records gift of land for the merit of the king to the temple of Lakshminārāyaṇa-Perumāḷ at Guṇḍalūr in Mērpakkai-nāḍu, a district of Adhirājendra-maṇḍalam. See Cd. 654 and 689.

667. 619 *of* 1907.—(Telugu and Grantha.) On a slab set up in the Agastyēśvara temple in the same village. Seems to record a gift for the merit of Pratāparudra (II ?).

668. 620 *of* 1907.—(Tamil.) On another slab set up in the same temple. Dated in the 21st year (Durmukha) of the Chōḷa king Tribhuvanachakravartin Rājarājadēva. Mentions the Tiruvagattīśvaramuḍaiya-Nāyanār at Kundalūr in Pottappi-nāḍu.

669. 621 *of* 1907.—(Grantha and Tamil.) On the south wall of the central shrine in the same temple. Ambadēva Mahārāja records in Ś. 1212, Virōdhin, gift of three lamps. See No. 654 above.

670. 622 *of* 1907.—(Tamil.) On the same wall. Dated in the reign of Sōmidēva. Records in Ś. 1206, expired, Tāraṇa, gifts for the merit of the king.

671. 623 *of* 1907.—(Tamil.) On the same wall. A damaged record of Ambadēva-Mahārāja (Śaka and cyclic years doubtful). Records gift of land for a lamp. See No. 654 above.

672-673. Close by the temple of Virabhadrasvāmi. (Grantha and Telugu.) Two records dated Ś. 1477 (A.D. 1555) and Ś. 1480 (A.D. 1558).

674. A C.P. grant referring to Guṇḍlūr Śīma (now in the Madras Museum) is described in *Ep. Rep.*, 1891, June, p. 5. It is in Nandinagari character and Sanskrit language, and records that in Ś. 1448, Sarvajit, Pushya, Makhara Saṅkrānti, Krishṇadēva Rāya gave the village of Māḍavara in Guṇḍlūr Śīma to a temple of Narasimha.

Hastavaram.

675. Near the ruined temple east of the village. (Telugu.) Records that Maṭla Anantachōḍa Dēva Mahārāja gave in Ś. 1522, Śārvari, to Kāśi Viśvanātha 3½ muṇṭas of land in the village. *Ins., Ced. Dts.*, p. 246, No. 21.

Itimārupuram.

676. On a stone in the pagoda of Rājēśvara. (Telugu.) Records that Annamarasu and Yellayya established brass images of the deity, the Āḷvārs, etc., in the Varadarājasvāmi temple in Ś. 1441, Vikrama. *Ibid.*, p. 249, No. 34.

677. Near the above. (Telugu.) Records the exemption of the local barbers from tax in Ś. 1468, Prabhava, by Guravarasu and Chinna Śiṅgarāsu Chōḍa Mahārāju, in the reign of Sadāśivarāya. (The village was also called Ōbasamudram.) *Ibid.*, p. 250, No. 35.

Jillellamaḍaka.

678. A C.P. in the hands of Tirumalakumāra Varadāchārya in the village. (Sanskrit and Devanagari.) Records that Tirumalarāya (I) granted in Ś. 1493, Prajōtpatti, on the first annual ceremony of his father Śrī Raṅgarāya, the village of Jillēllamuḍuku with 5 hamlets to Śrīnivāsāchārya. The village is said to be in Pulaganāḍ country of the Sidhout district. *Ins., Ced. Dts.*, p. 277, No. 116. A copy of this is also in *Ibid.*, p. 289, No. 152.

679. A C.P. in the hands of Dēvarājāchārya in the same village. (Telugu.) Records that the weavers of Anantarājappēṭa gave to Pinnatōṭa Śēsha (?) Pantulu in the year Viḷambi, an allowance of one *rūka* or gold paṇam for every marriage in every house of the weavers. *Ibid.*, p. 289, No. 153.

Cambhalakuṇṭa.

680. A Telugu P.G. in the hands of Aiyanaśāstri recording that Maṭḷa Kumāra Tiruvēṅgalanātha Dēva Chōḍa Mahārāja built an agrahāram in the eastern part of Tirumalāmbāpuram and granted it as free gift to Brahmans in Ś. 1678, Yuva. *Ins., Ced. Dts.*, p. 298, No. 176 and p. 273, No. 104.

Kampasamudram.

681. A Telugu P.G. recording in Ś. 1611, Pramōdūta, gift of land to a number of Brahmans in 12 shares by Maṭḷa Veṅkaṭarāmarāju, son of Kumāra Anantarāju Dēvachōḍamahārāju. *Ibid.*, p. 274, No. 108, also p. 299, No. 179.

Kiṭsamāmbāpuram (Krishṇamāmbāpuram).

682. A copper plate in the hands of the local Brahmans. (Sanskrit.) Records that in Ś. 1612, Veṅkaṭarāmarāja gave to 26 Brahmans the villages of Mandarum and Kitsamāmbāpuram. *Ibid.*, p. 262, No. 77, and p. 284, No. 140.

Kommūru.

683. On a stone in front of the Pōtarāju temple. (Telugu.) Records that Sālakarāja Perumāḷrāja, the prime minister of Achutarāya, granted to Chennakēśavasvāmi land for sinking a well, in Ś. 1452, Virōdhi. *Ins., Ced. Dts.*, p. 93, No. 141.

684. On a stone near the Hanumanta pagoda. (Telugu.) Records that the Dommaras granted the duties due to them from the village in Ś. 1443, Vishu, to Gods Tiruvēṅgalanātha and Rāmayyadēva. *Ibid.*, No. 142.

685. On a stone near the fortress. Telugu. Records that Narasimhapantulu of Jammalamaḍugu built a fort in Ś. 1631, Virōdhi, while he was managing the Awknāḍu. *Ibid.*, p. 94, No. 143.

Koṇḍūru.

686. A Telugu copper plate in the hands of Śēshādri Śāstri in the village. Records that Maṭla Tiruvēṅgalanātha Rāja Dēvachōḍamahārāja, son of Veṅkaṭapatirāja gave in S. 1729, Akshaya, some land in Koṇḍūr to Veḷḷakurichi Subbājōsyalu. *Ins., Ced. Dts.*, p. 266, No. 86, another copy p. 287, No. 147.

Kottapalli.

687. A P.G. Telugu in the hands of the local Brahmans. Records that Maṭla Tiruvēṅgalānātha Rāja Dēvachōḍamahārāja gave this village in Pottappināḍu to Veṅkāji Pantulu in Ś. 1629, Sarvadhāri. *Ibid.*, p. 292, No. 164.

Lepaka.

688. 413 *of* 1911.—(Tamil.) On the south wall of the Kharēśvara temple. A damaged and incomplete record of the Chōḷa king Tribhuvanachakravartin Vīrarājēndrachōḷadēva, dated twenty-sixth year, Raktākshi. Seems to record a gift of land to the temple of Karavīśvaram Uḍaiyār at Nenpākkai in Mēr-Pākkaināḍu, a subdivision of Ādhirājēndra-maṇḍalam. Below this is a record of Ś. 1209 which registers a gift of money to the same temple. Mr. Krishna Sastri attributes the inscription to Kulōttuṅga Chōḷa III.

689. 414 *of* 1911.—(Tamil.) On the same wall. A much damaged record, dated Ś. 1224, Śubhakrit. Refers to the temple of Karavīśvaramuḍaiya-Nāyanār at Neppākkai and mentions the Maṇḍalīka Brahmarākshasa Ambadēva-Mahārāja, the celebrated feudatory of Pratāparudra II and Governor of the Cuddapah country. See No. 654 above.]

690. 415 *of* 1911.—(Tamil.) On the same wall. An incomplete record of the Chōḷa king Rājarājadēva III (1216—48), dated twenty-fourth year, Vikārin. Seems to record a gift of lamps to the same temple.

691. 416 *of* 1911.—(Tamil.) On the same wall. An unfinished record, dated Ś. 1224, Śubhakrit. Gives only the date.

692. 417 *of* 1911.—(Tamil.) On the north wall of the same temple. An unfinished record of Tribhuvanachakravartin Vijayagaṇḍagōpāladēva (1250–83), dated twenty-ninth year Bahudhānya. Gives only the date.

693. 418 *of* 1911.—(Tamil.) On the east wall of the same temple. A record of the Chōḷa king Rājarājadēva III (1216—48). Records in his sixth year, Vishaiya (Vrisha), gift of one *māḍai* for a lamp by a Taṭṭān of Nenpākkai, to the temple of Karavīśuramuḍaiya-Nāyanār.

694. 419 *of* 1911.—(Tamil.) On the same wall. Dated in the reign of the Chōḷa king Rājarājadēva III. Records in his tenth year gift of paddy for three lamps by a native of Pottappi.

695. 420 *of* 1911.—(Tamil.) On the same wall. Records in the reign of the Chōḷa king Tribhuvanachakravartin Kōnērimaikoṇḍān Rājēndra-Chōḷadēva III "who took the head of two Pāṇḍya (kings)", gift of lands in the village of Nenpākkam to the temple of Tiruchchiṟṟambalam-Uḍaiyār. The royal secretary (ōlai) who wrote the order was Vīraśōḷappiramārāyan and the signatories were Viḷuppadarāyan and Munaiyadaraiyan. A Sanskrit passage at the beginning gives a long list of birudas similar to those of his Śrīraṅgam record. (64 of 1892.)

696. 421 *of* 1911.—(Telugu.) On a slab set up near the entrance into the Chennakēśava-Perumāḷ temple in the same village. Records in Ś. 1424, Dundubhi, gift of land to the temples of Chennakēśvaradēva and Kharavīśvaradēva by a certain Yaramanāyani-Timmayya, for the merit of Dēvi-Nāyaniṅgāru.

697. 422 *of* 1911.—(Telugu.) On another slab set up in the same place. A much-damaged record, dated Ś. 1330, Sarvajit. Mentions Mallā Reḍḍi with a long list of family titles and the temple of Kharavēśvara at Lembāka.

698. 423 *of* 1911.—(Tamil.) On the third slab set up in the same place. A record of Ambadēva-Mahārāja, damaged at the beginning. Registers that a certain Gaṅgadēva, son of Sarvādhikāri Irumaḍidēva induced a merchant (nagarattār) of Nellūr to present a lamp to the temple of Kēśava-Perumāḷ at Nenpākkam, for the success of the king. See Nos. 689 and 654 above.

699. 424 *of* 1911.—(Telugu.) On the fourth slab in the same place. Mentions Mallā Reḍḍi, son of Annā-Reḍḍi, and records in Ś. 1335, Vijaya, that a merchant of Nellore built the southern wall of the compound in the temple of Kēśava-Perumāḷ at Lembāka. See Cd. 880 and Gt. 634.

700. 425 *of* 1911.—(Tamil.) On the fifth slab in the same place. Records in the thirteenth year of the Pāṇḍya king Māravarman *alias* Tribhuvanachakravartin Sundara-Pāṇḍyadēva (I or II ?) that some land near the temple of Nenpākkai-Viṇṇagar *alias* Kēśava-Perumāḷ was assigned for a street called Pallavarāyan-tiruvīdi after Pallavarāyan, the chief of Tuñjalūr in Naḍuvir-kūṟṟu, a subdivision of Miḷalai-kūṟṟam. One of the faces bears the Pāṇḍya symbol of an *aṅkuśa* between two fish.

701. 426 *of* 1911.—(Tamil.) On a slab set up near the south wall of the same temple. A damaged record of the Chōḷa king Rājarājadēva III, dated twenty-second year. Records gift of twelve *māḍai* for a lamp to the temple of Kēśava-Perumāḷ. Another record of the same year of the king is inserted on the top of the slab and registers also the gift of a lamp.

702. 427 *of* 1911.—(Tamil.) On a pillar of the Mahā-maṇṭapa in the same temple. Records in Ś. 1198, Dhātri, gift of twelve *māḍai* for a lamp.

703. 428 *of* 1911.—(Tamil.) On the same pillar. Records in Ś. 1216, Jaya, gift of twelve *mādai* for a lamp to the temple of Kēśava-Perumāḷ at Nenpākkai.

704. 429 *of* 1911.—(Tamil.) On another pillar of the same maṇṭapa. A damaged record dated Ś. 1204, Chitrabhānu. Mentions the gift made for the success of "the Mahārāja's son," which may be tentatively read as Dāri(ta)kka-Tēvarasa, by his Sarvādhikāri. Another Śaka date 1217, Manmatha, is also found on the same pillar.

705. 430 *of* 1911.—(Telugu.) On a sluice of the Timmarasu tank in the same village. Records in Ś. 1634, Nandana, that Perumāḷḷarāja, son of Maṭla Veṅkaṭakrishṇamārāju-Dēvachōḍa-Mahārāju, built the sluice to the tank originally constructed by Bācharsu-Timmarasu. See C.P. Nos. 3 and 4 of 1908 and Pottappi Inscriptions.

Malaimārpuram.

706. On a stone of Kōdaṇḍarāmasvāmi pagoda. (Telugu.) Records that Maṭḷa Kumāra Anantaraju gave the duties and taxes of Pottappi village to the God in Ś. 1641, Vikāri. *Ins., Ced. Dts.*, p. 254, No. 50.

707. Near the above inscription. (Telugu.) Records that in the time of the same chief Raṅgareḍḍi and Anantareḍḍi, the chief persons of the village, erected a spire in the Kōdaṇḍarāma shrine and presented jewels to the various deities, besides establishing the images of Hanūman and the Āḷvārs. Same date as the above. *Ibid.*, p. 255, No. 51.

708. On the inner part of the gate wall of the Mādhavasvāmi pagoda. (Telugu.) Records that Miseragaṇḍa Kaṭhāri Śāḷuva Timmadēva Mahārāya gave in a Bahudhānya to the deity lands for building and a garden in the village. *Ibid.*, No. 52.

Mandapalle.

709. Near the temple. Records that Vasantarāja erected in a certain Manmatha an image of the Goddess Lakshmīdēvi in the village. *Ibid.*, p. 245, No. 16.

Maṅgampēṭa.

780. A Kanarese record of "Meeramaharājā" saying that he built the temple of the Goddess Dasalamma Śakti in the village. (The latter was also called Togūrupēṭa.) *Ibid.*, p. 245, No. 17.

781. Near the Pagoda of Chennakēśava. (Telugu.) Records that in the reign of Sadāśivarāya Śrīraṅgarāya and his brother, Tirumala, gave to God Raghunāthasvāmi, in Ś. 1472, Sādhāraṇa, the village of Pulapaṭūru in Pottappināḍ. *Ibid.*, p. 246, No. 18.

Mannūr.

782. On the wall of the Mukhamaṇṭapam in Chennakēśava pagoda. (Telugu.) Records that Gutti Tirumalarājayya erected a maṇṭapam in Ś. 1489, Prabhava, in the reign of Sadāśivarāya. *Ins., Ced. Dts.*, p. 259, No. 65.

783. In a stone south of the village. (Telugu.) Records that in Ś. 1495, Śrīmukha, in the reign of Śrīraṅgarāya of Penukoṇḍa, the Vīramushṭivāru, Dommaravāru, "Milardavaru and Coontatuvaru" gave away their annual fee from the village to God Chennakēśava. *Ibid.*, No. 66.

Nandalūr.

784. 570 *of* 1907.—(Grantha and Tamil.) On the south base of the maṇṭapa in front of the central shrine in the Saumyanāthasvāmin temple, first tier. Built in the beginning. Mentions Madhurāntaka-Pottappichchōḷa-Nallamsittaraśan. The village of Nirantanūr is called a Brahmapuri. Records the restoration by Nallamsittaraśan and his sons of a grant made jointly by Vatsarāja and a predecessor of the former.

785. 571 *of* 1907.—(Grantha and Tamil.) On the same tier. An incomplete record of the Chōḷa king Rājādhirājadēva (II), dated twelfth year, Hēmalamba. Records a gift of land. [Mr. Sewell examines the date of this inscription which is given as Saturday, Śravishṭā, Makara pūrvapaksha prathama, in *Ep. Ind.*, X, 126-7, and concludes that it should have been in the fifteenth year of Rājādhirāja II, on Saturday, January 21st, A.D. 1178, within six months of the accession of Kulōttuṅga III in July 1178.]

786. 572 *of* 1907.—(Grantha and Tamil.) On the second, third and fourth tiers of the same base. A record of the Chōḷa king Vīra-Rājakēsarivarman *alias* Chakravartin Śrī-Kulōttuṅga Chōḷa-dēva in his eighth year (day of Śivarātri, Śravaṇa, Friday, 14th tithi of the second fortnight of Kumbha). The temple is called Śrī-Kulōttuṅgachōḷa-Viṇṇagar-Āḻvār in Śrī-Kulōttuṅga-Chōḷa-Chaturvēdimaṅgalam, the agarabrahmadēya of Nirandanūr in Mērpākkaį-nāḍu, a subdivision Ādhirājēndramaṇḍalam. Madhurāntaka-Pottappichchōḷa-Siddharasa (unidentified) got the boundaries of the temple engraved on stone. [See *Ep. Ind.*, X, p. 125 and XI, p. 289, where Mr. R. Sewell points out that the date is suitable neither for Kulōttuṅga I or III. With regard to the second he describes four possible dates between 1135 and 1152 and eventually decides in favour of Friday, February 4th, A.D. 1144. He infers that the accession of Kulōttuṅga II should be between February 5th, A.D. 1136, and February 4th, A.D. 1137. Diwan Bahadur Swamikannu Pillai, on the other hand, fixes the date on Friday, February 7th, A.D. 1141.]

787. 573 *of* 1907.—(Grantha and Tamil.) On the fourth tier of the same base. A record in Virōdhikrit. Built in at the beginning.

788. 574 *of* 1907.—(Grantha and Tamil.) On the sixth tier of the same base. A damaged record of the Chōḷa king Tribhuvana-chakravartin Śrī-Kulōttuṅga Chōḷadēva (III), dated the fourth year, Plava. Seems to record a gift of land.

789. 575 *of* 1907.—(Grantha and Tamil.) On the lowermost portion of the south wall of the same maṇṭapa. Records gift of land in Pottappi to the temple of Śokka-Perumāḷ in Nirandanūr.

790. 576 *of* 1907.—(Grantha and Tamil.) On the same wall. A record of the Chōḷa king Tribhuvanachakravartin Śrī-Kulōttuṅga Chōḷadeva III, "who was pleased to take Madura and the crowned head of the Pāṇḍya," in his thirty-third year, Prajōtpatti. The temple is called Śokkapperumāḷ *alias* Śri-Kulottuṅgachōḷa-Viṇṇagar in Kulōttuṅga-Chōḷachaturvēdimaṅgalam, the agara-brahmadēya of Nirandanūr in Mēr-pākkaināḍu, a subdivision of Ādhirājēndra maṇḍalam.

791. 577 *of* 1907.—(Grantha and Tamil.) On the second, third and fourth tiers of the west base of the same maṇṭapa. Records a gift by Bhujabala Vīra-Nārāyaṇa Āhavamalladēva Mahārāja and mentions Bhāskarabhaṭṭōpādhyaya. See N.A. 498.

792. 578 of 1907.—(Tamil.) On the north base of the same maṇṭapa, first tier. A record of the Chōḷa king Tribhuvanachakra-vartin Śrī-Kulōttuṅga Chōḷadēva III, "who was pleased to take Madura and the crowned head of the Pāṇḍya." Records in his twenty-sixth year Raktākshi, that Nallan-Siddharasa, son of Madhurāntaka Pottappi-chchōḷan *alias* Erama-Siddharasan, exempted from certain taxes three villages, viz., Nandanūr *alias* the agara-brahmadēya Śrī-Kulōttuṅga-Chōḷa-chaturvēdimaṅgalam, Andappūr *alias* Tyāgasamudra-chaturvēdimaṅgalam, and Mantram *alias* Bhujabalasiddhi-chaturvēdimaṅgalam.

793. 579 *of* 1907.—(Grantha and Tamil.) On the second and third tiers of the north base and on three tiers of the west base of the maṇṭapa in front of the central shrine in the Saumyanāthasvāmin temple. Dated in the reign of the Chōḷa king Parakēsarivarman *alias* Tribhuvanachakravartin Śrī-Vikrama-Chōḷadēva (1118—35). Records in his eighth year and Ś. 1047, Viśvāvasu, the gift of a village (in seventy shares), by the Telugu-choḷa mahāmaṇḍalēśvara Vimalādityadēva, ruler of Pottappi, for the success of the king's arms. The donor was the son of Siddharasa and was called Madhurāntaka Pottappi-Chōḷa. See No. 798 below and No. 797 for another Telugu-choḷa feudatory of the same king.

794. 580 *of* 1907.—(Grantha and Tamil.) On the fifth tier of the north base, the north and west walls of the same maṇṭapa and the north wall of the central shrine in the same temple. A record of the Chōḷa king Vīrarājēndra-Chōḷadēva (III), in his thirteenth year, Piṅgaḷa. Gives a genealogy of the king's Telugu-Chōḍa feudatory chief Manmasiddha, the son of Tikka I and the patron of the poet Tikkaṇa Sōmayāji. The inscription records that the Brahman residents of Peruṅgaṇḍūru (unidentified) who had got that place in former times from Mukunti Kāḍuveṭṭi, once left it on account of a famine and, on return, found themselves deprived of their land and of their income from certain Veḷḷāḷas who had, owing to *Mārijavara* (plague), left their original habitation and settled in this village on condition of paying the produce (*arikaru*) of the fields over which they built their huts; and that Manmasiddhi, to whom the Brahmans appealed, inquired into the whole matter and restored the village to them under the name of Kōḍūr "in order to secure religious merit for his father Tirukāḷadēva-Mahārāja." The genealogy given in the epigraph is a little different from that given by Venkayya in *Ep. Rep.*, 1899-1900, p. 18. The epigraph is also interesting for the mention of the plague, the movement of the population on account of it and the occurrence of famine in a *Mīnaśani*. There seems to be reference to trial by ordeal.

795. 581 *of* 1907.—(Tamil.) On the fourth tier of the same base. Records in the thirty-first year, Vibhava, of the Chōḷa king Kulōttuṅga-Chōḷadēva gift of land for two lamps to the god Śokkapperumāḷ of the temple of Kulōttuṅgachōla Viṇṇagar Emberumān by Payirappi-Reḍḍi son of Pūmi-Reḍḍi, the manrāḍuvar of Taṅgatūr in Mērpākkai-nāḍu, a subdivision of Ādhirājēndramaṇḍalam.

796. 582 *of* 1907.—(Tamil.) On the first tier of the east base of the same maṇṭapa; right of entrance. Dated in the reign of the Chōḷa king Tribhuvanachakravartin Śrī-Kulōttuṅgachōḷadēva III, "who was pleased to take Madura and the crowned head of the Pāṇḍya." Records in his thirty-first year, Śukla, gift of lamps by Madhurāntaka Pottappichchōḷa Tirukkāḷattidēva for the merit of his father Manumasittarasan, and of Nallasiddharasa. [See *Ep. Ind.*, X, pp. 131-2, where Mr. Sewell discusses the date and calculates from the details given that it should be 24th March, A.D. 1209.]

797. 583 *of* 1907.—(Tamil.) On the second tier of the same base. Dated in the reign of the Chōḷa king Parakēsarivarman *alias* Chakravartin Śrī-Vikrama-Chōḷadēva. Records in his third year and Ś. 1044, Śārvarin, a gift by the Mahāmaṇḍalēśvara Bettarasa, who was ruling Pottappi-nāḍu, for the success of the king's arms. Built in at the beginning. [Bettarasa not yet identified.]

798. 584 *of* 1907.—(Tamil.) On the third and fourth tiers of the same base. Built in at the beginning. Records a gift by Madhurāntaka Pottappi-Chōḷa Vimalādityadēva, son of Siddharasa. See No. 793 above.

799. 585 *of* 1907.—(Tamil.) On the second and third tiers of the same base; left of entrance. Built in at the end. The Mahāmaṇḍalēśvara Madurāntaka Pottappi-Chōḷa-Siddharasa was ruling Pottappi-nādu. See No. 793 above.

800. 586 *of* 1907.—(Tamil.) On the fourth tier of the same base. Dated in the reign of the Chōḷa king Kulōttuṅga-Chōḷadēva (III?). Records in his third year, Plava, gift of two lamps by a native of Māṅgāḍu in Kulōttuṅgachōḷa-Vaḷanāḍu, a subdivision of Jayaṅgoṇḍa-Chōḷa-maṇḍalam. Built in at the end.

801. 587 *of* 1907.—(Tamil.) On the fifth and sixth tiers of the same base. A record of the Chōḷa king Kulōttuṅga-Chōḷadēva (III?), dated fifth year, Śubhakrit. Built in at the end.

802. 588 *of* 1907.—(Tamil.) On the south wall of the central shrine in the same temple. Records in Nandana, the seventeenth year of the Pāṇḍya king Sundara-Pāṇḍyadēva that a native of Toḷūr in Toḷūr-nāḍu, a district of Maṇavilkōṭṭam in Jayaṅgoṇḍa-Chōḷamaṇḍalam, had the god and goddess bathed. [See *Ep. Ind.*, X, p. 143, where Mr. Sewell discusses the date and considers that Wednesday, March 18th, A.D. 1293, in the reign of Jaṭāvarman Sundara Pāṇḍya (III, 1276—90) might be intended.]

803. 589 *of* 1907.—(Telugu.) On the north and west bases of the central shrine in the Saumyanāthasvāmin temple. Records in Ś. 1541, Siddhārthin, gifts by a woman belonging to the palace of Tiruvēṅgalanātharāju. The temple is called Saumyanāthasvāmin at Nelandalūru, which was another name of Nirantarapura. See *Ins., Ced. Dts.*, p. 244, No. 10.

804. 590 *of* 1907.—(Tamil.) On the north wall of the tiruchuttumāḷiga of the same temple. A damaged record of the Pāṇḍya king Jaṭāvarman *alias* Tribhuvanachakravartin Sundara Pāṇḍyadēva (III), dated in fifteenth year, Virōdin. [See *Ep. Ind.*, X, p. 142, where Mr. Sewell fixes the date from the astronomical details on Monday, February 20th, A.D. 1290, in the reign of Jaṭāvarman Sundara Pāṇḍya III.]

805. 591 *of* 1907.—(Tamil.) On the same wall. Belongs to the reign of the Pāṇḍya king Jaṭāvarman *alias* Tribhuvanachakravartin Sundara-Pāṇḍyadēva (III, 1276—90). Records in his tenth year, Vyaya, that Piḷḷai Pallavarāyar laid a flower garden.

806. 592 *of* 1907.—(Tamil.) On the same wall. A record of the Pāṇḍya king Jaṭāvarman *alias* Tribhuvanachakravartin Sundara-Pāṇḍyadēva (III, 1276—90), in his tenth year, Vyaya. Records a gift of land by Eḍuttakaiyaḻagiyar *alias* Piḷḷai Pallavarāyan of Tuñjalūr in Tirumiḻalai-kūṟṟam, a district Pāṇḍimaṇḍalam. See *Ep. Ind.*, X, p. 142.

807. 593 *of* 1907.—(Tamil.) On the same wall. A record of the Pāṇḍya king Jaṭāvarman *alias* Tribhuvanachakravartin

Sundara-Pāṇḍyadēva (III, 1276–90) in his tenth year, Vyaya. Records gift of gold for a flower garden by Piḷḷai Pallavarāyar.

808. 594 *of* 1907.—(Grantha and Tamil.) On the south wall of the same tiruchuttumāḷiga. A record of the Pāṇḍya king Jaṭāvarman *alias* Tribhuvanachakravartin Sundara-Pāṇḍyadēva (III, 1276—90). Records in his seventeenth year, Nandana, the laying out of a flower garden in the name of the Toṇḍaimān, Tirunelvēliyūḍaiyār Nandivarman, under orders from Mānaparipāla. See *Ep. Ind.*, X, p. 144.

809. 595 *of* 1907.—(Grantha and Tamil.) On the inner eastern gōpura of the same temple, right side. Mentions in Sādhāraṇa, Śrīraṅga-Nāyaka, minister of the Gaṇḍapeṇḍadara Gaṅgasāhaṇi (feudatory of Kākatīya king Gaṇapāti).

810. 596 *of* 1907.—(Tamil.) In the same place. A record of the Chōḷa king Rājarājadēva (III)[1] in his twenty-third year, Hēmalambi, and twenty-fourth year, Vikārin. Records a gift by a native of Muranōṭṭamaṅgalam in Vaḷḷuva-nāḍu, a district of Malai-maṇḍalam. See *Ep. Ind.*, X, p. 134.

811. 597 *of* 1907.—(Tamil.) In the same place. A record in Ś. 1193, Prajāpati. Gift by Perumāṇḍidēvarasa, younger brother of Prāsādi-Tikkarasa and son of Jagadobbagaṇḍan Kāmarasar.

812. 598 *of* 1907.—(Tamil.) In the same place, left side. Records in Ś. 1172, Saumya, gift of the proceeds of certain taxes to the temple, for recovery from some illness of Madhurāntaka Pottappichōḷa Gaṇḍagōpāla *alias* Manumasittarasar (i.e., the son of Tikka I and the patron Tikkaṇa Sōmayāji).

813. 599 *of* 1907.—(Tamil.) In the same place. A damaged record dated in Ś. 1194, expired, Āṅgirasa.

814. 600 *of* 1907.—(Tamil.) On the base of the same gōpura, left of entrance. A record of the Chōḷa king Rājakēsarivarman Chakravartin Kulōttuṅga-Chōḷadēva in his twenty-seventh year. The village is called Nirandalūr *alias* śrī-Kulōttuṅgachōḷa-chaturvēdimaṅgalam in Mērpākkai-nāḍu, a district of Ādhirājēndra-maṇḍalam.

815. 601 *of* 1907.—(Tamil.) On the base of the inner eastern gōpura of the Saumyanāthasvāmin temple, south side. A record of the Chōḷa king Kulōttuṅga-Chōḷadēva (III). Records in his twenty-fourth year Dundubhi, gift of ten *Bhujabala-māḍai* by Nukkamadēvi, queen of Madhurāntaka Poṭtappichōḷa Nallasiddharasa (not clearly identified). See *Ep. Ind.*, X, p. 129.

816. 602 *of* 1907.—(Tamil.) On the base of the same gōpura, right of entrance. An incomplete record of the Chōḷa king Tribhuvanachakravartin śrī-Kulōttuṅgachōḷadēva (III), dated thirty-sixth year, Śrīmukha. Records provision for offerings to the shrine of Vēdanāyaka-Perumāḷ.

817. 603 *of* 1907.—(Tamil.) On the east wall of the second prākāra of the same temple. A damaged record, dated in Ś. 1247, Rudhirōdgārin. Seems to register the levying of a fine.

818. 604 *of* 1907.—(Tamil.) On the same wall. A damaged record dated in Ś. . . . Records gift of two cows for lamps.

819. 605 *of* 1907.—(Telugu.) On a slab lying in the flower garden of the same temple. Belongs to the reign of the Vijayanagara king Vīrapratāpa Vīra-Sadāśivarāyadēva-Mahārāya. Records in Ś. 1490, Piṅgaḷa, gift of land by Vōbaḷarāju, son of Nandyāla Avubaḷarāju, for the God's ablution out of his "Nainkarum." See *Ins., Ced. Dts.*, p. 243, No. 6.

820. 606 *of* 1907.—(Telugu.) On a slab set up near the inner gōpura of the same temple. A record of the Vijayanagara king Vīrapratāpa Dēvarāya-Mahārāya (II) in Ś. 1355, Pramādin. Records a gift by the principal residents of five villages in Pottappi-nāḍu, viz., Prōlināḍu, Lembāka, Tāḷapāka, Taṅgatūru and Opili, to the temple of Chokkanātha Perumāḷ on the bank of the Bāhunadi (Cheyyāru). [See *Ins., Ced. Dts.*, p. 241, No. 3. The latter says that they gave a contribution of 1/16 of the revenues of Pottappi Nāḍu to God Chokkanātha.]

821. 607 *of* 1907.—(Telugu.) On another slab set up in the same place. Dated in the reign of the Vijayanagara king Vīrapratāpa Vīra-Achyutarāya Mahārāya. Records in Ś. 1456, Manmatha, the restoration of the village of Āṇḍupūru by Rāma-bhaṭḷayya on the request of Tāḷapāka Tirumalayyaṅgāru, with the permission of the king. [See *Ins., Ced. Dts.*, p. 242, No. 4, where this inscription is given.] See Ct. 21.

822. 608 *of* 1907.—(Telugu.) On a third slab set up in the same place. Dated in the reign of the Vijayanagara king Sadāśivadēva-Mahārāya. Records in Ś. 1478, Naḷa, gift of land in nine villages by a woman (daughter of Tippā Bhaṭṭuḍu, a resident). See *Ins., Ced. Dts.*, p. 242, No. 5, for a more detailed summary.

823. 609 *of* 1907.—(Telugu.) On a fourth slab set up in the same place. A damaged record of the Vijayanagara king Vīra-pratāpa Vīra Veṅkaṭapatirāya (I, 1586—1614), dated Ś. 1523, Plava. [The inscription is also given in *Ins., Ced. Dts.*, p. 243, No. 7.]

824. 610 *of* 1907.—(Tamil.) On the outer gōpura of the same temple, right of entrance. Records in Ś. 1186, Raktākshi, gift by Nāgarasa, minister (pradhāni) of the Gaṇḍapeṇḍara Jannigadēva (in the reign of Rudrāmbā whose feudatory Janniga was).

825. 611 *of* 1907.—(Grantha.) On the same gōpura, left of entrance. Records the building of the gōpura by Sōmīśvara, son of Vimalāditya, who belonged to the family of Pottappichōḷa. For Vimalāditya see No. 793 above. [The exact connection of Siddharasa, his son Vimala, and *his* son Sōmēśvara with the main Manmasiddhi line is unknown.]

826. 612 *of* 1907.—(Telugu.) On the same gōpura, left of entrance. A record in Viḷambi, mentioning Rāmabhaṭḷayyavāru.

827. 613 *of* 1907.—(Grantha and Tamil.) On a slab set up in the same place. A damaged record of the Pāṇḍya king Sundara Pāṇḍya (Jaṭāvarman I). *Begins samasta-jagad-ādhāra, etc.*

828. 614 *of* 1907.—(Tamil.) On another slab set up in the same place. Dated in the reign of the Pāṇḍya king Jaṭāvarman *alias* Tribhuvanachakravartin Sundara-Pāṇḍyadēva (III, 1276—90). Refers in his ninth year, Pārthiva, to the Rāmānujan-tirunandavanam founded by Piḷḷai Pallavarāyar. The god is called Śokkapperumāḷ of the temple called Kulōttuṅga-Chōḷa-Viṇṇagar-Emberumān at Nirandanūr in Mērpākkai-nāḍu, a district of Adhirājēndra-maṇḍalam.

829. 615 *of* 1907.—(Telugu.) On a third slab set up in the same place. An unfinished record of the Śāḷuva king Immaḍi-Naraśiṅgarāya-Mahārāya, son of Śāḷuva-Naraśiṅgarāya-Mahārāya (the usurper), dated Ś. 1423, Durmati. Records the gift of the village of Awkpāḍu for the merit of Narasanāyaka-Oḍayalu. [See *Ins., Ced. Dts.*, p. 241, No. 2, which says that the donor was Parvata Nāyuḍu, son of Dēva Nāyaḍu. Narasa Nāyak was the founder of the Tuḷuva dynasty.]

830. 616 *of* 1907.—(Telugu.) On a fourth slab lying near the outer gōpura of the Saumyanāthasvāmin temple. Dated in the reign of the Kākatīya king Pratāparudradēva-Mahārāja. Records in Ś. 1231, Kīlaka, gift of the proceeds of certain taxes from five villages, viz., Āṇḍapūru, Maudadamu, Mannūru, Astyapuram and Trumi-Nelandanūru. See *Ins., Ced. Dts.*, p. 241, No. 1.

831. On the other side of the above inscription. Records a grant of thirty kuṇṭas of land for planting a nandavanam or flower garden to the God Tiruvēṅgalanātha in the reign of Sadāśivarāya. *Ins., Ced. Dts.*, p. 243, No. 8.

832. On the north of the surrounding wall of the temple. (Telugu.) Records that Maṭṭakumārayya Dēva Chōḍa Mahāraja made a grant to the God of Chokkanāthasvāmi of (Nellundalore) in Ś. 1444, Chitrabhānu. A broken record. *Ins., Ced. Dts.*, p. 243, No. 9.

Obali.

833. 438 *of* 1911.—(Tamil.) On a slab set up near the Padmagirināthasvāmin temple. Records in *Vikriti* money granted for a number of lamps to the temple of Malaikinṛa-Perumāḷ at Vallōlam.

834. 439 *of* 1911.—(Telugu.) On a slab set up in front of the Saṅgamēśvara temple in the same village. A damaged record, dated Paridhāvin. Records that a certain Vīramushṭi Śiṅgāram Vīrayya presented the income which was due to him from Opili to the temple of Vīrēśvara in presence of Mandula Basavayya, the *muḍrakartā* of Vīraśaiva-Siddha-Bhikshāvṛitti Ayyavāru, who was a worshipper of Mallikārjuna-liṅga on the Śrīparvata mountain.

835. 440 *of* 1911.—(Tamil.) On a slab set up near the Vīrabhadrasvāmin temple, in the same village. Records in Ś. 1152, Vikriti, gift of money for lamps to Śaṅgīśuramuḍaiya-Nāyanār at Vallōlam.

836. 441 *of* 1911.—(Tamil.) On the back of the same slab. Records in the eighteenth year of the Chōḷa king Rājarājadēva gift of two lamps.

Paṭūru.

The following four records have been taken from *Mack. MSS.* and are in Telugu.

837. On the south side of the Pāṭūr village east of the temple of the Goddess Yellamma. Records that Paulammagāru established the temple of Mailār Dēva at Paṭūr and granted some land to the God, in Ś. 1274, Nandana. *Ins., Ced. Dts.*, p. 244, No. 11.

838. On the vicinity of the God Chennakēśavasvāmi temple west of the above temple at Pāṭūr. Records that a person Bhaṇḍārum Chavoonāyaniṅgāru planted the palm tree garden on the bank of the Bāhunadi river, in Ś. 1299, Piṅgaḷa. *Ibid.*, No. 12.

839. On the bank of the Bāhunadi river. Records that Mallayya Timmaṇa Timmarasu dug the channel between the river and Pāṭūr in Ś. 1596, Ānanda, in the time of Meer Saheb. *Ibid.*, p. 245, No. 13.

840. Between Paṭūr and Pulappaṭṭūr near the ruined Bhairava temple. Records that Manmaya Dēva Chōḍa Mahārāja, son of Brahmayadēva, the son of Madhurāntaka Pottappi Chōḷa, erected the Bhairava temple at Pulappaṭṭūr in Ś. 1256, Bhava. *Ibid.*, Nos. 14 and 15.

Pedda Ōrampādu.

841. A Telugu paper grant in the hands of Bukkaṇṇa in the village. Records that Nārāyaṇarāja, grandson of Nandyāla Anantarāja, son of Veṅkaṭapati Rāja, gave to Gaṇḍikōṭa Buchaṇa in Ś. 1699, Hēviḷambi, some lands. *Ibid.*, p. 300, No. 182.

842. A Telugu paper grant in the hands of Yellappa recording that Dēśūr Rāmareḍḍi and Subbareḍḍi gave to Ghaṇḍikōṭa Buchana some land in Ś. 1713, Virōdhikrit. *Ibid.*, No. 183.

843. A Telugu record of Maṭḷa Veṅkaṭarāya Dēva Chōḍa Mahārāya in Vikriti. *Ibid.*, No. 184.

844. A Telugu record of Śūra Chennagāru in Krōdhi, granting lands to evidently Ghaṇḍikōṭa Buchaṇa. *Ibid.*, No. 185.

Penagalūru.

845. A C.P. (Sanskrit, Dēvanagari) in the hands of the local Brahmans. Records that Matla Tirumalarāja made in Ś. 1493, Prajōtpatti, in the reign of Tirumalarāja (I), brother of Pedda Rāmarāya of Vijayanagaram, the village of Penagalūr in 128 shares, in the name of his father, called it Yellamarāsu-Samudram and granted it, in free gift, to Brahmans. *Ins., Ced. Dts.*, p. 272, No. 100, and p. 288, No. 149. See *Cuddapah Gazr.*, p. 247, where it is pointed out that the local Śrōtriyamdārs had their original grant confirmed by Tirumala I owing to their fear of losing their rights after Talikōṭa.

Poli.

846. 407 *of* 1911.—(Tamil.) On the south wall of the Śiva temple. A record of the Chōḷa king Rājarājadēva III in his twenty-seventh year Śubhakrit. Records gift of one *māḍai* for a lamp by a certain Reḍḍi to the temple of Uḷḷaṅkuḷunda-Nāyanār at Puḍōli in Mēr-Pākkaināḍu, a subdivision of Ādhirājēndra-maṇḍalam.

847. 408 *of* 1911.—(Tamil.) On the east wall of the Varadarājasvāmin temple in the same village. Records in Ś. 1204, Chitrabhānu, gift of two lamps to the temple of Karumāṇikka-Perumāḷ.

848. 409 *of* 1911.—(Telugu.) On the same wall. Records in Ś. 1482, Raudri, that the *balipiṭha* was presented by a certain Timmaṇa to the temple of Kariyamāṇikyarāya, for the merit of his uncle Ponna-nāyuḍu. See *Ins., Ced. Dts.*, p. 282, No. 134.

849. 410 *of* 1911.—(Telugu.) On a slab set up in the courtyard of the same temple. A much damaged record of (the Kāyastha feudatory) Ambadēva-Mahārāja, ruling at Vallūri-paṭṭaṇa, dated Ś. 1212, Virōdhin. The king has a long list of *birudas*. Records gift of 1,700 kuṇṭas of land in Poli to God Karumāṇikka Rāya Perumāḷ. See *Ibid.*, p. 259, No. 64.

Pondalūru.

The following local records have been taken from *Mack. MSS.* and are in Telugu.

850. In the temple. Records that Brahmmarākshasa Gaṇḍapeṇḍēra Janniga Dēva Mahārāsu gave the village of Pondalūru to Sadāśiva Kurukkaḷ in 1182, Krōdhi, in the reign of Gaṇapatidēvarāya (1213–59). *Ibid.*, p. 251, No. 38. See also No. 824.

851. South of the above. Exemption of barbers of Uṭukūr from tax in Ś. 1483, Dundubhi, by Rāmarājá in the reign of Sadāśivarāya. *Ibid.*, No. 39.

852. In the Varadarāja temple. Records rebuilding of the temple by Nādaṇḍla Appayyagāru in Ś. 1434, Āṅgirasa. *Ibid.*, No. 40.

853. West of the above. Records that Tirumalarāsu gave some land to God Varadarāja in Ś. 1492, Pramōdūta, in the reign of Sadāśiva Rāya. *Ins., Ced. Dts.*, p. 251, No. 41.

Pottappi.

This was the well-known headquarters of the Telugu-chōḷas * from the eleventh century.

854. 434 *of* 1911.—(Telugu.) On the entrance into the Mūlasthānēśvara temple. An unfinished record of the time of the Vijayanagara king Vīrapratāpa Sadāśivadēva-Mahārāya, date of which is lost. Registers a *daśavanda* charter granted to certain Reḍḍis by Varadayyadēva Chōḍamahārāja, son of Maṭla Pōcharājayyadēva-Chōḍamahārāja and mentions the Mahāmaṇḍalēśvara Rāmarāju-Tirumalarājayyadēva-Mahārāja (probably the same as Gutti Erra Timmayya dēva). This is the earliest of the Maṭla chiefs' records. Varadayya dug up an irrigation canal called Antaraṅgakālva at Pottappi, which was granted to him as an *amaranāyakam* by Tirumalarāja. He was evidently the son-in-law of Kṛishṇadēva Rāya and reputed ancestor of the chief Maṭla Ananta, son of Yella, or Kōnaya Yella, who was the author of the काकुत्स्थ विजय. See Cg. 762 and Cp. 863-A–B.

855. 435 *of* 1911.—(Tamil.) On a slab built into the floor of the *garbhagriha* in the same temple. A damaged and incomplete record of the Chōḷa king Tribhuvanachakravartin Kulōttuṅga-Chōḷadēva (III), date of which is lost. Mentions a certain Madhurāntaka Pottappichōḷa Sitti-Araiyan. [He must have been, like the Nīlagaṅgaraiyans, feudatory of Kulōttuṅga III.]

856. 436 *of* 1911.—(Telugu.) On the east wall of the Vēṇugōpālasvāmin temple in the same village. Registers in Ś. 1640, Viḷambi, that Maṭla Komāra-Kāntarāju-Dēvachōḍa Mahārāju ordered the dilapidated *nāsika* (i.e., śukhanāsika) of the Gōpālasvāmin temple at Pottappi, the headquarter of Pottappi-nāḍu in Siddhāvaṭṭam which was a subdivision of Udayagiri, to be renewed. See 854, 863-A and 863 for other Maṭla chiefs.

857. 437 *of* 1911.—(Tamil and Grantha.) On the east, south and north walls of the same temple. A much damaged and incomplete record of Manumasiddha, dated Ś. 1180, Kāḷayukti. Gives a list of *birudas* at the beginning. Mentions the Sōmēśvara temple. [Manma was the patron of the Telugu poet Tikkaṇa Sōmayāji.]

858. On a stone in front of the Gōpālasvāmi Pagoda. Records that Guravarāja and Chinna Śiṅgarāja exempted in Ś. 1468,

---

* The *Cuddapah Gasr.* gives three inscriptions in this place, one dated in S. 1115; the second dated in Ś. 1459 in the time of Maṭla Ananta, the author of *Kākusthavijayamu*; and the third in Ś. 1643.

Prabhava, in the reign of Sadāśivarāya the local barbers from all taxes and duties. *Ins., Ced. Dts.*, p. 253, No. 44.

859. On a stone in the same pagoda. (Telugu.) Records that in Ś. 1640, Viḷambi, in the reign of Maṭḷa Anantarasu Dēva Chōḍa Mahārāja, the Reḍḍis and Karṇams of the place granted two kuṇṭas to a stone cutter who carved the Gōpāla image. [This chief was, of course, later than the one referred to in Nos. 863-A and B.] *Ibid.*, p. 253, No. 45.

860. In the Śiva temple.—(Telugu.) Records that Varadarāsu and Yellamarāsu gave sixty kuṇṭas of land to certain people for digging a canal in the village in Ś. 1493, Prajōtpatti, in the reign of Sadāśivarāya. *Ibid.*, No. 46.

861. On the banks of the cheruvu west of the Śiva temple. (Telugu.) A damaged gift of the Mahājanas of Pottappi and Gudusupalli, dated in Ś. 1001 (?), in the reign of Rāmachōḍa Mahārāja. *Ibid.*, No. 47.

862. Near the ruined pagoda west of Pottappi. (Telugu.) A similar grant in the same date. *Ibid.*, No. 48.

863. On a stone north-west of the village. (Telugu.) Records that Timmarāju gave some land in Pottappi to a carpenter, in Ś. 1530, Sādhāraṇa, in the reign of Chandragiri Veṅkaṭapatirāya (I 1586–1614). *Ibid.*, p. 254, No. 49.

Pullampet.

863-A. *C.P.* 3 *of* 1907–8.—A Telugu record of Maṭḷa Veṅkaṭarāmarāju in Ś. 1609, Vibhava.

863-B. *C.P.* 4 *of* 1907–8.—A Sanskrit record of the same chief in Ś. 1612, Pramōda. [From the genealogy of this we understand that five generations or roughly 125 years, passed between Pedda Ananta (author of the *Kākusthavijyamu*) and Veṅkaṭarāmarāju, thereby showing that the former lived about 1565.

Puttanavāripalli.

864. A Telugu P.G. in the village. Records that Maṭḷa Veṅkaṭa Rāmarāju Dēvachōḍa Mahārāja gave the village in twelve shares to Brahmans for a favourable rent of eight gold chakrams or paṇams in Ś. 1678, Yuva. *Ibid.*, p. 292, No. 162, and p. 267, No. 88.

Rāghavarāsupuram.

865. A Telugu P.G. in the hands of the local Brahmans. Records that Maṭḷa Veṅkaṭarāmarāja, son of Tiruvēṅgaḷanātharāju, gave in Ś. 1681, Bahudhānya, the village of Veṅkaṭarāghavapuram (named after his brother) to Brahmans in eighteen shares. *Ibid.*, p. 302, No. 188.

866. Another Telugu P.G. in the village. Records that Chalu Chalamala Jayarāmareḍḍi, son of Awkumārareḍḍi, gave to

Veṅkaṭāchala Śāstri in Ś. 1712, Sādhāraṇa, some land in Akkampallacheruvu. *Ins., Ced. Dts.*, p. 302, No. 189.

Rāmamāmbāpuram.

867. A Telugu P.G. in the hands of the local Brahmans. Records that Maṭla Tiruvēṅgalanātha Rāja Dēvachōḍa established in the name of his mother the village of Rāmamāmbāpuram and granted it in Ś. 1677, Yuva, to sixteen learned Brahmans, in sixteen Vrittis. *Ibid.*, p. 271, No. 99, and p. 297, No. 173.

Rollamadugu.

868. A C.P. in Sanskrit in the hands of the local karṇam. Records that Achyutarāya, grandson of Dēvarāya, gave, in Ś. 1209 (?), Sarvajit, four villages to Brahmans. *Ibid.*, p. 260, No. 70. The record does not seem to be genuine.

Śeṭṭiguṇṭa.

869. On a stone below the tank. (Telugu.) Records that Nallama Kṛishṇamareḍḍi paid to one Tirumalanāyaḍu, son of Kṛishṇama, in Ś. 1606, Raktākshi, the value of the produce from the tank for digging a new tank at Kōttapaḷḷi. *Ibid.*, p. 282, No. 132. See also *Cuddapah Gazr.*, p. 245.

Śēshamāmabāpuram.

870. A P.G. in the hands of the local Brahmans. (Telugu.) Records that Kumāra Anantarāya Dēvachōḍa Mahārāja gave the village in free gift to sixteen Brahmans in Ś. 1642, Vikāri. *Ibid.*, p. 291, No. 159, and p. 261, No. 71.

Śiṅganamala.

871. A paper grant (Telugu) in the hands of Gaṅgaveṅkaṭarāju in the village. Records that Maṭla Kumāra Anantarāja Dēvachōḍa gave the village in Ś. 1637, to a Brahman named Śivarāy. *Ibid.*, p. 272, No. 102, and p. 297, No. 174.

872. A paper grant (in Sanskrit) at Śiṇganamala Chennarāyasamudram. Records that Kumāra Anantarāja Dēvachōḍa gave the agraharām in 15 shares to Brahmans in Ś. 1638, Hēviḷambi. *Ibid.*, p. 297, No. 175.

Śrinivāsapuram (Kotapalli).

873. Near the image of Hanumantarāya. (Telugu.) Records that Mādharāja and Nāgarāja granted the village of Ōbala Koṇḍapalli to Tirumala-Tātāchārya in Ś. 1482, Siddhārthi. *Ins., Ced. Dts.*, p. 258, No. 59. See By. 320.

874. A Telugu paper grant in the hands of the local Brahmans. Records that Maṭla Tiruvēṅgalanātha Dēva Chōḍa

Mahārāja gave 400 kuṇṭas of land to Brahmatantra Svatantara Vēdānta Rāmānujasvāmi in Ś. 1692, Vikriti, for distribution of food at Tirupati. *Ins., Ced. Dts.*, p. 280, No. 125, and p. 304, No. 104.

Śriraṅgarāsupuram.

875. A (Telugu) grant in the hands of the local Brahmans. Records that Maṭḷa Dēva Mahārāja gave the village as a free gift to Allūr Subbā Śāstri in Ś. 1648, Śōbhakrit. *Ibid.*, p. 262, No. 75, and p. 284, No. 138.

876. In the same hands. (Telugu.) Records that Maṭḷa Veṅkaṭarāma Rāja Dēvachōḍa Mahārāja granted the agrahāram for the annual rent of 20 Aparañji Chakrams to Allūr Gaṅgādhara Sōmayāji in Ś. 1721, Siddhārthi. *Ibid.*, p. 262, No. 76, also p. 284, No. 139.

Tāḷḷapāka.

877. On a stone south of the village. (Telugu.) Records that Apparachintala Peddachakrarāju gave to God Tiruvēṅgalanātha in a certain Krōdhana one kuṇṭa of land in this village. *Ibid.*, p. 280, No. 129.

Taṅgatūru.

878. 431 *of* 1911.—(Telugu.) On a slab set up in front of the Ādikēśavasvāmin temple. A much damaged record of the Vijayanagara king Dēvarāya I, son of Vīra-Harihara (II), date of which is lost. Mentions a *pradhāni* of the king.

879. 432 *of* 1911.—(Telugu.) On a slab set up near the ruined temple of Siddhēśvara in the same village. A much damaged record of the Kākatīya king Pratāparudradēva (II, 1295—1323), ruling at Oruṅgallupaṭṭaṇa, dated Ś. 1237, Rākshasa. Seems to record a gift of voluntary contributions *(magamai)* to the temple of Siddhanāthadēva at Taṅgatūru. [This inscription is given in *Ibid.*, p. 252, No. 43, and is more detailed. It says that the inhabitants of Pottappi Nāḍu granted the following taxes to the God:—(1) 4 *kāśu* on each buffalo-load; (2) 3 *kāśu* on each bullock-load; 2 *kāśu* on each bag of betel leaf, of other articles and grains.]

880. 433 *of* 1911.—(Telugu.) On a slab set up in the court-yard of the Kailāsanāthasvāmin temple in the same village. A damaged record dated Ś. 1328, Vyaya. Mentions Annā Reḍḍi and his son Mallā Reḍḍi. All the usual Reḍḍi titles are repeated at the beginning of the inscription. Annā Reḍḍi was the son of Mallā Reḍḍi, the younger brother of Vēma Reḍḍi of Addaṅki. Vēma was evidently the famous chief who fought against the Mahomedans, built the flight of steps at Ahōbilam and Śrīśailam, etc. [See 424 of 1911 at Lēpaka, 268 of 1897 at Amarāvati; *Ep. Ind.*,

VIII, p. 10. See also *Ins., Ced. Dts.*, p. 251, No. 42.] The inscription gives this genealogy :—

Vēma Reḍḍi of Addaṅki. — Malla Reḍḍi (I)

Mallā Reḍḍi (I)
|
Annā Reḍḍi
|
Mallā Reḍḍi (II)

Of these Annā Reḍḍi and Mallā Reḍḍi are new figures first brought to light in this epigraph.

[The following records taken from *Mack. MSS.* are in Telugu.]

881. A paper grant in the hands of Shaḍdarśana Somayājulu. Records that Maṭḷa Veṅkaṭarāmārazu Dēvachōḍa Mahārāja granted Chintaguṇṭa village in free gift to Sarasvati Sarvatōmukha Mahā vratayājulu, in Ś. 1662, Raudra. *Ibid.*, p. 269, No. 93, and p. 294, No. 167.

882. Another paper grant with the same person. Records that Maṭḷa Veṅkaṭa Rāmarāsu Dēvachōḍa Mahārāja granted 400 kuṇṭas dry field in Poli village and 100 kuṇṭas of paddy field in Munnur village in free gift to Shaḍdarśana Īśvar Sōmayājulu in 21 shares in Ś. 1682, Vikrama. *Ibid.*, p. 269, No. 94, and p. 295, No. 168.

883. Another paper grant with the same person. Records that Maṭḷa Anantarāju Dēvachōḍa Mahārāja granted 8 kuṇṭas of paddy field, 20 kuṇṭas of dry field in Labanka village, besides money, to Sarasvati Sarvatōmukhayājulu, in Ś. 1654, Paridhāvi. *Ibid.*, p. 270, No. 95, and p. 295, No. 169.

884. A paper grant in the hands of Shaḍdarśana Chūḍāmaṇi Sōmayājulu. Records that Maṭḷakumārarāju Dēvachōḍa Mahārāja granted the land of Brahmanapulla in the Bommavaram village in the Pulugulanāṇḍu, in free gift to Sarasvati Pauṇḍareekayājulu and Sōmēśvarayājulu in Ś. 1679, Īśvara. *Ibid.*, p. 270, No. 96, and p. 296, No. 170.

885. Another paper grant with the same person. Records that the inhabitants of Pottapināḍu and Pulugulanāḍu gave an annual charitable contribution at 30 pagodas in Pottapināḍ and at 10 pagodas in Pulugulanāḍ, to Sarasvati Sōmayājulu in Ś. 1652, Sādhāraṇa. *Ibid.*, p. 276, No. 97, and p. 296, No. 171.

886. Another paper grant with the same person. Records that Maṭḷa Veṅkaṭa- Rāmarāja granted 20 kuṇṭas of paddy field in different villages to the same scholar in Raudri. *Ibid.*, p. 98, No. 98, and p. 296, No. 172.

Timmayyapāḷem.

887. A Telugu paper grant in the hand of Śrōtriyamdār of the village. Records that Pullavole Reḍḍi and Karṇam granted the village to Rāmābhaṭlu Narasimhajosyalu in Ś. 1674, Āṅgirasa. *Ins., Ced. Dts.*, p. 305, No. 200.

Tiranampalli.

888. In the Vanhīśvara temple in the village. (Telugu). Records that Maningala Narasayyagāru granted 45 kuṇṭas of paddy fields in the Pennagalore village to the God of the place in Krōdhana. *Ibid.*, p. 250, No. 37.

Tiruvēṅgalanādharājupuram.

889. A (Telugu) paper grant in the hands of Pedutala Papamchutlu. Records that Maṭla Veṅkaṭarāmarāju, son of Tiruvāṅgalanātharāju, made an agrahāram in the country of Pulugalanāḍ on the north of Pareyavaram and in the south of Pulavage lake in the name of his father and granted it in free gift to the Brahmans in 10 shares in Ś. 1679, Dhātu. *Ibid.*, p. 299, No. 181, also p. 275, No. 110.

Ūṭukūr.

890. In the Nāgēśvara Pagoda. (Telugu.) Records the Sadāśivarāya exempted the tax on local barbers in Ś. 1484, Dundubhi. *Ibid.*, p. 260, No. 67.

891. Near the Gaṇēśa temple. (Telugu.) Records that "Gunnaswami Kumāraḍu Śrīrām" purchased 10 kuṇṭas of land in the village and granted it in Ś. 1428, Krōdhi, to Aḷagapperumāḷ, son of Śrīraṅgarāju. *Ibid.*, p. 260, No. 68.

892. A (Telugu) paper grant in the hands of Yerrapāpu Reḍḍi at Ūṭukūr. Records that the village of Obali became ruined and that Maṭla Veṅgalanātha Dēvachōḍa Mahārāja gave the headship of the village to one Nārāyaṇareḍḍi of Ūṭukūr with some additional endowments for populating and improving it in Ś. 1632, Virōdhi. *Ibid.*, p. 268, No. 91 and p. 293, No. 164.

893. A (Telugu) P.G. in the hands of the same. Records that in Ś. 1638, Jaya, the people of Taṅgatūru Rajyam and thirty-four towns issued a grant in Ś. 1638, Jaya, fixing a payment to Nārāyaṇareḍḍi and another at the rate of one "Purka" on each bullock load of the following goods:—Pepper, nuts, cotton, thread, wax, common seed, tin, lead, copper, sulphur; and also one visam on each load of the following goods:—Jaggery, tobacco, garlic, gunny, gingelly oil, tamarind, salt, rice, grains, etc., in the Pottappi and Puligula Nāḍus. *Ibid.*, pp. 268-9, No. 92 and p. 293, No. 166.

Vāsudēvapuram.

894. A (Telugu) P.G. in the hands of Venkaṭanārāyaṇ at Vāsudēvapuram (Yellaguṇḍa). Records that in Ś. 1630, Śukla,

Maṭḷa Veṅkāṭrāmarāju Devachōḍamahārāja granted the village in free gift to one Subbābhaṭṭu. *Ins., Ced. Dts.*, p. 274, No. 109, and p. 299, No. 180.

Mangamāmbāpuram (Velagachērla).

895. A P.G. in the hands of local Brahmans. Records that Maṭḷa Kumāra Anantarāja made a portion of Lembākka, a new village called Vengamāmbāpuram, in honour of his mother in Ś. 1642, Plava, and gave it to fourteen Brahmans in fourteen shares. There are four other copies of the same inscription, but dated in Ś. 1673, 1673 and 1691.

Vellelavārikanḍrika.

896. A (Telugu) P.G. in the hands of the local Brahmans. Records that Maṭḷa Tiruvēṅgalanātha Dēvachōḍa gave some land in Anantarājupēṭa to Vellēla Veṅkaṭarāmaśāstri. *Ibid.*, p. 303, No. 191.

Veṅgamāmbāpuram.

897. A (Telugu) P.G. in the hands of the local Brahmans. Records that in Ś. 1632, Virōdhi, Maṭḷa Tiruvēṅgalanātha built the village in the land of Śiṅgarapalla and gave it to Vēdānta Ayyavāru Bhaṭṭu and other Brahmans in eighteen shares. *Ibid.*, p. 273, No. 105.

898. In P.G. in the hands of Nallamaguṇḍa Reḍḍi in the same village. Records that Maṭḷa Chennarāja Dēvachōḍamahārāja granted to Nallama Raṅgappa in Śubhakrit some kuṇṭas of dry and wet lands. *Ibid.*, p. 298, No. 177.

Yemmanūru.

899. A P.G. in the hands of Chennubhaṭṭa of the place. Records that Maṭḷa Veṅkaṭarāmarāsu, son of Tiruvēṅgalanātharāsu, gave to Chennabhaṭṭa in Ś. 1678, Yuva, the waste land of Veṅgammāpaḷḷi in Pottappināḍu for favourable rent. *Ibid.*, p. 303, No. 192.

Rāyachōṭi.

900. 442 *of* 1911.—(Telugu.) On a slab set up in the courtyard of the Vīrabhadrasvāmin temple. Records in Durmukhi gift of the village of Mogapalampaḷḷi to a number of Śaiva priests to maintain 160 lamps in the temple of Vīrayyadēva at Rāchavīti by an agent of Veṅkaṭādri Nāyaniṅgāru and the trustees.

901. 443 *of* 1911.—(Telugu.) On the base of the east gōpura of the same temple. A damaged record of the Vijayanagara king Vīrapratāpa Vīra-Achyutadēva Mahārāya, dated Ś. 1456, Jaya. Records gifts by Veṅkaṭādri Nāyaniṅgāru to the temple of Vīrēśvara at Rāchavīti.

902. 444 *of* 1911.—(Telugu.) On the wall of the same gōpura. A damaged record of the Vijayanagara king Vīrapratāpa Kṛishṇadēvarāya-Mahārāya, dated Ś. 1442, Vikrama. Records gift by Kāma-Nāyaniṅgāru for the merit of the king. Mentions the two provinces Penugoṇḍa-Mārjavāḍa and Udayagiri Mārjavāḍa.

903. 445 *of* 1911.—(Telugu.) On the south wall of the central shrine in the same temple. A record of the Vijayanagara king Vīrapratāpa Vīra-Sadāśivadēva Mahārāya in Ś. 1484, Dundubhi. Records that Amarināyani Veṅgala-Nāyaniṅgāru, the agent of the Mahāmaṇḍalēśvara Jillēla Raṅgapatirājayyadēva-Mahārāja who was governing the Rāmadurgam-śīma, repaired the central shrine and the *śukanāśi* of the Vīrēśvara (also called Vīrabhadradēva) temple for the merit of his master. [This chief like Nāgarājayyadēva of Mārkāpūr and Voṇṭimiṭṭa was connected with the Aravīti brothers by his mother's side.]

904. 446 *of* 1911.—(Tamil.) On a slab set up in the hamlet of old Rāyachōṭi near the same village. Records that Niśśaṅka-pratāpa Rāyadēva-Mahārāya, "lord of Karkaṭapura," gave in Ś. 1155, Nandana, the village of Rāyanārāyaṇapputtēri which was named after himself to the temple of Janārdana-Perumāḷ built at Āṇḍappūr in Kīḷai-Mārāyapāḍi, a district of Raṭṭapāḍikoṇḍaśōḷa-maṇḍalam, by a private individual.

SIDDHAVATTAM TALUK.

Boddecherla.

905. On a stone situated on the bank of the river Gundala-kamma near the ruined pagoda of the village. (Telugu.) Records that Kākatiya Gaṇapatidēva granted some land in the village to Rāmanāthadēva in Ś. 1179, Piṅgaḷa. *Ins., Ced. Dts.*, p. 213, No. 1.

906. On a stone lying near the gate of the Āñjanēya Pagoda. (Telugu.) Records that Velugōṭi Kumāra-Yāchamanāyaḍu of Veṅkaṭagiri re-established in Ś. 1662, Raudri, the pagoda in the village and granted some land in Turlapāḍu in the district of Veṅkaṭagiri. *Ibid.*, p. 214, No. 3.

Bukkayapalli.

907. On a stone in the village. (Telugu.) Records that Gummaḍūr Aubaladēva Mahārāya gave in Pramādhi to a dancing woman in Śripatikoṇḍasvāmi temple three *tūms* of dry land. *Ibid.*, p. 495, No. 20.

Chenduvāyi.

908. On a stone in the Pagoda of Yellamma. (Telugu.) Records that the Reḍḍies and Karṇams of the place granted some land to Goddess Yellamma in Ś. 1694, Nandana, for daily worship. *Ibid.*, p. 492, No. 13.

909. On a stone on the bank of the Pinākini river, east of the village. (Telugu.) Records that in Ś. 1147 (Pārthiva ?), Kantamanāyak, granted the village as free gift to the Brahman Chaturmukabhaṭṭa. *Ins., Ced. Dts.*, p. 493, No. 14.

Chintarājupalli.

910. On a stone in the village. (Telugu.) Records that Maṭla Anantarāya gave in Ś. 1520, Vishu, in the reign of Śrīraṅgarāya some land in the village to one Chinnamanāyaḍu. *Ibid.*, p. 492, No. 11. See Cg. 762, Cp. 863-B, and Cp. 854.

Gaṅga-Pērūru.

911. On a stone north-east of the village. A grant in Ś. 1081 of some revenue to Rāmasvāmi temple at Voṇṭimiṭṭa. *Antiquities*, p.

912. In a field south-east of the village. An undated grant of Naraśiṇgarāya of Vijayanagar.

913. A C.P. in the local mosque recording in Ś. 1699 a grant of land at Mukundapuram by the Nawab of Cuddapah. *Antiquities*, p. and *Cuddapah Gazr.*, p. 240.

914. On a stone in the village. (Telugu.) Records that Nāgarājayya granted to God Raghunāyaka of Voṇṭimiṭṭa in Ś. 1484, Siddhārthi, in the reign of Sadāśivarāya the village of Gāṅgapērūru as a free gift. *Ibid.*, p. 500, No. 36.

Jonnavaram.

915. On a stone east of the local tank. (Telugu.) Records that Nāgarājayya Dēvamāharāja exempted in Śubhakrit, in the reign of Sadāśivamahārāya, the tax on local barbers. *Ibid.*, p. 496, No. 24.

916. On a stone in the Mādhava Dēvar temple. (Telugu.) Records that Pōtināyaḍu and Nāgamānāyaḍu granted to Rāmāyaṇam Mādhavayya three *tūms* of land at Mādhapuram village in Ś. 1451, Virōdhi. *Ibid.*, No. 25.

917. On a stone south of the above. (Telugu.) Records that Potināyaḍu granted Mādhapuram village to God Mādhavasvāmi in Ś. 1455, Nandana, in the reign of Achyutarāya. *Ibid.*, No. 26.

Koṇḍūru.

918. On a stone in the boundary of the place. (Telugu.) Records that peoples of Koṇḍukavi Liṅgayyappaḷḷi and Koṇḍūru settled the boundary in Ś. 1695, Vijaya. *Ibid.*, p. 497, No. 27.

Kōṭapāḍ.

918-A. On a stone near the gate of the *Āvula male.* Records that in Ś. 1500, in the time of Kōṭapōti Bhakki Reḍḍi, the karṇam and others gave six *kuntas* to one Bhīma Reḍḍi for the performance of *āvulaparupu*, i.e., worship of sacred cattle. See *Cuddapah Gazr.*, pp. 238–9 for very interesting details.

Maddūru.

919. On a stone near the Bhairava pagoda. (Telugu.). Records that Pāparāja Kundea, the manager in the custom house at Siddhāvaṭṭam, granted the fees of the custom house at Maddūru to God Ishṭakāmēśvara of Siddhāvaṭṭam in Ś. 1454, Khara, in the reign of Achyutadēva Mahārāya. *Ins., Ced. Dts.*, p. 494, No. 17.

Mallinānipaṭṭaṇam.

920. On a stone in the boundary of the village. (Telugu.) Records that Liṅgarāsayya granted four tūms of paddy field in the village to God Kumārasvāmi in Ś. 1457, Manmatha. *Ibid.*, p. 493, No. 15.

921. On a stone situated in a ruined pagoda. (Telugu.) Records that the Vipravinōdins and jugglers granted their allowance from the village to God Chennakēśava in Ś. 1496, Rākshasa. *Ibid.*, No. 16.

Pennapērūru.

922. On a stone west of the village. (Telugu.) Records that Nimmala Yelamallappareḍḍi dug a well and built it in Ś. 1693, Khara. *Ibid.*, p. 490, No. 5.

Raṅgampaḷḷi.

923. On a stone in the village. (Telugu.) Records that Perumāḷadēva, the minister of Murāri Nārāyaṇ Brahmarākshasa Jannayyadēva Mahārāja of Panugal, granted in Ś. 1118, Akshaya, to Śaṅkaradēva and Mallēśvara the village as free gift. *Ibid.*, p. 498, No. 29.

*Siddhāvaṭṭam.**

924. On the fort wall near the gate. Records that Anantarājayya erected the compound wall and dug a large tank in Ś. 1528, Viśvāvasu, in the reign of Vīraveṅkaṭarāyalu. *Ibid.*, p. 489, No. 1.

925. On a stone in the Siddhēśvara pagoda. Records that Jitti Rāmanāyaka erected the pagoda in Ś. 1169, Plavaṅga, in the reign of Akkarasa Gaṅgarasa Rājayya. *Ibid.*, No. 2.

926. On a stone in front of the Yellamma pagoda. Records that Timmarasayya's son granted a village in free gift to

---

* I regret that a large number of paper grants of this place were copied and included in the list of epigraphs. But having once made the list and assigned the serial numbers I have not thought it advisable to omit them. Of these Nos. 928, 929 and 930 are in Persian. The rest are in Telugu.

Vīraparamēśvara in Ś. 1443, Vishu, in the reign of Kṛishṇarāya. *Ins., Ced. Dts.*, p. 489, No. 3.

927. On a stone near the tank in the fort. Records that Tantrapati Pōlināyaḍu, the prime minister of Ādirājēndra, constructed the Siddhēśvara pagoda in Ś. 1155. *Ibid.*, p. 499, No. 31.

928. On the mosque of Bismalla on the rampart. (Persian.) Records that the mosque was built by Alam Khān in H. 1186. *Ibid.*, No. 32. Abdul Alam Khān was Nawab of Cuddapah about A.D. 1755.

929. On a stone in the mosque of Sekkulla in the fort. Records that Mayana Alam Khān, the Subadar of Cuddapah, built it in H. 1184. *Ibid.*, No. 33. See the previous epigraph.

930. On a mosque near the fort gate. Records that Sayud Mahomed, a darogar of Aurangazeb Padshah, built it in H. 1181. *Ibid.*, p. 34.

931. On a stone in the Kēśavasvāmi pagoda. Records that Attappa Nāyaḍu granted some land in Tikkala village to the deity in Ś. 1170 in the reign of Tikkarasa Gaṅgayyadēva. *Ibid.*, p. 500, No. 35.

932. In the hands of Sayud Abdul Futta. Records that in Ś. 1529, Sarvajit, the people of the villages of Siddhāvaṭṭam district, gave 100 *bigas* of land to "Peerjadahsaib." *Ibid.*, p. 501, No. 37.

933. With the same person. A grant similar to the above. *Ibid.*, No. 38.

934. In the hands of Shaik Ali and Hussain Makkuga? Records that the Reḍḍies and Karṇams of Siddhāvaṭṭam granted some land to Mulla Ali in a certain Bahudhānya. *Ibid.*, p. 502, No. 39.

935. In the possession of the astronomer Appa Bhaṭṭu. Records that Fatti Singh, Killedar, gave to Chandrasēkhara Jōsyalu in 1636, Jaya, four kuṇṭas at Siddhāvaṭṭam. *Ibid.*, No. 40.

936. In the possession of Naraśiṅgarāya. Records that twelve kuṇṭas of land in Boddecherla were given to Kannoji Bāpurāyaḍu by Maṭla Tiruvēṅgalanātha Dēvachōḍa Mahārāja in Ś. 1687, Pārthiva. *Ibid.*, No. 41.

937. A record of Maṭla Veṅkaṭadēva ordering the Reḍḍi and Karṇam of Kulakanāḍu Sīma to continue the above. *Ibid.*, No. 42.

938. A record of Maṭla Tiruvēṅgalanātha in Vyaya, continuing the above. *Ibid.*, No. 43.

939. A record of Musalināyaḍu in Bahudhānya, ordering Goppūri Śūrappa to continue the above. *Ibid.*, No. 44.

940. In the possession of the same Naraśiṅgarāyalu. An orde of Veṅkaṭarama Rāja Dēvachōḍa in Bahudhānya to the

Reḍḍis and Karṇams of Pottappināḍu to continue the above. *Ins., Ced. Dts.*, p. 502, No. 45.

941. With the same. An order of Dodore Musalināyaḍu to Kopparti Timmareḍḍi to pay twenty-three pagodas and four paṇams to Bāparāyaḍu from the revenue, *Ibid.*, No. 46.

942. With the same. The same Mussalman chief gives a grant to Naraśiṅgarao in Pramādhi. *Ibid.*, No. 47.

943. In the hands of the same person. An order of Maṭla Kumāra Veṇkaṭa Rāghavarāju to Gōṭṭūr Subbarāyalu to continue the grant of certain lands in Brāhmaṇappaḷḷi Agrahāram. *Ibid.*, No. 48.

944. With the same person. An order of the same Maṭla chief to Appaḷācharlu of Brāhmaṇappaḷḷi to continue the same. *Ibid.*, No. 49.

945. In the hands of the same person. Records that Jupulli Lakshma Rāyalu appointed Bāparāyaḍu to manage affairs on the former system in Yuva. *Ibid.*, No. 50.

946. With the same person. A record of the same chief giving twenty-four *gorrus* of land in the village of Poṅgūr to Kānajovi Bāparāyaḍu, in Ś. 1679, Bahudhānya. *Ibid.*, No. 51.

947. With the same person. Records that the same chief transferred his salary of 200 pagodas on Duttalūr and 50 pagodas in the Poṅgūr village in Yuva to Bāparāyaḍu. *Ibid.*, No. 52.

948. With the same person. Records that the same chief built a Pēṭah in the name of Appā Rao at Poṅgūr and divided the allowance of the Pēṭah between Appā Rao and another person. *Ibid.*, No. 53.

949. In the hands of the same Naraśingarow. Gift by the same chief to Bāparāyaḍu of the annual payment of 200 pagodas from several villages in Yuva. *Ibid.*, No. 54.

950. In the hands of the same person. Records that the Reḍḍis and Karṇams of Buggalapalli granted to Kānajovi Veṅkaṭarao Viśvāji 15 *tūms* of land and 40 pagodas in the village in Ś. 1673, Prajōtpatti. *Ibid.*, No. 55.

951. Records in Ś. 1637, Manmatha, lands of 50 pagodas in Yāpuḍipalli to the same man by the Reḍḍis and Karṇams of the village. *Ibid.*, No. 56.

952. In the hands of the same person. Records that the Reḍḍies and Karṇams of Yeppalappēṭa granted land for 66 pagodas to the same person in Ś. 1698, Dundubhi. *Ibid.*, No. 57.

953. With the same person. Records that the Reḍḍies and Karṇams of Boggulappalli gave in Ś. 1710, Saumya, 13 *tūms* of land for 25 pagodas to the same man. *Ibid.*, No. 58.

954. In the hands of one Chunchu. Records that Kanday Pōtunāyaḍu and Yellammanāyaḍu, etc., granted to Kadirayya in

Ś. 1686, Subhānu, three-fourths of the village of Panukuratti. *Ins., Ced. Dts.*, p. 502, No. 59.

955. In the hands of Nāgappareḍḍi. Records that the farmers and accountants of Jaṅgampalli paid certain money to Nāgappareḍḍi and another in Ś. 1708, Prabhava, to build the village of Mallappanpēṭa. *Ibid.*, No. 60.

956. In the hands of Rāmakrishṇabhaṭ. Records that Vīrūr Sītārāmayya, Sthala-Karṇam of Siddhāvaṭṭam, granted the village of Vīrapaḷḷi for 5 chakrams in Raudri to Gaḍiyāram Kōnambhaṭ. *Ibid.*, No. 61.

957. In the hands of the same person. Records that Sayud Amil granted a share in Vīrayyappaḷḷi village to Rāmakṛishṇabhaṭṭa for digging a tank. *Ibid.*, No. 62.

958. With the same person. Sayud Amin of Siddhāvaṭṭam Sirkar confirmed the above. *Ibid.*, No. 63.

959. With the same person. Mir Rasul granted to the same person in 1113, Sun, the village of Vīrayyappalli, for the Śrotriyam rent of five chakrams. *Ibid.*, No. 64.

960. With the same person. Records that Veṅkaṇṇa granted in Bahudhānya to the same person 4 kuṇṭas of land in the village of Pidatala Vīrayapaḷḷi. *Ibid.*, No. 65.

961. With the same person. Records that Visaji Nāganāth, Karodi levied on the above a rent of 15 paṇams. *Ibid.*, No. 66.

962. In the hands of Rāmakrishṇabhaṭ. Records that Sayud Gulam Shuriff of Siddhāvaṭṭam gave to Rāmakrishṇabhaṭ in 47 Zulu an order fixing five chakrams for Vīrayapaḷḷi village. *Ibid.*, No. 67.

963. With the same person. A record of Veṅkaṇṇa in Bahudhānya raising the above to six chakrams for the present year and reducing it to three for the next. *Ibid.*, No. 68.

964. In the hands of Gōpālabhaṭ and Śēshabhaṭ. Records that Abdul Ghani ordered in 1172, Fasli, some persons to adjust their accounts. *Ibid.*, No. 69.

Takkolu.

965. On a stone near a local a well. (Telugu.) Records that Raṅgarāja gave to God Tripurāntaka in Vijaya two *tūms* of land in the village. *Ibid.*, p. 490, No. 6.

Vārikuṇṭa.

966. On a stone near the local Chennakēśava pagoda. (Telugu.) Records that Choti Siddhēśvara Śāḷuvarāja and people rebuilt the pagoda of Kēśava and granted to the deity seven *tūms* of land in the village in Ś. 1454, Kara. *Ibid.*, p. 495, No. 21.

Virūru.

967. On a stone north of the local Vīrabhadra pagoda. (Telugu.) Records that Sarasvati Malladēvarāja and the people of the Vipravinōda community granted their allowance due in this village to God Vīrēśvara in Ś. 1449, Sarvajit. *Ins., Ced. Dts.*, p. 494, No. 18.

Vonṭimitta.

[Some scholars consider this place to be the Ēkaśilānagara of Poet Bommara Pōtaṇa, the author of the *Bhāgavatam*, while others identify it with Oragallu or Waraṅgal. The subject is one of fierce controversy to-day.]

968. 411 *of* 1911.—(Telugu.) On a slab set up near the eastern gōpura of the Kōdaṇḍarāmasvāmin temple. The Vijayanagara king Vīrapratāpa Sadāśivadēva-Mahārāya records in Ś. 1480, Kāḷayukti, that the village of Vonṭimiṭṭa in the Siddhāvaṭam Śīma of Udaiyagiri-rājya with its connected hamlets was granted to the temple of Raghunāyaka for offerings, repairs, festivals, etc., by Nāgarājayyadēva-Mahārāja, the son-in-law of Rāmarājayya-Guṭṭi-Yara-Tirumalarājayya of the Āravīḍu family. This chief was either the founder of the last Vijayanagara dynasty or one of his four brothers Timma Rāja. For another inscription of Nāgarājayya, see 161 of 1905 at Mārkāpūr. See also *Ins., Ced. Dts.*, p. 491, No. 7. For the description of the Kōdaṇḍarama temple see *Cuddapah Gazr.*, p. 237.

969. 412 *of* 1911.—(Telugu.) On a second slab in the same place. A record of the Vijayanagara king Vīrapratāpa Sadāśivadēva-Mahārāya, in Ś. 1477, Ānanda, Gutti Tirumalayyadēva Mahārāja of the Āravīḍu family is stated to have been the prime-minister of the king. Gift of three villages including Pulupaṭūru in Pottapināḍu and of some wet land in Vonṭi-miṭṭa to the same temple. Below this is inscribed a record of Ś. 1705, Sōbhakrit, registering gifts by certain Reḍḍis and Karṇams. See *Ins., Ced. Dts.*, p. 491, No. 8.

970. On a stone below the above. (Telugu.) Records that the Reḍḍis and Karaṇams of 18 villages fixed an allowance of one pagoda for each to God Kōdaṇḍarāmasvāmi in Ś. 1705, Śobhakrit. *Ibid.*, No. 9.

971. On a stone south of the above. Records that Peddanarasayya and Chinnanarasayya of Bōyanapaḷḷi fixed an allowance of 10 paṇams per year to the same deity in Ś. 1704, Śōbhakrit. *Ibid.*, No. 10.

GANJĀM DISTRICT.

The Mack. MSS. contain a number of inscriptions under the heading of Ganjām which are not to be found in the departmental list. They are in the following Telugu books:—

1. *No.* 535 (*No.* 14, *C.M.*, 983).—Forty-seven inscriptions on copper plates. Five taluks specified in the fly leaf. The O. MSS. Library No. of the volume is 15-6-2. I have gone through the volume and included the inscriptions in the list, except in regard to a few villages which I have not been able to locate.

2. *No.* 616 (*No.* 18, *C.M.*, 987).—One hundred and twenty-five inscriptions in Ganjām Province, Guṇṭūr and Nizampatam districts. It is a folio volume and has the Nos. 616 and Wp. 122 written with red pencil on cover. The Library No. of the book is 15-6-21. I have entered the inscriptions in their proper places, except in regard to two which I have not been able to identify.

3. *No.* 653 (*No.* 15, *C.M.*, 984).—One hundred and twenty-eight inscriptions in the Ganjām Province. The Library No. of this MS. book is 15-6-12. It has been copied in Brown's *Local Records*, Vol. 59, p. 169 ff.

A large number of these are not *epigraphs* in the strict sense of the term; because they are said to be copies of *grants* in the hands of the people of various agrahāras. The grants themselves are in some cases not in copper plates but in the form of title-deeds. Objection might be taken for the inclusion of these under the list of *inscriptions*; but having once made the list and having in view the identity of objects and the historic interest of these, I have retained them.

GENERAL.

Copper Plates.

1. *C.P. No.* 155 *of Mr. Sewell's List.*—(Graham's Plate No. I, discovered at Chicacole, now in Madras Museum.) This is an inscription of Nandaprabhañjanavarma, a king of Kalinga. "It is not dated, but it is decidedly ancient, and is probably pre-Chāḷukyan. The order is issued from the city of Sārapaḷḷi, to the Kuṭumbis at the village of Adeyavāṭa or Adeyavata, and records an agrahāra grant of that village," to the Charaṇas or branches of the Dēvarāṭa gōtra, for the benefit of a Brahman named Harischandrasvāmi. See *Tam. and Sans. Ins.*, pp. 159—161, where it is edited. Also *Ind. Antq.*, XIII, p. 48, and Vol. X, p. 243, where Dr. Fleet has summarised it.

2. *C.P. No.* 156 *of Mr. Sewell's List.*—(Graham's Plate No. II, now in the Madras Museum.) Records an inscription of Indravarma, king of Kaliṅga, of the Gaṅga family. "It is dated in numerical symbols, in the one hundred and twenty-eighth year of the victorious reign (of his dynasty), on the fifteenth day of the month Chaitra; the Saka year is not given. The order is issued from the city of Kaliṅganagara, and records a grant of the village of Tāmaracheruvu, in the district of Varāhavartani, on the occasion of an eclipse of the moon on the day of the full moon of the month Mārgaśira." See *Ind. Antq.*, X, p. 243; *Tam. and Sans. Ins.* and *Ind. Antq.*, XIII, p. 122.

3. *C.P. No.* 157 *of Mr. Sewell's List.*—(Graham's Plate No. III, now in the Madras Museum.) This is another record of Indravarman, of the Gaṅga family. "It is dated in numerical symbols, in the one hundred and forty-sixth year of the victorious reign of his dynasfy on the twelfth day of the month Māgha; the Śaka year is not given. The order is issued from the city of Kaliṅganagara, to the Kuṭumbis at the village of Talamula, in the Korosōṭaka Pañchali and records a grant of that village on the seventh day of the month Māgha." *Ind., Antq.*; X, p. 243, No. 3; *Tam. and Sans. Ins.*, pp. 164—66, and *Ind. Antq.*, XIII, p. 122.

4. *C.P.No.* 158 *of Mr. Sewell's List.*—(Graham's Plate No. IV.) This is an inscription in Sanskrit, of Dēvēndravarma, son of Anantavarma of the Gaṅga family. "It is dated, in words, in the fifty-first year of the victorious reign of the Gaṅga vamśa. The order is issued from the city of Kaliṅganagara, to the Kuṭumbis at the village of Tāmarachcheruvu, in the district of Varāhavartani, and records the grant of that village on the occasion of an eclipse of the Sun." See *Ind. Antq.*, Vol. X, p. 243, No. 4; *Ibid.*, Vol. XIII, p. 273; and *Tam. and Sans. Ins.*, pp. 167—70.

5. *C.P. No.* 159 *of Mr. Sewell's List.*—(Graham's Plate No. V, now in the Madras Museum.) This is an inscription of Satyavarma, son of Dēvēndravarma, of the Gaṅga family, and king of Kaliṅga. "It is dated, in words, in the fifty-first year of the centuries of years of Gāṅgēyavamśa; the Śaka year is not given. The order is issued from the city of Kaliṅganagara, to the Kuṭumbis at the village of Tārugrāma in the district of Galēla and records the grant of that village on the occasion of an eclipse of the sun." See *Ind. Antq.*, Vol. X, p. 243, No. 5; *Tam. and Sans. Ins.*, p. 168.

6. "The Chicacole Plates of Dēvēndravarman." These plates which were discovered at Chicacole by Graham with the previous five plates and which were long missing, form a record which is not very correct Sanskrit. They record the grant of the village of Poppaṅgika in Saraumantamba, a subdivision of Krōshṭukavartani as an agrahāra to six Brahman teachers who resided at

Kaliṅganagara and who belonged to the Chhāṇḍōgya school. The grant was made by Dēvēndravarman, son of Guṇārṇava, on the eighth tithi of the bright fortnight of Māgha, during the Sun's progress to the north (in the one hundred and eighty-third year of the dynasty). Another date is given as the twentieth day of the month of Sravaṇa, which is subsequent to the first by several months. Owing to the uncertainty in which the Gaṅga era is still involved, nothing can at present be said about Dēvēndravarman, the son of Guṇārṇava, but that he must be distinct from Dēvēndravarman, the son of Anantavarman, and that the name Guṇārṇava occurs twice in the list of the ancestors of Chōḍagaṅga of Kalinga. See *Ep. Ind.*, Vol. III, pp. 130—34.

7. *C.P. No.* 214 *of Mr. Sewell's List.*—In the Collector's office, Ganjām. Records a grant of two villages bringing an income of four *palas* in silver to a Brahman of the Kāśyapa gōtra, during an equinox, by Mahārāja Prithvīvarmadēva, ruler of Kaliṅga, of the Gaṅga dynasty, son of Mahēndravarmadēva, worshipper of Śiva on the Mahēndrāchala mountain, while seated on his throne in Kōlāhalapura (Kōlar). [The donee was a student of the Vājasanēya Vēda, the Kaṇva Śākhā and belonged to the five-fold pravara of Bhārgava, Chyāvana, Apnavāna, Aurva aud Jamadagni. He is called a Bhaṭṭaputra (cf. Rājaputra) and the inscription is written by the *Sandhivigrahin* "minister of peace and war". See *Ep. Ind.*, IV, pp. 198—201. Kielhorn attributes the epigraph on palæographical grounds, to the twelfth or thirteenth century A.D.]

8. *C.P. No.* 215 *of Mr. Sewell's List.*—In the Collector's office, Ganjām. (Uriya.) Records grant to the deity of the temple at Pūri of three villages by the Zamindar of Tārḷa in the reign of Mahārāja Vīrakēśavadēva, by permission of Harischandradēva. Mr. Sewell identifies the king with the sovereign of Orissa of that name who ruled from 1736 to 1773.

9. *C.P. No.* 216 *of Mr. Sewell's List.*—In the Collector's office, Ganjām. (Magadhi.) A record in the reign of a queen Daṇḍimahādēvi who succeeded her husband (her son probably being a minor), and who gave a village named Gōrasambha in the southern Kōsala country to a Brahman of the Kāśyapa gōtra. See *Ep. Ind.*, VI, pp. 140—42, where Dr. Kielhorn edits the inscription. He says that the language is Sanskrit, and the characters " In the northern alphabet peculiar to eastern India." The Queen's edict is addressed to her *Sāmantas*, *Mahārājas*, *Antaraṅgas*, *Kumāramātyas*, *Upārikas*, *Vishayapatis*, etc., of the Arttani Vishaya, and is to the effect that she gave the village of Gajrasambha in Dakshiṇakōsala in Koṅgōḍa Maṇḍalika, for the merit of her parents to Purushōttama Bhaṭṭar of the Kāśyapa gōtra, Vājasanēya-charaṇa and Kaṇva Śākha. The queen was then at her camp of victory at Guhēśvarapatāka.

10. *C.P. No.* 217 *of Mr. Sewell's List.*—In the Collector's office. A record of queen Daṇḍimahādēvi, the donor of the previous epigraph. The language of the grant is in Sanskrit and the characters in the style of the north-east India like the Nāgaḍam Plates of Vajrahasta (Ś. 979), the Būguḍa plates of Mādhavavarman, etc. The record gives No. 180 as the year of its issue. Dr. Kielhorn takes this to be the number of the Samvat year, but the plate itself is modern. The inscription gives the genealogy of the queen and says that, while staying in her camp of victory at Guhēśvarapatāka, she issued an edict to the chiefs and officers of Koṅgōḍamaṇḍala, that she gave, on the occasion of Saṅkrānti, the village of Villa to her minister Dhavala, and that he gave it in the fifth of the dark half of Mārgaśira of year 180 to a number of Brahmans. Kielhorn identifies Koṅgōḍa with Hieun Tsiang's Kong-u-t'o, "somewhere between Kuttack and Aska," but it has been palæographically objected to. See *Ep. Ind.*, Vol. VI, pp. 133—40.

11. *C.P. No.* 218 *of Mr. Sewell's List.*—(Discovered by the late W. DeN. Ramus, Esq., Assistant Commissioner, Salt Revenue, on the bank of a river in Chinna Kimedi Malias and presented by him to the Madras Museum. See the inscriptions of Madras for details.)

ASKA TALUK.

12. A C.P. of the time of Śaśānkarāja. Originally in the Collector's office, Ganjām, and now in Madras Museum. A record in the Sanskrit language but in the alphabet which is the "acute-angled type with nail-heads and which forms the transition from the Gupta to the Dēvaṇāgarị." Dated in Gupta Samvat 300 (A.D. 619-20). Mahārāja Mahāsāmanta Sainyabhīta Mādhavarman II, son of Yaśōbhīta and grandson of Mādhavarāja I, of the Śailōdbhava family, who was a feudatory of Śaśānka-Mahārāja (king of Karṇasvarṇa and the murderer of Rājyavardhana, the elder brother and predecessor of Harsha of Tanesvar), issued an order from his camp at Koṇgēḍa, granting to a Brahman the village of Chhavalakkaya in the Kṛishṇagiri with Nīlagiri or Puri in Orissa. Koṅgēḍa is referred to in Daṇḍimahādēvi's Inscriptions (See No. 3). The only other plate regarding the family of the present epigraph is the Būgaḍa plates of Mādhavavarman Sainyabhīta, but the latter is palæographically much more modern and therefore a grant of a later prince of the dynasty. See *Ep. Ind.*, VI, pp. 143—46.

13. *C.P. No.* 4 *of* 1914.—A record of the Eastern Gaṅga king Mahārāja Indravarman, son of Dānārṇava, in Sanskrit (Telugu), dated in Paurṇami, year 149, Pushya, Di. 20. Records the gift of the village of Bhukkukūra-Chchhēda in Kuraka-Rāshṭra, to a certain Bhavadhattaśarman of Triliṅga, by the king, whose capital was at Dantapura.

Aska (Asika).

Connected by tradition with Aśōka to whom the following epigraph is falsely attributed. The following is in Aska zamindari.

14. 186 *of* 1913.—On a stone built into the floor of the Tiruvidhēśvara svāmi temple at Aska. (Uriya.) Records (says Babu Sasi Bushan Palit) that the temple was constructed or dedicated on 100 Samvat, Kanyā, fifteenth day, a date which is disproved by the modern nature of the characters. [The temple is said to have been built by Aśōka. " The Aska estate originally formed a part of the Aska Zamindari; the latter was dismembered during the Moghul Government of the Northern Circars, 1560 to 1753, upon the death of Ramrowt Row, the last Zamindar, and divided amongst the neighbouring Atagadah." *Madras Manu*, III, p. 46.]

Budagulo.

15. 187 *of* 1913.—On the Boyrane-Kallikōṭa road. (Telugu, Sanskrit and Uriya.) A record of Mahammaṇḍu-kuḷḷi Kuḍupā Nijām Padasa (i.e., Muhammad Quli Qutbshah 1581—1611), dated in Ś. 1512, Virōdhi, Chaittra, first fortnight, 10, Thursday. Records that a general of the king named Sayud Sāha Sūkaralli Mōhana Parītu who was in command of the 84 forts of the Āndra *Trilinga-madhyama* country (conquered by Muhammaḍ Quli) dug a tank on the west bank of Lāṅgulya river called Śiṅgasāgaram evidently in honour of the then Gajapati ruler Narasimha or Śīṅgabhūpāla. The record says that Narasimha belonged to the lunar race and Sāḷva family and ruled over Utkala, including Rajamendry Kaliṅga and Saurāshtra countries. He was moreover a relation of Bāhu-balēndra, apparently a chief who lived after Mukundadēva usurpation which took place in 1551.

Chañcharāpalli alias *Malkitadēvipuram.*

16. A title-deed in the hands of the local people, dated in the fifty-fourth year of Vīrakēśvaradēva, Mesha 10, Vaiśakha Śuddha 3, Monday, gift of the village to Vidyākaradās by Marakatadēvi; the chief queen. *Local Records*, Vol. 59, pp. 267–68. [According to the list of Orissa kings given in Mr. Sewell's *Antiquities* ' Bir Kisor Deva ' ruled for 37 years from 1736 to 1773 or, according to another version, from 1743 to 1786. It was in his time that the Mahrattas established their rule over Orissa.]

Chandramahādēvipuram.

17. A title-deed of the sixty-fourth year of Vīrakēśvaradēva Mahārāja, Mīnam 8, Phālguna, Śuddha 10, Monday, relating to gift of a village to Lōkanātha and five others by the queen of Kṛishna Śiṅgadēva of Dhārakōṭa. See *Local Records*, Vol. 59, pp. 302—04, and note to No. 16.

*Dhārakōṭa.**

18. Records in the fifth year of Hari Kṛishṇadēva Mahārāja, Tulā 20, gift of land to Mahēśvara Tīyāḍi by Rāmachandra Simha dēva. See *Local Records*, Vol. 59, pp. 306–07. According to Sterling Hari Krishṇa ruled from 1715 to 1720 and according to another version from 1713 to 1718.

19. A record of the twelfth year of Mukundadēva, Vrishabha 3, Prabhava, Vaisākha Śuddha 7, Thursday, recording deed of sale of the above land by Gōvinda Tīyāḍi to Ghaṭṭa Rāmadās Pantulu. *Ibid.*, pp. 308–09. [Was this Mukunda dēva the usurper or one of the later chiefs of Khurda ?]

Dayānidhipuram.

20. A grant of Śrī-Vīrapurushōttama alias Bhīmadēva Mahārāja, in Samasta 37, Kārttika 9, Ashaḍha Śuddha 15, Thursday, Lunar eclipse, to "Śṛīgāri," of a village for himself and 13 other Brahmans. *Mack. MSS.*, Book XIV, 15-6-2. [The date of neither of the two Purushōttama dēvas 1479—1504 and 1607–28 agrees with the present record. It is doubtful whether *Samasta* refers to the regnal year or an era.]

21. Another grant of the same, in Samasta 44 ?, in Mēsham 30, Vaiśākha Śuddha 7, Wednesday, to the people of Viśvambarabhūmi, henceforth called Purushōttamapuram. *Ibid.* See note to the above.

Dharmarājapuram.

22. A grant of Vīraśrī-Vīrādhivīra-Śrī-Kalapāshaṇḍadēvara, in fourth year, Kumbhā 17, Pushya Śuddha 15, of the above village to Vāmadēvāchārya Bhaṭṭamiśra, who was to give 11 shares to 11 other Brahmans. The plate is said to bear the seals of conch and chakra.

23. A grant of Śrī Dharmadēva Rāja, of some lands in the village to Trilōchana Mahāpātra, son of the above donee in his third year, Kārttika Śuddha 5, Thursday. *Ibid.*

Ghāsipalle.

24. A record in Samasta 39, of Vīradēva Mahārāja, Tulā 5, Kārttika Śuddha 10, Tuesday, recording the gift of the village to three men by Aska Daṇḍapāṭi Naḷavamśarāju Dhārakōṭa chief Purushōttama Śinghadēva. See *Local Records,* Vol. 59, pp. 311–12. [The family of the Dhārakōta chiefs claim to be descended from Naḷa. The founder of it, Śōbhachandra Simha, is said to have

* This is the seat of an ancient Zamindari, adjoining Bodaguda on the north and Goomsur on the east. It was originally a part of Khidishīngy Zamindari, alleged to be founded by Sobab Chandra Singh in A.D. 1168—1206. It became a separate Zamindari in 1476, when "Boliyar" Singh divided the original estate into four divisions. See *Madras Manual*, III, pp. 269–70.

come from Jaipur and settled in Ganjām in the eleventh century. The estate of Kedi Singhi which he founded became divided in 1476 into four estates of which Darakōṭa was one. Purushōttama was evidently one of the chiefs of this estate.]

Gōpālakṛishṇapuram.

25. Records in the thirty-eighth year of Vīrakēśvaradēva Mahārazu, Tulā, Āśvija Śuddha 11, Tuesday, gift of forests (to be cleared) by Rājēndraśiṅga Rāzu Gāru. *Local Records*, Vol. 59, pp. 304–05. (*Mack. MSS.*, Bk. XV.) See No. 16 above.

26. Records in the seventeenth year of Divyaśiṅgadēva Mahārāja, Kumbha 18, Śuddha 14, Tuesday, gift by Rāmachandraśiṅga Rāja to Nīlāmbaradāsa in accordance with the desire of his grandmother. *Ibid.*, p. 305. [The king referred to here was evidently the first of the two Dirb Singh Dēvas who respectively ruled from 1692—1715 and 1786—98.]

27. Records in the same date another gift in accordance with the grant of Vīrakēśvaradēva's in Mēsha 4, Pramādīcha, Vaiśākha Śuddha 2, Friday, to Ghaṭṭa Gōpālakrishṇama Pantulu. *Ibid.*, p. 306. See note to No. 16.

28. Records in the thirty-eighth year of Vīrakēśvaradēva, (1743—86), Tulā 2, Āśvija Bahuḷa 10, Tuesday, sale of land to Ghaṭṭa Gōpālakrishṇama Pantulu for Rs. 3,345. *Ibid.*, pp. 313—15. The Dhārakōṭa chief Rājēndraśiṅga Rāja Gāru's consent.

29. Records in the reign of the same ruler, Samasta 61, Mīnam 28, Adhikachaitra Bahuḷa 7, Friday, sale of land to the above by Naraharidās of Dhārādēyipuram in Ārugaḍa Rājya. *Ibid.*, pp. 315-16. [If we take 61 to be the regnal year, we find inconsistency between this and the usual version as, according to the latter, he ruled only for 43 years from 1743 to 1786.]

30. Records in the reign of Divya Simha Mahārāja, Samasta 17, Kumbha 18, Śukla 14, Tuesday, gift of land to Nīlāmbaradās, son of Kapiladās, of Vīrabalabhadrapuram in Vāḍiśārājya (?) by Dhārakōṭa chief Rāmachandra Śīṅgadēva's consent. *Ibid.*, pp. 315—17.

31. Records in Samasta 71 of Vīrakēśvaradēva, Pramādīcha, Mēsham 4, Vaiśākha Śuddha (?), Friday, sale of land to Kṛishṇama Pantulu by Simharatha, a Mahājana of Dhārākōṭa Nārāyaṇapuram. *Ibid.*, pp. 318–19. See note to No. 29 above.

32. Records in Samasta 17, in the time of Vīraśrī Divya Simhadēva Mahārāja, Kumbha 18, gift of land to Chiri Ratha, with Dhārakōṭa Rājēndrasimha's consent. *Ibid.*, pp. 319–20. See note to No. 26.

33. Records in Samasta 38 of Vīrakēśvaradēva (1743—86), Tulā 2, Āśvija Śuddha 11, Tuesday, sale of land to the same donee. *Ibid.*, pp. 320—25.

Gudiśaṭhā (Gudisoro?).

34. Records in the reign of Śrī Mukundadēva, Samasta 23, Makaram 23, Pushyasuddha 13, Friday, gift of the village to two people by Purushōttama Śrīgadēva of Dhārakōṭa. *Loc. Rec.*, Vol. 59, pp. 336-7. See No. 19 above.

35. Records in Samasta 9 of Vīra Śrī Divya Simhadēva Rāja (1692—1715?) Simha 2, Bhādrapada Śuddha 10, Monday, gift of land to Jagannātha Ratha, son of Kēśavadīkshita, grandson of Sarvapada Pāṇigrāhi Nīlakaṇṭha Dīkshita. *Ibid.*, pp. 337-8.

Harikṛishṇapuram.

36. Records in the eighteenth year of Vīrakēśvaradēva (1743—86?) Mēsha 12, Vaiśākha bahuḷa 10, Wednesday, the gift of the village to Nītyānanda bhaṭṭa-miśra by Harikṛishṇa Śiṅgadēva Rāja. See *Loc. Rec.*, Vol. 59, pp. 341—7.

Jagannāthapuram.

37. A C.P. grant of Vīraśrī-Jagannātha *alias* Bhīmadēva Rāja in Kumbha 22, Phalguna-Suddha Daśami, Wednesday. Records that he gave various lands, gardens, etc., in a number of villages to " Chikkalupala " Jōsya. *Ibid.*, No. 7.

38. A grant of the same king in Tulā 12, Kārttika-Śuddha 15, Sunday. Records the gift of the village in 16 parts to one Gaṅgādhara. The village is said to be east of Viśvanāthapuram, west of Patripuram. *Ibid.*

Jagannāthapuram (near Guṇṭupadu, Dhārakoṭa).

39. Records in the reign of Mukunda Dēva, Samasta 14, Vrishabha 29, Āshaḍha Śuddha 12, Friday, gift of land in Guṇṭupaḍa to Anamapāḍi Gāru by Dharakōṭa chief Jagannātha Śiṅga Raja on condition that he was to supply two gold sacred threads during two full moons. *Loc. Rec.*, Vol. 59, pp. 326-7. Was Mukundadēva the Khurdā chief who ruled from 1692 to 1715?

Jagannāthapuram (near Śaśapuram).

40. Records in the fifth year of Mukunda Dēva, Mīnam 12, Chaitrabahuḷa 2, Friday, sale of land (815 bharaṇas) to Sadāśivamiśra and eleven others by Jagannātha Śiṅga. See *Loc. Rec.*, Vol. 59, pp. 295-6. See note to the above epigraph.

Kamalādēvipuram.

41. Records in Samasta 31 in the reign of Vīrakēśvaradēva, Mithuna 9, Ashāḍhabahuḷa 14, Friday, gift of land to Nityānandabhaṭṭa-miśra by Hari Kṛishṇa Śiṅgadēva Rāja. See *Loc. Rec.*, Vol. 59, pp. 350—2. See also No. 36 above.

Kaṭṭagaḍa (" Kuñjavihāripuram alias Kāṭhaguha ").

42. Records in the eleventh year of Mukundadēva Rāya, Tulā 24, Kārttika-Śuddha 15, Thursday, gift of the village to Gōpīnātha Mahāpātra, son of Trilōchana Mahāpātra, and grandson of Dibbaśiṅga by Kūnjavihāri Śiṅgadēvarāju. *Loc. Rec.*, Vol. 59, pp. 265-6. [This Mukundadēva was evidently the man who ruled from 1664 to 1692, according to Sterling.]

43. Records in Sam. 68 of Vīrakēśvaradēva, (1743—86), Tulā 9, Āśvija śuddha 15, Friday, gift of land to Ānanda Santarao by the same donor. *Ibid.*, pp. 269—70. See Nos. 29 and 30 above which seem also to show that *Samasta* should not be taken as regnal year.

Kāyirāpalli (Kadirāpalli ?).

44. Records in Samasta 58 in the time of Vīrakēśvaradēva Mahārāja, Mīnam 7, Phālguna Śuddha 13, Monday, the issue of a title-deed of the village to Bhayigō Mahāpātra, by Kṛishṇa Śingh of Dhārakōṭa. *Ibid.*, pp. 301-2. [Was Kṛishṇa Singh the Uriya scholar who had the *Mahābhārata* translated into Uriya verse ?]

Kāyira Rāmachandrapuram (Kora Rāmachandrapuram).

44-A. Records in the fourth year of Śrī Kṛishṇadēva Mahārāza, Kumbham 10, Phālguna Śuddha 15, Wednesday, gift of the village to Gurulōkanāthamiśra Gōsāyi. *Ibid.*, pp. 292-4.

Kirākhayiagrahāra.

45. Records in Samasta thirty-seven, in the reign of Vīrakēś-varadēva (1743—86 ?) Simham 14, Bhādrapada Śuddha 15, Friday, sale of the village to Purushōttama Mahāpātra for Rs. 220-4-0 in the presence of the Brindāvana deity. *Ibid.*, pp. 309—11.

Kirtipuram alias *Rājēndrapuram.*

46. Records in Samasta 37 in the reign of Vīrakēśvaradēva, Makara 1, Māghabahuḷa 30, Friday, gift of land to Madhu-praharāzu Gāru by Rājēndraśiṅgadēva Rāzu (Dhārakōṭa chief ?). *Ibid.*, pp. 276—9.

47. Records in the thirty-seventh year of the same king, Kumbha 17, Phālguna Śuddha 15, Monday, sale of land to Sarva-vāhanapād and Kṛishṇa Paṇḍa. *Ibid.*, pp. 280—4.

48. Records in Samasta 41 of Śrī Vīrakēśvaradēva, Mēsha 30, Vaiśākha Śuddha 3, Saturday, gift of land (Dāvugāvundi, renamed Rājēndrapuram) to Nārāyaṇakōṭa and three others by Rājēndraśiṅgadēva Rāja, the Chief of Dhārakōṭa. *Ibid.*, pp. 285—8.

Kaṇḍadēvuḷi Rāyaśiṅgapuram (Rasimhapuram).

49. Records in Samasta 5, in the time of Śrī Purushōttamadēva, Makaram 7, Māghabahuḷa 30, Monday, gift of the village to Balabhadramiśra by Rāyaśiṅgadēva Rājugāru. *Loc. Rec.*, Vol. 59, pp. 289—91. Was Purushōttama the Dhārakōṭa or Khurda chief (1690—30)? See No. 52 below.

Padmanābhapuram.

50. A grant of the village of Ekkalarēvu newly called Padmanābhapuram to Nāgalakoṇḍavāmana and his son Rāmabhaṭḷu by Padmanābhēndradēva in Samasta 18, Vrischika 17, Mārgaśira-Bahuḷa 30, Wednesday. The record says that Vāmana lived for sometime and then his son Rāmakṛishṇa sold it to others. *Ibid.*

51. Records in the reign of Harikṛishṇadēva, Samasta 3, Kumbham 15, Phalguna-śuddha 10, Monday, gift of Abhayapuram to Vasudēvarāzu Gāru by Padmanābha Śiṅgadēva, in twenty-two parts, as *Yagnadakshiṇa*. *Ibid.*, pp. 272—6.

Pāñchaśingipuram (Bhāriguḍa).

52. Records in the time of Dibbaśiṅgadēva, Samasta 3, Vaiśākhaśuddha 15, Monday, gift of the village to Sarva-Kavichandra, with the consent of the Dhārakōṭa chief Śrī Purushottama Śiṅgadēva. *Ibid.*, pp. 297-8. Dibbaśinga ruled from 1692 to 1715.

Purushōttamapuram (Gaṅgāpuram).

53. Records in the reign of Mukunda Dēva, in Samasta 15, Āshāḍha Śuddha 2, Wednesday, Mithuna 13, gift of the village of Purushōttamapuram to its mahājanas by the Dhārakōṭa chief Purushōttama Śiṅgadēva. *Ibid.*, pp. 299-301. [Mukunda Dēva was evidently the predecessor of Dibba Singh I, who ruled from 1664 to 1692.]

Rājēndrapuram.

54. Records in Samasta 54 in the reign of Vīrakēśvaradēva, Māghaśuddha 15, Wednesday, gift of village by Rājēndra Śiṅgadēva Rāzu to a number of Brahmans. *Ibid.*, pp. 328—33. See No. 43 above.

Rāmakṛishṇapuram.

55. Records in Samasta 18 in the reign of Śri Vīrakēśvaradēva, Simha 2, Bhādrapada-bahuḷa 9, Sunday, gift of 80 bharaṇas of land to Māguṇi Sāntarā Gāru by Hari Kṛishṇa Śiṅga Dēva Rājā. *Ibid.*, pp. 348-9. See Nos. 43 and 44 above.

Svarṇadēvipuram.

56. Records in the reign of Śrī Vīrakēśvaradēva, in Samasta 4, Karkaṭaka 12, Śrāvaṇabahuḷa 5, Friday, lunar eclipse, gift of the village to Mārkaṇḍāchārya Praharāja, son of Trilōchanāchārya and grandson of Vāmadēvāchārya, by the Cherugaḍa chief Kripāsindhu Dēvarāja Gāru. See *Loc. Rec.*, Vol. 59, pp. 338--40. Cherugaḍa was one of the four estates into which the Khedi Singi estate became divided in 1476.

Berhampur Taluk.

Bontomundali.

57. A C.P. recording gift to Viśvanātha Sāmanta Rāya of the above village by Pedda Padmanābhadēvara Gāru. *Mack. MSS.*, Bk. XIV.

Dabharu Purushōttapuram.

58. Records that in Sam. 58 (?), Kumbha 28, Phalguna-Śuddha 7, Wednesday, Vīraśrī-Purushōttama Anaṅga Bhīma Dēva Kēśari built the village anew and gave it to Brahmans, under the new name. *Ibid.*

Deviliyapada.

59. Records that king Padmanābha Anaṅga Bhīma Kēsari, in Sam. 5 (?), Makara 15, Māgha 12, Friday, renewed the grant of the above village to Narasimhapādi in place of the original donee, his father. *Ibid.*

Dēvipuram.

60. Records that Padmanābha Anaṅga Bhīma gave to Dharādhara Vāhanapati a number of villages under the name of Dēvipuram in year 18, Karkaṭaka 1, Āshāḍha Bahuḷa 1, Tuesday, Saṅkrānti. *Ibid.*

Dhānyarāśi.

61. Records that in year 45 (?), Vrishabha 4, Jyēshṭha-Bahuḷa 13, Purushōttama Mahārāja demanded from the people of the above village tax for the occupation of more lands in Īśānya direction. A list of people owning the lands is given. *Ibid.*

Gōvindupuram.

62. A C.P. recording gift of the village to a Brahman who was the court physician of Śrī-Mātaṅgadēva Mahārāja in Ś. 1528. *Ibid.*

Jagannādhapuram.

63. A C.P. recording that Jagannāthadēva Dhātri gave in Sam. 2, Simha 8, Bhādrapada-Śuddha 15, Monday, in lunar eclipse, the village of Bhīmapuram with the new name of Jagannāthapuram, to one Raghumiśra. *Ibid.*

Jaugada.

64 to 76. 84 *to* 96 *of* 1909.—On a rock in the hill at Jaugada. (Pali) Edict of the Mauryan Emperor Dēvānām Piye or Aśōka.

These were prepared for a revised edition of Vol. I, of *Corpus Inscriptionum Indicarum*, pp. 17—20. For an excellent bibliographical notice of the inscription and place, see *Antiquities*, Vol. I, pp. 4-5. For the latest work on the subject see Vincent Smith's Edicts of Aśōka 1909, pp. 59-61.]

Kabatamundali.

77. A C.P. which records that Ananta Anaṅga Bhīma Dēva Kēsari gave in Samasta 2, Vrishabha 17, Sunday, to Dharādhara Vāhanapati, the above village. *Ibid.* See No. 60 above.

Nongolodeyi.

78. A C.P. recording that Vīrēśvaradēva gave in year forty-five, Kanyā 10, Aśvija Bahuḷa 10, Jayavāram, the above village to Śrīdhara Mahāpātra. The price of the land is said to be 3,000 (Rupees ?). *Ibid.*

Pitāmbarapūr.

79. A C.P. which records that in Samasta 14, in Mituna 18, Āshāḍha Śuddha 7, Tuesday, Śrī-Vīra-Pītāmbara Anaṅga Bhīma Dēvara Kēsari Mahārāja gave his name to Gōpināthapuram, and gave it in charity to the people. *Ibid.*

Vijayapadmanābhapūr.

80. A grant of Padmanābha Anaṅga Bhīma, dated in Samasta 5, Mīna 29, Vaiśāka Bahuḷa 1, Wednesday, and recording the gift of Laḍḍigam and a few other villages, under the new name of Vijayapadmanābhapuram, to Prabhākhara Bhaṭṭamiśra and Bhavinikidāsa. *Ibid.*

CHATRAPUR TALUK.

Bhāgirathapuram.

81. A record of Vīra Śrī Durbha Śiṅga in Samasta 31, Vrishabha 30, Jyēshṭa 15, Thursday, lunar eclipse, relating that the Humma chief Sūra Śrī Bhagīratha Sāmanta Mahāpātra gave the village to Harinātha, in expiation of his son's death and for the increase of the family. See *Loc. Rec.*, Vol. 59, pp. 197-98. [Durbah Śiṅga was perhaps the Kurdha chief who ruled from 1692 to 1715.]

*Balaṅkēśavarapura Agrahāram.**

82. A C.P. of Śiṅgadēva Mahārāja in Samasta 2, Makara 5, to 18 Mahājanas. *Mack. MSS.*, Bk. 14.

Biridikōṭa.

83. A grant of land in the reign of Vīrakēśvaradēva Mahārāja in Samasta 52, Mithuna 10, Āshaḍha Bahūḷa 10, Sunday, to

* Spelt Balakēsarapuram in Postal Directory, 1893, formerly in the Ganjām taluk.

Ganjadiya Mahantu Balarām Dāsa, with the consent of Mahāratha Mahāpātra. *Loc. Rec.*, Vol. 59, p. 192 f., No. 32.

84. Gift of land to Mahant Balabhadrā Dās by the same. *Ibid.*, No. 33.

85. Records gift of land to Mahant Nārāyaṇa Dās in the reign of Mukundadēva Mahārāja, Samasta 19, in Kumbha 19, Phalguna Bahuḷa 12, Saturday. *Ibid.*, No. 34.

86. A record of Vīra Narasiṃhadēva Mahārāja in year seventeen, Vrischika 22, Mārgasira Śuddha 5, Friday, relating gift to Sēvaka Nārāyaṇa Paṇḍa, with the consent of Śrī Dharmacharaṇasūr Mahāratha Mahāpātra. *Ibid.*, p. 194, No. 35.

87. A record of the fifth year of Mukunda Dēva, in Mēsham 10, Vaiśākha Bahuḷa 2, Sunday, relating gift of land to Sēvaka Jagannātha Paṇḍa, with the consent of Śrī Rāmachandrasūr Mahāratha Mahāpātra. *Ibid.*, No. 36.

88. A record of Śrī Vīrakēśvara Mahādēva in year 55, Kanyā 26, Āśvija Bahuḷa 9, Sunday, relating gift of land to Nīḷā Paṇḍa, with the consent of Balaṅkēśvarasura Śrī Mahāratha Mahāpātra. *Ibid.*, No. 37.

Divyaśingapur (Durbaśingapuram).

89. A record of Vīra Śrī Divyaśiṅga Mahārāja, in year 32, Vrishabha 30, Jyēshṭa Śuddha 15, Thursday, lunar eclipse, relating that Dibbaśiṅga Sāmantarāya Mahāpātra gave some land to two Gōsāyis to worship God Mahādēva and feed Brahmans. *Ibid.*, pp. 199–200.

Gobba.

The following epigraphs have been taken from *Mack. MSS.*, Bk. XV (Oppert's No. 15–6–12) :—

90. Records that Mahāratha-Mahāpātralu gave in Samasta 68, Mēsham 12, Vaiśākha Bahuḷa 10, Sunday, some lands to Ānandamahāpātra. (Signed Mahāratha-mahāpātralu.)

91. Records that Mahāratha-mahāpātralu gave in Samasta 57, Makara 14, Māgha Śuddha 9, Wednesday, some lands to Ānandamahāpātra. (Signed Mahāratha-mahāpātralu.)

Humma.

92. A record of Vīrakēśvaradēva (1743—86) in Samasta 51, Mīna 10, Phalguna Śuddha 10, Wednesday, relating sale of 100 bharaṇas of land by Śrī Rāmachandra Sāmantarāya Mahāpātra to a person for Rs. 925, in the Mokāssa of Humma, on condition he was to pay a tax of Rs. 8 to Government. *Ibid.*, No. 40.

93. A sale of 20 bharaṇas of land to Jagannātha Pāda by Sāmantarāya in the reign of Mukundadēva (1664—92?) in Samasta 70, Mithuna 27, Śravaṇa Bahuḷa 3, Monday. *Ibid.*, No. 41.

94. Records that in Vīrakēśvara's reign (1743—86), in year 17, Dhanus 18, Sunday, that Humma Rājyādhipati Śūra Śrī Sāmantarāya Mahāpātra gave to Vāsudēva Bhaṭṭa (?) a mango grove. *Loc. Rec.*, Vol. 59, No. 42.

95. Records that in the tenth year of Balabhadra (1656—64?), Kumbha 25, the brother of Jagannātha Sāmantarāya Mahāpātra gave 60 bharaṇas to Narahari "Chod-Rao." *Ibid.*, No. 43.

96. Records in the reign of Vīra Śrī Gadādharadēva, Samasta 28, Vriśhabha 5, gift of 50 bharaṇas to Mukunda with the consent of Viśvēśvarabāhu Sāmanta Mahāpātra. *Ibid.*, No. 44.

97. Records that in the reign of Vīra Śrī Dubbasingh Mahārāya (1692—1715?), in Samasta 29, Kumbha 10, the Humma chief Sāmantarāya Mahāpātra gave 30 bharaṇas of land to Rāmachandra Gohar. *Ibid.*, No. 45.

98. A record of Vīra Śrī Rāmachandradēva Mahārāja in Samasta 12, Makara 25, recording gift by the same chief to Kripāsindhu Mahāratha. *Ibid.*, No. 46. The king was apparently the same as he who ruled from 1727 to 1743.

99. Records that in the reign of Vīra Śrī Vīrakēśvaradēva (1743—86?), Mahārāja, Samasta 5, Kumbha 5, Hummarājyādhipati Sāmantarāya Mahāpātra gave some land to Dīnabandhu Sētu Rao. *Ibid.*, 47.

100. Records that in the ninth year of Vīra Śrī Purushōttama Dēva Mahārāja, Mēsham 2, the same chief gave to Gahadali Jambu 20 bharaṇas of land on a tax of five Santas a bharaṇa. Consent of Humma Rājyādhipati Śūra Śrī Gadādhara Sāmanta Rāya Mahāpātra. *Ibid.*, p. 206, No. 48.

101. Records that in the eighth year of Vīra Śrī Rāmachandradēva Mahārāja, Mīnam 17, Tuesday, the Humma chief gave to Kapila Pātra 12½ bharaṇas of land. Consent of Bhāgīratha Sāmantarāya Mahāpātra. *Ibid.*, p. 207, No. 49.

102. Records that in the eleventh year of Vīrakēśvaradēva Mahārāja, Kanyā 3, Sāmantarāya Mahāpātra gave to Balabhadra Paṇḍa 10 bharaṇas of land. Consent of the same chief as in above. *Ibid.*, No. 50.

103. Records that in the twenty-first year of Mukunda Dēva, in Chaittra Śuddha 14, Monday, Humma Rājyādhipati Śūra Śrī Sāmantarāya Mahāpātra gave to Guṇḍamalla Śītārāma Pantulu 15 bharaṇas. Consent of Śūra Śrī Kṛishṇachandra Sāmantarāya. *Ibid.*, No. 51.

*Kamalādēvipuram.**

104. Gift of the village of Virasapuram under the new name of Vijaya Vinākshapuram by Kallikōḍa Rājyātipati Śrī Naḷiṇāksha

---

* According to the Postal Directory of 1893 it is in Ganjām taluk, in the post town of Kaḷḷikōṭa. Ganjām is now in Chatrapūr taluk.

Mardharājadēva in the reign of Hari Krishṇadē va Mahārāja in Aśvija Śuddha 5, Wednesday, to Janārdana Karagāri. *Mack. MSS.*, Bk. 14.

Kēśavapuram (Kēsapūr?)

105. A record of Vīrakēśvaradēva Mahārāja in Samasta 58, Śārvari, Kārttika Śuddha 2, Sunday, Krishṇa Sūr Harischandradēva gave to Jaganātha Mahāpātra, during lunar eclipse, the village of Kēśapuram. *Loc. Rec.*, Vol. 59, pp. 211–2.

Lokanādhapuram.

106. A record of Mukundadēva Rāya in year 23, Bhava, Pushya Bahuḷa 11, Friday, recording that Śrī Nārāyaṇa Sūr Harichandana Dēvagāru gave the village to Nīlakaṇṭha Paṇḍa of Kauṇḍinyagōtra and Yajus-Śākhā. *Ibid.*, pp. 216–67.

*Nārayaṇapuram.**

107. A record of Vīrakēśvaradēva Mahārāja, in Samasta 2, Pramādīcha, Makara 25, Māgha Śuddha 15, Sunday. Records that Krishṇa Sūr Harischandra Nārāyaṇa Sūr of Kauṇḍinyagōtra and Yajurvēda was given during a lunar eclipse this village as a Śrōtriyam. *Ibid.*, pp. 209—211.

108. A record of the same king in Samasta 55, Vikāri, Kumbha 13, Māgha Śuddha 5, Sunday. Records that Purushōttamasūri's wife Kamalādēvivoṇṭi Mahādēvi gave to Nagarampalli Veṅkayyabhaṭḷu the village of Nārāyaṇapuram in five parts. *Ibid.*, p. 214.

Raghunāthapuram.

109. A record of Vīra Rāmachandra dēva Mahārāja in year 7, Simha 30, Bhādrapada Śuddha 7, Friday, relating gift of the village of Vīra Raghunāthapuram in Aragaḍa Rājya to Dani paramaguru. *Ibid.*, pp. 227—30.

Rāmachandrapuram.

110. A record of Mukundadēva in year 5, . . . twenty-fifth day, Vaiśākha Śuddha 15, Saturday, relating that the Aragaḍa Rājyādhipati Srī Harichandana Jagadēvagāru gave the village in thirteen parts to the Brahman Purushōttama Bhaṭṭa and others. *Ibid.*, p. 233.

Rambha.

The following inscriptions have been taken from the *Mack. MSS.*, XV, No. 15-6-12:—

111. A record of Gajapati Gauḍēśvara Vīrakēśvaradēva in Samasta 32, Mēsham 3, Vaiśākha Śuddha 15, Saturday, relating

* There are at least seventeen villages of this name in the Ganjām district—four in Aska, two in Berhampur, etc.

gift of land to a person of Purushōttamapuram in Guruvāy Rājya in Kṛishnaprasarakōṭa under the new name of Charaṇapuram.

112. A gift by Mahāratha Mahāpātraluṅgāru.

113. A record of Vīra Śrī-Mukundadēva in Samasta 10, Kumbha 19, Śuddha 5, Friday, relating gift of a village to Jagannātha Rauth.

114. Records that Vīrakēśvaradēva gave in Samasta 52, Vrishaba 5, Jyēshṭha Bahuḷa 13, Friday, a piece of land for a person for holy bath in the Gōdāvari.

115. A record of the same king in Samasta 32, Vrishaba 29, Jyeshṭha Bahuḷa 1, Monday, relating a gift to a Brahman. See *Loc. Rec.*, Vol. 59, p. 180.

116. A record of the same king in Samasta 2, Karkaṭaka 25, Sravaṇa Bahuḷa 30, Friday, relating gift of land to the Brahman Mukunda. *Ibid.*, p. 181.

117. Records that Śrī-Mukundadēva gave some land to Nārāyaṇadāsa at Raṅga-grāmam (Rambha-grāmam ?) in Samasta 5, Mēsham 19, Jyēshṭha Bahuḷa 7, Friday.

118. A record of Śrī-Mukundadēva in Samasta 14, Vrischika 27, Ashāḍha Bahuḷa 12, Friday, making a gift to Gaṅgādaradās Pītāmbaradās.

119. Records that Vīrakēśvara gave in Samasta 22, Mēsham 24, Vaiśāgha-bahuḷa 2, Wednesday, some land to Naraśiṅgapanda.

120. Gift of land by the same king in Samasta 17, Karkaṭaka 42, Śravaṇa-bahuḷa 30, Tuesday, to Jōgimalk in Rambha-grāmam.

121. A record of Vīrakēśvara in Samasta 48, Vrishaba 2, Vaiśākha 12, Wednesday, relating gift to Nārāyaṇapanda.

122. A record of Śrī-Mahāratha Mahāpātra in Sam 69, Kumbha 22, relating gift of the temple lands to Raghunātha-panda for service therein.

123. A gift by the same king to Gōpinātha Subuddhi in Samasta 59, Mīnam 6.

124. A record of the same king relating gift to Bompa Sapu in Samasta 73, Mīna 10, in Rambha-grāmam to Dadhivāhanasvāmi.

125. A record of Vīrakēśvara, dated in Samasta 60, Karkaṭaka 8, Śravaṇa Śuddha 1, Friday, relating gift of land for Bālavēṅkaṭēśvarasvāmi in Rambha.

126. Records that Mukundadēva Mahārāja gave in Samasta 3, Makaram 3, Māgha-bahuḷa 2, Wednesday, some land to Bhagavānpanda.

127. Records that Mahārathamahāpātra gave in Samasta 21, Vrishabham 10, some lands to Gōpinātha-Subuddhi for God Chandraśēkharasvāmi's worship.

128. Records that Mahāratha-mahāpātra gave in Samasta 71, Tulā 11, some lands to Puripanda for God Balaṅkēśvarasvāmi's worship in Rambha village.

129. Records that Mahāratha-mahāpātralu gave in Samasta 33, Dhanus 18, some lands to Nārāyaṇapanda for Dadhivāhanasvāmi's worship in Rambha village.

130. Records that Śrimahāratha mahāpātra gave some land to Bhagavānpanda in Rambha village.

131. Records that Vīra-Śrī-Rāmachandradēva Mahārāja gave in Samasta 14, Kumbha 16, Chaitrabahuḷa 9, Saturday, some lands to Mahājana Bhagavān Tiyaḍu (Yatiayaḍu ?) of Dharmaśaraṇapura.

132. Records that Mahāratha-mahāpātruḍu gave in Samasta 37, Kumbham 14, some lands to a yati.

133. Records that Vīrēśvaradēva Mahārāja gave in Samasta 59, Mēsha 4, Vaiśākha Śukla 7, Monday, some lands to Pindak Yatiyaḍu. (Sd. Mahāratha-mahāpātrulu.)

134. Records that Mahāratha-mahāpātrulu gave in Samasta 22, Makaram 3, some lands to Ānanda Śaṭhapaṅkti.

CHICACOLE TALUK.

Araśavilli.

135. 387 *of* 1896.—(Telugu). On a slab built into the wall of the *Prākāra* of the Sūryanārāyaṇa temple. The Gaṅga king Anantavarmadēva (1074—1146) records in Ś. 1068, seventy-second year, the gift of a lamp. [This was the last year of the king.]

136. 388 *of* 1896.—(Telugu.) The Gaṅga king, Anantavarmadēva records in Ś. 1069, seventy-second year, the gift of a lamp. See note to the above epigraph.

137. 389 *of* 1896.—(Telugu.) On another slab in the same place. Records in the fifty-eighth year of the Gaṅga king Anantavarmadēva (1074--1146), a gift of land in Araśavilli to Brāhmaṇas for a *sattra* by a merchant.

Balaga.

138. A-G. In the maṭha of Jagannāthasvāmi, founded in 1693 by Purandara dās Bhāvāji, and supported by grants of villages and Government commutation for salt revenue. Mr. Sewell gives a list of seven grants in the maṭh, viz., (1) the village of Chidivilasa from Navāb Haji Hussein in 1693; (2) Gummapāḍu from Pratāparudra Nārāyaṇa dēva in 1728; (3) Taḷḷavalasa from Navāb Mafus Khan in 1754; (4) lands from Bādulla Khan in 1749; (5) Chinnalavānipalle from Raghunātha Jagadēva in 1755; (6) Lands from Nārāyaṇa Gajapati in 1757; and (7) lands from the Moghul Government of Delhi in 1757. The original *farmans* are said to be in the hands of settlement officers. *Antiquities*, p. 7.

Chicacole.

For an excellent account of the antiquities of this place, ancient and mediæval, Hindu and Muhammadan, see Mr. Sewell's *Antiquities,* Vol. I, pp. 7-8. The remains of Hindu temples, Muhammadan Darogas and mosques, etc., are given. Epigraphically the place is famous as the site of the six Gaṅga plates of Grahame described above under Nos. 1 to 6. Besides these, Mr. Sewell gives a number of inscriptions of which, however, the following only are definite enough to be included here.

139. In the wall of Jama Masjid.—(Persian.) Consists of sixteen verses narrating the virtues and valour of Shir-Muhammad Khan, a Sirdar of the Nizam, who resided at Kaliṅgapaṭṇam, who followed a severe iconoclastic policy, and who built this mosque, in 1641. *Antiquities,* pp. 7-8.

140. In the mosque of Agha Jan. (Built in 1620.) Contains a number of verses praising the greatness of the builder. *Ibid.,* p. 8.

141. In the tomb of Burhan-ud-din Aulya. Record shis death in H. 1103 (A.D. 1691). *Ibid.,* p. 8.

Dirghāsi.

142. 271 *of* 1896.—(Sanskrit and Telugu.) On a slab in a field north-east of the village. Records in Ś. 997, the building of a *nāṭyaśāla* in front of the temple of Durga and the gift of two lamps, by Vanapati, the son of a Brahman Gōkarṇa of Ātrēyagōtra and door-keeper *(Pratihārin)* and commander-in-chief of the Gaṅga king Rājarāja (A.D. 1068—76) as well as his wife Padmādēvi. He defeated the king of Veṅgi and other enemies, namely, the Chōḍa king, the Utkala, Kimiḍi (Ganjām district), Kōsala, Giḍrisiṅgi and Oḍḍa [Orissa, whose king was later on reinstated by Rājarāja's son Anantavarma (1075-1146)]. See *Ep. Ind.,* Vol. IV, pp. 314—8, where Mr. G. V. Ramamurti edicts the inscription. He points out that the Veṅgi king should be Vijayāditya VII.

Kōmarṭi.

143. The Kōmarṭi plates of Chandavarman of Kaliṅga (so-called because they were discovered at Kōmarṭi in the Narasannapēṭa taluk). The language is Sanskrit prose and the alphabet similar to the Kollēru plates of Vijayanandivarman (*Ind. Antiq.,* Vol. V, p. 176) and the Chicacole plates of Nandaprabhañjanavarman. (No. 2 above) and decidedly more ancient than the Achyutapuram Plates of Indravarman I which are the oldest *dated* inscription of the E. Gaṅgas. The inscription records the grant of the village of Kohetūra (unidentified), to a Brāhmaṇa of the Vājasanēya school, by Mahārāja Kaliṅgādhipati Chandavarman in his sixth year, while he was staying at Simhapura. [Dr. Hultzsch believes that Chandavarman might be the same as his namesake who is mentioned as the father of Vijayanandivarman of the Kollēru plates. See *Ep. Ind.*, IV, pp. 142—5. He also believes that he and Nandaprabhañjanavarman should have belonged to the same dynasty not only on paloægraphical grounds but on their bearing the same title Kaliṅgādhipati and the same legend *Pitrbhaktah* on the seals of their respective copper plate grants.]

Nadagam.

143-A. The Nadagam Plates of Vajrahasta, dated Ś. 979, Phalguna Śuddha 12, corresponding to 4th March, 1058. It is a Sanskrit record issued from Kaliṅganagara, recording the grant of twelve villages separated from Ēraḍavishaya and constituted into a new *Vishaya* called after Vēlpūra (one of the twelve). The donor was king Vajrahasta of the Kaliṅga Gaṅga line and the donee his son-in-law Daṇḍanāyaka Samaya. [Mr. G. V. Ramamurti Pantulu edits the record in *Ep. Ind.*, IV, p. 183 ff. Compare the genealogy of the line as shown by this epigraph with that of Dr. Fleet and note that he is Vajrahasta III according to one and Vajrahasta V according to the other. His parentage also is differently given. In any case the present epigraph is valuable as it gives the date of his coronation. It took place in Ś. 960, Vrishabha, Śukla 3, Sunday, corresponding to 3rd May, 1038, His immediate successor was Rājarāja (1068-76), the father of the celebrated Anantavarman Chōḍagaṅga.]

Rāgōlu.

144. 391 *of* 1896.—(Sanskrit and Telugu.) On a stone in a field. Records the gift of a lamp.

145. A C.P. grant of Śaktivarman, edited in *Ep. Ind.*, Vol. XII, pp. 1—3, by Professor E. Hultzsch. "The alphabet is of an early southern type and the language Sanskrit prose." A record of Mahārāja Śaktivarman, said to be the Lord of Kaliṅga and "son of Vāsishṭhi." While at Pishṭāpura (Piṭhāpuram, Gōdāvari district) he issued, in his thirteenth year, an edict to the people of Rākaluva (i.e., Rāgōlu) in the Kaliṅgavishaya that he gave it as an agrahāra to the Brāhmaṇa Kumāraśarman of the Sāvarṇa gōtra and Vājasanēyi Śākha and his eight sons. [Pishṭapuram is mentioned in the Allahabad pillar inscription of Samudragupta (Fleet's *Gupta Inscriptions*, p. 13) Aihole inscription of Puḷakēśin II (*Ep. Ind.*, VI, 11) and Timmapuram plates of Vishṇuvardhana I (*Ep. Ind.*, IX, 319).]

Rāyipāḍu.

146. 390 *of* 1896.—(Sanskrit and Telugu.) On a stone lying in the bed of the tank. The Gaṅga king, Anantavarmadēva records in Ś. 1070, fourth year, the gift of a lamp. See No. 355.

Rōnāṅki.

147. 392 *of* 1896.—(Telugu.) On a stone lying on the bank of the Vaṁśadhāra, first and second faces. Records in Ś. 1015, nineteenth year of the Gaṅga king Chōḍagangadēva a gift of land to the temple of Siddhēśvara by queen Lakshmīdēvi.

148. 393 *of* 1896.—(Telugu.) On the, same stone, third and fourth faces. Records in Ś. 1015, nineteenth year, the Gaṅga king, Chōḍagaṅgadēva of a gift of land by the same queen.

Śingupuram.

149. The Brihatprōshṭa grant of Umāvarman, published in *Ep. Ind.*, Vol. XII, pp. 4—6. Both the alphabet and the phraseology of the grant resemble those of the Komarti plates of Chaṇḍavarman, to whose family Umāvarman apparently belonged. The inscription records that Umāvarman granted in year 30 the village of Brihatprōshṭa to a Brāhman named Haridatta. The king is said to have resided at Simhapura which Dr. Hultzsch identifies with modern Śiṅgupuram between Chicacole and Narasannapēṭa. See *Ep. Ind.*, XII, p. 4, for the reference in the Buddhistic chronicles of Ceylon to Simhapura in the eleventh and twelfth centuries.

Śrikūrmam.

Dr. Hultzsch points out in the *Madr., Ep. Rep.,* 1896, that the inscriptions of this place are much better preserved than the other stone records of the Telugu country as they are inscribed in hard black stone which has withstood successfully the influence of the climate. Most of these inscriptions are about the successors of Anantavarman Chōḍagaṅga. Among these there were four Narasimhas, and four Bhānudēvas. "The first Narasimha was the son of Anaṅgabhīma (No. 307 of 1896). The second ascended the throne about A.D. 1275-76 (Nos. 272, 297, 304, 323, 335, 356, 363, 367 and 375 of 1896), and the third about A.D. 1322–23 (Nos. 300, 310, 319, 343, 355 and 358 of 1896). His queens bore the names Gaṅga and Sīta (Nos. 308, 309, 324, 343, 344 and 345 of 1896)." The first of the Bhānudēvas "appears to have reigned between the first and second Narasimhas (Nos. 351 and 353 of 1896). The second and the third were contemporaries of the third Narasimha (Nos. 302 and 324 of 1896) and the fourth reigned between the third and the fourth Narasimhas (Nos. 315 and 336 of 1896). A single inscription supplies the name of Jagannātha, perhaps a successor of the second Narasimhas (No. 332 of 1896)." According to sterling the Gaṅgavaṁśa of Kaliṅga commenced in A.D. 1131 and was in power for the next four centuries till 1451 when Kapilēndra came to the throne. Regarding the Gaṅgaṁśa rulers he points out that more than five Narasimhas and seven Bhānus ruled till 1451. Under these kings the invasion of Telingana and Karnāṭaka was very common. The literary and religious importance of some of the local inscriptions is referred to under each of them. Mr. Sewell notes (see his *Antiquities*) 16 inscriptions in this place; but as the departmental list contains more than 100 a comparison of the two sets is not necessary.

150. 272 *of* 1896.—(Sanskrit and Telugu.) On the first pillar from the left in the Tiruchuttumaṇṭapa in the Kūrmēśvara temple, south and east faces. A minister of Vīra-Narasimhadēva (II) recording in 1212, fourteenth year, a gift of gold. [According to W. W. Hunter's *Orissa* a Kēsari Narasimha ruled from 1282 to 1307. The present record shows that he came to the throne in A.D. 1276.]

151. 273 *of* 1896.—(Telugu.) On the same pillar, north and west faces. Anantavarma-Pratāpavīra-Narasimhadēva records in Ś. 1227, thirty-third year, a gift of land and gold. [See *Antiquities*, II, 207, where Pratāpa Narasimha is attributed to 1307 to 1327.]

152. 274 *of* 1896.—(Telugu.) On the second pillar in the same maṇṭapa, north and west faces. The Gajapati king, Pratāpavīra-Purushōttamadēva (generally ascribed to 1479—1504) records in Ś. 1393, seventh year, a gift for offerings. [The inscription settles the date of Purushōttama's accession to be A.D. 1464-5. See Nos. 198, 162 and 243 below.]

153. 275 *of* 1896.—(Sanskrit and Telugu.) On the same pillar, south face. Records in Ś. 1279, Hēmamlamba, gift of two lamps by Lakshmi, the queen of Narasimha of Bīragōṭṭa. See No. 232.

154. 276 *of* 1896.—(Telugu.) On the same pillar, east face. Records gift of a land.

155. 277 *of* 1896.—(Sanskrit.) On the third pillar in the same maṇṭapa, east face. Vīra-Bānudēva records in his twelfth year, a gift of gold.

156. 278 *of* 1896.—(Telugu.) On the same pillar, south face. Records in Ś. 1281, the gift of two lamps.

157. 279 *of* 1896.—(Sanskrit.) On the same pillar, north face. Records that king Narasimha provided for the supply of oil to the temple.

158. 280 *of* 1896.—(Telugu.) On the fifth pillar in the same maṇṭapa, east face. Records in Ś. 1314, the gift of a lamp.

159. 281 *of* 1896.—(Sanskrit and Telugu.) On the seventh pillar in the same maṇṭapa, east face. Records in Ś. 1349, Plavaṅga, the gift of a lamp by Śiṅgama, daughter of Jayantarāja and wife of Vatsarāja of the Śilāvamśa.

160. 282 *of* 1896.—(Sanskrit and Telugu.) On the same pillar, west face. Records in Ś. 1206, the gift of a lamp by a merchant.

161. 283 *of* 1896.—(Sanskrit and Telugu.) On the same pillar, north face. Records in Ś. 1569, Sarvajit, the setting up of an image of Lakshmi.

162. 284 *of* 1896.—(Telugu.) On the same pillar, west face. The Gajapati king, Pratāpa-Kapilēśvaradēva records in Ś. 1382, Vikrama, thirty-second year, the gift of a brass image carrying a lamp and of some land. [The inscription shows that Kapilēśvara was crowned about A.D. 1429–30. So the traditional version of 1452—1479 has to be given up. *Antiquities*, p. 207.]

163. 285 *of* 1896.—(Sanskrit and Telugu.) On the eighth pillar in the same maṇṭapa, east face. Records in Ś. 1198, gift of gold.

164. 286 *of* 1896.—(Telugu.) On the eighth pillar in the same maṇṭapa, east face. Records in Ś. 1336, the gift of a *chāmara* and of gold.

165. 287 *of* 1896.—(Telugu.) On the same pillar, north face. Records in Ś. 1198, gift of gold.

166. 288 *of* 1896.—(Sanskrit.) On the same pillar, west face. Records in Ś. 1220, the gift of a necklace by Purushōttama, the brother of Vijayarka (Vijayāditya II) and son of Rājarājadēva of the Sōmānvaya. See *Ep. Ind.*, V, 36–7 and note to No. 230 below.

167. 289 *of* 1896.—(Sanskrit.) On the same pillar, west face. Records in Ś. 1357, Rākshasa, the gift of the village of Kākatapallikā and of vessels by a Gaṅga king of the Śīlānvaya.

168. 290 *of* 1896.—(Sanskrit.) On the ninth pillar in the same maṇṭapa, east and north faces. A record in Ś. 1203, the eighth tithi of the bright half of Mēsha, corresponding to Saturday, the 29th March, A.D. 1281. Mentions the Mādhva teachers Purushōttamatīrtha, Ānandatīrtha and Naraharitīrtha. (An incomplete record.) [The inscription is very important as it fixes the date of Madhvāchārya and others. See *Ep. Ind.*, VI, 260—6, where Mr. H. Krishna Sastri edits the inscription. For a discussion of the date see also my article on Vēdānta Dēśika in *J.R.A.S. Bo.*, 1915—6.]

169. 291 *of* 1896.—(Sanskrit and Telugu.) On the same pillar, west and south faces. Records in Ś. 1215, Magha, Śukla-Pañchami, Sunday, corresponding, according to Kielhorn, to the 3rd January, A.D. 1294, that Naraharitīrtha, a pupil of Ānandatīrtha, set up images of Rāma, Sīta, and Lakshmaṇa, and made various gifts to them. *Ep. Ind.*, VI, p. 268.

170. 292 *of* 1896.—(Telugu.) On the same pillar, west face. Records in the thirty-fourth year of Vīra-Narasimha, the gift of two chāmaras. See No. 151 above.

171. 293 *of* 1896.—(Telugu.) On the same pillar, north face. Records in Ś. 1344, the gift of a lamp.

172. 294 *of* 1896.—(Telugu.) On the same pillar, east face. Records in Ś. 1341, the gift of an image carrying a lamp.

173. 295 *of* 1896.—(Nagari.) On the tenth pillar in the same maṇṭapa, north and west faces. A record in Śamvat 1459, Ś. 1325, Sarvadhārin (wrong).

174. 296 *of* 1896.—(Telugu.) On the same pillar, north face. Records in Ś. 1205, the gift of a lamp by the wife of Narasimhabhaṭṭōpādhyāya.

175. 297 *of* 1896.—(Telugu.) On the same pillar, west face. Records in Ś. 1211, fourteenth year of Vīra-Narasimhadēva, the gift of a lamp. [So Vīra-Narasimha came to the throne in A.D. 1276. See No. 150 above.]

176. 298 *of* 1896.—(Sanskrit.) On the same pillar, east face. Records in Ś. 1205, the gift of a lamp by the wife of Narasimhabhaṭṭōpādhyāya, who was a contemporary of king Anaṅgabhīma (1175—1202, according to Mr. W. W. Hunter) and had built an enclosure of black stone for the temple. See No. 60 above.

177. 299 *of* 1896.—(Telugu.) On the same pillar, east face. Records in the time of Vīra-Narasimhadēva in Ś. 1324, the gift of a lamp by a merchant. See No. 36 above. [Is 1324 a mistake for 1224?]

178. 300 *of* 1896.—(Sanskrit and Telugu.) On the eleventh pillar in the same maṇṭapa, east face. Records in Ś. 1263, eighteenth year of Pratāpavīra-Naranarasimhadēva, the gift of gold. [So the inscription proves that the king came to the throne in A.D. 1323.]

179. 301 *of* 1896.—(Telugu.) On the same pillar, west face. Records in Ś. 1367, Raktākshin, the gift of a lamp.

180. 302 *of* 1896.—(Telugu.) On the same pillar, west face. Records in Ś. 1243, the gift of a lamp by a military officer of Vīrādhivīra-Bānudēva.

181. 303 *of* 1896.—(Telugu.) On the twelfth pillar in the same maṇṭapa, east and north faces. Records in Ś. 1325, Svabhānu, the gift of an image carrying a lamp.

182. 304 *of* 1896.—(Sanskrit and Telugu.) On the same pillar, west and south faces. Records in Ś. 1214, seventeenth year of Pratāpavīra-Narasimhadēva, the gift of a lamp. See No. 178 above which gives a different date.

183. 305 *of* 1896.—(Telugu.) On the same pillar, west and east face. Records in Ś. 1207, the gift of a lamp.

184. 306 *of* 1896.—(Sanskrit and Telugu.) On the same pillar, west and north face. Records in Ś. 1221, the gift of a lamp.

185. 307 *of* 1896.—(Sanskrit and Telugu.) On the fourteenth pillar in the same maṇṭapa east, north, west and south faces. Records in Ś. 1172, the gift of land, etc., by a feudatory of Pratāpavīra-Narasimhadēva (I), who was the son of Anaṅgabhīma of the Gaṅga family. [Pratāpa-Narasimha is attributed in Hunter's *Orissa* to 1307—1327.]

186. 308 *of* 1896.—(Sanskrit and Telugu.) On the same pillar, east face. Records in Ś. 1265, the gift of an image carrying a lamp and of ornaments by Gaṅgamahādēvi for the merit of Pratāpavīra-Narasimhadēva.

187. 309 *of* 1896.—(Sanskrit and Telugu.) On the same pillar, north face. Records in Ś. 1244 the gift of ornaments, etc., by Gaṅgāmba, the wife of king Nrisimha.

188. 310 *of* 1896.—(Telugu.) On the same pillar, north and west faces. Records in the reign of Vīrādhivīra-Naranarasimhadēva in Ś. 1271, twenty-eighth year, gifts for offerings by Kommidēvamma.

189. 311 *of* 1896.—(Telugu.) On the same pillar, south face. Records in Ś. 1788, Krōdhana, a visit paid to the temple by the second son of "the late zamindar of Jeypore."

190. 312 *of* 1896.—(Telugu and Sanskrit.) On the seventeenth pillar in the same maṇṭapa, east face. Records in Ś. 1253 the gift of a garden by a follower of Rāmānuja.

191. 313 *of* 1896.—(Telugu.) On the eighteenth pillar in the same maṇṭapa, west face. The Gajapati king Pratāpa-Kapilēśvaradēva records in Ś. 1377, twenty-fifth year, the gift of land. [See No. 162 above.]

192. 314 *of* 1896.—(Telugu.) On the nineteenth pillar in the same maṇṭapa, east face. Records in the seventh year of Pratāpavīra-Naranarasimhadēva the gift of a lamp.

193. 315 *of* 1896.—(Telugu.) On the nineteenth pillar in the same maṇṭapa, east face. Records in Ś. 1276, third year of Pratāpavīra-Bānudēva, the gift of a lamp.

194. 316 *of* 1896.—(Sanskrit.) On the twentieth pillar in the same maṇṭapa, east face. Records in Ś. 1226 the gift of a lamp.

195. 317 *of* 1896.—(Sanskrit.) On the twentieth pillar in the same maṇṭapa, east face. Records in Ś. 1373, Prajāpati, the gift of a lamp during the reign of Kapilēndra. Mentions Kaliṅganagara. See No. 162 above.

196. 318 *of* 1896.—(Telugu.) On the same pillar, north face. Records in Ś. 1373, Prajāpati, a gift of land.

197. 319 *of* 1896.—(Telugu.) On the twenty-first pillar, in the same maṇṭapa, east face. Records in Ś. 1267, twenty-third year of Pratāpavīra-Naranarasimhadēva, the gift of a lamp.

198. 320 *of* 1896.—(Sanskrit.) On the twenty-second pillar in the same maṇṭapa, east face. Records in Ś. 1374, the erection of a Dōḷamaṇṭapa.

199. 321 *of* 1896.—(Telugu.) On the same pillar, north face. A record in Ś. (?) Pramōdūta.

200. 322 *of* 1896.—(Sanskrit and Telugu.) On the twenty-third pillar in the same maṇṭapa, north, west and south faces. Records in Ś. 1685, Svabhānu, the setting up of an image of

Lakshmaṇa, to replace another which had been taken away by the Mahrāttas.

201. 323 *of* 1896.—(Sanskrit and Telugu.) On the same pillar, south, east, north and west faces. Records in the reign of Vīra-Narasimhadēva in Ś. 1219, twenty-third year, the gift of gold and cows by the minister Garuḍanārāyaṇadēva.

202. 324 *of* 1896.—(Sanskrit.) On the twenty-fourth pillar in the same maṇṭapa, east face. Records that in Ś. 1254, third year of Vīra-Bhāṇudēva, that the king gave images of Vīra-Narasimhadēva and of Gaṅgāmbika, which were holding lamps, and some land in Eraḍavishaya.

203. 325 *of* 1896.—(Telugu.) On the twenty-fifth pillar in the same maṇṭapa, south face. Records in Ś. 1301 the appointment of a dancing girl for holding a chāmara.

204. 326 *of* 1896.—(Telugu and Sanskrit.) In the twenty-sixth pillar in the same maṇṭapa, north face. Records in Ś. 1301, third year of Vīra-Narasimhadēva, the gift of a lamp.

205. 327 *of* 1896.—(Sanskrit.) On the same pillar, south face. Records in Ś. 1227 the gift of a lamp.

206. 328 *of* 1896.—(Sanskrit.) On the same pillar, south face. Records in Ś. 1241 the gift of a lamp.

207. 329 *of* 1896.—(Sanskrit and Telugu.) On the twenty-seventh pillar in the same maṇṭapa, north face. Records in Ś. 1302, fourth year of Vīra-Narasimhadēva, the gift of an image holding a lamp.

208. 330 *of* 1896.—(Telugu.) On the same pillar, south and west faces. A record of Ś. 1732, Pramōdūta.

209. 331 *of* 1896.—(Sanskrit and Hindi.) On the same pillar, south, east and north faces. Records in Ś. 1252, fourth year of Pratāpavīra-Naranarasimhadēva, the gift of a lamp and gold.

210. 332 *of* 1896.—(Sanskrit and Telugu.) On the twenty-ninth pillar in the same maṇṭapa, south, east, north and west faces. Records 40 *Nishkas or gaṇḍamāḍas* for offerings to the God in Ś. 1231, third year of Jagannāthadēva (son of Purushōttamadēva), also known as Viśvanātha. [See *Ep. Ind.*, V, 35–6, where the date is said to be irregular and of no value. See also No. 230 below.]

211. 333 *of* 1896.—(Sanskrit and Telugu.) On the same pillar, south, east and north faces. Records in Ś. 1519, Hēmalamba, that a Brāhmaṇa had himself weighed against silver and brass.

212. 334 *of* 1896.—(Sanskrit and Telugu.) On the thirty-second pillar in the same maṇṭapa, east face. Records in Ś. 1236 the gift of a canopy.

213. 335 *of* 1896.—(Telugu.) On the same pillar, north face. Records in Ś. 1212, fifteenth year of Pratāpavīra-Narasimhadēva, the gift of a lamp.

214. 336 *of* 1896.—On the thirty-third pillar in the same maṇṭapa, west face. Records that in Ś. 1275, third year of Vīrabhānudēva, the gift of a lamp was made by an inhabitant of Kōḍūru.

215. 337 *of* 1896.—(Telugu.) On the same pillar, south and east faces. Records in the seventh year of Pratāpavīrādhivīra-Naranarasimhadēva, gift of gold for offerings.

216. 338 *of* 1896.—(Telugu.) On the same pillar, north face. Records in Ś. 1283 the gift of a lamp. Mention *Sikati.*

217. 339 *of* 1896.—(Telugu.) On the thirty-sixth pillar in the same maṇṭapa, east and north faces. A damaged record in Ś. 1731, Śukla.

218. 340 *of* 1896.—(Sanskrit.) On the same pillar, west face. Records in Ś. 1234 provision for singing and playing on the *viṇa.*

219. 341 *of* 1896.—(Sanskrit.) On the thirty-seventh pillar in the same maṇṭapa, east face. Records gift of a land for a flower garden. (Date doubtful.)

220. 342 *of* 1896.—(Sanskrit and Telugu.) On the same pillar, south face. Records in Ś. 1278 gift of gold for offerings.

221. 343 *of* 1896.—(Telugu.) On the thirty-ninth pillar in the same maṇṭapa, west face. Records in Ś. 1271, twenty-eighth year of Vīrādhivīra-Naranarasimhadēva that his queen Gaṅgādēvi and Sītādēvi appointed one dancing-master and two dancing girls.

222. 344 *of* 1896.—(Sanskrit.) On the same pillar, south face. Records in Ś. 1267 that Gaṅgamahādēvi, queen of Narasimha-dēva, provided for the blowing of a conch.

223. 345 *of* 1896.—(Sanskrit and Telugu.) On the same pillar, east and north faces. Records in Ś. 1263 the gift of an image holding a lamp by Kommidēvi for the benefit of her daughter Sītādēvi and gift of gold by Gaṅgamahādēvi.

224. 346 *of* 1896.—(Telugu.) On the forty-first pillar in the same maṇṭapa, north face. Records in Ś. 1425, Rudhirōdgārin in the reign of the Gajapati king, Pratāpa Rudradēva, the gift of an image holding a lamp. [He was the opponent of Kṛishṇadēva Rāya of Vijayanagar.]

225. 347 *of* 1896.—(Telugu.) On the same pillar, west and south faces. A record of the Gajapati king Pratāpa-Purushōttama-dēva in Ś. 1417, Rākshasa, thirty-second year, concerning a gift of land by a merchant from Raṅgōlu. See No. 152 above.

226. 348 *of* 1896.—(Sanskrit.) On the same pillar, east face. Records the gift of a lamp and ornaments.

227. 349 *of* 1896.—(Sanskrit.) On the same pillar, east, north, west and south faces. Records in Ś. 1177 the gift of certain land in Ippili, which king Anaṅgabhīma (1175—1202) had previously granted to Brāhmaṇas. See No. 176 above.

228. 350 *of* 1896.—(Sanskrit and Telugu.) On the same pillar, south face. Records in Ś. 1177 a gift of land in Ippili.

229. 351 *of* 1896.—(Sanskrit.) On the forty-second pillar in the same maṇṭapa, west, south and east faces. Records in Ś. 1193 gift of land by a minister of Bhānudēva.

230. 352 *of* 1896.—(Sanskrit.) On the forty-third pillar in the same maṇṭapa, east, north and west faces. Records in Ś. 1195 the gift of 25 cows for a lamp by Vijayāditya (II), whose father Rājarāja had been minister of Vīra-Nrisimha (I, Gaṅga king).* He is said to be a descendant of the (Eastern) Chāḷukya king Vimalāditya and of his son Rājarāja Narēndra who ruled at Rājamahēndri and who had the Mahābhārata translated into Telugu. [The inscription is very important as it confirms the traditions that Nannaya Bhaṭṭa first translated the *Mahābhārata* in Rājarāja Narēndra's court. See *Ep. Ind.*, V, pp. 32—4. Dr. Hultzsch considers the date, after changing Wednesday into Monday, to be 23rd October, A.D. 1273.]

231. 353 *of* 1896.—(Sanskrit.) On the forty-fourth pillar in the same maṇṭapa, east and north faces. Records in Ś. 1197 the gift of a lamp by a minister of Vīra-Bhānudēva.

232. 354 *of* 1896.—(Telugu.) On the same pillar, west face. Records in Ś. 1199 a gift of land. Mentions gold coins of Bīragoṭṭa. See No. 153 above.

233. 355 *of* 1896.—(Sanskrit and Telugu.) On the forty-fifth pillar in the same maṇṭapa, north face. Records in Ś. 1272, twenty-ninth year of Narasimhadēva, the gift of a lamp by a merchant.

234. 356 *of* 1896.—On the same pillar, west face. Records in Ś. 1201, third year of Pratāpa-vīra Narasimhadēva, the gift of land by a military officer.

---

* The inscription gives the connection between the descendants of Rājarāja Narēndra and the Gaṅga kings. It gives this genealogy :—

Vimalāditya (1015—22).
|
Rājarāja Narēndra (1022—63).
|
Vijayāditya I.
|
Rājarāja
Vasaal of the Gaṅga Vīra Narasimha I.
|
- Vijayāditya II or Vijayārka. (Ś. 1195).
- Purushōttama (Ś. 1199—1240).
  |
  Jagannātha or Viśvanātha (Ś. 1231) Vassal of Vīrabhānudēva II.

235. 357 *of* 1896.—(Telugu.) On the same pillar, south and east faces. Records in Ś. 1340 gift of land for a lamp.

236. 358 *of* 1896.—(Telugu.) On the forty-sixth pillar in the same maṇṭapa, west and south faces. Records in Ś. 1267, twenty-second year of Pratāpa-vīra-Naranarasimhadēva, gift of land. Mentions Chikati.

237. 359 *of* 1896.—(Sanskrit and Telugu.) On the same pillar, east face. Records in Ś. 1199 the gift of 50 ewes for lamp by Purushōttamadēva, son of Rājarājadēva and brother of Vijayāditya II, mentioned in No. 230. [See *Ep. Ind.*, V, pp. 34–5 and the genealogical tree given as note to No. 230.]

238. 360 *of* 1896.—(Telugu.) On the same pillar, west face. Records in Ś. 1327 gift of gold for offerings.

239. 361 *of* 1896.—(Sanskrit.) On the forty-seventh pillar in the same maṇṭapa, west face. Records in Ś. 1291 gift of land by Harichandana, son of Rāmadēva, of the race of the Sun.

240. 362 *of* 1896.—(Telugu.) On the same pillar, south face. Records in the thirty-third year of Vīra-Narasimhadēva gift of land.

241. 363 *of* 1896.—(Telugu.) On the forty-eighth pillar in the same maṇṭapa, west face. Records that in the reign of Vīra-Narasimhadēva in Ś. 1215, eighteenth year, the gift of a lamp was made by an inhabitant of Nagara.

242. 364 *of* 1896.—(Sanskrit.) On the same pillar, south face. Records in Ś. 1291 the gift of cows.

243. 365 *of* 1896.—(Telugu.) On the forty-ninth pillar in the same maṇṭapa, north face. A record of the reign of Pratāpavijaya-Purushōttamadēva in Ś. 1392, seventh year, regarding the gift of silver vessels and chāmaras by an inhabitant of Pālakoṇḍa. [According to Hunter Purushōttama ruled from 1379 to 1504. He was the man who invaded Conjeeveram and carried away the king's daughter as captive in order to be wedded to Jagannātha's sweeper. See No. 152 above.]

244. 366 *of* 1896.—(Telugu.) On the same pillar, west and south faces. Records in the seventh year of the Gajapati king, Pratāpa-Purushōttamadēva, in Ś. 1393, Khara, gift of land by the same person. See No. 243 above.

245. 367 *of* 1896.—(Telugu.) On the same pillar, west, south and east faces. A record of the eighteenth year of Vīra-Naranarasimhadēva, Ś. 1215, Thursday, fullmoon of Rishabha, corresponding, according to Kielhorn, to 21st May, A.D. 1293. Records gift of gold by Naraharitīrtha. See No. 168 above and *Ep. Ind.*, VI, pp. 267–8.

246. 368 *of* 1896.—(Telugu.) On the fiftieth pillar in the same maṇṭapa, north face. Records in Ś. 1393, Khara, the gift of land.

247. 369 *of* 1896.—(Telugu.) On the same pillar, south and east faces. Records in Ś. 1186 (Friday, Kanyā Krishṇa-Trayōdaśi) corresponding, according to Kielhorn, to 19th September, A.D. 1264, gift of gold by Naraharitīrtha. See Nos. 168 and 245 and *Ep. Ind.*, VI, p. 266.

248. 370 *of* 1896.—(Sanskrit.) On the same pillar, west face. A record in Ś. 1186, connected with the preceding inscription.

249. 371 *of* 1896.—(Telugu.) On the first pillar in the first row of the Asthānamaṇṭapa in the same temple, south face. Records in Ś. 1154 gift of a lamp by a merchant.

250. 372 *of* 1896.—(Telugu.) On the third pillar in the same row, east, north and west faces. Muhammad Quli Padshah (of Golkonda) records in Ś. 1526, Krōdhin, the gift of the village Kūrmum by a feudatory named Aśvarāya, who had defeated Mukunda-Bāhubalēndra, the famous Telugu usurper of the Gajapati sovereignty. See Gt. 764 and Cg. 1175. According to Sterling the usurpation took place in 1550. According to Hunter Mukunda-dēva ruled from 1551 to 1559.

251. 373 *of* 1896.—On the fourth pillar in the second row of the same maṇṭapa, south face. A Sanskṛit record in Ś. 1182. (Damaged.)

252. 374 *of* 1896.—(Telugu.) On a slab to the right of the north gate of the same temple. Records in Ś. 1163 the gift of gold for offerings.

253. 375 *of* 1896.—(Telugu.) On a slab to the right of the north gate of the same temple. A record of Vīra-Narasimha-dēva in Ś. 1204, seventh year. (Now damaged.)

254. 376 *of* 1896.—(Sanskrit and Telugu.) On a slab to the right of the north gate of the same temple. A damaged record, dated Ś. 1170.

255. 377 *of* 1896.—(Sanskṛit.) On a pillar at the second entrance to the temple from the south. Records in Ś. 1274, Śubhakrit (wrong), that a certain Narasimhabhārati made over certain land, which he had received from the king, to his pupils.

256. 378 *of* 1896.—(Telugu.) On a slab to the left of the south entrance to the Bhōgamaṇṭapa in the same temple, south face. Records in Ś. 1127 the gift of a lamp.

257. 379 *of* 1896.—(Sanskrit.) On a slab to the left of the south entrance to the Bhōgamaṇṭapa in the same temple, south face. Records the gift of a lamp.

258. 380 *of* 1896.—(Telugu.) On a slab to the left of the south entrance to the Bhōgamaṇṭapa in the same temple, south face. Records in Ś. 1035, thirty-eighth year of the Gaṅga king, Anantavarma-Chōḍagaṅgadēva (1075—1146), the gift of a lamp.

259. 381 *of* 1896.—(Telugu.) On the same slab, east face. Records in Ś. 1128, eleventh year of the Gaṅga king Anantavarmadēva, the gift of a lamp.

260. 382 *of* 1896.—(Telugu.) On a slab to the right of the same entrance. Records in Ś. 10 (71), ninth year of the Gaṅga king Anantavarmadēva, the gift of a lamp.

261. 383 *of* 1896.—(Telugu.) On a slab to the right of the same entrance. A record of the Gaṅga king Anantavarma-Madhukāmārṇavadēva in Ś. 1071, fourth year. (A much damaged record.) [See No. 355 below. *Madhukāmārṇava* was evidently a surname of Anantavarma. For another surname Jaṭēśvara see No. 329 below.]

262. 384 *of* 1896.—(Telugu.) On a pillar to the left of the first entrance to the central shrine in the same temple. Records in Ś. 1074, seventh year of Gaṅga king Anantavarmadēva, the gift of a lamp. [See No. 355 below.]

263. 385 *of* 1896.—(Telugu.) On a pillar to the left of the first entrance to the central shrine in the same temple. Records in Ś. 1074, seventh year of Gaṅga king Anantavarmadēva, the gift of a lamp. [See No. 355 below.]

264. 386 *of* 1896.—(Telugu.) On a pillar to the left of the first entrance to the central shrine in the same temple. Records in Ś. 1065, sixty-eighth year of Gaṅga king Anantavarmadēva (1075—1146), the gift of a lamp.

GOOMSUR TALUK.

Buguḍa.

265. The C.P. grant of Mādhavarman, Sainyabhīta II. A record in Nāgari character and Sanskṛit language, mentioning the grant of a village in "Guḍḍa" district and opening with the following genealogical account of the donor:—

Puḷindasēna
(ruler of Kaliṅga)
|
Śailōdbhava
(real founder of the family).
| |
Raṇabhīta.
|
Sainyabhīta I.
| |
Yaśōbhīta.
|
Sainyabhīta II or Mādhavavarman.

[The double line denotes mere descent and the single line a son or successor.] The inscription is to the effect that, from his residence at Kaingōḍa, Mādhavavarman informed his officials and people that, on a solar eclipse, he gave the village of Puipīna in Kadira *Paṭṭaka* in *Guḍḍavishaya*, to the Bhaṭṭa Vāmana, son of Ādityadēva and grandson of Vāmana. See *Madr. Ep. Rep.*, 1890 (October, p. 2) and *Ep. Ind.*, Vol. III, 41—6, and *Ibid.*, Vol. VII pp. 100—2, which corrects a mistake in the former.

Payakirāyapuram (Payakarapalli ?).

266. A record of Mukundadēva in Raudri, chaitra-bahuḷa 5, relating that Nārāyaṇa sur Harichandana gave the village to Gōḍamarti Kūrmāchāryalu of the Kāśyapa-gōtra and Kaṇva Śākhā. *Loc. Rec.*, Vol. 59, pp. 219-20.

ICHCHHĀPURAM TALUK.

Brindāvana Chandrapūr.

267. A C.P. grant of Vīra Śrī Purushōttama Anaṅgabhimadēva Kēsari in Sam. 52, Mithuna 5, Āshāḍhaśuddha 7, Friday, to Jōgidāsa Brahmachāri, of the above village. He built a maṭha there and settled a number of Brahmans each having his share. See *Mack. MSS.*, Bk. XIV (Brown's No. 983 and Oppert's No. 15-6-2).

Kulamaṇipuram.

268. A C.P. grant of Gajapati Gauravēśvara Karnāṭakula Baḍagēśvara, Indradyumnāvatāra, Mahāvīra Mantrapratāpa Śrī Vīra Viśvēśvara, in Mēsha 18, Vaiśākha Śuddha, Sunday, lunar eclipse. Records the grant of the above village with the eight kinds of enjoyment to Baṇḍāgara Gaṅgarāja of the Kauśika-gōtra, Rigvēda and Kaṇva Śākhā "with the consent of Kulamaṇi Rājēndradēva." *Ibid.*, No. I, pp. 1—3.

269. A grant of Vīrēśvaradēva Mahārāya in Samasta 53 (?) Kārttika 10, Śrāvaṇa Śuddha 11, Saturday, to Appikaṇṭla Kāmayya Bhukta of the Śāṇḍilyagōtra and Yajurvēda. A house and lands were granted, besides lands for other Brahmans with the consent of Śrīkṛishṇachandra Rājēndradēva. *Ibid.*

270. Another grant of the same king in Samasta 55 (?), in Dhanus 27, Pushya Śuddha 11, Sunday, to Viśvāvadhāni Sarvaṇṇabhaṭṭulu with the consent of the same chief. *Ibid.*

271. A grant of the same king in Samasta 88 (?), Mithuna 20, to Mallēśvara Bhaṭṭa. He was given lands in various villages with the consent of the same chief. *Ibid.*

272. Another grant of the same king in year 39 in Simha 21 to Amalēśvara Bhaṭṭa with the consent of Kulamaṇi Rājēndradēva. *Ibid.*

273. Records that Śrī-Pītāmbhara Dharēndradēva gave in Samasta 12 year (?), Kumbha 20, Phalguna Bahuḷa 6, Friday, two villages to Jagannāthabhaṭṭa and Subramaṇya Bhaṭṭa. *Ibid.*

Lōkonādhcpuram (Lōkanāthapuram).

274. A grant of Mukundadēva in Samasta 27, in Mēsha 16, Vaiśākha-amāvāsya, Sunday, solar eclipse to Gurukādhipati Gōsāyi for living there and blessing him and his people. The village was divided into six parts and allotted to six people. "The consent of Lōkanātha Ravutta Gāru." *Ibid.*

Muktāpuram.

275. A grant of Mukundadēva in Saṁasta 4 ? Mīnam 30, Chaitra Śuddha 15, Sunday, to Harisēvakhawantrarāya of the Bhāradvājagōtra and Rigvēda. The gift was really made by Muktamāla Śrīpatamahādēvi, the queen. The village was given for a Śrōtriyam rent of 8 rupees. *Ibid.*

Birojogonāthopūr.

276. A record of Vīrakēśvara Mahārāja in Samasta 12, Mēsham 20, Vaisākha Śuddha 8, Friday. Records gift of the village to Raghunātha Sāntarāya Mahāpātra by Aragaḍa Rājyādhipati Jagannātha Harichandana. *Loc. Rec.*, Vol. 59, pp. 250–51.

Boghadi Madhusūdanapuram.

277. A record of Vīrakēśvaradēva in year 25, Karkaṭaka Śravaṇa Śuddha 15, Saturday, lunar eclipse, relating that the Aragaḍa Rājyādhipati Madhusūdana Harichandana Jagadēva gave the village of Bogaḍa in his name to its people. See *Ibid.*, pp. 238–42.

Bono Raghunāthapuram.

278. A record of Śrī Rāmachandradēva Mahārāja in Samasta 4, Kumbha 20, Chaittra bahuḷa 2, Friday, giving to a Paramaguru the title-deed of the village. See *Ibid.* pp. 246—48.

Chondromādeipur (Chandramādevipuram).

279. Records in the reign of Vīrakēśvaradēva in year 11, Mēsha 20, Vaiśākha bahuḷa 30, Monday, solar eclipse, that the Aragaḍa Rājyādhipati Jagannātha Harichandana gave the village to Nandadāsa and people. *Ibid.*, p. 243.

Chodiāpoda Krustnodāsopur (Chadavaḍa alias Kṛishṇadāsapura).

280. A record of Purushōttamadēva Mahārāya, in year 5, Mēsham 30, Vaiśākha Śuddha 15, Wednesday, lunar eclipse, relating gift of the village to Chandraśēkhara Paramaguru and people with the consent of the Aragaḍa Rājyādhipati Kṛishṇa Niśśaṅkagāru. *Ibid.*, pp. 230—32.

Chhochina Jāgannāthapur (Chābinna Jāgannathapūr).

281. Records that in the fifth year of Vīrakēśvaradēva, in Vrischika 19, Mārgaśira-bahuḷa 30, Monday, a Dīkshita who was the son of Gōvindaratha Gōsayi and grandson of Śrīnivāsa ratha Dīkshita gave 100 *Bharaṇas* to Vasuratha Rāju Guru with the consent of Aragaḍa Rājyādhipati Śrī Jagannātha Harichandana Jagadēvagāru. *Loc. Rec.*, Vol. 59, pp. 222—26.

Chondi Ramochondropur (Tsundi Rāmachandrapuram).

282. A record of Dibba Śiṅgadēva Mahārāja in Samasta 5, Makaram 29, Māghaśuddha 15, Wednesday, lunar eclipse, relating the gift of the village to Guru Sāntarāyaḍu and other people. *Ibid.*, pp. 226–7.

Gowradeipūr (Gauridēvipuram).

283. A record of the Aṛagaḍa Rājyādhipati Rāmachandra Mahārāja in Samasta 5, Karkaṭaka 30, Śravaṇabahuḷa 5, Wednesday. Records that he gave the village to Vasurathagāru and people in twelve parts. *Ibid.*, pp. 244–5.

Jēmadeipur (Jāmadāyipuram).

284. A record of Divya Śiṅgadēva Mahārāya in year 9, Tulā 15, Kārttikabahuḷa 15, Saturday. Records that the Aragaḍa Rājyādhipati Rāmachandra Harichandana Jagadēva gave the village to Vanamāli Śatavastugāru and people. *Ibid.*, pp. 245–6.

Nenli Śrinivāsapūr.

285. A record of Rāmachandradēva Mahārāja in year 5, Tulā 17, Kārttikabahuḷa 30, Monday, recording gift of the village to Śrīnivāsaratha Dīkshita and people by Aragaḍa Rājyādhipati Dhanañjaya Harichandana dēva. *Ibid.*, pp. 252–3.

Nunighāṭi Gōpināthapuram.

286. Records that Gōpināthadēva Mahārāja gave in year 11, Mēsha 13, Vaiśākhabahūḷa 30, Monday, solar eclipse, lands to Dhanāñjaya Nedinānta Rao for effecting his cure from paleness. *Ibid.*, pp. 234–5.

Prāṇadēvipuram (Pranodeipur).

287. A record of Śrī Vīrakēśvara Mahāraya in year 5, Makara 3, Pushyaśuddha 15, lunar eclipse, recording gift to Dharma Paramaguru with the consent of Prāṇadēvi Santanagāri. *Ibid.*, pp. 235—7.

Sāntarāpūru.

288. A record of Vīraśri Rāmachandradēva Māhāraja in Samasta 11, Vrishabha 25, Jyēshṭhaśuddha 3, Wednesday, relating gift to Vāsuvatharāja Guru Mahāpātra and others of the village of Sāntarāpūru with the consent of Aragaḍa Rājyādhipati Raghunātha Harisyandana Jagadēva. *Loc. Rec.*, Vol. 59, pp. 260–2.

Sunyō Rāmachandrapurām.

289. A record of the second year of Narasimhadēva, Mahārāya, Mēsham 2, Vaiśākha-Śuddha 10, Tuesday, granting the village, for the donor's long life, to Dhaniratha Gāru and others. See *Ibid.*, pp. 249–50.

PARLĀKIMEDI TALUK.

Achyutapuram.

290. "The Achyutapuram plates of Indravarman I," so called because the plates were in the hands of a resident of Achyutapuram near Mukhaliṅgam. Records a gift of land made at Kaliṅganagara by the Kaliṅga-Gaṅga king Indravarma *alias* Rājasimha during the sun's progress to the north, on the new moon of Chaittra, in the eighty-seventh year of the dynasty. The object of the grant was a field in the village of Siddhārtaka in the District of Varāhavartini and it was given to a Brāhman of the Chāṇḍōgya school, with the privilege of using the Rājataṭāka (king's tank) for irrigation. See *Ep. Ind.*, Vol. III,pp. 127—30, where Dr. Hultzsch edits it. He believes that the king of this record is Indravarman I *alias* Rājasimha, whose inscription is published by Dr. Fleet in *Ind. Antq.*, Vol. XIV, pp. 131 f.]

Mukhaliṅgam.

This village has been identified by Mr. G. V. Ramamurti with Kaliṅganagara, the capital of the Gaṅga kings of Kaliṅga. See *Madras Journal*, 1889–94, p. 68. He shows that the two temples of Mukhaliṅgēśvara and Bhīmēśvara formerly bore the names of Madhukēśvara and Aniyaṅka—Bhīmēśvara, that the former was founded by the Gaṅga Kāmārṇava II and the latter by Vajrahasta II. See *Ep. Ind.*, Vol. IV, No. 24.

291. 140 *of* 1896.—(Telugu.) On a pillar to the left of the entrance to the central shrine of the Mukhaliṅgēśvara temple. A Telugu record of the Gaṅga king Anantavarmadēva (1075—1146), dated in Ś. 1024, twenty-eighth year. Mentions his E. Chāḷukya contemporary Vīra-Chōḍadēva. [Anantavarma came to the throne in A.D. 1075. He reigned for 72 years.]

292. 141 *of* 1896.—(Uriya.) On a pillar to the right of the same entrance, north face. A record of the Gajapati king Pratāpa Kapilēśvaradēva (1452—79). See *Antiquities*, II, p. 207 and No. 162 above.

293. 142 *of* 1896.—(Sanskrit.) On the same pillar, east face. Records in Ś. 1056 the gift of a lamp.

294. 143 *of* 1896.—(Telugu.) On the same pillar, east, face. Records in Ś. 1049, fifty-third year of the Gaṅga king Anantavarmadēva (1075—1146) the gift of a lamp.

295. 144 *of* 1896.—(Telugu.) On the same pillar, east face. Records in Ś. 1049, fifty-third year of the Gaṅga king, Sōḍagaṅgadēva the gift of a lamp.

296. 145 *of* 1896.—On the same pillar, east face. A damaged record in Nagari, of the Gaṅga king Anantavarman *alias* Chōḍagaṅgadēva (1075—1146).

297. 146 *of* 1896.—(Sanskrit and Telugu.) On the same pillar, east face. Records in Ś. 1030, in Sanskrit and Telugu, the gift of a lamp by Sōmaḷamahādēvi, queen of the Gaṅga king.

298. 147 *of* 1896.—(Telugu.) On the first pillar in the right row of the Asthānamaṇṭapa in the same temple, north face. The Gaṅga king Anantavarmadēva (1075—1146) records the gift of a lamp.

299. 148 *of* 1896.—(Telugu.) On the first pillar in the right row of the Āsthānamaṇṭapa in the same temple, north face. Dated in the reign of the Gaṅga king, Anantavarmadēva (1075—1146). Records the gift of two lamps by an inhabitant of Bikkivrōlu.

300. 149 *of* 1896.—(Telugu.) On the first pillar in the right row of the Āsthānamaṇṭapa in the same temple, north face. Records in Ś. 1054, fifty-eighth year of the Gaṅga king, Anantavarmadēva the gift of a lamp. Mentions Chōḍa-gaṅgadēva.

301. 150 *of* 1896.—(Telugu.) On the first pillar in the right row of the Asthānamaṇṭapa in the same temple, north face. Records in Ś. 1059, the gift of a lamp by Daṇḍanāyaka.

302. 151 *of* 1896.—(Telugu.) On the same pillar, east face. Records in Ś. 1050, fifty-fourth year of the Gaṅga king, Chōḍagaṅgadēva (1075—1146) the gift of a lamp.

303. 152 *of* 1896.—(Telugu.) On the same pillar, east face. Records in Ś. 1047, fiftieth year of the Gaṅga king, Chōḍagaṅga dēva (1075—1146) the gift of a lamp.

304. 153 *of* 1896.—(Telugu.) On the same pillar, east face. A record of the reign of the Gaṅga king, Anantavarmadēva (1075—1146). Records in Ś. 1055, his fifty-ninth year, the gift of a lamp by the wife of Chōḍagaṅgadēva's younger brother.

305. 154 *of* 1896.—(Telugu.) On the same pillar, east face. A record of the Gaṅga king. Anantavarmadēva (1075—1146) in Ś. 1056.

306. 155 *of* 1896.—(Telugu.) On the same pillar, south face. Records in fifty-seventh year (of the same king) the gift of a lamp. (Beginning lost.)

307. 156 *of* 1896.—(Telugu.) On the same pillar, south face. Records in Ś. 1051 (1075—1146) fifty-fifth year of the Gaṅga king, Anantavarmadēva, the gift of a lamp.

308. 157 *of* 1896.—(Telugu.) On the same pillar, south face. The Gaṅga king, Chōḍagaṅgadēva, records the gift of a lamp. (Date doubtful.)

309. 158 *of* 1896.—(Sanskrit.) On the same pillar, south face. Records in Ś. 1042 the gift of a lamp by a Brāhmaṇa.

310. 159 *of* 1896.—(Telugu.) On the same pillar, south face. A record of the Gaṅga king, Anantavarmadēva (1075—1146) *alias* Chōḍagaṅgadēva in Ś. 1033, thirty-seventh year. (End built in.)

311. 160 *of* 1896.—(Telugu.) On the same pillar, west face. The Gaṅga king, Anantavarmadēva (1075—1146), records in Ś. 1052 the gift of a lamp.

312. 161 *of* 1896.—(Telugu.) On the same pillar, west face. Records in Ś. 1048 the gift of a lamp.

313. 162 *of* 1896.—(Telugu.) On the same pillar, west face. Records in Ś. 1047, fifty-first year of the Gaṅga king, Anantavarmadēva, the gift of a lamp.

314. 163 *of* 1896.—(Telugu.) On the same pillar, west face. Records in the thirty-seventh year of the Gaṅga king, Anantavarmadēva, the gift of a lamp.

315. 164 *of* 1896.—(Telugu.) On the second pillar in the right row of the Āsthānamaṇṭapa in the same temple, north face. Records in Ś. 1062, sixty-fifth year of the Gaṅga king, Anantavarmadēva (1075—1146), the gift of a lamp.

316. 165 *of* 1896.—(Telugu.) On the second pillar in the right row of the Āsthānamaṇṭapa in the same temple, north face. Records in Ś. 1053, fifty-seventh year of the Gaṅga king, Chōḍagaṅgadēva (1075—1146), the gift of a lamp.

317. 166 *of* 1896.—(Telugu.) On the second pillar in the right row of the Āsthānamaṇṭapa in the same temple, north face. Records in Ś. 1048, fifty-third year of the Gaṅga king, Anantavarmadēva (1075—1146), the gift of a lamp. [The inscription shows that the king ascended the throne or became co-regent in Ś. 985, i.e., three years earlier than the date given in his copper-plate grant.]

318. 167 *of* 1896.—(Telugu.) On the second pillar in the right row of the Āsthānamaṇṭapa in the .same temple, north face. Records in Ś. 1020, twenty-third year of the Gaṅga king, Anantavarmadēva (1075—1146), the gift of a lamp.

319. 168 *of* 1896.—(Telugu.) On a second pillar in the right row of the Āsthānamaṇṭapa in the same temple, north face. Records in Ś. 1054 the gift of a lamp.

320. 169 *of* 1895.—(Sanskrit.) On the second pillar in the right row of the Āsthānamaṇṭapa in the same temple, north face. Records in Ś. 1055 the gift of a lamp by a superintendent of salt mines and minister of Vikrama-Gaṅga to the temple of Madhukēśvara at Kaliṅgavaninagara. See note to the next epigraph.

321. 170 *of* 1896.—(Sanskrit.) On the second pillar in the right row of the Āsthānamaṇṭapa in the same temple, north face. Records in Ś. 1068 the gift of lamp by another minister of Vikramagaṅga to the temple of Madhukēśvara at Kaliṅgadēśanagara [Vikramagaṅga was evidently a contemporary of Anantavarma.]

322. 171 *of* 1896.—(Telugu.) On the same pillar, east face. Records the gift of a lamp. (Beginning built in.)

323. 172 *of* 1896.—(Sanskrit and Telugu.) On the same pillar east face. Records in Ś. 1045 ? the gift of a lamp; mentions Chōḍagaṅga.

324. 173 *of* 1896.—(Telugu.) On the same pillar, east face. Records in Ś. 1043, forty-fifth year, in the reign of the Gaṅga king, Chōḍagaṅgadēva (1045—1146), the gift of a lamp.

325. 174 *of* 1896.—(Telugu.) On the same pillar, east face. Records in the fifty-ninth year of the Gaṅga king Anantavarmadēva (1075—1146), the gift of a lamp.

326. 175 *of* 1896.—(Telugu.) On the same pillar, east face. Records in the fifty-eighth year of the Gaṅga king, Anantavarmadēva, the gift of a lamp.

327. 176 *of* 1896.—(Sanskrit.) On the same pillar, west face. Records in Ś. 1061, the gift of a lamp.

328. 177 *of* 1896.—(Telugu.) On the same pillar, west face. Records in the forty-ninth year of the Gaṅga king, Anantavarmadēva (1075—1146) in Ś. 1045, the gift of a lamp.

329. 178 *of* 1896.—(Telugu.) On the same pillar, west face. A record of Jaṭēśvaradēva, dated in Ś. 1070, third year, about the gift of a lamp. [Jaṭēśvara was apparently the surname of that Anantavarma who succeeded Chōḍagaṅga in 1146.

330. 179 *of* 1896.—(Sanskrit.) On the same pillar, west face. A record of Ś. 1062. (Much damaged.)

331. 180 *of* 1896.—(Telugu.) On the same pillar, south face. The Gaṅga king, Anantavarmadēva, records in Ś. 1109, twenty-second year, a gift of land by the maṇḍalika Purushōttama.

332. 181 *of* 1896.—(Telugu.) On the third pillar in the right row of the Āsthānamaṇṭapa in the same temple, north face. Records the gift of a lamp by the Gaṅga king, Anantavarmadēva.

333. 182 *of* 1896.—(Telugu.) On the third pillar in the right row of the Āsthānamaṇṭapa in the same temple, north face. The Gaṅga king, Anantavarmadēva (1075—1146), records in his seventy-third year the gift of a lamp.

334. 183 *of* 1896.—(Telugu.) On the third pillar in the right row of the Asthānamaṇṭapa in the same temple, north face. The Gaṅga king, Anantavarmadēva (1075—1146), records the gift of a lamp. (Date doubtful.)

335. 184 *of* 1896.—(Sanskrit and Telugu.) On the third pillar in the right row of the Āsthānamaṇṭapa in the same temple, north face. Records in Ś. 1041 the gift of a lamp by a minister of Chōḍagaṅga (1075—1146).

336. 185 *of* 1896.—(Telugu.) On the third pillar in the right row of the Āsthānamaṇṭapa in the same temple, north face. Records in Ś. 1055, fifty-ninth year of the Gaṅga king, Anantavarmadēva (1075—1146), the gift of land in Varāhavartani.

337. 186 *of* 1896.—(Telugu.) On the third pillar in the right row of the Āsthānamaṇṭapa in the same temple, north face. The Gaṅga king, Anantavarmadēva (1075—1146), records the gift of a lamp.

338. 187 *of* 1896.—(Telugu.) On the same east face. The Gaṅga king, Anantavarmadēva (1075—1146), records in Ś. 1056, fifty-ninth year, the gift of a lamp.

339. 188 *of* 1896.—(Telugu.) On the same pillar east face. The Gaṅga king, Anantavarmadēva, records in his fifty-ninth year the gift of a lamp.

340. 189 *of* 1896.—(Telugu.) On the same pillar, east face. Records in Ś. 1056, fifty-eighth year of Anantavarmadēva, the gift of a lamp by a writer from Arśavilli.

341. 190 *of* 1896.—(Sanskrit.) On the same pillar, east face. Records the gift of a lamp by a merchant.

342. 191 *of* 1896.—(Telugu.) On the same pillar, west face. Records in the ninth year of the Gaṅga king, Anantavarmadēva, the gift of a lamp by an officer.

343. 192 *of* 1896.—(Telugu.) On the fourth pillar in the right row of the Asthānamaṇṭapa in the same temple, west face. A record of the Gaṅga king, Anantavarmadēva. (Damaged.)

344. 193 *of* 1896.—(Telugu.) On the fourth pillar in the right row of the Asthānamaṇṭapa in the same temple, west face. Records in Ś. 1058, sixty-first year of the Gaṅga king, Anantavarmadēva, the gift of a lamp.

345. 194 *of* 1896.—(Telugu.) On the same pillar in the right row of the Asthānamaṇṭapa in the same temple, west face. Records, in the fifty-seventh year of the Gaṅga king, Anantavarmadēva, the gift of a lamp.

346. 195 *of* 1896.—(Telugu.) On the same pillar in the right row of the Asthānamaṇṭapa in the same temple, west face. The Gaṅga king, Anantavarmadēva, records the gift of a lamp.

347. 196 *of* 1896.—(Sanskrit and Telugu.) On the same pillar, north face. Records in Ś. 1063, the gift of land in Varāhavartani by a military officer.

348. 197 *of* 1896.—(Sanskrit.) On the same pillar, north face. Records in Ś. 1062 the gift of a lamp.

349. 198 *of* 1896.—(Telugu.) On the same pillar, north face. Records in Ś. 1064 the gift of a lamp.

350. 199 *of* 1896.—(Telugu.) On the same pillar, north face. Records in Ś. 1064, sixty-eighth year of the Gaṅga king, Anantavarmadēva (1075—1146), the gift of a lamp.

351. 200 *of* 1896.—(Telugu.) On the same pillar, north face. Records in Ś. 1065 the gift of land.

352. 201 *of* 1896.—(Telugu.) On the fourth pillar in the left row of the Āsthānamaṇṭapa in the same temple, south face. Records in Ś. 1060, sixty-third year of the Gaṅga king, Anantavarmadēva, the gift of a lamp.

353. 202 *of* 1896.—(Telugu.) On the fourth pillar in the left row of the Āsthānamaṇṭapa in the same temple, south face. Records in Ś. 1057 the gift of lamp.

354. 203 *of* 1896.—(Sanskrit.) On the fourth pillar in the left row of the Āsthānamaṇṭapa in the same temple, south face. Records in Ś. 1062 the gift of a lamp by the queen of Gaṅgēśvaradēva.

355. 204 *of* 1896.—(Telugu.) On the same pillar, west face. The Gaṅga king, Anantavarmadēva, records in Ś. 1070, third year, the gift of a lamp. This king, points out Dr. Hultzsch, must have been the successor of Anantavarman Chōḍagaṅga who ruled for seventy-two years till Ś. 1069. See Nos. 261 and 329 above.

356. 205 *of* 1896.—(Telugu.) On the same pillar, west face. The Gaṅga king, Anantavarmadēva (1075—1146), records in Ś. 1060, sixty-fourth year, the gift of a lamp.

357. 206 *of* 1896.—(Telugu.) On the third pillar in the left row of the Āsthānamaṇṭapa in the same temple, south face. Records in Ś. 1050 the gift of a lamp.

358. 207 *of* 1896.—(Sanskrit and Telugu.) On the third pillar in the left row of the Āsthānamaṇṭapa in the same temple, south face. Records the gift of a lamp.

359. 208 *of* 1896.—(Sanskrit and Telugu.) On the third pillar in the left row of the Āsthānamaṇṭapa in the same temple, south face. Records in Ś. 1015 the gift of a lamp by a minister of Chōḍagaṅga (1075—1146).

360. 209 *of* 1896.—(Telugu.) On the third pillar in the left row of the Āsthānamaṇṭapa in the same temple, south face. A record in Ś. 1244.

361. 210 *of* 1896.--(Sanskrit.) On the third pillar in the left row of the Āsthānamaṇṭapa in the same temple, south face. Records in Ś. 1032 the gift of a lamp by Lakshmi, queen of a Gaṅga king (Anantavarman).

362. 211 *of* 1896.—(Sanskrit and Telugu.) On the third pillar in the left row of the Āsthānamaṇṭapa in the same temple, south face. Records in Ś. 1035 the gift of a lamp by Prithivīmahādēvi, another queen of Chōḍagaṅga (1075—1146).

363. 212 *of* 1896.—(Telugu.) On the third pillar in the left row of the Āsthānamaṇṭapa in the same temple, south face. Records in Ś. 1054, the gift of bells, etc.

364. 213 *of* 1896.--(Telugu.) On the same pillar, east face. The Gaṅga king, Chōḍagaṅgadēva (1075—1146) records in Ś. 1055 the gift of a lamp.

365. 214 *of* 1896.—(Telugu.) On the same pillar, east face. Records in the reign of the Gaṅga king, Chōḍagaṅgadēva, in Ś. 1089, the gift of a lamp by a dancing girl.

366. 215 *of* 1896.—(Sanskrit and Telugu.) On the same pillar, east face. Records in Ś. 1035 gift of a lamp by a queen of Chōḍagaṅga (1075—1146).

367. 216 *of* 1896.—(Sanskrit.) On the same pillar, east face. Records in Ś. 1100? the gift of a lamp to the temple of Madhukēśa on the bank of the Vamśadhāra.

368. 217 *of* 1896.—(Sanskrit.) On the same pillar, east face. Records in Ś. 1215, the gift of a lamp.

369. 218 *of* 1896.—(Telugu.) On the same pillar, west face. Records the gift of a lamp.

370. 219 *of* 1896.—(Telugu.) On the second pillar in the left row of the Āsthānamaṇṭapa in the same temple, south face. The Gaṅga king, Chōḍagaṅgadēva (1075—1146) records in Ś. 1057, fifty-ninth year, the gift of a lamp.

371. 220 *of* 1896.—(Telugu.) On the second pillar in the left row of the Āsthānamaṇṭapa in the same temple, south face. The Gaṅga king, Chōḍagaṅgadēva (1075—1146) records in Ś. 1053, fifty-seventh year, the gift of a lamp; mentions Varāhavartani.

372. 221 *of* 1896.—(Telugu.) On the second pillar in the left row of the Āsthānamaṇṭapa in the same temple, south face. Records in Ś. 1045, forty-eighth year of the Gaṅga king, Chōḍagaṅgadēva (1075--1146), the gift of a lamp by a military officer.

373. 222 *of* 1896.—(Telugu.) On the second pillar in the left row of the Asthānamaṇṭapa in the same temple, south face. The Gaṅga king Anantavarmadēva (1075—1146) records in Ś. 1046, forty-ninth year, the gift of a lamp.

89

374. 223 *of* 1896.—(Telugu.) On the same pillar, east face. Records in Ś. 1047, the gift of a lamp by a servant of Vīra Chōḍadēva, the E. Chāḷukyan.

375. 224 *of* 1896.—(Telugu.) On the same pillar, east face. The Gaṅga king Chōḍagaṅgadēva (1075—1146) records in Ś. 1045, forty-ninth year, the gift of a lamp.

376. 225 *of* 1896.—(Telugu.) On the same pillar, east face. A record of the Gaṅga king Anantavarmadēva (1075—1146) in his forty-fifth year. (End obliterated.)

377. 226 *of* 1896.—On the same pillar, east face. A damaged record in Telugu.

378. 227 *of* 1896.—(Sanskrit.) On the first pillar in the left row of the Asthānamaṇṭapa in the same temple, south face. Records in Ś. 1066, the gift of a lamp by a military officer.

379. 228 *of* 1896.—(Sanskrit.) On the first pillar in the left row of the Āsthānamaṇṭapa in the same temple, south face. Records in Ś. 1053, the gift of lamp to the temple of Madhu-kēśvara in Kaliṅgadēśanagara by a servant of the Chāḷukya-Gaṅga king.

380. 229 *of* 1896.—(Telugu.) On the first pillar in the left row of the Āsthānamaṇṭapa in the same temple, south face. The Gaṅga king Chōḍagaṅgadēva (1075—1146) records in Ś. 1053, fifty-seventh year, the gift of a lamp.

381. 230 *of* 1896.—(Sanskrit.) On the same pillar, east face. Records in Ś. 1052, the gift of a lamp by a minister of Chōḍa-gaṅga and inhabitant of Dākshārāma to the temple of Madhu-kēśvara at Trikaliṅgavaninagara.

382. 231 *of* 1896.—(Telugu.) On the same pillar, east face. The Gaṅga king Anantavarmadēva (1075—1146) records in his fifty-third year, the gift of a lamp.

383. 232 *of* 1896.—(Telugu.) On the same pillar, east face. A record of the Gaṅga king Anantavarmadēva in his fifty-eighth year. (Damaged.)

384. 233 *of* 1896.—(Telugu.) On the same pillar, east face. A record of Ś. 1291. (Damaged.)

385. 234 *of* 1896.—(Telugu.) Left of the entrance into the Āsthānamaṇṭapa in the same temple. The Gaṅga king Chōḍa-gaṅgadēva (1075—1146) records in Ś. 1043, forty-fifth year, the gift of a lamp.

386. 235 *of* 1896.—(Sanskrit and Telugu.) Left of the entrance into the Āsthānamaṇṭapa in the same temple. Records in Ś. 1015, the gift of a lamp by a military officer.

387. 236 *of* 1896.—(Telugu.) Right of the entrance into the Āsthānamaṇṭapa in the same temple. The Gaṅga king Ananta-varmadēva (1075—1146) records in Ś. 1061, sixty-fourth year, the gift of a lamp.

388. 237 *of* 1896.—(Sanskrit and Telugu.) Right of the entrance into the Āsthānamaṇṭapa in the same temple. Records in Ś. 1013 the gift of a lamp to the temple of Madhukēśvara at Gōkarṇa.

389. 238 *of* 1896.—(Sanskrit.) On the left door-pillar of the entrance into the Āsthānamaṇṭapa in the same temple. Records in Ś. 1077, the gift of a lamp.

390. 239 *of* 1896.—(Sanskrit.) On the left door-pillar of the entrance into the Āsthānamaṇṭapa in the same temple. Records in Ś. 1064, the gift of a lamp by Umāvallabha, the son of the Gaṅga king.

391. 240 *of* 1896.—(Sanskrit.) On the left door-pillar of the entrance into the Āsthānamaṇṭapa in the same temple. Records in Ś. 1065 the gift of a lamp.

392. 241 *of* 1896.—(Sanskrit.) On the left door-pillar of the entrance into the Āsthānamaṇṭapa in the same temple. Records in Ś. 1067, the gift of a lamp.

393. 242 *of* 1896.—(Telugu.) On the right door-pillar of the same entrance. The Gaṅga king Anantavarmadēva records in Ś. 1097, the gift of a lamp.

394. 243 *of* 1896.—(Telugu.) On the right door-pillar of the same entrance. Records in Ś. 1085, the gift of a lamp.

395. 244 *of* 1896.—(Telugu.) On a slab to the left of the second entrance into the same temple, west face. The Gaṅga king Anantavarmadēva (1075—1146) records in Ś. 1005, eighth year, the gift of a lamp.

396. 245 *of* 1896.—(Telugu.) On a slab to the left of the second entrance into the same temple, west face. Records in Ś. 1014, the gift of a lamp.

397. 246 *of* 1896.—(Telugu.) On the same slab, north face. The Gaṅga king Anantavarmadēva, records in Ś. 1004, eighth year, the gift of a lamp.

398. 247 *of* 1896.—On a slab to the right of the same entrance. A record in Uriya.

399. 248 *of* 1896.—(Sanskrit.) On a slab to the left of the main entrance into the same temple. Records in Ś. 990 the gift by the queen of Vajrahasta, who was the daughter of a Haihaya king. [Vajrahasta was the grandfather of Anantavarma.]

400. 249 *of* 1896.—(Sanskrit, Nāgari.) On a slab to the right of the same entrance. Records in the thirty-ninth year of the Gaṅga king Anantavarma-Vajrahastadēva, the gift of a lamp by the wife of a military officer.

401. 250 *of* 1896.—(Telugu.) On the south wall of the Kubēra shrine in the same temple. A record of the Gaṅga king

Anantavarmadēva. (A damaged record, the date of which is doubtful.)

402. 251 *of* 1896.—(Sanskrit.) On the east wall of the same shrine. Records in Ś. 1002, the gift of a lamp.

403. 252 *of* 1896.—(Telugu in old archaic characters.) On the south wall of the Vāyudēva shrine in the same temple. Mentions Samsārabhītadēva.

404. 253 *of* 1896.—On the east wall of the same shrine. A Telugu record in old archaic characters.

405. 254 *of* 1896.—(Telugu.) Left of the southern entrance into the Āsthānamaṇṭapa in the same temple. Records the gift of a lamp.

406. 255 *of* 1896.—(Telugu.) Left of the southern entrance into the Asthānamaṇṭapa in the same temple. Records in Ś. 1100, the gift of a lamp.

407. 256 *of* 1896.—(Telugu.) Right of the same entrance. Records in Ś. 1078, the gift of a lamp.

408. 257 *of* 1896.—On a slab in the Nṛisimhasvāmi Maṭha at Mukhaliṅgam. A Nāgari record of Anantavarma-Vajrahasta dēva of the Gaṅga dynasty, dated thirty-second year. (Damaged.)

409. 258 *of* 1896.—(Telugu.) Left of the east entrance into the Bhīmēśvara temple at Mukhaliṅgam. Records in Ś. 1107, the gift of a lamp to the temple of Aniyaṅkabhīmēśvara.

410. 259 *of* 1896.—(Telugu.) Right of the same entrance. Records in Ś. 1064, sixty-seventh year of Anantavarmadēva, the gift of a lamp to the same temple by a writer from Ippili.

411. 260 *of* 1896.—(Telugu.) Right of the same entrance. Records in Ś. 1014, the gift of a lamp to the same temple.

412. 261 *of* 1896.—(Sanskrit and Telugu.) On the third pillar in the right row of the Āsthānamaṇṭapa in the same temple. Records in Ś. 1062, the gift of a lamp to the same temple by a military officer.

413. 262 *of* 1896.—(Sanskrit.) On the third pillar in the right row of the Āsthānamaṇṭapa in the same temple. Records in Ś. 1065, the gift of a lamp to the same temple.

414. 263 *of* 1896.—(Sanskrit.) On the third pillar in the right row of the Āsthānamaṇṭapa in the same temple. Records in Ś. 1065, the gift of a lamp to the same temple.

415. 264 *of* 1896.—(Sanskrit.) On the second pillar in the right row of the Āsthānamaṇṭapa in the same temple. Records in Ś. 1062, the gift of a lamp to the same temple.

416. 265 *of* 1896.—(Telugu.) On a slab to the left of the southern entrance into the Āsthānamaṇṭapa in the same temple. The Gaṅga king Anantavarmadēva (1165—?) records in Ś. 1110, twenty-third year, the gift of a land to the same temple.

417. 266 *of* 1896.—(Telugu.) On a slab to the right of the same entrance. This Gaṅga king, Anantavarmadēva (apparently different from his namesake in No. 416) records in Ś. 1093, third year, the gift of a land to the same temple.

418. 267 *of* 1896.—(Telugu.) On the south face of No. 416. Records in Ś. 991, the gift of a lamp to the same temple.

419. 268 *of* 1896.—(Telugu.) On the west face of No. 416. The Gaṅga king, Anantavarmadēva, records the gift of a lamp to the same temple by an inhabitant of Dīrgāsi.

420. 269 *of* 1896.—(Telugu.) On a slab to the left of the second entrance into the central shrine of the same temple. The Gaṅga king, Anantavarmadēva, the successor of Anantavarma Chōḍagaṅga (1075—1146) records in Ś. 1070, third year, the gift of a lamp to the same temple. See No. 355 above.

421. 270 *of* 1896.—(Telugu.) On a slab to the left of the second entrance into the central shrine of the same temple. The Gaṅga king, Anantavarmadēva, records in Ś. 1077, tenth year, the gift of a lamp to the same temple. [The king was the successor of Chōḍagaṅga who ruled from 1075 to 1146. See No. 355 above.]

Parlākimedi.

422. A C.P. grant of the reign of a Gaṅga king, Vajrahasta (similar to the grants of the Gaṅga kings Indravarman, Dēvēndravarman and Satyavarman). Records that while he was residing at Kaliṅganagara, his minister (?) Dāraparāja, son of Chōḷa Kāmādhirāja and regent of "the five districts *(Pañchavishaya)*, issued an order to the cultivators and householders (kuṭumbis) of Laṅka-kōṇa to the effect that, on the occasion of his daughter's marriage, he gave away the village of Hossaṇḍi to a soldier who is said to be an ornament of the Naggari Sāḷuki family. [Dr. Kielhorn would assign the inscription on palæographical grounds to the eleventh century, to Vajrahasta V (*Circa* 1035—70), " the grandfather of Anantavarman Chōḍa Gaṅga who was anointed king on the 17th February A.D. 1078." See *Ep. Ind.*, Vol. III, pp. 220—224 and Gj. 143-A above.

SŌMPĒTA TALUK.

(Mandasa Zamindari.)

*Mahēndragiri.**

The Gōkarṇēśvara temple at the top of the hill was sacred to the early Gaṅga kings of Kaliṅga. Besides this there are the two temples of Yudhishṭhira and Bhīma.

* This historic place is situated 32 miles south-west of Berhampur and 4 miles off Harivaram in Mandasa Zamindari in Sōmpēṭa taluk. For the temples, the cairn-like huts and other antiquities of the place see *Antiquities*, pp. 5-6.

423. 394 *of* 1896.—(Sanskrit and Telugu.) On a slab to the right of the entrance to the Kunti shrine in the Gōkarṇēśvara temple. Records in Ś. 1045 the gift of a lamp to the temple of Mahēndrēśvara.

424. 395 *of* 1896.—(Telugu.) On a slab to the left of the same entrance. A record of the Gaṅga king, Anantavarma-Chōḍagaṅgadēva in Ś. 1055, sixtieth year. Details the gift of a lamp by an inhabitant of Araśavilli to the temple of Gōkarṇēśvara on the Mahēndra hill.

425. 396 *of* 1896.—(Sanskrit.) At the entrance to the Yudhishṭhira temple on Mahēndragiri. A record of the Chōḷa king Rājēndra Chōḷa saying that after defeating his brother-in-law Vimalāditya (1015—22),he set up a pillar of victory on the Mahēndra mountain. Emblems of the Chōḷa and the Pāṇḍyan feudatory (i.e., the tiger and two fishes) are engraved below the inscription.

426. 397 *of* 1896.—(Tamil.) On three stones lying near the Kunti shrine on Mahēndragiri. A record of the Chōḷa king Rājēndra Chōḷa. Tamil version of the preceding inscription.

TEKKALI TALUK.

Gōdāvaripuram.

427. A record of the third year of Śrī Mukunda dēva, Raudri, Chaittra Śuddha 15th Wednesday, lunar eclipse. Records that Śrī Nārāyaṇa Harichandana Dēvagāru gave the village of Gōdāvaripuram as Śrōtriyam to Kamalalōchanabhaṭṭamiśra of Kaṇva Śākhā and Lōhitāyanatasagōtra. *Loc. Rec.*, Vol. 59, pp. 218-9.

Śivarāmapuram.

428. A record of Śrī Mukunda dēva in year 23, Bhava, Māgha Śuddha 12, Tuesday, relating that Śrī Nārāyaṇa sūr Harischandra dēva gave the village to Viśvanapaḷḷi Hanūmān Bhaṭḷu of Kauṇḍinya Gōtra and Yajus-Śākhā as a Śrōtriyam. *Loc. Rec.*, Vol. 59, pp. 215-6.